EFFECTIVE LEGAL RESEARCH

A PRACTICAL MANUAL OF LAW BOOKS
AND THEIR USE

EFFECTIVE LEGAL RESEARCH

A PRACTICAL MANUAL OF LAW BOOKS AND THEIR USE

By

MILES O. PRICE, B.S., B.L.S., LL.B., LL.D.
LIBRARIAN, COLUMBIA UNIVERSITY LAW LIBRARY

And

HARRY BITNER, A.B., B.L.S., LL.B.
LIBRARIAN, UNITED STATES DEPARTMENT OF JUSTICE

PRENTICE-HALL, INC.
Englewood Cliffs, N. J.

L. C. Cat. Card No. 53-11286

First printing.....................................August, 1953

Second printing.............................January, 1954

Third printing...............................January, 1956

To

F. J. P.

and

A. B.

FOREWORD

We are told that ancient law was a secret law. In the days of the Romans, it was the secret of the pontifices. Japan, in more recent years, kept the people uninformed as to the essence of its criminal law. While such secretiveness is obviously not the intent of the American law-makers, the result is nevertheless the same. The labyrinth of our law, with its conglomerate mass, discordancies, and uncertainties, is such that even the initiated at times finds it incomprehensible, unwieldy, and esoteric.

While there have been many attempts to explain our legal situation, no satisfactory correctives have been adopted. The stream of legal materials which must be consulted by lawyers and judges continues to flow relentlessly and unabatedly. In addition to the bulk and the diffusion of case law, contradictions of prior rulings and lack of a fixed policy have increasingly added to the lawyers' difficult task of understanding and predicting the law.

Yet the anachronism of American law has been partially abated and its day of reckoning postponed by the extensive development and use of secondary aids in legal research. In fact, it is a common practice for lawyers and judges to cite or use those publications which summarily describe legal rules as though they were the final arbiters of the law. The disturbing failure of the courts to restrain the length and number of their published opinions appears to be the primary reason for this development. Unless the judges set some control over their product, both as to bulk and as to volume, it is inevitable, as Mr. Chief Justice Harlan F. Stone warned, that our system of making the judicial reports the chief repository of the common law will break down of its own weight.

Awareness of this problem which faces the courts today enhances the need for organized instruction in the use of legal research materials. Such instruction has become an integral part of American legal pedagogy, that of acquainting the neophyte with the vast literature of the law and directing him in research methodology.

Books on legal research can generally be categorized as: (1) comprehensive or reference publications, (2) laboratory manuals or outlines and (3) the intermediate books which steer a middle course. These approaches attempt to satisfy the various pedagogical needs; however, each manifests certain disadvantages which are recognized by the authors of this volume. Messrs. Price and Bitner attempt to meet this problem by including in their book desirable features of all three plans. They hope to satisfy the objections to a comprehensive treatise, such as limited class time, through the arrangement of materials and typography. "Must" reading is in large type, followed often by discussion in smaller type, which amplifies the main statement. This arrangement provides a manageable text (in large type) for standard instruction while offering detailed information for the more intensive course or reference needs. Thus, the lawyer whose time is limited need only study the large type to gain familiarity with the essentials of legal research. Further, occasionally under "Notes," the authors include historical and other explanatory material for the benefit of librarians and teachers. In this manner, the book assumes the characteristics of a students' and a teachers' manual. In addition, the book should also be of substantial assistance as a reference tool for attorneys and students with legal problems.

Another commendable feature of this publication is its simple and lucid style. The inclusion of the maximum information under each topic results in some duplication, especially as to digests and citators, but the benefit gained by complete explanations as to research procedure vouchsafe this repetition. The frequent use of tables is of further aid to the searcher and the detailed index, by gearing the problems to the tables, makes them easily accessible.

The appendices will be of immeasurable assistance to librarians and other reference workers, since they are, for the most part, extensive, current revisions of tested research findings. Only those who have worked on comparable bibliographic listings can appreciate fully the many hours of effort which have gone into these apendices. The accuracy, completeness, and currency of the bibliographic information will undoubtedly place this book in the forefront of law library reference tools.

The book lends itself to the use or omission of optional materials. Among these "optional" chapters are: 4: Treaties; 5: Legislative histories; 9: Statutes in other forms; 10: Court rules; 17: Administrative law; 23: Restatements; 24: Law dictionaries; 25: Form books; 26: Loose-leaf services; 27: Miscellaneous and non-legal publications; and 29: English and Canadian material. These chapters can be used or not, as desired; however, problem sets have been prepared for each of them.

The final chapter of the book incorporates the essentials of Mr. Price's, *A Practical Manual of Standard Legal Citations*, an invaluable aid to legal writing.

This volume will assume a position among the outstanding American treatises and reference books on legal research and bibliography. Its quality is especially unique since it is in part the full harvest of the rich pedagogical and research experiences of a most distinguished and much loved law librarian, Miles Price.

ERVIN H. POLLACK

The Ohio State University
College of Law

PREFACE

This book is the authors' answer to the countless questions concerning how to find the law, which during nearly a quarter of a century have been asked of them by lawyers and students, at the library loan desk and in the classroom. Because these questions have assumed a definite pattern, the answers in this book emphasize perhaps more than is customary in such books the function of legal literature rather than the special characteristics of specific books, although existing law books in all categories are herein adequately described. The attempt has been made to show that when a problem arises which should be solvable by a law book, that book exists, and that it functions along well-defined lines which are herein described. Because of the increasing importance of statute and administrative law, special effort has been made to describe with more than usual fullness the literature and techniques in these fields. The tabular approach to the law has likewise been emphasized throughout. The bibliographical appendices and the list of abbreviations have been compiled with care, to make them at once practical, up to date, and accurate. Believing that an index is a major factor in the usefulness of any work such as this, the authors have supplied one that is unusually detailed.

Like all reference books, this one is the product of many hands. Friends and colleagues have most generously given of their services and made suggestions which have materially increased the value of the book. Although it is manifestly impossible to acknowledge our debt to most of them, some must be singled out for mention.

Fred B. Rothman, erstwhile law librarian, read the manuscript, and the book is much the better for his frank and constructive criticisms. Meira Pimsleur, of the Columbia University Law Library staff, was the expert and untiring bibliographer of the book. Others who have been most helpful include Charles J. Zinn, Legislative Counsel of the House of Representatives Committee on the Judiciary; Minnie Wiener, Librarian of the United States Renegotiation Board; Jean Ashman, Librarian of the United States Railway Retirement Board; James B. Childs, of the Library of Congress; Maurice Maxwell and John Burke, of Sweet & Maxwell, Ltd.; Howard Drake, Secretary and Librarian of the University of London Institute of Advanced Legal Studies; George A. Johnston and Leonard G. Wrinch, of the Law Society of Upper Canada; William T. Hibbitt, of the Carswell Company, Ltd.; Pauline E. Gee, of the Yale Law Library; and Mortimer Schwartz, of the University of Oklahoma Law School Library. The staff of the Columbia University Law Library have at all times been most patient and helpful; especially Virginia Gray, Charlotte Sherr, Joseph Katz, William Wiedman, Dorothy Chamberlain, and Florence Zagayko.

The following publishers have graciously permitted the reproduction in this book of material published by them, and have been helpful in other ways: American Law Book Co.; Butterworth & Co., Ltd.; Callaghan & Co.; Carswell Co., Ltd.;

Commerce Clearing House, Inc.; Lawyers Co-Operative Publishing Co.; Little, Brown & Co.; Prentice-Hall, Inc.; Shepard's Citations, Inc.; Sweet & Maxwell, Ltd.; and West Publishing Co. The authors are also grateful to Frederick C. Hicks for permission to bring up to date the List of Anglo-American Legal Periodicals, from the third edition of his *Materials and Methods of Legal Research* (Lawyers Co-Operative Publishing Co.), and for permission to use the list of Anglo-American abbreviations in that work as a checklist in compiling their own list.

To all others who have so generously helped the authors, they say a blanket "Thank You!"

MILES O. PRICE
HARRY BITNER

Columbia University,
New York.

TABLE OF CONTENTS

TABLE OF CONTENTS

APPENDICES

INDEX

EFFECTIVE LEGAL RESEARCH

A PRACTICAL MANUAL OF LAW BOOKS AND THEIR USE

Chapter 1

INTRODUCTION

A. Nature of Law as It Affects Law Books and Their Use.

Lawyers are probably more dependent upon the literature of their profession than their prototypes in any other field. They simply cannot function away from a working law library, because law books are not merely the repositories of secondary reference materials, but are the actual and indispensable source material of the law.

Law books differ greatly in form and use from those in other fields. This is a difference based upon the nature of law, which must be considered if the differences are to be understood and the books used intelligently. The philosophy of the law, is beyond the scope of this *Manual*, but some comprehension of it is vital to an understanding of why law books are as they are.

A practical definition of law is that it is the aggregate of rules recognized and acted upon by courts of justice. Most of these rules are not written down as such in law books so as to constitute authority that a court is bound to obey, but must be gathered from diverse sources. The sources of Anglo-American law are, roughly, the common law and legislation. Common law in turn included originally the law merchant, canon law, military law, and equity — some of which are now largely taken over by statutes. Statutes include constitutions, treaties, enactments of formal legislative bodies and of such subordinate legislation as that of municipalities, administrative bodies, and courts.

There are few constants in this law, but continual change, and these changes and the means for keeping abreast of them vitally affect law book composition and use. Changes may be gradual, as in a common-law rule modified by judicial decision; or sudden and revolutionary, as in a statute changing the common law.

The rules of the common law (which in effect is custom judicially recognized, as distinct from local custom, which must be pleaded and proved), are taken from decisions of appellate courts of competent jurisdiction, and grow by a process of synthesis from these decisions. By the same token, they may be modified or changed by decisions.

The kind of law of which the layman usually thinks is legislation — the product of duly constituted bodies authorized to make rules which, within the competence of the body making them (whether legislature, court, administrative agency, or municipality) are binding upon those subject to them. These rules, once made, are subject to interpretation by a court which may consider their constitutionality as well as their application to the factual situation then before it; or to amendment, repeal, or extension by the body promulgating them.

The significance of this with respect to law books is that these decisions as made and these rules as enacted are not published and arranged on book shelves by subject matter, but by jurisdiction and date. Thus, there is an enormous and constantly changing mass of decisions and legislative rules. From these the lawyer must speedily and accurately extract the law applicable to his specific problem, so as to be able with some degree of certainty to predict the action of a court to which the problem may conceivably be presented. How the lawyer or student is enabled to do this is the subject of this *Manual*. He who understands the why and how of law books has a very substantial advantage over him who does not.

B. Aim of the Search: What is Authority?

Jurors may be swayed by eloquence, but what the lawyer must rely upon in convincing a court is *authority* which that court is bound to respect. Accordingly, practically all law books are either books of authority, indexes to authority, or means for appraising the present value and status of authority.

Kinds of Authority. Authority is of two kinds, primary and secondary. Secondary authority is at most persuasive, and strictly speaking is not authority at all. Mandatory primary authority is what the lawyer seeks; lacking that, he may find persuasive authority useful.

Primary Authority. There are two kinds of primary authority: (1) direct legislation in force; and (2) judicial decisions. These are further subdivided into mandatory (or imperative) and persuasive authority.

Mandatory authority. Direct legislation in effect in the jurisdiction where enacted or promulgated is mandatory; outside it, it is not even persuasive, though decisions construing it occasionally are. An example of the latter is when a statute which has been copied from another jurisdiction comes before a court for interpretation in a case of first impression. Then, a well-considered decision on a like statute from a court of another jurisdiction may be highly persuasive, though in no way binding or imperative. Judicial decisions, when direct or "square" holdings, are mandatory authority when from a higher court in the same jurisdiction or from the same court (except when that same court exercises its undoubted power to overrule its own prior decisions).

When a court of competent jurisdiction hands down a decision under our system of the common law, that decision establishes a precedent binding upon the court rendering it and upon courts subordinate to it, until and unless it is reversed on appeal to a higher court, or is overruled by the same court in another and later case, or the subject matter is changed by statute. The fact of subordination binds the lower court; the policy of uniformity binds the court making the decision. But when it is demonstrated that the original decision was a blunder in the first place, or that conditions have so changed that the earlier rule is now manifestly erroneous, the court has not only the power but the duty to overrule itself when a later case involving the same rule presents itself. More often, the court will so whittle away at its old decision, in later ones, that it in effect undermines the authority of that decision without in so many words overruling it. The citator discussed in Chapter 28 has for one of its functions the notation of later decisions overruling or modifying the authority, as precedent, of earlier ones.

Persuasive authority. Legislation of itself, from another jurisdiction, is not even persuasive authority, though, as noted above, a decision construing it may be. Decisions may be persuasive authority when (1) from coordinate courts of the same jurisdiction (as from one or more Circuits of the United States Courts of Appeals); (2) involving dictum from any court in any jurisdiction; and (3) from courts of another jurisdiction.

The rationale of considering the decisions of courts of other jurisdictions is that, since all are construing the same common-law system, decisions, except where local conditions or statutes vary the rule, should be in harmony. Accordingly, New York courts cite Texas decisions and American courts cite English decisions — but only as persuasive makeweights.[1] When a court in one jurisdiction necessarily construes a law of another, however, conflict of laws rules dictate that the decisions of that other jurisdiction as to its own law are controlling; but even here the court of the forum does not hold that authority to be mandatory.

Authority as between federal and state courts. A United States Supreme court decision may be either mandatory or only persuasive in a state court. If it interprets federal legislation, including the Constitution, it is mandatory on state and federal courts alike as to the principle stated; otherwise, it is mandatory on federal but only persuasive in the state courts. Conversely, the pronouncements of the highest state courts as to their law are binding on federal courts unless a Constitutional question is involved. In the absence of rulings by the highest state courts, those of the intermediate courts are of at least persuasive authority, but those of a state trial court which does not publish or index its reports are not binding precedent upon federal courts.[2]

Dictum as authority. The status of dictum as authority is discussed in Chapter 11. Strictly speaking, it has none, even persuasive, as its subject matter by definition was not necessarily raised and considered in the decision in which uttered. In actual practice, however, well-considered dicta are often persuasive, some so much so that their original status as dictum is overlooked or forgotten, and they are cited as authority.

Secondary Authority. Secondary authority, so called, is not really authority at all. It comprises instead indexes to authority (case finders, digests, encyclopedias, *etc.*); and means (as citators) for appraising the value of authority when found. It can be highly persuasive, however, and well-written treatises, law review articles, and legal encyclopedias are frequently cited in legal writing.

C. The Role of Stare Decisis in Law Book Making.

The significance of the various kinds and degrees of authority stems from the rule of stare decisis which under our comon-law system so largely controls judicial decisions. A brief statement of this rule (about which more is said in Chapter 11) is that, under a precise set of facts, "a deliberate or solemn decision of a court or judge, made after full argument on a question of law fairly arising in a case and necessary to its determination, is an authority or binding precedent in

---

[1] For example, the controversial New York case of *Mitchell* v. *Rochester Ry. Co.*, 151 N.Y. 107, 45 N. E. 354, 34 L. R. A. 791, 56 Am. St. Rep. 604 (1896), has been cited in the opinions of the courts of twenty-seven other states.

[2] *King* v. *Order of United Commercial Travelers*, 333 U. S. 153, 68 S. Ct. 488, 92 L. Ed. 608 (1948); and numerous law review comments thereon.

the same court, or in other courts of . . . lower ranks within the same jurisdiction, in subsequent cases where the very point is again presented. . . ." [3]

This doctrine (which is subject to many qualifications and variations) functions as a graph, upon which every decision in point is represented by a dot. When a line is drawn through all of these dots, a definite curve or trend is discernible, enabling the lawyer to predict judicial action upon a like set of facts in the future. The curve or trend is the statement of a legal principle distilled from the decided cases and applicable in like future cases.

Law books are affected when the very latest reported case, instead of following the line of the earlier ones, deviates one way or the other, or even reverses its field and heads in the other direction. Similarly, a new statute may modify or repeal an old one or in effect abolish an entire line of common-law decisions. Therefore, law publishing is geared to high-speed distribution and indexing of law reports and statutes. The lawyer and student alike must be constantly on the alert to make certain that his research has not been nullified by a later publication than he has seen. There are indeed few constants in the law.

D. Law Book Characteristics.

Because primary authority is usually published in chronological rather than in classified order, and because the latest statute or decision may substantially alter or affect a legal rule, law books have assumed certain quite definite characteristics, a knowledge of which is essential to the searcher. Most law books bear a striking resemblance to each other. The familiar National Reporter System "advance sheet," is to a considerable extent, the epitome of law books. It has a *table of cases* (the most nearly universal of all law book features); a *table of statutes construed* (also, in some form or other, a common law book feature); a list of "*words and phrases*" defined (found in most digests and in many other books); and a *digest* or elaborate index which is the lawyer's most necessary tool for extracting the rules of case law. Other features of law books are *transfer or conversion tables* (from one form of statute to another, or from one form of case citation to another).

What to Look for in a Law Book. The reader should first of all ascertain what the law book covers — by subject matter and date — and how it is put together. The *title page* tells who wrote or edited the book and what it is about. If it is a supplement to another book, dates covered are usually noted. The *table of contents* furnishes valuable clues as to the organization of the book. Frequently, a very useful feature is the *preface or introduction*, which may supply a background or history of the subject matter of the book which aids the reader in his understanding of what it is about. Other characteristics are mentioned in the paragraph immediately above, and their presence or absence in a book should be ascertained, and where in it they are situated.

Abbreviations. Lawyers cite thousands of authorities from hundreds of publications. In order to lessen the prohibitive labor involved in writing these citations out in full, an elaborate system of abbreviated citations has been evolved, which is followed in all legal writing. For a description of this, *see* Chapter 32. Nearly every book in which abbreviations are employed lists them, together with the

---

[3] D. H. Chamberlain, *The Doctrine of Stare Decisis* (New York, Baker, 1885), p. 19.

full title of the work abbreviated. These lists are a necessary part of the lawyer's equipment, and a very full one is found in this *Manual*.

Speed of Publication and Supplementation of Law Books. Nearly all types of law books except student and philosophical treatises and dictionaries aim to keep up with the very latest developments of statute or case law. Therefore, law books are geared to speed of original publication and to frequency of supplementation.

Importance of Publication Dates. The *date* of a statute, case, treatise, or citator is one of its most vital elements. A superseded bit of authority is not only useless but dangerous. A secondary book of index — as a digest, practitioner's book or citator — depends for much of its value upon how recent it is. The searcher should therefore acquire the invariable habit of looking at the date, the title page, the notation on a supplement — anything which will tell him whether the publication he is consulting will do the job for him.

Many annotated statutes and digests are supplemented by "recompiled" volumes incorporating supplementary material, so that the publication dates of the bound volumes composing the set (as distinguished from the pocket supplements in the back of those same volumes) may vary greatly. For example, in the *United States Code Annotated*, Title 25, "Indians," was published in 1928 and has not been recompiled because it is not a very active topic, legislatively. On the other hand, titles involving bankruptcy, railroads, labor, and taxation have been recompiled in that set several times. In either case, a preliminary to search should be a glance at the title page. One would hardly expect to find the 1946 statute setting up an Indian Claims Commission in the 1928 volume of Title 25, but any law librarian has repeatedly seen law students waste time in futile search through a main volume published years before the statute they are seeking was enacted, ignoring the pocket supplement.

Always make certain whether what is wanted is covered by the *main work* or by the *supplement*. In law books the supplement is quite likely to be a "pocket part," in the back of the main volume and keyed to that volume so as to bring its sections up to date and also to add new sections or other material. Often this new material consists of the *total revision or repeal of much that is in the main volume.*

Tools for Using Law Books. The fundamental materials of the law — the statutes and reported cases — are by far the best indexed of all professional literature. Through the available indexes it is possible, if not always simple, to extract the legal principles set forth in every reported American case from 1658 to a few days ago; to find such a case by its name; and to tell whether it is still good authority. Similarly, this can be done for statutes and for English material. These tools are known as indexes, tables, digests, citators, form books, treatises (including also legal encyclopedias and periodicals), and dictionaries. A knowledge of their resources and use is the subject of this *Manual*.

Chapter 2

TYPES AND IMPORTANCE OF LEGISLATION

A. Increasing Importance of Legislation.
B. "Conventional" and "Subordinate" Legislation.
C. Classes of Conventional Federal Legislation and Their Authority.

A. Increasing Importance of Legislation.

The first of the primary sources of legal authority to be considered here is legislation. Although formerly the lawyer almost always began his legal research in a given problem by going first to the decided cases and only later to the statutes, legislation has become so increasingly important in recent years, particularly since the advent of the "New Deal," that more and more often that order is reversed.

> Inevitably the work of the Supreme Court reflects the great shift in the center of gravity of lawmaking. Broadly speaking, the number of cases disposed of by opinions has not changed from term to term. But even as late as 1875 more than 40 per cent of the controversies before the Court were common-law litigation, fifty years later only 5 per cent, while today cases not resting on statutes are reduced almost to zero. It is therefore accurate to say that courts have ceased to be the primary makers of law in the sense in which they "legislated" the common law. It is certainly true of the Supreme Court that almost every case has a statute at its heart or close to it.[1]

B. "Conventional" and "Subordinate" Legislation.

"Legislation" is usually thought of by the layman as the enactments of the federal Congress and the various state legislatures. It does of course include these; but it also encompasses a great deal more, much of which has a considerably more direct impact upon the average citizen than the output of the legislatures.

Conventional Legislation. This, the output of the legislature, comprises not only the enactments of the federal Congress and the state legislature, but also constitutions, treaties, and interstate compacts, the latter two of which are not initiated by the legislatures but require their approval. Municipal ordinances are regarded in some states as conventional legislation (local laws), and in others as subordinate, delegated legislation.

Subordinate Legislation. This is issued within the framework of conventional legislation, and comprises rules and regulations of administrative bodies, the executive orders and proclamations of the President of the United States and of the governors of the states, municipal ordinances (in some states), and the rules of courts.

---

[1] Felix Frankfurter, Sixth Annual Benjamin N. Cardozo lecture delivered before the Association of the Bar of the City of New York, March 18, 1947; reprinted here by permission from 2 *The Record of the Association of the Bar of the City of New York*, No. 6 (1947).

Within its broad constitutional and statutory limitations, a rule of practice of the United States Patent Office, a schedule of utility rates by the New York Public Service Commission, a rule of the Vermont Supreme Court, or a rationing order of the Office of Price Administration is as truly legislation as an enactment of the federal Congress. In the aggregate, this subordinate legislation is vastly important and has given rise to law books (loose-leaf services, for example) unknown to earlier generations of lawyers.

C. Classes of Conventional Federal Legislation and Their Authority.

Although federal legislation is described in this chapter, nearly all that is written here applies equally to state legislation. For more detailed accounts of state legislation, *see* Chapter 7.

Constitutional Provisions as to Federal Laws.   The Constitutional provisions relating to federal legislation are Article I, § 7, paragraph 2; Article I, § 6, paragraph 18; and Article VI, paragraph 2. Judicial interpretation of these three paragraphs restricts the designation "law" to three categories of legislation: the act, the joint resolution, and the treaty. The approval of an interstate compact is by joint resolution. Whether or not the reorganization plan is formally designated as law, there can be no doubt that, when approved under the terms of a reorganization act, a plan has the force of law.

Conventional Federal Legislation Below the Constitutional Level. Federal conventional legislation below the Constitutional level comprises the following forms, most but not all of which are duplicated in corresponding state legislation:

Simple, concurrent and joint resolutions; acts, treaties, and interstate compacts.

The last two forms might be designated as "hybrid" legislation, since they require the action of an agency outside the legislature. Acts and joint resolutions for convenience are further subdivided into "public" and "private," but legally there is no distinction, as both have the force of law.

Simple resolutions. The resolution (popularly called "simple resolution") has no legislative effect outside the house in which it originates. It becomes operative upon passage by that house, requires no signature by the President, and concerns only the business of the one house. Creation and appointment of committees (other than joint, which are created by concurrent resolution), approval of the printing of copies of documents for which money has already been appropriated, inquiries addressed to government departments, expressions of sympathy or policy, and directing an investigation by a committee (other than a joint committee), are by simple resolution.

The investigations of the House Committee on Un-American Activities, for example, were launched by such a resolution. A really important legislative development is the calling up by simple resolution of specific bills for consideration at a definite time, which effectively expedites the business of the Congress. A less laudable use is as a sounding board for a legislator to propose legislation which he knows can not be enacted into law, but upon which he may force newsworthy debate. The enacting clause consists of the one word "Resolved." The text of many but not all, as passed, is found in the *Congressional Record* as of the day of passage. Later, all are printed in the *Journal* of the house passing them. They are not published as slip laws or in the *Statutes at Large*, but are indexed in the *Congressional Record Index*, and (by subject only) in the *Congressional Record Daily Digest*.

Concurrent resolutions. The concurrent resolution is, in form, one passed by both houses, as shown by its enacting clause: "Resolved in the House of Representatives (the Senate concurring)," or the converse when originating in the Senate. It is binding upon neither house until agreed to by both. Since in its modern form it does not contain a proposition of legislation, it is not sent to the President for his signature. Its purpose is to create and appoint joint committees, arrange for joint sessions of the two houses, and to express fact, as well as principles and purposes of the two houses.[2]

A modern use is to disapprove (as provided in the various reorganization acts) of reorganization plans submitted by the President. In its function of expressing policy, unsuccessful attempts have been made to extend its scope to the termination of existing legislation (to end the war with Germany in 1920, for example). In effect it enables the Congress to legislate without Presidential approval or veto.[3] Thus, by the Neutrality Act of 1939, the Congress by concurrent resolution was empowered to find the existence of a state of war putting the act into operation; and the Lend-Lease Act empowered the Congress by concurrent resolution to terminate the President's authority under the act, on or before a given date.

An important and frequently exercised purpose is to recall a bill from enrollment, subsequent to passage by both houses but prior to Presidential approval, for correction.

(In state legislation, petitions to Congress are normally by concurrent resolution, as are ratifications of amendments to the federal Constitution and proposals for amendments to the state constitutions.) Concurrent resolutions are printed in the *Statutes at Large* (from which it might be inferred that they do constitute legislation of limited scope), and their passage through Congress is indexed in the *Congressional Record Index* and in the *Congressional Record Daily Digest*.

Joint resolutions. In federal legislation the joint resolution is a law, just as is an act. Joint resolutions proposing constitutional amendments, having passed both houses, are not submitted to the President for his signature, but all others are. The procedure in both the House (Rule XXI)[4] and the Senate (Rule XIV)[5] is the same for bills (which become acts upon passage) and for joint resolutions. The enacting clauses are, respectively, "Be it enacted" and "Resolved," and it is said that the joint resolution more often has a preamble, but there the difference ceases.

Until the 77th Congress (January, 1941), acts and joint resolutions were numbered separately (but chronologically) as "Public, No. 844," and "Pub. Res., No. 106" (in succession on the same page of the *Statutes at Large*), but beginning with that Congress, in 55 *Statutes at Large*, both acts and joint resolutions have been listed as "Public Law No. . . ." without distinction.

Although the *House Manual* in Section 397 states that "At one time they [joint resolutions] were used for purposes of general legislation; but the two Houses finally concluded that a bill was the proper instrument for this purpose," examination of joint resolutions shows that little if any distinction is in fact observed. The joint resolution, however, is the usual vehicle for stating policies. Texas (5 Stat. 797) and Hawaii (30 Stat. 750) were annexed to the Union in that manner. Joint resolutions in both bill and slip law form are distributed to the public (if designated as public laws) through the Superintendent of Documents and are printed in the *Statutes at Large*.

The situation in state legislation is different, in that, in some states, the joint resolution is not law but occupies a lesser status.[6]

Acts of Congress. Acts are the common means of legislative expression, 90 per

---

[2] *House Rules and Manual*, H. Doc. No. 700, 75th Cong., 3d Sess. 396 (1938).
[3] Howard White, *The Concurrent Resolution in Congress*, 35 Am. Pol. Sci. Rev. 886 (1941).
[4] See footnote 2 above.
[5] Senate Manual, S. Doc. No. 11, 81st Cong., 1st Sess. 18 (1949).
[6] *Ex parte Hague*, 105 N. J. Eq. 134, 147 Atl. 220 (1929), aff'd N. J. Misc. 89, 150 Atl. 332 (1930); *People ex rel. Argus Co*, v. *Palmer*, 146 N. Y. 406. 42 N. E. 543 (1895).

cent of Congressional enactments taking that form. The enactment clause is "Be it enacted by the Senate and House of Representatives of the United States of America in Congress Assembled." Bills which have passed both houses, been prepared for the President's signature and then approved by him or passed over his veto, become acts.

Interstate compacts. There are sanctioned by Article I, Section 1, clause 3 of the Constitution, to the effect that "No state shall, without the consent of Congress . . . enter into any agreement with another state. . . ." Congressional consent is given directly by act (or occasionally by joint resolution), or by approval of a state constitution embodying the compact, or it may be inferred from legislative acts recognizing the validity of the agreement. Compacts thus are not a separate form of federal legislation. Approval may be given before or after the states have entered into their compact, which is done by parallel enactments of the several state legislatures concerned.[7] A list of all interstate compacts entered into up to 1949 is contained in the 1949 annual *Handbook* of the National Conference of Commissioners of Uniform State Laws; and later compacts have been listed in succeeding *Handbooks*.

Such compacts are commonly used to settle boundary disputes and to provide for various kinds of cooperative state action, particularly in the development of natural resources. The agreement between New Jersey and New York, setting up the Port of New York Authority was such a compact. (*See* Joint Resolution of August 23, 1921, 42 Stat. 822.) Although such compacts are not to be confused with uniform state laws, they are essential to the effective promotion of uniformity in certain fields, such as the control of river and harbor traffic between adjacent states, irrigation and flood control between contiguous states, certain aspects of fire and life insurance and taxation, reciprocal grants of penal and police jurisdiction, *etc*.[8]

Reorganization plans. Although reorganization plans are printed in the *Statutes at Large*, and require positive or negative action of the Congress or of one house thereof (provisions of the different acts vary), they are nearer to administrative than to conventional legislation, and so are discussed in Chapter 17.

Treaties. These are discussed in Chapter 4.

Notes

"Private" and "Public" laws. There are no hard and fast rules for determining whether a piece of legislation is to be designated as private or public. The final decision has been one for the Editor of Laws of the Department of State (whose duties in this respect were transferred to the Administrator of General Services by the amendment of September 23, 1951, by Section 112 of Title 1 of the *United States Code*). He has used as criteria the debates as published in the *Congressional Record;* the nature, effect, and scope of the legislation; whether it amends existing legislation (in which case it will be classed as was the original act); and his own best judgment.

[7] For example, the Ohio River Valley Water Sanitation Compact (1948), variously enacted as Ill. Laws 1939, p. 310; Ind. Laws 1939, c. 315; Ky. Acts 1940, c. 150; N. Y. Laws 1939, c. 945; Ohio Laws 1939, p. 447; Pa. Acts 1938, c. 117; and W. Va. Acts 1939, c. 38.

[8] The literature is extensive. Recommended are Andrew A. Bruce, *The Compacts and Agreements of States with One Another and with Foreign Powers*, 2 Minn. L. Rev. 500 (1918); Felix Frankfurter and James M. Landis, *The Compact Clause of the Constitution: a Study in Interstate Adjustments*, 34 Yale L. J. 985 (1925); William J. Donovan, *State Compacts as a Method of Settling Problems Common to Several States*, 80 U. of Pa. L. Rev. 5 (1931); *A Reconsideration of the Nature of Interstate Compacts*, Note, 35 Col. L. Rev. 76 (1935); *Constitutional Restrictions on Interstate Compacts*, Note, 50 Col. L. Rev. 994 (1950).

Private legislation is that which is passed for the benefit of an individual or group, not of direct or immediate interest to the government or the public. It includes for the most part pensions, authorization of the appointment of individuals to represent the United States on international bodies, the relief of a person (or his estate) injured by government action (as when a Navy truck damages his property), the removal of political disabilities, *etc.* Where there is doubt as to the proper classification, the public classification is usually assigned. In practice, there has been some inconsistency, particularly as to acts granting land to counties or municipalities, which have been classified both ways. The classification is important because private laws are not distributed to the public through the Superintendent of Documents, as are public laws, though individual ones may be secured from the General Services Administration. Assignment of "chapter" numbers to new laws ignores the distinction between public and private, so that chapter 1 may be a public law, chapter 2 private, *etc.*, and so published in different volumes of the *Statutes at Large.*

Definitions of Congressional legislation. The official statement of the nature of the various kinds of Congressional legislation is found in the *House* and *Senate Manuals,* of which new editions appear at the beginning of each Congress. The most concise statement of legislation and of the legislative process, derived from these sources, is on page 1507 of volume 1 of the *Checklist of United States Public Documents, 1789-1909.*[9] An excellent brief statement is in Charles J. Zinn, *How Our Laws are Made.*[10] For the most complete discussion of the three types of Congressional resolutions, *see* Denys P. Myers, *Joint Resolutions Are Laws.*[11] *The Concurrent Resolution in Congress,* by Howard White [12] is the most complete treatment of this type.

Legislation preceding the Constitutional period. It is frequently asked why, although this country cast itself adrift from England by the Declaration of Independence in 1776, our national legislation covers only the period from 1789 on. As a matter of fact, there was legislation prior to 1789, though superseded by that of the Constitutional period. State legislation has continued without interruption from Colonial days.

Pre-Confederation legislation. Most of the area now comprising the United States of America was for varying periods from 1492 governed by Spain, the Netherlands, England, France, or Mexico. Each governing power introduced many of its own laws and customs, and some of these have left a permanent impress upon our existing legislation. However, it is not the function of this book to trace this impress. An excellent collection of early charters, laws, and the like, relating to American law and history, can be found in Henry Steele Commager's *Documents of American History.*[13] These documents date from the statement of the privileges and prerogatives granted to Columbus on April 30, 1492, and include Colonial charters, British and other acts affecting the Colonies, the various declarations leading up to and including the Declaration of Independence, *etc.*

A concise account of the sources of American law is given by Richard R. Powell in his *The Law of Real Property,*[14] Vol. I, Chapter 4. Much of the common law and many of the statutes of the mother countries were adopted by the states of the United States and are still of some effect. In general, it may be said that the upper date limit set in these "reception" statutes is July 4, 1776, or that of the accession of the territory concerned to the United States, whichever is later.

Confederation legislation. From 1774 to 1789, this nation was governed by the Continental Congress; from March 1, 1781, by authority of the *Articles of Confederation.* Although it is seldom necessary to consult the legislation of the Confederation, the Continental Congress did legislate throughout its existence, and that legislation is still occasionally the subject of litigation. (*See* the "Table of Statutes Cited and Construed," in 14

---

[9] 3d edition, Washington, D. C., United States Government Printing Office, 1911.

[10] Issued as a special supplement to the *United States Code Congressional and Administrative Service,* 1952, and reissued as a separate pamphlet by the West Publishing Company, St. Paul, Minnesota.

[11] 28 A. B. A. J. 33 (1942).

[12] See footnote 3 above.

[13] 5th edition, New York, Appleton Century, 1949.

[14] New York, Matthew Bender & Co., 1949.

Digest of United States Supreme Court Reports 35, 67 (1950).[15] While this legislation in general shared the weakness of the *Articles*, some of the ordinances (as they were called) were of far-reaching and lasting effect. The most important of these was the *Ordinance of 1787*, which created the Northwest Territory from territories ceded by the states of the United States, set up its form of government, and provided for the formation of new states from it. It profoundly influenced the laws and government of those states north of the Ohio River. Other ordinances established the United States and state boundaries; still others set up the various governmental departments and regulations for their operation. Treaties with foreign governments were an imporatnt function of the Continental Congress.

The *Articles of Confederation* are printed in the *Journals of the Continental Congress*, in the *United States Code* as an "Organic Law of the United States," and in the statutes of several of the states of the United States.

Ordinances of the Confederation were printed in the *Journals of the Continental Congress* (*see* page 47), and have never been collected elsewhere. Unfortunately these ordinances are nowhere printed in their entirety, as finally enacted by the Congress. On the contrary, they are printed piecemeal, as part of the minutes of Congressional sessions during which they were debated and amended — a clause here, a section there — so that it is very difficult to determine the exact form of any given ordinance.

The Ordinance of 1787 is printed in all edition of the *United States Code* and in the statutes of some of the states north of the Ohio River.

Treaties. The text of the treaties concluded by the Confederation is found in the *Journals*.

Legislative proceedings. The *Journals of the Continental Congress*, 1774-1789, have appeared in several editions. *See* page 47.

Confederate States of America (1861-1865). The Confederacy throughout its existence legislated, and its statutes and those of the member states are found in law libraries. There has been litigation on some of these enactments, as noted in the "Table of statutes construed" in the *Digest of United States Supreme Court Reports, supra*.

---

[15] Rochester, Lawyers Co-operative Publishing Company, 1950.

Chapter 3

PUBLICATION OF
CONVENTIONAL FEDERAL LEGISLATION

A. Constitutions.
B. Slip Laws.
C. United States Statutes at Large.
D. Statutory Compilations.
E. Authority of Statutes as Publications.

A. Constitution.

The federal Constitution, with its amendments, is the broad statement of principles which since 1789 have guided and controlled the laws and lawmaking of the United States, and of the several states. Adopted after the failure of the weak Confederation, it is for most practical purposes the beginning of our national legislation.[1] The first ten amendments, the so-called "Bill of Rights," were proposed by Congress (along with two others not approved by the requisite three-fourths of the states and so not adopted), on September 29, 1789, and ratified by 1791.

Where Found. In printed form the Constitution is this country's most available piece of legislation, being found in almost every general encyclopedia, reference work, and compilation of federal or state statutes, whether official or unofficial; in most constitutional law treatises and case books; and in separate form in numerous official and unofficial single volumes or pamphlets. It is also printed in the biennial *House* and *Senate manuals.*

The Constitution as Consulted by Lawyers and Students. The government publishes a "literal print" of the Constitution and its amendments, which is in a convenient form for reference by those desiring only to examine the text unencumbered by other matter. Because the Constitution, probably above all other statutes, requires interpretation, those who consult it commonly desire an annotated edition. The annotation may be to the cases only or it may include more or less elaborate explanatory matter.

Library of Congress edition.[2] For many purposes, this is the most useful edition. This is particularly true when the searcher seeks a good basic knowledge of the principles of the Constitution and of its interpretation, rather than every case

---

[1] For pre-constitutional legislation, *see* page 10.

[2] The Constitution of the United States of America; analysis and interpretation. Annotations of cases decided by the Supreme Court of the United States to June 30, 1952. Prepared by the Legislative Reference Service, Library of Congress, Edward S. Corwin, editor. Washington, D. C., U. S. Govt. Print. Off., 1953. (82d Congress, 2d Session. Sen. Doc. No. 170.)

which has construed it. This edition is in effect an encyclopedic treatment of the Constitution, and though it is useful to lawyers, one need not be a lawyer to use it with profit and understanding. As compared to a privately published annotated edition, such as in the *United States Code Annotated* or *Federal Code Annotated,* it suffers from a lack of systematic supplementation.

This edition contains a "literal" print of the Constitution and amendments, for those who need only the text. There is a detailed account of the ratification of the several amendments. Then the Constitution is annotated, by article or amendment, section and clause, word for word. The edition is virtually a Constitutional history as well as an annotated Constitution, because under each clause or section there is set forth not only the current interpretation thereof, but also a history of the legal route which the courts have traversed in arriving at their present interpretation. The range of source materials in the annotations is wide, including citations to and quotations from both federal and state court decisions, as well as from commentaries and treatises on American constitutional law and government, arguments of counsel, and occasionally federal statutes.

As an aid to understanding the Constitution, Professor Edward S. Corwin, the editor, has contributed a prefatory essay which is a survey of the historical development of four major concepts by which the Supreme Court has been guided in interpreting the Constitution. These are: judicial review, dual federalism, separation of powers (including delegation of legislative power and the reign of law), and due process. There is also a good subject index.

In annotated editions of statutes. The practicing lawyer, although he will often refer to the Library of Congress edition for a quick brush up on the meaning of the Constitution and citations to leading cases interpreting it, will normally need to consult a fully annotated edition which cites not only *all* the United States Supreme Court cases reasonably in point, but also those of the state courts, as well as appropriate opinions of the Attorney General of the United States, Presidential executive orders and proclamations, Board of Tax Appeals and Tax Court decisions, and occasional law review articles. These are found in the *Federal Code Annotated* and in the *United States Code Annotated,* which have the added virtue of annual pocket part supplementation and frequent interim service pamphlets. In addition, most of the state statutory compilations annotate the federal Constitution.

Amendments. The amending process is described in Article V of the Constitution. Amendments are proposed by a joint resolution of the Congress passed by two-thirds of the quorum present and voting in each house, and must be adopted or ratified by at least three-quarters of the states, either by convention or by their legislatures, as the states decide. The language of the Constitution is so broad that many questions as to the scope and procedure of the amending process have arisen. These are discussed in Lester B. Orfield, *The Amending of the Federal Constitution.*[3] Annotated editions of the Constitution contain a brief statement as to the adoption of each amendment.

Judicial History of the Constitution and Amendments. The "Shephardizing" of the federal Constitution (that is, giving its legislative and judicial history subsequent to adoption) is described in Chapter 28. It is unique in that, of course, the Constitution can never be held to be unconstitutional.

---

[3] Ann Arbor, University of Michigan Press; Chicago, Callaghan & Co., 1942.

Notes

Proposed Constitutional Amendments. Proposed amendments, since they are in form joint resolutions, are printed in the *Statutes at Large* for the session of Congress which proposed them. The General Services Administration will furnish on request full data concerning the present status of pending amendments.

There are three compilations of *proposed amendments* covering the period to January 3, 1947. The first comprises volume II of the American Historical Association's *Annual Report* for 1896, and consists of a prize essay by Herman V. Ames on *The Proposed Amendments to the Constitution During the First Century of its History* [4] [to 1889], printed as House Document No. 353, part 2, 54th Congress, 2d Session. *Proposed Amendments to the Constitution of the United States . . . December 4, 1889 to July 2, 1926* [5] [and *December 6, 1926 to January 3, 1947*],[6] list chronologically the various proposals since submitted to the Congress. "Proposed" as used in the titles of these three documents means only that the proposals listed were introduced into the Congress, not that they were submitted to the states. Very few ever reached the latter stage.

Legislative History and Intent. This is to be found in the notes and journals of some of the delegates to the constitutional convention, particularly James Madison, Rufus King, William Paterson and James McHenry; in the variant texts of the proposed drafts; and in the record of the debates of the Federal Convention of 1787, especially again as reported by Madison. While the definitive edition of Madison's notes is that by Gaillard Hunt and James Brown Scott, *The Debates in the Federal Convention of 1787 which Framed the Constitution of the United States of America, Reported by James Madison,*[7] the most convenient and complete record of the convention and the resolutions leading up to it, is in the *Documents Illustrative of the Formation of the Union of the American States*, compiled by Charles C. Tansill.[8] It contains the important documents beginning with the declarations and resolves of the First Continental Congress of October 14, 1774, on through the records of the constitutional convention debates, texts of the various proposed drafts, the resolutions submitting the final draft and those of the first nineteen amendments to the Constitution. This compilation may be said to have superseded the cumbersome and less complete earlier *Documentary History of the Constitution of the United States of America*, 1786-1870.[9] Another standard work, though less complete in fundamental documents, is *The Records of the Federal Convention of 1787*, edited by Max Farrand.[10]

A secondary source of great importance is *The Federalist*, a series of contemporary essays by Madison, Jay and Hamilton, advocating the adoption of the Constitution, and explaining in considerable detail the intent of its framers. There have been numerous editions. Negatively significant is *Constitutional Chaff — Rejected Suggestions of the Constitutional Convention of 1787*, compiled by Jane Butzner from the notes of Madison, Pierce, King, and Yates.[11]

Foreign Constitutions. Although the United States lawyer has infrequent occasion to consult the constitutions of foreign countries, that necessity does arise. A three-volume compilation by Amos J. Peaslee, *Constitutions of Nations; the First Compilation in the English Language of the Texts of the Constitutions of the Various Nations of the World, Together with Summaries, Annotations, Bibliographies, and Comparative*

---

[4] House Doc. No. 353, part 2, 54th Cong., 2d Sess. Washington, D. C., U. S. Govt. Print. Off., 1897.

[5] Prepared by Library of Congress, Legislative Reference Service. Washington, D. C., U. S. Govt. Print. Off., 1926. Senate Doc. No. 93, 69th Cong., 1st Sess.

[6] Revised by Senate Library under direction of Carl A. Loeffler. Washington, D. C., U. S. Govt. Print. Off., 1947.

[7] New York, Oxford University Press, 1920.

[8] Prepared by Library of Congress, Legislative Reference Service. Washington, D. C., U. S. Govt. Print. Off., 1927; also as House Doc. No. 398, 69th Cong., 1st Sess.

[9] U. S. Bureau of Rolls & Library (of Department of State). Washington, D. C., Department of State, 1894-1905. 5 volumes.

[10] New Haven, Yale University Press, 1937. Revised edition. 4 volumes.

[11] New York, Columbia University Press, 1941.

Tables,[12] collects this material. *New Constitutions in the Soviet Sphere*, edited by Samuel L. Sharp; [13] and *The Constitutions of the Americas as of January 1, 1948*,[14] cover the areas named.
Chicago Press, 1948.

B. Slip Laws.

The first officially published form of federal Congressional legislation is of each enactment — whether in one paragraph or hundreds of pages — as a separate pamphlet, known as a "slip law." This is the same form as is later bound and indexed for each year as the *Statutes at Large*. Slip laws are issued in two series, the *Public* and *Private* Laws, containing together both the acts and joint resolutions. Through the 76th Congress (1940-42), the *Public* and *Private Joint Resolutions* were published as two series separate from the Acts, but with the beginning of the 77th Congress they were merged as above, as *Public* and *Private Laws*. A slip law is shown below, with numbered arrows pointing to its various parts.

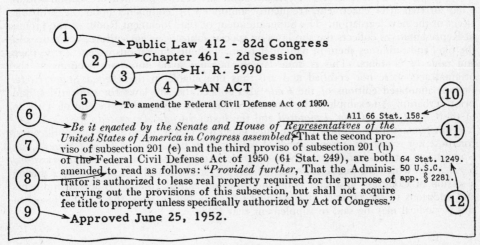

Public Law 412 - 82d Congress
Chapter 461 - 2d Session
H. R. 5990
AN ACT
To amend the Federal Civil Defense Act of 1950.

All 66 Stat. 158.

Be it enacted by the Senate and House of Representatives of the United States of America in Congress assembled, That the second proviso of subsection 201 (e) and the third proviso of subsection 201 (h) of the Federal Civil Defense Act of 1950 (64 Stat. 249), are both amended to read as follows: "*Provided further*, That the Administrator is authorized to lease real property required for the purpose of carrying out the provisions of this subsection, but shall not acquire fee title to property unless specifically authorized by Act of Congress."

64 Stat. 1249.
50 U.S.C.
app. § 2281.

Approved June 25, 1952.

Exhibit 1

1. *Law number* of a designated Congress.
2. *Chapter* and session number. (The session is important here and here only.)
3. *Bill number*. (Here, House of Representatives number 5990, not to be confused with House Report — "H. Rept.")
4. *Kind of legislation* (an Act here).
5. *Preamble.*
6. *Enacting clause;* "Resolved" in a resolution.
7. *Popular name* or short title. *See* page 56.
8. An example of *"perpetual revision." See* also page 26.

9. *Approval date.* If effective on a different date, that date is specified in the act. When passed over the President's veto, that is indicated.
10. *Statutes at Large* citation for the act as it will appear in bound form.
11. *The first section of any act is unnumbered.* In legal writing, however, the first section of an act containing more than one section is nevertheless cited as "Section 1."
12. *Editorial matter in the margin;* here, a citation to a statute amended.

The information given above "an Act" is for index or identification purposes only and is not a part of the enactment. As such it is useful and is repeated in the *Statutes at Large*. Until the publication of the bound volume of the *Statutes at Large* (about fourteen months after the slip law publication), the *Law* and *Bill* numbers together are

---

[12] Concord, N. H., Rumford Press, 1950.
[13] Washington, D. C., Foundation for Foreign Affairs, 1950.
[14] Edited by Russell H. Fitzgibbon, Cullen B. Gosnell, and others. Chicago, University of Chicago Press, 1948.

the law's identification tag. In the example above, the matter in the margin has been inserted in slip laws only since mid-1951. It corresponds to similar rubrics in the *Statutes at Large*. The *Statutes at Large* citation given there for each act, while subject to correction in the published volume, is undoubtedly correct. "All 66 Stat. 158" means that all the text is on page 158; when it begins elsewhere on a page, the exact place of beginning and the words at the top of the second and succeeding pages of the act in the *Statutes at Large* are indicated, corresponding to "star paging" as described on page 94.

Chapter simply fixes the order of approval, Chapter 1 being the first law (whether Public or Private) approved during a session, Chapter 2 the second, and so forth. It has no other significance. The bill or resolution number is useful in tracing legislative history, since the number is retained throughout the bill's progress in Congress, and into the *Statutes at Large*.

Other Forms of Publication of Federal Slip Laws. The Commerce Clearing House, *Congressional Legislative Reporting Service* supplies the unofficial but accurate text of both federal and state laws immediately after passage. Non-subscribers may buy individual enactments. Occasionally, unusually important laws are printed in the "Statutes" section of the *United States Law Week*, reaching subscribers within a week of approval. Loose leaf services often distribute the text of pertinent legislation within a day or two after enactment, frequently annotated by comments upon the probable effect of the new legislation. The Superintendent of the Document Room of the House of Representatives collects the slip laws on special subjects, as agriculture, veterans, and the like, and publishes them in pamphlet form, without annotations except a title page and table of contents. This is done largely because some important sections of the original acts were not codified and are thus unavailable in the *United States Code*. Private annotated editions of the *Code* also collect the slip laws for some titles, and print verbatim. An example is the internal revenue laws, printed at the end of Title 26 of the *United States Code Annotated* and the *Federal Code Annotated*.

From January 1939 on, perhaps the most generally useful form of slip law publication for those not requiring extreme speed of receipt, is in the unofficial *United States Code Congressional and Administrative News* (formerly the *United States Code Congressional Service*), in which the public laws are collected in semi-monthly pamphlet issues during a session of Congress, and later cumulated into an annual volume. Since amendments and additions to the *District of Columbia Code* are public laws, the current issues of this periodical may be said to supplement that *Code*.

Notes

Availability of Slip Laws. Both *Private* and *Public Laws* are individually listed in the *Monthly Catalog of United States Publications*, under the heading "Congress." Individual private laws may usually be secured free from the National Archives; the *Public Laws* are sold individually, usually at five cents apiece, or may be subscribed for at $3.00 a session. They are usually received about three weeks after approval date.

Numbering of Bills and Enactments. Through the 74th Congress, all bills and their resulting enactments were renumbered at the beginning of each *session* of a two-year *Congress*, so that not only the number of the Congress but also the session were necessary parts of a citation. Beginning with the 75th Congress (1937), however, all bills and acts are numbered consecutively throughout a *Congress*, and are not renumbered each *session.* Chapters renumber anew with each *session* however.

C. United States Statutes at Large.

These, the federal session laws, are the first permanent form of federal statutes. They are published after the end of each session of a Congress, and contain the legislation enacted during the calendar year of that session. *See* "Notes," p. 19 *infra*, for historical data on the publication of Statutes at Large.

Contents of Statutes at Large. Beginning with volume 65 (for 1951), the

Statutes at Large have contained only public and private laws, joint and concurrent resolutions, proclamations, reorganization plans, and Constitutional amendments. The treaties and executive agreements of international import, formerly published in the *Statutes at Large*, are now printed in a new series called *United States Treaties and other International Agreements*, volume 1 of which covers 1950. Treaties are discussed in Chapter 4.

Varying content over the years. There has been considerable variation. *Public laws, private laws, treaties* (including, through volume 17, those with the Indians), have been included regularly, beginning with volume 9, with compilations of this material before 1845 printed in the earlier volumes. *Concurrent resolutions were* first published in volume 29 (1893-95); *executive agreements* in volume 47 (1931-33). *Presidential proclamations* have been printed with more or less regularity since volume 3, but there is no complete collection in print. *Reorganization plans*, if approved, have been in the public law part, beginning with volume 53 (1939); all, whether approved or not, may be found in the *Congressional Record*.

The *Statutes at Large* from time to time have seen the publication of material not specifically within their field. The first edition of the *Revised Statutes* was volume 18, part 1; *Revised Statutes Relating to the District of Columbia, December 1, 1873*, was part 2 of that volume. (This made part 3 the repository of the public laws, an exception to the rule which has caused considerable confusion.) Volume 44, part 1 was the first edition of the *United States Code*, 1926. Volume 53, part 1, was the *Internal Revenue Code*, of 1939.

Status of the Statutes at Large. The practicing lawyer is chiefly interested in public laws (treaties are discussed in Chapter 4) and for him four things are emphasized:

1. With the exception of the *Revised Statutes* sections still in force, and those titles of the *United States Code* re-enacted into positive law, the *Statutes at Large* are still the "best evidence," to be cited in legal writing. Those titles of the *United States Code* not reenacted into positive law are only prima facie the law. In legal writing of all types, unless a statute has been reenacted as positive law in a code and repealed thereby in its original form, it is as a Statute at Large that it is cited, together with its title, if any (as "Immigration and Nationality Act of 1952"). The *United States Code* citation is usually added, but for convenience only, and the *section numbers cited in legal writing are those of the original act, not of the Code.* The Code is so much more convenient to use that law students at least tend to forget that, with the exception of a few of its titles, it is no positive law, but only prima facie the law.

2. If the original form of an act (including the numbering of its sections) is desired, the *Statutes at Large* is the best place to find it. To be sure, there are conversion tables from the original act and sections to the *Code* title and sections but they often lead to error in the transfer.

3. Many acts are not codified at all, and some which have been codified are only partly so, with other sections uncodified. Revenue acts are examples of the latter.

4. Tracing a *Statutes at Large* section into its corresponding *United States Code* section is achieved through use of Table *I b* of the *Code*, thus: the act of May 26, 1942, Chapter 319, § 11, 56 Stat. 303 (1943), is in 12 U.S.C. § 1743 (1946 ed.), as shown by that table.

Although for convenience the lawyer consults the *United States Code* for most purposes, he may not ignore the legal evidence from which it was derived, the *Statutes at Large*.

Form of Statutes at Large. The material in the *Statutes at Large* is copied verbatim from the original enrolled acts, treaties, reorganization plans, *etc.*, of which they are composed. The public and private laws are reprints of the slip laws, except that the identification material is in the margin instead of at the top.

---

606   PUBLIC LAWS—CHS. 563, 564, 573—DEC. 11, 12, 1945   [59 Stat.

[CHAPTER 564]

December 11, 1945
[H. R. 1123]
[Public Law 255]

AN ACT

To provide for a temporary increase in the age limit for appointees to the United States Military Academy and the United States Naval Academy

U. S. Military Academy.
10 U. S. C. §§ 1094, 1100.

Appointees; age limit, etc.

Be it enacted by the Senate and House of Representatives of the United States of America in Congress assembled, That section 1318 of the Revised Statutes, as amended by the Act of March 30, 1920 (41 Stat. 548), is amended to read as follows:

"Appointees shall be admitted to the United States Military Academy only between the ages of seventeen and twenty-two years, except in the following case: Any appointee who has served honorably not less than one year in the armed forces of the United States during any of the present wars, and who possesses the other qualifications required by law, may be admitted between the ages of seventeen and twenty-four years: *Provided*, That whenever any member of the graduating class shall fail to complete the course with his class by reason of sickness, or deficiency in his studies, or other cause, such failure shall not operate to delay the admission of his successor."

U. S. Naval Academy

Candidates; age limit, etc.

SEC. 2. Section 1517 of the Revised Statutes as amended (34 U. S. C. 1045), is amended to read as follows:

"Candidates allowed for Congressional districts, for Territories and for the District of Columbia, must be actual residents of the districts or Territories, respectively, from which they are nominated. All candidates for admission to the Naval Academy must be not less than seventeen years of age nor more than twenty-one years of age on April 1st of the calendar year in which they enter the Academy: *Provided*, That any candidate who has served honorably not less than one year in the armed forces of the United States during any of the present wars and who possesses the other qualifications required by law may be admitted between the ages of seventeen and twenty-three years."

Approved December 11, 1945

[CHAPTER 573]

December 12, 1945
[H. R. 694]
[Public Law 256]

AN ACT

To amend section 321, title III, part II, Transportation Act of 1940, with respect to the movement of Government traffic.

Transportation Act of 1940, amendment
54 Stat. 954.
49 U. S. C. § 65 (a).

Government traffic.

Be it enacted by the Senate and House of Representatives of the United States of America in Congress assembled, That subsection (a) of section 321 of title III, part II, of the Transportation Act of 1940, be, and the same is hereby, amended by striking out the following: "except that the foregoing provision shall not apply to the transpor-

---

Exhibit 2

a. *Index material in the margins.* This material is, as with the slip laws, intended for identification and index purposes. There are found the *bill and public or private law number*, and the date of approval. Also in the margin are rubrics comparable to the headnotes of a case: they *index* the matter in the paragraphs they adjoin. They may save much time when the searcher is interested in only one or a few sections of a long act and does not know the section number, as they lead swiftly to what he wants. They also identify by exact citation amended acts mentioned in the adjoining text only by name or date, and save the searcher from recourse to a transfer table.

b. *Chapter numbers.* Chapter numbers, by which the public and private laws are arranged, are consecutive, in a single series which includes both private and public laws. That is, in 59 *Statutes at Large,* for example, Chapter 564, a public law, is found in the public law section, but Chapters 565-572, private laws, are in another volume with private laws. The material is thus in chronological, not subject order. Chapter numbers begin anew with each volume of the Statutes at Large, while law numbers are consecutive through an entire Congress. Thus, in 66 *Statutes at Large,* covering the second session of the 82d Congress, Chapter 4 is Public Law 256 of the 82d Congress.

Through volume 38 (1913-15), joint resolutions, though laws, were not given chapter numbers, but a resolution number only, in brackets. Beginning with volume 39, joint resolutions were assigned chapter numbers, but not public or private law numbers. Beginning with volume 56, for the 77th Congress (1942), acts and joint resolutions alike are numbered as public or private laws, without distinction.

c. *Table and index.* Following the table of contents in each volume is the authentication of the legislation contained therein. Then follow the "List of Public Laws (or Private, in another table) Contained in This Volume," by *number,* title, approval date, and page where printed; and a list of reorganization plans, if any, is included therein. *This is the place to search when the citation is to the law by public law number, not chapter.* If, as seldom happens, the citation is to chapter only of a given Congress and session, no table is needed, since the chapters are consecutive. Each volume of the public laws is fairly well indexed, by subject, department, bureau, popular name of act, individuals named in acts, amendments to the *Internal Revenue Code* and other *Code* sections enacted into positive law, and reorganization plans. Congressmen connected with legislation are not indexed herein; but are indexed in the Congressional Record. Private laws are separately indexed, when published in a different volume from the public laws; otherwise there is a single index.

Notes

Historical Notes on the *Statutes at Large*. Through the 74th Congress (1935-36), the *Statutes at Large* contained the legislation of an entire *Congress* (two years' duration). The enactments of a *session* (there were usually two, but more, if necessary, in each Congress), were collected at its end in unbound volumes known as *Pamphlet Laws.* (Beginning with the first session of the 73d Congress, 1931-32, the title was *Session Laws.*) They were superseded at the end of each Congress by the *Statutes at Large,* and the publication was abandoned altogether with the close of the 74th Congress, when the *Statutes at Large* themselves became session laws.

The first edition, *Laws of the United States* (the Folwell edition), was published under the authority of the Act of March 3, 1795 (1 Stat. 443), and its twelve volumes covered the first four Congresses (1789-1813). It was superseded by the Bioren and Duane editi̶̶̶̶̶̶̶̶̶̶̶̶̶̶ ̶̶il 18, 1814 (3 Stat. 129), covering in its ten volumes the first ̶̶̶̶̶̶̶̶̶̶̶̶̶̶ (1789-1845), when again a new start was made with the series whi̶̶̶̶̶̶̶̶̶̶ed the entire nationhood period (1789-1949), through the first session of the 82d Congress.

In this series, the public laws for the first 28 Congresses, 1789-1845, were collected in volumes 1-5; volume 6 contained the private laws for the same period; volume 7, Indian Treaties, 1778-1845; volume 8, Treaties with foreign nations, 1778-1845, together with a general index to the first eight volumes. Volumes 9 to 17 were similar in form and content to the present volumes, but covered more time. Volume 9 covered three Congresses, volumes 10 to 12, two Congresses each; from which time until volume 49 (1936), one Congress was covered. Beginning with volume 18 (under the Act of June 20, 1874, 18 Stat. 113) publication, which up to that time had been by Little, Brown & Co., was taken over by the Government Printing Office.

Beginning with volume 64, covering the legislative year 1950, all material other than treaties and other international agreements has been compiled by the General Services Administration. The Department of State, as in the past, continues to be responsible for publishing the international agreements.

D. Statutory Compilations.[15]

Need for Compilations. Although the session law form of conventional legislation is the best published evidence of the majority of federal and state enactments, it is not the form most frequently consulted by the lawyer. There are four good reasons for this. *First*, the session laws, in all but two states are printed in volumes arranged chronologically by approval date, not by subject. *Second*, session laws commonly include private acts and those of only local interest. *Third*, and most important, a high percentage are soon repealed, amended, or expire by some date or event limitation within themselves (as the end of an appropriation year or of a war); or an act with such a limitation may be extended by later legislation. *Finally*, the session laws take up too much expensive shelf room.

All this results, after a very few sessions of a legislature, in a hopeless mass of legislation, the extent, meaning, and operative force of which it is not possible to determine. What the lawyer must have and does have is a throwing together of laws of public general interest in force, in a usable arrangement, constantly kept up to date. This has been done in several ways, the chief of which follow.

Forms of Compilation.

1. The acts of public general interest are thrown together, in the *same chronological order as originally passed*, but with temporary and repealed acts omitted. This, the form of the English *Statutes Revised*, is rare in the United States.
2. The repealed and temporary enactments are omitted, and the remainder are printed *verbatim in classified order, without change in text.*
3. The repealed and temporary acts are omitted; *the remainder combined and re-written as necessary*, and arranged in *classified* order. This is the form of the *United States Revised Statutes*, the *United States Code*, and of most state compilations. In this form the compilation may be in whole or in part re-enacted as positive law, superseding the original session law from which derived. Otherwise such compilations are only prime facie the law, rebuttable by reference to the original session laws. Even so, they are so convenient and well-done that they are the form of statute commonly consulted by lawyers.
4. The laws in force are *rewritten and classified; additional provisions and new legislation added;* and the final result enacted as *the complete and only law*, within the limitations of the act. A code may cover all the law of the jurisdiction, or only the substantive, adjective, or criminal, *etc.* The form is common in European systems but is rare in America, except for adjective, and to some extent, criminal codes.

The above compilations are given various titles by various st█████████ definite meaning. They may be called "Revisions," "Consolidations, ████████pila-tions," or "Codes," indiscriminately, but in the United States almost all have the form of paragraph 3, above.

United States Revised Statutes. The only complete revision of the "public general laws of permanent interest" in federal legislation was the *Revised Statutes of the United States . . . in Force on the First Day of December, One Thousand Eight Hundred and Seventy-Three* (1875). The existing mass of legislation from 1789 on was carefully analyzed, laws of temporary, private, or local interest (or those parts which were of such interest) discarded; the remainder was *arranged in classified order, rewritten as necessary, and re-enacted as the law, repealing*

---

[15] Although not legal words of art, "law" as applied to legislation often means a session law; and "statute" a revision, compilation or codification of laws of public general interest in force. The terms are often so employed in this book.

and superseding those Statutes at Large from which it was derived. However, the revision aroused so much dissatisfaction, because of errors and of the feeling that the revisers in many instances had exceeded their authority, that a second edition was published in 1878, under the authority of the Act of Congress of March 2, 1877 (19 Stat. 268) (1878).[16]

This second edition did two things. First, by authority of omnibus correction laws it corrected the errors of the first edition; second, it brought the edition down to date by notation of pertinent legislation up to January 1, 1878. However, *the status of the second edition is different from that of the first.*

Legal status of the first and second editions. Although the *Revised Statutes* is very old as United States statutes go, much of it is still the law of the land, either as enacted or, usually, as amended by later enactments; [17] and although in practice the lawyer may first learn of the existence of the pertinent *Revised Statutes* section upon which a *United States Code* section is based from the parallel citation always given in that *Code* section, the *Revised Statutes* as amended is the best authority, not the *Code* sections. Many sections of the *Revised Statutes* are still very much alive.

The first edition was re-enacted as the law, repealing and superseding the *Statutes at Large* or parts thereof from which it was derived. In citing it, therefore, it is neither necessary nor proper to cite these *Statutes at Large*, though of course *later amending* enactments should be cited.

The second edition, in so far as it corrects the errors in the first, has a different status: *the new sections or parts* are only prima facie the law, rebuttable by reference to the *Statutes at Large* from which derived. Because of the way corrections (including repeals) are printed in the second edition, however, there is no difficulty in determining which is which. As shown by the page reprinted below, it is done by means of brackets [] and *italics.*

---

216   TITLE XIV.—THE ARMY.—CH. 1

Civil employ-   SEC. 1224. [*Officers of the Army on the active list shall not be separated*
ment prohibited.   *from their regiments or corps for employment on civil works of internal im-*
5 July, 1838, c.   *provement, nor be allowed to engage in the service of incorporated companies,*
⬛⬛⬛⬛⬛ 5 p.   *or be employed as acting paymaster, or disbursing agent of the Indian depart-*
⬛⬛⬛⬛⬛⬛   *ment, if such extra employment require that he be separated from his regiment*
27 Feb., 1877, c   *or company, or otherwise interfere with the performance of the military duties*
69, c. 19, p. 243.   *proper.*] [No officer of the Army shall be employed on civil works or
                      internal improvements, or be allowed to engage in the service of any
                      incorporated company, or be employed as acting paymaster or disburs-
                      ing-agent of the Indian Department, if such extra employment requires
                      that he shall be separated from his company, regiment, or corps, or if
                      it shall otherwise interfere with the performance of the military duties
                      proper.] [See § 2062.]

Exhibit 3

In effect, the second edition *Shepardizes* the first, up to January 1, 1878: Material contained in the first edition but later repealed is bracketed in italics, and the repealer

---

[16] For a documented historical discussion of the two editions of this work, *see* Ralph H. Dwan and Ernest R. Feidler, *The Federal Statutes, Their History and Use,* 22 Minn. L. Rev. 1008, 1012 (1938).

[17] *See* for example, 59 Stat. 606, c. 564, *supra,* page 18.

cited in italics in the margin. New material is bracketed in roman type. Therefore, in consulting the second edition, particular attention should be paid to brackets and to italicized matter, whether in text or margin.

The first edition is still the standard for citation in some government departments, but it is seldom seen any more, except in its original form as volume 18, part 1, of the *Statutes at Large*, the second edition being usually cited instead. In either case, the edition cited (1875) or (1878) should form part of the citation.

Form and makeup of the Revised Statutes (1878). The revision is in 74 "titles" (the last one containing the repeal provisions), and most titles are subdivided into two or more "Chapters." The sections are numbered consecutively, from Section 1 in Title 1, to Section 5601, the last, in Title 74. This useful feature (abandoned in the *United States Code* to facilitate addition of sections where desired), simplifies citation, since only the section number is required.

As with the *Statutes at Large*, the *margins* contain identification and index material: the subject matter of the section, the *Statutes at Large* citation from which the section was derived (and, in the second edition, later repealers or modifying statutes), and some citations to cases interpreting either the original statute or the *Revised Statutes* section. There is a table of "Errors in Marginal References," at page 1099.

Index to Revised Statutes. There is a subject index.

Tables. As with nearly every law book where there has been a shift from one form of statute or text section numbering to another, there are indispensable parallel transfer tables. *Errors in Marginal References* has been referred to above. *Reference Index . . . from Statutes to Sections* is a table, arranged by *Statutes at Large* approval date, chapter, section, volume, and page, cross-referencing to the resulting *Revised Statutes* section. This table also serves as a *table of repeals*.

Tracing a Revised Statutes section into the United States Code. This is done through Table Ia of the *Code*, thus: R. S. § 2938 became 19 U. S. C. § 378. Table VIIIa of the *United States Code* (*Revised Statutes* repealed), however, reveals that this section was later repealed by an act of February 28, 1933, 47 Stat. 1349, c. 131, § 1 (1933).

Repeals of Revised Statutes sections. Table VIII, *supra*, lists repealed sections (whether ever in the *Code* or not), and cites the repealers.

United States Code. The lawyer as a practical matter consults either an official or a private edition of the *United States Code* (cited as U.S.C.) more often than any other form of federal statute. This is the current official compilation by subject of the public "general and permanent laws of the United States in force. . . . No new law is enacted and no law is repealed. It is prima facie the law. It is presumed to be the law. The presumption is rebuttable by production of prior unrepealed Acts of Congress at variance with the Code." [18] In other words, the *Code* is an informal rearrangement by subject, and a very restricted rewriting of the federal legislation from 1789 to date, of a public and permanent nature; discarding all but a few private acts, repealed and expired acts and those not of general interest. Treaties are not included, except as editorial matter where needed.

Authority of the Code. The *Code* is informal in that, while the selection, arrangement, and wording are done under the supervision of a committee of the House of Representatives by commercial publishing firms and the result is pub-

_____

[18] 44 Stat., part 1, Preface (1926).

lished by the government, Congress does not *re-enact* the *Code* as the law. It is a convenient editorial job, but with the exceptions noted below, of titles re-enacted into positive law, the law is still the *Revised Statutes* or *Statutes at Large* from which the *Code* titles and sections are derived.

Consequently, citation in legal writing is to the original statutes (with parallel reference to the *Code*). On the other hand, not to be academic about it, the work is so well done that as a practical matter the *Code* for most purposes of daily use has largely supplanted the statutes which are the real authority.

It was the original intention to take up the "titles" of the *Code*, one by one, and reenact them as positive law, as was done with the *Revised Statutes*, and about a fifth of the titles have been so treated, as noted in the preface of each *Code* volume or supplement.

Assignment of material to the *Code* is purely an editorial matter. Sections included in one edition may be omitted from the next; or may be changed from one title to another. That is one reason why the date or supplement number of the edition cited should be given. The rewriting is very slight, being confined almost entirely to the omission of introductory words of the original act, such as "Provided," or "That," at the beginning of a section; and the substitution of *Code* title and section numbers in the body of the text for the official title and sections of the act from which derived, when these are mentioned. Sometimes, as when an act affects a plurality of agencies, a section may be repeated *in toto* in several *Code* titles, except for the omission of the names of agencies not pertinent to the title wherein printed.

Title 26 is not listed in the Preface to the *Code* as among those enacted into positive law. This is because, through an oversight in drafting, the act of February 10, 1939, c. 2, 53 Stat. 1, nowhere mentions the *United States Code*. It provides instead that the new compilation "hereby enacted into law . . . be known as the Internal Revenue Code and may be cited as I. R. C." There is thus the anomaly that although the frequently-amended *I. R. C.* as a practical matter is kept up to date by Title 26 of the *United States Code*, that title is only prima facie the law, and the *I. R. C.* is the authority to be cited. The distinction, while academic, is always made. The error has been avoided in the enacting clauses of all later codifications, which are in the following form: "Title 14 of the United States Code, entitled 'Coast Guard' is hereby revised, codified and enacted into law, and may be cited as 'Title 14, United States Code, section —' as follows:"

Note that to avoid confusion, section numbers of the *codifying act* (as in the *Statutes at Large*) are spelled out: "Sec. 2, sec. 3"), while those of the *codified title* (of the *United States Code*) as printed in that act are designated as "§ 2, § 3." *The codified title is set out in the unnumbered Section 1 of the codifying act;* Sections 2 and following of that act are saving clauses, the repealers of prior legislation, *etc.*, but not part of the *Code* title.

Makeup of the United States Code: section numbers. The *Code* discards entirely the consecutive numbering of sections covering the entire work in one sequence, as found in the *Revised Statutes*. Instead, the material is divided into fifty "titles," for each of which the section numbers begin anew with number 1. Accordingly, a citation to a section of the *Code* must include also the title number, which was not necessary with the *Revised Statutes*. Depending upon the amount of material in a title, it may be subdivided as follows:

(1) Title; (2) Part; (3) Chapter; and (4) Section; of which only the title and section numbers need be given in the citation.

Several titles, as Title 29, Labor; Title 35, Patents; and Title 50: War and National Defense, have *appendices*, but the appendix is not properly an integral part of the *Code*. Usually the appendix prints only pertinent agency rules of practice, but in some, acts of a *temporary* nature are printed for convenience. An example is the Trading with the Enemy Act of 1917, in the appendix to Title 50.

Where, as frequently happens, it is desired to cite editorial matter (or an uncodified statute) contained in a note to a *Code* section, it is done by adding "note" to the section citation. Thus, 26 U.S.C. § 1100 note. There are many gaps in section numbering, so as to leave room for new sections within a title or chapter. Thus, Title 33, Chapter 10 (1946), ends with section 475, but the next chapter begins with section 491.

The titles of the Code, after the first six (which have to do with the organization and operation of the government), are roughly alphabetical by subject, though this is not a sure guide. Thus, Title 7 is Agriculture, 8 is Aliens and Nationality, 9 is Arbitration, *etc.*

Tables of contents. In one way the makeup of the *Code* resembles a typical case digest: each title begins with a table of contents—that is, a table of chapters by number and caption—and at the beginning of each chapter there is a similar expanded table for that chapter.

Text notes. (1) The text often is not identical with that of the act from which derived (as shown in the example on page 25), though the changes, except as noted below, are of form, not substance. (2) Substantive provisions of some statute sections may be altered by a Presidential executive order, under an enabling statute. Tariff rates are an example. (3) The consecutive order of the sections does not necessarily follow that of the statute. Consequently, the *Code* is not a very satisfactory source for the text of the original statute as a whole, though it may be for an individual section thereof. (4) Parts only of a statute may be codified, and not the entire statute. Thus, a purely procedural section may be omitted from the *Code*. An example is 26 U.S.C. § 1100 note, where that portion of the Revenue Act of 1942 relating to practice before the United States Tax Court is set forth in a note, but is not a part of the *Code* itself. The fact that material is thus included in a note most emphatically does not mean that it is not the law; it means merely that it is not part of the *Code*. (5) The provisions of a statute may be altered by a reorganization plan, as in the example shown above; this is especially true where there has been a change of the title or functions of an agency.

Editorial matter notes. Below the text of a *Code* section, editorial notes give all or part of the following information: (1) derivation of codified sections, where earlier statutes have been enacted into positive law (as in the *Revised Statutes*); (2) codification data; (3) revisers' notes, if any; (4) citations in which the substance of amendments to the section is set forth; (5) cross-references to related *Code* sections; (6) notes of transfer of functions to another agency; (7) citations to or texts of executive orders, proclamations, or reorganization plans by the President under specific legislative authority; examples are changes in tariff rates under reciprocal agreements, the enumeration of arms, ammunition, and implements of war; changes of title and transfer of functions of agencies under reorganization plans, and the like; (8) definitions of terms; and (9) the effective date and interpretation of the original act.

Perpetual revision. Although several enactments may be cited in parentheses as authority for any given section of the *Code*, under the system of "perpetual revision" prevailing in most legislatures, the latest amendment of a statute usually (1) supersedes the earlier forms by substituting the amendment itself (". . . is amended to read as follows"); or (2) adds an entirely new paragraph to it without disturbing the existing text (". . . is amended by adding at the end thereof the following new sentence"). In other words, although an individual statute section may be a synthesis of several antecedent enactments, its final form is usually either that of the latest enactment cited as a source (1 above); or the next-to-the-last enactment, plus the last (2 above). Few statute sections are amended any more by the mere substitution of one word or sentence for another, or by the deletion of a word or sentence; the section is more likely to be reenacted in its new form, *in toto*. Enough are still amended by substitution of one word for another, however, to require the comparison of the *Code* with the original laws. *See* page 18 for example of two types of amendment.

63 Stat. 864, to give effect to former provisions of section 778 of this title.

1 →

§ 778. Administration by Secretary of Labor; delegation of powers.

2 →

Sections 751–756, 757–791 and 793 of this title shall be administered by the Secretary. The Secretary is authorized to delegate to any officer or employee of the Department of Labor any of the powers conferred upon him by said sections. (As amended

3 →

Oct. 14, 1949, ch. 691, title II, § 205 (a), 63 Stat. 864; 1950 Reorg. Plan No. 19, § 1, eff. May 24, 1950, 15 F. R. 3178, 64 Stat. 1271.)

AMENDMENTS

4 →

1949—Act Oct. 14, 1949, cited to text, amended section generally to give effect to section 3 of 1946 Reorg. Plan No. 2, cited to text, which abolished the United States Employees' Compensation Commission and transferred its functions to the Federal Security Administrator.

TRANSFER OF BUREAU, APPEALS BOARD, AND FUNCTIONS

The Bureau of Employees' Compensation, established within the Federal Security Agency by Agency Order 58 of July 16, 1946, set out under this section, was, together with its functions, transferred to the Department of Labor to be administered under the direction and supervision of the Secretary of Labor, and the functions of the Federal Security Administrator, and of the Federal Security Agency, with respect to such Bureau and with respect to employees' compensation (including workmen's compensation), were transferred to the Secretary of Labor, all of such functions, except those not included in the transfer, to be performed by such Secretary or, subject to his direction and control, by such officers, agencies, and employees of the Department of Labor as he shall designate, by section 1 of 1950 Reorg. Plan No. 19, cited to text and set out below. Section 2 of such Plan transferred to the Department of Labor the Employees' Compensation Appeals Board which had also been established within the Federal Security Agency by said Agency Order 58, and transferred the functions of the Federal Security Administrator, with respect to such Board, to the Secretary of Labor. Such section 2 further provided that said Board shall continue to have authority to hear and, subject to applicable law and the rules and regulations of the Secretary of Labor, to make final decision on appeals taken from determinations and awards with respect to claims of employees of the Federal Government or of the District of Columbia.

REORGANIZATION PLAN NO. 19 OF 1950

15 F. R. 3178, 64 Stat. 1271

EMPLOYEES' COMPENSATION FUNCTIONS

§ 1. BUREAU OF EMPLOYEES' COMPENSATION

The Bureau of Employees' Compensation of the Federal Security Agency, together with its functions, is transferred to the Department of Labor and shall be administered under the direction and supervision of the Secretary of Labor. The functions of the Federal Security Administrator, and of the Federal Security Agency, with respect to the Bureau of Employees' Compensation and with respect to employees' compensation (including workmen's compensation) are transferred to the Secretary of Labor: *Provided,* That there are not transferred by the provisions of this reorganization plan (1) any function of the Public Health Service; (2) any function of the Federal Security Agency or the Federal Security Administrator under the Vocational Rehabilitation Act, as amended (including the function of assuring the development and accomplishment of State rehabilitation plans affecting beneficiaries under the Federal Employees' Compensation Act); nor (3) the function of developing or establishing rehabilitation services or facilities. The functions transferred by the provisions of this section shall be performed by the Secretary of Labor or, subject

1. Section number.
2. Text proper, showing an example of "rewriting" in the *Code:* the original act reads "This Act shall be administered by the Administrator."
3. Statutory authority for the *Code* section, including a reorganization plan. This section is an example of "perpetual revision," in which the latest amendment cited combines all the earlier forms in one current superseding enactment. *See* "Perpetual Revision," p. 24. The parenthetical citation affords an accurate means of determining the exact section of the original act (§ 205a here) from which the *Code* section was derived. This may also be done through Table I(b), "Statutes Included," of the *Code.*
4. Editorial matter, identified by its smaller type than the *Code* proper.

Exhibit 4

Indexes and tables. The *Code* has a voluminous subject index, a table of acts by popular name (as the Taft-Hartley Act), and a table of government agencies and their statutory set up. There are also extensive tables of statutes included in the *Code*, with their corresponding *Code* location (e.g., that the Act of September 19, 1922, c. 346, § 3, 42 Stat. 850, is 15 U. S. C. § 143); of statutes repealed; and of statutes eliminated. These and their use are described, along with other indexes and tables performing the same functions, in Chapter 8.

New editions and supplements to the Code. The first edition of the Code appeared in 1926. New editions have been issued approximately every six years since; cumulative supplements are published annually. The 1952 edition will be issued in 1953 in five or six volumes.

United States Code: Unofficial Annotated Editions. To the legal purist, a statute is not really authority, only a decision of an appellate court being that. Accordingly, the lawyer believes that a statute means only what the courts say it does, and for most of his work with statutes consults an annotated edition. In such an edition the text of the *Code* is of course identical with that of the official edition, and the editorial material is substantially so, but each section of the *Code* is followed by digests of judicial opinions and opinions of the attorneys general interpreting it. An annotated edition of a statute thus possesses some of the characteristics of both a digest and a citator, informing the lawyer of the statute's meaning and present value as authority.

There have been several private annotated editions of the *United States Code*, of which only those described below are of present interest.

United States Code Annotated.[19] The first annotated edition of the United States Code bore this title (cited U. S. C. A.)

Content: text of the official Code. The complete text of the official edition, with the same section numbering, and substantially the same notes and other subsidiary editorial material, is printed. Where the editorial material is not identical, it is usually because of a time lag between the publication of the *U. S. C. A.* pocket parts and the official edition. Since the same editorial staff compiles both sets of notes, the earlier-printed *U. S. C. A.* supplements, tables, and indexes often contain material not yet found in the official, but which will appear there later. Each of the more recent recompiled volumes has its own scope note, setting forth the contents and special features of that volume.

Content: additional material not found in the official edition. Verbatim *texts of pertinent statutes* are printed for some *Code* titles. For example, the revenue acts from 1924 to date are printed as a supplement to Title 26. *Court rules* are found in five different places, as shown by the index. For some titles, particularly when they have been revised, there is a *historical or critical essay* by a member of the Bar. Examples are commentaries on the federal organic laws, the Chandler Act, and the Lanham Trade-Mark Act.

Annotations. These are digests of official and unofficial federal and state reports, and of the opinions of the United States Attorney General. Whenever *Code* titles are revised and renumbered, annotations to the old sections are brought under the comparable section, if any, in the new edition.

Indexes and tables. These are very similar to those in the *United States Code; see* pages 26 and 59. An additional index, not found in the official edition, is the *Index to Legislative History and Congressional Comment,* in the final index volume,

---

[19] St. Paul, Minn., West Publishing Company, 1927-52 (current) 50 titles in 84 volumes.

which is in effect a subject index to Congressional committee reports on public laws enacted, as published since 1941 in the *United States Code Congressional and Administrative News.*

Supplementation. There is a thrice-yearly *pamphlet service*, cumulated at the end of the year into pocket parts, making it a quarterly service.

The pamphlets serve the dual purpose of printing the new enactments, as codified, and supplementing the annotations, tables and indexes of the complete *U. S. C. A.* Except for the annotations, the *U. S. C. A.* may be said to be supplemented by the semi-monthly (during sessions of Congress) issues of the *United States Code Congressional and Administrative News*, where the *conversion tables from slip law to Code* are unofficial but accurate. Frequently, when new legislation of a particularly important nature is enacted, a special pamphlet edition confined to that act, in codified form, is issued by the *U. S. C. A.* within a few days of enactment, together with all revisers' notes and other editional matter. This has also been done for some entire titles when re-enacted into positive law. For example, when Titles 18 and 28 were so re-enacted, pamphlets were issued for each, containing the full text of the statute and all historical and revisers' notes. *Re-compiled volumes* are printed as needed, combining all existing material for a given title or part thereof into a single new volume, to be supplemented in turn by pocket parts. Whatever the form of supplementation, the matter supplemented is indicated on the title page of the supplement, leaving no reason for the searcher to omit any of the units necessary to a complete search. *Always look at the publication date of any unit or pocket part consulted.*

Federal Code Annotated.[20] This edition of the Code differs from the official chiefly in that it is annotated by the cases and certain other opinions. It contains the usual tables and indexes.

Content: text of the official edition. The complete text of the organic documents and of the several titles and sections of the *Code*, as well as the various agency rules of practice as found in the official edition is printed, but the editorial notes of the official edition are not copied. Where the compilers of the official edition have in their rewording of the statutes altered (in the opinion of the compilers of the *F. C. A.*) the true meaning of the original, the *F. C. A.* "is either made to conform literally to the authoritative enactments, or explanatory notes are placed under all objectionable sections calling attention to what is editorial language as distinguished from the true wording of the enactment." In practice, these notes are for the most part explanatory rather than critical or corrective.

Content: additional material, not found in the official edition. *Magna Carta* is printed in the volumes of organic laws. The Revenue acts from 1913 to 1938 (preceding the *Internal Revenue Code)* are reprinted and annotated in material supplementary to Title 26. *The F. C. A. does not annotate the sections of the Internal Revenue Code as such,* but as part of a comprehensive "Income Tax Digest" which includes in one schematic arrangement (as set forth in volume 6) annotations of all income tax statutes, whether in Title 26 or not. However, for each *Internal Revenue Code* section for which there are cases, there is a cross-reference to the corresponding paragraph in the Income Tax Digest. *Uncodified laws, treaties and proclamations* (that is, legislation never placed in the *Code),* are

---

[20] Indianapolis, Ind., Bobbs-Merrill, 1937-52 (current) 13 volumes in 20.

annotated in a separate and unique volume. Citations include "superseded and repealed sections of the *Revised Statutes*, Public Acts and Resolutions of Congress which were not carried either in the United States Code or Federal Code Annotated, and Private acts; treaties with Indians and foreign governments; Proclamations of the President." The arrangement of statutes and treaties is chronological, with separate tables for each category. *United States court rules* are in a separate volume.

Annotations. Annotations are to official and unofficial federal and state reports, Attorney General's and Judge Advocate General's opinions, executive orders, proclamations, and occasionally to law review articles.

Indexes and tables. These are very similar to those of the official *United States Code*.

Supplementation. (1) "Current Service" is a pamphlet service for the legislation of the current year, unannotated, appearing bi-monthly during sessions of Congress, the issues of which are cumulated into annual annotated pocket supplements at the end of the legislative year. When an especially important statute is enacted, a special additional pamphlet edition is issued, in slip law form. (2) Bound supplements. There is a ten-year cumulative supplement covering the period through January 30, 1947. The pocket parts of the original volumes and the current service supplement these. (2) Recompiled volumes are issued as necessary, for the various titles. A complete search, then, may involve the original volume, 10-year supplement, annual pocket part, and the current service supplements to date.

E. Authority of Statutes as Publications.

The authority of the various published forms of statutes has already been discussed in describing those publications. A summary at this point seems convenient, however. The *style* of statutory citation is described at pages 326–331.

Enrolled act. In the federal government (and state practice is similar), after a bill has been passed by both houses of Congress, it is "enrolled" on parchment and sent to the President for approval. Experience has demonstrated the fallibility of the copyist, who often omits words or even whole sentences. If the error is discovered before the President has approved, or it has been re-passed over his veto, the enrolled bill may be recalled for correction, by a concurrent resolution of both houses. However, once it has been approved and thus become an act, the enrolled act, under the doctrine of *Harwood* v. *Wentworth* [21] is conclusive evidence both of its passage and its terms, even though it be shown that, as enrolled, it omitted vital clauses or in other ways differed from the act as passed by the Congress. The act stands and can only be corrected by another act. The same is true in many states, where the court must resort to the copy attested, enrolled, and deposited with the Secretary of State. It is a matter of the separation of powers—the court cannot undo the legisature's work for it. In some states, however, the enrolled bill is only prima facie evidence, and resort may be had to the legislative journals to discover the bill's true form.[22]

As a practical matter, the enrolled act is not cited, unless the accuracy of the printed copy is challenged, but it is available for reference in case of repugnance between it and a later printed copy. One of the following printed forms of the act is therefore cited.

---

[21] 162 U. S. 547, 16 S. Ct. 890, 40 L. Ed. 1069 (1896); *see also Gardner* v. *The Collectors*, 6 Wall 499, 18 L. Ed. 890 (U. S. 1868).

[22] For a discussion of the problem, *see* J. A. C. Grant, *Judicial Control of the Legislative Process: the Federal Rule*. 3 Western Pol. Q. 364 (1950).

Slip law. Cite only until the *Statutes at Large* or session law containing it is published. When state session laws are cited by chapter or number and section (as Ala. Laws 1943, No. 6, § 6), rather than by volume and page, laws found in unofficial advance sheets may be cited without mentioning the advance sheet.

Statutes at Large and Session Laws. Cite until and unless expressly repealed by a later codifying statute re-enacted into positive law, after which it should no longer be cited as authority. However, when a re-enacted code section has later been amended or a new section added, cite both the code and amending session law. Where the statute has been made part of a compilation which is only prima facie the law and not re-enacted into positive law, cite the session law from this, followed by the compilation form.

United States Revised Statutes. When still in force, cite without the statute from which derived, because that has been repealed; if it has been amended or added to, give both the *Statutes at Large* and *United States Code* citation for such amendment or addition. If the *Revised Statutes* section has been included in a later codification of its material into positive law, it was repealed by that codification, and should no longer be cited.

United States Code. When the section cited has not been re-enacted into positive law, cite the *Statute at Large* with the Code in parallel. Where it has been re-enacted into positive law, the session law from which derived has been repealed and should not be cited, but amendments should be noted.

Chapter 4

TREATIES AND OTHER INTERNATIONAL ACTS OF THE UNITED STATES[1]

A. Importance of in Law Practice.
B. Place in the Legislative Hierarchy.
C. Publication of the International Acts of the United States.
D. Lists, Subject Indexes, and Digests of International Acts.

A. Importance of in Law Practice.

To many people the treaty is an esoteric affair, reminiscent of high protocol, peace conferences, and the like. It is all of that, but it is also a matter of the disposition of the effects of a deceased national of Greece, domiciled in Iowa; the extradition to Missouri of a criminal from the Netherlands; the right of a Chilean to sue in a New York court on a contract; or the validity of a California statute prohibiting certain aliens from holding real property in that state. As long as the nationals of one country travel to, do business in, or settle down in another country, the treaty will be of interest, not only to the diplomat, but to the common man. As a matter of fact, most of the cases interpreting treaties are from state courts, not federal. For example, the Treaty of March 2, 1899, with the United Kingdom, has been adjudicated twenty-one times, sixteen of them by state courts. At home, the relations of the United States with most of the American Indians are still governed by treaty.

B. Place in the Legislative Hierarchy.

Whether or not both treaties and executive agreements are properly to be considered as conventional legislation is academic. As a practical matter, they are used interchangeably for many purposes and so are treated together here. While this *Manual* is not a book on legal theory, sufficient of the background of international acts is given herein to serve as a basis for understanding the makeup and functions of this material.

"Treaty" and "Executive Agreement" Defined. Article II, Section 2 of the Constitution provides that "The President . . . shall have power, by and with the advice and consent of the Senate, to make treaties, provided two-thirds of the Senators present concur; and he shall nominate and, by and with the advice and consent of the Senate shall appoint Ambassadors and other public Ministers and Consuls."

---

[1] The authors acknowledge the valuable assistance of Mrs. Florence Ferner Zagayko, librarian in charge of the John Bassett Moore collection of international law, of the Columbia University Law Library, in the preparation of this chapter.

The term "treaty" is not an exact word of art in either international or municipal law. In the United States it denotes an international compact concluded by the President with a foreign power, as above, but it may be designated as a treaty, convention, protocol, contract, or other term. Treaties may be bipartite, multipartite, bilateral, multilateral, *etc.* Under the municipal law a treaty is either executory or self-executing, and the distinction is important. An *executory* treaty is one requiring a subsequent legislative enactment by the Congress, to perform an act stipulated in the treaty. Examples are treaties calling for the appropriation of money, regulating extradition, and the protection of migratory birds. A *self-executing* treaty is one which by its terms is full and complete, requiring no further legislation for its enforcement. Examples are treaties adding territory, establishing immigration quotas, exempting Indians from certain custom duties, effectuating most-favored-nation clauses, *etc.*

Executive agreements are entered into by the President with a foreign state, in his capacity as United States representative with foreign nations. These agreements in turn may be under authority of specific acts of Congress (such as those which appoint the President as a fact finder with power to act); or they may be agreements entered into purely under those Constitutional powers possessed by the President as the Chief Executive of the United States.

Examples of the first type are reciprocal trade and tariff agreements and those respecting international copyright, trade-mark and postal money order regulations. Examples of the second type are agreements settling pecuniary claims of American citizens against foreign nations, the exchange in 1940 of United States destroyers for air bases in British possessions, *modi vivendi, etc.* Although executive agreements have been employed by the President from the beginning of our national existence (twenty-seven were entered into from 1789 to 1839, as against sixty treaties), their heaviest use dates from the preparations for World War II. Many more executive agreements are now entered into than formal treaties, the extreme having been reached in 1944, with one treaty and seventy-four executive agreements.

As the Law of the Land. **Under international law.** Both treaties and executive agreements are contracts between the United States and foreign nations having the requisite power to carry out the terms thereof, and at international law they are equally binding. Such an international pact may be invalid as part of the municipal law of the United States, but still binding as a contract between the United States and the other signatory. This is true of both executory and self-executing treaties; since the *Belmont* [2] and *Pink* [3] cases at least, it seems to be true of executive agreements as well.

At municipal law: as "the law of the land." Article VI of the Constitution provides that ". . . all treaties made, or which shall be made, under the authority of the United States, shall be the supreme law of the land; and the judges of every state shall be bound thereby, any thing in the Constitution or law of any state to the contrary notwithstanding." A formal treaty, therefore, negotiated and signed by the President and approved by the Senate, has the force of a federal statute, no more, no less. ". . . there is no principle of law more firmly established by the highest court of the land than that, while a treaty will supersede a prior act of Congress, an act of Congress may supersede a prior treaty. The latest expression controls, whether it be a treaty or an act of Congress." [4] Like any other statute, it is subject to Constitutional limitations and to judicial review,[5] but the courts

---

2 *United States* v. *Belmont*, 301 U. S. 324, 57 S. Ct. 758, 81 L. Ed. 1134 (1937).

3 *United States* v. *Pink*, 315 U. S. 203, 60 S. Ct. 562, 86 L. Ed. 796 (1942).

4 *United States* v. *Thompson*, 258 Fed. 268 (E. D. Ark., 1919).

5 Philip B. Perlman, *On Amending the Treaty Power*, 52 Col. L. Rev. 825, 843 (1952).

strive to avoid finding repugnance. It has been said that no treaty provision has ever been held unconstitutional.[6]

Even though superseded by a later statute, however, a treaty, as an international contract, may still be binding, though unenforceable in our courts, and a valid claim of the other signatory on behalf of itself or its nationals may be based upon it. A *state constitutional provision or statute* in conflict with a treaty is invalid and unenforceable. The question of the status of state legislation in conflict with the United Nations *Charter* has been raised but not yet litigated. There is a strong movement, supported by the American Bar Association, for a Constitutional amendment restricting the effect of treaties.

Executive agreements have been the subject of spirited debate, but in the *Belmont* and *Pink* cases cited above, the Supreme Court went far toward upholding them as the law of the land, even when opposed to the internal policy of a sovereign state. They are probably not, however, the "law of the land" to the extent that they can supersede an act of Congress except when made under the authorization of a later act,[7] and to this extent at least are not interchangeable with treaties.

C. Publication of the International Acts of the United States.[8]

Press Releases.   The first publication of a treaty or executive agreement is or may be in the form of a mimeographed press release of the Department of State (not all agreements are so published), usually issued at the date of signing. This, in the case of a formal treaty, is thus in advance of its presentation to the Senate for approval, and its later ratification by the President.[9] The text, in English only, is preceded by a Departmental statement tracing the history of the agreement.

Department of State Bulletin.   A *statement* concerning the agreement is then printed in the *Bulletin* (the information being made accessible through the tardily-published semi-annual indexes), but the *texts* of only the short notes are so published.

"Slip Law" form.   The next form of publication is comparable to the slip law. There have been three numbered series of these slip agreements, all issued by the Department of State.

Treaty Series. The first series was the *Treaty Series* (cited as T.S.), and bibliographically it is a very peculiar series indeed. It began in January, 1908, with number 489, and through number 814 published both formal treaties and executive orders. From 814 to 994, which ended the series, the series published only formal treaties. Executive agreements are indicated by "A" and half-numbers. Thus, 531-A was an executive agreement with Germany concerning prisoners of war; 531½ was an agreement concerning claims. The numbers preceding 489 were unnumbered as published, and there is no complete set; many in fact were never printed at all. The best set of these early acts is in the Library of Congress.

Executive Agreement Series. As of October 1, 1929, through March 16, 1945, 506 numbers of this series (cited as E. A. S.), comprising "the official texts of promulgated international agreements (other than treaties) to which the United States is a party, such as are entered into by an exchange of notes, or such as the President is empowered to ratify or proclaim without the advice and consent of the Senate," were issued. For

---

[6] But *see* Willard B. Cowles, *Treaties and Constitutional Law*, (Washington, D. C., American Council on Public Affairs, 1941), pp. 14, 103, 114–116, 294.

[7] Wallace McClure, *International Executive Agreements*, (New York, Columbia University Press, 1941), p. 343.

[8] The reader is referred to Florence Ferner Zagayko's *International Documentation and Treaty Problems*, 43 L. Lib. J. 85–93 (1950), for an excellent discussion of this topic.

[9] The Senate "approves" or "recommends ratification" of treaties; the President then "ratifiies."

the benefit of those who wished to continue filing this new set with the old *Treaty Series*, parallel numbers appropriate to the old set were supplied. Thus, *Executive Agreement Series* No. 67 "may be filed in the *Treaty Series* after *Treaty Series* No. 872." This arrangement, however, proved too cumbersome, and the combined series was resumed, as below.

Treaties and Other International Acts Series. This series (cited as T. I. A. S.), which began with the number 1501, as of December 27, 1945 (the 994 numbers of the *Treaty Series*, added to the 506 of the *Executive Agreements Series*, came to 1500), was "inaugurated to make available in a single series the texts of treaties and other instruments (such as constitutions and charters of international organizations, declarations, agreements effected by exchanges of diplomatic notes, *et cetera*) establishing or defining relations between the United States and other countries." It is now current, publication lagging about six months behind the effective date of the acts as printed.

These three series are indispensable for serious work with United States treaties and executive agreements. They present the full texts of the various acts, in English and any foreign language involved, and include the President's proclamations, if any, of these acts. The title page gives the title and critical dates. The series may be subscribed for through the Superintendent of Documents, or purchased individually from him at an average cost of about ten cents apiece.

Unofficial slip law treaty publication. Formal treaties are published also in the *United States Code Congressional and Administrative News* and in some looseleaf services. *Tax Treaties*, for example, is a Commerce Clearing House loose-leaf reporter, printing the full text of United States treaties covering income and estate taxes.

Statutes at Large. Both treaties and executive agreements of international import were published in the treaties volume of the *Statutes at Large* through volume 64.

Treaties were printed in this series, from 1778, but their appearance until volume 32 (1903) was highly irregular. Indian treaties were collected in volume 7 (covering the years 1778-1845), and printed thereafter through volume 16, as though treaties with foreign countries. Treaties with foreign countries, covering 1776-1845, were collected in volume 8, and since then have been published in the individual volumes. Beginning with volume 47 (1931-32), executive agreements of international interest were included.

United States Treaties and Other International Agreements. For the material covered, this series takes the place of the former publication of treaties and executive agreements in the *Statutes at Large*, as noted above. It is the annual, bound, form of publication of the *Treaties and other International Acts Series*, beginning with T. I. A. S. No. 2010, January 27, 1950. Each volume is indexed by country and subject.

League of Nations and United Nations Treaty Series. Although the United States never became a member of the League of Nations, most of its international acts, 1920 through 1945, were published in the *League of Nations Treaty Series:* and they are now published in the successor *United Nations Treaty Series*. Both of these series are well, if tardily, indexed.

Collections of United States Treaties. Numerous collections have been published, but for most practical purposes those described below are the ones currently consulted. Of these, for some purposes *Malloy* [10] is being gradually superseded

---

[10] William M. Malloy, *Treaties, Conventions, International Acts, Protocols, and Agreements Between the United States of America and Other Powers*, (Washington, D. C., U. S. Govt. Print. Off., 1910-1938) 4 volumes.

by *Miller*.[11] Unfortunately, the *Miller* series has been discontinued, at least temporarily, and its future is in grave doubt. Volume 3 of *Malloy*, covering the years 1910-23, was compiled by C. F. Redmond, and is often cited as III Redmond; similarly, the fourth and final volume (to date), covering 1923-37, was compiled by Edward J. Trenwith, and is often cited as IV Trenwith.

The *Malloy* set prints the English text only of the acts, without comment, though the first two volumes give some citations to cases interpreting them. Parallel citations to the various treaty series and to the *Statutes at Large* where these acts are published are given.

The *Miller* series at the present time ends with volume 9 (published 1948), covering the period through July 1, 1863. For this period it supersedes *Malloy* for scholarly purposes, though *Malloy* is still the most convenient for the English text. *Miller* annotates each act by extensive notes. There is as yet no index. Volume 1 is introductory, outlining the plan of the series and giving tables of documents from 1778 to 1931 included. The "Plan of the Edition" discusses briefly many aspects of treaties, their history, procedure, controlling dates, and their publication. There is also an extensive critical bibliography of treaty collections.

Indian treaties. As noted on page 33, these were originally published in various volumes of the *Statutes at Large*. For convenience, these as well as laws relating to American Indians were compiled by Charles J. Kappler in *Indian Affairs, Laws and Treaties*.[12] Treaties are in volume 2, the laws in the other four volumes. the material is reprinted in facsimile, chronologically arranged, as taken from the *Statutes at Large* and is indexed. The work is best used in conjunction with Felix S. Cohen's *Handbook of Federal Indian Law*,[13] and the *Compilation of Material Relating to Indians*.[14]

D. Lists and Subject Indexes of International Acts.

There are no good general indexes, covering all international acts, but the information can be pieced together.

Lists of International Acts in Force or Submitted to the Senate. The most complete and serviceable lists of international acts of the United States which at any time have been in force are the first two listed below. The two lists, one by series number (and indexed by subject), and the other by country, are best used together.

Numerical list of the treaty series, executive agreement series, and treaties and other international acts series. This list is contained in *United States Treaty Developments*, Appendix II, and was reprinted as Department of State *Publication* 3787 (1950), through *T.I.A.S.* 1965. It lists all international acts by series number, under which are given the country involved, date, subject or title of act, and place of publication — in the *Statutes at Large, Malloy, Miller*, etc. The list as

---

[11] David H. Miller, *Treaties and Other International Acts of the United States of America*, (Washington, D. C., U. S. Govt. Print. Off., 1931–1948) volume 8.

[12] Washington, D. C., U. S. Govt. Print. Off., 1904–1941. 5 volumes.

[13] Washington, D. C., U. S. Govt. Print. Off., 1945.

[14] U. S. Cong., House Committee on Public Lands. Subcommittee on Indian Affairs. *Compilation of Material Relating to Indians of United States and Territory of Alaska.* Washington, D. C., U. S. Govt. Print. Off., 1950.

printed in *United States Treaty Developments* is indexed by country and subject, and is kept up to date by loose-leaf releases. It is also kept up to date by the cumulative (from January 1, 1948) semiannual *Publications of the State Department*, which lists new treaties and executive agreements by serial number and indexes them by country and subject.

List of treaties and other international agreements contained in the United States statutes at large. This list, printed in 64 *Statutes at Large*, Part 3 (1953) — which is the last volume of the *Statutes at Large* to contain international acts — is a list by country. Under each country, the acts are arranged first by subject and thereunder chronologically. Series number, date, volume, and page references to where printed in the *Statutes at Large* are given. Indian treaties as found in volumes 7 to 18, inclusive, of the *Statutes at Large*, are not included.

Miscellaneous lists. McClenon and Gilbert's *Index to the Federal Statutes, 1874–1931* [15] (*see* Chapter 6); *Malloy* and *Miller*, and *Treaties in Force . . . on December 31, 1941* [16] are all good lists. The last named is an annotated list of international acts, arranged by subject and indexed by both country and subject. It is kept up to date by the loose-leaf *United States Treaty Developments*, which will eventually supersede it. *Malloy* (*IV Trenwith*) lists treaties submitted to the Senate for approval, 1789–1937. Lists are aslo tabulated in the Department of State *List of Treaties* Submitted to the Senate, 1935–1944.[17] This list (which includes submissions still lacking approval) is also kept up to date by *Treaty Developments*, Appendix I, and by information in the weekly *Department of State Bulletin*.

Status Tables of Treaties. Appendix I of *Treaty Developments* lists all treaties pending in the Senate, with information as to action taken or remaining to be taken by that body. The calendar of the Senate Committee on Foreign Relations has such a list, less convenient to use. Status tables are also contained in the C. C. H. *Congressional Index* and (for tax treaties) in the C. C. H. *Tax Treaties*.

Subject Indexes of International Acts. By far the best and most inclusive subject index is that in *Treaty Developments*, but since it covers only those developments since the beginning of 1944 (though eventually it is expected to include all international acts), it must be supplemented by other sources. *Malloy* and *Miller* are both indexed. There is also a very complete subject index covering the first 839 numbers of the *Treaty Series* (*Subject Index to the Treaty Series and Executive Agreements Series, July 1, 1931*),[18] which includes also a numerical table of the series, as well as a table of unperfected treaties. From January 1, 1948 current acts are indexed in the *Publications of the Department of State*, noted above.

Treaties by Popular Name. It sometimes becomes necessary to translate the popular name of a treaty, as the Hay-Pauncefote, Ashburton-Webster, or Sweden General Peace Treaty, into its official *Statutes at Large* citation. This may be done through the index found in IV *Trenwith*, the table of "Statutes by Popular Names"

---

[15] Walter H. McClennon and Wilfred C. Gilbert, *Index to the Federal Statutes, 1874–1931*, (Washington, D. C., U. S. Govt. Print. Off., 1933).

[16] U. S. Department of State. *Treaties in Force; a List of Treaties and Other International Acts of the United States in Force on December 31, 1941*, (Washington, D. C., U. S. Govt. Print. Off., 1944).

[17] Washington, D. C., U. S. Govt. Print. Off., 1945.

[18] Washington, D. C., U. S. Govt. Print. Off., 1932.

in the *Digest of United States Supreme Court Reports*,[19] and in *A Table of Federal Acts by Popular Names or Short Titles*.[20] Similar lists in the *United States Code* are not satisfactory for treaties.

Citators for International Acts. Since treaties and executive agreements of international import are statutes, they are subject to much the same process of amendment, repeal, extension, and the like, as are other statutes, and they are interpreted by the courts, both federal and state, in the same manner.[21]

United States treaty developments. The best citator, for developments beginning with 1944, is the Department of State loose-leaf service of this name. It gives in one place, for each international act, the following information: ". . . notes respecting the date and place of signature, effective date, duration, citations to text, signatories, ratifications, adherences, accessions, reservations, amendments, extensions, terminations, authorizing and implementing legislation, executive action, administrative interpretations, opinions of the Attorney General, court decisions, and other relevant action." Tables include lists of treaties pending in or submitted to the Senate for approval, treaties withdrawn from the Senate, numerical *lists of all the various treaty series to date*, lists by *subjects and regions*, and the most comprehensive subject and country index. It is kept up to date by replacement sheets. Unfortunately for its present usefulness, it covers only actions (on any agreement, no matter of what date) taken from the beginning of 1944, but eventually it is expected to expand backward to include all actions on such agreements from the beginning.

Statutes construed tables. These tables in the National Reporter System and in some West Publishing Company case digests include international agreements printed as *Statutes at Large*. The *Federal Code Annotated*, volume 12, annotates treaties, including those with the American Indians. Treaties which have been adjudicated by the Supreme Court of the United States (including those with foreign countries to which the United States was not a party, and Indian treaties) are listed in the table of statutes construed in the *Digest of United States Supreme Court Reports, supra.*

Subsequent legislative history of treaties. When the *Statutes at Large* citation of a treaty is given, and often when it is mentioned in a case only by name, *Shepard's United States Citations* (*see* Chapter 28) notes supersedings, amendments, *etc.* of international agreements exactly as for any other United States uncodified statutes. If the international agreement is not a *Statute at Large*, it is not listed in *Shepard. Treaty Information*, above, gives all changes beginning with 1944 in international agreements to which the United States was a party. For earlier information of the kind, there are two cumulative indexes, covering respectively the periods October 29–June 1935, and July 1935–June 1939. *Treaties in Force, 1941* [22] supplies some information about treaty changes, including many international agreements not *Statutes at Large*. The weekly *Department of State Bulletin* prints current treaty information (indexed in the semi-annual volumes), which occasionally notes alteration in the status of international agreements.

---

[19] Rochester, N. Y., Lawyers Co-operative Publishing Co., 1950. Volume 14.

[20] Colorado Springs, Colo., Shepard's Citations, issued from time to time.

[21] The reader is referred to Miles O. Price, *Citation Books for United States Treaties*, 41 L. Lib. J. 347–364 (1948), for an extended treatment of this topic.

[22] *See* footnote 13, above.

Judicial history of treaties. For the *federal* courts, *Treaty Developments* is the simplest source of such information, since the citations to cases are collected in one place. *Shepard's United States Citations* is the tool most lawyers would use, since all treaties to date are covered, if printed in the *Statutes at Large*. Only citing cases from federal courts are noted here, but *all* federal cases mentioning the treaty are listed, not just those directly construing it.

It should be noted that treaties in *Shepard* are arranged by date, rather than by *Statutes at Large* volume and page, though both citations are given. For example, the Act of December 2, 1919, 41 Stat. 1779, precedes in *Shepard* the Act of December 5, which is 41 Stat. 363, because the low page numbers are public laws and consequently printed in Part 1 of the *Statutes at Large;* while the high page numbers are for private laws and treaties, in subsequent parts of the *Statutes.* If the searcher using *Shepard* has only the name of the treaty, as Webster-Ashburton, he can translate it into the *Statutes at Large* citation by use of a popular-name table noted above.

The *Federal Code Annotated*, volume 12, annotates federal uncodified statutes, which include treaties. Citing cases include both federal and state cases, but only those *construing* the treaty. However, the treaty is *listed* whether cited by cases or not. Special attention is given to Indian treaties. The *Digest of United States Supreme Court Reports*, in its table of statutes construed, cites Supreme Court cases only. In this table, treaties, both with foreign countries and with the Indians, are listed twice (unless the United States is not a party, when only once); once alphabetically by country or tribe; and once by date, as a United States *Statute at Large*. State cases involving treaties, on appeal to the Supreme Court, are listed in volume 9, by state citation. The *Supreme Court Reporter* beginning with volume 37, 1916, has a table of statutes construed, which includes treaties.

For the state courts. Thirty-six state *Shepards* have a section citing federal statutes contrued, which of course includes treaties and executive agreements cited as *Statutes at Large*. In the *Federal Code Annotated*, state cases construing treaties are cited, even when not appealed to the United States Supreme Court. For the twelve states not covered by *Shepard* citations to federal statutes in the manner noted above, the *Federal Code Annotated* is one source of information about state courts in construing treaties. Another is through the "Tables of Statutes Construed," noted above. In these tables, treaties interpreted are listed under "Treaties," not under *Statutes at Large* citations.

Indian treaties. These are annotated by United States and state cases, in volume 12 of the *Federal Code Annotated*, where they are arranged first by date and under that alphabetically by *tribe*. In the index to this volume, on the other hand, the reverse arrangement is found: listing is by *tribe*, then *date*. The *Digest of United States Supreme Court Reports* lists treaty citations alphabetically by tribe, then chronologically; treaties cited often antedate our nationhood, being then with the English and French. Felix S. Cohen's *Handbook of Federal Indian Law* [23] pages 33–378, annotates Indian treaties by federal decisions. The "annotated table of statutes and treaties," arranged by *Statutes at Large* citation, at pages 485—608 of this work, covers treaties. This is the most complete statutory citation extant of Indian treaties and statutes to 1942. The last Indian treaty was signed in 1904; treaties from 1778 through 1842 were compiled and published as volume 7 of the *Statutes at Large*, later ones being published in volumes 8 to 16.

---

[23] *See* footnote 13, above.

Foreign treaties interpreted by American courts. Where there are treaties to which the United States is also a party, the citation may be translated into the *Statutes at Large* citation and so *Shepardized*. Treaties by specific countries are listed in volume 12 of the *Federal Code Annotated*. The *Digest of United States Supreme Court Reports* lists adjudicated treaties with foreign countries twice; alphabetically by country; and, if they are with the United States, by date and *Statutes at Large* citation.

Digests of International Law. There have been three United States digests of international law. These in essence are digests of treaties, court decisions interpreting them, and other official documents, together with a great deal of explanatory comment.

Wharton's Digest.[24] This is the old "standard" digest, though now largely superseded by the two later ones described below. The supplement to the third volume consists of material omitted from the first edition, either inadvertently or because discovered after the edition went to press.

Moore's Digest.[25] This is still an indispensable analysis of international law from the United States point of view, as embodied in official documents. Volume 8 comprises an index by subject, country and person; a list of cases cited; and a list of documents cited.

Hackworth's Digest.[26] This is an analysis of international law as applied by the United States, based upon material made available since the publication of *Moore*. The material in *Moore* is not duplicated in the later work, but with a few exceptions the order and style of treatment are the same. Volume VIII is a general index and table of cases.

Notes

Legal Status of Treaties and Other International Acts of the United States. The powers of the President in foreign relations are treated at length in many works on constitutional and international law. Of special interest in connection with treaties and and executive agreements are Wallace McClure, *International Executive Agreements;*[27] Henry S. Fraser, *Treaties and Executive Agreements: An Analysis Prepared for the Committee on Foreign Relations;*[28] and the spirited series of articles appearing in volumes 53 and 54 of the *Yale Law Journal*: E. M. Borchard, *Shall the Executive Agreement Replace the Treaty?*[29]; Myres S. McDougal and Ashar Lans, *Treaties and Congressional or Presidential Agreements: Interchangeable Instruments of National Policy;*[30] and E. M. Borchard, *Treaties and Executive Agreements—a Reply.*[31] Especially recommended as a non-controversial exposition is that by Hunter Miller on pages 3 to 14 of volume 1 of his *Treaties and Other International Acts of the United States of America.*[32] What may be regarded as the Department of State view is set forth at length in volume 5 of

---

[24] Wharton, Francis, *A Digest of the International Law of the United States.* 2d ed., Washington, D. C., U. S. Govt. Print. Off., 1887. 3 v. and appendix.

[25] Moore, John B. *A Digest of International Law . . .* Washington, D. C., U. S. Govt. Print. Off., 1906. 8 v. Also as H. Doc., No. 551, 56th Cong., 2d Sess.

[26] Hackworth, Green H., *Digest of International Law.* Washington, D. C., U. S. Govt. Print. Off., 1940-1944. 8 v.

[27] New York, Columbia University Press, 1941.

[28] Senate Document No. 244, 78th Congress, 2d session, 1944.

[29] Yale Law Journal 664 (1944).

[30] 54 Yale Law Journal, 181-351, 534-615 (1945).

[31] 54 Yale Law Journal, 616-664 (1945).

[32] *See* footnote 11 above.

Green H. Hackworth's *Digest of International Law*,[33] Chapter XVI. Executive agreements are discussed in Sections 514-517.

Dates of International Acts. There are or may be five critical dates in the progress of a formal United States treaty to adoption, those of the *signature* by the plentipotentiaries of the powers concerned, the *approval* by the Senate by a two-thirds vote of those present, the *ratification* by the President, the *exchange of ratifications*, and the President's *proclamation* of the treaty.

Date of a treaty. The *date when signed* is that by which a formal treaty is cited by the Department of State and by international lawyers, though it usually is not its effective date. For example, the treaty signed July 2, 1860, with Costa Rica was consented to by the Senate on January 16, 1861, ratified by the President January 21; ratifications were exchanged November 9, 1861, and it was proclaimed November 11, 1861; but this treaty is cited as of July 2, 1860. The date is for convenience in citation only. Municipal lawyers, in contrast, usually cite the *date of proclamation* (if it is proclaimed), or the *effective date* as noted in the treaty. It is by this date that it is printed in the *Statutes at Large*. The difference may be extreme, as in the case of the Isle of Pines treaty of March 2, 1904. This, instead of appearing in 32 *Statutes at Large* with other 1904 legislation, actually was printed in volume 44, because its effective date was March 23, 1925.

Effective date of a treaty. Unless otherwise indicated in the treaty itself, the effective date is that of United States ratification by the President (or, if exchange of of ratifications is called for, that date). Thus, the convention of February 10, 1925, between the United States and Great Britain (T. S. 744), though ratified by the United States on March 26, 1926, and proclaimed by the President on July 12 of that year, by its terms became effective upon the exchange of ratifications, which was July 8, 1926. The effective date can almost always be determined from the printed text, but it may vary, as to whether international or municipal law is concerned. It may be and often is specified in the body of the treaty itself, as noted, though for domestic purposes that date is not binding upon United States courts. It has been asserted that upon ratification the effective date becomes the date of signature, and this may be true if so stated in the text of a political treaty, but the doctrine of relation back has no application where rights of individual United States citizens are concerned. The Senate in advising ratification of a treaty may modify its terms, and as the treaty operates as a statute, no citizen can be put on notice as to its terms until final approval. In multilateral treaties and conventions, the effective date, which may be, and usually is, later than that of United States ratification, is to be determined from the text. United States treaties are usually, but not always, promulgated by the President, in a proclamation issued after ratification and published with the treaty; but this is not a necessary procedure.

In published treaties, the effective date is usually indicated at some point extraneous to the body of the treaty itself, as in a syllabus or on the title page. In official Department of State indexes to treaties and in the loose-leaf *United States Treaty Developments*, the date and the effective date of each act, whether treaty or executive agreement, are clearly stated.

Date of executive agreements. The *date* of an executive agreement is, like that of a treaty, that of the signature. The *effective date*, since such agreements do not require Congressional consent, is the one stated in the agreement itself. These dates, as with treaties, are indicated on the face, title page, or in a syllabus to the printed publication, and in the official indexes. Executive agreements are often proclaimed, especially if made under the authorization of an act of Congress, and occasionally their terms require ratification by the President.

---

[33] *See* footnote 26 above.

Chapter 5

LEGISLATIVE HISTORIES

A. The Need for Such Histories.

"The custom of remaking statutes to fit their histories has gone so far that a formal Act, read three times and voted on by Congress and approved by the President, is no longer a safe basis on which a lawyer may advise his client, or a lower court decide a case. This has very practical consequences to the profession. The lawyer must consult all the committee reports on the bill, and on all its antecedents, and all that its supporters and opponents said in debate, and then predict what part of the conflicting views will likely appeal to a majority of the Court. . . ." [1]

B. The Two Aspects of Such Histories.

There are two aspects to the making of legislative histories for federal legislation. The first is following every step of a bill from its introduction into the legislature through its final approval or rejection. The aim here is to ascertain the *status of a pending bill* at any given time. The second, paralleling the first, is the determination of *legislative intent* in the enactment of a statute *after it has been approved.*

C. Steps in the Passage of a Bill Through Congress.

The compilation of legislative histories is rendered easier by familiarity with the steps in the passage of a bill through the legislature, and with the pertinent materials available. A bill may take any of the following steps before becoming a federal law; the Senate procedure is somewhat more formal than that of the House of Representatives. The state legislative process is so similar as not to need any further comment here. [2]

The Bill is Introduced. The bill is drafted, usually by experts employed by the respective houses of the legislature for that purpose. (Revenue bills must originate in

[1] Mr. Justice Robert H. Jackson, of the United States Supreme Court, *The Meaning of Statutes: What Congress Says or What the Court Says*, 34 A. B. A. J. 535, 538 (1948).

[2] The outline of the legislative process below, though abridged, is correct in its essentials. For a more detailed account *see* Charles J. Zinn, *How Our Laws Are Made*, pages 11-31 (published as a special section of the *United States Code Congressional and Administrative Service*, 1952, No. 5). Mr. Zinn is Law Revision Counsel, Committee on the Judiciary, U. S. House of Representatives. The legislative process generally is described at length in J. G. Sutherland, *Statutes and Statutory Construction* (3d ed., 1943), chapters 4-20. An elementary account of federal law-making is by Clarence C. Dill, *How Congress Makes Laws* (1939). The state process is set forth in detail by Armand B. Coigne, *Statute Making* (1948), where differing procedures are described and tabulated. Legislatures, federal and state, are guided in their procedures by printed rules contained in the manuals described in Chapter 30.

the House of Representatives). It is first dropped into the "hopper," then read (by title), given a serial or bill number, assigned to its proper committee, and ordered to be printed. In the House, bills are rarely read even by title at this point.

The Bill is Considered in Committee. Most consideration of a bill is by standing or special committees of the respective houses, and a bill lacking such consideration stands little chance of passage. It is estimated that 90 per cent of all bills die in committee.[3] When the committee decides to study and report the bill, it may hold public hearings on it, at which time those who are interested advocate or oppose it, in person or through briefs, or both. Thereafter, the committee submits to the Congress a printed report, recommending passage or non-passage of the bill.

The Bill is Placed on the Calendar. When reported, the bill, which has probably been amended during the committee consideration, is placed upon a calendar (corresponding to a court docket), of the house where introduced. In the House, "bills raising revenues, general appropriation bills, and bills of a public character directly or indirectly appropriating money or property" are placed on the *Union* calendar. Here are placed most public bills, but there is also a *House* calendar for public bills not raising revenue or appropriating money or property. Bills may be removed from the above calendars if there is no objection, and placed on *Consent* calendar. If there is still no objection when brought up for consideraton, bills on the Consent calender are passed without debate, by unanimous consent. The *Private* calendar is for bills for claims against the United States, and private immigration bills. When the bill's turn is reached, it is read in full, section by section (unless, as usually happens, by unanimous consent the reading is dispensed with—in which case the entire bill is often printed in the Congressional Record at this point in the proceedings), and is then debated. This is the critical stage of a reported bill.

Third Reading of the Bill, and Vote. The bill is then read for a third time (by title), and voted upon. Ninety per cent of all enacted bills are voted by unanimous consent.[4] After passage in one house, the bill is sent to the other house for action.

Procedure in the Other House. After the bill passes one house, much of the same procedure is followed in the other house, where, however, the erstwhile bill is designated as an "Act." If the bill is amended by the second house, it is returned to the first, after passage, for further consideration.

Conference Procedure.[5] When there has been disagreement between the two houses as to any part of the bill, each house appoints a conference committee to determine its final form. Conferees may compromise differences, but no new matter may be added by them, nor may matters already agreed upon by both houses be touched. Conference reports are submitted to each house, together with the printed conference bill (which retains its original number). The conference report is invariably printed in the house in which the bill originated, and occasionally by the other house. These reports may be debated but not amended. Many are accepted and the resultant bills passed by unanimous consent. Such bills are usually printed in the *Congressional Record* at this point.

The Bill is Signed by the Speaker and Vice-President. After passage of a bill by both houses, it is signed, first by the Speaker of the House of Representatives, and then by the Vice-President, and forwarded to the President for approval.

The Approval of the Bill. A bill becomes law upon approval by the President, which may be by signature, or by his failing for ten days (within a session) to veto it. A veto is affirmative (returning it by the President to Congress with a message of disapproval), or by inaction (as a "pocket veto"); if a bill is received by the President less than ten days before the adjournment of Congress, his failure to sign the bill kills it. An affirmative veto can be overridden only by a two-thirds vote of a quorum voting in both houses, which seldom occurs.[6]

---

[3] Clarence C. Dill, *How Congress Makes Laws* (1939), p. 104.

[4] *See* note 3, above, p. 66.

[5] *See* Charles J. Zinn, *Conference Procedure in Congress*, 38 A. B. A. J. 864 (1952) .

[6] The subject is discussed at length, and clarifying legislation proposed, in a study made for the House Committee on the Judiciary, *The Veto Power of the President* (1951), by Charles J. Zinn, Legislative Counsel.

Fate of Bills at the End of a Congress. All *bills* which have not matured into law die at the end of a Congress, and must be introduced anew in a subsequent Congress if further action is desired. Bills retain their status from session to session of the same Congress. *Treaties*, however, remain in the Senate Foreign Relations Committee until disposed of, which may take years.

D. Materials for Federal Legislative Histories.

Before the Bill is Introduced. Most important legislation does not just happen. It usually evolves from a demonstrated need, from the pressure of interested groups, or, increasingly, as the result of legislative investigation into various areas of the law, to see if changes are advisable. The results of these investigations are usually published.

The Bill in its Various Forms.   A bill is shown on the opposite page.

Bills are numbered consecutively through an entire Congress. The bill number uniquely identifies the bill and all hearings and reports on it, throughout its history in Congress and when it is printed as a slip law or in the Statutes at Large.

To expedite the passage of a measure, an identical (or "companion") bill may be introduced simultaneously in both houses. In the progress of a bill through a house, amendments are frequently offered, each of which is separately printed in bill form and in the *Congressional Record*. When amendments are accepted by the committee in charge of a bill, the bill is reprinted, matter to be omitted from the original bill having a horizontal line through it, new matter being printed in italics. Sometimes the original bill becomes so unrecognizable that it is scrapped in favor of a new one, embodying all agreed upon changes, and called a "clean" bill.

Slip bills. The first printed form of publication of a bill, either as introduced or amended, is the "slip" bill shown on page 43. Slip bills may be subscribed to by the session, from the Superintendent of Documents; and many libraries designated as depositories of government publications have them. Individual bills may usually be secured free upon application to the committee to which assigned.

Committee print of a bill. The "Committee Print," prepared for use of the Committee in charge of it, shows in parallel columns, section by section, the provisions of the bill as compared to existing statutes; together with notes giving the purpose of projected changes made by the new bill. These prints are available only from the respective committees.

Hearings print of a bill. The bill is always printed as a part of the record of a hearing on it.

Congressional Record print of a bill. The *Congressional Record* prints *certain* bills, either in full or as amended, at second or third reading, but such texts are unreliable. Printing or not is a matter of editorial discretion.

Resolutions in bill form. All resolutions of any kind introduced are printed and distributed in slip form. Concurrent and simple resolutions are also printed in full in the *Congressional Record*. As passed, both of these latter are printed in the House and Senate *Journals*, and the concurrent in the *Statutes at Large* as well.[7]

Digest of Public General Bills.[8] This prints "in the form of a brief synopsis the essential features of the introduced public bills and resolutions and a little *fuller digest of reported measures*. . . . Each issue contains a section showing the status of all bills acted upon and another listing the public laws and resolutions enacted, with corresponding bill numbers." Short of the full text of a bill, this is the best source of information

---

[7] For the designation of the various types of resolution, see Chapter 2.

[8] Prepared by the U. S. Library of Congress, Legislative Reference Service. Washington, D. C., U. S. Govt. Print. Off., 1936 to date.

82D CONGRESS
1ST SESSION

H. R. 4601

IN THE SENATE OF THE UNITED STATES

JULY 27 (legislative day, JULY 24), 1951
Read twice and referred to the Committee on Finance

AN ACT

To provide that the admissions tax shall not apply in respect of admissions free of charge of uniformed members of the Armed Forces of the United States.

1   *Be it enacted·by the Senate and House of Representa-*
2   *tives of the United States of America in Congress assembled,*
3   That section 1700 (a) (1) of the Internal Revenue Code
4   is hereby amended by adding at the end thereof the follow-
5   ing new sentence: "No tax shall be imposed in the case of
6   admission free of charge of a member of the Armed Forces
7   of the United States when in uniform."
8   SEC. 2. The amendment made by this Act shall be
9   applicable to admissions on and after the first day of the
10   first month which begins more than ten days after the date
11   of the enactment of this Act.

Passed the House of Representatives July 26, 1951.

Attest·   RALPH R. ROBERTS,
                                                      Clerk.

Exhibit 5

as to its content. There is a subject index of digested bills. A green-paged section gives the *status* of bills acted upon during the session, together with a *new digest of amended bills.* The *list of public laws enacted* is by law number, with reference to corresponding bill numbers. The final of the approximately eight annual issues cumulates all previous digests, status, and public law tables and indexes.

Bills in commercial services. Public general bills are listed by number and title in the Commerce Clearing House *Congressional Index* (mentioned below). The *United States Code Congressional and Administrative News* has an "Index-Digest of Bills Introduced" during the period covered by each issue. Entries are by subject, followed by the bill number.

Legislative Calendars. These are the Congressman's inventories of business on hand and records of its present status. Each house, and almost every standing committee has its own calendar.

"Calendars of the House of Representatives and History of Legislation." This daily *cumulative* calendar is perhaps the most useful single tool for tracing the legislative history of a bill whether Senate or House. (Its Senate counterpart is not nearly as useful.) The history of every *Senate* bill which has been reported or passed by that house is also given. The following are regular features.

Bills in conference. These are listed by *date*, not bill number. Information includes the title of the bill, conference report number, and action taken by each house; bills through conference give the above information plus public or private law number and date of approval.

"Numerical order of bills and resolutions which have passed either or both houses, and bills now pending on the calendar." This list of bills reported out of committee by both houses is perhaps the most useful feature of the calendars. How it looks is shown below.

41

NUMERICAL ORDER OF BILLS AND RESOLUTIONS WHICH HAVE PASSED EITHER OR BOTH HOUSES, AND BILLS NOW PENDING ON THE CALENDAR

Complete history of all actions on each bill follows the number in chronological order. For subject of bill see index, using index key following bill number in this section

NOTE.—Similar or identical bills, and bills having reference to each other, are indicated by number in parentheses

No.	Index Key and History of bill	No.	Index Key and History of Bill
	HOUSE BILLS		HOUSE BILLS—Continued
	H. R. 1 (H. Res. 83).—Armed Forces, gratuitous indemnity. Reported from Veterans' Affairs Jan. 17, 1951; Report No. 6. Union Calendar. Passed House Jan. 24, 1951. Reported in Senate Feb. 14, 1951; Finance; Report No. 91. Passed Senate, amended Feb. 26, 1951. Senate asks for a conference Feb. 26, 1951. House agrees to a conference Feb. 27, 1951. Conference report filed Apr. 12, 1951. Report No. 319. House agrees to conference report Apr. 13, 1951. Senate agrees to conference report Apr. 13, 1951 Approved Apr. 25, 1951. Public Law No. 23.		H. R. 244 (S. 355) (H. Res. 419).—Postal service, pay increase. Reported from Post Office and Civil Service, Aug. 23, 1951; Report No. 958. Union Calendar. Laid on table Sept. 20, 1951. S. 355 passed in lieu. H. R. 301.—Veterans, female veterans, benefits. Reported from Veterans' Affairs June 13, 1951; Report No. 555. Union Calendar. Passed House June 20, 1951.

Exhibit 6

DOCKET No.	AUTHOR AND DATE OF INTRODUCTION	NUMBER OF BILL	TITLE	DATE OF REFERENCE TO SUBCOMMITTEE AND ACTION
		17		
33	Mr. Johnson of Colorado. Jan. 16, 1951. (Substantially the same as H. R. 5187 of 81st Cong., similar to H. R. 538 and H. R. 2321 by Mr. O'Hara, and identical to H. R. 2099 by Mr. O'Hara, 82d Cong.)	S. 508	To protect consumers and others against misbranding, false advertising, and false invoicing of fur products and furs.	Jan. 31, 1951.—Considered in executive session and ordered reported without amendment. Feb. 5, 1951.—Reported by Mr. Johnson of Colorado (S. Rept. 78). Feb. 22, 1951.—Amendment proposed by Senator Lodge and ordered to lie on table. Mar. 12, 1951.—Passed over by request of Senators Wherry and Hendrickson. Apr. 11, 1951.—Passed over on call of calendar on objection of Mr. Hendrickson. May 4, 1951.—Passed over by request of Senator Hendrickson. May 17, 1951.—Passed over by request of Senator Hendrickson. (NOTE.—Feb. 2, 1951.—H. R. 2321 was introduced by Mr. O'Hara and referred to House Interstate and Foreign Commerce Committee. Apr. 17, 1951.—Hearings held. (To be printed.) June 8, 1951.—Considered in executive session and ordered reported with amendments. June 11, 1951.—Reported by Mr. O'Hara. (H. Rept. 546.) June 18, 1951.—Passed House, with amendments. June 19, 1951.—Placed on Senate Calendar. June 21, 1951.—H. R. 2321 passed Senate with amendments, in lieu of S. 508. June 22, 1951.—House disagreed to amendments of the Senate and asked for conference. June 22, 1951.—House conferees appointed: Representatives Beckworth, Priest, Harris, Wolverton, and O'Hara. June 25, 1951.—Senate conferees appointed: Senators Johnson of Colorado, McFarland, Magnuson, Brewster, and Capehart. June 28, 1951.—Conferees met in executive session. July 26, 1951.—Conferees met in executive session and reached an agreement. July 27, 1951.—Conference report filed in House by Mr. O'Hara. (H. Rept. 769.) July 27, 1951.—Conference report agreed to in Senate. July 27, 1951.—Conference report agreed to in House. Aug. 8, 1951.—Signed by the President. (Public Law 110.)

94029—82—Senate Interstate and Foreign Commerce Cal——3

Exhibit 7

Calendars (union, House, private and consent). Here are noted the date of placing the bill on the calendar, the person and committee in charge of it, the subject matter, and the calendar (docket) number.

List of public and private laws and resolutions enacted.

The entry following the dash (Armed forces, gratuitous indemnity), is as the bill is listed in the subject index.

Subject index to the calendars.

Status table of major bills, by number, title, and steps through Congress.

"Final Edition" for a Congress. After the final adjournment of a *Congress* a "Final Edition" of the calendar is prepared, in readiness for the convening of the first session of the next Congress. This gives a complete resumé of actions on *all House and Senate bills and resolutions* during the entire Congress, and since it comes out in advance of the "History of Bills" of the *Congressional Record*, it is perhaps the single most useful repository of legislative history for a given Congress. It gives no information about bills and resolutions upon which no action was taken, and to this extent is thus less complete than the "History of Bills," which lists all which are introduced, whether or not acted upon. There is an index, and a complete statistical resumé of the activities of the last five Congresses. There is also a table of "Status of Major Bills" for each session of the Congress covered.

Committee Calendars. Nearly all standing committees of both houses have their own published calendars. The one described below, is fairly typical.

The calendar proper tells everything, including action in the other house, and the numbers of identical, similar or substitute bills. Thus (Exhibit 7, page 45):

Senate Committee on Interstate and Foreign Commerce Calendars. Committee and sub-committee personnel, their functions and statutory duties and powers are set forth. Senate and House bills pending before the committee are listed.

There are two indexes; by introducers of bills on the calendar, and by subject. Especially useful for discovery of legislative intent is the chronological list of *"executive communications . . ."* It is the custom of legislative committees to solicit the advice or attitude of interested agencies and many such communications are later published as Congressional Documents.

Printed *committee reports* (including committee prints) are listed by report number, with reference to bill number and title. *Public hearings* held are listed by docket and bill number, with the hearing date and statement of availability of printed hearings.

Committee Hearings. Legislative hearings are either related to specific pending bills, or those held pursuant to a House or Senate resolution calling for the investigation of some condition which may require the introduction of corrective bills. Advance notice of hearings is given in the *Daily Digest* of the *Congressional Record.* Committee calendars state whether printed or not; the Commerce Clearing House *Congressional Index* does the same, as does the annual "History of Bills Enacted into Law" of the *Daily Digest.*[9] A great deal of information, in the form of prepared and impromptu statements, elaborate briefs and even entire books, is printed in these hearings, but much of it is chaff and all must be read with an awareness of bias on the part of witnesses.

Committee Reports and Memoranda. Legislative committees issue numerous reports, each of which bears an identifying serial number (as H. Rept. No. 19, 81st Cong., 1st Sess., or S. Rept. No. 163, 72d Cong., 2d Sess.) The "History of Bills" in the *Congressional Record* and legislative *Journals,* and the status tables in the *Congressional Index* give the serial numbers of reports on each bill reported.

Reports on pending bills. Each bill reported to the floor of the House or Senate by the committee in charge is accompanied by a report setting forth the recommendations of the committee (and there may be a dissenting minority report) that the bill do or do not pass with the reasons therefor. The Legislative Reorganization Act of 1946[10] gave each committee a professional staff of four, plus adequate clerical help, and since then these reports have tended to be highly factual expositions of the background of the respective bills and the reasons for important new legislation. Reports on routine legislation are more perfunctory.

Reports of investigating committees. The results of exploratory investigations into such topics as juvenile delinquency, immigration, baseball and the like are often embodied in committee reports, though more often these are designated as *Documents.*

---

[9] The most complete source of information, giving prices, is the *Monthly Catalog of United States Government Publications.* The Senate Library has issued an *Index to Congressional Committee Hearings (Not Confidential in Character)* (1935), with 1941 and 1951 supplements. The index is both by subject and bill number. Hearings may often be secured free from committee members, and may be subscribed for en masse from the Superintendent of Documents, for about $750.00 per year.

[10] Act of August 2, 1946, 60 Stat. 812, c. 753, 2 U. S. C. § 31 *et seq.* (1946).

House and Senate Documents. Congressional *Documents*, so-called, comprise the enormous mass of papers ordered printed by either house of Congress, other than committee reports and hearings. Among them are reports of Congressional investigatory committees, or monographs on various topics. All *Presidential messages* are so printed. For the purposes of legislative histories, the printing as documents of *communications from government departments and agencies* relating to pending bills should be noted.

Legislative Debates and Proceedings. From 1774 on there has been some sort of official or unofficial publication recording the minutes and debates of Congress. Of current interest are the *Congressional Record* and the House and Senate *Journals*.[11]

Congressional Record.[12] This newspaper is probably the most useful single publication for the purposes of legislative history. Published during Congressional sessions Monday through Friday, except on days following a Congressional recess, it is supposed to be a full and faithful record of what takes place in Congress. As such it covers the following.

The introduction of all bills and resolutions and amendments.

Debates, which are reported verbatim.

The text of many bills and joint resolutions. Simple and concurrent resolutions are printed *as passed.*

Presidential messages.

Treaties, when debated.

An "**Index to the Proceedings**" **is printed fortnightly and cumulated annually.** It is in three parts: a combined "Index to the Proceedings," and a "History of Bills and Resolutions" for each the House and Senate. Entries under Congresmen cover every bill and amendment offered by each, and every motion or remark made. The "*History of Bills and Resolutions*" is a *status table,* probably

---

11 *Journals of the Continental Congress,* 1774-1789. These journals are the only really accessible sources of information as to United States legislation antedating the Constitutional period. They have been published in one official contemporaneous edition of thirteen volumes, and the following reprints, with extensive editorial notes: *Folwell,* 13 volumes, 1800-1801; *Way and Gideon* 4 volumes, 1823; and the *Library of Congress* edition, 34 volumes 1904-1937. The minutes, debates and enactments ("ordinances") of the Continental Congress appear in these *Journals.* Each volume of the definitive *Library of Congress* edition is separately indexed. *Annals of Congress,* (1789-1824, 42 volumes). The title of this series is the *Debates and Proceedings in the Congress of the United States* . . . but the set is better known and cited by its half-title, as above. The set was compiled in 1834 by Gales and Seaton, from various sources, and the proceedings are not given verbatim. The last volume for each Congress has an appendix containing the public laws for that Congress. *Gales and Seaton's Register of Debates* (1824-1837, 14 volumes in 29 books). This series, generally cited as *Register of Debates,* was contemporaneously published, but the proceedings are not verbatim. The last volume for each session contains the laws enacted. Each book has its own not very good index. *Congressional Globe* (1833-1873, 46 volumes in 109 books). As will be seen, this set overlaps the *Register of Debates.* The volume numbering following volume 14 is hopelessly confused, so that the entire set is best cited by Congress and session, rather than volume. Though the reports of proceedings in the earlier volumes are paraphrased and abridged, the later reports are almost verbatim. Each session has its own index for Senate and House proceedings. Messages of the President are printed for the years 1833-1867 (to the close of the 39th Congress), and from 1853 to 1873 (2d session of the 32d Congress to close of the 42d), the laws are printed.

12 *Congressional Record.* Washington, D. C., U. S. Govt. Print. Off., from March 4, 1873 to date.

the most widely available of any, and a good one. It is also a finding guide to the *text of simple and concurrent resolutions* as passed. There is no list of laws enacted, except as noted under bill number. All *bills* and *joint, concurrent* and *simple resolutions* are listed by number, with title and every action taken on them noted, up to and including approval by the President or enactment over his veto. However, it is difficult to follow debate on a bill through this "History," because it tends to list the first page where a bill was taken up but to ignore the skipping over many pages because of intervening motions. Checking debates is a laborious task. A specimen entry is shown below.

H. R. 4051—To grant to enlisted personnel of the armed forces certain benefits in lieu of accumulated leave
Referred to the Calendar of Motions to Discharge Committees, 3945.—Reported with amendment (H. Rept. 1990), 4782.—Made special order (H. Res. 631), 6479-6484.—Debated, amended, and passed House, 6484–6511, 6665.—Referred to Senate Committee on Military Affairs, 6620.—Reported with amendments (S. Rept. 1704), 8650.—Debated in Senate, 9206, 9643, 9708–9725, 9726–9735.—Amended and passed Senate; title amended, 9735.—House disagrees to Senate amendments and agrees to a conference, 9880.—Conferees appointed, 9980, 10218.—Senate insists upon its amendments and asks for a conference, 9839.—Conferees appointed, 9839.—Conference report (No. 2706) submitted in House and agreed to, 10573-10590.—Conference report submitted in Senate and agreed to, 10523.—Examined and signed, 10619, 10667.—Presented to the President, 10667.—Approved [Public, No. 704], 10789.

Exhibit 8

The Daily Digest.[13] This is a supplement in each daily issue of the *Congressional Record* but cumulated at the end of a session into a separate bound volume. It began with the first session of the 80th Congress, in 1947, and gives the "Highlights" of Congressional action the preceding day; bills introduced, bills and resolutions reported or passed in the respective houses; a resumé of business transacted, committee appointments, votes, debates; and committee hearings. The first issue of each month contains a cumulative statistical survey of the business transacted by Congress to date and a table of appropriation bills passed. The annual index cumulates the daily indexes but has also a *table of bills enacted into public law* during the session; a "*History of Bills Enacted into Public Law*," in which, arranged by law number, are given the bill, title, number, date of introduction, hearings, date reported, committee report number, *Congressional Record* page noting passage and approval; and an index which serves as a *status table, by subject,* for each bill and resolution *acted upon* during the session. A typical entry follows. Page references are to the *Daily Digest*, which in turn refers to the pertinent *Congressional Record* pages.

LABOR-FEDERAL SECURITY (H. R. 3333)
Committee, House D105, 423
House D109, 366, 424
Committee, Senate D140, 145, 148, 152, 156, 160, 163, 182, 202, 211, 232
Senate D228, 237, 243, 298, 427
Conference committee D400, 420
Public Law 141

Exhibit 9

---

[13] In Congressional Record since March 17, 1947. *See* footnote 12 above.

Note

The paging of the daily edition of the *Congressional Record* and of the *Daily Digest* differs from that of the bound volume. Since Congressmen are permitted to revise their remarks prior to final printing, the text may differ also. Cite the bound volume if available; otherwise give volume, page and *exact date* of the daily issue.

House and Senate Journals. The Constitution requires the keeping of journals by both houses of Congress.[14] Their content is essentially that of the *Congressional Record*, with the debates omitted.

Presidential Messages. When the President presents suggested legislation to Congress, or makes his annual report on the "state of the Union," or when he vetoes a bill (other than by a "pocket veto"), he writes a message to Congress explaining his reasons. These official statements have value in a legislative history. Since 1873 they have been currently printed in the *Congressional Record*, the House and Senate *Journals* (veto messages only in the *Journal* of the house in which the bill originated), as House or Senate *Documents*, and (since 1939) selected ones in the unofficial *United States Code Congressional and Administrative News.*[15]

United States Code Congressional and Administrative News.[16] Since 1939, this publication (under the names of *United States Code Congressional Service* and *United States Code Congressional and Administrative Service* previous to its present title) has aimed at supplying in one place verbatim copies of federal legislative materials less easily selected and accessible in official form. It is a very good tool not only for legislative history but for the collection and use of current federal legislation. Each issue (semi-monthly during sessions of Congress, cumulating into annual bound volumes) contains the following departments.

1. *Commentary on the legislative situation* (omitted from the bound volume). The final pamphlet issue for a session sometimes contains an extensive summary of legislation enacted.

2. *"Index-Digest of Bills Introduced."* It is omitted from the bound volumes.

3. *Biographical data of President, cabinet and Congress.*

4. *Verbatim text without margin notes of all public laws.*

5. *"Legislative history"* of nearly all public laws. For many, this is the most convenient *compilation of committee reports on bills enacted into law.* This material is indexed in the *United States Code Annotated.*

---

[14] The House *Journals* for the first thirteen Congresses were published all at one time in nine numbered volumes; thereafter they have appeared at the close of each session, for that session, in the numbered serial set of Government documents. The Senate *Journals* for the first thirteen Congresses were issued all at one time in five unnumbered volumes, and since then have appeared at the close of each session, in the serial set. There is also a set of Senate *Executive Journals*, containing the proceedings of executive sessions, seldom included in the Senate *Journals*. Formerly published at irregular intervals and released only long after the close of the sessions covered, they are, beginning in 1950, published and released annually.

[15] There is no complete collection of all the messages of the Presidents. Most of them have been printed in James D. Richardson's *A Compilation of the Messages and Papers of the President, 1789-1897* (10 volumes, with later supplements through March 4, 1929). *Veto Messages of the Presidents of the United States, with the Action of Congress Thereon*, a compilation by Ben Perley Moore, covers such messages up to August, 1886. Veto messages are separately listed in the *Congressional Record* index.

[16] St. Paul, Minn., West Publishing Co., 1942 to date. To May 1950 as *United States Code Congressional Service;* 1951-May 20, 1952 as *United States Code Congressional and Administrative Service.*

6. *President's legislative and state of the Union messages, verbatim.*

7. *Presidential proclamations and executive orders, verbatim.*

8. *Amendments to federal court rules, verbatim.*

9. *Important administrative rules and regulations, verbatim.*

10. *Tables.* These largely duplicate those in the *United States Code Annotated.* They include (1) *public laws enacted,* with *Statutes at Large* volume and chapter; (2) *United States Code* classification for public laws enacted. This is probably the earliest source of this information. The classification, assigned in advance of the *Code* publication, is unofficial, but is reliable. (3) *United States Code* sections *affected* by new legislation; (4) Bills enacted into law (by bill number); (5) proclamations and executive orders, by number, date, and title; (6) abbreviations of principal government agency titles, as NLRB, *etc.;* (7) titles and statutory origin of principal government agencies, substantially as those in the *United States Code.*

11. *Cumulative subject index to all material printed.*

Commerce Clearing House "Congressional Index." [17] This is a loose-leaf treatment of the legislative history material of a Congress, taken from diverse official sources and so arranged and published as to be more usable than the official. It is purely an index, containing no texts or abridgements of bills, committee reports or debates. Several of the indexes are in two parts, covering, first, the *latest bills,* and then all the rest; a complete coverage requires the examination of both parts.

1. *Pending public measures are indexed.* The headings are "Headline legislation"; "Name bills" (as Taft-Hartley); companion bills; by subject, with bills acted upon indicated by an asterisk; by author (introducer).

2. *Members of Congress are listed, with biographical information.*

3. *Bills and resolutions are listed by number.*

4. *Status tables are provided.* These tables show every Congressional action on each *reported* bill and resolution. Approved bills of the current session are indicated by a star. A useful feature of these tables is the information about *hearings.* The serial numbers of *committee reports* are given.

5. *Special reports* (those not relating to pending bills) of House and Senate committees are listed.

6. *Committee personnel are listed.*

7. *Public laws enacted are listed by number and subject.*

8. *Treaties pending at the beginning of each session of a Congress are listed with action taken.*

9. *Voting record of each Congressman.* The vote of each Congressman on any bill subject to a roll-call vote is given. Listing is (a) by bill number; and (b) by Congressman, thus noting both who voted for and against a given bill, and how a given Congressman voted on all roll-call bills.

E. Compiling a Legislative History.

The routine and materials employed in compiling a legislative history depend largely upon the organization served, the exact purpose of the history, and the time at which the compilation is begun. Some purposes require the entire process detailed below; others only a small part of it.

Contemporary Checking of Passage of a Bill through Congress. The fol-

---

[17] Congressional Index Service. Chicago, Commerce Clearing House. Begins with 75th Congress, 1937.

lowing procedure of a typical government agency for compiling legislative histories for its own purposes is perhaps somewhat more elaborate than most law offices would follow, and may be simplified to the extent desired.

FIRST SUPPLEMENT SURPLUS APPROPRIATION RESCISSION ACT, 1946 [18]
Public Law 301—79th Congress
Ch. 30—2d Session
*(H.R. 5158)
Approved February 18, 1946.

* This bill supersedes H. R. 4103 . . . and H. R. 4407 . . . H. R. 4407 . . . was vetoed . . . because it contained a rider to return . . . See appendixes for histories on H. R. 4103 and H. R. 4407.

H. R. 5604, a bill reducing or further reducing . . . was reported in the House on February 27, 1946.

APPENDIX A.

H. R. 4103, a bill reducing certain appropriations. . . . [the history of this companion bill is given as above]

Exhibit 10

1. Digest the *Congressional Record* and *Federal Register* daily, reporting on all legislation of interest to the agency, noting both new bills, the progress of previously noted bills, and regulations touching agency activities.

2. For each new bill of interest start a file; until the bill becomes law or dies, initial entries are made on a large index card calling for the following information:

[18] This history is greatly abridged, both as to number and fullness of entries, from one prepared by Miss Minnie Wiener, as Librarian of the General Services Administration.

bill number, companion and related bill numbers, name of introducer, title and subject matter of bill, hearings, action in Congress (dates, pages in *Congressional Record* where noted, committee reports, etc.), President's action, public or private law number. All bills, hearings, reports, Congressional documents and *Congressional Record* clippings of debates are collected, with the act as finally approved.

3. From the index card above, make a calendar or table of contents in final form, as follows, numbering each item in the margin. Collect, arrange by number all material listed, in order, and bind or file for permanent preservation.

4. Cross-references should be made to all companion and related bills, and the same process followed for them.

Status Tables. Numerous tables note the status of bills already introduced. If available, the best for pending legislation are the daily House and Senate *calendars*, and those of the individual committees; used in connection with the *Congressional Record* the date of each action is the key; if a less frequent check is sufficient, the fortnightly (cumulating annually) *Congressional Record* "History of Bills and Resolutions" and the status tables in the *Congressional Index* are excellent.

Summary of Citations to Legislative Intent Materials. Materials useful in determining legislative intent include Presidential messages, records of Congressional debates, hearings, reports, and numbered Congressional documents. *Messages* are printed in the *Congressional Record*, as Congressional numbered *Documents* (findable through the bill number), and in the *United States Code Congressional and Administrative News*. *Hearings* are listed by bill number in the *Congressional Index* status tables, in the *Daily Digest* of the *Congressional Record*, and in the committee calendars, where those to be printed are noted. *Committee reports* on specific bills are listed by number in all status tables. All the above, and numbered Congressional *Documents* are listed by committee in the *Monthly Catalog of United States Government Publications*, but not by bill number. Committee Reports for enacted public laws are cited and printed in the *United States Code Congressional and Administrative News*.

Finding the Bill Number of a Law. It often becomes necessary to trace the legislative history and intent of an existing law. To do this it is first necessary to learn its bill number, which may be done easily by two methods. (1) The *Statutes at Large* and slip laws each give the bill number, as shown at pages 15 and 18.

(2) When only the subject of a law is known, the above citations are obtainable through the statute subject index. A third but more laborious method is to trace the law through the table in the annual volume of the *Daily Digest*, which under the public law number gives the desired information. The same may be done through the *Congressional Index* table of enacted laws, but neither of these methods would be employed if the slip law or *Statute at Large were available*.

F. State Legislative Histories.

The materials for state legislative histories are scarce in print, but not altogether nonexistent. They are much more available for tracing the progress of bills through the legislatures than for determining the legislative intent of specific bills.

Materials Published During Sessions. Few state legislatures print their bills for general distribution. Individual bills, however, may usually be secured during term time on application to legislators. Amendments and often entire important bills are printed verbatim in the legislative journals of most states. Bills by title or synopsis are increasingly noted in state legislative "Bulletins," "Synopses and Digests," and the like, issued throughout a session. Though these publications vary in scope, most of them list the bills and resolutions by number and title or synopsis of contents, and give the legislative history from introduction to final approval. Customarily, interim bulletins are cumulated at session's end. Among the states providing this service are California (which has the most elaborate one), Connecticut, Illinois, Maine, Nevada, Massachusetts, Oregon, and Washington. Some of the journals described below are also available during legislative sessions.

Unofficial Advance Sheet Legislative Services. A promising recent development has been the publication for several states of advance sheet supplements to privately published annotated statutes, similar to the *United States Code Congressional and Administrative News* for federal statutes, but not so elaborate. For some states there are also unofficial legislative services, on the order of the *Legislative Index*, but not so complete.

Legislative Journals, Usually Published After a Session. Each house of every state legislature except that of New Mexico publishes a legislative journal. These are excellent for tracing the progress of bills through the legislatures, but, with two or three exceptions, of little value for determining legislative intent.

They fall into two categories. First are the journals of California, Maine, and Pennsylvania, which approximate in content the *Congressional Record*, with the addition of verbatim texts of many bills and more or less complete committee reports. Thus, these journals not only trace the legislative history of a bill, but provide considerable data bearing upon legislative intent as well. The journals in the second category, comprising the remaining states, parallel the House and Senate *Journals* of the Congress in giving the minutes and votes of legislative sessions. Most of them also print amendments to pending bills, either in full or by amending provisions; and many print committee reports on important bills, sometimes in full but usually in digest form. It is thus possible to trace the history of bills through these journals, and also, but to a very limited extent, to determine legislative intent.

State Legislative Documents. A small and diminishing number of states maintain bound document sets, corresponding roughly to the United States serial set, but this material contains little of legislative history interest. Occasionally an investigating committee report on a legislative matter is printed therein, but these latter reports are more readily available directly from the reporting agencies themselves.

State Legislative Research Organization Reports. Perhaps the most fruitful source of background information on state legislation is found in the reports and bulletins of the numerous law revision commissions, legislative research bureaus, legislative councils, and state university bureaus of government and public administration, which are described in Chapter 27.

G. Availability of Legislative History Materials.

Practically all the materials noted in this chapter are listed and priced in either the *Monthly Catalog of United States Government Publications*, the *Monthly Checklist of State Publications*, or the unofficial *Public Affairs Information Service Bulletin*, described in Chapter 27. Many may be subscribed for by the year, but individual bills, hearings, committee reports and calendars can often be secured free on application to legislators, legislative committees or document rooms.

CHAPTER 6

INDEXES AND TABLES: WORK WITH FEDERAL STATUTES

A. Subject Indexes to Statutes Generally.

Each session law volume and each compilation of statutes indexes the laws in it. Such indexes are less satisfactory than those to case law. Whereas practically all reported American cases from 1658 to date are thoroughly indexed in several ways, no similarly complete index exists in print for federal or state statutes. A detailed card index of federal and state statutes is maintained in the Library of Congress, but, due to expense, there is no prospect that it will be printed.

B. Subject Indexes to Federal Statutes.

With the exception of the Beaman and the McClenon and Gilbert indexes described below, subject indexes of any current value, to federal statutes, are to individual volumes of the *Statutes at Large* or to such compilations as the *Revised Statutes* or *United States Code*. Also, with the exception of the two indexes mentioned, statutory subject indexes are to statutes *in force* at the time the index was completed. What the lawyer is most interested in, usually, is an index of public general statutes in force, of general interest, such as those to the *Code*. The scope of the various indexes is pointed out below.

Subject Indexes to the Constitution. This charter is indexed separately in all editions of the *United States Code* and in annotated editions of the Constitution. It is also separately indexed in many state statutory compilations.

Subject Indexes to All Federal Statutes Ever Enacted. The only coverage here is through consultation of the subject index of each volume of the *Statutes at Large*. With a few exceptions, these volumes index private and public laws separately.

Subject Indexes to Federal Private Laws. Private laws are indexed in the individual volumes of the *Statutes at Large*, but no cumulative index of present value exists.

Subject Indexes to All Federal Public Laws Ever Enacted. There is no cumulative index of this kind.

Subject Indexes to All "Public General Laws of a Permanent Nature." An index of this nature would not index appropriation acts or others of only a temporary nature, but would include others which at any time had been in force. The only federal examples of present significance are the following:

1. **Index analysis of the Federal Statutes . . . 1789-1873.**[1] Compiled by Middleton G. Beaman and A. K. McNamara, this index combines with the McClenon and Gilbert index, below, to cover federal legislation through 1931. To the extent that legislation for 1789 to 1873 was incorporated in the *Revised Statutes* (which was indexed by McClenon and Gilbert), the two indexes overlap in coverage, but this is the only cumulative index covering *all* such legislation for the period given. This is a subject index in the usual form, plus a table of repeals and amendments to the *Statutes at Large*, and a table of acts by popular name. Neither table is of present value. Scott and Beaman's *Index Analysis of the Federal Statutes, 1873-1907,*[2] was superseded by *McClenon and Gilbert*, below.

2. **Index to the Federal Statutes, 1874-1931.**[3] Compiled by Walter H. McClenon and Wilfred C. Gilbert, and usually known by their names, this index covers also the *Revised Statutes*, so that to a considerable extent its scope actually is from 1789 to 1931. It aims to index all "general and permanent laws" enacted, whether still in force or not. Provisions no longer in force are starred; those repealed or superseded are in italics, as shown below.

INDEX TO THE FEDERAL STATUTES   875

PUBLIC PROPERTY—Continued.
  PURCHASE—Continued.
    of Land requires authority of law_____ R. S. 3736 (U. S. C. 41:14)
    *from Members of Congress, when allowable_____ *R. S. 3740; 19:249 Fb 27 1877*
    from Members of Congress, Delegates or Resident Commissioners, when allowable_____ 35:1109§116 Mr 4 1909
                                                                                        (U. S. C. 18:206)

Exhibit 11

A variety of information is given in footnotes, such as a list of statutes presented by states for Statuary Hall in the Capitol building; commemorative coins authorized; corporations federally chartered; acts passed over the Presidential veto, *etc.* There are several statutory tables, now obsolete.

The present value of the index. This is reduced by its age, but it is still the only one of wide scope, to all federal statutes of general and permanent interest which at any time were in force, through the year 1931. In tracing the history of earlier legislation, it is invaluable. For example, the history of federal legislation concerning banks, courts, railroads, *etc.*, through 1931, is readily followed through this index.

[1] Washington, D. C., U. S. Govt. Print. Off., 1911.
[2] Washington, D. C., U. S. Govt. Print. Off., 1908.
[3] Washington, D. C., U. S. Govt. Print. Off., 1933.

Subject Indexes to Permanent Federal Laws of a Public General Nature in Force. This is the most satisfactory index for most present purposes, and is the common type. Every general statutory compilation has such an index. That for the Revised Statutes is now of limited interest. Those to the various editions of the *United States Code* are the ones most consulted by lawyers. This type of index must be used with an awareness that enactments repealed, superseded or expired before its compilation are not indexed, so that it may be necessary to consult an earlier edition of the statutes for them; and that some statutes indexed therein may since have been amended, repealed, or superseded, requiring recourse to pamphlet supplements or to *Shepard's United States Citations* (described in Chapter 28), to make certain that the picture is complete and accurate.

United States Code subject indexes. All material in the *Code* — editorial as well as *Code* sections—is thoroughly indexed in a separate index volume. Entries are both by large topic (as Agriculture, Bankruptcy), and by catchword (as Staining, High Schools, and Jurisdictional Amount). There are also occasional references to acts by popular name or subject. The Federal Rules of Civil and Criminal Procedure and some court rules are indexed, as are those agency rules of practice which are printed in the Code appendices. The index to the *United States Code Annotated*, while essentially the same as that of the official edition, has some additional entries. *Recompiled volumes* have their own separate indexes, but the general index, since it covers overlapping subject matter from all titles of the *Code*, is often more satisfactory to use. The *Federal Code Annotated* has both a general index and one for each separate volume.

Subject Indexes to Federal Administrative Rules and Regulations. The indexes to the *Federal Register* and the *Code of Federal Regulations* are described in Chapter 17. Some of these rules are also indexed in some loose-leaf services, as noted in Chapter 26.

Indexes to Federal Court Rules. As described in Chapter 10, these rules are indexed in any volume printing them, whether it be a pamphlet from the court concerned, the *United States Code,* a special volume of a Supreme Court digest, in the *Federal Rules Service,* or in separate treatises or manuals on federal procedure.

C. Tables of Federal Acts by Popular Name.

Many acts are known by a popular name — as the "G. I. Bill of Rights" — which is conferred upon them by the public or by the enacting clause (". . . this Act may be cited as the 'Territorial Enabling Act of 1950.'"). Almost every edition of federal statutes lists enactments in this manner, either in the general subject index or more usually in a separate table. Below are notes on some of the more used tables.

Comprehensive Tables of Federal Statutes by Popular Name. For most purposes, a list such as one of the following would be first choice.

"Federal acts by popular names or short titles." This is perhaps the best known list. It is cumulated by Shepard's Citations, Inc., Colorado Springs, Colorado, at frequent intervals, and kept up to date by the red paper cumulative supplements and white paper advance sheets of *Shepard's United States Citations.* Complete citations are given to all forms of the acts cited, as below.

<table>
<tr><td colspan="2" align="center">TABLE OF FEDERAL ACTS   F-G</td></tr>
</table>

Federal Highway Act of 1938
June 8, 1938, c. 328, 52 Stat. 633
Code Title 16, §460b
Code Title 23, §2b, 7note, 8a, 10b, 13a,
   21b, 41b, 55b, c. 2note
 	
Federal Highway Act·of 1940
Sept. 5, 1940, c. 715, 54 Stat. 867
Code Title 15, §6061
Code Title 16, §§8-1, 460b, 460c
·Code Title 23, §§3b, 6a-1, 7note, 10b,
   10c, 20a, 21c, 23b, 54a, 55b
Code Title 25, §318b
	Firearms Act (Copeland)
	June 30, 1938, c. 850, 52 Stat. 1250
	Code Title 15, §§901-909
	
	First Deficiency Appropriation Act, 1940
	Apr 6, 1940, c. 77, 54 Stat. 82
	
	First Deficiency Appropriation Act, 1941
	Apr. 1, 1941, c. 32, Public No. 25
	
	First Deficiency Appropriation Act, Fiscal Year 1937
	Feb. 9, 1937, c. 9, 50 Stat. 8

Exhibit 12

"**Table of statutes by popular name.**" Volume 14 of the *Digest of United States Supreme Court Reports*[4] contains probably the most complete table of its kind. It is supplemented by annual cumulative pocket parts. The breadth of its scope renders it useful as a subject index; all legislation in many categories may be easily traced throughout. For example, all legislation concerning national forests, monuments, and parks is listed; all naturalization, pension, Indian, tariff, and merchant marine acts are listed, as are general peace treaties. Legislation, including appropriation acts relating to government departments and other agencies is listed, as are neutrality proclamations.

Tables of Codified Federal Statutes by Popular Name. The official *United States Code,* and the unofficial annotated editions of it all have tables of statutes by popular name, which at any time have been *included in the Code.* The coverage is thus not so broad as that in the two tables described above. The official and *Federal Code Annotated* tables tend to emphasize the official short title of the act as set forth in the enacting clause, rather than the popular title conferred by the public. For example, the official "Labor Management Relations Act of 1947," not the better known "Taft-Hartley Act," is thus cited.

Federal Statutes by Popular Name, for the Current Year. The tables noted above list legislation of the current year by official short title. The *United States Code Congressional and Administrative News*[5] also has such a table. The *Congressional Index*[6] lists "Name Bills," "Headline Legislation," and acts by official short title. The general index of the *United States Law Week*[7] and the American Digest System *Descriptive-Word Indexes*[8] frequently list litigated statutes by popular name.

D. Bill Status Tables.

In tracing the progress of pending legislation, tables giving the current status of individual bills and resolutions are indispensable. The notes below are intended to correlate more detailed descriptions of these tables in Chapter 5, on Legislative Histories.

---

[4] *See* page 113.
[5] St. Paul, Minn., West Publishing Company.
[6] Chicago, Ill., Commerce Clearing House, Inc.
[7] Washington, D. C., The Bureau of National Affairs.
[8] St. Paul, Minn., West Publishing Company.

Status Tables for All Bills Introduced. Status tables generally ignore un-reported bills, estimated at 90 per cent of the total. Omission of a bill from a cumulative status table indicates that it was never reported out of committee.

Congressional Record "History of Bills." All bills and resolutions are listed as intro-duced, in the fortnightly noncumulative indexes to the *Congressional Record.* There-after, they are listed only as action is taken on them during the period covered by the index. At the end of each session, all this information is cumulated into a "History of Bills" for each the House and the Senate, in which *every bill and resolution introduced,* whether acted upon or not, is listed, and its legislative history given. This is the only complete status table for Congressional legislation, and it is a good one, widely available.

Status Tables for Bills Acted Upon.

1. Congressional Record "Daily Digest." The *subject index* of bills acted upon, serves as a status table. *See* page 48.

2. Congressional Index. The status table in this unofficial loose-leaf service shows every action on every *reported public bill.*

3. Digest of Public General Bills. A green-paged section gives the status of bills acted upon during a session.

4. House Calendar. The daily "Numerical order of bills and resolutions which have passed either House, and bills now pending on the calendar" (*see* page 44) is a very good status table of *reported bills of both House and Senate.* The "Final Edition" for each Congress is perhaps the most useful single status table.

5. Committee Calendars. These calendars are perhaps the most useful of all status tables, since they give the status not only of the individual bills, but of *companion or substitute bills* as well.

Status Tables of Treaties. *See* Chapter 4, Treaties.

E. Chapter and Law Number Tables.

The official edition of the federal slip laws supplies the following critical num-bers: public or private law; Congress and session; chapter; bill; volume and page of the *Statutes at Large;* and date of approval. That is, for example, Public Law 415; 82d Congress, 2d Session, Chapter 478; S. 2610; 66 Stat. 282; June 27, 1952. (The *Statutes at Large* citation on the official slip law has been given only since mid-1951). Often, however, the slip law is not at hand and it becomes necessary by other means to translate a bill to a law number, or the reverse; a law number to a *Statutes at Large* citation; or a law number to a *United States Code* title and section. Tables are available to perform most of these tasks for public law, but seldom for private laws.

From Bill Number to Law Number. That is, *as from* H. R. 6539, 81st Con-gress, 2d Session, *to* Public Law Number 495 of the same Congress.

1. On the face of the slip law or Statutes at Large, as noted above, whether a public or private law.
2. Status tables. All the tables described above give the law number of bills enacted into law.
3. United States Code Congressional and Administrative News. The tables of "Senate and House Bills Enacted" give this for public laws.

From Law Number into Bill Number. That is, *as from* Public Law Num-ber 495, 81st Congress, 2d Session, *to* H. R. 6539 of the same Congress.

1. On the face of the slip law.
2. On the face of the Statutes at Large. The "List of Public Law" and "List of Private

Laws," arranged by law number, refer to the page where the law is printed and the bill number given.

3. Digest of Public General Bills. The "Public Laws" table.

4. Congressional Record "Daily Digest." There is an annual "History of Bills Enacted into Public Law," arranged by law number.

5. United States Code Congressional and Administrative News. In the "Table of Public Laws."

6. Congressional Index. In the table of "Enactments—Public Laws."

From Bill or Law Number to Chapter Number. That is, *as from* H. R. 6539, Public Law Number 495, *to* Chapter 139, 81st Congress, 2d Session.

1. On the face of the slip law or Statutes at Large.

2. United States Code Congressional and Administrative News. In the "Table of Public Laws."

From Bill or Law Number to Statutes at Large. That is, *as from* the above bill and law numbers *to* 64 Stat. 96 (1952).

1. On the face of the official slip law, since mid-1951.

2. Statutes at Large. In the "List of Public Laws," "List of Private Laws."

3. United States Code Congressional and Administrative News. The volume and chapter number are given in the "Table of Public Laws."

From Bill or Public Law to Revised Statutes or United States Code. That is, *as from* H. R. 4289, Public Law Number 493, § 1, 81st Congress, 2d Session, *to* 48 U. S. C. § 371 (Supp. III, 1951). (Public Law 495, used as an example above, was not codified.)

1. United States Code Congressional and Administrative News. The "Table of Classifications" is arranged by public law number.

2. All editions of the Revised Statutes or United States Code. By translating the bill or law number into the *Statutes at Large* citation, the equivalent *Revised Statutes* or *United States Code* citations is found through the tables of "Statutes Included" in the compilations.

F. Parallel Transfer Tables from One Form of Statute to Another: Where Published.

One of the most necessary tables is that which translates a citation from one form of enactment to another, as from session law to code, or the reverse. (One form of transfer table is the table of acts by popular name. If an act is cited by name, the table gives the complete formal citation in all forms). Where needed, these tables are usually supplied in both official and unofficial compilations of statutes, and sometimes in session law volumes as well. The most complete of such tables, of present interest, are those for the *United States Code*. With the exceptions noted below, the tables in all editions are substantially identical.

United States Code Tables. **Table I: "Statutes Included."** This table is in two parts: In (a), each section of the *Revised Statutes* included in the *Code* is listed, followed by the corresponding *Code* section. Thus, R. S. 107 is 2 U. S. C. § 203. In (b), each section of the *Statutes at Large* is similarly treated. Thus, the Act of March 18, 1935 (the table is arranged by date), c. 32, § 2, 49 Stat. 46, is 7 U. S. C. § 609. Frequently the *Code* citation is not to a section of the *Code*, but to a statute cited in an editorial note to a section cited.

Table II: "Executive Acts Included." In this table, executive orders, proclamations, and reorganization plans which in any way affect or implement *Code* sections are listed, together with the section affected or implemented. Most such *Code* references will be to editorial notes in which the executive act is paraphrased or reproduced verbatim. Thus, Executive Order No. 6260 is cited to 12 U. S. C. § 95a note, where the order, issued under authority of § 95a, is printed. Where, however, the executive act changes the text of the *Code* section, rather than implementing it (as an order changing tariff rates), it is cited without the "note," as one of the parenthetical statutory sources of the section. For example, Executive Order No. 7756 changed the duties of the Secretary of the Interior, as set forth in 5 U. S. C. § 485.

  Tables II-VII. These are parallel citations from certain fundamental laws — the bankruptcy act, criminal and judicial codes, internal revenue and interstate commerce acts — to the corresponding sections of the *United States Code*.

  Repeal tables. Tables VIII-XI are the reverse of tables I-II: they are of statutes and executive acts repealed, executed or eliminated. The *Revised Statutes* table lists sections which have been repealed, whether or not they were ever part of the *Code*, and this is the best source of such information. The remaining tables list only statutes which at one time were incorporated in the *Code* but have since been repealed or otherwise become ineffective.

  United States Code Annotated Tables. These are substantially like the official edition tables, but are often more detailed and are supplemented more frequently. There is an additional table which is very useful for finding legislative intent.

  Index to legislative history and Congressional comment. The final *U. S. C. A.* index volume contains this table, which is in effect a subject index to Congressional committee reports on public laws, as published since 1941 in the *United States Code Congressional and Administrative News.*

  Federal Code Annotated Tables. These are substantially like those of the official edition for the period preceding the *Revised Statutes,* but beginning with 1874 *a single table in effect combines the several tables of the official.* It is fuller, in that it shows the disposition of *all public acts,* whether or not part of the *Code,* indicating whether the provision is temporary, obsolete, executed, repealed (citing the repealer), or still in force but not codified; and if in the *Code,* the title and section.

G. Parallel Transfer Tables from one Form of Statute to Another: Use of.

  From Slip Law to Statutes at Large. See "From Bill or Public Law Number to Statutes at Large," above.

  From Slip Law to United States Code. That is, *as from* Public Law Number 814, 81st Congress, 2d Session, c. 994, § 208 (a) *to* 26 U. S. C. § 115 (g) (1), (2) (Supp. III, 1950).

  United States Code Congressional and Administrative News. The "Table of Classifications" makes the transfer. If the law is more than a year old, the citation should be found to the *Statutes at Large* first, and the transfer then made through a table in the *United States Code,* as described below.

  From Statutes at Large to Revised Statutes. That is, *as from* the Act of September 2, 1789, c. 12, § 1, 1 Stat. 65, *to* R. S. § 161.

"Reference Index to the Revised Statutes . . . from Statutes to Sections," in the *Revised Statutes*, makes the transfer.

From Statutes at Large to United States Code. That is, *as from* the Act of Feburary 10, 1939, c. 2, § 3261, 53 Stat. 393, *to* 26 U. S. C. § 3261.

United States Code. The official edition does this through "Table I—Statutes Included, (b) Statutes at Large," The *U. S. C. A.* does it through its "Chronological Tables," and the *F. C. A.* through its "Key to United States Statutes at Large." *See* the description of *Code* tables, above.

From Revised Statutes to United States Code. A table in all the editions of the *Code* supplies this information. For example, R. S. § 4178 is 46 U. S. C. § 46, as shown by such a table.

From Revised Statutes to Statutes at Large.

From United States Code to Statutes at Large. No tables are needed to translate sections of compilations back to the basic enactment, because that information is given in connection with the printed text of each section of the compilation. In the *Revised Statutes*, it is shown in roman type in the margin. In the *Code*, citations to statutory authority are in parentheses at the end of the *Code* section.

Tables for Administrative Rules and Regulations. These are described in Chapter 17.

H. Federal Agencies: Statutory Background and Organization.

A knowledge of how an agency is set up, of what its functions are, and who its chief personnel are, is often a necessary preliminary to finding the law applicable to a problem. Several means of varying scope are provided to supply this need, as described in Chapter 17.

I. Work with Statutes: Elementary Considerations.

The most important decision to make in work with statutes of any kind is to determine what is wanted. Is a particular statute or section sought? In its original or in codified form? What is known about it — date, subject matter, bill or law number, and the like? Are case or other annotations wanted, or just the text? Is it a matter of tracing the progress of a bill through the legislature or of determining the intent of the legislators in enacting a law? Has a certain regulation been amended since promulgation? Once the desired goal is determined, the rest is largely a matter of knowing the resources of statutory publication.

The next most important factor in an efficient search is to ascertain that the right materials are being used. Does the publication date of the volume being consulted exclude the particular statute, regulation or annotation sought? Are all the required units and supplements at hand? Is it certain that the statute is still in force, or should an earlier compilation be consulted?

J. Original and Compiled Forms Distinguished.

This matter is discussed at page 17. Compilations of statutes of public general interest, arranged by subject, are so much more convenient than the slip or session law form — and as a consequence lawyers and students so much prefer to work with them — that searchers are prone to forget that the compilation is usually only prima facie the law, and that the original form is then still the real authority. In legal writing of all kinds, the session law form of a statute is best cited, not the compilation, *unless the latter has been re-enacted as the positive law*, in terms repealing the original session law.[9] The preface of each volume and supplement of the *Code* lists the titles re-enacted into positive law. If the original act has not been amended, the *Code* text of any given section is probably identical with the original, but the safe procedure is to check with the original to make certain.

K. Finding the Earliest Printing of New Enactments.

Slip laws, as described in Chapter 3, commonly provide the promptest publication of new laws, except in loose-leaf services. *See* Chapter 26.

L. Finding a Particular Federal Statute.

The most common task in work with legislation is to find a particular statute. This may be done in a variety of ways, depending upon the information available.

By Subject. If only the subject matter of the desired statute is known, recourse must be had to a subject index. A preliminary division of the search is made by determining if possible whether the law is public or private.

The normal approach is through a subject index of *public general laws in force*, such as are found in all statutory compilations. If it turns out that the statute is no longer in force, the search leads to indexes of all public general acts which at any time have been in force; this means the index described at pages 54 to 56, supplemented for the period from 1932 to date by the annual indexes to the *Statutes at Large*. Care must be taken that all applicable statutes are consulted; often more than one is pertinent to a given set of facts.

In searching multi-volume unofficial editions of the *United States Code*, the indexes to individual volumes and titles are more convenient to use than the more bulky general index to the entire *Code*, but it is dangerous to restrict the search to them. The reason is that legislation very often overlaps, a topic being covered by more than one title of the *Code*. This is particularly true where adjective and substantive law impinge upon each other; often what seems logically to be substantive law is covered wholly or in part by a procedural provision. It is safest, therefore, to check with an index to the whole body of the law — the general index.

By Title. If the popular name of a law (as Taft-Hartley Law) is known, its official citation may be found through a table of statutes by popular name, as described at page 55.

By Bill, Law, or Chapter Number. When only this information is at hand. the act can be traced through tables described at pages 57 to 61. The *number of the Congress or the date* are necessary parts of data, because bills, law numbers, and chapters are renumbered from the beginning of each new Congress. These critical data are found on each slip law and in the *Statutes at Large*.

---

[9] Thus, the statutory provision that human labor is not a commodity is cited as "Section 6 of the Clayton Act" (with a footnote reference to the Act of October 15, 1914, c. 323, § 6, 38 Stat. 731, 15 U. S. C. § 17), and not as "Title 15, Section 17 of the United States Code."

Transfer Tables from One Form of Statute to Another. *See* pages 60 and 61.

Treaties. These are indexed by number and subject, as described in Chapter 4.

Statutes No Longer in Force. In using subject indexes, it should be remembered that the only complete coverage is by the indexes to each of the many session laws (*Statutes at Large*), from the beginning to date, and that compiled indexes all omit something — private laws, uncodified laws, temporary, repealed, and superseded laws. A law indexed in one such compilation of public general laws in force may be omitted from a later one because no longer in force. It is then often necessary to start with the index to the current compilation and to work back through the various earlier editions. If found in the 1940 compilation, for example, but not in that for 1946, a table of repeals in the 1946 and succeeding editions will show when and by what act the desired law was repealed. Whenever a law is found in a compilation, each section will contain a reference to the original session law from which derived. For indexes to all public general federal acts from 1789 to 1931, *see* page 55.

M. Finding Federal Administrative Rules and Regulations.

This material is described in Chapter 7, together with all tables and indexes.

N. Finding Federal Court Rules.

This material is described at page 87.

O. Work with the United States Revised Statutes.

Although covering codified laws only through December 1, 1873, much of the *Revised Statutes* is still in force, though usually as amended by later enactments. The lawyer's contact with this compilation, however, is generally to check the text of sections cited as authority for such sections of the *United States Code* as have not been re-enacted into positive law. Its makeup and use are described in Chapter 3. A table in the *United States Code* gives the location of all *Revised Statutes* which are a part of that compilation; if repealed another table cites the repealer.

P. Work with the United States Code.

The status of the *Code* as authority, and its makeup are described in Chapter 3. It is the form of federal statute most used by the lawyer, even though he will cite the original *Statutes at Large* in legal writing as his authority. Which edition of the *Code* — official unannotated or unofficial annotated — to consult, if all are available, depends largely upon whether only the text of a statute is wanted, or if case annotations also are required.

Official Editions. If only the text of a *Code* section is needed, the official edition is more convenient, since it does not require the reader to turn over page after page of digest paragraphs annotating the individual sections. Notes, tables, and indexes are largely the same in all editions. The official edition costs only a fraction of the unofficial. From that point on, however, the advantage is all with the unofficial editions, which are what the lawyer customarily uses.

Unofficial Annotated Editions. These also are described in detail in Chapter 3, together with the special features of each. The added value of the unofficial editions lies in the digests of cases interpreting each section of the Constitution and *Code*, and also in their more frequent supplementation.

Finding the Required Code Sections. Much of the difficulty which users of the *Code* experience is in finding a specific section when their citation is to a slip law or to the *Statutes at Large*. A careful examination of the *Code*, in connection with the reading of the material on indexes and tables in this chapter and the material cited herein in Chapter 3, will resolve nearly all such difficulties. Particular attention is called to the sections in this chapter on "Chapter and Law Number Tables" and "Parallel Tables for Statutes from One Form to Another." Care should always be taken to ascertain by scanning the publication date of the volume or supplement consulted, that it covers the desired dates and that the sequence of parts is complete.

Q. Citators for Federal Statutes.

Having found a statute section in point, the lawyer must yet determine two things: (1) That the section is still in force in the form found, not having been amended, repealed or superseded by later legislative action; and (2) whether it has been construed by a court of competent authority. Elaborate devices called citators or citation books aid the lawyer here. They are described in Chapter 28.

CHAPTER 7

STATE LEGISLATION AND ITS PUBLICATION

A. SIMILARITY TO FEDERAL LEGISLATIVE FORMS.
B. CONSTITUTIONS.
C. STATE SESSION LAWS.
D. STATE STATUTORY COMPILATIONS.
E. MUNICIPAL CHARTERS, ORDINANCES AND CODES.

A. Similarity to Federal Legislative Forms.

The characteristics of state legislative forms and their publication are so like their federal counterparts as to require little additional comment. The period covered, however, runs far back of 1789; the states in existence at that date had had more or less regular publication of their legislation, both for the Colonial period, and from 1776 to 1789.

B. Constitutions.

Constitutions of Individual States. The statutory compilations of each state contain the text of the state constitution and amendments. In addition, where the state was formed from another larger state or from a territory, the appropriate documents leading up to statehood are usually printed with the constitution. These documents may include the Ordinance of 1787, the enabling act setting up the territorial government or providing for statehood, or, in some cases, appropriate treaty provisions.

Editions vary considerably in content and completeness of annotations. An earlier constitution than the one presently in force may be included, with or without parallel conversion tables from one to the other; some, Arizona, for instance, contain compilers' notes; others, as the *Iowa Code Annotated*, present a historical essay on the various constitutions of the state and their interpretation.

State legislative manuals provided for the use of legislators contain the constitution. A few states, as California, publish official annotated editions of their constitutions.

Compilations of Constitutions of All States. There have been several compilations of the constitutions of all states, but, except for historical purposes, the only compilation of current value is the *Constitutions of the States and the United States*, issued in 1938 by the New York Constitutional Convention Committee as Volume III of its preliminary studies. A useful feature is a comprehensive combined subject index to the provisions of the constitutions of all states and of the United States.

65

Although some new state constitutions have been adopted since 1938 and others repeatedly amended, this compilation is still useful. There are three principal methods of bringing it down to date:

1. The safest, most laborious, is to check the latest editions of the session laws and compiled statutes of each state.

2. Citations to later revisions and amendments will be given in the biennial *Book of the States*,[1] kept up to date by the monthly *State Government*, both published by the Council of State Governments.

3. The same can be done through 1948 in the biennial *State Law Index*.[2]

4. The lawyer will commonly check the constitution citations in the state *Shepard's Citations*, which, for all states except Mississippi and Nevada, note amendments and proposed amendments, with citations to the session laws where printed. This of course requires the examination of the citator for each state. There is no royal road to complete coverage. The only advantage of methods "a" and "b" is that they give a conspectus in a page or two of what has been done in all states over a given two-year period.

Earlier compilations of state constitutions, now of only historical value, include: *The Federal and State Constitutions, Colonial Charters, and Other Organic Laws of the United States;*[3] *The Federal and State Constitutions, Colonial Charters and Other Organic Laws of the States, Territories and Colonies Now or Heretofore Forming the United States of America;*[4] *Index Digest of State Constitutions;*[5] and, *The State Constitutions and the Federal Constitution and Organic Laws of the Territories and Other Colonial Dependencies of the United States of America.*[6]

Amendments to State Constitutions. Since state constitutions are amended so much more often than the federal constitution, it is somewhat difficult to keep track of amendments. They are printed as part of the constitution in all editions of the statutes, but considerable time elapses between the ratification of an amendment and its printing in the statute supplement, so that the searcher will often consult the text of the amendment as submitted to the voters (or, in Delaware, to a second session of the legislature). The text is published in the state session laws as of the session when proposed, and is found through the appropriate *Shepard's Citations* unit. Since most proposed amendments *are not ratified*, the careful lawyer will check carefully, to make certain that the proposal was indeed adopted.

The *Shepard* notation form is illustrated by this Florida example:

Art VII

§ 5

PAd '49 [p. 1399]

meaning that the text of the proposed amendment (by adding a section to Article VII) was printed in the 1949 Florida Laws at page 1399. A revision of an existing section would have been cited PA '49 [1399]. If the proposed amendment

---

[1] Chicago, Published by Council of State Governments. 9 volumes to date, 1935-1952.

[2] 12 volumes covering 1926/26-1947/48. Washington, D. C., United States Government Printing Office, 1929-1949.

[3] Compiled by Ben Perley Moore. 2d ed., Washington, D. C., United States Government Printing Office, 1878. 2 v.

[4] Compiled by Francis Newton Thorpe. Washington, D. C., United States Government Printing Office, 1909. 7 v.

[5] Prepared for the New York State Constitutional Convention Commission by the Legislative Drafting Research Fund of Columbia University. Albany, New York State Constitutional Convention Commission, 1915.

[6] Compiled by Charles Kettleborough. Indianapolis, B. F. Bowen, 1918.

is rejected, the above entry will be dropped from the next *Shepard* supplement; if ratified, that supplement will note it as follows:

Art VII

5

A '49 p. 1399 [for a revision]; or

Ad'49 p. 1399 [for an added section].

Note that the date given in *Shepard* is that of the session law when *proposed;* actual *adoption* is usually a year or two later.

The biennial, now discontinued, *State Law Index* cited for all states amendments ratified, rejected, and pending.

The amending process has received much attention by the states. A table of procedures employed by the various states is found on pages 88-94 of the *Book of the States* for 1950-51. Except in Delaware, amendment of existing constitutions is by legislative proposal (usually in the form of a joint resolution), to be submitted to the voters at the next general election. In Delaware adoption is by two sessions of the state legislature. In state elections, adoption is by majority vote, except in Rhode Island, where three-fifths are required. Many studies of the amending process have been made, examples of which are: John P. Keith, *Methods of Constitutional Revision;* [7] Paul G. Steinbicker and Martin L. Faust, *Manual on the Amending Procedure and the Initiative and Referendum for the Missouri Constitutional Convention of 1943;* [8] Walter F. Dodd, *The Revision and Amendment of State Constitutions;* [9] Louisiana State Law Institute, *The Amending Process;* [10] Irby R. Hudson, *The Amending Process in State Constitutions.* [11]

Legislation Enacted in Accordance with a Constitutional Provision. When, as is frequently the case, a state legislative act mentions a particular article and section of the constitution, *Shepard's* state statutory citations note that fact, as shown by the following from *Shepard's Florida Citations:*

Art. V

§ 24

'49 C25066 § 1

meaning that Chapter 25066, § 1 of the Florida Laws for 1949 mentions the above section of the Florida constitution.

Judicial History of State Constitutions. The interpretation of these provisions by federal and state courts is traced through the various kinds of citators described in Chapter 18, certain Supreme Court digests, and the "Table of Statutes Construed" in all units of the National Reporter System.

C. State Session Laws.

Every state and territory publishes its session laws, under varying titles from state to state. There are, for example, the Massachusetts *Acts and Resolves;* the Rhode Island *Public Laws;* the South Carolina *Acts and Joint Resolutions;* the California *Statutes and Amendments to the Code;* the Kentucky *Laws;* etc. This is usually done at the end of each session, but often the laws of one or more special

---

[7] Austin, Texas, University of Texas Bureau of Municipal Research, 1949.

[8] Columbia, Mo., Missouri Constitutional Convention of 1943, 1943.

[9] Baltimore, Johns Hopkins Press, 1910.

[10] Louisiana State Law Institute, University Station, La. *Constitutional Problems,* no. 3 Prepared by Central Research Staff, Constitutional Revision Project, 1947.

[11] Irby R. Hudson. *The Amending Process in State Constitutions, in Tennessee.* University. Bureau of Public Administration. Papers on Constitutional Revision, volume 1, 1947.

sessions are combined with those of a regular session in a single volume. Regular sessions vary from state to state, from annual to quadrennial.

Slip Laws. The slip law form as an official publication is almost non-existent for state legislation. In several states (and the number is increasing), the first publication is in an advance sheet "session law service," usually by the publisher of the annotated "lifetime" edition of the statutory revision or code. These advance sheets are not to be confused with the current annotation service which is part of all annotated statute services, as the latter are in *code*, not slip law, form.

Content of Session Law Volumes. In makeup, session laws closely resemble the United States *Statutes at Large*. Often the state constitution and amendments are included. Most states publish public, private, and local laws and resolutions in a single volume; some publish only public laws; others, the public and private laws separately; usually the resolutions (which in some states lack the force of law) follow the acts and are separately numbered. The chapter or act numbers are almost always assigned chronologically by date of approval; but in some states (as Kansas and Oklahoma), a more or less successful attempt is made to follow exactly the titles and sections of the statutory revisions.

1. *Subject index.* All state session laws have subject indexes, but they vary greatly in size and quality.

2. *Table of chapters or acts included.* This table lists the legislation included, in the numerical order.

3. *Table of statutory revision or code titles and sections amended and repealed.* This table is aranged by code title and section, and may be included in the subject index under the heading "amendments and repeals," or it may be a separate table. In some states, as Massachusetts and New Jersey, it is cumulative from the latest official revision, and shows the combined effect of all later legislation. In other states the tables cumulate over long periods; California's, for example, covers the entire statehood period, from 1850.

4. *Table of amendments and repeals of uncodified laws.* In some states, as California, Idaho, and New York, this table covers the entire statehood period.

5. *Table of allocation of session laws into the revision or code.* This table traces current session laws into code titles and sections. It is not a common type.

6. *Table of bills maturing into laws during the sessions.* This is not a common type of session law table.

7. *Miscellaneous tables.* These may include the personnel of the legislature, personnel and calendars of the state courts, votes in the preceding elections, and the state auditor's and state treasurer's reports.

8. *Unofficial editions of session laws.* A development paralleling the session law services of unofficial statute compilations in some states is the publication of unofficial editions of the session laws in bound form. While their principal appeal is their more prompt publication, they usually have other features of utility. An example is *McKinney's Session Laws of New York*,[12] which combines the texts of the new laws (in which amendments, additions and deletions of older laws by the new are typographically indicated), with all the available legislative history reports and memoranda.

State Law Index. Compiled by the Library of Congress Legislative Reference Service, this was a biennial index of the session laws of public interest, of all states, during the years 1925 to 1948, after which it was discontinued for lack of funds. It was for most purposes the only comprehensive source of information as to legislation across state lines. Entries were alphabetical by rather broad subjects,

[12] Brooklyn, N. Y., Edward Thompson, Company, 1951 to date.

but with copious cross-references. Citations were to state, date of approval, and inclusive pages, chapter, and section of the acts. Entries under each heading were alphabetical by state. Thus, it was simple to find citations to the legislation of any or all states for a given period. A table of legislative sessions during each biennium covered gave the inclusive dates of each regular and special session of a state legislature, with the number of acts passed.

Public affairs information service bulletin. To a limited extent this *Bulletin* (*see* page 252) serves as a substitute for the discontinued *State Law Index* as a current index to the session laws of the Congress and of all states, since, in the fields of social science, economics and sociology it indexes important new laws as they are published in session law form. Entries are by subject, not by jurisdiction.

Authority of State Session Laws. The session laws are the best evidence (subject to comparison with the enrolled law), unless and until superseded by a codification which is positive law and not merely prima facie the law. In those states which have "perpetual revision," code sections are of course enacted as positive law by the session law itself.

In some states, most laws of public general interest are codified into positive law and for those laws the session low form of citation is seldom used, but only that of the consolidation or code. In actual practice in most states the lawyer consults the latest unofficial edition of the statutes (usually annotated), from which he gets the session law citation for each section cited. Where the revision as a whole has been enacted into positive law (as compared to the California — Louisiana — New York scheme of perpetual revision by section), the citation is of the revision "as amended by . . ." later session laws.

Notes

Publication of Session Laws. Keeping track of session laws is much more difficult than the same chore for law reports. This is partly because of the interpolation of special and extra sessions, but chiefly because of the extreme irregularity of publication procedure among the states. In the 1945-46 Ohio legislative session there were one regular and four special sessions. In thirty states and territories, the bound volumes are obtained from the office of the Secretary of State; in eleven from the state library; and in the remainder from a commercial printer or publisher designated by the legislature. The Council of State Governments, 1313 East 60th Street, Chicago 37, Illinois, issues a weekly mimeographed list of legislatures in session, about to convene, and adjourned (with dates), which is helpful. The subscription price is $3.00 per year.

Checklists of State Session Laws. There are four standard checklists of State Session laws:

1. State Library of Massachusetts, *Handlist of Legislative Sessions and Session Laws . . . to May, 1912,*[13] which in spite of some errors is still the most complete source of information about Colonial and state session laws of all states, constitutional conventions, and statutory revisions, for the period covered. It is out of print but obtainable second hand.

2. Grace E. Macdonald, *Checklist of Session Laws.* This covers the period through 1933, and was intended to supersede the *Handlist.*

3. Ervin H. Pollack, *A Supplement . . . to the Checklist of Session Laws Compiled by*

---

[13] Boston, Mass., Wright & Potter, 1912.
[14] New York, N. Y., H. W. Wilson, 1936.

Grace E. Macdonald. . . .[15] This is more than a supplement, as it corrects errors in *Macdonald.*

4. *Check List of Current American State Reports, Statutes and Session Laws.* The above lists are kept up to date by this regular feature of the *Law Library Journal*, though the information is less full.

D. State Statutory Compilations.

The problems of making available in convenient and up to date form the state legislation in force of a public, general, and permanent nature, are simliar to those met under federal legislation (described above), and are solved in much the same way. The resulting editions of the laws in classified form bear various titles in the several states—Codes, Revisions, Compilations, Consolidations, General Statutes, or Statutes—but these are not legal words of art, and all perform substantially the same function in the same way. Their status as law varies from state to state, but that is independent of title. Following is a checklist of features to be examined when consulting a state statutory compilation.

Status of the Compilation As Law. This is almost always shown by a certificate of the secretary of state, usually at the beginning of the set. It varies from that of positive law (repealing and superseding the original statutes from which derived), published and distributed by the state (as are the *Revised Statutes of Maine*, 1944), to a wholly informal private venture without state initiative, but indispensable (as *Purdon's Pennsylvania Statutes*).

a. **Enactment into positive law.** The highest authority of course is that of a compilation enacted as positive law, superseding and repealing the statutes from which derived, published and distributed by the state as the law. The federal prototype was the United States *Revised Statutes.*

The stigmata of this type are the enacting clauses: "It is enacted by the General Assembly [of Rhode Island] as follows . . ."; "*The Revised Statutes* [of 1937] is hereby adopted as all the public statute law of the State of New Jersey of a general nature. . . ." This type is fairly common but labors under the inherent disadvantage of early obsolescence caused by the reluctance of state legislatures to enact a successor or supplement to such a revision. Therefore, an unofficial, frequently-supplemented edition becomes necessary, and there is the anomaly of the lawyer consulting the unofficial edition as a practical matter, but citing the official, *as amended by later session laws*, as his authority.

A variant of this type of revision is found in the states which have "*perpetual revision*" of the separate codes and titles, rather than an overall revision of the entire body of public general laws at one time. After the enactment of a title or code as positive law, subsequent amendments and additions are in the form "Section 110 of [the Domestic Relations Law] is hereby amended to read as follows . . ."; "Chapter 64 [of the Village Law] is hereby amended by adding a new section, to be section 81a, to read as follows. . . ." In other words, in such cases the amendment may be said to be cumulative in effect, *the latest form superseding all earlier ones.* The annotated edition, however, cites the earlier forms, for historical purposes. Theoretically this keeps the public general law in force up to date; practically, dependence is upon unofficial editions of type c, below, because of the superior availablility and quality of their upkeep service.

b. **Official compilation of laws in force, in classified order, but without re-enactment as positive law.** This is a common form, exactly on the same plan as the *United States Code*, and the resulting classified statutes are prima facie the law, rebuttable by reference to the original laws from which derived, no new law

---

[15] Boston, Mass., National Association of State Libraries, 1941.

being enacted by the compilation. Usually the work is done by a state reviser, appointed under a statute. The Michigan *Compiled Laws* of 1948 and the Wisconsin *Statutes* are of this type. The historical notes in such an edition are apt to be very meager and the case annotations lacking. A parallel unofficial annotated edition often co-exists with this type (as in Missouri).

c. Unofficial and annotated edition of an official but obsolescent compilation of type a or b, above. This is perhaps the most common type. It is the type of *McKinney's New York Consolidated News;* of the *Mississippi Code of 1942 Annotated; Deering's California Codes;* the *Arkansas Statutes Annotated, Official Edition;* and many others.

d. Entirely unofficial compilation, without state initiative. This is the unusual type of *Purdon's Pennsylvania Statutes.* Pennsylvania has no general official compilation, and the classification in *Purdon's* is entirely that of the publishers. Otherwise, it is a typical "lifetime" statutory compilation, cited by and to all courts.

As a practical matter, while the latest official compilation re-enacted into positive law should be cited as authority in legal writing (perhaps as amended by later session laws), the title and section numbers in the private annotated editions are identical with those of the official. For a table of preferred citation forms, *see* page 321 ff.

Content: Statutes and Court Rules. The aim is to provide in a single volume or set all the statutes of a given state which are needed by the profession of that state in the usual course of practice, omitting obsolete material, appropriation acts, and those of no general interest. Court rules are a common component of state statutory compilations.

The "organic documents," federal and state, are usually included. The *New Mexico Statutes Annotated* of 1941 contains the *Kearney Code*, pertinent treaties with Mexico, and the organic and enabling acts leading to the state's admission to the Union. Surprisingly, Magna Carta is fairly common. In a few states the procedural law and the court rules are separately published because they are so often amended that frequent new editions are necessary. Occasionally some of the uncodified acts are separately printed, as *Deering's California General Laws* or *McKinney's New York Unconsolidated Laws.* These are for the most part "public laws," relating to the business of government.

Statute Section Numbering. In order to facilitate understanding and remembering, legislators and publishers have adopted more or less successful section numbering devices, three rather definite numbering patterns having emerged.

The simplest follows the *United States Revised Statutes* pattern of consecutive numbering from beginning to end of the compilation without reference to titles or chapters. In Throckmorton's *Ohio Code Annotated* (1948), § 14153 simply means a consecutive section number

The second pattern is based upon the division of the statute compilation into titles or chapters, and sections. Here the simplest numbering is that of the *Colorado Statutes Annotated* (1935): c.59, § 2. The *Iowa Code Annotated* (1949) has it as § 59.2; the *Virginia Code Annotated* (1949) § 59-2; and Purdon's *Pennsylvania Statutes Annotated* as 59 PS § 2.

In the third pattern, the tripartite division into title, chapter and section, or chapter, article and section is retained in the numbering. Thus, the *Arizona Code Annotated* (1939) § 11-201 means that the section indicated is chapter 11, article 2, section 1. Another way is § 11:2-1, as in New Jersey. In the *Alaska Compiled Laws Annotated* (1918), the number is § 11-2-1. The *Revised Codes of Montana* (1947) introduces the complication of very high section numbers. In it, § 94-3599 indicates title 94, chapter 35, section 99. To avoid confusion, when the final section number equals or exceeds 100, another dash is introduced: § 94-35-100. This is also done when the chapter number reaches 100; for example, 94-100-1: Successive chapters in the same title are numbered 101, 201, 301, *etc.* instead of 101, 102, 103, *etc.*

Content: Editorial Matter and Case Annotations.
State statutory compilations vary in size from one volume to as many as seventy, the difference in size being due almost entirely to the editorial matter and annotations.

In most officially published compilations—that is, those compiled and distributed by the state—the editorial matter in the text is very brief, being confined to a cryptic notation of the origin of the various statute sections, with an occasional cross-reference or note of amendment or repeal. An example is the Michigan *Compiled Laws* of 1948. This type is, for purposes of verifying the text only of a statute, often more convenient than the annotated edition, saving leafing through numerous pages of annotations, but for most purposes must be supplemented by an annotated edition.

The next step, as in the Vermont *Statutes Revised* of 1947, is to cite cases interpreting the statutes. The Missouri *Revised Statutes* type goes further and gives *case digests*. For real help in tracing the history of a statute section, that is, noting its evolution from the original session law and its subsequent amendment, one is almost always forced to the commercially published annotated editions. The editorial matter other than case annotations typically includes the derivation of each statute section from its earlier forms; perhaps excerpts from revisers' notes, explaining why changes were made; cross-references to other provisions; and the Bobbs-Merrill editions cite similar provisions in the laws of other states.

A late development has been the citation of pertinent law review, encyclopedia and *American Law Reports* comment; and the inclusion of historical or critical essays on various aspects of the law of the state, by members of the local Bar. The range of this historical comment is extreme, from none at all to a complete tracing back to the earliest session laws, with notes from revisers and law revision commissions as to the background and meaning of recent pertinent amendments.

There is a trend toward making the unofficial editions serve as practitioners' manuals. An example is the Lawyers Co-operative Publishing Company's treatment, in its *New York Consolidated Laws Service*, of the Workmen's Compensation Law. As a preliminary to the usual annotations to the Law itself, the *Service* prints a compilation of other applicable laws, rules of practice of official and unofficial boards, and forms, to be used in connection with the Law. Mortality, interest, and annuity tables, court-calendars, lists of state officials, *etc.*, are sometimes found.

Case annotations vary from none at all in certain official editions, to full-dress case digests. Annotations commonly cover the federal and local state courts and the opinions of the state attorney general. West Publishing Company and affiliated company editions copy or paraphrase National Reporter System case headnotes. When a statute changes its form or classification, the case digests are taken over from the old into the new classification. The annotated statute thus performs some of the functions of a citator. Where, however, a provision has been entirely repealed and not merely shifted in classification, the pertinent digest paragraphs are omitted from later editions because there is no place for them. That is one reason why law librarians save superseded editions, which often contains statutes and annotations not elsewhere available.

Indexes.
All state compilations are more or less well indexed by subject, and these indexes do not vary sufficiently for much comment.

In some indexes, local and special laws are separately indexed. Connecticut has an entry for "Words and Phrases," and New Mexico has a table of cases, most unusual in statutes. Separate tables of statutes by popular title are absent (some twenty-two of the state *Shepards* have them), but entries of individual acts by popular name are frequently found in the general index in their regular alphabetical order. Constitutions are usually indexed separately. In some states it is so difficult to distinguish adjective, substantive, codified or uncodified law, that there are general indexes for the whole body of the law, whether in the statutory compilation or not. The *Larmac Consolidated Index to Constitutions and Laws of California*,[16] and *Thompson's Laws of New York*[17] index are examples.

Statutory indexes and their use are further described at page 80.

Parallel Conversion Tables. The purpose of a statutory parallel table is to trace an earlier form of legislation (that is, a section of a session law or earlier compilation) forward into its place in the current compilation, and to determine if it is still law. (The reverse process, tracing backward to the legislative antecedents of a current code section, is through session law and statute citations found in parentheses or in a historical note at the end of the text of each section in the current compilation.) Since in most states there have been several statutory compilations, often involving a radical change in classification, the need of a table carrying the searcher from an earlier form to the current one is evident.

Such tables may be divided into two categories, those which trace from the original session law, through *all* earlier compilations to the current one; and those which trace only from the latest compilation which was re-enacted into positive law. The former are the more useful.

An example of the first type (which by definition includes also the second type) is the *New Mexico Statutes 1941 Annotated*, as shown herewith.

114   PARALLEL REFERENCE TABLES

Ch.	Section	Herein	Ch.	Section	Herein	Ch.	Section	Herein
100	2	58-608	109	1–4	Appn.	112	11	Emer.
	3	Rplg.	110	1	41-2201, n.	113	1	22-201
101	1–3	R '23,		2	Rplg.		2	R '29,
		c. 148, § 1431	111	1	3-1201			c. 127, § 2
102	1–11	R '35,		2	3-1202		3	22-101, 38-701
		c. 45, § 28		3	3-1203		4	Rplg.

Exhibit 13

These tables first list every chapter and section of every New Mexico session law, and its disposition in the 1941 *Statutes*. If not in the *Statutes*, because an appropriation, emergency or special act, or because repealed or obsolete, that fact is indicated in the table. (More common is the type exemplified by the *Minnesota Statutes Annotated*, listing only those session laws which at any time have been *codified*, and omitting mention of the rest.) The other tables show the disposition

---

[16] San Francisco, Calif., Recorder Printing and Publishing Co. Issued biennially on the odd year.

[17] Brooklyn, N. Y., Edward Thompson Co., 1939.

into the 1941 *Statutes* of sections from the 1915 *Code* and 1929 *Compiled Statutes*, and whether they are still in force.

An example of the second type, which goes back only to an *earlier revision*, is the *General Statutes of Connecticut, Revision of 1949*, below.

REVISION OF 1930

1930	1949	1930	1949	1930	1949	1930	1949
§1	§1	§54	§80	§107	§144	§159	Rd.
2	2	55	81	108	145	160	216
3	3	56	82	109	146	161	102
4	4	57	84	110	147	162	A-rd.
5	5	58	85	111	157	163	A-rd.
6	6	59	87	112	158	164	Rd.

Exhibit 14

This carries an earlier revision statute section into the current one, unless it has been repealed or is obsolete, in which case it is omitted. If it is desired to trace the original session law into the revision, in this type of table, the *earliest revision following the session law's enactment* must be consulted, where usually there is a table of session laws covered in the revision. Lacking such a session law table, the approach is through the subject matter of the specific session law section (in the subject index), through which its counterpart in the current revision may be located. This section will state the session law from which derived, thus providing a check. If the subject matter of the statute is unknown, the searcher is then helpless.

That is the present situation with the New York session laws; if the searcher has only the session law citation (as L. 1929, c. 315 § 2), and lacks a knowledge of the subject matter, there is no tabular or index method by which he can trace the law into the consolidated laws. By means of volume 6 of *The Consolidated Laws of the State of New York*,[18] the disposition of any session law from February 1, 1778, to December 31, 1909 (the consolidation date) may be found as of December 31. 1909—it is done much better in volume 6 of *Birdseye's Annotated Consolidated Laws* [19] — but there is no similar table for the consolidated laws since 1909, though there is for the *un*consolidated laws. Changes since 1909 in the Consolidated laws (amendments, repeals, renumbering, *etc.*), are noted in a table of "Changes in the Consolidated Laws" in the back of each session law volume, *cumulating* every ten years.

A variant of the above type of parallel statutory conversion table is one exemplified by the *Mississippi Code* of 1942, as shown below. This type of table (1) lists in order the sections of the latest compilation which was *reenacted as positive law* (the 1930 *Code* here); (2) the corresponding sections of *subsequent compilations which are only prima facie the law* (the 1942 *Code* and pocket supplements here); and (3) the disposition of session laws enacted since the latest

[18] Albany, N. Y., J. B. Lyon, 1909. This volume has title: *The Statutory Record of the Consolidated Laws.*

[19] New York, Banks Publishing Company. 1909.

positive law compilation, in the later prima facie compilation. This table enables the searcher to go at once from the statute section which is positive law and must still be cited in legal writing (as amended by later statutes, if any), to the corresponding section of the current compilation, which though only prima facie the law is the one lawyers commonly consult in their daily practice, because it is kept up to date. The third part of the table noted above of course traces session laws enacted since the latest compilation enacted into positive law (1930 here) into the current (1942 here) compilation. (For example, that Chapter 30 of the Mississippi *Laws* of 1935 was incorporated in § 5390 of the 1942 *Code*.) If the later session law modifies or repeals a *Code* section, the table shows that. The dates assigned to these state statutory compilations are often misleading, in that legislation for the year given in the title may not be included. As always, the title page and contents table should be carefully checked for actual coverage.

TABLE A

Code 1930 §§	Code 1942 §§	Sections of 1930 Code Omitted, with Reasons for Omission	Code 1930 §§	Code 1942 §§	Sections of 1930 Code Omitted, with Reasons for Omission
5025–5064		R 1934 ch. 120	5131	5633	
5065	9262		5132	5634	
5066	9263		5133	5635	
5067	9264		5134	5636	
5068	9265		5135	5637	

Exhibit 15

Where intervening compilations retain the same section numbers as the earlier one, conversion tables from the earlier to the intermediate are of course unnecessary.

Subsequent Amendments, Repeals, and the Like. These are indicated in various ways in the tables, as by a code letter or other signal in the conversion tables, from the old to the new statute form (as in the *Florida Statutes Annotated*), or by separate tables (as in the *Mississippi Code of 1942*), or both. The only general statement possible is that, with a few exceptions, such as the Connecticut *General Statutes* of 1949, there are tables enabling the searcher to trace the provisions of a session law or earlier compilation into the latest compilation, with information (often a citation to pertinent amendments or repealers) as to subsequent provisions.

Supplementation. Much of the value of a statutory compilation depends upon the frequency and completeness of its supplements. As often as not, the official edition is not supplemented at all by the state, the lawyer being therefore relegated to the consultation of subsequent volumes of session laws, or, where they exist, commercial annotated editions.

Supplementation, where it exists, is usually by annual pocket parts, cumulative bound supplements, re-compiled individual volumes, and the like. An increasing number of state statutes, however, are being further supplemented by a more frequent advance sheet service supplying the text of new session laws, together with tabular material giving their statute classification, citations to repeals, amendments, *etc.*, supplementing like tables in the bound set. In some of these advance sheets, material similar to that in the *United States Code Congressional and Administrative News* is added; such as the governor's budget and veto messages, and recommendations of official and unofficial bodies to the legislature concerning pending legislation. The Iowa and Pennsylvania advance sheets list bills maturing into laws.

Noting the date of publication of any statutory material should be routine, together with information given as to supplementation, so that the full sequence may be checked if necessary.

Which Edition of a Statute to Consult. In some states there are as many as three different editions of the statutes. Which to consult depends upon all the factors discussed above—purpose (whether to read the text only, or also for history and case annotations); fullness of editorial information and case annotations, content and arrangement of tables and indexes; and frequency of supplementation —and also the cost of the sets and their upkeep. The steady growth of the fully-annotated, frequently-supplemented, multi-volume sets seem to prove that their utility overbalances their much higher cost to the lawyer.

E. Municipal Charters, Ordinances, and Codes.

The creation of municipal corporations is a function of the state legislature. The modern practice is to enact a general law setting up standards and conditions for the creation of such corporations, and then to assign the duty to some officer or official body to determine whether these have been met in specific instances. Incorporation may be by special act, however, if not forbidden by the state constitution, or by the adoption of a home rule charter in states permitting them.

Charters. The charter granted by the legislature constitutes a limited delegation of its power over the government of the area covered. In form it may follow a special or general statute; or may be one selected from among a number of legislatively authorized forms ("optional charters"); or the commission or city manager form may be adopted. The charter is the city's fundamental document, judicially noticed by the courts. Unless contrary to the state constitution, the legislature may amend or repeal a municipal charter. Constitutional or home rule charters may, in some states, be amended by a vote of the electors.

Ordinances. These are the local laws of the municipalities, enacted by the duly constituted board of aldermen, council, or commission, under authority delegated by the state legislature, for application within the narrow limits of its jurisdiction. An ordinance must be in writing and enacted according to all the prescribed formalities. It may be in furtherance of the police power of the municipality and prescribe penalties for its violation; or it may grant franchises and special privileges; or be for the improvement of the physical facilities of the corporation, for the doing of public works or abatement of nuisances; or may correspond to a code of laws laying down rules for the conduct of public business. If duly voted, an ordinance is as binding upon those concerned as the general laws of the state are upon its citizens.

In some states, a general state statute provides for the enactment by the cities, counties, and villages of the state of "local laws" which are in effect ordinances but are published with the session laws of the state, often in separate volumes. In many localities ordinances are referred to as "resolutions."

In states where there is an "upstate" community overshadowed by a "down-state" overwhelmingly large city, the legislature is apt to keep more than usually close control over the ordinances of the metropolis. An example is New York City, operating under a home rule charter but governed through a huge administrative code enacted as Chapter 929 of the Laws of 1937, and amended by subsequent acts of the state legislature.

Publication of Municipal Charters and Ordinances. With the exception of such state-published local laws as those noted above, the only general rule concerning the publication of municipal charters and ordinances is that there is no rule. General legislation concerning municipal charters and ordinances is of course a part of the statutory compilation for each state, but it rarely contains any actual charters. Sample charters in full for six cities are found in W. K. Chute's *The Law of Modern Municipal Charters*.[20] In any general publication of a city code, the charter is included. Most large cities revise their charters or codes fairly frequently, though irregularly.

In the case of ordinances, there is greater regularity. Many large cities publish their ordinances in official journals, and in smaller communities they may be printed in an annual compilation which includes departmental reports and a résumé of official proceedings of the municipality. In some states, new ordinances or amendments must be published in local newspapers as adopted.

When published in collected form, charters and ordinances in force are printed together as a "code," somewhat analogous to the publication of the United States Constitution and *United States Code* together.

The definitive list of charters and ordinances of present interest is that published by the Bureau of the Census in 1948, as Number 27 of its "State and Local Government Special Studies." This is an alphabetical list of all United States cities which publish these documents, with bibliograhical entries for each publication. *The Municipal Yearbook*[21] devotes one extensive chapter to the publication of model ordinances, both general and by specific subject (as aeronautics, auditoriums, awnings). The place of publication and the price, if any, of each ordinance is given.

Legal notes on ordinances are made a part of the annual *Municipalities and the Law in Action*,[22] of the National Institute of Municipal Law Officers. In 1952, this same Institute began the publication of a loose-leaf Model Ordinance Service, covering every aspect of ordinance writing. In 1932, the Municipal Administration Service issued as its Publication No. 29, *The Codification and Drafting of Ordinances for Small Towns*,[23] which discusses in some detail both the technique of codification and the legal problems encountered in it. A useful part of this publication is a list of "Model Ordinances, Standards, Specifications, Bibliographies and Selected Articles Useful in Municipal Ordinance Making," by Gertrude Lucas. In some states, as Oregon, Virginia and Washington, municipal leagues, under the auspices of the state university, publish sample ordinances and information on ordinance drafting. The Michie City Publications Company (a subsidiary of the Michie Co., Law Publishers of Charlottesville, Va.), specializes in drafting, codifying, and publishing municipal codes. The problems involved and their solution are discussed by Charles W. Sublett, *Codification of Your City Ordinances*, distributed by the Company.

Citators for Charters and Ordinances. Charters and ordinances are amended, repealed, and adjudicated just as are conventional legislation, and are

---

[20] Detroit, Michigan, Drake, 1920.
[21] Chicago, Ill., International City Managers' Association.
[22] Washington, D. C., National Institute of Municipal Law Officers.
[23] By John F. Sly, Jefferson B. Fordham, and George A. Shipman. New York, Municipal Administration Service, 1932.

covered by the usual statutory citation books. However, the coverage is incomplete, due to failure of the municipalities to provide the necessary information as to amendment and repeal.

Shepard's Citations. In nearly all state *Shepard's*, charters and ordinances are covered, both as to amendments and repeals and as to adjudication. For some state citators there is a separate subject index of ordinances cited, because most ordinances are not numbered and must therefore be cited by subject and date. Otherwise the tabular treatment is exactly as for other statutes.

National Reporter System. The "Table of Statutes Construed" in the regional units cites charters, but apparently not ordinances, construed by cases in the various jurisdictions.

Digest of the United States Supreme Court Reports. City ordinances and codes construed by the Supreme Court are covered in the tables of this digest and of the *Lawyer's Edition* of the *United States Reports.*

CHAPTER 8

WORK WITH STATE STATUTES

A. General Considerations.

Much of what is said in Chapter 6 concerning work with federal statutes applies equally to work with state statutes.

B. Constitutions.

These are printed and indexed in state legislative manuals in compilations of statutes. Earlier constitutions and other organic documents pertaining to the state are also commonly included. There are some compilations of current interest, of the constitutional provisions of all states. Constitutions are covered as statutes by the state *Shepard's Citations*.

C. Session Laws.

Each state publishes its session laws; slip laws (usually as parts of unofficial advance sheet statute services) are found in only a few states. Unofficial editions usually contain added matter of interest, sometimes including legislative reports.

D. Local Laws.

In some states, laws applicable to individual towns or towns of a class are called local laws. They may be published at the end of the regular session law volumes or as separate volumes. In a few states the city council is empowered to enact local laws which are essentially city ordinances. Municipal charters, codes and ordinances are described in Chapter 7.

E. Statutory Compilations.

These are described in Chapter 7. They differ from their federal counterparts for the most part only in their more frequent editions.

F. Administrative Rules and Orders.

See chapter 17: "The State Aspect of Administrative Law."

G. Court Rules.

See Chapter 10: "Court Rules."

H. Statutes of Other States.

See Chapter 9.

I. Statutory Indexes and Tables.

Subject Indexes. **All laws ever enacted in a state.** The only compiled indexes to all legislation enacted are those in the individual session law volumes. The nearest to a complete index of the laws of any state is the *General Index to the Laws of the State of New York, 1777–1901*,[1] with a supplement through 1907, which indexes both public and private enactments.

All laws presently in force in a state. There is no such current index.

All public laws presently in force. This is an uncommon index, which, in a single alphabet, indexes codified, uncodified and procedural laws. Consolidated indexes commonly do not index uncodified laws, which are predominantly of a local nature. Examples of a type of index covering about everything but private laws and appropriation acts, are the *Larmac Consolidated Index to the Constitution and Laws of California*,[2] and the *Consolidated Index to Thompson's Laws of New York*.[3]

Public general laws presently in force. This is the common type of statutory index, which is an integral part of a consolidation of the laws. In some states the constitution and the procedural laws are separately indexed, which is inconvenient, because it is often difficult to ascertain in advance how a law is classified, and consequently which index to consult. That is why indexes of the *Larmac* type are so useful.

In using an index of laws in force to trace a particular enactment when the date is unknown, a sort of bibliographical game of tick, tack, toe is played, starting in with the current index and working back through indexes to earlier editions, until an entry covering the desired law is found. The section of statute when found will tell from what session law it was derived. Sometimes, however, the citation to source is to an earlier compilation, in which case that compilation must be searched for the desired session law citation.

Indexes to laws of more than one state. *See State Law Index*, page 68, and *Subject Collections Covering More than One Jurisdiction* in Chapter 9.

Popular Name Indexes to State Statutes. Such indexes are uncommon for state statutes, though some compilations have them; for example, the *Iowa Code Annotated*. *Shepard's Citations* for half the states have popular name tables for statutes.

---

[1] Albany, N. Y., J. B. Lyon, 1902. 3 v. Volume covering 1902-1907, Albany, N. Y., J. B. Lyon, 1908.

[2] San Francisco, Calif. Recorder Printing and Publishing Company, issued biennially on the odd year.

[3] Brooklyn, N. Y., Edward Thompson Company, 1939. 2 v. and supplements.

Parallel Tables from One Form of Statute to Another. Since new editions of state statutory compilations are comparatively frequent, and since these usually result in a more or less complete revision of the classification scheme, parallel tables are correspondingly important. These tables are discussed at pages 73 to 75.

From session law to code. Parallel tables for this transfer are found in a few session laws. Not many state compilations have such tables, either, though they are now found in a small but increasing number of annotated editions.

From code to session law. The various code sections cite their source. If an earlier compilation is cited as the source, it must be checked for the session law source from which derived.

From one edition of a code to another. This is a common and useful type of conversion table, showing in parallel columns, section by section, the various codes which have been in force in the state, with the equivalent sections (if any) in earlier or later codes. Many codes indicate in parenthesis the corresponding sections of earlier codes, if any. These tables are particularly useful in connection with those state *Shepard's* which are geared only to the *latest* compilation. For example, the *Revised Laws* of Minnesota of 1905, § 3920, can not be directly Shepardized in *Shepard's Minnesota Citations*, but the parallel tables in the *Minnesota Statutes Annotated* refer to the current equivalent, § 531.30, under which all cases construing that section *and its predecessors* are covered by *Shepard.* This method is not infallible, however, as some so-called equivalents are by no means equivalent. These tables also frequently note repeals and amendments of sections of an earlier code.

Bill Status Tables. Many states now publish tables showing the status during a session of pending bills. These tables are described at page 53. In a few states, session law volumes present a table of bills maturing into law during a session.

Chapter and Law Number Tables. The chapter and law numbers of an act are noted on the face of the session laws as published, and in tables in each session law volume. This information is also given in tabular form in most state legislative journals and the like, as described at page 53, noted above.

Interstate Compacts. These are listed in the annual *Handbook* of the National Conference of Commissioners of Uniform State Laws, beginning with 1949.

J. Citation Books for State Statutes.

These are described in Chapter 28. Most state session law volumes contain tables of amendments and repeals of existing legislation by new laws, but these tables are seldom cumulative. Similar tables are common in state compilations, especially the annotated ones. Annotated statutes digest cases construing the statutes printed therein.

K. Legislative Intent.

The means for determining this for state statutes are described in Chapter 5, under "State Legislative Histories."

CHAPTER 9

FEDERAL AND STATE STATUTES IN OTHER FORMS

A. The Need for Such Publication.
B. Speedy and Unofficial Publication of Session Laws.
C. Offically-Published Collections, by Subject.
D. Subject Collections Covering More Than One Jurisdiction.
E. Form Books.
F. Learning of Irregular Statutory Publications.

A. The Need for Such Publication.

Up to this time the publication of the *entire body* of the legislation of permanent and general interest, federal and state, has been considered. There are other important forms of publication, however, both official and unofficial. They are compiled and distributed to satisfy various needs, such as speed, convenience for staff use in an administrative agency, for the members of a trade or industry, or for citizens interested in certain limited aspects of the law, for instance, traffic or hunting laws. Below are listed some typical collections, for purposes of illustration only. In most categories there are many others.

B. Speedy and Unofficial Publication of Session Laws.

The text of session laws is often published immediately upon enactment, by unofficial agencies. Although these are distributed for information only, they may be relied upon for most practical purposes, and some of them are more convenient to acquire, store, and service than are the official ones.

Advance Sheets. The speediest and most complete advance sheet services for session laws, both federal and state, are probably those of the Commerce Clearing House *Congressional Legislative Reporting Service*[1] (for federal), and *Advance Session Session Law Reports*[2] (for state), which supply mimeographed copies of new legislation immediately following enactment, as received by teletype. Perhaps the most practical unofficial source of session laws for most people lies in the printed advance sheet services. For federal slip laws of public general interest this is the *United States Code Congressional and Administrative News* (formerly *United States Code Congressional Service*), the service of which is described on page 49. Few states have such services yet, but the number is growing, as noted at page 68.

Newspapers. Occasionally the complete or partial text of every important session law is published in a city newspaper the next day after approval, usually accompanied by a digest and comment.

---

[1] New York, N. Y., Commerce Clearing House.
[2] New York, N. Y., Commerce Clearing House.

Legal Periodicals. The unofficial *United States Law Week* [3] occasionally publishes the complete text of very important federal session laws, within a week of approval. Specialized legal periodicals often do the same for legislation affecting their specialty.

Loose-Leaf Services. These often supply their subscribers with the complete text of pertinent legislation within a day or two of approval.

C. Officially-Published Collections, by Subject.

Many federal and state agencies collect and publish (often annotated to court and departmental decisions) the laws relating to their work, for staff use. Especial attention should be paid to the publication date of these collections, as supplementation is usually infrequent or nonexistent. Federal examples are *Laws Relating to the Navy, Annotated*,[4] a loose-leaf service; the *Internal Revenue Bulletin*,[5] which publishes the laws and regulations relating to internal revenue; *Statutes and Decisions Pertaining to the Federal Trade Commission;* [6] and the *Interstate Commerce Acts Annotated*.[7] Of considerable interest are the compilations of session laws by the Superintendent of the House of Representatives Document Room, covering in all a wide range of subjects, such as veterans' affairs, civil service, pensions, *etc*.

Many state executive departments issue similar collections for their own use. More common, however, are those published for free distribution to interested citizens, containing highway, fish and game, education laws, and the like.

D. Subject Collections Covering More than One Jurisdiction.

There is frequent call for the laws of all or several states, covering a particular topic. Comparatively few such collections exist and fewer are so kept to date as to be safe for use. There is the further danger that the compiler may have selected only the obvious laws, as revealed by subject indexes, neglecting others of importance which are not so obvious. The safest way to effect such coverage is by arduous search in the statutes of each state. The collections do serve a purpose, however, at least for a limited time following their publication. They vary greatly in treatment. Some print the entire text of legislation, annotated or otherwise. Others are merely digests or paraphrases. Some typical collections are noted below.

Directories. The most general coverage is that of the *Lawyers' Directory*,[8] and the *Martindale-Hubbell Law Directory*.[9] These are described in Chapter 27.

Compilations on One Subject Only. Occasionally the federal or state governments issue collections of both federal and state laws on a specific subject. Examples are the Department of Commerce collection of federal and state laws relating to weights and measures; and the *Compilation of Laws and Proposals Relating to Federal Aid to Education* (1949), by the State College of Washington. Paraphrases are frequently made by state law revision commissions, legislative ref-

---

[3] Washington, D. C., Bureau of National Affairs.

[4] Washington, D. C., Office of the Judge Advocate General, Navy Department.

[5] Issued by the Office of Internal Revenue. Washington, D. C., United States Govt. Print. Off.

[6] Washington, D. C., Govt. Print. Off., 1930-51, 4 v.

[7] Prepared by the Interstate Commerce Commission. Published in Washington, D. C., U. S. Govt. Print. Off.

[8] Philadelphia, Sharp & Alleman.

[9] New York, Martindale-Hubbell Law Directory, Inc.

erence bureaus, or university bureaus of public administration, for the use of legislators. Compilations of state constitutions were noted in Chapter 7.

The Uniform Laws Annotated. As its title indicates, this is an annotated edition of those laws proposed by the National Conference of Commissioners of Uniform State Laws. They cover such topics as sales, negotiable instruments, warehouse receipts, criminal extradition, partnership, and so forth, and most of them have been adopted by from one to all states. The Uniform Law sections are annotated by decisions of the courts exactly as in any other annotated statute, and the other familiar features of a typical annotated statute are present. A list of all uniform laws and the date of their adoption by the Commissioners is found in each volume. In the appropriate volumes there are tables of states which have adopted the uniform laws annotated therein. Because few states in enacting these uniform laws retain the original section numbers, there is in the front of each volume a conversion table from the uniform law into the corresponding section of the statutes of all states which have enacted the law. Supplements are annual pocket parts, with recompiled volumes as necessary. The annual *Handbook* of the Conference is a mine of information about the Uniform Laws. States adopting any of the laws are listed by name, with the laws they have adopted and the date of adoption; conversely, uniform laws are listed, with states adopting, and dates. Before final acceptance and proposal of a draft law by the conference itself the tentative draft is published in the *Handbook*, together with comments on each section. For example, the proposed Uniform Securities Act (among others) was so treated in the 1951 *Handbook*. The *Handbook* also is a repository of the text of obsolete Uniform Laws, such as the Uniform Annulment of Marriage and Divorce Act. The Uniform Laws are Shepardizable as such through the National Reporter System tables of "Statutes Construed." As adopted by the various states, they are of course covered by *Shepard's Citations* and by annotated statutes.

Trade or Professional Organization Compilations. Many groups try to keep abreast of legislation affecting them. Their publications vary from the complete text of laws (as in the loose-leaf *Compilation of Federal and State Economic Poison Laws*, of the National Association of Insecticide Manufacturers, Inc.), to paraphrases (such as those on factors' liens, commercial crimes, assumed names, *etc.*, published annually in the *Credit Manual of Commercial Laws*, of the National Association of Credit Men); or the monthly *Consumer Finance Law Bulletin*, of the National Consumer Finance Association; to tabular summaries or citations (as the *Summary of State Liquor Control Laws and Regulations Relating to Distilled Spirits*, of the Distilled Spirits Institute). Perhaps the most useful publication of this kind covering the whole field of state government, is the *Book of the States*,[10] in effect a biennial cumulation of matter previously published in *State Government*, the monthly organ of the Council of State Governments. Among the tables and paraphrases of the 1950-51 edition, for example, are the record of uniform and model state laws enacted, purchasing practices in the various states, child-labor standards, and motor vehicle laws.

Private Compilations. Purely private enterprises are such as the *Corporation Manual*,[11] (usually referred to as "Parker's"), an annual compilation of corporation

---

[10] Chicago, Council of State Governments.
[11] New York, N. Y., United States Corporation Company.

and "blue sky" laws of the states, with the original text rearranged under a uniform classification; and Huston's *School Laws of the 48 States*,[12] containing the full original text of the statutes. Perhaps the most effective collections are those in loose-leaf services, which collect currently and annotate statutes of all jurisdictions on conditional sales, wills, labor regulation, and so forth.

Treatises Containing Statutes or Paraphrases. Treatises comprise one of the most prolific and best kept up to date repositories of legislation by subject. These are described in Chapter 21.

E. Form Books.

Many of the forms, both adjective and substantive, employed in drafting legal documents are prescribed by statute. They are described in Chapter 25.

F. Indexes Covering the Laws of All States.

See the *State Law Index*, page 68.

G. Learning of Irregular Statutory Publications.

Federal statutes of all kinds are listed currently as published, in the *Monthly Catalog of United States Government Publications*[13]; state statutes, in the *Monthly Checklist of State Publications*.[14] These and many unofficial compilations are listed in the weekly *Public Affairs Information Service*,[15] found in most large public and university libraries. *See* Chapter 27.

---

[12] Seattle, Wash., Wendell Huston Company.

[13] *United States Government Publications; monthly catalog.* . . . Issued by the Superintendent of Documents. Washington, D. C., U. S. Govt. Print. Off.

[14] Issued by U. S. Library of Congress, Documents Division. Washington, D. C., U. S. Govt Print. Off.

[15] New York, 11 W. 40th St.

Chapter 10

RULES OF COURTS AND ADMINISTRATIVE AGENCIES

A. Function.

Rules are necessary in the proper and expeditious transaction of business before courts and administrative agencies having quasi-judicial tribunals. For federal and state courts alike the rules are usually available in one or more printed forms, often annotated, or as the subject of a treatise on local practice. Similar rules, usually somewhat less technical, are promulgated and applied in proceedings before quasi-judicial administrative tribunals.

B. Federal Court Rules.

The rule making power of the federal courts is defined in 18 U. S. C. § § 3771, 3772 for criminal procedure; and in 28 U. S. C. § § 2072-2073 for federal courts generally and for civil procedure. As authorized by these and predecessor statutes, the Supreme Court of the United States has promulgated rules for its own court and separate lower federal courts; civil procedure and criminal procedure rules for use in federal district courts; and admiralty rules. The former equity rules have been merged with those for civil procedure.

District Courts and Courts of Appeals Rules for Individual Courts.
28 U. S. C. § 2071 authorizes the lower federal courts to make their own rules, not to be inconsistent with the rules of general application laid down for them by the Supreme Court. The district courts and the Courts of Appeals, which come into contact with special conditions requiring their own local rules, have formulated such rules, which are not to be confused with the general rules for civil and criminal procedure laid down by the Supreme Court.

C. State Court Rules.

State courts follow much the same procedure as the federal, in promulgating rules not inconsistent with the constitutions and enactments of the state legislatures. Many states have, since 1938, adopted rules of procedure modeled after the federal rules.

D. Rules of Practice of Quasi-Judicial Tribunals.

Many federal and state quasi-judicial tribunals hear appeals from decisions of examiners and others charged with carrying out the purposes of administrative agencies under the law. Among such are the Interstate Commerce Commission, National Labor Relations Board, United States Tax Court, and most state public utility and tax commissions and labor relations boards. Procedure before these tribunals, while apt to be somewhat less formal than that of full fledged courts, is parallel in nearly all respects. It follows that these tribunals have rules of practice, which have the same effect as statutes as rules of courts do, in both federal and state commissions.[1] The power to promulgate rules of practice is granted federal agencies by Section 3a of the Administrative Procedure Act, which provides also for their publication in the *Federal Register*. State statutes setting up administrative agencies commonly confer similar power.

E. Availability of Published Court and Agency Rules.

1. *From the Courts or Agencies.* Many courts and quasi-judicial tribunals distribute their rules in pamphlet form, free on application. For local court rules this is often the only source.

2. *In Statute Compilations.* Federal rules of court are printed in the *United States Code*, findable through its general index. Included are not only the rules for specific courts, but the rules of civil and criminal procedure applicable to district courts generally, and of some quasi-judicial tribunals. Local rules of the separate district courts and of the Courts of Appeals are not included. Both official and private editions of the *Code* supply much historical and other editorial matter, and the private editions are annotated by the cases, and opinions of the Attorney General. *State court rules* are found in more than half the state statutory compilations, the private editions usually being annotated. Some state statutory compilations print the rules of the circuit of the Court of Appeals and of the district courts covering such states. An example is *Burns' Indiana Statutes Annotated*.

3. *In Law Reports.* *Federal court rules* (not including those for the Courts of Appeals and for individual district courts), are printed in all editions of the *United States Reports*. The *Federal Rules Decisions* prints federal court rules and amendments of general application, but not those of individual courts other than the Supreme Court. *State Court rules* are found in about two-thirds of the official editions of state law reports (in a few states only amendments are printed). Rules are printed also in the advance sheets, but not the bound volumes, of the regional National Reporter System units, and furnish in most cases the promptest available printing of these rules. *Shepard's United States*, *Federal* and *State Citations* indicate where in the law reports court rules are printed.

4. *In Loose-Leaf Services.* *See* the *Federal Rules Service*, in this Chapter. Rules of practice of agencies and commissions are sometimes printed in tax or regulatory loose-leaf services.

5. *In Separate Treatises and Manuals.* Treatises and encyclopedias of practice and procedure, whether federal or state, being essentially commentaries on codes of procedure and court rules, commonly incorporate the rules falling within

---

[1] Roscoe Pound, *Regulation of Judicial Procedure by Rules of Court*, 10 Ill. L. Rev. 163, 164 (1915).

their scope. Every state or group of states has its own local practice books, which often print court rules. The most compact and inclusive collections of rules of court, however, are apt to be in separate rules manuals, often annotated to the rules of a given jurisdiction. The *Digest of United States Supreme Court Reports* [2] and the *Supreme Court Digest* [3] both have separate "Federal Court Rules" volumes, containing federal court rules (including those for the circuits of the Court of Appeals but not for individual district courts), admiralty, copyright, and general orders in bankruptcy. A similar manual, but annotated (including state court decisions on federal court rules), is the *Federal Court Rules Annotated*.[4] A less common repository is the separate volume of annotated rules of all courts, federal and state, within the jurisdiction, as in Ervin H. Pollack's *Ohio Court Rules Annotated*.[5]

6. *Finding List of Court and Agency Rules.* The index below refers to the paragraphs above in which the places of publication of the mentioned rules are noted. The relative value of these sources is largely a matter of the frequency and fullness of supplementation.

Admiralty	1, 2, 3, 5
Civil procedure, federal	2, 3, 4, 5
Copyright	1, 2
Court of Claims	1, 2, 5
Courts of Appeals, local rules	1, 5, In some State Statutes
Criminal procedure, federal	2, 3, 5
Customs Court	1, 2, 5
District Courts, local rules	1, 4, *Federal Rules Service*, in some State Statutes
District of Columbia Court of Appeals	1, 2, 5
Emergency Court of Appeals	1, 2, 5
Equity (merged with Civil Procedure rules)	
General Orders in Bankruptcy	2, 3, 5
Military Appeals Court	1, 2, 5
Supreme Court of the United States	1, 2, 3, 5
Tax Court of the United States	1, 2, 5
Quasi-judicial tribunals	1, 2, *Federal Register, Code of Federal Regulations, Administrative Law Service.*

F. Decisions Construing Court Rules.

Commonly, decisions of federal, state, and quasi-judicial tribunals construing their rules of procedure are printed in the same reporters that cover the decisions of such tribunals generally. There are two special reports, however, printing decisions on federal court rules.

Federal Rules Decisions. This is a unit of the National Reporter System, printing decisions of federal courts involving rules of both civil and criminal procedure. Although the decisions printed are only those not also printed in the *Federal Reporter* or *Federal Supplement*, each advance sheet and bound volume

---

[2] Rochester, N. Y., Lawyers Co-operative Publishing Co., 1949.

[3] *United States Supreme Court Digest, 1754 to date.* St. Paul, Minn., West Publishing Co., 1943-1946. 16 v.

[4] Indianapolis, Bobbs-Merrill Co., Inc., 1952.

[5] Buffalo, N. Y., Dennis, 1949.

RULE 2

ONE FORM OF ACTION

There shall be one form of action to be known as "civil action."

.1   Abolition of forms of action
    Cases vols. 11, 16—St. Cit. vol. 6
    .11   Status of "Theory of the Pleadings" doctrine under Federal
          Rules (see also FINDEX 8a.53)
         Cases vols. 1, 2, 3, 5, 7—L. R. 4, vol. 1—St. Cit., vol. 3—see also 3 Fed.
         Rules Serv. Comm. 8a.26
    .12   Retention of substantive law distinctions
         Cases vol. 16
    .13   Relation to statutes of limitation
         Cases vols. 1, 2—L. R. 23, vol. 3 ; L. R. 63, vol. 7
.2   Merger of law and equity
    L. R. 24, vol. 2—St. Cit. vol. 6
    .21   Abolition of formal distinctions
         Cases vols. 1-7, 10, 11, 14—L. R. 50, vol. 5 ; L. R. 63, vol. 7
    .22   Retention of substantive law distinctions
         Cases vols. 3, 6, 9, 10, 12, 16—L. R. 63, vol. 7
         .221   Requirement as to adequate remedy at law (see also
               FINDEX 18b.31)
         Cases vols. 5, 7, 9, 12
    .23   The problem of jury trial : see FINDEX 38a.
.3   Concept of "claim" under the Federal Rules
    Cases vols. 7, 10—Comm. vol. 5

II. COMMENCEMENT OF ACTION; SERVICE OF PROCESS, PLEADINGS, MOTIONS, AND ORDERS

RULE 3

COMMENCEMENT OF ACTION

A civil action is commenced by filing a complaint with the court.

.1   Filing of complaint
    .11   Effect of Rule on earlier statutes prescribing manner of
          commencing action
         Cases vols. 1, 10
    .12   Effect of commencement of action
         Cases vols. 9, 10, 11, 14
    .13   Necessity for payment of filing fees
         Cases vol. 11
    .14   Filing defined : see FINDEX 5e.

[For references to latest material, see green supplementary pages of FINDEX.]

Exhibit 16

cites cases in all federal courts construing each rule. Many articles on the federal rules are reprinted in this *Reporter*. A cumulative author and subject index to them is in Volume 12.

Federal Rules Service. This is a loose-leaf service devoted entirely to decisions construing the federal rules of civil procedure. Approximately annually the material for that period is cumulated into a bound volume of decisions. The loose leaves (except for certain indexes) cover only current material, though indexing all material from the beginning of the service in 1939. This service combines in one unit the functions of a law reporter, a digest (with all the usual constituents), and a citator.

The service is organized around a copyrighted device called the "Federal FindeX," which combines functions such as those of the West copyrighted Key-Number, the analysis at the head of the conventional case digest main topics, and an index. The FindeX is in effect an elaborate arrangement of the federal rules of civil procedure, very much in the manner of a case digest topical analysis.

The FindeX, as shown, comprises (a) the full text of each federal rule, as amended to date; (b) a FindeX figure, consisting of the rule number, followed by a decimal number, serving to classify the material (as 2.23); (c) the definition of each FindeX number; (d) cross-reference to similar material in other FindeX numbers; and (e) index references to volumes of the service printing cases under a given FindeX number; any editorial commentary on the topic; and citations to district court local rules. The FindeX is supplemented weekly. The service organized around the FindeX comprises a weekly news release; a cumulative table of cases; the text of federal decisions construing the rules; "Local Court Rules" in force—this being the most convenient repository of local district court rules; a word index giving a fact approach to the FindeX; and a "Federal Rules Digest" covering all federal court cases decided since the adoption of the Rules of Civil Procedure in 1938.

G. State Court Rules Modeled After Federal Rules.

Many states have since 1938 adopted rules of civil procedure modeled after the federal rules. The *Federal Rules Service Digest*, described above, contains comparative tables of such state rules and the federal rules serving as their source. Any differences between state and federal rules are also pointed out.

H. Citation Books for Court Rules.

Court rules are treated as statutes in citators.

Shepard's United States, Federal, and State Citations cover court rules in the same manner as other statutes. The place of publication of the latest revision and of subsequent amendments, in the official reports of the jurisdiction, is given. For example: "Supreme Judicial Court, 1926 (252 Mas85.)" Comments on the rules by law journals within the jurisdiction are also noted. Cases annotating earlier forms of rules are, as far as practicable, brought over to annotate the corresponding current form.

Statutory Compilations Printing Rules of Court. These customarily note amendments, repeals, and the like, of rules. Annotated editions digest decisions construing each rule.

Treatises and Rules Manuals. Practice treatises are in effect commentaries on the rules. The *Federal Rules Service* Findex is a citator.

Statutes Construed Tables. These National Reporter System tables, described at page 118, cover court rules.

Digests frequently annotate court rules. All federal court rules from the beginning, for example, are annotated in the *Federal Digest.*

The United States Supreme Court Bulletin. This Commerce Clearing House loose-leaf publication annotates the Supreme Court rules.

I. Suggested Routine of Search for Court Rules.

To Find the Rules of a Given Court or Agency. Consult the "Finding List," above. In most law libraries rules will be found either as part of a statutory compilation, or in a separate manual of court rules. Rules of quasi-judicial tribunals are often found in the rules of practice of the agency served.

To Ascertain the Latest Form of a Rule. Consult the latest supplement to the volume containing the rule. *Shepard's Citations* show amendments, repeals, revisions, and the place of publication (if in an official law report). Usually in other editions of rules an editorial note gives the date of any amendments.

To Find Citations to Decisions Construing a Rule. Shepard's Citations, the National Reporter System tables of statutes or court rules construed, annotated rules, treatises, and rules services list such cases.

To Find a Textual Discussion of a Rule. A treatise or "practice book" is best.

Notes

Rule-Making Power Generally. There has been much question as to the power to make court rules—whether and to what extent it resides in the legislatures or in the courts themselves. The courts stress their inherent powers and assert that the doctrine of separation of powers in this country limits the legislatures' control. In a given jurisdiction, the wording of the constitution and statutes made under its authority are to a great extent determinative. *See* T. Williams, *The Scope of Authority for Rules of Court Affecting Procedure,* 22 Wash. U. L. Q. 459 (1937); A. Gertner, *The Inherent Power of Courts to Make Rules,* 10 U. of Cin. L. Rev. 32 (1936). The weight of judicial authority is that the courts have inherent power to make reasonable rules for the conduct of business brought before them, (*In re Hien,* 166 U. S. 432, 17 S. Ct. 624, 41 L. Ed. 1066 (1896); *Petition of Florida State Bar Assn. for Promulgation of New Florida Rules of Civil Procedure,* 145 Fla. 223, 199 So. 57 (1940)), particularly as to local conditions not readily covered by rules of general application. On the other hand, the rules must conform to and are subordinate to legislation which is constitutional in the jurisdiction where enacted. [*De Camp.* v. *Central Arizona Light & Power Co.,* 47 Ariz. 517, 47 P. 2d 311 (1936).] Typical of the dual origin of the rule-making power are those of the Supreme Court of Indiana "Pursuant to its inherent rule-making power and the authority vested in it by the General Assembly, the Supreme Court of Indiana hereby adopts the following rules of court . . ."

Authority of Rules of Court. Rules of court, not inconsistent with enactments of the legislature, have the force and effect of statutes, but any rule inconsistent with a statute is inoperative, though the language of the courts differs as to this last. [*Lambert* v. *Lambert,* 270 N. Y. 422, 1 N. E. 2d 833 (1936).] However, rules prescribed by the United States Supreme Court by virtue of 18 U. S. C. §§ 3771, 3773, and 28 U. S. C. §§ 2072, 2073 (Supp. IV, 1951), can supersede existing statutes. Some courts speak of the rules as having the effect of rules promulgated by the legislature, or as being positive law. (14 Am. Jur. 355, 156, and cases cited.) Others state that rules set forth "under the express direction of the legislature have the force of mandatory statutes." [*Presho State Bank* v. *Northwest Mill Co.,* 45 S. D. 58, 185 N. W. 370, 23 A. L. R. 48 (1921)]. Rules of court made and published have the force of law and are binding on the court and the parties to the action. [*District of Columbia* v. *Roth*, 18 App. D. C. 547, 553 (1901)].

Nomenclature.   Rules of court are called by a variety of names, as rules of practice, rules of procedure, and the like. To make it more confusing, the term is often used interchangeably with federal or state codes of procedure, which are direct enactments of the legislature. Partly this is because, in some jurisdictions, the court rules are incorporated in the procedural codes, though adopted by the courts pursuant to a legislative directive providing for subsequent legislative approval before becoming effective. However, the distinction should be maintained between a code of procedure, enacted as law, and the rules of the courts operating under that code and implementing it.

CHAPTER 11

LAW REPORTS: RATIONALE, FORMAT, AND USE AS PRECEDENT

A. Importance of Law Reports.[1]

The most important material in a reasonably complete American working law library is its collection of published reports of judicial decisions, English and American. Except for statutes and the tools for their use, practically all other books in a law library are means for unlocking the store of rules found in these reports, or for ascertaining whether the rule of law of a given case is still good law. The elaborate machinery for making accessible these printed reports is necessary because the reports are printed according to decision date, not subject matter. The legal purist goes so far as to maintain that case law is the only real authority, in that a statute's meaning is fixed and determined only by a judicial decision.

B. Definition and Purpose of a Law Report.

A law report has been defined as ". . . the production of an adequate record of a judicial decision on a point of law, in a case heard in open court, for the subsequent citation as a precedent. A law report is a report of law, and not of fact. Only the issues and the facts relevant to the point of law should be recorded, since every judgment is founded on a situation of fact." [2]

"The purpose of a law report is the exposition of the law. It should show the parties, the nature of the pleadings, the essential facts, the arguments of Counsel, the decision, and the grounds for the judgment." [3]

C. What Judicial Decisions [4] are Reported.

With the exception of the reports of the federal district courts, the Court of

---

[1] For comment on the evolution of the law report, *see* Chapter 29.

[2] C. G. Moran, *The Heralds of the Law*, (London, Stevens, 1948).

[3] Gt. Britain, Lord Chancellor's Department, *Report of the Law Reporting Committee*, (London, H. M. S. O., 1940), p. 3.

Claims, the Customs Court, and those of some lower courts in a few states such as New York and Pennsylvania, printed reports are of cases appealed to a higher court on a point of law. Even in the reports of the courts of first instance mentioned, the cases reported have to do with the weight or admission of evidence, pleadings, or other matters of law, with only sufficient facts appearing in the opinion to make clear the point of law at issue. However, by no means all cases heard, even in appellate courts, are reported. The attempt generally is to print reports of decisions which make new law or are of general interest to the public, and to exclude those which lack these qualities and are merely routine.

Relatively few of the cases heard in lower courts are reported, though the decisions are matters of record in the courts where given, and exemplified copies of them may be had from the clerks of the courts. The value as precedents of decisions of state trial courts is dubious.[5] Selectivity of reporting of the decisions of appellate courts, aimed at reducing the vast bulk (about 30,000 a year) of reported cases, has not always worked out well, frequently requiring the private publication of collections of "unreported cases" which a later editor has deemed important. It provides also an important reason for such private editions as the National Reporter System, in which since 1879 many thousands of otherwise unreported appellate decisions have been printed.

D. Reporting Judicial Decisions.

In the United States, contrary to English practice, opinions of courts are read instead of being delivered orally, and there are official reporters who are responsible for making a record of all proceedings, including the opinion and judgment of each case. Some reports are "official" and other "unofficial," the difference being that the official are published under statutory direction and the unofficial usually are not. Both use identical texts of opinions and judgments as supplied by the courts, but the editorial matter (such as tables, indexes and, usually, headnotes) is different. Both official and unofficial reports are citable in court, though courts prefer the citation of their own official reports, with the permissible additional citation in parallel of the unofficial report.

Reasons for Unofficial Reporting. These are: the need for speedier and more frequent publication than is afforded by most official reports; for combined reports for a group of contiguous states having similar interests; for the selection and annotation of a group of cases covering all jurisdictions but of interest to lawyers everywhere; for special-subject cases as part of a special-subject service covering all the law, case and statutory, of that subject; and, finally, for the publication of cases not deemed worthy of publication by the official reporter.

"Star Paging" of Unofficial Editions. Except in facsimile reprints without

---

[4] In discussing law reports and their use as precedent, five terms are frequently but often erroneously employed interchangeably. These are "law report," "opinion," "decision," and "judgment" or "decree." Technically, the "report" is all inclusive — the case title, statement of facts, opinion, and the decision; the opinion is the statement of what the court says in reaching its decision; and the decision is the official determination of the rights of the parties, with accompanying order, if needed. In the above paragraph, "decision" is used as an inclusive term, because many cases are reported without opinion.

[5] South Carolina Court of Common Pleas for Spartansburg County, Judgment Roll No. 33, 454, July 19, 1946; *King* v. *Order of United Commercial Travelers,* 333 U. S. 153 (1948).

notes, the pagination of the official editions of law reports differs from that of the unofficial, and the unofficial are often "star paged," as follows:

of competition. From

* 464

its findings, the Com-

This indicates that page 463 of the official report ends with "From" and page 464 begins with "its." Unofficial editions of the *United States Reports*, and the *English Reports — Full Reprint* are examples of star paging. With the exception of the *Supreme Court Reporter*, National Reporter System reports are not star paged, because printed before the official edition.

Notes

Official Reporting. In nine states there are constitutional or statutory provisions requiring written opinions, but this has not worked well, and similar statutes have been repealed or held unconstitutional in some states. This is discussed by Max Radin in *The Requirement of Written Opinions.*[6]

In the period prior to 1790, English case reports were the only ones freely available to the profession in America, and they were cited in spite of statutes forbidding it. The first American reports were unofficial, the very first such published being Ephraim Kirby's *Reports of Cases Adjudged in the Superior Court of the State of Connecticut from the year 1785 to May 1788.*[7] Later, unofficial reporters in various states collected and published many earlier reports, a process which is still going on. The earliest were those of the Provincial Court of Maryland, printed as the first volume of Harris and McHenry's reports, covering the years 1658 to 1774. Naturally, most of these early reports were fragmentary. "Official" reporting began with the appointment in 1790 by the Supreme Court of the United States of an official reporter, resulting in the initial volume of the *United States Reports* (1 Dallas), which, however, contained nothing but Pennsylvania Supreme Court reports. In 1804, both Massachusetts and New York instituted official reporting, a system which spread to all states and territories except Alaska. A brief, well documented account of American reporting is by Francis R. Aumann, *American Law Reports: Yesterday and Today.*[8].

It was early decided that the opinion of the court is in the public domain and thus not copyrightable, but that the reporter or the state could copyright any and all editorial matter going to form a complete report. There is some doubt that the syllabi written by the court by direction of a statute are copyrightable.[9]

Both official and unofficial reports are citable in court, though courts prefer the citation of their own official reports; the additional citation in parallel of the unofficial is permitted.

E. Law Reports Cited by the Name of the Reporter.

Formerly, the reporter commonly gave his name to his series of reports, as Dallas, Pickering, or Wendell, regardless of the jurisdiction reported. About the middle of the nineteenth century this cumbersome practice was dropped in favor of naming the series after the jurisdiction, as United States or Massachusetts. In those official series still current at the time, the existing volumes were renumbered consecutively from the earliest one. Thus, there were then ninety such renumbered *United States*

---

[6] 18 Cal. L. Rev. 486 (1930).

[7] Litchfield, Conn., Collier, 1789.

[8] 4 Ohio St. L. J. 311 (1938).

[9] *See Wheaton* v. *Peters*, 8 Peters 591 (U. S. 1834); *Callaghan* v. *Myers*, 128 U. S. 617 (1898); and *West Publishing Co.* v. *Edward Thompson Co.*, 186 Fed. 833 (2d Cir. 1919).

Reports (Dallas through Wallace), ninety-six *Massachusetts Reports,* etc. However, in spite of the renumbering, these early "nominatives" are still cited in their original form. Thus, 90 U. S. is cited as 23 Wallace, but 91 U. S. is not 1 Otto but 91 U. S. Similarly for state reports. In this *Manual* and in most libraries, conversion tables from named reporter to consecutive numbering are provided. *Shepard's Citations* customarily provide such conversion tables where needed.

Many early series, no longer current, were not renumbered, and these of course are still cited by the name of the reporter, as shown in the bibliographical manual of state reports in this book. Since their titles are always abbreviated in citations, consultation of a table of abbreviations, such as the one in this *Manual,* is often necessary to identify the report.

F. Parts of a Reported Case.

A reported case may consist of the following parts.

Title. The title of the case designates the parties, as *Smith* v. *Jones, In re Brown, Matter of Murphy, People* v. *Graham, The Elizabeth,* or *United States* v. *34 Cases of Squareface Gin.* The plaintiff-defendant order is usually kept throughout, but in some courts the order is reversed on appeal when the defendant has lost in the court below and is the "Plaintiff in Error" in the court above.

Docket Number. This is the serial number assigned to a case when filed in a court and awaiting action, and is useful as identification, particularly in searching appeal papers relating to it, or when seeking information as to its present status. The term and dates when the case was argued and decided are usually given here.

Headnote or Syllabus. This is a convenient index to matter in the opinion, giving a short statement of the rule or rules of law laid down by the court in deciding the case. In the National Reporter System and some other reports, the headnote paragraphs are numbered, thus being keyed to like numbers in the text of the opinion, so that it is easy to find the matter referred to, in the opinions. The headnote may be propositional (that is, purely a statement of a legal principle), or factual (containing sufficient facts to tie it to the case at hand). In some states the headnote is written by the judge or court, when it will usually bear the notation "syllabus by the court," but usually it is written by the reporter. In some states, as Georgia, Ohio, and Oklahoma, the court is required by law to write a syllabus, which announces the law as decided by the court. The opinion then is the personal statement of the judge.

It cannot be too strongly emphasized that, with the possible exception of the syllabi by the courts in those few jurisdictions where by statute they are said to announce the law of the case, these headnote paragraphs are not authority but only indexes to it. Some cases have fifty or more headnote paragraphs, and a dozen are not uncommon, but both experience and common sense make it obvious that only a very few of these are statements of legal principles necessarily raised, considered, and decided in the case. The rest result from the practice of taking every piece of dictum or random statement of the court in its opinion, and making a headnote paragraph out of it. Since it is impossible in reading the headnote to separate authority from dictum, the case itself must be read.

Statement of Facts. As apart from the opinion, this statement is usually omitted from reports of decisions today, though in some states, as New York, and in the unofficial *American Law Reports,* it may occupy as much as a page of print.

Commonly today, the court states *in its opinion* as many of the facts as are deemed necessary to the decision.

Statement of How the Case Arose. In practically all published case reports, there is a preliminary brief statement of how the case came to the court which is deciding it. In considering a case as possible authority for a proposition of law, how it arose should always be borne carefully in mind, since that may be decisive of its applicability. For example, a case coming up on a prayer for a preliminary injunction is unlikely to be authority on the merits of a point of substantive law, though such point may be discussed as background for the decision.

Names of Counsel. Two principal functions are performed by these names. Counsel are often willing to supply briefs when these have not been printed. When the opinion in a case has not been published, counsel may be in a position to detail the arguments, the questions asked by the courts, and other possible factors influencing the decision and affecting its value as precedent.

Synopses of Briefs of Counsel. In the older reports it was common to set forth at some length the arguments of counsel and citations to authority, taken from counsel's briefs, but this is now done in only a few reporters. Potentially, if the case is in point, this is a useful tool in a search for authority in like cases.

Opinion of the Court. This is the court's explanation of why it decided as it did. In it, the court, speaking through the judge delivering the opinion, gives those facts of the case which are necessary for consideration and decision of the point of law raised; sets forth the errors charged by the appellant; and then proceeds to lay a foundation for the decision of the court. Frequently the judges agree on the decision of a case but disagree as to their reasons, and file *concurring opinions*, thus tending to dilute the value of the case as precedent. Many cases are decided by a divided court, when one or more *dissenting opinions* are usually filed and become part of the printed record. *Per curiam* and *memorandum decisions* are common in federal and some state courts in reporting routine decisions, especially those on motions. In these, the opinion is omitted, but the decision or order is set forth. Frequently, when a written opinion has been read but the court orders only the decision to be printed, the National Reporter System report of the case supplies the headnotes to the opinion as actually delivered, and the case is thus digested. Most per curiam decisions, however, lack these headnotes and are not digested.

Commonly, the opinion consists of a general statement of the points of law involved, and this is quite likely to be pure dictum. Then the law is applied to the specific circumstances of the case being decided, the statement of which usually involves *ratio decidendi*, the statement of an underlying principle leading inevitably to the decision. Professor Eugene Wambaugh put it in the form of a syllogism containing the following propositions:

(1) When the circumstances surrounding the parties are thus and thus, the rights of the parties are thus and thus; (2) in this particular case such circumstances do surround the parties; (3) in this particular case the other circumstances are not material; and (4) in this particular case the rights of the parties are as indicated in the first proposition. (In the phraseology of logicians, the first of these propositions is the major premise, the second and third taken together are the minor premise, and the fourth is the conclusion.)[10]

---

[10] *The Study of Cases,* (Boston, Little, Brown & Co., 1892), p. 16.

Decision of the Court. This is what the court *does*, as distinguished from what it *says* in its opinion. It is expressed in some such terse language as "Affirmed," "Reversed," "There is no error," and the like. It should be noted that the *decision is final*, but that the opinion, the formal statement of the reasoning leading up to the decision, may be and frequently is revised after delivery and before final printing, and occasionally is even withdrawn entirely.

G. The Role of Stare Decisis in Case Law.

The part which law reports play in Anglo-American jurisprudence can not be understood without reference to the doctrine of stare decisis, or precedent. Its influence on law books and their making was noted in Chapter 1, but further definition is needed here.

The Doctrine Defined. The term is derived from the legal maxim, *stare decisis et non quieta movere, to adhere to precedent and not to unsettle things which are settled.* The theory of Anglo-American law is that the principle underlying the decision in one case will be deemed of imperative authority, controlling the decisions of like cases in the same court or in lower courts within the same jurisdiction, unless and until the decision in question is reversed or overruled by a court of competent authority. Such decision will only be overruled for urgent reasons and in exceptional cases. A single decision does not necessarily create a precedent to be followed.

Decisions relied upon as precedent are commonly those of appellate courts. The value as precedent of decisions of state trial courts, as noted at page 3, is dubious, as the decision will probably be appealed to the higher courts and accordingly is not the best evidence of the rule of law laid down. The authority of decisions as between federal and state courts is discussed at page 3.

Res Judicata Distinguished. Stare decisis extracts a rule for general guidance, for like cases in the future. Res Judicata is quite different and has nothing to do with precedent; a case subject to the rule of res judicata may or may not also be a precedent. "The general principle . . . is that a right, question or fact distinctly put in issue and directly determined by a court of competent jurisdiction, as a ground of recovery, cannot be disputed in a subsequent suit between the same parties or their privies; and even if the second suit is for a different cause of action, the right, question or fact once so determined must, as between the same parties or their privies, be taken as conclusively established, so long as the judgment in the first suit remains unmodified." [11] Both rules aim at reducing litigation, but in different ways. Res judicata works as an *estoppel* between the parties; whereas stare decisis is applied without respect to the parties.

Reasons for the Doctrine. Since Anglo-American law is not one of established codes, in the Civil Law manner, judges need some other guide, and so they rely upon prior decisions as an aid in present deliberations. Chancellor James Kent stated the rationale as follows:

A solemn decision upon a point of law arising in any given case, becomes an authority in a like case, because it is the highest evidence which we can have of the law applicable to the subject, and the judges are bound to follow that decision so long as it stands unreversed, unless it can be shown that the law was misunderstood or misapplied in that

---

[11] *Southern Pacific Ry.* v. *United States,* 168 U. S. 1, 48 (1897).

particular case. If a decision has been made upon solemn argument and mature deliberation, the presumption is in favor of its correctness; and the community have a right to regard it as a just declaration or exposition of the law, and to regulate their actions and contracts by it. It would, therefore, be extremely inconvenient to the public, if precedents were not duly regarded and implicitly followed. It is on the notoriety and stability of such rules that professional men can give safe advice to those who consult them; and people in general can venture with confidence to buy and trust, and to deal with each other. If judicial decisions were to be lightly disregarded, we should disturb and unsettle the great landmarks of property. When a rule has been once deliberately adopted and declared, it ought not to be disturbed unless by a court of appeal or review, and never by the same court, except for very cogent reasons, and upon a clear manifestation of error; and if the practice were otherwise, it would be leaving us in a state of perpetual uncertainty as to the law.[12]

Analysis of the Doctrine. The doctrine is by no means exact in its meaning or application. The following, based upon the admirable analysis of Professor Eugene Wambaugh [13] raises some questions frequently presented.

Point must have been raised and considered. Precedents are based upon the consideration and decision of actual cases. The point of law for which a case stands must have been raised and considered by counsel and court in such a case. A point raised by counsel but not deemed by the court as necessary for the decision and not considered by it is not a precedent.

Indentity of essential circumstances. Kent's requirement of a "like case" is not taken literally, as no two cases are identical. Non-essential circumstances (parties, time, and place are usually such) may be stripped from a fact situation and still leave a case "on all fours" with the case sought to be used as a precedent; but at the point where elimination of an element changes the legal principle involved, the cases are no longer "like." The exact determination of these matters involves the delicate and complex art of the lawyer.

Doctrine of the case. It follows that there must be a rule in the case sought to be used as precedent, without which that case could not have been decided as it was; and that that rule must be of general application to the class of cases under consideration. This rule is ordinarily extracted from the opinions of the court, but by no means all that the court says in its opinions is usable as precedent. What the court says is an expression of why it reaches its decision. In it the court often discusses issues not raised or decided in the case, by way of illustration or for other purposes.

Ratio decidendi. The legal reasoning of the court which leads inevitably and necessarily to the decision is on a different basis from dictum. It is a statement of a doctrine precisely applicable to the case being decided, and necessarily involved in the decision. Usually this doctrine is expressed in so many words (not necessarily consecutive) of the court in its opinion; but all or part of it may be in the court's mind but so obvious to all concerned as not to require expression. To that extent it may be deducible from the context. As reasoning from a rule to its specific application, *ratio decidendi* is broader than the decision.

Dictum. An expression of opinion as to the state of the law, not necessarily raised by the case or necessary to its decision, is called dictum, and dicta are not regarded as precedents within the rule of stare decisis. This is because they are in effect merely the unofficial statements of rules of law—such as a text writer might make—and not definite, official decisions of a question at issue before the court. Not having been at issue before the court, they have not been argued by counsel or investigated fully. To that extent, the court in its remarks is really deciding a hypothetical case, and not the one before it. Only the specific case before the court is the basis of a precedent. The test is whether

---

[12] 1 *Commentaries on American Law* 476, (14th ed., Boston, Little, Brown & Co., 1896).

[13] Wambaugh, *op. cit.*, passim. The theories of Professors Wambaugh, Llewellyn, Goodhart and Glanville Williams are discussed and criticized by R. N. Gooderson, *Ratio Decidendi and the Rules of Law*, 30 Can. Bar. Rev. 892 (1952).

or not the court's statement is required in the consideration and determination of the issues necessarily presented to and decided by the court, or is merely illustration or background material.

Well considered dicta, nevertheless, are often highly persuasive and are frequently cited. When done, it should be with full awareness, however.

Points raised in argument but not considered in the opinion. A point not considered by the court is not precedent. The best way to learn what the court considered as a basis for its decision is the opinion, and if a point which has been raised in argument is ignored in the opinion, it is some evidence that the court ignored it. It is not conclusive evidence, however, and it is often possible to demonstrate that the court must have had a point in mind as a basis for decision, even though absent from the opinion. It is then precedent on that point. The doctrine may be so familiar and well settled as not to need laboring. On the other hand, a point which could have been raised by counsel in argument but was not is not precedent.

Application of the Doctrine: Opinions Analyzed.[14]

Per curiam opinions. These are not held in as high esteem as are opinions in which the reasons for the decision are carefully worked out. The decision stands, but it is difficult to show what was in the court's mind.

Where no reasons or citations are given. The same reasoning applies as to a per curiam opinion.

Equally divided court. Sometimes when a case comes up on appeal, one judge does not participate, and the remaining judges divide evenly. This, by not overturning the decision of the court below, leaves it in or affirms it. Such a case is not precedent.

Majority of a divided court. Often, though the case is decided by a majority of the court, one or more dissents are filed, which have the effect of diluting the authority of the case. However, it is said that when more than one point is involved, the authority of the case is undiminished for those points not covered by the dissent.

Concurring in the result but not the reasoning. When judges agree on a decision but disagree as to the reasons for it, "certainly it cannot be claimed . . . that it is to be regarded as authority."[15]

When a statute is involved. If a statute not declaratory of the common law controls the decisions, the decision lacks authority outside the jurisdiction where made, as stated in Chapter I; however, it may be highly persuasive in other jurisdictions.

Case not followed. If a single case is not followed, when opportunity offers, it has little or no standing. Similarly (as may be learned through citators), if a case has been freely criticized or distinguished by later cases, its authority may be diminished to the vanishing point, even if not openly overruled. In fact, that is the usual way of overruling a case in effect. Conversely, if a case is frequently followed and approved, its authority is thereby enhanced.

Overruled case. A case may be formally overruled by a later case in the same jurisdiction, thus eliminating it as authority. This may be done because conditions have changed, thus making the old rule harsh or unjust; or because the court is convinced that the original case was wrongly decided. *But see* "strict rule," below.

Cases from other jurisdictions. Cases in point from other jurisdictions are not imperative authority, but when well reasoned are highly persuasive and so are freely cited by counsel and courts. The standing of a case as precedent within its own jurisdiction is enhanced by the citation of cases in agreement from other jurisdictions.

Stare Decisis as a Rule from the Grave. The doctrine does not act as a dead hand, because the judges do not permit it to do so. It permits changes in doctrine as conditions warrant, and cases are constantly re-examined so that they do not constitute a "government of the living by the dead." Conditions so change that the precedent in time becomes only a starting point in the search for a new and

---

[14] An important function of the citators described in Chapter 18 is to note the presence of certain of the factors noted below in the cases checked upon as precedent.

[15] *Dubuque* v. *Illinois Central R. R.*, 39 Iowa 56, 80 (1874).

currently applicable principle. As a result, "the life of a rule is seldom more than a generation." [16]

The strict rule. The above states the "liberal rule," as usually applied to matters involving <u>human rights</u>. Where, however, there has been a long line of cases so decided as to create a <u>definite rule</u>, the courts seldom change the rule, rather leaving it to the legislature to do so.[17] It is not uncommon for the courts in such instances to suggest remedial legislation. An outstanding example is the abrogation of the common law fellow servant rule by legislation, following the refusal of the courts to upset a long line of decisions resulting in an admittedly harsh rule. <u>Where the rule involves property, the courts refuse to alter it and thus upset titles and vested rights.</u> To a somewhat lesser degree, this is true also of contract rights.

[handwritten margin note: only the leg. has prospective juris.]

Notes

Illustrative Case.   The opinion in *Hoffman* v. *Le Traunik*, 209 F. 375 (N. D. N. Y 1913), illustrates the distinction between dictum, *ratio decidendi*, and decisions. It is also a good example of the decisive effect on precedent of the manner in which a case reaches the appellate court. This particular opinion is also proof that an opinion need not be dull.

In Equity. Suit by Aaron Hoffman against Sam Le Traunik, for alleged infringement of copyright in the use of monologues. On motion for preliminary injunction pendente lite. Denied.

[*P.* charged *D*, a burlesque comedian, with using his copyrighted monologues. The opinion reproduced one monologue and discussed certain similarities of *D's* material; it then proceeded as follows] *see* p. 102.

Casting the proposition extracted from the above excerpt, in the form of a syllogism, we have:

1. Preliminary injunctions will not issue except in the clearest cases. [A general rule.]

2. Where, on a motion for a preliminary injunction, complainant makes affidavit one way, defendant the other; and the substantive issue will be tried on its merits within two months; no public interest being involved; and the damage to the complainant will not be very serious, no clear and satisfactory case is made. [Illustrating the rule.]

3. Therefore, these conditions existing here, the motion for a preliminary injunction to restrain D from using his monologues is denied.

All that is said above by the court about copyright and infringement is dictum, not required for the decision. The case decides nothing on the merits of any copyright infringement issue, but for reasons given refuses a preliminary injunction.

---

[16] Roscoe Pound, *The History and System of the Common Law*, (New York, P. F. Collier, c. 1939), p. 62.

[17] The matter is discussed at length in *Bricker* v. *Green*, 313 Mich. 218, 21 N.W.2d 105, 163 A. L. R. 697 (1946), which overruled a long and unbroken line of decisions on the imputation of a driver's negligence to his passenger.

378   209 FEDERAL REPORTER

378   HOFFMAN V. LE TRAUNIK

It may be proved on the trial that the complainant originated all these expressions, and the court may be of the mind that no one but the author and his licensees should be permitted to use them; but, so long as the defendants aver under oath that they were not new with complainant but common-property and used on the stage prior to the writing of complainant's monologues, it seems to me that a preliminary injunction should not issue. No public interest is involved, and the damage to the complainant will not be very serious. The answers are served, and a term of court will be held at Albany February 10th, when the suit can be tried if the parties desire.

[2] To be entitled to be copyrighted, the composition must be "original, meritorious, and free from illegality or immorality." And "a work, in order to be copyrighted, must be original in the sense that the author has created it by his own skill, labor, and judgment, without directly copying or evasively imitating the work of another." However, "a new and original plan, arrangement, or combination of materials will entitle the author to a copyright therein, whether the materials themselves be new or old."

[3] But here the defendants have not copied substantially the plan, arrangement or combination of materials found in complainant's monologues or in any one of them. Conceding literary or artistic merit in the complainant's monologues growing out of some original matter combined with old matter in a new and an original plan, arrangement, or combination, the defendants do not infringe, not having used that plan, arrangement, or combination, unless they have abstracted and used some of the complainant's new matter and so much of it as to authorize the finding that there has been a copying or a taking.

"Copying the whole or a substantial part of a copyrighted work constitutes and is an essential element of infringement. It is not confined to literal repetition or reproduction but includes also the various modes in which the matter of any work may be adopted, imitated, transferred, or reproduced with more or less colorable alteration to disguise the piracy. But, on the principle of de minimis non curat lex, it is necessary that a substantial part of the copyrighted work be taken." 9 Cyc. 939, 940.

If there is any piracy in this case, it consists in the taking and use of these isolated expressions or "gags," as they are called, and to constitute infringement it must be established by the complainant that they were original with him. The burden is on him to show this, and with complainant making affidavit one way and the defendants the other, and a sworn answer also interposed, a clear and satisfactory case on such a subject is not made for the drastic use of a preliminary injunction.

The motion is denied, but the defendants must be ready for trial at the Albany term of this court or the motion may be renewed on the same and additional papers.

Exhibit 17

CHAPTER 12

FORMS OF PUBLICATION OF LAW REPORTS

A. General Considerations.

Law reports may be published in any or all of the following forms. Except in a few legal periodicals and loose-leaf services, they are published in the order of the decision date, not by subject. This is why the elaborate indexes later to be described in this book are necessary.

B. Slip Decision.

This, a separate pamphlet or sheet for each opinion, usually unrevised and un-corrected, has only speed of publication to commend it. It is uncommon outside the federal courts, though an increasing number of state courts now issue such decisions. Sometimes, as for the Supreme Court of the United States, they are called "preliminary prints." The slip decision is released on decision day or close to it, and customarily is complete save for the syllabus. It is usually printed, but some states issue it in mimeographed form. Whether slip decisions are available for any given court may be ascertained from the clerk of the court.

C. Advance Sheets.

The advance sheet typically is a periodical pamphlet publication collecting all reports decided within the jurisdiction or jurisdictions reported since its preceding issue. It includes practically every feature contained in the bound volume into which it later cumulates.

According to series, it appears up to fifty-two times a year, as against once a year for the average official bound reports. Begun as a special feature of the National Reporter System, it has since spread to a considerable number of official reports. With the exception of the *Lawyers' Edition* of the United States Supreme Court reports, volume and page numbers are identical with those of the bound volumes, so that they can be cited directly by volume and page. Bound volumes, but not advance sheets, of the *Lawyers' Edition* are heavily annotated, which is why the pagination differs between the two.

Corrections in Advance Sheets. Because of the accent on speed of publication, advance sheets are subject to error. The judge writing the opinion can at any time prior to final publication in bound form withdraw it for revision, and there are instances where he has withdrawn it from publication entirely. Because of this, some libraries do not discard their unbound advance sheets upon receipt of the superseding bound volume.

D. Legal Newspapers and Periodicals Publishing Law Reports.

Publication herein may be of the full report, or the report minus the headnotes, or the report may be abridged. The legal newspaper may be a daily practioners' sheet, as the *New York Law Journal*, or a periodical of less frequency, as the *Washington Law Reporter*. The chief value of these reports lies in speed of publication, but occasionally the local newspaper publishes decisions not elsewhere reported, and the latter is searched for such cases, as a last resort. Legal periodicals are described in Chapter 22.

E. Loose-Leaf Services.

As described in Chapter 26, these publications print special-subject reports in tax and regulatory fields.

F. Bound Volumes of Law Reports.

The final form of a law report is the bound volume, which contains nearly all the essential features of a digest, plus the text of the report iself. The manifest impossibility of requiring the lawyer to search the many thousand volumes of reports, one by one, in order to find his law, has necessitated the appearance of the digest. This combines the index material of all the report volumes in much shorter, classified compass. The typical bound law report, official or unofficial, contains most of the following features:

1. *Title page*, giving the *title of the series*, the *jurisdiction*, and the *reporter's name*.
2. *Names of the judges* of the court or courts served.
3. *Table of cases* reported in the volume.
4. *Table of cases affected or cited* by decisions reported. This table is in the *United States Reports* and about half the official state reports.
5. *Table of statutes interpreted* by cases reported. This table is in the *United States Reports* in all editions, two-thirds of the official state reports, and in the National Reporter System.
6. *Written opinions*, in chronological order.
7. *Per curiam or memorandum opinions*, usually following the written.
8. *Subject index or digest* of opinions reported.
9. *Words and phrases* judicially defined.
10. *Court rules* adopted during the period covered by the report. *See also* Chapter 10.

G. Agency Publication of Law Reports.

Governmental agencies sometimes collect all reports, both judicial and quasi-judicial, of decisions affecting them and the laws they administer. These are of course special-subject reports.

CHAPTER 13

LAW REPORTS: DECISIONS OF FEDERAL
AND STATE COURTS

A. THE FEDERAL COURT SYSTEM AS IT AFFECTS LAW REPORT PUBLICATION.
B. UNITED STATES SUPREME COURT REPORTS.
C. LOWER FEDERAL COURT REPORTS.
D. LOWER FEDERAL COURTS FOR WHICH THERE ARE "OFFICIAL" REPORTS.
E. DATES OF FEDERAL JUDICIAL AND ADMINISTRATIVE REPORTS.
F. DIGESTS OF CASES DECIDED IN FEDERAL COURTS.
G. CITATORS FOR FEDERAL COURT REPORTS.
H. STATE COURT REPORTS.

A. The Federal Court System as it Affects Law Report Publication.[1]

The highest federal court is the Supreme Court of the United States. Beneath it are the Courts of Appeals (formerly the Circuit Courts of Appeals), and the Court of Appeals for the District of Columbia. These courts have jurisdiction of appeals from final decisions of United States and district courts (including in most instances those of Alaska, the Canal Zone, and the Virgin Islands). The general federal courts of original jurisdiction are the district courts, of which there is at least one in every state. Those for Alaska, the Canal Zone, and the Virgin Islands have, in addition to federal jurisdiction, local jurisdiction approximating that of state courts. There are also several special federal courts, which are mentioned below in connection with their reports.

Reporting Policy of Federal Courts. All written and nearly all per curiam decisions of the Supreme Court are officially or unofficially reported. This is true also of the reports of the intermediate appellate courts and those of the special courts. Only selected decisions of the district courts are published. Unpublished reports may usually be had, as typed manuscripts, from the court clerks, for about $1.00 a page.

B. United States Supreme Court Reports.

All written and most per curiam reports of decisions are printed in the official *United States Reports*, and in the unofficial *Lawyers' Edition* and *Supreme Court Reporter*. Many per curiam decisions not officially reported are published in the two unofficial editions. These latter decisions for the most part simply note the probable jurisdiction of the Court, extend time for filing various petitions, fix the

---

[1] This *Manual* is concerned with court systems only in so far as they affect the publication and use of law reports. The Constitutional and statutory bases of federal courts are discussed in standard works on federal practice and procedure. Wilber G. Katz, *Federal Legislative Courts*, 43 Harv. L. Rev. 894 (1930), is also recommended.

compensation of special masters, permit the filing of briefs as *amici curiae*, and similar matters not affecting the merits of a case. The decisions of the court are reported in "slip" form, advance sheets, and bound volumes.

Slip Decisions. Monday is "decision day" in the Supreme Court, though occasionally orders are handed down on other days. After the day's session, printed copies of decisions and orders are released in "slip" form, a separate publication for each opinion or order. An opinion as so printed contains only the docket number, the title *(Sherr* v. *Gray)*, how it came to the Court (by writ of certiorari, *etc.*), the date of the decision, and its complete text, with the judgment. There are thus no headnotes or other editorial matter. Their only virtue is speed of publication, and they are often corrected later. The official edition (which includes both written and per curiam decisions) is available from the Government Printing Office by subscription. Delivery ordinarily varies from two days to two weeks after the decision date. There are also two unofficial editions, facsimiles of the original, usually mailed to subscribers on decision date. They are in the *United States Supreme Court Bulletin*, and the *United States Law Week*, both described below. Loose-leaf services frequently mail to their subscribers on decision day decisions of outstanding interest.

United States Reports. This is the title of the official edition of the reports of the Supreme Court of the United States, dating nominally from 1774 but actually only from the first reported case of the Court, in the August term of 1791. This is a typical report series, published first in pamphlet "Advance Prints" with identical pagination to the bound volumes into which they cumulate. The advance sheets appear at irregular intervals of from a month to six weeks during term time, so that the time lag from decision to receipt date may be up to two months. The first ninety volumes of the set are cited by the names of the official reporters instead of as "United States Reports."

Lawyers' Edition of the Supreme Court Reports. This is an unofficial edition, covering the entire set of *United States Reports*. It contains many reports not reported originally in the early volumes, including those in the appendices to volumes 131 and 154, described below in the Notes. Although the text is identical with that of the official edition (except where errors in the official are pointed out and parallel statutory and case citations are supplied when lacking in the official), the editorial matter is quite different.

As presently published, each report is summarized. The headnotes are rewritten in somewhat expanded form and keyed both to the text of the opinion and to the *A. L. R. Digest* (*see* page 127). Briefs of counsel are summarized. The most significant difference, however, is that many cases are "annotated," increasingly so of late years, in the manner of the *American Law Reports*, to be described later. That is, the points of law decided are written up, often at considerable length, with citations to authority, much in the manner of a law review note. When not thus annotated, there are reference to annotations to the annotated reports series. There are extensive tables which are cumulated in the *Digest of the United States Supreme Court Reports*. These include a table of federal and state cases reheard, affirmed, reversed, *etc.*, by the Supreme Court; and of foreign, federal and state statutes construed. Each volume contains cross-reference tables from the official citation to the *Lawyers' Edition*. Certain per curiam orders, not officially reported, are reported.

Supreme Court Reporter. This is a unit of the unofficial National Reporter System (described in Chapter 14), with the conventional features of those reporters. The coverage is from 106 U. S. (October term, 1882) to date. The advance sheets appear semi-monthly. The time lag for decisions reported is usually from about ten days to three weeks. They cumulate into one annual volume, star paged to the official. The text is identical with that of the official, except as noted above for the *Lawyers' Edition*, but the headnotes and other editorial matter are different.

In addition to features common to all *Reporters* (as the units of the National Reporter System are popularly known), federal court rules and amendments are printed as adopted, and there are tables of rules construed by cases reported. Memorials to deceased Supreme Court justices are printed. A transfer table from official to *Reporter* citation is supplied, and there is a digest, identical in classification with that of the American Digest System. Reference is here made to the discussion of "Statutes Construed" tables, at page 118, because these tables are especially significant for their citations of state court decisions interpreting federal statutes.

United States Supreme Court "Services." Three services, one official and two unofficial, report on the work of the Supreme Court.

Journal of the Supreme Court. This daily publication contains a statement of the business transacted—attorneys admitted to practice, decisions and orders handed down, *etc.* It is not easy to use in searching for back information, as there is no index. It is printed also in the *United States Law Week*, below.

United States Supreme Court Bulletin. This is a Commerce Clearing House loose-leaf reporter mailed out on decision day. It contains: (1) a statement of all official actions taken by the Court for the week preceding; (2) facsimile reprints of decisions and orders; (3) a topical index to cases on the docket or decided during the term; (4) a table of cases on the docket; (5) the rules of the Court; (6) the docket (with a summary of docketed cases); (7) a weekly "United States Supreme Court Docket" (highlights of recently docketed cases and cases awaiting decision); and (8) a tentative calendar for argument.

United States Law Week. Also mailed on decision day, this contains the complete docket, summaries (by topic) of cases on the docket, a "Review of Supreme Court's Work," facsimile "slip" decisions, and an extensive index. The "Review" is a law-review-style treatment of various aspects of the Court's work. It contains exhaustive statements of important cases recently argued and awaiting decision, with arguments of counsel; or a review of the term's decisions on cases involving (for example) taxation. These articles are indexed both by subject and by docket number, and in the *Index to Legal Periodicals (see* Chapter 22). The Court's *Journal* for the week is also reproduced here. An elaborate subject, case and docket index is issued and cumulated periodically, with a final cumulated issue at the end of the term of the Court.

Cases pending, argued, and awaiting decision, and the latest decisions, are readily available through these services.

Notes

Background of the United States Reports. Dallas (1790) is regarded as the first official reporter, though there is evidence that Cranch (1801) was the first reporter regularly appointed; but the original editions of Dallas and Cranch probably lacked official sanction. The first legislation providing for the appointment of an official reporter and the printing of his reports was in the Act of March 3, 1817, Chapter 63, 3 Stat. 376 (1850).

It was not until 1834 that all opinions of the Court were required by order to be filed with the clerk. The manuscript record of the opinions in the clerk's office began with the January term, 1835, but the printed record did not begin until the December term, 1857 (J. C. Bancroft Davis, 131 U. S. Appx. xv, xvi, 1888). In the early years of the Court only important opinions were reduced to writing and read.[2] As a result, many early decisions were imperfectly reported or not at all. In 1888, J. C. Bancroft Davis, then reporter, collected and printed 221 of these unreported cases in an appendix to volume 131 of the *United States Reports*. In 154 U. S., Mr. Davis printed about two hundred additional hitherto unreported cases in an appendix.

The first volume of Dallas and three-quarters of the second contain only Pennsylvania Supreme Court Reports, and all Dallas volumes contain some such reports. There was a rump and unaccepted volume 17 of Peters, when Mr. Peters at first refused to be displaced as reporter by Mr. Howard. Volume 126 contains the report of only one case.

The first ninety volumes of the reports are entitled *Reports of Cases Argued and Adjudged in the Supreme Court of the United States*. In 1875, with volume 91, the title was changed to the present *United States Reports*. Few sets of the "original" officials are now available in usable condition. Instead, the edition by F. C. Brightly [continued by Steward Rapalje through 17 Howard (58 U. S., December term, 1854) and by the later easily obtainable "official" volumes] or the *Lawyers' Edition*, are usually acquired for the earlier cases. Both of these unofficial editions are star paged and contain added notes. There are other unofficial editions of some of the early reports (usually abridged by the omission of briefs of counsel). Notable among these are *Curtis' Decisions*, covering also through 17 Howard; and *Miller's Decisions*, covering 18 to 24 Howard and 1 and 2 Black (1855–1862). All these reports begin with 2 Dallas (2 U. S.).

C. Lower Federal Court Reports.

With the exception of the few special courts noted below, the lower federal courts have been reported *only unofficially*. However, the current reports of the decisions of the district courts are available in typewritten form from the various court clerks or official reporters, at a cost of about $1.00 per page. Each of the ten circuits of the Courts of Appeals, the Court of Appeals of the District of Columbia, and the special courts of appeal print and distribute slip decisions. Bound volumes of official reports are not available except for some special courts, since the intended use of the slip reports is of an interim character. An important difference in coverage is that these *slip decisions report per curiam decisions which may be omitted from the unofficial edition*. Other than that, the distinction is of only academic importance, since the unofficial reports are universally accepted. On the other hand, the special courts which issue their own reports in bound form prefer to be cited to them rather than to their unofficial counterparts, though parallel citation to the unofficial report is acceptable. For more on this, *see* Chapter 32, on citation form.

1789-1880: Federal Cases. In the period preceding the establishment of the Federal Reporter in 1880, some 233 different reporters at various times printed lower federal court decisions. This was an impossible situation for the practicing lawyer. Between the years 1894 and 1897 a unique series, *Federal Cases*,[3] appeared,

---

[2] Charles E. Hughes, *The Supreme Court of the United States*. New York, Columbia University Press, 1928, p. 65.

[3] St. Paul, West Pub. Co., 1894-97. 30 v.

combining and reprinting the cases so diversely published originally. This set is now used to the exclusion of the original reports.

Arrangement of Federal Cases. The arrangement of cases is not chronological, as in other reports, but by title and arbitrary case number. That is, Case No. 1 is *The Aalesund;* Case No. 26 is *Acker* v. *The Rainbow;* Case No. 18,222 is *In re Zug, etc.* This strict alphabetical arrangement was interrupted in the last volume, because by that time the publishers had accumulated "Additional Cases" Nos. 18,223 to 18,313, which were printed in an alphabetically arranged appendix. As nearly as possible, these reports were verbatim reprints of the originals, the citations of which were given also, together with the court deciding the case, the decision date, and a headnote. Certain citator material was added in brackets. Frequently, *unreported cases* cited to certain points in other decisions were noted by title; *e.g.,* Case No. 17,856. This set of reports is still useful for the many early important decisions found in it.

Citation of cases in Federal Cases. Citation to cases reprinted in this series before 1897, of course, was by the original series, and it is thus necessary to translate these citations to the *Federal Cases* citations. If the case name is known, the cases may be found in their alphabetical order, either in the main series or in the "Additional Cases." If not, a blue-paper section in the unnumbered digest volume is a conversion table in parallel from the original reporter volume and page citation to the Federal Cases number. Thus, 2 *Benedict's U. S. District Court Reports* (2 Ben.) 76, is Case No. 15,626. All these older abbreviations are noted in the table of abbreviations in this *Manual.*

Digests, case, and conversion tables for Federal Cases. There is an unnumbered digest volume, which contains a table of cases and the blue-paper conversion table noted above.

Miscellaneous material in Federal Cases. Volume 1 lists all circuit and district judges to 1880, or district, and alphabetically by name. Biographical notes of these and other judges, to 1894, are in volume 30. Descriptions of all principal series of federal reports reprinted are also in that volume, as are the Laws of Oleron, Wisby, the Hanse Towns, and the Marine Ordinances of Louis XIV.

1880 to Date: Federal Reporter, Supplement, and Rules Decisions. Although there have been other reports for the lower federal courts since 1880, for practical purposes today the lawyer consults the *Reporters,* except for the reports of some of the special courts described below. The *Reporters* are "unofficial" reports, but since (again with the exception of the reports of the special courts) there have been no official reports, the distinction is academic. As National Reporter System units, these reports contain all the features of that system, as described in Chapter 14.

Federal Reporter. This series reports the decisions of the federal intermediate appellate courts; that is, the Courts of Appeals, the United States Court of Customs and Patent Appeals (for patent cases), and the United States Emergency Court of Appeals. The District of Columbia Court of Appeals is reported both in the *Reporter* and in its own separate series. From its beginning in 1880 through volume 60, second series (October term, 1931), this *Reporter* reported also the district courts of the United States and the tax cases of the United States Court of Claims. *All written opinions of the appellate courts* (with the above-noted exceptions) are said to be reported. There are weekly advance sheets. Official "slip" reports covering both written and most per curiam decisions are also available from clerks of the courts.

Federal Supplement. Selected decisions of the United States district courts and the tax cases of the Court of Claims which are deemed to be of sufficient general interest to merit publication are reported here. The series began with the October term, 1932, the same courts having from 1880 to that time been reported in the

Federal Reporter. Customs Court decisions are not here reported, but there is an official reporter for that court.

Federal Rules Decisions. This newest unit of the National Reporter System (dating from 1940) is highly specialized. It reports decisions interpreting the federal rules of civil and criminal procedure (essentially federal district court decisions) *not elsewhere reported.* It is a typical *Reporter* in its essential makeup, but also prints speeches and articles on federal practice, for which there is a cumulative index in the set. *Federal rules are annotated to the cases* in all published report series, supplementing the references in Barron and Holtzoff, *Federal Practice and Procedure.*[4] New revisions and amendments of court rules are printed as adopted. Advance sheets are printed monthly.

Coverage of the Federal Reporter and Federal Supplement. The broad reporting policy of the unofficial *Reports* covering the lower federal courts is largely determined by the Judicial Conference of the United States. If that body (composed of the chief judges of the various circuits of the Courts of Appeals, meeting on call of the Chief Justice of the Supreme Court) were to request the West Publishing Company to report the customs cases of the Court of Customs and Patent Appeals and those of the Customs Court, the publishers would probably comply.

D. Lower Federal Courts for Which There Are "Official" Reports.

For all of the special federal courts named below there are "official" reports, printed by the government. With the exception of the following, all their decisions are also reported in the *Federal Reporter* or *Federal Supplement:* Customs Court decisions; customs decisions in the Court of Customs and Patent Appeals; and Court of Claims cases other than tax cases. In form, these official reports are all typical law reports, and a checklist of them appears in the bibliographical appendix in this book.

Court of Claims. This is a legislative court with jurisdiction to hear certain statutorily defined claims against the United States, as noted in 28 U. S. C. § 1491 (1946) There have been two series of official reports, the first, unnumbered, from 1855 to 1862; and the second (current), beginning 1863. Tax claims decisions of this court are also reported in the *Federal Reporter* (through Volume 60, Second Series), and the *Federal Supplement.* There are official slip decisions.

Court of Customs and Patent Appeals. This legislative court hears appeals from the Customs Court, the Patent Office tribunals, and, on questions of law, certain findings of the United States Tariff Commission. It is officially reported in two separate parallel series, the *Court of Customs and Patent Appeals Reports (Patent Cases)*, and the *Court of Customs and Patent Appeals Reports (Customs Cases).* Its patent decisions are also reported in the *Federal Reporter*, the *United States Patents Quarterly*, and the *Decisions* of the Commissioner of Patents.

Customs Court. This court was formerly the Board of General Appraisers, of the Treasury Department, but was transformed into a legislative court by the Act of May 28, 1926, c. 411, § 1, 44 Stat. 669, 19 U. S. C. 1518 (1946). Although it was called a true "court of the United States" in *Brooks* v. *Mandel-Witte Co., Inc.*,[5] there has been some confusion as to its status and consequently some confusion in searching its reports.

To 1890, these were printed in a series called *Synopses of Decisions.* From then through 1937, its decisions were published in thirty-seven volumes of *Treasury Decisions.* Since 1938 the series has been called *United States Customs Court Reports.* Within each volume at present there are *Customs Decisions, Customs Decisions Abstracts,* and

---

[4] St. Paul, West Pub. Co.; Brooklyn, E. Thompson, 1950-51. 7 v. Kept up to date by pocket supplements.

[5] 54 F. 2d 922 (2d Cir. 1932), cert. den. 286 U. S. 559, 52 S. Ct. 641, 76 L. Ed. 1292 (1932). *See also* the article by Judge George S. Brown, *The United States Customs Court*, 19 A. B. A. J. 332, 416 (1933).

Reappraisement Decisions. All these are first published in an advance sheet called *Treasury Decisions.* In 1936, the Treasury Department issued a *Digest of Customs and Related Laws and of Decisions Thereunder,*[6] to which there was a 1941 supplement. This is in effect an edition of the customs laws, annotated to judicial and administrative decisions.

Emergency Court of Appeals. This legislative court was set up during World War II to review orders of the Emergency Price Control Administrator. It had limited jurisdiction to hear cases against the Administrator by the defendant in civil or criminal proceedings instituted by the Administrator.[7] Its functions have been continued since that war by successor agencies. Its decisions are reported officially in "slip" form only, there being no official bound volumes. They are reported also in the *Federal Reporter.*

Court of Military Appeals. In spite of its title, this is not a true court, but a quasi-judicial agency located for administrative purposes in the Department of Defense. Accordingly, its decisions are not reported in the *Federal Reporter.* Official "slip" decisions are printed. These, together with the holdings and decisions of the Judge Advocates' General Boards of Review are cumulated into an unofficial reporter, *Court-Martial Reports.*[8] Headnotes bear classification numbers by which they will be filed to form a conventional digest. Each bound volume contains a table of cases and opinions cited, a table of orders, laws and regulations cited ,and a subject index, in addition to the usual table of cases reported.

Tax Court of the United States. This independent executive agency and its predecessor Board of Tax Appeals are not true courts, though their published reports of decisions resemble court reports. Loose-leaf services also print and annotate the reports. There is a conventional digest.

Departmental Editions of Federal Judicial Decisions. Some administrative agencies having quasi-judicial tribunals publish their decisions and pertinent decisions of courts, in series bearing their own name. An example is the *Decisions of the Commissioner of Patents and the United States Courts in Patent and Trade Mark Cases.* These are not particularly convenient to the general practitioner for their court decisions, which are more readily accessible elsewhere, but the specialized practitioner finds them useful.

E. Dates of Federal, Judicial, and Administrative Reports.

Because case citations in legal writing so frequently omit date of decision, it may be difficult to determine the date of a given cited decision with any degree of precision. When the printed report is not at hand, case tables in digests of course lead to digest paragraphs for such cases, where the year of decision is commonly given. I. J. Lowe's *Key to the Year of Decisions of Cases in the United States Supreme Court, Federal and State Reports and other Legal Reports,*[9] enables the searcher to find the year of decision. The title is a misnomer because as yet the material relating to state reports is omitted; it will be included at a later date. Through 1881 (volume 107), printed reports of the United States Supreme Court decisions were dated only by term, as "October Term, 1880," without month or day. The *Lawyers' Edition* supplies the exact date of decision.

F. Digests of Cases Decided in Federal Courts.

The reported cases of all federal courts are more or less completely digested in one or more conventional digests of varying scope. As the theory and construc-

---

[6] Prepared by the Bureau of Customs. Washington D.C., U. S. Govt. Print. Off., 1936. 3 v. Supplement covers Jan. 11, 1935-Dec. 31, 1940.

[7] Act of June 30, 1942, c. 26, Title II, § 204, 56 Stat. 31 as amended, 50 U. S. C. App. § 924(o) (1946).

[8] Rochester, N. Y. Lawyers Co-operative Pub. Co., 1951/52 to date.

[9] Senate Document No. 73, 79th Congress, 1st Session, 1945.

tion of digests and certain typical digests are described in Chapter 19, and as all the digests noted below are conventional, only their special features will be noted here.

Digests Covering All Federal Courts. *American Digest System.* This system digests all reported American cases except those of the Customs Court. It is described in Chapter 19.

Federal Digest. This is a set of seventy-six volumes, with annual pocket supplements, quarterly pamphlet supplements, and recompiled volumes as needed. It digests the reported decisions of the various federal courts, from 1754 to date, except those of the Customs Court. Included are the cases from the federal courts for Alaska and Hawaii, and the United States Court of Appeals for the District of Columbia.

While this is a typical Key-Number digest, as described in Chapter 19, with all the usual features of such digests, some special ones should be mentioned. Volume 2 has a brief *History of the Federal Judicial System.*

Supplemental tables of cases are supplied for certain new topics made from old ones, such as "Federal Civil Procedure." In this way cases digested earlier under another topic and Key-Number can be found in the new topic, along with all other federal cases in point. Such a table works in this way: The searcher has found a labor relations case, *Malone* v. *Gardner*, 62 F. 2d 15 (4th Cir. 1932) which is directly in point, and he wishes to find all similar federal court cases. The pertinent digest paragraph in the report bears the Key-Number "Master and Servant ⌖ 16," but the *Federal Digest* no longer has such a number, the pocket supplement saying "See topic LABOR RELATIONS." The special table of cases for that new topic shows that *Malone* v. *Gardner* is now digested under "Labor Relations ⌖ 47," where all federal cases point of any date are collected.

Where an old digest topic was greatly expanded *before* the compilation of the general table of cases for the digest in 1940, however, no separate case table as above is needed. The reason is that cases digested and classified under a now-obsolete Key-Number prior to that date are readily found through this general table of cases. Thus, the case of *Pontiac Commercial and Savings Bank* v. *Commissioner*, 41 F. 2d 602 (6th Cir. 1930), was originally classified as "Internal Revenue ⌖ 7 (3)." Since that case was decided before the revision of this topic in 1940, it will be listed in the general table of cases in the *Digest*, where its new classification number, "Internal Revenue ⌖ 321," will be given, and where all cases in point are now collected.

Patents adjudicated by federal courts are listed by number at the end of the "Patents" topic, and a similar table (by name) is found at the end of the title "Trade-Marks, Trade-Names, Etc." A recent trend in this digest is the printing of the text of pertinent *federal acts* at the end of the digest topic. For example, labor relations acts (in the *United States Code* form) are printed at the end of the main topic "Labor Relations."

This digest has the usual *descriptive-word index* and plaintiff-defendant, defendant-plaintiff *tables of cases.* There is also a table of *cases by popular names. Court rules* and *general orders in bankruptcy* are printed in a special volume.

Federal reports digested in state digests. State digests commonly digest all federal court decisions on their own state or on state cases up on appeal from the state courts.

Digests Covering the Supreme Court of the United States. Supreme Court cases are digested in the American Digest System and in the *Federal Digest*, but there are two special digests for that Court alone.

Digest of United States Supreme Court Reports.[10] This digest is a typical case digest, but with some distinguishing characteristics of its own. The *table of cases* is in a single alphabet for plaintiff-defendant, defendant-plaintiff, and popular name (Hot Oil case). References to additional cases and discussions in point are made through citations to *American Jurisprudence* and the *American Law Reports* annotations and digest. Annotations in the *Lawyers' Edition* are indexed separately. *Dissenting and separate concurring opinions* are separately listed in the tables. The *Table of Federal Statutes by Popular Name* (Morrill Act, Taft-Hartley Act) is perhaps the most complete of all such tables. *Words and phrases judicially defined* are not listed in the separate "Tables" volume, but under "Words and Phrases" in the digest proper.

Court rules. A separate, unnumbered volume prints and annotates the Constitution (briefly) and federal court rules, including those of specific courts other than the individual district courts. It is one of the few places in which to find the rules of the various circuits of the Courts of Appeals. *General orders in bankruptcy* are included, as is a schedule of fees established for the clerks of the United States Courts of Appeals.

Citator information. In the digest proper, whenever a point of law noted in a digest paragraph has been modified or commented upon by a later Supreme Court decision, that fact is noted in small type immediately under the paragraph, together with the precise holding of the later case. This is kept up to date by annual pocket parts. Volume 14 of the set is an unusual citator for Supreme Court cases. An extensive *Table of Cases Affirmed, Reversed, Reheard, Etc., in the Supreme Court* covers rehearings in that court, and lower court cases (both federal and state) considered by the Court. The arrangement is by volume and page of the report considered, not by case name, with the precise action by the Supreme Court stated. This table supplies perhaps the speediest means of determining whether a specific federal or state case or group of cases has been appealed to the Supreme Court, and its disposition there.

The Table of Laws Cited and Construed by cases digested is unique in some of its coverage, in that it includes constitutions, statutes, treaties, proclamations and regulations construed, not only of the federal and state governments, of the Confederate States of America, and of the American Indians, but also those of foreign countries. Thus, the Austrian Civil Code § 1425 was construed in 274 U. S. 253 (1927); the treaty of 1765 between England and the Creek Indians was construed in 9 Pet. 711 (U. S. 1835), *etc.* Treaties of the United States with Indians, and interstate compacts, are also construed. A useful feature of the citation of both state and federal statutes is that the form of the statute is listed as of the date of the original action, so that the title and section of an earlier code do not have to be translated into an uneasy equivalent to the current code. Thus, *Hoyt's Compiled Laws of Arizona*, of 1877, and the *Revised Statutes* of 1887 of that state are cited as such in the table, and not as the equivalent under the *Arizona Codes Annotates* of 1939 or later.

Supplementation. In addition to cumulative annual parts, supplementation is by the bi-weekly (during term time) advance sheets of the *Lawyers' Edition*, except that the table of cases reheard, *etc.*, is absent from the latter.

United States Supreme Court Digest.[11] A typical West Publishing Company Key-Number digest, this has the various features of such digests, such as *tables of cases, words and phrases* judicially defined, *cases listed by popular names*,

---

[10] Rochester, N. Y., Lawyers Co-operative Pub. Co., 1948-51. 16 volumes and an unnumbered volume of court rules. Kept up to date by annual cumulative pocket supplements.

[11] United States Supreme Court Digest 1754 to date. St Paul, West Pub. Co., 1943-1946. 16 v. Kept up to date by pocket supplements.

and a *descriptive-word index*. The final volume contains annotated federal *court rules* (including those for the Courts of Appeals), and *general orders in bankruptcy*. Both the digest paragraph and the table of cases give such citator information as is available at publication time, as it done in the American Digest System.

Digests Covering the Lower Federal Courts. Federal Cases. An unnumbered volume in this set digests reported decisions of lower federal courts through 1880. As a digest it is superseded by the *Federal Digest*, but *it is still useful for the conversion table* from the original reporter citation to the equivalent *Federal Cases* citation.

    Federal Digest. As noted above, at page 112, this digest covers *all* federal courts except the Customs Court.

    Court of Claims Digest.[12] This is a typical Key-Number system digest. Volume 1 contains a history of the court and of legislation involving it. Since the headnotes of the official reports are currently Key-Numbered, finding cases in point in the other Key-Numbered digests is simple.

    Customs Court Digest. The *Digest of Customs and Related Laws and Decisions Thereunder,*[13] is really an annotated edition of the customs laws rather than a typical digest.

    Digests in Individual Volumes and Advance Sheets of Reports. Each bound volume and advance sheet of any series of reports has its own digest for cases printed therein. Those in the National Reporter System employ the uniform copyrighted Key-Number classification as found in the American Digest System.

G. Citators for Federal Court Reports.

The function, construction, and use of citation books are described in Chapter 28.

H. State Court Reports.

Every state and territory (except Alaska, where the federal district court, reported in the unofficial *Alaska Reports,* has also substantially the powers and jurisdiction of a state court) has its own system of courts, with a supreme court (by whatever title) at the top. A substantial number (as California, Illinois, Indiana, Missouri, Ohio, and New York) have intermediate appellate courts as well. In a few states (as New York, Ohio, and Pennsylvania), selected reports of certain courts of first instance are printed.

    Official State Reports. What was said at page 94 about official and unofficial reporting of course applies to state reports. Publication of official state reports is typically only in bound volumes, but in some states there are slip decisions (normally distributed through the clerk of the court reported) and advance sheets. Citation form is described in Chapter 32.

    Unofficial State Reports. There are many editions of unofficial state reports. The distinction between them and the official is academic, except that in legal writing the official should always be cited first, if published, with the unofficial parallel citation following.

---

[12] United States Court of Claims Digest 1855 to date. St. Paul, West Pub. Co., 1950. 8 v., with annual supplements.

[13] See footnote 6 above.

Cases not officially reported. Many cases not officially reported are reported unofficially, sometimes in legal newspapers or special collections of "unreported" cases, but principally in the National Reporter System. This sometimes causes uncertainty, when the writer searches in vain for the official citation of such a report. The best test is the table of cases in a standard digest covering that jurisdiction: if it fails to give an official citation, the chances are overwhelming that the case was omitted from the official reporter (provided always that the official report volume had been published at the time the table of cases consulted was compiled). A further check is through the regional *Shepard* (as decribed in Chapter 28); if it fails to cite also the official report, then there is no official.

State and Territorial Courts: Digests. In one form or another, the reported decisions of all federal and state appellate courts and of some courts of first instance, from 1658 to date are covered by conventional digests, as described in Chapter 19.

American Digest System. This is described in Chapter 19. It covers all states.

Reporter Digests. State courts by groups are covered by the regional *Reporter* digests, which are typical Key-Number digests. Their coverage is not uniform, all cases reported in standard reporters for some states being digested, while for others only *Reporter* cases are covered. The coverage of the individual digests is shown in Chapter 14, on the National Reporter System. An added feature of these regional digests since about 1940 has been the cumulative *table of statutes construed*, taken from the tables in the *Reporters*.

Individual state digests. There are an increasing number of state Key-Number digests, utilizing the digests of state cases from the American Digest System, so that each state is covered from the beginning. In addition, *federal decisions on state law* or involving appeals of state cases to federal courts, are digested. Each of these state Key-Number digests, in addition to the characteristic features of such digests, incorporates something of special interest to that state. Examples are the enumeration and description of all New York state courts from the beginning, and the description of their reports, in Volume 2 of *Abbott's New York Digest;* and the "Table of Statutes Construed," in the *Massachusetts Digest Annotated.*

There are many state digests other than those which are Key-Numbered, though some of these, by permission, copy the Key-Number classification without the key symbol. Their composition, tables and methods of use so nearly coincide in all significant respects with other digests that the lawyer who can work with one digest is soon at home with them all. All of course seek to emphasize their local character. The *Indiana Decimal Digest*, for example, is keyed to *Burns' Indiana Statutes*, which in turn is keyed to the *Digest*. This digest is also a citator. The citation is given immediately following the digest paragraph, and is indicated by an eye-catching arrow. Wherever a plurality of cases can be grouped under a single digest statement of a legal principle in this digest, they are so listed. This arrow is carried into the composite "Table of Cases Judicially Noticed," which also, of course, serves as a case citator. There is a further "Table of Superseded Cases," as well as a "Table of Memorandum Decisions." *Page's Ohio Digest* employs the same arrow for citator data, and has a separate alpabetical table of "Cases Judicially Noticed." There are also both a subject and an author index to Ohio legal periodicals. *Callaghan's Wisconsin Digest* cites *A. L. R.* annotations, local practice treatises, and all law review comments on Wisconsin cases.

California Jurisprudence, Michigan Jurisprudence, Ohio Jurisprudence, and *Texas Jurisprudence,* are legal encyclopedias for those states.

Notes

Official State Reports. Without exception, there is statutory provision for "official" reporting and publication of judicial appellate decisions in all states. The reporting policies of the states are in all cases fixed by statute. In some states the official reporter is directed to include "all" appellate court decisions; in others, all for which there are "written opinions." In most states all deemed by the court (or, in Massachusetts, by the reporter) to be of "sufficient importance" are printed. In those states having intermediate appellate courts, selected reports of those courts are reported.

What makes a report official. This is not always clear. Those prepared by the statutorily appointed reporter and published under authorization of statute are certainly official, and this category includes all but a handful of the current state reports. Until about the middle of the 19th century, however, it was customary for the official reporter to publish and distribute reports at his own expense or profit, and the reports were known by his name. Whether or not these were official in the present day sense is academic; they exist and are acceptably cited in any legal writing. Current official reports are cited by a title—as Arkansas, Illinois, Vermont, and the like—reflecting the jurisdiction reported, rather than by the name of the reporter.

A fairly recent development is the adoption, wholly or in part, of National Reporter System reports as official, and the consequent dropping of the old official series designation to a greater or less degree. In some states, as Delaware, this takes the form of retention of the official reports in their old form, except for the use of the copyrighted Key-Number system headnotes (without the class numbers) and indexes of the National Reporter System. In others, as Alabama and Louisiana, the regional (*Southern* in these two states) *Reporter* cases for those states are printed verbatim in all respects, except that their own state volume and page designations, in continuation of the former official reports, are retained, and the whole then adopted by court rule as the official reporter. A further development, as in Kentucky, is the dropping entirely of all semblance of the official series and the collection under court authority of the state's reports from the *Reporter* covering the state, which is then called, for example, *Kentucky Decisions.* This type, however, bears the *Reporter* volume and page numbers throughout and is so cited.

Care should be exercised by the lawyer in citing such state reporters, to determine whether or not they have superseded the old official, or are just an additional and parallel report series. In general, when a series is called simply "Reports," as *Oregon, Virginia,* or *Indiana Reports,* it is likely to be an official series. When National Reporter System reports are adopted by a state, all the features found in the bound volumes of the regional *Reporters* from which they are taken are incorporated also.

LAW REPORTS: NATIONAL REPORTER SYSTEM

A. Scope.

By far the largest group of unofficial reports, covering all federal courts but the Customs Court, and the appellate courts of all states (and some of first instance), is the National Reporter System. Begun with the *North Western Reporter* in 1879, the system spread within a decade to cover all the courts noted above (including a special series, the *New York Supplement*, for the courts of record of New York).

Intermediate appellate courts have not always been reported. For example, the Illinois Appellate Court was not reported in the *North Eastern Reporter* until 1936, beginning with Volume 284 of the official. In 1940, the *Federal Rules Decisions*, reporting federal decisions *not elsewhere reported* which construe the Federal Rules of Civil and Criminal Procedure, was added. The coverage of the respective units of the System, and of the accompanying digests, is indicated in the Notes. There is thus a gap in law reporting for the period up to the *Reporters*, resulting in the frequent practice of working law libraries' acquiring the complete official reports for the local state, supplemented by the official reports of all other states up to the *Reporters*, and from then on by the National Reporter System units. Reprints of the first 108 volumes of the *United States Reports* are available to complete the coverage of those reports.

Coverage of Reporters and Reporter Digests.[1] **Atlantic Reporter** (1885 to date): #52 Connecticut; 12 Delaware (7 Houston); 6 Delaware Chancery; #77 Maine; #63 Maryland; #63 New Hampshire; #47 New Jersey Law; #40 New Jersey Equity; #108 Pennsylvania State; #102 Pennsylvania Superior; 15 Rhode Island; 58 Vermont; District of Columbia v. 31 2d Atl. Rep. (1942).

Atlantic Reporter Digest (1764 to date): All Connecticut, Delaware, Maine, New Jersey, and Rhode Island cases from the earliest time as reported in standard reports; Maryland, New Hampshire, Pennsylvania, and Vermont cases only from 1 *Atlantic Reporter* to date.

New York Supplement: 1 New York (Court of Appeals), 1847 to date; lower courts of record (including the Appellate Division), 1888 to date.

North Eastern Reporter (1885 to date): #112 Illinois; 284 Illinois **App.;** 102 In-

[1] # indicates that only part of this volume is covered.

diana; 1 Indiana App.; 139 Massachusetts; 99 New York; 43 Ohio State; 20 Ohio App.

North Eastern Digest (1817 to date): All Indiana cases from the earliest time as reported in standard reports, but Illinois, Massachusetts, New York and Ohio cases only from 1 North Eastern Reporter to date.

North Western Reporter (1879 to date): 1 Dakota; 51 Iowa; 41 Michigan; 26 Minnesota; 9 Nebraska; 1 Nebraska Unofficial; 1 North Dakota; 1 South Dakota; 46 Wisconsin.

North Western Digest (1836 to date): All *North Western Reporter* cases from the earliest time as reported in standard reports.

Pacific Reporter (1883 to date): 1 Arizona; 64 California; 1 California 2d; 1 California App.; 1 California App. 2d; #2 California Unreported; 7 Colorado; 1 Colorado App.; 2 Idaho; 30 Kansas; 1 Kansas App.; 4 Montana; 17 Nevada; 3 New Mexico; 1 Oklahoma; 1 Oklahoma Crim. App.; 11 Oregon; 3 Utah; 1 Washington; 2 Washington Territory; 3 Wyoming.

Pacific Digest (1850 to date): All *Pacific Reporter* cases.

South Eastern Reporter (1887 to date): #77 Georgia; 1 Georgia App.; #96 North Carolina; #25 South Carolina; #82 Virginia; 29 West Virginia.

South Eastern Digest (1729 to date): All *South Eastern Reporter* cases.

Southern Reporter (1887 to date): #80 Alabama; 1 Alabama App.; #22 Florida; 104 Louisiana; 39 Louisiana Ann.; 9 Louisiana App.; 64 Mississippi.

Southern Digest (1809 to date): All *Southern Reporter* cases and also early decisions of Florida prior to *Southern Reporter*.

South Western Reporter (1887 to date): 47 Arkansas; #84 Kentucky; #8 Kentucky Law Rep.; 1 Kentucky Decisions; 89 Missouri; #93 Missouri App.; #84 Tennessee; 16 Tennessee App.; 66 Texas; 21 Texas App.; 1 Texas Civ. App.; 31 Texas Crim. R.; 4 Willson Civ. Cas. Ct. App. (Texas).

South Western Digest (1887 to date): Only from Volume 1 of the *South Western Reporter* to date, except, all Texas cases prior to *South Western*.

Supreme Court Reporter (1882 to date): 106 *United States Reports* to date.

United States Supreme Court Digest (1754 to date): All cases from 2 Dallas (2 U. S.).

Federal Reporter (1880 to date): U. S. Circuit Court to 1912 (when abolished); U. S. Circuit Courts of Appeal (1891–1948), continued by Courts of Appeals (Sept. 1, 1948, to date); U. S. District courts to 1932; U. S. Commerce Court, 1910–1913 (entire life); U. S. Court of Customs and Patent Appeals (Patent cases), 1929 to date; U. S. Court of Claims (Tax cases, 1930–1932; U. S. Court of Appeals, D. C., 1919 to date.

Federal Digest (1754 to date): Federal courts, except Customs court cases, including cases from federal courts for Alaska and Hawaii and United States Court of Appeals for the District of Columbia.

Federal Supplement (1932 to date): U. S. District Courts and U. S. Court of Claims (tax cases).

Federal Rules Decisions (1940 to date): Federal court decisions, not elsewhere reported, interpreting the federal Rules of Civil and Criminal Procedure.

B. Rationale of the National Reporter System.

There have been numerous developments in this system since its beginnings, but as constituted for many years the philosophy and forms are substantially as follows. (The West Publishing Company, St. Paul, Minnesota, distributes a pamphlet which describes in detail the content, form, and working of the *Reporters*. What follows is, accordingly, only by way of emphasizing certain features of the *Reporters*.)

Speed of Publication: Advance Sheets. Speed of publication and distribution of law reports is of the essence in the practice of the law. In 1879, however, the official state reports were published only in bound form, usually more than a year and often several years after the decision date, and the situation today is little changed in most states. Thus, the "advance sheet" (weekly, except the semi-monthly *Supreme Court Reporter* and monthly *Federal Rules Decisions*) publication of decided cases was born and has continued to be an important feature of all *Reporter* units. Each issue is a complete report volume in itself, with nearly all the features which later cumulate into the various *Reporter* bound volumes.

Combining Reports of Contiguous States. The *Reporter* philosophy is that the law in certain fairly large groups of contiguous states has common elements of interest to all in each group. By combining contiguous states of similar interests for a *Reporter* coverage, enough decisions are available in the area to make practicable the weekly publication of the whole, at a reasonable cost.

Reporting More Cases. The editors feel that many decisions, unreported in the official reports, merit publication. As a result, many thousands of decisions elsewhere unavailable in print, are found in the *Reporters*. The fact that they were unreported in the official reports in no way lessens their authority as precedents.

Key-Number System. This device for the uniform classification of all points of law in reported cases, is an important element of the National Reporter System.

C. Content of the Reporters.

Opinions and Headnotes. The text of the opinions is identical with the official, being supplied by the courts reported. Errors discovered in the official edition are pointed out, and parallel statutory and case citations are supplied when lacking. In reporting the decisions of the courts which are directed by statute to supply a syllabus which shall state the law of the case, the *Reporters* regard that syllabus as an integral part of the official record, and print it verbatim, following their own headnotes. The *Reporter* headnotes are later incorporated in the Key-Number digests.

Words and Phrases. This is a feature found in all units of the National Reporter System, by which words and phrases (whether in common use or legal words of art) as defined by the court in its opinion in the case reported are set forth. This is described in Chapter 24.

Tables of Cases. For convenience in all *Reporters* except the *Supreme Court Reporter*, there are two case tables in the bound volumes: (1) of all cases in all states or Federal court circuits covered by the Reporter, combined in one alphabet; and (2) alphabetical case tables by individual states or circuits. The advance sheets tables are by state. The *Supreme Court Reporter* has a single table, in one alphabet.

Tables of Statutes Construed. These important tables list both conventional and administrative legislation construed by the courts in cases reported. They are found in advance sheets and bound volumes, and since about 1940 have cumulated into the respective regional *Reporter* and some state digests. As they fulfill a citator function, they are described in Chapter 28.

Judges. Each bound volume lists (by jurisdiction) the judges of the courts reported.

"Judicial Highlights." Occasional issues of advance sheets contain a blue-paged "synopsis of state and federal cases of current interest and importance."

Court rules. Of recent years, new rules (both revisions and amendments) of courts have been printed in the appropriate *Reporter units*, at the time of adoption.

Digests. Each advance sheet and bound volume contains a digest, formed from Key-Numbered digest paragraphs from the cases reported therein.

digest contains Key no. Paragraphs

D. Citation Books for Reporters.

Shepard's Citations cover all *Reporter units*, as described in Chapter 28.

E. The Key-Number Classification.

The most significant difference between the *Reporters* and the official editions of reports is the Key-Number classification of headnotes, because this is the basis of the classification of the entire American Digest System and allied digests. By this means, the points of law announced in the individual headnote paragraphs of reported cases in the published decisions of United States and state appellate courts from 1658 to date are readily found.

Philosophy of the Key-Number Classification. The system is based upon a detailed analysis of the legal relationships of individuals and government, as to property and contract rights, torts, crimes, and remedies. Within a framework of some 422 main heads or chapters (the number increases slowly over the years as the growth of the law requires the splitting of old chapters and the addition of new), there are many thousands of sub-heads, by which such large topics as Abandonment, Corporations, Landlord and Tenant, Torts, and Workmen's Compensation are reduced to workable dimensions. How this is done is explained in detail in Chapter 19, "Digests."

CITY OF TOLEDO v. JOHNSON   Ohio   675
50 N.E.2d 675

---

72 Ohio App. 46

CITY OF TOLEDO v. JOHNSON, Appellant.

Court of Appeals of Ohio, Lucas County
June 1, 1938.

1. Criminal law ☞304(21)

Court of Appeals cannot take judicial notice that the "number game" is a "game or scheme of chance" or gambling.

See Words and Phrases, Permanent Edition, for all other definitions of "Game of Chance" and "Number Game"

2. Gaming ☞94(1)

In a prosecution for operating a "number game" as a game of chance for money in violation of ordinance, there must be proof that a number game is such a game or scheme of chance or gambling in absence of statute or ordinance recognizing the number game as being in such classification.

3. Gaming ☞98(1)

Where there was neither statute nor ordinance defining the number game as a game of chance for money, and court was unauthorized to take judicial notice that the number game is a game of chance, evidence that defendant was maintaining the number game was insufficient to sustain a conviction under ordinance of maintaining a game of chance for money.

At the left of this page is a typical application of the Key-Number to a National Reporter System case report, taken from 50 N. E. 2d 675 (1938). (Where it is available at press time, the official citation is supplied, as here, rendering the use of conversion tables to find such citation unnecessary. Such is the time lag of official reporting, however, that this official citation is usually undetermined when the bound *Reporter* volume is made up.) The example is from a state requiring the court to prepare a syllabus, and so the two sets of headnotes, official and *Reporter*, afford an opportunity to compare headnote writing techniques. Usually there are more *Reporter* paragraphs than official, and the *Reporters* try to connect each note as directly as possible to the case reported, by including facts. Each note is a single sentence. In some cases a *Reporter* headnote is given, even though the opinion is not printed as part of the report, as in *Schmidt v. Langer*, 336 Ill. App. 158, 83 N. E. 2d 35 (1948).

In the example, the bold-face numerals (**1, 2, 3**) are not part of the headnote or Key-Number classification, but refer to like numerals, in brackets [**1**], in the text of the opinion, where the headnoted rule is stated. Criminal Law ☞ 304(21) is the Key-Number, each such number always being composed of *both a word or words (the main topic heading), and a number (indicating the sub-topic)*. In the digest at the back of the *Reporter* in which our case is

---

676   Ohio   50 NORTH EASTERN REPORTER, 2d SERIES

Syllabus by the Court.

1. A court may not take judicial notice that a "number game" is a game or scheme of chance or gambling.

2. In order to sustain a conviction on a charge of unlawfully engaging "in a game of chance for money, to wit, number game," in violation of an ordinance making it unlawful to engage in a game of chance, there must be proof that a "number game" is a game or scheme of chance or gambling, there being no such "game of chance" recognized by statute or ordinance as a "number game."

George Johnson was convicted of engaging in a game of chance for money, and he appeals.—[Editorial Statement]

printed, this subhead is defined as *Evidence: Judicial Notice, Presumptions, and Burden of Proof: Nature of certain games and terminology thereof.* This particular paragraph, verbatim, is printed in 13 *Fifth Decennial Digest* 668, along with six other paragraphs on the same topic, from six states. It is also printed in the *North Eastern Reporter Digest* under the same classification. By means explained in Chapter 19 like cases in point, if any, from 1658 to date may be found through this same Key-Number.

Exhibit 18

CHAPTER 15

LAW REPORTS:
SELECTIVE AND SPECIAL-SUBJECT SYSTEMS

A. Annotated Reports System.

Rationale. An estimated ninety per cent of the approximately 30,000 American law reports published each year interpret local statutes or otherwise relate to local practice; or decide no point of law but only concern the admission, exclusion, or weight of evidence; or merely decide again what has been decided before, without adding any new law. That states the reason for the selective and annotated reports system. The local lawyer in, say, Illinois, will of course need the complete Illinois reports, but he will also be interested in many cases decided in other jurisdictions, which are well decided, with well-reasoned opinions, and which are of general application. These cases, comprising but a small fraction of the total decided cases in all jurisdictions, merit expert selection and annotation, for the use of lawyers everywhere.

There have been some seven principal selective reports series, as described in the "Notes" below, the first three *(American Reports, American Decisions,* and *American State Reports)* being popularly known as the "Trinity Series." Only one, the *American Law Reports* (hereinafter referred to as *A. L. R.),* is still current. The *Lawyers Edition of the United States Reports* (see page 106), while by no means a selective reports series, is definitely a unit of the annotated reports system.

American Law Reports [1] *(1919 to date.) A. L. R.* is now in its second series, printing and annotating opinions of appellate courts in all jurisdictions (but with a minimum of United States Supreme Court cases, which are taken care of by the annotations in the *Lawyers' Edition).*

Selection and content of A. L. R. reports. Cases are selected on the basis of probable usefulness to lawyers generally and as illustrative of established principles, and are not necessarily "leading cases." Every opinion is printed in full, from the official text. Parallel official and *Reporter* citations are supplied. The decision is summarized at some length, especially beginning with the second series (1947); and the subject of the annotation is noted. Headnotes are written by the editors (except that any "syllabus by the court" is printed verbatim also), and classified according to the *Permanent A. L. R. Digest* classification. There are frequent cross-references to *American Jurisprudence,* a legal encyclopedia based largely upon annotated reports series cases. Thus:

---

[1] Rochester, N. Y., Lawyers Co-operative Pub. Co., 1919 to date.

250   AMERICAN LAW REPORTS, ANNOTATED   5 ALR2d

REUBEN BORDY
v.
ROBERT SMITH, Impleaded, etc., Appt.

SCHOOL DISTRICT OF OMAHA et al., Interveners, Appts.

METROPOLITAN UTILITIES DISTRICT OF OMAHA et al.,
Interveners

(three cases)

Nebraska Supreme Court — October 15, 1948
(150 Neb 272, 34 NW2d 331, 5 ALR2d 250)

SUMMARY OF DECISION

A clerk of a Nebraska district court, who was official custodian of the proceeds of tax foreclosure bids pending their ultimate disposition, invested part of them in United States Treasury Certificates on which he received a considerable sum as interest.

His contention that, as his accountability for the principal was absolute, he was entitled to the interest, was not accepted, nor was his contention that the difficulty of determining to whom the proceeds of the bid should go and the sharing of interest among the distributees was a reason for permitting him to keep the interest.

The court further held that the amount could not be claimed by the county under a statute requiring the clerk to turn over any perquisites of office to the county, but that interest is an increment of the fund which produces it and therefore should be shared by the distributees of the fund, who would be the bidders where the owners redeem, the taxing authorities where the sales are confirmed, and, after taxes, former owners or encumbrancers.

SUBJECT OF ANNOTATION
Beginning on page 257

Liability of public officer for interest or other earnings received
on public money in his possession.

HEADNOTES
Classified to ALR Digests

Officers, § 126 — liability for funds held officially.
1. The liability of a public officer in Nebraska for funds entrusted to his care by virtue of his office is that of an insurer, except as it has been modified by statute.
[See Am Jur "Public Officers," § 309.]

Officers, § 131.3 — right to interest earned on funds held officially.
2. That a clerk of a district court is absolutely accountable for funds received by him in virtue of his office does not entitle him to the interest from investments thereof pending their ultimate disposition.

Interest, § 1 — as part of fund producing it.
3. In the absence of a statute to the contrary, interest becomes a part of the fund by the investment of which it was produced.

Officers, § 131.3 — right to retain interest from unauthorized investment of funds held officially.
4. A criminal statute which upon

Exhibit 19

ANNOTATION

Liability of public officer for interest or other earnings received on public money in his possession

[See ALR Digests, Officers, § 131.3.]

INDEX

I. Introduction

§ 1. In general.

This annotation deals with the question whether a public officer who, having custody of public funds, receives interest from the use of such funds, may retain the interest as his own or has to account for it in the same manner as for the principal.

In order that the question as to the accountability of a public officer for interest received on public funds in his possession can arise, it must be assumed that the money in his possession is public money[1] and that the officer

[1] The general rule stated above has no application where the fund in the hands of the public officer is not a public fund. This limitation of the general rule was well brought out in United States v. MacMillan (1913; DC) 209 F 266 (affd (1917; CCA 7th) 251 F 55, which is affd (1920) 253 US 195, 64 L ed 857, 40 S Ct 540). It was held in this case that the Federal government had no claim to interest which had accrued on a fund

✦ **Consult ALR2d BLUE BOOK SERVICE for cases subsequent to publication date** ✦

[5 ALR2d]—17

Exhibit 20

Headnotes are numbered and keyed to corresponding numerals in the opinion text. The *statement of facts* and *summaries of arguments of counsel* are supplied.

The A. L. R. annotation. The annotation is a distinguishing point of *A. L. R.* worth extended comment. All cases are now annotated, though in the earlier volumes this was not always true. The annotations vary in length from half a page to several hundred pages, and are encyclopedic treatments of the topics discussed. An example is the 305-page annotation in 164 A. L. R. 8, "liability for accidents at street or highway intersection as affected by reliance upon or disregard of traffic sign, signal or marker." *(A. L. R.* annotations as treatises are discussed in Chapter 21.) They are keyed through the headnotes to *American Jurisprudence,* and *American Jurisprudence* cites *A. L. R.* annotations.

As will be seen *(see* Chapter 19), an annotation is organized in much the same manner as a digest topic. There is an *introduction, corresponding to the digest scope note,* in which the limits of the annotation are defined and the main and subsidiary questions to be considered are broadly stated. Then the *main topic is broken down into sub-topics,* each of which is considered in turn, with majority, and jurisdictional rules set forth and analyzed, together with discussion of supporting authority. Variations and departures from the various rules and the reasons assigned therefor are pointed out. *Where the result depended upon a statute, that is noted.*

All cases in point are said to be considered in the annotation.

Authority citation is as follows, to facilitate the *jurisdictional approach:* Following the statements of the general rules, all cases in point are cited, by jurisdiction; then for the textual analyses following the general statements, where majority and minority rules and variations are stated and discussed, *individual supporting cases are analyzed.* Here there are no formal digests in the usual manner, but the illustrative comment on individual supporting cases in effect analyzses them, often at considerable length. Jurisdictions are emphasized by printing the name part of a report citation in heavy type, as 84 **Wis.** 473. Of late years, *law review comments* on a point of law are occasionally cited.

There are no advance sheets, and the cases printed are usually over a year old at publication date. For this reason *the parallel A. L. R. citation is often omitted from digest tables of cases* made up before the selection for annotation is made.

The net result of the annotation is that the student or lawyer who can find one in point has had a preliminary, arduous task of case finding and analysis done for him. Annotations are particularly effective in analyses of narrow subjects not yet adequately treated in text books. They are also effective where a new decision has upset an old rule and the treatises and encyclopedias have not yet adequately discussed its probable effect. An example of the first is the annotation in 1 A. L. R. 2d 802, on "liability for loss of hat, coat or other property, deposited by customer in place of business." Typical of the second is the annotation in 143 A. L. R. 1294, on the effect on foreign divorce of *Williams* v. *North Carolina,* which overruled the old case of *Haddock* v. *Haddock.* The *annotation, of course, is in no sense authority,* but only an elaborate index to authority. The case analyses are sufficiently detailed in most instances to tell the searcher in advance whether or not he should read the entire case.

Noting up A. R. annotations: A. L. R. Blue Book. As with other law books and the tools for their use, the *A. L. R.* annotation's obsolescence begins with publication. It is stated that in compiling the annotation, all existing cases in point are read, but how about cases decided since?

A. L. R. takes care of this by its *Blue Book* and supplements. The *Blue Book* is a *citator* to *A. L. R.*, arranged by *A. L. R.* volume and page (that is, the page cited is that upon which the annotation begins, not of the case annotated), as shown below.

---

56 ALR　　　　　SUPPLEMENTAL DECISIONS　　　　　**582**

56 A.L.R. 1039–1042.
Wilkinson v. B. S. (Cal. App.) 269 P. 705.
Tallwater v. B. (TexComApp) 156 SW(2d) 142.

56 A.L.R. 1056–1058.
Supplemented in 81 A.L.R. 1415, and 87 A.L.R. 735.◆
Superseded in 109 A.L.R. 550.◆

Graf v. M. County W. D. 75 Cal. App. Dec. 271, 26 P.(2d) 29.
Chavoya v. I. A. C. (Cal. App.) 72 P.(2d) 236.
Stakonis v. U. A. Co. (Conn.) 148 A. 334.
Duval Engineering & Contracting Co. v. J. (Fla) 16 So(2d) 290.
F. Becker Asphaltum Roofing Co. v. I. C. 333 Ill. 340, 164 N. E. 668.
Atlantic Refining Co. v. F. (Md) 25 A(2d) 667.

Fedas v. S. Ins. Co. (Pa.) 151 A. 285.
Patriotic Order Sons of America Hall Assoc. v. H. F. Ins. Co. 305 Pa. 107, 157 A. 259, 78 A.L.R. 899.
Gardull v. R. I. Co. (Pa. Super.) 2 A.(2d) 504.
Weems v. S. F. I. Co. (Tenn) 178 SW(2d) 377.
Newark Fire Ins. Co. v. M. (TennApp) 170 SW(2d) 927.
Third Nat. Bank v. A. E. I. Co. (TennApp) 178 SW(2d) 915.

Exhibit 21

In the *Blue Book*, currently, each *A. L. R.* case annotation is brought up to date by later cases in point, cited by National Reporter System and official citation. In the *Blue Book* to the first series, matching these later cases to a large annotation may be quite laborious, since there is no indication as to the page or section of the annotation which is being supplemented by the later case. The second series *Blue Book*, however, keys the later cases to the appropriate annotation section number. Furthermore, beginning with 1953, each case so cited will have an accompanying digest line to indicate its subject matter. The *Blue Book* will then resemble an "index-digest." Below, note section numbers.

ALR2d BLUE BOOK

COVERING

VOLUMES 1–21 ALR2d

SUPPLEMENTING BLUE BOOK MATERIAL IN ALR2d DIGEST FOR VOLS. 1–18

CASES ARE CLASSIFIED TO ANNOTATION SECTION NUMBERS

1 ALR2d 167–174
Overman v. F. C. O. Co. (Mo) 238 SW2d 34 (§ 4).

1 ALR2d 365–370
Carson v. M. L. Ins. Co. 156 Ohio St 104, 100 NE2d 197.

1 ALR2d 1060–1075
Liberty Title & Trust Co. v. P. (NJ) 77 A2d 219 (§§ 3, 5, 9).
Re Hubbell's Will (NY) 97 NE 2d 888 (§ 3).

Exhibit 22

When sufficient additional cases in point have been decided, a *supplemental annotation* is frequently compiled, as noted for 56 A. L. R. 1056–1058, above, this being indicated by the [*] accompanying the citation. When this is done, two things happen: (1) Citations to all later cases previously noted as in point to 56 A. L. R. 1056-1058 are cancelled out, as indicated by the [*], because they are now included in the supplemental annotation; and (2) citations to all future cases in point are listed under the supplemental citation instead of under the original one. Thus, in the example, later annotations are at 81 A. L. R. 1415, 87 A. L. R. 735, and 109 A. L. R. 550.

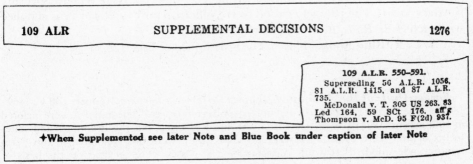

109 ALR   SUPPLEMENTAL DECISIONS   **1276**

> 109 A.L.R. 550–591.
> Superseding 56 A.L.R. 1056, 81 A.L.R. 1415, and 87 A.L.R. 735.
> McDonald v. T. 305 US 263. 83 Led 164, 59 SCt 176, aff'g Thompson v. McD. 95 F(2d) 937.

✦When Supplemented see later Note and Blue Book under caption of later Note

Exhibit 23

The Blue Book itself is supplemented for the 175 volumes comprising the first series of *A. L. R.* by an annual cumulative blue pamphlet of *Supplemental Decisions*. In our example above, for instance, the annotation in 109 A. L. R. 550 has been supplemented by a still later annotation in 175 A. L. R. 1333, where a search in the pamphlet shows numerous later cases in point. A complete search, therefore, would require perusal of annotations in all the annotations cited above, and in the cases cited as supplementing the latest annotation. The blue pamphlet appears annually. *The Blue Book for the second series of A. L. R.* appears as blue-paged sections of bound volumes and annual pamphlet supplements to the *American Law Reports, Second Series Digest*. Eventually there will be a separate *Second Series Blue Book.*

Digests for the Selective Case System. *"Trinity Series" and Lawyers Reports Annotated.* As listed in the "Notes," there were conventional digests and other aids to the use of these four series of reports. The digest for the *Lawyers Reports Annotated (L. R. A.)* is still of current utility.

Permanent Digest of American Law Reports Annotated, covering volumes 1-175 A. L. R.[2] This otherwise conventional digest has no word index, but that need is largely supplied by the *A. L. R. Word Index to Annotations.*[3] Some paragraphs in the digest have references to *A. L. R.* annotations, others do not. This is because, while all points in an *A.L.R.* case are fully *digested*, only a few closely connected one are *annotated*. Thus, *Egner v. States Realty Co.*, 170 A. L. R. 500, has twenty-nine headnotes (all digested). But only the first six (relating to the termination of partners' agency by partnership dissolution) are the subject of the annotation, and are so indexed in the *Word Index.*

There are three approaches to the cases in *A. L. R.*: the table of cases, the fact approach (through the *Word Index)*, and the analytical, through the topic head-

[2] Rochester, N. Y., Lawyers Co-operative Pub. Co., 1949-1951. 12 v.
[3] Rochester, N. Y., Lawyers Co-operative Pub. Co., 1937-1943. 4 v.

ings in the digest. An *A. L. R. Table of Cases with Parallel References to Official Reports,* issued to legal writers at irregular intervals, lists all cases published in *A. L. R.,* in order of official citation. These approaches generally are described in Chapters 19 and 30.

American Law Reports, Second Series Digest. This covers the period beginning with 1947.

Citators for Selective Cases System Cases. **Shepard's Citations.** All cases in the system are covered by the appropriate *Shepard* units but there is none especially for the system. The parallel citation to the official report or *Reporter* is supplied with each *A. L. R., L. R. A.,* or other system report.

A. L. R. Blue Book. This citator is described at page 126.

Notes

Earlier Units of the Annotated Reports System. **American Reports** (60 v., 1869–1887). The first series published reported only state cases. The reports were printed in full, except such parts as related only to local practice, but the headnotes and statements of fact were carefully rewritten. While they were not annotated as that term is now understood, there were occasional notes. Cases were selected on the basis of probable usefulness and as illustrative of established principles, and were not confined to "leading cases."

American Decisions (100 v., through 1868). Because of the success of American Reports, another set was published, covering American cases of interest from the earliest time through 1868. The same selection criteria were employed, except for more emphasis on "leading cases," but there were more and longer notes, though nothing approaching the modern annotation. An added feature was the more elaborate statement of facts and the resumé of the arguments of counsel.

American State Reports (104 v., 1887–1911).

Lawyers Reports Annotated (First Series, 70 v., 1888–1905; New Series, 52 v., 1905–1914; dated series, 24 v., 1914 A-F to 1918 A-F).

American and English Annotated Cases. (21 v., 1906–1911), merging into **American Annotated Cases** (32 v., 1912–1918).

The four series above were competing, finally merging in 1918 into the current *American Law Reports.* The same general editorial policy was followed as with the earliest series, except that important federal decisions were added, and that the notes or annotations became an increasingly major feature. In 1913, an edition of *Lawyers Reports Annotated* (L. R. A.), first series, was published with a supplement of "Extra Annotations," in which each *L. R. A.* case was annotated to decisions subsequent to those in the original annotations or notes.

Digests and other Aids in Using the Earlier Units. All units of the selective cases system have their own digests, together comprising digests of these cases from 1760 to date. They are:

1760–1888. Stewart Rapalje's *Digest of the Decisions of the Courts of Last Resort of the Several States . . . Contained In the 160 Volumes of the American Reports.*[4]

1887–1911. Edmund S. Green's *Digest of the Decisions . . . Contained In the American State Report*[5] 1888–1918. *Complete Digest of All Lawyers Reports Annotated.*[6] This is a conventional digest. There is, however, a separate and additional *Complete Index to All L. R. A. Notes* (1930), arranged by topics and sections keyed roughly but not exactly to the digest. If, as is usually true, the searcher is interested in an annotation, he should begin with this *Index*, which is usually called the *Desk Book.*

---

[4] San Francisco, Bancroft-Whitney Co., 1891. 3 v.

[5] San Francisco, Bancroft-Whitney Co., 1904-1912. 5 v.

[6] Rochester, N. Y., Lawyers Co-operative Pub. Co., 1921-1924. 10 v.

Notes on the American Reports and *Notes on the American Decisions* [7] are citators to cases reported in these two series, arranged by volume and page of *American Reports* and *Decisions*, respectively, as commented upon by later cases in all courts.

Table of cases Alphabetically Arranged as to the Several States in the [Trinity Series]. [8]
Numerical Table of Cases Reported in the [Trinity Series and American Annotated Cases]. [9] These two tables still have some utility. The first is a conventional table of cases, except that it is arranged by states, with parallel official and *Trinity Series* citations. The second translates from official to unofficial citation, as from 111 Md. 53 to 134 A. S. R. 586.

L. R. A. Green Book. [10] This is a citator in which all *L. R. A.* cases cited in later *L. R. A.* or *A. L. R.* annotations (through 70 *A. L. R.*) are noted.

B. Special-Subject Reporters.

The objective of the special subject series is the selection from all jurisdictions involved of the reports of decisions of appellate courts and, as appropriate, of quasi-judicial tribunals, bearing upon that subject. These may relate to labor, taxation, public utilities, or bankruptcy. While the decisions thus reported are usually available in conventional law reports, the special subject reports often collect and report federal and state commission reports as well, some of which are not otherwise conveniently accessible. Usually these special subject reports offer some additional feature not found in the conventional reports — notes, annotations, or cross-references to a treatise on the subject covered. Most such series have been relatively short lived and few are now current, except those published in conjunction with loose-leaf services. They are listed in the Bibliographical Reference Manual.

C. Loose-Leaf Reporting Services.

These are described in Chapter 26.

---

[7] San Francisco, Bancroft-Whitney, 1909-1912. 20 v. Vol. 1-13, Notes on the American Decisions; v. 14-20, Notes on the American Reports.

[8] By William S. Torbert. San Francisco, Bancroft-Whitney Co., 1905.

[9] Comp. and Verified by George J. Martin. San Francisco, Bancroft-Whitney Co., 1912. 5th ed.

[10] *L. R. A. Cases Cited (L. R. A. Green Book).* Rochester, Lawyers Co-operative Pub. Co., 1932.

CHAPTER 16

LAW REPORTS: TABULAR MEANS FOR FINDING

A. Need for Tables.

Once a citation to a case has been found, there remains the task of actually finding the case among the thousands of books on the shelves. While this is usually simple, the enormous mass of cases and the fact that a given case may be reported in several different standard series, necessitate tabular means for facilitating the search. Information about these is correlated below.

B. Tables of Abbreviations.

Because legal writers cite hundreds of cases and other authorities, selected from among thousands of different publications, they abbreviate titles, to save time and space. While the meanings of most of these abbreviations are fairly obvious, others would be incomprehensible without a table of abbreviations. Many such tables are available in digests, loose-leaf services, citators, dictionaries, encyclopedias, *etc.*, as well as in works on legal bibliography. Probably the most complete list is that in the "Bibliographical Reference Manual" in this book.

C. Tables of Cases.

The most common as well as one of the most useful indexes to reported cases is the ubiquitous table of cases. Since the table of cases approach to the law is available through nearly every law book printing or discussion cases (except the general law encyclopedias), it is described in a separate chapter, Chapter 30.

D. Parallel Citation Tables from Official to Unofficial Reports, and Reverse.

Lawyer and student alike have frequent occasion to write parallel citations from the official to the unofficial reports, or the reverse; or to find a case in one series when cited to another series. Thus, to translate from 102 *Missouri* 57 to 14 *South Western* 813; or from 17 *Atlantic* 316 to 81 *Maine* 411. There are several means for doing this, and the best one to employ depends upon the circumstances in each case.

Tables of Cases. All digest tables of cases give parallel citations, including the official, *Reporter*, and annotated reports series. Thus, *Kritzer* v. *Moffat*, 136 Wash. 410, 240 P. 355, 44 A. L. R. 681 (1925). The name of the case is a prerequisite to the use of these tables. The omission of the official citation in a table means that the case was not officially reported. The omission of the annotated reports citation is not proof, however, that the case was not in such a series; the table may have been compiled before the case was selected for inclusion.

Official to Reporter Citation. As *from* 102 Mo. 57 *to* 14 S. W. 813.

National Reporter Blue Book (1928, with 1936 and 1948 Permanent Supplements, and annual cumlative pamphlet supplements.)[1] "A complete table showing volume and page of the *Reporter* for every case found in the corresonding state [and United States Supreme Court] reports." This is a very simple table, printed on blue paper and bound in blue, to make it easily findable. It is arranged by volume and page of the official reports, as follows:

---

142 TEXAS REPORTS

Tex. Pg.	S.W.2d Vol.	S.W.2d Pg.	Tex. Pg.	S.W.2d Vol.	S.W.2d Pg.	Tex. Pg.	S.W.2d Vol.	S.W.2d Pg.	Tex. Pg.	S.W.2d Vol.	S.W.2d Pg.	Tex. Pg.	S.W.2d Vol.	S.W.2d Pg.	Tex. Pg.	S.W.2d Vol.	S.W.2d Pg.
1	175	249	124	176	310	216	176	932	324	177	954	432	179	958	589	180	135
5	175	230	127	176	311	222	177	264	332	177	951	439	179	288	594	180	616
19	175	247	129	176	730	228	177	249	337	178	117	444	179	239	600	180	131
23	175	243	134	176	729	232	177	49	344	178	114	451	179	283	608	180	619
29	175	957	138	176	562	238	177	56	350	178	510	460	179	269	616	180	334
36	175	407	141	176	564	243	177	52	358	178	261	476	179	291	624	180	339
41	175	401	152	177	962	251	177	600	365	178	264	486	179	278	630	180	906

Exhibit 24

State Blue and White Books. These, a separate one for each state and sold for use only in the state covered, are in two parts, the "Blue Section" and the "White Section." The first is the counterpart (for the one state only) of the *Blue Book* above described, translating the official state report citation to the *Reporter*. The White Section reverses this process, and translates the *Reporter* to the official citation, for the one state only.

Official to Federal Cases citation. As *from* 1 Ben. 15 *to* F. C. No. 16,510. "Official" here means only the original report series cumulated as of 1880 into *Federal Cases*. A blue-paged section in the digest volume of the set translates from these original series to *Federal Cases* citations.

Vols. 1–30.]   TABLE OF CITATIONS.

BANNING & ARDEN'S PATENT CASES—Cont'd.			BENEDICT'S UNITED STATES DISTRICT COURT REPORTS.		
Vol. 5, Ban. & A.—Cont'd.			**Vol. 1, Ben.**		
Page. F.C.No.	Page. F.C.No.		Page. F.C.No.	Page. F.C.No.	Page. F.C.No.
484 (2 F. 899)........ —	572 (3 F. 222)........ —		1......... 5,339	225.........13,202	397.........17,474
486 (3 F. 338)........ —	575 ....17,579a		8......... 2,617	226......... 6,416	398......... 7,892
488 (3 F. 335)........ —	577 (3 F. 143)........ —		15.........16,510	228......... 1,556	402......... 6,189
491 (2 F. 855)........ —	584 (3 F. 151)........ —		19......... 4,472	234.........12,218	406......... 8,577
509 (3 F. 95)........ —	586 (3 F. 298)........ —		19 (note).. 8,412	241.........14,012	407......... 1,543
511 (3 F. 636)........ —	590 (3 F. 599)........ —				

Exhibit 25

---

[1] St. Paul, Minn., West Pub. Co.

Shepard's United States and State Citations. The first tabular entry under the official citation of a case is the parallel citation to the "same case" in both _Reporter_ and annotated case series. Thus:

UNITED STATES SUPREME COURT REPORTS						Vol. 209
d 67 LE 313	Injunction	123 Ten 564	218 Mas 154	j 29 SC 219	32 F2d 716	136 P 1164	—264—
d 43 SC 148	State	133 SW1013	105 NE1020	230 US 407	95 F2d 693	131 Wsh416	(52 LE783)
262 US 509	Officer–	125 Ten 215	137 Md 411	57 LE1544	2 FS 705	230 P 845	(28 SC561)
67 LE1097	Effect	141 SW 753	112 At 573	33 SC 743	4 FS 443	146 Wsh 25	s 28 ADC355
43 SC 644	177 F 7	131 Ten 340	32 ND 246	248 US 162	Statutes	261 P 799	Wills
275 US 270	TD44697	174 SW1141	155 NW 67	63 LE 189	Executive	26 Lns279n	Testamen-
f 72 LE 275	180 Ala 530	166 Ten 428	32 ND 261	39 SC 37	Interpre-	65 AR 528n	tary
f 48 SC 111	61 So 901	62 SW 55	155 NW 73	204 US 524	tation–	—258—	Capacity–
d279 US 104	8 Ca2d292	172 Ten 202	121 NJL420	79 LE1039	Weight	(52 LE782)	Proof–
d 73 LE 630	65 P2d 795	110 SW 482	3 A2d 166	55 SC 501	Accorded	(28 SC487)	Declara-
d 49 SC 294	106 CaA594	174 Ten 497	157 Ap 858	300 US 638	289 US 351	s105 NW	tions–Ad-
j279 US 109	289 P 916	127 SW 115	143 NYS164	81 LE 854	77 LE1249	[1130	missibility
j 73 LE 632	—CaA—	—TxCi—	157 Ap 866	57 SC 510	53 SC 614	s135 Ia 717	78 F2d 219

Exhibit 26

This parallel citation is given only in paper supplements leading up to the first bound volume, and in that first bound volume following the publication of the report cited. It is not given in later supplements or bound volumes. Note that all the earlier editions of the _Shepard_ units designated "same case" in another report series by a lower case "s" instead of by the parentheses. In the above example, the "s" refers to the appealed case when it was in the Iowa Supreme Court, not to a parallel citation of the Supreme Court case. Note that the appealed case, 105 N. W. 1130, was not officially reported; that the Iowa Supreme Court reheard the case (105 Iowa 900), and that it was again appealed to the United States Supreme Court (215 U. S. 591). An example of the use of "s" to mean the same case in a parallel report series is in 174 Mass. 212, below.

MASSACHUSETTS REPORTS				Vol. 174
—570—		6MQ(2) 20, —129—	195Mas²115 —212—	259Mas ²462
s 54NE 257	Vol. 174	16MQ(5)224 s 54NE 338	196Mas 220 s 54NE 539	265Mas 3386
177Mas¹193		—68— .33AIR 1748n	197Mas²483 s 75AS 300	267Mas 2522
180Mas 119		s 54NE 358 —132—	199Mas¹572 s161Mas 558	269Mas 393
180Mas¹147	s 54NE 339	s176Mas 433 s 54NE 502	201Mas¹300 j184Mas¹155	275Mas 5335
184Mas¹129	—1— 178Mas 463	183Mas¹556, 206Mas 568	d204Mas 227 d226Mas¹491	228US 8274
190Mas 183	194Mas⁴180	186Mas 42, 231Mas⁵581	215Mas 135 100AS 520n	57LE 8833
192Mas 144	210Mas⁷156	195Mas 54 14Lns 102n	f219Mas 190 45Lns 1305n	33SC 8460
193Mas 166	211Mas⁴133	210Mas¹298 —144—	219Mas 291 AC'18D 5n	229US¹²377
206Mas 179	226Mas8453	—74— s 54NE 490	250Mas¹371 —216—	57LE¹²¹235

Exhibit 27

In this parallel citation, the s. 161 Mas. 558 refers to the same case at its first hearing before the Supreme Judicial Court, while the 174 Mas. 212 is the rehearing of that case. Thus, 161 Mas. 558 is not a parallel citation to 174 Mas. 212.

Official to Trinity Series Citation. _See Numerical Table of Cases Reported in the_ [_Trinity Series and American Annotated Cases_], in "Notes" to Chapter 15.

Official to A. L. R. Citation. The _A. L. R. Table of Cases with Parallel References to Official Reports_, issued at irregular intervals and circulated only to authors, lists all cases published in _A. L. R._, in the order of official citation. The "n" means the case was annotated in _A. L. R._

A.L.R. PARALLEL TABLE   31

224 Iowa.	A.L.R.	104 Kan.	A.L.R.	108 Kan.	A.L.R.
829–832	115: 725n.	1–2	3: 268n.	204–205	15: 658n.
844–847	116: 242n.	57–59	13: 744n.	320–327	19: 90n.
913–924	115: 169n.	141–144	2: 880n.	379–385	16: 1488n.
1035–1041	118: 801n.	159–165	5: 483n.	667–673	14: 604n.
1190–1197	116: 89n.	198–203	10: 1165n.		
		301–311	3: 1283n.	109 Kan.	

Exhibit 28

Unofficial to Official Citation. As *from* 107 N. E. 439 *to* 219 Mass. 566.

State Blue and White Books. The White Section of this table makes this transfer.

Shepard's Reporter Citations. These follow the same procedure as in the State *Shepards*, above, to translate from *Reporter* to official citation. There are of course many *Reporter* cases for which there is no official report and consequently no parallel official citation.

Sometimes the official citation is given at the beginning of the *Reporter* report. But usually the *Reporter* is printed before the official citation is known.

Chapter 17

ADMINISTRATIVE LAW

A. Administrative Rules and Regulations.

The Need. "Administrative law" is based upon the common-sense recognition of the fact that business has to be transacted with reasonable expedition. And in the enormously complicated affairs of the government this can be done only by the delegation by Congress of some authority to the agencies and people who actually must transact business.

For the purposes of this *Manual*, administrative law may be divided into that which is solely of internal or intra-agency effect; and that which concerns the relationship between the agency and citizens, or between citizens as regulated by the agency. With the first we are not here concerned, as that is primarily a matter of office routine and of little general significance.

The extent to which legislatures, under the Constitution, may delegate their powers is a complex matter of constitutional law outside the scope of this book. However, both rule-making powers and the preliminary power to enforce decisions under the rules are, within wide limits, given to the various agencies of the executive branch of the government, to counties and municipalities, and to courts. Thus there are rules covering the following activities: setting the hours of opening of post offices and the number of mail deliveries a day; the regulation of prices and wages, and rationing in wartime; the formalities of the preparation of income tax returns; the rates charged by public utilities; automobile parking regulations; the changing of some tariff rates; the creation or transfer of functions of governmental agencies; the taking over and operation of railroads in emergencies, and so forth, by regulation and order rather than by direct legislation. Furthermore, there is the preliminary enforcement of these orders and regulations by tribunals which are not courts but which function in much the same manner.

The Scope and Basis of Administrative Regulation. Administrative or sub-legislation includes rules and regulations made by the President and state governors, heads of lesser government agencies, and by courts. Some of the rules thus promulgated are by virtue of the *inherent power of such agencies to get work done*, matters with which the legislatures do not wish to be bothered. For the most part these concern matters of orderly procedure in the transaction of agency business. Most sub-legislation, however, is by *authorization and direction of specific legislation which delegates the power* to the officers and bodies designated, to put into effect and administer it. The President's power to conclude executive agreements with foreign governments derives from the Constitution, which defines his control over foreign regulations. A tariff act or reciprocal trade agreement authorizes the President to order limited changes in tariff rates; or the Interstate Commerce Commission is given wide latitude in setting railroad rates and specifications for equipment.

Basis of the Rule-Making Power. Both the law and the practice of federal rule making power have been described at length in the United States Attorney General's Committee on Administrative Procedure's *Final Report;* [1] and in K. C. Davis, *Administrative Law.* [2] Chapters I and II of the first, and V and VI of the latter work are especially in point. The pertinent statutory provision is the Administrative Procedure Act, Section 3 (a), 60 Stat. 237, 238 (1946), 5 U. S. C. § 1003(a) (1946).

B. Publication of Rules: The Federal Register System.

By far the most inclusive publication of federal administrative legislation is through what is known as the Federal Register System. This was established as a result of the Federal Register Act of 1935 (as amended by the Administrative Procedure Act of 1946). The three publications comprising this system are the *Federal Register, Code of Federal Regulations*, and the *Government Organization Manual.*

Notes

Genesis of the Federal Register System. The difficulty in keeping track of the many thousands of administrative rules promulgated every year is multiplied by the number of agencies issuing them. This is further complicated by the numerous births, deaths, and transfers of functions of such agencies. Before the early 'Thirties,' this was not an insurmountable problem, but it then speedily became impossible for either government or ordinary citizens affected by the rules to learn of their existence, amendment, or revocation.

The situation was brought to a head in 1935 when, in argument of the *Hot-Oil* case *(Panama Refining Co.* v. *Ryan*, 293 U. S. 388, 412), before the Supreme Court of the United States, it was learned that, unknown to either the oil industry, the rationing enforcement officials, or the lower courts, the regulation sued upon had been revoked. Under the lash of Mr. Justice Brandeis' comments and an aroused public opinion, corrective legislation was enacted, providing for the speedy publication of rules and regulations of general application. This was the Federal Register Act of 1935, which, as amended and in conjunction with the Administrative Procedure Act of 1946, provides the legislative basis for what is known as the Federal Register System.[3] The rules relating to the system, together with their statutory authority, are set forth in Title 1 of the *Code of Federal Regulations* (1949).

The Federal Register. The first place of publication of rules of general application is almost always in the *Federal Register*, issued five days a week except

---

[1] Washington, D. C., U. S. Govt. Print. Off., 1941. Published as Senate Document No. 8, 77th Cong., 1st Sess.

[2] St. Paul, West Pub. Co., 1951.

[3] For a highly critical account of how this has worked out, *see* Frank C. Newman, *Government and Ignorance — a Progress Report on Publication of Federal Regulations*, 63 Harv. L. Rev. 929 (1950).

on a day following a holiday. It is in effect the daily supplement to the *Code of Federal Regulations.* It began publication on March 14, 1936.

Under the statute, the following kinds of rules are required or authorized to be filed and published: (1) Presidential proclamations and executive orders of general interest in the numbered series, and any other documents which the President submits or orders to be published. (2) Every document, issued under proper authority, prescribing a penalty or a course of conduct, conferring a right, privilege, authority or immunity, or imposing an obligation, and relevant or applicable to the general public, the members of a class or the persons of a locality. (3) Documents or classes of documents required by act of Congress to be filed and published. (4) Other documents deemed by the Director of the *Federal Register* to be of sufficient interest.[4] The text as published in the *Federal Register* is prima facie evidence of the filing and text of the original document, and courts are required to take judicial notice of it. The *Federal Register* covers only executive orders and administrative regulations. It does not include the rules of Congress or of courts.

Arrangement of material. Documents published are arranged under four principal headings, in the following order:
> The President.
> Rules and Regulations.
> Proposed Rule Making.
> Notices.

Presidential proclamations and orders. See "B," below, "The President as Lawmaker."

Rules and regulations. The arrangement of rules in each issue is by a classification in which titles and organization to some extent follow that of the *United States Code.* For example, Title 7 is Agriculture in both. This classification is also that of the *Code of Federal Regulations,* into which the *Federal Register* rules cumulate annually.

Compilations of Rules in the Federal Register. From time to time, when all or most of the rules of an agency are revised or recodified for publication in a single issue of the *Federal Register,* they are published out of their regular order, as a special supplement, which is a most convenient arrangement. Examples are the Civil Aeronautics Board rules, published as a unit in 14 Fed. Reg. 4033–4477 (1949); the Veterans' Administration rules, in 13 Fed. Reg. No. 231, part II (Nov. 27, 1948); the rules of practice in patent cases, in 13 Fed. Reg. 9575 (1948); and others. These complete recodifications are the temporary end-product of a process which constantly goes on in rule making. A rule is made, amended, and expanded. Then the chapter or the title of which it is a part becomes so cumbersome because of the amendments that the chapter is completely revised—whereupon the process begins anew. In time, the whole title is such a hodgepodge of amendments and revocations that it is completely done over in one of these supplements. Before it is printed, it is already out of date, and the process starts all over again. This is one of the *raisons d'être* of the loose-leaf service, which keeps track of these changes for its subscribers.

Rule of practice. The rules of practice adopted by federal administrative agencies prescribe the procedure which must be followed in transacting business with these agencies. Failure by the practitioner to observe them may prejudice or defeat the client's cause. The rules are printed in the *Federal Register* and later in the *Code of Federal Regulations.*

Some of these rules are also printed in the *United States Code,* and many agencies print them separately and send them free on request. Pike and Fischer's *Administrative Law,* Second Series (*see* page 151) prints perhaps the most complete collection of "Agency Rules." Some of the loose-leaf services described in Chapter 26 also print

---

[4] 1 C. F. R. §§ 31-1.35 (1949).

agency rules of practice. Finally, treatises (as those on taxation, patents, or trade-marks) frequently print the rules as appendices.

Some ingenuity is necessary to find the rules in the *Code of Federal Regulations* indexes, as they are not always listed where one would expect. For example, the rules of practice of the United States Maritime Commission are entered under that agency, under "Organization, procedure, and delegations"; those of the Internal Revenue Bureau under "Records and Procedure." There is no general index heading for "Rules of Practice."

Proposed rule making. Proposed changes in rules of general application, including rate changes, are published in the *Federal Register* a suitable time in advance of adoption, to permit interested parties to be heard in opposition. Such proposed changes are listed in the appropriate places in the "Codification Guide."

Notices. Changes in statements of agency organization and functions are printed in this section, as are notices of agreements filed for approval, notices of opinions and orders, applications for relief, Office of Alien Property Custodian vesting orders, *etc.*

Indexes and tables. These are described, *post*, under indexes and tables to the Federal Register System as a whole.

Since rule changes may be very frequent and drastic, and since only the latest form of rule, as actually in force, is printed in the *Code of Federal Regulations*, the *Federal Register* issues should be retained, as often they are the only repository of the text of an earlier form of rule, repealed during the year. *Rules proposed but not adopted are found only in the Federal Register.*

Code of Federal Regulations. This code (hereinafter cited as *CFR*) is the cumulation of *rules in force* of federal administrative agencies, of general application, most of which were first published in the *Federal Register*.

These rules cover a very wide range of interest. Therein one may find the Attorney General's list of subversive organizations, Treasury regulations on tax matters, a list of unhealthful posts in the foreign service, the average value of farms in every county and territory, the interest rates on government bonds, postal rates, visa regulations, all sorts of commodity standards, and so forth. The *Code* is not so inclusive as the *Federal Register*, however: (1) Descriptions of agency organization are omitted, in favor of digests of such statements (with citations to the full statement in the *Federal Register*), in the *United States Government Organization Manual*. (2) Many miscellaneous rules are omitted or cited by reference only. (3) Preliminary statements of policy reasons for the adoption of certain rules are omitted. These often contain statements useful to the public concerned. (4) Proposed rules are omitted.

Status of editions of Code. The authority and scope of the *CFR* are set forth in detail in the General Preface to the 1949 edition, where the 1939 edition preface is also reprinted. For all actions arising under rules as of December 31, 1948 or later, the second edition supersedes the first. For actions arising prior to that date, the first edition is still in effect. The second edition is the one herein described.

Format of the Code. The *CFR* is divided into fifty titles, alphabetically arranged except the first three (which concern the organization of the government). Many of these titles correspond in numbering and title to those of the *United States Code*. The basic subdivision is into chapters, parts and sections. The *chapters* bear the names of the agencies administering the rules included therein, as the Civil Aeronautics Administration. The *section numbers* are formed from the chapter numbers, plus a decimal point and a subsection number. Thus, § 202.13 is subsection number 13 of Chapter 202. There are annual supplements, some cumulative, others not.

The above chapter numbering can be the cause of a great deal of confusion, since agencies and their functions are continually being shifted from one department or bureau to another. When this is done, a new agency often falls heir to the old chapter and section numbers. Thus, 24 C. F. R. § 202.13 (1939 ed.) relates to an entirely different agency and subject matter from the same section in the second edition, 1949. Therefore, the date of edition or supplement should form part of the citation of a section.

Current status and statutory basis of CFR sections. The *CFR* is a compilation of rules *actually in force at the date of printing* the bound volume or pocket supplement. Any which have been amended, superseded, terminated or repealed during the calendar year covered by a pocket supplement are cited in a brief "Prior Amendments" note, together with the page in the *Federal Register* printing the original. Thus:

(Secs. 3, 11, 52 Stat. 1061, 1066 as amended;
29 U. S. C. 203, 211) [Reg. 31, 15 F. R. 4220,
July 1, 1950]

Prior Amendments

1949: 14 F. R. 3588, June 30.

Exhibit 29

Also, a "List of Sections Affected" in the supplement cites all sections of regulations in both bound volume and supplement which were affected either directly or indirectly during any calendar year following the publication of the bound volume. *Statutes* upon which rules are based are cited with the rules in the *CFR*. Their first place of publication (usually in the *Federal Register*, in which case the exact minute of filing is given), is also cited, as below ("Source").

MARKETING QUOTA REGULATIONS, BURLEY
AND FLUE-CURED TOBACCO 1950–51 MAR-
KETING YEAR

AUTHORITY: §§ 725.112 to 725.128 issued
under sec. 375, 52 Stat. 66; as amended; 7
U. S. C. 1375. Interpret or apply secs. 301,
313, 363, 52 Stat. 38, 47, 63, as amended; 7
U. S. C. and Sup., 1301, 1313, 1363.

SOURCE: §§ 725.112 to 725.128 contained in
MQ–21–Tobacco (1950), 14 F. R. 5037, Aug.
16, 1949.

Exhibit 30

United States Government Organization Manual. The purpose of the third member of the Federal Register System trinity is to keep users abreast of the current organization and functions of governmental agencies and of selected quasi-official agencies (National Research Council, American Red Cross), and international organizations. To that end, it prints digests of more complete statements already printed in the *Federal Register*, setting forth for each agency its mode of creation and authority (under statutes, executive orders, and reorganization plans), organization (including major personnel), and functions. Often an organization chart is included. (Condensed statements of the statutory background of most of these agencies are also printed in the tables of the *United States Code and the United States Code Congressional and Administrative News*.)

This annual publication is a guide to how the government agencies are set up and operate — how the government keeps house. An understanding of the mechanics of the government and a knowledge of the names of officials are often of great assistance in starting a search.

Indexes to the Federal Register System. The indexes include the following:

United States Government Organization Manual Index. It contains (1) "List of Names" of all personnel mentioned in the *Manual;* and (2) "Index," which is a subject index to government organizations and the statutes applicable. This is an index not only of active organizations, but also to Appendix A, "Executive agencies and functions . . . abolished, transferred, or terminated subsequent to March 4, 1933." *This index is the best starting place in the search for the statutory origin, organization, function, and principal personnel of government agencies.*

Federal Register Index. The daily index is cumulated monthly, quarterly and annually, covering the calendar year. It is not an easy index to use. The bulk of the entries are by agency, thereunder by sub-agency and function, thus requiring considerable knowledge of governmental organization for efficient use. However, there are also many catchword entries, as "subversive organizations," synthetic liquid fuels," and "instalment credit." This index, because it covers all the material published in the *Federal Register,* is more inclusive than that of the *Code of Federal Regulations,* which indexes only regulations adopted and presently in force. The "Codification Guide," described under "Tables," *infra,* is a vital part of the index.

Code of Federal Regulations Index. There is a "General Index," supplemented by annual pocket parts, but also a separate one for each bound volume, for the individual titles of the *CFR.* These indexes are largely by agency, but contain many catchword entries. The catchword entries in the separate volumes are only cross-references to the agency issuing the regulation, making the "General Index" more convenient to use. Each bound volume pocket part has a "List of Sections Affected," which is that part of the annual "Codification Guide" covering regulations printed in such volume. The first edition of the *CFR* had only a general index, none for each volume. It has been supplemented by the cumulative supplement of June 1, 1938, and in the succeeding annual supplements, up to the publication of the second edition, as of December 31, 1948.

Tables for the Federal Register System. Since federal regulations are so closely tied up with statutes, conversion means are supplied whereby it is possible to tell: (a) what rules have been promulgated under the authority of a given statute, proclamation or executive order; (b) for any rule, its statutory basis; (c) changes in the form of any published rule; and (d) the subsequent legislative history of Presidential proclamations and executive orders, and of some administrative regulations.

1. **Conversion tables from statute to rule, including Presidential documents:** as *from* 46 U. S. C. § 921 *to* 19 C. F. R. § 333.

(i) "United States Code sections which are authority for rules codified in the Code of Federal Regulations." This is a table, in Title 2 of the *CFR* and supplements, arranged by *United States Code* citation, with parallel citation to the *CFR* rule for which the *USC* is cited as authority. Thus:

7 U. S. C. 162	Title 2—The Congress	
United States Code	**Code of Federal Regulations**
7 U. S. C. 162	7 CFR Part 352
166	7 CFR Part 323
167	7 CFR Part 302
228	9 CFR Part 201
	Part 202

Exhibit 31

(ii) Statutes into Presidential documents. Beginning with the 1949 supplements, Title 3 of the *CFR*, Table 5 lists "Statutes cited as authority for Presidential documents," Thus:

Tables

Statutes at Large—Continued

Date	Citation	Title of act	Document
1945 ·			
——	59 Stat. 410		EO 10082.
July 5	Secs. 2, 3, 59 Stat. 410, 411		Proc. 2829, 2865, 2867.
——	Sec. 8, 59 Stat. 515	Bretton Woods Agreement Act.	EO 10033.
Aug. 11	59 Stat. 530		Proc. 2855.
Dec. 29	Sec. 1, 59 Stat. 669	International Organizations Immunities Act.	EO 10083, 10086.

Exhibit 32

2. **Conversion from Presidential proclamations, executive orders or other orders or reorganization plans, to *CFR*;** as *from* Executive order no. 5644 *to* 5 *CFR* 301.61. In three tables to Title 3 of the *CFR*, Presidential documents are listed by number, with their subject matter, *CFR* reference, and the nature of that reference. Thus:

			Title 3—The President	Chapter II—Executive Orders	
E. O. No.	Date	F. R. Citation	Subject	Reference	Comment
	1939	**4 F. R.**			
8202	July 13	3243	Authorizing and requesting the Federal Power Commission to perform certain functions relating to the transmission of electric energy between the United States and foreign countries and to the exportation and importation of natural gas from and into the United States.	18 CFR Part 32; 32.30; 32.50; Part 153; 153.1; 153.10; 33 CFR 209.130	Cited as authority. Cited in text. Do. Interpreted or applied. Cited in text. Do. Do.
8216	July 25	3430	Alaska, land and water withdrawn for naval purposes	32 CFR 702.4	Cited in table.
8232	Sept. 5	3812	Control of the Panama Canal and the Canal Zone	35 CFR 5.64	Cited in text.
8234	Sept. 5	3823	Prescribing regulations governing the passage and control of vessels through the Panama Canal in any war in which the United States is neutral.	35 CFR 4.161	Cited in note preceding 4.161.
8238	Sept. 6	3835	Extending the limits of the customs port of entry of Baltimore, Md., in customs collection District No. 13 (Maryland), to include Sparrows Point, Md.	19 CFR 1.1	Cited in table.
8250	Sept. 11	3890	Revocation of Executive Order No. 2006 of July 30, 1914, placing certain land under the jurisdiction of the Secretary of the Navy for use as a Naval Radio Station.	35 CFR 21.4	Do.
8251	Sept. 12	3899	Regulations governing the entrance of foreign and domestic aircraft into the Canal Zone, and navigation therein.	35 CFR 5.1–5.64	Superseded.

Exhibit 33

3. **Conversion from Presidential proclamations, executive or other orders, and reorganization plans, to *United State Code* sections affected by the orders;** as *from* Executive order no. 6084 *to* 12 U. S. C. § 1026. This is done through Table II ("Executive Acts Included") of the *United States Code* and similar tables in the *United States Code Annotated* and in the *Federal Code Annotated*. *See* page 59.

4. **Conversion from *CFR* to Presidential or statutory authority:** as *from* 29 C. F. R. 654.1 *to* 52 Stat. 615, 29 U. S. C. § 205(e), 9 F. R. 12510.

(i) Authority is cited either as a footnote (for a single section), or as a note preceding a group of sections. *See* page 138.

(ii) In Title 3 of the first edition of the *CFR*, a table, arranged by *CFR* title and section number, gives in parallel columns the proclamation or executive order included or cited in the regulation. No statutory authority is cited, and this table was omitted from all supplements and from the second edition, since the same information now accompanies the text of each regulation, as above. Thus Title 3 of the first edition should be retained for reference purposes.

5. **Changes in the form or status of published rules.** Federal administrative rules and regulations (including Presidential documents) are so frequently modified or revoked that it would be impossible to ascertain the present status of any given rule without something similar in function to the *Shepard* citator "legislative history" notations. Tables performing such functions have been provided.

(i) "Table of Documents Affected by Later Documents." This table, in the annual supplement to each *CFR* (1949 edition) title, lists sections affected by any document published in the *Federal Register* during the year, including of course all Presidential documents. It includes amendatory documents codified in full in the supplement containing the table, but also documents which were revoked, superseded or otherwise terminated during the year, and so not published in the supplement; and proposed rules. Reference is made to the page of the *Federal Register* where the document was originally printed. This serves as a *Shepardizer* for the legislative history of a rule.

List of Sections Affected—1949

All sections of Chapters II to VIII of Title 7 which were affected by documents published in the FEDERAL REGISTER during 1949 are enumerated in the following list. The list includes amendatory documents codified in full in this Pocket Supplement. It also includes documents which were revoked, superseded, or otherwise terminated during 1949. Page numbers refer to FEDERAL REGISTER pages. Page numbers of documents affecting sections but not specifically amending the text thereof appear in brackets.

TITLE 7—Continued	Page	TITLE 7—Continued	Page
Chapter II:		Chapter IV:	
Appendix ____ 1513, 2657, 4817, 5364		Part 415 [revised]_____	4543
Chapter III:		*Prior to revision:*	
Part 301:		415.4 _____	1393
Proposed rules_____ 1176,		Part 416 [revised]_____	5290
1285, 1384, 5231, 6334, 6335, 6793		416.6 _____	6674
301.38—301.38–11 _____	999	416.16 _____	6675
301.38a _____	1866	416.17 _____	6675
301.38–5a _____	1866	*Prior to revision:*	
301.48–2 _____	1866	416.1 _____	4547
301.48–4 _____	1867	Part 417 [revised]_____	5298
301.48–5 _____	1867	417.16 _____	6675
301.48–8 _____	1867	Part 418:	
301.48–9 _____	1867	418.151–418.168 [revised]__	1457
301.52–2 _____	2059	418.154_____ 6675,	7701
301.52–4a _____	5733	418.156 _____	4548
301.58–3—301.58–12 _____	[335]	418.167 _____	4548,

Exhibit 34

The supplements for 1943-47, to the first edition, noted changes in form or status of regulations printed therein. For Presidential documents this was done under a heading "Related Presidential Documents of Subsequent Date," which listed the affecting document without telling the nature of the effect. For the remaining *CFR* titles, changes were noted by bracketing entries in the Chapter and part tables of contents for each title. Thus, the entry for a table of contents would indicate that a particular section has been [Added], [Amended], *etc.*

(ii). Codification Guide. Each daily issue of the *Federal Register* now contains a checklist of *CFR* title and section numbers affected by documents published in that issue. The "Guide" began in July, 1944. (There was also a cumulated one for the calendar year 1944, in the 1943 *CFR* supplement.) The codification guide lists not only regulations in force which have been published or modified, but those revoked, terminated or superseded, as well as proposed rules. All forms of a regulation in effect at any time during the period covered are listed, showing their disposition and where published in the *Federal Register*. This guide is cumulated in all Federal *Register* indexes, so that the annual index combines, in one place, the tables above which are distributed throughout the *CFR* volumes according to title. Usually the annual index table is issued substantially in advance of the pocket supplement tables, however. Perhaps because of this, it contains more errors than the corresponding *CFR* table. Below is a specimen entry.

272		**CODIFICATION GUIDE, 1950**			
TITLE 14—Continued	Page	**TITLE 14—Continued**	Page	**TITLE 14—Continued**	Page
Chapter I—Continued		Chapter I—Continued		Chapter I—Continued	
Part 24—Continued		Part 42—Continued		Part 60—Continued	
24.10	[4939]	42.6	4263	60.17-11—60.17-18—Con.	
24.22	5837	42.9	4264	60.17-15	1482, 4888, 4913
24.25	5838	42.11	4264	60.17-16	1482
24.29	5838	42.16-1	83	60.17-18	3253, 4913
24.40-24.42	5043	42.21	31	60.17-101—60.17-109	152, 461
Part 25	5043	42.25-2	3151	60.17-101	3253
Proposed rules	603	42.29—42.29-2	8924	60.17-102	1482

Exhibit 35

(iii) Tables of documents published in the Federal Register. The *CFR* supplements for 1945-47 listed every document printed in the *Federal Register* for those years. Presidential documents were listed following Title 3; the remainder following Title 50.

(iv) "Related Documents Tables" in the Federal Register. Each of the first three volumes of the *Federal Register* contains a "Related Documents Table," in which all documents published during the year are listed, together with an indication of all "Related Documents Amended." That is, the list in volume 3 (1938), for example, shows that Executive Order 7862, published on page 734, amends in some respect an executive order printed on page 601 of volume 1.

(v) U. S. Code tables of Presidential documents repealed or eliminated. Tables IXa and XIa of the *U. S. C.* (and similar tables in the *U. S. C. A.*) note, respectively, repeals or elimination for other reasons, of Presidential documents which were at any time a part of a *Code* section or editorial note.

By means of tables i-iv, above, it is feasible to determine changes made in Presidential or agency documents from March 14, 1936, on. Beginning with the Codification Guide in July, 1944, the tables of changes in the *FR* and *CFR* duplicate each other for the most part, but those in the *CFR* are somewhat more accurate and easier to use.

Determination of the Present Form of a Rule. The search would normally begin with the bound volume of the appropriate title of the *CFR*, proceeding to the "Table of Documents Affected by Later Documents" in the annual supplement, thence to subsequent *Federal Register* "Codification Guides" to date. Though somewhat laborious, the procedure is simple.

Subsequent Judicial History of Federal Administrative Rules. Tracing the *judicial* history of the rules by tabular or other positive means is for the most part impossible or at least impracticable, but there are some exceptions.

Shepard's Citations. If a rule is cited in connection with a *Statute at Large*, it is covered under that heading in *Shepard's United States Citations*, but few are so cited. Presidential proclamations and reorganization plans, and executive agreements may be so identified through Table II in the *United States Code* and a similar table in the *United*

States Code Annotated. The procedure is to consult the table listing Presidential documents included in the *Code,* and then to Shepardize the *Code* section with which the document is identified. This is indirect but effective.

National Reporter System *"Tables of Statutes Construed."* Presidential executive orders and proclamations, and such administrative regulations as are the subject of litigation are covered by these tables. *See* page 118.

Digest of United States Supreme Court Reports. The material mentioned above is also covered in the table of statutes construed, in this digest, when it has been the subject of a Supreme Court decision. *See* page 113.

Loose leaf services. Tax and some other agency regulations are annotated in services. *See* Chapter 26.

Other Sources of Federal Rules Publication. Many official agencies print and distribute on request their rules of practice and other regulations administered by them. They may be printed in company with the laws under which the agency operates, and contain annotations to agency or court decisions interpreting them. Loose-leaf services frequently print these regulations and rules of practice. The most complete current unofficial publication of Presidential proclamations and executive orders is in the *United States Code Congressional and Administrative News,* which also publishes occasional administrative regulations of general interest.

C. The President as Lawmaker.

Both directly and indirectly, the President of the United States is an important lawmaker. This book is not concerned with how the Constitutional and public law aspects of the President's legislative powers emanated. It considers these powers only in so far as they relate to the publication and finding of the resulting subordinate legislation, as part of the sum total of federal law.

The powers are derived from the Constitution, by delegation from Congress, and from the power of the President as chief executive and Commander in Chief of the Armed Forces to get things done. As a practical matter, they are also implemented strongly by his control of patronage, and from his immense influence as head of the political party in power. On the negative side, there is the practically decisive Presidential veto or threat of veto of unwanted legislation. In the years 1789 through 1931, only forty-nine acts were passed over the Presidential veto, of which seven were purely personal in nature, and most of the rest were of only local or temporary interest.[5] Franklin D. Roosevelt vetoed 136 bills, of which only five were repassed over his veto.[6]

Congress, within the very wide Constitutional limitations of the doctrine of separation of powers, may authorize the President to conclude reciprocal trade agreements with other nations; raise or lower tariff rates; withdraw public lands from private entry; fix certain prices; realign or create new federal agencies below the rank of department, and the like. In turn, under the Act of August 8, 1950, c. 646, 64 Stat. 419, 3 U. S. C. §§ 301-303 (Supp. V, 1952), which regularized a situation which had long existed, much of this rule-making power is delegated by the President to various executive agencies under his jurisdiction. House

---

[5] McClenon and Gilbert, *Index to the Federal Statutes, 1874-1931.* Washington, D. C., U. S. Govt. Print. Off., 1933 p. 825.

[6] C. Perry Patterson, *Presidential Government in the United States* (Chapel Hill, N. C., University of North Carolina Press, 1947), p. 54.

Report No. 1867 of the 81st Congress explains the purpose of the Act, and an appendix lists illustrative "provisions of law vesting functions in the President." Examples of delegation are the Public Land Orders (P.L.O.) issued by the Secretary of the Interior, Canal Zone Orders (C. Z. O.), and Transfer Orders (T. O.). The form of delegated order is "By virtue of the authority vested in the President and pursuant to Executive Order No. . . ."

Forms of Presidential Legislation. Aside from the treaties and executive agreements of international interest for which the President is responsible (discussed in Chapter 4), the President's legislative output consists of reorganization plans, proclamations, executive orders, and several categories of less important miscellaneous orders.

Reorganization plans. The reorganization plan for government agencies is a legislative hybrid, requiring both Congressional and Presidential action. It is in effect an executive order issued by direction of and under the authority of a specific act of Congress (as the Reorganization Act of 1949). It combines, shifts, and even abolishes designated agencies of the executive branch of the government below the rank of department (or their functions); the order to become effective only if not disapproved by Congress. The scope of reorganization and the mode of veto or approval vary considerably from act to act. The practice prescribed in the later acts has been to set a date limit within which such plans are to be submitted, and to make the plans effective only if, within a specified period after submission to Congress (usually sixty days), it is not disapproved by a *majority of the elected membership of either House.*

Proclamations and executive orders. The most frequent and pervasive manifestation of the President's legislative activities in the issuance of proclamations and executive orders. They are the medium through which the President exercises a great deal of his authority, especially that delegated to him by Congress through specific legislation. In importance they vary from the order authorizing the appointment of a minor government employee without regard to Civil Service rules, to those establishing war emergency agencies such as the Office of Price Administration and fixing its functions. Revocation, superseding, or amendment of an order is by another such order. The authority for issuing is stated, usually in a preamble, substantially as follows: "By virtue of the authority vested in me by section 10 of the Railway Labor Act . . . I hereby create . . ."; or "By virtue of the authority vested in me as President of the United States . . .".

There is no difference in legal effect between the proclamation and the executive order.[7]

Senate Bill 2190, of the Eighty-second Congress, provided that "Executive Order No. 10290 . . . is hereby repealed." *Staff Memoranda* 81-1-59 and 60, of the Senate Committee on Expenditures in the Executive Departments, record the results of a searching inquiry into the President's rulemaking power and the power of Congress to repeal a rule.

OUTLINE FOR USE OF EXECUTIVE ORDERS [8]

I. Locating By Serial Number or Date.

[7] Message of President William H. Taft to Congress, July 26, 1911 (47 Cong. Rec. 3207), citing *Wood* v. *Beach*, 156 U. S. 548, 550 (1895).

[8] The authors are indebted to Miss Jean Ashman, Law Librarian of the United States Railroad Retirement Board Library, for permission to use this outline (as modified by them).

a Slip copies. *See* page 148.

b. In the *Code of Federal Regulations*, Title 3. There are two tables, largely but not entirely duplicating each other, which *list* all executive orders to date which have been included or cited in the *CFR*. They do not print the text. They are as follows:

Through no. 7926, Feb. 9, 1835-July 7, 1938: In 3 *CFR* 216-330 (1st ed.).

Through no. 10025, and continued to date by pocket supplements: In 3 *CFR* 160–241 (1949 ed.). Both lists include unnumbered as well as numbered orders. They are not complete lists of all published executive orders, but only those "included or cited in the *CFR*." For a complete list of all published through number 8030 (by which time the complete text of all orders of a public general nature were being printed in the supplement to *CFR*) see the Historical Records Survey publications described on page 148.

7906-9347, June 6, 1938-May 27, 1943: Cumulative supplement, pages 1339-1387. This supplement to the first edition and all succeeding ones listed below *not only list all orders for the period covered, but print the full text*.

9348-9412, June 3, 1943-Dec. 27, 1943: In 1943 Supplement.

9413-9508, Jan. 4, 1944-Dec. 27, 1944: In 1944 Supplement.

9509-9670. Jan. 8, 1945-Dec. 28, 1945: In 1945 Supplement.

9153A, 9671–9817, April 30, 1942–Dec. 29, 1945–Dec. 31, 1946: In 1946 Supplement.

9818-9915, Jan. 7, 1947-Dec. 30, 1947: In 1947 Supplement.

9916-10025, Dec. 1947-Dec. 30, 1948: In 1948 Supplement.

10026-10094, Jan. 4, 1949-Dec. 22, 1949: In 1949 Supplement.

10095-10199, Jan. 3, 1950-Dec. 21, 1950: In 1950 Supplement.

10200-10315, Jan. 3, 1951-Dec. 19, 1951: In 1951 Supplement; and so on, in every succeeding supplement to Title 3.

c. In the *Federal Register*. The first executive order printed herein was number 7316, of March 13, 1936. Beginning with that one, the numbers and dates provided in the table above will lead to the proper volumes of the *Federal Register* with the reservation that, as seen below, the last order issued in a given year may be the first printed in the *Federal Register* for the *succeeding* year. There is no numerical table of executive orders in the *Federal Register*, the only listing being alphabetically by subject under "Presidential Documents" or "President of the United States," in the general index. For the text of orders preceding those printed in the 1943 Supplement to the *CFR*, as printed in the *Federal Register*, as noted above *see* the table *below*.

Beginning with 7316, Mar. 13, 1936: 1 *Federal Register*.
" " 7530, Dec. 31, 1936: 2 " "
" " 7780, Dec. 30, 1937: 3 " "
" " 8031, Jan. 9, 1939: 4 " "
" " 8317, Jan. 10, 1940: 5 " "
" " 8623, Dec. 31, 1940: 6 " "
" " 9006, Jan. 2, 1942: 7 " "
" " 9292, Dec. 31, 1942: 8 " "
" " 9413, Jan. 4, 1944: 9 " "

d. In the *Historical Records Survey*. The two publications of the *Survey*, as described on page 148, list and index all executive orders in the numbered series through number 8030, 1862-1938; and all those in the unnumbered series, 1789 through 1941.

e. In the *United States Code Congressional and Admiinstrative News*. See page 148. This service *lists and prints the complete text* of all executive orders of public general interest (which includes nearly all), beginning with number 9292. The annual cumulation of the *News* printing a given order may be found through the table above, of material included in the *CFR* Supplements, where the issue date is given.

II. Locating by Topic.

a. *Historical Records Survey*. The indexes noted at page 148, covering through 1938 (number 8030) for the numbered series and through 1941 for the unnumbered series, are the only reasonably complete subject matter indexes for this material.

b. *Index to the Federal Statutes, 1874–1931* (McClenon and Gilbert). A very few orders are indexed under "President of the United States."

c. *Code of Federal Regulations.* The various supplements printing the orders (from number 7906 to date) also index them by subject. The index to the main text of Title 3 does not index them. There is no cumulative index.

d. *Federal Register.* The indexes to this periodical list the orders by subject matter under the heading "Presidential Documents," or "President of the United States."

e. *United States Code Congressional and Administrative News.* Executive orders are indexed in the general index to each issue and bound volume printing the orders.

f. *United States Code.* The general index notes executive orders by subject, as it does statutes, and in the same alphabet. When such orders have become a part of a codified statute or are mentioned in an editorial note under a *Code* section, the order is designated by number in the subject entry in the *U. S. C.* and *U. S. C. A.* indexes.

III. Determining the Present Form and Effect of an Order. *See* page 139 for a description of the various tables showing the amendment, revocation, termination, superseding, *etc.*, of executive orders.

IV. Shepardizing Executive Orders. See pages 268–270.

Miscellaneous Presidential orders. As Commander in Chief of the Armed Forces, the President issues "Military Orders" (M.O.), an unnumbered series. The Office of Strategic Services was set up by such an order; appointments and promotions of officers are by military order. Administrative orders (A. O.), called "Directives," comprise a dated but unnumbered series by the President as Chief Executive. They may direct conservation of motor fuel by federal agencies, or the preservation of the confidential status of certain official records. In a similar series, entitled "Designations of Officials," the President appoints a Coordinator of Government Films, delegates certain functions to the Secretary of the Treasury, or appoints a Maritime War Emergency Board. There are also "Presidential Letters" to subordinates, directing that certain acts be performed. Many of these might just as well have been given a number, as executive orders.

Notes

The President's Powers as Legislator. Rankin M. Gibson, *The President's Inherent Emergency Powers* [9] discusses a controversial aspect of these powers.

Reorganization Plans' Genesis. The reorganization plan is not new as a device for consolidation of agencies and functions of the federal government in the interests of efficiency and economy. In 1798 there was already a call for such reorganization, and as early as February 14, 1903 (5 U. S. C. § 602), the President was empowered by Congress to transfer certain named bureaus. The first really general reorganization act was that of June 30, 1932, amended and superseded by the Act of March 3, 1933, as further amended by the Act of March 20, 1933 (5 U. S. C. § § 124-132). By it the President was authorized to reorganize a large variety of executive agencies, by executive order, either house of Congress retaining a veto power by resolution within sixty days of the date of the order.

The first reorganization act to provide for reorganization plans, as distinct from from executive orders, was that of April 3, 1939 (53 Stat. 561-565). This act authorized the President to submit numbered plans to Congress, to become effective thirty days after submission unless within that time disapproved by concurrent resolution. The literature is extensive, the most complete bibliography being in W. Brooke Graves' *Reorganization of the Executive Branch of the United States; a Compilation of Basic*

---

[9] 12 Fed. Bar J. 107 (1951).

Information and Significant Documents, 1912-1948.[10] A brief but useful discussion is in *Reorganization of Government Agencies*.[11] The whole problem is analyzed in Lewis Meriam and Laurence F. Schmeckebier, *Reorganization of the National Government: What Does it Involve?* [12] *Senate Action on Hoover Commission Reports; Report of the Committee on Government Operations* describes in detail the Hoover Commission plans, the resulting reorganization plans, and congressional action on them.[13]

Functions of Proclamations and Executive Orders. Many *proclamations* have no legal effect, being merely appeals to the public to observe certain "days" or "months" as Armed Forces Day, or Cancer Control Month. Actions involving foreign nations or nationals are usually announced by proclamation, such as treaty approval, copyright extension, trade agreements, matters settling immigration quotas, changing tariff rates, or setting Panama Canal toll rates. National emergencies are proclaimed, as are usually but not always the setting aside of national parks and monuments. Usually land is withdrawn from or restored to the public domain by proclamation. If there is any criterion at all, it is that of widespread public interest in the subject matter of the proclamation, as compared to the usually more restricted scope of the executive order, but that is not always a safe guide nor is the distinction important. Sometimes a "day" or a change in toll rates, or other Presidential activity usually initiated by proclamation is by executive order instead.

Executive orders are the medium through which the President exercises a great deal of his authority, especially that delegated to him by Congress through specific legislation. Prior to 1939, reorganization of government agencies was done by executive order. Emergency boards to investigate labor disputes of national impact are set up by executive order; regulations are thus promulgated. The present form of these orders was substantially fixed in 1873, but it was not until 1907 that the State Department, which was the custodian of the orders, began to number them in series. President Hoover, by Executive Order No. 5220, of November 8, 1929, set up a routine for the issuance, numbering, and preservation of the orders. The present procedure for both proclamations and executive orders is that established by Executive Order No. 10,006, October 6, 1948, as codified in 1 *CFR* §§ 1.91—1.97 (1949 ed.).

Publication and Availability of Presidential Documents. Reorganization Plans. The plans are not printed as bills, but as House and Senate numbered *Documents;* as such, they are also printed in the *United States Code Congressional and Administrative News.* These are the only available places of publication of *plans proposed but not approved.*

After approval, the plans are printed in several places. Beginning with Plan Number 1 of 1939, reorganization plans, if approved, have been published in the *Federal Register* on the day after their effective date. Beginning with the Cumulative Supplement to the first edition of the *CFR* (covering 1938 to 1943, inclusive), plans have been printed as Presidential documents in Title 3. They are also published in the *Statutes at Large,* and in two places in Title 5 of the *United States Code* ("Executive Departments and Government Officers and Employees"), though they are not part of the *Code.* The plans are indexed in any publication printing them.

First, they are printed, along with historical and other notes, as annotations to the codified sections of the *enabling act* under which they were issued. *Normally the search for organization plans will begin here,* for only here are *all* the documents, such as the enabling act, the text of the plan, Presidential messages pertaining to it, any necessary

---

[10] U. S. Library of Congress, Legislative Reference Service, Public Affairs Bulletin No. 66, February, 1949.

[11] Senate Report No. 638, 79th Cong., 1st Sess. (1945).

[12] Washington, D. C., The Brookings Institution, 1939.

[13] H. Rept. No. 4, 83d Cong., 1st Sess. (1953).

executive orders implementing it, and editorial notes and cross-references, assembled in one place, *for all plans in force*. Second, such reorganization plans or parts thereof as applied to *each individual agency* concerned are printed in Title 5 as notes to the appropriate sections affected by the plans. Furthermore, *where a function has been transferred* away from an agency by a plan, that fact is noted, together with all necessary editorial matter, in a "Transfer of Functions" note relating to the *agency from which* the functions were transferred, in its appropriate *Code* title or section.

Executive orders, proclamations, and other orders. The most usable current repositories of Presidential documents other than treaties and executive agreements (for which *see* under "Treaties") are the following:

"Slip" proclamations and executive orders are published separately as pamphlets, when not of sufficient interest for publication in the *Federal Register*, and as such are listed in the *Monthly Catalog of United States Government Publications*. There are few such.

Federal Register **and** *Code of Federal Regulations.* All Presidential documents of general interest as above described are published and indexed in the *Federal Register*, from which they are cumulated into the annual supplements to Title 3 ("The President") of the *CFR* (beginning with the supplement covering 1936 to 1943, inclusive). Strangely enough, they appear in the main volume of neither edition of this *Code*, but only in the supplements. Normally, the search for such documents, except collected reorganization plans a year old or more, would begin with these publications.

United States Code Congressional and Administrative News. From its beginning in 1939, this unofficial periodical published selected proclamations and executive orders. Beginning with Proclamation No. 2575 and Executive Order No. 9292, it has printed the complete text of all which are published in the *Federal Register*. It is perhaps the most convenient current repository for these two series, supplemented for the most recent numbers by the *Federal Register*. Reorganization plans and formal treaties are also published in this periodical.

Statutes at Large. Proclamations, but not executive orders, have been printed in each volume, beginning with volume 11; volumes 3, 4, 10, and 11 are supposed to contain all issued from 1789 to 1859, but in fact many are missing. Reorganization plans, treaties, and executive agreements of international interest also appear in the *Statutes at Large*.

Indexes to Presidential Documents. Most documents (all that are of general interest) are currently indexed by subject in the volumes or issues wherein printed; they are also listed alphabetically by subject under the heading "Presidential Documents" or "President" in such places. Those directly affecting *United States Code* sections are indexed in the general index to the *Code; see*, for example, under "Collection Districts" and "Coast Guard." The definitive indexes to executive orders through 1938 are those compiled by the Historical Record Survey of the Works Progress Administration. *Presidential Executive Orders*,[14] volume 2, indexes the numbered series order through 8039 (1938). Volume 1 lists the orders numerically. *List and Index of Presidential Executive Orders, Unnumbered Series*,[15] in one mimeographed volume, both lists and indexes the available unnumbered series order. This is no complete list or file of such orders available. The list of unnumbered series refers to where the orders were published or cited.

There is no general index to all proclamations.

Tables of Presidential Documents. See "Tables for the Federal Register System," at page 139.

D. Administrative Agency Rulings and Opinions.

Governmental agencies are called upon in particular cases to construe and apply

---

[14] New York, Books, Inc. Distributed by Archives Pub. Co., a division of Hastings House, 1944. 2 v.

[15] Newark, N. J., n.d.

the laws and regulations they administer, and commonly do so in a written order or decision of some kind. The whole machinery thus set in motion, in both federal and state agencies, rather closely parallels that of the law courts.

Scope of Administrative Agency Rulings. There is the widest variation in the scope and application of agency rulings. Such rulings, in any given agency may relate only to the internal affairs of the agency itself, or may regulate the relations of the government with private citizens, or of citizens with each other.

As to the former, a ruling may be an office opinion or memorandum, effective only as to matters of *internal agency procedure*, and with these the lawyer (and this book) are little concerned. Or the Solicitor, as chief law officer of an agency, may in informal opinions, lay down agency advisory interpretations for *outside application*. Similarly, the Attorney General, as the chief law officer of the federal or state government, is called upon by other departments for opinions in matters of law affecting them. These opinions, while advisory only, exert great influence in the administration of government affairs. Decisions and orders *effective outside the government* proper range from limited monopoly grants (patents, trade-marks, copyrights), through public utility rate making, to regulatory decisions under specific statutes.

Appendix L of the *Final Report* of the Attorney General's Committee on Administrative Procedure,[16] sets forth the "Form and Content of Intermediate Reports and Final Administrative Decisions."

Publication of Administrative Rulings. When printed in full, administrative decisions so closely resemble reported court decisions in form as to require little additional comment here. (For the role of precedent in these decisions, *see* the Notes, page 152. By no means all agencies, particularly state, publish their rulings, and the lawyer seeking them may be relegated to consultation of the records in the agency office itself. In such a case, he should ascertain whether the decision may properly be cited as authority. For example, many rulings of the United States Patent Office are unpublished "manuscript decisions," on file in the Office. But only those relating to trade-marks, and to patent applications which have matured, are open to the public and may be cited.

Rulings may appear in any or all of the following forms.

Press releases. These are ordinarily mimeographed and circulated to newspapers and others interested within a day or two of the decision. They commonly contain a brief statement of facts, followed by a paraphrase of the arguments of counsel, an abridgement of the opinion, and the decision. They are for information only. Most federal agencies maintain mailing lists for press releases.

Mimeographed reports of decisions. These reports, usually issued within a day or two of the decision date, give either long abridgments of the full opinion, or, more commonly, the complete decision and order, minus syllabus but with all footnotes. There is some serial designation by which they may be cited, which usually includes the volume number of the report series in which the reports will eventually appear, and a case number (since the page number is as yet undetermined). Thus, 97 N. L. R. B. No. 72. Mailing lists are maintained for these reports.

Printed slip decisions. Less common than other published forms are the individually printed opinions, decisions and orders. These (examples are those of the Attorney General of the United States and of the United States Maritime Commission) are usually in final complete form as found in the later-published bound cumulations. They include number, title or other case designation, headnote, opinion, order, *etc.*; except that though the volume number is supplied, the page number may be lacking. Citations of a ruling may thus be made from a slip decision by volume and page, or by volume and docket or other serial number, according to the information supplied.

Advance sheet pamphlets and bulletins. A more usual form of intermediate

---

[16] *See* note 1, above.

printed publication of administrative rulings is in periodical advance sheets or agency bulletins. These vary in content from agency to agency.

The *Decisions of the Comptroller General of the United States* appear in monthly advance sheets, which at the end of the year cumulate into a bound volume having the same pagination (and so may be cited from the advance sheet). Some, as the Department of Agriculture *Agriculture Decisions*, appear as advance sheets which include *both Department and court decisions*. Others publish not only agency rulings of various kinds, and court decisions, but also regulations promulgated by authority of statutes, applicable to agency business. Such is the bi-weekly *Internal Revenue Bulletin* (cumulating semi-annually), containing all decisions of the Treasury Department pertaining to internal revenue matters (including regulations), court decisions, opinions of the Chief Counsel of the Bureau, and Bureau rulings and decisions pertaining to taxes. In still others, this material, plus perhaps new rules of practice, dockets of impending hearings and the like, appears as a department in an agency-wide periodical. Occasionally, as in the *Official Gazette* of the United States Patent Office, this part is also extracted and published as a separate bulletin.

Bound volumes of agency rulings. The preliminary, unbound form of agency ruling is almost always superseded by a bound volume, duplicating in all essential features the bound volumes of court reports. (A checklist of federal agency reports appears in the Bibliographical Reference Manual in this book.) That is, it contains a table of cases reported (which in the Department of Justice *Administrative Decisions under Immigration and Nationality Laws* may be by initial only); occasionally a table of cases cited; the text of opinions and orders; and a digest of decisions printed in that volume.

Unofficial publication of agency rulings. In business and regulatory fields, the speediest printed publication of these rulings is often commercial, as in loose-leaf services and legal periodicals. This is particularly true in labor, taxation, patents, and public utilities. A common practice is to collect statutes, administrative regulations, court decisions, and agency rulings in one *loose-leaf service* as described in Chapter 26), according to an elaborate classification devised to bring together in one place all the law on a given topic. At the end of the year the agency and court adjudications in a special-subject law report series, as labor or tax cases and the like are extracted and published. Often these unofficial series print reports unavailable in officially printed form. Occasionally the only publication of any kind is unofficial, as the *Office of Price Administration Service* during World War II.[17]

Legal periodicals frequently publish federal or state (or both) court and agency adjudications. For state regulatory agencies these may be the best or even the only printed reports available. Examples are the *Public Utilities Fortnightly*, the *Journal of the Federal Communications Bar Association*, and *Taxes*. Some trade or professional associations publish bulletins containing this material, usually in abridged form. An example is the *Consumer Finance Law Bulletin*, of the National Consumer Finance Association.

Administrative Law Digests. The conventional digests of case material relating to administrative law correspond so exactly to those digests described in Chapter 19 that little further comment is called for here. *Court decisions involving administrative law* are of course digested under appropriate subject headings in conventional case digests covering these courts.

American Digest System. The title "Administrative Law and Procedure" first appeared in the *Fifth Decennial Digest*, and comprises digests of federal and state *court* decisions formerly classified under a variety of other heads. *No agency decisions are included.* Since perhaps not all material deemed by the searcher as classifiable under this title may in fact be digested here, the searcher would still do well to rely in part upon the "Descriptive-Word Index."

Agency special-subject digests. Most official and unofficial publication series of agency rulings (which for the most part print also *court* decisions on appeals from such rulings) have digests of some kind. Often it is only the index-digest found in each bound

---

[17] Prepared under the general direction of Ervin H. Pollack, Rochester, N. Y., Federal Regulation Publishers. 1944–47. 5 v.

volume, so that a coverage requires the examination of numerous single volumes. Some federal agencies cumulate this digest material at irregular intervals, and for the periods covered such digests are extremely useful. But the conventional officially-published digest suffers from the lack of a continuous and consistent publication policy to keep it up to date. Therefore, the most useful digests of official agency decisions are apt to be commercial ventures. Such are the Lust series for Interstate Commerce Commission Reports,[18] and the Lois G. Moore *Tax Court Digest*,[19] which are regularly supplemented and kept up to date.

More common are the digests which are part of unofficial editions of agency rulings. Examples are the cumulative digests of the *United States Patents Quarterly*, and the *Labor Relations Cumulative Digest and Index* of the unofficial Bureau of National Affairs. Of much wider scope in the aggregate, and of greater publication frequency, are the loose-leaf special-subject services.

A variant of the official digest is the digest of statutes and rules applicable to a particular agency, usually annotated to court and agency decisions interpreting them. Examples are the *Interstate Commerce Acts Annotated*,[20] and the *Digest of Customs and Related Laws and the Decisions Thereunder*.[21] Since these are arranged by statute section they serve the same citator function as any other annotated statute, but the careful lawyer will always bring them down to date through conventional citators. They are intended primarily for agency use, but for the period covered are useful also to practitioners.

Library holdings of digests. The catalog or other inventory record of each law library will tell whether there is a digest for a given report series.

Pike and Fischer Administrative Law Service.[22] The first series of this service started in 1941, as a " 'horizontal' analysis of principles common to the procedure of all administrative agencies." In other words, it was a service on administrative procedure, not on the substantive aspects of the law. It collected and analyzed both court and agency decisions, arranged according to an elaborate functional "guide." Now out of print, it has been superseded by a second edition, beginning with 1951 cases. This series is devoted to the collection and speedy dissemination of current cases, but *also digests cases printed in the first series*. It consists of three units:

Digest. All cases in the first series are digested, as well as later ones. The digest is supplemented by a fortnightly "Current Digest," cumulating into an annual cumulative pocket supplement. The detailed classification, quite different from that of the first edition, is based upon the Administrative Procedure Act. There are a "word index" and a table of cases.

Annual bound volumes of new cases. These collect reports of court and agency decisions on administrative procedure, beginning with 1951. Each volume has its own digest and case table.

"Current Material." This is a loose-leaf collection containing: (1) The Administrative Procedure Act; (2) House and Senate Committee reports for the Act; (3) Administrative agency rules of practice. This is the most convenient and up to date collection of such rules, and it suffices for most purposes, but, being confined to some twenty-one "major" agencies, lacks some which are printed in the *Federal Register*. It contains also: (4) Reports of new cases, with headnotes keyed to the digest classification; (5) "Current

---

18 *Consolidated Digest of Decisions under the Interstate Commerce Act (1887-1924)* Fowler, Ind., H. C. Lust Co., 1925. 2 v. and supplements to date.

19 Indianapolis, Ind., Bobbs-Merrill, 1951 to date.

20 Washington, D. C., U. S. Govt. Print. Off., 1930 to date.

21 Prepared by the Bureau of Customs. Washington, D. C., U. S. Govt. Print. Off., 1936. 3 v. and supplement to Dec. 1940.

22 [First Series] Albany, M. Bender, 1941-48. 5 v. Second Series. Albany, M. Bender, 1952 to date. "Decisions," "Digest" and "Current Material" in separate volumes.

Digest," for the current year; (6) Table of cases for the current year; and (7) "Release" or report letter, commenting briefly on outstanding new cases.

Citators for Agency Rulings. These are noted at page 270.

State Agency Rulings. See "D," "E," *supra.*

Notes

Importance of administrative agency rulings. In the aggregate, these decisions probably affect every citizen, often more so than those of courts. This is true because, although in proper case (as in matters of law), appeal from final administrative rulings lies to the courts, the expense and delay involved are often so great as to render appeal impracticable. Then the administrative agency decision becomes the final one. For example, in the fiscal year 1950, the National Labor Relations Board closed 20,640 cases, of which 2951 were appeals from subordinate examiners to the full Board; but only 101 cases during that year were decided by federal courts on appeal from the Board. In the same fiscal year, the Federal Trade Commission disposed of 1172 complaints, while there were only eleven federal court decisions on appeal from Commission orders. The annual reports of the agencies concerned usually analyze in considerable detail their legal activities and present a good picture of the enforcement functions of such agencies.

Role of Precedent in Agency Rulings. Although in most respects rulings of administrative bodies resemble those of courts, application of the doctrine of precedent differs somewhat from the practice of courts.

Whereas courts seek a system of rules universally applicable to given classes of causes and tend to hold themselves bound by their own prior decisions in like situations (the rule of stare decisis), administrative agencies, faced with an infinitude of slightly varying fact situations in their interpretation of the mandates of a given statute, *emphasize the achievement of justice in the actual cause* before them. Consequently, adherence to the rule is frequently specifically disavowed in agency opinions. The following policy statement by the Bureau of Internal Revenue, printed in each issue of the *Internal Revenue Bulletin,* expresses a typical attitude:

> . . . Each ruling embodies the administrative application of the law and Treasury Decisions to the entire state of facts upon which a particular case rests. It is especially to be noted that the same result will not necessarily be reached in another case unless all the material facts are identical with those of the reported case. . . . It may be observed that the rulings published from time to time may appear to reverse rulings previously published.

On the other hand, the role of precedent in administrative rulings is important, and constant reference to it may be found in the opinions of most agencies. (However, a few, as the Federal Trade Commission, do not cite their own prior rulings.) Agencies do seek some means of ensuring consistency in their rulings, but emphasize the distinction between a binding rule of decision of general application and a guiding principle which may or may not be useful in the resolution of problem involving a specific state of facts under a statute.

Appendix M of the *Final Report* of the Attorney General's Commission on Administrative Procedure [23] sets forth the "Reliance upon Precedents" in nineteen federal administrative agencies. The matter is discussed at length by William H. Pittman in *The Doctrine of Precedents and the I. C. C.;* [24] and *The Doctrine of Precedents and Public Service Commissions;* [25] and in K. C. Davis, *Administrative Law.*[26] Court and agency decisions in point are collected in Pike and Fischer, *Administrative Law.*[27]

---

[23] *See* footnote 1, above.

[24] 5 Geo. Wash. L. Rev. 543 (1937).

[25] 11 Mo. L. Rev. 31 (1946).

[26] *See* footnote 2, above.

[27] 2d series, Decisions volume. Albany, M. Bender, 1952 to date.

Machinery of Administrative Adjudication. For federal agencies the process is largely regulated by the Administrative Procedure Act, which is followed fairly closely under state procedure. The theory and practice of federal agencies are authoritatively treated in the *Final Report* of the Attorney General's Committee on Administrative Procedure, *supra, and its accompanying fourteen Monographs*.[28]

The immediate agency or division thereof issuing an administrative ruling may be a single officer, as the Attorney General, or a departmental solicitor, or a field law examiner; or it may be one of a hierarchy of quasi-judicial tribunals within a larger agency. For example, in the United States Patent Office, in the denial or grant of a patent or patent claim, appeal lies from a subordinate divisional examiner, to the primary examiner of the division, to the Board of Examiners in Chief (or, in proper case, to the Board of Interference Examiners or the Commissioner of Patents), thence to the Court of Customs and Patent Appeals, a court ranking as a federal Court of Appeal.

Procedure before such an agency ranges in formality from man-to-man discussion at an examiner's desk, up to hearings before a black robed tribunal, conducted with all the panoply of a court trial, except that a somewhat wider latitude is permitted here than under the rules of courts. Most agencies have their own strict rules of practice and many their own roster of attorneys or agents who alone may represent clients before them. The right of laymen to appear in a representative capacity before federal and state agencies and commissions is a constant bone of contention between them and lawyers. All but perhaps three federal agencies permit lay representation. In most of the few state cases involving lay representation which have reached the courts, the right has been denied, as constituting unlicensed practice of the law.

The topic, as to federal agencies, was discussed in detail, with a consideration of the earlier literature, by J. S. Waterman, *Federal Administrative Bars: Admissions and Disbarment*.[29] A later article by John W. Cragun, *Admission to Practice: Present Regulation by Federal Agencies*,[30] presents a detailed chart covering all principal agencies, with an extensive review of disbarment, suspension and grievance procedures. Being a lawyer is not of itself always sufficient qualification for admission to agency practice, as before the Patent Office, for example. The right to appear before governmental boards or commissions generally is treated extensively in annotations in 111 A. L. R. 32 (1937), 125 A. L. R. 1179 (1940), 151 A. L. R. 787 (1944), and in notes in 32 Iowa L. Rev. 543 (1947), 95 U. of Pa. L. Rev. 218 (1946), 35 Mich L. Rev. 442 (1937), 5 L. & Contemp. Prob. 89 (1938), and 52 Harv. L. Rev. 1185 (1939). There are several professional journals devoted to the problems of such practice, notably the *Journal of the Patent Office Society* and the *I. C. C. Practitioners' Journal*. And both the *George Washington Law Review* and the *Georgetown Law Journal*, published in the national capital, specialize in administrative law topics. On the state side, an article worth reading is George M. Morris, *Practical Aspects of Practice Before Administrative Agencies*.[31]

There are also numerous treatises. An especially practical work in small compass is *A Manual on Trial Technique in Administrative Proceedings and Illustrative Federal Administrative Agencies*.[32]

E. The State Aspect of Administrative Law.

Importance. The impact of administrative law upon the average citizen is perhaps greater in state than in federal relations. But, because it has been so all-pervasive for so long, the citizen is hardly conscious of its presence except when he pays his income tax. But the barber, the plumber, the teacher—all practitioners of the many trades or professions subject to licensing—the housewife who pays her gas and telephone bills (utility rates are administrative legislation), the man who

---

[28] Monographs have title: *Administrative Procedure in Government Agencies. Monograph[s]* Washington, D. C., U. S. Govt. Print. Off., 1941. Also published as Senate Document No. 10, 77th Cong., 1st Sess.

[29] 3 U. of Chi. L. Rev. 261 (1936).

[30] 34 A. B. A. J. 111 (1948).

[31] 15 Conn. B. J. 106 (1941).

[32] Prepared by the Junior Bar Section of the Bar Association of the District of Columbia, 1950.

drives an automobile, the theatre owner, the farmer selling milk or the packer shipping oranges, the laborer injured on the job or out of a job—all these and many more are affected in one way or another by rules, regulations, rate schedules, and decisions of state administrative agencies and commissions.

Although the problem of promulgating and publishing agency rules and decisions is much the same as in the federal government, it has been less satisfactorily handled. This is probably due to the editorial and publication expenses, which are so great that few states have been willing to assume them.

State Manuals. With two exceptions, each state has a publication fulfilling more or less the same functions as the *United States Government Organization Manual,* describing the governmental setup of the state, the courts, the legislature, and the administrative organization. Their relevance to the subject matter of this book is that they tell the lawyer what agency and which officials are responsible for regulatory matters of interest to his client.

State Administrative Rules and Regulations. Most state licensing or regulatory agencies and commissions publish the regulations governing licenses, and give them to the licensee with his license. Similarly, tax and equalization boards, workmen's compensation hearing officers, and the like are apt to print their regulations.

Efforts at systematic publication. Many states have attempted to systematize the filing and publication of their agency and commission rules of public general interest, so that persons affected may know what they are. Inspired by the example of the Federal Register Act of 1936, these states have attempted by enabling legislation to provide for the filing and publication of their rules. (The best account of this is *State Administrative Rules,* by Carroll C. Moreland, in the biennial issues of the *Book of the States.*)

Central filing and publication legislation. A weakness of the early legislation was its absence of provision for central control. In 1937, South Carolina provided for filing (with the Secretary of State) and publication (with the session laws of each regular session) of all regulations of public general interest. Since then many other states have adopted measures of similar intent, though of varying form. Central filing and some means of publication are universal provisions. Some rules form appendices to annual reports, others are incorporated with the administrative codes. To date, the most comprehensive program of publication, on a par with that of the Federal Register System, is that of the California *Administrative Code,*[33] a loose-leaf project paralleling the titles of the California *Codes.*

Unfortunately, the enactment of enabling legislation has not always meant carrying out its purposes, and the publication of state rules has had a checkered career. Some states which started in blithely have found it too expensive, and have simply ignored or repealed their legislation.

State codes of administrative procedure. A parallel activity has been the enactment of state codes of administrative procedure, and the National Conference of Commissioners of Uniform Laws in 1946 adopted a Model Act, which has been enacted, with modifications, by several states. The aim of this act is to provide for the drafting and publishing of agency rules, and for equitable hearing and appeal procedures.

State Administrative Agency Opinions and Decisions. State agency decisions follow the pattern of the federal, but official publication of them is somewhat rare, except in the two categories below.

Attorney Generals' Opinions. The attorney general, as the chief law officer of the

---

[33] Sacramento, Distributed by Bureau of Printing (Documents Division), 1945 to date. 23 Titles in 7 loose leaf binders.

state, is asked by other state officials for opinions on questions of law confronting them. Every state publishes these opinions—which, though advisory only, have considerable weight—in bound form, and in some states there is a preliminary pamphlet publication as well. A variant is the "informal" opinion, roughly paralleling the memorandum decision of the courts. Some large cities publish the opinions of their city attorneys. The opinions usually follow closely the form and technique of the judicial opinion; and when they comment on cases or statutes they are noted in some of the state *Shepard's Citations*, as *citing cases*. They are similarly noted in the annotated statutes of some states. A checklist of these published opinions, by L. W. Morse, was published in 30 Law Library Journal 39 (1937). The Council of State Governments has published since March, 1937, a weekly *Digest of Opinions of Attorneys General*, with semi-annual indexes. Opinions published are selected and digests are arranged by subject.

There is a National Association of Attorneys General, the annual Proceedings of which are published.

Public Utility Commission decisions. Every state has its public service, public utility, commerce commission, or the like. These approve or initiate rate schedules, grant certificates of convenience and necessity, and issue order to effectuate their decisions. The opinions and orders follow closely the form of judicial opinions, and are published, usually in conjunction with the routine periodic reports of the respective commissions. Two series of special-subject reports, the *Public Utilities Reports*, and *Public Utilities Reports (New Series)* [34] have published court and agency decisions. The accompanying *Annual Digest* performs the usual function of such a tool. It contains also a "List of Appeals, Rehearings, and Modifications" relating to prior rulings.

Miscellaneous commission decisions. Except for the two categories above, there is little official publication of state commission decisions. Probably the most frequently published are those of workmen's compensation or unemployment commissions, and labor relations boards. In a few states these are printed, resembling law reports, but most states which publish them at all mimeograph them. Other agencies sometimes publishing their decisions are those relating to veterans' affairs, rent control, *etc*. New York has for many years printed a series called *Department Reports*, including decisions of its Education, Conservation, Labor, Taxation and Finance Departments, and the State Tax Commission.

Loose-Leaf Services. The most convenient, expeditious and complete collection of state administrative rules and decisions on any given subject is usually in loose-leaf services. As in all such services, these are a "package" cumulation of statutes, orders, decisions, and commentary on the subject matter of the individual service, such as labor, insurance, taxation, public utilities, or other subject of interest to business men across state lines. *See* Chapter 26.

Checking on Publication of State Administrative Material. Through the *Monthly Checklist of State Publications*, of the Library of Congress, this should take no more than half an hour per month. This list carefully notes the inclusion in any publication of regulations or decisions.

---

[34] Rochester, N. Y., Lawyers Co-operative Pub. Co., 1915-33. 101 v. New Series, Washington, D. C., Rochester, N. Y., Public Utilities Reports. In 94 v., from 1934 to date. Kept current in Public Utilities Fortnightly.

CHAPTER 18

INDEX AND SEARCH BOOKS

A. Purpose.

Up to this point this *Manual* has described and discussed the source materials of Anglo-American law. As incidental thereto it has also described those aids to the use of this material which are integral parts of the official and unofficial volumes of statutes and reports as published. These auxiliary tools — such as indexes, tables, and annotations—are for the most part sufficient guides to the use of statutes, except that citation books, as described in Chapter 28, are necessary in order to keep abreast of subsequent legislative and judicial treatment of a given statute. They are quite inadequate, however, as indexes to the great mass of decided cases which form the basis of our common law jurisprudence or which construe statutes. To be sure, it is conceivable that, by search through the indexes in each volume of the many thousands of law reports, the state of the law on a particular point could be determined. But as a practical matter it would be impossible by individual effort to keep up with even the thirty thousand or so new opinions published each year, to say nothing of extracting with any certainty the rules of law from the backlog of nearly 3,000,000 reported cases.

B. Kinds of Indexes and Search Books.

This situation calls for cooperative effort, and it has been supplied by law publishers to such a degree that legal literature is the best indexed of all professional or scientific literature. Several distinct categories of indexes and guides have been developed, partly mechanical but all requiring the most expert technical and editorial skill, to enable the lawyer to practice his profession. These include case digests, treatises, encyclopedias, annotations, restatements, legal periodicals, dictionaries, form books, loose-leaf services, and citation books. They are generically known as books of index and search books. They do not relieve the lawyer of the necessity of finding, appraising and applying authority—the statutes and decisions of competent jurisdiction—but they lead him to it.

C. Authority of Index and Search Books.

These books are not themselves authority of any kind, a fact which should never be overlooked. To be sure, certain of them, such as treatises, encyclopedias, and legal periodicals, are cited both by judges and advocates because of the excellence and completeness of their analysis. Accordingly, they have a definite formative influence on the law. They are, however, in no sense mandatory, in that a court is bound by any statement of the law in them. They are only persuasive, and when they are cited it is because the citer approves and adopts them as a convenient analysis and statement of that which is authority—the cases and statutes upon which they are based. Accordingly, when a judge in his opinion says that a certain rule of law is as stated in *American Jurisprudence, Corpus Juris Secundum, Wigmore,* or a *Columbia Law Review* article by Chaffee (as is very frequently done), he is not citing them as authority which he or any future judge is bound to obey. He is merely saying that the authors cited have read and analyzed the cases and statutes carefully and have written down a statement of the law extracted from them which he, the judge, believes to be a proper interpretation of this authority. Much less is the statement of a rule of law in a digest to be accepted as applicable to any given situation, without careful study of the case digested. None of these index and search books is an end in itself, but only a means to an end. As such, they are indispensable.[1]

---

[1] A critical analysis of this topic is by W. M. Lile, *The Uses and Abuses of Secondary Authority,* 1 Va. L. Rev. 604 (1913).

Chapter 19

DIGESTS

A. Function of Digests.
B. The Distinguishing Feature of Digests.
C. Authority of Digests.
D. Scope of Digests.
E. The American Digest System.
F. Techniques of Use of the American Digest System.
G. Digests of Less Scope than the American Digest System.
H. Coordinating the Digest with Other Case Finders.

A. The Function of Digests.

A digest is a subject index to the rules of law raised or discussed in the reported cases. It is arranged according to familiar legal principles and with cognizance of statutes and fact situations. As such, it is the most important and necessary single tool of the lawyer for getting at the law as stated in judicial opinions. The statements of rules (called digest paragraphs) are commonly those set forth in the individual headnote paragraphs to reported cases. In the American Digest System, described below, they are, for cases reported in the National Reporter System, the actual Key-Numbered headnote paragraphs taken from the various *Reporters*, with added citator material. The example below is from the *Fifth Decennial Digest.*

Wis. The state court had jurisdiction to proceed to confirm foreclosure sale and execute judgment of forcelosure even though farm debtor's petition under Frasier-Lemke Act was pending, where there was no stay of proceedings granted, since the stay of proceedings provided by the Frasier-Lemke Act is a "judicial stay" not a "statutory stay" and requires application to state or federal court in which foreclosure proceedings are pending for a stay. Bankr.Act § 75(n), as amended, 11 U.S.C.A. § 203(n).—Kalb v. Luce, 279 N.W. 685, 228 Wis. 519, rehearing denied 280 N.W. 725, 228 Wis. 519, appeal dismissed 59 S.Ct. 107, 305 U.S. 566, 83 L.Ed. 356, followed in 285 N.W. 431, 231 Wis. 186, reversed 60 S.Ct. 343, 308 U.S. 433, 84 L.Ed. 370, mandate conformed to 291 N.W. 481, 234 Wis. 509.

Exhibit 36

The many millions of these headnote paragraphs, taken from reported cases published in chronological, not classified order, are arranged to form the digest, under an elaborate classification by subject which brings like cases together. Although the classification schemes vary somewhat, they are so similar to that of the American Digest System in organization and effect that no further description of them is needed here.

B. The Distinguishing Feature of Digests.

As compared with treaties and encyclopedias, the digest is distinguished by its literary form, or, rather, the lack of it. The digest is a collection of separate paragraphs, each of which is related to its fellows only because they belong in the same subject class. There is no editorial comment on the case, no synthesis of rules from a group of cases, no statement as to jurisdictional rules, historical developments, majority and minority views, *etc.* Each rule is there on its own. It leaves to the reader the task of determining its place within the hierarchy of decisions on the point, and its applicability to his own specific problem. Presupposing possession on his part of all the skills and techniques necessary for its proper use, that is why the digest is peculiarly the lawyer's tool.

Even for the lawyer the digest may be a dangerous tool, however, if he is not constantly on the alert to the law's changes, both by decision and by statute. For example, common-law marriages contracted in New York after 1933 no longer have any legal validity there, but no comment in the digests calls attention to that fact, as do treatises on marriage in New York. Nevertheless, the earlier New York cases on the point are left in the digest, though their authority as to fact situations since 1933 is for most purposes *nil.*

C. Authority of Digests.

The digest emphatically is not authority, but only a guide to it. There is no presumption that the rule of law as stated in a digest paragraph is the rule of the case.

In the first place, *no editor can compress in one sentence the rule of a case,* including the fact situation, how the case arose, relevant statutes, and the like. The statement as made may seem to be "on all fours" with the searcher's own case, but upon a careful reading of the entire opinion and statement of facts, other factors may appear, rendering it useless for his purposes. Secondly, *no digest confines its statements to square holdings.* Cases supplying as many as forty different digest paragraph statements of rules of law are common, making it obvious that practically every statement as to the law made by the court, whether by way of ratio decidendi or obiter dictum, is taken from the opinion. Since there is no indication in the digest as to which is which, and no attempt to assess the value of any statement as precedent, it follows that the lawyer must read, or at least examine, each case cited in the digest, for its pertinence to him. In practice, the great majority of cases taken from the digest will be discarded as unsuitable, but the remaining few may be sufficiently in point to justify their inclusion in a brief. It is not uncommon, when no case directly in point is found, to cite a case for its dicta, but it should be done with full awareness. Thirdly, human *errors inevitably occur* (though fortunately they are few), causing the digest to state the reverse of the true rule of a case. This is particularly true of technical rules, as in patents, with the practical application of which the digester may be unfamiliar.

D. Scope of Digests.

Digests vary greatly in scope. The American Digest System, said to cover all printed opinion in all American jurisdictions, from 1658 to date, is the most comprehensive. Others cover the various units of the National Reporter System, separate states, or individual courts, as the Supreme Court of the United States, or single topics, as patents.

Notes

Digests are necessary because law reports, the basis of our common law and the interpreters of statutes, are published in chronological rather than subject order. At a rough estimate, there are printed reports extant of some three million decisions of American courts, with new ones issued at the rate of nearly thirty thousand a year. Nevertheless, under the Anglo-American system of jurisprudence, a major portion of our law must be extracted promptly and accurately from this great mass, dating back to 1658 in this country and much further in England. The lawyer must be enabled to assess the legal effect of a given set of facts and predict with some degree of assurance the probable decision of a judicial tribunal thereon; and the court, in order that its adjudications may be consistent with settled law, must have ready access to the guideposts provided by earlier decisions in point. The answer to the needs of practitioner and court alike is the digest, which extracts the rules of law from each case, and speedily and systematically arranges them in usable fashion.

E. The American Digest System.[1]

The most comprehensive of all American digests is the group with this title. Since, except in scope and for its copyrighted Key-Number system (which in purpose and effect is emulated by various other classification symbols in other digests), these digests are the prototypes of nearly all American digests, they are here described in detail, as examples of digests generally.

Scope of the American Digest System. In its various units these digests are said by the publisher to cover all standard law reports from appellate courts rendering written opinions, from 1658 to date, as well as those from certain courts of first instance, as federal district and some state courts.

Units of the American Digest System. The front part of each *General Digest* volume contains the table shown at the top of page 161.

The *Century Edition* (covering the years 1658-1896) does not have the Key-Number classification, but all other units do. The *Decennials*, as the table and their names show, are cumulated every ten years, the *Digest* year being a fiscal year corresponding to court terms. The *Decennials* are supplemented by monthly pamphlets of the *General Digest*, which cumulate about every four months into bound volumes which in turn are superseded at the end of ten years by the next *Decennial*. The digests in each advance sheet of the various *Reporters* supplement the latest *General Digest* pamphlet, so that a complete search carries through the Century, *Decennials*, *General* (bound and unbound), and *Reporter* advance sheets.

Table showing reports digested in each unit. Tables appear in the front of each digest volume, beginning with the *Third Decennial*, giving the inclusive volumes and pages of each *Reporter* digested therein. Thus, it shows that the

---

[1] This system and its use are ably described in a pamphlet distributed gratis by its publishers, the West Publishing Company, St. Paul, Minnesota. While that description is much fuller than space permits in this chapter, the authors of this *Manual* believe it advisable to single out some aspects of the American Digest System for comment here, because their experience with both lawyers and students has shown that additional emphasis on these points is needed for complete comprehension.

TABLE
SHOWING PERIOD OF TIME

COVERED BY EACH UNIT OF THE

AMERICAN DIGEST SYSTEM

TOGETHER WITH

VOLUMES OF DIGEST WHERE TABLES OF CASES WILL BE FOUND

YEARS	DIGEST UNIT	TABLE OF CASES WHERE FOUND
1658–1896	Century	First Decennial, vols. 21–25
1897–1906	First Decennial	First Decennial, vols. 21–25
1907–1916	Second Decennial	Second Decennial, vol. 24
1916–1926	Third Decennial	Third Decennial, vol. 29
1926–1936	Fourth Decennial	Fourth Decennial, vol. 34
1936–1946	Fifth Decennial	Fifth Decennial, vols. 48–49
1946–to date	General Digest, Second Series	General Digest, vol. 1–to date

Exhibit 37

Fifth Decennial Digest covers the *Atlantic Reporter* from 181 Atl. 545 to 45 A.2d 927; volume 17 of the *General Digest*, 2d Series, covers 12 *Federal Supplement*, pages 38 to 267. The *Decennial* Digest tables also list all other "current standard reports" digested, but without inclusive volumes and pages.

Classification Scheme. An elaborate arrangement by which all *rules of law announced* in cases digested are placed according to subject, is based upon the division of the law into that of persons, property, contracts, torts, crimes, remedies, and government. These seven great divisions are expanded into some 422 chapters or main topic headings, as "Abandonment," "Chattel Mortgages," "Landlord and Tenant," and the like. They correspond to the lawyers' conventional conception of the divisions of the law as taught him in law school. (The number increases gradually from *Decennial* to *Decennial*, as new topics are added and old ones are split.) A *list of these main topics* is printed in the front of every volume, beginning with the *Fourth Decennial*. These main topics are arranged *alphabetically* in the digests, not grouped by subject relationships. In spite of the extreme detail of the *Digest* coverage, there are some blind spots. For example, there is no topic or sub-topic for conflict of laws, though cases involving it, as scattered through various main topics, may be found through "Conflict of Laws" in the *Descriptive-Word Indexes*.

Scope Note and Analysis. Each main topic has a "Scope Note" and "Analysis," as shown in the specimen page copied on page 162.

The Scope Note is necessitated by the overlapping of subjects, many of which, upon cursory analysis, might seem to belong as well in one topic as another; the

1–5th D—1415

AGRICULTURE.

Scope-Note.

INCLUDES promotion and regulation of agricultural pursuits in general; public aid and protection to those engaged therein; agricultural societies; agricultural liens; and other incidental rights and remedies.

Matters not in this topic, treated elsewhere. see Descriptive-Word Index.

Analysis.

1. Constitutional and statutory provisions.
2. Agricultural boards and officers.
3. Public aid.
4. Agricultural societies.
     (1). In general.
     (2). Nature and powers.
     (3). Liabilities.
5. Agricultural exhibitions and fairs.
6. Co-operative corporations or associations.
7. Fertilizers.
8. Weeds and other noxious plants.
9. Destructive insects, birds, and other animals, and diseases of plants.
10. Agricultural liens.
11. —— Right to lien.
12. —— Proceedings to perfect.
13. —— Operation and effect.
14. —— Waiver, discharge, release, and satisfaction.
15. —— Enforcement.
16. Illegal traffic in agricultural products.

---

1. Constitutional and statutory provisions.

a. In general—p. 1415
b. What constitutes agriculture—p. 1415
c. Validity of statutes in general—p. 1416
d. Due process and equal protection.
e. Delegation of power—p. 1420
f. Repeal of statutes—p. 1421
g. Retroactivity of statutes—p. 1422.
h. Purpose of statutes—p. 1422
i. Construction of statutes in general—p. 1423
j. Quantity and price; parity payments— p. 1424
k. Actions and proceedings—p. 1425

---

a. *In general.*

C.C.A.Or. 1938. It is within the police power of Congress in its area of regulation of interstate commerce to remove or ameliorate economic evils in the walnut industry. Agricultural Adjustment Act §§ 1, 8c, subd. (15), 7 U.S.C.A. §§ 601, 608c, subd. (15); U.S. C.A.Const. Amend. 5.—Wallace v. Hudson-Duncan & Co., 98 F.2d 985.

C.C.A.Tenn. 1944. The Agricultural Adjustment Act is an exercise of the power of Congress to regulate commerce. Agricultural Adjustment Act of 1938, § 1 et seq., 7 U.S.C.A. § 1281 et seq.—Rodgers v. U. S., 138 F.2d 992.

Ala. 1945. Legislative power to regulate and to establish markets for agricultural products is within police power of the state. —In re Opinion of the Justices, 22 So.2d 521, 247 Ala. 66.

Ark. 1942. Since broad use may be made of the state's police power, if the treatment of rice by grower, miller, seller, or others dealing with it creates a hazard against which there should be protection, then any agency through which the rice passes may be subjected to regulation and a tax laid for the reasonable cost.—Stuttgart Rice Mill Co. v. Crandall, 157 S.W.2d 205, 203 Ark. 281.

b. *What constitutes agriculture.*

Colo. 1938. As respects use of the word "agriculture" in a statute, "agriculture," in its common and appropriate sense, is used to signify that species of cultivation which is in-

Exhibit 38

note sets forth the content of each topic. It serves as an eliminator of potential search topics. For example, if the searcher were interested in damage to crops, the relation of a farmer to his employees, or reorganization of agricultural corporations, the above scope note would save his time, by at once eliminating the topic "agriculture" from his consideration. The Analysis splits a topic into workable concepts, by which one skilled in the law is enabled speedily to arrive at the proper Key-Number. The main analysis is usually subjected to a further breakdown into sub-analyses. For example, Key-Number Agriculture ☞ 1, as shown, is broken into eleven subdivisions for easier handling. "Agriculture" is a small digest topic, but the principle is the same as in the large ones (where "Internal Revenue's" thirty-point analysis, for example, is further subdivided into 2484 separate Key-Number divisions, the whole analysis occupying forty pages). It is this analysis which forms the basis of the analytical approach to the case law.

Use of the analysis in other digests. Since the *Reporter* syllabi are all Key-Numbered under this same analysis, the actual compilation of the *Digest* is largely mechanical, once the *Reporter* editor has written and classified the various headnote paragraphs. It is a matter of filing from then on, applicable alike to all Key-Number digests, and requiring only the selection of the identical classified digest paragraphs on a jurisdictional basis for the various digests. Thus, the headnote number of the case in 37 Atl. 335 (1944), bears the Key-Number "Municipal Corporation ☞ 513(3)." Under that number this headnote has been used in the following digests: *Atlantic Reporter* advance sheets and bound volume, when the case was reported there; *General Digest; Fifth Decennial Digest; Atlantic Reporter Digest;* and West's *Maryland Digest.* Each of these digests is as a whole substantially uniform with the others as to all significant features, though the state digests often contain additional material of local interest.

Digest Paragraphs. Following the Analysis, the digest paragraphs are arranged by Key-Number classification, and under that by jurisdiction and date. United States Supreme Court cases, if any, come first; then come Courts of Appeals cases, followed by district court cases, alphabetically by state district; then the state cases, alphabetically by state. These digest paragraphs differ from the syllabi of the *Reporter* cases from which they are taken only in that they often contain additional citator information not available when the case was first printed. That is, if the case digested has been the subject of later court treatment on rehearing or appeal, before the publication of the digest in which it is digested, that fact is noted, with citation to later cases. An example is shown at page 158.

Auxiliary Tables and Indexes. Every digest unit is equipped with additional tables and indexes, necessary as aids to finding the rules of law in the digest paragraphs composing it. American Digest System tables, typical of them all, are described below.

Tables of cases. Each *Decennial* unit has a Plaintiff-Defendant case table, giving the information shown in the example below.

> **Schmidt v. Wolf Contracting Co** 269
> AD 201, 55 NYS2d 162, foll Van
> Gorder v. Binghamton State Hospital 269 AD 798, 55 NYS2d 847,
> Marovoski v. Socony-Vacuum Oil
> Co 269 AD 798, 55 NYS2d 847 and
> Knobb v. Leon Neon Service Corp
> 269 AD 798, 55 NYS2d 848, appeal
> den 269 AD 870, 57 NYS2d 261, and
> 294 NY 973, 63 NE2d 709, aff 295
> NY 748, 65 NE2d 568—Const Law
> 70(3), 113, 117, 154(1), 253, 301;
> Statut 181(1, 2), 183, 184, 188, 189,
> 215, 217; Work Comp 2, 6, 9, 10,
> 11, 15, 16, 34, 51, 73.

Exhibit 39

It will be noted that the table not only gives parallel citations to the respective series reporting the case, but also serves as a citator to the extent noted below.

TABLE OF CASES DIGESTED

ABBREVIATIONS

aff...............affirmed	mod............modified
am...............amended	overr............overruled
cert.............certiorari	rearg............reargument
den.............denied	reh.............rehearing
dism.............dismissed	rev.............reversed
foll.............followed	sugg error sus...suggestion of error sustained
gr...............granted	transf..........transferred
	vac............vacated

References are to Digest Topics and Key Numbers

M

Maahs v. Maahs 307 Mich 549, 12 N W2d 335—Bills & N 527(1); Joint Ten 3.
Maas v. Dermody 257 AD 898, 12 NYS 2d 408, aff 285 NY 828, 35 NE2d 500—Towns 70.
Maas v. Harvey, LaApp, 4 So2d 21 aff 200 La 736, 8 So2d 683—Autos 193(10); Insurance 435.4, 435.14.

Maass v. Higgins, NY, 61 SCt 631, 312 US 443, 85 LEd 940, 132 ALR 1035—Int Rev 158, 1016.
Maass v. Sefcik, TexCivApp, 138 SW 2d 897—App & E 1050(1), 1060(1), 1175(1); Chat Mtg 230; Libel 7 (2), 33, 114, 118, 129.
Mabardy v. Railway Exp Agency, D CMass, 26 FSupp 25—Fed Civ Proc

Mabry v. Hartford Ins Co 26 Tenn App 463, 173 SW2d 169—Insurance 335(3), 665(4).
Mabry v. Knabb 151 Fla 432, 10 So 2d 330—Atty & C 24, 189, 190(1, 4); Compromise 15(1), 23(1, 3); Equity 394; Judgm 720; Land & Ten 137; Tax 531(2), 708(1, 7).
Mabry v. Mabry 65 GaApp 132, 15

Exhibit 40

All the actions noted under "Abbreviations," above, concern court actions directly connected with the precise case listed, and do not include comment on that case in opinions involving a different case. For example, "overruled" here does not mean that a designated case was overruled by a later decision (as *Haddock* v. *Haddock* by *Williams* v. *North Carolina*), but that a motion in that exact case was overruled by the court.

Case tables, but without the citator information, are found in the respective units of the supplementing *General Digest* and in the *Reporter* advance sheets. Combined, these tables form by far the most complete of all American case tables. A separate "Table of Cases Affirmed, Reversed, Etc . . ." by cases digested in the *General Digest* is printed for every ten volumes of that digest (about every three years) in the supplemental *Descriptive-Word Index* for these volumes, and in separate blue pamphlets for every succeeding bound volume, of which there are three a year.

The same case name may be listed several times in a table of cases, each appearance representing a different stage of its progress through the courts. In such a listing, the case on appeal to the Supreme Court of the United States is listed first, even though decided later than the state court actions. Thus, *Kalb* v. *Luce*, a Wisconsin case, is listed six times in the table of cases in the *Fifth Decennial*, because of a variety of appeals and rehearings, culminating in an appeal to the United States Supreme Court, which issued an order to the Wisconsin court to conform its final order to an earlier decision. Care must be taken, therefore, in searching the table of cases, to ascertain the final disposition of the case being searched.

Kalb v. Feuerstein 234 Wis 507, 291 NW 840—Bankr 213; Mtg 529(10).
Kalb v. Luce, Wis, 60 SCt 343, 308 US 433, 84 LEd 370, conformed to 234 Wis 509, 291 NW 841—Bankr 1, 20(1), 213; Const Law 70(3); Courts 97(5), 359; Judgm 470; States 4.
Kalb v. Luce 228 Wis 519, 279 NW 685, reh den 228 Wis 519, 280 NW 725, appeal dism 59 SCt 107, 305 US 566, 83 LEd 356, foll 231 Wis 186, 285 NW 431, rev 60 SCt 343, 308 US 433, 84 LEd 370, conformed to 234 Wis 509, 291 NW 841—Assault 10; Bankr 213; Courts 97 (5).
Kalb v. Luce 228 Wis 519, 280 NW 725—Bankr 213, 217.

Kalb v. Luce 231 Wis 186, 285 NW 431, foll'g 228 Wis 519, 279 NW 685, reh den 228 Wis 519, 280 NW 725, appeal dism 59 SCt 107, 305 US 566, 83 LEd 356, rev 60 SCt 343, 308 US 433, 84 LEd 370, conformed to 234 Wis 509, 291 NW 841.
Kalb v. Luce 234 Wis 509, 291 NW 841—Action 50(6); Consp 18; Judges 36; Plead 34(1); Princ & A 159(1); Sheriffs 98(1), 137(1).
Kalb v. Luce 239 Wis 256, 1 NW2d 176—App & E 544(1), 901, 1031(1), 1032(1), 1043(8); Consp 8, 18, 20; Venue 42, 50, 78.
Kalb v. State 195 Ga 544, 25 SE2d 24 —Crim Law 407(2), 762(1), 778 (11), 781(7), 784(7), 825(1), 1036 (1), 1129(3), 1172(9); Homic 204, 215(2), 216, 250, 289; Witn 246(2).

Exhibit 41

Special case tables for new Digest topics. Special case tables are compiled for certain new titles of the *Digest* that are made up of cases taken from other topics in earlier *Digest* units. An example is "Workmen's Compensation," first appearing in the *Fourth Decennial*, and comprising for the most part earlier cases taken from the topic "Master and Servant" in all units. All cases digested under this new topic were listed in a separate table accompanying the "Workmen's Compensation" title. How this operates is described below, under "Key-Number change through new or expanded classification topic."

Popular name case tables. Beginning with the table of cases volume of the *Second Decennial Digest*, each table of cases volume has a table of cases often known or cited by popular name, as the "Apex Case," "Danbury Hatters' Case," "Hot Oil Case," and the like. These tables give the same information as do the other case tables described above.

Parallel transfer tables from Century to Decennial or reverse. Since the topic and section numbers in the *Century Digest* (1658-1896) are not identical with the Key-Numbers of the *Decennial Digests*, means are provided for converting one classification number into the other, to ensure finding cases on the same point of law in both digests. Pink-paged "Tables of Key-Number Section for Century Digest" are found in the tables of cases of the *First* and *Second Decennials* only, citing in parallel from the *Century* topic and section number to the corresponding *Decennial* Key-Number. Thus:

CENTURY DIGEST SECTIONS WITH CORRESPONDING KEY-NUMBERS													A 51
CONTRIBUTION													
Dec. & Cent. Key No.		Dec. & Cent. Key No.		Dec. & Cent. Key No.		Dec. & Cent. Key No.		Dec. & Cent. Key No.		Dec. & Cent. Key No.		Dec. & Cent. Key No.	
Sec.	Sec.	Sec.	Sec.	Sec.	Sec.	Sec.	Sec.	Sec.	Sec.	Sec.	Sec.	Sec.	Sec.
1	1	5	3	9	5	13	7	17	9(3)	18	9(2)	21	9(6)
2	3	6	5	10	6	14	9(1)		Lim. of	19	9(4)	22	9(8)
3	4	7	5	11	6	15	8		Act.	20	9(5)		
4	4	8	5	12	6	16	Eq. 44		49(1-8)				

Exhibit 42

"Contribution 20" of the *Century* is seen to be equivalent to "Contribution ⌖ 9(5)" of the *Decennial*. Conversely, if the Key-Number is known and it is desired to find the equivalent *Century* topic and section number, this may be found through "See" references beneath the black-letter Key-Number in the *First* and *Second Decennials* only. (The *Second Decennial* is far superior to the *First* in this respect.) See Exhibit 43.

If the case to be pursued into the *Century Digest* is found in the *Third* or later *Decennials*, the search involves simply the additional step of checking *the same Key-Number in the Second Decennial*, which will give the required *Century* topic and section number, as above. It is thus a simple mechanical matter, once a case in point is found, to find its classification number in both the *Century, Decennial*, and *General Digests*, where all other cases in point, from 1658 to date, are filed.

Key-Number change through new or expanded classification of topics. The procedure just described will not work when an entirely new digest topic has been formed out of an old one, or where an old one has been greatly expanded. An example of the former is "Workmen's Compensation," formed in the *Fourth Decennial* from cases previously digested under the last few sections of "Master and Servant." All pertinent cases from the earliest date through part of 1936 were combined in this one title, in a single volume. The expansion in the *Fifth Decennial* of "Internal Revenue" from 48 to 2484 Key-Numbers is an example of the latter; all tax cases previously classified under the earlier scheme, were reclassified and printed in a single volume under the new classification. In these topics it is therefore necessary to translate the old Key-Number to the new, or the reverse, in order to search all digest units.

For some of the new topics (as distinguished from old ones expanded), special tables of cases have been provided in the volumes covering them. These case tables embrace all case names from the earlier digest topics now included in the new. An example is "Workmen's Compensation," above mentioned. It works in this way: The searcher has found an Oregon case exactly in point, *King v. Union Oil Co. of California*, 144 Ore. 655, 24 P. 2d 345 (1933), digested in the *Third Decennial* under "Master and Servant ⌖ 354," but he wants later cases in point in this and other jurisdictions. So he goes to the *Fourth Decennial Digest*, following the normal procedure, where, however, he fails to find any section ⌖ 354 under "Master and Servant." He is referred there to "Workmen's Compensation," where, in the special table of cases bound with this topic, in the *Fourth Decennial*, a search under "King" leads to the Key-Number "Workmen's Compensation ⌖ 2180," where he finds the *King* case and other cases in point. Similarly, special case tables are provided for "Administrative Law," "Declaratory Judgments," and "Labor Relations." Some new topics for which there are no special case tables in the *Decennials* do have them in the *Federal* Digest, among them "Federal Civil Procedure."

Some such topics, especially old ones which have been greatly expanded, lack these special case tables, or any other mechanical means for noting parallel Key-Numbers. One of these, "Internal Revenue," which was greatly expanded after the adoption in 1938 of the *Internal Revenue Code*, is covered by the general table of cases for the *Federal Digest*, because that table was compiled in 1940 after the expanded classification was adopted. Topics lacking the table of cases approach, however, must be worked analytically or through the *Descriptive-Word Index*. If one wonders why parallel tables of old and new Key-Numbers are not provided, it should be remembered that when forty-eight numbers are expanded to 2484, there really are no parallels, and that such a table would be confusing.

```
21. Operation and effect.
See 11 Cent. Dig. Conversion, §§ 56-65.
Effect on right to maintain partition, see Parti-
tion, 21.
```

Exhibit 43

Key-Number tables in the General Digest. This is a table, cumulated in the bound volumes of the *General Digest Descriptive-Word Index* and supplemented by a pamphlet "Cumulative Table of Key Numbers," at irregular intervals. It is designed to avoid searching through an interim volume for cases for which there are no digests therein. A specimen is shown below.

For example, the above table shows that, if the searcher were interested in Abatement and Revival 56, he would need to examine only two of the first ten volumes of the *General Digest*.

TABLE OF KEY NUMBERS

GENERAL DIGEST, VOLUMES 1–10 2d

A Time Saver For Locating The Latest Cases

Example: Having found a proposition of law under the topic Abandonment 4 refer to the same topic and Key in table which will show that other cases appear in the General Digest, Second Series 5, 7, 8 and 9. Search is therefore unnecessary in Volumes 1, 2, 3, 4, 6, and 10, of the General Digest, Second Series.

ABANDONMENT	ABATEMENT AND RE-VIVAL—Cont'd	ABSENTEES	ACCOUNT—Cont'd
2—1, 2, 3, 5, 7, 8, 9, 10	56—5, 10	2—9	6—4, 5, 6, 7, 9, 10
3—3, 5, 7, 8, 10	57—4, 6, 7, 9	3—7	7—6, 9
4—5, 7, 8, 9	58—1, 4, 5, 6, 9, 10	4—4	8—4, 5
5—3, 4, 5, 6, 7, 8, 9	58(1)—5, 7	5—1, 2, 4, 8, 9	9—7
6—1, 4, 9	58(2)—9	6—4, 5	11—1
7—9		7—2, 4, 9	12—1, 3, 4, 6, 8, 10

Exhibit 44

Descriptive-Word Index. This is an enormous table, aimed at finding the least common denominator of a given fact situation to lead to the desired Key-Number, when the analytical method is difficult to apply. In it, each of the 422 main topics of the *Digest* (as "Damages," and "Landlord and Tenant") is broken down into an alphabetical arrangement of sub-topics listing facts involved in cases digested. In addition, there are catch words, as "Demotion," "Conductors," "Dizziness," "Doghouses," "Atomic," and the like. Each entry gives the Key-Numbers of digested cases involving the word or term desired. These tables, bound in blue cloth or blue paper for easy finding are supplied for the various units of the American Digest System. The index for the *First* and *Second Decennials* is cumulated in one alphabet, as are those for the *Third* and *Fourth Decennials*. Supplementing the latest *Decennial's Descriptive-Word Index* are similar indexes for the *General Digest*. For every ten volumes these *General Digest* indexes are bound in blue cloth, and supplemented for each succeeding volume up to ten by non-cumulative indexes for each volume.

F. Techniques of Use of the American Digest System.

Preliminary Problem Analysis. The first thing to do is to analyze the facts so as to clear away dead wood and restrict consideration to those elements necessary to the solution of the problem.

    a. What parties are involved?
    b. How did the case arise, how did it find its way to this court?
    c. What is the subject matter—tort, contract, crime?
    d. Is a statute involved?
    e. What is the cause of action?
    f. What remedy is sought?

Not all these elements are likely to be vital in any single problem. In a contract case the fact that the plaintiff is an infant may be controlling, whereas it might be of no importance in a tort. Whether a case involves the admissibility of evidence, want of jurisdiction, or an improper charge to a jury may determine the applicability of digested cases to the problem at hand. A case decided on a statute is unlikely to be a useful precedent where no such statute is involved. Nor is a prayer for a preliminary injunction apt to lead to a decision on the merits of a substantive fact situation.

Approaches to Case Law through the Digest. There are four standard procedures for finding cases in point in the American Digest System. Since these procedures are so typical of those employed in using other case digests, they will be described here for them all. The specific illustrations given in the discussion below, while simple, are typical of the reasoning and routines to be followed in pursuing the respective techniques. On the other hand, the student should remember that in actual practice a case exactly on all fours as to facts and law of his own problem is uncommon; and that he must usually be content with a reasonable approximation of the fact situation as applicable to the rule of law involved; and that very often the cases in *several* classifications must be fully searched before the right one is found.

Table of Cases Approach. The simplest technique in work with digests is, by means of a case known to be in point, to locate other like cases. The citation to the original case may have been found in a variety of ways — through a casebook, treatise, annotation, encyclopedia, *etc.* Through it the required Key-Number may be found by going to the full report of the case in the National Reporter System. A quicker way is to consult the digest table of cases, which will list *all* Key-Numbers under which the case has been digested. If the date of the case is unknown, it may be necessary to search through several of the *Decennial Digest* units. Going to the actual case in the *Reporter* is surer, since the pertinent Key-Number is then determined with entire exactitude. Having found this number, the searcher may then go through the various *Digest* units and find all other cases in point, regardless of date. Since the table of cases technique is common to nearly all case finders, and since there are a number of problems common to all, it is further described in Chapter 30, "The Table of Cases Approach to the Law."

Fact or Descriptive-Word Index Approach. Lacking a case in point, the first place of search, even for the seasoned lawyer, is usually through the *Descriptive-Word Index* which is a part of every American Digest System Unit, and of practically all other digests. Many situations, while susceptible of analysis according to the legal concepts involved (as described below under "Analytical or Topical Approach,") are more readily workable by seizing upon some salient and perhaps rather uncommon fact involved. It is for these situations that the descriptive-word index has been developed. The rationale of this tool is that often the *legal analysis* not only involves very large and complex main topics, but is not sufficiently clear so that the pertinent Key-Numbers can be readily and certainly pinpointed. However, if a *special fact* can be made the least common denominator in the analysis, the search can frequently be drastically limited.

For example, a woman brings an action to recover for injuries received when she jumped from a stalled automobile at a railroad crossing and was struck by one of a line of box cars which was suddenly discovered to be backing toward the automobile. Several main topics are involved here—railroads, torts, negligence, automobiles, and damages—but they are all very large and the analysis to the desired point is not very obvious, though it can be made. However, two special facts are present—that the accident ocurred at a *railroad crossing*, and that a train *backed* into the plaintiff at that crossing. Further thought reveals that the totality of crossing accidents is greater than those caused at such crossings by backing trains. Therefore, by a process taking much less time to carry out than to describe, "backing" is determined to be the smallest significant fact, the least common denominator. Examination of "Backing" in the *Fifth Decennial Digest Descriptive-Word Index* leads to the sub-entry "Trains," with a further sub-division under "Crossing accidents," where fact situations are noted, with pertinent Key-Numbers. Thus:

BACKING (Cont'd)

TRAILER into highway, contributory negligence of motorist. **Autos 245(67)**

TRAINS—
   Contributory negligence of motorist crossing. **R R 327(1), 333(1)**
   Crossing accidents, **R R 310**
     Absence of license signals as negligence as jury question. **R R 350(8)**
     Amendment of pleading affecting limitations. **Lim of Act 127(14)**
     Contributory negligence of—
       Automobile guest. **R R 350(21)**
       Motorist, reliance on precautions on part of railroad. **R R 330(1–3)**
     Gross negligence. **R R 310**
     Instruction, conformity to pleadings and issues. **R R 351(2)**
     Last clear chance. **R R 338**
     Question for jury. **R R 350(8)**
       Darkness. **R R 350(26)**
       Proximate cause. **R R 350(32)**
     Pleading cause of action under last clear chance doctrine. **R R 344(10)**
   Duty as to lookout for employees in yard. **R R 369(3)**

Exhibit 45

The *Descriptive-Word Index* so meticulously picks out all pertinent fact situations, however, that the probable Key-Numbers could have been found in the example above through several entries under "Automobiles," "Crossings," "Railroads," *etc.*, but not quite so quickly as under "Backing."

The above is purely a catchword problem, depending upon the unusual situation of "backing" for its easy solution. In numerous instances, however, no such decisive catchword is available, and a closer scrutiny of the facts must be made, requiring the examination of the detailed alphabetical analyses under the main topics in the *Descriptive-Word Index*. For example, the guest knowingly riding in an automobile driven by an intoxicated driver, to his consequent injury in an accident, seeks recovery. The significant words here are "passenger," "guest," "intoxicated driver," and "automobile" (under all of which, directly or indirectly, the the proper Key-Numbers can be found), but proper legal analysis shows that the real point at issue is the passenger's contributory negligence in knowingly riding with an intoxicated driver. Under the main topic of "Contributory Negligence," the pertinent Key-Numbers are given under half a dozen sub-heads (as "Automobiles"; "Intoxicated driver, driving with"; "Guest, driving with intoxicated host"; "Intoxicated persons, riding with"; *etc.),* with cross-references to other pertinent topics. The proper Key-Number is thus speedily found.

Since there are several different units of the *Descriptive-Word Index,* covering as many different periods of time, common sense must be employed in using them. For example, as few people were purchasing radios and automobile tires on the installment plan between 1896 and 1916 (the period covered by the *Descriptive-Word Index* for the first two *Decennials),* a search in this unit for a case involving such transactions would probably be useless. However, in the next unit (covering the *Third* and *Fourth Decennials)* such a search would be fruitful. Similarly, atomic energy was not involved in any cases digested in the *Fifth Decennial,* but the *Descriptive-Word Index* covering a later period does include such entries.

   Analytical or Topical Approach. For the skilled lawyer this is often the speediest method of finding cases in point, but with practice the law student also can develop it into a valuable part of his equipment.

Having a known set of facts but no case in point, how is the pertinent Key-Number to be found? First, a preliminary process of analysis should be followed, to determine whether the problem is one of persons, property, contracts, torts, crimes, remedies, or government. An added step will further break it down into a much smaller subdivision of the law—admiralty, damages, husband and wife, or tenancy in common. These are recognizable as logically belonging to one of the 422 subjects in the "List of Digest Topics" found in the front of each volume of the *Fourth* and subsequent *Decennial Digests.* Most of them are pretty obvious. For example, a contract of insurance leads to "Insurance" rather than "Contracts," because that is a workable subdivision of the law of contracts. Similarly, a problem on the admissibility of evidence falls within the topic "Evidence." Others are not so obvious, and require more careful analysis. The proper recipient of the proceeds of deceased's life insurance might be a problem in insurance, equity, or marshaling of assets. Perhaps it can be found under all. In this, the "Scope Note" and "Analysis" at the head of each main topic help.

By running down the analysis, bearing carefully in mind the particular factual, substantive and procedural circumstances of his problem, the lawyer selects one or more Key-Numbers as the most likely to be applicable, and the digest paragraphs thereunder are read for leads. Facts especially to be observed are: how the exact case at hand arose; is procedural or substantive law involved; is there a statute concerned; what remedy is sought; what is the basis of appeal?

Suppose the plaintiff, who occupies a loft building for manufacturing purposes, has had some of his goods damaged through the overflow of water from that part of the premises in the same building occupied by the defendant and under his control. The defendant admits the overflow. Damages are involved, but liability must first be established. Since the parties are fellow tenants of a building, the topic "Landlord and

Tenant" is at once suggested. Checking the main analysis of that topic enables the lawyer to discard at once all sub-topics but VII: "Premises and Enjoyment and Use Thereof."

LANDLORD AND TENANT

Scope-Note.

INCLUDES nature and incidents of estates for years and tenancies from year to year, at will, or at sufferance; leases and agreements for the occupation of real property in general, the relation between the parties thereto, and their rights and liabilities as between themselves and as to others incident to such relation; and remedies relating thereto.

Matters not in this topic, treated elsewhere, see Descriptive-Word Index.

Analysis.

I. CREATION AND EXISTENCE OF THE RELATION, ⬤1–19.

II. LEASES AND AGREEMENTS IN GENERAL, ⬤20–49.
    A. Requisites and Validity, ⬤20–36.
    B. Construction and Operation, ⬤37–49.

III. LANDLORD'S TITLE AND REVERSION, ⬤50–69.
    A. Rights and Powers of Landlord, ⬤50–60.
    B. Estoppel of Tenant, ⬤61–69.

IV. TERMS FOR YEARS, ⬤70–112½.
    A. Nature and Extent, ⬤70–73.
    B. Assignment, Subletting, and Mortgage, ⬤74–81.
    C. Extensions, Renewals, and Options to Purchase or Sell, ⬤81½–92.
    D. Termination, ⬤93–112½.

V. TENANCIES FROM YEAR TO YEAR AND MONTH TO MONTH, ⬤113–116.

VI. TENANCIES AT WILL AND AT SUFFERANCE, ⬤117–120.

VII. PREMISES, AND ENJOYMENT AND USE THEREOF, ⬤121–180.
    A. Description, Extent, and Condition, ⬤121–125.
    B. Possession, Enjoyment, and Use, ⬤126–144.
    C. Incumbrances, Taxes, and Assessments, ⬤145–149.
    D. Repairs, Insurance, and Improvements, ⬤150–161.
    E. Injuries from Dangerous or Defective Condition, ⬤162–170.
    F. Eviction, ⬤171–180.

VIII. RENT AND ADVANCES, ⬤181–274.
    A. Rights and Liabilities, ⬤181–216.
    B. Actions, ⬤217–238.
    C. Lien, ⬤239–262½.
    D. Distress, ⬤263–274.

IX. RE-ENTRY AND RECOVERY OF POSSESSION BY LANDLORD, ⬤275–318.

X. RENTING ON SHARES, ⬤319–333.

Exhibit 46

A check of sub-topic VII, in the sub-analysis, as speedily suggests that E: "Injuries from Dangerous or Defective Conditions," be examined.

17—3d Dec.Dig., Page 1139   LANDLORD AND TENANT

VII. Premises and Enjoyment and Use Thereof—Continued.
 (E) Injuries from Dangerous or Defective Condition.
   ⌒162. Nature and extent of landlord's duty to tenant.
      163. Mutual duties of tenants of different portions of same premises.
      164. Injuries to tenants or occupants.
         164 (1). Injuries due to defective or dangerous condition of premises in general.
         164 (2). Injuries due to failure to repair.
         164 (3). Injuries due to negligence in making repairs.
         164 (4). Injuries due to unlighted passageways.
         164 (5). Liability for injuries to subtenant.
         164 (6). Liability of landlord as dependent on knowledge of defects.
         164 (7). Notice to or knowledge of tenant as to defects.
      165. Injuries to employé of tenant.
         165 (1). Injuries due to defective or dangerous condition of premises in general.
         165 (2). Injuries due to failure to repair.
         165 (3). Injuries due to unlighted passageway.
         165 (4). Liability of landlord as dependent on knowledge of defects.
         165 (5). Failure to guard dangerous places.
         165 (6). Operation or condition of elevators.
         165 (7). Notice to or knowledge of tenant as to defects.
      166. Injuries to property of tenant on premises.
         166 (1). Nature and extent of the duties of landlord and tenant respectively.
         166 (2). Injuries due to defective condition of premises in general.
         166 (3). Injuries due to failure to repair.
         166 (4). Injuries due to negligence in making repairs.
         166 (5). Injuries due to defective water pipes or drains.
         166 (6). Injuries due to negligent acts of landlord.
         166 (7, 8). Injuries due to negligence of third persons in general.
         166 (9). Injuries due to negligence of cotenant.
         166 (10). Liability of landlord as dependent on knowledge or notice of defects.
      167. Injuries to third persons and their property.
         167 (1). Duties of landlord and tenant to third persons.
         167 (2). Injuries due to defective or dangerous condition of premises in general.

Exhibit 47

The sub-analysis under letter suggests Key-Numbers ⌒ 163 and ⌒ 166, especially ⌒ 166(9). A search of these numbers in the *Third Decinnial Digest* reveals at least three cases apparently in point and worth reading in full. A search through other units of the system discloses similar cases in point, for the most part under "Landlord and Tenant ⌒ 166(9)." The "Table of Key-Numbers" covering the first seventeen volumes of the *General Digest* discloses that only volumes 7, 9, 13, and 15 digest any cases under either number above, making it unnecessary to search any other of these interim volumes for cases in point. A complete search, as noted below, would include the advance sheets of all Reporters not yet covered by the monthly pamphlets of the *General Digest.*

Words and Phrases Approach. A fourth approach to the law through digests is by means of words and phrases judicially defined in the opinions of the courts, and almost every digest has a table of these terms. These tables and the approach to the law through them are discussed in Chapter 24, "Law Dictionaries."

Progress from Unit to Unit of the Digest, for Full Coverage. The process of finding like cases in all units of the American Digest System is described in this Chapter at pages 165, 166, and 167. It should be remembered that a full search may include: (1) The *Century Digest;* (2) all units of the *Decennial Digests;* (3) all bound volumes and monthly pamphlets of the *General Digest;* and (4) National Reporter System advance sheets.

G. Digests of Less Scope than the American Digest System.

Nearly all the reported cases digested in the American Digest System are also included in other digests of less scope. Since in construction and use these smaller digests so closely resemble the American Digest System, no detailed description of them individually is needed. However, some of their specialized features are pointed out at the pages indicated below, where the reports covered by them are described.

Federal Court Digests. Included are those for the Supreme Court (at pages 113 and 114; for lower federal courts generally (at page 112; and for individual federal courts — as the Court of Claims (at page 114).

State Court Digests. Included are those for individual states (at page 115), and for the National Reporter System regional *Reporters* (at page 119).

Full Coverage in Other Digests. The process of search (including where the classification has been changed) is the same as for other digests, except that it is easier, because usually the only units to be consulted are (a) the bound volume; (b) the cumulative pocket supplement; and (c) the *Reporter* advance sheets (digest portion) to date. The common practice of publishers is, when the pocket supplement grows too bulky, to issue a "recompiled" volume, incorporating all the material; or, less satisfactorily, to issue, say, a ten years' "second series" digest supplementing the original set.

H. Coordinating the Digest with Other Case Finders.

Digests, while the most comprehensive and generally useful of all case finders, are by no means the only ones. Secondary works of index, such as treatises, encyclopedias, legal periodicals, annotations, and citators, are fruitful sources of cases in point and provide starting points for searchers. The technique of coordinating the various indexes usually involves working from a treatise or other discussion of the law (wherein a case in point is found), forward to the digest. This is done by means of a table of cases supplying a Key-Number or similar classification device. However, a most useful process reverses this: Having found a case in point through the digest, a search in the table of cases of a treatise or in the *Index to Legal Periodicals* frequently makes available a discussion of the points of law involved, together with the citation of additional cases and other literature. A citator such as *Shepard's Citations* lists all cases which have cited a given case, thus not only determining the value of the case as precedent, but supplying other cases in point. This material is described in the succeeding chapters. If a case gleaned from a digest or other source has been annotated in the *American Law Reports,* the table of cases usually (but not always) supplies that information. (Of course the *A. L. R. Digest* would list all *A. L. R.* cases).

Chapter 20

ENCYCLOPEDIAS

A. Function.

Ideally, the legal encyclopedia provides within its announced scope the following material: (1) a complete and integrated statement of all the applicable law; (2) citation to the authority relied upon, which may include not only references to cases in point but digests of cases and excerpts from standard treatises and American Law Institute *Restatements;* (3) exhaustive analytical and subject indexes; and (4) frequent supplements, in which the main text may be rewritten in view of later cases than those forming the basis of the original discussion.

The encyclopedia is best used as a starting point in a search for the law, to provide a "frame of reference." The cases cited act as conduits between the encyclopedia and the brief paragraphs in the digests which tell the searcher whether or not he should read the entire case. By giving the reader an elementary statement of the law applicable to his problem, as extracted from the cases cited as supporting the text, the encyclopedia places those cases selected for reading in their proper perspective.

Since the primary purpose of the encyclopedia is to help judges decide and lawyers to win cases, it is, like the practitioners' text book, the exponent of the law as it is. The men for whom it is designed are little concerned for the moment with the history of the past or speculation as to the future; these they can glean, if desired, from scholarly treatises or law review articles on history or jurisprudence. The encyclopedia resembles student books, however, in that it is careful to state and explain majority, minority, and jurisdictional rules; and in that its statements of the law begin with an elementary exposition of each point covered.

B. Authority.

Legal encyclopedias are neither primary nor mandatory authority, but only guides to it; they are at most persuasive, and what has been said of other secondary works as authority applies to them. As indexes, however, they have been very influential. Some years ago the publisher of one legal encyclopedia noted that in five recent volumes of the reports of each of the forty-eight states, that encyclopedia had been cited 10,395 times, ranging from seven in Massachusetts to 879 in Alabama. Always, however, the encyclopedias and the courts citing them are careful to base their statements of the law upon the authority of the cited cases.

C. Form.

Like the conventional treatise, the encyclopedia states the law in literary form, as extracted from the authorities cited. *Like the digest*, the encyclopedia is alphabetically arranged by topics under a classification system almost exactly like that of the digest, even to the scope note, "analysis," and "sub-analyses." The *scope note* is an eliminator. By stating briefly what is covered by a topic, it also tells by implication what is not, and thus prevents the searcher from wasting his time. The *analysis* may be compared to an unusually detailed table of contents. For the most part, the encyclopedia consists of about 400 alphabetically arranged students' and practitioners' treatises, which vary in length from a few lines to hundreds of pages. It resembles the digest in having a descriptive-word index, but no general encyclopedia has a table of cases, though some of the special ones do. The digest page is typical of those of law books generally—the text discussion above the line, supported by citations to authority below.

There are two current "general" legal encyclopedias, which are described below.

D. American Jurisprudence.[1]

This "comprehensive text statement of American case law as developed in the cases and annotations in the annotated reports" (hereinafter cited as *Am. Jur.)* aims at complete coverage of both adjective and substantive law of general application, as modified by statute, and with strong emphasis on American law as found in the annotated reports. It does not attempt to serve as a law dictionary in the usual form, and maxims are defined only when mentioned in a decision, as noted under "Maxims" in the "General Index." Under "Words and Phrases" in the "General Index," however, a great many words, terms, and maxims are listed, with topic and section references to where discussed and defined in the main text. For example, "Alluvion" is defined under the main topic "Waters," § 476; "Sweet cider" under "Intoxicating Liquors," § 13; rather than under "Alluvion" and "Sweet cider," in the A's and S's, as in a formal dictionary. But they are listed in alphabetical order under "Words and Phrases" in the index.

Scope of Citations to Authority. *Am. Jur.* makes no attempt to cite every case in point in support of its text; it relies heavily but by no means exclusively upon cases printed and annotated in the annotated selective case series, including *all* United States Supreme Court cases. It also cites and quotes pertinent American Law Institute *Restatements*. It does not compete with local annotated statutes. It does note, however, when a statute is necessarily involved in a cited decision, and discusses,

---

[1] San Francisco, Calif., Bancroft-Whitney Co., Rochester, N. Y., Lawyers' Co-operative Pub. Co., 1936-1952. 58 volumes and 4 "General Index" volumes, with annual cumulative pocket supplements.

where pertinent, the theory and interpretation of legislation and of individual statutes. The fundamentals of procedure are treated, but individual local rules are not emphasized. English cases of significance are cited.

In practice, this permits a wide citation of cases. Thus, while this encyclopedia stands entirely on its own feet as an independent work, it incorporates by reference all annotated reports, series annotations of current interest, and is most useful when read in that connection. These annotations, of course, are available to readers of any other encyclopedia, through parallel citations to *A. L. R.* cases used as authority. It is the belief of the publishers that this reduces the bulk and expense of the encyclopedia, while affording fuller discussion (through the annotations) of such individual statements in the main text as the reader wishes to pursue more exhaustively than is practicable within the bounds of a treatise. How that works is shown by the example on page 177 of the original text of an *Am. Jur.* page as brought up to date by annual cumulated supplements. The text statement here of "Divorce and Separation," Section 751, is supported by footnote authorities (for example, notes 5 and 6). It includes references to a more expanded treatment in an annotation, in the making of which all cases in point are cited and many are analyzed. The supplement cites later authority and annotations, rewriting the original text when required by the later decisions. *See* page 178.

Arrangement, Indexes, and Tables. The work consists of some 443 separate treatises, alphabetically arranged. The analyses and sub-analyses preceding the text are typical, and are the basis of the analytical approach to the law through *Am. Jur.* Each volume has its own subject index, for topics in that volume. This index, together with suitable cross-references, is also consolidated into a four-volume "General Index" to the entire set. The text material in the "Annual Cumulative [pocket] Supplements" to each volume, however, is indexed neither in the supplements themselves nor in the "General Index," but in a separate annual cumulative "Index to the . . . Cumulative Supplement." Because of the inevitable overlapping in the coverage of subject matter in the various "treatises" composing the encyclopedia, it is more satisfactory to use the "General Index" as supplemented by the "Index to the . . . Cumulative Supplement" than those for the individual topics in each volume of the text. Then, every pertinent entry for every treatise topic is collected under appropriate heads, even though the main treatment is under a single one of those heads. For example, the nine entries in the "General Index" under "Carriers: Theft, loss by," refer to four different main topics, though the main treatment is under "Larceny."

Instructions in the use of the indexes, and a list of main titles indexed, precede the subject index proper. *There is no table of cases.* Each volume has a parallel table of *Ruling Case Law* (predecessor to *Am. Jur.*) topics and sections.

Supplementation. Annual cumulative pocket parts supplement each volume, and these are indexed by a single cumulative supplement index, mentioned above. Since the paragraphs (and corresponding footnotes) of each main title are numbered, proceeding from the main text to the supplement, or the reverse, is simply a matter of matching title, section, page and footnote numbers. Thus, later material on "Divorce and Separation," § 751, p. 565, note 5 of the main text, is found under the same notation in the cumulative pocket supplement. Moreover entirely new material necessitated by developments of the law is often included in the supplementary notes, and *Am. Jur.* has adopted a special system of typographical styles to call attention to it. This is explained in an "Explanatory Note" at the beginning of each pocket supplement.

ceedings were taken, although the decree was founded upon causes which would not be considered sufficient in a Canadian court.[4]

§ 751. **Application of Full Faith and Credit Provision.**—A decree of a state in which the plaintiff only is resident and in which the parties have never cohabited or had their matrimonial domicil is not entitled to recognition in the courts of other states under the requirements of the full faith and credit guaranty of the Federal Constitution where the defendant is served only constructively.[5] At least, the decree is not within the guaranty so far as it purports to affect the marital status of a citizen of the state in which recognition is asked.[6] Nor is recognition required by a state statute declaring that the records and judicial proceedings properly authenticated shall have such faith and credit given to them in every court within the United States as they have by law or usage in the courts of the state from which they are taken.[7]

In some states it is declared by statute that if an inhabitant of the state goes into another state or country to obtain a divorce for a cause which occurred in the former state while the parties resided there or for a cause which would not authorize a divorce by the laws of the former state, a divorce so obtained shall be of no force or effect in that state. A divorce obtained in this manner in one state is not entitled to recognition in the state having such a statute, notwithstanding the defendant to the divorce proceeding entered her appearance in the action and, upon a settlement, withdrew her answer.[8] To hold such a divorce invalid does not violate the full faith and credit clause of the Federal Constitution.[9]

§ 752. **Comity.**—The fact that the degree of a court of a state in which the plaintiff only resides and in which jurisdiction is obtained by constructive service is not within the jurisdiction of the full faith and credit guaranty of the Federal Constitution does not mean that it will not be given recognition in other states; it may still be given recognition on the principles of comity.[10]

[4] Rex v. Hamilton, 22 Ont. L. Rep. 484, 20 Ann. Cas. 868.

[5] Haddock v. Haddock, 201 U. S. 562, 50 L. ed. 867, 26 S. Ct. 525, 5 Ann. Cas. 1; Delanoy v. Delanoy, 216 Cal. 27, 13 P. (2d) 719, 86 A.L.R. 1321; Bruguiere v. Bruguiere, 172 Cal. 199, 155 P. 988, Ann. Cas. 1917E. 122; Durden v. Durden, 184 Ga. 421, 191 S. E. 455, citing R. C. L.; Perkins v. Perkins, 225 Mass. 82, 113 N. E. 841, L.R.A. 1917B, 1028; Corvin v. Com. 131 Va. 649, 108 S. E. 651, 39 A.L.R. 592.

A wife who was not successful in having a divorce decree set aside on the ground of want of jurisdiction in the state in which it was rendered may not thereafter, in a sister state, claim that the decree is, because of want of jurisdiction, not entitled to full faith and credit. Chamblin v. Chamblin, 362 Ill. 588, 1 N. E. (2d) 73, 104 A.L.R. 1183, writ of certiorari denied in 299 U. S. 541, 81 L. ed. 398, 57 S. Ct. 24; Walker v. Walker, 125 Md. 649, 94 A. 346, Ann. Cas. 1916B, 934; Sewall v. Sewall, 122 Mass. 156, 23 Am. Rep. 299; Larrick v. Walters, 39 Ohio App. 363, 177 N. E. 642, citing R. C. L. Annotation: 39 A.L.R. 603, s. 86 A.L.R. 1329.

Some early cases seem to have assumed the contrary, see infra, §§ 754, 755.

[6] People v. Baker, 76 N. Y. 78, 32 Am. Rep. 274.

[7] Joyner v. Joyner, 131 Ga. 217, 62 S. E. 182, 18 L.R.A.(N.S.) 647, 127 Am. St. Rep. 220.

[8] Andrews v. Andrews, 188 U. S. 14, 47 L. ed. 366, 23 S. Ct. 237.

[9] Ibid.

[10] Haddock v. Haddock, 201 U. S. 562, 50 L. ed. 867, 26 S. Ct. 525, 5 Ann. Cas. 1; De Bouchel v. Candler (D. C.) 296 F. 482; Crimm v. Crimm, 211 Ala. 13, 99 So. 301, citing R. C. L.; Delanoy v. Delanoy, 216 Cal. 27, 13 P. (2d) 719, 86 A.L.R. 1321; Gildersleeve v. Gildersleeve, 88 Conn. 689, 92 A. 684, Ann. Cas. 1916B, 920; Joyner v. Joyner, 131 Ga. 217, 62 S. E. 182, 18 L.R.A. (N.S.) 647, 127 Am. St. Rep. 220; Voorhies v. Voorhies, 184 La. 406, 166 So. 121, citing R. C. L.; Walker v. Walker, 125 Md. 649, 94 A. 346, Ann. Cas. 1916B, 934; Howard v. Strode, 242 Mo. 210, 146 S. W. 792, Ann. Cas. 1913C, 1057; State ex rel. Sparrenberger v. District Ct. 66 Mont. 496, 214 P. 85, 33 A.L.R. 464; McNamara v. McNamara, 99 Neb. 9, 154 N. W. 858, L.R.A.1916B, 1272; Felt v. Felt, 59 N. J. Eq. 606, 45 A. 105, 49 A. 1071, 47 L.R.A. 546, 83 Am. St. Rep. 612; Ball v. Cross, 231 N. Y. 329, 132 N. E. 106, 39 A.L.R. 600; Larrick v. Walters, 39 Ohio App. 363, 177 N. E. 642, citing R. C. L.; Kenner v. Kenner, 139 Tenn. 211, 700, 201 S. W. 779, 202 S. W. 723, L.R.A.1918E, 587; Toncray v. Toncray, 123 Tenn. 476, 34 L.R.A.(N.S.) 1106, 131 N. W. 977, Ann. Cas.

Exhibit 48

17 Am Jur   DIVORCE AND SEPARATION   §§ 744–751

§ 751. Application of Full Faith and Credit Provision.

Am Jur cited in Roberts, v. Roberts, 137 Me 194, 17 A (2d) 140.

McFarland v. McFarland, 179 Va 418, 19 SE (2d) 77.

For a summarization of the status of divorce decree rendered by a sister state since the decision in Williams v. North Carolina, see infra, § 751.5 (Supp).

p. 565, notes 5, 6.

The full faith and credit clause of the Federal Constitution requires the extraterritorial recognition of the validity of a divorce decree obtained in accordance with the requirements of procedural due process in a state by a spouse who under the law of such state had acquired a bona fide domicil there, although the spouse who remained in the state of the original matrimonial domicil did not appear in the divorce suit and was not served with process in the state in which the divorce was granted. Williams v. North Carolina, 317 US 287, 304, 87 L ed 279, 289, 63 S Ct 207, 143 ALR 1273, expressly overruling Haddock v. Haddock, 201 US 562, 50 L ed 867, 26 S Ct 525, 5 Ann Cas 1.

Anno: 157 ALR 1400.

The courts of one state are bound by the full faith and credit clause of the Federal Constitution to recognize a decree of courts of another state granting to a person there domiciled a divorce from an absent spouse. Re Holmes, 291 NY 261, 52 NE (2d) 424, 150 ALR 447.

§ 751.5 (New text) — Status of Foreign Decree Since Decision in Williams v. North Carolina.

The holdings of the cases in the Supreme Court of the United States, beginning with and including Williams v. North Carolina,[1] which govern the extent to which a divorce decree must be given effect in other states under the full faith and credit clause of the Federal Constitution if considered apart from the reasons given in support thereof, are easily intelligible, if divorce decrees rendered solely upon constructive service are distinguished from divorce decrees rendered in proceedings in which the defendant appeared and participated, and if as to the former, the nature of the rights affected by a divorce are taken into consideration.[2] These Supreme Court decisions may be summarized as follows:

(1) A divorce decree obtained upon constructive service in proceedings in which the nonresident defendant did not appear and participate is entitled to full faith and credit if the plaintiff, at the time of instituting the proceedings, was domiciled in the state grant-

Exhibit 48 — Part II

American Jurisprudence has been meticulous in calling attention in its supplements to changes caused by decisions overruling or modifying established rules, and rewriting the original text as required. The sample page shown illustrates this in their treatment of the case of *Williams* v. *North Carolina*, which expressly overruled an earlier case on the application of the full faith and credit provision of the Constitution. In all, four pages of new material, largely rewriting the main text in view of these decisions were added in the supplement.

E. Corpus Juris-Corpus Juris Secundum System.[2]

These two encyclopedias combine to form "a complete restatement of the entire American law, as developed by all reported cases"; an annotated legal dictionary; and an annotated dictionary of legal maxims. The arrangement of legal topics, word, and maxims defined is in a single alphabet: that is, "Actions," "*Actors non probante absolvitur reus,*" and "Actual."

Scope of Citation to Authority. Both encyclopedias emphasize the citation of *all* cases in point, differing in this respect from *Am. Jur. Corpus Juris* (hereinafter cited as *C. J.*) cites many English and Canadian cases, but these, with few exceptions, are omitted from *Corpus Juris Secundum* (hereinafter cited as *C. J. S.*). *C. J. S.* cites (and often quotes) pertinent *Restatement* provisions, treatises and law review articles. The theory of legislation and of statutory construction is treated, and where a statute is involved in a decision cited as authority, that is brought out in the footnote citation of the case, but there is no attempt to treat local statutes generally. Where statutes are important controls, their effect is analyzed in the main text. No attempt is made to serve as local practice books, but these encyclopedias cover in detail the fundamentals of procedure.

---

[2] The publishers issue a free pamphlet "Legal Research by the Use of Corpus Juris Secundum and Corpus Juris," describing in detail the organization and use of these encyclopedias.

F. Corpus Juris.[3]

Form. This is a typical "general" legal encyclopedia, in content, organization, and use, as described above.

Arrangement, Indexes, Tables. The 449 individual treatises are arranged in alphabetical order. Each has exactly the same sort of analysis and sub-analyses as in a typical digest, together with cross-references to related topics. Individual volumes are not indexed, but volume 72 is a "Descriptive-Word Index and Concordance" for the entire set. It fulfills the same function as its digest counterpart, and is the avenue for the fact approach. Although the topics and section numbers in *C. J.* are not identical with those in *C. J. S.*, they are sufficiently similar to be useful in searching the latter encyclopedia, until such time as there is a consolidated index for it. *There is no table of cases* for the set. There are, however, "Parallel Tables Showing Where the *Cyc* References Are Found in Corpus Juris," which are typical transfer tables. For example, the subject matter of "Chattel Mortgages," 6 *Cyc.* p. 1051, note 51, is the same as that in 11 *C. J.* 438, note 43. There is as yet no similar transfer table from *C. J.* to *C. J. S.*, because *C. J. S.* is not complete.

Quick Search Manual. This combines in one volume all the topical analyses of the entire set, and is a means of approach through the analytical method, though of diminishing importance to the extent that *C. J. S. supersedes C. J.* The *Manual* also contains the "Law Chart," showing the division of the subject matter of the encyclopedia into the seven categories of persons, property, contracts, torts, crimes, remedies, and government. It includes subdivisions, under the formula governing the compilation of the encyclopedia. This is designed to aid in the preliminary analysis of a problem by concepts of law.

Supplementation. Keeping the text and supporting case citations up to date in *C. J.* is done by annual bound (not pocket part) supplements. The supplements for the years 1921 to 1931, covering both *Cyc* (the precedessor of *C. J.*) and *C. J.* were cumulated for convenience into three units called "Permanent Annotations." These do three things, as shown by the specimen below.

1962 [33 C. J. 225] *INTEREST—INTEREST REIPUBLICÆ UT SIT FINIS LITIUM*

225–64 Ark 31SW(2d)521(2dcase). [c] Statute limiting rate has no application after maturity. 107Conn276, 140A202. **225–66** 16F(2d)654: TexCivA 6SW(2d)186. But see Ark 31SW(2d)521(2dcase). [b] (2) 84Mont285, 275P743. **226–69½–New.** Where note and mortgage provide for stated rate until maturity and greater rate thereafter, mortgagee declaring whole debt due before maturity can recover only lesser rate until decree. Ark 31SW(2d)521(2dcase).

on money laid aside for building installments from date of note. 112 OhSt219, 147NE641, 40ALR819. (11) Notes for money, laid aside for holding installment bearing interest only on amount actually advanced after maturity of notes. 112 OhSt219, 147NE641, 40ALR819. [g] Money due.–316 Ill 488, 147NE459, 464. **231–10½–New.** Where vendor's suit for specific performance is necessary to establish his title to property by prescription, interest has been held allowable

were made parties, county is not liable for interest during time when collection was enjoined though it was not expressly restrained from making payment. 161Ga287, 130SE580. **247–81** 43F(2d)358(1stcase). **247–82** 239Mich575, 215NW13. **248–93** But see 319Mo 104, 274SW770. **250–19** Fla 1298589. **250–20** [a] (2) In action on supersedeas bond for recovery of rentals by plaintiffs in whom title to land was

Exhibit 49

New cases involving new material are labeled "New" and are digested; new *cases supporting the C. J. text* are merely cited, with perhaps a brief added

---

[3] New York, N. Y., American Law Book Co., 1914-1937, 72 volumes; Permanent Annotations Volumes, 1922-26; 1927-31; Annual Annotations Volumes 1932 to date.

comment; new *cases significantly at variance with the original text* are cited with a "but see" notation. Parallel reference to the main encyclopedia is by volume, page, and note (not section) number. Thus, in the example above, the first citation supplements 33 *C. J.* 225, note 64.

Beginning with 1932, annotations have been published in annual volumes, but with a change of style, as shown by the example below.

MOTOR VEHICLES
§ 671
D.C.Fla. Under Florida law, driver of automobile who fails to stop his automobile if he cannot see another automobile on highway ahead of him going in same direction because of bright lights of approaching automobile, and who by such failure has collision with automobile in front of him, is guilty of negligence and is liable for damages.—Spell v. U. S., 72 F.Supp. 731.

Exhibit 50

In this new style, all supplementary references are by *Reporter* digest paragraphs, and without other comment; reference to the encyclopedia proper is by *topic* and *section* number, not by volume, page, and note. Supplements beginning with 1932, therefore, are in effect digests. Since *C. J. S.* probably will not be completed until about 1958, *C. J.* annotations are still necessary for a diminishing number of titles.

Supplementation as affected by C. J. S. The volumes containing material supplementing *C. J.* appear in two series. The first, intended for non-subscribers to *C. J. S.* who wish to keep their case references up to date, covers new material for *all C. J.* titles, whether superseded by *C. J. S.* or not. The second covers only so much of that set as is not yet superseded by *C. J. S.* Since each volume of *C. J. S.* as it appears cites all cases from the time of publication of the original volume of *C. J.* (that is, it incorporates all the annotations from the *C. J.* supplements), *C. J.* supplements are no longer printed for topics now covered by *C.J.S.*—that it, for superseded topics. Therefore, the annual "annotations" to *C. J.* in this second series cover fewer topics, and with the last volume of *C. J. S.* they will be discontinued. For example, the "Annotations" for 1951 in this series start with "Prohibitions," since all preceding topics were covered at that date by *C. J. S.* Similarly, those for 1952 start with "Schools and School Districts." Notwithstanding this, the label on the spine of each annotated volume states that it covers from "Abandonment to Workmen's Compensation"—from beginning to end. This is to save the searcher from wasting time looking in the "Annotations" for superseded topics included in *C. J. S.*, confusion being avoided by a cross-reference in the "Annotations," to the *C. J. S.* topics; thus, "Abandonment to Process, see *Corpus Juris Secundum.*"

G. Corpus Juris Secundum.[4]

The Relationship of Corpus Juris and Corpus Juris Secundum. The *text* of *C. J.* is entirely superseded by the corresponding text of *C. J. S.* volumes as they appear, and should not be read as a statement of the present law for these topics. The *C. J. notes*, on the other hand, are incorporated into *C. J. S.* by reference, and are still alive. That is, citation of authority by *C. J. S.* is (1) to cases decided

---

[4] Brooklyn, N. Y., American Law Book Co., In 79 volumes, 1936 to date. Kept up to date with annual cumulative pocket supplements.

since *C. J.* — including all case citations in the "Annotations" for superseded *C. J.* titles; and (2) for earlier cases — those cited as authority for the original *C. J.* text — to designated volumes, pages and notes of *C. J.* A complete search of authority, accordingly, for a non-superseded *C. J.* title would be to *C. J.*, as supplemented by the "Permanent Annotations" through 1931 and the "Annotations" beginning with 1932. For a superseded title of *C. J.* it would be *C. J. S.*, supplemented by *C. J.* notes as cited in *C. J. S.*, and *C. J. S.* pocket supplements.

Arrangement. The 433 treatises comprising the major portion of the work are arranged in alphabetical order as in a digest. The digest analogy is carried still further by the scope notes, analyses and sub-analyses of each topic, by which the content and the breakdown of the discussion into workable units are shown. Anybody who can use a digest by means of the analytical approach can do the same with *C. J.S.* Four hundred ten of the four hundred thirty-three main topics in the encyclopedia are identical in name with those of the American Digest System; and while the section numbers of the encyclopedia are not identical in most cases with the Key-Numbers of the digest, the organization of matter under the various topics of the two works is so similar that it is not difficult to go from one to the other. In a topic where a statute is influential, as in "Forgery" or the "Statute of Frauds," the parallel is striking. Where the encyclopedia and the digest chiefly differ is in that the encyclopedia always starts out with an elementary introduction, for which there is no digest parallel.

Page format. A typical *C. J. S.* page is shown at page 182.

In the specimen page, the black-letter statement of the prevailing law (1), expanded in the discussion proper (2), is analogous to that in the *Hornbook* series of student texts. Points to be emphasized in the notes are in black-letter also (3). The topic ("Conflict of Laws" here), and the title, section, page, and note numbers are keyed to like notations in the annual pocket supplements, where later citations to authority (occasionally calling for the revision of the main text) are found under the same numbers. Authority is often directly quoted in the exact language of the opinion (4), A. L. I. Restatement (5), or treatise; or a *Reporter* headnote may be substantially copied (6). There are cross-references to related topics (7), and to notes citing cases as authority in *C. J.* (8)

Dictionary Function of C. J. S. The encyclopedia is also an annotated legal dictionary, as shown by the example below.

---

§ 15 *ADULTERATION—ADULTERIUM NON PROBET, ETC.* 2 C. J. S.

ADULTERINE. Begotten in an adulterous intercourse,[1] the offspring being known as adulterine bastards.[2]

ADULTERINE GUILDS. Traders acting as a corporation without a charter.[3]

ADULTERIUM NON PROBET CONTRA ALIUM SOLA MULIERIS CONFESSIONE.[4]

---

of the section.—Peninsular Naval Stores Co. v. State, 93 S.E. 159, 20 Ga. App. 501.

1. Black L. D.

2. Kotzke v. Kotzke's Estate, 171 N W. 442, 443, 205 Mich. 184.

"Bastards" distinguished

In the Roman and canon law, adulterine bastards were distinguished from such as were the issue of two unmarried persons, and the former were treated with more severity, not being allowed the status of natural children, and being ineligible to holy orders.—Black L. D.

3. Black L. D.

4. A maxim meaning "Adultery is not proved against another by the confession of the woman."—Adams Gloss., cited in Betts v. Betts, 1 Johns. Ch.(N.Y.) 197. 199.

Exhibit 51

found in the cases where the positive law of the domicile makes void certain kinds of marriages by its citizens although celebrated elsewhere, and although they would otherwise be valid where celebrated, in which case such a marriage is held to be void not only in the domiciliary state,[29] but in every other state.[30]

For an extended discussion of the foregoing and an exhaustive collection of the authorities, the C.J.S. title Marriage § 4, also 38 C.J. p 1276 note 24–p 1279 note 45, should be consulted.

A distinction should be made at this point between the creation and existence of the marriage status and the incidents attached thereto. Hence while a foreign contracted marriage will be recognized everywhere, the rights and duties flowing therefrom will be governed by the law of the place where the parties are[31] or by some law other than that of the state creating the status, depending upon the nature of the problem involved.[32] Appropriate sections of the title Husband and Wife should be consulted for the treatment of the law governing the particular rights growing out of the marriage relation.

See § 16 c infra for a discussion of the foregoing rules in so far as they involve the capacity of the parties to enter into the marriage status. See § 20 e

infra for a discussion of the law governing the formal requisites of a marriage.

d. Parent and Child

While ordinarily the relation of parent and child is governed by the law of the domicile of the parent having custody, any state in which a minor child is found has jurisdiction to determine questions of custody and control in the interest of the child.

As stated in the C.J.S. title Parent and Child § 1, also 46 C.J. p 1220 note 3, the term parent and child indicates the relation existing between husband and wife or either of them and their legitimate offspring. It is a status, not a property right.[33]

A Conflict of Laws problem involving this relationship may arise when the right to, and jurisdiction to determine, the custody and control of a minor child is involved. While basically the domicile of the parent having custody of the child is the place which has control of the status of parent and child, because the domicile of the parent is that of the child, see the C.J.S. title Domicile § 12, also 19 C.J. p 411 note 29, only such state having the right to adjudicate any change in the relationship,[34] because every state has an interest in the welfare of children within its confines, the law of the domicile of the parents is not necessarily a factor in determining questions of the custody and control of a child,[35] the state within which the child is found

Mass.—Atwood v. Atwood, 8 N.E.2d 916.
N.Y.—In re Seymour, 185 N.Y.S. 373, 113 Misc. 421.
Okl.—Eggers v. Olson, 231 P. 483, 104 Okl. 297.

29. **Mass.**—Atwood v. Atwood, 8 N. E.2d 916—Hanson v. Hanson, 191 N.E. 673, 287 Mass. 154, 93 A.L.R. 701.
N.Y.—Bell v. Little, 197 N.Y.S. 674, 204 App.Div. 235, modifying 189 N. Y.S. 935, and affirmed 143 N.E. 726, 237 N.Y. 519—Bays v. Bays, 174 N. Y.S. 212, 105 Misc. 492.
Okl.—Eggers v. Olson, 231 P. 483, 104 Okl. 297—Ross v. Bryant, 217 P. 364, 90 Okl. 300.
Wis.—Lyannes v. Lyannes, 177 N.W. 683, 171 Wis. 381.
Prohibiting evasion of local law
The legislature can declare out-of-state marriage of Massachusetts residents void in Massachusetts, if marriage was consummated in another state to avoid provisions of Massachusetts laws forbidding marriage in Massachusetts.—Atwood v. Atwood, Mass., 8 N.E.2d 916.
Law of domicile governs
Where citizens of one state go to another state, and there contract a marriage prohibited by the statutes

of the former state governing public policy as to persons competent to enter into such status, and return forthwith to the place of domicile, the validity of their marital status, when drawn in question therein, will be determined by the law of domicile under the rule that the law, not of the place of contract, but of the domicile of the parties, governs.— Ross v. Bryant, 217 P. 364, 90 Okl. 300.

"A marriage which is against the law of the state of domicil of either party, though the requirements of the law of the state of celebration have been complied with, will be invalid everywhere in the following cases: (a) polygamous marriage, (b) incestuous marriage between persons so closely related that their marriage is contrary to a strong public policy of the domicil, (c) marriage between persons of different races where such marriages are at the domicil regarded as odious, (d) marriage of a domiciliary which a statute at the domicil makes void even though celebrated in another state." —Restatement, Conflict of Laws § 132.

30. **Mich.**—People v. Steere, 151 N. W. 617, 184 Mich. 556.
Wis.—Hall v. Industrial Commission.

162 N.W. 312, 165 Wis. 364, L.R.A. 1917D 829.
31. **Wis.**—Forbes v. Forbes. 277 N. W. 112, 226 Wis. 47
12 C.J. p 459 note 25.
32. **S.D.**—Calhoun v. Bryant, 133 N. W. 266, 271, 28 S.D. 266.
"We believe a substantially correct statement of the proposition is that the law of the state where the marriage is consummated establishes the 'relationship' of one to the other as husband and wife or parent and child which is universally recognized, but that the mere incidents flowing from that 'status' or relationship are controlled by the law of the domicile of the parties or the situs of the property."—Calhoun v. Bryant, supra.

33. **Pa.**—In re Rosenthal, 157 A. 342, 103 Pa.Super. 27.
34. **Iowa.**—Kline v. Kline, 10 N.W. 825, 57 Iowa 386, 42 Am.R. 47.
Minn.—State v. Larson, 252 N.W. 329, 190 Minn. 496.
N.Y.—Finlay v. Finlay, 148 N.E. 624, 240 N.Y. 429.
Tex.—Lanning v. Gregory, 99 S.W. 542, 100 Tex. 310, 10 L.R.A.,N.S., 690.
35. **N.Y.**—Finlay v. Finlay, 148 N.E. 624, 240 N.Y. 429, 40 A.L.R. 792.

Exhibit 52

Some definitions, with their citations to authority, are exhaustive. "At," "In," and "Public," for example, occupy, respectively, fifteen, nineteen, and fourteen pages.

Indexes and Tables. Each main topic (as "Agency," or "Conflict of Laws") is separately indexed in the volume containing it. When the set is completed, there will be a consolidated descriptive-word index of the whole. In the meantime, the text proper of *C. J. S.* takes care of this to a considerable extent by cross-references to related topics and sections. *There is no table of cases.* There is as yet *no transfer table* to and from *C. J.* Reference from sections in *C. J. S.* to coresponding subject matter in *C. J.*, however, is usually simple, through the citation by *C. J. S.* of *C. J.* notes. Thus, "Public Lands" § 119, note 72 in *C. J. S.* refers to 50 *C. J.*, p. 1004, note 5 for earlier authority. Going from *C. J.* to *C. J. S.* is feasible in most instances through the *C. J. Descriptive-Word Index and Concordance*, since the topics and section numbers, while not identical, are nearly enough so, usually, as to lead to the proper sections in *C. J. S.* This is best done through the individual volume indexes, however. In the front of each volume of *C. J. S.* there is a *table of abbreviations* of reports, treatises, and legal periodicals cited as authority in the set. Though by no means a complete table of abbreviations, it is useful beyond the immediate confines of the encyclopedia itself.

Words and Phrases Defined in C. J. S. This table is an index to the dictionary function of the encyclopedia. The words are listed, with references to the text pages where defined, in a table at the back of each volume (for that volume), preceding the indexes.

Supplementation. Each volume is supplemented by annual cumulative pocket parts, in which the new references are keyed to the main text by *volume, page, title, section,* and *note* numbers. Matching up original text and supplement is done very simply. For example, to bring up to date the text and corresponding citations to authority for the topic "Commerce," Section 142, note 99, which is on page 512 of volume 15 of *C. J. C.*, it is only necessary to go to the pocket supplement in volume 15, under § 142, page 512, note 99, where later citations in point are collected, as seen in the specimen page below.

---

§ 142 Pages 512–514	*COMMERCE*	15 CJS 76

Purchases of operating rights
U.S.—Falwell v. U. S., supra—Shein v. U. S., D.C.N.J., 102 F.Supp. 320, affd. 72 S.Ct. 1043, 343 U.S. 944, 96 L.Ed. —.
99. U.S.—Schenley Distillers Corporation v. U. S., supra, n. 97—I. C. C. v. Isner, D.C.Mich., 92 F.Supp. 582.

Since the publication of Corpus Juris Secundum the case cited therein has been reversed and the court has been held not required to determine whether applicant is entitled to a certificate under other provisions of the Motor Carrier Act of 1935.99.1

99.1 U.S.—U. S. v. Maher, Or., 59 S.Ct. 768, 307 U.S. 148, 83 L.Ed. 1162, reh. den. 59 S.Ct. 831, 307 U.S. 649, 83 L.Ed. 1528—A. E. McDonald Motor Freight Lines v. U. S., supra, n. 97—A. B. & C. Motor Transp. Co. v. U. S., D.C.Mass., 69 F.Supp. 166.

In this example, the added text material shows that the cases relied upon in the original note have been reversed, states the new rule, and cites the reversing case, together (in note 99.1) with later cases in point. *C. J. S.* is thus to a limited extent a citator. Although *C. J. S.* makes such comments as this, often at considerable length, its policy is not to speculate (in the manner of law reviews) on the *probable* effects of new rulings or statutes.

Exhibit 53

H. State Legal Encyclopedias.

California,[5] *Michigan*,[6] *Ohio*,[7] and *Texas*[8] *Jurisprudence* are legal encyclopedias of the states mentioned, on the plan of *American Jurisprudence*.

I. Special-Subject Legal Encyclopedias.

There are special encyclopedias for insurance, automobiles, corporations, municipal corporations, banks and banking, oil and gas, and for federal and state procedure, among other topics. The difference between them and the ordinary practitioners' books is that they aim to cover the subject exhaustively in all aspects, and that commonly they have annotated forms. For example, John A. Appleman's *Insurance Law and Practice*[9] discusses every kind of insurance from every point of view. These special encyclopedias are essentially casefinders, with a running text commentary and aimed-at-complete citation to authority. Majority, minority, and variant rules are set forth, and much of the authority cited is digested or abridged from the original cases and statutes. Most of them differ from general legal encyclopedias in having tables of cases, making this approach to the law available. The descriptive-word index is also available but the analysis of topics, while present at the beginning of each chapter, is seldom so detailed as that in the general encyclopedias. Through the case tables it is possible to pursue the discussion from the general legal encyclopedias into the more detailed treatment of the special ones.

Notes

Advantages and Disadvantages of Encyclopedias. The principal advantages claimed for the encyclopedia over a collection of treatises covering the same topics are many. (1) a saving of overall total expense; (2) more complete coverage; (3) a continuity of editorial policy always alert to the growth and change of the law; and (4) assured, complete, and regular supplementation.

One major defect of the conventional treatise is that while there is a great deal of duplication (in that several authors write substantially the same things about the same things), there are also gaps, covered by nobody at all. The aggregate of these unrepresented topics is large and important, though individually many are not commercially feasible as subjects for treatises. It is the claim of the encyclopedias that their analyses give complete and uniformly expert treatment of all topics of the law, and that purchasers need not worry about gaps; furthermore, that the cost of the entire set is a small fraction of that of individual treatises covering less ground. The editorial staffs, reading all cases, are said to follow the law in all its growth and changes. It is also said that the individual author of treatises can not hope to have at his command anything approaching the mass of expertly digested and arranged material that is routine on an encyclopedia staff. Equally important is the continuous supplementation, so that in theory the one-set law library is never out of date. It is further claimed that the combined index is a much better guide to the body of the law than the sum total of the

---

[5] San Francisco, Calif., Bancroft-Whitney Co., 1921-26. 27 volumes; 10-year Supplement 1926-1936, 12 v.; annual supplements to date. Second edition, 1952 to date, in progress.

[6] Santa Barbara, Calif., Michigan Jurisprudence Co., 1953 — projected in 25 volumes.

[7] Rochester, N. Y., Lawyers' Co-operative Pub. Co., 1928-49. 45 volumes; 1943 Cumulative Supplement, 3 volumes.

[8] San Francisco, Calif., Bancroft-Whitney Co., 1929-51. 48 volumes. 10-year Supplement, 1937-47. 10 volumes; Index to the whole, 2 volumes, 1951. Kept up to date by pocket supplements.

[9] Kansas City, Mo., Vernon Law Book Co.; St. Paul, Minn., West Pub. Co., 1941-1948, 25 v., with annual cumulative supplements.

indexes to individual treatises. There is a considerable degree of analogy between the expert editorial service of the encylopedia staff and that of the loose-leaf service.

The disadvantages of the encyclopedia, assuming that the purchaser needs a treatise covering the entire law, are said to be largely inherent in the size of the encyclopedia and its necessary staff. The ground to be covered is so enormous that it must be gone over gradually and the product sold volume by volume to finance the operation. *Corpus Juris* was twenty-three years from first to last volume, about the length of time Dean Pound has allotted to the life of a decision as precedent, and *Corpus Juris Secundum* will take somewhat longer. It took sixteen years to complete *American Jurisprudence,* though the fifty-eight volumes preceding the general index were done in twelve. A great deal of law can build up and change in that time particularly, in a period of social and economic flux. The value of an encyclopedia, accordingly, would seem to depend quite largely upon the supplementation policy—*i.e.* to what extent the supplements are merely routine records of later cases decided; or, on the other hand, to what extent they rewrite the main text; or comment at sufficient length on later cases which overturn or substantially alter the law as described in that text.

Another disadvantage ascribed to the encyclopedia is that, while the standard of anonymous authorship is admittedly high and even, the encyclopedia does not enjoy the prestige of that of an independent work by a man of known high standing as a lawyer or teacher and author.

A criticism sometimes voiced by teachers of law is that encyclopedias tend to find certainty where none exists, and state as settled law principles which are subject to uncertainty and jurisdictional variations. That danger, if it exists, is, of course, found in any secondary work commenting on the law of the cases. It is guarded against, as it always should be, by the searchers' reading the cases cited as authority and considering their application to the problem under consideration.

Other American Legal Encyclopedias.   As pointed out in the notes to Chapter 29, on English materials, the legal encyclopedia stems from the abridgment, the first of which (Statham's) was published in 1488. Bacon's and Viner's *Abridgments,* the later editions of which were popular in the United States into the nineteenth century, were legal encyclopedias approaching the modern style.

The first American legal encyclopedia was Thornton's *Universal Cyclopaedia of Law.*[10] There seems to be some doubt that it was ever intended for lawyers' use, as it cited no cases, but it contained the germ of an idea which resulted in the ambitious project of the *American and English Encyclopaedia of Law,*[11] which was a modern legal encyclopedia of substantive law. This proved to be so popular with the profession that an encyclopedia of adjective law was started in 1895, the *Encyclopaedia of Pleading and Practice.*[12] In 1896, two encyclopedias were started. The first was a second edition of the *American and English Encyclopaedia of Law.*[13] This was not a true second edition, but a complete revision. To the substantive law of the first edition it added evidence. To take care of the remainder of the adjective law, the *Encyclopaedia of Forms and Precedents*[14] was published. In 1909 it was sought to combine adjective and substantive law in one work (as is the present style) in the *American and English Encyclopaedia of Law and Practice,*[15] but the work was abandoned.

The *Cyclopedia of Law and Procedure,*[16] known as *Cyc.,* and the predecessor of *Corpus Juris* and *Corpus Juris Secundum,* combined adjective and substantive law, and was very successful. Although it has been entirely superseded by *Corpus Juris-Corpus Juris Secundum,* it is still occasionally consulted by readers who regard its discussions of common-law actions as superior in some ways to those of its successors.

---

[10] Northport, N. Y., E. Thompson, 1883. 2d ed., 2 v. 1885.

[11] Northport, N. Y., E. Thompson, 1887-1896. 31 volumes.

[12] Northport, N. Y., E. Thompson, 1895-1902, 23 volumes, with supplements, 1903-1905, 4 volumes.

[13] Northport, N. Y., E. Thompson, 1896-1905, 32 volumes; supplements 1905-1908, 5 volumes.

[14] Northport, N. Y., J. Cockcroft, 1896-1904, 18 volumes.

[15] Northport, N. Y., E. Thompson, 1909-1910, 5 volumes, covering A — Assignment.

[16] New York, N. Y., American Law Book Co., 1901-1912, 40 volumes.

Ruling Case Law,[17] the predecessor of *American Jurisprudence*, was "at once a digest of particular reports and a compendium of the entire body of the law as developed by the United States Supreme Court Reports—Lawyers' Edition, *A. L. R. Annotated*, English Ruling Cases, L. R. A., American Decisions, American Reports, American Annotated Cases, English Ruling Cases, and British Ruling Cases . . ." Because of the length and expertness of its digests it was very useful.

The *Encyclopedia of United States Supreme Court Reports*,[18] was an encyclopedic treatment of the law as taken from United States Supreme Court cases.

There have been numerous other works dubbed "encyclopedia of law," some written as elementary texts for correspondence schools of law, but they need not be considered here.

J. Techniques of Using Legal Encyclopedias.

Except that general legal encyclopedias lack tables of cases commented upon or used as authority in them (precluding the case approach), the approaches to the law through these works are identical with those to the digest, as already described in Chapter 19. They are easier, in fact, since the compilers have done most of the preliminary work for the reader, by their statements of the law as extracted from the decided cases. Thus, use of annotations in conjunction with encyclopedias often affords a much more exhaustive treatment of narrow points (and especially jurisdictional variations in rules) than is provided by the encyclopedias alone. During the intervals between annual supplements to the encyclopedias, conventional digests and *Reporter* advance sheets serve to supply citations to the latest cases in point.

Encyclopedias as Elementary Treatises. The encyclopedia presentation of a main topic (as "Evidence" or "Landlord and Tenant") leads off with a general and elementary statement of the law involved, a technique also followed for each principal subdivision or chapter of this main topic. Terms are defined and the scope limited. Then the subject matter is developed at length, point by point, following the analysis and sub-analyses which precede each topic, as in a digest. As a result, the encyclopedia serves both as an elementary quick review book and as a detailed analysis and casefinder for the law involved.

Encyclopedias as Casefinders. The most important function of an encyclopedia, of course, is to give the lawyer cases in point. The most lucid text is useless without the backing of authority. How the encyclopedia leads to the cases is shown in the solution of the problem below.

> **Problem.** At the time of their marriage in 1939, *H* took out a $15,000 life insurance policy in favor of *W* as named beneficiary. There was a double indemnity provision in case of accidental death. The policy also provided that "In the event of death of any beneficiary before insured, the interest of such beneficiary shall vest in the insured"; and "Double indemnity death benefits shall not be payable if death resulted . . . from having been engaged in aviation or aeronautics."
>
> In 1941, *H* borrowed $7500 from *F* (his father), giving *F* a note for that amount, secured also by the assignment of "all his right, title and interest" in the policy, the insurer indorsing the assignment on the policy. In 1946, *H* and *W* were killed in the crash of a regularly licensed carrier airplane, in which they were passengers. What are the rights of the administrators of the estates of *H* and *W*?
>
> Four problems are involved, each of which must be separately solved.

---

[17] Northport, N. Y., E. Thompson; San Francisco, Calif., Bancroft-Whitney Co., 1914-1921, 28 volumes, with permanent supplement 1929-1930, 8 volumes, and pocket supplements to 1945.

[18] Charlottesville, Va., The Michie Co., 1908-1923, 13 v. (v. 12-13: Supplement), with supplements to 1949.

1. The insurer denies liability for double indemnity, on the ground that *H* was "engaged in aviation or aeronautics." 2. *F* claims that *H*'s assignment to him of "all his right, title, and interest" in the policy entitles him to the proceeds. This has two aspects, assignment and security. 3. *H*'s administrator claims that the "death of beneficiary before insured" provision entitles him to the proceeds, because of a presumption of *H*'s longer survival in case of death by common disaster. 4. A final question is whether, where *H*'s estate is able to pay his note without recourse to the collateral security of the policy, *F* must attack that source, rather than the proceeds of the policy.

Since all four of the sub-problems are solved by like processes in the encyclopedias, only the first one will be solved here, as an example. In order to save duplication, the solution will be first by the fact method, through *C. J. S.*, and then through the analytical approach in *Am. Jur.*, with mention of two specialized subject encyclopedias. Each approach is, of course, equally available to users of any of these encyclopedias.

1. The insurer denies liability for double indemnity, on the ground that *H* was "engaged in aviation or aeronautics."

a. Index approach. Since this is obviously an insurance problem, the "Index to Insurance" in volume 46 of *C. J. S.* is consulted, which yields the following applicable entries, all leading to "Insurance § 938."

INDEXING

Airplanes and aeronautics
  Life Insurance, death from engaging in
  aviation, § 938
Double Indemnity
  Death resulting from particular risks, § 938
  Passenger
    Double Indemnity for death, § 938
    Participating in aviation within exception, § 938
    Public conveyance, death of passenger riding in, § 938
Life Insurance
  Accidental death benefits, § 938
  Aviation, liability for death while engaging in, § 938
Passengers
  Airplane
    Double indemnity clause exception applicable to passenger of, § 938
    Double indemnity for death, § 938

Exhibit 54

Section 938 leads, through several sub-analyses, to page 1086, where the precise question involved in the problem is discussed, with citations (in footnote 92) to authority from all jurisdictions which have considered it. (Normally at this point, the *C. J. S.* text would refer to earlier cases in point in *C. J.*, but there is no such citation in this example. This is because, when the "Insurance" title of *C. J.* was compiled in 1924, people were not yet riding as passengers in commercial air lines, and so there were no cases to which to refer back.) Turning to the annual cumulative pocket supplement in the back of volume 45, a search under *45 C. J. S. 1086, § 938, note 92,* will reveal any later authorities in point.

b. Analytical approach. In solving the same problem through the analytical approach in *Am. Jur.*, preliminary analysis of course determines it to be one of insurance, and that therefore the topic "Insurance" in *Am. Jur.* be searched. As in digests, there is first a main analysis, with only the principal chapter headings, but with references to pages where each main head is expanded into a detailed sub-analysis. "Insurance" is divided into twenty-four of these main heads. After scanning the twenty-four main heads of the analysis, the searcher discards as inapplicable such heads as "Insurance Companies," "Insurance Agents and Brokers," "Insurable Interest," *etc.* But he finds that "XIV: Risks and Causes of Loss," seems worth examining, particularly "D4: Accident insurance: Particular kinds of accidents or provisions." Accordingly the detailed outline of this sub-head, as shown below, is examined, where § § 968 and 969 seem to be in point.

INSURANCE   29 Am Jur

XIV. D,   4. PARTICULAR KINDS OF ACCIDENTS OR PROVISIONS.

      b. ACCIDENTS IN CONNECTION WITH VEHICLES, CONVEYANCES, OR AIRCRAFT,
           OR WHILE WALKING OR ON HIGHWAY

      § 953. *Generally.*
      § 954. *Death or Injury in Public or Passenger Conveyance.*
      § 955. *—What Constitutes "Passenger."*
      § 956. *—What Constitutes Being "In" or "On" Conveyance.*
      § 957. *—Walking as Incident to Journey.*
      § 958. *What Constitutes Public or Passenger Conveyance.*
      § 959. *—Taxicabs; Hired Automobiles.*
      § 960. *Exceptions as to Entering or Leaving Moving Conveyances.*
      § 961. *Exceptions concerning Place Where Riding on Conveyance.*
      § 962. *Provisions as to Train Wrecks.*
      § 963. *Exception while on Railway Roadbed, Bridge, etc.*
      § 964. *Death or Injury while on Public Highway.*
      § 965. *"Vehicles."*
      § 966. *Accidents in Connection with Automobile or Motorcycle.*
      § 967. *—Motorcycle as "Motor-driven Car."*
      § 968. *Participation or Engagement in Aviation or Aeronautics.*
      § 969. *—Where Insured Is Passenger.*
      § 970. *Death or Injury in Elevator.*
      § 971. *—What Constitutes "Passenger Elevator."*

Exhibit 55

On page 730, § 968, a brief introductory statement to aviation clauses is found. This is amplified by § 969, where the exact point of the problem is covered, with citations to authority (footnotes 6 and 7). The pocket supplement digests a new case in point. In both the main text and the supplement, *A. L. R.* annotations to cases on the aviation clause involved are cited.

    c. Use of Special Legal Encylopedias. The insurance problem above is solved in exactly the same two ways — through the index and the analytical approaches — in John A. Appleman's encyclopedia of *Insurance Law and Practice, with Forms,*[19] and the *Cyclopedia of Insurance Law (Couch on Insurance).*[20] No difference in technique from those already described is involved, but the treatment of the various topics is considerably more detailed than in the general legal encyclopedias. In addition, *Couch* cites pertinent *A. L. R.* annotations. There is an added approach, however, because each of these special encyclopedias has a table of cases. Therefore, a case in point leads directly from the case table to the discussion of the law desired.

    d. *Finding the law in Corpus Juris.* Those topics at the end of the alphabet, not yet superseded by *C. J. S.*, must still be searched in the *C. J.-C. J. S.* system through *C. J.*, where the process is the same as that already described for *C. J. S.*, with one exception. That, there is a consolidated "Descriptive-Word Index and Concordance" for the entire set, instead of separate indexes for each volume, and that the process of supplementation is as described at pages 179 and 180. The following illustrative problem is typical.

    1. An employee working on a highway sought protection from a storm, in a farm building fronting on the highway, where he was injured. Was he injured in an

---

[19] Appleman, *op. cit.* footnote 9.
[20] Couch, George J. *Cyclopedia of Insurance Law.* Rochester, N. Y., Lawyers' Co-operative Pub. Co., 1929-31 9 v., with annual pocket supplements.

accident "arising out of and in the course of his employment" so as to be compensable under the workmen's compensation acts?

a. *Index approach.* The problem is obviously one in "Workmen's Compensation" under a statute. It was not an accident on a highway, but one caused by seeking shelter from a storm. The index search leads to "Workmen's Compensation Acts: Shelter: Injury sustained while seeking shelter as arising out of and in course of employment. § 414." A search beginning with "Shelter" in the index would give the same result.

b. *Analytical approach.* The "Analysis" on page 181 of volume 71 of *C. J.* has twenty-six main heads, but "XII: Injuries for which compensation may be had" seems the only pertinent one. A sub-analysis of that topic, beginning on page 190, leads to "C: Arising out of, and in the course of employment." A rundown of that sub-analysis leads to "4b(4): Particular acts for personal comfort or convenience of employee: Seeking warmth or shelter. § 414." Section 414 gives a brief statement of the divergent rules applicable, with footnote citations to authority.

c. *Finding the latest authorities in point in C. J.* This problem in general is described at page 179. As applied to this specific problem ,v. 7, "Workmen's Compensation Acts," of the encyclopedia was published in 1935 (although the annual bound supplements to *C. J.* go back to 1921), and of course included all cases in point up to within a year or two of that time, when the compilation was completed. Examination of the "Annual Annotations" reveals that 1934 is the first volume containing a "Workmen's Compensation Acts" title, so that the supplementary search for authority begins with that volume. Cases in point are naturally found under "Workmen's Compensation Acts. § 414."

If the American Digest System is available, its use provides a quicker method of finding the digest paragraphs comprising the *C. J.* supplements. A case in point cited by *C. J.* in our problem above was *Ryan* v. *City of Port Huron*, 234 Mich. 648, 209 N. W. 101 (1926). The *North Western Reporter* syllabus shows that the pertinent Key-Number classification for our point was "Master and Servant ⟷ 375," but a search of the *Fourth Decennial Digest* under that number reveals that this material has been collected under a new title, "Workmen's Compensation." As explained at page 167, a separate table of cases in the "Workmen's Compensation" volume of the *Fourth Decennial* indicates that the *Ryan* case is now digested under "Workmen's Compensation ⟷ 655: Seeking warmth and shelter," under which number later cases in point will be found as digested.

The Legal Encyclopedia as Dictionary. *Am. Jur.* definitions are listed in its "General Index," under "Maxims" and "Words and Phrases." They are defined as part of the discussion of a subject matter in the text proper, not in alphabetical order as in a dictionary. In *C. J. S.*, words, terms, and maxims are defined and annotated in their regular alphabetical order, interspersed with the main text topics, as in a dictionary.

Integration of Annotations and Digests with Encyclopedias. Both *A. L. R.* annotations and digests frequently serve as valuable auxiliaries to legal encyclopedias.

A. L. R. annotations. Annotations consider at length minute points touched upon more broadly in treatises and encyclopedias. They cover by no means every desired point, but when there is an available annotation, it serves both an expository and a casefinder function. While *Am. Jur.* emphasizes its connection with the annotations and cites them directly, the parallel citations in other encyclopedias also lead to *A. L. R.* cases and their annotations. How this works out in the insurance problem above is shown by the following list of annotations in point. Such annotations as are listed are of course kept up to date by later annotations and cases as cited in the *A. L. R. Bluebook*, the function of which is described at pages 124 to 170.

"Engaged in aviation or aeronautics." Section XIV (Insurance Questions) of the annotation on "Aeroplanes and Aeronautics" in 99 A. L. R. 173, 199, continues earlier annotations. Under "participation in aeronautics," it cites, briefs, and discusses cases in point. An annotation in 155 A. L. R. 1026, "Construction and application of provisions of life or accident policy relating to aeronautics," discusses at length the cases interpreting seven different double indemnity aviation clauses.

Assignment of "all his right, title and interest." The annotation in 83 A. L. R. 77, on "Rights and remedies of beneficiary after death of insured who had pledged policy to secure debt," devotes a sub-division to the "Rights and remedies as between beneficiary and pledgee," which is continued in 160 A. L. R. 1389, 1393.

Survivorship when a common disaster clause. This is treated in the annotation, "Disposition of life insurance which, by terms of policy, is dependent upon survivorship . . . ," in 113 A. L. R. 881, which discusses also the burden of proof.

Duty to exhaust other collateral or other assets of insured. Two pages of the annotation in 160 A. L. R. 1393, 1393, cited above, discuss this point.

Chapter 21

TREATISES

A. Functions of Treatises.
B. Authority of Treatises.
C. Kinds of Treatises.
D. Form of Treatises.
E. Supplementation of Treatises.
F. Techniques in the Use of Treatises.

A. Functions of Treatises.

The reader of a treatise usually has one or more of the following purposes: to brush up or refresh his memory on the present state of the law covered by the book; to study minutely an aspect of the law less thoroughly treated in any other medium; or to take from it citations to leading cases in point which will lead to other cases.

The treatise, as an index to the law, applies the expert knowledge and research facilities of the author to an exhaustive consideration of the decided cases and statutes of competent jurisdiction in point, and then sets down in connected literary style an exposition of the law as found therein. It thus goes a step beyond the digest, which supplies no comment. The encyclopedia is said to be an alphabetically arranged collection of treatises, but, according to its scope and purpose, the treatise may be expected to do things that the encyclopedia does not usually attempt. It traces the history of the law covered, and its development along varying lines. In its best form it is apt to be more assiduous than the encyclopedia to point out the effect of statutes or of cases overruling a line of earlier cases, and to call attention to majority, minority, and jurisdictional rules, and trends or needed changes. It is less a frame of reference from an elementary exposition, to cited cases to be read; and more an exhaustive treatment of the law, with a detailed study of the cases. Whereas the encyclopedia is rarely critical, the treatise is quite apt to be so, and it thus exerts a definite formative influence upon the law.

Effective means of supplementation are provided for practitioners' books.

The kind of treatise consulted will depend upon the lawyer's problem, and there are works of a kind to satisfy most of his needs. He may be interested in the history of the law; or, if a student or lawyer who has never studied the particular branch of the law upon which he is now required to advise, he seeks an elementary exposition, with citation to leading cases; or he may want a practitioners' text which is little more than a digest of all cases, in literary form. A candidate for admission to the Bar studies review or "cram" books of a single jurisdiction. Many books on the law are written for the layman — business or professional men, taxpayers, housewives, authors, *etc.* The needs and the varieties of books to provide for their interests are endless.

191

B. Authority of Treatises.[1]

The textbook is to be used, not as authority, but as a guide to the finding of authority or as a means of refreshing the searcher's memory of the principles of law governing his problems. It is a paradox. It is at once the first book consulted by most lawyers and law students when starting to "work up" the materials on a point of law; and it is without standing as authority. Contrary to the situation in most learned fields, the textwriter in common law, no matter what his eminence, is not authority, though he may be influential to the degree that his analyses and statements of the law as extracted from the cases and statutes seem valid. When treatises are mentioned in opinions and briefs it is because the judge or attorney citing them adopts their reasoning or statements, with accompanying citations to authority, as his own. But it is the *cases* which are the authority, *not* the author's analysis. Author Cooley's comment, in his treatise on *Torts,* upon Mr. Justice Cooley's opinion in a Michigan Supreme Court decision, is not authority, though the opinion may be.

Within these limitations, the treatise may be extremely useful, and is often cited by court and attorney. While no court is bound by a statement in *Wigmore* or *Williston,* or any other treatise, it is just as true that it will be influenced by a carefully reasoned analysis of a line of cases by these authors, especially if that analysis has stood up for a number of years. While no treatise has ever achieved the dignity of mandatory authority, some have approached it. Henry Bracton's *De Legibus et Consuetudinibus Angliae;*[2] Ranulf de Glanville's *Tractatus de Legibus et Consuetudinibus Regni Anglie;*[3] Thomas Littleton's *Tenures;*[4] and William Blackstone's *Commentaries on the Laws of England,*[5] are examples.

C. Kinds of Treatises.

Treatises are classified according to their purpose, as histories of the law, works on jurisprudence, commentaries, monographs, and textbooks proper. Naturally, in the actual writing there is considerable overlapping of these categories. Since treatises are published in such great numbers, the works listed below are merely illustrative examples of various types.

Histories of Anglo-American Law. These vary in size and scope from the multi-volume work aiming to treat exhaustively the whole subject (such as William S. Holdsworth's thirteen-volume *A History of English Law*),[6] to an elementary student's book like Max Radin's *Handbook of Anglo-American Legal History.*[7] The literature of legal history is well outlined in such books as Winfield's *Chief Sources of English Legal History.*[8]

---

[1] Numerous examples of the citation and influence of treatises in court are collected by Borris M. Komar in *Probative Force of Authoritative Law Works,* 3 B. U. L. Rev. 175 (1923), and 5 B. U. L. Rev. 32 (1925); and by W. M. Lile, *The Uses and Abuses of Secondary Authority,* 1 Va. L. Rev. 604 (1913).

[2] London, Richard Tottell, 1659.

[3] London, Richard Tottell, 1554.

[4] London, Lettour & Machlinia, 1480.

[5] Oxford, Clarendon Press, 1765-1769. 4 v.

[6] London, Methuen, 1903-1952. 13 v.

[7] St. Paul, West 1936.

[8] Cambridge, Harvard Univ. Press, 1925.

Works on Jurisprudence. Such works include studies and speculation on what is law and where it comes from; the philosophy of law; the growth of the law and of legal science. They are apt to be scholarly and highly technical, and of more immediate interest to the scholar and teacher than to the elementary student and practitioner. Examples are Carleton K. Allen, *Law in the Making;*[9] John Austin, *The Austinian Theory of Law;*[10] Jeremy Bentham, *Theory of Legislation;*[11] Benjamin N. Cardozo, *The Paradoxes of Legal Science;*[12] Roscoe Pound, *Social Control Through Law;*[13] and Julius Stone, *The Providence and Function of Law.*[14]

Commentaries. Commentaries are seldom written any more, because the law has grown much too complicated to be expressed in the manner of a commentary. They are broad in scope, as Blackstone's *Commentaries on the Laws of England,*[15] Kent's *Commentaries on American Law,*[16] or (in much smaller compass) Coke on *Littleton's Tenures.*[17] They are expositions of the principles of a large subject matter, in which the author's views are set forth, reinforced by such authority as he deems it advisable to adduce. The purpose of the commentary is to instruct the reader in the fundamentals of the law (in which aim it resembles the elementary student's book). It is not primarily a case finder and commonly cites comparatively few cases. It is thus at the opposite pole from a work on the law of long-term leases in New York, for example, which is very limited in scope and short on general theory, but aims to be an exhaustive casefinder for the subject covered.

Monographs. As the name suggests, such a book takes for its subject a single legal topic and deals with it exhaustively. This subject may be very narrow, as the rule against perpetuities, or a law review article on equitable mortgages in New York; or it may comprise a major sub-division of the law, such as a multi-volume work on contracts, evidence, or real property. Few monographs in this technical sense are now written, particularly on large topics, since the requirements are so great as to discourage all but those few authors with special facilities. As distinguished from the textbook proper, the monograph aims at a thoroughly scholarly exposition of the topic within its scope. It considers that topic's historical and theoretical background and development; its divergent rules and the reasons therefor; and present trends and probable or needed changes by way of statute or decision. This is all backed by exhaustive citation to and analysis of authority. Such a book, if frequently supplemented, is also a good practitioners' book. Examples of such works are Samuel Williston, *Contracts;* John H. Wigmore, *Evidence;* and R. R. Powell, *Real Property.* Student editions have been made from some monographs by eliminating all but the most important footnote citations, while retaining most of the text discussion.

Textbooks Proper. These are intended for instruction or as casefinders, and most treatises fall within this category. They may be subdivided into student

---

[9] 5th ed. Oxford, Clarendon Press, 1951.

[10] London, Murray, 1931.

[11] *The Works of Jeremy Bentham,* vol. 1. Edinburgh, W. Tait, 1843.

[12] New York, Columbia Univ. Press, 1928.

[13] New Haven, Yale Univ. Press, 1942.

[14] Sydney, Australia, Associated General Publications, 1946.

[15] *See* Footnote 5, above.

[16] New York, O. Halsted, 1826-30. 4 v.

[17] Coke, Sir Edward. *The First Part of the Institutes of the Laws of England; or, A Commentarie upon Littleton.* London. Printed for the Societie of Stationers, 1628.

books (including bar review books), practitioners' books, encyclopedias on a single large topic (as corporations or insurance), and law books for the layman. The emphasis in all of them is on the practical rather than the scholarly, though some, especially some of the more recent student books, combine the two. Some of the varieties of textbooks are described below, together with criteria of their value.

Varieties of Treatises. Below are comments on the makeup of various kinds of treatises, with examples. The examples are in no sense to be regarded as a list of "best books."

1. *Student Books.* The student book offers an elementary exposition of the principles of the topic covered — such as contracts, torts, or insurance — for the purpose of instructing its readers or refreshing their memory. Like the monograph, it traces the historical development of the topic, though usually with less detail, discusses the divergent rules, criticizes cases, and tries to provide an overall picture of the law involved. Often it is the best available book on the topic. Not being intended as an exhaustive case finder, it makes no attempt to list all in point, but confines itself to a relatively few leading cases — though in recent years the number cited has tended to increase. Theory and trends are emphasized, elements which are commonly omitted from practitioners' books. A generation ago this type of book found few readers among practitioners, but now it is recognized as an excellent starting point, both for a brush-up and for good cases in point. Furthermore, it often supplies the most convenient survey of the more scholarly aspects of the subject treated, since it tends to follow the techniques of modern law school instruction. A substantial part of some of these books first appeared as leading articles in law review. An example is K. C. Davis, *Administrative Law*.[18]

The student book's value for the student lies, not in substituting it for a careful reading of his casebook, but in putting him straight as to the meaning of a case in the overall picture of the law, when the case has not been clear to him when read. Since some casebooks are keyed to popular student books, and vice versa, there is always a fair chance that a search of the table of cases of the text will lead to a discussion of the points raised in the case.

2. *Cram and bar review books.* A variation of the student book is the cram book, which is an outline of a restricted topic, for a single jurisdiction, such as criminal law, family law, or practice, and is intended only for review purposes. It mentions local peculiarities, collects a minimum number of outstanding cases and statutes, but is worthless for general instructional purposes. In the fulfillment of its own very limited function, however, it is useful.

3. *Practitioners' books.* Most law books are written neither for students nor for scholars, but to help practicing lawyers win cases. Accordingly, the majority of these books emphasize the casefinding function of the treatise and the practical aspects of the existing law, rather than historical development and theories. They assume a sufficient background in the law to permit the text to concentrate on bare essentials. Some practitioners' books are little more than digests. They are apt to disappoint the seeker after an adequate picture of the meanderings of the law or the reasons behind them, but if they cite all cases in point and extract from them a valid statement of the law as it now stands, as a basis for prediction by judge or advocate, they serve their purpose; always provided, of course, that they are supplemented often enough. It should be understood that there is no hard and fast dividing line between the scholarly books and the practitioners' books; some of the better ones are both.

4. *Annotations as treatises.* *A. L. R.* annotations assume increasingly the character and proportions of practitioners' treatises on comparatively limited topics usually not treated at length in separate textbooks. An example is in two successive annotations by W. E. Shipley in 16 A. L. R. 2d (1951) on the topics of (1) excessive and (2) ade-

---

[18] St. Paul, West, 1951.

quate damages for personal injuries not resulting in death. Together, these two annotations occupy 453 pages and consider 162 separate types of injury. They are indexed to the extent of fififteen pages.

5. *Local books.* Many practitioners' books are "local" in character, confined as narrowly as practicable to the law of the jurisdiction for which they are written. Thus, there are books on the New York law of landlord and tenant; Delaware, New Jersey and other state books on corporations; Maryland and other state books on marriage and divorce; *etc.* Similarly, there are "United States" books, such as those on the federal law of contracts and on federal practice. These local books, as might be expected, are most common in procedural law, nearly every state or group of states having one or more such, well and frequently supplemented. The procedural books run the gamut, from the massive encyclopedia of twenty-five volumes to the tiny bar cram book.

6. *Encyclopedias.* In some fields, such as insurance, corporations, automobiles, municipal corporations, and federal procedure, practitioners' books, encyclopedic in scope and treatment, aim at complete coverage of every aspect of the topic, substantive and procedural, with annotated forms. As with general legal encyclopedias, these are in effect collections of smaller treatises, so integregated as to cover the entire topic without undue overlapping.

7. *Noncommercial works.* Many topics are of such limited appeal, because of their nature or because an adequate treatment requires such an excessive amount of research in relation to their probable sales, that the commercial publishers can not afford to publish treatises on them at all, or at least not without substantial subsidy. Fortunately, university presses and endowed foundations or funds have stepped into this breach and many books falling within the above category are published. Often these works are not only of scholarly worth but are of value to the practitioner as well, affording the only adequate treatment of a subject. Examples are:

Abbott, Grace. *The Child and the State.* Chicago, Univ. of Chicago Press, 1947. 2 v.

Berger, Morroe. *Equality by Statute.* New York, Columbia Univ. Press, 1952.

Carpenter, Jesse T. *Employers' Associations and Collective Bargaining in New York City.* Ithaca, Cornell Univ. Press, 1950.

Cooper, Frank E. *Administrative Agencies and the Courts.* Ann Arbor, Univ. of Michigan Law School, 1951.

Daggett, Harriett S. *Mineral Rights in Louisiana.* Baton Rouge, Louisiana State Univ. Press, 1949.

Mangum, Charles S. *The Legal Status of the Negro.* Chapel Hill, Univ. of North Carolina Press, 1940.

————*The Legal Status of the Tenant Farmer in the Southeast.* Chapel Hill, Univ. of North Carolina Press, 1952.

Orfield, Lester B. *The Amending of the Federal Constitution.* Ann Arbor, Univ. of Michigan Press, 1942.

Rabel, Ernst. *The Conflict of Laws.* Ann Arbor, Univ. of Michigan Press, 1945-50. 3 v.

Ragland, George, Jr. *Discovery Before Trial.* Chicago, Callaghan, 1932.

Uhler, Armin. *Review of Administrative Acts.* Ann Arbor, Univ. of Michigan Press, 1942.

Vanderbilt, Arthur T. *Minimum Standards of Judicial Administration.* New York, National Conference of Judicial Councils, 1949.

Wood, Virginia L. *Due Process of Law, 1932-1949.* Baton Rouge, Louisiana State Univ. Press, 1951.

Government publications, discussed in Chapter 27 are, of course, in this category.

8. *Institutes and symposia.* Not all non-commercial publications emphasize the research or learned aspects of the law. On the contrary, many are intensely practical. The latter are likely to be the published papers of an increasing number of institutes and symposia. Although these are in book form, they perhaps resemble more the legal periodical article, being composed for the most part of groups of comparatively short

essays on the topic of the institute or symposium. In fact, the symposia are often published in law reviews. Typical of the institutes are those of the Practising Law Institute, giving brush-up courses for lawyers; the New York University annual institute on federal taxation; the Southwestern Legal Foundation annual institute on oil and gas, and its institute on personal injury litigation; the University of Notre Dame convocations on natural law; the University of Oklahoma institute on tax procedure; the University of Illinois institute on legislation on collective bargaining; and the copyright institute of the Federal Bar Association of New York, New Jersey, and Connecticut.

9. *Essays.* Essays in honor of a distinguished lawyer, judge, or teacher are occasionally published, the contributors being almost always among the most distinguished men in their fields. Essay contests are also a source of useful contributions. These essays, on a general theme related to the principal activity of the person honored or in whose name the contest is held, usually, but by no means always, emphasize the scholarly, and often discuss topics not elsewhere treated so well or so fully, if at all. An example is, "Our Non-Citizen Nationals, Who Are They?," by Dudley O. McGovney,[19] which discusses the status of Puerto Rican, Hawaiians, *etc.* The Henry L. Doherty Memorial Fund was responsible for a volume of essays on petroleum conservation. The essays of the annual Nathan Burkan competition produce essays on copyright law which are needed in a field in which too little is written. The Association of American Law Schools has compiled volumes of *Selected Essays* on contracts, family law, constitutional law, comprising reprints of law review articles of outstanding merit. The New York University School of Law has published (through the New York University Press) a three-volume work, *Law: a Century of Progress 1835-1935* (1937); and has more or less continued this study since 1942 with its *Annual Survey of American Law.*

10. *Trade or professional association publications.* Some organizations of attorneys in specialized fields, as municipalities and credit men, publish compilations of data of interest to them. These may consist of essays or of annotated abridgments of laws of all states on, for example, replevin, and are of a highly practical nature. Usually these compilations are open to the public, but occasionally, because of the possibility of danger inherent in the subject matter, they are restricted.

11. *Specialties.* Below are a few examples of treatises on rather narrow topics:

Bishop, Frank P. *Advertising and the Law.* London, E. Benn Ltd., 1928.

Bugan, Thomas G. *When Does Title Pass as Between Shipper and Consignee?* Chicago, Scheffer Print. Co., 1948.

Dunham, Allison. *Property Tax Exemption of Colleges and Universities.* New York, Commission on Financing Higher Education, 1951.

Lindey, Alexander. *Plagiarism and Originality.* New York, Harper & Bros, 1952.

Loss, Louis. *Securities Regulation.* Boston, Little Brown & Co., 1951.

Magill, Roswell F. *Taxable Income.* Revised Ed. New York, Ronald Press, 1945.

Norris, Martin J. *The Law of Seamen.* New York, Baker, Voorhis & Co., 1951.

Philos, Conrad D. *Handbook of Court Martial Law.* Chicago, Callaghan, 1951.

Pollak, Otto. *The Criminality of Women.* Philadelphia, Univ. of Pennsylvania Press, 1950.

Sage, George H. *Basing-Point Pricing Systems Under the Federal Antitrust Laws.* St. Louis, Thomas Law Book Co., 1951.

Thomas, Aaron J., Jr. *Economic Regulation of Scheduled Air Transport.* Buffalo, Dennis, 1951.

Warner, Harry P. *Radio and Television Law.* Albany, Bender, 1948.

Wiener, Frederick B. *Effective Appellate Advocacy.* New York, Prentice-Hall Inc., 1950.

Yankwich, Leon R. *It's Libel or Contempt if You Print It.* Los Angeles, Parker, 1950.

12. *Law books for the business or professional man.* "Everyman his own law-

---

[19] In *Legal Essays in Tribute to Orrin Kip McMurray.* Berkeley, Univ. of California Press, 1935.

yer" books are always with us, but are without the purview of this *Manual*. However, there are numerous works written for business or professional men, which, though not typical law books, are of value to the lawyer because they tell him something about the special problems of these people, and of the applicable law. Commonly these books are written for the benefit of the hotel man, the undertaker, the publisher, the minister, the accountant, or the engineer, to apprise and warn him of some of the situations confronting him which might lead to legal liability. They cite few cases, but those are sufficient, with the help of the text, to set a skilled lawyer on the right track. Their value to the people for whom primarily written is lessened usually by the lack of supplementation to keep them up to date. Examples of books for professional and business men are:

Arthur, William R. *The Law of Drugs and Druggists*. 2d ed. St. Paul, West, 1940.
Brothers, Elmer D. *Dental Jurisprudence*. St. Louis, Mosby Co., 1926.
Edwards, Newton. *The Courts and the Public Schools*. Chicago, Univ. of Chicago Press, 1936.
Hannah, Harold W. *Law on the Farm*. New York, Macmillan, 1948.
McCullough, Conde B. and John R. *The Engineer at Law*. Salem, Ore., State Print. Dept., 1946. 2 v.
Street, Arthur L. H. *The Miller and the Law*. Minneapolis, Minn., Miller Pub. Co., 1926.
Thomas, Edward. *Chemical Inventions and Chemical Patents*. Albany, Bender, 1950.
Zollman, Carl. *American Church Law*. St. Paul, West, 1933.

A useful series intended to give the intelligent layman a brief survey of his rights and duties in various areas of the law is the inexpensive "Legal Almanac Series,"[20] small pamphlets on such subjects as marriage and divorce, immigration and naturalization, rent regulation, *etc.*

13. *Business books for the lawyer.* Some specialties are published for the lawyer himself. There are books telling him or his managing clerk how to run the business of a law office; the mechanics of writing legal communications on a typewriter; how to set up a calendar; how to write fee contracts, *etc.* Also there are books for him to read about the business side of patents, and how to understand the accounting problems arising in his practice. Some of these books are:

Ambert, Roy T. *Lawyers' Practice Time Table*. New York, Baker, Voorhis & Co., 1936.
Antus, John J. *Law Office Secretary's Manual*. New York, Prentice-Hall, Inc., 1940.
Horowitz, Jacob I. *Manual for Lawyers and Law Clerks*. 2 ed. New York, Central Book Co., 1936.
McCarty, Dwight G. *Law Office Management*. Rev. ed. New York, Prentice-Hall, Inc., 1946.
Oehler, Christian. *Lawyer's Accounting Handbook*. Albany, Bender, 1952.
Schmutz, George L. *Condemnation Appraisal Handbook*. New York, Prentice-Hall, Inc., 1949.
Shannon, William H. *Legal Accounting*. St. Paul, West, 1951.
Shugerman, A. L. *Accounting for Lawyers*. Indianapolis, Bobbs-Merrill, 1952.
Wood, Earl W. *Fee Contracts for Lawyers,* New York, Prentice-Hall, Inc., 1936.

14. *Comparative law.* Somewhat akin to works on jurisprudence but usually of more immediate interest to the practitioner are those works discussing and comparing the laws across national lines, such as studies of international trade-mark or copyright registration, constitutional law, divorce laws, press laws, and the like. Examples are:

Fitzgibbon, Russell H. *The Constitutions of the Americas as of January 1, 1948*. Chicago, Univ. of Chicago Press, 1948.

---

[20] New York, Oceana Publications.

Galenson, Walter. *Comparative Labor Movements*. New York, Prentice-Hall, Inc., 1952.

Gutteridge, H. C. *Comparative Law*. Cambridge, University Press, 1949.

Hereward, P. O. *Handbook on Trade Mark Laws Throughout the World*. London, Sweet & Maxwell, 1951.

Ireland, Gordon and Galindez, Jesús de. *Divorce in the Americas*. Buffalo, N. Y., Dennis, 1947.

Kruse, Louis F. V. *The Right of Property*. London, Oxford Univ. Press, 1939.

Ladas, Stephen P. *International Protection of Industrial Property*. Cambridge, Harvard Univ. Press, 1930.

————*International Protection of Literary and Artistic Property*. New York, Macmillan, 1938.

————*International Protection of Trade Marks*. Cambridge, Harvard Univ. Press, 1929.

Terrou, Fernant and Lucien Solal. *Legislation for Press, Film and Radio*. Paris, UNESCO, 1951.

United Nations. Secretariat. Dept. of Social Affairs. *Probation and Related Measures*. New York, 1951.

Foreign Law Books for the American Lawyer. More and more, the American lawyer's practice brings him into contact with foreign law. While he will usually retain a specialist to advise him in such circumstances, there are times when a knowledge of the existence of foreign codes or commentaries in English (usually in his Bar library) will be helpful. There are English translations of many foreign codes, and some legal directories abridge such laws as pertain to business and domestic relations; there are treaties on divorce in the Americas, patents, trademarks, and copyright throughout the world, and of the right of property. The United Nations has published documents in English relating to many aspects of the laws of all countries. On the purely business side, there is an extensive income tax law service for some Latin-American countries, and the semi-official Inter-American Development Commission has published for each of several Latin-American countries "A Statement of the Laws . . . in Matters Affecting Business in its Various Aspects and Activities."

D. Form of Treatises.

The typical legal treatise differs from any other kind of treatise only in having a table of cases, and occasionally a table of statutes commented upon; and, particularly in practitioners' books, in its frequency of supplementation. Some treatises (W. R. Schneider's *Workmen's Compensation* [21] is an example) collect and print the statutes in point, either verbatim or abridged. Prefaces, tables of contents and subject indexes perform their usual functions. The prefaces, particularly in student books, may be very much worth reading, as placing the subjects of the books in their proper setting.

Criteria of the Value of Treatises. Treatises range from the excellent and indispensable to the worthless. The great flood of decided cases combines with the increasing impact of statutory changes of settled law to render it next to impossible for any single man to cover adequately and continuously any large area of the law. For this reason, treatises are written "more and more about less and less." In other words, commentaries on the whole law are no longer written,

---

[21] 3d or Permanent ed. St. Louis, Thomas, 1941-51. 9 v.

and monographic treatments of large topics are rare. For example, no new (as distinguished from a new edition) extensive treatment of corporations has appeared since 1917; but a great many treatises on such minute topics as "Corporate Meetings, Minutes and Resolutions," "Modern Corporate Reports to Stockholders, Employees and the Public," and "Corporate Charter Amendments Affecting the Interests of Stockholders in the Properties of the Corporation" have appeared. Textbook writing of any considerable scope is and must be a business carried on by or with the help of a publisher's editorial staff. Of course exceptional circumstances turn up a man who, as teacher, reporter for an American Law Institute topic, or the retiring counsel and executive of (say) an insurance organization, makes available as a by-product the many years of his research and practice.

Some criteria are noted below.

1. *Purpose of the book.* This is most important. Is the book a monumental treatise like *Williston,* or a student book like *Anson?* Is it a practitioners' all-inclusive work like Walker's *Patents,* or an abstruse book on a minute topic like patent claim drafting? Is it intended for the use of a student, lawyer, or research professor? To be useful, the book must be designed for the reader consulting it. A book on copyright law written for and useful to the author and publisher as a guide to how to copyright a book, and allied problems, might be valueless to the lawyer with an infringement problem; and the reverse.

2. *Timeliness.* This as a factor depends upon the topic covered. Real property law in general changes slowly, but a statutory change may render indispensable for the moment a treatise on cooperative apartments which will be obsolete in five years. There was a rash of books on the 1938 Federal Rules of Civil Procedure, useful at the time as comparing the new with the old, but of no value now, because speculation has been superseded by the authority of decided cases interpreting the rules.

3. *Availability of other books on the subject.* A book on a subject not elsewhere treated in print may be of some value, at least as a casefinder, even if not well done.

4. *Age of the book.* This as a factor also depends upon the nature of the book. Cardozo's works on jurisprudence are as useful and valid today as when written; a student book expository of broad principles of a subject like torts or contracts, ages slowly as a general thing, but needs occasional revision to keep abreast of gradual change; a practitioners' book — a case finder — on the other hand, requires frequent supplementation to maintain its value.

5. *Editions.* Lawyers are conservative about their books, and prefer old friends to new ones. Consequently, long after the original author or compiler of a successful text is dead, new editions continue to come out in his name. John Norton Pomeroy's *Equity Jurisprudence* [22] was first published in 1881, but continues to be a standard work. Obviously, in such a case, the contribution of the original author is diluted by the years and the real value of the current edition depends largely upon its editor. If it is a true new edition, well done, that is fine; if, as often happens, it is merely brought up to date by citing supplementary cases without integrating them into the text, a digest may be better.

6. *Author and publisher.* Text writing involves infinite labor as well as wide knowledge and deep scholarship. Some authors have achieved such a reputation for work well done that almost anything of theirs may be accepted without question. Of others, questions may well be asked. What is the author's professional standing; is he a well known teacher; has he been a reporter for the American Law Institute; a successful practitioner; an outstanding judge; or is the work the joint product of the editorial staff of a publishing house known for the soundness of its output? Or has it been published by a university press, a learned foundation or a government agency which in the past has published reliable books? The publisher is apt to be an important factor in the evaluation of a law book. One with an established reputation for producing works

---

[22] 5th ed., San Francisco, Calif., Bancroft-Whitney; Rochester, N. Y., Lawyers Co-operative Pub. Co., 1941. 5 v.

of high excellence may usually (though not always) be relied upon to protect that reputation and to demand and attract good manuscripts. This does not mean that a lesser known publisher does not likewise publish good law books, but it does place a little more burden of proof on him. Again, some publishers have staffs which enable them to specialize in case-finder-type works which the lawyer may buy with the reasonable assurance that they will be regularly supplemented and so protected against speedy obsolescence — a service other publishers may be less equipped to render. Some publishers put out the best "local books" for their areas. Some publish only a few law books, but these of a uniformly high grade of scholarly and practical excellence. A few place a bar sinister upon their imprints.

. **7. *A survey of the available material in a single subject.*** An example of the variety of works on single topic of the law is in the annotated bibliography on patent law, by Miles O. Price, in 42 Law Library Journal 47 (1949). A shorter list, for evidence, follows.

Chamberlayne, Charles F. *A Treatise on the Modern Law of Evidence.* Albany, M. Bender, 1911–1916. 5 v. (A somewhat shorter treatment than Wigmore's)

Cohn, Alfred and Joseph F. Chisholm. *Take the Witness.* New York. F. A. Stokes, 1934.

Cornelius, Asher L. *Cross-Examination of Witnesses.* Indianapolis, Bobbs-Merrill, 1929.

Curtis, Arthur F. *New York Law of Evidence.* Albany, M. Bender, 1926. (a local practice book)

Greenman, Frederick F. *Wire-tapping.* Stamford, Conn., Overbrook Press, 1938.

Harvard Law Review. *Selected Essays on the Law of Evidence.* 2d ed. Cambridge, Harvard Law Review Association, 1941.

Herzog, Asa S. *Camera, Take the Stand!* New York, Prentice-Hall, Inc., 1940.

Sandifer, Durward V. *Evidence Before International Tribunals.* Chicago, Foundation Press, 1939.

Scott, Charles C. *Photographic Evidence.* Kansas City, Vernon Law Book Co., 1942.

Stephens, Harold M. *Administrative Tribunals and the Rules of Evidence.* Cambridge, Harvard Univ. Press, 1933.

Stern, William A. *Getting the evidence.* Albany, M. Bender, 1936.

Wigmore, John H. *The Principles of Judicial Proof.* Boston, Little, Brown & Co., 1931.

Wigmore, John H. *A Students' Textbook on the Law of Evidence.* Chicago, Foundation Press, 1935.

Wigmore, John H. *A Treatise on the Anglo-American System of Evidence in Trials at Common Law.* 3d ed. Boston, Little, Brown & Co., 1940. 10 v.

E. Supplementation of Treatises.

In general, a practitioners' book is no better than its supplementation service. A major disadvantage of the treatise, as compared to the digest or encyclopedia, is its tendency to obsolescence. Publishers employ several devices to overcome this. Entirely new editions are fairly frequent, especially in local practice books. (In England the lawyers tend to reject the treatise supplement in favor of frequent new editions.) Bound or pamphlet supplements, usually annual, are usual, the most common type being the cumulative pocket supplement or "part." A recent development which overcomes most of the disadvantages of other kinds of supplements is the loose-leaf binder, permitting the preparation and insertion of new pages or pamphlets in their proper places when called for, but doing away with the pocket parts and (to a considerable extent) recompiled volumes. An example is Richard R. Powell's *Real Property.*[23]

---

[23] Albany, M. Bender. v. 1–3 pub. to date, 1949–52.

A technique the student should acquire early is to examine the date both of the main work and of the supplement of any treatise he is consulting, as the date may largely determine its value.

F. Techniques in the Use of Treatises.

While the manner of use of treatises is fairly obvious, the discussion below may be helpful.

Purpose of the Search. Most important is the purpose for which the books is to be used. A learned doctoral dissertation on the history and theory of insurance would perhaps ill serve the lawyer seeking the latest cases on injury to employees in atomic energy laboratories; nor would the student desiring a brief discussion of the theory of insurable interest first consult a comprehensive insurance law encyclopedia. The truck fleet owner desiring a general guide to the principles of automobile liability insurance under the National Standard Policy provisions; or a travel agency interested in a study of aviation accident law applicable to international air transportation, might be best served by one of several books written for him as a business man — and the lawyer needing a refresher could profitably read the same book. Defining the purpose also serves to narrow the search. Although the lawyer with a case on collective bargaining could extract much of profit from a large treatise on contracts generally, a specialized treatise by an experienced labor lawyer, on that precise topic, probably would be better.

Learning What is Published and Available. Legal treatises are published by many agencies, as commercial publishers, university presses, foundations, trade associations, and government bureaus. The commercial publishers keep both law library and private practitioner apprised of their current publications, but the other agencies have little contact with the practitioner. By far the best source of information for him is a good law library catalog by author, title, and subject, as administered by a competent librarian. Usually these librarians may be reached by telephone and are glad to give advice.

The possibility that a book other than a legal treatise is available either in the law library or in a nearby university or public library should not be overlooked. Many agencies have legal departments which compile guides of various kinds for the conduct of their own business, which may be just what is needed to answer a specialized question. It is not always clear, however, without examination of the books themselves, just what they contain. There may be a chapter on a topic not elsewhere covered, but not brought out in the catalog. It is therefore best to examine a likely book carefully, especially the table of contents and the subject index, since even a single section or paragraph may supply a valuable lead.

Tables. The *table of contents* fulfills an obvious function and should be examined for the author's analysis. The *subject index* provides a much more detailed analysis, but the reader must realize that indexers may not think the way he does, and that considerable ingenuity is often required to find a topic's listing. The *table of cases*, found in nearly all law books, emphasizes the secondary nature of a treatise, and is a factor in the makeup of the text pages. In varying degree these pages are composed of text commentary above the line, supported by citations to authority below. In a book on legal history or the philosophy of law, these footnote references are usually comparatively few; in a student text most of the "leading" cases are cited; while in a practitioners' work, substantially all cases in point are cited, as in a digest, often taking up more space on a page than the main text above the line. *The table of cases has two principal functions.* It leads to the page or pages (or sections) in the treatise where the significant points of law in a case are discussed; and the case citations in the footnotes on the designated pages give parallel references to all standard reports printing the case, thus leading the reader to annotations or digests of other cases in point. Some student books are deliberately keyed to popular casebooks, to enable the student to find a discussion of the meaning and effect of the cases in them.

Correlation of Treatises with other Books of Index. Having found the discussion he wants, through the table of cases, the reader, if he wants to go on from there, has various resources at his command, particularly through the Key-Number given in the *Reporter* cited, or through the digest table of cases; and he can find annotations if the case was reprinted in *A. L. R.* Through the *A. L. R. Digest* he can find the treatment of the applicable point of law in *American Jurisprudence.* If the case has been decided since 1916, the reader may also be able to find it discussed in a law review, through the *Index to Legal Periodicals* case table; or, in many cases, the law review article is directly cited by the footnote in the text, or in *Shepard's Citations.* It is an endless chain. Conversely, having found a case in point in some other manner, the searcher can often find it listed in the table of cases in a treatise, leading to the text discussion and the citations of other authority. When a case in point has been found in one treatise but the discussion there is inadequate, it is often simple to locate a like discussion on the subject in another treatise, through its case table.

Forms. Many treatises print pertinent forms, either in a separate section or in the text proper. These are usually well indexed and are often annotated to the statutes and cases as well. Form books are discussed in Chapter 25.

CHAPTER 22

LEGAL PERIODICALS

A. Function.

The legal periodical is at once a student's book, a practitioner's book, and the foremost outlet of the research scholar in law. It is the most versatile of all the books in a law library. It is flexible, represents many points of view, and discusses legal topics ranging from the elementary, through the eminently practical, to the most learned and abstruse. As is true in other professional fields, new developments in the law are usually first discussed in the professional periodical and often discussed there only. As a forum for the critical analysis of legal topics it is pre-eminent. In articles of differing purposes it discusses the law as it *was*, as it *is*, as it *is tending*, and as it *ought to be* — with a thoroughness and thoughtfulness found nowhere else.

Many proposed reforms in the law got their first airing through this medium, including those relating to corporate reorganization, the new Federal Rules of Civil Procedure, "Heart-Balm" legislation, fair trade laws, and the undistributed profits tax.

B. Authority

Legal periodicals are only persuasive, as are treatises and encyclopedias.

No court ever cites a law review article as mandatory authority, but they are frequently referred to in opinions and footnotes in such a manner as to leave no doubt as to their persuasiveness. An example is the frequent mention of law review articles written by Samuel C. Wiel, on the theories of water use, in the opinion in *United States* v. *Gerlach Live Stock Co.*[1] The court in *Rahorn* v. *Hayton*[2] cites no less than twelve law review articles in its opinion. Perhaps the practice of citing this material stems from the presence of former law teachers on the Supreme Court bench. Among others this would include Justices Stone, Frankfurter, Rutledge, Burton, Holmes, Douglas, and Roberts.

---

[1] 339 U. S. 725, 70 S. Ct. 955, 94 L. Ed. 1231 (1950).
[2] 34 Wash. 2d 105, 208 P. 2d 133 (1949).

C. Varieties.

Legal periodicals are of many kinds, published under many auspices and for many purposes. The principal varieties are mentioned below.

Practice Periodicals. Some legal periodicals or newspapers have as almost their only function keeping their subscribers abreast of the legal business transacted within their area. Commonly these print court dockets and reports, comments on pending cases, and legal advertising. Some of the reports published are of cases of purely local interest, reports perhaps not elsewhere printed. Some legal newspapers are in part official organs for courts in their areas. (An example is the *New York Law Journal.*) The appeal of these periodicals is almost wholly temporary, but they are nevertheless indispensable for their time and purpose. Those described below are for purposes of example only; there are many others.

1. The United States Law Week. This loose-leaf periodical consists of an unnumbered federal statutes section and four numbered sections, some of which have already been described adequately in connection with statutes and law reports. "The *statute section* is issued only as laws of general interest or importance are passed by Congress." Numbered *Section 1*, entitled "Summary and Analysis," is a four-page news comment on recent federal statutes, federal and state court decisions, and federal agency rulings. *Section 2* publishes digests of varying length, of selected new federal and state court decisions, and of federal agency rulings. *Section 3* contains the "Journal of proceedings of the Supreme Court, summary orders of the Court, cases docketed and summary of cases recently filed, calendar of hearings scheduled, and special articles on Supreme Court work; including summaries of arguments in important cases, periodical reports on cases argued and awaiting decision, *etc.*" *Section 4* contains "opinions . . . in full text, supplemented by Digest-headnotes, and with cumulative table of opinions for current term of the Court."

Index to the United States Law Week. There are two indexes. A green-paper one covers the statutes and Section 2; it is issued monthly and cumulates for six months, after which there are two "permanent" six-months indexes which together cover the entire yearly volume. That is, there are indexes covering July-December and January-June (since the volume year begins in July). A red-paper index covers sections 3 and 4 — the United States Supreme Court. It is issued in the same manner as the green index, except that a final single index covers the entire court term. This index serves as a subject index to the Court's work, a docket, and a status table.

2. Legal newspapers. There are numerous newspapers, published several times a week for the use of practising lawyers in the area covered by each. They contain reports of local interest (some, from lower courts, not published elsewhere), court dockets and calendars, editorials, original and reprinted articles, and legal advertising. Examples are the *New York Law Journal, Washington* (D.C.) *Law Reporter, Los Angeles Journal, Denver Journal, Chicago Law Bulletin,* and the *St. Paul Legal Ledger.*

Independent Scholarly Reviews. These reviews, examples of which are the *Law Quarterly Review* and the *Modern Review,* emphasize scholarly research but are of considerable practical value to the lawyer as well. In composition and policy they are very similar to the law school reviews.

Law School Reviews.[3] Most scholarly law reviews are sponsored by law schools, where they serve as outlets for both the scholarly and technically expert writings of teachers, practitioners and judges, and for the closely supervised minor research of the scholastically elite students of the sponsoring schools. Aside from his own specialized practice journal, the practitioner, as well as the student and

---

[3] Law reviews, their function, makeup and varieties, are described, with citations to the literature, by John E. Cribbet, *Experimentation in the Law Reviews,* 5 J. Legal Ed. 72 (1952).

teacher, is more likely to be interested in law school reviews than in any other type. The typical law school review is divided into four parts.

1. Leading articles. The first part of a typical issue, occupying more than half the total space, prints leading articles by law school teachers, practioners and judges. A leading article usually runs to about thirty pages. It is likely to be monographic in character, aiming at exhaustive analysis of a single narrow topic, with full citations to authority. Often this topic has been nowhere else treated, or at least not adequately.

2. "Notes" or "Comments" section. The work here is contributed by student editors, and is often of the utmost value. Commonly limited to eight or ten pages for each note (but one on "Tort Liability of Municipal Corporations in Illinois," for example, took twenty-two), each note treats narrow aspects of the law, often those nowhere else discussed in print. Typical topics discussed are "Reaching the Out-of-State Mail-Order Insurer," "Recovery by Employee Spouse under Workmen's Compensation Acts," "Fire Insurance Recovery on a Limited Interest in Property," "Enforceable Arbitration of Commercial Disputes in the Textile Industries," "Deposits in Contracts to Sell Immovable Property in Louisiana," and "Admissibility of Scientific Tests for Intoxication."

3. Recent cases. A junior editor studies an assigned case and in two or three pages discusses it, with its relation to and effect upon existing law. These cases (from seven to ten in each issue) are carefully selected from a reading of all advance sheets, and in the aggregate they probably comprise those most worth reading. They are valuable to the student, as doing a fairly exhaustive treatment of a minute point of law and explaining the meaning of particular cases. They help the practioner keep abreast of significant new cases.

4. Book reviews. While the reviews are useful, the time lag between book publication and review is much too long.

5. Special features of law school reviews. A common variant of the conventional law review program as described above is a lengthy review (up to one hundred fifty pages) of the work of the Supreme Court of the United States or of a state, for the year just ended; or an exhaustive study of a developing field of the law, as damages or declaratory judgments; or a detailed analysis of new legislation, as a revenue or bankruptcy act or a commercial code. Once a year some reviews study the development of the law in their state for the year, noting the influence of statute or decision in each area of the law, as constitutional law, contracts, or torts.

Symposia in law school reviews. Beginning with Duke University's *Law and Contemporary Problems*, in 1933, entire issues of law reviews have frequently been devoted to articles on a single topic. All issues of the periodical just named (which contains no student work) are so dedicated, and a like policy, except that there are notes and case comments by students, was adopted in 1949 by the *University of Illinois Law Forum*. A more common use of the symposium is in occasional issues of conventional law reviews. The articles in these symposia represent a cross-section of comment by teachers, practitioners and judges, on such topics as "Minors and Incompetents in Illinois"; "Private Insurance"; and "Air Cargo." An unusual variation is the *Williamette Series of Legal Handbooks*, on such topics as "Instructions to Juries," and "A Handbook of Oregon Appellate Procedure."

Geographical slant of law school reviews. All but a few "national" law school reviews emphasize to some extent the law of their own state or locality. Some of these, as the *Oregon Law Review* and the *Indiana Law Journal*, also serve as the organ of the state bar association. The *Revista Jurídica* of the University of Puerto Rico has an obvious local interest; while the contents of the *University of Toronto Law Journal*, the *Cambridge Law Journal*, and the *Annual Law Review* (of the University of Western Australia) reflect their regional origin.

Specialization of law school reviews. Some school reviews specalize in a particular aspect of the law. The *Louisiana Law Review* and the *Tulane Law Review*, and to some extent the *Georgetown Law Journal*, emphasize civil law in America. The *George Washington Law Review*, in the nation's capital, has a very strong federal and administrative law slant, shared also by the *Georgetown Law Journal*, published in the same city. The Far Eastern and Russian Institute of the University of Washington publishes *Soviet Press Translations*. Emory University's *Journal of Public Law* emphasizes federal, state, and international aspects of the law. New York University School of Law's *Tax Law Review* is another specialty, as are Northwestern University's *Journal of Air Law and Commerce*, and *Journal of Criminal Law and Criminology* (which contain no student work). The Catholic University of America School of Canon Law publishes the *Jurist*, with an annual special number called the *Seminar*. It also publishes *Canon Law Studies*, consisting of dissertations submitted toward the Doctor of Canon Law Degree.

6. **Intramural law school reviews.** Reviews composed entirely of student notes and case comments are a recent and very lively development. They are designed primarily as outlets for the best work of students in legal bibliography or legal writing courses; though in some schools, as Duke, where there is no student work in the principal law review, they take the place of the notes and comments sections of the conventional law school review. Among the schools having such reviews are Hastings, St. Louis, Duke, Ohio State, and New York University. Different in purpose but also supplying an outlet for student work are the book reviews in the *Reading Guide* at the University of Virginia Law School; and the *University of Miami Lawyer*, a news magazine.

Professional Law Reviews. Some of the best legal periodicals are published by associations of scholarly specialists. Among these are the *Journal of Legal Education, Journal of the Society of Public Teachers of Law*, and the *American Journal of Comparative Law*. More common are those of associations of practitioners, of which the bar association journal is the outstanding example. These vary in quality from the scholarly few like the *Canadian Bar Review*, to mimeographed news letters. National groups are represented by the *American Bar Association Journal*, the *Lawyers' Guild Review*, the *National Bar Journal*, and the *Women Lawyers' Journal*. Below the national level, bar journals are of all types. The *Federal Bar Journal* specializes in federal practice. Many federal agencies have their own bars, some of which publish professional journals. Examples are *The Journal of the Patent Office Society*, and *The I. C. C. Practitioners' Journal*.

On the state level, bar association journals are for the most part of the news and trade journal type, but some publish other useful material, such as the opinions of the attorneys general of the state. Several bar journals digest recent state supreme court opinions.

D. Abridgments of Periodical Articles.

Abridgments of legal periodical articles provide an overall picture of available material for libraries not subscribing to all the English language periodicals; they also permit a compromise style of reading more articles than would otherwise be possible, even by those who have the complete articles in the original.

Legal Periodical Digest.[4] This loose-leaf service digests at considerable length *selected* articles published in most current English language legal periodicals. It also lists cases commented upon and digests selected notes. Each digest is filed under a paragraph number by a broad listing in which commercial law topics are numbered from 1001 to 1500; constitutional law from 1501 to 2000, *etc.* While exact numbers are not retained from year to year for the various sub-topics, this numbering scheme ensures that if a useful article on negligence is found under, say, paragraph 7003 one year, similar articles will be found at about that paragraph number in other years' digests. The index is described under "Indexes," below.

---

[4] New York, Commerce Clearing House, 1928 to date.

Law Review Digest.[5] This bi-monthly periodical of the Readers' Digest type condenses a selection of articles, no attempt being made at complete coverage. It fulfills the same function as its predecessor *Current Legal Thought*.[6] The index is described under "Indexes," below.

E. Indexes to Legal Periodicals.

Since the material in legal periodicals is as heterogeneous as that in digests and encyclopedias, indexes are necessary. These are of two principal types: consolidated indexes of a great number of periodicals, and the indexes prepared by the publishers of each periodical for their own publications. They fall considerably short, for the most part, of the excellence and fullness of the indexes to digests and encyclopedias.

Jones-Chipman Index to Legal Periodical Literature.[7] The first three volumes of this index, covering the period preceding the start of the *Index to Legal Periodicals* in 1908, are indispensable, but the last three are little used by libraries possessing the latter work, because the *Index to Legal Periodicals* is considerably more inclusive in its coverage and is better kept up to date. The Jones-Chipman index is a subject and author index to the principal English language legal periodicals from 1803 to 1937, when it was apparently discontinued. The arrangement of subject entries is alphabetical by rather large topics. Few notes or case comments, and no book reviews are indexed.

Index to Legal Periodicals.[8] For the period covered, this is the most inclusive index to English language legal periodicals. The principal American, British and British colonial periodicals, many bar association publications, and some judicial council reports are indexed. Entries are alphabetical by subject, under a scheme based (by permission of the West Publishing Company) upon that of the American Digest System, though less elaborate.

All leading articles, notes, case comments, and book reviews published in the publications indexed are covered. Searching through the numerous units of the *Index* may be laborious and often requires considerable ingenuity. Since not more than two or three subject entries are made for an article, indexing is not so close as it should be. There are *author, book review,* and (beginning with 1917) *case indexes.* In the latter table, cases commented upon in both leading articles, notes and case comments are listed. Through 1925, the Index cumulated annually, but beginning with 1926 it has cumulated both annually and triennially. From year to year, the frequency of publication has varied, usually being bi-monthly.

An Interim Supplement to the Index to Legal Periodicals. This mimeographed index is "issued every three weeks and is noncumulative, being intended only for use between issues of the *Index to Legal Periodicals.*" Although indorsed by the American Association of Law Libraries, it has no connection with the *Index to Legal Periodicals,* but is entirely a non-profit cooperative enterprise of the staffs of the law libraries of Columbia University and New York University. Its coverage in periodicals indexed is greater than that of the *Index to Legal Periodicals.* It indexes a wide selection of foreign language, international law, comparative law, and nonlegal periodicals not indexed by the *Index to Legal Periodicals,* as well as Congressional hearings and reports. By permission

---

[5] Boonton, N. J., Kimball-Clark Pub. Co., Nov. 1950 to date.
[6] New York, Current Legal Thought, Inc., 1935-1948. 14 v.
[7] 1888–1939, in 6 v. Various imprints, the latest being Los Angeles, Parker & Baird Co.
[8] New York, H. W. Wilson, 1908 to date.

of the West Publishing Company, it employs the same system of West subject headings as that of the *Index*. It indexes leading articles and student "Notes" or "Comments," but, with an occasional exception, no case comments. Neither does it index book reviews. Since it is entirely a voluntary effort, its future is uncertain.

Legal Periodical Digest Index. A consolidated topical index to this looseleaf service covers the years 1928 to 1941, and is continued by the current indexes to date. Each biennial "edition" of the *Digest* has its own subject, author, and case indexes; a table of articles by title; and a parallel "Citation Reference Table," from the original law review volume and page to the *Digest* year and paragraph. If, for example, an article was originally published in 29 Georgetown Law Journal 809, the table shows that it was digested in 1941, at paragraph 3571. There is a consolidation of this table, also covering the years 1928 to 1941, which is supplemented in the biennial new "editions."

Law Review Digest Index. A "Subject-Matter Index" covers "all articles, comments and notes in the current issues of [thirty-five or more] leading law reviews."

Miscellaneous Legal Periodical Indexes. Individual law reviews provide their own indexes to each volume, which, though varying greatly in completeness and quality, are usually considerably more detailed than other periodical indexes. From time to time, most of the reviews publish cumulative indexes covering several years. These indexes commonly note statutes or American Law Institute *Restatements* commented upon at any length. The *Michigan Law Review* in each issue indexes a few selected articles from other reviews. *Page's Ohio Digest* indexes Ohio legal periodicals. Most *Shepard's (state) Citations* now note comment by law reviews of the individual state covered, on cases decided by the courts of that state and, beginning with May, 1953, the American Bar Association Journal case comments are noted in *Shepard's United States* and *Federal Citations*. Some looseleaf services index legal periodical articles of interest. Examples are the Prentice-Hall and Commerce Clearing House federal income tax services.

Bar association proceedings indexes. In 1942 the *Index to State Bar Association Reports and Proceedings* [9] appeared. It also indexes American Bar Association, Canadian Bar Association, and some local bar association proceedings. It is the best place to search for biographical information concerning lawyers, for the period covered. It has not been kept up to date, but the *Index to Legal Periodicals* currently indexes many bar publications. The American Bar Association annual *Reports* index the *American Bar Association Journal*.

Indexes to English Legal Periodicals. Practically all English legal periodicals are currently indexed in the *Index to Legal Periodicals*, but there are also some periodical indexes published in England, as noted in Chapter 29, "English Material."

E. Approach to the Law Through Legal Periodicals.

The problems in the use of legal periodicals nearly all relate to finding an article in point. Once having found that, there is no special technique, except careful reading and the checking up of authorities cited. More and more, leading articles and long notes are *self-indexed*, in that they are divided and sub-divided into small units, each with its own subject caption. Commonly the first division of an article is the introduction, which states the problem and gives a historical and perhaps a

---

[9] New York, Baker, Voorhis, 1942.

bibliographical summary of the topic. This writing technique is particularly useful in a long article when the reader is interested in only part of it. For example, in an article on *Intoxication and Criminal Responsibility*, by Jerome Hall,[10] the minute but important sub-topic of involuntary intoxication is thus pinpointed.

It should also be observed that legal writers are meticulous in giving credit to other writers for material used or suggested. In practice, this means that the finding of one article in point frequently leads to the best of the earlier literature, as cited in footnotes. This is particularly true at the beginning of an article, where this earlier literature is likely to be collected. When the topic discussed is one upon which comparatively little has been written, this is a very useful technique. *See*, for example, Alan F. Westen, *The Wire-Tapping Problem*,[11] where a dozen articles and reports on this topic are cited. One value of this approach is that it operates as an endless chain: parallel citations to annotated cases are turned up, cases in point cited in the articles or comment may be traced (through the *Reporter* Key-Number) into the digests, and so on.

How to Find Material in Point.

1. *Subject indexes.* The best leads normally are found through the use of periodical indexes described above. The procedure is the same as that used for a digest or encyclopedia descriptive-word index, except that there are far fewer words in the periodical index and the task is correspondingly more difficult. Since the subjects in these indexes are seldom fully broken down, it may be necessary to search several pages of entries in each unit of the index to ascertain whether or not the topic is covered. Sometimes the topics under which to search are fairly obvious, such as "Contracts," "Patents," or "Finding Lost Goods," but more often they are not. Perhaps more than in any other kind of law book, plain downright industry is necessary, but the results are frequently worth it.

2. *Author indexes.* If the name of the author of a leading article is known, it is a simple matter of searching the right (by date) index unit. References from authors in the *Index to Legal Periodicals* are not to pages of the Index, but to main topics under which the authors' articles are indexed. To help locate these articles by title under a given main topic, the initial letter of the first word of the title is encircled in the reference, as below.

Surrency, Erwin C.
Restatement of the Law (P).

This means that Mr. Surrency wrote an article classified under the main topic "Restatement of the Law," and that the title of the article indexed begins with the letter "P."

3. *Treatise, encyclopedia or annotation approach.* Footnote citations in treatises and annotations frequently list periodical articles in point. The technique is to find a discussion in point in such a treatise or annotation, and then to see if a periodical article is cited. Very seldom are tables of such citations provided.

4. *Judicial opinions and briefs approach.* Periodical articles are frequently cited by judges and lawyers, usually in footnotes, but there is no tabular means for finding references to them. If examination of the case or brief reveals such citations, all well and good.

5. *Shepard's state Citations approach.* Most state *Shepards* now cite local state periodical articles or case comments on particular cases. For example, 226 Iowa 977, 285 N. W. 664 (1939), was discussed in 32 Iowa Law Review 575, as noted in the Iowa *Shepard*. No similiar notation is found in the *Northwestern Shepard*, covering Iowa, nor would any *Shepard* note it, if this same case were to be discussed in an Illinois or other out-of-state law review.

---

[10] 57 Harv. L. Rev. 1045 (1944).
[11] 52 Col. L. Rev. 165, 167 (1952).

6. *Table of cases approach.* This is a particularly useful approach for the student or practitioner wishing to keep abreast of late case developments. The cases listed in the *Index to Legal Periodicals* table are for the most part those discussed in individual "case comments." But if a case is commented upon at any length in a leading article or note, it also is listed, no matter when decided. For example, the tax case of *Dobson* v. *Commissioner* [12] has been the subject of endless leading articles and comments over the years.

The table of cases approach is available through the *Jones-Chipman Index* (volume 3, page 536, for the years 1898 through 1907); through the *Index to Legal Periodicals* from 1917 to date; and, for selected cases, through the *Legal Periodical Digest* index, from 1928 to date. Individual law review indexes carry the approach much further back.

Perhaps the student may not understand the meaning of a case cited for outside reading. If it has been discussed in a law review within the above dates, he will find this helpful. Or the practitioner may desire an exhaustive treatment of a recent case on labor law, divorce, or contracts. Perhaps it has been the subject of a leading article, note, or case comment. Sometimes a case may be commented upon by as many as thirty-five different law reviews. The searcher can then choose his favorite review or the one (as indicated by inclusive pages in the citation) which devotes a suitable number of pages to the case.

---

[12] 320 U. S. 489, 64 S. Ct. 239, 88 L. Ed. 248 (1943).

CHAPTER 23

AMERICAN LAW INSTITUTE RESTATEMENTS OF THE COMMON LAW

A. Function.

The Restatements aim is "to present an orderly restatement of the general common law of the United States, including in that term not only the law developed solely by judicial decision, but also the law that has grown from the application by the courts of statutes that were generally enacted and were in force for many years." [1] They are definitely not codes: they are statements of the law, *not as the Institute would like to make it, but as it believes the law is.* A code is backed by legislative authority and can only be changed by such; the *Restatements* have only the persuasive authority of the men who agreed to them, and they are designed to change as the law changes.

The *Restatements* aim to clear away the verbiage of existing statements of the common law and instead to state agreed-upon "best rules" as applied in the United States generally. They attempt to check the growing diversity of the rules of the common law among the states. They try to give to the judges — especially the rapidly changing trial judges — a statement of common-law rules which has more scholarship and study behind it than is found in the conventional treatise or legal encyclopedia. To the lawyer they give a rule of decision backed by the prestige of the Institute and a high degree of acceptance by the courts. To the student they give a statement of principles, backed by commentaries and numerous illustrative examples to set him straight in his study.

B. Form and Scope.

Restatements have been adopted for agency, conflict of laws, contracts, judgments, property, restitution, security, torts, and trusts. The Institute has also drafted a *Code of Evidence*, a *Code of Criminal Procedure*, and (with the National Conference of Commissioners on Uniform State Laws) a *Code of Commercial Law.*

---

[1] *See* Wolkin, *Restatements of the Law,* in the Notes to this chapter.

Each *Restatement* begins with an introduction, describing the organization and purpose of the Institute, and an elaborate schematic table of contents showing the organization of the material. The treatment of this material closely resembles that in the *Hornbook Series* of treatises, in that it is in three distinct parts, as follows.

First, there is a black-letter statement of a principle (which may be more or less elaborately subdivided). This is the *Restatement* proper. *Second,* there is a comment for most sections. This is designed to explain the meaning of the black-letter section, and to limit its application. *Third,* there are "illustrations" of the various sections and subsections. These correspond to the footnote digests of cases supporting text statements in treatises, but are not citations to cases, though any lawyer will recognize many familiar cases in the illustrations. In the preliminary drafts, supporting cases were cited.

The *Restatements* differ from treatises in that they state only the "best" rule, and *cite no authority.* The rule stated, however, has been found to be the applicable rule in nearly 98 per cent of the decided cases mentioning *Restatements* since their adoption.

C. Indexes.

Each *Restatement* has its own detailed index, and there is also a *General Index* [2] to all *Restatements*, which not only combines the individual indexes but contains many additional catchwords and cross-references.

D. Keeping the Restatements up to Date.

It is no part of the Institute's policy to embalm legal rules in the *Restatements.* As the law changes, it is hoped that a restudy of the Restatements can be made so as to reflect those changes. The first such study was embodied in the *Restatement of the Law, 1948 Supplement (see Notes).* This volume, for such sections as are changed, gives the entire new text or comment, noting how the old is changed, and the reasons for making the change. Here, decided cases and statutes causing the change are cited (being the only instances in which the *Restatements* cite authority), and treatises and law review articles discussing the change are also noted. Changes, however, have been surprisingly few, and most of them have been only in clarification of language.

E. Authority of the Restatements.

While the *Restatements* are in no way primary authority, they have proved to be persuasive in the extreme. As of December 31, 1948, a total of 16,192 published appellate decisions had cited them. They had been cited by federal courts, including the Supreme Court of the United States, 3253 times during that period. Disagreement with the *Restatements* have been only about 2 per cent varying from 1.4 per cent for Agency, to 2.6 per cent for Conflict of Laws and Contracts.[3] The effect has been that the *Restatements* are presumed to state the common-law rule,

---

[2] Restatement of the Law. Permanent General Index. St. Paul, Minn., American Law Institute Publishers, 1946.

[3] Goodrich, Herbert T., Restatement and Codification [In *David Dudley Field, Centenary Essays.* (New York University School of Law, 1949) p. 246]. As of April 1, 1952 there were 20,639 citations (*Report* of the Director, 1952).

and that the party opposing them has the burden of proof to the contrary. This of course does not make the *Restatements* in any sense mandatory on the court, but it does indicate that they are becoming accepted as the authoritative statement of the common law in the United States.

F. Shepardizing the Restatements.

Although the *Restatements* are not statutes but only a private statement of the rules of common law, they have achieved sufficient prestige to be covered (in the same manner as statutes) in more then a third of the state (but not *Reporter*, *United States* or *Federal*) *Shepards*. Presumably this coverage will be expanded to other state *Shepards* as well. For states covered, this is the best means of completely tracing citations of cases commenting on the *Restatements*, though considerably more information is given in the *Restatement in the Courts*.

Restatement in the Courts. The American Law Institute has compiled the citations to the *Restatements* by appellate courts, in three volumes, as listed in the *Notes*. The first, the *Restatement in the Courts*, Permanent Edition . . . (1945), was supplemented by later volumes, in 1948 and 1953. Citations are in the form of digests of decisions, arranged by *Restatement* (as Agency or Contracts) and section. The first volume cited thousands of law review comments also, but these were omitted from the supplements. Parallel citations to section numbers in the tentative drafts and the final official *Restatements* are given in a table in the first volume. The history of the Institute and its *Restatements*, in the first volume, is definitive.

State Annotations. Decisions in point with the *Restatement* sections, but which had been handed down by the respective courts *preceding* the adoption and publication of the *Restatements*, were lined up by state bar associations, and the results published in local law reviews and bar journals. Later, this work was put on a systematic basis through the cooperation of these state bar associations with the Institute. State annotations are published and kept up to date by the American Law Institute Publishers, and sold through them, as listed in the West Publishing Company catalogs. The future of the state annotations program, however, is in doubt. Only about 2 per cent difference has been noted between *Restatement* and local rules, but there are many gaps in state adjudications of *Restatement* sections. From 10 to 50 per cent of the sections have not been adjudicated yet, and while the courts seldom repudiate the *Restatement* rules, they often fail to mention them. The purpose of the state annotations is to state correctly the local rule; or, if there is no local rule, to formulate one which appellate courts generally recognize.

Law Review and Treatise Comment. By December 31, 1948, there had been more than 15,000 law review comments on the *Restatements* and these, through 1944, were annotated to the respective topics and sections in the first volume of the *Restatement in the Courts*. Such annotations were dropped by later supplements, except where the rule was changed, but most individual law review indexes and some bar association journals cite comments on the *Restatements* in such reviews. The index volume (volume 8) of Williston's *Contracts* (rev. ed. 1938), lists *Restatement* sections commented upon in the text.

English Use of the Restatements. English courts have been reluctant to use the *Restatements*, regarding them as on a par with treatises, but they have been cited, quoted and followed, in both trial and appellate courts, and the practice is increasing. (*See Denning*, in the *Notes.*)

G. Glossary of Terms Defined in the Restatement.

A sixty-eight-page glossary is included in the *Restatement in the Courts, Permanent Edition* (1945), beginning at page 43. Definitions included are from all the *Restatements*, and refer to the *Restatement* titles and sections where the terms are defined.

H. Techniques for Using the Restatements.

Order of Search. If the searcher lacks a citation to a specific topic and section of a *Restatement*, the combined *Index* should first be consulted. In its 1100 pages it covers in great detail, analytically and by catchword, the entire subject matter of all *Restatements*. Each *Restatement* also has its own index, but as there is some overlapping of subject matter, the combined index is better to start with. Having decided upon an appropriate topic and section, and studied the comment and examples there found, the searcher's next step is to consult the *Restatement in the Courts,* 1948 (and Supplements), to see if any changes have been made in text or comment. Then state annotations for his state should be consulted. If there are none for his state, the annotations in the *Restatement in the Courts* and its supplements should then be searched for the rules in other states in which the courts have construed the topic and section in point.

The *Restatement in the Courts* (but not the Supplements) is also annotated to law review articles, and most individual law review indexes refer by topic and section to discussion in those reviews. *American Jurisprudence* and *Corpus Juris Secundum* often cite and occasionally quote the *Restatements*.

Notes

History and Methods of Compiling the Restatements. The definitive statement of the history, purposes and writing of the *Restatements* is contained in the *Restatement in the Courts, Permanent Edition* (1945). Most of the work of compiling the *Restatements* was done by Reporters for each topic, men eminent in their respective fields; helped by staffs of advisers. After each group of specialists determined for itself the proper statement of the "best rule" of law in each case, the tentative draft or parts of it were submitted to the Council of the American Law Institute for debate and final approval. The Reporters were teachers of law, of the caliber of Williston, Powell, and Beale. The advisers were eminent teachers, practitioners and judges. What constituted the "best" rule was the occasion of many historic battles before the final form was agreed to. No study of comparable exhaustiveness or scholarship was ever made of American law before.

The *Restatement of Contracts*, for example, took nine years to complete. The numerous preliminary treatises and drafts have been listed by Long and Surrency, as noted below. It is to be regretted that the numerous tentative drafts, working papers, and annotated reports of statutes and other materials used in the preparation of the *Restatements* as adopted, were not published and distributed more widely. As evidences of what might be called "legislative intent" in the drafting of the *Restatements*, and as compilations of comments and authorities on the common law as modified by statute, they are most useful to those fortunate enough to have them. For a brief statement which includes a note on each *Restatement* the last paper listed below is suggested.

American Law Institute. *Glossary of Words and Phrases Defined in the Restatement. History of the American Law Institute and the First Restatement of the Law* (in *Restatement in the Courts, Permanent Edition*). St. Paul, Minn., American Law Institute Publishers, 1945; Supplements, 1948, 1953.

Denning, Alfred D., *The Restatement of the Law in the English Courts*, 37 A. B. A. J. 329 (1951).

Glasier, Gilson G., *Work of the American Law Institute and What it Means to the Law Librarian*, 18 L. Lib. J. 96 (1925).

Goodrich, Herbert F., Restatement and Codification (In *David Dudley Field, Centenary Essays*). New York, New York University School of Law, 1949. p. 241.

Long, Mariana, *A Bibliographical Check List of Publications of the American Law Institute* . . . 32 L. Lib. J. 159 (1939); 41 L. Lib. J. 50 (1948).

Owens, Edwin J., *The Judicial Process, Stare Decisis and the Restatements*, 21 J. St. B. Calif. 116 (1946).

Ransom, William L., *What and Where is the Law: The Restatement in the Courts*, 32 A. B. A. J. 168 (1946).

Surrency, Erwin C., *A Bibliography of the Tenative Drafts of the Restatements*, 44 L. Lib. J. 11 (1951); 45 L. Lib. J. 26 (1952).

Wolkin, Paul A., *Restatements of the Law; Origin, Preparation Availability*, 21 Ohio B. A. Rept. 663 (1949).

CHAPTER 24

DICTIONARIES — WORDS AND PHRASES — MAXIMS

A. FUNCTION AND VALUE OF LAW DICTIONARIES.
B. AUTHORITY AND TECHNIQUES OF USE.
C. SCOPE.
D. SOME UNITED STATES DICTIONARIES DESCRIBED.
E. ENGLISH LAW DICTIONARIES.

A. Function and Value of Law Dictionaries.[1]

Roscoe Pound has written: "My first advice to the beginner in the study of law has always been to buy a good law dictionary and turn to it constantly. . . . The sure way of acquiring an enduring grasp upon legal terminology is to look up every word as it is encountered in the student's reading, get its meaning concretely in view of the context, and keep up this process until there is an assured conviction that it is no longer necessary.[2]

This is advice echoed by every law teacher. Working in the law without knowledge of the exact meaning of the terms employed is to play a game of blind man's buff. There is no excuse for being mistaken or hazy as to the exact meaning of legal terminology.

The law dictionary defines and illustrates the meanings of words, terms, and phrases which are legal words of art or have a legal slant. Most of these are English, but because the early language of the law was Latin and law French, many words from these languages are defined. Since there have been many elements of more modern French and Spanish law in America, terms from these languages are plentiful too. Canon law terms are defined also. All dictionaries of any kind or size, except some pocket dictionaries, cite or quote authority for their definitions; law dictionaries do this probably more than any other.

B. Authority and Techniques of Use.

A law dictionary is not a work of legal authority. At most, when it quotes from a judicial decision, it has the status of a digest. It is not intended to state the law, but to define the common meanings of words and terms of legal import. Even when it cites authority, it is not to be relied upon entirely, as the authority cited

---

[1] The authors have carefully studied all the dictionaries described or listed in this chapter. They also acknowledge indebtedness to the following: S. A. Alibone, *Bouvier's Law Dictionary*, 93 N. Am. Rev. 71 (1861); William C. Anderson, *Law Dictionaries*, 28 Am. L. Rev. 531 (1894); J. D. Cowley, *Some Early Dictionaries of English Law*, 36 Jur. Rev. 65 (1924); and James A. H. Murray, *The Evolution of English Lexicography*. Oxford, Clarendon Press, 1900.

[2] Foreword to James A. Ballentine, *Law Dictionary with Pronunciations* (Rochester, N. Y., Lawyers Cooperative Pub. Co., 1930).

defines each word or term *only in its special context*, and the meaning may be modified as conditions change.

Nevertheless, the law dictionary is indispensable, because it gives workable definitions, useful and sufficient under most circumstances. Because most definitions cite their authority, the dictionary may provide a starting point in the finding of cases, when the meaning of legal terminology or of words of common import is an issue. The only technique needed is diligence and industry.

C. Scope.

There are six recognizable types of dictionaries, of which the second described below is by far the most widely used.

The Glossary. Words herein are defined rather briefly, perhaps with citations to cases or other authority, but without illustrative examples or quotations. These are relatively uncommon, because they so often lack sufficient detail to satisfy the needs of their users.

The Semi-Encyclopedic Type. Such are *Ballentine, Black,* and *Shumaker.* Variorum definitions are provided as called for; more words are defined than in the glossary; and citations to authority are given or perhaps quoted verbatim. Maxims are defined and there are various tables, particularly of abbreviations.

Concise Encyclopedias of the Law. *Bouvier,* described later herein, is now the only example of this type.

The Words and Phrases Type. This dictionary takes as its entire definition the sense and often the exact words of judicial opinions in which such words and phrases are construed.

The Legal Maxim Definer. This, a vanishing type, is devoted entirely to defining and commenting upon legal maxims. Maxims are also defined in encyclopedic and semi-encyclopedic dictionaries and in some legal encyclopedias.

Legal Encyclopedias. As noted in Chapter 20, law encyclopedias also serve a definite dictionary function.

Auxiliary Information. Practically all legal dictionaries supply auxiliary information of various types. Most common is the *table of abbreviations.* Other tables are of *English regnal years, statutes of limitations, mortality and interest tables, etc.* Not all dictionaries have all of these tables. Some of the tables are separately placed — at the beginning or end of the book; others appear in their regular alphabetical place in the dictionary proper. As with every other law book, the individual dictionary should be carefully examined for its resources and arrangement the first time used.

D. Some United States Dictionaries Described.

The dictionary is such a familiar book that little time need be spent describing any one of them. For this reason, *Black, Ballentine,* and *Shumaker,* probably the most used of them all, will not be described here at all, though listed in the bibliography. Those below are singled out because of some special features thought to make individual treatment worth while.

American Law Institute Restatements Glossary. A sixty-eight-page "glossary of terms defined in the Restatements" is found in the *Restatement in the*

Courts, Permanent Edition (1945), beginning on page 43. Definitions included are from the *Restatements* of Agency, Contracts, Conflict of Laws, Property, Restitution, Torts, and Trusts.

Bouvier's Law Dictionary and Concise Encyclopedia.[3] All other American law dictionaries are inevitably compared with this one. It is a concise encyclopedia of Anglo-American law. An outstanding characteristic, compared to its American predecessors, is its emphasis on the American elements in the law. Authority is cited for definitions when available, and often it is quoted as well. Long sections of statutes or treatises are also occasionally quoted. Many words or topics are treated encyclopedically. Three pages are thus given to "Ejectment," nine to "Elections," and ten to "Railroad." In a word or topic where the law is subject to frequent change, such a treatment has the effect of a digest not kept up to date, but in others, especially for matters essentially historical (as the *Year Books*), it is very useful. There are no separate tables, as in most later dictionaries, but there are some in their proper alphabetical places. Regnal years, for example, are tabulated under "Regnal Years"; maxims are defined under the topic "Maxims"; abbreviations are collected under "Abbreviations."

Because of the greater portability and convenience of small dictionaries, as well as the development of legal encyclopedias which supplant much that is in Bouvier, that dictionary is less used than formerly, though retaining its old prestige.

Words and Phrases Dictionaries. Law dictionaries characteristically cite the authority for their definitions. A variant is the words-and-phrases-judicially-defined type, in which the definition is taken from a judicial opinion wherein the word or phrase is defined by the court. Sometimes the language is quoted verbatim, but usually it is paraphrased from the opinion by the compiler. It can be a very useful approach to the law when the meaning of a word or phrase, whether of special legal import or in common use, is important. The words and phrases approach is frequently a useful starting point in the search for cases.

Words and Phrases.[4] In 1894, the West Publishing Company issued the first edition of this work, which aims to cover words judicially defined in cases from 1658 to date which are digested in the American Digest System. Words defined include not only those of legal art, such as are defined in law dictionaries generally, but also words in more common use which have been employed in statutes or elsewhere and have been the subject of judicial consideration. An example is "parallel," in a statute regulating parallel railroads; or "accessible," or "yard limits." In effect, this is a digest of words instead of points of law. An example is shown on page 219 opposite, exhibit 56.

Relation to National Reporter System. This set is kept up to date by annual pocket parts, which in turn are compiled from the advance sheets of the respective *Reporters*. Each advance sheet has its own table of words and phrases, as do each *Reporter* bound volume and each *Reporter* digest (but not the American Digest System). These tables, however, differ from *Words and Phrases*, above, in that *they only list, but do not define* the words—which are defined in the headnotes and in the opinion on the pages referred to in the tables.

Miscellaneous words and phrases dictionaries. In addition to the titles listed above, nearly all other digests have tables of words and phrases defined. Most of these tables do not themselves define the terms listed, but only refer to the page in the digest where they are defined. *American Jurisprudence* also has such a table in its "General Index."

---

[3] 3d Revision, being the eighth edition, by Francis Rawle. Kansas City, Mo., Vernon Law Book Co., 1914. 3 v.

[4] Permanent Edition. St. Paul, West Pub. Co., 1940–52. 45 v. Kept up to date by cumulative pocket supplements.

PARALLEL

Railroads—Cont'd

two roads which connect two important cities, and are natural competitors for the traffic between such cities. Louisville & N. R.
Co. v. Commonwealth of Kentucky, 16 S.Ct.
714, 719, 161 U.S. 677, 40 L.Ed. 849.

The term "parallel line," in the clause
of the Constitution forbidding any railroad
corporation to in any way control any other
corporation having in its control a parallel
or competing line, is not limited in its operation to a railroad completely constructed, but
includes a projected road surveyed, laid out,
and in the process of construction. Pennsylvania R. Co. v. Commonwealth, Pa., 7 A. 368,
373.

"Parallel railroads," as used in Const.
art. 15, § 6, providing that no railroad corporation shall consolidate with any other railroad
corporation owning or having under its control a parallel or competing line, etc., means
railroads running in one general direction,
traversing the same section of country, and
running within a few miles of one another
throughout their respective routes, and does
not include exact parallelism. State v. Montana R. Co., 53 P. 623, 627, 21 Mont. 221, 45
L.R.A. 271.

Exhibit 56

General English Language Dictionaries.   English legal words and terms
are defined in ordinary English dictionaries, but usually without the detail or
citations to authority found in the law dictionaries. *The New English Dictionary
on Historical Principles* [5] defines many words not elsewhere defined, especially
obscure ones.

Special-Subject Dictionaries of Interest to Lawyers.   Dictionaries intended
for non-lawyers often have a legal slant or define words of interest to the lawyer.
Among these are Paul H. Casselman's *Labor Dictionary;* [6] Albert Crew's *A Dictionary of Medico-Legal Terms;* [7] Charles W. Fricke's *5000 Criminal Definitions;* [8]
Erskine Pollock's *Legal Medical Dictionary;* [9] E. W. A. Tuson's *Vocabulary
of International and Maritime Law and Insurance;* [10] and Eric L. Kohler's *A Dictionary for Accountants.* [11]

---

[5] *Murray's Oxford English Dictionary.* Oxford, Clarendon Press, 1888-1928. 10 v. and supplement, 1933.

[6] New York, Philosophical Library, 1949.

[7] London, Pitman, 1937.

[8] Los Angeles, O. W. Smith, 1941.

[9] London, Butterworth, 1935.

[10] In his *The British Merchant's, Shipowner's and Master Mariner's Practical Guide.* London,
Richard Griffin, 1858. pp. 307-382.

[11] New York, Prentice-Hall, Inc., 1952.

Loose-Leaf Services as Dictionaries.   Some loose-leaf services list definitions of technical terms employed in the subject matter covered. Examples are "Words and Phrases Used in Collective Bargaining" (In the Prentice-Hall *Union Contracts and Collective Bargaining Practice Service*), and "Labor Terms" (in the Commerce Clearing House *Labor Law Reporter*).

E. British Law Dictionaries.

Those of historical interest are described below in the Notes. Of the currently useful ones, John J. S. Wharton's *Law Lexicon* [12] is outstanding of the semi-encyclopedic type. Except for its natural slant toward British and Indian law, it differs little from American law dictionaries. Smaller, desk-type books are H. A. C. Sturgess and Arthur B. Hewitt's *A Dictionary of Legal Terms and Citations*,[13] and H. N. Mozley and G. C. Whiteley's *Law Dictionary*.[14] There are also dictionaries intended for use in India, Australia, and other countries now or formerly British dependencies. Some are mentioned in the Notes.

Words and Phrases. The British claim to have originated this type of dictionary, with Frederick Stroud's *Judicial Dictionary*,[15] in 1890. The Third edition of this work (1952) is in five volumes, and differs from its American counterparts in having tables of cases and of statutes involved in the definitions. Cases on the construction of repealed statutes are listed, as well as some from Scottish, Irish, and Dominion sources. A similar work is Roland Burrows' *Words and Phrases Judicially Defined*.[16] A. W. Dalrymple's and Andrew D. Gibb's *Dictionary of Words and Phrases*,[17] is especially designed for Scottish use; and there are similar works for some of the Dominions, as G. D. Sanagan and G. K. Drynan's *The Encyclopedia of Words and Phrases, Legal Maxims: Canada 1825-1940;*[18] and Leonard G. Wrinch's *The Canadian Abridgment Index of Words and Phrases Judicially Noticed in Canadian Reports*.[19]

Scottish Dictionaries.   Most law dictionaries define some Scottish terms. Andrew D. Gibb's *Students' Glossary of Scottish Legal Terms* [20] has an obvious use.

Statutory Definitions. At intervals the Office of the Parliamentary Counsel of Great Britain issues an *Index to Statutory Definitions*,[21] in which the words listed are not defined but bear a citation to the act and section defining them.

Maxims. Most law dictionaries and encyclopedias define maxims. Herbert Broom's *A Selection of Legal Maxims, Classified and Illustrated*,[22] is a treatise or commentary on maxims. Although there is an alphabetical table of maxims, with pages where defined, the text arrangement is by ten broad topics, such as maxims relating to public policy, the Crown, contracts, evidence, *etc.*

[12] London, Spettigue and Farrance, 1848.
[13] 2d ed. London, Pitman, 1945.
[14] 5th ed. London, Butterworth, 1930.
[15] London, Sweet and Maxwell, 1890.
[16] London, Butterworth, 1943-45. 5 v. and pocket supplements to date.
[17] Edinburgh, W. Green, 1946.
[18] Toronto, Richard De Boo Ltd., 1940-41, 5 v., with supp. 1940-46.
[19] Toronto, Burroughs & Co., Ltd., 1952.
[20] Edinburgh, W. Green, 1946.
[21] London, H. M. Stationery Office, 1936.
[22] 10th ed., London, Sweet and Maxwell, 1939.

Notes

Development of English Law Dictionaries. In England, the law dictionary preceded in point of time the general English dictionary as we now know it, the respective dates being 1527 for John Rastell's *Termes de la Ley*, and 1538 for Sir Thomas Elyot's *Dictionarie.*

Prior to *Elyot* there were many glossaries in England, but up to 1521 they were all English-Latin or Latin-English. Latin was still the language of the educated world, and readers were presumed to be familiar with its words without outside help. But, somewhere between 600 and 700 A.D. it became customary for English scholars to write an easier Latin word over a harder one, when reading a manuscript. This formed part of a general practice of writing comments between the lines, the added writings being called glosses; in time, as manuscripts were copied and recopied, it often became impossible to distinguish between the gloss and the original text.

As English established itself as a respectable language, English words, instead of Latin, came to be used to define the hard Latin words, and Latin-English and English-Latin word lists or dictionaries developed. But, as English has always been a borrowing language, especially since the Norman Conquest, the necessity of defining these borrowed words arose, and they were gradually added to dictionaries and defined in English. At first no words presumed to be understood by most educated men were defined, but only "hard" words. The first dictionary of English words only, Robert Cawdry's *Table Alphabetical of Hard Words,*[23] was such a dictionary. By 1721, England was ready for an English dictionary designed to include both easy and hard words, and Nathan Bailey's *Universal Etymological English Dictionary*[24] was published, upon which Dr Samuel Johnson's famous *Dictionary of the English Language*[25] was based.

Law Dictionaries Proper. Although there have been upwards of seventy-five English law dictionaries published, only five were of outstanding importance up to the publication of John Bouvier's famous dictionary in 1839. These were by John Rastell, John Cowell, Thomas Blount, Giles Jacob, and Timothy Cunningham.

1527. Rastell, John, *Expositiones Terminorum Legum Anglorum.*[26] There is some dispute as to whether this was written by John, or by his son, William, but scholarship seems to favor the former. In 1567, William certainly translated the work, giving it its more common title of *Termes de la Ley.* Originally written in law French and based upon Littleton and other law books of the time, it achieved at least twenty-nine editions. By 1579 it was printed in parallel columns, Norman-French and English. It cited no authority.

1607. Cowell, John, *Nomothetes: The Interpreter, or Books containing the Signification of Words.*[27] This was written entirely in English, much of it plagiarized from Rastell, and because of political statements in it, was the cause of much controversy. For the first time in law dictionaries it cited authorities. It appeared in numerous editions, later ones by Thomas Manley and White Kennet being considerably revised and enlarged. It and the law dictionaries following it included many common words and words not of especial legal connotation. The "educated man" concept of dictionaries was being discarded.

1670. Blount, Thomas, *Nomo-Lexikon; a Law Dictionary and Glossary.*[28] This dictionary (not to be confused with his *Glossographia,* of 1656) devoted more space to etymology and the description of ancient customs than to the explanations of common-law terms, but it was reprinted in 1691, and a revised edition by William Nelson appeared in 1717.

1729. Jacob, Giles, *New Law Dictionary.*[29] Appearing first in a single large folio

[23] Cawdry, Robert, *Table Alphabetical . . . of Hard Usual Words.* Printed by I. R. for Edmund Weaver, 1604.

[24] London, 1721.

[25] London, 1755.

[26] London, 1527.

[27] Cambridge, John Legate, 1607.

[28] London, In the Savoy, Tho. Newcomb, 1670.

[29] London, In the Savoy, E. & R. Nutt, 1729.

volume, it was reprinted down to 1835. Beginning with the 11th edition, of 1797, it was edited and enlarged by Thomas E. Tomlins. It was more of an encyclopedia than a dictionary, containing writs, precedents, forms, *etc*. It has value to this day for its descriptions of writs and common-law actions, for which in some instances it provides the only readily accessible source of information.

1764-1765. Cunningham, Timothy, *A New and Complete Law Dictionary*.[30] This dictionary was the first aiming at the inclusion of all legal terms, not just the easy ones. It treated by preference, however, "obsolete words, in charters, *etc*."

Bouvier's Law Dictionary. With the publication of this work in 1839, the evolution of the English law dictionary was complete, but of course new ones are frequently published, to satisfy more modern needs. Some of these, both English and American, are listed below.

The complete title of John Bouvier's work was *A Law Dictionary Adapted to the Laws of the United States, and of the Several States of the American Union; with References to the Civil and other Systems of Foreign Law*.[31] The compiler of this greatest of American law dictionaries came to this country from France in 1802, at the age of fifteen, and settled with his parents in Philadelphia. There, in due time he became in turn a successful publisher, lawyer, and judge. Becoming dissatisfied with existing English legal dictionaries, based upon the jurisprudence of another country and partially obsolete even there, he set about compiling a modern dictionary suitable to the United States, with special relation to American statutes. Real property and mercantile law words as employed in America were a special study. However, occasional comparison of terms of civil, canon, and other systems of foreign law with our own were made. It was Bouvier's claim that he had not merely brought old dictionaries up to date, but had written a new dictionary. The statement of his policy and of his difficulties is set forth in the preface to his first edition, as reprinted in the third Rawles edition. There have been many editions (including "student" editions). That of 1883 was the fifteenth, though the Rawles edition of 1914 calls itself the eighth. The later ones have been named rather than numbered, as the "Century" edition.

List of British and American Law Dictionaries, Including Maxims. In the list below, the date in parentheses is of the first edition. For many of these titles there have been later editions. Those titles which are still of current utility (usually through the publication of later editions) are marked with an asterisk. While this list is believed to contain most of the works of past or present significance, it makes no claim of completeness. The entries are not bibliographically complete, but contain sufficient data for identification. Those of more than usual historical or current value have been noted in the text. Some non-legal dictionaries are included, for their occasional legal definitions.

Abbott, Benjamin V., *Dictionary of Terms and Phrases* (2 v. Boston, 1879).

Adams, Henry C., *Juridical Glossary*. (Albany, 1886. v. 1, A-E only).

* Aiyar, P. R., *Law Lexicon of British India* (Madras, 1940).

* Alsager, C. M., *Dictionary of Business Terms* (Chicago, 1932).

* American Institute of Accountants. *Accounting Terminology*. (New York, 1931).

Anderson, William C., *A Dictionary of Law* (Chicago, 1889).

* Arndt, E. H. D., *Economic and Legal Dictionary, English-Afrikaans* (Pretoria, 1933).

Bacon, Francis, *Maxims of the Law* (London, 1636) (In his Elements of the Laws of England).

Baldwin, W. E., *Baldwin's Dollar Law Dictionary* (Cleveland, 1924).

* Ballentine, James A., *The College Law Dictionary* (Rochester, N. Y., 1948).

————,*Law Dictionary* (San Francisco, 1916).

Bell, Robert, *Dictionary of the Law of Scotland* (Edinburgh, 1807-08).

Bell, William H. S., *South African Legal Dictionary* (Grahamstown, 1910).

Best, William M., *Dictionary of English Law* (London, 1846).

* Black, Henry C., *Dictionary of Law* (St. Paul, 1891).

Blount, Thomas, *Nomo-Lexikon: a Law Dictionary* (London, 1670).

---

[30] London, S. Crowder, 1764-65. 2 v
[31] Philadelphia, 1839. 2 v.

Bouvier, John, *Law Dictionary* (2 v. Philadelphia, 1839).

Branch, Thomas, *Principia Legis et Aequitatis* (London, 1753. Maxims).

* Brooks, W. Collin, *Concise Dictionary of Finance* (London, 1934).

* Broom, Herbert, *A Selection of Legal Maxims* (London, 1845).

Brown, Archibald, *New Law Dictionary* (London, 1874).

Browne, I., *Judicial Interpretation of Common Words* (San Francisco, 1883).

Burn, Richard, *New Law Dictionary* (2 v. London, 1792).

* Burrill, Alexander M., *New Law Dictionary* (2 v. New York, 1950-51).

* Burrows, Roland, *Words and Phrases Judicially Defined* (5 v. London, 1943-45).

Byrne, W. J., *Dictionary of English Law* (London, 1923).

Caldwell, Frederick P., *Kentucky Judicial Dictionary* (3 v. Cincinnati, 1919-20).

————*Virginia and West Virginia Judicial Dictionary* (6 v. Cincinnati, 1922-23).

* Casselman, Paul H., *Labor Dictionary* (New York, 1949).

Cochran, William C., *Students' Law Lexicon* (Cincinnati, 1888)

Corfield, William A., *Laconic Law Dictionary* (London, 1856).

Costello, L. W. J., *Pocket Law Lexicon* (London, 1921).

Cowell, John, *The Interpreter* (London, 1607).

* Craigie, William A., *A Dictionary of American English* (4 v. Chicago, 1938-44).

* Crew, Albert, *Dictionary of Medico-Legal Terms* (London, 1937).

Cunningham, Timothy, *New and Complete Law-Dictionary* (2 v. London, 1764-65).

Dalrymple, A. W., *Dictionary of Words and Phrases (see* Gibb)

Dutcher, Salem, *Expressions of Law and Fact Construed by the Courts of Georgia* (Atlanta, 1899).

* Egbert, Lawrance D., *Law Dictionary; English-Español-Francais-Deutsch* (New York, 1949).

English, Arthur, *Dictionary of Words and Phrases* (Washington, D. C., 1899).

Finch, Henry, *Description of the Common Laws of England* (London, 1612) (Maxims).

* Fricke, Charles W., *5000 Criminal Definitions* (Los Angeles, 1941).

* Glover, E. H., *Police Encyclopedia of Legal Terms* (London, 1934?)

* Ghose, Lalit M., *Judicial Interpretations of Terms and Laws of British India* (2 v. Calcutta, 1917).

* Gibb, Andrew D., *Students' Glossary of Scottish Legal Terms* (Edinburgh, 1946).

* Gibb, Andrew D., and A. W. Dalrymple, *Dictionary of Words and Phrases* (Edinburgh, 1946) (Scottish).

* Great Britain. Office of the Parliamentary Counsel. *Index to Statutory Definitions* (London, 1925).

Halkerston, Peter, *Collection of Latin Maxims* (London, 1823).

* Hartford Accident and Indemnity Company. *Glossary of Casualty and Surety Terms and Phrases* (Hartford, 1946).

* Hartford Fire Insurance Company. *Short Glossary* (Hartford, 1946).

* Henius, Frank, *Dictionary of Foreign Trade* (New York, 1949).

Hore, P. H. *An Explanation of Ancient Terms and Measures of Land* (London, 1874).

* Horton Byrne J., and others, *Dictionary of Modern Economics* (Washington, D.C., 1948).

* Hyamson, Albert M., *Dictionary of International Affairs* (Washington, D. C., 1947).

Jacob, Giles, *New Law Dictionary* (London, 1729).

Jagadisa Aiyer, Krishna. *Manual of Law Terms* (Calcutta, 1927). (India).

Judicial and Statutory Definitions (23 v. St. Paul, 1904-33).

Kelham, Robert, *Dictionary of the Norman or Old French Language* (London, 1779).

Kinney, Jonathan K., *Law Dictionary* (Chicago, 1893).

* Kohler, Eric L., *A Dictionary for Accountants* (New York, 1952).

Lawson, John D., *Concordance of Words and Phrases* (St. Louis, 1883).

Leigh, Edward, *Philological Commentary* (London, 1652).

Lewis, Timothy, *Glossary of Mediaeval Welsh Law* (Manchester, 1913).

Livingston, Edward, *Definitions of All the Technical Words Used in the System of Penal Law . . . of Louisiana.* (New Orleans, 1824).

Lofft, Capel, *Maxims and Rules of the Law of England* (London, 1876).

Marriot, William, *New Law Dictionary* (4 v. London, 1798).

Montefiore, Joshua, *Commercial Dictionary* (London, 1803).

Mozley, H. N., and G. C. Whiteley, *Concise Law Dictionary* (London, 1876).

* Narotam, Desai, *Manual of Legal Maxims, Words, Phrases* (Bombay, 1911). (India).

* *New English Dictionary on Historical Principles* (Murray's Oxford English Dictionary, 10 v., 1888-1928 and suppl. 1933).

Norton-Kyshe, James W., *Dictionary of Legal Questions* (London, 1904).

Noy, William, *Treatise on the Principal Maximes* (London, 1634).

O'Dougherty, Harold St. L., *Eagle Legal Definitions . . . Underworld Terms and Their Meanings* (Brooklyn, 1937).

* Osborn, P. G., *Concise Law Dictionary* (Toronto, 1927).

Paterson, James, *Dictionary of Parallel Terms and Phrases in the Laws of England and Scotland* (Edinburgh, 1860) (In his *Compendium of English and Scottish Law*).

* Pollock, Erskine, *Legal Medical Dictionary* (London, 1935).

Pope, Benjamin W., *Legal Definitions* (2 v. Chicago, 1919-20).

Potts, Thomas, *Compendious Law Dictionary* (London, 1803).

Rapalje, Stewart, and Lawrence, Robert L., *Dictionary of American and English Law* (2 v. Jersey City, 1883).

Rastell, John, *Expositions Terminorum Legum Anglorum* (London, 1527). (Termes de la Ley).

Rawson, Henry G., *Pocket Law-Lexicon* (London, 1882).

Ryman, Dean E., *Compilation of Words and Phrases . . . Georgia* (Atlanta, 1910).

* Sanagan, Gerald D., and Drynan, George K., *Encyclopedia of Words and Phrases, Legal Maxims: Canada, 1825-1940.* (5v. Toronto, 1940-41).

* Shumaker, Walter A., *Cyclopedia Law Dictionary* (Chicago, 1912).

Skene, John, *De Verborum Significatione* (London, 1597).

* Sloan, Harold S., and Arnold J. Zurcher, *A Dictionary of Economics.* (New York, 1949).

Spelman, Henry, *Archaeologus* (London, 1626).

Stimson, Frederic J., *Glossary of Technical Terms* (Boston, 1881).

* Stroud, Frederick, *Judicial Dictionary* (London, 1890).

Student's Law Dictionary (London, 1740).

Students' Law Dictionary (New York, 1879).

* Sturgess, H. A. C., and Arthur B. Hewitt, *Dictionary of Legal Terms, Statutory Definitions and Citations* (London, 1934).

Sweet, Charles, *Dictionary of English Law* (London, 1882).

Tayler, Thomas, *Law Glossary.* (London, 1819).

Thomas, William B., *Kentucky Words and Phrases* (Louisville, 1915).

Tomlins, Thomas E., *Popular Law Dictionary* (London, 1838).

Tuson, E. W. A., *Vocabulary of International and Maritime Law and Insurance.* (In his *The British Merchant's Shipowner's and Master Mariner's Practical Guide.* London, 1858).

* Webster, Richard, *Dictionary of Marketing Terms, United States Usage.* (Basle, 1952).

Wharton, John J. S., *Law Lexicon* (London, 1848).

Whishaw, James, *New Law Dictionary* (London, 1829).

Widifield, Charles H., *Words and Phrases Judicially Defined* (Toronto, 1914).

Williams, Thomas W., *Law Dictionary* (London, 1816).

Wilson, Horace H., *Glossary of Judicial and Revenue Terms* (London, 1855). (India).

Wingate, Edmund, *Maxims of Reason* (London, 1658).

* *Words and Phrases* (Permanent Edition) 45 v. St. Paul. 1940).

* Wrinch, Leonard G., *The Canadian Abridgment Index of Words and Phrases Judicially Noticed in Canadian Reports.* (Toronto, 1952).

CHAPTER 25

FORM BOOKS

A. Function and Scope.
B. Annotated Forms.
C. Varieties.
D. Techniques of Using Form Books.

A. Function and Scope.

Drafting legal documents is a test of exact knowledge. The lawyer may know, or think he knows, all there is to know about contracts, wills, or complaints; but when he sits down to write out a document which may be attacked in the courts, he is beset by doubts. Is this clause too broad; does that proviso properly protect; does this declaration state a cause of action; is the manuscript properly typed, and with all the necessary squiggles where they belong?

The allayer of these doubts is the form book, which is as indispensable to the lawyer as a cookbook to a bride. One of the most treasured possessions of a law firm is often its collection of private forms, carefully locked away in the office safe. Great care is essential in copying or adapting forms, however, to make certain that they exactly fit the precise situation for which they are being used. A carelessly adopted form is potentially very dangerous.

B. Annotated Forms.

A form which has not been adjudicated has somewhat the same weak status as an unadjudicated statute. Therefore, it is customary to include in form books forms which have withstood attack in court. Many forms, of course, both business and procedural, but particularly the latter, are statutory. The fact that a form is not annotated does not necessarily condemn it, however. It may be one of such age and universal acceptance that it is protected by a sort of judicial notice.

C. Varieties.

Forms are broadly classified as business (or substantive) and procedural; and form books usually are one or the other, though some are both. An example of the latter is *Medina's Bostwick* (5th ed., 1951), three-quarters of which pertain to New York procedure, and the final quarter "Common Forms of Instruments." Most business forms other than statutory, unlike procedural forms, are of pretty general application. There are, however, form books designed for specific geographical areas, where special problems of law (as irrigation, oil and gas, *etc.*) may be encountered. An example is *Cowdery*, which, while of general application, emphasizes a western-state interest. *Statutory forms*, both substantive and pro-

225

cedural, are commonly printed in state statutory compilations, where they are findable through the general index. Commercial editions of the statutes sometimes interpolate forms, whether statutory or not. An example is the *New York Consolidated Laws Service*.[1] Many statutory forms (including some from foreign countries) are printed in both the *Martindale-Hubbell Law Directory* and *The Lawyers Directory* (*see* Chapter 27). Procedural forms are so much the creatures of state statutes that they are usually applicable only in one jurisdiction. By the same token, procedural form books are commonly loose-leaf or appear in frequent new editions, to keep abreast statutory changes; while business forms are standard to a much greater degree and do not normally call for such frequent revision.

D. Format.

Forms are published in an endless variety of styles, some of which are noted below. Individual titles are listed in the *Notes*. A useful feature preceding the forms themselves for each main topic in most form books is *a brief commentary and analysis of general and specific problems encountered, with drafting suggestions, and perhaps a checklist of suggested inclusions*. Such a checklist is printed in the end-papers of *American Jurisprudence Legal Forms Annotated*.

Business or Substantive Forms

Encyclopedic collections. *Nichols*, and *Modern Legal Forms* are examples of business form books which aim to cover the entire field. They print both standard and statutory forms, annotated by the decisions; are well indexed; and are kept up to date by pocket supplements. In addition to both long- and short-form complete forms, special attention is paid to particular clauses. The arrangement is alphabetical by broad topic, as far as possible; for example, "Abandonment," "Arbitration and Award," *etc.* (with analytical sub-divisions thereunder). But the index should be consulted, since topics overlap in unexpected ways, and the desired form sometimes is found under an unthoughtof main topic. A recent innovation in forms publication is American Jurisprudence Legal Forms Annotated, in which the forms are keyed to the text of American Jurisprudence.

Briefer collections. Numerous single- or double-volume books print a good selection of standard forms, with less attention to special contracts and particular clauses than is possible in the encylopedic compilations.

Special-subject forms. Many forms are collected for particular topics, such as corporations, wills, real property, workmen's compensation, *etc.* These have the advantage of saving a search through unwanted material on other topics. Some of these are published separately. Examples are, *Gordon's* annotated compilations on real property, agreements, and wills; the *Doris-Friedman-Spillman* series of corporate forms; and Rollinson's *Clauses in Wills and Forms of Wills*. More commonly, however, they are adjuncts of treatises or encyclopedias on the special subject covered (in which case some procedural forms may also be included). *It is so common for practitioners' treatises to print appropriate forms that they should be looked for as a matter of course.* Sometimes the forms are collected at the end of the complete text (as in Fletcher's *Corporations*); or at the end of a chapter; or they may accompany the pertinent text sections, thus being scattered through the book containing them. In either case, they are indexed, and often the word "Forms" appears on the spine of the volume collecting them. The treatises printing these forms may be of general application, as Page or Thompson's *Wills*; or they may cover the statutes of all jurisdictions, as the forms in Parker's *Corporation Manual*. Or they may be restricted to a particular jurisdiction, as Klipstein's *Drafting New York Wills*; or they may cover a minute subdivision of a large topic, as Charles S. Rhyne's *The Law of Municipal Contracts, with Annotated Model*

---

[1] Rochester, N. Y., Lawyers Co-operative Publishing Co., 1950-52. 12 v., kept to date by pocket parts.

Forms.[2] An advantage of having forms in practitioners' treatises is that they are usually supplemented at regular intervals.

Statutory forms. As noted above, many forms are statutory and are printed as parts of the statutory compilations and of legal directories. Commonly these are indexed in compilations of statutes.

Practice or Procedural Forms. Because these are so largely statutory, they are almost always restricted in scope to a particular jurisdiction or even to a particular action; or (especially in practice before federal bodies) to a single tribunal, such as the Supreme Court, Interstate Commerce Commission, or Patent Office. An exception is Bancroft-Whitney's *Code Pleading in the Western States.* As with business forms, they may appear as compilations of forms only, but most frequently they are published as integral parts of treatises. Most treatises on practice and procedure include printed forms, which are usually annotated by the decisions. Treatises on topics of substantive law which are peculiarly the creatures of statutes (such as bankruptcy or patents) usually print procedural forms also.

Briefs as form books. Appeal papers are a good and frequently used source of procedural forms. Where a complaint or the like has been attacked as defective, but upheld on appeal, it is often copied from the appeal papers by lawyers having a like problem.

Foreign Law Forms. Forms, principally business, in use in foreign countries, are printed in the *Martindale-Hubbell Law Dictionary* and in the *Lawyers Directory*, described in Chapter 27.

Lawyers' Work Books Containing Forms.

For judicial officers. There are several manuals for justices of the peace and notaries, which contain forms. *Reed's Branson's Instructions to Juries* contains numerous examples of instructions in both civil and criminal causes, which have been sustained on appeal.

Instructions for writing legal forms. The mechanics of writing legal documents, including typing, are set forth in sufficient detail by *Antus, McCarty*, and *Horowitz*, mentioned in the *Notes.*

D. Techniques of Using Form Books.

There are three principal problems in the use of forms: (1) finding the proper form; (2) selecting the applicable clauses; and (3) properly typing the resulting document.

Selecting the Proper Form. The first choice is as between procedural and business forms, since they are seldom printed in the same volume or set. The *index* to the proper form book or treatise should then direct to the desired form, but often considerable ingenuity is required to place the searcher *en rapport* with the indexer. The *analytical contents tables* found in every form book often aid in this search. *Supplements* should not be neglected, especially for procedural forms, where statutory changes are frequent. Also, if the form is procedural, care should be taken that it is *applicable in the searcher's jurisdiction*. In addition to form books and treatises, *statutes and appeal papers are good sources to search.*

Selecting the Applicable Clauses. Form books commonly print (1) a long form of document; (2) a short form; and (3) a variety of particular clauses. The preliminary comment on the problems peculiar to a particular legal topic, and on particular clauses, which is almost always a preliminary part of the treatment of a particular form book topic, is often helpful. In fitting in particular clauses, inconsistent or contradictory ones should be avoided. Few forms can be taken verbatim from a form book, and common sense, caution, and professional skill

---

[2] Washington, D. C., National Institute of Municipal Law Officers, 1952.

must be employed in adapting or synthesizing them for a specific set of facts. A form book is never a substitute for sound legal training. If a form or clause is annotated to the searcher's own jurisdiction, that is helpful. Finally, a *checklist* previously prepared by the searcher should be compared with the completed form, to ensure that nothing has been omitted. Some special-subject form books supply suggested checklists; Klipstein's *Drafting New York Wills* is an example.

Typing the Form Acceptably. A neat and technically correct paper is important. The lawyer's work books cited above provide the draftsman and the typist with the requisite models and instructions.

Notes

Below are listed a few form books. They are intended as illustrative examples only, of the variety of materials available.

Business or Substantive Forms.

Encyclopedic. *Modern Legal Forms* (Kansas City., Mo., Vernon Law Book Co., 1938-50. 4 v.)

American Jurisprudence Legal Forms Annotated (Rochester, N. Y., Lawyers' Co-operative Publishing Co; 1953 —. Projected in 14 v. V 1, June, 1953).

Nichols, Clark A., *Cyclopedia of Legal Forms, Annotated* (Chicago, Callaghan, 1936. 9 v.)

Single Volume Editions. Jones, Leonard A., *Legal Forms Annotated* (Indianapolis, Bobbs-Merrill. 9th ed., 1946)

Nichols, Clark A., *Nichols' Annotated Forms* (Chicago, Callaghan, 2d ed., 1945)

Geographical Slant. *Cowdery's Forms* (Western) (San Francisco, Bancroft-Whitney. 6th ed., 1951. 3v.)

Special-Subject Form Books.

Doris, Lillian, and Friedman, Edith J., *Corporate Meetings, Minutes and Resolutions.* (New York, Prentice-Hall, Inc., 3d ed., 1951)

Doris, Lillian, Friedman, Edith J., and Spillman, Howard H., *Corporate Secretary's Manual and Guide.* (New York, Prentice-Hall, Inc. Rev. ed., 1949).

Fletcher, William M., *Corporation Forms and Precedents, Annotated.* (Chicago, Callaghan. 3d rev. ed., 1938. 5 v.).

Friedman, Edith J., ed., *Encyclopedia of Corporate Forms.* (New York, Prentice-Hall, Inc., 1937-40. 4 v.).

Gordon, Saul, *Modern Annotated Forms of Agreement.* (New York, Prentice-Hall, Inc. 1940).

———*Standard Annotated Real Estate Forms.* (New York, Prentice-Hall, Inc., 1945).

———*Standard Annotated Forms of Wills.* (New York, Prentice-Hall, Inc., 1947).

Rollinson, William D., *Clauses in Wills and Forms of Wills.* (Albany, M. Bender, 1946).

White, Frank, *White on Corporations.* (Albany, M. Bender. 12th ed., 1947–50. 6 v.).

Treatises Having Forms.

Beer, Henry Ward, *Federal Trade Law and Practice.* (Chicago, Callaghan, 1942)

Bogert, George G., *The Law of Trusts and Trustees.* (Kansas City, Mo., Vernon Law Book Co., 1935-51. 8 v.).

Callmann, Rudolf, *The Law of Unfair Competition and Trade Marks.* (Chicago, Callaghan. 2d ed., 1950. 5 v.).

Collier, William, *Collier on Bankruptcy.* (Albany, M. Bender. 14th ed., 1940-47. 9 v.).

Grossman, Milton L., *The New York Law of Domestic Relations.* (Buffalo, Fred Dennis, 1947).

Klipstein, Harold D., *Drafting New York Wills; Law and Clauses.* (New York, Baker, Voorhis, 1948).

Larson, Arthur, *The Law of Workmen's Compensation.* (Albany, M. Bender, 1952).

Page, William H., *A Treatise on the Law of Wills.* (Cincinnati, W. H. Anderson, 1941-42. 5 v.).

Thompson, George W., *The Law of Wills.* (Indianapolis, Bobbs-Merrill. 3d ed., 1947).

————*Commentaries on the Modern Law of Real Property.* (Indianapolis, Bobbs-Merrill, 1939-41. 12 v.).

Annotated Statutes Having Substantive and Procedural Forms.

Florida Statutes Annotated. (Atlanta, Ga., Harrison; St. Paul, West, 1943-52. 31 v., kept to date by cumulative annual pocket parts).

New York Consolidated Laws Service. (Rochester, N. Y., Lawyers Co-operative Publishing Co., 1950-52. 12 v., kept to date by pocket parts).

There are many others.

Procedural Forms.

FORM BOOKS.

Bender's Forms of Pleading of the State of New York. (Albany, M. Bender, 1946-48. 8 v.).

Bender's Forms for the Civil Practice Acts of the State of New York. (Albany, M. Bender, 1937-49. 8 v.).

Bradbury, Harry F., *Lawyers' Manual.* (New York, Baker, Voorhis. 5th ed., 1942).

Guandolo, John, and Kennedy, Robert B., *Federal Procedure Forms.* (Buffalo, Dennis, 1949).

Medina's Bostwick: Common Practice Forms. (Albany, M. Bender. 5th ed., 1951 revision.) (This also contains substantive forms.)

TREATISES CONTAINING FORMS.

Bancroft-Whitney's *Code Pleading in the Western States.* (San Francisco, Bancroft-Whitney, 1926).

Barron, William W., and Holtzoff, Alexander, *Federal Practice and Procedure, with Forms.* Rules ed. (St. Paul, West, 1950-51. 7 v.).

Ohlinger, Gustavus, *Jurisdiction and Procedure of the Courts of the United States* (binder's title: *Federal Practice*) (Cincinnati, W. H. Anderson. Rev. ed., 1938-50. 6 v.).

LAWYERS' WORK BOOKS.

Anderson's Manual for Notaries Public. (Meier ed., Cincinnati, W. H. Anderson, 1940).

Antus, John J., *Law Office Secretary's Manual.* (New York, Prentice-Hall, Inc., 1940).

Branson, Edward R., *The Law of Instructions to Juries.* (Indianapolis, Bobbs-Merrill. 3d ed., by A. H. Reid, 1936. 5 v.).

Horowitz, Jacob I., *Manual for Lawyers and Law Clerks.* (New York, Central Book Co., 2d ed., 1936).

John, Edward M., *John's American Notary and Commissioner of Deeds Manual.* (Chicago, Callaghan. 5th ed., 1942).

McCarty, Dwight G., *Law Office Management.* (New York, Prentice-Hall, Inc. Rev. ed., 1946).

Miller, B. M., *The Legal Secretary's Complete Handbook.* (New York, Prentice-Hall, Inc., 1952).

Morrison, Alfred A., *A Guide for Justices of the Peace: New York.* (Albany, M. Bender, 1949).

CHAPTER 26

LOOSE-LEAF SERVICES

A. Background and Purpose.[1]

Loose-leaf services (as Prentice-Hall, Inc., and some other publishers designate their publications) or reporters (the term employed by Commerce Clearing House, Inc. — hereinafter referred to as C.C.H.), had their inception in the Sixteenth — income tax — Amendment to the Constitution in 1913, which precipitated such a flood of administrative rules and orders in tax and other regulatory fields that no individual lawyer or firm of lawyers could cope with it.

The modern loose-leaf service is the embodiment of that colloquial term, the "package deal," as applied to law book publication. It collects and reports *all* the pertinent material in a specialized field of law in which the continuous reporting of new developments is necessary; no matter how and where the material originates; and *coordinates* and presents all the essential data from it promptly, in a highly usable form; each editorial comment being backed by the latest pertinent authority of all kinds.

B. Scope of Loose-Leaf Services.

Services cover virtually all those fields of business in which administrative law plays an important role, and they have branched out into other areas as well. Roughly, these fields can be broken down into three principal categories.

1. Federal and state tax laws of all kinds.
2. Business regulation on both the federal and state level.
3. Miscellaneous services, such as the *Congressional Index, United States Supreme Court Bulletin,* and the Pike and Fischer *Administrative Law* and *Federal Rules* services, which have been described elsewhere in this *Manual.*

C. Specialization and Consolidation.

Each service covers one specific field of law and aims to do it completely *in one*

---

[1] The principal publishers of loose-leaf services distribute guides to the use of their publications. The authors of this *Manual* have (with permission) taken material for this chapter from guides issued by Prentice-Hall, Inc., and Commerce Clearing House, Inc. However, although each guide describes in detail the special features of its publisher's services and how to use them, that material is not duplicated here, the aim being only to set forth the general philosophy of loose-leaf services and to discuss those characteristics which are more or less common to all. Emphasis is placed herein upon matters in connection with services which in the experience of the authors have most perplexed their users.

place. All types of legal authority — statutes, administrative regulations, executive orders, rulings, court decisions, and agency interpretations and memoranda affecting the specific field of law covered — are collected and coordinated in one spot, with editorial comment and explanations as needed.[2] As statutes and regulations are amended or new ones promulgated, or as new agency rulings and court decisions are rendered, the material in the service is likewise amended, superseded or rewritten wholly or in part, as called for. How that is done is shown by specimen on page 232 from the Prentice-Hall *Federal Tax Service*.

In exhibit 57 the arrows are added for the purposes of the following explanation.

First, the Pilot Paragraph [¶ 13.001], indicated by the arrow, gives a birds-eye view of the entire topic of deductibility of interest. Cross-references and "additional references" are made to paragraphs treating other phases of the interest problem. The second arrow points out the exact text of the *pertinent statute* (always indicated by the vertical line), [¶ 13.002]. Third, the exact text of *pertinent regulations*, in full [as indicated by ¶ 13.003, arrow 3], identified by the "key" symbol, follows. The key always means that the material is an official regulation. Then comes the *editorial text* [¶ ¶ 31.005 *et seq.*], explaining the law on each point involved, supported by full *citation to all rulings and decisions*. These may include, as here, United States Supreme Court, lower federal court, and Tax Court decisions, both reported and memorandum; and also such informal expressions of agency policy as releases, and letters or telegrams to the editors replying to specific questions. In a substantial number of services, the complete court and agency reports of decisions are also collected behind a separate tab.

The Commerce Clearing House *Standard Federal Tax Reporter* prints the full text of the law and pertinent regulations, as above, with one or more "CCH Explanations," followed by digests of material cited in support, as shown on page 233.

D. Basic Organization.

While the service or reporter retains in one form or another most of the familiar indexes, tables, *etc.*, of the conventional law book, its organization, being geared to both *coordination of diverse materials and speed of publication*, is quite different. Although the organization varies considerably from publisher to publisher and from service to service of the same publisher, certain fundamentals are common to most of them, which are as follows.

Binders. Each service is delivered to the subscriber in a binder, either ring or post style.

Instructions for Use. Marked by conspicuous tabs at the front of each service are complete instructions on its scope, organization and use. These are carefully and graphically worked out, with specimen pages and problems, and a few minutes' perusal of them will save a great deal of time over aimless searching.

Basic Text or Compilation. The basic information on the topic covered by the service is usually but not always set forth in a "treatise," which is revised at intervals varying with the subject matter. Where, as in federal income taxation, the changes in statute and decision are frequent and drastic, the basic compilation may be revised annually. If, on the other hand, the topic is relatively stable, as in labor, wills or trusts, there is a continual partial revision, with complete revision only after several years' accumulation of changes.

---

[2] The most important types of materials collected and synthesized in a typical loose-leaf service are enumerated and described briefly in the *Notes* to this chapter.

1

INTEREST   **13.011**

[¶ 13,001] With the minor exceptions noted below, the law [¶ 13,002] allows a deduction for interest on indebtedness "paid or accrued within the taxable year." Generally speaking, "interest" corresponds to the business man's conception of the term [¶ 13,005 et seq.]. To justify a deduction, it must be shown that there was an indebtedness [¶ 13,030 et seq.; 13,096] and that the indebtedness was that of the taxpayer [¶ 13,051 et seq.].

● Pilot ●
Paragraph

No distinction is made between interest on business debts and interest on personal debts. Thus a taxpayer can deduct interest on a mortgage on his residence or interest on money borrowed from a bank to purchase a pleasure automobile.

Taxpayers on the cash basis deduct interest in the year it is paid [¶ 13,062 et seq.]; taxpayers on the accrual basis in the year liability to make payment arose [¶ 13,076 et seq.].

Interest on indebtedness incurred to purchase or carry certain wholly tax-exempt securities is not deductible [¶ 13,060 et seq.].

The rule that substance, rather than form, is controlling [¶ 28,201 et seq.] may be applied to disallow deduction of amounts that are called interest but are in fact something else, e.g., capital expenditures [¶ 13,015] or dividends [¶ 13,096].

Additional references.—

Deduction of interest in computing adjusted gross income—¶ 4141.

Disallowance of interest or indebtedness incurred to purchase single premium life insurance or endowment contracts—¶ 11,550.

Deduction of amount representing interest paid to coöperative apartment corporation —¶ 11,451.

2

L
A
W

[¶ 13,002] I.R.C., SEC. 23. DEDUCTIONS FROM GROSS INCOME. In computing net income there shall be allowed as deductions: • • •

(b) **Interest.**—All interest paid or accrued within the taxable year on indebtedness, except on indebtedness incurred or continued to purchase or carry obligations (other than obligations of the United States issued after September 24, 1917, and originally subscribed for by the taxpayer) the interest upon which is wholly exempt from the taxes imposed by this chapter.

3

[¶ 13,003] REG. 111, SEC. 29.23(b)-1 (As amended by T.D. 5458, June 15, 1945). Interest.—Interest paid or accrued within the year on indebtedness may be deducted from gross income, except that interest on indebtedness incurred or continued to purchase or carry obligations, such as municipal bonds, Panama Canal loan 3 percent bonds, or (in case of a taxpayer not an original subscriber) obliga-

---

[¶ 13,004] Blank.

INTEREST DEFINED

[¶ 13,005] General.—"Interest" is the amount which one has contracted to pay for the use of borrowed money and as used in Sec. 23(b) [¶ 13,002] the term has the usual, ordinary and everyday meaning given to it in the business world. Old Colony R.R. Co. v. Comm. (1932), 284 U.S. 552, 76 L.Ed. 484, 52 S.Ct. 211, 10 AFTR 786, Ct.D. 456, CB June 1932, p. 274; Deputy v. DuPont (1939), 308 U.S. 488, 84 L.Ed. 416, 60 S.Ct. 363, 23 AFTR 808, Ct.D. 1435, CB 1940-1, p. 118.

[¶ 13,006] Interest calculated for cost-keeping.—A taxpayer may not charge his business with interest on money that he has invested [¶ 13,003].

Example: An individual proprietor who has invested $100,000 in his business may charge that business $4,000 each year for cost-keeping purposes. That charge is not deductible. Even if it were, the effect would be nil, since the same amount would have to be included in gross income.

A similar rule applies to partnerships [¶ 15,525].

[¶ 13,006-A] Bookkeeping entries.—An erroneous bookkeeping entry does not preclude a deduction. Court Holding Co., 2 TC 531, affirmed without discussion of this point (1945), 324 U.S. 331, 89 L. Ed. 981, 65 S. Ct. 707, 33 AFTR 593, Ct. D. 1636, CB 1945, p. 58, which reversed (CCA-5), 143 F.2d 823, 32 AFTR 1088; Northwestern Penn. Gas Corp., ¶ 44,017 P-H Memo TC.

A general discussion of the effect of book entries is at ¶ 28,212.

Exhibit 57

CCH *Explanation*

.28 Rented residential property.—If residential property is rented furnished, a reasonable amount of depreciation may be deducted on the furniture and other furnishings of the property. If a taxpayer's personal residence is rented for a short time during the year during the taxpayer's absence from his home, as for instance, for the summer months or the winter months, the Commissioner probably would have denied any deductions as offsets under the 1941 law and prior law, because depreciation and expenses were deductible only on property used in trade or business, and such leasing would probably not be considered a trade or business. However, for 1939 and later years, depreciation and other expenses are deductible against the income from such leasing of income-producing property. A similar conclusion would be reached in the case of property which is sublet. If only a part of the taxpayer's residence is rented, a proportionate part of the depreciation, repairs, and maintenance may be deducted as an offset against the income from the rented portion. For illustration of the method of determining the basis on residential property converted to rental use, see "Example (1)" in the regulation at ¶ 189.—CCH.

.281 Corporation may deduct depreciation on residence property owned by it and occupied rent-free by its president.

Reynard Corp., 30 BTA 451. Dec. 8522 (Acq.).

.2815 Taxpayer was allowed depreciation on an apartment building for that portion not occupied rent-free by her son.

L. M. Buchwach, TC memo. op., 9 TCM 835, Dec. 17,887(M).

.282 Depreciation of residential property is denied in the absence of evidence as to the fair market value of the property when converted from use as the petitioner's residence to rental property.

Thatcher, 24 BTA 1130, Dec. 7330.

.283 Depreciation was allowed as to a residence which had been effectively converted to the production of income, even though unproductive.

H. I. Fagan, TC memo. op., 9 TCM 44, Dec. 17,468(M).

¶ 216.2761   § 29.23(1)-2

Exhibit 58

Arrangement Within the Basic Compilation. This follows somewhat the philosophy expressed above. Generally, since services are founded upon *statutes and the regulations* promulgated thereunder, this fundamental material is printed first as enacted, for quick reference purposes, even though it may be printed and annotated by subject matter later on in the service. Then come the *basic compilation proper*, the *decisions and orders* interpreting the statutes and regulations, the *new materials, indexes, tables,* and so forth.

Where, as in taxation or bankruptcy law, the basis of the service topic is *one outstandingly important statute*, the arrangement of the service is likely to be by section of that statute. The Pike and Fischer *Administrative Law* service, for example, is in effect an elaborate section-by-section annotation of the Federal Administrative Procedure Act. Where, however, as in labor law or trade regulation, there are *numerous statutes of coordinate importance*, often overlapping in coverage, the arrangement is usually by topic, with ample cross-references to related topics. Similarly, where the subject matter of the service follows *common-law rules* closely (as in trusts and estates), the material is developed by *subject or topic*.

Uniform Arrangement of State Statutes. Where there are statutes in many states on the same topic, they are customarily rearranged in the services by states under a classification system of captions and paragraph numbers uniform for all, so that the same precise subject is found in each state under the same paragraph number.

Here is how it works. The problem of unemployment contribution payment by an interstate salesman is covered in the Prentice-Hall *Social Security Service* by Par. 27.126 (as found through the topical index). A search under that number in the laws of each jurisdiction automatically turns up the pertinent statutory provision. Similarly, in the C.C.H. *Labor Law Reporter* "Yellow Dog" contract statutory provisions are found for each state that has them, under Par. 41.005.

"New Matter" or "Current Matter": Speed of Supplementation. Depending upon the service, supplementation of the basic compilation is as frequent as weekly, but when a particularly important statute is enacted, judicial decision rendered, or regulation adopted, overnight distribution to subscribers is often made.

Perpetual Revision. A loose-leaf service not only distributes new basic material, but when *a new statute or regulation* causes the obsolescence of existing material, the editors analyze anew the topic or sub-topic affected, and immediately incorporate the result into the body of the service, the out-dated pages then being discarded. New statutes, amendments, regulations, and proposed regulations are mailed out shortly after approval or promulgation.

Report Letter or Bulletin. A newsletter reporting the *latest legislative and judicial developments* of interest to subscribers accompanies mailings of new matters. In this letter *pending legislation* may be listed, together with its present status. *Law charts* and *synopses of certain characteristics of pertinent laws of all states*, are a feature of some services.

Guide Cards or Tabs. The major divisions or sections of the text and other sections of the service are separated by celluloided guide or tab cards. Upon these are noted the subject matter of the section, and the paragraph numbers included in it.

Paragraph Number Arrangement. All material is identified and indexed by *paragraph*, not page, number. In most cases these numbers are enclosed in brackets to avoid confusion with official numbers assigned to laws and regulations. Each page of the service is also numbered for ease and accuracy in filing. Index and other references throughout are to paragraph numbers. *These are not fixed classification numbers*, and usually are changed with each new edition.

Indexes. A major approach to any loose-leaf service is through its subject or topical indexes and their supplements. As these indexes vary greatly from service to service, the excellent and full instructions for their use, preceding in each service the indexes themselves, should be mastered.

Coverage by date. Indexes are divided into at least the following units, on the basis of lateness of material indexed: (i) *Index to the basic compilation* or treatise; and (ii) *Index to new matters* published since the original compilation. Some services have, in addition, (iii) a *super-late index* to the material in the latest releases of supplementary sheets, not yet incorporated into the cumulative index to new matters.

Coverage of subject matter. The basic topical index may cover the entire service and be the only index to the basic compilation; or it may refer to topics in a more detailed topical index to each major subdivision of the service. For example, in the C. C. H. *Trade Regulation Reporter*, the Sherman, Clayton,

Robinson-Patman and other regulatory acts, each has its own topical index. A variant, usually confined to services filling several binders and covering a rather wide variety of subdivision, is the *Answer Finder, Problem Solver,* or *Rapid Finder* index. This has for its purpose the coordination of references to the complete service. Thus, in the Prentice-Hall *Labor Equipment,* discharge of employees is discussed in several of its five volumes. It saves time to look first in the "Answer Finder" or its supplement, under "Discharge," where over eighty different aspects of the topic are listed. The C.C.H. "Rapid Finder Index," preceding the "Topical Index," provides a quick approach to the main phases of a broad field, for example, labor law.

Some services have all types of indexes mentioned above. Most do not.

Supplementation of main topical index. The main topical index to the basic compilation leads to the desired paragraph numbers in the compilation. All new matter is keyed to the same paragraph numbers. Supplementary indexes are or may be of two kinds.

1. *"Current Topical Index."* This is a counterpart in brief to the main topical index, and indexes new matters by subject.

2. More common (some services have both) are *numerical supplementary tables, arranged by paragraph number of the basic compilation,* by means of which, through a simple matching of numbers, all the new material supplementing a given paragraph is collected. In the Prentice-Hall services these are called "Cross-Reference Tables," and "Supplementary Cross Reference Tables"; in the Commerce Clearing House reporters, "Cumulative Indexes" and "Latest Additions." In some services these tables are purely numerical, as from *main text* ¶ 52.101 to *supplement* ¶ 98.377, without more. In others, there is a brief digest of the new material:

¶ 59.217   .25. Sec. 722 and the net loss provision ¶ 61.095 are separately applicable; E. P. C. 29 is erroneous—Nivison-Weiskopf, T. C.

In each instance these tables are cross-references from a paragraph number in the basic compilation (¶ 52.101 or ¶ 59.217 above) to (a) later and (b) latest supplementary material exactly in point. (*See also* page 240.)

Bureau of National Affairs Labor Relations Reporter indexes. These are typical periodical indexes, because this service resembles more closely a co-ordinated group of periodicals and law reports than a typical loose-leaf service.

Tables. Tables vary greatly according to the subject matter of the service. Practically all services have case tables, some in the form of citators. Most tax services have *court dockets.* An important table is the finding list, which *cross-references from official statute or regulation citation to the corresponding paragraph number of the service.* Most services have lists of the *personnel of the agency* or agencies principally covered. As noted above, cross-reference tables lead from the basic compilation to the new materials in point.

Citator Functions of Services. Tax and regulatory services note amendments, repeals, and other legislative and judicial changes affecting statutes and regulations covered, and are annotated by judicial decisions and agency rulings, and so to that extent they perform a definite citator function. With respect to administrative regulations and rulings, this information is often unavailable elsewhere, or not so promptly.

The citator function may be rendered by a separate publication, as the Prentice-Hall *Federal Tax Service Citator* (for court and agency decisions and rulings); or by a separate division of a service, as in the C.C.H. *Standard Federal Tax Reporter* and *Federal Estate and Gift Tax Reporter* "Citator Tables." Finding lists lead to notations of amendments or repeals of statutes and regulations, and to annotations of cases or agency rulings.

Tax citators in loose-leaf services render a complete citator service for court and tax court cases, treasury decisions and rulings, and executive orders commented upon. Commonly citator case tables are divided into two sections: (1) court and tax court decisions by *case name;* and (2) Treasury decisions and rulings and executive orders, by *serial number.* The *Internal Revenue Code* and *Treasury Regulations* have no loose-leaf citator, as such; but inasmuch as changes in form are indicated, and case and other comments upon them are made in the annotations to the *Code* sections, certain citator information is available, as it is in any annotated statute.

E. How to Use Loose-Leaf Services.[3]

The approaches to the solutions of legal problems through loose-leaf services parallel those to the digest, the annotated statute, and the encyclopedia. Any one familiar with the use of those works can use a loose-leaf service.

Fact or Index Approach: Three-Step Method. This method corresponds to the *Descriptive-Word Index* approach to case digests.

Sample Problem. Johnson purchases a piece of real estate from Adams. The contract provides that Johnson pay the accrued real estate taxes. Who is entitled to deduct these real estate taxes from his income, in computing the federal income tax, Johnson or Adams?

First step: The index. First, consult the main topical index to the basic compilation, as it leads to the fundamental discussion of the topic in point, and, through cross-references to the supplementary material. A variety of salient facts should be selected from the analysis of the problem for search in the index. In the above example, for instance, the Prentice-Hall *Federal Tax Service* supplies entries under "Property," "Purchaser," "Real Estate," and "Vendor," with sub-entries leading to the precise set of facts. The C.C.H. *Standard Federal Tax Reporter* indexes this same fact situation under "Real Property," "Sales of Property," and "Taxes," with appropriate sub-entries under each.

References are to paragraph numbers, and usually more than one potentially applicable one will be turned up by the index. In the above example, the various catchwords in the Prentice-Hall service all turn to ¶ 13.123, which pinpoints it as probably the proper one. In the C.C.H. *Reporter,* the corresponding paragraphs are ¶ 181.0657, ¶ 181.12, ¶ 181.177. Since there is over-lapping in statutes, it is usually best to examine more than one possibly pertinent paragraph before completing the search. Shown on page 237 is a part of the Prentice-Hall *Federal Tax Service* index applicable to the tax problem above.

---

[3] In both Prentice-Hall and the Commerce Clearing House services there is a heavy manila sheet, with tab projecting at the top of the binder, labeled "How to Use This Service (or Reporter)," indicating where complete, detailed and graphic information as to the scope, organization, indexes, with sample problems worked out. Publishers of other services all provide similar aids. They remove whatever mystery there might otherwise be as to the techniques and procedures required.

Master Index

```
PROPERTY:
. abandonment of: See "Abandonment"
. accounts receivable as..10,292-A
. acquisition for tax avoidance purposes
    ..6921-6940
. assignment of, income taxable to whom
    ..7201-F
```
```
. taxes: See also "Real estate, taxes"
.. accrual..7888; 13,145-13,148
.. adjusted gross income..4101; 4121; 4139;
    4140
.. attorney's fees litigating..11,146; 11,805
.. beneficiaries..13,124
.. cancellation, income..7253-A
.. contested..6407-A; 13,131
.. delinquent..11,264-A; 13,123-A—13,123-E;
    13,825-B
.. estates and trusts..13,124; 15,085; 15,088
.. excess accrual..7378
.. expenses connected with..11,140-A
. life insurance company..16,002(c); 16,-
    015; 16,017-16,022
.. mutual insurance companies other than
    life or marine..16,095(b)(c); 16,112;
    16,116
.. oil and gas wells, paid by lessee, deple-
    tion..14,623
.. paid by mortgagee..13,120
.. paid by tenant..12,003; 12,013
.. paid by trust, effect on income of bene-
    ficiaries..15,128
.. paid for another..13,120
.. priority of Federal taxes..19,898
.. purchaser and seller..13,123-13,123-B;
    13,825-B
.. refunds..7351 et seq.; 13,134
. title to: See "Title, property" and "Real
    estate, title to"
```

Exhibit 59

Second step: The basic text. The index in the sample problem has led to the precise paragraph (¶ 13.123, or ¶ 181.177) covering the problem. Out of the general tax situation involving the deductibility of taxes, it has led to the exact *situation* surrounding that tax (deductibility as between purchaser and seller). As on page 238, the text lays down the general rule covering the precise situation, and cites the source of that rule—in this case a decision of the United States Supreme Court. It states the facts on which that general rule was based, and quotes the Court's reasons for arriving at the rule. The general rule is supported by citations to additional cases (*see* arrow 2). Furthermore, citations to cases decided before the Supreme Court set up the rule, but which can be used as references because they are consistent with the rule, are provided (*see* arrow 3).

Working the same problem in the C.C.H. *Standard Federal Tax Reporter*, ¶ 181.0657 is a *C.C.H. Explanation* on state and local property tax aspects generally, in which our problem is discussed; ¶ 181.13 is a similar *Explanation* on deductibility of taxes, with a specific ¶ (as shown) on real estate taxes; ¶ 181.177 (as shown) discusses the principal authority, followed by other paragraphs ¶ 181.178–181.179 treating similar tax situations. *See* page 239.

Third step: Current matter. The first two steps have led to a discussion of the exact fact situation as of the date of the distribution of the basic compilation of the service. Collecting later decisions and agency rulings in point requires only the mechanical matching up of the paragraph numbers (¶¶ 13.123 and 181.177 respectively, for the two services) by means of the supplementary indexes de-

1 　**13,118**　Taxes—Who May Claim Deduction　(§ 23(c) — ¶ 13,102)

➡ 　**[¶ 13,123]** Deduction of property taxes as between purchaser and **seller.**—In 1942 the U. S. Supreme Court laid down the rule that, *if prior to the sale,*

(1)　the tax was a lien against the property, or

(2)　the seller was personally liable for the tax,

the purchaser is not entitled to deduct the tax even though he pays it. The payment represents taxes imposed upon the seller, and, from the standpoint of the purchaser, constitutes part of the purchase price. <u>Magruder v. Supplee</u> (1942), 316 U.S. 394, 62 S.Ct. 1162, 86 L.Ed. 1555, <u>29 AFTR 196</u>, Ct.D. 1559, CB 1942-1, p. 173. reversing 123 F.(2d) 399, <u>28 AFTR 325</u>, which had affirmed 36 F. Supp. 722, 26 AFTR 565.

The facts in the above case were that during 1936 and 1937 the taxpayers purchased various parcels of real estate in Maryland upon which State and city taxes for the current year had not been paid at the time of purchase, and, pursuant to contract, paid the amount of such taxes; the vendors undertook to bear the burden of that portion of the taxes arithmetically allocable to the fraction of the year that had expired prior to the date of purchase, and adjustments were made in the purchase price to reflect this arrangement. In holding that the amounts so paid by the purchasers did not constitute "taxes paid" within the meaning of section 23(c) but were part of the cost of the properties, the Court stated:

Thus either a pre-existing tax lien or personal liability for the taxes on the part of a vendor is sufficient to foreclose a subsequent purchaser, who pays the amount necessary to discharge such payment as a "tax paid". Where both lien and personal liability coincide, as here, there can be no other conclusion than that the taxes were imposed on the vendors. Respondents simply paid their vendors' taxes; they cannot deduct the amounts. or any portion thereof, paid to discharge liabilities so firmly fixed against their predecessors in title by the laws of Maryland.

The view of the court below that the parties' contractual arrangement for apportionment of the tax burden was controlling is untenable. Parties cannot change the incidence of local taxes by their agreement.

2

➡ 　The above decision was followed in:

Helvering v. Johnson County Realty Co., (CCA-8; 1942) 128 F.(2d) 716, 29 AFTR 696, reversing 44 BTA 121 (Iowa taxes for 1935, which became a lien in September of that year, held not deductible by one who purchased the property on December 23, 1935, and paid such taxes in 1936)

George E. Warren Corp., ¶ 42,333 P-H Memo BTA (Massachusetts)

Harbor Building Trust, ¶ 42,350 P-H Memo BTA (Massachusetts)

3　Ezra Brudno et al., ¶ 42,581 P-H Memo TC, affirmed 138 F.(2d) 779, 31 AFTR 835

➡ 　(a)　Decisions prior to the Supplee case.—Prior to the Supplee decision, above, the term "accrual date" was used to designate both the time for deduction of the taxes by a taxpayer reporting income on the accrual basis and the date which controlled (regardless of accounting method) on the question of whether the tax was imposed upon the purchaser or seller. The following earlier decisions, in which the tax had become a lien at the time of the sale, though using somewhat different language, are consistent with the Supplee case in their conclusions disallowing the deduction on the part of the purchaser or grantee:

Grand Hotel Co., 21 BTA 890 (Washington)

Leamington Hotel Co., 26 BTA 1004 (Minnesota)

¶ **13,121**　FOR LATEST RULINGS consult the Cross-Reference Table, page 73,001 ➡

Exhibit 60

4088   Deductions: Taxes—Sec. 23(c) [page 4051]

[¶ 181.13]—Deductible by Whom—Continued
CCH Explanation

> See the discussion below.) An individual who elects to take the optional standard deduction may deduct only those taxes which are

> **Real estate taxes** are deductible only by the owner against whom they are assessed. The purchaser of real estate who paid the taxes after they had become a lien against the property or a personal obligation of the previous owner may not deduct such payments as taxes. They are a part of the cost of the property. They are deductible by the seller but must also be included in the sale price of the real estate. See ¶ 181.0657.

¶ 181.13   § 29.23(c)-2   Copyright 1951, Commerce Clearing House, Inc.

4094   Deductions: Taxes—Sec. 23(c) [page 4051]

[¶ 181.176]—Deductible by Whom—Continued

though nontaxable, and the predecessor's taxes paid by petitioner were additional cost to it of the property.

Merchants Bank Bldg. Co. v. Helvering, (CCA-8) 36-2 USTC ¶ 9378, 84 Fed. (2d) 478.

Similarly, where property to which the lien for Ohio property taxes had already attached was transferred by the owning corporation to the taxpayer, in return for assumption of certain liabilities and issuance of some stock (which transfer was a sale and not a statutory merger under applicable Ohio statutes) payment of the taxes by taxpayer constituted a part of the cost of acquiring the land and the taxes are not deductible.

Cable Co., 46 BTA 85, Dec. 12,237.

.177 **Purchase of real estate during year.** —Contractual agreement for apportionment of real property taxes between the vendor and the purchaser has no effect in determining the deductibility of the tax. Either a pre-existing lien against the property at the time of purchase or personal liability for the taxes on the part of a vendor is sufficient to foreclose a subsequent purchaser from deducting as a tax any payments made by him to discharge such pre-existing liability. Here, both the state (Maryland) and the city (Baltimore) had liens for taxes for the calendar year 1936 from the due date, January 1, 1936, and taxpayer, who purchased the property on May 10, 1936, could deduct no part of the 1936 taxes paid by him as taxes. The portion of the taxes paid by him was a part of his contractual cost of the property.

Magruder v. Supplee, 316 U. S. 394, 42-2 USTC ¶ 9498.

Followed:

Helvering v. Johnson County Realty Co., (CCA-8) 42-2 USTC ¶ 9537, 128 Fed. (2d) 716.
Harbor Building Trust, BTA memo. op., Dec. 12,570-A.

California Sanitary Co., Ltd., 32 BTA 122, Dec. 8889.
Gatens Investment Co., 36 BTA 309, Dec. 9170.
Banfield, 42 BTA 769, Dec. 11,317.
American Liberty Oil Co., 43 BTA 76, Dec. 11,414 (Nonacq.).
Pyramid Metals Co., 44 BTA 1087, Dec. 12,009.
Cable Co., 46 BTA 85, Dec. 12,237.
Woodlaw Investment Co., BTA memo. op., Dec. 11,888-A.
Hall C. Smith, 11 TC 174, Dec. 16,531 (Nonacq.).
R. K. Steele, TC memo. op., 7 TCM 558, Dec. 16,548(M).
G. C. M. 7235, VIII-2 CB 197.

Such accrued taxes may not offset rental income.

Brown, BTA memo. op., Dec. 11,782-A.

Where the record does not show exactly when New York town, county and school taxes became a lien, purchaser with agreement to pay pro rata share of taxes for the current year is denied any deduction.

Mattes et al., TC memo. op., 1 TCM 220, Dec. 12,915-D.

Although taxes had been assessed on the realty prior to its purchase by taxpayer, payment of said taxes did not constitute a capital expenditure, as contended by the Commissioner, but was deductible as an expense. Under New York law, the vendor was not personally liable for said taxes because he was a non-resident of the district in which the property was located; and the tax did not become a lien on the property until after its acquisition by taxpayer. Thus, taxpayer's payment of the tax was in discharge of a lien which became effective upon his own property after taking title to it, and constituted a payment of his own taxes; and he was entitled to the deduction.

Com. v. LeRoy, (CCA-2) 45-2 USTC ¶ 9441, 152 Fed. (2d) 936.

Followed.

Com. v. Lawrence Operating Corp., (CCA-2) 45-2 USTC ¶ 9442.

Exhibit 61

scribed on page 235. How this operates is shown below, but note that there is still a later supplementary index *for the very latest materials*, not shown here, which must also be consulted.

Cross Reference Table

DEDUCTIONS—INTEREST, TAXES

13,033......74,169   Accrual of bond interest covering pre-incorporation period (TC). (NA). Pending before CCA-3.

13,036......72,398   Liability for interest on deficiencies not extinguished by application of carry-back provisions (DC).

13,037......76,145   Lucas, Mabelle T. (A).
         76,145   Toy, Harvey M. (A).
         76,146   Partial deduction for interest transferee paid on estate tax deficiency —IT 3156 modified (IT).

13,054......72,242   Prior law—divorced wife not taxable on interest received on hus-
13,121......71,026   Goodman, Chas., pending before CCA-2.

13,123......74,002   N. Y. City real estate taxes paid on property purchased before taxes became due deductible in full (TC). (A; NA). Ed., ¶ 70,202. Gov't. author. appeal.

         74,277   Second installment of N. Y. City taxes paid on real estate purchased before installment due deductible (TC). Pending before CCA-6.

[¶ 74,002] 9 TC No. 33—N. Y. City real estate taxes paid by purchaser on property purchased before taxes became due deductible in full [See also ¶ 13,123]— amount called "interest" not deductible without proof of accrual in taxable year [See also ¶ 6404; 13,061]—Commissioner's allocation of purchase price between land and building sustained [See also ¶ 14,096]—useful economic life of inadequate building held less than structural life [See also ¶ 14,124].—

(ADDA, INC., v. COMMISSIONER; Docket No. 8883; August 18, 1947. Deficiency for 1942 redetermined.)

1. On August 5, 1940, the taxpayer purchased a building in New York City and on October 1, 1940, received a real estate tax bill for the year July 1, 1940, to June 30, 1941, which it paid in full. The amount paid, held, deductible in full because under New York law there was neither a lien on the property nor personal liability on the seller for payment of the taxes at the time of the "interest" to the seller for a certain period under the terms of a mortgage deed, held, not sustained by the evidence.

3. The Commissioner's allocation of purchase price between land and building sustained.

4. The useful economic life of a building of two stories and penthouse erected on a site in New York City several times more valuable than the building, held, on the evidence to be 21 years from time of the taxpayer's

Exhibit 62

Analytical Approach. While this approach is more complicated and less uniform than for case digests, it is probably the most effective of all when mastered. As in case digests, the problem is analyzed through its legal implications rather than by fact or catchword situations.

Tables of contents. Services have a wide variety of such tables, including those for the service as a whole and also for many of the tabbed subdivisions. The approach to the law through them corresponds to that of the "Analysis" in a case digest. For example, the question arises of the seller's right to a fixture under a conditional sales contract where he claims a material man's or mechanic's lien on the realty. Running down the table of contents of the C.C.H. *Conditional Sale-Chattel Mortgage Reports* treatise reveals that this topic is discussed generally under Conditional Sales ¶ 360.

If the text of statutes and annotations to cases in point in any state, as Arkansas or Wisconsin, are desired, they will, under the uniform arrangement of statutes, be found back of the tabs for each of those states, with the same paragraph number in each state. In the example above, that number happens to be the same paragraph as in the basic compilation (¶ 360). More often, the paragraph numbering of the uniform state classification will differ from that of the treatise. But the pertinent number is found in the same way, through the table of contents analysis, leading to the same material in all states.

Analytical tables. A variant of the table of contents analysis is provided in some services by so-called analytical tables. On each subject covered by such a

---

Analytical Tables — Real Estate — Acquisition,   **29,173**
Ownership and Disposition

REAL ESTATE — ACQUISITION, OWNERSHIP AND DISPOSITION

[¶ 29,154] Many sections of the income tax law affect real estate. Almost everything you do from the time you buy it until you sell it affects the amount of your income tax bill. Some things that just happen affect it too, e.g., real estate is damaged, destroyed or condemned Each time you do something or something happens, check the lists below to find the effect on your income tax bill.

The following broad subjects relating to or including real estate are covered in other tables or paragraphs in this section:

Depletion ....¶ 29,078
Depreciation ....¶ 29,079
Obsolescence ....¶ 29,140

(d)   Sale or other disposition.—Gain or loss is recognized on every sale or exchange of real estate unless excepted by statute [¶ 10,202]. The amount of the gain or loss is the difference between the adjusted basis of the property (generally cost plus improvements less depreciation) and the amount realized [¶ 10,003]. Whether the gain or loss upon a sale or exchange is treated as a capital gain or loss or as an ordinary gain or loss depends upon the nature of the property transferred [¶ 5061 et seq.].

Abandonment ....¶ 13,524; 13,540
Casualty—fire, flood, storm, etc. ....¶ 4951; 13,440 et seq.

Residential property sold ....¶ 10,696-B; 13,391
Tax sale ....¶ 5103; 13,488
Taxes accrued prior to sale but paid by purchaser ....¶ 13,123
Time for reporting gain or loss ....¶ 6253 et seq.
Voluntary removal of buildings ....¶ 13,507
Voluntary surrender to mortgagee ....¶ 5105; 5106

Exhibit 63

table, the table enumerates the various fact situations involved, and refers to paragraphs in the service explaining the effect of those situations under the law. Exhibit 63, above, from the Prentice-Hall *Federal Tax Service*, shows how such a table functions in the analysis of the real property tax problem considered above.

Pilot charts and correlators. Similarly, the "Pilot Chart" found in Prentice-Hall services gives a bird's-eye view, in chart form, of the scope of the subject. It provides general answers to basic questions on the subject, and routes the searcher to specific paragraphs in the service where he will find the answers to his problem. The illustration below, again from the Prentice-Hall *Federal Tax*

[¶ 13,100] ● Pilot Chart—Deduction of Taxes.—

DEDUCTIBLE

General rule is that all taxes paid or accrued within the taxable year are deductible, whether or not connected with the taxpayer's business or investments. Exceptions, stated in ¶ 13,102, are summarized below.

NOT DEDUCTIBLE

Federal	State	Foreign
Income. War-profits. Estate. Gift. Excess profits tax. Import duties, excise and stamp taxes (but such items deductible if expense under Sec. 23(a). See ¶ 13,171.	Estate, inheritance, legacy, succession, and gift. Local benefit assessments [¶ 13,197].	Income, war-profits and excess-profits, if the taxpayer chooses to take to any extent the benefit of Section 131 (relating to credits for foreign taxes) [¶ 13,-103; 13,195].

WHO MAY CLAIM DEDUCTION

General rule.—Deductible only by person upon whom imposed [¶ 13,103; 13,120].
  State excise and sales taxes—¶ 13,125; 13,126.
  Federal taxes—¶ 13,172.

Exceptions.—Certain taxes of shareholder paid by corporation [See ¶ 13,239-13,248], and state and local retail sales taxes stated as separate item [see ¶ 13,125].
  Taxes paid by mortgagee.—¶ 13,123-A.
  Taxes paid by purchaser.—¶ 13,123.

As to deductions of payments to a cooperative apartment corporation by a tenant stockholder, see ¶ 11,451 et seq.

TIME FOR CLAIMING DEDUCTION

General rules [¶ 13,128].
Cash basis taxpayer—year in which paid [¶ 13,129].
Accrual basis taxpayer—year in which accrued [¶ 13,130].
  State income taxes—¶ 13,140.
  State sales taxes—¶ 13,143.
  State property taxes—¶ 13,145.
  State franchise, excise and miscellaneous taxes—¶ 13,149.
Time for deduction of Federal taxes [¶ 13,181].

Exhibit 64

Service, shows how this applies to the real estate deduction problem already considered.

The C.C.H. device is the "Correlators," as shown below, in which a specific topic is surveyed, with references to applicable *Reporter* paragraphs.

Correlator
DEDUCTIONS FOR INTEREST AND TAXES

**Taxes—
Deduction
By Whom**

In general, taxes are deductible only by the person upon whom they are imposed. However, state or local *retail* sales taxes, and, for taxable years beginning after 1950, gasoline taxes, separately stated and passed on to the consumer, are deductible by the consumer (¶ 180). At ¶ 181.243 is a discussion of deductibility of federal taxes in general and by whom the allowable deductions may be made for each of the various tax levies, and at ¶ 181.815 appear a summary and tabulation showing, for each state, who is entitled to the deduction for state tax levies. Special rules apply to import duties, lessees, liquor taxes, predecessor's taxes, taxes involved in purchases of real estate during the year (¶ 181.169-181.177), and certain taxes of a shareholder paid by a corporation without reimbursement (¶ 186-187).

Correlator   Copyright 1951, Commerce Clearing House, Inc:

Exhibit 65

Table of Cases Approach. The table of cases, familiar to all lawyers, fulfills its usual function in the service, and the approach to the law through it is the same. The following information is usually given.

1. The full citation to the case, including parallel citations to standard report series.
2. The paragraph number where found in the service.
3. Citator information is often given.
4. In some services (as for taxation) where the basic compilation is frequently revised, citations to prior-year paragraph numbers in earlier editions of the service are given, at which the case appears in full text.

Finding List Approach. An approach somewhat similar to the table of cases type is that through finding lists. The important function of Finding Lists is to lead the searcher *from the official citation* of statutes, regulations, agency rulings, releases, forms, and opinions of attorneys general, *to the paragraph numbers* in the services where these matters are printed, discussed, or annotated. They serve to coordinate information about a statute, the regulations carrying out its mandates, and agency or office policy statements pertinent thereto. Since the statutes are by no means always printed in a service in the order of their original section numbering, and since regulations are commonly printed in connection with pertinent statutes rather than in the order of their original numbering, the value of these tables is obvious.

Usually these lists are in *tabular form*, following the official statute or regulation as cited, but they are *alphabetical* when the material so indexed is not numbered. An example of the latter is the "Arbitration Clause Finding List" in the Prentice-Hall *Labor Arbitration Service*. Sample pages from finding lists are shown below.

1152   Finding Lists—U. S. Code Reference Table   (3) 8-1-51
Report 99

United States Code			United States Code			United States Code		
Title	Section	Par.	Title	Section	Par.	Title	Section	Par.
49 (Cont'd)			49 (Cont'd)			50	151	3325
	649....2443;	19,540		1106	2973		151b	3328a
	671....2468;	20,001		1107	2974		151c	3328b
	672....2469;	20,002		1108	2975		151d	3328c
	673....2470;	20,003		1109	2980		151e	3328f

Copyright 1951, Commerce Clearing House, Inc.

5-20-46   79,731

P-H ARBITRATION CLAUSE FINDING LIST

[¶ 79,731] Clauses on particular subjects can be located quickly and easily by referring to the following P-H Arbitration Clause Finding List showing paragraph in Service at which the clause appears. Main topics are indicated by bold face type.

— A —
Adjustment Committee..64,012.2
Alternate Tribunal:
   See **ARBITRATION TRIBUNAL**

Arbitration (continued):
. initiation (continued):
.. reference to arbitration..64,111
.. time limit..64,114
.. withdrawal prohibited..64,112
. lockout by company prohibited
  ..64,113

Exhibit 66

Working with finding lists in very simple. If all that the searcher knows is the section number of a part of a law, an article number of a regulation, the series and serial number of an administrative order or memorandum, or a similar citation, he matches that up with the number in the finding lists, which direct him to the appropriate paragraph in the service. Alphabetical finding lists, of course, are arranged in the manner of subject indexes. Not all services have finding lists. Where the service cuts across state laws, the uniform arrangement scheme is usually sufficient. If the service does have finding lists, *they are plainly tabbed.*

Notes

Below are brief descriptions of varieties of materials collected and analyzed by typical tax and regulatory loose-leaf services.

1. Common-law rules: The services have text material based upon common-law rules, underlying legal principles, and historical developments.

2. Statutes: Complete and up-to-date texts of all relevant statutes, including constitutions, are printed.

3. Regulations: The full, up-to-date texts of administrative regulations are printed. *Rules of practice* are included in some services.

4. Rulings: Rulings of administrative agencies made in applying the law and regulations to specific sets of facts are included.

Example.—The relationship of law, regulation and ruling is shown as follows:

The law says:

"The term wages means all remuneration for employment including the cash value of all remuneration paid in any medium other than cash . . ."

The regulation says:

"The medium in which remuneration is paid is . . . immaterial. It may be paid in cash or something other than cash, as for example, goods, lodging, food, or clothing."

The ruling says:

"When an employee accepted a negotiable promissory note as remuneration for employment, the fair market value of the note at the time of delivery to the employee constituted wages subject to the Act."

Thus, the *law*, gives the general policy of the legislature; the *regulations* give the enforcement policy of the administrative agency; and the *rulings* give the application of these policies to specific sets of circumstances.

5. Court decisions: All decisions of all state and federal courts on the subject are reported.

6. Administrative decisions: If an administrative agency has quasi-judicial powers, the service reports the decisions of the agency.

7. Legislative committee reports. Extensive excerpts from reports of legislative committees are reported. These are of particular value in understanding the meaning of new legislation. Sometimes the entire report is separately supplied.

8. Attorney generals' opinions: Opinions of the federal and state attorneys general are reported.

9. Special rulings and interpretations: Through their wide contacts, services are able to obtain hundreds of special rulings of administrative agencies not otherwise made public. These are reported in the services. While not binding in any situation other than the one to which they refer, they are valuable in showing to the lawyer the trend of administrative thinking and the possible interpretation that will be placed on a case he is handling at the moment.

10. Forms: Forms pertinent to the subject of the services are reproduced. These include official forms, such as tax return forms, and forms developed by the editors and other legal authorities to cover matters such as wills, trust agreements, corporate forms, and many others. Many of these are completely filled in and are accompanied by step-by-step explanations and instructions to assist the lawyer in their use.

11. Editorial analyses — Law notes: The editors of loose-leaf services prepare editorial analyses and law notes that are helpful to the lawyer in making his own interpretation of the law and in indicating how a particular law may be applied.

Special Notes on Statutes and Regulations

Since most tax and regulatory law services are based upon statutes and the regulations promulgated for their administration, exact means are provided for locating this legislation in the services. Most of these means have been described in the text of this chapter, and so will merely be referred to here.

Finding Lists. These present the simplest and most accurate means of locating statutory material where a single outstanding statute and the regulations pertaining to it are concerned. They are described at page 243.

Law Charts. In services cutting across state lines, the uniform arrangement leads readily to most of the important points covered. However, there are numerous factual matters for which the searcher may appreciate a quicker run-down than this gives.

Law charts are provided in some services to take care of this need. Sometimes they are in a section tabbed "Law Charts." Or they may be in the "Report Letter"; or in an appropriate place in the treatise. All have explanatory footnotes, not shown in the examples below.

Vol. X—No. 4
7-24-52

LABOR REPORT

Page
5

No. 4—5

P-H EMPLOYMENT LAWS CHART

| State | Discrimination | Women | | Minors | | | Medical Examinations |
		Hours	Wages	Hours	Wages	Work Permits	
Ala.	No	No	No	Yes	No	Yes[1]	No
Alaska	Yes[3]	Yes	Yes[8]	Yes	No	No	Yes[4]
Ariz.	Yes[2]	Yes	Yes[8]	Yes	Yes	Yes[1]	No
Ark.	Yes[3]	Yes	Yes[8]	Yes	No	Yes[1]	Yes[4]
Calif.	Yes[5]	Yes[6]	Yes[3]	Yes	Yes	Yes[7]	Yes[4]

[see page 6 for footnotes]

¶ 4.3

24,112   Charts—Statutes of Limitations

[¶ 9161]   TABLE OF STATUTES OF LIMITATIONS

State	Years Contract Under Seal	Years Ordinary Contracts	Years Promissory Notes	Years Open Accounts	Years Domestic Judgments in Courts of Record	Years Domestic Judgments in Courts not of Record	Years Foreign Judgments in Courts of Record	Years Foreign Judgments in Courts not of Record
Alabama	10	6	6	3	20	6	20	6
Arizona.	6 See (t)	3 oral 6 written See (t)	6 See (t)	3	5	5	4	4
Arkansas...	5	5 written 3 oral	5	3	10	10	10	10

¶ 9161   **Commerce Clearing House, Inc.**

Exhibit 67

Special-Subject Services by State. Some large topics, as taxation and corporations, are divided into separate state services or editions. Here the services aim to index and annotate every state statute relating in any way to the main topic. For example, in the Prentice-Hall *Corporation Service*, the index to New York statutes in point covers not only the various corporation laws proper, but sixteen other statutes, from the Civil Practice Act to Workmen's Compensation, which touch upon corporations. Similarly the C.C.H. *State Tax Reporter* for New York covers not only the Tax Law but twenty other consolidated laws and numerous unconsolidated laws.

CHAPTER 27

MISCELLANEOUS MATERIALS

A. VARIETIES.
B. BRIEFS AND RECORDS ON APPEAL.
C. DIRECTORIES.
D. GOVERNMENT PUBLICATIONS.

A. Varieties.

The obvious and most important fundamental materials and secondary books of reference and index have now been discussed in this *Manual*, but no lawyer's equipment would be even reasonably complete without a knowledge of several additional categories of legal and non-legal books. Among these are government publications, briefs and records on appeal, and legal directories. Some of these will be lacking in many law libraries, but will almost always be available in some library in the community. In the aggregate they are very useful.

B. Briefs and Records on Appeal.

In most jurisdictions appellants and appellees must submit to the appellate court printed briefs and transcripts of the record from the court below. These printed papers represent the results of the best legal knowledge and research on the part of counsel.

They have two principal functions after they have served their original purpose: (1) Lawyers with similar legal problems study them for their analyses, arguments, and for the authority adduced in support thereof. (2) When a form of complaint or indictment has withstood attack on appeal, it is frequently copied by other lawyers in their own practice.

Few libraries have extensive collections of appeal papers, as few copies are printed. Bar, court, and larger law school libraries are their most likely repositories, and in some states their fortunate possessors lend them freely. A more recent development as to the appeal papers of the Supreme Court of the United States is their reproduction for subscribers on microfilm or microprint; the appeal papers of some state courts are also being so reproduced.

C. Directories.

Legal directories perform the obvious function of listing lawyers and giving certain information about them. Most are confined to active practitioners but some types, as law school alumni directories, for example, list others than active lawyers. Some are general, for all lawyers; other are jurisdictional or list lawyers in a specified branch of practice, or members of a particular association.

Martindale-Hubbell Law Directory.[1] This is both an annual directory of lawyers and a digest of laws.

Lawyers. Lawyers are listed alphabetically by state and town, and thereunder by name, making it necessary to know the residence of a listed lawyer in order to find his name. The date of birth, college and law school graduation, and of admission to the bar are given, together with any specialty, membership in the American Bar Association and a "confidential" rating. "Professional cards" are printed both in the directory proper (for individual lawyers), and in a so-called "Biographical Section" at the end of the main directory, for law firms. In the latter, the partners' names and some additional data are given, with bank references, the nature of the practice, and usually a list of clients. A selection of foreign lawyers is also listed.

A special listing is made of lawyers admitted to practice before the United States Patent Office. Another section is devoted to the American Bar Association, its organization, officers, activities, and canons.

Law digests. The final volume of this directory is devoted to digests of laws of all states and territories, and of foreign countries. Special *forms* of statutory instruments favored in the various jurisdictions are often included. Statutory forms are frequently a part of the texts. The federal section is confined to digests of United States copyright, patent, tax and trade-mark laws. For many lawyers this and the *Lawyers Directory*, described below, represent their only readily available source of knowledge of foreign law.

Uniform and model acts and codes are printed in full in an appendix.

Court calendars. A court calendar section gives the jurisdiction, personnel and terms of federal, state, territorial, District of Columbia, and Canal Zone courts.

The Lawyers Directory.[2] This annual directory gives the same information as the one described above. More emphasis is placed upon the listing of foreign lawyers, and the foreign embassies and legations in Washington and United States embassies, legations and consular offices throughout the world are listed. *Forms* are in a separate section, by jurisdiction.

The American Bar.[3] This annual publication is essentially a directory of firms, after the fashion of the "Biographical Section" of the *Martindale-Hubbell Law Directory*.

Local and Special-Practice Directories. In some jurisdictions, directories are published for local use, containing a variety of information concerning practice matters and personnel. More common are directories of special-subject practitioners. *Recommended Probate Counsel*[4] is one of many such. Because of the canons of ethics concerning permissible advertising by attorneys, these lists are carefully regulated. A list of all kinds of them, including foreign, is published annually in the American Bar Association *Reports*.

Bar Association, Alumni, and Legal Fraternity Directories. Most bar associations print a roster of their members, either in their annual reports or as separate pamphlets. Many law schools print directories of their alumni, and legal fraternities, as Phi Alpha Delta and Phi Delta Phi, do the same.

Who's Who in Law.[5] Only one issue of this directory has appeared, so that it is chiefly useful historically. The biographies are exceedingly brief, but do contain information not found in other directories.

---

[1] Summit, N. J., Martindale-Hubbell, Inc., 1931 to date.
[2] Cincinnati, O., The Lawyers Directory, Inc., 1883 to date.
[3] Minneapolis, Minn., J. C., Fifield Co., 1918 to date.
[4] Chicago, Ill., Central Guarantee Co., 1942 to date.
[5] New York, J. C. Schwarz, 1937.

Digest of Women Lawyers and Judges.[6] The editor, Laura Miller Derry, has collected brief biographies, often with photographs, of women lawyers and judges. There is a section of "interesting facts" and a bibliography of publications by women lawyers.

"The Bench and Bar Of." A popular form of subscription book is the collection of laudatory biographies of lawyers of a particular county, city or state.

Official Register of the United States.[7] The United States Civil Service Commission publishes this annual directory of all government officials occupying administrative and supervisory positions in the three branches of the government. Armed services personnel are not listed. Listing is by department and agency, with a complete alphabetical index by person at the end. Information given includes the position occupied, the home state and district of the official, and his salary.

Statistical Abstract of the United States.[8] An annual volume of political, social, industrial, and economic statistics of the United States, with references to other literature on the subject, this work deserves a place in any law library. Statistics are generally comparative, over a period of fifteen or twenty years.

D. Government Publications.[9]

These, federal and state, comprise one of the potentially most fruitful sources of legal information, but one which is too frequently neglected by the lawyer. The government, as author, has at its command practically unlimited resources for the production, compilation, analysis, and publication of data on every conceivable topic of interest to its citizens, including lawyers and their clients. Government publications are generally presumed to be objective and to present the official viewpoint. They have the additional merits of covering much material which the commercial publisher could not profitably publish, and of being free or relatively inexpensive. Frequently authorities from private life are drafted to work in conjunction with government experts in doing the actual writing.

Categories of Government Publications. Government publications (frequently called government documents) as those produced at public expense, by tax-supported institutions. They thus include not only those put out by federal and state legislative, executive and judicial bodies, but also those issued under the auspices of state educational institutions and experiment stations.

Statutory material and law reports. The most important government publications to the lawyer have already been described in this *Manual.* They are the officially published federal and state statutory materials (including laws, bills, hearings, reports and legislative journals), and reports of the decisions of courts and quasi-judicial administrative tribunals.

---

6 Louisville, Ky., Dunne Press. 1st ed., 1949.

7 Washington, D. C., U. S. Govt. Print. Off., 1907 to date.

8 Prepared by the Bureau of the Census. Washington, D. C., U. S. Govt. Print. Off., 1879 to date.

9 The definitive work on all aspects of federal documents is Anne M. Boyd, and Rae E. Rips, *United States Government Publications*, New York, Wilson. 3d ed., 1949. State publications are similarly covered by Jerome K. Wilcox, *Manual on the Use of State Publications.* Chicago, Ill., American Library Association, 1940. A scholarly work, principally on federal documents but covering also state, is Laurence F. Schmeckebier, *Government Publications and Their Use* (Washington, D. C., Brookings Institution. 2d ed., 1939). It contains much information not elsewhere available, but is unfortunately out of print.

Congressional reports and documents of general interest. As noted in Chapter 5, Congressional committee report on their activities, either in connection with specific pending bills or to set forth the results of investigations authorized by resolutions in either house. Most of these are of routine interest, but many explore various fields of existing law so thoroughly as to be of wide interest, quite apart from the original purpose of the investigations producing them. For example, the most complete and authoritative treatise on *The Immigration and Naturalization Systems of the United States*, costing $400,000 in editorial expenses alone, was such a report.[10] Other reports cover such topics as juvenile delinquency (with special reference to the effect of comics magazines), revenue revision, labor-management relations, holding companies, *etc.*

Government agency reports and bulletins. As part of their administrative duties or by legislative direction, most federal and state departures issue regular or special publications of legal interest. Examples are the annual reports and opinions of federal and state attorneys general, labor relations boards, public utilities commissioners, *etc.;* the *Monthly Labor Review* of the Department of Labor; the *Monographs* of the United States Attorney General's Committee on Administrative Procedure; and the *Monographs* of the Temporary National Economic Commission.

Legislative reference service and law revision agency publications. Nearly all states have organizations to aid the legislatures in the intelligent formulation of needed legislation. Their functions are to collect and compile accurate, complete and unbiased data of aid to legislators; to seek out areas of the law requiring legislative revision; and to prepare and propose needed corrective legislation. To do this there are legislative reference services, legislative councils, judicial councils, and law revision commissions. Nearly every state has such an organization. The names mean little by way of differentiating them; their functions vary and overlap so that it is impossible clearly to distinguish between them,[11] but they are essentially permanent joint legislative committees which meet during the legislative interim to consider the program of the next session. Many formulate and propose bills for legislative consideration (together with their reasons for such proposals), and to assist them they have permanent research and bill drafting staffs.

Important to the lawyer is the fact that these organizations commonly publish the results of their legal research, covering, in the aggregate, practically every topic made the subject of legislation; and that these can be made readily available in the average law library, free or at small cost.

The quality of the product averages high, serving as well reasoned and authoritative statements of the limited areas of the law covered. For example, the *Second Annual Report* of the New York State Law Revision Commission,[12] contained a 294-page treatise on seals and considerations, 80 pages on liability for injuries resulting from fright or shock, 186 pages on the Rule against Perpetuities, as well as many shorter studies. Some of the shorter reports concern topics so limited as seldom to be treated adequately or at all elsewhere. Since these reports are usually accompanied by proposed remedial legislation and reasoned recommendations for its enactment, their value in determining legislative intent is evident.

Constitutional convention studies. Before the convening of a state constitutional convention, a preparatory commission commonly makes extensive comparative studies

---

[10] S. Rept. No. 1515, 81st Cong., 2d Sess. (1950), made in response to S. Res. 137, 80th Cong., 1st Sess.

[11] In some states, the legislative council advises on matters of substantive law, and judicial council on adjective law, but the distinction is uncommon. An extensive study of *The Legislature: The Legislative Council* was made by William Miller for the Governor's Committee on Preparatory Research for the New Jersey Constitutional Convention (Trenton, N. J., 1947). Other studies are by George D. Smith, *Aids for Lawmakers: a Survey of Legislative Reference Services and Legislative Councils* (Seattle, Washington, University of Washington Bureau of Public Administration Report No. 68, 1946); and *Law Revision Agencies* (Springfield, Ill., Illinois Legislative Council Research Department, 1949). *A Checklist of State Judicial Council Reports from their Beginning Through 1947*, by Harry B. Merican, appeared in 41 L. Lib. J. 135 (1948).

[12] Albany, N. Y., Lyon, 1936 (Leg. Doc. [1936] No. 65.)

of every aspect of state government, and publishes the results for the use of the delegates. Outstanding examples were the publications prepared for the New York 1938, the New Jersey 1942, and the Missouri 1943-1944 conventions.

State university bureaus of public administration, and the like. A recent and rapidly expanding development is that of state university bureaus of public administration or government. More than half the states now have such bureaus, with functions closely analogous to the research duties of the legislative council. They specialize rather closely in the problems of their own states. Some pay particular attention to the needs of local government administrators. An example is the University of Washington Bureau of Governmental Research and Services, *Local Ordinances; The Drafting, Compilation, Codification, and Revision of Ordinances in Third and Fourth Class Cities.*[13] On the other hand, the publication may be a comparative study of the recent labor legislation of all states, a textbook for practicing lawyers on trying negligence actions, a detailed manual of state government functions, a collection of the housing laws of all states, a study of state-federal relations, a manual of municipal court procedure, an annotated edition of the state constitution, a study of the regulation of taxicabs by municipalities, or a series of studies on the legislative processes of a given state.

Comparative studies of state laws. The agencies and their publications discussed in the three sections above constitute one of the best sources of comparisons of legislation on specific topics, across state lines.

State university research publications. The university publications noted above are nearly all on the practical side. However, scholarly publications emanating from the graduate schools or faculties of state universities are common, particularly in the fields of constitutional and administrative law. Often these are doctoral dissertations, published in a learned journal or monograph series of the university, or the publication of a professor's scholarly work, subsidized by a foundation.

The Use of Government Publications. Government publications are those which some government agency puts out, and are treated in a law library just as those of any other publisher. That is, a government report, periodical, or other serial publication is catalogued and shelved just as is the *Harvard Law Review;* while a separate government pamphlet or treatise is bibliographically identical with one published by West, Bender, or Bobbs-Merrill. Therefore, in any organized library, the use of government publications presents no different problems than those of periodicals or treatises generally. Most government publications have printed Library of Congress catalog cards, which easily resolve any difficulties of form. All are found under both author and subject.

As when consulting any unfamiliar material, the lawyer or law student, if in doubt, should call upon the librarian for help with government publications.

Availability of Government Publications. Although many government publications are issued serially, most are irregular separates, so that some effective means of promptly learning of their appearance is necessary for effective use of them. The following are the best sources of such information.

United States Government Publications Monthly Catalog.[14] This publication is usually called "Monthly Catalog of Government Publications" or simply, the "Monthly Catalog." It is the sales list of the Superintendent of Documents, and the bulk of official federal governmental publications, processed as well as printed, are listed in it. In theory, all are listed here, but many processed ones escape. (Not all documents are received by the Superintendent of Document for listing promptly after publication. To take care of this situation, three biennial *Supplements* to the *Monthly Catalog,* which listed material received too long after publication to be regarded as "current publications, were issued during the calendar years 1941-42 to 1945-46. Beginning with 1947,

---

[13] Seattle, Wash., University of Washington, 1948.
[14] Washington, D. C., U. S. Govt. Print. Off., 1895 to date.

however, documents have been listed *as received, regardless of publication date*.) Publications are listed by issuing agency, with complete bibliographic information, including the serial number of the Library of Congress printed cards cataloging them (if any), the price, and a notation of whether sent to depository libraries. There is an extensive annual author and subject index. The *Monthly Catalog* costs $3.75 a year, and each issue contains full information as to how to order documents and Library of Congress cards.

Price lists of United States Government publications.[15] The subject price lists issued at frequent intervals show all publications available for sale in each category. These are sent free on application. Price list 10 is for laws; 10A, decisions of courts, boards and commissions; 49, proceedings of Congress; and 54, political science. Individual agencies, as the Departments of Agriculture and State, occasionally issue lists of their own publications.

Monthly Checklist of State Publications.[16] This list (commonly known as the "Monthly Checklist,") is incomplete, representing only those publications received from month to month by the Library of Congress, but it is the best list available. Documents are listed by state, and thereunder by issuing agency. Full bibliographical entries are given, including the printer and the Library of Congress catalog card number, but the price is rarely noted. There is an annual author and subject index.

Public Affairs Information Service Bulletin. This weekly bulletin indexes by subject federal, state, municipal, and foreign documentary material of interest to political scientists, economists, and lawyers. It also lists many commercially printed books and periodicals of like interest. It gives full bibliographic information about each entry. It is published at 14 West 40th Street, New York 18, and costs $100.00 per year.

Distribution of Government Publications.[17] The United States Superintendent of Documents maintains the largest bookstore in the world, for the sale of federal publications deposited with him for distribution. These are supposed to include all printed publications and take in as well much of the processed material. The entire sales process, including how to remit and to order Library of Congress printed catalog cards, is fully described in each issue of the *Monthly Catalog.*

Each Senator and Representative is entitled to designate a library in his district as a "depository library" to receive government publications, and at present there are about 560 such libraries, though only about a quarter of them elect to receive all documents available for distribution (including, since 1938, House and Senate *Journals,* hearings, bills, and committee reports). Confidential publications, advance sheets of decisions, reprints from bound volumes, processed publications, patent specifications, and maps are not sent to depository libraries. Many depository libraries have also the "Serial Set" of Congressional documents (Senate and House *Reports, Documents* and *Journals*), a set bound up (since the 15th Congress) in consecutively numbered volumes. Publications distributed to depositories are marked in the *Monthly Catalog* with a small black circle.

State documents have no such centralized distribution as do federal, though some twenty-two states individually have central control systems. Exchange and distribution to libraries is described in *Wilcox,* Chapter 21. Individuals seeking such publications had best write to the issuing agencies, as noted in the *Monthly Checklist.*

---

[15] Washington, D. C., U. S. Govt. Print. Off., nos. 1-79, frequently revised.

[16] Prepared by the Processing Dept. of the Library of Congress. Washington, D. C., U. S. Govt. Print. Off., 1910 to date.

[17] For a detailed discussion of this topic, see *Boyd and Rips,* Chapter II, and *Wilcox,* Chapters 20 and 21, note 9 above.

Indexes to Government Publications. There have been several comprehensive indexes to government publications,[18] but only one is of current interest to the practicing lawyer. This is the annual index to the *Monthly Catalog.* It is detailed, by author, agency, and subject. In 1953, a *Decennial Cumulative Index*[19] covering the years 1941-1950 was issued. It is more than a consolidation of the constituent indexes. Especial effort has been made "to bring consistency into the treatment of similar materials, and to establish patterns of subject subhead treatment for the broader main subjects." References are to specific entries in the *Monthly Catalog* and Supplement, by year and page number (1940- September 1947), or page and entry number (October 1947, to date).

---

[18] These are fully described in *Boyd and Rips,* note 9 above, Chapter III. Of special interest to lawyers are Benjamin Perley Poore, *A Descriptive Catalogue of the Government Publications of the United States, Sept. 5 1774 to Mar. 4 1881* (Washington, D. C., U. S. Govt. Print. Off., 1885); John Griffith Ames, *Comprehensive Index to the Publications of the United States Government 1881-1893* (Washington, D. C., U. S. Govt. Print. Off. 2d ed., 1905. 2 v.); Documents Office, *Catalog of the Public Documents of the Congress and of all Departments of the Government of the U. S. . . . March 4, 1893 to December 31, 1940* (Washington, D. C., U. S. Govt. Print. Off., 1896-1945. 25 v.); and the annual indexes to the *Monthly Catalog,* 1895 to date, above referred to. These are to be found in most large public and university libraries.

[19] Washington, D. C., U. S. Govt. Print. Off., 1953.

Chapter 28

CITATORS

A. Functions.
B. Scope of Citators.
C. Shepardizing a Case: State Shepards.
D. Shepardizing a Case: National Reporter System Shepards.
E. Case Citators other than Shepard's.
F. Shepardizing Legislation.
G. Supplementation of Citators.
H. Subordinate Legislation and Decisions: Administrative Law.

A. Functions.

The citator or citation book tells the lawyer whether statutes and cases to be cited by him as authority are in fact valid for that purpose. The status of this material as authority constantly changes through later legislative or judicial action, and there is no assurance on its face that the long-sought-for statute or case exactly in point is of any value whatsoever when found. The careful lawyer, therefore, checks upon the present value of each authority sought to be used by him. The citator is also one of the best means of collecting other cases in point, and performs several useful subsidary functions.

Evaluating a Statute or Case as Authority. **Statutes: Amendment, repeal, court interpretation.** A statute may be amended, repealed, extended in time, revised, superseded, or otherwise affected, wholly or in part, by later legislative action. Or a court of competent jurisdiction may declare it constitutional, void, or invalid, or the reverse. Citators note these things.

Cases: "History." A case may be affirmed, reversed, or modified on appeal, or the appeal may be dismissed. There may be rehearings by the same court. Thus, the *same case* with which you are working may have numerous vicissitudes in its progress through the courts, and all of these are noted in citators. An example is the *Kalb* case, the history of which is shown on page 165. In each such instance, the *identical* case is directly affected by court action.

Cases: "Treatment." A court in a subsequent action in a *different case* often affects the value of an earlier case as precedent. By overruling a case, it destroys its value as a rule applicable to later cases, though in no way affecting the *holding* of the overruled case as between the parties to it. More frequently, by comment on the earlier holding, the court may *criticize, distinguish, explain, follow,* or *question* it with respect to the case then under consideration, and so diminish or enhance its value as precedent.

"Cited" and "citing" material. Since these terms are frequently employed in legal writing, they are explained here. "Cited" material in a citator is simply the

254

statute or case which is being "Shepardized," [1] and "citing" material is that which is cited as affecting its validity. To put it another way, the "cited" material is the case or statute with which you are starting, and the "citing" material is that which refers to the cited material.

Thus, in the examples shown on pages 263 and 257, Ch. 228, § 5 and 296 Mass. 275 (respectively the statute and case Shepardized there), are "cited" material, while everything else is "citing." Citing material has a wide range, comprising (for our Massachusetts example) (1) all Massachusetts legislation amending, repealing or otherwise affecting existing legislation (as 1933 Laws, c. 221 in the example); (2) all Massachusetts and Federal Court reported decisions construing Massachusetts legislation or cases (as 301 U. S. 573); (3) opinions of the Attorney General of Massachusetts affecting existing legislation or cases; (4) Massachusetts law review comments on Massachusetts legislation or cases; and (5) annotated reports system comments on Massachusetts legislation or cases.

Collecting other Cases in Point. Some citators (as Shepard's), by listing all cases commenting upon a case known by the searcher to be in point, thus collect additional references of value. Since the courts have regarded these cases as worthy of comment as to the point of law involved, such cases assay unusually high as precedent. Cases commenting upon a statute, even though not directly construing it, aid the lawyer in ascertaining the statute's meaning.

Other Citator Functions. **Parallel citations to other standard reports or editions of statutes are given.** This is one of the best means for translating one form of citation to another. (Thus, in our example, the citator translates 296 Mass. 275 to 5 N. E. 2d 720).

Court rule publication notation. Citators tell in which volumes of reports court rules and amendments thereto are published.

Tables of statutes and cases by popular names. Statutes and cases are often cited by a popular name—as Taft-Hartley Act or *Hot Oil* case—which must be translated to the official citation before they can be Shepardized. Tables (for which *see* the Index) are provided for this purpose.

B. Scope of Citators.

In one form or another, citators cover all federal and state statutes and reported cases (except as noted below). They also cover the *Uniform Laws* and for some states, the American Law Institute *Restatements.*

Scope of Shepard's Citations.[2] By far the most complete American citator system, in both geographical scope and fullness of treatment, is Shepard's Citations. Each unit of the National Reporter System is covered by its Shepard (including *Shepard's United States Citations* and *Federal Reporter Citations,* for federal statutes and cases); and each state except Mississippi and Nevada has a separate

---

[1] Throughout this *Manual,* "Shepardize" and "Shepardizing" are employed as words of art, to describe certain essential operations in assessing the current value of statutes and cases as authority. These terms are used herein by the express permission of Shepard's Citations, Inc.

[2] Shepard's Citations, Inc., Colorado Springs, Colorado, issues a pamphlet, *How to Use Shepard's Citations,* for free distribution. It describes in considerably more detail than can this *Manual* the content and techniques of use of the various *Shepard's Citations.* Some of the material in the following discussion is taken by permission from this and other Shepard publications, with the intent to emphasize certain aspects of these publications which the experience of the authors of this *Manual* has shown to need such emphasis.

Shepard. The exact coverage of each of the more than sixty different units is noted in the "Table of Contents" in each unit. Material included in the citators differs somewhat from unit to unit and from edition to edition of the same unit, so that new editions should always be examined carefully, but is substantially uniform.

Miscellaneous Citators. Although *Shepard* dominates the citator field, there are other repositories of citation information. No one of these citators, however, except in loose-leaf services on federal taxation, has the completeness of treatment found in *Shepard.* This is particularly true of the subsequent judicial treatment of legislation and cases. Therefore, their use is normally supplementary to *Shepard.* On the other hand, if the *Shepard* is not at hand, some or all of the desired information often may be obtainable in one or more of these other publications. Certain of them may temporarily give a more recent judicial history of a statute than *Shepard;* or, for states for which there is no *Shepard,* or for subordinate legislation, give pertinent information not elsewhere available. Some of these citators are described at pages 261-263.

District of Columbia, Mississippi, and Nevada Citators. There are no conventional citators for these political units exclusively. The District of Columbia *Code* is covered by *Shepard's United States Citations;* the Court of Appeals of the District of Columbia (a federal court) is covered by *Shepard's Federal Reporter Citations;* the Municipal Court of Appeals, beginning with 31 A. 2d (1942), by *Shepard's Atlantic Reporter Citations.* Mississippi and Nevada statutes are covered to some extent by the citator functions of the compiled statutes of these states, while *Shepard's Southern Reporter Citations* cover cases beginning with 64 Mississippi (1886), and *Shepard's Pacific Citations* does the same for cases beginning with 17 Nevada (1883). Statutes of these two states are currently covered by the tables of "*Statutes Construed,*" as noted on page 266.

Territories Citators. These are outside the scope of the usual citators, but there is a *Citario de las Decisiones de Puerto Rico* [3]; and *Hawaiian Citations* [4] covers Hawaiian cases, but has not been kept up to date. Tables of statutes construed in the statutes of Alaska and Hawaii give some citator information.

Administrative law material. *See* Chapter 17.

C. Shepardizing a Case: State Shepards.

Shepardizing a case is as simple as it is effective. Let us suppose that the searcher has found a case in point—296 Mass. 275—which he wishes to use as authority in his brief. First, however, he must ascertain that it is still good law. Therefore he Shepardizes it.

Explanatory material in each Shepard unit. The technique of Shepardizing is explained in detail in a section in the front of each *Shepard* unit, with illustrative cases and statutes especially applicable to that unit. In order to find the specimen case below in *Shepard's Massachusetts Citations,* the searcher simply looks for "Volume 296" (in large type above the line in the *Shepard* volume), and for the figure "275" below the line. If his citation is to the unofficial *North*

---

[3] San Juan, P. R., Negociado de Materiales, Imprenta y Transporte, 1950-51. The volumes published to date cover the years 1899-1942.

[4] Prepared by Elizabeth Finley and Bernhard Knollenberg. New York, 1942. There are 2 supplements covering the years 1931-41.

ILLUSTRATIVE CASE

Massachusetts Reports Vol. 296		Northeastern Reporter, Second Series Vol. 5

Massachusetts Reports

Vol. 296

—275—
s 5NE 720
s300US 657
s 81LE 867
s 57SC 434
298Mas[2]500
299Mas 410
d300Mas[6]637
e301Mas[1]212
302Mas[3]567
302Mas[6]614
303Mas[4]647
303Mas[3]658
304Mas[4]181
304Mas 189
304Mas 293
304Mas 649
305Mas 235
305Mas 292
306Mas 30
307Mas[1]274
307Mas[3]419
309Mas 447
309Mas[3]567
309Mas 582
309Mas[3]593
309Mas 623
310Mas[3]552
312Mas[6]493
e313Mas[1]730
314Mas 438
315Mas[3]340
315Mas[4]372
317Mas 56
317Mas[1]508
319Mas[7]306
320Mas 340
322Mas[3]736
301US [8]573
81LE[8]1283
57SC [8]884
89F2d[4]211
e 89F2d[3]380
23FS [8]995
31FS [2]604
38FS 867
39FS [3]666
47FS [8]498
1938AG 82
1939AG 69
1942AG 135
'42-44AG 5
19BUR663
22BUR 89
25BUR 61
33MQ(1) 38
108AR [8]613n
108AR [1]617n
118AR[3]1221n

Citations to the case of Howes Brothers Company v. Unemployment Compensation Commission reported in Volume 296 Massachusetts Reports at page 275 are shown in the left margin as they appear in this volume.

An examination of the history of this case shows that the same case "s" (see tables of abbreviations, *infra*) is reported in 5 Northeastern Reporter, Second Series "NE" page 720. Upon appeal to the United States Supreme Court, a petition for writ of certiorari was denied in 300 United States Reports "US" 657, 81 Lawyers Edition of United States "LE" 867, 57 Supreme Court Reporter "SC" 434. The arrangement of these citations is an example of the grouping that is used wherever there are parallel sets of reports covering the same citing case.

An examination of the treatment of this case indicates that it has been distinguished "d" and explained "e" in subsequent cases in the Massachusetts Reports and Federal Reporter, Second Series.

The first citation is found in 298 Massachusetts Reports "Mas" 500. The superior figure "2" appearing in advance of the citing page number 500 indicates that the principle of law brought out in paragraph two of the syllabus of 296 Mas 275 is also dealt with in 298 Mas 500. If you are especially interested in this paragraph of the syllabus, the citing authorities indicate that this point of law has been cited to in a case reported in 31 Federal Supplement "FS" 604.

There are references analyzed to other paragraphs of the syllabus of the cited case in cases reported in the Massachusetts Reports, United States Supreme Court Reports (three editions), Federal Reporter, Second Series "F2d", Federal Supplement and in the notes of the American Law Reports "ALR". Thus, the citations dealing with a point of law in any particular paragraph of the syllabus may be referred to instantly without examining every citation to the case.

This case has also been cited in the Opinions of the Attorney General of Massachusetts "AG", Boston University Law Review "BUR" and Massachusetts Law Quarterly "MQ".

By reference to the citations to the corresponding decision in the Northeastern Reporter division of this volume, which are reproduced in the right margin it is possible to trace the history and citations to this decision in the parallel Massachusetts decisions in the Northeastern Reporter and in cases in the United States Supreme and lower Federal Courts.

Thus, in the most compact and convenient form, the complete judicial history of every Massachusetts case is shown; where else reported; whether affirmed, reversed, dismissed or modified; and the mode of its citation, whether followed, explained, distinguished, overruled, etc., and the extent to which each of the points decided in the case has been regarded as an authority.

Northeastern Reporter, Second Series

Vol. 5

—720—
s296Mas 275
s300US 657
s 81LE 867
s 57SC 434
11NE [6]590
12NE [4]855
d 15NE[13]818
e 16NE [2]667
19NE[13]814
20NE [3]457
22NE 960
22NE 361
22NE [1]865
22NE 766
23NE [4]136
23NE [5]137
23NE [9]161
23NE [5]668
24NE[18]676
25NE [5]380
25NE 762
27NE [4]268
30NE 2220
30NE [3]275
34NE 536
34NE[12]537
34NE 7541
35NE 74
35NE 14
35NE[28]252
39NE [3]107
45NE 472
e 49NE [1]226
49NE [5]595
52NE [6]571
53NE 109
57NE [15]18
59NE 22
65NE [9]532
68NE [4]188
79NE [3]729
301US[29]573
81LE[29]1283
57SC[29]884
89F2d[9]211
e 89F2d[7]380
23FS[29]995
31FS[12]604
38FS 867
39FS 7666
47FS [2]498

9

Exhibit 68

Eastern Reporter (5 N. E. 2d 720), he first turns to that section of the citator entitled "Northeastern Reporter (Massachusetts Decisions")," as shown in the right margin of the sample page on page 257 where he will be given the official citation ("s 296 Mas 275"). The rest of the process is described in the above instruction page from *Shepard's Massachusetts Citations, 1933-1949 Supplement*. Particular attention is called to the initials in the left margin of the tabulated "citing" material, and to the superior figures preceding the page references; these are explained in the instruction page.

Parallel case citations. *Shepard's Citations* provide one of the best means of translating an official citation to a *Reporter* citation, or the reverse. The parallel citation is supplied, whether or not other cases have later cited the main case. Note that "same case in another report series" is denoted in the older *Shepards* by the "s" preceding the case citation. In the newer ones it is done by enclosing the case citation in parentheses, the "s" then being reserved for the main case in other stages of its progress through the courts. *Once the parallel citation has been printed in a bound volume, it is no longer given in succeeding supplements.*

Parallel reference tables of reports in Shepard. There are two kinds of cross-reference tables, one or both of which appear in some *Shepards*. One is a parallel table of reports from original nominative (as Black, Pickering, or Dallas) to the consecutively renumbered volumes. Part of such a table is shown below. This is useful because, while these reports are listed in *Shepard* by the consecutive numbered volume, they are often still cited by the old nominative series, and so the citation must be translated.

MASSACHUSETTS REPORTS
Vols. 18–96

Cross Reference Table

14 Allen ....96 Massachusetts	12 Metcalf ....53 Massachusetts
1 Cushing.............55 Massachusetts	13 Metcalf ....54 Massachusetts
2 Cushing.............56 Massachusetts	1 Pickering ....18 Massachusetts
3 Cushing.............57 Massachusetts	2 Pickering ....19 Massachusetts
4 Cushing.............58 Massachusetts	3 Pickering ....20 Massachusetts
5 Cushing.............59 Massachusetts	4 Pickering ....21 Massachusetts
6 Cushing.............60 Massachusetts	5 Pickering ...,.......22 Massachusetts
7 Cushing.............61 Massachusetts	6 Pickering ....23 Massachusetts

Exhibit 69

The second table (in *Shepard's United States Citations* it is combined with the first), is useful where, because of large size, the *Shepard* for a jurisdiction is split into more than one volume. This table tells in which volume a given report is Shepardized. See page 259, exhibit 70.

Page references to citing material in Shepard. Two things should be noted about page citations of citing or commenting material: (1) they are to the actual page of the case where the main case is cited by the commenting opinion, and this ordinarily will not be the first page of a case. Thus, the specimen case above was

```
Table of Reports in Shepard's United States
         and Federal Reporter Editions

Abstracts ...................................................United States
Abstracts, New Series ......................................United States
American Bankruptcy Reports ................................Federal
American Bankruptcy Reports, New Series ....................Federal
American Maritime Cases ....................................Federal
Appeal Cases, District of Columbia Reports .................Federal
Black's Reports (66–67 U. S.)...............................United States
Board of Tax Appeals Reports ..............................United States
Court of Claims Reports ...................................Federal
```

Exhibit 70

"distinguished" at 300 Mass. 637, but the official citation to the case is 300 Mass. 630. (2) This citation is to the *first time* that case is mentioned in the citing case; it may be mentioned again on later pages, but no later page citations are given *unless other points are cited*, when they *are* noted.

Comments by courts of another jurisdiction. Often the searcher is interested in comments on his case by courts of other jurisdictions. These can be found in the *Shepard* system only through the use of National Reporter System citations, which *Shepards* treat as follows.

On cases decided before the National Reporter System. Thirty-one state *Shepards* note comments in the National Reporter System on cases decided before that System began. For eleven of these states there is a separate section in the *state citator* ("Massachusetts Reporters—Vols. 1-38—cited in the National Reporter System"), which notes every comment on these earlier cases by reported cases in all jurisdictions. Fourteen *state Shepards* supply this information, not in a separate section, but by *Reporter* citations following the citations of cases of the forum, in the citator proper. Thus, in *Shepard's Illinois Citations*, as shown below, 102 Ill. 359 (an 1882 pre-*North Eastern Reporter* case) was commented upon by 362 Ill. 58, 60, which is also 198 N. E. 703, 704; and by 106 P. 2d 163, 175, which is a Utah case. Six states include citations through the *Reporter* unit which covers that state, but not for all jurisdictions.

ILLINOIS SUPREME COURT REPORTS   **Vol. 102**

```
—359—
362 Ill  160
198 NE1704
106 P2d 175
```

Exhibit 71

On National Reporter System cases. The search here must be made through *Shepard's* regional *Reporter Citations*. In our Massachusetts example, taking the citation 5 N. E. 2d 720 into Shepard's *Northeastern Citations*, the searcher will find there every *Reporter* citation of cases mentioning 5 N. E. 2d 720, together with the state of the court making the decision. First, Massachusetts commenting cases are cited for a Massachusetts main case, then other states in that *Reporter* unit *(Northeastern* here), and then, alphabetically by state, cases from other regional *Reporters*.

Reporter sections in state Shepards. The section in the state *Shepards* covering pre-*Reporter* cases is described *supra*. In addition, every state *Shepard* except the one for New York (for which there is a separate *New York Supplement Shepard)*, has a section in which all cases for that state, from the beginning of the National Reporter System, are listed by *Reporter* citation ("Northeastern Reporter, Massachusetts Decisions," here), together with citations to comments thereon, but *by courts of that state only*. This is as shown in the right hand margin of the illustrative case, *supra*. Since some *Reporter* cases are not officially reported, this section lists more cases than does the official section.

D. Shepardizing a Case: National Reporter System Shepards.

The process of Shepardizing cases through *Reporter Shepards* is exactly the same as for the state units, but in addition to citing the Massachusetts cases (for example), commenting upon the main case, all commenting cases in all *Reporters* are cited, thus giving nationwide coverage. Our main case is shown to have been cited by the courts of eighteen other states. No statutes are covered by *Reporter* Shepards (except *Shepard's United States Citations)* and no law review comments are noted, as in the state *Shepards*.

Shepardizing State Cases Not Officially Reported. Regional *Reporters* (as *North Western)* include many cases not officially reported, and so not Shepardizable in the state *Shepards* except in the section covering local cases reported in the *Reporter*. The absence of a parallel official citation in its proper place in a *Reporter* Shepard is, except in the *Atlantic Reporter Shepard*, almost infallible proof of the lack of an official report. *For cases beginning with the National Reporter System*, the *Reporter Shepard* is more complete than the state *Shepard* "official" section to the extent that the cited material is fuller. Cases antedating the National Reporter System, if commented upon by *Reporters* at a later date, are listed in the "Reports cited in the National Reporter System."

Federal Court Decisions. **Supreme Court cases.** Citations to reports in *Shepard's United States Citations* are in three parallel series: (a) by *United States Reports* Citation; (b) by *Supreme Court Reporter* citation; and (c) by *Lawyers' Edition* citation. If the searcher's reference is to one of the first ninety volumes, by the reporter's name, a "Parallel Reference Table" in the front of the unit translates from the nominative (Dallas, Peters) to the *United States Reports* citation. Similarly, each unofficial citation is translated into the official citation ("same case"), and, to save space, all actual Shepardizing information is given only under the official—with the following exception: The unofficial listings show cases not officially reported, and if such cases have been the subject of Shepardizable action, that action is indicated under the unofficial citation, since there is no place for it under the official.

Lower federal courts. *Shepard's Federal Reporter Citations* covers these. Included in the coverage are cases adjudicating patents and trade-marks; these are listed both by case citation and by patent number or trade-mark name. Since some of the material in the two *Shepards* covering the federal courts might just as logically perhaps have been included in one as well as the other, a reference table at the front of each unit tells in which unit that particular series is Shepardized.

E. Case Citators other than Shepard's.

Digests Most digests, through their tables of cases or in their digest paragraphs, or both, state whether the cases digested therein have been affirmed, reversed, or modified on appeal—corresponding to the *Shepard* "History of the Case." The subsequent "Treatment of the Case" (comment on the case by later decisions in other cases) is given in only a few digests, and then only as of the date of compilation and not kept up to date.

Decennial Digest tables of cases. The "Tables of Cases Affirmed, Reversed, or Modified," containing in the "Descriptive-Word Index" of the *General Digest* supplementing the *Decennials* is a citator table. It lists cases which, during the publication period of the table, have been affected by later decisions. Only the *judicial history* of the identical case is given, not comment on it by other cases. This separate table is not continued in the *Decennials*, because the same information is then given both in the general *table of cases* and in the *digest paragraphs*.

"Digest of United States Supreme Court Reports": Table of cases affirmed, reversed, reheard, etc. The scope of cases includes: (1) United States Supreme Court cases reheard in that court, beginning with the October 1916 term. (2) Lower federal court cases affected. (3) State, territorial, and District of Columbia cases. (4) *L. R. A.* and *A. L. R.* cases affected by subsequent Supreme Court decisions are listed.

In the *Digest* proper, the subsequent *judicial treatment* (that is, whether a case was followed, distinguished, explained, *etc.)* is given as part of the digest paragraph. *The table itself affords the quickest means of checking up on all cases in any jurisdiction or over any given time span, which have been directly affected by subsequent decisions of the Supreme Court.* It is supplemented only annually; though each bound volume of the *Lawyers' Edition* of the *United States Reports* contains this table for its term of court, it is not found in the bi-weekly advance sheets.

Tables of cases judicially noticed. There are several case citators arranged by Plaintiff-Defendant case table. *Haviland and Greene's Citations* for New York aims at complete case citation service, as do such digest tables as those in the *Indiana Decimal Digest* and *Page's Ohio Digest.*

Loose-leaf Services as Case Citators. These are discussed in Chapter 26.

Law Reports as Case Citators. Each volume of the *United States Reports* and about half the official state reports have tables of cases cited or affected by decisions therein.

Law Reviews as Case Citators. Beginning with 1917, the *Index to Legal Periodicals* has listed cases commented upon in most English language legal periodicals.

Rose's Notes.[5] The *United States Reports*, volumes 2-283, were covered by a citator, arranged in the usual volume-and-page citation order, but in its case treatment resembling law review notes or case comments on an extended scale. Cited material included not only cases from federal courts, but also state reports and those from the various annotated reports series. Although apparently discontinued in 1932, it is still useful in connection with the earlier Supreme Court decisions. A similar series covered Texas reports through 1910.

F. Shepardizing Legislation.

The purpose of this process is to trace subsequent legislative action on a piece of legislation — amendments, repeals, additions, extensions, and the like; and to determine whether a court has held it constitutional or valid, or the reverse. Because legislation is apt to change its form, the process of Sheparardizing is more complicated than the parallel process with cases. Some of the difficulties are discussed in the "Notes" at page 266.

Shepard's Citations Coverage of Legislation. The Shepard system covers federal and state (except Mississippi and Nevada) constitutions, session laws, compiled statutes, city charters and ordinances, and court rules. Charters and ordinances are subject-indexed in each unit. Changes in the form of legislation covered are noted, and the judicial construction of statutes is shown.

Arrangement of legislation in Shepards. Finding the legislation to be Shepardized is a little more difficult sometimes than with cases. Legislation is arranged by article and section for constitutions; date, chapter, and session for session laws; title and section for compiled statutes; city, date, and section for charters and ordinances; and by court, date, and section for court rules. Arranging by date sometimes causes confusion in *Shepard's United States Citations* when (as in treaties, for example) a group of earlier but hitherto unpublished acts are collected in a later volume of the *Statutes at Large.* Since the date controls the order of listing, the Act of January 23, 1792, c. 5, which is 1 Stat. 229, follows in *Shepard* a treaty of July 2, 1791, published in a compilation of treaties in 7 Stat. 39.

Citation information supplied in Shepards. The wide range of information provided by Shepard is shown in the illustrative statute, page 263. The abbreviations employed in the example, and others for statutes, are found and explained in the front of every Shepard unit covering statutes. In practice, the example, taken by permission from *Shepard's Massachusetts Citations, Supplement 1933-1949*, would be brought down to date by examination of any later bound supplements, red-paper cumulative supplements, and white-paper "Advance Sheets." Occasionally, still later cases construing a statute may be found through the National Reporter System and *Lawyers' Edition* advance sheets table of "Statutes Construed."

Federal court construction of state legislation.

State court construction of federal legislation. Federal court decisions construing state legislation and state court decisions construing federal legislation are both noted in forty-two state *Shepards*.

Statutory Citators other than Shepard's. Numerous publications perform

---

[5] Rose, Walter Mallins, *Rose's Notes on the United States Supreme Court Reports.* San Francisco, Bancroft-Whitney, 1917–1920 in 20 v., with 2 supplements, 1925–26 in 5 v. and 1932–35 in 10 v.

ILLUSTRATIVE STATUTE

1933 Bound Volume

General Laws (Ter. Ed.) 1932

Ch. 228

§ 5
195Mas 261
81NE 312
242Mas 66
136NE 173
251Mas 372
146NE 696
265Mas 108
163NE 883
265Mas 295
164NE 85
267Mas 350
166NE 831
44F 586
123F 349
292F 810
16MQ(5) 60

1933-1949 Bound Supplement

General Laws (Ter. Ed.) 1932

Ch. 228

§ 5
A1933C 221
A1937C 406
287Mas 246
191NE 387
295Mas 7
2NE1018
297Mas 483
9NE 375
C305Mas 5
C 24NE 677
305Mas 27
24NE 682
310Mas 722
39NE 757
311Mas 6
39NE 970
312Mas 32
43NE 4
20BUR338
18MQ(1) 51
19MQ(1) 99
22MQ(2) 36
1938C 16

8

Citations to Chapter "Ch." 228, section "§" 5 of the General Laws, Tercentenary Edition, 1932 are shown in the left margin as they appear in the 1933 bound volume and in this volume. This particular section imposes a one year limitation upon a citation to compel an executor or administrator to appear and prosecute or defend an action.

The first two references given in this volume indicate that this section has been amended "A" by the Massachusetts Acts of 1933 chapter "C" 221 and by 1937 C 406. These are followed by a reference in Volume 287 Massachusetts Reports "Mas" page 246 and in the corresponding report of this decision in 191 Northeastern Reporter "NE" page 387. Wherever there are parallel sets of reports covering the same citing case, these citations immediately follow each other.

The references to this section, appearing in both volumes, include other citations by the Massachusetts Supreme Judicial Court and by the lower Federal Courts in cases reported in 44 Federal Reporter "F" 586, 123 F 349 and 292 F 810. The abbreviation "C" in advance of the reference 305 Mas 5 indicates that the Supreme Judicial Court has declared this section to be constitutional.

This section has also been cited in the Boston University Law Review "BUR," Massachusetts Law Quarterly "MQ" and in the Massachusetts Acts of 1938.

Wherever possible all references to prior editions of Massachusetts Statutes and Laws and to the Acts, by the Massachusetts Supreme Judicial Court since 1902, and by the Federal Courts from the earliest times, have been transposed to the appropriate chapter, section and subdivision of the General Laws, Tercentenary Edition, 1932.

Citations to the Acts and Resolves not included in the General Laws, Tercentenary Edition, 1932 are shown in a special division of this work.

The method of treatment in all divisions of the statutes is essentially the same. Whenever any part of the statute law has been amended, repealed, superseded, etc., by subsequent acts passed by the General Court this information is immediately available. The next group includes citations by the Massachusetts and Federal Courts. These are followed by citations in the Opinions of the Attorney General of Massachusetts, Harvard Law Review, Boston University Law Review, Massachusetts Law Quarterly and subsequent Acts and Resolves.

Exhibit 72

one or more citator functions for statutes, though none approaches the overall fullness of the Shepard system. Most of them are best used to supplement a *Shepard* by connecting an older form of statute to the current one, or, in the case of some tables of statutes construed, by supplying a later case construing a statute. These auxiliary citators may be found as integral parts of session law volumes, compilations of federal or state statutes, and in tables of statutes construed. Certain of these citators are described at page 266, in the "Notes" section.

Notation of amendments, repeals, etc. Many state session law volumes contain lists of legislation affected by new legislation. *See also* Chapters 7 and 8.

Notation of change in form of legislation. Tables in some session laws and in most statutory compilations have parallel conversion tables from (1) the session law form to the compilation title and section; and (2) from an earlier compilation citation to the current form. These tables are often necessary when the *Shepard* is based only upon the current form of statute, but the citation is to an earlier form. *See* also Chapters 6-8.

Tables of statutes judicially construed. These are found in bound volumes and advance sheets of National Reporter System units, and cumulate into similar tables in the regional *Reporter* digests and in some state Key-Number System digests (as for Massachusetts). Other digests have them, as described below in the "Notes." These tables serve various purposes. Temporarily the advance sheets may supply a later citation than the *Shepard;* sometimes they cover material not included in Shepard. About two-thirds of the official law reports have tables of statutes construed, and those state reports now published by West incorporate "Statutes Construed" tables. These tables are not cumulated; *Shepard's* are.

Special Comment on Shepardizing Federal Legislation. The difficulties encountered in Shepardizing legislation are discussed at page 266. As a result of them, finding the citation to a statute section in the form in which it is listed in a citator frequently involves translating an earlier form of statute into the current one, which usually is the only form under which it is Shepardizable. As applied to federal statutes, the effect is as noted below.

Statutes at Large. *Shepard's United States Citations* covers this form of federal statute only if it has not been incorporated into the *United States Code.* If a given section has been so incorporated, it is listed and covered by *Shepard* only as a *Code* section. These statutes covered in the *Statutes at Large* part of Shepard receive the full *Shepard* treatment for all amendments, repeals, *etc.*, and for cases construing them. Otherwise, the information must be sought elsewhere. Repeals of *Statutes at Large* included in the *Code* are noted in the *Code* tables. The *Federal Code Annotated* does this for *all Statutes at Large* beginning with volume 18 (1874); that is, after the *Revised Statutes* date.

Cases construing the Statutes at Large. Shepards (*United States and forty state units*) cover both federal and state cases construing the *Statutes at Large.* Tables of statutes construed in some digests, and in the National Reporter System do this to some extent. The *Federal Code Annotated,* as above noted, digests cases construing the *Statutes at Large* since 1874.

Revised Statutes. *Shepard* omits this, except insofar as included in the *Code,* to which statute form a citation must be translated for Shepardizing. *Code* transfer tables give the *Code* citation required. That is, if it is desired to Shepardize *Revised Statutes* § 5232, Table Ia in the *United States Code* shows that this section is now part of 12 U. S. C. § 135, which is directly Shepardized. *Repeals* of all *Revised Statutes* sections, whether or not codified, are noted in the *Code* tables of repeals. Tables of statutes construed cover this compilation. The *Federal Code Annotated* "annotations to uncodified laws and treaties" cover the *Revised Statutes*, as do the tables of the *Digest of United States Supreme Court Reports*.

United States Code. Shepards (*United States* and forty-two states) cover the *Code* interpretations by both federal and state courts. No statutory changes back of the *latest Code Supplement* are shown. Changes subsequent to the latest *Code Supplement* appear in the current cumulative (paper bound) *Shepard* supple₁ ment. Thus, no such changes (amendments, repeals, *etc.*) back to December 31, 1940, are shown in the 1943 *Shepard's United States Citations*. Intervening changes are shown in the latest bound supplement to this edition, and current changes later than that are noted in the paper bound supplements to date. If earlier amendments and the like are wanted, they may be traced through the parenthetical citations at the end of *Code* sections, and in such historical notes as are there provided. All construing *cases*, however, regardless of date, are noted for these sections in force. *Tables of statutes construed* in digests and *Reporters* cover the *Code*, as do the annotated editions of the *Code*.

Treaties and executive agreements. *See* Chapter 4.

Proclamations, executive orders, etc. *See* "Subordinate Legislation and Decisions," *infra*.

Special Comment on Shepardizing State Legislation. The same difficulties encountered in Shepardizing federal legislation arise in state legislation, and are solved in the same way. *See* page 266 and Chapter 8.

Session laws. The current Shepard policy is to cover as session laws only those not incorporated into the state compilation. Tables of statutes construed cover session laws. Session law volumes themselves usually note changes in existing legislation, by the new laws. Some state statutory compilations have tables showing all amendments, repeals, *etc.*, of session laws for varying periods.

Compiled statutes. The Shepard trend is to cover only the latest form of statute. *See* page 266. However, all citations to cases construing the predecessor forms of the statutes are transferred to the new form, as far as possible. Annotated statutes are themselves of course a form of citator, noting both statutory changes and digesting cases construing statutes.

Miscellaneous Shepardizable Material. **American Law Institute Restatements of the Law.** About one-third of the state *Shepards* are *Restatements* citators, in the same manner as for statutes. The *Restatements in the Courts* (*see* Chapter 23) are citators.

Uniform laws. These are noted in the *Uniform Laws Annotated*, and in the tables of "Statutes Construed" in the National Reporter System. By use of the *Federal Acts by Popular Name* table (*see* page 56), and the *Acts by Popular Name* in twenty-six state *Shepards*, translating the Uniform Laws into the corresponding federal or state statutory citation, these laws are also fully covered in the usual manner by the respective *Shepards*.

Interstate compacts. As session laws of the states concerned, these are covered by *Shepard*. As adjudicated by the Supreme Court of the United States, they are listed as "Compacts with States" in the table of statutes construed in the *Digest of United States Supreme Court Reports*.

Court rules. *See* Chapter 10.

Notes on Difficulties in Shepardizing *Legislation*

Once a case is decided and the opinion published, its form is fixed. Subsequent judicial action may affect its value as precedent but not its form. Statutes, however, change in form: constitutions are amended or new ones adopted; session laws are codified into sections of "codes" or other compilations, and they are amended and repealed; codes themselves are revised at intervals (Iowa has had a dozen such in its history).

In the older *Shepards* every form of statute was listed. Both the session law and its codified form were given, together with all subsequent legislation and judicial action affecting the text, duplicated under each form. But bulk and costs alike skyrocketed under that system, so that as a matter of expediency (providing the lawyer with a citator not too expensive to buy or too bulky to handle, and which would at the same time answer his needs reasonably well) certain compromises were adopted, as the result of careful polling of lawyers as to their preferences. These compromises are not in effect for all *Shepards* but are coming to be, and will be described here.

Under this policy, the latest compilation in a given jurisdiction is taken as a starting point for noting legislative changes in the form of a codified statute, and no amendments, repeals, and the like are shown for legislation preceding that date. Such legislative change *after* the starting point is fully noted. As far as possible, all cases construing the present statute in any of its earlier forms are transferred to the current section. A repealed statute of course is not so represented. Uncodified statutes (session laws), however, are covered from the earliest times.

The rationale is somewhat as follows: The lawyer ordinarily is interested only in the current form of a statute, and it is a needless waste of his money to pay for a compilation covering earlier forms. In the comparatively few instances in which he must trace the earlier forms of a statute, he can do it through annotated statutes and their tables, which will lead him also to the present, Shepardizable, form of the statute.

In pursuance of this policy, *Shepard's United States Citations*, as noted above, no longer lists a *Statute at Large* as such if it has been made a part of the United States Code, but only in its *Code* form. Citations in the *Statutes at Large* form must accordingly be transferred to the *Code* form. The same is true for most states, where an earlier form has been superseded by a later one. Parallel tables in most state statutes compilations aid in this, as do the historical notes and annotations to the statutes themselves. The tables of statutes construed in the National Reporter Sysem and in some digests still list statutes by the form as of the time the cause of action arose.

The advice of the authors of this *Manual* to law librarians is never to discard superseded *Shepard* bound volumes covering statutes, but to keep them as an aid to Shepardizing earlier forms of statutes than those in the superseding edition.

Notes on Other Publications Serving as Statutory Citators

Tables of Statutes Construed in Digests. *Key-Number System digests.* Material from National Reporter System tables of "Statutes Construed" as described below, is cumulated in regional *Reporter* digests and those for some states.

"Digest of United States Supreme Court Reports": Laws Cited and Construed. This 630-page table and its annual supplements cover only Supreme Court cases. Some of the citator information given is nowhere else readily available. The table is divided into the following parts:

1. Foreign (including Roman) laws.
2. Indian laws and treaties with foreign nations.
3. Federal statutes: (a) Articles of Confederation; (b) United States Constitution; (c) Continental Congress acts; (d) Congressional acts and joint resolutions (as *Statutes at Large*); (e) *United States Revised Statutes;* (f) United States Judicial Code; (g) *United States Code;* (h) Treaties and executive agreements with foreign nations; (i) Compacts between states; (j) Proclamations and executive orders; and (k) Confederate States statutes.

4. State and territorial statutes. Statutes are listed in the form set forth in the case construing them. Ohio statutes, for example, are thus cited for codes as far back as 1833.

Compiled Statutes as Citators. Some official unannotated and most annotated editions of statutes serve a citator function, though they are best used in conjunction with *Shepard's Citations* to cover earlier forms of statutes than the current one treated in *Shepard*. Such editions give a certain amount of the history of each section of a statute. Annotated statutes cite or digest federal cases and cases of the state covered, which construe each section of the statutes.

National Reporter System Tables of "Statutes Construed." Since approximately January 1936, each advance sheet and bound volume of each unit of the National Reporter System has contained a table of federal and state statutes construed by decisions printed during the publication period of the unit. However, the *citation is by no means confined to decisions printed in the unit containing the table*, but covers statutes interpreted by decisions reported in other units for the same period.

For example, the table in the *Atlantic Reporter* notes the interpretation of Maryland statutes by all federal courts covered by the *Supreme Court Reporter, Federal Reporter,* and *Federal Supplement;* and by Maryland courts reported in the *Atlantic Reporter.* "Statutes Construed" include not only federal and state constitutions, session laws, compilations and treaties, but municipal charters, court rules and executive rules regulations, such as Presidential proclamations and executive orders. Where a federal act has been codified, it is listed in this table both under the *Statutes at Large* and *United States Code* citations. *Uniform Laws Annotated* are covered by this table. In the *Federal Rules Decisions* table, all statutes construed are federal or state practice acts or rules of practice.

The table aids in tracing the judicial history of the statutes noted, and since the advance sheets (and occasionally the bound volumes) of the *Reporters* containing the table appear at considerably more frequent intervals than the conventional citation books, the table should be searched for the very latest decisions on a statute. This is a technique often overlooked, but which on occasion may be most useful. It is of especial value of course for the statutes of Mississippi and Nevada—for which states there are as yet no *Shepards*—for supplementing the citation function of the compiled statutes of those states.

The table is particularly useful in connection with Presidential proclamations and executive orders which have not been published as *Statutes at Large* or been incorporated into the editorial matter of the *United States Code* (and so covered by *Shepard's United States Citations*). The table is cumulated into the regional *Reporter* digests and into some Key-Number System state digests. West's *Massachusetts Digest Annotated,* for example has such a table.

These tables note only that a statute has been construed, not the nature of the action taken, as in *Shepard*. Statutes construed are listed as cited in the cases, and not according to the current form of the statute. Thus, if the statute construed is one of the Massachusetts *Revised Laws* of 1902, 1882, or 1860, it is so listed in the table, not under its current equivalent. Where the statutes of a state have been recompiled rather recently, however, these tables as cumulated in the digests do not always carry cases back of them, but serve rather as current supplements to the annotated statutes.

G. Supplementation of Citators.

Shepard's Citations. A complete *Shepard* unit consists of the following parts: (a) One or more bound volumes; (b) a quarterly red-paper cumulative supplement; and (c) for the *United States, Federal Reporter,* and about one-fourth of the state *Shepards*, a quarterly white-paper "Advance Sheet Edition." The Advance Sheet Edition appears six weeks after the red-paper supplement, so that for units containing this edition, supplementation is about every six weeks. The exact coverage of a complete unit, usually on the cover binding, is shown as below.

Occasionally, still later cases construing a statute may be found through the National Reporter System advance sheets table of "Statutes Construed," and in the bi-weekly *Lawyers' Edition* advance sheets of Supreme Court reports.

WHAT YOUR LIBRARY SHOULD CONTAIN

1933 Bound Volume   1933-1949 Bound Volume

Supplemented with

May, 1952 Cumulative Supplement Vol. XLV No. 2
June, 1952 Advance Sheet Vol. XIX No. 4

DESTROY ALL OTHER ISSUES

Exhibit 73

Other forms of Citators. These are supplemented in the same manner and frequency as the main work of which they are a part.

H. Subordinate Legislation and Decisions: Administrative Law.

There are no citators of wide scope for this material, and most of it is not thus covered in any way as yet. When Shepardizable at all it is (with the exceptions noted below) almost always as a subsidiary function of some other kind of law book. Most of the available material in this field has been described in Chapter 17, and so will only be alluded to here.

Rule Changes: "Legislative Action." See Chapter 17. Amendment and repeal of federal administrative rules and regulations are all noted in the *Federal Register* "Codification Guide," and in the *Code of Federal Regulations* pocket supplement "List of Sections Affected." No *Shepard* covers this subject matter. A more convenient means of tracing changes of agency rules and regulations, for some subjects, is through loose-leaf services.

Presidential Legislation: Proclamations, Executive Orders, Reorganization plans. **Proclamation and reorganization plans.** As *Statutes at Large*, these are covered by *Shepard's United States Citations*, as are any other statutes printed therein. As proclamations and reorganization plans they are covered by the "Statutes Construed" tables in the National Reporter System reports and in digests having such tables. As proclamations and reorganization plans interpreted by the Supreme Court, they are covered by the statutory tables of the *Digest of United States Supreme Court Reports*. When they affect *United States Code* sections, they may be related to those sections (and so indirectly Shepardized) through the *United States Code* Table II — "Executive Acts Included." *See* the specimen on page 269.

Executive orders. Executive orders are not published in the *Statutes at Large*, and so are not directly covered by *Shepard's Citations*. However, many are integral parts of *Code* sections or are discussed or printed in the notes to the *Code* sections. Since all such sections are covered by *Shepard's United States Citations*, the order is then indirectly Shepardizable in many instances through the Code, if it can be directly related to an executive order. Relating an executive order, proclamation, or reorganization plan to a *Code* section is easily accomplished through Table II of the *Code*, noted above, or through a similar *U. S. C. A.* table.

Thus, in the example below, if it is desired to Shepardize executive order 6084, the various *Code* sections of which it is a part are found through the table, and sections are Shepardized. It is indirect and not altogether satisfactory, but it can be done. This is true whether, as in our example, the order becomes an integral part of the *Code* section, or is mentioned in an editorial note to the section.

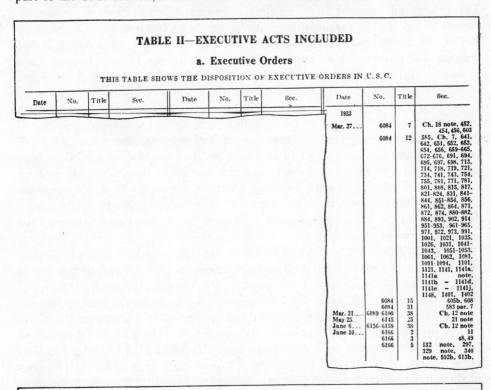

TABLE II—EXECUTIVE ACTS INCLUDED

a. Executive Orders

THIS TABLE SHOWS THE DISPOSITION OF EXECUTIVE ORDERS IN U. S. C.

Date	No.	Title	Sec.	Date	No.	Title	Sec.	Date	No.	Title	Sec.
								1933			
								Mar. 27...	6084	7	Ch. 18 note, 452, 454, 456, 603
									6084	12	585, Ch. 7, 641, 642, 651, 652, 653, 654, 656, 659-665, 672-676, 691, 694, 695, 697, 698, 713, 714, 718, 719, 721, 734, 741, 743, 754, 755, 761, 771, 781, 801, 808, 815, 817, 821-824, 831, 841-844, 851-854, 856, 861, 862, 864, 871, 872, 874, 880-882, 884, 893, 902, 914, 951-953, 961-965, 971, 972, 973, 991, 1001, 1021, 1025, 1026, 1031, 1041-1043, 1051-1053, 1061, 1062, 1081, 1091-1094, 1101, 1121, 1141, 1141a, 1141a note, 1141b - 1141d, 1141e - 1141j, 1148, 1401, 1402
									6084	15	605b, 608
									6084	31	583 par. 7
								Mar. 31...	6089-6100	38	Ch. 12 note
								May 25..	6145	25	21 note
								June 6...	6156-6159	38	Ch. 12 note
								June 10...	6166	2	11
									6166	3	48, 49
									6166	5	132 note, 297, 329 note, 340 note, 592b, 613b,

---

§ 1026   TITLE 12.—BANKS AND BANKING   **Page 1130**

Stat. 1454, and amended Ex. Ord. No. 6084, Mar. 27, 1933.)

§ 1026. Application for charter.

The charters to such Federal intermediate credit banks shall be granted upon application of the directors of the Federal land banks, which application shall be in such form as the Farm Credit Administration shall prescribe. (July 17, 1916, ch. 245, § 201 (f), as added Mar. 4, 1923, ch. 252, § 2, 42 Stat. 1454, and amended Ex. Ord. No. 6084, Mar. 27, 1933.)

DISCOUNTS AND LOANS

§ 1031. Lending powers; purchase and sale of debentures of intermediate credit banks; loans to cooperative associations.

Exhibit 73-A

When the order is not so related to a *Code* section, it is not included in *Shepard's Citations*. However, if construed by the courts, it is covered by the tables of "Statutes Construed" and in the statutory tables of the *Digest of United States Supreme Court Reports*.

State Administrative Rules and Changes. *See* Chapter 17, the State Aspect of Administrative Law.

Agency or Court Rulings on Statutes and Administrative Regulations. The only instance of systematic treatment of decisions interpreting administrative rules and orders is in citators in loose-leaf services covering the United States Tax Court (an administrative agency). Agency interpretations of a strictly internal nature are more frequently available. Examples are those in the *Cumulative Bulletin* of the Internal Revenue Bureau, and the table of "Civil Aviation Rules, Policies and Interpretations" in the Commerce Clearing House *Aviation Law Reporter.* Agency rules of practice as interpreted by the agencies and courts are sometimes annotated in the digest portions of the reporters reporting such agencies.

Two agencies, however, provide rather extensive citators in connection with their published decisions. The Comptroller General, in his *Index Digest of the Published Decisions . . . with Statutes, Decisions and Opinions Cited Therein,*[6] lists all statutes cited in his decisions; all of his own decisions cited in his later decisions; opinions of the Attorney General; and court decisions (arranged by case name) cited. The citator covers both the Comptroller General's decisions and those of the Comptroller of the Treasury. The *Index Digests* cover the period July 1, 1894-June 30, 1946, and kept up to date by similar citator tables in the annual volume of *Decisions.*

Agriculture Decisions, "decisions of the Secretary of Agriculture under regulatory laws administered in the United States Department of Agriculture," have a citator in each bound volume, listing "statutes, orders, *etc.,* cited in *Agriculture Decisions,*" and "Decisions cited in *Agriculture Decisions.*" It is a citator for statutes, regulations, orders and court decisions relating to matter printed in Agriculture Decisions.

Administrative Agency Decisions Generally. These are better taken care of by citators than are the rules and regulations. *Shepard's United States Citations* cover reports of decisions of the Interstate Commerce Commission; the Opinions of the United States Attorney General; customs and internal revenue decisions of the Treasury Department; Tax Court decisions; Interior Department, Customs Court, and Court of Customs and Patent Appeals (Customs). *Shepard's Federal Reporter Citations* covers Commissioner of Patents *Decisions* (official and in the *United States Patents Quarterly*); Court of Customs and Patent Appeals (Patents); patents by number or name; and *General Orders in Bankruptcy.*

Loose-leaf services cover agency decisions more thoroughly than they do the rules and regulations. Official reports of agency decisions may contain citator tables, covering federal statutes, agency regulations, and court and agency decisions.

An example is the "Cumulative Citations" sections of the *Agriculture* Decisions. The Federal Communications Commission Reports have a "Table of Cases, Statutes, and other Authorities Cited," which includes both court and Commission rulings.

Patents and Trade-Marks. These are covered in *Shepard's Federal Reporter* Citations, and also in tables in the *Federal Digest,* and in the *United States Patents Quarterly.*

---

[6] U. S. General Accounting Office. *Index Digest of the Published Decisions of the Comptroller General of the United States with Statutes, Decisions, and Opinions Cited Therein, 1894-1946.* Washington, D. C., U. S. Govt. Print. Off., 1929-50. 3 v.

CHAPTER 29

ENGLISH AND CANADIAN MATERIALS[1]

A. Authority of English Statutes and Decisions in America.

Every law student is constantly made aware in his courses, especially in the first year, of the contribution of English statutes and case law to the development of the basic concepts of the common law. The question of their continued weight arises, however, and whether they are cited merely as background, or as mandatory authority. The problem is two-pronged: To what extent are English statutes of any date authority in the United States; and to what extent are English decisions interpreting the English common law binding authority? In each state this is a matter of statute.

English Decisions Interpreting Common Law. Although the English common law, as modified by English statutes up to the time of the American Colonial settlement and as interpreted by English decisions up to the separation of the Colonies from England, is regarded as the basis of American jurisprudence, these decisions are not binding as actual authority, but are only highly persuasive. They are often highly effective, however, and are frequently cited by courts and in briefs. They are not applicable to Constitutional questions.

English Decisions Interpreting English Statutes. These are persuasive when such statutes have formed the basis of specific American statutes (as those on the law of sales or civil procedure), and a case of first impression involving them confronts an American court. The court will then pay close attention to well-considered English decisions interpreting their own statute, and will frequently adopt their reasoning. Such precedents are of course only persuasive, however. In *conflict of laws* situations, where the American court is asked to adopt an English court's construction of an English statute the presumption is in favor of that construction, but this will not be permitted to prevail against what the American courts regard as a plain and obvious policy to the contrary.

[1] The authors gratefully acknowledge the advice of Messrs. Maurice Maxwell and John Burke, of Sweet & Maxwell, Ltd.; and of Mr. Howard Drake, Secretary and Librarian of the University of London Institute of Advanced Legal Studies, who read and criticized this chapter in manuscript. They are, however, in no respect responsible for the statements made herein.

Study of English materials and of their authority in America is by no means an academic matter, as courts are constantly being asked to decide questions of American law upon the basis of the English law from which it was so largely derived. Since there is no national American common law, each state has to decide for itself the degree of adoption of the English common law within its borders, and with the exception of civil law Louisiana, every state has some sort of "reception statute," relating to the legal effect of English decisions, or statutes, or both.

No general statement can be made as to the provisions of these statutes. They have been analyzed with special reference to their effect upon the law of real property, by R. R. Powell, in Volume I, Chapter 4, of his treatise on *Real Property*.[2] As to English decisions as evidence of the common law, most reception statutes place July 4, 1776, as the limit up to which such decisions are authority here. Others specify the date of the state's admission into the Union. English statutes enacted after the settlement of the colony out of which a state was formed are generally stated in the reception statutes to be of no effect, since the common law as received in America at the time of settlement was that of England at that time, as modified only by English statutes then in force. Thus, in Virginia, the upper limit on statute reception was 1607, in Massachusetts 1620.

These American reception statutes and the American decisions all pay lip service to the binding authority of English statutes and common law, but as interpreted by American courts they all leave what Professor Powell calls an "escape valve." That is, the opinions, while holding English precedents to be binding, do so only to the extent that they are "suitable to American conditions"; or are "not in conflict with American indigenous law"; or where later changes in conditions have not made them inapplicable. An interesting analysis of conditions inviting the citation of cases across national lines is by Albert Kiralfy, *The Persuasive Authority of American Rulings in England*.[3]

B. English Statutes.

Because American statute forms are for the most part copied from English protoypes, the American practitioner will find little difficulty with the latter. Although for most practical purposes today the practitioner uses a compilation of statutes in force, occasionally he must consult a collection of annual statutes, similar to American session laws. Both are decribed below.

The Statutes Revised.[4] This officially published work, covering the years 1235 to 1948, prints all acts in force (exclusive of those of a local, personal or private nature), in *chronological, not classified, order*. Parts of included acts which are of local, personal or private nature are omitted, but the omission is noted. Acts relating exclusively to Northern Ireland are also omitted. An unnumbered volume contains Church Assembly Measures, 1920-1948. There are extensive notes. Each volume has its own subject and chronological index, but the set has no cumulative index of its own, relying for this upon the annual *Index to Statutes in Force*[5] and the *Chronological Table of the Statutes*,[6] described below. Because England is in process of consolidating many of its acts (analogous to our codification process), this set was out of date before printed, and must be carefully used in connection with the indexes referred to, and the annual *Statutes* containing the consolidation acts. This checking is greatly facilitated by conspicuous

---

[2] Albany, M. Bender, 1949-52, v. 1-3 published to date.

[3] 23 Tulane L. R. 209 (1948).

[4] London, H. M. Stationery Off., 1950. 3d rev. ed. 32 v. and 1 v. of Church Assembly Measures.

[5] London, H. M. Stationery Off. To 1949 as *Chronological Table and Index of the Statutes*. Beginning 1949 issued separately as *Index to the Statutes in Force* (in 4 v. to date).

[6] London, H. M. Stationery Off. To 1949 as *Chronological Table and Index of the Statutes*. Beginning 1949 issued as *Chronological Table of the Statutes* (in 2 v. to date).

stars in the *Chronological Table*, which point out all statutory changes since the publication of the *Statutes Revised* in 1948. In addition the annual noncumulative *Annotations to Acts; Directions for Noting the Amendments Made by the Acts, Statutory Instruments, and Church Assembly Measures* note for the year covered the exact changes in wording made by later enactments. Gummed labels containing the text of longer passages of amending acts are supplied, to be pasted in the respective volumes of the *Statutes Revised*.

Halsbury's Statutes of England.[7] There is no American counterpart of this encyclopedic treatment of the statutes of England and Northern Ireland (which must not be confused with *Halsbury's Laws of England, infra*). Statutes of public general interest in force are classified under 174 alphabetically arranged titles, as "Actions," "Husband and Wife," and "War Damage." Each of these main titles begins with a table of contents, corresponding to the analysis in a conventional American case digest or encyclopedia. Then there is a chronological table of all statutes printed under that title. Following this is a "Preliminary Note" (an essay on the subject matter of the title), after which the texts of the various acts are printed verbatim. Following the text of each section of an act are "Notes," in small type, which Shepardize the act, by both subsequent legislative and judicial action. *See* the specimen page below, at page 274.

Paragraph key numbering in Halsbury's. A special feature, common to *Halsbury's Statutes, Halsbury's Laws* and the *English and Empire Digest*, is the keying of paragraphs to later cumlative supplements. At the end of each statute paragraph there is a number in heavy brackets, as **[1037]**, called the key number. *This is not a classification number, but the volume and bracketed number* (3-1037 in the example below) identify that statute paragraph in all future cumulative supplements. It is a very neat device for Shepardizing a statute.

Tables for Halsbury's Statutes. *Each volume* and supplement has a *table of the statutes* which are in part or in full printed therein; a *table of cases* interpreting such statutes; and a *table of abbreviations* employed in the volume. It has its own *subject index* also. The *final tables volume of the set* cumulates the chronological tables of statutes and adds an alphabetical list of statutes; it also cumulates and expands the subject index, but omits the table of cases.

Supplementation of Halsbury's Statutes. There are three supplements, which serve different purposes and should not be confused with each other; (1) *Annotated Current Statutes*. This is a five-times-a-year loose-leaf annotated "slip law" service. (2) *Continuation Volume*. This cumulates the preceding year's "slip laws" and classifies and indexes them as in the main set. (3) *Cumulative Supplement*. This is an annual citator volume to the main set, to which it is keyed by paragraph number, as shown below, page 274. It brings the "Notes" down to date for each statute section number.

Acts and Ordinances of the Interregnum, 1642-1660.[8] The searcher will look in vain for any English statutes covering the period of the Commonwealth. There was a legislature, however, and it did legislate, as evidenced by several fragmentary collections. The definitive edition is the one named here, in which those pieces of legislation deemed of importance are printed. Volume three contains a *chronological list of acts and ordinances* printed, a *subject index*, and an *index of names, places, and things legislated about;* together with an essay on the content and validity of legislation of the Interregnum period.

Slip Laws and Annual Statutes. The more important older collections are described in the "Notes" below. Sessional or annual volumes have been published continuously by the King's (or Queen's) Printer from 1 Richard III (1484) to

---

[7] Editor-in-chief, Sir Roland Burrows. London, Butterworth, 1848–52. 2d ed. 31 v. to date.
[8] Collected by C. H. Firth and R. S. Rait. London, H. M. Stationery Off., 1911. 3 v.

518   VOL. 3—COMPANIES

(3) Where a company is ordered to add to its name the words " and reduced ", those words shall, until the expiration of the period specified in the order, be deemed to be part of the name of the company.   [1037]

NOTES

This section corresponds to s. 57 of the 1929 Act, which corresponded to s. 50 of the 1908 Act.

May make an order confirming reduction.   The court has a wide discretion to sanction a reduction (*Re Credit Assurance and Guarantee Corporation, Ltd.*, [1902] 2 Ch. 601), but will not sanction a reduction which would work unfairly as against any shareholders who do not consent to it (*Bannatyne* v. *Direct Spanish Telegraph Co.* (1886), 34 Ch.D. 287 ; 9 Digest 149, *843*).   The court will consider whether the sanction to the proposed reduction ought to be refused out of regard to the interest of members of the public induced to take shares in the company and whether the reduction is fair between classes of shareholders ; see *Poole* v. *National Bank of China, Ltd.*, [1907] A.C. 229, H.L.; 9 Digest 149, *842* ; and see also *Carruth* v. *Imperial Chemical Industries, Ltd.*, [1937] A.C. 707 ; [1937] 2 All E.R. 422 ; Digest Supp.   Where there are several classes of shareholders and there has been a loss of capital, the loss should be made to fall upon that class of shares which according to the constitution of the company ought to bear it (*Re Floating Dock Co. of St. Thomas, Ltd.*, [1895] 1 Ch. 691 ; and cf. *Re Direct Spanish Telegraph Co.* (1886), 34 Ch.D. 307 ; 9 Digest 148, *836*).   The court has refused to confirm a reduction by the surrender of paid up deferred shares, the holders of which were to receive a larger amount in paid up ordinary shares, by which amount the capital was to be increased (*Re Development Co. of Central and West Africa*, [1902] 1 Ch. 547 ; 9 Digest 153, *868*).   For further cases on this topic, see 9 Digest 148 *et seq*.

See also *Re Chatterley-Whitfield Collieries, Ltd.*, [1948] 1 All E.R. 911, C.A., where the court, having regard to the rights of the preference shareholders under the Coal Industry Nationalisation Act, 1946 (c. 59), s. 25, title Mines, Minerals and Quarries, Vol. 16, refused to sanction a petition by a company to reduce its share capital by returning to preference shareholders all capital paid up on their shares.

Creditor entitled to object.   See s. 67, p. 516, *ante*.   Generally with regard to proof of consent, see 9 Digest 165, 166.

And reduced.   Before the 1929 Act the addition of these words was obligatory, unless dispensed with by the court.   They need not now be added unless the court so directs.

Company to publish reasons for reduction.   For a case where the company was not required to publish the reasons for the reduction, see *Re Llynvi, Tondu and Ogmore Coal and Iron Co.* (1877), 37 L.T. 373 ; 9 Digest 155, *883* ; for a case where it was required to do so, see *Re Truman, Hanbury, Buxton & Co., Ltd.*, [1910] 2 Ch. 498 ; 9 Digest 168, *1038*.

Definitions.   For " company " and " the court ", see s. 455 (1), p. 788, *post*.

Northern Ireland.   Cf. the Companies Act (Northern Ireland), 1932 (c. 7) (N.I.), s. 57.

Vol. 3—919–1061   HALSBURY'S STATUTES (2ND EDN.)—SUPPT.
KEY
NOS.

1037   **Section 68.—**

May make an order confirming reduction.   After " *Re Chatterley-Whitfield Collieries, Ltd.*, [1948] 1 All E. R. 911 " delete " C. A."   This decision was reversed by the Court of Appeal, whose decision was affirmed (*sub nom. Prudential Assurance Co., Ltd.* v. *Chatterley-Whitfield Collieries Co., Ltd.*) by the House of Lords, [1949] A. C. 512 ; [1949] 1 All E. R. 1094.   See also *Scottish Insurance Corporation, Ltd.* v. *Wilsons and Clyde Coal Co., Ltd.*, [1949] A. C. 462 ; [1949] 1 All E. R. 1068.

Exhibit 74

date, except during the Commonwealth, when the Acts and Ordinances were issued separately as slip laws soon after enactment.[9] These laws are now currently available in several forms.

Slip laws. These are issued by Her Majesty's Stationery Office as approved —each act a separate pamphlet, as in the United States.

Public General Statutes. At the end of the year the slip laws are cumulated, with indexes and tables, under the above title (which has varied somewhat over the years), a series issued by the public printer since 1831. The printer makes the laws available to other publishers, who commonly distribute them as part of a law report or other subscription service. When so issued, they are usually mailed at intervals of about a month.

Current Law Statutes.[10] These have been published in parts since 1948 (annotated since 1950), as a separate companion service to *Current Law*, a digest.

Halsbury's Statutes of England, "Interim Service of Annotated Current Statutes." As noted above, this is a loose-leaf slip law service, issued five times a year.

Scotch Statutes. The Scotch statutes consist of: *Scots Statutes Revised; the Acts of the Parliaments,*[11] 1424-1707—*Scots Statutes Revised; the Public General Statutes affecting Scotland,* 1707-1900 [12]—*Scots Statutes,* 1901-1948 [13]—continued currently by *Scottish "Current Law" Statutes,* 1949 to date.[14] *Blackwood's Scots Statutes,* 1707-1947 [15] has been discontinued.

Statutory Instruments.[16] Through 1947 these counterparts of our own *Code of Federal Regulations* were known as *Statutory Rules and Orders.* Beginning with 1948, they took their present title. They consist of rules, regulations and orders implementing formal legislation, including treaties. The statutory authorization and effective date of each instrument are stated. There are the usual tables and indexes in each of the annual volumes of instruments, as well as additional tables showing, respectively, the effect on acts of Parliament of the new instruments adopted during the year; and of the year's legislation on previous instruments. Instruments are numbered serially by year. Thus, 1937 (No. 252); 1938 (No. 18). The headings of law correspond to those in the *Index to Statutes in Force.* Under each subject entry, (as "War Charities,") are listed, first the *Power* (that is, the act of Parliament under which the order is issued), then the *Exercise* (that is, the regulation or order issued under the power).

The Statutory Rules and Orders and Statutory Instruments Revised, to December 31, 1948.[17] This official edition reprints all statutory instruments (with certain minor exceptions) of a "general and permanent character," and certain Orders in Council and Letters Patent. Omitted are such instruments as temporary defence regulations, court rules, and regulations of Eire and Northern Ireland. The first three volumes print both the original form of the instrument and any amendments, but in the remaining

---

[9] But *see* Percy H. Winfield, *The Chief Sources of English Legal History*, Cambridge, Mass., Harvard Unvi. Press, 1925, p. 91, note 3.
[10] London, Sweet & Maxwell, 1947 to date (monthly issues).
[11] Edinburgh, Green, 1908.
[12] Edinburgh, Green, 1899-1902. 10 v. (v. 10 is Index).
[13] Edinburgh, Green, 1901-48. 12 v.
[14] Edinburgh, Green, 1949 to date.
[15] Edinburgh, Blackwood's edition, 1848-1947.
[16] London, H. M. Stationery Office, 1904 to date. In 81 v.
[17] London, H. M. Stationery Off., 1948-52. 25 v.

volumes only the current form, as amended, is given, with footnote citations to the amendments. Although the title of the set reads as of "December 31, 1948," many entries are through December 31, 1951. It is kept up to date by the annual volumes of *Statutory Instruments*. The arangement of material is by subject, as in the annual volumes.

Tables. The last volume of the set contains extensive tables, which include chiefly: (1) an alphabetical *list of titles* or subject headings for the set; (2) a numerical *table of instruments*, for finding a given instrument by year and number; and (3) a *Table of Effects*, which Shepardizes the instruments by noting all amendments, revocations, and the like of earlier instruments by later ones.

Index. *See* "Indexes to English Statutes," *infra.*

Halsbury's Statutory Instruments.[18] This is a classified encyclopedic treatment, on the same plan as *Halsbury's Statutes.* It prints and annotates a selection of instruments, with references to those in force but not printed. There are quarterly supplements and an annual noter-up volume.

Treaties. British treaties and agreements of international effect (including un-ratified treaties) are published officially in separate form as Command Papers, all of which appear in the bound volume of the *Parliamentary Papers* for each session entitled *State Papers*—a volume which precedes the sessional index volume. Treaties are indexed in the monthly and annual lists of government publications, of Her Majesty's Stationery Office.

Those treaties which are ratified, and most of the agreements and exchanges of notes, are issued as a numbered *Treaty Series* [19] (in which a new numbering commences every year). The last *Treaty Series* number of each year is an *Index*, and the one preceding it a *List of Ratifications, Accessions, Withdrawals, Etc.* for the current year. Biennial or triennial indexes are also issued within the series itself. The numbered series began in 1892.

British treaties are also included in the collection of *British and Foreign State Papers,*[20] covering the period from 1812, and in Hertslet's *Commercial Treaties.*[21] The first volume of each of these series included pertinent treaties in force at the time the set was begun. *Hertslet* was incorporated with the *British and Foreign State Papers,* beginning with volume 116 (1922) of the latter. British treaties from 1919 are also printed and indexed in the *League of Nations Treaty Series* and the *United Nations Treaty Series.*

C. Indexes to English Statutes.

Available indexes are superior to their American counterparts. Each annual volume of session laws has its conventional index; those noted below are to collections of statutes.

"Chronological Table of the Statutes, 1235 to Date." [22] In this annual cumulative table all statutes are listed in chronological order (regnal year, chapter, and section), together with short title (if any). Repeals and modifications are noted in italics, with citations to the act repealing or modifying. Since 1949, action later than 1948 affecting any act printed in the Statutes Revised (3d ed.) is designated by a heavy black star. References to Irish acts since 1923 are italicized.

---

[18] London, Butterworth, 1951-52. 25 v.

[19] London, H. M. Stationery Off., 1892 to date.

[20] London, H. M. Stationery Off., 1812 to date.

[21] London, v. 1-19 pub. by Butterworth, 1827-95; v. 20-31 pub. by H. M. Stationery Off., 1898-1925.

[22] *See* footnote 6, *supra.*

"Index to Statutes in Force." [23] This annual (since 1870) cumulative subject index to public acts is a companion volume to the *Chronological Table*, and the two together form the indexes to the third edition of the *Statutes Revised* as well as to all annual statutes.

Statutes of the Realm (1225-1713). [24] There are two elaborate index volumes to these early statutes, the "alphabetical," and the "chronological." The value of these indexes today is that they *index many statutes long since repealed*, which are not indexed in the *Index to Statutes in Force*, though noted in the *Chronological Table*.

Index to Local and Private Acts. Bramwell's *Analytical Table of Private Statutes, 1727-1812*, and *Salt's Index to Private Acts Passed in the Reign of Anne, George I and George II* (with a supplement covering 1801-1899) cover this little-used material.

Index to Local and Personal Acts." [25] This consists of classified lists of the local, personal and private acts, special orders, and special procedure orders, 1801-1947.

"Guide to Government Orders, Indexing S. R. & Os. and S. Is in Force." [26] This annual cumulative index *lists all statutes under which orders have been issued*, with the subject heading under which the order is found in the index. The subject index is arranged substantially under the same headings as those of the *Index to Statutes in Force*. Under each "Power" (that is, the title and citation of the *enabling act*) there is the "Exercise" (that is, the *instrument's* short title, subject matter, and place where printed). This index serves as the index to the *Revised* edition. *Halsbury's Statutory Instruments* also has such an index.

D. Dates of English Statutes.

English statutes are conventionally cited by *regnal year*, that is, by the year of the sovereign's reign during which they were enacted (as 1 Geo. V, 15 Vict.) The simplest way to translate this to the calendar year is through the *Chronological Table of the Statutes*. Exact days of the month covered by each regnal year are given in a table in Sweet and Maxwell's *Guide to Law Reports and Statutes*,[27] at page 56. For most purposes, the table printed in the Bibliographical Reference Manual, herein, will suffice.

Although the regnal year is still a necessary element in the *citation* of English statutes, it has ceased to be of vital importance in the actual *finding* of those statutes enacted since about 1875. This is because nearly all significant statutes during that period bear a "short title," part of which is the year of passage. Thus, "Housing Act, 1949"; "Medical Act, 1950." Under the Short Title Act, 1896, 59 & 60 Vict., c. 14, s. 1; and the Statute Law Revision Act, 1948, 11 & 12 Geo. 6, c. 62, s. 5, it is legal to cite an act by short title only, but the regnal year and chapter are added in most legal writing, as in this sentence.

Notes on English Statute Collections

There have been numerous collections of English statutes, all the way back to Magna Charta, but those listed below are the ones usually consulted today, if available.

---

[23] *See* footnote 5, *supra.*

[24] London, G. Eyre & A. Strahan. Alphabetical, 1824; Chronological, 1828.

[25] London, H. M. Stationery Off., 1949.

[26] London, H. M. Stationery Off., 1952. Annual, this is first issue.

[27] London, Sweet & Maxwell, 1948. 2d ed.

Statutes of the Realm (covering 1225-1713).[28] This is indispensable, as the fullest and most accurate edition of the statutes for the period covered. Printed from original and authentic manuscripts, there are nine large folio volumes in ten, published between 1810 and 1822, with an alphabetical index in 1824 and a chronological index in 1828. It includes verbatim copies (in parallel translations from Latin or Law French where necessary) of statutes as enacted, even though later repealed; and the Private Acts up to 31 Henry VIII (1539). Titles of private acts from then on were printed, but not the text. The "Charters of Liberties" (Magna Charta, *etc.*) are printed in volume 1, which also contains historical material on various early editions of the statutes. Each volume has its own index and there are two cumulative index volumes. Editorial notes accompany many of the statutes.

Pickering's Statutes at Large (Magna Charta to 1869).[29] Because of its octavo size, this is the most popular edition of the English statutes. Published in various series under various titles, it was finally discontinued in 1869. The *Pickering* set proper, to 1792, prints many acts by title only, making it rather irritating to use, though most such omitted acts are of little importance.

Tomlins and Raithby's Statutes at Large (Magna Charta to 1800).[30] This is also an octavo edition, continued to 1869 by an anuual edition printed by the King's Printer — when it, like Pickering's, was discontinued. Based upon Ruffhead's edition below, it printed every public act that had not been repealed or had not expired.

Runnington's edition of Ruffhead's Statutes at Large (Magna Charta to 1800).[31] Although it may be regarded as the "standard" edition for most purposes, because it is in quarto volumes and thus inconvenient to use, it is not as popular as those named above. It is the preferred edition from the period covered by the *Statutes of the Realm.* The text is said to be excellent and to include many hitherto unpublished statutes. On the other hand, many acts, local or private in nature, or obsolete, were omitted.

Chitty's Statutes of Practical Utility.[32] The aim of this edition was to select and publish statutes in force which were of use to the practicing lawyer. Arrangement was by subject and there were many notes and annotations, together with useful tables. There were five editions through 1910, with annual continuation volumes through 1945 when *Chitty's* was discontinued.

Classification of English Statutes. Acts of the English Parliament currently are: "public general," "local and personal," "private and personal including estates," and (since 1919) "Church Assembly Measures." The classification and authority of English statutes are discussed in 31 *Halsbury's Laws of England* (2d ed.) 455, and in 24 *Halsbury's Statutes of England* (2d ed.) 128. Treaties are published separately as "Command Papers," and in various treaty series. Private, local, and personal acts are little used in American practice and collections of them are scarce. They are issued in "slip" form or as bills, and copies of individual acts may be obtained, if in print, from the Copyright Office, House of Lords.

E. English Law Reports.

These reports are so similar in construction and purpose to American that the American user is at once at home with them. The development of the law report and some of the principal series of reports are described in the "Notes," *infra.*

F. English Law Reports Through 1865.

The three hundred or more different series of law reports through 1865 have been compressed, in reprints, from their original many hundreds of lineal feet of

---

[28] London, G. Eyre & A. Strahan, 1810-22. 9 v.
[29] Cambridge, 1726-1807. Various publishers. 46 v.
[30] London, Eyre & Strahan, 1801-1826. 10 v.
[31] London, Baskett, 1769-1800. 18 v.
[32] London, Sweet & Maxwell. 6th ed., 1911-13. 16 v. Continued, v. 17-42, to 1948.

shelf space to about forty, by printing only the best of several duplicating reports.

"English Reports, Full Reprint" (covering 1378-1865).[33] This set reprints practically all reports of value for the years covered, as contained in some 274 different report series. About one hundred thousand cases are reprinted, verbatim (hence the "Full Reprint," which means that every case in the set is reprinted in full), with parallel citations to reports of the case in other series. Some editorial notes are provided. The parallel citations are in the following form (the "S. C." meaning "Same Case in another Report."):

> *Mayor of Ludlow* v. *Charlton*, 6 M. & W. 815 (1940). [S. C. 10 L. J. Ex. 75; 3 Jur. 657; 8 Car. & P. 242. Followed, *Arnold* v. *Poole Corp.*, 4 Man. & G. 860; Referred to, *Wells* v. *Kingston-Upon-Hull*, 1875, L. R. 10 C. P. 409.]

The reprint volumes are arranged by courts (as House of Lords, Chancery, Nisi Prius, *etc.*), and are *star paged* to the original. Many "unauthorized" *(see* "Notes," *infra)* series of reports were not reprinted at all, but most cases reported in these series were reprinted in this set from authorized reports. A *wall chart*, listing alphabetically all report series reprinted, with parallel references to the corresponding volumes of the *Reprint*, is provided. Those experiencing difficulty in finding cases through the abbreviations in this chart should consult Glanville L. Williams, *Addendum to the Table of English Reports*, 7 Camb. L. J. 261 (1941), where the deficiencies of the set are discussed and a supplementary table of abbreviations is provided. There is a two-volume *table of cases.*

"Revised Reports" (covering 1785-1865).[34] This set reprints most of the cases for the period covered. In general, for these years, it duplicates the *English Reports, Full Reprint,* but it *reprints many collateral (unauthorized) report series* not represented in that reprint, and so contains occasional reports not printed in the *Full Reprint*. An example is *Wardell* v. *Usher*, 3 Scott's New Reports 508 (1841). There is a *table of cases.*

G. English Law Reports, 1865 to Date.

"Law Reports" (1865 to Date). This is the principal current body of English reports. A chart, with instructions for proper citation of the different series in which these reports have been published, is printed in this *Manual* at page 353. Not mentioned in that chart is the *Indian Appeals* series, issued under the auspices of the publishers of the *Law Reports* through 1950, when it was discontinued.

Authority of the "Law Reports." This series is not "official," but it has been called semi-official.[35] The judges revise and approve the reports of their own decisions before they are published, and it is the general custom of the courts to require citation of the *Law Reports* only, when a case has been published in one of its series.[36] (This rule has been somewhat relaxed in Rent Act cases). Every report is initialed or signed by the barrister who wrote it — which is common in other English reports also.

Different series of "Law Reports." There are currently four series: *Appeal Cases* (covering the House of Lords and the Judicial Committee of the Privy Council); *Queen's Bench Division* (including cases appealed to the Court of Appeal, and decisions of the Court of Criminal Appeal); *Chancery Division* (equity, lunacy, and, on appeal,

---

[33] Edinburgh, W. Green, 1900-1930. 176 v.

[34] London, Sweet & Maxwell; Boston, Little, Brown, 1891-1917. 149 v.

[35] Lord Chancellor's Department, *Report of the Law Reporting Committee*, London, H. M. Stationery Off., 1940. p. 17.

[36] *Ibid.*, p. 17.

cases heard in the Court of Appeal); and the *Probate, Divorce, and Admiralty Division* (with appeals in the Court of Appeal and decisions in the Ecclesiastical Courts).[37] The *Law Reports* are issued in monthly parts, with annual indexes and tables. Each volume contains a "Table of Cases Judicially Noticed," and of "Statutes Judicially Considered" by cases printed therein—case and statutory citators, in other words—which tables cumulated in the *Law Reports Digest*, discontinued in 1951.

"**Weekly Notes**" (**covering 1860-1952**). This periodical printed reports of cases decided in all courts covered by the *Law Reports*. Most of these cases were later fully reported in the *Law Reports* themselves, but many others (marked by an asterisk) were not, so that the periodical reported more cases than the main *Law Reports* series. Part II of the periodical noted the titles of newly enacted statutes, printed new court rules, and gave other miscellaneous information of interest to practitioners.

"**Weekly Law Reports**" (**1953—**). Probably the most complete of all current series in its coverage of "general" reports is this one, which superseded the *Weekly Notes*. It is said to cover *every decision likely to appear in any general series of reports*. Each issue is in two parts, bound together. Part I prints reports (starred) which will not later appear in the *Law Reports*. These are prepared by barristers but are not revised by the judges. Part II prints the reports as they will later appear in the *Law Reports*, except that arguments of counsel are omitted. These reports are revised by the judges. Reports are published about three weeks after decision date. Each issue has a cumulative table of cases for the volume, and an "Index of Subject Matter" digesting cases in that particular issue. These indexes cumulate annually.

Beginning January, 1953, this series absorbed the *Times Law Reports*.

Inclusiveness of "Law Reports" and "Weekly Law Reports" coverage. These current reports aim to report "every reportable case of general interest." The editor is the final arbiter, and according to his criteria, questions of fact alone are not reportable at all; cases of temporary interest, or which are a fresh illustration of an old principle, are not included in the *Law Reports* but may be printed as starred cases in the *Weekly Law Reports*. The cases printed in the *Law Reports* "consist of new points of law and are therefore cases of permanent interest to the legal profession." [38]

Miscellaneous English Law Reports. Although the old "authorized" reports dropped out soon after 1865, some other reports continued and a few new ones started. These were of two kinds: "general," as the *Law Journal, Law Times,* and *Times Law Reports;* and special, as *Patent, Design, Trade Mark and other Cases.* The general reports competed directly with the *Law Reports*, and published many reports not contained in that series; but most of the cases printed in the special reports were *not* elsewhere reported. Of the four principle series of general reports covering all the superior courts *(Law Times Reports, Law Journal Reports, Times Law Reports,* and *All England Law Reports)*, only the last mentioned is now current. In addition, the *Solicitors' Journal* (1875 to date) prints rather brief reports of some four hundred cases each year. A similar function is performed by the *Estates Gazette* (1903 to date), while the *Law Times* and the *Law Journal*, though they have discontinued their separate *Reports* still publish in the periodicals themselves brief reports of cases. The *Estates Gazette Reports* are unusual in that they are not reported by barristers.

The curtailed reports enjoy less prestige than the full reports. The relative value of the different series of English reports as authority is set forth in cases digested in 30 *English and Empire Digest* [Replacement, 236-239, cases 837-907 (1951)].

---

[37] In connection with these reports, reference should be made to *The Criminal Appeal Reports*, 1908 to date (London, Stevens & Kaynes, 1909 to date), which include cases heard on assize and in the Divisional Courts. There is a combined table of cases and subject index for the first thirty-four volumes (through 1950). (London, Sweet & Maxwell, 1952).

[38] Letter to the authors, by F. Hudson, Secretary of the Incorporated Council of Law Reporting for England and Wales.

"**All England Law Reports**" (1936 —). Appearing weekly, these reports cover the superior courts and courts of special jurisdiction; they report about eight hundred cases a year (as compared to about three hundred in the Law Reports proper). Through 1946 they were "annotated" by brief notes. Beginning with October 23, 1952, the first issue of each month cross-references from the cases to the appropriate sections of *Halsbury's Laws of England*. The case reports are briefer than those in the *Law Reports*, in that no attempt is made to give counsel's arguments. Each weekly issue contains a cumlative table of cases for the year to date, and a table which "notes up" (Shepardizes) cases and statutes referred to in the decisions. There are an annual *table of cases* reported, *subject index*, *tables of cases and statutes referred to*, and of *words and phrases* judicially defined. All tables are cumulated in an annual *Index and Noter-Up*, covering all reported cases and statutes from 1936 to date. There is thus readily available at all times a combined table of cases, subject index, and citator for the period covered. The *Index and Noter-Up* may be purchased separately from the reports.

American reprints of English reports. Many English reports antedating 1865 were reprinted in the United States, but these, like the original editions, have been superseded for practical purposes by the reprints.

Annotated reports series. Several such series have been published in the United States, usually combined with American cases (such as the *American and English Annotated Cases*). Others were entirely British in content (as *English Ruling Cases*). There have also been combined English and American special-subject series, as *American and English Corporation Cases*. All have now ceased publication. *A. L. R.* does not print English cases, though occasionally one is digested in an annotation.

Notes on English Courts and Early Law Reports.

The English Court System as it Affects Law Reporting. Because English law reporting reflects the court system under which it operates, it can best be understood against the background of that system. English courts in effect combine in one hierarchy those courts which in the United States are federal and state tribunals. The court system was greatly simplified by the Judicature Acts of 1873 and 1875, and further clarified by the Acts of 1881, 1885, and others.

Courts prior to the Judicature Act of 1873. Just prior to the enactment of the Judicature Act of 1873, English superior courts comprised:

Present High Court Jurisdiction	1. High Court of Chancery. 2. Court of King's Bench. 3. Court of Common Pleas at Westminster. 4. Court of Exchequer. 5. Probate Court. 6. Court of Divorce and Matrimonial Causes. 7. High Court of Admiralty. 8. Courts of Assizes.

On the Appellate side were the following courts:

Present Court of Appeal Jurisdiction	9. Court of Exchequer Chamber (common-law appeals). 10. Lords Justices in Chancery (for Chancery appeals). 11. Appellate jurisdiction of the Privy Council, in Lunacy, and from instance jurisdiction of Admiralty.

The highest appellate courts, then as now, were the:

12. House of Lords.
13. Judicial Committee of the Privy Council.

Courts under the Judicature Acts of 1873 and later. The legislation of 1873 to 1875 set up a Supreme Court of Judicature, divided into the *High Court* and the *Court of Appeal.*

The High Court. By its "divisional courts" this court was given jurisdiction formerly exercised by the first eight courts above. In 1881, the Queen's Bench, Common

Pleas and Exchequer Divisions were combined as the *Queen's Bench Division*. Since that time the High Court therefore has consisted of *Chancery; Queen's* (or *King's*) *Bench;* and *Probate, Divorce, and Admiralty Divisions*. These divisions of the courts before and after 1873 are important today because the *Law Reports* have followed them.

The High Court has wide original and appellate jurisdiction, which was modified in 1938, with respect to the criminal side.

The Court of Appeal. Under the above legislation, this court took the appellate jurisdiction of the courts numbered 9 to 11, above. Its appellate jurisdiction is over a wide variety of appeals, including those from the High Court and its divisions. Its original jurisdiction is extremely limited.

It should be mentioned here that though cases decided on appeal by the Court of Appeal are marked "C.A." in the reports, *there is no Court of Appeal series of reports,* the decisions of the court being reported in the appropriate "divisional" series. That is, if the case comes up from the King's Bench Division, for example, the decision of the Court of Appeal is reported as a King's Bench (C.A.) report. Thus, *Milmo* v. *Carreras,* [1946] 1 K. B. 306 (C.A.), arose originally in the King's Bench Division, was decided on appeal to the Court of Appeal, and is reported in the King's Bench Division of the *Law Reports.* The *Law Reports Appeal Cases* series, not to be confused with those of the Court of Appeal, reports the decisions of the House of Lords and of the Judicial Committee of the Privy Council.

The House of Lords. This is the final court of appeal for Great Britain and Northern Ireland. Any member of that House may sit, but only lawyers do sit, and a minimum number of highly placed judicial officers is required by the Act of 1876, 39 & 40 Vict., c. 59, s. 5. Original jurisdiction is unimportant to American lawyers. Appellate jurisdiction is over appeals from judgments and orders of the Court of Appeal and from Scottish or Northern Ireland reports; and over appeals of public importance from the Court of Criminal Appeal. The final appeal for dominions, colonies, protectorates, mandated territories, prize courts and Ecclesiastical courts is the Judicial Committee of the Privy Council.

Criminal appeals. These follow this path: Appeals from petty sessions are either (a) by way of rehearing to Quarter Sessions; or (b) on a point of law, by "case stated," to a divisional court of the Queen's Bench Division. Appeals from Quarter Sessions and from Assizes (including the Central Criminal Court), are to the Court of Criminal Appeal. There is no appeal in criminal matters from the Divisional Court. Appeal lies from the Court of Criminal Appeal to the House of Lords only on the fiat of the Attorney General that the case involves a point of law of public importance.

Specialized courts. There are numerous other courts, with which the American lawyer is not likely to be concerned sufficiently to require description here. Among them are Ecclesiastical, children's, colonial, local government, and referees' courts.

HISTORICAL.

The Court of Exchequer. The oldest of the English courts of which there are today direct descendants was the Exchequer, probably dating from the twelfth century. Purely a revenue court originally, it became under Elizabeth I a common-law court of first instance, withdrawing many cases from the Court of Common Pleas. It was also a court of equity. On the common-law side there developed a separate Exchequer of of Pleas, with (from 1358) a Court of Exchequer Chamber to hear common-law appeals from it. The Court of Exchequer in 1873 became the Exchequer Division of the High Court, and in 1881 was merged into the Queen's Bench Division, where cases involving the Treasury are heard. The appellate jurisdiction was taken over at the same time (1873) by the Court of Appeal.

The Court of Common Pleas. This was also established as a common-law court by the close of the twelfth century, with jurisdiction between subject and subject. In the constant pressure by King's Bench and Exchequer, it lost most of its exclusive jurisdiction, and is now a part of the Queen's Bench Division of the High Court.

The Court of King's Bench. It grew out of the King's Council, to which were referred errors of the Common Pleas and pleas to the Crown (criminal cases). Eventually, at the expense of the Common Pleas, it so extended its jurisdiction as to become a court of general jurisdiction, not only in criminal but in civil matters. Today, as the Queen's Bench Division of the High Court, it has wide civil jurisdiction, but in practice, since 1938, its criminal jurisdiction has been reduced.

The Court of Chancery. This resulted from the need for some procedure to soften the rigid rules of the common-law courts. First came petitions to the King and Council, by those aggrieved. These were turned over to the Chancellor, an ecclesiastical officer and delegate to the Council, for his recommendations. As the work of the Chancellor grew in volume, his tribunal gradually took on the character of a court of equity, with its own system of jurisprudence. At the time of the Judicature Act of 1873, it consisted of the High Court of Chancery, with appeal to the Lords Justices in Chancery. Under the Act and its successors, it became the Chancery Division of the High Court, with appeals to the Court of Appeal and to the House of Lords.

Admiralty jurisdiction. Originally a matter of local port courts, by the middle of the fourteenth century a well-defined court of maritime jurisdiction had developed, though regular records go back only to 1524. For the present jurisdiction, *see* below.

Marriage, divorce, and probate. Originally they were matters for the Ecclesiastical courts, but in 1857 a Probate Court and a Divorce Court were established. Under the Judicature Acts, admiralty, divorce, and probate matters were made a division of the High Court.

English courts, past and present, are described in the following works, among others:

R. M. Jackson, *The Machinery of Justice in England;* [39]

G. R. Y. Radcliffe and Geoffrey Cross, *The English Legal System;* [40]

W. L. Burdick, *The Bench and Bar of Other Lands*, pp. 3-193; [41]

T. F. T. Plucknett, *A Concise History of the Common Law;* [42]

Harold G. Hanbury, *English Courts of Law*.[43]

The authors are also indebted to Captain W. Holden, Librarian of Gray's Inn.

Development of the English Law Report. The law report as we now know it was substantially fixed in form by 1765, but the process of development was a long and haphazard one. This was in large measure because there probably never has been "official" reporting of decisions in England (except for a few special courts, as patents and taxation), and because English opinions are almost always delivered orally and not read from manuscript. This has led to a multiplicity of duplicating and often inaccurate reports. Reporting is selective, and though there have been some three hundred different series of reports, not only does no one of them report all decided appellate cases, but not all of them combined do so. Furthermore, reports are only of those parts of the opinion deemed by the reporter to be useful to the lawyer. This confusion, duplication, and variance in law reports is furthered by the fact that any written report signed or initialled by a barrister, or any oral report vouched by a barrister, is citable in court.[44]

Pre-Year Book Reports. The earliest reports of any kind were probably scant records of legal proceedings in contemporary documents, such as the *Domesday Book* and chronicles. In 1879, M. M. Bigelow published a number of these, covering the years 1066-1189, in his *Placita Anglo-Normanica*.[45] They were not at all real reports as now understood, but only scraps of writs and pleas—interesting only historically. The *Rotuli Curiae Regis* (Plea Rolls),[46] in two volumes covering the period 1194 to 1199, were published in 1835. Beginning 1189 (the first year of Richard I), the plea rolls were made a part of the official record. As such, they contained little more than the place and date of the trial, the names of the parties, the nature of the proceedings, and the date. A collection containing reports of criminal trials as far back as 1163 is T. B. and T. J. Howell's *Complete Collection of State Trials . . . from the Earliest Period* to

---

[39] Cambridge, University Press, 1940.

[40] London, Butterworth. 2d ed., 1946.

[41] Brooklyn, Metropolitan Law Book Co., 1939.

[42] London, Butterworth, 4th ed., 1948.

[43] London, Oxford University Press, 1944.

[44] Lord Westbury, Lord Chancellor, 171 Parl. Deb. 778 (Hansard's, 3d Ser. 1863).

[45] Boston, Little, Brown, 1879.

[46] London, Eyre & Spottiswoode, 1835. 2 v.

1873,[47] which superseded several earlier attempts to gather reports of these trials from various sources.

Year Books, *1282-1537.* The beginning date of this series of reports in variously given as 1282, 1285, and 1293. Just how they came to be written and why they ceased (unless the latter was because of the coincident invention of printing) has been the subject of much speculation, but it is generally believed that the reports, such as they were, were originally written down by students or practitioners in open court, for educational purposes. On the other hand, it was long believed that they were done by court officials, though this view is now generally discredited. Most of the *Year Books* have now been printed, but not all. Modern editions, as those by the Selden Society and the Ames Foundation of Harvard University, are admirable examples of careful editing, with copious notes, but they are still books for the scholar rather than the practitioner. As such, they are invaluable as affording glimpses of medieval court rooms, with their writs and pleas. They also profoundly influenced the progress of the law for over three hundred years, through their use in treatises and digests. Henry de Bracton, in his *De Legibus et Consuetudinibus Angliae* (about 1250-1260),[48] digested some five hundred cases from the Plea Rolls, and in the *Note Book* ascribed to him collected about two thousand. Cases from the *Year Books* provided the basis for such forerunners of the modern digest as Statham's (1489), Fitzherbert's (1516), and Brooke's (1570) *Abridgments,* Many cases from the latter part of the *Year Books* were later published in the reports of Bellewe, Moore, Dyer, Brooke, and Benloe.

Named Reporters, *1537-1785.* During the period beginning with the end of the *Year Books* and roughly coinciding with the beginning of the popularity of the printed book, the law report as known today was developed. It was a period of more than one hundred different series of reports, varying in quality from the unreliable to the magnificent. In the early part of this period the reports were made for the personal use of the reporter—a practitioner or judge—and were not intended for publication. Garbled copies, from manuscripts stolen from the author and published without his knowledge and often many years after his death, were frequent. Some reports were illiterate translations from the original Latin or Law French. Plowden's (covering 1550-1580) and Coke's (1572-1616) reports, which were prepared with great care, were as much commentaries as reports. Otherwise, they closely approached the modern report form, though lacking headnotes. The eleven volumes of Coke's reports published during his lifetime enjoyed such prestige that they were known simply as *The Reports,* but the two posthumous volumes were not so highly regarded. The publication of the various reports was highly irregular. New Benloe and Anderson cover a period of one hundred thirty years; Owen, Saville, Brownlow, Gouldsborough, Popham, and Lane, from fifty to one hundred years. Several reporters would report the same case, with widely divergent results. Following the English Revolution there was a gradual improvement in reporting, culminating in the first really modern reports, those of Burrow (covering 1757-1771), who in 1765 introduced the headnote.

Named Reporters, *1785-1865.* Although Burrow in effect standardized the form of the law report, publication lagged far behind decision. The great contribution of Durnford and East's reports (1785-1800) was that they were compiled and published regularly at the end of the King's Bench term covered (and hence were known as the *Term Reports).* From 1785 on, English law reporting has been more or less standardized, accurate, and prompt. The period to 1865 (the *Law Reports*) was also one of duplicating and overlapping reports.

"Authorized" Reports. In an attempt to reduce the number of reporters, some judges, beginning about 1785, appointed "authorized" reporters. They were not "official" or salaried, as in America, but they were afforded special privileges in that the judges appointing them aided them in setting down oral opinions and provided copies of written ones for the reporter. Though it is disputed, it seems probable that from 1785 to about 1832 these reports enjoyed the monopoly of exclusive citation.[49] As is likely to be the case in monopoly, this system carried with it the seeds of its own destruction. The

---

[47] London, T. C. Hansard for R. Bagshaw [etc.] 1809-1826.
[48] The first printed edition was published by Richard Tottell in 1569. *See* Dict. Nat. Biog.
[49] C. G. Moran, *The Heralds of the Law* (London, Stevens, 1948), p. 16; William S. Holds-

authorized reports were expensive, and publication lagged intolerably. Other reports (as the *Jurist, Law Times Reports, Law Journal Reports,* and the *Weekly Reporter*), sprang up and won the right of citation. More important, the Council of Law Reporting in England and Wales was formed for the purpose of publishing the *Law Reports.*

The Law Reports, 1865 to date. When the *Law Reports* began publication, there were twelve series, corresponding to the existing court setup, as follows: (1) *House of Lords, English and Irish Appeals;* (2) *House of Lords, Scotch and Divorce Appeals;* (3) *Privy Council Appeals;* (4) *Privy Council Indian Appeals* (beginning 1873); (5) *Chancery Appeal Cases;* (6) *Crown Cases Reserved;* (7) *Queen's Bench Cases;* (8) *Common Pleas Cases;* (9) *Exchequer Cases;* (10) *Equity Cases;* (11) *Admiralty and Ecclesiastical Cases;* and (12) *Probate and Divorce Cases.* As a result of the reorganization of courts under the Judicature Act of 1875, these twelve report series were reduced, beginning January 1876, to seven, as follows: (A) *Appeal Cases* (combining numbers 1-3, above); (B) *Indian Appeals;* (C) *Queen's Bench Division;* (D) *Common Pleas Division;* (E) *Exchequer Division;* (F) *Chancery Division;* and (G) *Probate Division* (comprising numbers 5–12, above, corresponding to the divisions of the new High Court). In 1881, C, D, and E, above, were combined as sub-divisions of the *Queen's Bench Division,* leaving as current series, A, B, C, F, and G. It so continued until 1950, when the *Indian Appeals* (B, above) were discontinued with volume 77 of the set, leaving as the four current sets *Appeal Cases, Queen's Bench Division, Chancery Division,* and the *Probate, Divorce, and Admiralty Division.*

H. English Search Books and Indexes.

Auxiliary aids to finding English law parallel in general their American counterparts, with perhaps greater emphasis on statutory indexes and citators.

Current Law and Current Law Year Book.[50] This publication, begun in 1947, does its best to live up to its subtitle *"All* the law from *every* source." In its monthly issues (cumulating annually, with a "Current Law Consolidation," 1947-1951), it is, for the period covered, at once a statutory digest and citator, a case digest and citator, and an index to British legal periodicals and treatises. As such, it is a complete and convenient single index to current English law. *There is a separate Scottish edition,* duplicating the English, but with the addition of a blue-paper section covering statutes, statutory instruments and cases applicable to Scotland only. The *Consolidation* omits this Scottish material.

Digests. In a single alphabet of about two hundred main topics (the number varies somewhat from year to year), *Current Law* digests (a) statutes, (b) statutory instruments, and (3) cases construing them. New statutes are digested at some length; older ones only to the extent necessary to understand the digested cases construing them. Cases digested include not only those from English superior courts, but also a selection from Irish, Dominion, and English county courts.

Statute lists. Under "Statutes and Orders," acts receiving the Royal Assent during the year are listed, by title; there is a separate "Table of Statutory Instruments."

Citators: statutes. Each paragraph digesting a statute or case gives pertinent citator data. In addition, a single table in the *Year Book* and in the *Current Law Consolidation, 1947-1951,* arranged by regnal years and chapters, lists all statutes passed during the period; statutory instruments issued under designated statutory power; cases construing each statute; periodical articles or books in point; and all amendments, repeals and the like, of listed statutes. This statute citator appears also in *Current Law Statutes.*

Citators: cases. The "Case Citator," in a single table "gives cases digested, cases judicially considered, cases affected by statute, and cases commented on in legal

worth, *Law Reporting in the Nineteenth and Twentieth Centuries* (New York, New York University School of Law, 1941), p. 1.

[50] London, Sweet & Maxwell. Monthly issues cumulated into annuals, 1947 to date. Five-year "Consolidation," 1947-51, London, Sweet & Maxwell, 1953.

periodicals." A *cumulative* table of cases for the current year is printed also in each of the monthly issues.

Index to legal literature. The final numbered paragraphs under each main topic list legal periodicals and books in point. Any case which has been the subject of an article or case comment is noted in the "Case Citator."

Subject index. Each volume contains a cumulative subject index to topics covered, continued by a similar cumulative table for the current year, in the monthly issues.

Digests of English Case Law. English case digests differ in only one essential respect from American digests: they also serve as citators, some of cases only, others for both statutes and cases. The same approach to case law through the table of cases, legal analysis, and fact situation is applicable for that as made through American digests. Although there have been numerous digests, those of current practical interest are limited to the following.

English and Empire Digest.[51] This has the most complete coverage of all English digests, though it does not quite live up to its subtitle: "A complete digest of every English case . . . with additional cases from the courts of Scotland, Ireland, the Empire of India, and the dominions beyond the seas." The digests are typical, with one important exception: Following the title of the case and parallel citations to all series reporting it, is an "annotation," which is a case citator, as seen in the specimen below.

---

346   DEEDS AND OTHER INSTRUMENTS.

Sect. 4.—Admission of extrinsic evidence: Sub-sect. 11, G. (a) & (b).]

1570. —— —— Enlarging scope of warranty.]— Where a written contract exists, parol evidence may be given to prove a verbal warranty respecting a matter on which the written contract is wholly silent. Such evidence is not admissible so far as to enlarge the scope of a warranty which is contained in the written contract.—LLOYD (EDWARD), LTD. *v.* STURGEON FALLS PULP CO., LTD. (1901), 85 L. T. 162.
*Annotations :—*Refd. Harrison v. Knowles & Foster, [1917] 2 K. B. 606. Mentd. *Re* Crighton v Law Car & General Insce. Corpn., [1910] 2 K. B. 738.

—— —— Sale of animals.]—*See* ANIMALS, Vol. II., p. 264, Nos. 422–424.

—— Bills of Exchange.]—*See* BILLS OF EXCHANGE, PROMISSORY NOTES & NEGOTIABLE INSTRUMENTS, Vol. VI., pp. 80–85, 88, 90, 284, Nos. 613, 614, 619, 621, 626, 628, 630, 632, 637, 649, 656, 1884.

(b) *Non-Contradictory of Contract.*

sion into effect.—VOUILLON *v.* STATES (1856), 25 L. J. Ch. 875 ; 27 L. T. O. S. 268 ; 2 Jur. N. S. 845.
*Annotation :—*Refd. North v. Loomes, [1919] 1 Ch. 378.

1575. —— Warranty.]—LLOYD (EDWARD), LTD. *v.* STURGEON FALLS PULP CO., LTD., No. 1570, *ante.*

1576. —— —— Condition of drainage in a house.] —Upon the execution of a lease of a dwelling-house, the landlord verbally warranted that the drains were in good condition. The lease contained covenants by the lessee to do the inside, & by the lessor to do the outside repairs, but was silent as to the then condition of the drains :—*Held :* the parol warranty was collateral to the lease & admissible in evidence, & the tenant was entitled to maintain an action for the breach of it.— DE LASSALLE *v.* GUILDFORD, [1901] 2 K. B. 215 ; 70 L. J. K. B. 533 ; 84 L. T. 549 ; 49 W. R. 467 ; 17 T. L. R. 384, C. A. ; *revsg.* S. C. *sub nom.* LASALLE *v.* GUILFORD, 17 T. L. R. 264.
*Annotations :—*Refd. Lloyd v. Sturgeon Falls Pulp Co. (1901), 85 L. T. 162 ; Milch v. Coburn (1910), 27 T. L. R. 170. Mentd. Heilbut, Symons v. Buckleton, [1913] A. C. 30.

Exhibit 75

A case is digested in only one place, but with cross-references to that place from other pertinent topics where the case is listed but not digested. Some cases, not digested at all, are listed and given case numbers and are annotated. *All digest paragraphs are numbered consecutively for each separate topic.* Each numbered paragraph above the line is tied to an identically numbered paragraph below the line when there is a dominion or colonial case in point. However, this number (as our "Deeds 1576") *is not a classification number covering a group of cases (as is the West Key-Number) but a serial number, uniquely identifying a single case.*

---

[51] London, Butterworth, 1919–1930. Supplemented to date.

Classification is done by an elaborate system of one hundred sixty-four main topics and many sub-topics.

Supplementation of the English and Empire Digest. "Volume 17, Deeds 1576," leads directly to the place in the cumulative supplement in which (a) later cases in point are digested; and (b) later annotations to the original case are given; and it is a reference point from *Halsbury's Laws of England* (as described *post*), where this and like cases are discussed. There are two supplements, one cumulative through 1940, and the other one an annual cumulative supplement covering 1941 to date.

As the cumulated material of a title becomes unwieldly, it is incorporated with that in the main volume, to form a recompiled volume. Then the old identification numbers of paragraphs are abandoned for new ones, with a cross-reference table from the old number to the new. Thus, in recompiled volume 30, old "Landlord and Tenant 76," is Replacement Volume "Landlord and Tenant 496." A further check is through the *Replacement Volume table of cases*, giving the current paragraph number of each case. Two other changes in the Replacement Volumes are (1) the abandonment of the horizontal dividing line between English and colonial cases (and the placing of the latter at a point following the English cases at the end of each classification sub-division); and (2) preceding the case digests in each sub-division there are cross-references to *Halsbury's Laws.*

How simply the supplements work is shown by the following supplementary material to the specimen printed above.

Cases 1534—1678a. ENGLISH AND EMPIRE DIGEST SUPPLEMENT.

1534. *Add. Annotation :*—Refd. Smith, Hogg *v.* Bamberger (1928), 97 L. J. K. B. 725.

1537. *Add. Annotation :*—Consd. Jacobs *v.* Batavia & General Plantations Trust, [1924] 2 Ch. 329.

1562. *Add. Annotation :*—Consd. Allen *v.* Royal Bank of Canada (1925), 41 T. L. R. 625.

1576. *Add. Annotations :*—Folld. Miller *v.* Cannon Hill Estates, Ltd., [1931] 2 K. B. 113. Refd. Collins *v.* Hopkins, [1923] 2 K. B. 617; Jameson *v.* Kinmell Bay Land Co.' (1931), 47 T. L. R. 410.

1576a. —— —— Condition of houses on building estate.]—A representation by builders in conversation with a prospective buyer, that all houses on the estate are of the best material & workmanship, may amount to a warranty collateral to a subsequent formal contract, for breach of which an action will lie.—MILLER *v.* CANNON HILL ESTATES, LTD., [1931] 2 K. B. 113; 100 L. J. K. B. 740; 144 L. T. 567; 75 Sol. Jo. 155.

Annotations :—Consd. Hoskins *v.* Woodham, [1938] 1 All E. R. 692. Refd. Perry *v.* Sharon, [1937] 4 All E. R. 390.

Exhibit 76

Since the supplement volume and paragraph numbers match those of the main volume, all the searcher has to do is to look in the supplement for volume 17, "Deeds 1576," and he will find later annotations to the main case, and later cases in point (1576 a in the example above).

English and Empire Digest Table of Cases. This table is the *most complete single listing of English cases.* References are to the volume and page of the

Digest where each case is digested. Each volume of the Digest also has its own table of cases, for that volume.

English and Empire Digest Descriptive-Word Index. The two-volume "Index" is a typical index of its kind, not, however, carried over into the supplements. In using it, it should be remembered that English terminology frequently differs from American. Examples are "Running down cases," for injuries to pedestrians on highways; "Winding up," for liquidation; and "Death duties," for inheritance tax.

English and Empire Digest Practice Manual. A separate, unnumbered, volume (continued in the supplements) contains "a complete digest of every live English case on pleading, practice and procedure." Supreme Court rules are printed verbatim, in the order of the *Digest* classification.

Mews' Digest . . . to the End of 1924.[52] This is a selective digest. In all respects but two it is a typical digest after the American fashion: it is a *case citator;* and, beginning with 1925, it is a *statute citator.* Cases are Shepardized by a table of "Cases Judicially Noticed." Statutes are Shepardized in a table by regnal years. Beginning in 1952 it has been supplied on order to subscribers to the *Law Reports,* in place of the discontinued annual *Law Reports Digest.*

All England Law Reports Digest. An annual cumulative "Index and Noter-Up" to all cases reported in this set from its beginning in 1936 is published. Since it is not a true digest, but an alphabetical subject index, it is best used in connection with the annual digest supplementing *Mews'.* Words and phrases are indexed, and there are tables of statutes and cases judicially considered.

Law Reports Digest of Cases and Statutes.[53] From their beginning in 1865, through 1951 when the digest was discontinued, the *Law Reports* were covered by a good digest. Through 1910 it digested only *Law Reports* and *Weekly Notes* cases, but from 1911 on it included cases from other reports. It was the first English digest to cover statutes. From the beginning it served both as a statute and case citator. The sixth cumulated unit (1931-1950) was the last such.

Current Law. The digest functions of this legal periodical are described at page 285.

Notes on the Forerunners to the Digest: Abridgments

The definitive bibliographical work on the early statutory and common-law abridgments and dictionaries is John D. Cowley's *Bibliography of Abridgments, Digests, Dictionaries and Indexes of English Law to the Year 1800.*[54] It forms an extra volume of the Selden Society *Publications;* and from it the authors have drawn freely while examining all the works described below. Those not having access to the various abridgments themselves will find them described by Percy H. Winfield in *The Chief Sources of English Legal History.*[55]

Abridgments. The forerunner of not only the digest but the legal encyclopedia and the dictionary was the "abridgment." The earliest of these were abridgments of statutes, beginning with the first published one, that of John Lettou and William Machlinia, about 1481. Similar abridgments continued on through the final attempt

---

[52] London, Sweet & Maxwell. 2d ed., 1925-28. 24 v.; continued by annual supplements, 1925-51. 27 v., and two ten-year supplements, from 1925-1935 (1936, 2v.) and from 1936-1945 (1949, 2v.)

[53] London, Incorporated Council of Law Reporting for England and Wales, 6 units covering 1865/1890; 1891/1900; 1901/1910; 1911/20; 1921/30; 1931/50.

[54] London, Quaritch, 1932.

[55] Cambridge, Harvard University Press, 1925.

at statute publication of this sort, Thomas Walter Williams' *Compendious Digest*.[56] Abridgments of cases were a somewhat later development (the first four were abridgments of *Year Book* cases), the earliest being published about 1488.

Nicholas Statham's *Abridgment of the Law* [57] was essentially a "briefing," as the law student would express it, of *Year Book* cases, under some two hundred fifty alphabetically arranged subject headings. It consisted of brief paragraphs stating the circumstances of the cases and the courts' holdings. Printed in "secretary" type to simulate manuscript, it was translated into English by Margaret C. Klingelsmith, Librarian of the University of Pennsylvania Law School, and published in an annotated edition in 1915. In the original it enjoyed but a short life, being quickly superseded by *Fitzherbert*.

Anthony Fitzherbert's *Graunde Abridgment*,[58] in three large folio volumes, which went through several editions, abridged some 14,039 cases, or four times as many as Statham. There were two hundred sixty main subject titles. Both Statham and Fitzherbert abridged many cases not found in the *Year Books*, but Fitzherbert was so far superior to Statham that it soon superseded it. In 1517 Rastell published an elaborate *Tabula* or index to Fitzherbert, which was necessary to make the work usable. Together, they had a major part in fixing the classification of the common law and form of its books.

Robert Brooke's *Graunde Abridgment*,[59] though conforming to Fitzherbert's general plan, divided its 20,717 cases into four hundred four titles, thus making it much easier to use. It is said that many of these cases were taken from treatises and other sources, and from cases decided after the later *Year Books*, as late as the reign of Henry VIII. Like its predecessors, it was printed in Law French. Copious marginal rubrics helped index the text material. There were several editions, including one in 1578, by Richard Bellewe, known as *Brooke's New Cases*, which was very popular.

Post-Year Book Abridgments. By this time, post-Year Book reports were being published in considerable volume, and the abridgment was losing some of is popularity. William Sheppard's *Epitome of All the Common and Statute Laws Now in Force* [60] was in English and included both statute and case law. His *Grand Abridgment* [61] was in English and of encyclopedic scope, though based upon the *Epitome*. It enjoyed little prestige. William Style's *Practical Register* [62] was originally a practice book, but when bought by John Lilly in 1710 it was changed in form, and in 1719 became known as Lilly's *Abridgment*.[63] It was an influential work. William Hughes' *The Grand Abridgment of the Law . . . from 1 Elizabeth to This Present Time* [64] was a supplement to *Brooke*, and the first abridgment of any worth to include seventeenth century cases. It was superseded by Henry Rolle's *Un Abridgment des Plusiers Cases et Resolutions del Common Ley*.[65] Though written in Anglo-Norman, it became very popular, partly because it was edited after Rolle's death by Sir Matthew Hale. It was in fact much better than any preceding work, and it is still cited for matters relating to legal history. For the first time, large topics were divided into sub-topics, for easier use. Furthermore, by also summarizing Parliamentary records and statutes, it became a digest of the whole law. It was translated into English by Knightly D'Anvers, as *A General Abridgment of the Common Law*,[66] as far as "Extinguishment." William Nelson's *Abridgment of the Common Law of England* [67] is a digest of cases subsequent to *Fitzherbert* and *Brooke*, but this work enjoyed small repute, being stigmatized as a poor copy of *Hughes*.

---

[56] London, H. M. Law Printers, for G. Kearsley. 2d ed., 1788.

[57] Printed without title-page, date or author's name; supposed to have been printed at Rouen, by Guillaume Le Talleur, for Richard Pynson.

[58] London, Wynkyn de Worde?, 1516.

[59] London, Richard Tottell, 1573, 2 v.

[60] London, Printed for W. Lee, *etc.*, 1656.

[61] London, Printed by E. Flesher, *etc.*, 1675. In 4 parts.

[62] First published under title: Regestum Practicale; or, The Practical Register. London, Charles Adams, 1657.

[63] London, In the Savoy, 1719. 2 v.

[64] London, H. Twyford, etc., 1660-1663. 3 v.

[65] London, A. Crooke, etc., 1668. 2 v.

[66] London, J. Walthoe, 1705-1737. 3 v.

[67] London, Gosling, 1725-1726. 3 v.

Charles Viner's *A General Abridgment of Law and Equity, Alphabetically Digested under Proper Titles, with Notes and References to the Whole* [68] may be considered to have brought the digest to full growth, the only substantial difference from the present day form being the lack of a descriptive-word index. In addition to the conventional arrangement and digest paragraphs, it had rather extensive explanatory notes to many of the cases, thus forming a connecting link to the modern legal encyclopedia. Though based on Rolle's *Abridgment*, it made use of other sources, and has some value as a case finder even today. The "index," issued in 1758, is almost wholly a table of cases, but also lists the digest topics.

Matthew Bacon's *A New Abridgment of the Law*,[69] originally published anonymously as "By a Gentleman of the Middle Temple," was as much a legal encyclopedia as a digest. Though the source of much of the material used is in dispute, there seems no doubt that Bacon took what he wanted from several treatises on the law, and that he made considerable use of compilations left by Lord Chief Baron Gilbert. Bacon's chief contribution was the merging of source material with exposition. He did not complete the work beyond the "Sheriff" title, the later work having been done by Joseph Sayer and Owen Ruffhead. There were several American editions, and the work is still of some value for its descriptions of common-law actions and writs.

John Comyn's *A Digest of the Laws of England*,[70] though primarily a digest, followed Bacon in that "the Author lays down Principles or Positions of Law and illustrates them by Instances, which he supports by Authorities . . ." Because of the high prestige of Comyn as a jurist, and of the excellence of his work, the *Digest* was frequently cited in the courts as authority. There were several American editions, the first enjoying especial prestige. The notation employing a main topic, subdivided under letters and numerals (as Evidence B.3 "When Proof is Necessary,") by which material in later supplements was keyed to the main work, foreshadowed the Key-Number, as employed in current American Digest System digests.

Charles Petersdorff's *A Practical and Elementary Abridgment*.[71] This is primarily a case finder, suited to the modern analytical method and resembles current digests. With mention of Petersdorff, the tracing of the development of the digest may properly be concluded, though there have been many other works of this type.

Encyclopedias of English Law. The purpose, organization and use of the English legal encyclopedia are so like those of its American counterpart that one familiar with one will have no difficulty with the other. With the exception of *Halsbury's*, all general encyclopedias of English law became casualties of the first or second World War.

Halsbury's Laws of England, being a complete restatement of the whole law of England.[72] **Organization.** The encyclopedia is put together and used exactly as are similar American works, but a great deal more attention is paid to statutes. Also, cases cited as authority are cross-referenced to the *English and Empire Digest*, as an aid to working up the whole law on a given case or point. For example, *Warren* v. *Murray* is cited as authority for a statement in *Halsbury's Laws*, with a footnote cross-reference to 32 Digest 453, 1194 (meaning volume 32, page 453, paragraph 1194), where that case is digested and "annotated" by refer-

---

[68] Aldershot in Hampshire, Pub. by the Author, 1742-53, with later additions to 1896, and an index volume in 1758.

[69] London, Printed by E. & R. Nutt & R. Gosling for H. Lintot. First ed., 1736-40 incomplete in 4 v. Later eds. in 5 v. (to 7th ed., in 1832).

[70] London, Printed by H. Woodfall, etc., for J. Knapton, etc. 1762-1767. 5 v. (through 5th ed. in 8 v., 1822).

[71] London, Baldwin, Cradock and Joy, 1825-30. 15 v., with five supplementary volumes to 1841; and 2d ed., 1861-1864, 6 v., with 1870 supplement.

[72] London, Butterworth. 3d ed., 1952 to date, 42 v. of which one volume is tables and two are consolidated index. First volume appeared Nov. 1952, there will be four each year thereafter.; 2d ed., 1931-1939, 37 v., with annual cumulative supplements; 1st ed., 1907-1917, 31 v.

ence to later cases. Conversely, if this case is first found in the *Digest*, it can easily be traced into the encyclopedia by means of the table of cases; or, in the *Replacement Volumes* of the *Digest*, and in the volumes of the third edition, through direct citations to *Halsbury's*.

Tables. Each volume contains a *table of statutes cited;* the tables do not cumulate in a single one for the entire set. Contrary to American encyclopedia practice, there is a *table of cases cited,* in each volume and cumulating into a "Consolidated Table of Cases" for the entire set. There is also a "General Index," which is a descriptive-word index in the usual form.

Supplementation. The supplementation scheme is similiar to that already described for the *English and Empire Digest.* An annual cumulative supplement, arranged by the same *volume, page,* and *paragraph* notations as those in the main work, keeps the encyclopedia up to date. As the volumes of the third edition appear, they will incorporate in their main text all corresponding supplementary material from the cumulative supplement up to the date of their compilation. The new volumes will of course be covered by the supplement. Tracing supplementary material is thus a simple matter of matching figures. For example, bringing up to date the discussion of the liability of a principal for misrepresentation of an agent, from the main volume to date, requires only the matching of Volume 1, page 289, paragraph 475, with the same numbers in the cumulative supplements. In the example at page 292 note how the supplement Shepardizes cases and statutes, in paragraphs 472 and 473.

Approach to the Law Through Halsbury's. The analytical approach (by means of the topical analysis or classification scheme) to the discussion of a point of law is exactly the same as in American encyclopedias. So is the fact (descriptive-word index) approach. The table of cases approach also is available, however, which is not true of American encyclopedias. If the general topic of law decided in a given case is known, as "Landlord and Tenant," "Companies," or "Deeds," a search in the case table in the volume covering that topic leads to the exact page in the encyclopedia where the case is used as authority for a statement in the text. Since at that point a cross-reference is made also to the exact topic and paragraph in the *English and Empire Digest* where that case and like cases are digested (information available of course through the *Digest* table of cases also), later cases in point may easily be found. Also, if it is desired to find a discussion of a statute, the tables of statutes in the respective volumes refer to the proper page. *Halsbury's Complete Statutes of England* also contains cross-references to *Halsbury's Laws.*

Encyclopaedia of forms and precedents other than court forms.[73] While this work is not, strictly speaking, a general legal encyclopedia, but an elaborate collection of forms, with "preliminary notes," many of the latter are so full that they take on the substance of encyclopedia treatment. For example, the "preliminary note" by W. J. Williams to volume 14, on the sale of land, occupies 355 pages and is a treatise on conveyancing. The complete work is made up of the preliminary notes, the illustrative forms (which are annotated to the statutes and cases), tables of statutes and cases cited (in each volume and not cumulated into a consolidated table for the set), and subject indexes in each volume (cumulated also into a "General Index" volume). This work is keyed to *Halsbury's Complete Statutes of England,* the *English and Empire Digest,* and the *All England Law Reports.*

Encyclopaedia of court forms and precedents in civil proceedings.[74]

---

[73] London, Butterworth. 3d ed., 1939-1950, 20 v., with cumulative supplements; 2d ed., 1926-1926, 20 v., with cumulative supplements; 1st ed., 1902-09. 17 v.

[74] London, Butterworth, 1937-1950. 16 v., with cumulative supps.

474. Where a ship is in charge of a duly qualified pilot, the owner or master is responsible for any loss or damage caused by the vessel by any fault of the navigation of the vessel. The fact that the pilotage is compulsory is not a defence to the owner or master (*o*), whether the pilotage is made compulsory by a public, general, or a local Act or by some other method (*p*).

SECT. 4.
Principal's Liability for Agent's Torts.

Compulsory pilotage.

SUB-SECT. 3.—*Misrepresentations.*

475. Where an agent is personally guilty of fraudulent misrepresentation (*q*) in the course of his employment, the principal is responsible as for any other tort, and an action of deceit lies against him (*r*).

Where agent knows representation to be false.

Where the agent makes a representation which he honestly believes to be true, but which the principal knows to be false, the principal is responsible (*s*). Where the principal makes through an agent a representation which the principal believes to be true, but which the agent knows to be false, the principal is also responsible (*t*). The principle of responsibility is that principal and agent are one, and if between them a misrepresentation is made it does not matter which of them made the representation or which of them possessed the guilty knowledge (*u*).

Where agent believes representation.

(*r*) *Barwick* v. *English Joint Stock Bank* (1867), L. R. 2 Exch. 259, *per* WILLES, J., at p. 265; 1 Digest 594, *2282*; *Lloyd* v. *Grace, Smith & Co.*, [1912] A. C. 716; 1 Digest 595, *2284*; *Byrne* v. *Rudd*, [1920] 2 I. R. 12. C. A. (Ir.).

(*s*) *Ludgater* v. *Love* (1881), 44 L. T. 694, C. A.; 1 Digest 589, *2254*.

(*t*) *Pearson* (*S.*) *& Son, Ltd.* v. *Dublin Corporation*, [1907] A. C. 351; 1 Digest 588, *2250*.

(*u*) *Ibid.*, *per* Lord LOREBURN at p. 354, and *per* Lord HALSBURY at p. 359. But in the converse case of a statement made to the agent and by him communicated to the principal, the knowledge of the agent of the untruth of the statement is not necessarily imputed to the principal (*Wells* v. *Smith*, [1914] 3 K. B. 722; 1 Digest 613, *2415*).

L.E.—I. U

---

472. **Trade Union.**
TEXT and NOTE (*e*).—Delete; repd. 1946.

473. **Local Authority.**
NOTE (*n*).—*Hillyer Case* as to nurses is not to be followed; **see** *Gold* v. *Essex C.C.*, Vol. XXII., Par. 737, notes, *post*.

474. *No change.*

475. **Where Agent Believes Representation.**
NOTE (*u*).—Applying the text, see also *London Cty. Freehold, etc., Ltd.* v. *Berkeley, etc., Co.*, [1936] 2 All E. R. 1039 (fraudulent information by one agent handed on to third party by innocent agent; principal liable); expld. in *Anglo-Scottish Beet Sugar Corp.* v. *Spalding U.D.C.*, [1937] 2 K. B. 607; [1937] 3 All E. R. 335.

Exhibit 77

Within its scope, the organization, tables and indexes of this work parallel those of the work described above. It is essentially an annotated collection of civil procedure forms, but the preliminary notes are brief treatises on the many aspects of English practice. For example, the description of English courts and their modes of doing business, in volume 1, is perhaps the most satisfactory for the American desiring only a quick resume. In addition to the case and statute tables and the subject index, there is a consolidated table of rules, with references to forms and annotations. The work is keyed to the same publications as the *Encyclopaedia* described above.

The annual practice.[75] This is an elaborate practice manual for English court rules, which are printed verbatim, heavily annotated to the statutes and cases. There are a table of cases, one of statutes, and a subject index.

Encyclopaedia of Scottish Legal Styles.[76] Except that for the most part it lacks the "preliminary notes," this collection of forms is the Scotch counterpart of the two encyclopedias of forms and precedents noted above. However, the annotations, when present at all, are meager. Included are both business and practice forms.

Notes

The development of the English legal encyclopedia, as an incident to that of the digest, is discussed at page 288. Among the English and Scotch legal encyclopedias now no longer published or discontinued temporarily, are the following: Green's *Encyclopaedia of Scots Law;*[77] *Encyclopaedia of the Laws of England;*[78] *The Scots Digest,*[79] which covered "Scots appeals in the House of Lords from 1707 and the cases decided in the Supreme Courts of Scotland," 1800 to 1947, when it was discontinued.

The Table of Cases Approach to English Case Law. What is said in Chapter 30 about the table of cases approach to the law applies for the most part to English materials also. The case tables listed herewith have all been noted in describing the sets of which they are a part.

From the earliest times to date:

English and Empire Digest. (The most complete table.)

Mews' Digest. (A selective table.)

Halsbury's Laws of England. (Cases cited as authority.)

Limited period coverage:

English Reports, Full Reprint (1378-1866.).

Revised Reports (1785-1866).

Law Reports Digest (1865-1951).

All England Law Reports (1936 to date).

Current Law (1947 to date).

Law review comments on cases:

Index to Legal Periodicals (1917 to date).

---

[75] London, Sweet & Maxwell, annually since 1881.

[76] Edinburgh, W. Green, 1935-1940. 10 v.

[77] Edinburgh, W. Green, 1896-1904, 14 v.; 1909-14, 12 v.; 1926-35, 16 v., with cumulative supplements (5th Cum. Supp., 1950-51, 2 v.)

[78] Under the editorship of of A. Wood Renton. London, Sweet & Maxwell, 1897-1903. 13 v.; 2d ed., 1906-18. 17 v., 3d ed., 1938-1940. 5 v., through "Eyre."

[79] 1700-1873: Edinburgh, W. Green, 1908-1812. 4 v.; 1873-1904: Edinburgh, W. Green, 1905. 2 v.; 1904-1930: Edinburgh, W. Green, 1915--931. 3 v.; Oct. 1930-Oct. 1947: Edinburgh, W. Green, 1930-1947. 11 v.

Law Quarterly Review (Volume 2, 1887, to date).
Current Law (1947 to date).

Words and Phrases. All current digests described above have as a feature "words and phrases judicially defined." These works, with their American counterparts, are discussed in Chapter 24, on dictionaries.

Citators for English Statutes and Cases. There is no tabular system in England for noting the legislative and judicial treatment of statutes and cases, similar to *Shepard's Citations*, but these are numerous means for doing this. All are incidental functions of some other work, such as a digest, encyclopedia or table of cases. In general they fall within three categories: (a) those, like the *English and Empire Digest,* in which the annotations are printed as part of a digest paragraph or syllabus; (b) those in the form of case and statute tables, in which the citation material follows the name of the case or statute, much in the manner of the *Decennial Digest* tables of cases; and (c) those in which the citation is part of a legal encyclopedia footnote. Citators for English cases and statutes are described at length by Miles O. Price in *Noting up British Statutes and Cases,* 40 Law Library Journal 251-70 (1947).

Citators listed below have been noted earlier in this chapter, in describing the works of which they are a part; they are coordinated here for convenience of reference.

1. Statute citators generally.
   Current Law and Current Law Statutes. (Perhaps the most satisfactory table, 1947 to date, for all aspects of statute citation)
   Halsbury's Statutes is good for all statutes in force.
2. Showing repeal, amendment, *etc.,* of statutes.
   Annotations to Acts [Amending] the Statutes Revised.
   Chronological Table of the Statutes (1235 to date).
   Public General Statutes (for current year tables only).
   Halsbury's Statutes of England (for statutes in force and for the current year).
3. Cases construing statutes.
   Digests (all but the *English and Empire Digest* have tables of statutes judicially construed; the *All England Law Reports Index* "notes up" ecclesiastical measures, Northern Ireland and Scotch statutes, and those of the dominions, dependencies, and mandated territories).
   Encyclopedias. (*Halsbury's Statutes* footnotes).
4. Statutory instruments citators. The tables in both the official and unofficial editions of these instruments are citators. Digests (except the *English and Empire*), have citator tables, covering various periods from 1891 to date.
5. Cases judicially considered. All digests described in this chapter serve as case citators. The *English and Empire does it through the* "annotations" to each digest paragraph (findable through the table of cases); the rest through alphabetical tables of "cases judiciallly noticed." *Current Law* is published most frequently of all case digests (five times a year).
6. English cases in Canadian courts. English cases cited in Canadian decisions are noted in the "Index of Cases Judicially Noticed in Canadian Reports," in the *Canadian Abridgment,* as described at page 298.

Statutory Forms. Forms based upon statutes are presented and discussed in the *Encyclopaedia of Forms and Precedents* and in *The Encyclopaedia of Forms and Precedents in Civil Proceedings.* In order to find a form corresponding to a given statute, the proper volume must be located (by subject matter), and the statute checked to see if there is a form.

I. Outline of Canadian Material.[80]

Canadian legal publications of all kinds so closely parallel their English and United States counterparts as to need little additional comment. Accordingly, only a bare outline of Canadian legislation, law reports, and search books of current interest is attempted here. The principal Canadian and provincial law reports from the beginning are listed in the Appendix II of this *Manual*. Because of the federal character of Canada's political organization — with both federal and provincial legislatures and courts — much the same problems are encountered as in the United States.

Federal Legislation. The United States lawyer in his search for the national legislation of Canada would probably begin with the *Revised Statutes of Canada, 1952.* He would then proceed to the *Statutes of Canada* (the session laws), and thence, if an administrative order were involved, to the *Statutory Orders and Regulations, Consolidation, 1949,* and its current supplementation through the quarterly consolidated indexes and tables of the *Consolidation* and the fortnightly issues of the *Canada Gazette,* Part II.

The Revised Statutes of Canada, 1952.[81] This work (cited as R. S. C. 1952) is a "consolidation," a verbatim reprint of public general statutes in force, including the Criminal Code, the British North America Acts, and certain other statutes and orders in council dealing with the admission to the Dominion, of provinces and territories. Many of the statutes printed herein are themselves consolidations of acts formerly in force, but reenacted as positive law, in the manner of *United States Code* reenactments of certain *Code* titles, repealing in the process the earlier statutes from which derived. In other words, the *R. S. C. 1952* has the status of the first edition of the *United States Revised Statutes,* and is not merely prima facie the law. The arrangement of material is by subject. The last volume is a subject index. Appendices list all prior acts consolidated in this edition, with parallel citations to the *R. S. C. 1952.*

Acts of the Parliament of Canada.[82] These session laws are typical of their kind. Part I prints "Public General Acts," and Part II "Local and Private Acts, Not Including Divorce Acts." Divorce acts are listed in a separate table however. Through 1946 they were printed in Part II, "Local and Private Acts," but since then they appear in a separate second volume. Tables in the session laws include an alphabetical list of "acts proclaimed," an index of public general acts for the session, and table of "Public Statutes 1907 [to date]" with amendments thereto, and their effect upon the current edition of the *Revised Statutes of Canada.*

Statutory orders and regulations, consolidation 1949.[83] This work is very similar to its English counterpart. *Acts* upon which orders are based are listed alphabetically by subject, beneath which are printed the *orders and regula-*

---

[80] The authors are indebted to Mr. George A. Johnston, of the Law Society of Upper Canada, Osgoode Hall, Toronto, for reading these notes in manuscript, and for numerous helpful comments. The responsibility for statements made and appraisals of Canadian publications and for errors is, however, entirely that of the authors. The viewpoint throughout is that of the United States, rather than the Canadian lawyer or law student.

[81] Ottawa, Queen's Printer, 1953. 6 v. (in process). There were other editions in 1886, 1906 and 1927. *See* Maurice Ollivier, *The Revised Statutes of Canada,* 26 Can. Bar. Rev. 7979 (1948).

[82] Ottawa, E. Cloutier, Queen's Printer, 1841 to date. The title varies; that on the spine currently is "Statutes of Canada."

[83] Ottawa, E. Cloutier, Queen's Printer, 1950. 5 v.

tions issued thereunder, as in force in 1949. There is a brief subject index, and there are quarterly consolidated indexes and tables. New orders and regulations are currently printed in Part II of the fortnightly official *Canada Gazette*. Not all orders are printed, but only those regarded by the editors as of sufficient public general interest to justify it.

Proclamations and orders in council passed under the authority of the War Measures Act R. S. C. (1927), chap. 206.[84] War orders were separately published in this series.

Criminal code. Official editions [85] appear at rather long intervals, but private annotated editions are issued frequently, and are the ones consulted by the legal profession. The *Criminal Code* also forms Chapter 36 of the *R. S. C. 1952*.

Provincial and Territorial Legislation. The provinces and territories have their own session laws, provincial ones usually being entitled "Statutes," and territorial ones ordinances. There are also the following compilations of current interest.

a. Alberta, 1906-1915, 1922, 1942. Ordinances of the North-West (now Northwest) Territories applying to Alberta through 1905 were separately published in 1907, 1911, and 1915.
b. British Columbia, 1871, 1888, 1897, 1911, 1924, 1936, 1948.
c. Manitoba, 1880, 1891, 1902, 1913, 1924, 1940.
   (Those for 1924 were "Consolidated Amendments.")
d. New Brunswick, 1877, 1903, 1907.
e. Newfoundland, 1872, 1892, 1916.
   Local and Private Acts, 1873.
f. Northwest Territories, 1888, 1898, 1931. The annual "Sessions Ordinances" were formerly designated as of the "North West Territories," but are now uniformly "Northwest." The ordinances are published irregularly in mimeographed form, but some are later printed, as those for 1948 and 1949.
g. Nova Scotia, 1873, 1884, 1900, 1923.
h. Ontario, 1877, 1887, 1897, 1914, 1927, 1937, 1950.
i. Prince Edward Island. There are no consolidations, but several indexes: *Crandall's Index to Statutes in Force 1845; Fraser's Index to Statutes 1869-1918; Fraser's Index to Statutes 1818-1928;* and *O'Donnell's Index to Statutes 1929-1944;*
j. Quebec, 1888, 1909, 1925, 1941.
k. Saskatchewan, 1909, 1920, 1930, 1940.
l. Yukon Territory, 1902, 1914.

Statutory Indexes. Although there have been numerous subject indexes to the federal legislation of Canada, few are of current value. For most practical purposes, the index to the *R. S. C. 1952*, as supplemented by the indexes to the *Statutes of Canada* to date, is used. A card index of both Dominion Local and Private Acts and Ontario Statutes has been kept since 1916 in the library of Osgoode Hall, in Toronto. A useful printed index covering all of Canada is the *Index to Dominion and Provincial Statutes from the Earliest Period down to 1916.*[86] This index may be said to have been brought down to date by the *R. S. C. 1952*. Two other indexes are the *Index to Eastern Provinces and Dominion Statute Amendments to 1926*, and *Index to Western Provinces and Dominion Statute Amendments to*

---

[84] Ottawa, E. Cloutier, 1940-September 1942. 8 v., continued by *Canadian War Orders and Regulations*. Ottawa, E. Cloutier, Oct. 12, 1942-1946. 13 v.
[85] *The Criminal Code and other Selected Statutes of Canada*. Ottawa, Queen's Printer.
[86] Montreal, Lovell, 1918.

1926.[87] These are not subject indexes in the usual manner, however, but rather alphabetical lists of statutes by short titles, with citations to the original and amending acts.

Index, local and private Acts, Dominion of Canada 1867-1941.[88] This index, compiled by Maurice Ollivier, is a subject index under very broad headings. An appendix contains a "Table of Public Statutes, 1907 to 1942"; and an alphabetical subject index to the *R. S. C. 192*7, showing amendments thereto; and certain other public acts and amendments.

Law Reports. All Canada is covered by conventional law reports, and there are in addition legal periodicals printing reports, either in full or abridged. All are listed in the appendix to this *Manual.* There is a present tendency to discontinue individual provincial reporters, in favor of combined reporters for several provinces, as in the National Reporter System in the United States. The following reports are current.

Covering all jurisdictions. The *Dominion Law Reports* are said to be "reports of all reportable Canadian cases from all the courts of Canada . . . and Canadian decisions in the Privy Council," from 1912 to date. Through volume 70 (1922), the volumes were numbered consecutively, but since then have been renumbered each year, and are cited in the manner of the English *Law Reports.* Thus, [1950] 3 D. L. R. 118; [1951] 1 D. L. R. 361.

Covering all criminal courts. *Canadian Criminal Reports Annotated* is a "series of reports of important decisions in criminal and quasi-criminal cases in Canada . . . of the Dominion and of the provinces thereof," since 1898. The annotations consist of statements of "cases judicially considered," and "statutes considered," —in other words, the annotations serve a citator function. There are also occasional brief annotations in the *A. L. R.* manner. *Criminal Reports (Canada)* is a "series of reports with annotations and practice notes on criminal cases arising in the courts of the various provinces of Canada," 1946 to date. There are notations of cases referred to in the opinions, and of statutes construed. About half the cases are, in addition, briefly annotated in the *A. L. R.* manner. Volume 14 (1952) contains a cumulative subject index of the first thirteen volumes.

Supreme Court of Canada. This court is covered both by the *Dominion Law Reports*, as noted above, and by *Canada Law Reports, Supreme Court of Canada.* The latter, dating from 1923, continues the *Reports of the Supreme Court of Canada* covering 1876 through 1922. Cases "referred to" are noted following the syllabi and are indexed in a separate table. Statutes construed are listed under "Statutes" in the index-digest of each volume.

Exchequer Court. *Canada Law Reports, Exchequer Court of Canada*, is a reporter dating from 1923, continuing the older *Reports of the Exchequer Court of Canada*, covering 1891 through 1922. The *Dominion Law Reports* series also covers this court.

Special-subject reports. Current special-subject reports include *Canadian Bankruptcy Reports Annotated*, 1920 to date; *Canadian Railway and Transport Cases*, 1902 to date; *Canadian Tax Cases Annotated*, 1938 to date; *Dominion Tax Cases*, 1920 to date; *Canada Tax Appeal Board Cases*, 1949 to date; *Canadian Patent Reporter*, 1941 to date; *Fox's Patent, Trade Mark, Design and Copyright Cases*,

---

[87] Toronto, Garrett, 1927.
[88] Ottawa, E. Cloutier, 1942.

1941 to date; *Insurance Law Reporter*, 1934 to date; *Canada Tax Cases*, 1917 to date; as well as several reports series published in connection with loose-leaf services.

Provincial courts. Reporters cover all provinces. The *Maritime Provinces Reports*, 1929 to date, cover reports of cases from the courts of New Brunswick, Nova Scotia, and Prince Edward Island, and, since 1947, Newfoundland. The *Western Weekly Reports* series (1911 to date), reports cases from Alberta, Saskatchewan, Manitoba and British Columbia. Both also report some Privy Council, Supreme Court of Canada and Exchequer Court of Canada cases. Individual provincial reports are also currently issued for the courts of Manitoba, Ontario, and Quebec. All provincial reporters, current and otherwise, are listed in the appendix to this *Manual*.

Digests. There have been many such, some covering all of Canada, others restricted in scope to Dominion cases or to those of individual provinces. The following are of current interest.

Canadian Abridgment system. The most complete digest, in jurisdictions and time covered, is a group composed of the *Canadian Abridgment*,[89] the *Canadian Abridgment Consolidation 1936-1945*[90] and the *Canadian Abridgment Annual*.[91] Through 1935 this system digests "decisions of the provincial and Dominion courts from the earliest times including appeals therefrom to the Privy Council, but excluding decisions based upon the Quebec Civil Code." Beginning with 1936 it includes Quebec Civil Code decisions.

This is a conventional digest except that it lacks a descriptive-word index. Cases are abridged at some length, rather than digested, for their point of chief legal interest, with cross-references to that abridgment from other points considered in the opinion. The *Consolidation* is keyed to the main work, by parenthetical references to *topic, chapter* and *section* of that work, thus enabling the searcher to find all cases in point in all units of the system, since this same cross-reference scheme is continued in the *Canadian Abridgment Annual*. Occasionally there are also cross-references to *Mews' Digest* (2d edition), where English cases in point may be found. Each volume has its own *table of cases*, and there is a consolidated table for the entire set through 1945. This is probably the most complete of all Canadian tables of cases. There is an index of *words and phrases* judicially defined. The *Index of Cases Judicially Noticed in Canadian Reports*, by Leonard G. Wrinch, is perhaps the most complete Canadian case citator, kept up to date by cumulative pocket supplements. This "Index" includes references to English as well as Canadian cases judicially noticed in Canadian courts. Beginning with the Consolidation (1936), there is also a *Table of Statutes Judicially Considered*, a statute citator. The *Canadian Abridgment Annual* supplements the *Abridgment* and the *Consolidation*.

All-Canada Digest system. From 1910 to date, this system purports to be "the key to every Canadian case and every current series of Canadian reports." It consists of the *All-Canada Digest 1910-1934*,[92] the *First Decennial Supplement*

---

[89] Toronto, Burroughs, 1935-1946. 35 v.
[90] Toronto, Burroughs, 1946-48. 4 v.
[91] Toronto, Burroughs, 1936-1951. 16 v. to date.
[92] Title varies. Toronto, Canada Law Book Co., 1935. 4 v.

1935-1944,[93] and the *Canadian Annual Digest.*[94] For the period covered, therefore, it traverses the same ground as the *Canadian Abridgment* system, though in considerably shorter compass. It is a conventional digest. The *Supplement* and the *Annual Digest* list *words and phrases, cases judicially noticed,* and Dominion and provincial statutes judicially considered.

Canadian Current Law.[95] This monthly digest of cases in all Canadian courts has the unusual feature of *digesting cases not yet reported.* Each issue has a cumulative table of cases for the current year and there is a subject index. Changes in federal legislation are noted, but since there is no tabular index to such statutes, material pertaining to them must be searched for through the subject index. Pertinent material from the *Canada Gazette* is noted, such as new statutory rules and orders. References are made under the respective subject headings to Canadian law review articles in point.

Dominion Report Service.[96] This is a *loose-leaf* digest, without English or United States counterpart in that form. In scope it is "a consolidation of the living law from the earliest times to date," purporting to digest "every reported Canadian Case . . . by the 11th of the month following" publication of the decision digested. In addition, it gives *advance* digests "of the important decisions of the highest courts . . ." Digests include a statement of facts, and a fairly long digest of the case, with cross-references to allied topics.

Digest paragraphs are arranged under sixteen main topics, under each of which there are several sub-topics, the whole numbered consecutively. Thus, "Commercial Law" 1-8; "Contracts" 9-14; "Criminal Law" 15-20, *etc.* Case digests are numbered consecutively under each topic and are filed thereunder by a paragraph number made up of the topic number, a hyphen, the case number, and a jurisdiction abbreviation. Thus, ¶ 1-482 Q denotes general commercial law, case number 482, from Quebec. Similar abbreviations indicate the Privy Council, Supreme or Exchequer Court of Canada, and the various other provincial courts.

Two or more units must be consulted for complete coverage: the "Consolidation" and one or more dated current volumes. In 1953 the "Consolidation" comprised five numbered volumes (including a now-discontinued "Current Volume" covering 1950-51), and a dated 1952-53 volume. There is a "periodic transfer of cases" from the current volumes to the "Consolidation," by which the latter is kept up to date.

Subject indexes. In the "Consolidation" there is a "Cumulative Topical Index" following each of the sixteen main topic tables, which is revised whenever material is transferred from the current volumes. In the current volumes there is a combined index for all topics, revised monthly.

Case tables. There are two case tables, a cumulative one covering the "Consolidation" and revised whenever transfers of new material are made to it; and one covering the current volumes and revised monthly. Together these tables purport to cover all Canadian reported cases "from the earliest times."

Finding lists, statutory citators. The current volumes contain "finding lists"

93 Toronto, Canada Law Book Co., 1946. 2 v.
94 Annual Supplement to the All-Canada Digest, 1910-1945 and Consolidated Supplement 1935-41. Toronto, Canada Law Book Co., 1935-51. In 11 v. to date.
95 Toronto, Burroughs, 1948-51. 4 v. to date.
96 Toronto, C. C. H. Canadian, Ltd.

of abbreviations employed in Canadian case reports; and "Code Citators," by which the Canadian Criminal Code, Bankruptcy Act, Winding-Up Act, and Companies Act, and the Quebec Civil, Civil Procedure and Municipal Codes may be Shepardized for cases construing them. As of 1953, these citators were only partially available in the "Consolidation."

Supreme Court of Canada cases. There are two index-digests of Supreme Court cases. *Index to Supreme Court* Cases (1923-1950)[97] is a one-volume digest of "all decisions of the Supreme Court of Canada, published in the *Canada Law Reports* from 1923 to 1950, inclusive, with relevant annotations regarding appeals to the Privy Council." There is also an index of statutes and codes cited or discussed, a citator. The *Index to Supreme Court of Canada Reports, 1876-1950*[98] is a two-volume index digest. It contains a consolidated table of cases and a subject index of Supreme Court of Canada cases for the whole period.

Chitty's Abridgment . . . Canadian Criminal Case Law.[99] This is a digest of *Canadian Criminal Cases*. Both the main volume and the 1925-1949 supplement contain a "Criminal Code Citator."

Repertoire General de Jurisprudence Canadienne.[100] This is a conventional digest of Federal, Privy Council, and Quebec cases through 1937, continued to date by the *Annuaire de Jurisprudence du Québec*.[101]

Index Judiciaire 1900-1947.[102] As its title indicates, this is a subject index to Quebec cases, rather than a digest.

Digest of Cases . . . in the Exchequer Court of Canada.[103] This group of digests covers the Exchequer Court from its beginning.

Encyclopedias. There is no exact Canadian counterpart of *Halsbury's Laws of England, American Jurisprudence*, and *Corpus Juris Secundum*, but there are current works which approach the conventional legal encyclopedia.

Canadian Encyclopedic Digest. There are two editions of this work (commonly referred to as C. E. D.): The *Canadian Encyclopedic Digest (Ontario)*, now in its second edition[104] and the *Canadian Encyclopedic Digest (Western)*[105]. The Ontario edition, covering cases from all *Ontario* and *Maritime Provinces* courts as well as from the Privy Council and Supreme Court of Canada applicable to this area, is an encyclopedia of the law as reflected in these cases. Federal law is treated when applicable. The digest, second edition, has a separate *statute citator* volume covering Ontario statutes judicially considered. There is *no table of cases* nor *table of words and phrases*, reliance for these being placed upon *Canadian Abridgment* tables. There is a loose-leaf cumulative annual supplement, keeping up to date the main work and the statute citator, as well as setting out the Ontario Rental regulations. The Western edition covers all West-

---

[97] Montreal, Wilson et Lafleur, 1951.
[98] By John Southall and Gerald D. Sanagan. Toronto, Butterworth, 1952.
[99] An Abridgment of the Canadian Criminal Case Law, 1892-1925. Toronto, Canada Law Book Co., 1925, with supplement 1925-30.
[100] Montreal, Wilson & Lafleur, 1914-15. 4 v.; Suppl. 1913-25. 2 v.; Supp. 1926-Jan. 1937. 3 v.
[101] Montreal, Wilson & Lafleur, 1937-1951. In 14 v. to date.
[102] Montreal, Denis, 1948. 2 v.
[103] From the beginning to 1922, Toronto, Carswell, 1924; 1922-1946, compiled by Redmond Quain, 1948, with supplement to 1950.
[104] Toronto, Carswell. 2d ed. begun in 1950 and projected in approximately 18 volumes.
[105] Calgary, Burroughs, 1919-1925. 7 v., with supplements to 1951. A second edition is announced to begin at the close of 1953.

ern Canada decisions and those of the Supreme Court of Canada and of the Privy Council applicable to the area.

Dominion Law Annotations Revised.[106] This is not, strictly speaking, an encyclopedia, but it performs much the same function for the material covered by the annotations. It is a rewriting of the annotations originally printed in the *Dominion Law Reports*, incorporating changes necessitated by later decisions and statutes. Since the annotations are arranged in classified order, the work resembles a somewhat fragmentary legal encyclopedia.

Citators. There are numerous Canadian citators, most of which are tables of statutes or cases "judicially considered." The following list includes those of current interest.

Federal statutes. The *Canadian Statute and Criminal Code Citator*, with its predecessor, *Tremeear's Canada Statute Citator*,[107] covers Dominion statutes from 1906 to date. It is now published annually. Amendments, additions, and repeals are noted, including those pertaining to the *R. S. C. 1927* (and, presumably the *R. S. C. 1952* in time), and cases construing federal legislation are cited. The nature of the action taken by the construing court, however, is not indicated. The Criminal Code is also covered in the "Code Citator" in *Chitty's Abridgment of Canadian Criminal Case Law, 1925-1949*, and in those citators noted below which purport to cover all Canadian statutes, both Dominion and provincial. Tables in the *Revised Statutes of Canada 1952* list consolidated acts contained in that revision, and their subsequent legislative history through 1952. The annual *Statutes of Canada* note all amendments of Dominion legislation from 1907 to date, by subject.

Federal and provincial statutes. The "Statute Citator" in the *All-Canada Digest 1935-1944* consolidation notes both statutory changes and cases construing Dominion and provincial statutes. This is continued in the *Canadian Annual Digest*. The *Canadian Abridgment Consolidation 1936-1945* and the *Canadian Abridgment Annual* have tables of statutes judicially considered, but these do not show statutory changes. Statutory changes for the current year are noted, by subject, in the monthly *Canadian Current Law*. As construed by the Supreme Court, foreign, Imperial, Dominion and provincial statutes are conveniently covered by the *Index to Supreme Court Cases* (1923-1950) "Index of Statutes and Codes Cited or Discussed."

Quebec statutes are covered by the "Table de Reference aux Codes" in the *Annuaire de Jurisprudence de Quebec*. *Ontario Statutes Judicially Considered* and the *Ontario Statute Citator 1950* cover Ontario statutes. Both are kept up to date by loose-leaf supplements. *Ontario Statutes Judicially Considered* briefly notes the effect of amendments; the *Ontario Statute Citator* sets out the amendments in full. The table in the *Canadian Encyclopedia Digest (Ontario)* second edition, notes Ontario statutes judicially considered. References to regulations under statutes are given in the *Canadian Statute Citator*, *Ontario Statutes Judicially Considered*, and the *Ontario Statute Citator*. *Citations of the Statutes of Alberta and Saskatchewan, 1886-1924*[108] covers those provinces.

---

[106] *Annotations Consolidated from Dominion Law Reports, 1911-1928.* Toronto, Canada Law Book Co., 1928-51. 3 v.

[107] Toronto, Burroughs, 1929; with 2 supplements, 1941 and 1952.

[108] Compiled by A. L. McLean, Toronto, Carswell, 1924.

Case citators. The most complete case citator is in the "Index of Cases Judicially Noticed in Canadian Reports . . . from the Earliest Times to [date]," by Leonard G. Wrinch, in the *Canadian Abridgment*, as kept up to date by pocket supplements. *English cases* judicially noticed are also included. Cases are listed by title, with citations to cases questioning, overruling, referring to, *etc.* The *All-Canada Digest 1935-1944* supplement also has such a table, continued in the *Canadian Annual Digest*. Both citators cover Dominion and provincial courts.

Loose-leaf services as citators. Particularly for statutes, the loose-leaf services for Canada are useful citators.

How to Shepardize a Canadian statute. The citators to be consulted are noted above. In these citators, the statutes are commonly listed by the "short title" of the original act or its consolidation—as "County Courts Act," "Dentistry Act," and the like. Exceptions are codes, as the Canadian Criminal Code and the Quebec Civil Code, which are cited by code and section. Having found the required statute and section in the citator, the searcher there sees that amendments, repeals, *etc.*, are cited first under each section, followed by citations to cases construing the section. There is no indication of what action the construing court took, so the cases must each be examined.

A feature of Canadian statute citators not found in those in the United States is the notation of statutory rules and orders promulgated under the authority of the statutes listed, and cases interpreting them. To find the interpretation of the *order* it is first necessary to look under the *basic act* under the authority of which the order was issued. Where a statute is involved in a decision, it is noted in the digests in *Canadian Current Law*, findable under the subject matter, as "Debtor and Creditor," "Real Property," *etc.*, thus bringing the citation down to within a month or two. Ontario statute citators have loose-leaf supplements.

How to Shepardize a Canadian case. Case citators are described above. The approach is through the case title, as *Smith* v. *Jones,* rather than through jurisdiction and law reporter, as 5 D. L. R. 78. Thus, any Canadian case may be Shepardized through the "Table of Cases Judicially Noticed," in the *Canadian Abridgment* system by consulting the bound volume and its pocket supplement. Other citators are of somewhat smaller scope as to jurisdictions or period covered.

While Canadian digests note other cases referred to in the opinions digested, the digest paragraph is not itself a citator *for the case digested*. It thus differs from the *English and Empire Digest*, where the "annotations" following the digest paragraph Shepardized the digested case. A separate case table is thus necessary for Shepardizing a Canadian case. With the exception noted below, citator material is not supplemented oftener than annually. The exception is of the reversing or affirming of a decision by a court on appeal. Such action may be found through the cumulative table of cases in the monthly *Canadian Current Law*. For example, *Canadian Indemnity Co.* v. *Andrews & George Co.*, a case then as yet unreported, was noted in the November 1952 issue of this monthly as reversing the decision of the lower court as reported in 4 W. W. R. (N. S.) 37. In other words, action corresponding to the *Shepard* "history of the case" is available monthly, but that relating to the "treatment of the case"—whether referred to, applied, followed, *etc.*, by another case—is supplemented only annually.

Loose-Leaf Services. Tax and regulatory loose-leaf services perform the same functions in Canada, and in the same manner, as those for the United States, described in Chapter 26. The principal publishers of such services are C. C. H. Canadian Limited, and Richard DeBoo Limited. The subject matter covered includes Dominion and provincial taxation, succession duties, companies, corporations, emergency control regulations, insurance, and labor. As in the United States, in connection with some of the services, the cases reported are later bound separately to form special-subject reports series.

Treatises. The following, selected from many perhaps equally good, are regardless of publication date, recommended to the United States lawyer.

PRACTICE BOOKS.

Audette, Louis A., *The Practice of the Exchequer Court of Canada.* 2d ed. Ottawa, Copeland-Chatterson-Crain, 1909.

Brierley, James C., *The Code of Civil Procedure of the Province of Quebec.* Montreal, Wilson, 1947.

Cameron, Edward R., *The Supreme Court of Canada Practice and Rules.* 3d ed. Toronto, Carswell, 1924.

Chitty, R. M. W., *The Ontario Annual Practice,* 1952. Toronto, Cartwright, 1952.

Holmested, George S., *Holmested and Langton on the Judicature Act of Ontario.* 5th ed., by Donald A. MacRae. Toronto, Carswell, 1940.

Snow's Criminal Code of Canada. 5th ed. Toronto, Carswell, 1939, with 1952 Supp.

Tremeear, William J., *Tremeear's Annotated Criminal Code.* 5th ed., by Alan B. Harvey. Toronto, Carswell, 1944 (with loose-leaf supplement).

Annual Practice, an English manual, is much used by Canadian lawyers. London, Sweet & Maxwell, 1881 to date.

SUBSTANTIVE BOOKS.

The following were recommended by a Canadian lawyer as being twenty-five books for first purchase:

Anger, William H., *A Digest of the Mercantile Law of Canada.* 16th ed., by Frederick R. Hume. Toronto, Cartwright, 1952.

Bradford, Samuel H. & Greenberg, Jacob H., *A Consolidation of the Canadian Bankruptcy Act, Annotated.* 3d ed. Toronto, Burroughs, 1951.

Crysler, Alfred C., *Labour Relations and Precedents in Canada.* Toronto, Carswell, 1949.

Falconbridge, John D., *Law of Banks and Banking.* 5th ed., Toronto, Canada Law Book Co., 1935.

———*The Law of Mortgages of Land.* 3d ed. Toronto, Canada Law Book Co., 1942.

Fox, Harold G., *Canadian Law and Practice Relating to Letters Patent for Inventions.* 3d ed. Toronto, Carswell, 1948. 2 v.

———*The Canadian Law of Copyright.* Toronto, Carswell, 1944.

Fraser, William K., *Canadian Company Forms.* 3d ed. Toronto, Carswell, 1947.

Hall, Frank C., *Digest of Automobile Accident Cases.* 2d ed. Toronto, Carswell, 1948.

Laverty, Francis J., *Insurance Law of Canada.* Toronto, Carswell, 1936.

Macaulay, Robert W. & H. M. Bruce, *Handbook on Canadian Mechanics' Liens.* Toronto, Carswell, 1951.

Maclaren, John J., *Bills, Notes and Cheques.* 6th ed., by Frederick Read. Toronto, Carswell, 1940.

Manning, Harold E., *Assessment and Rating.* 3d ed. Toronto, Cartwright, 1951.

Marriott, Alfred S., *Practice in Mortgage Acts in Ontario.* Toronto, Carswell, 1938.

Masten, Cornelius A. & William K. Fraser, *Company Law of Canada.* 4th ed. Toronto, Carswell, 1941.

O'Brien, Arthur H., *Conveyancing Law and Forms.* 8th ed. Toronto, Carswell, 1942.

O'Connor, Austin, *Highway Traffic Act.* 5th ed. Toronto, Carswell, 1951.

Power, W. K., *Law and Practice Relating to Divorce and Other Matrimonial Causes in Canada.* Calgary, Burroughs, 1948.

Quigg, Samuel, *Law Relating to Succession Duties in Canada.* 2d ed. Toronto, Carswell, 1937.

Robson, Hugh A. & Jabez B. Hugg, *Municipal Manual.* Toronto, Carswell, 1920.

Sheard, Terence, *Canadian Forms of Wills.* Toronto, Carswell, 1950.

Stikeman, Harry H., *Income Tax Act, Annotated.* Toronto, DeBoo, 1927-1948 consolidated. Annual, 1949 to date.

Wegenast, Franklin W., *Law of Canadian Companies.* Toronto, Burroughs, 1931.

Widdifield, Charles H., *Executors' Accounts.* 4th ed., by Thomas H. Barton. Toronto, Carswell, 1944.

Williams, Esten K., *Notes on Canadian Law of Landlord and Tenant,* 2d ed. Toronto, Carswell, 1934.

Legal Directories. In Canada these are called Law Lists. They perform the same function as in the United States, including the printing of abridgments of provincial laws. Both listed below are annual publications.

Legal Diary and Directory of Legal Correspondents in Canada. (On cover: *Carswell's Legal Diary*) Toronto, Carswell, 1900 to date.

Canadian Law List. Toronto, Cartwright, 1883? to date.

Legal Periodicals. These include the scholarly *Canadian Bar Review,* and the *University of Toronto Law Journal;* practitioners' professional journals like *Chitty's Law Journal;* those which serve a law reporter function, as the Quebec *Revue Legale;* bar association publications; and student law school reviews. They are currently indexed in *Canadian Current Law,* and those in the English language (and also the Revue du Barreau de la Province de Quebec) in the *Index to Legal Periodicals.*

Lists of Current Canadian Publications. *Chitty's Law Journal,* beginning with the issue for January 1953 (volume 3, number 1) has a list of "Canadian Legal Publications" of all kinds, designed to be complete. Publishers and prices are given. The list in the January issue of each year will consolidate all the monthly lists for the preceding year. The Carswell Company Limited, of Toronto, has for many years issued a monthly list of law publications of the entire British community of nations and dependencies, giving prices and publishers.

CHAPTER 30

THE TABLE OF CASES APPROACH TO THE LAW

A. Scope.

Case tables are found in almost every publication which either prints, discusses, or cites reported cases. This of course is because a case in point is usually the ultimate objective of the lawyer's search. One case in point leads, through a digest, to other cases in point; or to a detailed analysis of that and similar cases in a treatise, law review, or annotations. Two important exceptions to the prevalence of case tables are general legal encyclopedias and annotated statutes, which commonly lack them. However, even here there are exceptions, particularly among special-subject encyclopedias. There are several categories of case tables, as described below.

B. Plaintiff-Defendant Tables.

This is the usual type, as found in law reports, treatises, case books, legal periodical indexes, loose-leaf services, *etc.* Except in digest case tables, the only information commonly given in such tables is the page where the listed case is printed or referred to in the work containing the table. On that page, one may expect to find complete parallel citations to all standard reports of the case. In a digest case table the information commonly given includes parallel citations, the digest classification topics, and sections under which the digest of the case is classified. In many digests it also includes certain citator information—*i.e.* whether the case, within the period of time covered by the table, has been affirmed, reversed, *etc.* An example is the following, from the *Fifth Decennial Digest table of cases.* Sometimes a digest table of cases fails to record the *A. L. R.* citation of a case. This happens when the case was not printed in *A. L. R.* until after the digest table of cases was compiled. A surer parallel citation guide is in *Shepard's Citations.*

Not all published reports of decisions print the courts' opinions. Where there

```
Kalb v. Feuerstein 228 Wis 525, 279
NW 687, reh den 228 Wis 525, 280
NW 726, appeal dism 59 SCt 107,
305 US 566, 83 LEd 356, foll in
231 Wis 185, 285 NW 431, rev 60
SCt 343, 308 US 433, 84 LEd 370,
conformed to 234 Wis 507, 291 N
W ·840—Mtg 529(10).
```

Exhibit 78

is no opinion, there is nothing to digest and thus no reason for listing the case in a digest case table. However, most digests include names of even memorandum cases which are not digested. The *Decennial Digests'* policy is to list such a case when (as usually is true) the memorandum decisions is connected with another case which is digested.

C. Defendant-Plaintiff Tables.

A comparatively recent development is the separate defendant-plaintiff table of cases. It frequently supplies less information than its counterpart plaintiff-defendant table, perhaps simply referring to the plaintiff-defendant table entry, which must then be searched for full information. A convenient variant in some digests is the cross-reference in the plaintiff-defendant table itself. Thus, Ernest, McComb v., [referring to *McComb v. Ernest*].

D. Popular Name Case Tables.

Frequently the only available reference to case is by some such title as the *Hot-Oil Case*, *Gravel-Pit Case*, or *Goat Case*. *Shepard's Citations Table of Cases Cited by Popular Names, Federal and State* is a very convenient annual cumulative pamphlet which gives parallel citations to all standard report series for such cases. Beginning with the *Second Decennial Digest*, all *Decennials* have had such a table, in the table of cases volume, and many regional and local digests have it, though in some it takes the form of a cross-reference in the regular plaintiff-defendant table. Thus: "*Hot-Oil Case*. See *Panama Refining Co. v. Ryan*."

E. Official-to-Reporter and Reporter-to-Official Citation Tables.

Where only the official or the Reporter citation is known, parallel citations may be found in the appropriate *Shepard's Citations*, as described at pages 130-133. Similarly, there is an official-citation table for the *Trinity Series* and one for *A. L. R.*, as there described. The transfer tables in the National Reporter System *Blue Book* and *Blue and White Books* are described in Chapter 16.

F. Patents and Trade-Marks.

Tables of adjudicated patents and trade-marks are found under "Patents" and "Trade-Marks," respectively, in the *Federal Digest* proper, and in the *Federal Supplement, Federal Reporter*, and *Supreme Court Reporter*. For example: "Patent No. 1,403,046. Box-supporting shelf, claim 3, held not infringed. D.C.N.Y., 4 F. 2d 726." *Shepard's Federal Citations* has a similar table, as do the digests of the *United States Patents Quarterly*.

Since digest tables differ but little from one another in form and content, only the following will be described, as they are typical in everything but extent of coverage.

G. American Digest System Case Tables.

By far the most complete tables of American cases are those in the units of this system, purporting as they do, to list every case digested (or connected with a case which is digested) in report series covered, from 1658 to date. There is one unavoidable drawback to the use of these tables: if the case date is unknown, it may be necessary to search in all units. All cases, 1658 to 1906 (covering the *Century* and *First Decennial Digest*), are listed in volumes 21 to 25 of the *First Decennial Digest*. From 1906 (the digest period splits in the middle of the year ending with the digit 6), there is a table for each succeeding *Decennial Digest*, comprising the last volume of the unit; this is followed by a table in each monthly pamphlet and bound volume of the supplementing *General Digest* which cumulates into the next *Decennial*, so that a complete search may involve all the units above described. Citation information given in the table of cases may include notice of affirmance, reversal, certiorari grant or refusal, dismissal, rehearing, and several other court actions on the listed case, within the decennium. Beginning with the table of cases volume of the *Second Decennial Digest*, each *Decennial* has also had a table of cases by popular name, for cases digested in that decennium.

Special Case Tables for New Digest Topics. From time to time the development of the law, because of sociological pressure, scientific discovery, or statutory revision, requires either a new digest topic or the radical expansion and revision of an existing one. In such cases, an entirely new system of Key-Numbers usually is required, superseding those in preceding *Decennial* units, and some simple means of reference from the old to the new is necessary. For some topics this has been provided by special tables of cases for the new digest topic and bound with it, embracing all case names from earlier digest topics now included in the new. How this works is described in detail on page 112.

H. Legal Periodical Tables of Cases.

Since 1917 (as printed in the 1918 annual cumulation), cases commented upon in law reviews have been listed in the *Index to Legal Periodicals*. The same has been done for case comments, by the *Legal Periodical Digest* since 1928; and by individual periodicals, in both their annual and cumulative indexes. Some of these latter go far back beyond 1917.

I. Loose-Leaf Services.

Most loose-leaf services have tables of cases, plainly tabbed for easy finding.

J. Utility of Tables of Cases in the Search for Law.

Case tables have many uses. Their most obvious one is to supply the page number in the volume or advance sheet of law reports, case book, periodical, treatise, or annotation containing the table, where a particular case is printed or commented upon. Another simple but valuable service is to provide parallel case citations. In a digest table this is done directly, as part of the case listing. Tables lacking the volume and page citation but referring to the place where the case is printed or commented upon, of course lead, by this one additional step, to the full citation, which is usually given on the page where the case is printed or referred to in the work served by the table. Perhaps the most valuable service rendered is as a guide to the digest topic and section number of like cases in point. (If the *Reporter* report is available, of course this is given in the headnote, from which the digest is compiled. The searcher, in some way, has found a case or the name of a case in point, and wants to read other like cases. The digest table of cases supplies the topics and section numbers under which these are digested).

Student and practitioner alike profit by the tables of cases leading to the discussion of a case in a treatise, legal periodical or an annotation. The torts student, for example, not clear as to the point in *Pokora* v. *Wabash R. R.* in his case book, uses the table of cases in Prosser's *Torts* in order to learn what that author has to say about it; the trusts student, similarly disturbed about the more recent case of *Matter of Halpern*—decided too recently to be discussed in a treatise—uses the *Index to Legal Periodicals* or the *Legal Periodical Digest* table to find out what half a dozen law review authors think of it. Similarly, the practitioner, interested in the problem of the liability of a person supplying information upon which another was wrongfully arrested, and learning of *Gogue* v. *MacDonald*, a California case, searches the *A. L. R.* table of cases, to see if it was annotated. Or he may be interested in arguments of counsel in a case recently heard before the Supreme Court of the United States; perhaps the proceedings were reported in the *United States Law Week* and can be found through its table of cases. Or he may search the table of cases in a labor loose-leaf service for all arbitration cases involving the *International Harvester Company*. The possibilities are endless.

The table of cases method, however, is not available for most legal encyclopedias and annotated statutes, though cross-references are made from *A. L. R.* cases to *American Jurisprudence*.

K. Alphabeting in Case Tables.

Not the least of the lawyer's difficulties in using tables of cases is making certain that he has not missed a case by failure to search in the right place in the table. The variations in case names themselves are endless and complicated, and the alphabeting practice in case tables lacks uniformity and consistency. Some frequently applied principles are described below, but the searcher must always be prepared to find that his particular case table does not apply to them, and thus exercise his ingenuity in imagining other forms under which the case he is searching for may have been indexed. The material below follows the presentation order, though not the content, of the very full "Explantory Notes" at pages v and vi of the table of cases volume of the *A. L. R. Permanent Digest*.

Corporations, Associations, and Partnerships. Alphabeting is by the full corporate or partnership name, as *American Brake Shoe Co.* v. *Bowles*. However, where such a name begins with the name of a person, as *E. I. Du Pont de Nemours & Co.*, there are three variant practices. (1) Index exactly as written above. (2) Place the initials at the end of the surname, and index by the surname. Thus, *Du Pont de Nemours (E. I. & Co)*. (3) Cross-reference from (1) above: *E. I. Du Pont de Nemours & Co.* See *Du Pont de Nemours (E. I.) & Co.* Sometimes duplicate entries are made, using both forms. Note that here as elsewhere in alphabeting when initials precede a name, filing is done as though the initials were part of the succeeding word. Thus, *E. I. Du Pont de Nemours & Co.* alphabets as though the first word were EIDUPONT, so that in the case table it follows *Eidson* v. *State* but precedes *Eierman* v. *Eierman.*

Banks. There is still less uniformity in the treatment of names beginning with such titles as "Bank," "National Bank," "Savings Bank," *etc.*, followed by a geographical name—as *Bank of Baton Rouge* v. *Hendrix.* One practice is to file exactly as written, with no cross-reference from Baton Rouge. The other, diametrically opposite, is to file under the geographical name, as *Baton Rouge Bank* v. *Hendrix*, with no cross-refernce from "Bank." Prudence would dictate a search under both forms, if the first results in failure. Where, however, a geographical name is absent in the title, as *Bank of Commerce* v. *Brown*, the name is filed as written, with no cross-reference from "Commerce." The same is true of *Bank of Commerce of Oregon City* v. *Ryan*, though here again, prudence would indicate a search, if necessary, under the geographical name before giving up.

Railroads, Street Railways, Insurance Companies. The common practice here is to give the full name, always spelling out the first word of the title but perhaps abbreviating or using initials for all or part of the remaining title components. Thus, *Chicago, R. I. & P. R. Co.* v. *Sampson; New York L. Ins. Co.* v. *Alexander.*

Lodges, Societies, Orders. Case tables are utterly inconsistent in alphabeting titles beginning with such expressions as "Grand Lodge," "Sovereign Camp," *etc.* One group files the title as written, as *Sovereign Camp, W. O. W.* v. *Serten*, with no cross-reference from "Woodmen of the World." The other, on the contrary, files the title as *Woodmen of the World* v. *Serten*, ignoring the preliminary expression, but cross-referencing from it; "Sovereign Camp: See particular order, society, *etc.*"

Cities, Counties, States, Territories. The same inconsistency is found here, the one school filing as written and the other by the geographical word. Thus, "City of New Orleans" in one table is filed under "City"; in the other as "New Orleans." The first seems somewhat preferable, as avoiding possible confusion between a public corporation and a private one beginning with a geographical word. For example, there are, respectively, a New York city, county, state, and innumerable business entities beginning with the word "New York." In public corporation case names, however, most case tables are fairly liberal with cross-references from one form to the other.

Cross-References and Reversed Tables. Most case tables are fairly liberal with cross-references or reversed tables. Thus, *Katz* v. *Wiedman* is listed also as *Wiedman, Katz* v. in some tables. Others, however, as the *Decennials*, do not give reversed entries for case names. Still others, as noted, have separate defendant-plaintiff tables.

Ex Rel., Use Of. These cases are variously treated, but are usually cross-referenced from the relator's name; that is, *State of New York ex rel. Zagayko* v. *Hartley* is filed under State of New York, but cross-referenced from *Zagayko* v. *Hartley.* *Use of* cases are similary treated. Titles beginning with "State . . . ex rel." are filed at the end of other "State" cases, and thereunder are alphabeted by relator. Thus, *State* v. *Zolantikis* precedes *State ex rel. Adams* v. *Lee.* However, in some tables, *ex rel.* titles other than *State ex rel.* ignore the *ex rel.* in filing Thus, *Commonwealth ex rel. Jones* v. *Smith* would ignore the "ex rel. Jones" and file as *Commonwealth* v. *Smith.* Here, again, the careful searcher will try all forms if necessary.

Ampersand (&). This is alphabeted as "and" in most tables, but in some, titles containing it are filed after all others bearing the words preceding it. Thus, *Borden's Will, Re* precedes *Borden & Co.* in such tables.

Abbreviations. These are treated as though spelled out: Ft-Fort; St.-Saint; Mt.-Mount. M', Mc, and Mac, all mean "Mac" and are usually so alphabeted, but some tables follow the telephone directory practice and file by the letters with a cross-reference from "Mac."

Ex Parte, In Re, Matter Of, Estate Of. All are filed under the party's name, with cross-reference from the prefix. Thus: Ex parte *Lottenville,* is filed as *Lottenville,* Ex parte; Matter of *Chamberlain,* as *Chamberlain,* Matter of.

Numerals. These are filed as though spelled out: thus, 1690 Longfellow Ave. Corp. (one thousand six hundred *n*inety) precedes 1676 Claremont Ave. Corp. (one thousand six hundred *s*eventy-six). An exception is made for numbers (principally dates) which are commonly expressed in another manner than the above. Thus, the following dates are alphabeted under "nineteen" instead of "one thousand nine hundred," because that is the way people habitually express a date: 1942 Chevrolet Motors Co., 19 Rector St. Corp., 1935 East 71st St. Corp. Note that everything following the "19" is spelled out, making 1942 file before 1935. This is confusing, as illustrated by the table below, but that is the way many case tables are constructed.

> 1690 Longfellow Ave. Corp.
> 1676 Claremont Ave. Corp.
> 1942 Chevrolet Motors Co.
> 19 Rector St. Corp.
> 1935 East 71st St. Corp.

The Apostrophe: 's. The practice with 's varies. One rule regards the 's as an integral part of a company or corporate name, and files "Borden's Farm Products" after all plain "Borden" titles; but ignores the 's in "Borden's Will" or "Borden's Estate," which are filed as though the 's were not there. The other practice is to file as though the 's were part of the name under all circumstances, as follows: "Borden," "Borden's Estate," "Borden's Farm Products," "Borden's Will." Here, again, the searcher may have to try all forms.

Filing by "Letter" or by "Word." Most case tables file according to the *exact succession of letters,* regardless of any ensuing word division, which is called "filing by letters." "Filing by words," recognizing the word division, is more customary in scholarly writing. The resulting differences in filing order are illustrated below.

By Letters.	*By Words*
N. E. Wentworth Co.	N. E. Wentworth Co.
Newhart Mfg. Co.	New Haven.
New Haven.	New York.
Newman.	Newhart Mfg. Co.
New York.	Newman.

"De," "Du," "Van," "Von." Most case tables ignore the usual scholarly practice when alphabeting names preceded by the above prefixes, and treat the prefix as an integral part of the name in all cases. Thus, "De Groot," "Dennis," "Devlin," "De Witt," "Van Cott," "Vancouver," "Van de Carr," in that order.

Chapter 31

COORDINATING THE TECHNIQUES

A. Need for Coordination.

Up to this point, this *Manual* has described the fundamental materials of the law, such as statutes and law reports; the various types of indexes to them, such as digests, encyclopedias, *etc.*; and the means of appraising the present status of any authority found by citators. In so doing, it has set down the techniques of use and described the tabular approach to each of these sources and indexes, so that individual tasks such as finding specific laws and law reports and their evaluation should be simplified.

However, finding the law may be compared to playing golf: seldom does a player make a hole in one, or cover the course by the use of a single club, no matter how expert he is with that club. Similarly, most law-finding problems require the use of more than one source and index to the law. The skillful and imaginative interplay of the various means of finding the law is the mark of the successful searcher. Since the various techniques involved in finding and evaluating specific legislation and cases have been described in the preceding chapters, particularly in Chapters 6, 8, 9, and 16, a knowledge of them is assumed here. The aim of this chapter, accordingly, is to suggest some of the many possibilities of combining techniques in the solution of typical problems.

B. Approaches to the Law.

These have been described, particularly in connection with digests and encyclopedias, but will be reviewed briefly here. The approaches commonly thought of are the table of cases, fact (descriptive-word index), the topical or analytical, and the words and phrases. Three others of the utmost importance should be mentioned, however: the approaches through statutes, annotated reports, and the National Reporter System Key-Number.

It must be strongly emphasized that seldom is one approach a sufficient check upon either the scope or completeness of a search. Editors, compilers, and authors of digests, annotations, encyclopedias, treatises, and legal periodical articles are fallible and make errors of omission and commission; the differing points of views

311

of compilers of search books may turn up for the searcher cases in one work ignored in another. Within reason, several or all varieties of case finders or commentaries should be checked for each problem.

A Case in Point as the Chief Aim of Most Searches. Even when a statute is involved, the lawyer usually searches for a case in point interpreting that statute, and uses that as his rallying point. All else is likely to be incidental. Therefore, once the case is found, some of the other approaches to the law may usually be abandoned or modified. There is no point, except as a check, in traversing in another way ground already covered. One case in point inevitably leads to others, through digests and annotations.

Statutes through the Case Approach. A statute search usually carries over into the case law, because the lawyer wants to know how the courts have construed legislation applicable to his problem. A statute must be evaluated through judicial construction, which may be arrived at through annotated statutes or citators, but also through digests and other case indexes. It must be remembered that digests do not afford a direct lead to the construction of specific statutes (with a few exceptions, such as the "Table of Statutes Construed" in the regional *Reporter* digests since about 1940, and similar tables in the *Digest of the Supreme Court Reports*). However, cases construing statutes are digested by subject matter in the usual way; whenever a statute is involved in a decision, it is cited in a headnote paragraph. This often leads to statutes, the applicability of which was unsuspected by the searcher, and so yields a better result than a statute search alone. Needless to say, the avenue is by way of the conventional digest approaches.

Table of Cases Approach. This, as described in Chapter 30 and in connection with law reports and their indexes and search books, is perhaps the most nearly universal of all approaches. Having the name of a case in point, the searcher can find all others. Nearly every law book which prints, digests, analyzes, or describes cases has a table of cases covered.

The most comprehensive case tables are those in the American Digest System, as described at page 163, leading through the *Century Edition*, the *Decennials*, *General Digest*, and National Reporter System advance sheets to all cases decided from 1658 to within a few weeks of the publication of the latest case table, for all jurisdictions. Other digests of lesser scope have similar tables. Treatises, specialized encyclopedias, and law reports have case tables, as does the *Index to Legal Periodicals beginning* with 1917. Most law reviews have published separate cumulative indexes, with tables of cases commented upon. Most loose-leaf services likewise have them.

Statutes, general encyclopedias, and A. L. I. *Restatements* usually lack case tables, though state annotations to the various *Restatements* have them. English material, including legal encyclopedias and annotated statutes, commonly has case tables.

Key-Number Approach. Where the table of cases or some other approach has led to a *Reporter* case, the Key-Number found in the pertinent headnote leads directly to the applicable sections in the Key-Number digests, with a few exceptions noted at page 167, where the classification has been changed. Care must be exercised in this approach, however, that additional applicable Key-Numbers, findable through other approaches, are not overlooked.

Annotated Reports System Approach. If the subject matter of the search has been annotated, as it frequently has, the searcher may go immediately to the annotation. The publishers, through their editorial staff, aim to examine the digests and all the cases, as well as treatises, encyclopedias, and other sources and reference books, so as to bring together on one place the cases in which this point has been adjudicated. Since the editor carefully analyzes and criticizes the cases, and comments on the various rules and variations extracted from them, a great deal of preliminary work has thus been done already for the searcher.

Fact Approach. This, the descriptive-word index approach, is usually thought of in connection with digests, and is described in detail under that topic in Chapter 19. Its efficacy is by no means confined to digests, however. Every statutory index affords a fact approach, including those indexes in the Federal Register System and its state counterparts, for administrative regulations.

Annotated statutes combine a fact approach to the statutes directly through their general subject indexes, with a similar approach to the cases interpreting many of the individual sections of the statutes. This is done in connection with any statute section which contains a great many case digest paragraphs, through a special subject index to the cases construing that particular section. That is, the mass of digest paragraphs for that section is arranged according to a more or less detailed subject classification, and then indexed by catchword references to such minute subtopics as "change of basis," "death," "exhaustion," "severance damages," *etc*. An example, from the *United States Code Annotated* is shown on page 314.

In case law, the approach is just as applicable to encyclopedias, treatises, loose-leaf services, legal periodicals, and A. L. I. *Restatements* as it is to digests.

Analytical or Topic Approach. Here, too, one thinks of digests, and the approach is therefore described most fully in Chapter 19. Statutory compilations, however, also make full use of the device, and the analysis preceding the text of the various titles and sub-titles saves much time in arriving at the applicable section. It is less used in treatises, but encyclopedias employ it in the same manner as digests. As noted in Chapter 26, it is perhaps the speediest approach to loose-leaf services.

Words and Phrases Approach. Nearly all digests and encyclopedias use this device. The West *Words and Phrases*, described with other examples in Chapter 24, is a *dictionary* of common words and legal words of art, as judicially defined; but in most other works *Words and Phrases* is an alphabetical *index* to the page where the listed word is defined. Usually the words are listed in separate "words and phrases" tables, but in some books the words defined are listed in their regular alphabetical order in the general index to the work or in the main text. In most digests the table fills one or more separate volumes, usually at the beginning or end of the set, so as to be easily found.

C. Application of the Techniques: Order of Search.

Although the mode of search is a matter of common sense, the following outline is suggested as a checklist of factors to bear in mind. There are many others but these will cover most situations. The order given is logical, but often the circumstances of the search will dictate a different attack and the omission of some

———◇———

VII. SUBD (f). OBJECTIONS TO CLAIMS

Subdivision Index

---

251. Law governing

Where claim on note payable in Missouri was filed in bankruptcy court in Arkansas, statute of limitations governing note was the statute of Arkansas and not Missouri. In re Mays, D.C.Ark.1941, 38 F.Supp. 958, affirmed, 1942, 125 F.2d 693, 48 Am.Bankr.Rep.N.S. 716.

255. Evidence—Admissibility

In proceeding under this section, where claimant has attempted to establish by evidence the allegations of his proof of claim, he cannot be permitted to use such allegations to supply a deficiency in his evidence. In re Annin & Co., C.C.A.N.Y. 1938, 95 F.2d 381, 36 Am.Bankr.Rep.N.S. 381.

The general rule of law that a party can recover only on the cause of action alleged in his pleading, applies to claims presented in bankruptcy, and a claimant who has filed a statement of his demand under oath, as required under this title, cannot sustain it by evidence of an indebtedness arising in a different manner from that stated. In re Lansaw, D.C.Mo. 1902, 118 F. 365, 9 Am.Bankr.Rep. 167. See, also, Orr v. Park, Ga.1910, 183 F. 683, 106 C.C.A. 33, 25 Am.Bankr.Rep. 544.

The transcript of testimony taken during ancillary hearing before special master, pursuant to order of court before whom bankruptcy petition was filed, for purpose of ascertaining facts necessary to proper administration of bankrupt's estate with respect to claim against it was admissible in evidence at hearing on bankruptcy trustee's objection to allowance of claim. Hutson v. Coffman, C.C.A. Cal.1938, 100 F.2d 640.

Exhibit 79

of the steps. As the searcher grows in skill and experience, he will learn when it is feasible to eliminate certain steps; and to manipulate his materials so as to attack his problem in the most effective manner. All the steps in the outline herewith are necessary at one time or another; seldom are all necessary in the solution of a single problem.

Outline of Search

1. *Analysis of the Problem.* Separation into aspects involved, including parties, procedure, and substantive issues.
2. *Preliminary Review of the Subject Matter.* Where needed for orientation, through treatises, encyclopedias, *Restatements*, and the like.
3. *Search of Statutes and Administrative Regulations Involved.*
    a. Federal statutes.
    b. Home-state statutes.
    c. Other-state statutes: collections and indexes across state lines; persuasiveness of cases construing.
    d. Administrative regulations implementing statutes.
    e. Finding legislative intent where helpful.
4. *Search for Cases in Point.*
    a. Reading cases and orders cited by annotated statutes, treatises, *etc.*
    b. Finding additional cases through digests.
        i. Through Key-Numbers in *Reporter* cases read.
        ii. Tables of cases approach.
        iii. Analytical or topical approach.
        iv. Fact approach.
        v. Words and phrases approach.
    c. Search of the Annotated Reports System. (If desired this may precede "b," above.)
    d. As cited in administrative rulings.
5. *Search of Encyclopedias and Treatises.* To refresh the memory, to supply additional cases, and for subject matter analysis.
6. *Search of Legal Periodicals.* For a more detailed analysis of theoretical and controversial points, and for discussion of individual cases.
7. *Search of Loose-Leaf Services.* To coordinate all material in tax and regulatory fields.
8. *Search of Miscellaneous Material.* Study of A. L. I. *Restatements*, form books, government publications, *etc.*
9. *Completing the Search.* Making certain that the latest editions and supplements have been consulted, including the digest portions of National Reporter System advance sheets covering later cases than the *General Digest.*
10. *Appraising the Authorities Found.* Shepardizing statutes and cases.

Resourcefulness. Since few extended legal searches progress smoothly, and flank attacks must be made where the frontal fails, a most important weapon of the searcher is resourcefulness. In the use of indexes he must remember that perhaps the indexer had a different point of view than he has, and cast about for other words or terms under which his fact situation might have been listed. The same is true of the analytical approach. Often what seems to the searcher a perfectly obvious classification for his point of law did not seem so at all to the digester, with his much broader view of the whole topic. Seldom can the searcher be certain that, even when he has found cases in point through either the fact or analytical approach, other cases just as applicable are not lurking under other entries or classifications. It does not pay to be either too easily discouraged or satisfied.

Other Factors to be Considered. It must always be borne in mind that the digest paragraph, text exposition, or annotation, is not the law, and that the cases should always be read. In this connection, note should be taken of the parties, how the case arose, pertinent statutes involved, *etc.* In case work there is much chaff and little wheat.

Care and Accuracy. The searcher should provide himself with some sort of checklist or reminder of things to look out for in his search, to ensure completeness and accuracy. Prominent in that list should be an admonition to *copy citations and other data accurately*. More time has probably been lost by lawyers and students in inaccurate and incomplete copying of various data during searches than in any other way. That cryptic notation of yours which saves a few seconds and is so crystal clear to you when made will probably be incomprehensible at your desk later on when you wish to incorporate it in your brief or memorandum of law. Write it down as though you expected somebody else to have to decipher it.

By the same token, try as hard as you can to copy with reasonable fullness. That may sound like unnecessary advice, but it is very far indeed from being so. A check on accuracy is to copy down a complete statutory or case citation, including all parallel references. Thus, *Wypyski* v. *Keller*, 599 N. Y. 301, 201 N. E. 2d 518, 275 N. Y. S. 93, 201 A. L. R. 18 (1970), instead of only 599 N. Y. 301. The more checks in the way of parallel references you have, the more chances there are that one or more of them will be correct. Care should be taken that all necessary units—including supplements, advance sheets, *etc.*—of a publication consulted are covered. In this connection, the careful searcher will find it helpful to *preserve a precise record of each publication and part thereof covered in a search*, as a measure of the completeness of the search and check against having to search the same publication twice.

D. Illustrative Problem Involving Statutes.

Your client, executor of the estate of a deceased partner, wishes to know his rights and duties, the partnership agreement having a clause providing for the carrying on of the business by the remaining partners after the death or retirement of one of them. There is also the matter of the tax treatment of the partnership income. There are thus involved the right, duties, and personal liabilities of the executor, as well as the rights of the deceased partner's estate, of the partners, and of the federal Government. No question of procedure is involved.

Preliminary Review of the Subject Matter. Through an elementary treatise or legal encyclopedia you learn that in the United States, partnership, income taxation, and the liabilities of an executor are largely regulated by statute. You therefore begin by examining the statutes.

Search of Applicable Federal and Home-State Statutes.

Federal: Partnership income tax aspect. This is a matter of both federal and state jurisdiction, but for the purpose of this problem only the federal aspect is considered. The index to the *United States Code* leads to Title 26, Sections 181-190, where a reading of the law shows the tax of partners to be covered by Section 182. The annotations in *U. S. C. A.* and *F. C. A.* digest several promising cases, which are read in full, including *Guaranty Trust Co. of N. Y.* v. *Commissioner*, 303 U. S. 493, 58 S. Ct. 673, 82 L. Ed. 975 (1938).

Continuing the partnership business. The subject index of the annotated statutes of your state leads to the applicable section covering your problem, but the absence of case annotations shows that your courts have never construed these sections.

Executor's personal liabilities aspect. The search here might begin with the annotated statutes of your state, with a "local" book on executors and administrators, or with a loose-leaf service on wills, trusts, and estates. As for the other aspects of the problem, the techniques are the same throughout and will not be further commented upon here.

Search of the Statutes and Decisions of other States. You have failed to find cases construing the partnership act of your state applicable to the death of a partner, but you wonder if other states have similar statutes which their courts have construed; and if so, whether their decisions have any weight as precedent in your state. From your reading of Chapter 9 of this *Manual* you remember that there are numerous collections and indexes of statutes across state lines, and that one of them is the *Uniform Laws Annotated*. From volume 7, "Partnership," you learn that your state statute is copied from the Uniform Partnership Act.

Authority of decisions of other states. Before spending any more time on out-of-state precedents, you search under "Statutes" in *Am. Jur.* and *C. J.*, where you learn of a general rule of law to the effect that where a question of statutory construction is one of first impression in a state, the courts will consider the construction of like statutes in other states. You therefore return to the *U. L. A.*, where the index discloses that either § 41 or § 42 might be construed as covering the continuation of your partnership after the death of a partner. You observe that in searching the statutes (as well as digests and other search books), it is advisable to examine the material of more than one possibly applicable provision— that in practice your problems are rarely pinpointed.

The annotations turn up several cases reasonably in point, in as many different states. One, *Froess* v. *Froess*, 289 Pa. 69, 137 Atl. 124 (1927), seems especially promising, and you read it.

Search of other Indexes. Your experience has taught you that since there is so much overlapping of subject matter in the law, there may be applicable cases not digested under the exact statutory section which in your opinion logically covers the matter. Also, some points raised by inconsistent cases are not clear, so you decide to search other indexes to the law.

Search of the Digests.

Key-number approach. If you read the *Froess* and *Guaranty Trust* cases in the *Atlantic Reporter* and *Supreme Court Reporter*, the headnotes there give you the pertinent Key-Numbers, and you proceed directly to any West digest employing those numbers. An exception is when the Key-Number classification has been expanded or a new title has been added to the classification since the publication of your case, so that the Key-Number as found in the headnote no longer applies. Thus, in the American Digest System, the original Internal Revenue ⬥ 7(3) of the *Guaranty Trust* case has been changed to Internal Revenue ⬥ 834, following the great expansion of that title after the adoption of the *Internal Revenue Code* in 1938. How to find the current classification in such cases is described on page 167.

Table of cases approach. This is described generally in Chapter 30. No matter what digest is consulted, the table of cases will note all classification numbers under which a case is digested. In the American Digest System, with its many units, knowing the date of the decision is a time-saving lead to the proper table of cases unit.

Fact and analytical approaches. The problem here presents no especial difficulties. Note that in the income tax aspect, the Key-Number found (Internal

Revenue ☞ 834) turns up a case in point, *Heiner* v. *Mellon*, decided, not under the *Internal Revenue Code* § 182, but under a section of the Revenue Act of 1918 not in the *Code* at all. This shows that even in searching statutes, the digest subject analysis often leads to cases in point involving unsuspected applicable statutes or sections.

Words and phrases approach. This problem does not seem to hinge in any way upon the judicial definition of a word or term.

Search of the Annotated Reports. Hoping that your task has been partly performed for you by industrious annotators, you turn to the *A. L. R. Digests* and *Word Index to Annotations*. Here, by methods described in Chapter 15, you find several annotations on partnership taxation. One in particular, "Construction of § 42 of the Uniform Partnership Act as to the rights of parties where business is continued after a partner retires or dies," in 2 A. L. R. 2d 1084, seems exactly in point. In it, the cases are analyzed from various aspects, including the effect of consent to continuation of the business (§ 2 of the annotation), and the effect of particular agreements (§ 4). The *A. L. R. 2d Blue Book* lists later cases in point on those precise sections.

Search of Encyclopedias and Treatises. No special problems are posed here.

Search of Legal Periodicals. After reading the cases and treatises found through the above means, you are still not clear in your mind as to some aspects of your client's problem. In particular, *Guaranty Trust* and *Heiner* seem inconsistent and you are not certain of the doctrine applied. Your reading of Chapter 22 has told you that the forum of discussion of the finer points of legal theory is the legal periodical. A search of the *Index to Legal Periodicals* brings to light Weyher and Flom, *Death and Income Taxes—The Demise of a Partner*, 52 Col. L. Rev. 695 (1952), in which these and other cases in point are analyzed and the issues discussed at length. As is common in law review articles, this one in its footnotes gives a fairly extensive review of the earlier literature. The *Index to Legal Periodicals* also lists by name cases in point, as discussed in law review case comments.

Search of Loose-Leaf Services. Because your problem involves both tax and estate matters, loose-leaf services, as described in Chapter 26, are perhaps the most obvious search points.

Completing the Search for Authorities.

Appraising the Value of Authorities Found: **Shepardize all cases and statutes, searching all supplements to date.**

E. Illustrative Problem Involving Administrative Law.

Your client has purchased a dairy farm and dairy which until the purchase had distributed general milk products in the New York area. Desiring to add a line of frozen desserts, your client asks whether this new activity affects his legal status. You consider only the federal aspect.

Analysis. This problem involves the production, processing, and marketing of milk and milk products in a given area. Among other possible issues is whether this marketing activity is regulated by federal legislation.

Search of Statutes and Administrative Regulations Involved.

Federal statutes. As this is a matter of "public general interest," you examine the index of the *U. S. C.*, where, under "Milk and Cream," you note several entries which lead you to 7 U. S. C. § 608c. The text of § 608c(5) suggests that your client, because of his new activity, may be subject to regulation as a "handler" of milk products. Annotations in *U. S. C. A.* and *F. C. A.* turn up cases close to the point, but you are still doubtful as to whether a processor of his own milk into frozen desserts is a "handler" under the statute. Perhaps the regulations of the Government regulatory agency are more explicit, but how do you find them?

Administrative regulations. Through the *United States Government Organization Manual (see* Chapter 17) you learn that the regulatory body here is the Products and Marketing Administration (PMA) of the Department of Agriculture, so you know that the regulations will be in the *Code of Federal Regulations*, Title 7, "Agriculture." This title, however, fills hundreds of pages, so that you shorten the search through the subject index and the various tables of contents of the title. These lead to § 927.4(5) (regulating the New York area), covering frozen desserts. A quicker lead is through the parallel table from the *U. S. C.* to the *C. F. R.* (found in Title 2 of the *C. F. R.*, as described in Chapter 17 of this *Manual*), where the entry under 7 U. S. C. § 608c cites the regulations issued under the authority of the statute. Checking the *C. F. R.* pocket supplement, the "List of Sections Affected," and the *Federal Register* "Codification Guide" (as described in Chapter 17), you find that the regulation section has been renumbered and somewhat revised, so that in "Shepardizing" for later cases, as shown below, this must be borne in mind.

***Search of Agency and Judicial Rulings.* "Agriculture decisions."** This series of reports prints both agency and court rulings construing both the above statute and regulations issued under it. Volume 9 (1950), for example, has an elaborate cumlative citator, by both statute and regulation construed, and by subject, covering all these decisions. The agency rulings give both the agency interpretation of "handler," and citations to Congressional hearings, reports, *etc.*, in support, as to legislative intent. These citators, however, are found in but few reports of administrative rulings, and construction of regulations must ordinarily be sought indirectly through digests, unless a tax or regulatory loose-leaf service covers the subject matter.

Remainder of the Search. This follows the outline given above. Note, however, that since this case involves the judicial definition of what constitutes a milk "handler," the *words and phrases approach*, as described in Chapter 24, is available. Although the statute here and the court decisions construing it are Shepardizable in the usual manner, the regulations are not directly covered by *Shepard*.

F. Illustrative Problem Involving Treaty—State Law Conflict.

A, B, and *C,* brothers residing and doing business in your state, were killed in an accident, leaving wills bequeathing their property situated therein to their mother, a national and resident of Denmark. *A* was an American citizen; *B* a national of Denmark; and *C* a national of Belovia, a newly constituted political entity. Your state inheritance tax imposes a discriminatory tax on personal property passing to alien non-resident beneficiaries. Your client, the mother, resists this tax.

Analysis of the Problem. Consider only the state inheritance tax aspect. (a) The property passing is physically within the state, but is to be removed to Denmark. (b) *A* was an American citizen, but *B, C,* and their mother were aliens. (c) There was a mother-son relationship between the parties. (d) Is the state law valid, and does it affect all parties alike?

Preliminary Review of the Subject Matter. Treatises and legal encyclopedias agree that the state where the decedent's property is situated may discriminate in inheritance taxation against alien beneficiaries, but there is a caveat to the effect that the right has been impaired to a considerable extent by treaty. Through encyclopedias, and annotations on the relation of treaty to state and federal law in 4 A. L. R. 1377, 1382; and in 134 A. L. R. 882, 885, you learn that where there is a conflict between a treaty and a state constitution or statute, whether enacted prior or subsequently to the making of the treaty, the treaty controls.

Search of the Statutes Involved. **Federal statutes.** Although this is a state tax matter, the treaty caveat sends you in search of an applicable treaty between the United States and Denmark. Through means described in Chapter 4 of this *Manual* (Treaties), you find and read the Treaty of April 26, 1826, with Denmark, on friendship, commerce, and consular rights, 8 Stat. 340, T. S. 65, 3 Miller 239, I Malloy 373. Article 7 of that treaty, concerning inheritance taxation and the removal of property from one country by resident nationals of the other country, seems repugnant to your state inheritance tax statute, but you seek judicial construction.

In practice, at this time, you would now skip several steps in the search outline, and Shepardize this treaty to see if the United States Supreme Court had ever construed it. How this is done for treaties is shown in Chapter 4. You discover that the Court has construed this section three times, and you read the cases. Two of them, *Nielsen* v. *Johnson,* 279 U. S. 47, 49 S. Ct. 223, 73 L. Ed. 607 (1929); and *Petersen* v. *Iowa,* 245 U. S. 170, 38 S. Ct. 109, 62 L. Ed. 225 (1917), both involving Iowa statutes, seem to be in point. Since treaties are uncodified, this one is not covered by the annotations in *U. S. C. A.,* but the special volume of "Annotations to Uncodified Laws and Treaties," of the *F. C. A.,* digests cases in point, including the two above.

Search of home-state statutes. A search of the annotated statutes reveals that this inheritance tax provision has not been construed by your state courts. You therefore seek a like statute in another state, which has been construed.

Search of other-state statutes in point. These may be found in at least four ways. Since this problem involves state inheritance taxation, the speediest is through loose-leaf services covering the topic. Here the uniform classification scheme for state statutes (*see* page 323) leads to the appropriate section for each state having inheritance taxes discriminating against aliens. In the services, all the law—federal and state, statutory and case—relative to this situation, is collected in one place.

Second, treatises frequently cite the pertinent statutory provisions. Third, and hardest, the statutes of the various states may be checked. Fourth, as in our problem, if a treaty is involved, the cases found through Shepardizing it cite the state statutes construed.

An Iowa statute is cited in the two cases above, but one is § 1467 of the 1907 *Iowa Code,* and the other includes § § 7311, 7313, and 7315 of the 1927 *Iowa Code,* making it necessary to translate them into the current citation, so as to compare all with your state statute. Transferring into the present citation form may be done through the *Iowa Code Annotated* subject index, and through the elaborate parallel transfer tables in volume 58, from earlier to corresponding current statute forms. Both of these methods lead to § § 450.10 and 450.11 of the present *Iowa Code*, the latter section being exactly in point. Since the substance of the earlier *Code* provisions is set forth in the opinions in the two cases above, it is unnecessary to go to the 1907 and 1927 *Codes* for a direct comparison of the three texts.

Reading the section, you find it like that of your home state (in which the mother-son relationship is immaterial), and you scan the *Iowa Code Annotated* annotations, which digest both state and federal decisions. In addition, a "History and Source of the Law" note cites all earlier forms of the sections, affording another check as to the correspondence of the 1907 and 1927 sections to the present form. Furthermore, *Iowa Law Review* comments in point are listed (as they are in *Shepard's Iowa Citations*). The transfer table technique enables you to convert the 1907 and 1927 *Code* sections into the later forms as found in the current *Shepard's Iowa Citations* (*see* page 73) where *all cases* construing *all forms* of the statute are listed.

Search for other Cases in Point.

Reading cases found. From the digest paragraphs, the *Petersen* and *Nielsen* cases seem irreconcilable. A careful reading of the full reports, however, indicates that Section 7 of the treaty seems to protect the *estate of the transferor* who was a national of the country to which the property is to be transferred (Denmark here), rather than the *transferee* (the mother). Therefore is would seem that the estate of *A*, the American citizen, is not protected, as he is not a national of Denmark who seeks to remove property, and so that the transfer of his property by succession is subject to the discriminatory tax; that the estate of *B*, a national of Denmark, is so protected, and that his property is not subject to the tax; and that the estate of *C*, with whose country the United States has not yet concluded such a treaty as is here involved, has no such transfer protection.

Remainder of the search. The remainder of the search follows conventional lines. The Key-Number covering the topic is Treatises ⬥ 11: "Operation as to laws inconsistent with or repugnant to treaty provisions" where all such cases are digested. As the treaty has been thoroughly Shepardized, it is doubtful that more cases reasonably in point will be found. In the *Digest of United States Supreme Court Reports* statutory tables (in volume 14), cases construing this treaty are listed both under the laws of Denmark construed and under United States treaties construed. *A. L. R.* annotations in point have already been noted. Note also the comments on loose-leaf services and Shepardizing, above.

CHAPTER 32

STANDARD LEGAL CITATION FORMS [1]

The Function and Construction of a Good Citation.

The lawyer makes thousands of citations. The use of so many dictates a curtailed form, replete with abbreviations, one which, though lacking in the bibliographical niceties found in other learned fields, is wonderfully effective. As such it needs no apologies.

A legal citation has only one purpose: to lead its reader to the work cited, and this without enforced recourse to any other source of information, for data which should have been given in the citation itself. This chapter hopes to provide rules and examples sufficient to enable the user to combine utility with good form so as to produce the perfect citation.

A good citation, no matter what its form, possesses the following elements: an abbreviation of recognizable meaning, a date, the notation of the court deciding a cited case (if not evident on its face), and a parallel citation. Too many abbreviations are meaningless out of their context. The date is both a check against error (and errors in citations are unbelievably frequent) and a means of appraising the cited reference. The parallel citation serves the dual purpose of a check against error (one citation may be incorrect in detail but probably not all) and an assurance that the reader will have available one of the forms cited. The time and space saved by curtailing are as nothing compared to the trouble caused by an insufficient reference.

---

[1] This chapter is abridged from Miles O. Price, *A Practical Manual of Standard Legal Citations,* New York, Oceana Publications, 1950, by permission of the publisher and copyright owner.

Many times in this chapter it is said "The Supreme Court preference is this; for lower federal courts that; the state court briefs customarily do thus and so; and law review practice is as follows." As a matter of fact, there are few hard and fast rules. However, some three hundred briefs and as many opinions, about evenly divided among federal and state courts and federal administrative agencies, have been examined, as well as the output of some forty different law reviews; and the resulting analysis is responsible for what is believed to be a statement of good standard practice. In addition, courts, attorneys general, and administrative agencies, have cooperated by supplying forms of citations perferred by them (which are noted in their proper places by asterisks). The *United States Government Printing Office Manual of Style* (1945) has been the arbiter wherever pertinent, and any departures from it have been noted.

Law review practice, as frequently referred to, for practical purposes means the rules formulated in the pioneer citation manual, *A Uniform System of Citation, Form of Citation and Abbreviations*, a joint publication of the law reviews of Columbia, Harvard, Pennsylvania and Yale, now in its eighth edition. These rules are observed by the majority of American law reviews.

Examples shown in the following pages are all dated and many are in parallel. Where office practice omits these elements or either of them, it can be without hurt to the remainder of the citation.

CONGRESSIONAL PUBLICATIONS

A. Congressional Bills.

House and Senate bills	H. R.	S.
House and Senate resolutions	H. Res.	S. Res.
Concurrent resolutions	H. Con. Res.	S. Con. Res.
Joint resolutions	H. J. Res.	S. J. Res.

H. R. 70, 81st Cong., 1st Sess. (1949), p. 3.
S. 1201, 81st Cong., 1st Sess. (1949), p. 2. [For page references generally, *see* page 361. Date and page references are usually omitted for bills].

Repeating Citations. . . . hereinafter cited as H. R. 70 [*or* S. 1201].

B. Congressional Hearings.

1. **Government Preference:** Hearings before Senate Committee on H. R. 5327 (Import Duty on Virgin Copper), 81st Cong., 1st Session. (1949), p. 56. [Majority.]

2. **Title Page Form:** Import Duty on Virgin Copper. Hearings before Senate Committee . . . [This form, following the title page, seems preferable.]

C. Congressional Committee Reports.

Official United States abbreviates "Report" as "Rept.," which seems preferable to the law review "Rep."

    a. Government Style: H. Rept. No. 19, 81st Cong., 1st Sess. (1949), p. 7.
    b. Law Review Style: H. R. Rep. No. 19, 8st Cong., 1st Sess. 7 (1949).

D. Congressional Debates and Proceedings.

1. **Annals of Congress** ("Debates and Proceedings in the Congress of the United States"), 1789-1824.

18 Annals of Cong. 1763 (1819).

2. *Register of Debates* ("Gales and Seaton's"), 1824-1837.

    a. Preferred form: 11 Reg. Deb. 127 (1835) [following title page].
    b. Common form: 11 Cong. Deb. 127 (1835).

3. *Congressional Globe, 1833-1873.* Cite by Congress and Session.

    Cong. Globe, 41st Cong., 1st Sess. (1869), p. 499.

4. *Congressional Record, 1873 to date.* The page numbers of the daily edition and of the bound edition do not match. Cite the bound volume of available. In citing the daily edition, give the full date.

    a. Daily edition: 94 Cong. Rec. 9917 (Aug. 4, 1948).
    b. Bound volume: 94 Cong. Rec. 9761 (1948). [The same material.]

5. *Journals of the Continental Congress, 1774-1789.* The name of the printer or publisher is a necessary part of the citation, as is the date of publication, if different from that of the volume coverage, as in the Library of Congress edition.

    8 J. Cont. Cong. 972 (Oct. 9, 1783, Claypoole). [Contemporary.]
    25 J. Cont. Cong. 661 (Oct. 9, 1783, Library of Congress 1922).

6. *House Journal.*

    a. 1st 13 Congresses: 8 H. Jour., 12th Cong., 1st Sess. 217 (1812).
    b. Later Congresses: H. Jour., 78th Cong., 2d Sess. (1944), p. 291.

7. *Senate Journal:*

    S. Jour., 79th Cong., 2d Sess. (1946), p. 209.
    Senate Executive Journal. 25 S. Exec. Jour. . . .

E. Congressional Documents.

Official practice follows style A; law reviews favor style B, as being clearer.

    A. H. Doc. No. 75, 81st Cong., 1st Sess.(1949), p. 25,
    B. H. R. Doc. No. 75, 81st Cong., 1st Sess. 25 (1949).

    A. S. Exec. Doc. No. 23, 81st Cong., 1st Sess. (1949), p. 19.
    B. S. Exec. Doc. No. 23, 81st Cong., 1st Sess. 19 (1949).

F. Bulletin or Report Bearing a Document Number.

    Parking Lots in the District of Columbia. Report . . . (S. Doc. No. 209, 81st Cong., 2d Sess. 1949), p. 56.

SECTION AND CHAPTER DESIGNATION IN STATUTE CITATIONS

A. In General.

There is little uniformity in the treatment of chapter, article and section designations in statute citations, either in abbreviation or capitalization, but the following are believed to follow the preferred practice.

B. United States Supreme Court Preference.

Quotations follow copy exactly; otherwise spell out "section" in citing a statute when it is the first word of a sentence, but use the symbol "§" for other section references, both in the main text and footnotes.

> Section 811(c), as well as § 821 . . . but the former § is . . .

Law reviews, except when quoting (when they follow copy), commonly spell out and capitalize *text* references to a particular section of a particular act. *Footnote* references, except the first word of a sentence, employ the "§" symbol.

C. Suggested Form.

1. *Quotations:* Follow copy quoted as to section designations.

2. *Main Text:* Spell out and capitalize "section" as the first word of a sentence, and in references in a sentence to a specific section and act.

> Section 321 of the Act provides . . .
> It was provided in Section 321 of the Act . . .
> It was provided (Section 321) that . . .

In casual text references to a section formerly cited:

> In referring to that section he said . . .

In parenthetical full citations, use the "§" ("§ §" for "sections").

> This provision, 58 Stat. 631, § 8, that . . .
> . . . of this statute, 58 Stat. 631, § 8.
> This provision (58 Stat. 631, § 8), that . . .
> . . . does not constitute reversible error. Rev. Civ. Code, § 2414.

3. *Footnote Citations:* Spell out "section" as the first word of a sentence; otherwise use "§" except in *comment on a section*, when follow the same form as for text references.

D. Section References to the United States Code.

The Supreme Court preference in its opinions is in the style of 28 U. S. C. § 18 (no comma), which is recommended.

E. "Sec."

"sec.," uncapitalized, is seldom used except in quotations. "Sec.," capitalized, is more common. Uniformity and the majority rule both indicate the forms suggested above, however.

F. Chapter and Clause Designations.

In practice there is no unformity in the chapter designation, it being variously cited as c., C., Ch., Chap. and Chapter. This manual adopts "c." as the prevailing practice, but "ch." is clear and is acceptable in any citation, capitalized or otherwise. The plural of "c" is "cc." "Clause" is abbreviated "cl.," seldom capitalized except as the first word of a sentence, or as a proper noun: "Commerce Clause."

CONSTITUTIONS

A. General Considerations.

Constitutions are cited by article, section and clause (if given). In text references when set off by parentheses or by commas, and in footnotes, the symbol "§" is frequently used.

"Constitution" is capitalized only when a proper name; *i.e.* when the United States Constitution or that of a particular state is clearly indicated. Conservative practice is to capitalize "article," "section," and "clause" (or their abbreviations) only when they form the first word of a sentence, or in headings. In parenthetical citations, "§" for section is the majority rule.

The date of the United States Constitution is not given in citing it. Although the prevailing rule in citing state constitutions is to give the date only of those not presently in force, it would seem better to date all.

Amendment citations or citations of particular clauses by name are spelled out in full except in parenthetical or footnote references, but are not capitalized when used with the word "Constitution."

B. Text References.

the Constitution [meaning of the United States].
the United States Constitution.
Article V, section 18, of the Constitution of Indiana.
the New York Constitution of 1847, Article 8, section 1.
the fourteenth amendment of the Constitution provides.
the Fourteenth Amendment provides.
the commerce clause of the Constitution.
the Commerce Clause.
the Constitution provides (Art. I, § 8, cl. 8) for a patent system.
the Constitution provides for patents. Art. I, § 8, cl. 8.

C. Footnote References.

For typography, *see* page 374.

U. S. Const., Art. I, § 8, cl. 8.
U. S. Const., Amend. XVIII.
Ind. Const., Art. IV, § 5.
N. Y. Const., Art. 2, § 1 (1847).

D. Abbreviations.

"Constitution" is not abbreviated in the main text (except in parenthetical references or quotations), or in indexes, but it is in footnotes.

CONGRESSIONAL LEGISLATION

A. Current or Slip Laws.

Give the public or private law number, Congress and session, date of approval. The *Statutes at Large* citation is now printed in the margin of the official slip laws and may be *added* to the slip law citation if desired, for convenience in future reference. However, since the *Statutes at Large* are not published for more than a year after the end of the session covered by them, the slip law citation should be given if the *Statutes at Large* are not available at the time the citation is made.

Pub. L. No. 101, 80th Cong., 1st Sess. (June 23, 1947).
Priv. L. No. 111, 80th Cong., 1st Sess. (July 30, 1947).

B. Statutes at Large.

As soon as the *Statutes at Large* form is published cite it instead of the law number. Since the *Statutes at Large* (with the exception of such sections of the *Revised Statutes* as are still in force, the *Internal Revenue Code,* and such titles of the *United States Code* as have been reenacted into positive law) are the only permanent printed repositories of federal laws which are positive law rather than prima facie the law, they should be cited, in addition to the Code (with the exceptions noted in parentheses in this sentence).

> 47 Stat. 1470 (1933), 11 U. S. C. § 909 (1946 ed.)

Here the *Code* is cited only for additional convenience. However, those *Code* titles reenacted into positive law supersede and expressly repeal the *Statutes at Large* from which derived. Therefore, for them it is neither necessary nor proper to cite the *Statutes at Large,* except for historical purposes, since they are no longer in force in that form. For example, the *Copyright Code* (title 17 of the *U. S. Code*) repealed the Act of March 4, 1909, c. 320, 35 Stat. 1075, from which most of it was derived. The proper citation, therefore, is simply by title, section, and edition of the *Code.*

In citing the *Statutes at Large,* it is customary to cite also the act from which derived, by date, unless it can be readily identified from the context. The chapter number also is a necessary part of the citation, unless the particular act is sufficiently identified in other ways. Where footnotes are employed, the full citation of a statute is rarely found in the main text, but usually only the name and section of the act, as the Clayton Act, Section 7, *etc.;* the volume and page references being footnoted. Where, as is usually true, the section number of the *Code* is cited as part of the complete footnote citation, the section number of the act is usually omitted, to avoid needless repetition.

1. *Dating Statutes at Large Citations.* When the *Statute* citation alone is given, it should be dated, as 61 Stat. 37 (1947). Where the date of the *Statute* and of the cited edition of the *United States Code* is the same, give only the latter when citing both forms; otherwise give both dates.

> 47 Stat. 1470 (1933), 11 U. S. C. § 908 (1946 ed).
> 60 Stat. 89, 47 U. S. C. § 506 (1946 ed.). [A 1946 act.]

2. *Citing an Untitled Act.*

> Act. of July 23, 1947, c. 302, 61 Stat. 413 [Date is in the act here.]
> The act for payment of fees, 61 Stat. 413 (1947), provided that . . . [Context identifying the statute.]

3. *Citing a Particular Section or Page. See also* page 363.

> The Second Decontrol Act of 1947, Section 6(a), 61 Stat. 321, 323, empowered the Secretary . . . [The reference to page 321, where the act begins, is usually omitted. In a footnoted brief, 61 Stat. 321, 323 would appear as a footnote.]

4. *An Earlier Act Amended.*

> The salary was increased . . . Act of March 4, 1934, c. 84, § 7, 48 Stat. 460, as amended Aug. 2, 1946 c. 753, § 601(a), 60 Stat. 850.

5. *Citing an Act by Popular Name.*

The Labor Management Relations Act, 1947 (Taft-Hartley Act), Act of June

23, 1947, c. 120, 61 Stat. 136, hereinafter cited as LMRA (or, the Act). [With footnotes, only the title would appear in the main text].

6. Treaties. Treaties are cited in briefs as *Statutes at Large*, through volume 64, which is the last volume containing treaties. Beginning with 1950 (printing T.I.A.S. No. 2010), treaties and executive agreements of international import are published in a new series, *United States Treaties and Other International Acts*. The Department of State suggests the citation form "UST," which seems confusing. Clearer is "U. S. T. I. A." The "U. S." is added to distinguish the bound series from the "slip" treaties in the unbound "Treaties and Other International Acts Series," cited as "T. I. A. S." The Department of State suggests that in citing to the new publication, the volume-and- page notation be employed, as given below (b), but the conventional form is here recommended. In periodical articles, the various Department of State series in which they appear are also cited. The component parts of a treaty or executive agreement citation should ordinarily include the short title or a paraphrase thereof, the type of agreement (*i.e.*, treaty, convention, *etc.*), subject (peace, commerce), countries signing, and date of signature, *not* of Senate approval, the designated "effective date," or the date proclaimed.

a. *Cited as a Statute at Large in a brief.*

Treaty of Peace with Rumania, Feb. 18, 1947, Part II, 61 Stat. 1801 (1948).

b. *Cited as United States Treaties and Other International Acts.*

1 U. S. T. 1 [Department of State form.]
1 U. S. T. I. A. 1 (1952) [Recommended form.]

c. *Cited in a periodical.*

Treaty of Friendship, Commerce and Consular Rights, with Germany, Dec. 8, 1923.[1]
1. 44 Stat. 2132, U. S. Treaty Ser. 725, IV Trenwith 4191. [Footnote.]

7. Reorganization Plans, as Printed in the Statutes at Large.

Reorganization Plan No. 1 of 1947 . . . [Main text reference.]

8. Presidential Proclamations, as Printed in the Statutes at Large. For executive orders, *see* page 330. Both may also be cited to the *Federal Register* and to the *Code of Federal Regulations*.

Proc. No. 2899, Aug. 8, 1946, 61 Stat. 1033.

9. Concurrent Resolutions, as Printed in the Statutes at Large.

H. Con. Res. 49, 80th Cong., 1st Sess., 61 Stat. 1023 (1947).
S. Con. Res. 21, 80th Cong., 1st Sess., 61 Stat. 1023 .(1947).

10. Chapter Designation in Statutes at Large. In the main text, follow the same rules as for section designation. In parenthetical or footnote references, "chapter" is commonly abbreviated to a lower case "c." "Ch." is clearer, however.

Act of March 10, 1942, c. 178, 56 Stat. 152, 7 U. S. C. § 610 (1946 ed.).

C. United States Revised Statutes.

As far as still in force, the *Revised Statutes* is positive law and the original statute should not be cited as authority, though it may be cited for other purposes. Although most sections still in force have been included in the *United States Code*, the latter is not cited in Government briefs, unless to show a later amendment; it is, however, cited in legal writing generally. The edition is a necessary part of the citation (1875; or second, 1878). In briefs addressed to the United States Supreme Court, if the *Revised Statutes* is cited without a date or edition note, the second, 1878, edition is meant. *Do not* cite "1873" as the date of the first edition.

Since section numbering is consecutive, chapter and page references are omitted. "U. S." is omitted, except in such states as Illinois, Kentucky, Maine, and others which themselves have "Revised Statutes." Then it should be included to avoid ambiguity. In briefs, the usual abbreviation is R. S.; in legal periodicals, Rev. Stat., but either is acceptable in briefs. For typography, *see* page 374.

> Congress expressly provided, R. S. § 1(1875), 1 U. S. C. § 1 (1946 ed.) . . .
> Congress by the Act of May 26, 1790, c. 1, as amended, R. S. § 905 (2d ed., 1878), 28 U.S.C. § 687 (1946 ed.), declared . . .

D. United States Code.

Except where the title has been reenacted into positive law, include the original act, since it, not the *Code*, is then the authority. The date and supplement number of the edition cited are necessary parts of the citation. The authority and citation form of the *Code* are set forth in the Act of July 1, 1947, c. 388, § 1, 61 Stat. 633, 1 U. S. C. § 204 (Supp. II, 1949), which is followed in this *Manual*. In citing the supplement, the date only is usually given, which is insufficient to avoid ambiguity, because the publication date is not that of the legislation included. Give the supplement number also. (The 1952 supplement, for example, contains only 1951 legislation.)

1. *Code Citation to Latest Edition, with Supplement Citation.* In the citations below, if the "Act" citation is omitted, date the *Statutes at Large* citations instead. For typography of citations, *see* section on that subject.

> Act of June 2, 1946, c. 373, § 4, 62 Stat. 286, 15 U. S. C. § 328 (Supp. II, 1949), hereinafter cited as Code § 328.
> 62 Stat. 286 (1948), 15 U. S. C. § 328 (Supp. II, 1949).
> R. S. § 4119 (1875), 22 U. S. C. § 148 (1946 ed.).
> 18 U. S. C., 1946 ed., Supp. I § 48. [Favored by Supreme Court.]

2. *Code Citation Where Original Act Has Been Once Amended.*

> Act of June 8, 1948, c. 326, § 1(c), 52 Stat. 633, as amended Sept. 5, 1940, c. 715, § 11, 54 Stat. 876, 23 U. S. C. § 10b (1946 ed.).

3. *Code Citation Where Original Act Has Been Several Times Amended.*

> Act of Nov. 9, 1921, c. 199, § 11, 42 Stat. 214, as amended 23 U. S. C. § 12 (1946 ed.).

4. *Code Citation of Legislation of Current Year.* No official supplement covers the legislation of the same calendar year as printed, but the unofficial *United States Code Annotated* and *Federal Code Annotated* pamphlet supplements may be cited when covering a period for which there is as yet no official supplement.

> 63 Stat. 98, 18 U. S. C. A. § 3771 (Aug. 1949 pam.).

5. *Code Titles Enacted into Positive Law.* The edition date should form part of the citation, to avoid confusion, but usually it is omitted.

    a. Usual form: I. R. C. § 3157(a).
       Int. Rev. Code § 811(g). [Law review form.]
    b. Preferred: Int. Rev. Code § 811(g) (Sec. 404, Revenue Act. of 1942).
       I. R. C. § 3157(a) as amended by Pub. L. No. 261, 81st Cong., 1st Sess. (Aug. 23, 1949).

The Treasury Department, in its briefs, solves the problem by an appendix to each brief, in which the exact provisions of the *Internal Revenue Code* relied upon are quoted in full, a good practice followed by other agencies.

Internal Revenue Code.
   Sec. 713.
      (d) [as amended by the Excess Profits Tax Amendment of 1941, c. 10, 55 Stat. 17, Sec. 4].
      [Then quoting the statute.]

6. *Quoting the Act in a Footnote.* Where the cited provisions are short, it is common Government brief practice to copy them in a footnote, the first time cited, and thereafter to refer to them by section number. *(See* discussion of quotations in briefs, *infra.)* Thus:

   1. The pertinent provisions are as follows:
     "Sec. 5(a)" [quoting the section].
     "Sec. 12" [quoting the section].

SUBORDINATE LEGISLATION: ADMINISTRATIVE RULES AND REGULATIONS

A. Federal Register.

   Off. Alien Prop., Vesting Order No. 13843, 14 Fed. Reg. 6190 (1949). [F. R. or F.R. is common, but not clear.]

B. Code of Federal Regulations.

The number or date of the edition or supplement to the *C. F. R.* should be given, but seldom is. Changes in regulations are excessively frequent and devastating, so that, as in the examples below, identical title and section numbers may refer to quite different subject matters.

The form "CFR" is common and is acceptable to the Supreme Court. A more formal one is "C. F. R.," which is a form common in abbreviations generally.

   24 C. F. R. § 202.13 (1st ed. 1939).
   24 C. F. R. § 202.13 (1944 Supp.).
   24 C. F. R. § 202.13 (1949 ed.).

C. Presidential Proclamations and Executive Orders.

   Proc. No. 2855, 14 Fed. Reg. 5413 (1949). [Pre-*Statute* citation.]
   Proc. No. 2454, 55 Stat. 608 (1941).
   Exec. Order No. 9662, 10 Fed. Reg. 14653 (1945).

D. Rules of Practice.

In briefs intended for courts, the initial citation should make the name of the agency clear. Agencies themselves frequently cite the *Federal Register* or *Code of Federal Regulations* form of a rule.

   Patent Office, Rule 122 (Patents 1949).

Patent Office, Rule 141 (Trade-Marks 1948).
F. T. C. Rules and Regs., § 3.35. [Footnote form.]
F. T. C. Rules of Practice, Rule 7(c), 16 C. F. R. § 2.7(c) (1949 ed.).
Rules of Practice, Sept. 2, 1926, Rules 74, 76. [A good form.]

E. Administrative Regulations.

Begin the citation with the agency's name or abbreviation thereof, giving also the date. "Official form" below means only that this form has been used by the agency itself. For citations in briefs addressed to federal courts, the prefixed "U. S." is unnecessary, but for other legal writings it should be used for the first citation at least.

U. S. Treas. Regs. 105, § 81.24 (1943). [Footnote form.]
Section 19.322-7, Regulations 103, as amended by Treasury Decision 5645, approved July 20, 1948 (26 CFR 19.322.6). [Official.]
Regulations 105 (1943, Section 81.24. [Official form.]
Bureau of Land Management, Classification Order, Aug. 24, 1949, 14 Fed. Reg. 5346.

F. Court Rules.

The citations below are from official briefs.

Federal Rules of Civil Procedure, 6 (as amended 329 U. S. 843, Dec. 27, 1947).
Federal Rules of Criminal Procedure, Rule 18. [Preferred.]
General Orders in Bankruptcy, No. 26.
Admiralty Rules, No.54 (as amended July 21, 1948).
Mich. Court Rules, No. 51.
Rules, No. 51 (318 Mich. XII). [Giving the place of publication.]
Ill. Sup. Ct. Rule 49.

STATE LEGISLATION

A. Legislative History.

1 Calif. Senate Jour. 317, 56th Sess. (1945).
Neb. Legis. Jour., 68th Sess. (1947), p. 793.

B. Miscellaneous Documents.

Reports of state departments, when cited by numbered volume, follow the form of volume and page citation of law reports and periodicals; where not numbered by volume, the page citation follows the date, preceded by a comma, or follows the same form as the multi-volume citation (law review form), as desired.

Louisiana Revenue Code Comm., *Project of a Revenue Code* (1949), p. 916.
N. Y. Law Revision Comm., *Act, Recommendations and Study* . . . Legis. Doc. No. 65(F) (1949). [New York official usage places the date after "Doc."]
Sixth Annual Report of the Judicial Council of the State of New York, Legis. Doc. No. 48 (1940). [Not recommended.]

C. Chapter, Article and Section Designation.

See page 325.

D. Dating State Session Law and Statute Citations.

Dating state statute citations is usual, even in briefs addressed to federal courts which might not date federal statute citations. Session laws (except perhaps in

Ohio, where the volumes are numbered consecutively and are often so cited) are always dated.

1. Dating at the beginning. This is sometimes done in citing long strings of session laws, where the date is of historical importance.

> 1947 Ill. Laws; 1946 N. Y. Laws; 1930 N. C. Code.

2. Dating in the Middle. This is usual and recommended for session laws, with no comma between the title and date.

> Wash. Laws 1941, Chapter 1, § 9, p. 8.

3. Dating Statutes. Most state briefs place the date following the title, but for uniformity, the date and edition may be placed in parentheses, as below, following the section number.

> Mont. Rev. Codes (1935), § 7769. [Majority state style.]
> Mont. Rev. Codes, § 7769 (1935). [Law review style.]

D. State Constitutions.

See page 326.

E. Slip Laws and Session Laws.

Advance sheets are usually cited as if bound volumes. Page references are not usually given when the chapter or section number is also cited, but are convenient. If the law cited is not a "public law," indicate what it is. Standardization on the following abbreviations is recommended: c. for chapter, cl. for clause, § for section, and p. for page.

> Maine Laws 1945, P. & S., c. 96.
> Mass. Resolves 1945, c. 35 *[for Acts:* Stat. 1938, c. 136].
> Tenn. Private Acts 1945, c. 69.
> Ohio Laws 1947, c. 119, 113 O. L. 179.

1. Extra Sessions. These should be clearly indicated.

> Ala. Laws, 2d E. S. 1947, No. 16.
> Ga. Laws, E. S. Nov. 1948, No. 2.

2. Advance Sheet Citations. These may be shown if desired.

> N. Y. Laws 1950, c. 11 (1950 N. Y. Sess. L. Serv. 91).

3. Earlier Editions of Session Laws. Some of these are cited by the name of their editor, and by volume and page.

> N. Y. Laws 1779, c. 25, 1 Laws of New York 26 (Greenleaf, 1792).
> Va. Acts of Assembly 1647, Act 11, 1 Laws of Virginia 341 (Hening, 1823).

4. State Statutes. Where they exist, the latest official statutes, as amended by session laws, are usually cited in briefs, rather than the unofficial anotated editions, even when the latter bear a much later publication date. For example, though the Massachusetts lawyer as a practical matter uses the *Massachusetts Annotated Laws of 1944* and supplements, in briefs and legal opinions the much earlier official *Tercentenary Edition* is cited, as "amended in St. 1943, c. 529, § 3." In legal writing generally, however, the tendency is to cite the unofficial, if later. Often both editions are cited in parallel, in both briefs and opinions.

State, edition, and date as part of the citation. Except in a brief addressed to the court of the forum, the name of the state as well as the edition and date should always form part of the citation. For clearness, this *Manual*, as do the law reviews, places the date and edition name (if any) in parentheses at the end of the citation; but *most State briefs and opinions omit the parentheses.* The law review practice has much to commend it: it is uniform and easy to remember. In citing an edition of the statutes by date, use that date which is an integral part of the title; lacking that, the imprint date at the bottom of the title page; and lacking that, the copyright date. In New York, lawyers, in citing the *Consolidated Laws*, omit the editor's name (as McKinney's or Consolidated Laws Service) from the citation.

Recommended standard form for state statutes. What is required is a reference clearly stating to the reader exactly what is intended by the citation. If this is provided, the placing or misplacing of a comma or parentheses or date will not render a brief or other legal writing unacceptable. A neat and uniform job creates a better impression, however. In briefs addressed to your own state courts, follow their preferred form; in citing statutes of other states, the standard citation style below is advised.

> Ore. Comp. L. Ann. § 102.1773 (1940), as amended by . . .
> Ky. Rev. Stat. § 402.120 (Baldwin 1943).
> Wash. Rem. Rev. Stat. § 814 (Supp. 1943, P. P. C. § 979-493).

Table of state statute citations. The table below shows the citation form for both session laws and compilations, of the various states; those marked by asterisks (*) are the preferences expressed by official letters to the authors, but are not to be regarded as requirements. The Harvard Law Review Association, Cambridge, Massachusetts, issues an annual mimeographed chart showing current titles and suggested citation forms for statutes of all states, with which this list may be kept up to date.

TABLE OF STATE STATUTE CITATIONS

	Session Laws	*Statutes*
ALA.	Laws 1943, No. 6, § 8	Ala. Code 1940, Tit. 47, § 47
ALASKA	Laws 1949, c. 41	Alaska Comp. L. Ann. 1949, § 56:4-9
* ARIZONA	Laws 1950, Chap. 10	Sec. 46-2903, A. C. A. 1939
* ARK.	Act No. 59 of 1949, Section 6	Ark. Stats. (1947), Section 81-1327
* CALIF.	Stats. 1935, ch. 330, p. 1123, § 2 Deering's General Laws, Act. 3796	Gov. Code, § 11512 Insurance Code, § 10723 Code Civ. Proc., § 1955
* COLO.	Session Laws 1931, c. 95, p. 136, § 2	Sec. 200, Ch. 48, 1935 Colo. Stat. Ann., *or* '34 C. S. A. c. 73, § 31
* CONN.	Pub. Acts 1921, c. 109. *Since 1945:* Pub. Acts 1949, No. 49. *Preferred:* Gen. Stats. Supp. 1949, § 382a	Conn. Gen. Stats. 1949, § 1069 [No chapter necessary.]
* DEL.	Ch. 62, 47 Laws of Delaware, p. 102	Del. Rev. Code 1935, § 607, as amended by . . .
* FLA.	Sec. 1, Chapter 21820, Acts of 1943. Chapter 187, Special Acts of 1925	Sec. 32:01 F. S. 1949, *or* F. S. A.
* GA.	Ga. L. 1913, p. 112, sec. 1	Code, § 2706, *or* Code, Ann. Supp.

* Asterisk in the table above means officially-expressed preference.

Session Laws		*Statutes*
* HAWAII	Act. 40, S. L. 1949	Section 1420, R. L. H. 1945
* IDAHO	Session Laws 1949, c. 50, p. 2	Idaho Code 1947, § 5-905, *or* I. C. A.
* ILL.	Laws of 1945, p. 118	Ill. Rev. Stat. 1949, chap. 38, par. 119
* IND.	Acts 1881 (Spec. Sess.), Ch. 38, Sec. 803, Pg. 240	Burns' Anno. Ind. Stats., 1933, 1950 Replacement, Sec. 21:801
* IOWA	Chapter 73, Section 4, Acts 53d General Assembly	Section 232.17, Code of Iowa 1950, *or* Section 232.17, Code of Iowa 1950 (I. C. A.)
KAN.	Laws 1933, c. 320, § 12	Kan. Gen. Stat. 1935, § 60-705, Fourth, *meaning* 4th Supplement
* KY.	1948 Acts, C. 39, Sec. 6	KRS 402:120
LA.	Acts 1942, No. 147	Rev. Civ. Code, Art. 1588
* ME.	Ch. 10, P. L. 1949 [*or* Res.]	Sec. 133 of Ch. 22, Rev. Stat. Maine, 1944, amended by P. L. 1949, c. 349
* MD.	Chapter 501, Acts of 1947	Md. Code Article 2b, Section 63
* MASS.	St. 1938, c. 136, § 8	General Laws (Ter. Ed.) c. 215, § 11
* MICH.	PA 1949, No. 300, § 901	CL 1948, § 612.17 (Stat. Ann. 1949 Cum. Supp.)
* MINN.	L. 1933, c. 286	M. S. A. 555.01(3)
* MISS.	Chapter 267, Miss. Laws of 1950	Section 3957, Miss. Code of 1942
* MO.	Laws Mo. 1946, v. II, p. 156	R. S. Mo. 1939, Sec. 847, *or* Rev. Stat. Ann.
* MONT.	Section 2, Chapter 42, Montana Session Laws 1947	Section 4-1907, Revised Codes of Montana 1947
* NEB.	Laws 1935, c. 100, sec. 1, p. 329	R. S. 1943, c. 60, art. 4 *or* R. S. Supp. 1945
* NEV.	1941 Stats. 355, § 10	NCL 1919 § 8220, *or* NCL 1943-1949 Supp.
* N. H.	Laws 1949, *c.* 150, *s.* 2	Revised Laws (1942), *c.* 1, *s.* 1
* N. J.	L. 1945, *c.* 49 (R. S. 18:22-15.1)	Unchanged from the *R. S.* of 1937: *R. S.* 52:14-30; amending *R. S.* of 1937: *R. S.* 47:3-2, as am. *L.* 1941, *c.* 77; entirely new provision since 1937: *L.* 1945, *c.* 49 (*R. S.* 18:22-15.1)
* N. M.	Ch. 58, Laws 1941, § 8(b)	Sec. 18-101, N. M. S. 1941 anno.
* N. Y.	L. 1903, c. 147, § 3. Local Laws 1948, City of N. Y.	Conservation Law § 613
* N. C.	P. L. 1941, Ch. 189; *since 1943:* Session Laws	G. S. 1-180, as amended by Session Laws 1949
* N. D.	Chapter 286, Session Laws N. D. 1941	Section 6-0931 North Dakota Revised Code of 1943
* OHIO	Laws 1947, c. 199, 113 O. L. 179	Section 3294 General Code of Ohio
* OKLA.	Session Laws 1949, Title 70, Chapter 1A, Sec. 1	11 O. S. Supp. 1949, Sec. 83
* ORE.	Oregon Law 1935, § 11, Chap. 530	Section 40:1302, Oregon L. A., as amended
* PA.	The General County Law, Act of May 2, 1929, P. L. 1278, as amended, 16 P. S. § 1	Same.

---

* Asterisk in the table above means officially-expressed preference.

* P. R.	Act No. 230 of 1942 [(1) p. 1298]. [(1) for regular session, (2) for special.]	Civil Code (1930 ed.) § 299
* R. I.	Public Laws 1950—Jan. Sess. Chap. 1, p. 1	General Laws R. I. 1938, Chap. 1, p. 1
* S. C.	Act No. 1138 of Acts and Joint Resolutions, 46 Statutes, p. 2868, 1950	Section 37-42-86, Code of 1942 as amended
* S. D.	Session laws 1949, Ch. 24, Sec. 18	South Dakota Code 32:0101, *or* SDC
* TENN.	Pub. A. 1945, c. 20, *or* Priv. A.	Code of Tennessee, Section 8430, *or* Williams Tenn. Code 1934, § 8430
* TEX.	Acts 45th Leg., R. S. 1937, ch. 17, p. 25	Tex. Civ. Stat. (Vernon 1948) Art. 476 1925 R. C. S. Art. 1435
* UTAH	Chap. 15, Laws of Utah 1949	Utah Code Ann. 1943, Sec. 21-0-5
* VT.	Section 68 of No. 221, Acts of 1945	V. S. 47, § 119, *or* Vermont Statutes Revised
* VA.	Acts of Assembly 1950, p. 10	Virginia Code of 1950, Section 8-758
* WASH.	Laws 1949, Chapter 34, § 15, p. 43	Rem. Rev. Stat. § 814 (P.P.C. § 55-9) Rem. Supp. 1943, § 11265 (P. P. C. § 979-493)
* W. VA.	Section 1(b), Article 2, Chapter 17, Acts of the Legislature of 1915, Regular Session	Code, 1943, 57-3-1
* WIS.	Ch. 567, Laws of 1949	Sec. 70.47(7), Stats.
* WYO.	Section 5, Chapter 10, S. L. of Wyoming, 1949	Section 34-204, Wyoming Compiled Statutes, 1949

ENGLISH AND CANADIAN STATUTORY MATERIAL

A. Parliamentary Debates.

In some fashion, these are published from 1066 to date. The first publication was in *The Parliamentary History of England* (also known as *Cobbet's* and *Hansard's*). The second, now in its fifth series, is *The Parliamentary Debates*. There are weekly advance sheets (the *House of Commons* and *House of Lords Weekly Hansards*, respectively) for each House, having the same volume number and page number as the cumulated bound volumes. The debates reported therein are cited as of the bound volumes. The series number and date are part of the citation. The citations below are alternative, the first in each case being preferred.

> 7 Parl. Hist. of Eng. 356 (Hansard's 1716).
> 7 Hansard's Parl. Hist of England 356 (1716).
> 118 Parl Deb. 678 (Hansard's 3d Ser. 1891).
> 118 Hansard's Parl. Deb. 678 (3d Ser. 1891).
> 230 H. C. Deb. 721 (Hansard's 5th Ser. 1929).
> 133 Hansard's H. L. Deb. 62 (5th Ser. 1944).

B. English Statutes.

1. *Session Laws.* Cite by title (if any), regnal year, date, chapter, section,

---

* Asterisk in the table above means officially-expressed preference.

and schedule, (if any). Unofficial editions of the statutes are not cited as such.

> Supreme Court of Judicature Act, 1925, c. 49, s. 226, Sched. 6.

Where the title of the statute is not otherwise given, add the date, in parentheses.

> 19 & 20 Geo. V, c. 34, s. 2(2) (1929).

In tabular citations, by year, the title is enclosed in parentheses.

> 12 & 13 Geo. 6, c. 38 (Companies Act, 1948), s. 101.
> 12 & 13 Geo. 6, c. 58 (Criminal Justice Act, 1948), s. 38(2).

2. *Statutory Rules and Orders and Instruments.* Cite by year, number, volume, and page.

> S. R. & Order 1914 (No. 1629).
> S. I. 1948 (No. 2357) I, p. 101 [in which I is the volume number].

3. *Supreme Court Rules*

> R. S. C., Ord. 46, r. 4 (English).
> Rules of the Supreme Court, Order IV, rule 1 (Alberta).

C. Dominion of Canada Statutes.

Citation of Dominion statutes generally is much the same as for English, but in Canada *revised statutes,* as in the United States, are the rule, and are cited very much as here. The citations below are from official opinions.

> Emergency Gold Mining Assistance Act, 1948, 11 & 12 Geo. VI, s. 4(1).
> Section 37 (24) of the Interpretation Act, 1927 Rev. Stats. Canada, c. 1, as amended by . . .
> Ontario Rev. Stat. (1937), Chap. 18, as amended, 1939 Stats. c. 25.
> Farm Security Act (Sask 2d Sess.), c. 30, as amended 1945 (Sask.).

CASE MATERIAL

A. Italics.

Italics are employed in the following examples of case citations, as is the majority practice with respect to briefs. For the use of italics generally in citations, *see* Typography, noting there law review styles.

B. Elements of a Case Citation.

Case reports are commonly cited by names of the parties, volume, and page of reporter, the date of the decision, and when not otherwise entirely clear from the citation, the court deciding the case.

C. Case Names.

1. *Common Form.* Give only so much of the case name as makes the name entirely clear. Thus, *Francis Joseph Gryger, Petitioner,* v. *C. J. Burke, Warden, Eastern State Penitentiary,* becomes *Gryger* v. *Burke.* The official edition of the United States Supreme Court reports frequently omits the first name of the defendant *(e.g., United States* v. *United Mine Workers* becomes *United States* v. *Mine Workers,* not recommended for brief work).

2. *Abbreviations of Case Names.*

a. "United States" as a party. Abbreviate only when forming part of the name of a Government vessel.

United States v. *Maryland & Va. Milk Assn.*
The U. S. S. Texas.

b. The first word of a corporate or trade name. Write out in full. But *see also* "ommissions," *infra*.

State Life Ins. Co. v. *Board of Education.*

c. Exception. In legal writing other than briefs, the initials of Government administrative agencies and organizations such as labor unions, commonly known by these initials, may be substituted for the complete name where there is no danger of confusion. Legal periodicals and frequently the agencies themselves omit periods in the case title, but seldom in the series abbreviation.
Preferred form where initials are used:

N. L. R. B. v. *Hearst Publications.*
United States v. *C. I. O.*

Common, but not approved for briefs:

NLRB v. *Hearst Publications.*
United States v. *CIO.*
CAB v. *Brown,* 1 C. A. B. 814 (1945) [not 1 CAB 814].

3. *Railroads' First Names.* Spell out the first name. Law reviews omit the "Co," included in briefs. Supreme Court usage sanctions "R. Co." for both "Railway Company" and "Railroad Company."

Chicago, R. I. & P. Ry. Co. v. *Chicago, M. & St. P. R. R. Co.*

4. *Ex Parte, In Re, Matter Of.* Cite as written, but index under party. The Supreme Court preference is for *in re*, rather than *In the Matter of*.

Ex parte Sterba. [Text or footnote reference.]
Ex parte. See name of party. [Index reference.]
Sterba, Ex parte. [Index reference.]

5. *Ex Rel.* *United States ex rel. Greathouse* v. *Smith* is so cited. State practice sanctions the omission of the relator's name, *People ex rel. Wiseman* v. *Nierstheimer* being cited as *People* v. *Nierstheimer*, but the full form is better. For alphabeting, *see* page 374. There is no comma between State and *ex rel.*, and there is a period after *rel.*, an abbreviation.

6. *Abbreviated Parts of Case Names.* The following are commonly abbreviated in case titles except when they form the first word of the name of a party.

Administrator (Admr.)	Company (Co.)	Limited (Ltd.)
Association (Assn.)	Corporation (Corp.)	Railroad (R.R.)
Commission (Commr.)	Incorporated (Inc.)	Railway (Ry.)

Contractions (Comm'r for Commissioner, Dep't for Department, *etc.*) are frequently employed instead of abbreviations, and require no period because they end with the same letter as the full word. However, because of compactness and ease of remembering, the abbreviated form is preferred. Law reviews favor the contraction when appropriate. For comments on points and spaces in abbreviations, *see* pages 371 and 372.

7. *Corporate Titles Beginning with an Initial.* Give the corporate name in full, but alphabet under both the initial and the surname.

> *H. J. Heinz Co.* v. *N. L. R. B.*
> *Heinz Co.* v. *N. L. R. B.* [Supreme Court preference.]

8. *Omissions from Case Names.*
a. *"Et al.," "et ux.," "deceased," and the like.* Omit.
b. *Title containing both "Inc." or "Ltd." and "Co."* Use "Co."

> *Brown Co.* v. *Jones,* not *Brown Co., Inc.,* v. *Jones.*

c. *Title of the position occupied by a party.* Omit.

> *Durkee Foods, Inc.* v. *Harrison* [Omitting "Collector of Internal Revenue."]

d. *"City" and "State."* Omit unless to avoid ambiguity.

> *City of Washington* v. *Hodges. Washington* v. *Oregon.*
> *Coyle* v. *New York. Morral* v. *City of New York.*

e. *The first word of a party's name.* Do not omit generally. The Supreme Court does it, however, for names coming after the "v," as below.

> *McElroy* v. *Boise Valley Traction Co.* ["Traction Co."]
> *United States* v. *United Mine Workers.* ["Mine Workers."]

9. *Case Name Changes on Appeal.* Where the name has been altered or reversed on appeal or certiorari granted, it is cited as follows:

> *Colver* v. *Skeffington,* 265 F. 17 (D. Mass. 1920), reversed sub nom. *Skeffington* v. *Katzoff,* 277 F. 129 (1st Cir. 1922).

Exceptions to the "sub nom." device are (1) where certiorari has been denied or the appeal dismissed under another name; and (2) where one of the parties was an official, replaced by the time the case on appeal is argued. For example, if Robertson were replaced by Ooms as Commissioner of Patents.

> *Jones* v. *Robertson,* on appeal would be *Ooms* v. *Jones.*

10. *Popular Title Case Citations.* Capitalize "case" only when it is part of the official title. Once a case has been fully cited, later text references may be made by short title.

> *Nitro-Glycerine Case.* [Official title.]
> *Slaughter-House cases.* [Popular title.]
> *Williams* v. *North Carolina* . . . the *Williams* case.

11. *Chinese and American Indian Case Names.* Give the full name.

> *United States* v. *Wong Kim Ark. Ne-Kah-Wah-She-Tun-Kah* v. *Fall.*

12. *Japanese Case Names.* Omit the first name, as in English names.

> *In re Yamashita. Kiroka* v. *United States.*

D. Citing Judicial Opinions.

It is customary to cite both official or unofficial reports in most courts except the United States Supreme Court, where only the official reports of *federal* courts are preferred.

1. Unreported Decisions. Cite by name, court, date, docket number.

Jones v. *Smith*, no. 152, U. S. Sup. Ct., Jan. 10, 1950.
Eber v. *Katz*, no. 137, S. D. Ill., Feb. 10, 1950.
Scott v. *Jackson*, U. S. D. C. N. D. Ill., Nov. 16, 1948.
[The Supreme Court preference. *Eber* v. *Katz* above, is usual]
Cohen v. *Murphy*, no. 1738, Sup. Ct. Mo., Feb. 23, 1950.

2. Slip Decisions. Cite advance sheets or bound volumes if available. Citation is by docket number, court, and date (not term).

Wade v. *Mayo*, no. 40 U. S. Sup. Ct., June 14, 1943. [Official.]
Trupiano v. *United States*, no. 427, U. S. Sup. Ct., June 14, 1948 (8 CCH Sup. Ct. Bull. 2052).
Brown v. *Western Ry. of Alabama*, no. 43, U. S. Sup. Ct., Nov. 21, 1948 (18 U. S. Law Week 4029).

3. Legal Newspapers. Cite the standard reports if available.

Ferry v. *Settle*, 73 N. J. L. J. 1 (App. Div. Jan. 19, 1950).
Smith v. *Jones*, 124 N. Y. L. J. 1709, col. 2 (N. Y. 2d Dept. Nov. 19, 1950). [Date is of decision. In New York, omit the "N. Y.," as superfluous.]
Audino v. *Harris*, 24 Lab. Rel. Rep. (Labor-Management) 2043 (N. Y. Sup. 1949). [The National Labor Relations Board frequently cites as a law report: 24 L. R. R. M. 2043.]

4. Advance Sheets. With the exception of the *Lawyers' Edition* of the United States Supreme Court reports, advance sheets have the same volume and page numbers as the bound volume, and are customarily cited as bound volumes. If it is wished to signal an advance sheet citation, it is done as in the first example below. For federal court briefs cite the official *United States Reports* advance sheets, if available.

Loy v. *Kessler*, 39 N. W. 2d 260 (N. D. Aug. 26, 1949), or "N. D., decided August 26, 1949."
Commissioner v. *Estate of Church*, 335 U. S. 632 (1949).
United States v. *Capital Transit Co.*, 70 Sup. Ct. 115 (1949).
Eisler v. *United States*, 93 Law. ed. Adv. Ops. 1326 (1949).
Ross v. *Leuci*, 149 Misc. 345, 85 N. Y. S. 2d 497 (N. Y. City Ct. Jan. 4, 1949).

E. United States Supreme Court Reports.

1. Official Edition. Cite the first ninety volumes by reporters' names. It is not customary in federal court briefs to give parallel citations, nor in law reviews, but most state court briefs do.

Smith v. *Orton*, 21 How. 241 [Supreme Court preference.]
Smith v. *Orton*, 21 How. 241 (1858). [Majority.]
Smith v. *Orton*, 21 How. 241 (U. S. 1858). [Preferred.]
United States v. *United Shoe Machinery Co.*, 247 U. S. 62, 38 Sup. Ct. 473, 63 L. Ed. 968 (1918). [Common in state court briefs, and the most useful form. Government briefs omit the parallel citations.]

a. *Dating Supreme Court decisions.* In Supreme Court briefs, date only unpublished decisions. Date all forms, for other legal writing.

F. Lower Federal Court Reports.

1. *Early Circuit Courts (abolished January 1, 1912).* Cite the district but not the division thereof, including where one district comprises a whole state or the District of Columbia. The Supreme Court prefers "U. S. C. C. S. D. N. Y.," but the "U. S." is customarily omitted.

> *Micon* v. *Lamar*, 1 Fed. 14 (C. C. S. D. N. Y. 1880).
> *Smith* v. *Jones*, 21 Fed. Cas. 770, No. 12,505 (C. C. D. Pa. 1812).
> *Runaways . . .* 21 Fed. Cas. 1, No. 12,137 (C.C.D. C. 1834).

2. *District Courts.* Cite the district, but not the division thereof.

> *Edwards* v. *Brown*, 85 F. Supp. 290 (N. D. W. Va. 1949).
> *Smith* v. *Merrill*, 85 F. Supp. 104 (W. D. Ark. 1949), *not* W. D. Ark., Ft. Smith Div.
> *Houston* v. *Escott*, 85 F. Supp. 59 (D. Del. 1949).

3. *Federal Cases. A* below is the preferred form.

> A. 24 Fed. Cas. 784, No. 14,1441 (C. C. D. Mass. 1845).
> B. 24 Fed. Cas. 784 (C. C. D. Mass. 1845). [Uncommon.]
> C. 24 Fed. Cas. No. 14,441 (C. C. D. Mass. 1845).
>   [Perhaps the most common form. Spot paging here is as follows: "24 Fed. Cas. No. 14,441 at 787."]

4. *Circuit Courts of Appeals (to August 31, 1948).*

> 143 F. 2d 531 (9th Cir. 1944). [Preferred.]
> 143 F. 2d 531 (C. C. A. 9th 1944). [Old form.]

5. *Courts of Appeals (beginning September 1, 1948).* Cite by circuit number and year. There is no confusion with the old circuit courts.

> 185 F. 2d 437 (5th Cir. 1949).

6. *United States Court of Appeals for the District of Columbia. United States District Court of Appeals for the District of Columbia Circuit (new name adopted September 1, 1948).* The separate reporter, until November 10, 1941 (volumes 1-74), was known as *Appeal Cases,* but is better known as *United States Court of Appeals, District of Columbia.* Prefer the *Federal Reporter,* except when citing to the Court itself, because of its superior availability.

> 61 F. 2d 404 (D. C. Cir. 1932). [Formerly cited as "App. D. C. 1932."]
> 175 F. 2d 364 (D. C. Cir. 1949).

The Court prefers its own reporter. The first 74 volumes are cited by it as "App. D. C.," the later ones as "U. S. App. D. C." As there is also a Municipal Court of Appeals (reported in the *Atlantic Reporter*), the latter form would avoid possible confusion.

> *Bacon* v. *Bacon*, 83 U. S. App. D. C. 313 (1948).

Washington Law Reporter. When citing, give the full date of decision.
> *Abbot* v. *Bralove*, 77 Wash. L. Rept. 1299 (D. C. Cir. June 27, 1949).

7. *Emergency Court of Appeals.*
> *Herman* v. *Woods*, 175 F. 2d 781 (Em. App. 1949).

8. *Court of Claims.* For court briefs, cite the first form below.

> *Joseph Meltzer, Inc.* v. *United States*, 111 Ct. Cl. 389 (1949).
> *Joseph Meltzer, Inc.* v. *United States*, 77 F. Supp. 1018 (Ct. Cl. 1949).

9. *Court of Customs and Patent Appeals.* These reports are in two series. In Supreme Court briefs, cite the official reports if available; briefs to the Court itself usually give parallel citations, if available. Law reviews cite only the *Federal Reporter* reports, if available.

> *In re Lobdell,* 35 C. C. P. A. (Patents) 1091 (1948).
> *United States* v. *Field,* 12 C. C. P. A. (Customs) 543, T. D. 40738 (1936).
> *Burstein* v. *Seven-Up Co.,* 27 C. C. P. A. (Patents) 1202, 111 F. 2d 902 (1940).
> [C. C. P. A. preference.]
> *Burstein* v. *Seven-Up Co.,* 111 F. 2d 903 (Patents 1940). [Law reviews.]

10. *Federal Rules Decisions.*

> *Ratner* v. *Paramount Pictures,* 6 F. R. D. 618 (S. D. N. Y. 1942).

G. State Court Reports.

1. *Official Reports by Names Reporters.* Note the state and court in parentheses, with the date. The state of the forum usually omits the state designation for its own reports.

> *Shivers* v. *Wilson,* 5 Harr. & John. 130 (Md. App. 1820).
> *Forward* v. *Adams,* 7 Wend, 204 (N. Y. Sup. 1831).

2. *Official State Reports Covering Several Courts of the State.* Where a plurality of courts are covered by a single reporter, the court deciding the case should be indicated in parentheses.

> *Sharp* v. *Hayes,* 43 Del. 494 (Super. Ct. 1946).
> *Burlington* v. *Martin,* 129 N. J. L. 92 (Err. & App. 1942).
> *Smith* v. *Fulton,* 31 Ohio N. P. (N. S.) 49 (C. P. 1933).
> *Sinclair* v. *Rareshide,* 23 Del. Co. Rep. 194 (Pa. 1948).

3. *Parallel Citation of State Reports. See also* page 346.
State, court and date are noted at some point. The official citation, if any, precedes the unofficial. When no court is mentioned, the highest is meant. In some states the "Supreme Court" is not the highest

> *Bollenger* v. *Wagaraw,* 18 N. J. Misc. 1, 11 A. 2d (C. P. 1939).
> *Wynn* v. *Sullivan,* 294 Mass. 562, 3 N. E. 2d 235 (1936).
> *Martin* v. *Post,* 92 Hun 133, 36 N. Y. Supp. 554 (Sup. Ct. 1895).

For all legal writing, parallel citations to state reports should be given. Some states, however, prefer parallel citations *for out-of-state reports only*.

4. *Cases Officially Reported Without Opinion.* If only the unofficial report prints the opinion, cite as follows:

> *Blank* v. *Blank,* 59 Hun 1000, opinion in 5 N. Y. Supp. 200 (Sup. Ct. 1889).

5. *More than One Unofficial Reporter.* Prefer the current report.

> *Corrigan* v. *Ritter,* 15 N. Y. Supp. 163 (Sup. Ct. 1891), *not* 21 N. Y. Civ. Pro. Rep. 82 (no longer published).

6. *Case Not Officially Reported but Reported Unofficially. A,* below, is preferred, but *B* is common if the case will later be officially reported. *C* is employed when it is known that the case will not be officially reported.

> A. *Lipman* v. *Martin,* 39 N. W. 2d 69 (Mich. 1949).
> B. *Lipman* v. *Martin* . . . Mich. . . . 39 N. W. 2d 69 (1949).

C. *Lipman* v. *Martin*, 39 N. W. 2d 69 (Mich. Sup. Ct. 1949, not officially reported).

7. Annotated Reports Series. These are not cited in federal court briefs or in law reviews, as case reports, but frequently are in state courts. They are cited for their notes, however, preceded by "See."

Lively v. *Munday*, 201 Ga. 409, 40 S. E. 2d 62, 173 A. L. R. 1295 (1946).

Lively v. *Munday*, 201 Ga. 409, 40 S. E. 2d 62 (1946). *See* Annotation, 173 A. L. R. 1309, 1318 (1948). [Meaning, that part of an annotation beginning on page 1309 which is at page 1318. Law reviews use the form "See Note . . ."]

H. Federal Administrative Agency Rulings as Cited by the Agencies Themselves.

Below is a representative list of federal agencies, with their preferred practice (as indicated in letters to the authors) of citation of their own opinions. Almost without exception when the agency is a party, it spells its name out; when it is abbreviated, points and spaces (N. L. R. B., *not* N.L.R.B. or NLRB) are used. Law reviews compress the agency's initials when it is a party, (or, see below, omit it altogether), but not when it is the tribunal: *NLRB* v. *Hearst*, but 3 N. L. R. B. 18. In brief work where there is possible ambiguity, the agency name should begin the citation: "Comp. Gen. Ms. decision of December 18, 1949." Where the federal agency is itself a party, often the agency and law reviews omit the agency name as a party. Thus, *National Labor Relations Board* v. *Macy, Inc.*, would be cited as *Macy, Inc.*, 67 N. L. R. B. 418 (1945). Similarly, in Tax Court cases, *Basse* v. *Commissioner of Internal Revenue* would become *H. R. Basse*, 10 T. C. 119 (1948). It is a questionable practice for briefs, especially in Tax Court decisions, since the Court is not a party, and the Commissioner of Internal Revenue is not always the adverse party. In briefs to courts, especially, the agency's name as a party should form part of the case name. "***" indicates an official preference.

* *Agriculture Department: Miller* v. *Spence*, 9 A. D. 976; *Anonymous*, 9 A. D. 978 [where names of parties not used.] [For reports prior to the Agriculture Decisions: PACA Docket No. 109, S. 286.]

Attorney General: See *Justice Department.*

* *Comptroller General:* (Before July 1, 1921, *Comptroller of Treasury.*) Published decisions: 28 Comp. Gen. 547. *Or,* B-93924, July 26, 1950 (30 Comp. Gen. 28). Unpublished decisions: A-17476, March 16, 1937; B-92533, February 28, 1950. *Comptroller of Treasury* decisions: 21 Comp. Dec. 633.

* *Federal Communications Commission:* Officially published; *Station WHIP*, 9 FCC 139. Unpublished: WPAY, docket No. 5367, decided September 10, 1950. Published in *Pike & Fischer* only: *Peoria Broadcasting Co. (EMBD)*, 6 Pike & Fischer, R. R. 555.

* *Federal Power Commission:* Unpublished: *In the Matter of Mississippi River Fuel Corporation*, Federal Power Commission Opinion No. 198 in Docket No. G-1281, issued July 28, 1950, 85 P. U. R. (N. S.) 1. Officially published: *Columbian Fuel Corporation*, 2 F. P. C. 200, 35 P. U. R. (N. S.) 3.

* *Federal Trade Commission: American Optical Co.*, 28 F. T. C. 169. [Commission docket numbers, or dates, or both, may be included: *Federal Trade Commission* v. *Bradley*, 22 F. T. C. 915, Docket No. 1694 (1948).]

* *Interior Department:* Public-land appeals (unreported): *James P. Kelly*, A-25775 (April 11, 1950); (reported): *United States* v. *Dawson*, 58 I. D. 670 (1944). ["L. D." is used for volumes 1-52; "I. D." for succeeding volumes.] Solicitor's opinions, unreported: Solicitor's opinion M-36099 (September 5, 1950). Reported: Solicitor's opinion, 58 I. D. 378 (1943). Solicitor's determination under the Federal

Tort Claims Act: (unreported): *Richard S. Stuart*, T-167 (January 17, 1949); (reported): *John Doe*, 63 I. S. 700 (1949): Unreported appeals from tort claim determinations from other bureaus: *Evelyn McInnis*, TA-24 (December 2, 1949). Departmental decisions on contract appeals: (unreported): *Luther Brothers*, CA-19 (May 11, 1948); (reported): *American Company*, 58 I. S. 362 (1943). Solicitor's opinions in patent cases: (Unreported): Solicitor's opinion P-26 (July 19, 1949); (reported): Solicitor's opinion, 58 I. S. 374 (1943).

* *Interstate Commerce Commission:* 265 I. C. C., dated September 6, 1946; 186 I. C. C. 1, decided in 1931; Finance Docket No. 16259; 14 M. C. C. 473; 47 Val. Rep. 541; *Ex Parte No. MC-43. Electric Railway Mail Pay*, 58 I. C. C. 455 (August 7, 1920).

* *Justice Department:* Administrative decisions under Immigration and Nationality Laws: (published): *Matter of V.*, 1 I. & N. Dec. 160 (mimeographed): *Matter of F.*, Interim Decision No. 210. Attorney General's opinions: 39 A. G. 541 [39 Op. Atty. Gen. 541 is the predominant form outside the Department.]

* *National Labor Relations Board:* (published decisions): *Anchor Mills, Inc.*, 86 NLRB 1120; (not yet published): *Dameral-Allison Co.*, 91 NLRB No. 195; (unpublished): *Service Products Corp.*, 35-RC-386, July 11, 1950. [An advance sheet citation with citation to an unofficial reporter is: 86 N. L. R. B. No. 145, decided March 30, 1948, 21 L. R. R. M. 1280.]

* *Office of Contract Settlement:* (if published in Volume 1 of Reports): *American Brake Shoe Co.* v. *War Dept.*, 1 App. Bd. OCS No. 13, decided October 26, 1945; (reported in Volume 2 or later volumes): *Portage Co.* v. *Army*, 2 Ap. Bd. OCS No. 185, p. 104. [Note the departure from the usual citation practice.]

Patent Office:
Patents. Cite by patentee (a person, not italicized), patent number, and exact date of grant. If a foreign patent, the country of issue is noted.
The references relied upon are:
Dietz, 1,974, 808, Sept. 25, 1934.
Trade Marks: Cite by name, number and date.
"Paraselt," No. 358, 492, registered July 19, 1938.
Office Decisions:
Manuscript decisions: Citation of unpublished decisions is restricted to those open to the public, as when the application concerned has matured into a patent, or is a trademark application.
Ex parte Lyndale Farm, 171 Ms. D., Dec. 29, 1948. Official Gazette:
Ex parte Lawrence, 588 O. G. 519 (1946). [In court briefs: O. G. Pat. Off.]
United States Patents Quarterly:
Munsingwear, Inc. v. *Levenson*, 80 U.S.P.Q. 464 (1946). [Or, USPQ.]
Commissioner's Decisions.
Ex parte Wilcox, 417 O. G. 3 (1933), 1935 C. D. Patents 1.
Court Decisions: The patent Office rule is, on appeal to the Court of Customs and Patent Appeals, or the District Court, to cite that Court's reports when available; otherwise the *Federal Reporter*, but in practice both are usually cited and often the *USPQ* in addition.
Official Gazette: Court decisions relating to Office decisions.
Fearon v. *Krasnow*, 620 O. G. Pat. Off. 1255 (C. C. P. A. 1949).
Commissioner's Decisions: These are not normally cited for court decisions.
In re Mason, 33 C. C. P. A. (Patents) 930, 154 F. 2d 294, 62 USPQ 96, 588 O. G. 522, 1946 C. D. 268.
Court of Customs and Patent Appeals:
In re Slate, 27 C. C. P. A. (Patents) 810, 108 F. 2d 268.
Securities and Exchange Commission: 5 S. E. C. 112 (1939).
Detroit Edison Co. c. *Securities and Exchange Commission.*
Tax Court: 10 T. C. 388.

Treasury Department: The following is only an outline making no claim to completeness. Treasury Department rulings and regulations, in addition to the decisions of the Customs Court and those decisions of the Court of Customs and Patents Appeals pertaining to customs matters appear in *Treasury Decisions under Customs and Other Laws,* and in the weekly *Internal Revenue Bulletin* and its semi-annual *Cumulative Bulletin.* The Tax Court decisions also appear in the *Internal Revenue Bulletin,* in the *Cumulative Bulletin,* and in its own series of slip decisions, monthly advance sheets and bound volumes. Both series, customs and internal revenue, are officially cited by T. D. (Treasury Decisions) numbers and date.

> *(1947) T.D. 51726, 82 Treas. Dec. 190. [Volume citation is rare.] 36 Treas. Dec. Int. Rev. 225, T. D. 5052 (1941).

"T. D." may mean either customs or internal revenue decisions or regulations, and the serial numbers are duplicated in each series. The Department customarily dates the Decisions in some manner, usually by reference. "Tax Matters." Treasury decisions in tax matters concern the promulgation or interpretation of Regulations, and have force outside the Department. Though much of it is out of print, tax lawyers like to cite the *Cumulative Bulletin,* but official briefs prefer the volume and page of the *Treasury Decisions,* with the T. D. serial number if available. Cite the *Internal Revenue Bulletin* when the matter has not yet appeared in the *Cumulative Bulletin.* Court decisions should be cited from the Courts' own advance sheets or bound volume.

> * *Treasury practice:* I. T. 3934 (I.R.B. 1949-1,2). [The numeral after the comma is the page.]
>
> *Law Review practice:* I. T. 3934, Int. Rev. Bull. No. 1 at 2 (1949).

The *Cumulative Bulletin* is cited as follows:

> * *Treasury practice:* (1941) T. D. 5079, 36 Treas. Dec. Int. 282 [The volume and page reference usually is omitted.]
> I. T. 3934 (C. B. 1949-1, 54).
>
> *Law review style:*
>
> 1919-21: T. D. 3010, 3 Cum. Bull. 25 (1920). [Arabic numbers.]
> 1922-36: T. D. 4648, XV-I Cum. Bull. 489 (1925). [Roman numbers.]
> 1937-date: T. D. 5653, 1948-2 Cum. Bul. 140 [Unnumbered.]

Treasury Regulations. Their citation, both in text and footnote is formal in official briefs.

> Treasury Regulations 112, Section 35.722-2 [as amended by T. D. 5560, 9174-1 Cum. Bull. 72].
> U. S. Treas. Reg. 112, § 35.722-2 (1947). [Law review style.]

Tax Court.

> *Slip Decisions.*
> Basse v. *Commissioner of Int. Rev.,* no. 3370, Feb. 19, 1948 (10 T. C. No. 41).
> *Advance Sheets and Bound Volumes.*
> Beneditti v. *Commissioner of Int. Rev.,* 11 T. C. 308 (1945).
> * *Tax Court Practice: Fred B. Snite,* 10 T. C. 523
> Where the page has not been determined, leave a blank for it.
> * *Wooster Rubber Co.,* 14 T. C. . . . . (June 20, 1950).

Customs Matters: The weekly *Treasury Decisions under Customs . . . Laws,* is cumulated into the annual *Treasury Decisions under Customs and Other Laws,* but the pagination of the two series is not identical. Included are:

> *Treasury Decisions:* Departmental rulings, cited before 1938 as T. D.
> *Classification Decisions:* Customs Court decisions, cited since 1938 as C. D.
> *Abstract Decisions:* Cited as Abstract Dec., with city where decision was rendered.
> *Court of Customs and Patent Appeals:* Cited here as C. A. D.

Parallel citations in customs matters. The Customs Court is now a court of the United States. It and the Court of Customs and Patent Appeals prefer citations to their official reports, with parallel citations to the *Treasury Decisions* permitted.

Ringk v. *United States*, 12 Ct. Cust. Appls. 40, T. S. 39980 (1924).
Boone v. *United States*, 19 Cust. Ct. 62, C. D. 1068 (1947).
United States v. *Pyrometer Co.*, 21 C. C. P. A. (Customs) 169, C. A. D. 188 (1941).
[The post-1939 form.]

Court of Military Appeals. The opinions of this agency and of the Judge Advocates General Boards of Review, are cited by court martial number, surname of the accused, and date. When published in the *Court-Martial Reports*, the volume and page citation are added.

    a. Army cases: C. M. 346591, *Slozes*, 1 C. M. R. (1950).
    b. Navy cases: N. C. M. 6, *Eckenrod*, 1 C. M. R. 451 (1950).
    c. *Coast Guard cases:* C. G. C. M. 9736, *Yerger*, 1 C. M. R. 569 (1951).
    d. *Air Force cases:* A. C. M. 51438, *Black*, 1 C. M. T. 599 (1951).
    e. *Court of Military Appeals: United States* v. *McCrary* (No. 4), 1 C. M. R. 1 (1950).

I. Administrative Material Cited from Legal Newspapers.

Give the exact date of decision and docket number if known.

In re Transportation Activities of Midwest Transfer Co., 18 U. S. L. W. 2003 (I. C. C. June 13, 1949).
In re Ryan Aeronautical Co., 85 N. L. R. B. No. 200, decided Sept. 6, 1949, 24 L. R. R. M. 1547.

J. Collateral Elements of Case Citations.

Three parts of a case citation, often omitted but important, are the *date* of decision, designation of the deciding *court*, and the *parallel citation*. All are important.

1. *Dating Case Report Citations.* Case citations should be dated because, other things being equal, the value of a case as authority is likely to be inversely as its age, and dating the citation provides an important element of appraisal; and it is a check upon error in citations. Briefs for the United States Supreme Court do not customarily date citations of published federal court decisions, but dating is acceptable. For unpublished decisions, both the docket number and the exact date are given. State court decisions are customarily dated and the court indicated in parentheses, if that is not obvious from the citation proper. Briefs for lower federal courts customarily date all cited decisions in whatever form. State court briefs usually do not date cited cases. Some date those of out-of-state-courts.

Place of the date notation. Place in parentheses at the end of the citation, for published reports. The parentheses are often omitted in dating unpublished reports. Where report volumes are dated but not numbered, the date precedes the series designation. Note the paucity of commas.

In re La Porte, 54 F. Supp. 911 (W. D. N. Y. 1943).
People v. *Roth*, 128 Misc. 550 220 N. Y. Supp. 167 (Gen. Sess. 1937).
1927 C. D. (Patents). 193 [an unnumbered but dated series].
Wade v. *Major*, no. 40 U. S. Sup. Ct., June 14, 1948. [Unpublished.]

2. *Designating the Court Deciding the Citing Case.* Clearly indicate the court deciding the case when any chance of ambiguity exists. Usually the court is evident from the citation itself — 318 U. S. 118; 195 Mass. 25 — but often it is not. This is particularly true of the so-called nominatives (Howard, Wendell, and Pickering); of those states having reports covering more than one court (as

Delaware, New Jersey, and Ohio); and of the regional National Reporter System *Reporters* covering several states each.

a. Place for indicating the court. This is in parentheses at the end of the citation, preceding the date. In parallel citations, indicate court only in one.

Alexandria Canal Co. v. *Swann*, 5 How. 83 (U. S. 1847);
Application of Jacoby, 33 N. Y. S. 2d 621 (Sup. Ct. 1942);
Brady v. *Brooklyn*, 1 Barb 584 (N. Y. Sup. Ct. 1847);
De Bekker v. *Stokes*, 219 N. Y. 573, 114 N. E. 1064 (1916);
Greble v. *Morgan*, 26 S. E. 2d 494 (Ga. App. 1943).
Smith v. *Jones*, Pa. Super. Ct., Jan. 17, 1950.
 [An unreported case, with parentheses omitted.]

b. Named reporters. These reports are discussed at page 95. In spite of the fact that most of the "nominatives" have been renumbered as parts of consecutive series, it is still customary to cite them by their original designation (2 Cranch instead of 6 U. S., for example.) Since the jurisdiction of the majority of these reports is not evident from the citation, it should be supplied, with the date, but often it is not.

Supreme Court Reports.

Watts v. *Waddle*, 6 Pet. 389 [Supreme Court preference.]
Watts v. *Waddle*, 6 Pet. 389 (1832). [Majority practice.]
Watts v. *Waddle*, 6 Pet. 389 (U. S. 1832). [A good compromise.]
Watts v. *Waddle*, 6 Pet. 389 (32 U. S., 1832). [Sensible, but never seen.]

Lower federal court reports to 1880. Cite as *Federal Cases*, omitting the original reporter's name.

State Reports. *See* Supreme Court Reports, above. In some briefs the jurisdiction is omitted from the reports of the forum but given for out-of-state reports.

3. *Parallel Citations*. With the exceptions hereinafter noted, these are not common in federal court briefs but are found to a limited extent in most state court briefs and in law reviews.

a. Briefs to Supreme Court. Parallel citations are not given for Supreme Court cases, are permissible for lower federal court decisions, and are desired for state court decisions.

b. Lower federal court briefs. Parallel citations are supplied for state reports, but not usually for the Court of Claims or Court of Customs and Patent Appeals, where the official only is preferred. Adding the *Reporter* citation is recommended, however, for accessibility.

c. Administrative agency briefs. Here, parallel citations are customary.

d. State court briefs. Parallel citations are customary, but may be omitted for the courts of the home state.

e. Law reviews. Official Supreme Court reports only are cited, except that *Supreme Court Reporter* advance sheets are cited. *Reporter* citations only are customary for lower federal courts, but parallel citations are given for state reports.

K. Punctuation in Case Citation.

1. *Commas*. Commas separate the case name from the volume, page, and date citation, but are not used in the volume-and-page element itself except in multi-page references, as in citing dicta, or to separate this from the date and court notation in parentheses. They are not used to separate a cardinal and an ordinal (C. C. A. 9, 1946; *but* C. C. A. 9th 1946).

Doe v. *Roe*, 154 F. 2d 859 (9th Cir. 1946). [Preferred.]
S. E. C. v. *Bourbon.*, 47 F. Supp. 70, 73 (W. D. Ky. 1942).

2. *Citation in the Main Text*. Whether to set off a citation in the main text by commas, parentheses, period or semicolon, is partly a matter of taste, but depends also upon the number, location, and completeness of the citations to be set off. Note the punctuation below.

a. *These objections prevailed. Brown* v. *Coumanis*, 135 F. 2d 163 (9th Cir. 1943). [Preferred main text form.]
b. *These objections prevailed (Brown* v. *Coumanis*, 135 F. 2d 163 (9th Cir. 1943)). [Awkward dual parentheses.]
c. *These objections prevailed in Brown* v. *Coumanis.*[1] [Text.]
   [1] 135 F. 2d 163 (9th Cir. 1943). [Footnote. This, the law review form, avoids any awkwardness.]

3. *Parentheses*. The parenthesis at the end of a citation is a catchall device for imparting information. At the end of a citation of a bill, it names the introducer; at the end of an act, it gives the popular name. It is a useful device.

a. In the middle of a sentence. Use a comma if it would have been necessary if the parentheses were not there.

The case cited (401 Ill. 262) is not in point.
The case cited (401 Ill. 262), not being in point . . .

b. Parenthetical matter closing a sentence. Place the period outside and after the final curve, with no comma preceding the curves.

These objections prevailed *(Brown* v. *Coumanis*, 135 F. 2d 163).

c. More than one parenthetical citation. Note punctuation.

The Court so said in that case (66 Mont. 100), but was reversed on appeal (264 U. S. 560).

d. A complete citation in the middle of a sentence. Setting off by commas is preferred to parentheses, especially when the date or court deciding forms part of the citation, itself requiring parentheses.

These objections prevailed, *Brown* v. *Coumanis*, 135 F. 2d 163 (9th Cir. 1943), but that case is not in point.

e. In a separate sentence. Place the period within the curves.

These objections prevailed. *(Brown* v. *Coumanis.)*

f. Miscellaneous comments. Except with "semble" and "passim," brief comments made upon a case but not bearing upon its authority as precedent, may be enclosed in parentheses.

Bridges v. *Wixon*, 326 U. S. 135 (1945) (deportation);
Wood Paper Co. v. *Heft*, 8 Wall. 333 (U. S. 1869), semble.
See Gulf Oil Corp. v. Gilbert (Mr. Justice Black dissenting).

4. *Semicolons*. These are used to set off citations in a string.

Hargrave v. *Turbeville*, 114 F. 2d 33, 36 (2d Cir. 1940); *Salmon* v. *Leverett*, 201 F. 99, 100 (2d Cir. 1912).

L. Purpose of Citations: Signals and Subsequent Case History.

Both primary and secondary material may be cited as being directly in point; or it may not be in point precisely but still be worth citing. For these and other situations, an elaborate system of conventional signals has been adopted generally, carried to its highest point of development by law reviews. Because not used to a high degree in briefs, the system is not described fully here; a complete statement of it is made in the *Uniform System of Citations*, a joint publication of the law reviews of Harvard, Columbia, Pennsylvania, and Yale.

Briefs confine themselves for the most part to noting that a cited case was affirmed or reversed, was dismissed on appeal, or was a square holding or dictum, or should be compared with another case. In much theoretical writing, however, a more elaborate system is needed to indicate the degree of authority. Law review footnotes (where these signals are commonly placed), italicize them for case citations, but not for secondary material citations. Other legal writing, including briefs, prints in roman type.

1. *Square Holding: No Signal.* For a plurality of holdings, cite the initial page and the pages announcing each holding.

> *Hart* v. *Picou*, 147 La. 1017, 86 So. 479 (1920).
> *Boileau* v. *Williams*, 121 Con. 432, 440, 185 Atl. 429, 431 (1936).

2. *Square Holding: Contra.* A comma separates "contra" from the case cited.

> *In re La Porte*, 54 F. Supp. 911 (W D. N. Y. 1943); contra, *In re Danby* [giving citation]. [Law reviews capitalize "contra" and precede it by a period, not a semicolon.]

3. *Accord.* A square holding substantially in point but in some respects distinguishable is indicated by "accord," not often seen in briefs.

> *Cross* v. *Cross*, 110 Mont. 300, 102 P. 829 (1940); accord, *Doe* v. *Roe*, 212 Minn. 54, 2 N. W. 2d 426 (1942).

4. *See: Dictum.* Precede the citation by "see," giving both the first page of the report cited and that (or those) upon which the dictum (or dicta) begins. Note the punctuation.

> See *Wright* v. *Cummins*, 109 Kan. 667, 668, 196 Pac. 246, 247 (1921).
> Mr. Justice Brandeis stated the rule as follows [quote], *Canada Malting Co.* v. *Paterson.* [In quoting or paraphrasing dictum, the "see" is omitted.]
> *Townsend* v. *Goodfellow* (dictum). [Spelling out the "dictum."]

5. *But See: Dictum Contra.* Note the absence of a comma here.

> But see *Northern Pacific Ry Co.* v. *Sanders.*

6. *Cf. But Cf.* Where the dictum, though deriving from substantially different facts, is sufficiently in point as fairly to be cited in the discussion, substitute italicized "*cf.*" for "See."

> Cf. *Thomas* v. *Collins*, 232 U. S. 516, 540 (1945). But *cf. Bailey* v. *Alabama*, 219 220 (1911).

7. *E.G. See, E.G.* Where only one or a few of many cases available are cited, use "e.g.," always beginning a sentence, always italicized, and always followed by a comma.

E.g., Smith v. *Jones.* [Square holding]. See, *e.g., Smith* v. *Jones.*

8. *Subsequent History of a Case in the Courts.* Citations usually note later court action on a cited case. Law review footnotes italicize such words as point out the court action, since that action bears upon the weight of the case as authority. Briefs print in roman.

> *Travis* v. *American Cities Co.,* 192 App. Div. 16, 182 N. Y. Supp. 394 (1st Dept. 1920), affirmed without opinion, 233 N. Y. 510, 135 N. E. 896 (1922).

a. Abbreviating or contracting signals. A clear majority of federal and state court briefs examined spelled the signal words out in full.

M. Citation Order.

Primary authority is cited before secondary; higher courts before lower (in the same jurisdiction); a statute before the case interpreting it; and in citing secondary authority, the descending order is from a book to a leading article, to a note, to a case comment.

1. *Primary Authority.*

a. Statutes. Cite in chronological order from earlier to later forms.

> Act of March 3, 1873, c. 234, § 1, 17 Stat. 567, 38 U. S. C. § 155 (1946 ed.)

Cite a statute which is positive law before one which is not.

> 49 Stat. 449 (1935), 29 U. S. C. § 151 (1946 ed.)

In parallel citation, cite the official before the unofficial.

> Ohio Law of October 14, 1931, 114 O. L. 843, Section 3294 General Code of Ohio (Throckmorton 1940).

Cite the statute before the case interpreting, separating by a comma.

> N. Y. Decedent Estate Law Ill, *Stark* v. *National City Bank,* 278 N. Y. 388, 16 N. E. 2d 376 (1938).

b. Case citations. Cite the official, *Supreme Court Reporter, Lawyers' Edition,* and *A. L. R.,* in that order.

> *Kommes* v. *Liddell,* 332 U. S. 590, 68 Sup. Ct. 300, 92 L. Ed. 220 (1948).

In a string of citations, cases are usually cited in the descending order of accord, dictum, contra, etc., but briefs seldom go beneath square holding, dictum, and *cf.*

2. *Secondary Authority.* The citation order in briefs is of little significance. It is customary to regard a treatise or other separately published work as more important than a periodical; a periodical leading article above a note; which is of more importance than a case comment.

a. Purpose signals. Unless the material cited is in support of a settled point of law, "see" should precede the citation of such material.

N. Repeating Citations.

Legal writers have adopted the devices of *ibid., id., supra., infra, op. cit. supra,* etc. (always italicized) as short cuts, but they are to be used with great caution so as not to lead to confusion.

1. *Text References.* Once a case has been fully cited in the main text (or cited there by name, with appropriate footnote reference to the reporter), it may thereafter within reasonable intervening space limitations be referred to by short title only. But if a particular page is referred to in the later reference, the full name must be given.

> In the *Hot Oil* case, the court said . . .
> As noted in *Halvey* v. *Halvey, supra* at 613.

a. *Supra.* Use to refer to a case previously cited on the same or preceding page, but if more pages than that intervene, repeat in full.

> *Halvey* v. *Halvey, supra.*

b. Quotation containing a citation. Where the citation to a case in the text is in a quotation, cite the case fully in further references.

c. *Ibid., Id.* Where, in a text or footnote reference, there is a complete case citation and upon the same page and without intervening citations (in footnotes, in succeeding notes), another reference is made to that case, "*ibid.*" is sufficient. Where the citation is to a different page, cite "*id.* at 119." This short cut is restricted to references on the same or opposite page of the text so that both references are visible to the reader at the same time. Note the punctuation below.

> "For this Court has declared in *Guaranty Trust Co.* v. *York*, 326 U. S. 99,108, that a right without a remedy is no right . . . The *York* case says this precludes a resort to the Federal court . . . [ibid.], so that Bullington's chance to get to the Federal court on such a basis was practically nil. [*id.* at 109]"

In a footnoted brief the volume and page citation above, and the following "*ibid.*" and "*id.*" would be footnotes.

> 1. 326 U. S. 99, 108 (1946).
> 2. *Ibid.*
> 3. *Id.* at 109.

2. *Footnote References.* When a case is cited in a footnote relative to a statement in the main text but has not been mentioned in the text directly, repeat the citation in full in a later text reference to it.

If a case has been cited in a footnote and is referred to again in the same footnote, the case name, with *supra*, is sufficient, as in the text, for a square holding. Indicate dictum by the usual means for a spot citation.

> *Quigg* v. *Newgrass Co., supra.*
> *Quigg* v. *Newgrass & Co.,* supra at 900, 286 N. Y. Supp. at 928.

A group of cases previously cited in a footnote may be indicated in another footnote by references to that note; if the note as a whole is referred to, omit the "cases cited."

> Note 16 *supra*, and cases cited.

In a footnote reference to a single case cited in the footnote immediately preceding, the case name is sufficient.

> 17. *Halvey* v. *Halvey, supra* note 16.

3. *Secondary Material Citation.* A limited use of "*op. cit. supra.*" is permissible, but the device should never be employed where ambiguity is possible, as when two different works by the same author have been cited. Do not use to repeat the title of a periodical, but only as referring to the work of an author, whether separately or in a periodical article.

> *Robertson, op. cit. supra* note 3, at 15.

If desired, periodical articles previously cited in footnotes may be cited simply as *Hale, supra* note 43, at 933, but *op. cit.* is usual.

4. *Shortened Citations to Avoid Full Repetition.*

> *Hearings before Senate Committee on Finance on H. R. 5327 and S. 1358 (Import Duty on Virgin Copper)* 81st Cong., 1st Sess. (1949), p. 56 (hereinafter cited as *Hearings* on H. R. 5327 and S. 1358). [*Or* simply as *"Hearings."*]

5. *Punctuation.* *Id.* at, *supra* at, *infra* at, *supra* note 17 at, require no comma following the italicized words.

O. English Law Reports Citation.

1. *Indicating the Court Deciding the Case.* As in American reports, this should be done except in report series where the court is plainly indicated in the series title. In the *Law Reports* series the title usually indicates the court, but Court of Appeal cases (C. A.) and Judicial Committee of the Privy Council cases (P. C.) are exceptions.

> *Comber* v. *Jones*, 3 Bos. & Pull. 114, 127 Eng. Rep. 62 (C. P. 1802).
> *Fyfe* v. *Garden*, [1946] 1 All. E. R. 366 (H. L.).
> *Lawrence* v. *Hartwell*, 115 L. J. R. (N. S.) 481 (K. B. 1946).

2. *Dating English Case Decisions.* American practice, contrary to the English, is to put dates in parentheses at the end of the citation. Exceptions are those *Law Reports* beginning in 1891, and the *All England Reports*, in which the date, in brackets, is an integral part of the citation, preceding the series volume and page notation.

> *Bain* v. *Central Vermont Ry. Co.*, [1921] 2 A. C. 412.
> *Fyfe* v. *Garden*, [1946] 1 All. E. R. 366 (H. L.).

When the actual *decision* date differs in year from the bracketed *publication* or imprint date, then and only then is the decision date added, in parentheses, at the end of a bracketed date citation.

> *Petrie* v. *Mac Fisheries, Ltd.*, [1940] 1 K. B. 258 (C. A. 1939).

3. *Volume Numbers.* Since 1891, be certain to cite both the bracketed date and the volume number of the *Law Reports*, as each series renumbers annually.

> *Hill* v. *Regem*, [1945] 1 K. B. 329.

4. *Parallel Citations of English Cases.* American practice is to give parallel citations for reports up to the *Law Reports* (through 1865); since then citing only the *Law Reports* if the case is printed therein. If not so printed, then cite other reports in parallel, if any.

> a. *Original and Full Reprint parallel citation. Campbell* v. *French*, 6 T. R. 200, 101 Eng. Rep. 510 (K. B. 1795).
> b. *Law Reports and other report, parallel citation. See above. Smith* v. *Jones*, [1946] P. 31; 115 L. J. (N. S.) 29 (P.) 62 T. L. R. 16, 173 L. T. R. (N. S.) 305. [Note punctuation].

5. *Citing the English Reports — Full Reprint.*

Scarsdale v. *Curzon*, 1. I. & H. 40, 70 Eng. Rep. 653 (Ch. 1860).

6. *Citing the Law Reports.* Citation is rather complicated. In the accompanying chart, note particularly the use or omission of "L.R." as part of the citation, the use of square brackets for dates, and, since 1891, the renumbering of volumes each year when there is more than one volume in any series for that year. English practice in each of the examples below would place the date at the beginning of the series, citation, whether in parentheses or in brackets.

Hargrave v. *Turbeville*, L. R. 2 Ex. 130 (1867).
Leverette v. *Salmon*, L. R. 2 Ch. App. 100 (1866).
Stonaker v. *Fiordalisi*, 7 Ch. D. 680 (1877).
Breuer v. *Bloomfield*, L. R. 6 Q. B. 130 (1870).
Borner v. *Nolan*, [1946] 1 K. B. 480.

Cite the present Queen's Bench Division reports as Q. B., not Q. B. D., as was done from 1876 to 1891. The "D." was dropped in 1891 for Probate and Chancery Division citations also.

7. *Law Journal, Law Times, Times Law, and All England Reports.* With the exception of the *All England Reports*, these have ceased publication, but are still cited.

Rex. v. *Knockaloe Camp*, 87 L. J. K. B. (N. S.) 46 (1918), or
Rex. v. *Knockaloe Camp*, 87 L. J. R. 46 (K. B. 1918).
   [The "N. S." is usually omitted in England.]
Beard v. *Beard*, 174 L. T. R. (N. S.) 65 (C. A. 1845).
Dyer v. *Southern Ry.*, 64 T. L. R. 225 (K. B. 1948).
Lemon v. *Lardeur*, [1947] 2 All E. R. 329 (C. A. 1946).

8. Court of Appeal Cases. As noted on page 282, there is no such series, though there is such a court. English and American styles are shown below.

E. *Milmo* v. *Carreras*, C. A. [1946] 1 K. B. 306
E. *Milmo* v. *Carreras*, C. A. 1946. [Utterly insufficient.]
A. *Milmo* v. *Carreras*, [1946] 1 K. B. 306 (C. A.) [Preferred.]
A. *Lemon* v. *Lardeur*, [1946] 2 All. E. R. 329 (C. A.).

9. *Appeals Cases.* Do not confuse these House of Lords and Judicial Committee of the Privy Council cases with the *Court of Appeal* cases, above. Their citation form is shown in the chart, page 353.

P. Dominion of Canada Law Reports.

Canadian case citation form, as employed in Canadian law reports, differs from the United States style in that the decision date precedes rather than follows the series citation. Where, as in the *Canada Law Reports* beginning with 1923, and the *Dominion Law Reports*, volumes are numbered anew each year instead of in a consecutive series, the date is in brackets, following the *English Law Reports* style. Where the numbering is consecutive, the date is in parentheses.

[1926] S. C. R. 412 [1926 has only one volume.]
[1951] 3 D. L. R. 86; *but*
(1906) 23 R. P. C. 666.
(1951) 3 W. W. R. (N. S.) 169.

The Law Reports, 1865 to Date

It is suggested in the interest of uniformity that for the United States, the last two citations above read

23 R. P. C. 666 (1906).
3 W. W. R. (N. S.) 169 (1951).

Reporter	1865–1875	1876–1881	1881–1891	1891–1926	1926–date
Admiralty & Eccles. Cases	L. R. A. & E.				
Chancery Appeal Cases	L. R. Ch. App.				
Chancery Division		1 Ch. D.	16 Ch. D.	L. R. [1891] Ch.	[1926] Ch.
Common Pleas Cases	L. R. C. P.	1 C. P. D.			
Crown Cases Reserved	L. R. C. C.				
English & Irish App. Cases	L. R. H. L.				
Equity Cases	L. R. Eq.				
Exchequer Cases	L. R. Ex.	1 Ex. D.			
Privy Council App. Cases	L. R. P. C.				
House of Lords Cases		1 App. Cas.	6 App. Cas.	[1891] App. Cas.	[1926] App. Cas.
Privy Council Cases					
Probate & Divorce Cases	L. R. P. & D.	1 P. D.	6 P. D.	L. R. [1891] P.	[1926] P.
Queen's Bench Cases	L. R. Q. B.				
Queen's Bench Division (inc. Crown Cases Reserved)		1 Q. B. D.	5 Q. B. D.	L. R. [1891] 2 Q. B.	
King's Bench Division				L. R. [1902] 2 K. B.	[1926] 2 K. B.

FOREIGN LAW

While there is no uniform citation for all Civil Law countries, the following forms are suggested to the American user by Dr. Bruno H. Greene, formerly of the Vienna Bar, Professor of Law and Law Librarian of Syracuse University School of Law.

A. Statutes.

Cite: (1) Country. (2) The word "Law." (3) Exact Date. (4) Number of official gazette or collection in which published.

France: Law, July 14, 1819, Sec. VII — [Bulletin des Lois] 294.
Germany: Law, March 30, 1892, R. Ges. Bl. [Reichsgesetzblatt] 369.

B. Codes.

Cite: (1) Country. (2) Article or Section. (3) Code name. If the edition is important, add date in parentheses at the end of the citation.

Italy: Art 54, Cod. di Commercio.

C. Law Reports.

Cite: (1) Country. (2) The word "Decision." (3) Name of court and/or place (if given). (4) Date. (5) Docket number (if given). (6) Name and number of collection in which contained. Parties' names are usually omitted.

Belgium: Decision, Bruxelles, April 5, 1913, Pas [icrisie Belge], 1013, II, 334.
Austria: Decision, March 17, 1914, R II 64, G [lasier] U (nger) 6865.

D. Periodicals.

Cite: (1) Author. (2) Country (in parentheses). (3) Title of article. (4) Volume number. (5) Name of periodical. (6) Date. (7) Number of issue. (8) Page or other subdivision.

Pogoda, Benon (Poland), *Niesluszne Zbogacenie*, 62 Gaseta Sadvowa Warzawska, Ja. 29, 1934, n. 5, pp. 65-67.
Braun Rudolf (Austria), *Zur Frage der Reformbeduerftigkeit des Dritten Rueckstellungsgesetzes*, J [uristische] B [laetter], Jan. 7, 1950, n.1, pp. 1-3.

In all the above, cite full title of source in the first citation used. In subsequent citations, abbreviate in the form suggested in 1 Hyde, *International Law* lxxiii (2d ed. 1945), or Gutteridge, *Comparative Law* (1946), pp. 185-203.

E. Treatises and Commentaries.

Cite: (1) Author. (2) Title. (3) Place of publication. (4) Date. (5) Volume. (6) Page or other subdivision.

Demogue, *Les Notions Fondamentales du Droit Privé*, Paris, 1911, I, n. 246.
Neumann, Georg, *Kommentar zu den Zivilprozessgesetzen*, Wien, 1927, I, 15.

LOOSE-LEAF AND OTHER "SERVICES."

A. Prentice-Hall Services.

1. *Annual New Editions.* Some services, as the *Tax Court Memorandum*

Decisions, are recompiled annually. The year, volume, and edition, if any, are then part of the citation.

> *Estate of George H. Moses,* P-H 1949 T. C. Mem. Dec. ¶ 49,171 (1949). [P-H suggests: ¶ 49,171 P-H Memo TC.]

2. *Volumes Numbered, but Not the Edition, with Undated Binder.*

> *Connors v. Ahearn,* 3 P-H Wills, Est. & Trust Serv. ¶ 9679 (Pa. 1941).

3. *Uniform Classification Numbers for State Statutes.* In some services, uniform classification numbers have been adopted for state statute compilations covering certain topics. Thus, in the above service, ¶ 13,501 relates to inventory and accounts, in all States, but each state is separately paged under the classification number. Both the classification paragraph number and the state page number are necessary elements of the citation.

> Inventory and accounts, 3 P-H Wills, Est. & Trust Serv. ¶ 13,501 (Ky. 13).

B. Commerce Clearing House Reporters.

1. *Annual New Editions.* Services such as the *Federal Tax Reporter* are cited to the title of the reporter, the year, volume number and edition number, if any and the paragraph.

> *Gage Bros. & Co.,* 5 CCH 1950 Fed. Tax Rep. ¶ 7017 (T. C. 1949). [CCH itself adds the volume number to the date and cites Volume 5 of 1950 as 505 CCH Fed. Tax Rep., omitting the date reference.]

2. *Numbered Editions.*

> 5 CCH Lab. Rep. ¶ 51,434 (4th ed., 1946).

3. *Volumes Numbered, but Not the Edition.*

> 2 CCH State Tax Rep. (N. Y.) ¶ 72-924 (1947).

C. Federal Rules Service.

This Pike & Fischer service is cited by volume and section.

> *Strachman v. Palmer,* 13 Fed. Rules Serv. § 18a41, Case 2 (1st Cir. 1949).

Citing Local Federal Court Rules.

> 13 Fed. Rules Serv. D. Hawaii Rules (1949). [Loose-leaf volume.]
> 2 Fed. Rules Serv. 779 (1940). [Bound volume.]

D. Pike & Fischer Administrative Law.

> 1 Pike & Fischer Ad. Law § 35a.2 (1941).
> *Brown v. Hecht Co.,* 5 Pike & Fischer Ad. Law § 81a.11 (D. C. Cir. 1943).
> *Simon v. Porter,* 5 Pike & Fischer Ad. Law (Decision Notes) No. 814 (O. P. A. 146).

E. Labor Relations Reporter.

This may be cited either as a periodical—or as sets of case reports. The National Labor Relations Board in its opinions cites it as a law reporter.

> *Audino v. Harris,* 21 Lab. Rel Rep. (Labor-Management) 2043 (N. Y. Sup. 1949). [As a periodical.]

Audino v. *Harris*, 24 L. R. R. 2043 (N. Y. Sup. 1949). [As a law report.]

Pratt v. *Alaska Packers Assn.*, 24 Lab. Rel. Rep. (9 Wage & Hour Cas.) 61 (N. D. Cal. 1949).

In re George W. Borg Cor., 25 Lab. Rel. Rep. (13 Lab. Arb. Cas.) 525 (1929) [as a periodical, with law report note.]

In re George W. Borg Corp., 13 Lab. Arb. Cas. 525 (1949). [As a reporter.]

TREATISES, REPORTS, PERIODICALS, ETC.

A. Generally.

This material is cited by volume (if more than one), author (personal or corporate), title, page or section, edition, editor (when important), and date.

> 2 Pomeroy, *Equity Jurisprudence* 428 (5th ed., Symonds, 1941). [5th ed. 1941, if no editor is named, omitting comma.]

B. Page or Section References.

See pages 361 and 362.

C. Author Entry.

Authors are personal (as Wigmore, Powell), or corporate (as Columbia University, Department of State, New York Law Revision Commission). Many works have both kinds. The table below shows these forms.

Volume	Author	Title	Imprint, Etc.
6	Williston	*Contracts*	(rev. ed. 1936)
	American Jewish Congress	*Survey of . . . Admissions*	(1947)
	Harvard Research in International Law	*Draft Convention of Covenants . . . Foreign States*	(1932)
33	U. S. Dept. of Labor	Annual Report [no italics]	(1945)
	A. B. A. Special Comittee on Assistance to Lawyers	Report	(1944)
6	N. Y. Judicial Council	Annual Report	(1940)

1. *Personal Author*. Legal citation practice omits given names or initials unless their inclusion is necessary for clarity: Wigmore, but T. R. Powell, R. R. B. Powell. A good compromise is the Government brief practice of giving only the surname in text or footnote references, but the full name in the index. Lawyers cite as W. E. Hamilton, *not* Hamilton, W. E., in text or footnote references, but not in the index to a brief.

> Stieber, *Ten Years of Minnesota Labor Relations Act* (1949), p. 9. [Text or footnote reference.]
>
> Stieber, Jack W., *Ten Years of Minnesota Labor Relations Act* (Bull. No. 9, University of Minnesota Industrial Relations Center 1949), p. 9. [Index to brief.]

2. *Corporate Author*. Many reports and pamphlets lack a personal author. In such cases, treat the impersonal issuing agency as the author. You would not cite Williston as "A Treatise on the Law of Contracts, by Samuel E. Williston," and there is no more reason for citing the "Sixth Annual Report of the Judicial Council of the State of New York." The reader is interested first in its being a New York agency, then that it is the Judicial Council, then that it is the sixth annual report, or some other similar title. Cite the significant author, whether personal or corporate, first. Note that in the table above, all but Williston are Corporate authors.

Occasionally a report which is better known by title than by the agency producing it may be cited by title, but this is not recommended. The title may be forgotten, while the agency continues.

> *Investment Trusts and Investment Companies: Part 5, Conclusions and Recommendations* (S. E. C. 1942). [Law review form.]

3. *Where Both a Personal and a Corporate Author.* Generally cite by the personal author, with a parenthetical reference to the publishing agency.

> Walton Hamilton, *Patents and Free Enterprise* (T. N. E. C. Monograph No. 31, 1941), p. 19. [Note that the name is not inverted.]

If several T. N. E. C. Monographs are to be cited in the same brief and collected in the index as such, cite as Monographs, by number.

> Temporary National Economic Committee: Monograph No. 31 (Walton Hamilton, *Patents and Free Enterprise,* 1940), p. 19.
> Monograph No. 36 [giving title, etc.]

4. *Title.* Cite by title only when it is better known than the author. Cite the title as on the title page, giving it in full, with "A," "An," and "The," except where unduly long or complicated, or where it is so well known that "Contracts" or "Evidence" or the like is all that is necessary to identify the work. "Treatise on" is usually omitted. Do not cite as "Williston on Contracts," or the like, unless that is the exact title. Cite as Williston, *Contracts.*

a. Editor's name as part of the title. Cite by the editor's name only when it becomes better known than the original author's.

> Brannan. *Negotiable Instrument Law* (7th ed., Beutel, 1948), but *Medina's Bostwick's Forms.*

b. Annual reports. These, especially when bearing a document serial number, are sometimes cited by title, but the practice has nothing to commend it.

> *Sixth Annual Report of the Judicial Council of the State of New York,* Leg. Doc. No. 48 (1940), p. 17 [Law review style], *instead of the preferred*
> 6 N. Y. Jud. Council Ann. Rept. 17 (Leg. Doc. No. 48, 1940).

6. *Edition.* Note the capitalization and punctuation, below.

> Gray, *Rule against Perpetuities* (4th ed., Roland Gray, 1942).
> Williston, *Contracts* (rev. ed. 1936) [No comma here.]
> Walker, *Patents* (Deller's ed. 1937). [No comma here.]

Cite Blackstone and a very few similar classics as to the first edition, with page references starred as in the edition cited from.

> 4 Blackstone, *Commentaries* *298. [Bl. Comm., in footnotes often.]

7. *Translators.* These are shown in parentheses.

> Hatschek, *An outline of International Law* (Manning trans. 1930).

8. *Periodic Reports.* The decreasing majority rule is to cite as "Report of the Department of Agriculture," but an increasing number of Government agencies cite correctly by agency and title. The tradition of citing the publications of the Attorney General by title (Ops. Atty. Gen.) is still too strong to break, however.

A periodic report is cited as in a law report, not italicizing the title.

a. If the volumes are numbered.

> 73 A. B. A. Report 207 (1948).
> 33 Dept. of Labor Annual Rept. 19 (1948). [Preferred.]
> 33 Annual Rept. Dept. of Labor 19 (1948). [Law review and diminishing majority.]

b. If the volumes are not numbered.

> Ann. Rept. Atty. Gen. 49 (1947). [Majority, law review.]
> 1947 Attorney Gen. Ann. Rept. 49. [Suggested, as for unnumbered law review volumes.]

9. *Numbered Bulletins Lacking a Personal Author.*

a. If cited singly.

> *Characteristics of Company Unions* (U. S. Bureau of Labor Statistics, Bull. No. 634, 1935), p. 37.

b. If cited as one of several.

> Bull. No. 634 (*Characteristics of Company Unions*, 1935), p. 37.
> Bull. No. 770 [giving title, etc.]

10. *Numbered Bulletins Having a Personal Author.* See page 362.

11. *Collected Essays.*

a. Those of one author.

> Bohlen, *Landlord and Tenant*, in his Studies in the Law (1926), p. 202.

b. Collected essays of several authors.

> Corwin, *Judicial Review in Action*, in 1 *Selected Essays in Constitutional Law* 449 (1938).

12. *American Law Institute Publications.*[2] These are almost invariably cited by title, but as the output of the Institute becomes more and more varied in nature, this will lead to ambiguity, and it is suggested that the usual form of citation of legal literature be adopted, even for the Restatements. For citation purposes in briefs the Restatements should be assimilated to statutes, and not italicized. Both forms, the usual and the suggested, are shown below.

> 21 A. L. I. Proceeding 157 (1944). [Suggested.]
> 21 Proceedings A. L. I. 157 (1944). [Usual and law review.]
> A. L. I. Restatement, Torts § 18 (1934). [Suggested.]
> Restatement Torts § 18 (1934). [Usual and law review.]
> A. L. I. Restatement, Property § 53 (Tent. Draft. No. 2, 1930). [Suggested.]
> A. L. I. Restatement, Trusts, N. Y. Annot. § 57 (1947).
> A. L. I. Restatement, Agency § 390, comment (1933).
> A. L. I. Model Code of Evidence, Rule 399 (1942).
> Uniform Commercial Code § 76 (1949).

13. *Legal Encyclopedias.*

a. When citing to subject headings. Cite to the desired section.

> 47 C. J., Partnership, Section 7, n. 30 (1929). [Text and index.]
> 47 C. J., Partnership § 7, no. 30 (1929). [Footnote reference.]
> C. J., Partnership § 7 (1941 Annot.).
> 43 C. J. S., Injunctions § 156 (Ann. Cum. Part 1949).
> 36 Am. Jur., Mechanics' Liens § 206 (Cum. Supp. 1949).

---

[2] In chapter 23 of this *Manual*, "Restatement" is italicized as is the title of a book, but in *legal writing* generally it is, as here recommended, assimilated to a statute, and not italicized.

b. When omitting the subject heading. Cite to the desired page.

47 C. J. 644, n. 30 (1929).
36 Am. Jur. 136 (1941).

14. *Briefs*. Parts of the briefs, transcripts of the record below, etc., are usually cited in parentheses in other briefs. Do not italicize the references. Examples of citations in briefs are given below.

The formula in Appellant's brief (p. 4) is not operable.
The Appellant's formula is alleged to contain kaolin (Br. 4).
It is alleged that this is fully operable (Appellant's Brief 17), but ....
Brief for the United States as *amicus curiae*, p. 17, *Smith* v. *Jones* ...
Brief for Appellees, pp. 17, 27, *Doe* v. *Roe*, 300 N. Y. 19 (1948.)
Transcript of Record, p. 10, *Jackson* v. *Clayton & Durante*, 60 F. 2d 18 (1932).
Appellant is licensed to do business in Canada (R. 17).
Appellant is licensed to do business in Canada. (R. 17.)
Appellant does business in Canada (R. 17) and in ...
Appellant argues (Brief 53) that ...
The agreement (Appellant's Exhibit 19, not printed in the record) was ...
... were assigned against Defendant (Defendant's Exhibit 27, R. 29, f. 1).
Is it true that Defendant's formula contains kaolin? (R. 21.)

15. *Department of State Publications*. Routine "Publications" are cited by series number and title. *See also* index under "Treaties."

Dept. of State Pub. No. 1288, *Communications to the Mexican Ambassador at Washington of August 22, 1939* (1939).

More important publications may be cited by title.

United States Relations with China, with Special Reference to the Period 1944 to 1949 ... (U. S. Dept. of State, Pub. No. 3673, Far Eastern Series No. 30, 1949).

Foreign Relations of the United States.

Foreign Rel. U. S. 1912 (Dept. of State 1937), p. 616
2 Foreign Rel. U. S. 1932, at 473 (Dept. of State 1947).

Department of State Bulletin.

20 Dept. of State Bull. 577 (1949).

16. *Press Releases*. These are usually cited by title, and if mimeographed, the citation should so indicate.

Proposed New Rules of Practice, Treasury Dept.
Press Release No. 793, Nov. 27, 1949 (mimeographed).

17. *Purpose Signals*. Use sparingly in briefs, in the same manner as in case citations. *See* pages 348 and 349.

18. *Law Reviews*.

a. Volume and page references.

49 Col. L. Rev. 344 (1949).
1948 Wis. L. Rev. 528. [Where volumes are unnumbered.]

b. Leading articles. Cite by author, title, volume and page. In the main text, the author's name may be copied there in full, but in footnote references cite as below, with initials given only when their omission might cause uncertainty.

Browder, *Testamentary Conditions Against Contest* ... 49 Col. L. Rev. 321, 327 (1949). [Spotting material on page 327.]

W. A. Hamilton, *Safety in Airline Maintenance*, 9 J. Air L. 275 (1938).

c. Notes. As distinguished from case comments, these are variously called "Notes," "Comments," "Notes and Comments," and the like. When citing, follow the periodical's own nomenclature. Notes are cited with or without title.

> Note, 34 Va. L. Rev. 944 (1948). [Footnote style.]
> Note, *Constitutionality of Proposed Legislation*, 34 Va. L. Rev. 944 (1948). [Footnote, but giving title of Note.]
> Notes, 49 Col.L. Rev. 363 (1949), 27 Tex. L. Rev. 337 (1949). [In consecutive notes from different law reviews, all are designated as "Notes."]

d. Legislation notes.

> Legis., *Merger and Consolidation in Iowa*, 34 Iowa L. Rev. 67 (1948).

e. Case comments. Cite either by volume and page alone or by the case commented upon. In the latter instance, the case comment citation is given as a parallel citation to the case itself. Give both the law review publication date and the decision date if they differ. Follow the review's own nomenclature.

> Recent Decisions, 47 Mich. L. Rev. 109 (1948).
> *Pope* v. *Garrett*, 204 S. W. 2d 867 (1947), 37 Ky. L. Rev. 113 (1948).

f. Book reviews. These are rarely cited in briefs. A signed book review worthy of mention in a law review footnote is cited to the *reviewer's* name, not the book author's.

> J. A. Franck, Book Review, 27 Tex. L. Rev. 405 (1949).

19. *Non-Legal Periodicals.*

> E. P. Allen, *The Teacher of Government*, 41 Am. Pol. Sci. Rev. 527 (1947).
> *Buried Frontier*, The Lamp, Nov. 1948, p. 25 [Where repaged each issue.]

20. *Newspapers.* Cite by title, page, column and date. When there are several sections not continuously paged, add the section number.

> *Smith* v. *Jones*, U. S. Sup. Ct., New York Times, Feb. 5, 1950, p. 6, col. 3.
> *Harris* v. *Scott*, N. Y. Sup. Ct., New York Herald Tribune, Aug 6, 1950, § 3, p. 3, col. 7. [Sunday edition.]
> Krock, *How the Super-Bomb Was Disclosed*, New York Times, Feb. 2, 1950, p. 26, col. 5 [A signed article.]

21. *Typography.* *See* page 374.

22. *Capitalization of Titles of Leading Articles and Notes.* Capitalize first words, pronouns, adjectives, adverbs and verbs. Do not capitalize, except as first words, articles, conjunctions or prepositions.

> *Bargain and Sale under Power in Deeds of Trust.*
> *Distress and Execution in Pennsylvania.*

23. *Government Periodicals.* Cite as any other periodical.

> 94 Cong. Record 9761 (1948).

24. *Purpose Signals.* Law reviews are little cited in briefs as authority, but as embodying reasoning with which the cited does or does not agree. Signals are used for much the same purposes as in case citations.

PAGE CITATIONS
(*See also* Index references.)

A. Multi-Volume Works.

Where the reference is to sections rather than pages, the same principles govern as in page citations, with no comma separating the title of the reporter, treatise, or the like from either the page or section designation.

> 330 U. S. 219 (1947).
> 49 Col. L. Rev. 927 (1949).
> 4 Walker, *Patents* 28 (Deller's ed. 1947).
> 6 Fed. Res. Bd. Ann. Rept. 36 (1919).
> 8 Wigmore, *Evidence* § 2195 (3d ed. 1940).

B. Single-Volume Works.

1. *Law Reports*. Pages are referred to in the same manner as in multi-volume works.

> *Gilbert* v. *Cooley*, Walk. Ch. 494 (Mich. 1844).

2. *Unnumbered Treatises, Bulletins, Reports, etc.* Most law reviews cite pages in treatises and the like exactly as they do other legal literature having numbered volumes. It is uniform, it is easily remembered, and it is usually (but not always) clear. Legal writers and Government practice generally have adopted a different style, as follows.

> S. Rept. No. 1631, 77th Cong., 2d Sess. (1942), p. 51, *not*
> S. Rept. No. 1631, 77th Cong., 2d Sess. 51 (1942).

It is suggested that anybody using this *Manual* as a guide decide for himself or his organization which course to follow, A or B below, and stick to it. This Manual has adopted style B, as more common in briefs.

> A. Prosser, *Torts*, 193 (1941).
> B. Prosser, *Torts* (1941), p. 193. [Or pp. 193-198.]
> A. Prosser, *Torts* § 95 (1941).
> B. Prosser, *Torts* (1941), § 95. [Or §§ 95-108.]
> A. Secretary of Labor Ann. Rept. 40 (1946).
> B. Secretary of Labor Ann. Rept. (1946), p. 40.

Citations of more than one page.

> Where numbers are consecutive. 69-83 *(Or* pp. 69-83).
> Where numbers are not consecutive. 69, 70, 73. *(Or* pp. 69, 70, 73.)
> Where numbers are consecutive and above 100. 169-173, *not* 169-73.

C. Spot Page References.

1. *Law Reports*. *Edmonds* v. *Heil*, 333 Ill. App. 497, 77 N. E. 2d 863 (1948), is to the entire case beginning on the pages noted. 333 Ill. App. 497, 501, 77 N. E. 2d 863, 866 (1948), is to the matter on pages 501 and 866 of the reports cited.

2. *"At" in Spot Page Citations*. This convention is now usually confined to one of the following situations, to avoid the use of "p." or "page" as a part of a citation.

a. In case citation, further references to a different page of a case already fully cited may be made as follows. Note the punctuation.

297 N. Y. 315. [Formerly common, now unusual.]
id. at 319.
Jones v. *Smith, supra* at 321.

b. In further citation to a different page of a treatise or periodical article or the like *which has already been fully cited,* cite as follows. Note the punctuation.

4 Wigmore, *op. cit. supra* note 23, at 18.
4 Wigmore, *op. cit. supra* note 23, § 2817. [Since the "section" symbol is necessary here anyway, no purpose is served by adding "at."]

c. When referring to a specific page of a numbered bulletin or a current unbound number of a periodical not cumulating so as to be citable by volume and page in the usual advance sheet manner (the Lawyers' Edition Advance Opinions are an example), the use of "at" prevents two different kinds of numbers from coming together in a citation. However, it would be simpler just to use "p" instead of "at," since to most people "at" is an unfamiliar convention and "page" is not.

T. N. E. C. Monograph No. 31, at 78.
1950 Int. Rev. Bull. No. 3, at 15.

d. Supra, infra, ibid., id., op. cit. supra. See page 350.

e. Annotations. The citation is to the first and other page of the *annotation,* not to the case.

Annot., 157 A. L. R. 315, 321 (1945). [The date is the imprint of the volume, not of the decision. The annotation, not the case, is being cited. ("Note" in place of "Annot." is common.]

3. *Parenthetical Page Citations.*

a. A citation which is a sentence by itself. The period in the parenthetical sentence is inside the curves.

The formula is copied from Appellant's brief. (See p. 17.)

b. A page citation at the end of a sentence, but a part of it. The period follows the curves.

This was cited in the Appellant's brief (page 17).

c. A page citation in the middle of a sentence.
The case cited (401 Ill. 262) is not in point.
The case cited (401 Ill. 262), not being in point . . .

d. Where there is more than one parenthetical page reference in a sentence.

The court held (p. 319) as the State claims, but the Appellant's brief denies it (p. 2).

e. Where the parenthetical citation follows a question. Avoid ambiguity as follows.

Did the formula in Appellant's brief contain kaolin? (See page 4.)

4. *Briefs.* For page references in briefs, *see* page 359.

5. *Statutes.* Except in some state session laws and in the *United States Statutes at Large,* statutes are seldom cited by page.

a. United States Statutes at Large. Cite by volume and page, plus something else, which may be the title of the act, the chapter, section, or a specific page, if the context does not identify the reference.

> 38 Stat. 730 (1914). Alone it is not sufficient. This refers to the entire act.
> 38 Stat. 730, c. 323 (1914), refers to the entire act.
> The Clayton Act, 38 Stat. 730 (1914), identifies the act by name.
> Section 6 of the Clayton Act, 38 Stat. 731 (1914), refers to the exact page where the section is printed.
> 38 Stat. 730, 731 (1914), refers to page 731 of an act beginning on page 730. It is not a common citation form.
> 38 Stat. 731, § 6 (1914).

b. United States Code. Page citations are rare. Citation of collateral material printed in the *Code* but not part of it, is as follows.

> Rules of Practice in Trade-Mark Cases, effective July 31, 1948, 14 U. S. C. A. fol. § 1127 (1948). [Meaning that the rules as printed follow Section 1127 and that they were not printed with the official *U. S. C.,* or it would have been cited.]

When an uncodified section of an otherwise codified statute, or other material is mentioned in a *Code* footnote, cite the Code section to which it is a note.

> Revenue Act of 1942, § 504 (b), 26 U. S. C. § 1100 n. (1946 ed.).

c. State session laws. See pages 332-334.

NUMERALS

A. Cardinal and Ordinal.

One, two, six are cardinals; first, second, sixth, are ordinals. The contractions 1st, 2d, 6th, etc., are not abbreviations, and need no following period except as they close a sentence. The suggestions below have been paraphrased from the *United States Government Printing Office Style Manual* (rev. ed. 1945), pages 103-106.

B. Figures.

1. *Serial Numbers.* Cite in figures.

> Bulletin 725   Document 71   pages 352-357, *not* 352-57

2. *Quantities and Measurements Are Expressed in Figures.*

> June 1935, *not* June, 1935   March 6 to April 15, 1935   1st day of the month, *but* the last of May.   6 acres

3. *Isolated Numbers of 10 or More Are Expressed in Figures.*

> 50 ballots   10 times as large   about 40 men

C. Numbers Spelled Out.

1. *At the Beginning of a Sentence.* Spell out, generally.

2. *Repetition in Figures.* Spelled out numbers should not be repeated in figures, except in legal documents, when the form is as follows.

> five (5) dollars, *not* five dollars (5), *but* ten dollars ($10), *not* ten ($10) dollars.

3. *In a Sentence in the Main Text.*

Eighty-first Congress, *but* in a statute or report, 81st Cong., 1st Sess.

4. *Numbers Less than 10 Are Spelled Out.*

six horses   eight times as large   *but* 3 1/3 cans

5. *Fractions Standing Alone Are Generally Spelled Out.*

three-fourths of an inch *but* ½ to 1¾ cans

QUOTATION IN BRIEFS

A. In General.

Quoted matter is reproduced verbatim, even to errors in spelling, etc. Some matter, however, is usually deleted in a quotation, page references may be added, emphasis supplied, and obvious errors noted (but not corrected).

B. Citing the Source, Cases.

In quoting from an opinion not previously cited, the quotation is preceded or followed by a citation to the quoted source, including the exact page upon which the quotation begins.

> "It is likewise generally recognized . . . that negligence exists toward a pedestrian using a passive path . . ." *Erie Railroad Co.* v. *Tompkins*, 304 U. S. 64, 70 (1938).

a. *Location of page references.* Generally page references should precede the quotation.

> Mr. Justice Holmes stated in his dissent (page 273) that the doctrine was outmoded: [quoting].

C. Short Quotations.

Set off in the main text by quotation marks.

> The defendant contended "that by the common law . . . the only duty owed to the plaintiff was to refrain from wilful or wanton injury" (*id*. at 80).

D. Long Quotations.

A quotation of more than three or four lines becomes cumbersome in the body of a brief and should be set off by itself, by a wide indentation. The sentence introducing the matter had best start a new paragraph. The quotation is dropped two spaces and itself printed single-space, with double spaces between paragraphs quoted, if more than one. Omit quotation marks.

> Mr. Justice Reed in his dissent discussed the application of *Swift* v. *Tyson* (p. 9):
>
> The "doctrine of *Swift* v. *Tyson*," as I understand it, is that the words "the laws," as used in § 34, line one, of the Federal Judiciary Act of September 24, 1789, do not include in their meaning "the decisions of the local tribunals." Mr. Justice Story, in deciding that point, said . . .
>
> To decide the case now before us and to "disapprove" the doctrine of *Swift* v. *Tyson* [continuing the quotation].

E. Omissions from Quoted Matter.

In omitting, do not change or garble the text. Anything omitted should be clearly indicated. Ellipsis may be by three periods or by asterisks.

1. *Ellipsis within a Sentence.* Separate dots from the rest of the matter by one space.

> We do not question the . . . holding of this court . . . that "the laws of several states . . . do not include state court decisions as such."

2. *Omissions at the Beginning of a Sentence.*

> . . . that the state courts . . . would regard the question as foreclosed.

3. *Omission of an Entire Sentence.*   At the beginning of a quotation this is indicated by the three dots, followed by a sentence beginning with a capitalized word.

> . . . There is no federal common law . . .

4. *When the Final Sentence of the Quotation is Incomplete.* Show this by the dots; if it is complete, no dots are necessary.

5. *When an Ellipsis Occurs Following a Complete Sentence.* Give the complete sentence its usual period, followed by the three dots.

> Jones alleged he was not there. . . . However, he was there.

F. Introducing a Quotation.

1. *In the Main Text.*   When the quoted matter is made a part of the sentence but is not itself a sentence, only the quotation marks are necessary.

> The doctrine assumes "a transcendental body of law . . ." and . . .

2. *A Longer Quotation.* Where this is set off by itself by wide indentation, the three dots are necessary when the quotation does not begin with the first word of a sentence.

> The court said in part (p. 82) that—
> . . . as a general rule this court [continuing the quotation].

G. Dropping a Paragraph in a Quotation.

Indicate by using five dots to separate the paragraphs actually quoted, to take the place of the one or ones not quoted. Double space between the five dots and the paragraphs above and below.

. . . . .

H. When the Quoted Matter Has Dropped Matter.

Indicate by "sic."

> Mr. Justice Butler quoted Mr. Justice Holmes to the effect that "a court of the United States was bound . . . [*sic*] before the state courts had rendered an authoritative decision."

I. "Sic."

Extraneous matter supplied by the commentator is placed in brackets, and within the quotation marks. Such matter (as page citations, for example) when it is outside the quotation marks is placed in parentheses. When using both brackets and parentheses together, brackets always enclose the parentheses: [()]. *Sic*, a word, not abbreviation, requires no period.

J. Errors in Quoted Matter.

Indicate by "*sic*," in brackets and italicized, following the error.

The statutes was [*sic*] held vaid [*sic*].

K. Emphasis.

Matter italicized in the quoted matter is of course italicized when quoted. If it is desired to italicize quoted matter not italicized in the original text, do so as follows: At the end of the quotation, or in a footnote, use one of these forms, or something like them, in brackets.

[Emphasis supplied.] [Emphasis added.] [Italics supplied.]

L. Position of Punctuation Marks, Relative to Quotation Marks.

The United States Government Printing Office rule is: The comma and the final period will be placed inside the quotation marks. Other punctuation marks should be placed inside the quotation marks only if they are a part of the quotation.

Mr. Justice Holmes said that "I dissent from the decision. . . ."
Was it "just one of those things"?
Who asked, "Why?" [A question part of the quotation.]
The appellant said, "No!"
He said that that belonged to "The Star"; that it was his.
. . . as reported in "The Star": He declined to run.

M. Citing the Source: Statutes.

1. *In the Main Text.*   References are likely to be casual, as part of a sentence.

Section 303 requires notice "in writing."

2. *In Parenthetical Citations in the Main Text.*   Whether set aside by parentheses or commas, or as a separate citation at the end of the sentence, use the form of section designation (Sec., sec., §) used in printing the act itself.

According to that section (Sec., sec., § 303) "notice is required to be in writing."
". . . notice is required to be in writing" (Sec. 303).
"notice is required to be in writing." (Sec. 303.)

3. *A Verbatim Quotation of a Statute in the Main Text.*   Where this requires more than three or four lines, it is blocked off by deep indentations, the whole is dropped two spaces below the preceding text, as below. In federal briefs, it is common to make a footnote of the first reference to an act, quoting verbatim, and referring to it thereafter only by section. In such footnote citations quotation marks for the cited matter are common.

The pertinent provisions are as follows:

"Sec. 5(a). Unfair methods of competition [quoting] 52 Stat. 111-112, 15 U. S. C. § 15(a) (1946 ed.)."

Where several rather lengthy sections are to be quoted, a common federal brief practice is to place them all together in an appendix, without quotation marks.

APPENDIX I

Relevant provisions of Sec. 5, Sec. 12, and Sec. 15 of the Federal Trade Commission Act (Act of September 26, 1914, 38 Stat. 717, as amended by Act of March 21, 1938, 52 Stat. 111-115, and by Sec. 1107 (f) of Act of June 23, 1938, 52 Stat. 1028, 15 U. S. C. Sec. 45, Sec. 52, and Sec. 55):

Sec. 5(a). Unfair methods of competition [quoting].
Sec. 12 (a). It shall be unlawful [quoting].
Sec. 15. For the purposes of section 12 [quoting.]

INDEXES TO BRIEFS

A. Scope.

The so-called index is really (a) a table of contents, followed by (b) a resumé of counsel's argument, and closing with (c) a list of authorities cited. Exhibits are best listed in the table of contents part.

B. Table of Contents.

This follows the order of the brief.

C. Capitalization.

The first word of each new entry is capitalized, thereafter only words capitalized in the brief itself. Section, chapter and clause references, however, are not capitalized except in tabular citations. (*See* the Fair Labor Standards Act in the index following, compared with other statutory citations there.)

D. Table of Authorities Cited.

1. *Cases.* List alphabetically, in the same form as in the brief. Court action (usually certiorari granted or denied, or affirmance on appeal) is noted. If certiorari is pending, give the case's docket number and term of court. Dates and note of the court deciding are sometimes omitted. Pages in the brief where the case is cited are noted in the right hand margin. Case names are italicized or not, as in the brief itself.

Alphabeting cases. Alphabet by significant name, ignoring corporate initials, *ex parte, in re*, etc., but make cross-references as needed.

Ex parte. See name of party. [Also for Matter of, *In re*.]
Ex rel. See page 375.
M', Mc., Mac. Alphabet as if spelled "*Mac.*"
By words, not letters. See page 310.
Ship names. The Mary Jane, U. S. S. Raymond are given exactly, but alphabeted under the first significant name.
Foreign names with prefixes. De, della, di, la, van, von; the prefix is an integral part of the name; that is, DeGaulle is alphabeted under "D," not "G." This is contra to scholarly practice, but is the practice in briefs generally.

2. *Federal Constitution and Statutes.* List the Constitution, then statutes chronologically.

Act of June 23, 1947, c. 120, 61 Stat. 136, 29 U. S. C. (1946 ed.) (Labor Management Relations Act of 1947).

Most federal agencies list acts by title, if any. Note the Fair Labor Standards Act of 1938, *infra*.

3. *State Constitutions and Statutes.* List constitutions alphabetically by states, followed by statutes listed alphabetically by states.

4. *Miscellaneous Material.* List alphabetically by author or title, whichever form is used in the brief. It is common to give the author's full name in the index, however, even though cited only by surname in the brief.

E. Typography.

Follow the form used in the brief itself. Briefs printed all in roman except the case names are common in all courts.

INDEX

AUTHORITIES CITED

CAPITALIZATION

A. In General.

The tendency to capitalize too much; be conservative. The suggestions below are paraphrased from the chapter on capitalization in the *United States Government Printing Office Manual* (1945).

B. Proper Nouns and Their Derivatives.

Capitalize unless the derivative has acquired an independent meaning no longer closely identified with the original.

Italy, Italian, *but* italics.
Rome, Roman, *but* roman type.

C. "The."

Capitalize as part of an official name.

The Queen Mary [in a case name];
the Attorney General.

D. Names of Organized Bodies.

Congress, House, Senate, Committee on the Whole, *but* the committee.
Virginia Assembly, the assembly. State Highway Commission, the highway commission.

E. First Words of an Independent Clause or Sentence.

The question is, Shall the bill pass?

1. *Following a colon, exclamation point or interrogation point.* The first word is not capitalized if merely a supplementary remark follows.

Revolutions are not made: they come.

2. *Where the first word following a colon is an independent passage or sentence, or where it is tabular matter.*

The decision was as follows: That Jones is liable.

This I do not believe: That Section 8 so provides.
Section 8 provides for these things:
1. For notice in writing.
2. For a hearing.
3. For an appeal.

SUGGESTED CAPITALIZATION OF WORDS FREQUENTLY USED

ACT — The Merrill Act, Section 13 of that Act; *but* the act, an act of Congress.

AMENDMENT — When used as an exact title, as the Fourteenth Amendment; *but* the fourteenth amendment to the Constitution.

ARTICLE — *see* page 326.

BILL — Bill of Rights; *but* the Ives bill, a Congressional bill.

BRIEF — Brief for Respondent; *but* as said in Appellant's brief.

CIRCUIT — Circuit Court of Appeals; *but* the circuit courts.

CLAUSE — as a heading or title: the Commerce Clause, *but* the commerce clause of the Constitution.

COURT — the Supreme Court of the United States, the Court; *but* the Court of Appeals, Ninth Circuit, the court.

DISTRICT — United States Court for the Southern District of New York; *but* the district courts.

EX PARTE — in a case name: *Ex parte Smith; but* an ex parte hearing.

FEDERAL — majority: when referring unmistakably to the United States or its functions, or when part of a proper noun: the Federal Constitution, Federal courts, Federal judges; *but* a federal question, federal agents. In this *Manual*, it is capitalized only when part of a proper noun: Federal Constitution, *but* federal courts, federal judges. This is the minority practice.

GOVERNMENT — *see* above; the majority practice is the United States Government, the Government; *but* state governments.

IBID. ID.—only when beginning a sentence.

IN RE (no period) — only when part of a case report: *In re Perkins*.

LAW — as a heading or title: Public Law No. 1.

NUMBER — only as a heading or as part of a title: House Document number 17, page 3; *but* H. Doc. No. 17, 81st Cong., 1st Sess.

REPORT — only as a title or a proper name: Attorney General's Report, House Report No. 18; *but* the report of the Attorney General for 1949.

SECTION — *see* page 325.

SESSION — as part of a title: Eighty-first Congress, first session, 81st Cong., 1st Sess.; *but* a special session of Congress. [Many Government agencies do not capitalize session but do Congress.]

VOLUME — as a heading only: Volume 2: Rule against Perpetuities; *but* volume 2 of Williston, *supra*.

ABBREVIATIONS

A. Caution.

In employing the short cut which abbreviations provide, the legal writer must never lose sight of the sole object of a citation—to lead its reader to the work cited, without error, ambiguity, or the necessity of consulting additional conversion tables, case tables or the like, for data which the citation itself should have provided. There is never a legitimate choice between brevity and time saving for the writer on the one hand and clarity for the citation user on the other.

B. Contractions.

Distinguish these from abbreviations. Dep't, Adm'r, Ass'n, and the like are contractions, not followed by a period. Dept., Admr., Assn., *etc.*, are abbreviations, requiring a period. A contraction begins and ends with the same letter as the full word; an abbreviation often ends on a different letter: Jour., Rev., Stat., La., Wis., *etc.*, are examples. Law reviews favor contractions where at all feasible, as does the Government Printing Office. This *Manual* has used abbreviations, as more compact, less conducive to error, and uniform throughout.

C. Spacing Abbreviations.

There are three common practices in spacing the abbreviations used for case and other series citations.

1. *Space between all elements of the abbreviations.* Federal court briefs, nearly all state court briefs seen, and the majority of law reviews favor this rule, which is the style consequently adopted by this manual. However, most law reviews in 1949 adopted rule two, below, which in the future may be expected to control their citation practice. Rule one is in accordance with Government Printing Office Practice in legal references: While points and spaces are omitted in abbreviations of names of organized bodies, both points and spaces are used "in citing such legal references as *C. C. P. A., F. R., F. Supp., U. S. C., Yale L. J.,* etc." [3]

301 U. S. 15   175 S. E. 81   *N. L. R. B.* v. *Jones.*

2. *Omit the spacing, except between elements of the abbreviation each consisting of more than one letter.* This is favored by a strong minority of law reviews and a very small minority of state court briefs.

301 U. S. 15   175 S. E. 81   *N.L.R.B.* v. *Jones.*
C.C.S.D.N.Y. *but* Sup. Ct.   Fed. Cas.

3. *Space the initials of a personal name.* Space before and after unabbreviated words. This rule is universal.

United States v. *H. J. Heinz Co.*   *S. D. Ohio.*

For the practice of eliminating both points and spaces in certain abbreviations, such as Government and labor union agencies, *see* page 337. Where a word or an ampersand is an element of such an abbreviation, points and spaces are not omitted by the Government Printing Office.

D. Second Series of Law Reports.

Some second series are quite differently abbreviated than the first: Atl., A.2d; N. Y. Supp., N. Y. S. 2d, etc. The majority usage in briefs and opinions is style D, below, but the Government Printing Office favors style A, while law reviews use style B. Some unofficial reports designate their second series as "new series."

    A. 69 S. W. (2d) 404 (1934).
    B. 69 S. W.2d 404 (1934).
    C. 69 S.W.2d 404 (1934).
    D. 69 S. W. 2d 404 (1934).
       29 P. U. R. (N. S.) 18 (1948).

---

[3] Letter to authors by P. L. Cole, Deputy Public Printer, December 5, 1952.

4. *Periods.* With a few exceptions, every abbreviation which stands for a single word is followed by a period.

N. Y.   Ind. App.   App. Div.   LL.B.

The exceptions are: (a) Some words formerly written as two words but now as one: R. R. (for railroad), S. S. (for steamship; (b) symbols and call letters, as WGY for a radio station, SOS for a distress signal; (c) alphabetical designations of Government agencies, labor unions, *etc.*, so well known by their initials that there can be no ambiguity: NLRB, ICC, FTC, CIO. These last are too informal for briefs.

5. *Words Not Abbreviated.* Some words are not abbreviated in legal writing. A few of them follow.

day   mount   months: March, April, May, June, July
point   *infra*   states: Alaska, Hawaii, Idaho, Iowa, Ohio, Utah
supra   United States [exceptions: 328 U. S. 415; as the name of a Government vessel (U. S. S. Chicago); and in writing other than briefs in footnote references: U. S. Treas Regs.]

The Government Printing Office does not abbreviate Maine. It abbreviates Kansas as Kans., the Dakotas as N. Dak., and S. Dak. Legal writing prefers "Me.," "Kan.," "N. D.," and "S. D."

6. *Corporate, Firm and Railway Names.* *See* page 337.

7. *Ampersand (&).* Use this in place of "and" only where it is part of the corporate or firm name, as found in legal documents (incorporation or partnership papers and the like) or letterheads.

8. *Table of Frequently Used American Abbreviations.* This is a table from the word to the abbreviation. The complete table from abbreviation to word abbreviated is in the Appendix.

A

affidavit .... aff.
amendment .... amend.
and others .... *et al.*
and the following .... *et seq.*
and the following pages .... f., ff.
annotated .... ann.; Note.
answer .... answ.
appellant, appellate .... app.
appendix .... appx.
article (s) .... art., arts.
associate .... assoc.
association .... assn.
Atlantic Reporter .... Atl.
   Second Series A.2d
Attorney General .... Atty. Gen.

B

Bachelor of Laws .... LL.B.
bankruptcy .... bankr.
Blackstone's Commentaries .... Bl. Comm.
brief .... br.
bulletin(s) .... bull., bulls.

C

chapter(s) .... c. cc.

[or less common, ch., chs.]
Chief Justice .... C. J.
Circuit Court .... C. C.
Civil Appeals .... Civ. App.
Coke's Institutes .... Co. Inst.
Coke on Littleton .... Co. Litt.
column .... col.
commission .... comm.
commissioner .... commr.
Common Pleas .... C. P.
compare .... *cf.*
compiled .... comp.
Congress .... Cong.
Congressional Debates .... Cong. Deb.
Congressional Globe .... Cong. Globe.
consolidated .... cons.
Constitution .... Const.
corporation .... corp.
court .... C., Ct.
Court of Appeals for District
   of Columbia .... App. D. C.
Court of Claims .... Ct. Cl.
Court of Customs and Patent
   Appeals .... C. C. P. A.
Court of
   Customs Appeals .... Ct. Cust. App.

criminal .... cr.

D

defendant .... dft.
department .... dept.
district .... dist.
District Court .... D. C.
District Court (state) .... Dist. Ct.
District Court,
  District of Columbia .... D. D. C.
District of Columbia Court of
  Appeal Cases .... U. S. App. D. C.
document .... doc.

E

edition .... ed.
English Reprint .... Eng. Rep.
Equity .... Eq.
Exchequer .... Ex.
Exchequer Chamber .... Ex. Ch.
Executive Document .... Exec. Doc.
Executive Order .... Exec. Order.
exhibit .... ex.

F

Federal Register .... Fed. Reg.
Federal Reporter .... Fed.
  Second Series .... F. 2d
figure (s) .... fig., figs.
first .... 1st (no period)
folio .... fol.
footnote(s) .... n., nn.
for example .... e.g. (no space).

H

House bill .... H. R.
House concurrent
  resolution .... H. Con. Res.
House document ....H. Doc.
House joint resolution .... H. J. Res.
House of Lords .... H. L.
House resolution .... H. Res.

I

In the place cited .... loc. cit.
in the same place .... ibid.
incorporated .... inc.

J

journal .... jour., j.

L

Law .... L.
Lawyers' Edition .... L. Ed.
limited .... Ltd.

M

manuscript(s) .... ms., mss.
Manuscript decisions ....
  Ms. D. (Patents)

Ms. D. (Comp. Gen.)
Miscellaneous document .... Misc. Doc.

N

namely ....viz (no period)
New York Supplement .... N. Y. Supp.
  Second Series .... N. Y. S. 2d
North Eastern Reporter .... N. E.
  Second Series .... N. E. 2d
North Western Reporter .... N. W.
  Second Series .... N. W. 2d
number(s) .... no., nos.

O

on the relation of .... ex rel.

P

Pacific Reporter .... Pac.
  Second Series .... P. 2d
page(s) .... p. pp.
paragraph(s) .... par., pars.
part(s) .... pt., pts.
petitioner .... pet.
plaintiff .... pltf.
public resolution .... Pub. Res.

R

Railroad .... R. R.
  [Supreme Court permits Ry.]
Railway .... Ry.
record .... R.
Resolution .... Res.
respondent .... resp.
review, revise, revised .... rev.

S

same .... id.
Second .... 2d (no period)
section(s) .... sec., sec., §, § §
Senate bill .... S.
Senate joint resolution .... S. J. Res.
Senate report .... S. Rept.
Senate resolution .... S. Res.
series .... ser.
sic (no period)
South Eastern Reporter .... S. E.
  Second Series .... S. E. 2d
South Western Report .... S. W.
  Second Series .... S. W. 2d
Statute .... Stat.
Statutes at Large .... Stat.
Superior Court .... Super. Ct.
supplement .... supp.
Supreme Court, Supreme Court
  Reporter .... Sup. Ct.
Surrogate's Court .... Surr. Ct.

T

that is .... i.e. (no space)
third .... 3d (no period)

transcript .... tr.			
Treasury Regulations .. U. S. Treas. Regs.		**V**	
(usually plural)		Vice Chancellor .... V. C.	

U	**W**
under the name of .... sub. nom.	work cited above .... *op. cit. supra.*

TYPOGRAPHY

A. Function of Type Styles.

The refinements of type style, whether roman or italic, large or small capitals, and the like, are not particularly important in legal writing other than in learned treatises and law reviews. The great majority of briefs print only the case names (except the "v.") in italics, whether in text, footnote or index references, with everything else in roman, and a brief so printed is acceptable in any court or quasi-judicial tribunal. This is simple, easy, and error-proof.

The use of italics to make more vivid on the printed page the titles of secondary material cited is growing in briefs, however, especially those presented to federal agencies and courts, and that is the style adopted in this *Manual*. The only problem involved is the determination of what, for the purpose of italics, is a title. Some suggested rules are stated below. In typing, italics are indicated by underlining.

B. Statutes and Session Laws.

All references to section, article, chapter, clause, session laws, statutes, *etc.*, are customarily printed in roman, without large and small caps in most legal writing. The *United States Government Printing Office Style Manual* favors the following, however: "The words *article* and *section* at the beginning of paragraphs are abbreviated and set in caps and small caps, except that the first of a series is spelled out." In quoting a statute, the typographical style of the matter quoted is adopted.

Law review footnote style is to print the titles of session laws in roman ("New York Laws 1942, c. 387"), but titles of statutes in large and small caps ("CONST.," *not* "Const.," "STAT.," *not* "Stat.," "INT. REV. CODE," *not* "Int. Rev. Code."). This *Manual*, following the more usual style, prints both in roman, without small caps. (Large and small caps are indicated by double underscoring the part to be in small caps.)

CONST.   STAT.   INT.   REV.   CODE.

C. Case Reports. Case Names.

Italicize (except the "v."), whether in the main text, footnote or index references. Law reviews italicize case names *when commented upon*, whether in main text or footnote—including the "v."—but not when cited merely and not commented upon, in the footnotes.

Piacenza v. *Brosnan* [Majority.]

1. *Initials Standing for Persons.* "A," "B," etc., standing for persons, are capitalized and italicized: *A. B.*

2. *Ex parte, Ex rel., In re, Matter of.* In briefs which italicize case names in text or footnote, these terms are also italicized. If case names are not italicized, the Latin terms, but not "Matter of" are italicized. *Ex rel.* (an abbreviation) requires a period. *In re* does not.

Law reviews differentiate Latin elements of case names typographically from the rest. Ex parte *Sterba* in the text becomes *Ex parte* Sterba in the footnote. *United States* ex rel. *Greathouse v. Smith* in the text becomes United States *ex rel.* Greathouse v. Smith in the footnote. However, "Matter of," being English, is treated as is the rest of the case name: *Matter of Pennock's Estate* in the text becomes Matter of Pennock's Estate in the law review footnote.

D. Case Reports. Subsequent History of a Case.

When noting that a cited case was later *affirmed, reversed, reversed on other grounds, affirmed* or *reversed sub nom.*, or that *certiorari* or *rehearing* was *denied* or *granted*, the significant words may be italicized. Briefs practically never do this, however. Law reviews, because these are factors bearing directly upon the value of the cited case as authority, italicize such words when (as in footnotes) the case name is in roman, but put them in roman where (as in text references) the case name is italicized. In other words, in law reviews, comment upon the subsequent history of a case is in reverse type to the case name. Briefs normally italicize only the case name in either situation. Similarly, other elements affecting the authority of a case, as *see, but see, compare . . . with, contra, semble*, and the like, may be indicated in roman in the main text and italics in the footnotes, by law reviews, but briefs print them in roman.

> *Joseph A. Holpuch Co.* v. *United States*, 104 Ct. Cl. 67, 67 F. Supp. 949 (1945), certiorari granted sub nom. *United States* v. *Joseph A. Holpuch Co.*, 327 U. S. 772, reversed, 328 U. S. 237 (1946). [Brief style.]

E. Treatises, Bulletins, Reports.

Most briefs print the entire entry, author and title, in roman type, which is simple and acceptable to courts. Many Government briefs, however, italicize the title (not including the edition note and the editor's name), with the rest of the entry in roman. This *Manual* recommends this style as being effective and easy to remember.

> Gray, *Rule against Perpetuities* (4th ed., Roland Gray, 1942).

Law reviews generally adopt that style for text references only, but the one below, in large and small caps, for footnotes.

> Gray, Rule Against Perpetuities (4th ed., Roland Gray, 1942).

Where the title is that of a periodic report or of a publication assimilated to a statute, print the whole entry in roman; that is, do not italicize "Report," "Annual Report," "Restatement," and the like.

> 1947 Atty. Gen. Ann. Rept. 49
> A. L. I. Restatement, Agency § 18 (1933).

Where the title of a series, other than a periodical, forms part of a citation, print in roman.

> Walter Hamilton, *Patents and Free Enterprise* (T. N. E. C. Monograph No. 31, 1941), p. 19

F. Periodicals and Newspapers.

Cite the name of the author of a cited article in roman type, whether the author is a person or an impersonal agency. Probably the majority of briefs cite the title in roman also, properly enclosed in quotation marks. A substantial number of government briefs, however, italicize the title, wherever appearing, as in text, footnote or index, and that form is recommended and used by this *Manual*. Law reviews citing in the main text print the title in quotation marks in roman, but in italics, less quotation marks, in footnotes.

> Lathrop, *The Racial Covenant Cases*, 1948 Wis. L. Rev. 509. [Preferred.]

Law review "Notes" titles, when given in a footnote, follow the above rules as to typography.

Everything about a newspaper citation is printed in roman, except that the title of a signed article is italicized, as though a periodical article.

G. Congressional Publications.

Titles of hearings, committee reports with titles other than "Report," Congressional documents and the like, are italicized.

1. *What is a Title, for Capitalization.*

a. Hearings. The title is everything which precedes the Congress and session notation.

> *Hearings before Senate Committee on Finance on H. R. 5327 and S. 1358 (Import Duty on Virgin Copper)*, 81st Cong., 1st Sess. (1949).

b. Committee reports. The title is everything which precedes the report number.

> *Progress on Hoover Commission Recommendations. Report of the Committee on Expenditures in the Executive Departments*, S. Rept. No. 1158, 81st Cong., 1st Sess. (1949).

c. Documents bearing a Congressional serial number. The title is everything preceding the document number.

> *Parking Lots in the District of Columbia. Report . . .* (S. Doc. No. 209, 81st Cong., 2d Sess. 1949).

H. Italics

For the use of italics in case names, treatises, periodicals and Congressional publications, *see* pages 375 and 376. Italics are indicated in manuscript by underscoring. Do not overdo it.

1. *Capital Letters Indicating Persons.*

> *A* went to see *B* about it.

2. *Conventional Words in Legislation and Legal Documents.*

> *Whereas, Resolved, Resolved further, Provided, Ordered, Be it enacted, Be it resolved.*

3. *Latin and other Foreign Words or Phrases.* Few foreign legal words or phrases are now italicized, as most of them have been taken over into the language, and it is unnecessary affectation to italicize.

a. Do not italicize the following.

ad valorem	in toto	nisi	res judicata
bona fide	in transitu	nol-pros	stare decisis
certiorari	ipso facto	pendente lite	subpoena
circa	laissez faire	post mortem	sub nom.
contra	mandamus	pro rata	ultra vires
habeas corpus			

b. Italicize the following.

ab initio	*ex parte*	*i.e.*	*in re*	*nunc pro tunc*
a fortiori	*ex rel.*	*in extenso*	*in rem*	*op. cit.*
amicus curiae	*ibid.*	*infra*	*inter se*	*sic*
ante	*id.*	*in limine*	*inter sese*	*sua sponte*
coram nobis	*idem*	*in loco parentis*	*loc. cit.*	*sui generis*
et seq.				*supra*

INDEX TO STANDARD LEGAL CITATION FORMS

BIBLIOGRAPHICAL MANUAL [1]

---

[1] This bibliographical manual has been the responsibility of Meira G. Pimsleur, Supervisor of Acquisitions of the Columbia University Law Library, with the help of the authors and of other members of the staff. Where other credit is due, it is given in footnotes to the individual appendices herein. As far as possible, the reports, digests, and other items listed were examined and their critical characteristics determined. Where dates of coverage differ from those given in similar bibliographies, it is believed that this one is the more accurate. Entries to May 30, 1953, have been included where the information was available.

Appendix I.

AMERICAN LAW REPORTS AND DIGESTS

A. Federal Law Reports
B. State and Territorial Law Reports
C. State and Territorial Case Law Digests
D. Special Subject Law Reports
E. National Reporter System
F. Annotated Reports System
G. Federal Administrative Decisions Officially Published or Sponsored

A. Federal Law Reports [1]

United States Supreme Court

"Official" Edition

Reporter	Nominative Citation	United States Reports	Dates Covered
Dallas	1–4 Dall.	1–4 U.S.	1790–1800
Cranch	1–9 Cr.	5–13 U.S.	1801–1815
Wheaton	1–12 Wheat	14–25 U.S.	1816–1827
Peters [2]	1–16 Pet.	26–41 U.S.	1828–1842
Howard	1–24 How.	42–65 U.S.	1843–1860
Black	1–2 Black	66–67 U.S.	1861–1862
Wallace	1–23 Wall.	68–90 U.S.	1863–1874
United States Reports		91–[345]	1875–[1953]

Unofficial Editions

Curtis' Reports of Decisions	22 v.	2–58 U.S.	1790–1854
Miller's U. S. Supreme Court Decisions	4 v.	59–67 U.S.	1855–1862
United States Reports, Lawyers' Edition	[97] v.	1–[345] U.S.	1790–[1953]
Myer's Federal Decisions	30 v.		1790–1884
Peters' Condensed Reports	4 v.	1–25 U.S.	1791–1827
Supreme Court Reporter	[73] v.	106–[345] U.S.	1882–[1953]
Morrison's Transcript (See also Chapter XIII B.)	5 v.		1880–1883

---

[1] The latest volume numbers and dates of sets still current are enclosed in brackets [ ].

[2] A 17th volume of Peters is not considered as part of the official set. The cases in it are reported in 1 Howard.

Lower Federal Courts [3]

Various Circuit Courts, Circuit Courts of Appeals, Courts of Appeals, and District Courts

	Volumes	Period Covered
Alaska Federal Reports	5	1869–1937
(Continued by Alaska Reports, 9–date)		
Federal Cases [4]	30, Digest	1789–1879
Federal Reporter	300	1880–1924
Federal Reporter, 2d Series	[200]	1924–[1953]
Federal Rules Decisions	[12]	1939–[1953]
Federal Supplement	[110]	1924–[1953]
Myer's Federal Decisions	30	1790–1884
U. S. Courts of Appeals Reports	63	1892–1899
U. S. Circuit Courts of Appeals Reports	171	1892–1919
(Continued by Federal Reporter, v. 260–date)		

Reports Covering Various Old Circuits or Districts

	Volumes	Period Covered
Abbott's Circuit and District Court Reports	2	1863–1871
American Law Register		
(Through v. 41 N. S. this predecessor of the University of Pennsylvania Law Review printed many lower federal court reports not elsewhere published.)		
Banning and Arden's Reports . . . Patents	5	1874–1883
Brunner's Reports . . . Collected	1	1791–1860
Fisher's Reports . . . Patents	6	1848–1873
Monthly Law Reporter (Boston)	27	1838–1866

Circuit Court, First Circuit

Gallison, Reports . . . First Circuit	2	1812–1815
Mason, Reports . . . First Circuit	5	1816–1830
Sumner, Reports . . . First Circuit	3	1829–1839
Story, Reports . . . First Circuit	3	1839–1845
Woodbury and Minot, Reports . . . First Circuit	3	1845–1847
Curtis, Reports . . . First Circuit	2	1851–1856
Clifford, Reports . . . First Circuit	4	1870–1878
Holmes, Reports . . . First Circuit	1	1870–1875
Lowell, Judgments (*see* Massachusetts District)		

Circuit Court, Second Circuit

Paine, Reports . . . Second Circuit	2	1810–1840
Blatchford, Reports . . . Second Circuit	24	1845–1887

Circuit Court, Third Circuit

Wallace, J. B., Reports . . . (Wall. Sen.)	1	1801

---

[3] For a discussion of the reports of these courts, *see* Chapter 13, C, D.

[4] Nearly all of the approximately 230 different series reporting lower federal court cases up to 1880 are reprinted in *Federal Cases,* and the series are listed alphabetically in the green-paged "Table of Citations" in the Digest volume of that set. Few libraries have the original reports. However, a few reporters were so well known (though unofficial) that for convenience they are listed below. The dates of coverage given differ occasionally from those assigned in other bibliographies, but are believed to be correct.

	Volumes	Period Covered
Peters, Reports ... Third Circuit	1	1803–1818
Washington, Reports ... Third Circuit	4	1803–1827
Baldwin, Reports ... Third Circuit	1	1827–1833
Wallace, Jr., Cases ... Third Circuit	3	1842–1862
Dallas 2–4 (2–4 U. S.) contains Circuit Cases.		

Circuit Court, Fourth Circuit

	Volumes	Period Covered
Brockenbrough (*see* Marshall, below)		
Hughes, Reports ... Fourth Circuit	5	1792–1883
Marshall, Reports ... by Brockenbrough	2	1802–1836
Taney, Reports ... by Campbell	1	1836–1861
Chase, Reports ... by Jobson	1	1865–1869
Call's Va. Reports, v. 6, pp. 241–376		1793–1825

Circuit Court, Fifth Circuit

	Volumes	Period Covered
Woods, Cases ... Fifth Judicial Circuit	4	1870–1883
(*See also* 35 Ga. 285–365)		

Circuit Court, New Sixth and Seventh Circuits

	Volumes	Period Covered
Bond, Reports ...	2	1856–1871
Brown, Reports of Admiralty ...	1	1856–1875
Flippin, Reports ... Sixth Judicial Circuit	2	1859–1881

Circuit Court, Old Seventh Circuit

	Volumes	Period Covered
McLean, Reports ... Seventh Circuit	6	1829–1855
Bissell, Cases ... Seventh Judicial Circuit	11	1851–1883

Circuit Court, Eighth Circuit

	Volumes	Period Covered
Miller, Cases ... Eighth Circuit ... by Woolworth	1	1863–1869
Woolworth (*see* above.)		
Dillon, Cases ... Eighth Circuit	5	1870–1880
McCrary, Cases ... Eighth Circuit	5	1873–1883
Hempstead A*see* Ninth Circuit.)		

Circuit Court, Ninth Circuit

	Volumes	Period Covered
Hempstead (*see* Ninth Circuit.)		
McAllister, Reports ... Districts of California	1	1855–1859
Deady, Reports ... Oregon and California	1	1859–1869
(Although the title page reads "1859–1869," the first case reported is for January 8, 1861.)		
Sawyer, Reports ... Circuit and District Courts, Ninth Circuit	14	1870–1891

Circuit Court, District of Columbia Circuit

	Volumes	Period Covered
Cranch, Reports ...	6	1801–1841
(*See also* "State and Territorial Courts," *post*.)		

District Courts

District of Arkansas

	Volumes	Period Covered
Hempstead	1	1820–1856
(Territory Reports, 1820–1836; District Court, 1836–1849; Circuit Court, 1838–1856.)		

Districts of California and Oregon

	Volumes	Period Covered
Hoffman, Reports of Land Cases	1	1853–1858
Deady (*See* Ninth Circuit.)		
Sawyer (*See* Ninth Circuit.)		

	Volumes	*Period Covered*

District of Columbia District
(*See* under "State and Territorial Courts.")

District of Kansas
(*See* under "State and Territorial Courts.")

District of Maine

Ware, Reports ... District of Maine	3	1822–1866
Haskell, Reports ... District of Maine ("by Fox")	2	1866–1881

District of Massachusetts

Sprague, Decisions ... in Admiralty	2	1841–1864
Lowell, Judgments ... District of Massachusetts	2	1865–1877

District of New Hampshire
(*See* Smith's New Hampshire Reports, p. 432.)

District of New York

Van Ness, Reports of Two Cases ... Prize Court	1	1814
Blatchford and Howland, Reports ... S. Dist. of N. Y.	1	1827–1837
Olcott, Reports ... in Admiralty, S. Dist. of N.Y.	1	1843–1847
Abbott, Reports ... Admiralty	1	1847–1850
Blatchford, Reports ... of Cases in Prize	1	1861–1865
Benedict, Reports ... Second Circuit	10	1865–1879

District of Pennsylvania

Hopkins, Judgments in Admiralty	1	1779–1788
(*See* John W. Wallace, *The Reporters*, 4th ed., 1882, p. 567.)		
Peters, Admiralty Decisions	2	1780–1807
Fisher, Cases ... [in Prize]	1	1812–1813
Gilpin, Reports, Eastern Dist. of Pa.	1	1828–1836
Crabbe, Reports ... Eastern Dist. of Pa.	1	1836–1846
Cadwalader's Cases	2	1858–1879

District of North Carolina
Martin's Decisions
(*See* North Carolina, "State and Territorial Courts.")

District of South Carolina

Bee, Reports ... District Court of South Carolina	1	1792–1805
(Also known as Bee's Admiralty Reports, because of an appendix covering 1779–1809, by Francis Hopkinson.)		

District of Vermont
(*See* 20–25 Vermont Reports at page 408.)

District of Virginia
(*See* Hughes' Circuit Court Reports, p. 7.)

Pacific State Districts

Hoffman's Land Cases	1	1853–1858
Deady (*See* Ninth Circuit.)		
Sawyer (*See* Ninth Circuit.)		

Western Districts

Newberry, Reports of Admiralty Cases	1	1842–1857
Brown, Reports of Admiralty and Revenue Cases	1	1856–1875
(The Circuit Court Reports of Bissell, Bond, Flippin and Hempstead also contain Western District cases.)		

	Volumes	Period Covered
Separate Federal Courts. *See also* Chapter 30 D.		
Commerce Court		
Opinions of the U. S. Commerce Court	1	1911–1913
Court for China		
Extraterritorial Cases (Lobingier)	2	1920–1924
Court of Claims		
Reports . . . Submitted to the House of Representatives. (Unnumbered reports bearing Congressional serial numbers 871, 872, 915, 970–972, 1021, 1072–1076, 1108–1110, 1146, 1147, 1173)	18	1855–1863
Cases Decided in the Court of Claims	[122]	1863–[1953]
Devereux, Reports and Digest	1	1855–1856
Court of Customs Appeals		
Cases Decided	16	1919–1929
Court of Customs and Patent Appeals (Name since April 1929)		
Customs Cases Adjudged	17–[40]	1929–[1953]
Patent Cases Adjudged	17–[40]	1929–[1953]
(Beginning with v. 17 there are two parallel series, cited as C. C. P. A. (Customs); C. C. P. A. (Patents.)		
Court of Military Appeals		
(*See* Federal Administrative Agencies and Tribunals, *post.*)		
Customs Court		
(To May 1926, Board of U.S. General Appraisers) Reappraisement Decisions (From January 1900 to December 1933, as Treasury Department Circulars; from January 1934 to June 1938, in Treasury Decisions, v. 65–73; from July 1938 to date in Customs Court *Reports.* Currently they appear also in the weekly Treasury Decisions advance sheets, but no longer in the bound *Treasury Decisions.*)		1900–[1953]
Reports	[29]	1938–[1953]
Emergency Court of Appeals		
Official "slip" decisions are published Reported in the *Federal Reporter.*		1943–[1953]
Tax Court		
(*See* Federal Administrative Agencies and Tribunals, *post.*)		

B. State and Territorial Law Reports

This bibliography includes a few reprints or unofficial parallel reports, where the authors have thought it would be helpful to do so. It should be noted that in Arkansas, California, Connecticut, Kentucky, Maryland, Massachusetts, Michigan, Missouri, Oklahoma, Pennsylvania, Tennessee and Texas, the West Publishing Company publishes parallel series of reports, called "Reporters" or "Decisions," taken from the National Reporter System units covering the respective States. They have all the usual Reporter tables and other features.

Entries enclosed in brackets [ ] are still current, in which case the volume number given is the latest published when this list was compiled.

State Report Series	Period Covered	No. of Vols. to date
ALABAMA		
Minor	1820–1826	1
Stewart	1827–1831	3
Stewart and Porter	1831–1834	5
Porter	1834–1839	9
Smith's Condensed Reports	1820–1879	10
(new ed. of decisions including Minor, Stewart, Stewart & Porter, Porter and 1–8 Alabama)		
Alabama Reports	1840–[1952]	257
Shepard's Select Cases	1861–1863	1
(published in 37, 38, 39 Alabama)		
Alabama Appeals	1910–[1950]	35
ALASKA		
Alaska Federal Reports	1869–1937	5
Alaska Reports	1867–[1952]	13 vols. to date

(1867–87 appear only in Index-Digest vol. 1, since cases can be found in full in Federal Cases, reprint, and in Federal Reporter v. 1-118)

ARIZONA		
Arizona Reports (Supreme Court)	1866–[1952]	73
ARKANSAS		
(Terr.) Hempstead (Superior Court)	1820–1836	1
(State) Arkansas Reports	1837–[1950]	218
Martin's Decisions in Equity	1895–1900	1
Arkansas Law Reporter	1911–1916	17
The Law Reporter	1919–1937	63
CALIFORNIA		
California Decisions; the standard for over fifty years. Continues California Appellate Decisions, and California Decisions (Supreme Court), q. v.	1940–1941	7
Western Reports: Decisions of California Merged with the above	1940	1

DISTRICT COURTS AND DISTRICT COURTS OF APPEAL

Labatt	1857–1858	2
California Appellate	1905–1934	140
California Appellate (2d)	1934–[1952]	112
California Appellate Decisions	1905–1940	103
"Official organ of District Courts of Appeal" Succeeded by Advance California Appellate Reports, Dec. 6, 1940 to date, which in some libraries are bound up from advance sheets.		
California Appellate Decisions Supplement	1929–1940	3

PROBATE

Myrick	1872–1879	1
Coffey	1883–1915	6
Coffey (ed. Lyons and Tauszky)	1883–1896	2

SUPERIOR

Ragland (Superior Court Decisions)	1921–1926	2
(Work done on a third volume, but never published)		

State Report Series	Period Covered	No. of Vols. to date
CALIFORNIA (cont.)		
Appellate Departments	1929–[1952]	
(in California Appellate, v. 106–140; California Appellate (2d) 1–[112] as Appendix "California Supplement")		

SUPREME

Late Political Decisions of the Supreme Court	1855	1
("State Journal" Office, Sacramento)		
California Reports	1850–1934	220
California Reports (2d)	1934–[1952]	38
California Decisions	1890–1940	100
"Official organ of the Supreme Court"		
succeeded by		
Advance California Reports, Dec. 4, 1940 to date, which in some libraries are bound up from advance sheets		
California Unreported Cases	1855–1910	7
Unwritten Decisions (Ragland)	1878–1879	1

PERIODICALS, ETC., CONTAINING REPORTS

California Legal Record (Supreme Court)	1878–1879	2
California Jurisprudence		27
California Jurisprudence (2d ed.)		7
Pacific Coast Law Journal	1878–1883	12
San Francisco Law Journal	1877–1878	1

COLORADO		
Colorado Reports	1864–[1951]	124
Another ed. (Chicago, Callaghan)		
(1–4 as Annotated ed.)	1864–1932	91
Court of Appeals	1891–1905; 1912–1915	27
Colorado Law Reporter	1880–1884	4
Colorado Decisions (Annotated)	1900–1902	4
Colorado Nisi Prius Decisions. Repr. from Legal Adviser, v. 3, no. 13 – v. 6, no. 3 (Mills)	1900–1902	1

CONNECTICUT		
Particular Court: Records (Andros) (1935)	1687–1688	1
Particular Court: Records (Conn. Historical Society Collections, v. 22, 1928)	1639–1663	1
Superior Court Diary of William Samuel Johnson (American Historical Association. American Legal Records, v. 4, 1942)	1772–1773	1
Kirby (Waterbury, Dissell, 1898)	1785–1788	1
Kirby (Litchfield, Collier, 1789)	1785–1788	1
Kirby (Supp.)	1785–1789	1
(from a MSS vol. by Case, Lockwood & Brainard. Acorn Club, 1933)		
Root (with a variety of cases 1774–1789)	1789–1798	2
Day	1802–1813	5
Connecticut Reports	1814–[1952]	138
Connecticut Supplement	1935–[1952]	17

DAKOTA		
Dakota Reports	1867–1889	6

State Report Series	Period Covered	No. of Vols. to date
DELAWARE		
Delaware cases (Boorstin) [West]	1792–1830	3
v.3 has tables and digest		
Harrington 1–5 Del.	1832–1854	5
Houston 6–14 Del.	1855–1892	9
Marvel 15–16 Del.	1893–1897	2
Pennewill 17–23 Del.	1897–1909	7
Boyce 24–30 Del.	1909–1920	7
W. W. Harrington 31–39 Del.	1919–1939	9
Terry 40–[45] Del.	1939–[1950]	5
Houston's Criminal (Delaware Criminal Cases)	1856–1879	1
Delaware Chancery	1814–[1952]	30
DISTRICT OF COLUMBIA		
Cranch 1–6 D. C. (v.6: Index)	1801–1840	6
District of Columbia 6–7 D. C.	1863–1872	2
MacArthur 8–10 D. C.	1873–1879	3
MacArthur & Mackey 11 D. C.	1879–1880	1
Mackey 12–20 D. C.	1880–1892	9
Tucker & Clephane 21 D. C.	1892–1893	1
Hayward and Hazleton	1840–1863	2
MacArthur's Patent Cases	1841–1859	1
Appeal Cases	1893–[1952]	90
v.1–62 as District of Columbia Court of Appeals (1893–Dec.1933)		
v. 63–[90] as United States Court of Appeals for the District of Columbia (1934–[1952])		
Additional Cases	1901	1
McCormick (Supreme Court, N. S.)	1933–1935	2
Washington Law Reporter	1874–[1953]	81
Municipal Court of Appeals, Municipal Court, and a variety of other lower courts		
FLORIDA		
Florida Reports	1846–1948	160
continued as Southern Reporter, Florida Cases (2d) v. 37–		
Florida Supplement (lower courts of record and State commissions	1952–[1953]	2
GEORGIA		
Charlton, T. U. P.	1805–1811	1
Charlton, R. M.	1811–1837	1
Gault, Joseph	1820–1846	1
Dudley	1830–1833	1
Georgia Decisions	1842–1843	1 (2 pts.)
Georgia Reports	1846–[1952]	208
Georgia Reports Supplement to Volume 33	1864	1
Georgia Law Reporter	1885–1886	1
Georgia Appeals Reports	1907–[1952]	85

GUAM

"There are no printed reports for the decisions of the courts for Guam, Mariannas. They are either handed down and entered in the record or occasionally are mimeographed and sent to the Navy Dept., Washington. If the name of a particular case is known, an interested person may write to the Governor of Guam, who will send a copy of the particular decision." Letter from the Chief of the Law Division, Army Library, to the Columbia University Law Librarian, May 9, 1949.

State	Report Series	Period Covered	No. of Vols. to date
HAWAII			
Hawaii Reports (Supreme Court)		1847–[1950]	38
Ke Alakai o Ki Kanaka Hawaii (Poepoe)		1849–1889	1
District Court (U. S.)		1900–1917	4
IDAHO			
Cummins		1866–1867	1
Idaho Reports		1866–[1952]	72
Reports (Bancroft-Whitney)		1893–1932	51
ILLINOIS			
Illinois Reports (Supreme Court)		1819–[1952]	412 (see below
Breese	1 Ill.	1819–1831	for reporters)
Blackwell v. 1		1819–1841	1
Reports (no reporter)		Dec. Term 1832	1
Forman (continuation of Breese; contained in 1 Scammon)		1832–1838	
Scammon	2–5 Ill.	1832–1843	
Gilman	6–10 Ill.	1844–1849	
Illinois	11–	1850–	
Illinois Appellate Court		1877–[1952]	347
Illinois Circuit Court (Matthews and Bangs)		*1905–1912	4
Court of Claims		1889–[1951]	20
Chicago Law Journal (Barber)		1876–1878	1
INDIAN TERRITORY			
Indian Territory Reports		1896–1907	7
INDIANA			
Blackford (Supreme Court)		1817–1847	8
Smith's Supreme Court		1848–1849	1
Indiana Reports (Supreme Court)		1848–[1952]	230
Wilson's Superior Court		1871–1874	1
Indiana Appellate		1890–[1952]	122
IOWA			
Bradford		1838–1841	3 (in 1)
Morris		1839–1846	1
Greene		1847–1854	4
Iowa Reports (Supreme Court)		1855–[1952]	242
KANSAS			
McCahon		1858–1868	1
Kansas Reports (Supreme Court)		1862–[1951]	171
Kansas Appellate		1895–1901	10
Randolph		1895–1896	2
Dewey		1895–1896	2
Clemens		1896–1897	2
Dewey		1897–1901	4
Dassler (Supreme Court)		1862–1868	1†
KENTUCKY			
Kentucky Reports (Court of Appeals)		1785–1951	314
Continued in South Western Reporter 2d. v. 237–			(See below for reporters)

* Current case reports begin with 1905; some unreported and other earlier cases as far back as 1866 are reported, however.

† Intended to take the place of Kansas Reports v. 1, o.p. McCahon's Reports revised and appended to this volume.

State Report Series	Period Covered	No. of Vols. to date
KENTUCKY (cont.)		
Hughes 1 Ky.	1785–1801	1
Kentucky Decisions		
(Sneed) 2 Ky.	1801–1805	1
Hardin 3 Ky.	1805–1808	1
Bibb 4–7 Ky.	1808–1817	4
Marshall, A. K. 8–10 Ky.	1817–1821	3
Littell 11–15 Ky.	1822–1824	5
Littell's Selected Cases 16 Ky.	1795–1821	1
Monroe, T. B. 17–23 Ky.	1824–1828	7
Marshall, J. J. 24–30 Ky.	1829–1832	7
Dana 31–39 Ky.	1833–1840	9
Monroe, Ben 40–57 Ky.	1840–1857	18
Metcalfe 58–61 Ky.	1858–1863	4
Duvall 62–63 Ky.	1863–1866	2
Bush 64–77 Ky.	1866–1879	14
Kentucky Reports 78–314	1879–1951	237
Kentucky Opinions (Court of Appeals)	1864–1886	15
v. 14–15: Digests		
Kentucky Law Reporter	1880–1908	33
LOUISIANA		
Martin (Louisiana Term Reports. Old Series)	1809–1823	12
v. 1–2 (1809–1812) called Orleans Term Reports;		
v. 3–12 (1813–1823) as Louisiana Term Reports.		
Martin (Louisiana Term Reports, New Series)	1823–1830	8
Louisiana Reports (Supreme Court)	1830–1841	19
Miller 1–5	1830–1833	
Curry 6–19	1833–1841	
Robinson (Supreme Court)	1841–1846	12
Louisiana Annual (Supreme Court)	1846–1900	52
Manning's Unreported Cases	1877–1880	1
Louisiana Reports, Annotated Reprint Edition,		
1 Martin - 48 Louisiana Annual		100 vols. in 55 books
Louisiana Reports (Supreme Court)	1901–[1952]	v.104–220
		to date
(first vol. following 52 La. Ann. (1900) num-		
bered 104, since Martin, Louisiana, Robinson,		
Annuals and Manning totalled 103 vols.)		
McGloin (Court of Appeal)	1881–1884	2
Harrison, Condensed Reports (Supreme Court)	1809–1830	4
Gunby's Reports (Circuit Court of Appeals)	1885.	1
Teissier, Orleans Court of Appeals	1903–1917	14
Court of Appeals Reports	1924–1932	19
MAINE		
Province and Court Records	1636–1692	3
Circuit Courts Martial (F.O.J. Smith)	1831	1
Maine Reports (Supreme Court)	1820–[1950]	145 (see below for reporters)
Greenleaf 1–9 Maine	1820–1832	9
Fairfield 10–12 Maine	1833–1835	3
Maine 13–	1836–	
MARYLAND		
(Colony) Provincial Court; Judicial and Testa-		
mentary Business	1637–1670	5

State	Report Series	Period Covered	No. of Vols. to date
MARYLAND (cont.)			
Proceedings: Kent County		1648–1676	
Talbot County		1662–1674	
Somerset County		1665–1668	1
Proceedings: Charles County		1666–1674	2
Proceedings: Court of Chancery		1669–1679	1
Proceedings: Court of Appeals		1695–1729	1
(American legal records . v.1)			
Harris and M'Henry (General Court)		1658–1799	4
Harris and Johnson (Court of Appeals)		1800–1826	7
Harris and Gill (Court of Appeals)		1826–1829	2
Gill and Johnson (Court of Appeals)		1829–1842	12
Gill (Court of Appeals)			
(v. 8–9 completed by Miller)		1843–1851	9
Maryland Reports (Court of Appeals)		1851–[1949]	194
Bland (High Court of Chancery)		1811–1832	3
Maryland Chancery Decisions (or Reports)		1847–1854	4
Baltimore City Reports		1888–1928	4
MASSACHUSETTS			
(Colony) Records of the Court of Assistants (Noble)		1630–1692	3
Records of the Quarterly Courts Essex County		1636–1683	8
Records of the Quarterly Courts Suffolk County		1671–1680	2
Abstract and Index of the Records of Inferiour Court of Pleas (Suffolk County) (Historical Records Survey, 1940)		1680–1698	1
Records of the Court of General Sessions of the Peace (Worcester County)		1731–1737	1
(Province) Quincy (Superior Court of Judicature)		1761–1772	1
Massachusetts Reports (Supreme Judicial Court)		1804–[1951]	327(see below for reporters)
Williams	1 Mass.	1804–1805	1
Tyng	2–17 Mass.	1806–1820	16
Pickering	18–41 Mass.	1820–1839	24
Metcalf	42–54 Mass.	1840–1847	13
Cushing	55–66 Mass.	1848–1853	12
Gray	67–82 Mass.	1854–1860	16
Allen	83–96 Mass.	1861–1867	14
Browne (Reporter numbering ceases with v. 4)			
	97–100 Mass.	1867–1872	13
Thacher's Criminal Cases		1823–1842	1
Cushing's Contested Elections		1780–1852	1
Loring & Russell's Contested Elections		1853–1885	1
Russell's Contested Elections		1866–1902	1
Howard's Contested Election Cases		1903–1922	1
Davis, Land Court Decisions		1898–1908	1
Department Reports . . . "affecting business, with Supreme court decisions in full"		1915–1920	9

State Report Series	Period Covered	No. of Vols. to date
MASSACHUSETTS (cont.)		
Boston Municipal Court, Appellate Division	1935	1
Appellate Division Reports (District Courts)	1936–[1950]	15
Massachusetts Appellate Decisions (District Courts)	1941–[1951]	3
MICHIGAN		
Woodward, Unreported Cases in "Some Unreported Opinions of a Territorial Judge, 1805–1823," by Olive C. Lathrop. Law Library Journal 21:66–77, October 1928	1805–1823	
Blume, Supreme Court Transactions	1805–1836	6
Blume, Unreported Opinions	1836–1843	1
Harrington's Chancery	1836–1842	1
Walker's Chancery	1842–1845	1
Douglass (Supreme Court)	1843–1847	2
Michigan Reports (Supreme Court)	1847–[1952]	333
Howell's Nisi Prius Cases	1868–1884	1
Brown's Nisi Prius Reports	1869–1871	2
McGrath's Mandamus Cases	1891–1897	1
Fuller's Practice Reports (Supreme Court)	1896	1
Fiske's Overruled Cases (Supreme Court)	1925	1
Court of Claims	1939–1942	2
MINNESOTA		
Minnesota Reports (Supreme Court)	1851–[1951]	234
MISSISSIPPI		
Mississippi Court Records	1799–1859	1
Mississippi Reports	1818–[1952]	213 (see below for reporters)
Walker 1 Miss.	1818–1832	1
Howard 2–8 Miss.	1834–1843	7
Smedes & Marshall 9–22 Miss.	1843–1850	14
Mississippi 23–	1851–	
Freeman's Chancery	1839–1843	1
Smedes & Marshall's Chancery	1840–1843	1
Morris' State Cases	1818–1872	2
Mississippi Unreported Decisions (Hemingway & McDonald)	1820–1885	2
MISSOURI		
Missouri Reports (Supreme Court)	1821–[1952]	362
Missouri Appeal Reports	1876–[1950]	240
MONTANA		
Montana Reports (Supreme Court)	1868–[1951]	124
State Reporter, mimeographed advance sheets, issued by Chief Justice's Secretary	1947?–[1952]	
NEBRASKA		
Nebraska Reports (Supreme Court)	1860–[1952]	155
Nebraska Unofficial	1901–1904	5
NEVADA		
Nevada Reports (Supreme Court)	1865–[1950]	67
NEW HAMPSHIRE		
Smith (Cases printed out of chronological order)	1796–1816	1
New Hampshire Reports (Supreme Court)	1816–[1951]	96
New Hampshire Law Reporter (Supreme Ct.)	1897	1

State	Report Series	Period Covered	No. of Vols. to date
NEW JERSEY			
(Colony)			
Journal of the Courts of Common Right and Chancery of East N. J.		1683–1702	1
(Princeton Univ. Thesis, P. W. Edsall)			
Burlington Court Book of West N. J., Reed and Miller (American Legal Records, v. 5)		1680–1709	1
(State)			
Bloomfield, Manumission Cases		1775–1793	1
New Jersey Law Reports (Supreme Court)			
Coxe	1 N. J. Law	1790–1795	1
Pennington	2–3 N. J. Law	1806–1813	2
Southard	4–5 N. J. Law	1816–1820	2
Halsted	6–12 N. J. Law	1796–1804; 1821–1831	7
Greene, J. S.	13–15 N. J. Law	1831–1836	3
Harrison	16–19 N. J. Law	1837–1842	4
Spencer	20 N. J. Law	1842–1846	1
Zabriskie	21–24 N. J. Law	1847–1855	4
Dutcher	25–29 N. J. Law	1855–1862	5
Vroom, P. D.	30–35 N. J. Law	1862–1872	6
Vroom, G. D. W.	36–85 N. J. Law	1872–1914	50
Gummere	86–125 N. J. Law	1914–1921	41
Abbott	126–137 N. J. Law	1940–1948	10
Continued by New Jersey Reports (Supreme Court)		1948–[1952]	9
New Jersey Equity Reports			
Saxton	1 N. J. Eq.	1830–1832	1
Green	2–4 N. J. Eq.	1834–1845	3
Halsted	5–8 N. J. Eq.	1845–1853	4
Stockton	9–11 N. J. Eq.	1852–1858	3
Beasley	11–12 N. J. Eq.	1856–1861	2
McCarter	14–15 N. J. Eq.	1861–1863	2
Green, C. E.	16–27 N. J. Eq.	1862–1876	12
Stewart	28–45 N. J. Eq.	1877–1889	18
Dickinson	46–66 N. J. Eq.	1889–1904	21
Robbins	67–70 N. J. Eq.	1904–1905	4
Buchanan	71–85 N. J. Eq.	1906–1916	15
Stockton	86–101 N. J. Eq.	1916–1927	16
Backes	102–142 N. J. Eq.	1926–1948	41
Continued by New Jersey Superior Court Reports		1948–[1952]	21
New Jersey Miscellaneous		1923–1949	26

NEW MEXICO

Acknowledgment is made to Professor Arie Poldervaart, Librarian of the University of New Mexico College of Law, for information leading to the listing of the early New Mexico Reports. Confusion has been caused by designating 3 and 4 Gildersleeve as "official" or "unofficial." Strictly speaking, the distinction is only between the publishers of these volumes. Original Gildersleeve 3 and 4 (published by Bancroft-Whitney) are sometimes cited as "Unofficial, "whereas the E. W. Stephens reprint of these volumes was declared "Official" by the Territorial Supreme Court. The Stephens edition of these volumes differs in pagination and content from the original Bancroft-Whitney edition. No Johnson volumes are official. Citation of cases in 3 and 4 New Mexico as follows avoids all confusion:

Chisum v. Ayers, 3 N. M. (Gild., B.-W. ed.) 538, 4 N. M. (Gild., E. W. S. ed.) 89, 4 N. M. (John.) 48, 12 Pac. 697 (1887).

State	Report Series	Period Covered	No. of Vols. to date

NEW MEXICO (cont.)

New Mexico Reports (Supreme Court)		1852–[1951]	55
Gildersleeve	1	1852–1879	
Gildersleeve	2	1880–1883	
Gildersleeve	3 (Brancroft-Whitney)	1883–1886	
Gildersleeve	3 (reprint, E. W. Stephens)	1883–1886	
Johnson	3	1883–1886	
Gildersleeve	4 (Bancroft-Whitney)	1887–1889	
Gildersleeve	4 (reprint, E. W. Stephens)	1887–1889	
Johnson	4 (includes more cases than Gildersleeve)	1887–1889	
Gildersleeve	5	1888	

NEW YORK

Acknowledgment is made to Lawyers Cooperative Publishing Company and West Publishing Company for permission to use material from volume 2 of Abbott's New York Digest in this list.

New York State Reporter	1886–1896	75
New York Supplement	1888–1937	300
New York Supplement 2d series	1938–[1953]	118

LAW AND SUPREME

Coleman's Cases	1791–1800	1
contains 2 Supreme Court Orders, 1791 & 1793, but no cases prior to 1794.		
Coleman & Caines' Cases	1794–1805	1
Johnson's Cases	1799–1803	3
Caines' Cases	1796–1805	2
Caines' New York Term Reports	1803–1805	3
Johnson's Reports	1806–1823	20
Anthon's Nisi Prius	1807–1851	1
Yates Select Cases	1809	1
Coleman's, Coleman & Caines', Caines,' Yates Select Cases, Reprint ed. Diossy, 1883	1794–1809	4 in 1
Cowen	1823–1829	9
Wendell	1826–1841	26
Hill	1841–1844	7
Denio	1845–1848	5
Hill and Denio Supp., Lalor	1842–1844	1

New York Common Law Reports, Lawyers' Edition, (from Coleman through Denio v. 5)

- v. 1:   Coleman's Cases, 1 v.; Coleman & Caines' Cases, 1 v.; Johnson's Cases, 3 v.
- v. 2:   Caines' Reports, 3 v.; Caine's Cases in Error, 2 v.
- v. 3–6: Johnson's Reports, 20 v.
- v. 7:   Anthon's Nisi Prius, Yates' Select Cases, Lockwood's reversed cases, Cowen's Reports, v. 1–2.
- v. 8:   Cowen's Reports, v. 3–6.
- v. 9:   Cowen's Reports, v. 7–9; Wendell's Reports, v. 1.
- v. 10–14: Wendell's Reports, v. 2–26.
- v. 15:   Hill's Reports, v. 1–4.
- v. 16:   Hill's Reports, v. 5–7; Denio's Reports, v. 1.
- v. 17:   Denio's Reports, v. 2–5.
- Index

Edmond's Select Cases	1834–1853	2
Lockwood's Reversed Cases	1799–1847	1
Barbour's Supreme Court	1847–1877	67

NEW YORK (cont.)

State	Report Series	Period Covered	No. of Vols. to date
Lansing's Supreme Court		1869–1873	7
Thompson and Cook		1873–1875	6
Hun		1874–1895	92
Appellate Division		1896–[1951]	278
Silvernail's Supreme Court Reports		1889–1890	5
Winer, Unreported Opinions (In Dennis Buffalo City Court Act Annotated, 1940)		1912–1940	1

CHANCERY

Johnson's Chancery		1814–1823	7
Hopkins		1823–1826	1
Lansing's Select Cases		1824, 1826	1
Paige		1828–1845	11
Edwards		1831–1850	4
Hoffman		1839–1840	1
Clarke		1839–1841	1
Saratoga Chancery Sentinel		1841–1847	6 in 1
Sandford's Chancery		1843–1847	4
Barbour's Chancery		1845–1848	3
New York Chancery Reports Annotated Reprint		1814–1847	7

    v. 1: Johnson's Chancery, v. 1–5.
    v. 2: Johnson's Chancery, v. 6–7; Hopkins Chancery,
         v. 1; Paige's Chancery, v. 1–2.
    v. 3: Paige's Chancery, v. 3–6.
    v. 4: Paige's Chancery, v. 7–10.
    v. 5: Paige's Chancery, v. 11; Barbour's Chancery,
         v. 1–3; Chancery Sentinel, v. 1–6.
    v. 6: Edward's Chancery, v. 1–4; Hoffman's Chancery.
    v. 7: Clarke's Chancery; Sandford's Chancery, v. 1–4.

COURT OF APPEALS

New York			1847–[1952]	303
Comstock	1–4	N.Y.	1847–1851	4
Selden	5–10	N.Y.	1851–1854	6
Kernan	11–14	N.Y.	1854–1856	4
New York	15–			
Howard's Appeal Cases			1847–1848	1
Keyes			1863–1868	4
(Unofficial; cited as 40–43 N.Y.)				
Abbott			1850–1869	4
Selden's Notes			1852–1854	1
Tiffany, Transcript Appeals			1867–1868	7
New York Condensed Reports			1881–1882	1
Silvernail			1886–1892	4
New York Court of Appeals Reports (Reprint)			1847–1888	22

PRACTICE AND CODE

Howard's Practice		1844–1884	67
Howard's Practice, N.S.		1884–1886	3
Code Reporter		1848–1851	3
Code Reporter, N.S.		1850–1852	1
Abbott's Practice Cases		1854–1865	19
Abbott's Practice Cases, New Series		1865–1875	16
Abbott's New Cases		1876–1894	32
Civil Procedure Reports		1881–1907	40

    (vol. 40 is Table of cases to v. 1–39, Civil Pro-

State	Report Series	Period Covered	No. of Vols. to date

NEW YORK (cont.)

cedure Reports, and v. 1–3, New York Monthly Law Record)

Civil Procedure Reports, New Series	1908–1913	4
McCarty's Civil Procedure Reports (Unofficial, cited as 2 N. Y. Civ. Pro. Rep. (McCarty)	1882	1
New York Monthly Law Record	1896–1898	3
New York Miscellaneous	1892–[1951]	199
New York Annotated Cases	1894–1908	20
New York Leading Cases Annotated	1912–1914	2
Noble's Current Court Decisions	1908–1910	3
Bradbury's Pleading and Practice Reports	1910–1919	5

SURROGATE

Bradford	1849–1857	4
Redfield	1857–1882	5
Tucker	1864–1869	1
Demarest	1882–1888	6
Connoly	1888–1891	2
Power	1890–1894	1
Gibbons	1893–1898	2
Mills	1899–1917	18

SUPERIOR COURT

Hall	1–2 N. Y. S. Ct.	1828–1829	2
Sandford	3–7 N. Y. S. Ct.	1847–1852	5
Duer	8–13 N. Y. S. Ct.	1852–1857	6
Bosworth	14–23 N. Y. S. Ct.	1856–1863	10
Robertson	24–30 N. Y. S. Ct.	1863–1868	7
Sweeny	31–32 N. Y. S. Ct.	1869–1870	2
Jones and Spencer	33–61 N. Y. S. Ct.	1871–1892	29
Sheldon, Buffalo Superior Court		1854–1875	1

COMMON PLEAS

Livingston, Judicial Opinions	1802	1
Smith, E. D.	1850–1858	4
Hilton	1855–1860	2
Daly	1859–1891	16

CITY COURT

Select Cases of the Mayor's Court of New York City (American Legal Records, v. 2)	1674–1784	1
Marine Court; City Court Reports	1874–1889	2
v. 1 Robertson; Supplement, Jacobs, 1879–1884 in v. 1.		
v. 2. Jacobs		
Skillman's New York Police Reports	1828–1829	1

ADMIRALTY

Hough, Vice-Admiralty Reports	1715–1788	1

CRIMINAL

Criminal Recorder	1822–1823	1
Wheeler's Criminal Cases	1791–1825	3
Rogers' New York City Hall Recorder	1816–1822	6
Bacon, New York Judicial Repository	1818–1819	1
Parker Criminal Cases	1823–1868	6
Cowen's Criminal Reports	1867–1878	2
New York Criminal Reports	1878–1924	41

State	Report Series	Period Covered	No. of Vols. to date

NEW YORK (cont.)

COURT OF CLAIMS

Court of Claims Reports — 1907–1910, 1915–1918 — 7
(The first 10 years issued only in pamphlet form without decisions; merely reports to the legislature of the awards made. After 1918 continued in the State Department Reports.)

ELECTIONS

Armstrong's Contested Election Cases — 1777–1871 — 1
Baxter's Contested Election Cases — 1777–1899 — 1

MISCELLANEOUS COURTS

Armstrong's Cases of Breaches of Privilege — 1777–1871 — 1
State Department Reports — 1913–1914 — 4
  Continued by
Department Reports — 1914–[1952] — 72

PERIODICALS, ETC., CONTAINING NEW YORK REPORTS

Albany Law Journal — 1870–1908 — 70
Brooklyn Daily Record — 1882
Business Law Journal — 1923 to date
City Hall Recorder — 1816–1822 — 6
City Hall Reporter and New York General Law
  Magazine — 1833 — 1
Daily Record — 1908–
Daily Register — 1872–1889 — 37
  Continues New York Daily Transcript;
  continued by New York Law Journal
Livingston's Law Magazine — 1853–1855 — 4
Monthly Law Bulletin — 1879–1883 — 5
Monthly Legal Examiner — 1850 — 2 issues
New York Daily Transcript (Old Series) — 1859–1872 — 28
New York Daily Transcript (N. S.) — 1868–1872 — 17
New York Judicial Repository — 1818–1819
  Succeeded by Rogers' City Hall Recorder
New York Law Gazette — 1858 — 65 numbers
New York Law Journal — 1882–[1953] — 129
New York Legal News — 1880–1882 — 3
New York Legal Observer — 1842–1854 — 12
New York Legal Register — 1850 — 1
New York Monthly Law Bulletin — 1878–1883 — 5
New York Municipal Gazette — 1841–1846
New York Reporter (Barent Gardenier) — 1820 — 2
New York Transcript Reports — 1858–1868 — 11
New York Transcript Reports, N. S. — 1868–1872 — 17
  Continued by
Daily Register
New York Weekly Digest — 1876–1888 — 28
Weekly Transcript — 1861 — 11 numbers

NORTH CAROLINA
North Carolina Reports (Supreme Court) — 1778–[1952] — 235 (see below for reporters)

Martin	1 N. C.	1778–1797	1
Taylor	1 N. C.	1798–1802	1
Conference by Cameron & Norwood	1 N. C.	1800–1804	1

State Report Series		Period Covered	No. of Vols. to date
NORTH CAROLINA (cont.)			
Haywood	2–3 N. C.	1789–1806	2
Carolina Law Repository	4 N. C.	1813–1816	2
Term Reports	4 N. C.	1816–1818	1
Murphey	5–7 N. C.	1804–1819	3
Hawks	8–11 N. C.	1820–1826	4
Devereux's Law	12–15 N. C.	1826–1834	4
Devereux's Equity	16–17 N. C.	1826–1834	2
Devereux & Battle's Law	18–20 N. C.	1834–1839	4
			v. 3, 4 are
			N.C. v. 20
Devereux & Battle's Equity	21–22 N. C.	1834–1839	2
Iredell's Law	23–35 N. C.	1840–1852	13
Iredell's Equity	36–43 N. C.	1840–1852	8
Busbee's Law	44 N. C.	1852–1853	1
Busbee's Equity	45 N. C.	1852–1853	1
Jones' Law	46–53 N. C.	1853–1862	8
Jones' Equity	54–59 N. C.	1853–1863	6
Winston	60 N. C.	1863–1864	2
Phillips' Law	61 N. C.	1866–1868	1
Phillips' Equity	62 N. C.	1866–1868	1
North Carolina	63–	1868–	

NORTH DAKOTA

For Territorial Reports, 1867–1889 see Dakota, above.

North Dakota Reports (Supreme Court)		1890–[1951]	77

OHIO

(For a detailed description of Ohio Decisions see Ervin H. Pollack and J. Russell Leach, "Ohio's Reported Decisions — an Integrated Survey," in Ohio State Law Journal, volume 2, p. 413–435, Autumn 1950. Acknowledgment is hereby made to that article.)

SUPREME COURT

Ohio Reports	1821–1852	20
Succeeded by Ohio State Reports		
Ohio Reports, Century Ed. (Laning, publisher)	1821–1852	20
Ohio Reports Extra Annotated		
Longsdorf (Anderson, publisher)	1821–1852	20
Wilcox's Condensed Reports		
(Reprint of 1–7 Ohio Reports)	1821–1831	5
Hammond's Condensed Reports		
(Reprint of 1–2 Ohio Reports)	1821	1
Wright	1831–1834	1
Ohio State Reports		
Suceed Ohio Reports	1852–[1952]	157
Ohio State Reports, Extra Annotated		
(Anderson, pub.)	1852–1912	1–84 of Ohio State
Ohio Unreported Cases	1889–1899	1
No decisions, merely statement of facts and briefs of counsel without report.		

VARIOUS COURTS

Ohio Unreported Judicial Decisions (Pollack)	1807–1823	1
Ohio Federal Decisions	1809–1811	16
Tappan (Common Pleas)	1816–1819	1
Contains one Supreme Court opinion, 1817.		
Annals of Cleveland, Court Record Series	1837–1877	10

State	Report Series	Period Covered	No. of Vols. to date

OHIO (cont.)

Ohio Decisions, Reprint		1840–1855	13

Reprints from:

Western Law Journal, 10 vol.	Reprint vol.	1	
Western Law Monthly, 5 vol.	" "	2	
Weekly Law Gazette, 6 vol.	" "	3	
Daily Law and Bank Bulletin, 3 vol.	" "	3	
American Law Register, 34 vol.	" "	3	
Ohio Law Journal, 5 vol.	" "	3	
Cleveland Law Record, 1 vol.	" "	4	
Cleveland Law Reporter, 2 vol.	" "	4	
American Law Record, 15 vol.	" "	5–6	
Weekly Law Bulletin, 30 vol.	" "	7–11	
Handy's Reports, 2 vol.	" "	12	
Disney's Reports, 2 vol.	" "	12–13	
Cincinnati Superior Court Reporter, 2 vols.	" "	13	

REPRINT OF DECISIONS OF OHIO COURTS (BELOW SUPREME COURT)

	1840–1893	5
American Law Record, 15 vols.	1872–1886	
Cleveland Law Record, 1 vol.	1855–1856	
Cleveland Law Reporter, 2 vols.	1877–1879	
Cleveland Law Register, 1 vol.	1893	
Cincinnati Daily Court Bulletin, 1 vol.	1857	
Weekly Law and Bank Bulletin, 1 vol.	1857–1858	
Weekly Law Gazette, 4 vol.	1856–1860	
American Law Register, 34 vo˙	1853–1885	
Western Law Journal, 10 vol.	1840–1853	
Western Law Monthly, 5 vol.	1858–1863	
Dayton Reports, 3 Ohio Miscellaneous Decisions (Gotschall)	1865–1873	1
Goebel's Probate Reports	1885–1890	1
Ohio Circuit Court Reports (Jahn)	1885–1901	22
Merged with Ohio Circuit Decisions		
Ohio Circuit Decisions	1885–1901	12
Reprinted opinions from Ohio Circuit Court Reports, with added cases there omitted. With v. 13, merged with it.		
Ohio Nisi Prius Reports	1893–1901	8
Ohio Nisi Prius Reports, N. S.	1902–1934	32
Ohio Decisions (Ohio Lower Decisions)	1894–1896	3
Ohio Decisions	1894–1920	31
Iddings' Term Reports	1899–1900	1
Ohio Circuit Court Decisions	1901–1918	22
Successor to Ohio Circuit Court Reports (Jahn) and Ohio Circuit Court Decisions; consists of v."13–23"O.C.C.–"13–45"O.C.C.		
Ohio Circuit Court Reports, New Series	1903–1917	26
Ohio Courts of Appeals Reports	1915–1922	27–32
Ohio Appeals	1913–[1952]	90
Ohio Law Reporter	1903–1934	40
v. 21–40 as continuation of Ohio Court of Appeals Reports. v. 22– contain some cases not elsewhere reported.		
Ohio Law Abstract	1923–[1952]	62
Ohio Opinions (lifetime ed.)	1934–[1952]	48

State	Report Series	Period Covered	No. of Vols. to date

OHIO (cont.)

Kept to date by weekly supplement called
Ohio Law Reporter, v. 49– continuing numbering
of bound volumes

CINCINNATI SUPERIOR

Handy	1854–1856	2
Disney	1854–1859	2
Cincinnati Municipal Decisions	1862–1875	1
Cincinnati Superior Court Reporter (Taft and Storer)	1870–1873	2
Hosea	1903–1907	1

PUBLICATIONS CONTAINING REPORTS

American Law Record	1872–1886	15
American Law Register	1853–1885	34
Cincinnati Daily Court Bulletin	1857	1
Cleveland Law Record	1855–1856	1
Cleveland Law Register	1889–1893	1
Cleveland Law Reporter	1877–1879	2
Gongwer State Reports (current mimeograph service)		
Ohio Bar (advance opinions of Supreme Court, Court of Appeals, Nisi Prius and Federal Courts)		
Ohio Bar Association Report	1928–[1950]	23
Ohio Jurisprudence	1928–1938	43
Weekly Law and Bank Bulletin	1857–1858	1
Ohio Law Bulletin	1876–1921	66
Weekly Law Gazette (Continues Weekly Law and Bank Bulletin)	1856–1860	2–5
Ohio Law Journal	1880–1884	5
Ohio Legal News	1894–1896	3
Western Law Journal	1840–1853	10
Western Law Monthly	1858–1863	5

OKLAHOMA

Oklahoma Reports (Supreme Court)	1890–[1952]	205
Oklahoma Criminal Reports	1908–[1950]	92
The Journal; pub. by Oklahoma Bar Association	1930–[1953]	24

OREGON

Oregon Reports (Supreme Court)	1853–[1952]	194

PANAMA CANAL ZONE

Canal Zone Reports (Supreme Court)	1905–1926	3

PENNSYLVANIA

For a detailed description of Pennsylvania Reports *see Research in Pennsylvania Law*, by Carroll C. Moreland and Erwin C. Surrency. New York, Oceana Publications, 1953. Acknowledgment is hereby made to that publication.

Dallas	1754–1806	4
Yeates	1791–1808	4
Binney	1799–1814	6
Sergeant and Rawle	1814–1828	17
Grant's Cases	1814–1863	3
Rawle	1828–1835	5
Penrose and Watts	1829–1832	3
Watts	1832–1840	10
Wharton	1835–1841	6
Watts and Sergeant	1841–1845	9
Pennsylvania State	1845–[1952]	370

State Report Series	Period Covered	No. of Vols. to date
PENNSYLVANIA (cont.)		
Walker	1855–1885	4
Pennypacker	1881–1884	4
Sadler	1885–1888	10
Monaghan	1888–1890	2

SUPERIOR

Pennsylvania Superior Court Reports	1895–[1952]	170

VARIOUS COURTS

Addison	1791–1799	1
Ashmead	1808–1841	2
Beaver County Legal Journal	1939–[1951]	12
Berks County Law Journal	1908–[1949]	41
Blair County Law Reporter	1898–1903	2
Blair Law Reports, 2d series	1940–[1947]	2
Brewster	1856–1873	4
Brightly Nisi Prius Reports	1809–1851	1
Browne	1801–1814	2
Bucks County Law Reporter	1951–	
Bucks County	1684–1700	1
Cambria County Law Journal	1917–1928	1
Cambria County Reports	1929–[1950]	15
Campbell's Legal Gazette Reports	1869–1871	1
Chester County Court Records	1681–1697	1
Chester County Reports	1870–1885	2
	1947–[1953]	3–[7]
Clark, Pennsylvania Law Journal Reports	1842–1852	5
Common Pleas Reporter	1879–1887	4
Cumberland Law Journal	1950–[?]	not yet pub.
Dauphin County Reports	1897–[1952]	61
Delaware County Reports	1881–[1952]	38
Department Reports	1916–[1951]	37
District Reports	1892–1921	30
District and County Reports	1921–[1952]	78
Docket, The (Lebanon County)	1897–1898	2
Erie County Law Journal	1919–1945	27
continued as		
Erie County Legal Journal	1945–[1953]	28–[36]
Fayette Legal Journal	1938–[1950]	13
Fiduciary Reporter	1951–[1953]	3
Fisher's Prize Cases	1812–1813	1
Hazard's Legal Register	1828–1835	16
Hopkinson's Judgments in Admiralty	1779–1788	1
Hopkinson's Judgments in Admiralty	1785–1789	1
Journal of Law	1830–1831	1
Justice of the Peace	1899–1907	8
Justices' Law Reporter	1902–1918	16
Kulp (see Luzerne Legal Register Reports)		
Lackawanna Bar	–1878	1
Lackawanna Bar Reports	1906	1
Lackawanna Jurist	1888–[1953]	54
Lackawanna Law Times (see Luzerne Law Times)		
Lackawanna Legal News	1895–1903	8
Lackawanna Legal Record	1878–1879	1
Lancaster Bar	1869–1883	15
Lancaster Law Review	1883–[1951]	52

State Report Series	Period Covered	No. of Vols. to date
PENNSYLVANIA (cont.)		
Law Times (see Luzerne Law Times)		
Lawrence Law Journal	1941–[1951]	10
Lebanon County Legal Journal	1946–[1952]	4
Legal and Insurance Reporter	1859–1867	9
Legal Chronicle Reports (Foster)	1873–1875	3
Legal Gazette	1869–1876	8
Legal Gazette Reports (see Campbell's Legal Gazette Reports)		
Legal Intelligencer	1843–[?	?
Legal Opinion	1870–1873	5
Legal Record Reports	1879–1882	2
v. 1–2 of Schuylkill County Legal Record Reports		
Lehigh County Law Journal	1903–[1948]	22
Lehigh Valley Law Reporter	1885–1887	2
Luzerne Law Journal	1881	1
Luzerne Law Times (Old Series)	1873–1878	6
v. 1, no. 1 to v. 2, no. 4 as Scranton Law Times		
v. 2, no. 5 through vol. 4, and v. 6 as Law Times		
Luzerne Law Times (New Series)	1879–1885	7
Luzerne Legal Observer	1860–1864	4
Luzerne Legal Register	1872–1886	14
Luzerne Legal Register Reports	1882–[1951]	41
Lycoming Reporter	1947–[1950]	2
Magistrate and Constable	1895	2
Miles	1825–1841	2
Monroe Legal Reporter	1938–[1950]	12
Montgomery County Law Reporter	1885–[1951]	67
Municipal Law Reporter	1909–[1952]	43
Northampton County Reporter	1887–[1948]	31
Northumberland County Legal News	1888–1889	1
Northumberland Legal Journal	1913–[1951]	23
Olwine's Law Journal	1849–1850	1
Parson's Select Equity Cases	1842–1851	2
Pearson	1850–1880	2
Pennsylvania Corporation Reporter	1914–1939	28
Pennsylvania County Court Reports	1885–1921	50
Pennsylvania Law Journal	1842–1848	7
Pennsylvania Law Journal Reports (see Clark)		
Pennsylvania Law Record	1879–1880	3
Pennsylvania Law Record	1898–1901	4
(Listed in some bibliographies; not located. Included for the record.)		
Pennsylvania Law Series	1894–1896	4
Pennypacker's Colonial Cases	1683–1700	1
Philadelphia Reports	1850–1891	20
Pittsburgh Legal Journal	1853–[1950]	98
Pittsburgh Reports	1853–1873	3
Registrar's Book of Governor Keith's Court of Chancery	1720–1735	1
Schuylkill Legal Record	1879–[1951]	46
Schuylkill Register	1933–1945	10
Singer's Probate Cases	1901–1904	1
Somerset Legal Journal	1920–[1952]	15
Susquehanna Legal Chronicle	1878–1879	1

State	Report Series	Period Covered	No. of Vols. to date
PENNSYLVANIA (cont.)			
Vaux's Record's Decisions		1841–1845	1
Washington County Reports		1920–[1952]	32
Weekly Notes of Cases		1874–1899	44
Westmoreland County Law Journal		1911–[1951]	33
Wilcox, Lackawanna County Reports		1887–1889	1
Woodward's Decisions		1861–1874	2
Workmen's Compensation Cases, Court Decisions		1916–[1949]	29
York Legal Record		1880–[1951]	65

PHILIPPINE ISLANDS (including only to the beginning of Philippine Independence.)

Philippine Island Reports (Supreme Court) Printed also in Spanish.		1901–1946	75
Official Gazette Supplement (unpublished decisions of the Supreme Court and the Court of Appeals)		1939–1941	1
Official Gazette (beginning with v. 40, July 5, 1941, contains decisions of Supreme Court and Court of Appeals)		1941–	v. 1–
Philippine Decisions, (reprint of leading and important cases in 1–54 Philippine Island Reports.		1933–1934	10

PUERTO RICO

Castro, Decisiones de Puerto Rico; o, Compilación de Sentencias y Resoluciones		1899–1906	3
Puerto Rico Reports (Supreme Court)		1899–[1950]	71
Porto Rico Federal Reports (U. S. District Court)		1900–1924	13
Tax Court Decisiones		1943–[1947]	5

RHODE ISLAND

(Colony) Rhode Island Court Records, Court of Trials		1647–1670	2
Records of Court of Trials (Warwick) (Helen Capwell, Providence, 1922)		1659–1674	1
Records of Vice-Admiralty Court (Dorothy S. Towle, American Legal Records, v. 3)		1716–1752	1
Rhode Island Reports (Supreme Court)		1828–[1951]	77
Rhode Island Superior Court Rescripts		1917–1919	2
Rhode Island Decisions (Superior Court)		1924–1935	12

SOUTH CAROLINA

(Colony) Court of Chancery Records contains Minutes and Case Papers		1671–1779	1
South Carolina Law		1783–1868	49 as follows
Bay		1783–1804	2
Brevard		1793–1816	3
Treadway (incl. in 3 Brevard)		1812–1816	2
Mill (Constitutional)		1817–1818	2
Nott & McCord		1817–1820	2
McCord		1821–1828	4
Harper		1823–1830	1
Bailey		1828–1832	2
Hill		1833–1837	3
Riley (Law and Equity)		1836–1837	1
Dudley		1837–1838	1
Rice		1838–1839	1
Cheves		1839–1840	1
McMullan		1840–1842	2

State	Report Series	Period Covered	No. of Vols. to date
SOUTH CAROLINA (cont.)			
Speers		1842–1844	2
Richardson		1844–1846, 1850–1868	15
Strobhart		1846–50	5
South Carolina Equity		1784–1868	35 as follows
Desaussure		1784–1816	4
Harper		1824	1
McCord		1825–1827	2
Bailey		1830–1831	1
Richardson's Cases		1831–1832	1
Hill		1833–1837	2
Riley (Law and Equity)		1836–1837	1
Dudley		1837–1838	1
Rice		1838–1839	1
Cheves		1839–1840	1
McMullan		1840–1842	1
Speers		1842–1844	1
Richardson (for v. 12 see S. C. Law)		1844–46, 1850–1868	14
Strobhart		1846–1850	4
South Carolina Reports (Supreme Court)		1868–[1951]	220
South Carolina Reports, Annotated ed., unabridged		1783–1840?	38 as follows

v. 1	Bay, 1–2
v. 2	Brevard, 1–2
v. 3	Brevard, 3; Treadway, 1–2
v. 4	Mill, 1–2; Nott & McCord, 1
v. 5	Nott & McCord, 2; McCord, 1
v. 6	McCord, 2–3
v. 7	McCord, 4; Harper, 1.
v. 8	Bailey, 1–2.
v. 9	Hill, 1–2.
v. 10	Hill, 3; Riley, 1; Dudley, 1; Rice, 1; Cheves, 1.
v. 11	McMullan, 1–2; Speers, 1.
v. 12	Speers, 2; Richardson, 1.
v. 13	Richardson, 2; Strobhart 1
v. 14	Strobhart, 2–3.
v. 15	Strobhart, 4–5; Richardson, 3
v. 16	Richardson, 4–6
v. 17	Richardson, 7–9
v. 18	Richardson, 10–11
v. 19	Richardson, 12–15
v. 20	Desaussure, 1–3
v. 21	Desaussure, 4; Harper's Equity, 1; McCord's Equity, 1
v. 22	McCord's Equity, 2; Bailey's Equity, 1; Richardson's Equity Cases, 1
v. 23	Hill's Equity, 1–2
v. 24	Riley's 1; Dudley's, 1; Rice's, 1; Cheves', 1; and McMullan's, 1 Equity Reports
v. 25	Speers' Equity, 1; Richardson's Equity Reports, 1–2
v. 26	Strobhart's Equity, 1–4
v. 27	Richardson's Equity, 3–5
v. 28	Richardson's Equity, 6–9
v. 29	Richardson's Equity, 10–13
v. 30	Richardson's Equity, 14; South Carolina Reports, 1–2
v. 31	South Carolina, 3–4
v. 32	South Carolina, 5–7
v. 33	South Carolina, 8–10
v. 34	South Carolina, 11–13

State	Report Series	Period Covered	No. of Vols. to date
SOUTH CAROLINA (cont.)			
v. 35	South Carolina, 14–16		
v. 36	South Carolina, 17–19		
v. 37	South Carolina, 20–22		
v. 38	South Carolina, 23–25		

SOUTH DAKOTA

For Territorial Reports, 1867–1889 *see* Dakota

South Dakota Reports (Supreme Court)		1890–[1949]	72

TENNESSEE

Legal Reporter (Supreme Court) N. S.		1877–1879	3
Tennessee Reports (Supreme Court)		[1791–1951]	193 (see below for reporters)

Overton	1–2	Tenn.	1791–1817	2
Cooke	3, 3a	Tenn.	1811–1814	
	See also 158 App.			
Haywood	4–6	Tenn.	1816–1818	3
Peck	7	Tenn.	1821–1824	1
Martin &				
Yerger	8	Tenn.	1825–1828	1
Yerger	9–18	Tenn.	1818–1837	10
Meigs	19	Tenn.	1838–1839	1
Humphreys	20–30	Tenn.	1839–1851	11
Swan	31–32	Tenn.	1851–1853	2
Sneed	33–37	Tenn.	1853–1858	5
Head	38–40	Tenn.	1858–1859	3
Coldwell	41–47	Tenn.	1860–1870	7
Heiskell	48–59	Tenn.	1870–1874	12
Baxter	60–68	Tenn.	1872–1878	9
Lea	69–84	Tenn.	1878–1886	16
Pickle	85–108	Tenn.	1886–1902	24
Cates	109–127	Tenn.	1902–1913	19
Thompson	128–153	Tenn.	1913–1926	26
Smith	154–164	Smith	1925–1932	11
App. v. 158 same as 103a				
Tennessee	165–		1931–	
Tennessee Chancery (Cooper)			1872–1878	3
Tennessee Chancery Appeals (Wright)			1901–1904	2
Tennessee Chancery Appeals Decisions (Reprint)			1895–1907	7
Tennessee Civil Appeals (Higgins)			1910–1918	8
Thompson's Unreported Cases			1847–1869	1
Shannon's Unreported Cases			1847–1894	3
Tennessee Appeals			1925–[1951]	34

TEXAS

Dallam's Opinions (Supreme Court)		1840–1844	1
Texas Reports (Supreme Court)		1846–[1951]	149
v. 25 has supplementary volume			
Texas Criminal Appeals		1876–[1950]	154
Texas Civil Appeals Reports		1892–1911	62
Texas Civil Cases of Court of Appeals (White & Willson)		1876–1892	4
Texas Unreported Cases (Posey)		1879–1884	2
Texas Court Reporter		1900–1908	20
King's Conflicting Civil Cases		1840–1911	3
Robards' Conscript Cases		1862–1865	1

State	Report Series	Period Covered	No. of Vols. to date
TEXAS (cont.)			
Texas Law Reporter		1882–1884	3 [1–3
(Supersedes Texas Law Journal (not found))			(no. 9)]
UTAH			
Utah Reports		1855–[1949]	116
v. 1: 1855–1876; appendix to v. 3 has cases 1861–1877			
VERMONT			
Chipman, N. (Supreme Court)		1789–1791	1
Chipman, D. (Supreme Court)		1789–1824	2
Tyler (Supreme Court)		1800–1803	2
Brayton (Supreme Court)		1815–1819	1
Aikens (Supreme Court)		1825–1828	2
Vermont Reports (Supreme Court)		1826–[1951]	116
VIRGINIA			
(Colony) Minutes of the Council and General Court		1622–1632, 1670–1676	1
Virginia Colonial Decisions	1728–1753 (t.–p. 1728–1741)		2
Randolph and Barradall (Boston, Boston Book Co., 1909)			
Jefferson (General Court)	1730–1740, 1768–1772		1
Wythe's Chancery		1788–1799	1
Virginia Reports (Supreme Court of Appeals)		1730–[1952]	193 (see below for reporters)
Washington	1–2 Va.	1790–1796	2
Va. Cases, Criminal	3–4 Va.	1789–1826	2
Call	5–10 Va.	1797–1825	6
Hening & Munford	11–14 Va.	1806–1810	4
Munford	15–20 Va.	1810–1820	6
Gilmer	21 Va.	1820–1821	1
Randolph	22–27 Va.	1821–1828	6
Leigh	28–39 Va.	1829–1842	12
Robinson	40–41 Va.	1842–1844	2
Grattan	42–74 Va.	1844–1880	33
Virginia	75–	1880–	
Virginia Reports, Annotated, from Jefferson to 33 Grattan		1730–1880	26
Virginia Appeals		1907–1826	35
(Reprint ed. of Reports beginning with 106 Va.)			
Howison, Criminal Trials		1850–1851	1
Patton and Heath, Special Court of Appeals		1855–1857	2
Virginia Decisions (Unreported)		1870–1900	2
WASHINGTON			
Washington Territory Opinions		1854–1864	1
Washington Territory Reports		1854–1888	3
Washington Territory Reports, Reprint ed. (New Series)		1854–1888	3
Washington Reports (Supreme Court)		1890–1939	200
Washington Reports (2d)		1939–[1952]	40
WEST VIRGINIA			
West Virginia Reports (Supreme Court of Appeals)		1864–[1950]	134
Title page reads Aug. Term 1863; First case is Jan. Term, 1864.			

State Report Series	Period Covered	No. of Vols. to date
WISCONSIN		
Burnett (Supreme Court)	1841	1
(Bound with Session laws for Dec. 1841)		
Burnett (Supreme Court)	1842–1843	1
Chandler (Supreme Court)	1849–1852	4
Pinney (Supreme Court)	1839–1852	3
Reprints Burnett & Chandler		
Wisconsin Reports (Supreme Court)	1853–[1952]	260
Dixon and Ryan Supreme Court		
Selected Opinions (Roe)	1859–1878	1
Chicago, Callaghan, 1907		
WYOMING		
Wyoming Reports	1870–[1951]	68

C. State and Territorial Case Law Digests

Federal Case Law Digests. *See* Chapter 13.

National Reporter System Digests. *See* Chapter 14.

Annotated Reports System Digests. *See* Chapter 15.

State and Territorial Case Law Digests.

(With the few exceptions noted, only digests currently published are listed below. Publication dates and volume numbers given are as originally published. In some instances additional volumes have been published at a later date. All states and the District of Columbia are also covered by National Reporter System regional digests, to the extent described beginning at page 119, 120.)

State	Publisher	Publication Date	Vols.
ALABAMA			
Alabama Digest	West	1936	21
ALASKA			
Alaska Digest	West	1938	5
ARIZONA			
Arizona Digest	Bancroft-Whitney, & West	1937	8
ARKANSAS			
Arkansas Digest	West	1937–38	18
CALIFORNIA			
California Digest (McKinney)	Bancroft-Whitney	1930	28
West's California Digest	West	1951–52	50
California Jurisprudence	Bancroft-Whitney	1921–26	29
———Ten-Year Supplement	Bancroft-Whitney	1926–1936	12
California Jurisprudence 2d	Bancroft-Whitney	1952	1
			(in process)
COLORADO			
Colorado Digest	West, & Courtright	1938	15
CONNECTICUT			
Connecticut Digest (Richard H. Phillips)	State Pub. Hartford	1945	3
West's Connecticut Digest	Boston Law Book Co.	1950–51	16
DELAWARE			
Atlantic Reporter Digest	*See* page 117		

State	Publisher	Publication Date	Vols.
DISTRICT OF COLUMBIA			
District of Columbia Digest	Washington Law Book Co., and West	1936–37	12
Torbert, W. S.			
Index-digest of D. C. Cases	Wash., D. C., Byrne	1908–31	4

Federal Digest covers all D. C. cases except decisions of the Municipal Court of Appeals for D. C., which are digested in D. C. Digest, Maryland and Atlantic Reporter Digest.

State	Publisher	Publication Date	Vols.
FLORIDA			
Florida Digest	West	1936	12
Florida Encyclopedic Digest (Michie & Stedman)	Harrison	1933–34	15
GEORGIA			
Georgia Digest	West	1942	23
HAWAII			
Hawaii Digest	Terr. of Hawaii, and West	1939	6
IDAHO			
Idaho Digest	Bancroft-Whitney, and West	1939	6
ILLINOIS			
Illinois Digest	West, and Smith-Burdette	1940	36
Callaghan Illinois Digest	Callaghan	1913–26	15
——2d Series	Callaghan	1938–39	12
INDIANA			
Indiana Decimal Digest	Bobbs-Merrill	1933–38	16
Callaghan's Indiana Digest	Callaghan	1933–34	17
IOWA			
Iowa Digest	West	1941	20
Callaghan's Iowa Digest	Callaghan	1921–23	6
——Cumulative Supp., 1921–40		1941	6
KANSAS			
Kansas Digest	West	1932	11
Hatcher's Kansas Digest	Lawyers Co-op.	1952	6
KENTUCKY			
Kentucky Digest	West	1931	21
LOUISIANA			
Louisiana Digest	West	1936	20
Dart's New Louisiana Digest Annotated	Bobbs-Merrill	1951–52	9
MAINE			
Atlantic Digest	*See* page 117		
MARYLAND			
Maryland Digest	West	1940	16
MASSACHUSETTS			
Massachusetts Digest	West, and Little, Brown	1933–34, 1936	21
MICHIGAN			
Michigan Digest	West	1945	16
Callaghan Michigan Digest	Callaghan	1941–42	20
Michigan Jurisprudence	Michigan Jurisprudence Co., Santa Barbara, Calif.	1951	1 (in process)

State	Publisher	Publication Date	Vols.
MINNESOTA			
Minnesota Digest	West	1918	18
Dunnell's Minnesota Digest	Mason	3d ed. 1951	4
			(in process)
Mason's Digest Service	Mason	1952	v.24
			current
MISSISSIPPI			
Mississippi Digest	West	1936	15
MISSOURI			
Missouri Digest	West	1930	31
MONTANA			
Montana Digest	West, and Bancroft-		
	Whitney	1937	10
NEBRASKA			
Nebraska Digest	West	1939	12
NEVADA			
Pacific Digest	*See* page 118		
NEW HAMPSHIRE			
West's New Hampshire Digest	Boston Law Book Co.	1951	10
NEW JERSEY			
Atlantic Digest	*See* page 119		
NEW MEXICO			
New Mexico Digest	West	1948	6
NEW YORK			
Abbott New York Digest	West, and Lawyers Co-op.,		
	and Baker, Voorhis	1929–51	46
—Bound Supplement		1944	8
Clark's Surrogate's Annotations	Kimball-Clark	1942	1
New York Law Jist	New York Law Jist	1936	v.17
			current
Clark's Digest Annotator	Kimball-Clark	1937	v.17
			current
NORTH CAROLINA			
North Carolina Digest	West	1937	20
NORTH DAKOTA AND SOUTH DAKOTA			
Dakota Digest	West		12
OHIO			
West's Ohio Digest	West	1949	30
Page's Ohio Lifetime Digest	Bobbs-Merrill, and		
	Anderson	1934–35	15
Ohio Jurisprudence	Lawyers Co-op.	1928–38	43
—Cumulative Supp. to v. 1–43	Lawyers Co-op.	1943	3
Ohio Jurisprudence 2d	Lawyers Co-op.	1953	1
			(in process)
Bates Compact Ohio Digest	Banks-Baldwin	1926, 36, 46	3
OKLAHOMA			
Oklahoma Digest	West	1934	16
OREGON			
Oregon Digest	Bancroft-Whitney, and		
	West	1933	11
PENNSYLVANIA			
Vale Pennsylvania Digest	West	1938–39	45

State	Publisher	Publication Date	Vols.
PHILLIPINES			
Digest of the Reports of the Supreme Court of Phillipine Islands	Lawyers Co-op.	1927–52	13
PUERTO RICO			
Digesto de las Decisiones del Tribuno Supremo (Pasarell & Cruz)	San Juan, Negociado de Materiales	1930–51	5
RHODE ISLAND			
Atlantic Digest	See page 118		
SOUTH CAROLINA			
West's South Carolina Digest	West	1952	20 (in process)
SOUTH DAKOTA	See North Dakota		
TENNESSEE			
Tennessee Digest	West	1950	20
Michie's Digest of Tennessee Reports	Michie	1935	18
TEXAS			
Texas Digest	West	1935–36	42
Texas Jurisprudence	Bancroft-Whitney	1929–37	45
—Ten-Year Supp.	Bancroft-Whitney	1937–47	10
UTAH			
Pacific Digest	See page 119		
VERMONT			
Vermont Digest Annotated	West	1911–44	5
VIRGINIA			
Virginia & West Virginia Digest	West		20
Michie's Digest of Virginia and West Virginia Reports	Michie	1929–31	11
—Permanent Supplement	Michie	1941	6
Michie's Jurisprudence of Virginia and West Virginia	Michie	1948–52	24
WASHINGTON			
Washington Digest Annotated	West, and Bancroft-Whitney	1934–40	13
WEST VIRGINIA	See Virginia		
WISCONSIN			
Wisconsin Digest	West	1941	18
Callaghan's Wisconsin Digest (2d ed.)	Callaghan	1950	20
WYOMING			
Pacific Digest	See page 118		

D. Special Subject Law Reports

These are court reports, but some also include administrative tribunal decisions. Most such agency decisions, however, are listed below, under "Federal Administrative Decisions Officially Published or Sponsored." Where dates are enclosed in brackets [ ], entries are still current, in which case the volume number given is the latest published when this list was compiled.

Title	Dates Covered	No. of volumes
American and English Corporation Cases	1883–1894	48
—— New Series	1896–1904	19
American and English Decisions in Equity	1894–1904	10
American and English Patent Cases (Brodix)	1662–1890	20
English Courts, 1662–1843 (v. 1–3)		
Supreme Court U. S., 1754–1890 (v. 4–20)		
American and English Railroad Cases	1879–1895	61
—— New Series	1894–1913	68
Vol. 24–68 as Railroad Reports, 1902–1913		
American Bankruptcy Reports, Annotated	1889–1923	49
—— New Series	1924–1945	57
American Corporation Cases	1868–1887	10
American Criminal Reports	1877–1903	15
American Electrical Cases	1873–1908	9
American Federal Tax Reports (Prentice-Hall)	1796–[1953]	41
American Insolvency Reports	1878–1883	1
American Labor Arbitration Awards	1946–[1952]	4
American Labor Cases	1947–[1953]	7
American Maritime Cases	1923–[1953]	30
American Negligence Cases	1789–1897	17
American Negligence Reports	1897–1909	21
(continued by Negligence and Compensation Cases)		
American Practice Reports	1897–1898	1
American Probate Reports	1875–1895	8
American Railroad and Corporation Reports (Lewis)	1888–1896	12
American Railway Cases (Smith)	1854–1856	2
American Railway Reports	1872–1881	21
American Trade Mark Cases (Cox)	1825–1871	1
American Trade Mark Cases (Price & Stewart)	1879–1887	1
Automobile Cases (CCH Insurance Case Series)	1938–[1952]	37
Aviation Cases	1822–[1950]	2
Baldwin's Patent, Copyright, Trade-Mark Cases	1790–1928	10
Banking Cases Annotated (Michie)	1898–1903	5
Bankrupt Register		
(See National Bankruptcy Register Reports)		
Banning, Reports of Patent causes (Banning and Arden)	1874–1881	5
Bigelow, Life & Accident Insurance Cases	1810–1876	5
Compensation Review	1925–1932	15
Contested Election Cases (Clarke & Hall)	1789–1834	1
Contested Elections in Congress (Bartlett)	1834–1865	1
(See also Senate Election Cases)		
Copyright, Decisions of the U. S. Courts	1909–[1950]	10
(Copyright Office Bulletin no. 17–24, 26–27)		
Croswell, Collection of Patent Cases	1888	1
Death Tax Cases (CCH)	1898–1936	1
Federal and State Tax Cases (Supreme Court) "Report		
to the Joint Committee on Internal Revenue Taxation"	1938–1943	1
Federal Anti-Trust Cases, Decrees and Judgments		
(Shale)	1890–1918	1
Federal Anti-trust Decisions	1890–[1931]	12
Federal Carrier Cases (CCH)	1936–[1953]	8
Federal Contract Cases (CCH War law service, v. 2:		
Government contracts, supp.)	1942–1944	2
Federal Rules Decisions	1940–[1952]	12

Title	Dates Covered	No. of volumes
Fire and Casualty Cases (other than Automobile) (CCH Insurance Case Series)	1938–[1949]	6
Fisher's Patent Cases (Circuit Courts)	1848–1873	6
Fisher's Patent Reports (Supreme and Circuit Courts) ("all patent cases of the U. S. Supreme and Circuit Courts not included in Robb's Patent Cases and Fisher's Patent Cases."	1821–1850	1
Green, Criminal Law Reports	1874–1875	2
Insular Cases (Howe)	1900	1
Insurance Decisions (Indianapolis, Rough Notes Co.)	1931–1942	11
Insurance Law Journal	1871–1938	91
Labor Arbitration Awards (See American Labor Arbitration Awards)		
Labor Arbitration Reports (B.N.A.)	1946–[1952]	18
Labor Cases (CCH)	1937–[1952]	21
Labor Relations Reference Manual (includes opinions of the courts and decisions of the National Labor Relations Board)	1935–[1951]	28
Labor Relations Reporter	1937–1946	17
Life Cases (incl. health & accident) (CCH Insurance Case Series)	1938–[1951]	14
McArthur's Patent Cases (District of Columbia)	1841–1859	1
McMaster's Commercial Cases	1905–1923	29
Morrison's Mining Reports	1749–1906	22
Municipal Corporation Cases Annotated (Michie)	1894–1903	11
National Bank Cases (Thompson) (v. 1)	1864–1878	1
National Bank Cases (Browne) (v. 2–3)	1878–1889	2
National Bankruptcy News and Reports	1898–1901	4
Merged into American Bankruptcy Reports Annotated		
National Bankruptcy Register Reports	1868–1882	19
Vol. 1–4 # 10 as Bankrupt Register		
NLRB (National Labor Relations Board) Decisions (Prentice-Hall)	1937–1939	1
Negligence and Compensation Cases, Annotated (continuing American Negligence Reports)	1911–1936	39
——— New Series	1936–[1952]	30
Negligence Cases (other than automobile) (CCH Insurance Case Series)	1938–[1951]	18
New York State Tax Cases (Prentice-Hall)	1890–1926	1
New York Tax Cases v. 1–2 (CCH)	1903–[1947]	1
Patent Cases (Baldwin) (See Baldwin)		
Patent Cases (Robb) (See Robb)		
Patent Cases (Whitman) (See Whitman)		
Patent Office Decisions (see Federal Administrative Decisions list under Patent Office)		
Personal Injury Law Journal	1910–1911	2
Prize Cases (U. S. Supreme Court) (Carnegie Endowment for International Peace, 1923)	1789–1918	3
Probate Reports Annotated, continuing American Probate Reports	1896–1909	14

Title	Dates Covered	No. of volumes
Public Health Service		
Court decision holding U. S. Public Health service milk ordinance valid (Reprint no. 1629, Public health reports)	1934	1
Court decisions pertaining to the public health (Reprints no. 342, 410, Public health reports)	1913–1916	2
Court decisions relating to the public health (Fowler) Public health reports supplement 56, 84, 110	1919–1932	3
Court decisions relating to morbidity reports (Reprint no. 205, Public health reports)	1914	1
Public Utilities Reports Annotated	1915–1933	101
——— New Series	1934–[1952]	95
Railroad Reports		
See American and English Railroad Cases New Series		
Rate Research (National Electric Light Assn.)	1912–1930	2–35
Robb, Collection of Patent Cases	1789–1850	2
Selective Service System, National Headquarters Opinions	1941?–1943	3
Senate Election Cases (Taft)	1789–1885	1
State Tax Cases (CCH)	1918–1944	1
Street Railway Reports Annotated	1903–1913	8
Tax Cases decided by the Supreme Court "Report to the Joint Committee on Internal Revenue Taxation"	1942–1945	1
Tax Court Memorandum Decisions (Prentice-Hall)	1928–[1951]	20
Tax Court Memorandum Decisions (CCH)	1942–[1952]	11
Tax Court Reported Decisions (Prentice-Hall)	[1952]	1
Trade Cases (CCH)	1944–[1951]	4
Trade Mark Reporter	1911–[1951]	41
United States Aviation Reports	1822–[1953]	25
United States Patents Quarterly	1929–[1952]	95
United States Supreme Court, Business Law Decisions (CCH)	1934–[1943]	9
U. S. Tax Cases (CCH)	1935–[1953]	35
Consolidated volumes (to beginning of above)	1913–1934	4
Consolidated volume 5 (Excess Profits)	1917–1940	1
Wage and Hour Cases	1938–[1952]	10
Whitman, Patent Cases	1810–1874	2
Workmen's Compensation Law Journal	1917–1922	10

E. National Reporter System

See Chapter 14, where the various series are described and listed.

F. Annotated Reports System

See Chapter 15, where the various series are described and listed.

G. Federal Administrative Decisions

Some official series which publish also court reports are listed above, under "Special Subject Law Reports." Where the dates are enclosed in brackets [ ], entries are still current, in which case the volume number given is the latest published when this list was compiled.

Title	Dates Covered	No. of volumes
Agriculture Decisions		
See Department of Agriculture		
Assistant Attorney General for the Post Office Department		
See Post Office Department		
Attorney General Opinions	1789–[1948]	40
Bituminous Coal Division (Dept. of the Interior) Decisions and Orders	1940–1941	1
Board of Contract Adjustment (War Dept. Claims Board)		
See War Dept. Claims Board. Decisions of the Appeal Section		
Board of General Appraisers		
See Treasury Department		
Board of Immigration Appeals		
See Department of Justice		
Board of Tax Appeals Reports	1924–1942	47
(Continued as Tax Court Reports)		
Brainard's Legal Precedents in Land and Mining Cases	1883–1889	7
Bureau of Animal Industry		
Dockets (Processed)	1934–1940	1
Monthly Record (Processed)	1924–1939	16
Bureau of Employment Security		
Unemployment Compensation Interpretation Service. Benefit Series	1937–1949	12 in 26 books
Continued by its Benefit Series Service, Unemployment Insurance		
Benefit Series Service, Unemployment Insurance	[1950]	3 (loose-leaf)
Bureau of Labor Statistics		
Decisions of courts and Opinions affecting labor (Bulletins of the Bureau of Labor Statistics, Labor Laws of the U. S. Series)	1912–[1932]	
Civil Aeronautics Authority		
See Civil Aeronautics Board		
Civil Aeronautics Board Reports	1939–[1952]	10
Vol. 1 by Civil Aeronautics Authority		
Civil Service Commission		
Comptroller General, General Accounting Office		
Hatch Act Decisions (political activity cases) (Irwin)	1949	1
Claims Decision; (Court of Claims and Comptroller General)	1944	2
Comptroller General, General Accounting Office Decisions	1921–[1951]	30
Comptroller in the Department of the Treasury		
Decisions of the Second Comptroller	1817–1894	4
Decisions of the First Comptroller	1880–1894	7
Decisions of the Comptroller	1894–1921	27
Copp, Mining Decisions		
See General Land Office		
Court of Military Appeals		
Opinions (Processed) no. 1–[413]	1951–[1952]	2
Department of Agriculture		
Agriculture Decisions (Secretary of Agriculture)	1942–[1951]	10
Decisions of Courts in cases under the Federal Food and Drugs Act (Gates)	1908–1933	1
Food Inspection Decisions no. 1–212	1905–1934	1

Title	Dates Covered	No. of volumes
Laws, decisions and opinions applicable to the National Forests (Feagons)	1916	1
Notices of Judgment under Food and Drugs Act	1908–1943	no.1–31156
——— under Caustic Poison Act	1931–[1951]	no.1–[128]
——— under Federal Food, Drug and Cosmetic Act: Cosmetics	1940–[1951]	no.1–[189]
——— ——— Drugs and Devices	1940–[1951]	no.1–[3500]
——— ——— Foods	1940–[1951]	no.1–[17450]
——— under Insecticide Act	1912–[1951]	no.1–[2066]
——— summarizing judicial review of orders under Sec. 701(F)	1944–[1950]	no.1–[10]
——— under Federal Insecticide, Fungicide and Rodenticide Act	1950–[1951]	no.1–[76]
——— under Naval Stores Act	1929–[1946]	no.1–[11]
Department of Commerce and Labor		
Opinions of the Solicitor dealing with Workmen's Compensation	1908–1915	1
Department of the Interior		
Decisions in Appealed Pension and Bounty-Land Claims	1887–1930	22
Continued by Decisions of the Administrator of Veterans' Affairs, in appealed pension and civil service retirement cases		
See Veterans		
Decisions in Public Land Cases (Lester) (Philadelphia, Small)	1860–1870	2
Decisions relating to Public Lands	1881–[1947]	59
Department of the Interior. Bituminous Coal Division		
See Bituminous Coal Division		
Department of the Interior. General Land Office		
See General Land Office		
Department of the Interior. Petroleum Labor Policy Board		
See Petroleum Labor Policy Board		
Department of Justice		
Administrative Decisions under Immigration and Nationality Laws	1940–[1950]	3
(includes decisions of Board of Immigration Appeals)		
See also Attorney General Opinions		
Employees Compensation Appeals Board Decisions (Dept. of Labor)	1946–[1949]	2
Farm Credit Administration		
Summary of Cases relating to Farmers' Cooperative Associations	1939–[1951]	no.1–[51]
Feagons, National Forests		
See Department of Agriculture		
Federal Communications Commission		
Decisions (Processed)	1931–1940	8
Reports	1934–[1948]	12
Federal Emergency Administration of Public Works. Board of Labor Review. [Decisions]	1934–1936	1
Federal Maritime Board Cases, Decisions, Reports and Orders	1947–[1953]	v.3–[4]
(for v.1–2 see Maritime Commission Decisions)		
Federal Power Commission		
Opinions and Decisions	1931–[1940]	9
Federal Radio Commission		
Opinions of General Counsel	1928–1929	1

Title	Dates Covered	No. of volumes
Federal Reserve Bulletin (Board of Governors of Federal Reserve System) "Law Dept." contains opinions of counsel for the Board and decisions of the higher courts and opinions of the Attorney General	1915–[1951]	37
Federal Trade Commission		
Statutes and Decisions pertaining to F.T.C.	1914–[1948]	4
Decisions	1915–[1950]	46
Court Decisions	1930–1934	1
General Accounting Office		
See Comptroller General		
General Land Office Decisions (Copp)	1866–1872	1
Interstate Commerce Commission		
Reports	1887–[1952]	284
——Motor Carrier Cases	1936–[1952]	57
——Valuation Reports	1918–[1951]	51
Vol. 1–22 in Interstate Commerce Commission Reports; with vol. 22 separately numbered.		
Judge Advocate General (Air Force)		
Court-martial Reports	1948–1951	4
Judge Advocate General (Army)		
Opinions	1917–1919	3
Memorandum Opinions when acting upon applications for relief under Article of War 55	1949–1950	1
Judge Advocate General (Navy)		
Compilation of Court-martial Orders	1916–1937	2
Judge Advocate General (Defense Dept.)		
Court-martial Reports; holdings and decisions of Judge Advocate General Boards of Review and U. S. Court of Military Appeals	1951–[1952]	5
Land Cases		
See Department of the Interior		
Lester, Public Land Cases		
See Department of the Interior		
Maritime Commission		
Decisions of the U. S. Shipping Board, Dept. of Commerce, U. S. Shipping Board Bureau, and U. S. Maritime Commission	1919–1947	2
Continued as Federal Maritime Board Reports, v. 3– q. v.		
National Defense Mediation Board		
[Cases] no. 1–112	1941–1942	
Mimeographed. (May be found in Bulletin 714, Bureau of labor statistics. Report on the work of the National defense mediation board, p. 89–262)		
National Forests, Laws, decisions and opinions applicable to National Forests		
See Department of Agriculture		
National Labor Relations Act		
Court decisions relating to National Labor Relations Act	1928–[1949]	6
National Labor Board		
Decisions	1933–1934	2
Continued by National Labor Relations Board Decisions		

Title	Dates Covered	No. of volumes
National Labor Relations Board		
Decisions	1934–1935	2
Continuation of Decisions of National Labor Board. Continued by Decisions and Orders (no decisions June 16–Dec. 7, 1935)		
Decisions and Orders	1935–[1952]	98
Continuation of Decisions of National Labor Relations Board		
Decisions affecting Radio Broadcasting Stations (v. 1–48)	1943	1
National Mediation Board		
Certifications or Withdrawals. (Processed) Cases no. R1–R1299	1934–1944	4
Mediation Agreements. (Processed) Cases no. A215–A1139	1938–1942	1
National Railroad Adjustment Board Awards		
First Division no. 1–[15830]	1936–[1952]	109
Second Division no. 1–[1487]	1934–[1951]	13
Third Division no. 1–[6000]	1936–[1952]	57
Fourth Division no. 1–[700]	1936–[1950]	7
National Recovery Administration. Advisory Council.		
Decisions no. 1–233	1934–1935	5
National Recovery Administration. Industrial Appeals Board		
Decisions no. 1–40	1934–35	4
National War Labor Board		
Decisions and Orders (Processed) no. B1–B2224	1942–1945	22
Regional Decisions and Orders Region 1–12 (Processed)	1942–1945	22
Second Regional Board Decisions (Processed)	1945	3
War Labor Reports	1942–1945	28
Succeeded by Labor Arbitration Reports, *See* Special subject reports		
Office of Contract Settlement		
Decisions, Appeal Board	1945–1950	4
Office of Internal Revenue		
Bulletin. Income Tax Rulings	1919–1921	5
Decisions relating to the law of Conspiracy. Alcohol Tax Unit.	1938	1
Internal Revenue Bulletin		
Weekly issues cumulated semi-annually into Cumulative Bulletin	1922–[1953]	
Treasury Decisions under Internal Revenue Laws (after July 9, 1942 published in Internal Revenue Bulletin, Weekly and Cumulative Issues)	1898–1942	36
Office of Price Administration		
Opinions and Decisions (Pollack)	1942–1947	5
Patent Office		
Official Gazette, U. S. Patent Office		
Decision Leaflets; cumulated in Decisions of the Commissioner of Patents and of the U. S. courts in patent and trademark and copyright cases	1869–[1951]	81
Pension and bounty-land claims		
See Department of the Interior. Decisions in appealed pension and bounty-land claims		

Title	Dates Covered	No. of volumes
Petroleum Labor Policy Board Decisions		
(Dept. of the Interior)	1934–1935	1
Post Office Department		
Official opinions of the Solicitor	1873–[1936]	8
Vol. 1–5 as Official opinions of the Assistant Attorneys-General for the Post Office Department		
Processing Tax Board of Review		
Decisions (Processed)	1939–[1941]	
Public Land Cases		
See Department of the Interior		
Public Lands Decisions		
See Department of the Interior		
Railroad Labor Board Decisions	1920–1926	7
Railroad Retirement Board Law Bulletin	1939–1940	2
Reappraisement Decisions		
See Federal Reports list under Customs Court		
Securities and Exchange Commission Decisions	1934–[1946]	23
Securities and Exchange Commission		
Judicial Decisions (court decisions involving statutes administered by the S.E.C.)	1934–1939	1
Vol. 2 & 3 issued in limited processed edition.		
Shipping Board Decision		
and		
Shipping Board Bureau Decisions		
See Maritime Commission		
Solicitor for the Post Office Department		
See Post Office Department		
Tax Court		
Reports	1942–[1952]	17
Continues Board of Tax Appeals Reports		
Treasury Decisions under Customs and other laws	1868–[1951]	86
1868–1898 have title: Synopsis of the decisions; 1898–1903, Treasury decisions under tariff and navigation laws.		
Treasury Department — Office of Internal Revenue		
See Office of Internal Revenue		
Treasury Department		
Sales Tax Rulings	1920–1921	2
Veterans Administration		
Decisions in appealed pension and civil service retirement cases	1930–1932	1
Continuation of Decisions of Department of Interior in Appealed pension and bounty-land claims		
Decisions of the Administrator no. 1–715	1931–[1946[	2
Supplement 1–[6] to v. 1 no. 716–[905]	1946–[1952]	6
War Department Claims Board		
Decisions of Appeal Section	1919–1921	8
Vol. 1–6 as Decisions of Board of Contract Adjustment, War Department		
War Labor Reports		
See National War Labor Board		
Workmen's Compensation Opinions		
See Department of Commerce and Labor		
Opinions of the Solicitor, dealing with Workmen's compensation.		

BRITISH AND CANADIAN MATERIAL

A. Regnal Years of English Sovereigns

English statutes, cases in the Yearbooks, and occasionally others of the older English cases are cited by the year of the reign of a sovereign; hence the necessity for such tables as the following, adapted and abridged from the *Guide to Law Reports, Statutes and Regnal Years* (2d ed., London, Sweet & Maxwell, 1948), by permission of the publishers. For two reasons there is disagreement between various regnal year tables.

(1) Until January 1, 1752, while the common and historical year dated from January 1, as at present, the civil, ecclesiastical and legal year dated from March 25. Therefore, in that period, all dates between January 1 and March 25 belong, according to the civil computation, to one year earlier than the historical year. Thus, Edward III's reign is sometimes said to have begun on January 25, 1326, instead of January 25, 1327, and is accordingly cited as January 25, 1326/27.

(2) Frequently there was an interregnum between the death of one sovereign and the beginning of the actual reign of his successor. Unless this interregnum was long, it is usual for historical purposes to consider the succeeding reign as beginning simultaneously with the close of the preceding one, but for legal purposes it was formerly customary to reckon the regnal year as beginning on the date of coronation or the assumption of power. On the other hand, the regnal years ascribed to Charles II ignore the Interregnum, and are computed from the death of his father, January 30, 1648/49. Therefore, although he was not actually King until May 29, 1660, that year is designated as the twelfth of his reign.

Table of Regnal Years of English Sovereigns

King	Inclusive Dates
William I	14 Oct. 1066 - 9 Sept. 1087
William II	26 Sept. 1087 - 2 Aug. 1100
Henry I	5 Aug. 1100 - 1 Dec. 1135
Stephen	26 Dec. 1135 - 25 Oct. 1154
Henry II	19 Dec. 1154 - 6 July 1189
Richard I	3 Sept. 1189 - 6 April 1199
John	27 May 1199 - 19 Oct. 1216

King	Inclusive Dates
Henry III	28 Oct. 1216 - 16 Nov. 1272
Edward I	20 Nov. 1272 - 7 July 1307
Edward II	8 July 1307 - 20 Jan. 1327
Edward III	25 Jan. 1327 - 21 June 1377
Richard II	22 June 1377 - 29 Sept. 1399
Henry IV	30 Sept. 1399 - 20 March 1413
Henry V	21 March 1413 - 31 Aug. 1422
Henry VI	1 Sept. 1422 - 4 March 1461 (deposed by Edward V.)
Henry VI	9 Oct. 1470 - about April 1471 (regained Throne.)
Edward IV	4 March 1461 - 9 April 1483
Edward V	9 Apr. 1483 - 25 June 1483
Richard III	26 June 1483 - 22 Aug. 1485
Henry VII	22 Aug. 1485 - 21 April 1509
Henry VIII	22 April 1509 - 28 Jan. 1547
Edward VI	28 Jan. 1547 - 6 July 1553
Mary	6 July 1553 - 24 July 1554
Jane	6 July 1553 - 17 July 1553
Philip and Mary	25 July 1554 - 17 Nov. 1558
Elizabeth I	17 Nov. 1558 - 24 Mar. 1603
James I	24 March 1603 - 27 March 1625
Charles I	27 March 1625 - 30 Jan. 1649
Charles II	30 Jan. 1649 - 6 Feb. 1685
Interregnum	30 Jan. 1649 - 29 Jan. 1661
James II	6 Feb. 1685 - 11 Dec. 1688
William and Mary	13 Feb. 1689 - 8 Mar. 1702
Anne	8 March 1702 - 1 Aug. 1714
George I	1 Aug. 1714 - 11 June 1727
George II	11 June 1727 - 25 Oct. 1760
George III	25 Oct. 1760 - 29 Jan. 1820 (Regency 25 Oct. 1810 - 29 Jan. 1820)
George IV	29 Jan. 1820 - 26 June 1830
William IV	26 June 1830 - 20 June 1837
Victoria	20 June 1837 - 22 Jan. 1901
Edward VII	22 Jan. 1901 - 6 May 1910
George V	6 May 1910 - 20 Jan. 1936
Edward VIII	20 Jan. 1936 - 11 Dec. 1936
George VI	11 Dec. 1936 - 6 Feb. 1952
Elizabeth II	6 Feb. 1952 -

B. Terms of English Courts

Until November 1, 1875, by the Supreme Court of Judicature Act of 1873, § 26, terms of English common-law courts were named from ecclesiastical festivals, and cases were cited by name, festival and year. For such a citation, accordingly, a parallel table is necessary to set the approximate date of the decision. These dates differ, according to whether the year date was before or after 1831.

Hilary Term.

Before 1831, began Jan. 23 or 24;
Before 1831, extended from January 23 or 24 to February 12 or 13;
1831-1875, extended from January 11 to January 31.

Easter (or Paschal) Term.

Before 1831, began from April 8 to May 12 (17 days after Easter), and ended from May 4 to June 7 (26 days later).

1831-1875, began April 16 and ended May 8.

Trinity Term.

1264-1540, began May 27 to June 30, and ended June 17 to July 21.
1541-1830, began May 22 to June 15, and ended June 10 to July 14.
1831-1875, began May 22 and ended June 2.

Michaelmas Term.

Before 1641, began October 9 or 10 and ended November 28 or 29.
1641-1751, began October 23 or 24, and ended November 28 or 29.
1752-1830, began November 6 or 7, and ended November 25.
1831-1874, began November 2 and ended November 25.

C. Alphabetical List of English, Scotch, and Irish Law Reports

The following list is designed as an index to standard English, Scotch and Irish law reports, and only sufficient information is given to identify the various reports. Further description is supplied by the Library of Congress printed author catalog, and by W. Harold Maxwell and C. R. Brown's *A Complete List of British and Colonial Law Reports and Legal Periodicals*.[1] The latter is especially recommended to those requiring additional information within its scope. Nearly all English reports prior to 1865 are published in the *English Reports—Full Reprint*[2] and are listed alphabetically on a wall chart hung adjacent to where this set is shelved, in most law libraries. Many so-called collateral ("unauthorized," for which *see* page 279) reports not reprinted in the above set however, are in the *Revised Reports*[3] to which there is a complete table of cases.

In the following entries, dates in parentheses are publication dates (given only when considerably later than the dates covered by the reports), while all other dates represent the coverage of the cases reported. These latter dates will often differ from those given in other bibliographies, but were arrived at after careful comparison by the authors with the reports themselves. Where no volume numbers are given, there is only one volume.

Current series are indicated by an asterisk (*); where there is some doubt as to such currency, it is indicated thus:*?

For the meaning of such abbreviations as are employed, *see* Appendix VI.

Abbott's Jurisdiction of Court of Great Sessions. 1795

Abridgment of Cases in Equity. *See* Equity Cases Abridged.

Abstract of Cases & Decisions on Appeals Relating to Tax on Servants. 1781

Accountant (periodical) 127v. 1874–1952*

Accountant Law Reports. 14v. 1922–35*?

"Accountant" Tax Cases. *See* Annotated Tax Cases.

Acta Dominorum Concillii. 1501–03 (Stair Society, v.8; cited as A.D.C. v.3) *Scot*

Acton's Prize Cases. v.1–2 pt. 1. 1809–11

[1] 3d ed., Toronto, Canada, Carswell, 1937, with 1946 supplement. The authors gratefully acknowledge the permission of the publishers to consult this work in the compilation of their list. Additions and some modifications were made through search in the catalogs of the Library of Congress and of the Columbia University Law Library.

[2] As described at page 279.

[3] As described at page 279.

Acts Lawting Ct., Orkney, Shetland.
1612–16

Acts Lords, Auditors of Causes & Complaints (Scots Parliamentary Court).
1466–94 [1839]

Acts Lords of Council in Civil Causes
(Scots Parl. Ct.) 2v. 1478–1501

Acts Lords of Council in Public Affairs
(1932). (Scots Parl. Ct.) 1501–44

Acts Privy Council, James I, N.S. 8v.
1613–26

Acts Privy Council, Colonial Series
(1909–12). 6v. 1613–1783

Adam's Scotch Justiciary Case, 7v.
1893–1916

Addam's Ecclesiastical. v.1–3 pt. 1
1822–26

Additional Cases on Duties 1752–82

Admiralty Cases

Admiralty Cases (High Court of Admiralty). 2v. 1831–50 (Volume 1
cases selected from 2–3 Knapp's
Privy Council Reports, and Moore's
Privy Council Reports, v.1–4, 6, 7.
Volume 2 cases collected from v.1–7
of Notes of Cases.)

Shelton's Admiralty Examinations.
1637–38. (High Court of Admiralty
examinations collected by Dorothy
O. Shilton & Richard Holworthy.
London, Anglo-American Records
Foundation, 1932)

Admiralty Transport Arbitration Board
Judgments. 1923–27

Adolphus & Ellis' Q. B. 12v. 1834–42

Adolphus & Ellis' (N.S.) K.B. & Q.B.
18v. 1841–42

Alcock's Registry. 18v. 1832–41   *Ir*

Alcock & Napier's K. B. 1831–33   *Ir*

Aleyn's K. B. (1688). 1646–48

All England Law Reports. 45v.
1936–52*

Allwood's Weights & Measures.
1801–1906

Ambler's Chancery, 1828. 2v. 1716–83

Amphlett's Court Rolls of Manor of
Hales 1272–1307 (1919–34).

Anderson's Agriculture. 1800–1883
Scot

Anderson's Common Pleas. 2v.
1534–1606

Andrews' King's Bench. 1737–38

Annaly. *See* Lee's Cas. *temp.* Hardwicke.

Annotated Cas., Amer. & Eng., 1906–18.
53v.

Annotated Tax Cases. 31v. 1922–52/3*

Anstruther's Exchequer, 1817. 3v.
1792–97

Appeals from Fisheries Commission.
1861–93   *Ir*

Appeals Relating to Tax on Servants.
1778–81

Archbold's Poor Law. 1842–58

Architect's Law Reports. 4v. 1904–09

Arkley's Justiciary. 1846–48   *Scot*

Armstrong, Macartney, & Ogle's Nisi
Prius. 1840–42   *Ir*

Arnold's Common Pleas. 2v. 1838–39

Arnold & Hodges' Q.B. Practice Cas.
1840–41

Aspinall. *See* Maritime Cases.

Atcheson's Petersfield Petition (1831)
1820–21

Atkinson's Q. S. Records, Yorkshire
(North Riding) (1884–92). 9v. 1605–
1786

Atkyns' Chancery. 3v. 1736–54

Ault's Court Rolls of Ramsey Abbey
(Seignorial Courts) (1928).

Austen-Cartmell's Abstract of Trade
Marks (1893). 1876–92

Austin's County Court. 1867–69

Axon's Manchester (Quarter) Sessions
(1901) 1616–1739

Ayr's Registration Cases 1839–41   *Scot*

Ayr & Wigton's Regis. Cas. 1839–41
Scot

Bacon's Decisions, ed. Ritchie (1932).
1617–21

Baigent & Millard's History of Basingstoke (Municipal Courts) (1889).
1390–1588

Baildon's Select Cases in Ch. (1896).
1364–1471 (Selden Society, v. 10.)

Baildon's Select Civil Pleas, Curia Regis.
(1889). 1200–93

Baildon's Yorkshire Star Chamber Proc.
(1893)

Baildon & Lister's Court Roll of Man or
of Wakesfield (Seignorial Courts)
(1901–30). 4v. 1274–1317

Bailey's Precot Court Leet Records
(Seignorial Courts) (1937). 1510–
1600

Baldwin, J. F., Records of Privy Council
Cases, Rich. II–Henry VI. (1913).
1383–1457

Ball & Beatty's Chancery. 2v. 1807–14   *Ir*

Ballard's Somerton Court Rolls (1906)
1482–1573

Bamber's Mining Cases. 1923–24

Bankruptcy & Company Winding-Up Reports. 20v. 1915–42*

Bankruptcy & Insolvency Rep.(Dasent). 2v. 1853–55
30

Bar & Legal World (periodical). 1903

Bar Reports. (v.12–23 of Law Times Reports.)

Barbour's Cas. on Contract (1914). 1413–81

Barbour's Chancery Cases. Same as above.

Barnardiston's Chancery. 1740–41

Barnardiston's K. B. 2v. 1726–34

Barnes' Notes of Cases, Com. Pl. 1732–60

Barnewall & Adolphus' K. B. 5v. 1830–34

Barnewall & Alderson's K. B. 5v. 1817–22

Barnewall & Cresswell's K. B. 10v. 1822–

Barrister (legal periodical). 1824

Barron's Barony of Urie Court Records (1892). 1604–1747   *Scot*

Barron & Arnold's Elect. Cas. 1843–46

Barron & Austin's Elect. Cas. 1842

Bartholoman's Yorkshire Assize Cas. N.P. 1811

Bateson's Leicester Records (1899–1905). 3v. 1103–1603

Batty's King's Bench. 1825–26   *Ir*

Beames' Costs (1840). 1719–1822

Beames' Gen. Orders in Chancery. 1815

Beatty's Chancery. 1813–30   *Ir*

Beavan's Rolls Court. 36v. 1838–66

Beavan & Walford's Ry. Cas. 2 pts. 1846

Bell's Crown Cases. 1858–60

Bell's Dict. Ct. of Session Cas. 1842 *Scot*

Bell's House of Lords. 7v. 1842–50 *Scot*

Bell's Ct. of Session Cases. 1790–92 *Scot*

Bell's Ct. of Session Cas. 1794–95 *Scot*

Bellewe's King's Bench (1869). 1378–1400

Belt's Supplement to Vesey Senior. 1746–56

Bendloe (or Benloe), K. B. (1661). 1530–1627

Benloe & Dalison's Com. Pl. (1689). 1486–1579

Bennett & Dewhirst's Q. S. Rec., County Palatine of Chester (1940). 1559–1760

Bernard's Church Acts Cases. 1870–75 *Ir*

Best & Smith's K. B. 10v. 1861–69

Bidder's Locus Standi (Court of Referees on Private Bills in Parliament) v.1 in 7 pts. 1920–36*

Bigelow's Cases from William I–Richard I (1879). 1066–1195

Bigelow's Placita Anglo-Normannica. *See* above.

Bingham's Common Pleas. 10v. 1822–34

Bingham's Motor Claims Cas.(1946).

Bingham's New Cases, Com. Pl. 6v. 1834–40

Birkenhead's H. L. Judgments. 1919–22

Bittleston's Chambers Rep. 2v. 1875–84

Bittleston, Wise, & Parnell's Magistrates'. 5v. 1844–51

Black's Digest, Scottish Shipping Cas. 1865–90

Blackerby's Magistrates'. 1505–1734

Blackham, Dundas, & Osborne's Nisi Prius. 1846–48   *Ir*

Blackmore's Speaker's Dec. 2v. 1857–95

Blackstone's (H.) Com. Pl. 2v. 1788–1796

Blackstone's (W.) K. B. 2v. 1746–1779

Bligh's House of Lords. 4v. 1819–21

Bligh's New Series, H. L. 11v. 1827–37

Bohun's Election Cases. 1628–99

Booth's Chester Palatine Courts. 1811

Borthwick's Defamation. 1748–1824 *Scot*

Bosanquet & Puller's Com. Pl. 3v. 1796–1804

Bosanquet & Puller's New Rep., Com. Pl. 2v. 1804–07

Boscawen's Magistrates' Cases. 1735–83

Bott & Pratt's Poor Law. 3v. 1560–1833

Bourke's Parliamentary Precedents. 1842–56

Bowler's London (Quarter) Sessions Records (1935). 1605–85

Bracton's Note Book, Curia Regis (1887) 3v. 1218–40

Bradford's Somerset Star Chamber Cases (1911). 1485–1547

Brett's Dec. Grand Jury Acts. 1895 *Ir*

Brett's Grand Jury Law Decisions. 1895 *Ir*

Brewing Trade Review Licensing Reports. 22v. 1913–35*?

Bridgman (Sir. J.), Com. Pl. Rep. 1613–21

Bridgman (Sir. Orlando), Com. Pl. (1823). 1660–67

Brinkworth's Archdeacon's Ct., Oxford: Liber Actorum (1942–45). 1584 (Oxfordshire Record Ser., 33, 34)

British & Colonial Prize Cas. 3v. 1914–22

British Ruling Cases. 16v. 1905–31

Broderip & Bingham's Com. Pl. 3v. 1819–22

Broderick & Freemantle's Eccles. 1840–64

Brooke's Ecclesiastical. 1850–72

Brooke's New Cases, K. B. (1873). 1515–58

Broun's Justiciary Cas. 2v. 1842–45 *Scot*

Brown's Ch. (by Eden). 4v. 1778–94

Brown's Ch. (by Belt). 4v. 1778–94

Brown's H. L. (by Tomlins). 8v. 1701–1800

Brown's General Synopsis, Court of Session. 4v. 1540–1827 (A digest of Morison's Dictionary & Brown's Supplement.)   *Scot*

Brown's Baron Bailie Courts. 1816   *Scot*

Brown & McCall's Yorkshire Star Chamber Proc. (1909–27). 4v. 1485–1551

Browne's Compendious View (Eccles.) (2d ed., 1803.)   *Ir*

Browne & Macnamara. *See* Railway Cases.

Browning & Lushington's Admiralty. 1863–65

Brownlow & Gouldesborough's Com. Pl. 1569–1624

Brown's Supplement to Morison, Court of Session. 5v. 1620–1768   *Scot*

Bruce's Court of Session. 1714–15   *Scot*

Brunskill's Landlord & Tenant. 6v. 1891–95   *Ir*

Buchanan's Remarkable Cases, Court of Session. 1810–13   *Scot*

Buck's Bankruptcy. 1816–20

Bulstrode's King's Bench. 3v. 1609–26

Bunbury's Exchequer (1802). 1713–41

Burn's High Commission Court. 1865

Burn's Star Chamber Proceedings. 1495–1639

Burne's Staffordshire Q.S. Rolls. 5v. 1581–1606

Burrell & Marsden's Admiralty. 1584–1839

Burrow's King's Bench. 5v. 1756–1772

Burrow's Settlement Cases. 1732–76

Burton's Cases . . . Law, Equity, Conveyancing. 2v. 1700–75

Butterworth's Rating Appeals. 4v. 1913–31*?

Butterworth's Workmen's Compensation Cases. 41v. 1908–48

Butterworth's Workmen's Compensation Cases, Scotch & Irish Cases (Supplement to above). 18v. 1931–49

Cababé & Ellis' Q. B. 1882–85

Caldecott Magistrates' & Settlement Cases. 1777–87

Calendar of County Court, City Court & Eyre Rolls of Chester, Curia Regis. 1259–97 (Chetham Soc., v.84.)

Calendar Justiciary Rolls (1905–14). 2v. 1295–1307   *Ir*

Calendars Proc. in Ch. *temp.* Eliz. I (1827–32). 3v. 1377–1600

Calendars of Proceedings (Sup.) 1545–1625

Calthrop's K. B. (1872). 1609–1618

Cameron's Justiciary (Argyll). 1664–1705   *Scot*

Campbell's Nisi Prius. 4v. 1808–16

Cantwell's Tolls & Customs. 1596–1829 *Ir*

Carpmael's Patent Cases. 3v. 1602–1842

Carrington & Kirwan's N. P. v.1-3, pt. 2 1843–53

Carrington & Marshman's N. P. 1841–43

Carrington & Payne's N.P. 9v. 1823–41

Carrow, Hamerton, & Allen's New Sessions Cases. v. 1–4, pts. 1–4. 1844–51

Carshalton Ct. Rolls (1916). 1359–1506

Carter's Common Pleas. 1664–76

Carthew's King's Bench. 1686–1700

Cartmell's Trade Marks. 1876–92

Cary's Chancery. 1557–1604

Cases Concerning Actions on the Case. 1741

Cases (in Taxation) for Opinions of Law Officers (1907). 1880–82   *Scot*

Cases in Chancery (1735). 1660–1698

Cases in Law & Equity. 1720–73. *See also* Chancery Cases.

Cases in K. B. *temp.* Hardwicke (ed. Lee) (1815). 1733–38

Cases in Spiritual & Maritime Cts. 1822–23

Cases of Practice, Bail Court (1778). 1584–1775

Cases of Practice, Common Pleas. 1702–27

Cases of Settlement. 1685–1733

Cases on Appeals Concerning Duties. 1779–80

Cases on Appeals under Land Valuation Acts. 1858–79   *Scot*

Cases on Appeals under Land Valuation Acts (New Series). 1880   *Scot*

Cases on Duties on Houses, Windows or Lights. 1767–86

Cases on Duties on Inhabited Houses. 1779–86

Cases on Duties on Servants, Horses & Carriages. 1785–87

Cases on Houses, Windows, etc. 1779

Cases on Houses, Windows, etc. 1782

Cases on the Duties of Excise. 1715

Cases on the Six Circuits. 1841–43   *Ir*

Cases Respecting Assessed Taxes. 1823–65

Cases *temp.* Talbot, Chancery. 1730–37

Cases with Opinions of Eminent Council (Burton) 2v. 1700–75

Casson's Local Government Board. 14v. 1902–16

Cay's Registration Cases. 2 pts. 1837–40

Counsellors' Magazine 1795–1800

County Council Cas. 51v. in 57 1890–1950*   *Scot*

County Court Cas. (Cox, Macrae, & Hertslet). 3v. 1847–58

County Courts' Chronicle & Gazette of Bankruptcy. 47v. 1847–1920

County Court Reports (Cox). 34v. 1860–1919

Couper's Justiciary Cases 5v. 1868–85
                                      Scot

Court of Session Cases   *Scot*
    Shaw, 16v. in 17 1821–38
    Dunlop, 2d Ser., 24v. 1838–62
    Macpherson, 3d Ser. 11v. 1862–73
    Rettie, 4th Ser. 25v. 1873–98
    Fraser, 5th Ser. 8v. 1898–1906
    New Series, 30v. 1906–50*

Courthope, Court Rolls . . . Rape of Hastings (1934). 1387–1747 (Seignorial Courts).

Cowper's King's Bench. 2v. 1774–78

Cox's Chancery. 2v. 1783–96

Cox's Company Cases. 1 pt. 1848–49

Cox's County Ct. Rep. (N.S.) 34v. 1860–1919

Cox' Criminal Law Cas. v.1–31, pt.8 1843–1941.

Cox' Magistrates & Municipal Cas. 27v. 1859–1919

Cox' Mercantile Cases. 1pt. 1861

Cox, Macrae & Hertslet's County Court Cases. 3v. 1843–46

Cox & Atkinson's Registration Appeal Cases. 2pts. 1843–46

Craig & Phillips' Chancery. 1840–41

Craigie, Stewart, & Paton's H. L. Cases. 6v. 1726–1822   *Scot*

Crawford & Dix' Abridged Cas. 1837–38
                                      Ir

Crawford & Dix' Circuit Cas. 3v. 1839–46
                                      Ir

Creswell's Insolvency Cas. 1827–29

Criminal Appeal Reports (Cohen). 35v. 1908–51*

Cripps' Church & Clergy Cas. 2pts. 1847–50

Crockford. *See* Maritime Law Cases.

Croke's K.B., ed Leach (1790–92). 4v. 1582–1641

Crompton & Jervis' Exchequer. 2v. 1830–32

Crompton & Meeson's Exchequer. 2v. 1932–34

Crompton, Meeson, & Roscoe's Exchequer. 2v. 1834–36

Cruise on Dignities (Peerage). 1823

Curia Regis Rolls (1922–52). 10v. 1196–1222

Curteis' Ecclesiastical. 3v. 1834–44

Dale's Ecclesiastical. 1868–71

Dalrymple's Ct. of Session. 1698–1718
                                      Scot

Daniell's Exchequer Equity. 1817–20

Daniels' Compensation Cases (Land Clauses Act). 1892–1902

Danson & Lloyd's Mercantile Cases. 1828–29

Dasent's Acts & Proceedings (P.C.) (1890–1907). 32v. 1542–1604

Dasent's Bankruptcy. *See* Bankruptcy.

Davies' Bankrupt Laws. 1744

Davies' K. B., Irish & English. 1604–1612

Davies' Land Valuation Appeals. 3v. 1910–14

Davies' Patents. 1785–1816

Davies, Welsh Assize Roll (No. 147, 1940).

Davison & Merivale's King's Bench. 1843–44

Day's Election Cases. 1892–93

Deacon's Bankruptcy. 4v. 1834–40

Deacon & Chitty's Bankruptcy. 4v. 1832–35

Deane's Blockade Cases. 1854

Deane & Swabey's Ecclesiastical. 1855–57

Dearsly's Crown Cases. 1852–56

Dearsly & Bell's Crown Cases. 1856–58

Deas & Anderson's Session Cas. 5v. 1829–33   *Scot*

Decisions from the Chair (Parliament) 1857–72

De Colyar's County Courts. 1867–82

De Gex. (The Chancery cases included Bankruptcy; Bankruptcy also issued separately.)

De Gex' Bankruptcy. v1–2, pt.1. 1844–50

De Gex & Jones' Bankruptcy. 1857–59

De Gex & Jones' Chancery. 4v. 1857–59

De Gex & Smale's Chancery. 5v. 1846–52 *(Temp.* V.C. Knight, Bruce, Parker, & Stuart.)

De Gex, Fisher, & Jones' Bankruptcy. pt. 1 1859–61

De Gex, Fisher & Jones' Chancery. 4v. 1859–62

De Gex, Jones, & Smith's Bankruptcy. 1862–65

De Gex, Jones, & Smith's Chancery. 4v. 1862–65

De Gex, Macnaghten, & Gordon's Bankruptcy. pts. 1–9. 1851–55

De Gex, Macnaghten & Gordon's Chancery. 8v. 1851–57

Delane's Revision Courts. 1832–35

Denison's Crown Cases. 2v. 1844–52

Departmental Decisions (Local Government). Nos. 1–170 1905–48

De-Rating Appeals (Rowe, etc.) 16v. 1930–45*

Dickens' Chancery. (1803). 2v. 1559–1798

Dickinson, Court Book, Barony of Carnwath (1937). 1523–42   Scot

Dickinson, Sheriff Court Book of Fife (1928). 1515–22   Scot

Digest of Militia Laws, with Adjusted Cases. 1814

Diprose & Gammon's Friendly Societies. 1801–97

Dirleton's Session Cases. 1665–77 Scot

Dodson's Admiralty. 2v. 1811–22

Donnell's Land Cases. 1871–76

Donnelly's Chancery. v.1–2, pt. 1. 1836–37

Douglas' Elections. 4v. 1774–76

Douglas' King's Bench. 4v. 1778–85

Dow's House of Lords. 6v. 1812–18

Dow & Clark's House of Lords. 2v. 1827–32

Dowling's Bail Court. 9v. 1830–41

Dowling, New Series, Bail Ct. 2v. 1841–43

Dowling & Lowndes' Bail Ct. 7v. 1843–49

Dowling & Ryland's K. B. 9v. 1822–27

Dowling & Ryland's Magistrates' Cas. 4v. 1822–27

Dowling & Ryland's Nisi Prius. 1pt. 1822–23

Drewry's Chancery. 4v. 1852–59 (*Temp.* Shadwell and Kindersley.)

Drewry & Smale's Chancery. 2v. 1859–65

Drinkwater's Common Pleas, pts.1–5 1840–41

Drury's Ch. *temp.* Sugden. 1843–44 *Ir*

Drury's Sel. Cas. *temp.* Napier. 1858–59   *Ir*

Drury & Walsh's Chancery. 2v. 1837–40   *Ir*

Drury & Warren's Chancery. 4v. 1941–43   *Ir*

Duke, Charitable Uses (1805). 1555–1804

Duncan's Commercial Cases. 2v. 1885–86

Duncan's Entail. 1856   Scot

Dundee Law Chronicle (Sheriff's Ct.) 3v. 1856–58   Scot

Dunlap's Chancery, Amer. Reprint. 46v. 1843–71

Dunlap's Chancery (Phila. 1843–71). 46v.

Dunning's King's Bench. 1753–54

Durie's Court of Session. 1621–42 Scot

Durnford & East's K. B. ("Term Reports"). 8v. 1785–1800

Dyer's King's Bench (1794). 3v. 1513–82

Eagle & Young's Tithe Cases. 4v. 1204–1825

Earwaker's Court Leet Records of Manchester (1884–90). 12v. 1552–1846

East's King's Bench. 16v. 1801–12

Ecclesiastical Cts. Commission (1883). 2v. 1465–1872

Eden's Chancery. 2v. 1757–66

Edgar's Court of Session Cases. 1724–25   Scot

Edwards' Prerogative Ct. Abridgments. 1846

Edwards' Admiralty. 1808–12

Edwards' Cases on Vessels under British Licenses. 1812

Edwards' Flint Pleas, Chester Palatine Courts (1922). 1283–85

Elchies' Court of Session. 2v. 1733–54   Scot

Elder's Food & Drug Cases. 1876–1905

Election Cases. 1784–96   Scot

Ellis & Blackburn's K. B. 8v. 1851–58

Ellis, Blackburn, & Ellis' K. B. 1858

Ellis & Ellis' K. B. 3v. 1858–61

Elmes' Dilapidations (1829). 1616–1828

English Judges, Court of Sessions Decisions (1762). 1655–1661   Scot

English Reports, Full Reprint. 178v. 1220–1865

English Reports Annotated. 10v. 1866–69, 1900

Equity Cases Abridged. 2v. 1677–1744

Equity Reports, H.L. 3v. 1853–55

Erck's Ecclesiastical Register. 1608–1825   Ir

Espinasse's Nisi Prius. 6v. 1793–1807

Evans' Dec. Lord Mansfield (1803). 2v.

Exchequer Reports (Welsby, Hurlstone, & Gordon). 11v. 1847–56

Faculty of Advocates Rep., Ct. of Session   Scot
14v. 1752–1808 (v.14 in 2 volumes.)
7v. 1808–25
16v.(n.s.) 1825–41

Falconer's County Courts (1870).

Falconer's Ct. of Session. 2v. 1744–51
Scot

Falconer & Fitzherbert's Elections 1835–39

Farren's Insurance. 1807–23

Farrer, Court Rolls of Clitheroe (1897–1913). 3v. 1377–1567 (Seignorial Cts.)

Farrer, Court Rolls of Earl of Lancaster's Manors (1901). 1323–24 (Seignorial Courts.)

Farresley, Modern Cases, K. B. 1702–03 (See v. 7 Modern Reports)

Fawcett's Court of Referees. 1865

Fearne's Posthumous Works (1797).

Fergusson's Divorce Cases (Consistorial Court) 1811–17 Scot

Ferrall's Cases on Privilege (1837) Parliament.)

Finch's Contract Cases (1896).

Finch (Sir.H.), Chancery. 1673–1680

Finch (T.) Precedents in Chancery. 1689–1722

Finlay's Digest (original cases) 1769–71
Ir

First Book of Judgments (1655).

Fisheries Commission Appeals (3 pamphlets). 1868, 1871

Fisheries Commission Judgments. 1863–65 Ir

Fishwick, Pleadings & Dispositions, Lancaster Palatine Cts. (1896–99). 3v. 1489–1558

Fitzgibbon's Irish Land Cases. 25v. 1895–1920

Fitzgibbon's Registry Cases. 1894 Ir

Fitzgibbon's King's Bench. 1727–32

Fitzgibbon's Local Gov't. Dec. 17v. 1899–1919 Ir

Flanagan & Kelly's Rolls Court. 1840–42 Ir

Flenley, Register of Council of Marches (1916). 1569–91

Foley's Poor Law. 1556–1730

Forbes, Cases in St. Andrews Bishop Court (1845). Scot

Forbes' Court of Session. 1705–13 Scot

Forrest's Exchequer. 1800–01.

Forsyth's Cases & Opinions. 1704–1856

Fortescue's King's Bench. 1695–1738

Foster's Crown Cases. 1743–61

Foster & Finlason's N.P. 4v. 1856–67

Fountainhall's Ct. of Session. 2v. 1678–1712

Fowler, Roll of Justices in Eyre in Bedfordshire (1939). 1247

Fox & Smith's King's Bench. 2v. 1822–24

Fox & Smith's Registration. 1886–95

Francillon's County Court. 1847–52

Fraser's Election Cases. 2v. 1776–77

Frazer's Admiralty Cases (1814). Scot

Freeman's Chancery (1823). 1660–1706

Freeman's King's Bench (1826). 1670–1704

Furnivall, Depositions in Trials in Bishop's Court, Chester (1897). 1551–56

Gale's Exchequer. 2v. 1835–36

Gale's New Forest Decisions (1858).

Gale & Davison's K. B. 3v. 1841–43

Gardiner's Star Chamber (1886). 1631–32

Gazette of Bankruptcy. 4v. 1861–63

Giffard's Chancery. 5v. 1857–65 (Temp. Knight, Bruce, Parker, & Stuart.)

Gilbert's Chancery. 1705–27

Gilbert's Cases in Law & Equity. 1714–15

Gilmour & Falconer's Ct. of Session. 2v. in 1 1661–1686 Scot

Glanville's Election Cases (1875). 1624

Glascock's Reports (all courts). 1831–32 Ir

Glover's Municipal Corporation Cases (1841).

Glyn & Jameson's Bankruptcy. 2v. 1821–28

Godbolt's K. B. & C. B. 1575–1638

Gollanz, Rolls of Northampton Sessions (1940). 1314–20 (Northern Record Society, v.11).

Gomme, Court Minutes of Surrey & Kent Sewer Commission (1909). 1569–79

Gomme, Court Rolls of Tootgin Bec. (1909) 1394–1422

Goodeve's Patent Cases. 1785–1883

Gouldesborough's King's Bench. 1586–1602

Gow's Nisi Prius. 1818–20

Graves, Proceedings of King's Council (1877). 1392–93 Ir

Green's Land Cases. 1898–99 Ir

Greer's Land Cases. 5v. 1899–1903 Ir

Greer's Leading Cases (Land). 1v. & Appendix. 1872–98

Gretton, Oxford Q.S. Records (1934). 1687–89

Griffin's Patent Cases. 2v. 1866–87

Griffith's Poor Law. 1821–31

Gross, Select Cases from Coroners' Rolls (1896). 1265–1413
4v. 1431–1654

Guilding, Reading Records (1892–96).

Gunn, Stitchill Baron Court Records (1905). 1655–1807 *Scot*

Guthrie, Select Cases, Sheriff's Court. 2v. 1861–92 *Scot*

Gwillim's Tithes Cases. 4v. 1224–1824

Haggard's Admiralty. 3v. 1822–38

Haggard's Consistory. 2v. 1788–1821

Haggard's Ecclesiastical. v.1–4, pts. 1–2. 1827–33

Hailes' Court of Session. 2v. 1766–91 *Scot*

Hale's Ecclesiastical Criminal Precedents (1847). 1475–1640

Hale's Ecclesiastical Precedents (1841). 1583–1736

Halkerston's Compendium or General Abridgment of Faculty Decisions. 1752–1817 *Scot*

Hall, Sheffield Manorial Court Rolls (1926–28). 2v. 1384–1627 (Seignorial Courts.)

Hall & Twells' Chancery. 2v. 1848–50

Hamilton, Records of Court Leet, Manor of Dunluce (1934). 1798–1847 (Seignorial Courts.)

Hamlin's Copyright. 1891–1903 *Ir*

Handbook for Magistrates (Magistrates' Cases, Session Cases, Election Cases, Registration Cases). 1853–55

Hansell's Bankruptcy. 3v. 1915–17

Harbin, Somerset Q.S. Records (1907–19). 4v. 1607–77

Harcarse's Court of Session. 1681–91 *Scot*

Harcourt, His Grace the Steward & Trial of Peers (1907). 1206–1521

Hardres' Exchequer. 1655–69

Hardy, Calendar to Session Books, Middlesex Session Records (1905). 1689–1709

Hardy, Court Rolls of Tattenhill (1908). 2v. 1336–1650 (Seignorial Courts).

Hardy, Doncaster Court Rolls. 2v. 1454–1604

Hardy, Hertford Session Rolls. 9v. 1581–1894

Hardwicke, Cases *temp. See* Cunningham, Lee, Ridgeway, West.

Hare's Chancery *(temp.* Wigram, Turner, & Wood). 11v. 1841–53

Harland, Court Leet Records of Manchester (1864–65). 2v. 1552–1602

Harrington, Criminal Cases. 1887–89 *Ir*

Harris, Coventry Leet Book (1907–13). 1420–1555 (Seignorial Courts.)

Harrison & Rutherford's Com. Pl. 1865–66

Harrison & Wollaston's K. B. & Bail Court. 2v. 1835–36

Hatsell's Precedents . . . House of Commons. 4v. 1290–1818

Hawarde, Star Chamber (1894). 1593–1609

Hay, Liability for Accidents (1860).

Hay, Negligence (1860). *Scot*

Hay, Poor Law (1859). 1711–1859 *Scot*

Hay & Marriott's Admiralty (1801). 1776–79

Hayes' Exchequer. 1830–32 *Ir*

Hayes & Jones' Exchequer. 1832–34 *Ir*

Healey & Landon, Somerset Pleas (1897–1929). 4v. 1200–1280 (Curia Regis.)

Hearnshaw, Southampton Court Leet Records (1905–08). 4v. 1550–1624 (Seignorial Courts.)

Hector, Selections from Judicial Records of Renfrewshire (1876–78). 2v. *Scot*

Hemming & Miller's Vice-Chancellors. 2v. 1862–65

Hermand (Lord), Consistorial Decisions (1940). 1684–1777 *Scot*

Herne, Charitable Uses. 1578–1639

Hetley's Common Pleas. 1627–31

Hewitson, Preston Court Leet Records (1905). 1653–1813 (Seignorial Courts.)

Hobart's King's Bench. 1603–25

Hodges' Common Pleas. 3v. 1835–37

Hogan's Rolls Court. 2v. 1816–34 *Ir*

Holt's Admiralty. 1863–67

Holt's King's Bench. 1688–1710

Holt's Nisi Prius. 1815–17

Holt's Vice-Chancellors. 2v. 1845

Home (Clerk), Session Cases. 1735–44 *Scot*

Hood-Barrs, Married Women's Debts. 1890–95

Hopwood & Coltman's Registration. 2v. 1868–78

Hopwood & Philbrick's Registration. 1863–67

Horn & Hurlstone's Exchequer. 2v. 1838–39

Hough, Martial Law. 1808–54

House of Lords Cases (Clark) 11v. & Index. 1814–66

Hovenden's Supplement to Vesey's Ch. Rep. 2v.

Howard's Equity Pr. Cas., Exchequer. 2v. 1793 *Ir*

Howard's Popery Cases. 1720–73 *Ir*

Howard's Practice Cases, Chancery. 1775

Howell's State Trials (with Index). 34v. 1163–1820

Hudson, Building, 2v. 1869–1912

Hudson, Leet Jurisdiction in Norwich (1892). 1288–1391 (Seignorial Courts.)

Hudson & Brooke's K. B. 2v. 1827–31
Ir

Hughes' Extents (1811).

Hughes' Registration of Title. 1893–1915
Ir

Hume's Court of Session. 1781–1822
Scot

Humphreys, Wellington Court Rolls (1819). 1277–1908

Hunt's Annuity Cases. 1776–96

Hurlstone & Coltman's Exchequer. 4v. 1862–65

Hurlstone & Norman's Exchequer. 7v. 1856–62

Hurlstone & Walmsley's Exchequer. 1840–41

Hutton's Common Pleas. 1612–38

Hutton, Birmingham Court of Request (1808).

Huxley, Second Book of Judgments (1675)

Illingworth's Monopolies. 1273–1800

Important Cases in Bankruptcy. 1 pt. 1846

Industrial Court & Civil Service Tribunal Awards. 2v. 1937–38

Industrial Court Awards. 18v. 1919–36

Ingraham, Ecclesiastical Cases. 7v.

Ingraham's Eccles. Cas. (Phila. 1831–45). 7v.

Ingraham's Condensed . . . Chancery (New York, 1840). *Ir*

Insolvent Debtors' Court Rep., N.S. 1822

Ireland, Law Reports (all courts). 32v. 1878–93

Irish Chancery Rep. 17v. 1850–66

Irish Common Law Rep. 17v. 1849–60

Irish Equity Reports. 13v. 1838–50

Irish Jurist. 18v. 1848–66

Irish Jurist Rep. 17v. 1935–51*

Irish Law Reports. 13v. 1838–50

Irish Law Recorder. 4v. 1827–31

Irish Law Recorder, 2d Ser. 6v. 1833–38

Irish Law Times & Solicitors' Journal Reports. 69v. 1867–1953*

Irish Local Government Quarterly Orders & Legal Decisions. 17v. 1899–1919

Irish Petty Sessions Journal. 6v. 1893–99

Irish Petty Sessions Jour. N.S. 2v. 1899–1901

Irish Reports. 92v. 1894–1952*

Irish Reports, Common Law Ser. 11v. 1866–78

Irish Reports, Equity Series. 11v. 1866–78

Irish Reports, Land Cases Reserved. 1872–73

Irish Reports, Registry App. & Land Cases Reserved. 1868–76

Irish Rep., Verbatim Reprint. 12v. 1894–1912

Irish Weekly Law Reports (and Journal). 8v. 1895–1902

Irvine's Justiciary Cases. 5v. 1852–67
Scot

Jacob's Chancery. 1821–22

Jacob & Walker's Chancery. 2v. 1819–21

James' Martial Law. 1795–1820

Jeaffreson, Selected Middlesex Session Records (1886–92). 4v. 1549–1688

Jeayes, Court Rolls, Borough of Colchester. 3v. (1921–42) 1310–1379.

Jebb's Crown Cases. 1822–40 *Ir*

Jebb & Burke's Queen's Bench. 1841–42 *Ir*

Jebb & Symes' Queen's Bench. 2v. 1838–41 *Ir*

Jedburgh, Registration Cases (1847).
Scot

Jenkins, Calendar of Roll of Justices on Eyre (1945). 1227 (Curia Regis.)

Jenkins' Centuries (Exchequer) (1885). 1220–1623

Johnson's Vice-Chancellors *(temp.* Wigram, Turner, & Wood). 1858–60

Johnson & Hemming's Vice-Chancellors. 2v. 1859–62

Joint Stock Companies' Law Journal. 1848–49

Jones' Exchequer. 2v. 1834–38 *Ir*

Jones, Exchequer Proceedings Concerning Wales (1939).

Jones (T.) K. B. & Comm. Pl. 1667–84

Jones (W.) K.B. & Comm. Pl. 1620–41

Jones & Carey's Exchequer. 2 pts. 1838–39 *Ir*

Jones & La Touche's Chancery, *temp.* Sugden. 3v. 1844–46 *Ir*

Journal of Auctions & Sales. 1853–54

Journal of Jurisprudence & Scottish Law Magazine Reports. 35v. 1857–91

Joyce's Ecclesiastical. 1865–81

Judgments in Election Petitions. 1869–1929*

Judgments in Upper Bench & Comm. Pl. *(cited as* First Book of Judgments). 1655

Judgments under Criminal Law Act. 1882–1902   *Ir*

Judicial Decisions Affecting Building Societies. 8v. 1893–1909

Jurist (all courts). 31v. 1837–54

Jurist (New Series). 24v. 1855–66

Justice of the Peace & Local Government Review. 117v. 1837–1953*

Justiciary Cases. 7v. 1916–50*   *Scot*

Justiciary Records of Argyll & the Isles (1949). 1664–1705 (Stair Society, Publications, No. 12).   *Scot*

Kames' Remarkable Decisions. 2v. 1716–52   *Scot*

Kames' Select Decisions. 1752–68   *Scot*

Kames & Woodhouselee's Dictionary, Court of Session. 5v. 1540–1796   *Scot*

Kay's Vice-Chancellors (*temp.* Wigram, Turner, & Wood). 1853–54

Kay & Johnson's Vice-Chancellors (*temp.* Wigram, Turner, & Wood). 4v. 1854–58

Keble's King's Bench. 3v. 1661–79

Keen's Rolls Court. 2v. 1836–38

Keilwey's King's Bench (1688). 1496–1531

Kelyng (J.), Crown Cases (1873). 1662–69

Kelynge (W.), Chancery (1873). 1730–34

Kenyon's K. B. & Ch. (ed. Hanmer). 2v. 1753–59

Kilburn's Justice of the Peace (1715).

Kilkerran's Court of Session. 1738–52   *Scot*

Kimball, Rolls of Gloucestershire Sessions (1942). 1361–69 (Justices of the Peace.)

Kimball, Rolls of Warwick & Coventry Sessions (1939). 1377–97 (Justices of the Peace.)

King's Bench Cases. 1690–1701 (Usually cited as 12 Modern Reports.)

King's Bench Cases. 1709–25 (Usually cited as 10 Modern Reports.)

King's Bench Cases. 1694–1705 (Manuscript; title from Henry Singleton's Brief Catalogue of the Manuscript English Law Library. 1937.)

King's Bench Cases. 1715–18. 2v. (From Singleton, *supra.*)

Knapp's Privy Council. 3v. 1829–36

Knapp & Ombler's Elections. 1834–35

Knowles, Turton Manor Court Records. 1737–1850 (Seignorial Courts.)

Konstam's Rating Appeals. 2v. 1904–08

Konstam & Ward's Rating Appeals. 1909–12

Lailey's Hampshire County Courts. 1917–20

Lane's Exchequer (1884). 1605–12

Latch's King's Bench. 1624–27

Law & Equity Reporter (N. Y. 1876–78). 4v. (American, English, Irish.)

Law & Equity Reports (Boston, 1851–58). 1850–57. 40 v.

Law Chronicle. 4v. 1829–32 (V.1, nos. 1–4, called Scots Law Chronicle.)   *Scot*

Law Chronicle & Auction Register. 25v. 1813–37

Law Journal (all courts). 9v. 1822–31

Law Journal Cases on Assessed Taxes. 1824–26

Law Journal County Courts Reporter. 22v. 1912–33

Law Journal (Morgan & Williams). 2v. 1803–04

Law Journal Newspaper & County Court Appeals. 14v. 1933–47

Law Journal Reports (N. S.) 118v. in 127. 1831–1949

Law Journal (Smith). 3v. 1804–06

Law Recorder (v. 1 as Irish Recorder). 4v. 1827–31

Law Recorder, Second Series. 6v. 1833–38   *Ir*

Law Reporter (all courts). 2v. 1821–22

Law Reporter (sub-title of Law Times Reports). 11v. 1859–64

Law Reports (all courts). 194v. 1865–90

Law Reports, New Series. 358v. 1891–1952 (does not include Indian Appeals).

First Series, November, 1865, to December, 1875:

Admiralty and Ecclesiastical Cases. 4v. 1865–75

Chancery Appeal Cases. 10v. 1865–75

Common Pleas Cases. 10v. 1865–75

Crown Cases Reserved. 2v. 1865–75

English and Irish Appeals. 7v. 1866–75

Equity Cases. 20v. 1866–75

Exchequer Cases. 10v. 1865–75

Privy Council Appeals. 6v. 1865–75

Probate and Divorce Cases. 3v. 1865–75

Queen's Bench Cases. 10v. 1865–75

Scotch and Divorce Appeals. 2v. 1866–75

Registration Cases.# 3pts. 1868–71

Sessions Cases.# 1v. 1869–72

These were cases collected and reprinted, and do not form part of the regular series. They are rarely met with. The three parts of Registration Cases contain 367 pages.

Second Series, 1876–1890:

Appeal Cases. 15v. 1875–90

Chancery Division. 45v. 1875–90

Common Pleas Division. 5v. 1875–80

Exchequer Division. 5v. 1875–80

Probate Division. 15v. 1875–90

Queen's Bench Division. 25v. 1875–90

Third Series, 1891–1952*

Appeal Cases. 65v.

Chancery Division. 105v.

Probate Division. 63v.

Queen's and King's Bench. 125v.

Law Reports, Indian Appeals, Supplemental (Privy Council.) 1872–73

Law Reports, Indian Appeals. 77v. in 60. 1873–1950

Law Reports (Ireland). 32v. 1878–93

Law Reports, Registration Cases. 3 pts. 1868–71

Law Reports, Scotch & Divorce Appeals, House of Lords. 2v. 1866–75

Law Reports, Sessions Cases. 1869–72

Law Times (O. S.) (all courts). 34v. 1843–59

Law Times Reports (all courts). 177v. 1859–1947

Laws Concerning Elections. 1628–1779

Laws of the Stanneries of Cornwall (Municipal Courts). 1824

Lawson's Irish Registry Cases. 4v. 1885–1914

Lawyer (legal periodical). 1900

Lawyer & Magistrate. 6 pts. 1898–99 Ir

Lawyers' & Magistrates' Magazine. 6v. 1790–94

Leach's Club Cases (1879).

Leach's Crown Cases. 2v. 1730–1815

Leadam, Select Cases, Court of Requests (1898). 1497–1569 (Selden Society, v. 12).   Scot

Leadam, Star Chamber (1903–11). 2v. 1477–1544

Leadam, Select Cases before the King's Council (1918). (Selden Society, v. 35).

Leading Ecclesiastical Cases. 1849–74

Lee's K. B. Cas. temp. Hardwicke. 1733–38

Lee's Ecclesiastical. 2v. 1752–58

Legal Chronicle. 1844

Legal Examiner. 3v. 1831–33

Legal Examiner & Law Chronicle. 5v. 1833–35

Legal Guide. v.1–9, nos. 1–12. 1838–43

Legal Register. 1807–08

Legal Reporter. 3v. 1840–43   Ir

Le Hardy, Calendar to Buckingham Sessions Records (1933–36). 2v. 1678–1705

Le Hardy, Calendar, N. S. (Middlesex Session Records) (1935–36). 2v. 1612–15

Leigh & Cave's Crown Cases. 1861–65

Le Marchant, Legitimacy (1828).

Leonard's King's Bench. 1540–1615

Levinz' K. B. ed. Vickers. 3v. 1660–96

Lewin's Crown Cases on the Northern Circuit. 2v. 1822–38

Ley's King's Bench. 1608–29

Liddell's Martial Law (1805).

Lilly's Cases in Assize (N. P.) 1688–93

Lister, West Riding Session Rolls (1888–1915). 2v. 1597–1642

Littlejohn, Aberdeen Sheriff Court (1904–07). 3v. 1503–1660   Scot

Littleton's Common Pleas. 1627–31

Lizars, Legacy Duty Cases (Exchequer). 1840–50

Lloyd & Goold's Chancery, temp. Plunkett. 1834–39   Ir

Lloyd & Goold's Chancery, temp. Sugden. 1835   Ir

Lloyd & Welsby's Mercantile. 3pts. 1829–30

Lloyd's List Law Reports. 88v. 1919–52*

Lloyd's Prize Cases. 10v. 1914–22

Lloyd's Prize Cases (2d Ser.) v.1, nos. 1–26 1940–52*

Local Government Chronicle. 80v. 1855–1935

Local Government Reports (Knight's). 45v. 1903–47*

Lofft's King's Bench. 1772–74

Longfield & Townsend's Exchequer. 1841–42   Ir

Longstaffe, Durham Convent Manor Rolls (1889). 1296–1384 (Seignorial Courts.)

Longstaffe, High Commission Court (1858). 1626–39 (Surtees Soc., v. 34.)

Lowndes & Maxwell's Bail Court. 1852–54

Lowndes, Maxwell, & Pollock's Bail Court. 2v. 1850–51

Luder's Elections. 3v. 1785–87

Lugard, Eyre & Assize Rolls (1938). 1256–72 (Curia Regis.)

Lugard, Trailbaston (1934–35). 3v. 1306 (Curia Regis.)

Lumley's Poor Law. 2v. 1834–42

Lushington's Admiralty. 1859–62

Lutwyche (A.) Registration Appeals. 2v. 1843–53

Lutwyche (E.), Common Pleas. 2v. 1683–1704

Lutwyche (T.), Select Cases, King's Bench. (Bound with 10 Modern Reports and issued also as 11 Modern Reports.)

Lyne's Leases for Lives. 1716–1837 *Ir*

MacCarthy's Land Cases. 1887–92 *Ir*

McCleland's Exchequer. 1824

McCleland & Younge's Exchequer. 1824–25

McDevitt's Land Cases. 1882–84 *Ir*

McFarlane's Jury Court. 1838–39 *Scot*

McGillivray's Copyright. 8v. 1901–49*

Mackenzie, Pleadings in Some Remarkable Cases (1704). *Scot*

MacLaurin's Remarkable Cases (Justiciary). 1670–1773 *Scot*

Maclean & Robinson's House of Lords Appeals. 1839 *Scot*

Macnaghten, Select Cases in Chancery, *temp.* King. 1724–33

Macnaghten & Gordon's Chancery. 3v. 1849–52

McQueen's Scotch Appeal Cases. 4v. 1847–65

Macqueen's Peerage. 1856–57.

Macqueen's Probate & Divorce (1842).

Macrae & Hertslet's Bankruptcy. 2v. 1847–54

Macrory's Patents. 1847–60

Maddock's Vice-Chancellors. 6v. 1815–22

Magisterial Cases. 52v. 1896–1947*

The Magistrate. 5v. 1848–53

Magistrates' Cases. 18v. 1892–1910

Maitland, Gloucester Pleas of the Crown (1884). 1221 (Curia Regis.)

Maitland, Records of Parliament of 33 Edw. I (1893). 1305

Maitland, Select Pleas in Manorial Courts (1889). 1216–72 (Seignorial Courts.)

Maitland, Select Pleas of the Crown (1888). 1200–25 (Curia Regis.)

Maitland, Three Rolls in King's Court (1891). 1194–95 (Curia Regis.)

Maitland & Baildon, The Court Baron (1891). 1285–1327 (Seignorial Courts.)

Manchee, The Westminster City Fathers (1924). 1585–1601 (Municipal Courts.)

Mandley, Salford Court Leet Records (1902–03). 2v. 1597–1669 (Seignorial Courts.)

Manning's Digest, N.P., with Some Original Cases. 1790–1820

Manning's Revision Cases. 1832–35

Manning & Granger's Comm. Pl. 7v. 1840–45

Manning & Ryland's King's Bench. 5v. 1827–30

Manning & Ryland's Magistrates' Cases. 3v. 1827–30

Manson's Bankruptcy. 21v. 1894–1914

Manuscript Notes of Cases, K. B. 4v. 1735–39, 1748–54

Manwood, Forest Laws (1615, 1665). 1334–36

March's New Cases, K. B. 1639–42

March's Translation of Brooke's K. B. (1873). 1515–58

Marcham, Court Rolls, Bishop of London's Court of Hornsey (1929). 1603–1701

Maritime Cases, O.S. (Crockford). 3v. 1860–71

Maritime Cases, N.S. (Aspinall). 19v. 1870–1943*

Maritime Notes & Queries. 14v. 1873–1900

Marrack's Reports, Decisions of Lord Westbury (European Assurance Arbitration). 1872–74

Marsden, Select Admiralty Pleas (1892–97). 2v. 1527–1602 (Selden Society, v.6, 11.)

Marshall's Common Pleas. 2v. 1813–16

Marshall, Law of Insurance (1865).

Massingberd, Ingoldmell's Court Rolls (1902). 1291–1578 (Seignorial Courts)

Matthews, Cardiff Records (1898–1911) 6v. (Municipal Courts.)

Maule & Selwyn's K. B. 6v. 1813–17

Maxwell's Irish Land Purchase Cas. 1904–11

May's Parliamentary Procedure (1906).

Meeson & Welsby's Exchequer. 17v. 1836–47

Megone's Company Cases. 2v. 1888–91

Merivale's Chancery. 3v. 1815–17

Middlesex Session Records, Quarter Sessions. *See* Jeaffreson; Le Hardy; Hardy.

Millin's Petty Sessions Cases. 1875–98　*Ir*

Milward's Ecclesiastical. 1819–43　*Ir*

Miner's Guide (1810). (Mineral Court.)

Minister of Transport's Decisions on Restriction of Ribbon Development Act, 1935. 3v. 1937–39

Minton-Senhouse, Compensation Cases (Workmen's Compensation Acts.) 9v. 1898–1907

Miscellaneous Cases in Parliament. 1725–37

Mitchell's Maritime Register. 28v. 1856–83

Modern Cases, Q. B. *temp.* Holt 1703–04 (Attributed to W. Salkeld; *see* v.6 Modern Reports)

Modern Cases in Law and Equity 2v. 1721–1726 (*See* v.8–9 Modern Reports).

Modern Reports, K.B. (1793–96). 12v. 1663–1755

Molloy's Chancery. v.1–3, pt.1 1807–32　*Ir*

Monro, Acta Cancellariae (1847). 1545–1625

Montagu's Bankrupt Laws (1827). 2v.

Montagu's Bankruptcy. 2v. 1829–32

Montagu, Partnership. 2v. 1586–1821

Montagu, Set-Off Cases. 1728–1818

Montagu & Ayrton, Bankruptcy. 3v. 1833–38

Montagu & Bligh, Bankruptcy. 1832–33

Montagu & Chitty, Bankrupty. 1838–40

Montagu & M'Arthur, Bankruptcy (1830)

Montagu, Deacon, & De Gex, Bankruptcy. 3v. 1840–44

Monthly Law Magazine. 10v. 1838–41

Moody's Crown Cases. 2v. 1824–44

Moody & Malkin, Nisi Prius. 1826–30

Moody & Robinson, Nisi Prius. 2v. 1830–44

Moore (A.) *See* Bosanquet & Puller

Moore's Common Pleas. 12v. 1817–27

Moore's East India Appeals. 14v. 1836–72

Moore's King's Bench (1688). 1512–1621

Moore's Privy Council, Selected (In English Admiralty Reports, v. 4.) 6pts. in 1. 1836–50

Moore's Privy Council. 15v. 1836–62

Moore's Privy Council, N.S. 9v. 1862–73

Moore, The Gorham Case (P. C.) 1850

Moore & Payne, Comm. Pl. 5v. 1827–31

Moore & Scott, Comm. Pl. 4v. 1831–34

Morison's Dictionary of Decisions, Court of Session. 21v. & Supp. 1540–1815　*Scot*

Morison's Dictionary of Decisions, Synopsis. 2v. 1808–16　*Scot*

Morrell's Bankruptcy. 10v. 1884–93

Mosley's Chancery (1803). 1726–30

Mundy's Star Chamber (1913). 1500–58

Municipal Corporations Circular. 51v. 1878–1929

Municipal Law Reports. 3v. 1903–13 *Scot*

Munitions of War Acts, Appeals from Tribunals. 16pts. 1916–20　*Scot*

Munitions of War Acts, Appeals from Tribunals. 4v. 1916–20

Murphy & Hurlstone's Exchequer. 1836–37

Murray, Jury Courts. 5v. 1815–30　*Scot*

Mylne & Craig's Chancery. 5v. 1835–41

Mylne & Keen's Chancery. 3v. 1832–35

National Arbitration Tribunal Awards. Nos. 1-1660 in 3v. 1940–51*

National Health Insurance, Memoranda of Decisions. 1912–31

National Health Insurance, Reports of Decisions on Appeals. 2v. 1913–23

National Health Insurance, Reports of Inquiries & Appeals, Medical Benefit Regulations. 3v. 1913–24

National Health Insurance, Reports of Decisions on Appeals . . . Act of 1911. 1932–35*

National Health Insurance Commission, Reports of Decisions. 1913–16　*Ir*

Nelson's Chancery. (1872). 1625–93

Nevile & Manning's King's Bench. 6v. 1832–36

Nevile & Manning's Magistrates. 3v. 1832–36

Nevile & Perry's King's Bench. 3v. 1836–38

Nevile & Perry's Magistrates. 1836–37

Neville, Brown, & Macnamara. *See* Railway & Canal Cas.

New County Courts Cases. *See* Roberts.

New Forest Abstract of Claims (Forest Courts). 1670

New Irish Jurist (all courts). 5v. 1900–05

New Magistrates' & Municipal Corporation Cases. 5v. 1844–51

New Magistrates' Cases. *See* Bittleston.

New Practice Cases (Welford, Bittleston, *etc.*) 3v. 1844–48

New Reports (all courts). 6v. 1862–65

New Sessions Cases. *See* Carrow, Hamerton & Allen.

New Term Reports. 34 pts. 1835–41
   Arnold, C.P. 2v.
   Arnold & Hodges, K.B.
   Drinkwater, C.P.
   Gale, Exchequer. 2v.
   Harrison & Wollaston, K.B. 2v.
   Hodges, C.P. 3v.
   Horn & Hurlstone, Exchequer. 2v.
   Hurlstone & Walmsley, Exchequer.
   Murphy & Hurlstone, Exchequer
   Willmore, Wollaston & Davison, K. B.
   Willmore, Wollaston & Hodges, K. B. 2v.
   Wollaston, Bail Court.

Newbon, Court of Referees on Private Bills in Parliament. 2v. 1895–96

Newbon, Private Bills & Locus Standi Reports. 3v. 1899

Nicholl, Hare, & Carrow. *See* Railway Cases.

Nicolas, Legitimacy (1936). 1282–1813

Nicolas, Proceedings & Ordinances, Privy Council (1834–37). 7v. 1386–1547

Nicolson's Registration Appeal Court Digest. 1868   *Scot*

Nolan's Magistrates' Cases. 1791–92

Northern Ireland Law Reports. 28v. 1925–52*

Northumberland Pleas (1922). 1198–1272 (Curia Regis.)

Notes of Cases Decided by the Central Tribunal (Nos. 1-103). 12pts. 1916–18

Notes of Cases, Ecclesiastical & Maritime Courts. 7v. 1841–50

Notes of Decisions at Inverness (Registration Cases). 2v. 1835–53   *Scot*

Noy's Bench. 1559–1649

Official Gazette, County Councils Association. 6v. 1908–13

Old Bailey Sessions Papers, Central Criminal Court. 1715–1834

O'Malley & Hardcastle's Election Petitions. 7v. 1869–1929*?

Orders & Resolutions on Controverted Elections. 1628–1734

Owen's Common Pleas (1656). 1556–1615

Oxley, Railway & Canal Commission, Railway Rates Tribunal, Road Licenses Tribunal. 2v. 1897–1903

Page, Three Northumberland Assize Rolls (1891). 1256–79 (Curia Regis.)

Palgrave, Rotuli Curiae Regis (1835). 2v. 1194–99

Palmer, Assizes at Cambridge (1930). 1260

Palmer's King's Bench (1721). 1619–29

Parish Councils' Journal. 16v. 1895–1909

Park, Insurance (1842). 2v.

Parker, Calendar of Lancashire Assize Rolls (1904–05). 2v. 1241–85 (Curia Regis.)

Parker's Exchequer. 1743–67

Parker, Laws of Shipping & Insurance. 1693–1774

Parker, Plea Rolls, County Palatine (1928). 1401

Patents, Designs & Trade Mark Cases. 70v. 1884–1953*

Paterson's House of Lords (Scots) 2v. 1851–73

Paterson's Poor Law. 1857–63

Paton, Sheriff Court Book of Perth (1914).   *Scot*

Peake's Evidence. 1776–1809

Peake's Nisi Prius. 2v. 1790–1812

Peckwell's Election Cases. 2v. 1802–06

Peere Williams' Chancery. 3v. 1695–1735

Perry's Insolvency Cases. 1831

Perry & Davison's King's Bench. 4v. 1838–41

Perry & Knapp's Elections. 1833

Peter's Jessel's Decisions, Rolls Ct. 1883

Petitions Presented to Court of Claims. 1821

Peyton & Kesteven's Q. S. Minutes (1931). 2v. 1674–95

Phillips' Elections. 1780–81

Phillimore's Ecclesiastical. 3v. 1809–21

Phillimore's Ecclesiastical Judgments. 1867–75

Phillimore, Pleas of the Court of King's Bench (1898). 1297 (Curia Regis.)

Phillips' Chancery. 2v. 1841–49

Pigott & Rodwell's Registration. 1843–45

Placita de Quo Warranto, Edw.I–Edw.III (1818)

Placitorum Abbrevatio (1811) 1189–1327 (Curia Regis.)

Pleading & Practice Cases. 8pts. 1837–38

Plowden's King's Bench (1816). 2v. 1548–79

Plowden's Quaeries (1662).

Pollexfen's King's Bench. 1669–85

Popham's King's Bench. 1592–1627

Powell, Surrey Q.S. Records. 4v. –1666

Power, Rodwell, & Dew, Elections. 2v. 1847–56

Practical Register, Comm. Pl. 2v. 1705–42

Practical Register (Wyatt Chancery.) 1800

Pratt's Contraband of War (1861). 1740–50

Pratt's Ships' Light & Rule of the Road Cases. 1839–57

Precedents in Chancery. *See* Finch.

Pretty, Appeals Concerning Taxes on Land Values. 1911–16

Price's Exchequer. 13v. 1814–24

Price's Notes of Practice, Exchequer. 1830–31

Prince, Patents. 1842–43

Private Legislation Rep. 12v. 1901–18 *Scot*

Proceedings & Judgments, War Courts. 8v. 1920–29

Proceedings of Land Court, Small Landholders' Act. 23v. 1912–34*? *Scot*

Proceedings under Conciliation (Trade Disputes) Act, 1896. 16v. 1896–1920

Property Lawyer. 15v. 1826–30

Putnam, Kent Keepers of the Peace (1933). 1316–17

Putnam, Proceedings before Justices of the Peace (1938). 1338–1477

Putnam, Yorkshire Sessions of the Peace (1939.) 1360–64 (Yorkshire Archaeol. Soc. Record Ser., v. 100.)

Queen's Bench (Adolphus & Ellis, New Series) 18v. 1841–52

Railway & Canal Commission (in Law Reports, Court of Appeal) (1875).

Railway & Canal Commission, Railway Rates Tribunal, Road Licenses Tribunal. 7v. 1835–55

Railway, Canal & Road Traffic Cases. 28v. 1855–1948*

Raine, Depositions from Castle at York (1861). 1640–90

Raine, Ecclesiastical Proceedings in Durham Courts (1845). 1311–1591 (Surtees Society, v. 21.)

Ramshay, Practice (1838).

Ratcliff & Johnson, Warwick W.S. Books (1936–46). 7v. 1625–82

Rating & Income Tax (periodical). 46v. 1924–53*

Raymond (Lord), King's Bench. 3v. 1694–1732

Raymond (Sir. T.), King's Bench. 1660–82

Rayner, Digest of Law Concerning Libels. 1344–1769

Rayner's Tithe Cases. 3v. 1575–1782

Real Property & Conveyancing Cases. 2v. 1843–48

Records, Borough of Nottingham (1882–1914). 6v. 1155–1702

Register, Privy Council of Scotland.
1st Series (1877–98). 14v. 1545–1625
2d Series (1900–08). 8v. 1625–1660

3d Series (1909–33). 14v. 1661–1689*

Reilly's Reports of Decisions of Lords Westbury & Romilly (European Assurance Arbitration). 1pt. 1872–75

Reilly's Reports of Lord Cairns' Decisions (Albert Assurance Arbitration). 3pts. 1871–75

Reinstatement in Civil Employment. Selected Decisions by Umpire. (War Courts). 19v. 1944–45*

Reported Cases on Costs. 1867–91 *Ir*

Reports (The). (All courts). 15v. 1893–95

Reports (1st to 5th) of Defence of the Real Losses Royal Commission, with Appendices of Cases. 1916–20

Reports in Chancery. 1615–1712

Reports of Cases, Comm. Pl. *See* Cooke.

Reports of Cases on Income Tax and Inhabited House Duties. 33v. 1875–1953*

Reports of Inquiries (Wreck Commission). 1895–1935

Reports of Real Property Cases. *See* Real Property.

Reports of Patents, Designs, & Trade Marks Cases. 70v. 1884–1953*

Reports of Selected Compensation Cases. 3v. 1865–67

Reserved Cases (Circuit Cases). 1860–64 *Ir*

Revised Reports (All courts). 152v. 1785–1866

Rich, Staple Court Books of Bristol (1934). 1509–1601 (Bristol Record Society, v.5.)

Richardson & Styles, Select Cases of Procedure without Writ. 1224–69

Rickards & Michael, Locus Standi. 1885–89

Rickards & Saunders, Locus Standi. 1890–94

Ridgeway's Reports, *temp.* Hardwicke (1794. Chancery. 1744–45. King's Bench. 1733–36

Ridgway's Appeal Cases. 3v. 1784–96 *Ir*

Ridgway, Lapp, & Schoales, K. B. 1793–95 *Ir*

Rigg, Plea Rolls of Jewish Exchequer (1905–29). 3v. 1218–77 (Jewish Historical Society, v.3.)

Rigg, Select Pleas, Jewish Exchequer (1902). 1218–86 (Selden Soc. v.15.)

Ritchie's Reports. *See* Bacon.

Ritson, Savoy Court Leet Proceedings. 1682–1789

Roberts' Divorce Cases. 1816–1905 *Ir*

Roberts, Ruthin Court Rolls (1893). 1294–96

Roberts, Leeming, & Wallis, County Courts. 5pts. 1849–51

Robertson's Ecclesiastical. v.1–2, pts. 2–3. 1844–53

Robertson's Scotch Appeal Cases. 1707–27

Robinson Scotch Appeal Cases. 2v. 1840–41

Robinson (C.) Admiralty. 6v. 1798–1808

Robinson (W.) Admiralty. 3v. 1838–50

Roche, Dillon & Kehoe, Land Cases. 1881–82 *Ir*

Rogers, Oxford Pleas of the Crown (1891) 1285

Rolle's King's Bench. 2v. 1614–25

Rolls of Waltham Forest Court of Attachment. 5v. 1713–1848

Romanes, Court Books of Melrose Regality (1914–17). 3v. 1605–1706 *Scot*

Romilly (Sir S.) Notes of Ch. Cas. 1767–87

Roscoe, Cases on Damages in Collisions. 1898–1908

Roscoe's Prize Cases. 2v. 1745–1859

Rose's Bankruptcy. 2v. 1810–16

Ross' Leading Cases (Land). 3v. 1638–1849 *Scot*

Rothery's Wreck Commissioners' Judgments. 1876–80

Rotuli Parliamentorum (1765–1832) 8v. 1278–1553

Rotuli Parliamentorum Hactenus Inediti (1935). 1279–1373

Rowe's Re-Rating Appeals. 16v. 1930–45*

Rowe's Interesting Cases (English & Irish Martial Law). 1798–1823

Ruling Cases (English Ruling Cases). 27v. 1894–1908

Rural District Councils' Association Official Circular. 41v. 1895–1935*?

Rushworth's Historical Collections (Parl. & Star Chamber) (1721). 8v. 1618–48

Russell's Chancery. v.1–5 pts 1–2. 1823–29

Russell & Mylne's Chancery. 2v. 1829–33

Russell & Ryan's Crown Cases. 1799–1823

Ryan & Moody's Nisi Prius. 1823–26

Ryde's Rating Appeals. 3v. 1871–93

Ryde & Konstam's Rating Appeals. 1894–1904

Ryley's Pleadings in Parliament (1661). 1290–1327

Sachse, Minutes of Norwich Mayoralty Court (1942). 1630–31

Salkeld's K. B., ed. Evans. 3v. 1689–1712

Salter, Registrum Cancellarii Oxoniensis (1935). 2v. 1434–69

Samle & Giffard's Vice-Chancellor (*temp.* Knight, Bruce, Parker, & Stuart.) 3v. 1852–57

Saunders' King's Bench, ed. Williams. 3v. 1666–72

Saunders & Austin's Locus Standi. 2v. 1895–1904

Saunders & Bidder's Locus Standi. 2v. 1905–19

Saunders & Cole's Bail Court. 2v. 1846–48

Sausse & Scully's Rolls Court. 1837–40 *Ir*

Savile's Common Pleas (1688). 1580–94

Sayer's King's Bench. 1751–56

Sayles, Select Cases in K. B. (1936). 1273–1320 (Selden Society, v. 55).

Sayles, Select Cases in K. B. under Edw. I. 3v. 1273–1307 (Selden Society, v.55, 57, 58.)

Schoales & Lefroy's Chancery. 2v. 1802–09 *Ir*

Scots Law Times. 58v. 1893–1952*

Scots Law Times Reports (all courts). 73v. 1895–1952*

Scots Law Times Poor Law Rep. 10v. 1932–41

Scots Law Times Sheriff Ct. Rep. 31v. 1922–52*

Scots Revised Reports. 45v. 1707–1873

Scott's Common Pleas. 8v. 1834–40

Scott's New Reports, Comm. P. 8v. 1840–45

Scott-Moncrieff, Edinburgh Justiciary (1905). 2v. 1661–78

Scottish Jurist (all courts). 46v. 1829–73

Scottish Land Court Reports. 40v. 1913–52*

Scottish Law Journal & Sheriff Court Record. 3v. 1858–61

Scottish Law Magazine & Sheriff Court Reporter. 6v. 1861–67

Scottish Law Reporter (all courts). 61v. 1865—1924

Scottish Law Review & Sheriff Court Cases. 51v. 1885–1953*

Searle & Smith's Probate & Divorce. 2pts. 1859–60

Second Book of Judgments (1675).

Select Cases in Communal Courts (Anglo-Saxon). 734–1082

Select Cases Concerning Law Merchant. 3v. (Selden Soc., v.23, 46, 49.)

Select Cases in Chancery, *temp.* King, ed. Macnaghten (1850). 1724–33

Select Cases in Exchequer Chamber (1933–48). 2v. 1377–1509 (Selden Soc. v. 51, 64.)

Select Cases in Exchequer of Pleas (1931). 1236–1304 (Selden Soc. v. 48.)

Select Cases Relating to Evidence. 1698–1732

Select Collection of Cases (1825).

Select Collection of Cases Concerning Parliament (1792). *Ir*

Selected Decisions by Umpire for Northern Ireland Respecting Claims to Benefit (1932).

Selected Decisions by the Umpire under National Service Act, 1939. 1940–45*

Selection of Cases Affecting Solicitors. 1779–1896

Session Notes, Court of Session. 21v. in 9. 1925–48

Sessions Cases, K. B. (1873). 2v. 1710–48

Sessions Papers, Central Criminal Court. 158v. 1834–1913

Sessions Papers, Old Bailey. 1715–1834

Sharpe, Calendar of Coroners' Rolls (1913). 1300–78

Shaw, Cases Decided in House of Lords. 2v. 1821–24 *Scot*

Shaw, Teind Court. 1821–31 *Scot*

Shaw (John), Justiciary Cases. 1848–52 *Scot*

Shaw (Patrick) Justiciary Cases. 1819–31 *Scot*

Shaw & Maclean, H. L. Cases. 3v. 1835–38 *Scot*

Shearer, Selected Cases from Acta Dominorum Concilii et Sess. 1951. 1532–33 (Stair Society, v. 14.)

Sheriff Court Books of Argyll. 2v. *Scot*

Shillman, Workmen's Compensation. 1934–38 *Ir*

Shower, House of Lords (1876). 1694–99

Shower, King's Bench. 2v. 1678–94

Siderfin's K. B. 2v. 1657–70

Sillem, Records of Lincolnshire Sessions (1937). 1360–75 (Lincoln Record Society, v. 30.)

Simons' Vice-Chancellors. 17v. 1826–52

Simons' Vice-Chancellors. 2v. 1850–52

Simons & Stuart's Vice-Chancellors. 2v. 1822–26

Singleton, Notebook of Cases, Chancery & Exchequer. 1716–34

Skiller's King's Bench. 1681–98

Smale & Gifford's Chancery. 3v. 1852–57

Smee, Taxes (1797). 2v.

Smethurst's Locus Standi. 1867

Smirke, Case of Vice (1843.) (Stannaries). 1355–1631.

Smith's Leading Cases (1929). 2v.

Smith (J.P.), King's Bench. 3v. 1803–06

Smith's Registration. 3v. 1896–1915

Smith & Batty's King's Bench. 1824–25 *Ir*

Smyth & Bourke's Marriage Cases (1842). *Ir*

Smythe's Common Pleas. 1839–40 *Ir*

Solicitors' Journal & Reporter 96v. 1856–1952*

Sopwith, Dean Forest Mining Commissioners' Award (1841).

Special & Selected Law Cases (1648).

Spinks' Ecclesiastical & Admiralty. 2v. 1853–55

Spinks' Prize Cases. 1854–56

Staffordshire Suits, Star Chamber, Henry VII & VIII. 1516–35

Stair, Court of Session. 2v. 1661–81 *Scot*

Star Chamber Cases (1641).

Star Chamber Proceedings, Henry VII, no. 24. 1503 (Royal Hist. Soc. Trans., n.s. v. 16.) *Scot*

Star Session Cases. 1824–25

Starkie's Nisi Prius. 3v. 1814–23

State Trials (Cobbett & Howell, 1809–28). 34v. 1163–1820

State Trials, N.S.(Macdonnell, 1888–98), 8v. 1820–58

Stenton, Lincolnshire Assize Rolls (1926). 1202–09

Stenton, Northamptonshire Assize Rolls (1930). 1202–03

Stenton, Pleas before the King or His Justices (1952). 1198–1202 (Selden Soc. v. 68.)

Stenton, Rolls of Justice in Eyre for Yorkshire. 2v. 1218–19 Selden Soc., v. 53, 56.)

Stenton. Rolls of Justices in Eyre in Lincolnshire (1934). 1218–19, 1221 (Selden Soc. v. 57.)

Stenton, Rolls of Justice in Syre for Gloucestershire, Warwickshire & Staffordshire (1940). 1221–22 (Selden Soc. v. 59.)

Stewart-Brown, Chester Palatine Courts (1925). 1259–97

Stewart-Brown, Star Chamber (1916). Hen. 7 & 8

Stillingfleet, Ecclesiastical (1702–04). 2v.

Stone, Digest of Insurance Cases. 2v. 1700–1913

Stone & Graham's Court of Referees on Private Bills. 1pt. 1865

Strange's K. B., ed. Nolan. 2v. 1715–48

Stuart, Milne, & Peddie, Court of Session. 2v. 1851–53 *Scot*

Stubbing, Appeals from Munitions Tribunals (1916–20). 4v.

Style's King's Bench. 1648–55

Sugden's Laws of Property. 1814–48

Swabey's Admiralty. 1855–59

Swabey & Tristram's Probate & Divorce. 4v. 1858–65

Swanston's Chancery. 3v. 1818–19

Sweet, Wife's Separate Estate. 1838–40

Swinton's Justiciary Cases. 2v. 1835–41
          Scot

Swinton's Registry Cases. 1835–43 *Scot*

Syme's Justiciary Cases. 1826–29 *Scot*

Tait, Index to Session Cases *Scot*

Tait, Lanchashire Q.S. Rolls (1917). 1590–1606

Talbort, Cases *temp.*, ed. Williams. 1730–37

Talbot, Manorial Roll, Isle of Man (1924). 1511–15 (Manorial Courts.)

Tamlyn's Rolls Court. 1829–30

Taunton's Common Pleas. 8v. 1807–19

Tax Cases. 33v. 1875–1952*

Taxation Reports. 9v. 1939–52*

Taylor, Sessions of the Peace in Cambridge (1942). 1330, 1380–83

Temple & Mew's Criminal Appeal Cases. 1848–51

Term Reports. *See* Durnford & East; New Term Reports.

Thomas, Calendar of Mayor's Court Rolls (1924). 1298–1307

Thomas-Stanford, Court Rolls of Preston (1921). 1562–1702

Thompson, Northumberland Pleas. *See* Northumberland Pleas.

Thomson, A Lincolnshire Assize Roll (1945). 1298

Thornton. *See* Notes of Cases.

Times Law Reports (all courts). 68v. 1884–1952

Tomlins' Elections. 1689–1795

Torr, Wreyland Manor Court Rolls (1910). 1437–1727

Tothill's Chancery (1872). 1559–1646

Tout & Johnstone, State Trials of Edw.I (1906). 1289–93

Traffic Cases. *See* Railway.

Trehern & Grant. *See* British & Colonial.

Tristram's Consistory Judgments. 1872–90

Turner, Select Pleas of the Forest (1901). 1400 (Selden Soc., v. 13.)

Turner & Russell's Chancery. 1822–24

Twemlow, Liverpool Town Books (1918). 1550–71 (Municipal Courts.)

Tyrwhitt's Exchequer. 5v. 1830–35

Tyrwhitt & Granger's Exchequer. 1835–36

Unemployment Insurance, Decisions of Umpire.
 1911 Act. 4v. 1912–21
 1920 Act. 17v. 1921–38 (plus 1939–45 pamphlet.)*
 Demarcation of Trades. 1912–17
 Out-of-Work Donation. 3v. 1912–20
 Prior to April, 1928. 1912–28
 1928–34. 2v. 1928–34*

Urban District Councils' Association Official Circular. 45v. 1890–1935*?

Vaughan's Common Pleas (1706). 1665–74

Ventris' King's Bench & Common Pleas. 1668–91

Vernon's Chancery (1828). 2v. 1680–1719

Vernon & Scriven's King's Bench. 1786–88   *Ir*

Vesey, Jun.'s Chancery, and Hovenden's Supplement. 22v. 1789–1817

Vesey, sen.'s Chancery, and Belt's Supplement. 3v. 1746–55

Vesey & Beames' Chancery. 3v. 1812–14

Wade, Acta Curiae Admirallatus Scotiae (1937). 1557–61 (Stair Soc., No. 2.)

Wake, Northampton Q.S. Records (1924). 1630–58

Walker's De-rating Appeals. 1929–30
           Scot

Wallis' Chancery, by Lyne (1839). 1766–91

War Compensation Court Judgments. 8v. 1920–29

War Pensions Appeal Cases (Special Review Tribunal), Notes & Digest (1947).

Watson, Bristol Pleas of Crown (1902). 1221

Webster's Patents. 2v. 1601–1855

Weekly Law Reports (all courts). 1953*

Weekly Notes (all courts). 84v. 1866–1952

Weekly Reporter (all courts). 54v. 1853–1906

Wellstood, Records of Manor of Henley in Arden (1919). 1546–1918

Welsby, Hurlstone, & Gordon. *See* Exchequer Reports.

Welsh's Registry Cases. 1830–40 *Ir*

West, Law of Extents. 1686–1817

West's House of Lords. 1839–41

West's Chancery, *temp.* Hardwicke. 1736–39

Western's Tithe Cases (London). 1592–1822

White's Justiciary Cases. 3v. 1886–93 *Scot*

Wight's Election Cases. 2v. 1687–1803 *Scot*

Wightwick's Exchequer. 1810–11

Willes' Common Pleas, ed. Durnford. 1735–58

Williams. *See* Peere Williams.

Willis-Bund, Calendar of Worcestershire Q.S. Papers (1900). 1591–1643

Willmore, Wollaston, & Davison's K.B., Bail Court. 1837

Willmore, Wollaston, & Hodges' K. B., Bail Court. 2v. 1838–39

Wilmot's Notes & Opinions, K. B. 1757–70

Wilson's Chancery. 4pts. 1818–19

Wilson's Exchequer in Equity. 1805–17

Wilson's K.B. & Comm. Pl. 3v. 1742–74

Wilson & Shaw's Scotch Appeal Cases. 7v. 1825–34

Wimbledon Manor Rolls. 2v. 1461–1864

Winch's Common Pleas. 1621–25

Wolferstan & Bristowe's Elections. 1859–65

Wolferstan & Dew's Elections. 1856–58

Wollaston's Bail Court. 1840–41

Wollaston, Court of Claims (1936). 1901–11

Wollstein, Friendly Societies (1892).

Woman's Lawyer (Dodridge) (1632).

Wood, Court Book of Liberty of St. Sepulchre, Dublin (1931.) 1586–90 *Ir*

Wood, Court Book of Regality of Broughton & Canongate (1937). 1569–73 *Scot*

Wood, Dean Forest Awards (1878).

Wood's Tithe Cases. 4v. 1650–1798

Workmen's Compensation & Insurance Reports. 22v. 1912–33

Wyatt's Practical Register, Chancery (1800).

Year Books, ed. Maynard (1679–80). 11v. 1307–1537

ed. Horwood (1866–79). 5v. 1292–1307

ed. Horwood & Pike (1883–1911). 15v. 1337–1346

Selden Society (1903-date). 65v.*

Ames Foundation (1914–37). 3v. 1388–90

Yeatman, Ashford-in-the-Water Court Rolls. 1442–1711 (Seignorial Courts.)

Yelverton's King's Bench (1803). 1602–13

Younge's Exchequer, Equity. 1830–32

Younge & Collyer's Exchequer, Equity. 4v. 1834–42

Younge & Collyer's Chancery. 2v. 1841–44

Younge & Jervis' Exchequer. 3v. 1826–30

D. Chronological List of English Law Reports. By Courts

This list, while not as inclusive as the alphabetical list above, contains nearly all standard and collateral English (and some Irish) law reports. It is copied, by permission of the publishers, from *Guide to Law Reports, Statutes and Regnal Years*.[1]

Reports in all the Courts.

English Reports
The Revised Reports
Law Journal
———— Reports, New Series
Jurist
Law Times (Old Series)
Law Times Reports
Weekly Reporter
Common Law and Equity Reports
New Reports
The Law Reports
Times Law Reports
Weekly Notes
The Reports

All England Law Reports
Weekly Law Reports

House of Lords.

Shower, 1876
Colles
Brown, by Tomlins, 1803
Dow
Bligh
Bligh. New Series
Dow and Clark
Clark and Finnelly
Maclean and Robinson
West
House of Lords Cases (Clark) (with Index)
Birkenhead's Judgments, 1923

---

[1] 2d ed., London, Sweet & Maxwell, 1948.

Privy Council.

Acton. (And Vol. II. Part I.)
Knapp
Moore
Moore (New Series)
Moore. East India Appeals
Law Reports, Indian Appeals, Supplemental

Chancery.

Cary, 1872
Choyce Cases in Chancery, 1870
Tothill, 1872
Dickens
Reports in Chancery, 1736
Bacon, ed. Ritchie, 1932
Nelson, 1872
Equity Cases Abridged
Cases in Chancery
Freeman
Finch (Sir H.)
Vernon
Precedents in Chancery
Peere Williams
Gilbert
Select Cases, temp. King
Moseley
Kelynge, W., 1873
Cases, temp. Talbot
West, temp. Hardwicke
Atkyns
Ambler
Barnardiston
Ridgeway, temp. Hardwicke (*See also* K.B.)
Vesey, sen., and Belt's Supplement
Eden
Brown, by Eden
Brown, by Belt
Cox
Vesey, jun., with index, and Hovenden's Supplement
Vesey and Beames
Cooper, G., temp. Eldon
Merivale
Swanston
Jacob and Walker
Jacob
Turner and Russell
Russell
Russell and Mylne
Mylne and Keen
Mylne and Craig
Craig and Phillips
Phillips
Macnaghten and Gordon
De Gex, Macnaghten and Gordon

De Gex and Jones
De Gex, Fisher and Jones
De Gex, Jones and Smith

Collateral Reports.

Romilly's Notes of Cases
Wyatt's Practical Register
Wilson, 4 parts
Cooper, temp. Brougham
Donnelly
Cooper, C. P.
Cooper, temp. Cottenham
Hall and Twells

Rolls Court.

Tamlyn
Keen
Beavan

Vice-Chancellors' Courts.

Maddock	
Simons and Stuart	temp.
Simons	V.-C.s Shadwel
	and
Simons (New Series)	Kindersley
Drewry	
Drewry and Smale	
Younge and Collyer	temp. V.-C.s
Collyer	Knight, Bruce,
De Gex and Smale	Parker, and
Smale and Giffard	Stuart.
Giffard	

Hare	temp. V.-C.s
Kay	Wigram,
Kay and Johnson	Turner, and
Johnson	Wood
Johnson and Hemming	
Hemming and Miller	

Collateral Reports.

Holt

King's Bench & Queen's Bench.

State Trials (Cobbett and Howell)
State Trials (New Series)
Bracton's Note Book
Year Books (Horwood)
Year Books (Selden Society)
Year Books (Maynard)
Year Books (Horwood and Pike)
Bellewe
Keilway
Moore
Dyer
Brooke's New Cases
Brooke's New Cases
March's Translation of Brooke } 1873

Benloe
Leonard
Plowden
Owen
Noy
Coke
Godbolt
Croke
Gouldesborough
Popham
Yelverton
Hobart
Davies (Ireland)
Ley
Calthrop
Bulstrode
Rolle
Palmer
Jones, W.
Latch
March (New Cases)
Style
Aleyn
Siderfin
Raymond, Sir T.
Levinz
Keble
Kelyng, J.
Saunders
Jones, T.
Ventris
Pollexfen
Modern
Freeman
Shower
Skinner
Comberbach
Carthew
Holt
Salkeld
Raymond (Lord)
Fortescue
Comyns
Sessions Cases
Gilbert's Cases in Law and Equity
Strange
Barnardiston
Fitzgibbons
Barnes' Cases of Practice
Ridgeway, temp. Hardwicke (*see also* Chancery)
Cunningham, 1871
Lee, temp, Hardwicke
Andrews
Wilson
Blackstone, W.
Sayer
Kenyon

Wilmot's Notes and Opinions
Burrow
Lofft
Cowper
Douglas
Durnford and East
East
Maule and Selwyn
Barnewall and Alderson
————————— Cresswell
————————— Adolphus
Adolphus and Ellis
Queen's Bench (Adolphus and Ellis, New Series)
Ellis and Blackburn
Ellis, Blackburn and Ellis
Ellis and Ellis
Best and Smith
Cababé and Ellis

Collateral Reports.

Dunning
Smith, J. P.
Dowling and Ryland
Manning and Ryland
Nevile and Manning
Nevile and Perry
Perry and Davison
Gale and Davison
Davison and Merivale
Harrison and Wollaston
Willmore, Wollaston and Davison
Willmore, Wollaston and Hodges
Arnold and Hodges' Practice Cases

Bail Court.

Chitty
Dowling
Dowling (New Series)
———— and Lowndes
Saunders and Cole
Lowndes, Maxwell and Pollock
———— and Maxwell
Harrison and Wollaston
Willmore, Wollaston and Davison
Willmore, Wollaston and Hodges
Wollaston
New Practice Cases (Welford, Bittleston and Parnell)

Common Pleas.

Benloe and Dalison
Anderson
Brownlow and Gouldesborough
Saville
Hutton
Bridgman, Sir J.
Winch

Littleton
Hetley
Bridgman, **Sir O.**
Carter
Vaughan
Lutwyche
———— translated **1718**
Cooke, 1872
Barnes
Willes
Blackstone, H., **1827**
Bosanquet and Puller
Taunton
Broderip and Bingham
Bingham
Bingham (New Cases)
Manning and Granger
Common Bench (with Index)
————New Series (with Index)

Collateral Reports.

Marshall
Moore
Moore and Payne
Moore and Scott
Scott
——New Reports
Hodges
Arnold
Drinkwater
Harrison and Rutherfurd

Exchequer.

Jenkins, 1885
Lane, 1884
Conroy's Custodiam Reports
Hardres
Bunbury
Parker
Anstruther
Forrest
Wightwick
Price
McCleland
———— and Younge
Younge and Jervis
Crompton and Jervis
———— and Meeson
———— and Roscoe
Meeson and Welsby (with Index)
Exchequer Reports (Welsby, Hurlstone and Gordon)
Hurlstone and Norman
———— and Coltman

Collateral Reports.

Price's Notes of Practice Cases (1 Part)
Tyrwhitt

———— and Granger
Gale
Murphy and Hurlstone
Horn and Hurlstone
Hurlstone and Walmsley

Exchequer Equity.

Wilson (1 Part)
Daniell
Younge
———— and Collyer

Nisi Prius.

Clayton
Lilly, Assize
Peake
Espinasse
Campbell
Starkie
Dowling and Ryland (1 Part)
Carrington and Payne
Carrington and Marshman
Carrington and Kirwan
Foster and Finlason

Collateral Reports.

Bartholoman
Holt
Gow
Ryan and Moody
Moody and Malkin
Moody and Robinson

Ecclesiastical.

Lee
Haggard (Consistory)
Phillimore
Addams
Haggard
Curteis
Robertson
Spinks (Ecclesiastical and Admiralty)
Deane and Swabey
Phillimore's Ecclesiastical Judgments

Collateral Reports.

Brodrick and Fremantle
Joyce
Brooke
Dale
Notes of Cases in the Ecclesiastical and Maritime Courts
Cripps' Church and Clergy Cases (2 Parts)
Tristram's Consistory Judgments

Probate and Divorce.

Swabey and Tristram
Searle and Smith (2 Parts)

Admiralty and Shipping.

Hay and Marriott
Robinson, C.
Edwards
Dodson
Haggard
Robinson, W.
Spinks (Ecclesiastical and Admiralty)
Spinks' Prize Cases
Swabey
Lushington
Browning and Lushington

Collaterals and Extra Volumes.

Burrell and Marsden
Parker
Roscoe's Prize Cases
Lloyd's Prize Cases
British and Colonial Prize Cases
Notes of Cases in the Ecclesiastical and
    Maritime Courts
Holt's Admiralty Cases
Maritime Cases (Crockford)
————————— (Aspinal)
Lloyd's List Law Reports

Bankruptcy.

Rose
Buck
Glyn and Jameson
Montagu and M'Arthur
Montagu
Montagu and Bligh
Deacon and Chitty
Montagu and Ayrton
Deacon
Montague and Chitty
Montagu, Deacon and De Gex
De Gex
Fontblanque
Morrell
Manson (Bankruptcy and Companies
    Cases)
Bankruptcy and Winding Up Cases

Company Cases.

Megone
Manson (also under Bankruptcy)
Bankruptcy and Winding Up Cases

Railway and Canal Cases.

Nicholl, Hare, Carrow
Beavan and Walford's Railway Cases
    (2 Parts)
Neville, Browne and Macnamara, Rail-
    way, Canal & Road Traffic Cases

Election Cases.

Glanville
Tomlins
Douglas
Phillips
Luder
Fraser
Clifford
Peckwell
Corbett and Daniell
Cockburn and Rowe
Perry and Knapp
Knapp and Ombler
Falconer and Fitzherbert
Barron and Austin
Barron and Arnold
Power, Rodwell and Dew
Wolferstan and Dew
Wolferstan and Bristowe
O'Malley and Hardcastle (Election
    Petitions)

Registration Cases.

Cox and Atkinson's Registration Appeal
    Cases (2 Parts)
Pigott and Rodwell
Lutwyche
Keane and Grant
Hopwood and Philbrick
Hopwood and Coltman
Coltman
Fox and Smith
Smith

Revision Courts

Delane
Manning

Locus Standi Cases.

Clifford and Stephen
Clifford and Rickards
Rickards and Michael
Rickards and Saunders
Saunders and Austin
Saunders and Bidder
Bidder
Newbon, Private Bills Reports

Crown and Criminal Cases.

Kelyng, Sir J., 1873
Foster, 1792
Leach
Russell and Ryan
Lewin's Crown Cases on the Northern
    Circuit
Moody
Denison

Temple and Mew's Criminal Appeal
  Cases
Dearsley
Dearsley and Bell
Bell
Leigh and Cave
Central Criminal Court Sessions Papers
Cox's Criminal Law Cases
Criminal Appeal Reports

Local Government Cases.

Justice of the Peace
Local Government Reports
Cox's Magistrates Municipal and
  Parochial Cases

Patents and Trade Marks.

Davies
Carpmael
Webster
Macrory
Goodeve, 1884
Griffin, 1887
Reports of Patent, etc., Cases

Tax Cases.

Reports of Cases on Income Tax
Taxation Reports
Annotated Tax Cases

Commercial Court.

Commercial Cases

E. List of Canadian Law Reports

Entries in this list are arranged, first by Dominion and then alphabetically by province or territory; thereunder the listing is chronological by dates covered by the various reports.[1]

Dominion

Canadian Reports Appeal Cases. 24v.
  1807–1913
Coutlee's Supreme Court Cases. 1875–
  1906
Supreme Court Reports. 64v. 1876–1922
Supreme Court Reports (Annotated Reprint. 64v. & 2v. index 1876–1922
Cameron's Supreme Court Cases. 1877–
  1905
Canada Exchequer Court Reports. 21v.
  1895–1922
Canada Criminal Cases. 104v. 1898–1952
Canadian Commercial Law Reports. 4v.
  1901–05
Canadian Railway Cases. 68v. 1902–52
  (v.50–68, as Canadian Railway &
  Transport Cases.)
Dominion Law Reports. 70v. 1912–22
Dominion Law Reports, New Series.
  120v. 1923–52
Canadian Bankruptcy Reports. 32v.
  1921–52*
Canada Law Reports, Supreme Court.
  30v. 1922–52*
Canada Law Reports, Exchequer. 30v.
  1922–52*
Criminal Reports. 15v. 1946–52

Parliamentary Reports

Laperriere's Speaker's Decisions. 1841–
  72
Gemmill, Parliamentary Divorce. 1867–
  88
Desjardins, Speaker's Decisions. 1867–
  1900

Railway Commission

Board of Railway Commissioners for
  Canada, Report. 48v. 1904–52
  Judgments, Orders, etc. 41v. 1911–52

Miscellaneous Reports

Fox's Digest of Canadian Patent & Trade
  Mark Cases. 2v. 1845–1940
Cameron's Legal Opinions. 1859–76
Hunter's Torrens Cases. 1865–93
Cameron's Constitutional Decisions of the
  Privy Council. 2v. 1867–1929
Masters' Canadian Appeals. 1868–94
Cartwright's (Constitutional) Cases on
  the British North America Act. 5v.
  1868–96
Conciliation & Arbitration, Proceedings
  under Industrial Disputes Investigation Act of 1907. 28v. 1907–34
Insurance Law Reporter. 17v. 1933–50

[1] Acknowledgment is made to The Carswell Company, Limited, Toronto, Canada, for permission to use W. Harold Maxwell and C. R. Brown's *A Complete list of British and Colonial Law Reports and Legal Periodicals* . . . (Toronto, Canada, Carswell, 3d ed. 1937, with 1946 supplement) in the compilation of this list; and to William Hibbitt, of The Carswell Company, for supplying supplementary material up to May, 1953.

(continued by CCH Reporter, 1951 /52—)

Plaxton's Constitutional Decisions of Privy Council. 1930–39

Gordon's Digest of Excess Profits Tax Cases (British Empire) (1942).

Gordon's Digest of Income Tax Cases (British Empire), 1939, 1940, 1943. 3v.

Canada Tax Cases Annotated. 12v. 1938–52

Fox's Patent, Trade Mark, Design & Copyright Cases. 12v. 1940–51*

Canadian Patent Reporter. 15v. 1939–52*

Tax Appeal Board Cases. 6v. 1949–52*

Dominion Tax Cases. 6v. 1920–52*

Dominion Reports Service (continued by CCH loose-leaf service, 1946—). 10v. 1936–45

Dominion of Canada Labour Service (loose-leaf). 1943–52

Wheeler, Confederation Law of Canada. Privy Council Cases on British North America Act, 1867 (1896).

Provincial Law Reports

Alberta

Alberta Law Reports. 26v. 1909–32
Western Law Reporter. 34v. 1905–16
Western Weekly Reports. 108v. 1912–50
Western Weekly Reports, N.S. 6v. 1951–52

British Columbia

British Columbia Law Reports. 63v. 1867–1947
Martin's Mining Cases. 2v. 1853–1908
Western Law Reporter. 34v. 1905–16
Western Weekly Reports. 108v. 1912–50
Western Weekly Reports, N.S. 6v. 1951–52

Manitoba

Carey's Reports. 1875
Manitoba Reports, temp. Wood. 1875–83
Manitoba Law Reports. 59v. 1883–1952
Western Law Times & Reports. 6v. 1890–95
Western Law Reporter. 34v. 1905–16
Western Weekly Reports. 198v. 1912–50
Western Weekly Reports, N.S. 6v. 1951–52

New Brunswick

Chipman's M. S. (1 N.B.R.) 1825–35
Berton. (2 N.B.R.) 1835–39
Kerr's Reports. (3–5 N.B.R.) 3v. 1840–48
Allen's Reports. (6–11 N.B.R.) 6v. 1848–66
Hannay. (12–13 N. B. R.) 2v. 1867–71
Pugsley. (14–16 N.B.R.) 3v. 1872–77
Pugsley & Burbridge. (17–20 N.B.R.) 4v. 1878–82
New Brunswick Reports (21–54 N.B.R.) 34v. 1883–1929
Maritime Provinces Reports. 29v. 1929–52

Equity

Trueman's Equity Cases. 1876–93
New Brunswick Equity Reports (Trueman) 4v. 1894–1911

Admiralty

Stockton's Vice-Admiralty Cases. 1879–91

All Courts

Eastern Law Reporter. 14v. 1906–14

Newfoundland

Tucker's Select cases. 1817–28
Supreme Court Reports. 14v. 1817–1949
Maritime Provinces Reports. (Since April 1, 1949, has contained Newfoundland Reports.)

North-West Territories

Supreme Court Reports. 2v. 1887–98
Territories Law Reports. 7v. 1885–1907

Nova Scotia

Supreme Court

Thomson (N.S.R. 1). 1834–51
James (N.S.R. 2). 1853–55
Thomson (N.S.R. 3). 1856–59
Cochran (Part 1) (N.S.R. 4). 1859
Oldright (N.S.R. 5, 6). 2v. 1860–66
Nova Scotia Decisions (N.S.R. 7–9). 3v. 1866–75
(This is Geldert & Oxley, v.1–3).
Russell & Chesley (N.S.R. 10–12). 3v. 1875–79
Russell & Geldert (N.S.R. 13–27). 15v. 1879–95
Geldert & Russell (N.S.R. 28–39). 12v. 1895–1907
Wallace (hitherto unreported) (N.S.R. 40).

Geldert & Russell (N.S.R. 41–60). 20v.
1907–29

Maritime Provinces Reports. 29v. 1929–
52*

Equity

Ritchie's Equity Rep. by Russell. 1872–
82

Election

Russell's Election Cases. 1874

All Courts

Eastern Law Reporter. 14v. 1906–14

Admiralty

Stewart. 1803–13
Young, Vice-Admiralty. 1865–80

Ontario (Upper Canada)

Appeals

Error & Appeal Reports (Grant). 3v.
1846–66

Ontario Appeal Reports. 27v. 1876–1900

King's Bench

Taylor. 1823–27
Draper. 1829–31
Upper Canada K.B. Rep., Old Ser. 6v.
1831–44
Upper Canada Q.B. Rep., N.S. 46v.
1845–82 (since when, *see* Ontario Reports).

Common Pleas

Upper Canada Common Pleas Reports.
32v. 1850–82

Chancery

Grant's Upper Canada Chancery Reports.
29v. 1849–82 (since when, *see* Ontario Reports).

Chambers and Practice Cases

Upper Canada Chambers Reports. 2v.
1846–52
Practice Reports. 1850–1900 (Continued
by Ontario Law Reports.)
Chancery Chambers Reports. 4v. 1857–
72
Lefroy & Cassel's Practice Cases. 1881–
83

Election Cases

Patrick. 1824–49
Hodgins. 1871–79

Ontario Election Cases. 2v. 1884–1900
(Continued by Ontario Law Reports.)

Miscellaneous Law Reports

Upper Canada Court Records. 1789–94
Harrison & Hodgins' Municipal Rep.
1845–52
Local Courts & Municipal Gazette. 8v.
1865–72
Clarke & Scully's Drainage Cases. 2v.
1898–1903
Smith & Sager's Drainage Cases. 1904–
14
Price's Mining Commissioner's Cases.
1906–10
Godson's Mining Commissioner's Cases.
1911–17

Reports in All Courts

Ontario Reports. 32v. 1882–1900
Ontario Law Reports. 66v. 1901–31
Ontario Reports, N.S. 22v. 1931–52
Ontario Weekly Reporter. 27v. 1902–16
Other Law Reports (v.38–39 in one)
1917–18
Ontario Weekly Notes. 41v. 1909–32
Ontario Weekly Notes, N.S. 20v. 1933–
52*
Fraser, Records of the Early Courts of
Justice of Upper Canada (1918).

Prince Edward Island

Peters. 1850–72
Hazzard & Warburton. 2v. 1850–82
Eastern Law Reporter. 14v. 1906–16
Maritime Provinces Reports. 29v. 1929–
52

Quebec (Lower Canada)[1]

Judgments du Conseil Souverain de la
Nouvelle France (1885–89). 4v.
1663–1704
Judgments du Conseil Supérieur de Que-
bec (1889–91). 2v. 1705–16
Perreault Prevosté de Quebec. Extraits
ou Precedents, Tirés des Registres
(1824). 1726–58
Revised Reports, Province of Quebec.
29v. 1726–1891
Perreault Conseil Supérieur de Quebec.
Extraits ou Precedents, Tirés des
Registres. 1717–59
Pyke's K.B. Reports, District of Quebec.
1809–10
Stuart's Reports . . . with Appeals to
Privy Council. 1810–35

---

[1] There was no regular series of Quebec reports until 1892, but many sporadic series.

Lower Canada Reports. 17v. 1850–67
Montreal Condensed Reports. 1853–54
Seignorial Reports. 2v. 1856
Ramsay's Appeal Cases. 1873–86
Quebec Law Reports. 17v. 1874–91
Dorion Decisions de la Cour d'Appel. Q. B. Reports. 4v. 1880–86
Causes Célèbres sur les Taxes sur les Banques. 1883–85
Montreal Law Reports, Q.B. 7v. 1884–91
Montreal Law Reports, Superior Ct. 7v. 1865–91
Quebec Official Reports (Rapports Judiciares Officiels), K. B. 82v. 1892–1952 (Numbered volumes ceased with v.71, 1941.)
————Superior Court. 90v. 1892–1952 (Numbered volumes ceased with v.79, 1941.)
Quebec Practice Reports. 56v. 1897–1952

Admiralty

Stuart's Vice-Admiralty Rep. 2v. 1836–74

Cook. 1873–84

Parliamentary

Desjardins, Speaker's Decisions. 1867–1901
St. Maurice, Parliamentary Decisions. 1868–85

Saskatchewan

Western Law Reporter. 34v. 1905–16
Saskatchewan Law Reports. 25v. 1907–31
Western Weekly Reports. 108v. 1912–50
Western Weekly Reports, N. S. 6v. 1951–52

Yukon

Western Law Reporter. 34v. 1905–16
Western Weekly Reports. 108v. 1912–50
Western Weekly Reports, N. S. 6v. 1951–52

ANGLO-AMERICAN LEGAL PERIODICALS[1]

Accountant. London. 127 v. Oct. 1874–Dec. 1952* *W.*

Administrative Law Bulletin. Chicago. 4 v. Jan. 10, 1949–Sept. 1952* Pub: Section of Administrative Law, American Bar Assn. *Irreg.*

Advocate. British Columbia, Can. 10 v. 1943–Dec. 1952*.

Advocate. Minneapolis, 2 v. Jan. 1889–July 1890. *Semi-M.* (v. 1); *W.* (v. 2).

Advocate. Cleveland. 2 nos. Oct.–Nov. 1929. Official Journal, Cuyahoga County Bar Assn.

Advocates' Chronicle. Royapettah, Madras, India. v. 1, no. 1. Oct. 1932.

Aeronautical Law Journal. New York. 1 v. (2 nos.) Nov.–Dec. 1933. Pub: Meyers' Stationery & Print. Co.

Air Affairs. Washington, D.C. 3 v. Sept. 1946–Dec. 1950*. Pub: International Society of Air Affairs. *Irreg.* (v. 1–3 no. 2 Q.)

Air Commerce Bulletin. Washington, D.C. 11 v. July 1929–Dec. 15, 1939. Pub: U. S. Dept. of Commerce, Aeronautics Branch. Superseded by Civil Aeronautics Journal. *Semi-M.* (v. 1–4); *M.* (v. 5–11).

Air Hygiene Foundation of America. Legal Series, Bulletin. Pittsburgh. 3 v. 1936–1937*? After Oct. 1940 as Industrial Hygiene Foundation. Irreg. Bulletin 1, 7 nos.; bulletin 2, 1 no.; bulletin 3, 1 no.

Air Law Review. New York. 12 v. Jan. 1930–Oct. 1941. Pub: Board of Air Law Review of New York University School of Law. *Q.*

Ajmer-Merwara Law Journal. Ajmer, India. 26 v. Aug. 1926–1952*; 1934–35, v. 7–9 not numbered; 1936 is v. 10; supps. 1924–1927. *Irreg.*

Akron Bar Communications. Akron, Ohio. 5 v. 1948–May 1953* *M.*

Alabama Bar Bulletin. Birmingham. 1 v. (3 nos.) Apr., July, Oct. 1939. Pub: Alabama State Bar Assn. Merged with Alabama Lawyer.

Alabama Law Journal. Montgomery. 4 v. Apr. 1882–Apr. 1885. *M.* (v. 4, 1 no.).

Alabama Law Journal. Tuscaloosa. 5 v. Oct. 1925–May 1930. Pub: Board of Commissioners of State Bar and Law Dept. University of Alabama. *Q.*

Alabama Law Review. University. 5 v. Fall 1948–Spring 1953*. *Semi-A.*

Alabama Lawyer. Montgomery. 13 v. Jan. 1940–Oct. 1952*. Organ of State Bar of Alabama. Absorbed Alabama Bar Bulletin. *Q.*

Albany Law Journal. Albany, N. Y. 70 v. Jan. 8, 1870–Dec. 1908. *W.* (v. 1–62); *M.* (v. 63–70).

---

[1] This list is the work of many hands. Compiled originally in the Columbia University Law Library by Elsie Basset and continued by Pauline E. Gee in the Yale Law Library, it was published in the three editions of F. C. Hicks' *Materials and Methods of Legal Research*. It has since been supplemented by Miss Gee in the *Law Library Journal*. Through the courtesy of Mr. Hicks and Miss Gee, and the Lawyers' Co-Operative Publishing Company, this list, as revised and augmented by the staff of the Columbia University Law Library under the direction of Meira G. Pimsleur, is printed here as a public service. The information supplied is the best available to the compilers as of May 30, 1953. Much of it is fragmentary, and is given only as a matter of record.

Current periodicals are marked by an asterisk (*), the date given being that of the latest complete volume known to the compilers. Where there is some chance that a periodical may still be alive, that is indicated by an asterisk followed by an interrogation point (*?).

Albany Law Review. Albany, N. Y. 16 v. Nov. 1931–June 1952*. v. 1–11 as Albany Law Review of Recent Decisions. Suspended 1943–47. *Semi-A.*

Albany Law School Journal. Albany, N. Y. 1 v. 1875–76.

Alberta Law Quarterly. Edmonton. 5 v. Nov. 1934–June 1945. Pub: Students of the Faculty of Law University of Alberta. *Irreg. 8 issues to a vol.*

Allahabad Law Journal and Reports. Allahabad, India. 51 v. 1904–1953*. *W.* (v. 1–24 fortnightly).

Allahabad Law Times. Lahore, India. 17 v. Jan. 1923–1941. *Q.*

Allahabad Law Weekly. United Provinces, India. 5 v. 1941–1945*.

Allahabad Weekly Notes. Allahabad, India. 28 v. 1880–1908. Supp. volumes, 1912–14. 2 v.

Allahabad Weekly Reporter. Lucknow, India. 5 v. 1933–35.

Alumni Newsletter (Yale). *See* Yale Law School Association. Alumni Newsletter.

American Bankruptcy Review. New York. 14 v. Aug. 1924–Aug. 1937. (v. 1, no. 1 pub. at Savannah, Ga.) Superseded by Corporate Reorganizations Combined with American Bankruptcy Review. v. 14, 1 no.

American Bar Association Journal. Chicago. 38 v. Jan. 1915–Dec. 1952*. Continues Annual Bulletin of Comparative Law Bureau, American Bar Assn. *M.* (*Q.* to July 1920).

American Bar Association. Comparative Law Bureau. Annual Bulletin. nos. 1–7. 1908–1914. Unnumbered "Bulletin", 1933. Continued by American Bar Association Journal.

American Bar Association Standards. *See* Notes on Legal Education.

American Bar Association. Standing Committee on Public Relations. Public Relations Bulletin. *See* Public Relations Bulletin.

American Civil Law Journal. New York. 1 v. (4 nos.). Jan.–Apr. 1873. *M.*

American Consular Bulletin. Washington, D.C. 6 v. Mar. 1919–Sept. 1924. Continued by American Foreign Service Journal, later Foreign Service Journal. *M.* (v. 6, 9 nos.).

American Foreign Law Association Bulletin. New York. Spring, 1950–Spring 1951*.

American Foreign Service Journal. *See* Foreign Service Journal.

American Institute of Criminal Law and Criminology. Journal. *See* Journal of Criminal Law, Criminology and Police Science.

American Journal of Comparative Law. Ann Arbor, Mich. 2 v. Winter, 1952 — Winter 1953* *Q.*

American Journal of International Law. Washington, D. C. 46 v. Jan. 1907–Oct. 1952* *Q.*

American Journal of Medical Jurisprudence. Boston. 2 v. Sept. 1938–Sept. 1939. Organ, American Medico-Legal Assn. v. 1 (4 nos.); v. 2 (6 nos.)

American Journal of Police Science. Chicago. 3 v. Jan. 1930–Ap. 1932. Pub: Scientific Crime Detection Laboratory. Merged with Journal of Criminal Law and Criminology. *Bi-M* (v. 3, 2 nos.)

American Judicature Society. Bulletin. Chicago. 15 nos. 1914–20.

American Judicature Society. Journal. Chicago. 36 v. June 1917–Ap. 1953* *Bi-M.*

American Jurist and Law Magazine. Boston. 28 v. Jan. 1829–Jan. 1843. Merged into American Law Magazine. *Q.*

American Labor Legislation Review. New York. 32 v. Jan. 1911–Dec. 1942. Includes Proceedings and Papers of American Assn. for Labor Legislation, previously pub. in the two series: Proceedings and Legislative Review. *Q.*

American Law and Lawyers. Cincinnati. 9 v. Jan. 7, 1939–Sept. 23, 1947. *W.* (*Bi-W* July–Sept.)

American Law Journal. Columbus, O. 2 v. May 17, 1884–May 9, 1885. *W.*

American Law Journal (Hall's). Philadelphia. 6 v. Jan. 1808–1817. Title, v. 1–3: American Law Journal and Miscellaneous Repertory. For v. 7 *see* Journal of Jurisprudence (Hall's).

American Law Journal (N. S.) Philadelphia. 4 v. July 1848–May 1852. Continues

Pennsylvania Law Journal; also numbered v. 9–11 as such. Superseded by American Law Register. *M.*

American Law Magazine. Chicago. 2 v. Mar. 1882–Feb. 1883. Merged into Central Law Journal. *M* (v. 2: 2 nos.)

American Law Magazine. Philadelphia. 7 v. Ap. 1843–Jan. 1846. Supersedes American Jurist and Law Magazine. *Q.*

American Law Record. Cincinnati. 15 v. July 1872–June 1887. *M.*

American Law Register. *See* University of Pennsylvania Law Review.

American Law Review. *See* United States Law Review.

American Law School Review. St. Paul, Minn. 10 v. Oct. 1902–Dec. 1947. Pub: West Pub. Co. *Irreg.*

American Law Times. Washington and N. Y. 10 v. 1868–77. In conjunction with this were issued American Law Times Reports. Old Series 6 v. Washington. 1868–Ap. 1873 (v. 6: 4 nos.); New Series 4 v. New York. Jan. 1874–77. *M.*

American Law Times. New York. 1 v. (5 nos.) Sept. 1905-June 1906.

American Law Times. New York. 1 v. (2 nos.) Sept.–Dec. 1909. *Bi-M.*

American Lawyer. New York. 16 v. 1893–July 1908. *M* (v. 16: 7 nos.)

American Legal News. Detroit. 35 v. Oct. 1899–Mar. 1925. Title, v. 1–11, Collector and Commercial Lawyer. *M* (v. 35: 3 nos.)

American Legislator. *See* State Government.

American Life Convention. Legal Bureau. Legal Bulletin. 67 v. 1906?–Dec. 1952* *M.*

American Municipal Law Review. Chicago. 7 v. Mar. 1936–Oct. 1942. Title, v. 1–6, Legal Notes on Local Government. *Q* (v. 1, 2 nos. Mar; May; v. 2–5, *Bi-M.*)

American Slavic and East European Review. v. 4 (no. 8/9)–11 Aug. 1945–Dec. 1952* Issues for 1941–43 (v. 1–3) pub. as v. 20–22 of Slavonic and East European Review, American Ser. *Q.*

American Society of Military Law. *See* Journal of Criminal Law, Criminology and Police Science.

American Taxpayers' Quarterly. New York. v. 1, no. 1, Nov. 1931.

American Themis. New York. 1 v. (2 nos.) Jan.–Feb. 1844.

American University Intramural Law Review. Washington, D. C. 2 v. May 1952–Dec. 1952* Pub: Washington College of Law, American University. v. 1: 1 no.; v. 2: 1 no.

Annals of British Legislation. London. 18 v. 1856–68. O. S. v. 1–14 (1856–65); N. S. v. 1–4 (1865–68).

Annals of the Organization of American States. 3 v. 1949–51* Pub: Dept. of Public Information, Pan American Union. *Q.*

Annotated Legal Forms Magazine. New York. 5 v. Oct. 1927–Jan. 1930. *M.* (v. 5: 4 nos.).

Annual Law Register of the United States (Griffith's). Burlington, N. J. v. 3–4, 1821–22. v. 1–2 never pub.

Annual Law Review. Nedlands, Western Australia. 3 v. Dec. 1948– Dec. 1950* Pub: Univ. of Western Australia Law School.

Annual Review of the Law School of New York University. *See* New York University Law Review.

Arbitration in Action. *See* Arbitration Magazine.

Arbitration Journal. New York. 6 v. 1937–42. Pub: American Arbitration Assn. in colloboration with Chamber of Commerce of State of New York and American Arbitration Commission. Continued by Arbitration Magazine. *Q.*

Arbitration Journal, N. S. New York. 8 v. 1946–53* "New Series" dropped after volume 2. *Q.*

Arbitration Magazine. New York. 3 v. Jan. 1943–Oct. 1945. Vol. 1 as Arbitration in Action. Combined with International Arbitration to form Arbitration Journal, N. S. *Q.*

Arbitrator: Journal of Institute of Arbitrators Incorporated. *See* Institute of Arbitrators. Journal.

Architects' Law Reports and Review. London. 4 v. 1904–09. *Q.*

Arkansas Law Bulletin. *See* Arkansas. University. School of Law. Law School Bulletin.

Arkansas Law Journal. Fort Smith. 1 v. (4 nos.) 1877.

Arkansas Law Review and Bar Association Journal. Fayetteville, 6 v. Winter 1946/47–Fall 1952* Pub: School of Law, University of Arkansas and Bar Association of Arkansas. Continues University of Arkansas Law School Bulletin. *Q.*

Arkansas. University. School of Law. Law School Bulletin. Fayetteville. 11 v. Nov. 1929–May 1946. Sub-series of Univ. of Arkansas Bulletin. Publication suspended June 1933–Nov. 1936, June 1942–April 1946. Continued by Arkansas Law Review and Bar Association Journal. *Irreg.*

Articled Clerk. London. 13 nos. 1867–68.

Articled Clerks' Annual. Halifax, Nova Scotia. 1912–1935*?

Articled Clerks' Journal. New South Wales. 3 v. 1899–91. Continued by Law Chronicle.

Articled Clerks' Journal and Examiner. London. 3 v. Sept. 1879–81. *M.* (v. 3: 1 part).

Association of Casualty and Surety Executives. Bulletin. New York. 47 nos. Nov. 1923–March 1937. Title, no. 1–20: Workmen's Compensation Bulletin.

Association of Practitioners before the Interstate Commerce Commission. Bulletin. Washington, D.C. 3 v. Ap. 1931–Oct. 1933. Title, v. 1, no. 1, I.C.C. Practitioners' Quarterly Bulletin. Continued by I. C. C. Practitioners' Journal. *Q.*

––––**Journal.** *See* I. C. C. Practitioners' Journal.

Association of the Bar of the City of New York. Bulletin. 12 nos. Feb. 1920–March, 1923. *Irreg.*

Association of the Bar of the City of New York. The Record. *See* Record.

Auction Register and Law Chronicle. *See* Chronicle and Auction Register.

Australian Conveyancer and Solicitors Journal. Sydney. 1 v. Jan.–Nov. 1948*? *Bi–M.*

Australian Jurist. Melbourne. 5 v. Feb. 21, 1870–Dec. 22, 1874. In conjunction with this were issued Australian Jurist Reports. *W.* (*Irreg.*)

Australian Law Journal. Sydney. 25 v. May 5, 1927–Ap. 1952* Report of proceedings at the Australian Legal Convention, 1935 — issued as supplement to v. 9–. *M.*

Australian Law Times and Notes of Cases. Melbourne. 49 v. July 1879–Dec. 1928. Section Notes of Cases was published separately. *Bi–W.*

Australian Outlook; Journal of Australian Institute of International Affairs. Sydney. 6 v. Mar. 1947–Dec. 1952* Incorporating Austral-Asiatic Bulletin. *Q.*

Baltimore Law Transcript. Baltimore. 3 v. Oct. 17, 1868–Feb. 26, 1870. Individual nos. of v. 3 have title: Daily Law Transcript. *D. & W.* (v. 3, 19 nos.)

Banker and Tradesman. Boston and Cambridge. 32 v. 1872–1929; N. S. 27 v. 1929–1941*? Absorbed Massachusetts Law Reporter 1884. Title, v. 29, no. 44– v. 32, Review and Record: Banker and Tradesman. New series begins Oct. 8, 1929. Issued in 2 eds. Legal edition, and regular or general edition. To 1941 there were 27 vols. in Legal ed., and 106 vol. in regular ed. No more information available.

Banking Law Journal. New York. 69 v. May 1889–Dec. 1952* Absorbed Business Law Journal, May 1932. Subtitle, v. 60 to date: Combined with Bankers Magazine. *M.* (*Bi-M.* May 1889–Ap. 1894).

Bankrupt Register. *See* National Bankruptcy Register.

Bar. New York. 8 v. Fall, 1934–Dec. 1941. Pub: School of Business and Civic Administration, College of the City of New York. *Semi–A.* (v. 1, no. 2, Ap. 1935 numbered in error v. 2, no. 1; v. 3, no. 1, Dec. 1936 numbered in error v. 3, no. 2; v. 8, 1 no.)

Bar (West Virginia). *See* Virginia Law Review.

Bar and Legal World. London. 2 nos. Nov. 1903. *Fortn.*

Bar Association Bulletin (Los Angeles.) *See* Los Angeles Bar Bulletin.

Bar Association Bulletin (Ohio). *See* Ohio State Bar Association. Bulletin.

Bar Association of Nassau County. Bulletin. New York. 2 v. Nov. 1939–June 1940. *M.* (v. 1, 2 nos; v. 2, 6 nos.)

Bar Association of Tennessee. Memphis. 9 v. 1923–June 1931. Pub: Central Council. *Q.* (*Irreg.*)

Bar Association of the District of Columbia. Journal. Washington, D. C. 19 v. Mar. 1934–Dec. 1952* Title, March 1934–March 1935, Bulletin of the Bar Association of the District of Columbia; April 1935–June 1940, Journal of the District of Columbia Bar Association. *M.* (v. 1, 6 nos.)

Bar Association of the State of Kansas. Journal. Wichita. 21 v. Aug. 1932–May 1953* *Q.*

Bar Association Paragraph Digest. *See* Ohio State Bar Association. Bulletin.

Bar Briefs (North Dakota). *See* North Dakota Law Review.

Bar Bulletin. Boston. 23 v. Jan. 1924–Dec. 1952* Pub: Bar Assn. of the Council and Standing Committee. 1938 to date include list of officers, standing committees and members, formerly pub. separately. No. 1–167 without volume numbering. Numbering begins with v. 12, no. 1, Jan. 1941. *Irreg.*

Bar Bulletin (Los Angeles). *See* Los Angeles Bar Bulletin.

Bar Bulletin, New York County Lawyers Association. New York. 10 v. May 1943–Mar. 1953* *Irreg.*

Bar Examination Annual. London. 2 v. 1893–94. Supersedes Bar Examination Journal.

Bar Examination Guide. London. 5 v. 1895–99.

Bar Examination Journal. London. 10 v. 1871–92. Superseded by Bar Examination Annual.

Bar Examination Papers, Questions and Answers. *See* Kelly's Bar Examination Papers . . .

Bar Examiner. Denver. 21 v. Nov. 1931–Nov. 1952* Pub: National Conference of Bar Examiners. *M.* (v. 1–8); *Q.* (v. 9–).

Barrister. London. 4 nos. (120 pages) May 1824.

Barrister. Newark, N. J. 10 v. Ap. 1927–May 1936. Pub: Student Council of New Jersey Law School. Vol. 10: 8 nos.

Barrister. Toronto. 3 v. Dec. 1894–Dec. 1897. *M.*

Baylor Law Review. Waco, Texas. 4 v. Summer, 1948 — Summer 1952* *Q.*

Bell Yard. London. 22 nos. Nov. 1927–May 1939. Pub: Law Society's School of Law. *Irreg.*

Bench and Bar. Chicago. 5 v. Oct. 1869–Jan. 1874. O. S. v. 1–2 (Oct. 1869–Mar. 1871); N. S. v. 1–3 (Ap. 1871–Jan. 1874). *Q.*

Bench and Bar. Detroit. 6 v. Jan. 1921–May 1926. Pub: Lawyers Club of Detroit. *M.* (v. 6: 5 nos.)

Bench and Bar. Montreal. 15 v. Oct. 1931–May 1945. Oct.–Dec. 1931 called v. 1, no. 1–3; Jan. 1932 (forming first no. of v. 2) called v. 1, no. 4; Feb. 1932 called v. 2, no. 2. V. 10, no. 4–v. 15, no. 5, Ap. 1940–May 1945 pub. in Dominion Reports Service. *M.* (v. 1, 3 nos.; v. 15, 5 nos.)

Bench and Bar. New York. 43 v. Ap. 15, 1905–Nov. 1920. O. S. v. 1–28 (Ap. 1905–Mar. 1912), N. S. v. 1–15 (May 1912–Nov. 1920). No issue for Ap. 1912. *M.*

Bench and Bar of Minnesota. Minneapolis. 8 v. Nov. 1931–June 1940. Official pub. of Minnesota State Bar Assn. *Irreg.* (v. 1–2, 4 nos. ea.; v. 3, 3 nos.; v. 4, 1 no.; v. 5, 2 nos.; v. 6–7, 1 no. ea.; v. 8, 4 nos.) There were also eight prelimin. unnumb. issues. viz., Oct., Dec., 1928, May, Dec., 1929, Feb., March, June and Dec. 1930, the last six issued as supplements to Minnesota Law Review.

Bench and Bar of Minnesota. Minneapolis. 9 v. Dec. 1943–Nov. 1952* Official publication of Minnesota State Bar Assn. Continues Bench and Bar of Minnesota pub. from Oct. 1928–June 1940. *M.*

Bench and Bar, Official Publication of the Lawyers' Association of the Eighth Judicial Circuit of Missouri. St. Louis. 7 v. July 1935–Oct. 1942. Superseded by Official Publication of the Lawyers Association of St. Louis. *Irreg.* (v. 1, 6 nos.; v. 2, 4 nos.; v. 3, 5 nos.; v. 4, 2 nos.; v. 5, 1 no.; v. 6, 2 nos.; v. 7, 1 no.)

Bench and Bar Review. *See* Forum

Bibliography of Legal Science. Berlin. 4 v. 1910–13. American ed. of Journal of the International Institute of Legal Bibliography. Material identical with Zentralblatt der Rechtswissenschaft.

Bill of Rights Review. New York. 2 v. Summer, 1941–Summer, 1942. Pub: Bill of Rights Committee of American Bar Assn. *Q.*

Bi-monthly Law Review of the Law Department of the University of Detroit. *See* University of Detroit Bi-monthly Law Review.

Blackstone Law Bulletin. Chicago. 5 v. (12 nos.) Dec. 1925–Mar. 1931.

Bombay Law Journal. Bombay. 24 v. June 1923–Dec. 1946. *M.*

Bombay Law Reporter. Bombay. 41 v. 1899–1939*? Vol. 1 contains Reports only, the other volumes contain Journal and Reports with separate pagination. *Fortn.*

Bona Fides. Washington, D. C. v. 1, no. 1, May, 1939. Pub: George Washington University Student Bar Assn.

Boston Bar Association Bulletin. *See* Bar Bulletin.

Boston Law School Magazine. Boston. 1 v. Nov. 1896–Sept. 1897. *M.*

Boston Legal News. Boston. v. 1, no. 1, Feb. 27, 1897.

Boston University Law Review. Boston. 32 v. Jan. 1921–Nov. 1952* *Q.*

Bradford Law Students' Journal. London. 3 v. 1902–05.

Brainard's Legal Precedents in Land and Mining Cases. Washington, D. C. 7 v. Mar. 1883–1889. v. 7: 6 nos.

Brief. (Baird). New York. 1 v. (5 nos.) Oct. 1887–1888. *Bi-M.*

Brief (Los Angeles). 3 v. Jan. 1939–Dec. 1941. Pub: Hollywood Bar Assn. *Irreg.* (v. 1, 4 no.; v. 2, 8 no.; v. 3, no. 12 only).

Brief; a Legal Miscellany. St. Louis, Mo. 47 v. 1887–Summer 1952* Organ International Fraternity of Phi Delta Phi. Imprint varies. *Q.*

Brief: Business Magazine for the Practising Lawyer. Chicago. 1 v. June 1947.

Brief Case. Detroit. 6 v. Nov. 1926–May 1932. Pub: Detroit College of Law. *Irreg.* (v. 1, 7 nos.; v. 2, 8 nos.; v. 3, 8 nos.; v. 4, 6 nos.; v. 5, 7 nos.; v. 6, 5 nos.)

Brief Case; The Lawyers' Monthly. New York. 2 v. Ap. 1930–Mar. 1931.

Brief Case; a Monthly Magazine of Law for Everybody. Chicago. 1 v. July–Dec. 1923.

Brief Case, National Legal Aid Association. *See* Legal Aid Brief Case.

British Columbia Law Notes. Victoria. 1 v. (2 nos.) Feb.–Mar. 1894.

British Index Nazir Sanagraha (Barrisaul). India. No further information.

British Institute of International Affairs. Journal. *See* International Affairs.

Brooklyn Bar Association. Journal. Brooklyn, N. Y. 2 v. Oct. 1939–Feb. 1942. Vol. 1, 2 nos., Oct. 1939, Feb. 1940; v. 2, 1 no., Feb. 1942.

Brooklyn Barrister. Brooklyn, N. Y. 3 v. Mar. 1950–May 1952* Pub: Brooklyn Bar Assn.

Brooklyn Law Review. Brooklyn, N. Y. 18 v. April 1932–April 1952* Publication suspended July 1943–Feb. 1947. *Irreg. Bi-M* beginning with v. 11.

Buffalo Law Review. Buffalo, N. Y. 2 v. Spring 1951–Spring 1953* v. 1, 3 nos.; v. 2, 2 nos.

Bulletin, American Bar Association Section of Legal Education. *See* Notes on Legal Education.

Bulletin for International Fiscal Documentation. Bulletin de Documentation Fiscal. Amsterdam. 6 v. 1946–1952* Pub: International Bureau of Fiscal Documentation. Contents partly English, partly French.

Bulletin of International News. London. 22 v. Feb. 1925–June 23, 1945. Continued as The World Today.

Bulletin of the Bar Association of the District of Columbia. *See* Bar Association of the District of Columbia. Journal.

Bulletin of the Bureau of Criminal Investigation. Schenectady, N. Y. 17 v. Aug. 1936–1952* Pub: New York State Executive Dept., Div. of State Police, Bureau of Criminal Investigation. *M.* 1936–45; *Bi-M.* with 1946. (v. 1, 5 nos.)

Bulletin of the Commercial Law League of America. *See* Commercial Law Journal.

Bulletin of the Law Forum. *See* Consumer Finance Law Bulletin.

Burma Law Journal. Rangoon. 6 v. 1922–Oct. 1927.

Burma Law Times. Rangoon. 13 v. May 1907–1920. *M.*

Business Law. *See* Rosenberger's Pocket Law Journal.

Business Law Journal. New York. 19 v. Feb. 1923–Ap. 1932. Merged with Banking Law Journal. *M.* (v. 19, 4 nos.)

Business Law World. *See* Current Business Reports Plus Business Law World.

Business Lawyer. Portland, Ore. 8 v. July 1946–Jan. 1953* Pub: Section of Corporation, Banking and Mercantile Law, American Bar Assn. *Irreg.* (v. 1, 2 nos.; v. 2, 3 nos.)

Butterworth's Fortnightly Notes. *See* New Zealand Law Journal.

Calcutta Criminal Rulings. 39 v. 1896–1935*? Reprinted from Calcutta Weekly Notes.

Calcutta Law Journal. 70 v. Feb. 16, 1905–Dec. 1940*? *Fortn.*

Calcutta Legal Observer. 1 v. Nov. 1839–May, 1840. *W.*

Calcutta University Law College Magazine. Bengal. 5 v. 1931–1935*?

Calcutta Weekly Notes. 54 v. Nov. 1896–1941*?

Calendar of the Council of Legal Education. *See* Council of Legal Education.

California Law Journal. San Francisco. 2 v. Oct. 1862–July 1863. *W.* (v. 1, 26 nos.; v. 2, 7 nos.)

California Law Review. Berkeley. 40 v. Nov. 1912–Winter 1952/53* Pub: University of California School of Law. *Q.* (*Bi-M.* v. 1–30).

California Legal Record. San Francisco. 2 v. Mar. 30, 1878–Ap. 1879. Continues, together with Pacific Coast Law Journal, San Francisco Law Journal. *W.*

California State Bar Journal. *See* State Bar of California. Journal.

Cambridge Law Journal. London. 11 v. 1921–1952* Pub: Cambridge University Law Society. *A.* (3 nos. comprise a volume).

Canada Law Journal.Montreal. 4 v. July 1865–Oct. 1868. Title, v. 1–2: Lower Canada Law Journal. *Irreg.* (v. 1, 4 Q., 2–3 M.)

Canada Law Journal. Toronto. 68 v. Jan. 1855–Dec. 1922. O. S. v. 1–10, Jan. 1855–Dec. 1864; N. S. v. 1–58, Jan. 1865–Dec. 1922. Title, O. S.: Upper Canada Law Journal and Local Courts Gazette. Continued, together with Canadian Law Times, as Canadian Bar Review. *M.* and *Semi-M.*

Canadian Bar Review. Toronto. 30 v. Jan. 1923–Dec. 1952* Pub: Canadian Bar Association. Incorporated Canada Law Journal and Canadian Law Times and Review. *M.* (except July and Aug.)

Canadian Commercial Law. Montreal. 1 v. 1901.

Canadian Criminal Procedure Annotations. Toronto. 9 v. 1944–52* Preceded by same 3 v. loose-leaf, 1940–42.

Canadian Current Law. Toronto. 5 v. 1948–1952* *M.*

Canadian Green Bag. Montreal. v. 1, no. 1. Jan. 1, 1895.

Canadian Law Review. Toronto. 6 v. Oct. 1901–Dec. 1907. Merged into Canadian Law Times. *M.*

Canadian Law Times. Toronto. 42 v. Jan. 1881–Dec. 1922. Absorbed Canadian Law Review Jan. 1908. Joined Canada Law Journal to form Canadian Bar Review 1923. *M.*

Canadian Municipal Journal. Toronto. 2 v. 1891–92. *M.*

Canadian Patent Reporter. Toronto. 16 v. July 1941–Sept. 1952* *M.*

Canadian Police Gazette. Vancouver, B. C. 26 v. 1926–1952*.

Canadian Tax Foundation. Tax Bulletin. *See* Tax Bulletin to Members of the Canadian Tax Foundation.

Cape Law Journal. *See* South African Law Journal.

Capitol Daily. Washington, D. C. 5 v. Jan. 14, 1937–June 24, 1938. Pub: Capitol Daily News Service. v. 1, 119 nos.; v. 2, 125 nos.; v. 3, 126 nos.; v. 4, 125 nos.; v. 5, 119 nos.

Caribbean Law Journal. Jamaica, B. W. I. v. 1, no. 1, April 1952*.

Carolina Law Journal. Columbia, S. C. 1 v. (4 nos.) July 1830–Ap. 1831. *Q.*

Carolina Law Repository. Raleigh, N. C. 2 v. Mar. 1813–Sept. 1816. *Semi-A.*

Case and Comment. Rochester, N. Y. 57 v. May 1894–Dec. 1952* Pub: Lawyers Co-operative Pub. Co. Suspended for duration of war. *Q.* (*M.* to June 1918; *Bi-M.* v. 26, no. 1, Nov. 1919 to v. 35, Dec. 1929).

Catholic University of America Law Review. Washington, D. C. 2 v. May, 1950–May 1952* *Irreg.*

Caveat Emptor (England). 2 nos. 1932.

Central Hanover Estate Bulletin. New York. 13 v. Dec. 15, 1939–Dec. 1952* Pub: Central Hanover Bank & Trust Co. *M.*

Central Law Journal. St. Louis, Mo. 100 v. Jan. 1874–Mar. 25, 1927. Merged into Lawyer and Banker. *W.* (v. 100, 10 nos.)

Central Law Monthly. St. Louis, Mo. 3 v. 1880–82. Cont. as Chicago Law Journal.

Ceylon Law Journal. Colombo. 1 v. (7 nos.) Mar.–Oct. 1892. *M.* (issued with Supreme Court Reports).

Ceylon Law Journal (embodying Reports and Notes of Cases). Colombo. 9 v. June 18, 1936–1947* 40 nos. to a vol.

Ceylon Law Recorder. Colombo. 18 v. 1919–Aug. 1939*? *M.*

Ceylon Law Review. 7 v. Mar. 1899–1912. Includes "Tambyah's Reports." *M.* (*Irreg.*)

Ceylon Law Weekly. 30 v. 1931–1943*?

Ceylon Weekly Reporter. Colombo. 8 v. 1915–20.

Chancery Lane. London. 2 v. (16 nos.) 1909–11.

Chicago Bar Record. 33 v. May 9, 1910–Sept. 1952* Title, v. 3: Bar Association Record. Suspended publication Ap. 1932–Oct. 1934. *M.* (*Irreg.*)

Chicago Crime Commission. Bulletin. *See* Criminal Justice.

Chicago Guild Review. v. 1, no. 1, Feb. 1949. Pub: Chicago Chapter, National Lawyers Guild. Intended to supersede Lawyers Guild Monthly, and pub. during the latter's suspension.

Chicago-Kent Law Review. Chicago. 30 v. 1922–Sept. 1952* Pub: Chicago-Kent College of Law. 4 times during college year (*M.* v. 6–7).

Chicago Law Institute. Bulletin. 54 nos. Nov. 1, 1948–Ap. 1, 1953* *M.*

Chicago Law Journal. 2 v. 1876–77. v. 2: 192 pages.

Chicago Law Journal. 41 v. 1880–1907. Title, v. 1–3, 1880–82, Central Law Monthly. Ser. 3, v. 7–16, 20 omitted in numbering. *M.* (O. S. v. 1–10, 1880–89; N. S. v. 1–7, 1890–96); *W.* (3d ser. v. 1–24, 1896–1907).

Chicago Law Review. *See* University of Chicago Law Review.

Chicago Law Times. 3 v. Nov. 1886–Oct. 1889. *Q.*

Chicago Legal News. 57 v. Oct. 1868–July 16, 1925. *W.*

China Law Journal. Shanghai. 3 v. (no. 1–28.) Sept. 27, 1930–Dec. 15, 1931. *Fortn.*

China Law Review. Shanghai. 10 v. Ap. 1922–June 1937. Pub: Comparative Law School of China, Law Dept. of Soochow Univ. *Q.* (v. 1: 9 nos.; v. 10: 1 no).

China New Law Journal. Shanghai. Chinese Title: Hsin fa hsueh. Text in Chinese; added t.–p. in English. 1 v. (5 nos.) 1948 (no. 1, July).

Chitty's Law Journal. Toronto. 2 v. Nov. 1950–Dec. 1952* *M.* (10 issues per annum).

Chronicles of Kent. New York. 2 v. Feb. 1940–Dec. 1941. Pub: Columbia University Law Library, listing non-routine accessions to the library. Mimeo. *Irreg.* (supp. to v. 2 # 4, Dec. 1941).

Chronology of International Events and Documents. London. 8 v. June 19, 1945–Dec. 17, 1952* Suppl. to World Today. *Semi-M.*

Cincinnati Law Review. *See* University of Cincinnati Law Review.

Cincinnati Weekly Law Bulletin. *See* Ohio Law Bulletin.

Citator. *See* Indian Law Journal.

City-Hall Reporter and New York General Law Magazine. New York. 1 v. (3 nos.) Oct.–Dec. 1833 *M.*

City-State-Nation. Legislative Review. New York. 8 v. 1918–Dec. 1925. Pub: New York State League of Women Voters. *W.* (Jan.–June), *M.* (July–Dec.)

Civil Aeronautics Administration Journal. Washington, D. C. 13 v. Jan. 1940–

July 1952. Title, v. 1–v. 5 # 7, Jan. 1940–July 15, 1944, Civil Aeronautics Journal. Pub: U. S. Civil Aeronautics Authority. Supersedes Air Commerce Bulletin. Advance opinions of Board pub. in Journal through July 1940, after which only abstracts of opinions are pub. *M.* (*Semi-M.* to May 15, 1942. v. 13, 7 nos.)

Civil and Criminal Law Notes. Madras. 5 v. 1901–Jan. 1907. Title, v. 1–4: Madras Legal Companion. *M.*

Civil Law Journal. New Orleans. 1 no., June 1874?

Civil Liberties. New York. 110 nos. June 1931–March 1953* No. 1–73 have title: Civil Liberties Quarterly. With # 74 combined with Monthly Bulletin. Pub: American Civil Liberties Union. *M.* (*Q.* # 1–73).

Civil Liberties Quarterly. *See* Civil Liberties.

Civil Liberties Reporter. New York. v. 1, no. 1, Sept. 11, 1950*.

Civil Service Law Reporter. New York. v. 1. June 1951. Pub: National Civil Service League. *M.*

Clerk's (Monthly) Gazette. 5 v. 1899–1904. No further information available.

Cleveland Bar Association Journal. 23 v. Sept. 1927–Dec. 1952* Pub. suspended Feb. 1933–Oct. 1936; replaced during this period by Cleveland Bar Journal, Daily Legal News and Cleveland Recorder. *M.* (*Irreg.*)

Cleveland Bar Journal, Daily Legal News and Cleveland Recorder. Cleveland. 3 v. Jan. 19, 1934–May 8, 1936. An interim publication issued while Journal of the Cleveland Bar Association was suspended. v. 3, 5 nos.

Cleveland Law Reporter. Cleveland, Ohio. 2 v. 1878–79.

Cleveland Law School Journal. Cleveland, Ohio. v. 1, no. 1. Jan. 1916. Pub: Students of Law Dept. of Baldwin-Wallace College.

Cleveland Marshall Law Review. Cleveland, Ohio. 1 v. 1952*.

Clevenger's Monthly Practice. New York. 1 v. (4 nos.) Ap.–Dec. 1923.

Club, Bench, Bar, and Professional Life of Rhode Island. Providence. 3 v. 1896.

Coal Mining Law Journal. Belleville, Ill. 2 v. Mar. 1907–June 1908. *M.* (v. 2, 4 nos.)

Cochin Law Journal. Ernakulam. 11 v. June, 1934–Aug. 1943. v. 1, no. 3 contains separately paged section: Cochin Legislation. *M.* (v. 11, 4 nos.)

Code Reporter. New York. 4 v. July, 1848–1852. O. S. 3 v. July, 1848–June, 1851. N. S. 1 v., 1850–52. Title, N. S.: Reports of Decisions on the Code of Procedure (New Series).

Collector and Commercial Lawyer.*See* American Legal News.

College of Law Journal, Nagpur. *See* University College of Law Journal.

Colonial Law Journal. New Zealand. 1 pt. 1865–75. Collation: Table of cases i–iv; Reports 1–140; Journal 1–40.

Colorado Law Reporter. Denver. 4 v. Sept. 1880–Aug. 1884. *M.*

Columbia Journal of International Affairs. *See* Journal of International Affairs.

Columbia Jurist. New York. 3 v. Feb. 1885–Jan. 1887. Pub: Columbia College Law School. *W.*

Columbia Law Review. New York. 52 v. Jan. 1901–Dec. 1952* Pub: Columbia University Law School. Suspended Nov. 1918–Feb. 1919. *M.*, Nov.–Je.

Columbia Law School News. New York. 6 v. Ap. 22, 1947–Sept. 1952* Pub: Students of School of Law. Columbia University. *Bi-W.* (during college year except during vacation and examination weeks).

Columbia Law Times. New York. 6 v. Oct. 1887–May 1893. Pub: Students of Law and Political Science, Columbia College. *M.* during academic year.

Columbia University. Law School. Alumni Association. Bulletin. New York. 3 v. May 19, 1928; May 22, 1929; March 1930.

Commercial Law Annual. London. 4 v. 1871–74.

Commercial Law Journal. Chicago. 57 v. 1888–Dec. 1952* Title, 1888–1921, Bulletin of Commercial Law League of America; 1922–23, Commercial Law League Bulletin; Sept. 1923–July, 1930 Commercial Law League Journal. *M.*

Commercial Law Journal. Delhi. v. 1 # 1–11. Oct. 1947–Aug. 1948*? *M.*

Commercial Law Reporter. Capetown, South Africa. v. 1, 1948*?

Commercial Law Review. New York. 3 v. Sept. 1924–June 1927. *M.* (except July–Aug.)

Commercial Lawyer. St. Louis, Mo. 15 v. 1894?–1902. Merged with Legal News. *W.* and *M.*

Common Cause. Chicago, Ill. 4 v. July, 1947–July 1951* Pub: Committee to Frame a World Constitution. *M.*

Commonwealth Law Review. Melbourne. 6 v. Oct. 1903–Aug. 1909. *Bi-M.*

Compensation Review. New York. 15 v. Jan. 1925–June 1932. *M.*

Conference on Personal Finance Law. Quarterly Report. New York. 6 v. Fall, 1946–Fall, 1952*.

Congressional Digest. Washington, D. C. 31 v. Oct. 1921–1952* Title, Oct. 1921–1922, Capitol Eye. *M.*

Connecticut Bar Journal. Bridgeport. 26 v. Jan. 1927–Dec. 1952* Pub: State Bar Association of Connecticut. *Q.* (v. 8, 1 no.; v. 15, 5 nos.)

Connecticut Law Journal. Hartford. 17 v. Feb. 1935–Feb. 1952* v. 1 includes Advance sheets of Connecticut Supplement. v. 1–13 no. 48, pub. in Bridgeport by Connecticut Law Journal Pub. Co. *W.*

Constitutional Review. London. 1 v. 1909.

Constitutional Review. Washington, D. C. 13 v. Ap. 1917–Oct. 1929. Pub: National Association for Constitutional Government. Combined with George Washington Law Review, 1932. *Q.*

Consumer Finance Law Bulletin. Washington, D. C. 6 v. June 5, 1947–Dec. 15, 1952* Pub: National Consumer Finance Assn. Title, v. 1–4, Bulletin of the Law Forum. *Q.* (v. 1, 3 nos.).

Contemporary International Relations. Cambridge, Mass. 2 v. 1949/50–1950/51* Supersedes Current Reading on International Relations. *A.*

Contemporary Law Review. Madras. 5 v. July 1912–Sept. 1916. *M.* (v. 5, 1 pt.).

Conveyancer. (England). 1 v. 1836–42. No more information available.

Conveyancer and Property Lawyer. London. 16 v. Sept. 1936–Dec. 1952* Supersedes Conveyancer. *Q* (later *Bi-M.*).

Co-operator. Rochester, N. Y. 1 v. (12 nos.) Oct. 1915–Feb. 1918. Merged with Case and Comment.

Copp's Land Owner. Washington, D. C. 18 v. Ap. 1874–Nov. 15, 1891. Title, Ap. 1874–Mar. 1875, Western Land Owner. *M.* (v. 1–10); *Semi-M.* (v. 11–18).

Copyright Society of the U. S. A. Bulletin. New York. v. 1, #1, June 1953* To be issued 6 times a year.

Cornell Law Forum. Ithaca. 2 v. Mar. 1949–Dec. 1949* *M.*

Cornell Law Journal. Ithaca. v. 1, #1, June 1894.

Cornell Law Quarterly. Ithaca. 37 v. Nov. 1915–Summer 1952* Pub: Faculty and Students of Cornell Law School. *Q.*

Coroners' Society Reports (England). 1890–1935*? No more information available.

Corporate Practice Review. New York. 4 v. Oct. 1928–May 1932. *M.* (v. 4, 5 nos.).

Corporate Reorganizations. New York. 4 v. Aug. 1934–Aug. 1937. Superseded by Corporate Reorganizations combined with American Bankruptcy Review. *M.* (v. 4, 1 no.).

Corporate Reorganizations . . . combined with American Bankruptcy Review. New York. 6 v. Sept. 1937–Oct. 1947. Vols. numbered A1, A2 etc. Continues American Bankruptcy Review and Corporate Reorganizations.

Corporation Bulletin. New York. 8 v. 1903–June 1911. *Q.* (v. 8, 2 nos.).

Corporation Journal. New York. 19 v. 1908–Oct. 1951* Title, v. 1: Corporation Trust Company Journal. Vol. 1, 46 nos., 1908–Mar. 1915; v. 2 begins with no. 47, Apr. 1915. *M.* (except July–Aug.) (*Irreg.* to Mar. 1915).

Corporation Trust Company Journal. *See* Corporation Journal.

Council of Legal Education. Calendar. London. 53 v. 1901–1952/53*.

Councillor and Guardian. (England). 10 v. 1895–1904.

Councils Journal. London. 16 v. 1895–1909. Title, v. 1–5, Paris Councils Journal. Organ of Parish and District Councils' Assn. Cont. by Official Circular and then by Local Government Review.

Counsellor, The New York Law School Law Journal. New York. 5 v. Oct. 1891–May 1896. *M.* during school year.

Counsellor: Official Journal of National Council of Law Students. Cambridge, Mass. 2 nos. May, Sept. 1941. No. 1 has title: Bulletin.

Counsellors' Magazine (England). 1 v. 1795–1800.

County and Local Government Magazine. 2 v. 1890–91. Preceded by County Council Magazine, v. 1–2, 1889–90.

County and Municipal Record. Edinburgh. 80 v. Ap. 1903–1945*? Supersedes Municipal Record and Sanitary Journal.

County Council Gazette. *See* County Councils Association. Official Gazette.

County Council Magazine. 2 v. 1889–90. Cont. by County and Local Government Magazine, v. 3–4, 1890–91.

County Councils Association. Official Gazette. London. 25 v. 1908–Dec. 1932.

County Courts' Chronicle and Gazette of Bankruptcy. London. 47 v. June 1847–Ap. 1920. *M.*

County Courts Gazette. London. 3 v. 1912–17.

Cranenburgh's Criminal Cases, 1890–92. 2 v. 1864–76. Reprinted from Sutherland's Weekly Reporter.

Cream of the Law. Crawfordsville, Ind. 3 v. Jan. 1905–Oct. 1907. *Q.*

Creighton Brief. Omaha, Neb. 1 v. 1909. Pub: Creighton Univ. College of Law.

Crime Annual. London. 1931.

Crime Review. London. v. 1, no. 1. Dec. 1946.

Crime Survey. New York. 1 v. (3 nos.) Ap.–June 1935.

Criminal Justice: Journal of Chicago Crime Commission. 77 nos. Feb. 1919–Jan. 1950* Title, no. 1–46: Bulletin of Chicago Crime Commission. Publication suspended 1930–1934. *Irreg.*

Criminal Law Journal of India. Lahore. 53 v. 1904–Dec. 1952* *M.* (v. 3–10 *Fortn.*)

Criminal Law Magazine and Reporter. Jersey City, N. J. 18 v. Jan. 1880–Nov. 1896. *Bi-M.* (1880–85); *M.* (1886); *Bi-M.* (1887–93); *A.* (1894), *Bi-M.* (1895–96).

Criminal Law Notes. *See* Civil and Criminal Law Notes.

Criminal Law Reporter. Austin, Tex. v. 1. no. 1. Oct. 2, 1886.

Criminal Law Reporter. Parvatipuram, India. 12 v. 1911–1923. Vol. 12, 6 pts.; None pub. 1913; 1914, 2 pts.

Criminal Law Review. Madras. 10 v. Feb. 1913–1918. Vol. 10: 4 nos. (24–104 p.)

Criminal Lawyer. Vizagaptam, Madras. 3 v. May 1928–June 1930. Vol. 1 pub. at Parvatipuram. *M* (v. 1, 6 nos.; none pub. Nov.–Dec. 1928).

Criminal Recorder. London. 4 v. 1804–10.

Criminal Recorder (England). 2 v. 1815.

Criminological Research Bulletin. New York. 9 nos. 1931–1939*? Pub: Bureau of Social Hygiene, no. 1–5; Beginning no. 8, Committee on Criminal Statistics of American Prison Assn.; no. 6–7 appear only in Journal of Criminal Law and Criminology (v. 27–28). *Irreg.*

Criminologist. London. v. 1, no. 1. May 15, 1927.

Cumulative Digest of International Law and Relations. *See* International Law and Relations.

Current Business Reports plus Business Law World. Chicago. 3 v. May, 1926–June 1928. Title, May 1926: Business Law World combined with Current Business Reports. Continued in loose-leaf form as part of Commerce Clearing House Business Law Reference Service. *M.*

Current Comment and Legal Miscellany. Philadelphia. 3 v. Jan. 15, 1889–Ap. 15, 1891. *M* (v. 3, 4 nos.)

Current Law. Jan. 1947–Dec. 1952* Pub: Sweet & Maxwell.

Current Legal Problems. London. 5 v. 1948–1952* *A.*

Current Legal Reading. Rochester, N. Y. 1 v. (12 nos.) Sept. 1930–May 1931.

Current Legal Thought. New York. 14 v. Mar. 1935–Ap. 1949. *M.; Irreg.* (v. 14, 4 nos.)

Current Readings on International Relations. *See* Contemporary International Relations.

Cuttack Law Times. Cuttack, India. 16 v. 1935–1950*.

Cuyahoga County Bar Association Bulletin. Cleveland, Ohio. 14 v. 1928–Dec. 1941*? *M.*

Daily Law Record. Boston. 5 v. Oct. 6, 1884–Jan. 3, 1887.

Daily Law Transcript. *See* Baltimore Law Transcript.

Daily Record. Rochester, N. Y. 32 v. Mar. 15, 1908–Dec. 31, 1940*? *D* (except Sunday and legal holidays).

Daily Register. Official Law Journal of the City and County of New York. New York. 37 v. 1872–89. Continues New York Daily Transcript. Continued by New York Law Journal.

Dakota Law Review. Grand Forks, N. D. 4 v. Jan. 1927–Dec. 1932. Pub: North Dakota University Law School in co-operation with State Bar Assn. 4 times a year.

Dalhousie Law Association. Bulletin. Halifax, Nova Scotia. 1 v. (6 nos.) Dec. 1923–Mar. 1925.

Dayton Bar Bulletin. Dayton, Ohio. 2 v. 1944. Last issue Dec. 16. Pub: Dayton Bar Assn. *M.*

Decalogue Journal. Chicago. 2 v. Sept. 1950–July 1952* Pub: Decalogue Society of Lawyers. 5 times a year.

Decalogue Society of Lawyers. Bulletin. Chicago. 5 v. Last issue July 1944. *Irreg.*

Decision. Manila, Philippines. 8 v. 1945?– Dec. 31, 1952* *M.*

Delta Chi Quarterly. Ithaca, N. Y. 16 v. Ap. 1903–May 1919? v. 16, 2 nos.

Delta Theta Phi Paper Book. *See* Paper Book.

Denver Law Journal. Denver. 2 v. 1883–84. v. 2, 20 nos.

Denver Legal News. Denver. 2 v. Dec. 7, 1887–1889. *W* (v. 2, 48 nos.)

De Paul Law Review. Chicago. 2 v. Autumn/Winter 1951–Spring/Summer 1952* Pub: De Paul University School of Law. *Semi-A.*

Detroit Bar Quarterly. *See* Detroit Lawyer.

Detroit Law Journal. A Weekly Newspaper of Legal and Business Information. 19 v. 1898–1917. Title, v. 1–9, Detroit Legal Journal.

Detroit Law Review. 9 v. June 1931–June 1948. Pub: Detroit College of Law. Suspended pub. June 1938–Dec. 1947. 3 times a year (v. 1, 1 no.; v. 8, 1 no.)

Detroit Lawyer. 20 v. June 1931–Dec. 1952* Pub: Detroit Bar Assn. Title, v. 1–13, Detroit Bar Quarterly. *M.*

Detroit Legal Journal. *See* Detroit Law Journal; a Weekly Newspaper.

Detroit Legal News. 23 v. 1894–Oct. 7, 1916. vol. 23, 28 nos.

Dickinson Law Review. Carlisle, Pa. 57 v. Jan. 1897–June 1953* Title, v. 1–12, Forum of Dickinson School of Law. Pub: Students of Dickinson School of Law. *Q* (*M* Jan. 1897–May 1918; *Bi-M* Oct. 1918–July 1919; *M* Oct. 1919–June 1928).

Dicta. Denver. 29 v. Dec. 1923–Dec. 1952* Title, v. 1–5: Record. Pub: Denver Bar Association. *M.*

Dicta (Virginia Law Weekly). *See* Virginia Law Weekly; Dicta.

Digest. Lahore. 5 v. 1901–06. *M.*

District of Columbia Bar Association Journal. *See* Bar Association of the District of Columbia. Journal.

District of Columbia Young Lawyer. Washington, D.C. 6 v. 1947?–Oct. 1952* Pub. Junior Bar Section, District of Columbia Bar Assn.

Divorce Court and Breach of Promise Record (England). 10 nos. 1864.

Docket. Lebanon, Pa. 2 v. May 1897–Nov. 1898. *M* (v. 2, 5 nos.)

Docket. New York. 1937–1952* Pub: St. Thomas More Law Society of Manhattan College. 1937–1951 mimeographed; 1952, the only issue printed is called v. 2, no. 1. *A.*

Docket. San Antonio, Tex. 1 v. 1896. *M.*

Docket. St. Paul. 6 v. Jan. 1909–Winter 1941/42. Title, v. 1–5, West Publishing Co's Docket.

Documents of International Organization. Boston. 3 v. Nov. 1947–Sept. 1950. Pub: World Peace Foundation.

Drake Law Review. Des Moines, Ia. 2 v. Nov. 1951–May 1953* Pub: Students of Law School of Drake University. *Semi-A.*

Duke Bar Association Journal. Durham, N. C. 10 v. Mar. 1933–Ap. 1942. Pub:

Section of Publications, Duke Bar Association, School of Law, Duke University. *Semi-A.*

Duke Bar Journal. Durham, N. C. 3 v. Mar. 1951–Spring 1953* Pub: Duke University School of Law. *Semi-A* (Fall and Spring).

E. S. C. Quarterly. Raleigh. Summer 1942–Fall 1952* Pub: Employment Security Commission of North Carolina. Title, 1942–46, U. C. C. Quarterly and pub. by North Carolina Unemployment Compensation Commission.

East Anglican Law Clerks' Journal. Ipswich, England. v. 1, pt. 1. June 1909.

Economic Bulletin Issued by Trust Company of New Jersey. Jersey City, N. J. 1 v. (7 nos.) Dec. 22, 1930–Ap. 15, 1931. *Semi-M.*

Edinburgh Law Journal. Edinburgh. 2 v. Jan. 1831–1837.

Editorial Research Reports. Washington, D. C. Jan. 8, 1924–1952* Not numbered. *W.*

Educational Law and Administration. Columbus, Ohio. 7 v. Jan. 1932–Oct. 1939. Combined with Ohio School Board Magazine, Jan. 1936. Imprint varies. v. 7, 1 no.

Engineering Law. New York. 2 v. July 1912–June 1913. *M.*

English Historical Review. London. 67 v. 1886–1952* *Q.*

Erie County Bar Bulletin. Buffalo, N. Y. 13 v. Jan. 19, 1934–Jan. 1950. Vol. 5, no. 1, printed in Buffalo Daily Law Journal. Title varies. Suspended 1943–45. Pub: Research Committee of Erie County Bar. Continued by Buffalo Law Review. *Irreg.*

Estate Digest. New York. 1 v. Jan. 1950–Jan. 1951* Pub: Fiduciary Publishers. Prepared by Chemical Bank Trust Co. in collaboration with editors of Trusts and Estates. *M.*

Everybody's Law Magazine. New York. 1 v. (2 nos.) Jan./Mar.–Ap./June 1928.

Examination of Articled Clerks. See Leguleian.

Examiner. New York. 5 v. Oct. 25, 1813–May 1816. Continued as County Courier. (no information available on this title.)

Examiner (L'Observateur). Quebec, Can. 3 nos. Jan.–Mar. 1861. *M.*

External Affairs. Ottawa, Can. 4 v. Nov. 1948–Dec. 1952* Pub: Dept. of External Affairs. *M.*

F. E. U. Law Quarterly. Manila, Philippines. v. 1, no. 1. Jan. 1953* Pub: Far Eastern University Institute of Civil Law.

Federal Bar Association Journal. Washington, D. C. 12 v. Sept. 1931–Nov. 1952* Pub: Federal Bar Assn. *Q* (*Semi-A,* v. 1–5).

Federal Bar News. Washington, D. C. v. 1, no. 1–4. Mar. 1952–Dec. 1952* Pub: Federal Bar Assn., National Headquarters. *Irreg.*

Federal Communications Bar Journal. Washington, D. C. 12 v. 1937–Autumn 1952* None pub. 1946–47. v. 3 irregularly numbered: no. 1, without number; no. 2 called no. 1. *Q* (*M* ex. July–Aug., v. 1–7).

Federal Juror. New York. 23 v. Oct. 1929–Feb. 1952* Bulletin of Federal Grand Jury Assn., Southern District of New York. *Irreg.* v. 23, 1 no.

Federal Law Journal. New York. v. 1, no. 1. May 1939. Pub: Federal Bar Association of New York, New Jersey and Connecticut.

Federal Law Journal of India. *See* Supreme Court Journal (India).

Federal Law Quarterly. Indianapolis. 1 v. (3 nos.) Ap.–Oct. 1918.

Federal Probation. Washington, D. C. 16 v. May 1937–Oct./Dec. 1952* Title, 1937: Federal Probation News Letter; Mimeographed. Pub: U. S. Probation System, Bureau of Prisons, Dept. of Justice. *Q* (v. 1, 3 nos.)

Federal Register. Washington, D. C. 17 v. March 12, 1936–Dec. 31, 1952* Pub: National Archives of the United States. *D* (Tues.–Sat.)

Federation Bulletin. Buffalo, N. Y. 6 nos. Feb. 1933–June 1935. Pub: Federation of Bar Assns. of Western New York. *Irreg.*

Fiduciary Law Chronicle. New York. 3 v. Dec. 1929–Ap. 1932. *M* (v. 3, 2 nos.)

Fiduciary Reporter of Current Decisions on Wills, Estates and Trusts. Ithaca, N. Y. 12 v. Jan. 1940–Dec. 1952* Pub: Tompkins County Trust Co. Supersedes Recent Decisions Affecting Wills. Issues not numbered. *M.*

Fiduciary Review. Norristown, Pa. 69 nos. Nov. 1933–Sept. 1939?* Review, Digest and Comment of Cases Involving Trusts and Decedents' Estates Decided Recently in Pennsylvania. *M* (none pub. July–Aug. 1934.)

First District Bar Journal of Texas. Houston. 1 v. (7 nos.) June 1932–May 29, 1933. Pub: Bar Assn. of First Supreme Judicial District of Texas. Supersedes Houston Bar Journal. *M. Irreg.*

Florida Justice. Miami. 1 v. (6 nos.) Nov. 1938–Ap. 1939. Pub: Legislative Committee, Justice Peace and Constables' Assn. *M.*

Florida Law Journal. Lakeland. 26 v. Aug. 1927–Dec. 1952* Title, v. 1–8, no. 1: Florida State Bar Association Law Journal, pub. at Jacksonville. *M*, Oct.–July. (v. 1, 9 nos.)

Florida State Bar Association Law Journal. *See* Florida Law Journal.

Flugel's List. *See* Lawyers and Bankers Quarterly of St. Louis.

Food, Drug, Cosmetic Law Journal. New York. 7 v. Mar. 1946–Dec. 1952* Pub: Commerce Clearing House. Title, v. 1–4; Food, Drug, Cosmetic Law Quarterly. *M.*

Fordham Law Review. New York. 21 v. Nov. 1914–Nov. 1952* Vol. 1 contained in Fordham Monthly, (v. 33, no. 2–8). Vol. 1–3 pub. Nov. 1914–June 1917. Ceased June 1917. Publ. resumed Jan. 1935, with v. 4, no. 1 *Semi-A* (3 issues a year through v. 12).

Foreign Affairs. London. 13 v. July 1919–Ap. 1931. Pub: Union of Democratic Control. Continued as supplement to Time and Tide. *M.* (v. 13, 7 nos.)

Foreign Affairs. New York. 30 v. Sept. 15, 1922–July 1952* Pub: Council on Foreign Relations, Inc. Supersedes Journal of International Relations. *Q.*

Foreign Commerce Weekly. Washington, D. C. 47 v. Oct. 1940–Dec. 1952* Pub: U. S. Bureau of Foreign and Domestic Commerce. *W.*

Foreign Notes. Chicago. 18 v. Ap. 29, 1925–Dec. 20, 1941*? Vol. 1, no. 1–2 have title: News Bulletin. Pub: Chicago Council on Foreign Relations. *Bi-W (Irreg.)*

Foreign Policy Bulletin. New York. v. 1–2 # 3, Mar. 1920–July 1921; N. S. 31 v. Nov. 18, 1921–Sept. 1952* Title varies: v. 1–2, no. 1, 1920–Mar. 1921, League of Free Nations Association. Bulletin: v. 2, no. 2–3, Ap.–July 1921. Foreign Policy Association Bulletin; N. S. v. 1–10, 1921–Oct. 30, 1931, Foreign Policy Association, New York. News Bulletin. *W.*

Foreign Relations Bulletin. New York. 9 nos. 1927–31. Title, no. 2–6, Foreign Relations, Bulletins on Occasion. Pub: American Foundation, Inc., Maintaining the American Peace Award. *Irreg.*

Foreign Service Journal. Washington, D. C. 29 v. Oct. 1924–Dec. 1952* Supersedes American Consular Bulletin. Title, Oct. 1924–July 1951: American Foreign Service Journal. *M.*

Foreign Tax Law Semi-Weekly Bulletin. New York. 3 v. June 24, 1950–June 20, 1953* Title varies: v. 1, no. 1 to v. 3, no. 56, Foreign Tax Law Weekly Bulletin; v. 3, no. 57, Jan. 10, 1953 title changed to Foreign Tax Law Semi-Weekly Bulletin. *Semi-W (W* to Mar. 24, 1952).

Fortnightly Law Journal. Toronto. 17 v. June 1, 1931–Mar. 15, 1948.

Forum. Baltimore and New York. 3 v. (8 nos.) Jan. 1874–Oct. 1875. Title, v. 1 # 1, Jan. 1874, Forum Review.; v. 1 # 2, Ap. 1874, Forum Law Review.

Forum Law Review. *See* Forum.

Forum Review. *See* Forum.

Forum of the Dickinson School of Law. *See* Dickinson Law Review.

Gavel. *See* Milwaukee Bar Association Law Review.

Gazette and Bankrupt Court Reporter. New York. 1 v. July 15, 1867–May 1868. *Semi-M.*

Gazette des Tribunaux: Recueil des Jugements des Tribunaux Egyptiens. Alexandria. 6 v. 1875–Aug. 20, 1881. v. 6, 59 nos.

Gazette des Tribunaux Mixtes d'Egypte. Alexandria. 35 v. Nov. 10, 1910–July 1945. Contains reports of cases. *M.*

Gazette for Zanzibar and East Africa. Zanbizar. 31 v. Feb. 1892–Dec. 1922. *W.*

Gazette of Bankruptcy. London. 5 v. (185 nos.) Oct. 19, 1861–July 29, 1863. *Semi-W.*

Gazette Legale Italo-Americana (Italo-American Legal Gazette). New York. 31 v. Feb. 1922–Dec. 1952* Title, Feb. 1922–Feb. 1929, Gazette del Notaio Italo-Americano (Italo-American Notarial Gazette). *M.*

George Washington Law Review. Washington, D. C. 21 v. Nov. 1932–June 1953* Absorbed Constitutional Review. *Irreg.*

Georgetown Law Journal. Washington, D. C. 41 v. Nov. 1912–May 1953* Not pub. 1918–19. *Q* (with variations).

Georgia Bar Journal. Macon. 15 v. Ap. 1938–May 1953* Pub: Georgia Bar Assn. *Q.*

Georgia Law Journal. Atlanta. 3 nos. 1884.

Georgia Law Reporter. Atlanta. 1 v. Mar. 1885–1886. *Semi-M.*

Georgia Law Review. Athens. 3 nos. Mar. 1927–June 1928.

Georgia Lawyer. Macon. 2 v. June 1930–Jan. 1932. Pub: Georgia Bar Assn. *M* (v 1, no. 12 not issued. v. 2, 6 nos.)

Gibson's Law Notes. *See* Law Notes (London).

Glim. London. 15 nos. Trinity Term 1947–Hilary Term, 1953* Pub: Inns of Court Students' Union. *Q.*

Graya: A Magazine for Members of Gray's Inn. London. 34 nos. Sept. 1927– Michaelmas 1951* *Semi-A* (Easter and Michaelmas).

Green Bag. Boston. 26 v. Jan. 1889–Dec. 1914. *M.*

Griffith's Law Register. *See* Annual Law Register of the United States.

Grind Law Journal. Belfast. 1 v. (21 nos.) 1930. Each no. has separate t.-p. Unpaged.

Guild Law Student. New Haven, Conn. 5 v. 1947?–1952* Pub: Student Division, National Lawyers Guild.

Guild Lawyer. New York. 4 v. Dec. 1938–Dec. 1942. Pub: New York City Chapter, National Lawyers Guild. Continued by New York Guild Lawyer. *M (Irreg.)*

Guild Lawyer. Washington, D. C. 5 v. 1945?–Spring 1950. Pub: National Lawyers Guild, Washington, D. C. *Q* (v. 5, 1 no.)

Handbook for Magistrates. (England) 1 v. 1855.

Harvard Law Library Information Bulletin. Cambridge, Mass. 5 v. 1947–1952* *Bi-M.*

Harvard Law Review. Cambridge, Mass. 66 v. Ap. 1887–June 1953* Pub: Harvard Law Students. *M* (Nov.–June).

Harvard Law School Bulletin. Cambridge, Mass. 3 v. Ap. 1948–Dec. 1952* *A.*

Harvard Law School Record. Cambridge, Mass. 16 v. July 17, 1946–Ap. 30, 1953* 2 vols. (24 issues) per year.

Hastings Journal, an Intramural Law Review. San Francisco, Calif. 4 v. Fall 1939–Spring 1953* Pub: Hastings College of Law. *Semi-A* (Fall, Spring).

Hennepin Lawyer. Minneapolis, Minn. 20 v. Feb. 1933–July 1952* Pub: Hennepin County Bar Assn. *M* (with variations).

Hindu Law Journal. Triplicane, Madras. 7 v. May 1918–Ap./May 1925. *M.*

Hindu Law Quarterly. Bombay. 5 v. Jan. 1930–1936.

Hongkong University Journal of Law and Commerce. Hongkong. 2 v. Ap. 1928– Ap. 1929?

Hongkong University Law Journal. Hongkong. 1 v. (3 nos.) Jan. 1926–Jan. 1927, Ap. 1927.

Honorary Magistrate. Adelaide. 32 v. August, 1904–Dec. 1950* Pub: Justices' Assn. Incorp. (South Australia) *M.* (*Q.* to Aug. 1924).

Houston Bar Journal. Houston, Texas. 1 v. (10 nos.) Nov. 1930–Dec. 1931. Superseded by First District Bar Journal. *M.*

Hoya: Law School Number. Washington, D. C. 9 nos. June 12, 1933–May 13, 1936. Issued as separate issues of Hoya, and numbered according to it. Superseded by Res Ipsa Loquitur. *Irreg.* (v. 1, no. 1; v. 15, no. 12, 21, 28; v. 16, no. 8a, 22–A, 28; v. 17, no. 10, 27).

Hsin fa hsueh. *See* China New Law Journal.

Human Side of the People's Case. New York. 4 nos. Spring 1936–May 1937. Pub: New York County District Attorney's Office.

I & N Reporter. Washington, D. C. 1 v. July 1952–Ap. 1953* Pub: U. S. Dept. of Justice, Immigration and Naturalization Service. *Q.*

I. C. C. Practitioners' Journal. Washington, D. C. 20 v. Nov. 1933–Sept. 1953* Title, v. 1, no. 1, Practitioners' Journal. Pub: Association of Practitioners before the Interstate Commerce Commission. *M* (except July–Aug.)

I. C. C. Pracitioners' Quarterly Bulletin. *See* Association of Practitioners before the Interstate Commerce Commission. Bulletin.

I. L. O. At Work. Montreal. 7 nos. May 1941–June 1947* Supersedes I. L. O. Month by Month. Pub: International Labour Office. *Irreg.*

I. L. O. Month By Month. Geneva. 2 v. Jan./May 1939–Jan./Mar. 1940. Supersedes Monthly Summary of International Labour Office which ceased Dec. 1938. Superseded by I. L. O. At Work, May 1941. *M* (v. 2, 3 nos. in 1).

Idaho Law Journal. Moscow. 3 v. Feb. 1931–Nov. 1933. Pub: College of Law, University of Idaho. *Q.*

Il-Law-Ni News. Urbana, Ill. 3 nos. Dec. 5, 1952–May 7, 1953* Pub: University of Illinois College of Law. *Irreg.*

Illinois Bar Journal. Springfield. 41 v. 1912–June 1953* Title, v. 1–20, no. 1; Quarterly Bulletin pub. by Illinois State Bar Assn. *M* (Sept.–June; *Q*, 1912–Oct. 1932).

Illinois College of Law Weekly. Chicago. 2 v. Sept. 13, 1905–1906.

Illinois Law Bulletin. *See* Illinois Law Quarterly.

Illinois Law Quarterly. Urbana. 6 v. Feb. 1917–June 1924. Title, v. 1–2: Illinois Law Bulletin; v. 3: University of Illinois Law Bulletin. Merged into Illinois Law Review, 1924. Pub: University of Illinois College of Law.

Illinois Law Record. Chicago. 2 v. 1880. vol. 2, 2 nos.

Illinois Law Review. *See* Northwestern University Law Review.

Illustrated Legal News. Triplicane, Madras. v. 1, pt. 1, Aug. 3, 1935.

Immigration and Naturalization Service Monthly Review. Washington, D. C. 9 v. July 1943–June 1952. Continued by I & N Reporter. Pub: U. S. Dept. of Justice, Immigration and Naturalization Service.

Immigration Bar Bulletin. New York. 5 v. Dec. 1947–Dec. 1952* Pub: Assn. of Immigration and Nationality Lawyers. *Irreg.*

Income Tax Gazette. India. 8 v. 1941–1949* *M.*

Income Tax Law Journal. Allahabad, India. v. 7–14, no. 3. 1932/33–Mar. 1940. vols. 1–6 never published. *M.*

Income-Tax Payer. London. 27 v. July 1923–Feb. 1950* Pub: Income-taxpayers' society. *Q.*

Incorporated Law Society. Calendar. London. 16 v. 1881–93.

Incorporated Law Society. Gazette. Dublin. 1923–1936*?

Indian Advocate. Lahore. 1 v. (31 nos.) Jan. 27–Dec. 1937. *W.*

Indian Case Notes. 1910. (Possibly never issued; no information available).

Indian Jurist. Calcutta. 4 v. Sept. 1862–1867. O. S. 2 v. Sept. 1862–Jan. 1863 (v. 1: 8 nos., v. 2: 1 no.); N. S. 2 v. 1866–67.

Indian Jurist. Madras. 17 v. 1877–93. O. S. 7 v., 1877–83; N. S. 10 v. 1884–93. Supersedes Madras Jurist. *Semi-M.* and *M.*

Indian Law Herald. 1 v. 1905.

Indian Law Journal. 1878.

Indian Law Journal. Madras. 19 v. 1906–14. Title, v. 1–16, no. 1: Citator. *Fortn.*

Indian Law Magazine. Bombay. 1 v. (4 nos.) 1878.

Indian Law Magazine. Calcutta. 1895.

Indian Law Quarterly. Madras. 3 v. Ap. 1914–1917. vol. 3, 2 pts.

Indian Law Review. Calcutta. v. 6 #1. Feb. 1947–1952*.

Indian Law Times. Madras. 40 v. 1906–May 1928. Title, v. 1–39: Madras Law Times. vol. 36–37 never issued. *W.* (v. 35, 11 nos.; v. 40, 17 nos.)

Indiana Law Journal. Bloomington. v. 1 (4 nos.) June–Dec. 1925; N. S., 27 v. Jan. 1926–Summer 1952* *Q.* (*M.* v. 1–10; *Bi-M.*, v. 11–17).

Indiana Law Journal. Indianapolis. 3 v. Jan. 1898–June 1899. Pub: Indiana State Bar Assn. *M.* (v. 3, 6 nos.)

Indiana Law Magazine. Indianapolis. 5 v. May 1883–Mar. 1885. *Irreg.* (*M.* v. 1; vol. 5, 5 nos.)

Indiana Law Reporter. Indianapolis. 2 v. 1881.

Indiana Law Student. Indianapolis. v. 1, no 1. June 1896. Pub: Indiana Law School, University of Indianapolis.

Indiana Legal Register. 3 nos. 1871–72.

Industrial and Labor Relations Review. Ithaca, N. Y. 6 v. June 1946–July 1953* Pub: New York State School of Industrial and Labor Relations, Cornell University. *Q.*

Industrial Bulletin. Albany, N. Y. 31 v. Jan. 1922?–Dec. 1952* Pub: New York State Dept. of Labor. Continues New York State Industrial Commission. Bulletin. *M.*

Industrial Gazette. Western Australia. 15 v. 1921–1935*?

Industrial Law Review. London. 7 v. June 1946–Ap. 1953* Pub: Engineering–Legal Society. *Q.*

Industry and Labour. Geneva. 8 v. Jan. 1949–Dec. 1952* Supersedes Industrial and Labour Information, 1922–1940, which was incorporated in the International Labour Review, 1940. Pub: International Labour Office. *M.*

Institute of Arbitrators, Incorporated. Journal. London. 17 v. Oct. 1927–Dec. 1951* Title, N. S. no. 1–7: Arbitrator: Journal of the Institute of Arbitrators Incorporated. *Irreg.*

Insurance Counsel Journal. Birmingham, Ala. 19 v. Ap. 1934–Oct. 1952* Pub: International Assn. of Insurance Counsel. *Q.* (v. 1, 3 nos.)

Insurance Decisions. Indianapolis. 13 v. July 1, 1931–Sept. 1943. Pub. suspended Nov. 1931–Jan. 1932. Absorbed Insurance Digest, Mar. 1932. Merged into Insurance Law Journal. *M.* (*Semi-M.*, July–Oct. 1931, pub. in New York; v. 13, 3 nos.)

Insurance Law Journal. New York. 91 v. Sept. 1871–Dec. 1938. v. 21–60 also called N. S. v. 1–40. Continued by Commerce Clearing House Insurance Case Series: 1. Automobile; 2. Fire and casualty; 3. Life, health and accident; 4, Negligence. *M.*

Insurance Law Journal: Advance Digest of Full-Text Decisions Currently Reported in CCH Insurance Law Reporting Service. Chicago. 359 nos. Jan. 3, 1939–Dec. 1952* Keeps Insurance Law Reporting Service (CCH) up to date, and with the loose-leaf service continues Insurance Law Journal, 1871–1938, listed above.

Insurance Law Reporter. Montreal. 8 v. Jan. 1934–Dec. 1941*? *M.* (v. 1, 11 nos.)

Insurance Reporter. *See* Legal and Insurance Reporter.

Inter-American. Washington, D. C. 5 v. May 1942–Nov. 1946. Formed by Union of Inter-American Quarterly and Pan-American News. Title, v. 1, May–Dec. 1942, Inter-American Monthly. Merged into United Nations World. *M.*

Inter-American Monthly. *See* Inter-American.

Inter-American Quarterly. Washington, D. C. 3 v. Jan. 1939–Oct. 1941. Title, v. 1; Quarterly Journal of Inter-American Relations. United with Pan American News to form Inter-American (v. 1, Inter-American Monthly).

Intercollegiate Law Journal. New York. 2 v. Nov. 1891–Sept. 1893. Continued by University Law Review. *M.* (during school year. v. 2, 7 nos.)

Internal Revenue News. Washington, D. C. 6 v. July 1927–Sept. 1932. Pub: Bureau of Internal Revenue. *M.* (v. 6, 3 nos.)

International Affairs. London. 28 v. 1922–Dec. 1952* Title varies: 1922–Ap. 1926, Journal of British Institute of International Affairs; May 1926–Nov. 1930, Journal of Royal Institute of International Affairs. Vol. 19, June 1940–Sept. 1943 called International Affairs, Review Supplement comprising only the Book Review Section. *Q.*

International Affairs as Presented in Recent Periodicals, Books and Pamphlets. *See* Selected List of Recent Articles on International Affairs.

International Affairs, Review Supplement. *See* International Affairs.

International and Comparative Law Quarterly. London, 1 v. Jan. 1952–Oct. 1952* "The Journal of Society of Comparative Legislation." Supersedes Journal of Comparative Legislation and International Law Quarterly merged in one. *Q.*

International Arbitration Journal. New York. 1 v. Ap.–Dec. 1945. Pub: American Arbitration Assn. During suspension of Arbitration Journal, 1943–45 inclusive, the Association issued Arbitration Magazine, 3 v., 1943–45 and International Arbitration Journal. *Q.*

International Bar Association. Bulletins. New York. 1947, 1948, 1950, 1952. Numbered separately for each year beginning with no. 1. Mimeographed.

International Bar News. New York. v. 1, no. 1–v. 3, no. 1. Sept. 1947–May 1952* Pub: International Bar Assn.

International Bulletin of Agricultural Law. Rome. 1st year. 1940, no. 1–2*? Pub: International Institute of Agriculture.

International Conciliation, Documents. New York. 42 v. (nos. 1–486) 1907/08–1952* Pub: Carnegie Endowment for International Peace.

International Digest: a Monthly Review of Foreign Affairs. Forest Hills, N. Y. 2 v. Oct. 1930–May 1932. *M.* (except Aug. vol. 2, 5 nos.)

International Journal. Toronto. 7 v. Jan. 1946–Autumn 1952* Pub: Canadian Institute of International Affairs. *Q.*

International Journal of Law and Legislation relating to Food and Agriculture. Rome. no. 1–3 Jan./June 1947–Jan./June 1948* Title, no. 1–2 International Law Journal. Continues International Bulletin of Agricultural Law. Pub: Food & Agricultural Organization of the United Nations. *Semi-A.*

International Juridical Association. Monthly Bulletin. New York. 11 v. May 1932–Dec. 1942. Merged into Lawyers Guild Review. *M.* (v. 11, 6 nos.)

International Juridical Association Review. Berlin. v. 1, no. 1–4. Apr.–June 1930. Pub. also in French and German.

International Labour Review. Geneva. 66 v. Jan. 1921–Dec. 1952* Industrial and Labour Information included from 1940 to 1948, then pub. separately under title Industry and Labour. Pub: International Labour Office. *Bi-M.*

International Law and Relations. Washington, D. C. 6 v. June 1930–June 1937. Title varies: v. 1–4, no. 17, June 1930–Mar. 13, 1935, Cumulative Digest of International Law and Relations; v. 4, nos. 18–20, Ap. 3–10, 1935, International Law and Relations Digest. Pub: American University Graduate School. *Irreg.*

International Law Association. Bulletin. London. 5 nos. Dec. 1936–Nov. 1938.

International Law Notes. London. 4 v. (30 nos.) Jan. 1916–Dec. 1919. *Q.* 1916–17; *Irreg.* 1918–19.

International Law Quarterly. London. 4 v. Spring 1947–Oct. 1951. Jan. 1952 merged with Journal of Society of Comparative Legislation to form International and Comparative Law Quarterly.

International Lawyer. Chicago. v. 1, no. 1. Aug. 1949. Pub: International and Comparative Law Section, American Bar Assn.

International Organization. Boston. 6 v. Feb. 1937–Nov. 1952* Pub: World Peace Foundation. *Q.*

International Political Science Abstracts. Oxford. v. 1, no. 1–4. 1951*.

International Review. London. 75 nos. Oct. 1913–Dec. 1919. Title, Oct. 1913–Nov. 1918: War and Peace. Merged into Contemporary Review. Irregularly numbered.

Intramural Law Review, American University. *See* American University, Intramural Law Review.

Intramural Law Review of New York University. 8 v. Sept. 1945–May 1953* *Q.* (v. 1–3 *Semi-A.*)

Intramural Law Review, St. Louis University. *See* Saint Louis University Law Journal.

Iowa Bar Review. Iowa City. 6 v. 1934–40. Issued as supp. to Iowa Law Review, v. 20–25. Continues Iowa State Bar Association Quarterly. Superseded by Iowa State Bar Association News Bulletin.

Iowa Law Bulletin. *See* Iowa Law Review.

Iowa Law Review. Iowa City. 37 v. Jan. 1915–Summer 1952* Title, v. 1–10: Iowa Law Bulletin. Supersedes Law Bulletin of State University of Iowa. Vol. 20–25, 1934–40 contain supp. section called Iowa Bar Bulletin, v. 1–6. Pub: State University of Iowa, College of Law. *Q.*

Iowa Legal Inquisitor. Burlington. 2 v. Aug. 1851–May 1853. *M.* (v. 2, 5 nos.)

Iowa State Bar Association News Bulletin. Des Moines. 8 v. 1940–1948* Supersedes Iowa Bar Review. *M.* (*Irreg.*)

Iowa State Bar Association Quarterly. Des Moines. 3 v. Dec. 1929–June 1932. Continued by Iowa Bar Review. vol. 3, 3 nos.

Irish Jurist. Dublin. 18 v. 1848–66. Vols. 8–18 also called N. S. v. 1–11. Vol. 19, no. 1, January 1867 is believed to have been issued. *Semi-M.*

Irish Jurist. Dublin. 17 v. 1935–1951* In conjunction with this are issued Irish Jurist Reports.

Irish Jurist and Local Government Review. Dublin. 5 v. Nov. 15, 1900–Oct. 27, 1905.

Irish Law Times and Solicitors Journal. Dublin. 86 v. Feb. 2, 1867–Dec. 27, 1952* Title varies. *W.*

Irish Local Government Quarterly, Orders and Legal Decisions. Dublin. 17 v. 1899–1919. A quarterly supplement to Fitzgibbon and Johnston's "Law of Local Government on Ireland."

Irish Petty Sessions Journal. Dublin. 6 v. 1893–99. New Series, 2 v. 1899–1901.

Irish Weekly Law Reports and Journal. Dublin. 8 v. 1895–1902. Vols. 7–8 also called N. S. v. 1–2. Vol. 8: 3 pts. Title varies.

JAG Journal. Washington, D. C. 4 v. 1948–Dec. 1952* Pub: Office of Judge Advocate General of the Navy. *M.*

J. P. Sydney. 20 v. 1914–1933. Continues Magistrate. Pub: Official organ New South Wales Justices' Assn.

January Journal. St. Louis, Mo. v. 1, no. 1. Sept. 1941. Pub: Law Library Staff of Washington University. Mimeographed.

Japan Science Review—Law and Politics. Tokyo. no. 1, 1950*? Pub: Union of Japanese Societies of Law and Politics.

Jealous Mistress. Denver, Colo. 1 v. (9 nos.) June 1925–July 1926. Title, no. 1: Unchristened Notes of Colorado Bar Assn. Pub: Official organ, Colorado Bar Assn.

John Marshall Law Journal. Jersey City, N. J. 6 v. Dec. 1930–Sept. 1949. *Irreg.* (v. 1, 1 no.; v. 2, 1 no.; v. 3–4, 3 nos. each; v. 5, 1 no.; v. 6, 1 no.)

John Marshall Law Quarterly. Chicago. 8 v. Dec. 1935–June 1943. *Q.* (v. 1, 3 nos.)

Joint Stock Companies' Law Journal. London. 11 nos. 1848–49. Cox's Joint Stock Companies Cases, 1 pt., was issued with this Journal.

Journal, Oklahoma State Bar Association. *See* Oklahoma State Bar Association. Journal.

Journal of African Administration. London. 4 v. Jan. 1949–Oct. 1952* Pub. for the Secretary of State for the Colonies.

Journal of Air Law and Commerce. Chicago. 19 v. Jan. 1930–Autumn 1952* Title, v. 1–9: Journal of Air Law. Ed. by the Law Schools of Northwestern University, University of Southern California and Washington University, St. Louis in conjunction with Air Law Institute. Pub. suspended 1943–1946. *Q.*

Journal of Auctions and Sales. London. 94 nos. Aug. 6, 1853–Aug. 23, 1856. Issued as supp. to Law Times.

Journal of Banking Law. New York. 7 v. 1882–88. *Q.* (v. 3, 143 pages).

Journal of Comparative Legislation and International Law.. London. 2 v. Aug. 1896–Dec. 1897; N. S. 18 v. March 1899–Dec. 1918; 3d Ser. v. 1–33½. Ap. 1919–May 1951. Title varies. Merged with International Law Quarterly to form International and Comparative Law Quarterly.

Journal of Conational Law. New York. 3 v. July 1920–Oct. 1922. *Q.* (v. 3, 4 nos.)

Journal of Criminal Law. London. 16 v. (no. 1–62). Jan. 1937–June 1952* *Q.*

Journal of Criminal Law, Criminology and Police Science. Chicago. 42 v. May 1910–June 1952* Title, v. 1–31, Journal of American Institute of Criminal Law and Criminology; v. 31–41, Journal of Criminal Law and Criminology. Absorbed American Journal of Police Science, Ap. 1932. Pub: Official organ American Prison Assn. and American Society of Military Law. *Bi-M.* (*Q.* v. 9–12).

Journal of Criminal Science. London. 2 v. 1948–1950* Pub: Dept. of Criminal Science, Cambridge Univ. *Irreg.*

Journal of International Affairs. New York. 6 v. Spring 1947–Spring 1952* Title, v. 1–5 (1947–51): Columbia Journal of International Affairs. Pub: School of International Affairs, Columbia University. 2 issues a year.

Journal of International Law and Diplomacy. Tokyo. 51 v. 1902–Dec. 1951* Title, v. 1–25: Revue (mensuelle) de Droit Internationale et Diplomatique. Pub: Faculty of Law, Imperial University. Text chiefly in Japanese. *M. (Irreg.)*

Journal of Jurisprudence (Hall's). Philadelphia. 1 v. 1821. Cited as v. 7, American Law Journal.

Journal of Jurisprudence and Scottish Law Magazine. Edinburgh. 35 v. Jan. 1857–Dec. 1891. Title, v. 1–32: Journal of Jurisprudence. Absorbed Scottish Law Magazine and Sheriff Court Reporter, 1868. *M.*

Journal of Juristic Papyrology. New York, and Warsaw. 5 v. Ap. 1946–1951* Pub: Polish Institute of Arts and Sciences. None pub. 1947.

Journal of Land & Public Utility Economics. *See* Land Economics: a Quarterly Journal of Planning, Housing & Public Utilities.

Journal of Law. Philadelphia. 1 v. July 7, 1830–June 22, 1831. *Semi-M.*

Journal of Law & Politics. Nishinomiya, Japan. 2 v. Dec. 1949–Nov. 1951* Pub: Law and Politics Assn., Kwansei Gakuin University.

Journal of Legal and Political Sociology. New York. 4 v. Oct. 1942–Ap. 1947. Pub: Philosophical Library. Each vol. has special t.-p.

Journal of Legal Education. Durham, N. C. 5 v. Autumn 1948–Summer 1953* Pub: Assn. of American Law Schools; ed. by Faculty of Law, Duke University. *Q.*

Journal of Planning Law. London. [5v.] Ap. 1948–Dec. 1952* Volumes not numbered. *M.*

Journal of Political Science. Wellington, N. Z. v. 1, no. 1. Sept. 1948*? Pub: Victoria University College. Political Science Society.

Journal of Psychological Medicine; a Quarterly Review of Diseases of the Nervous System, Medical Jurisprudence and Anthropology. New York. 6 v. 1867–72. Title, v. 1–3: Quarterly Journal of Psychological Medicine and Medical Jurisprudence.

Journal of Public Law. Emory Univ., Ga. 1 v. Spring 1952–Fall 1952*.

Journal of Radio Law. Chicago. 2 v. Ap. 1931–Oct. 1932. Ed. by Law Schools of Northwestern University and University of Southern California in conjunction with Air Law Institute. *Q.* (v. 1, 3 nos.)

Journal of Social Philosophy and Jurisprudence. New York. 7 v. Oct. 1935–July 1942. Title, v. 1–6: Journal of Social Philosophy. *Q.*

Journal of Society of Commercial and Industrial Law. London. 1 v. (2 nos.) July–Sept. 1926. *Q.*

Journal of the American Institute of Criminal Law and Criminology. *See* Journal of Criminal Law, Criminology, and Police Science.

Journal of the American Judicature Society. *See* American Judicature Society. Journal.

Journal of the Law-School and of the Moot-Court attached to it, at Needham in Virginia. Richmond. 1 v. 1822.

Journal of the Missouri Bar. Jefferson City. 8 v. Jan. 1945–Nov. 1952* Supersedes Missouri Bar Journal. None pub. July 1945–Aug. 1946. *M.* (except July–Aug.)

Journal of the Parliaments of the Commonwealth. London. 33 v. Jan. 1920–Oct. 1952* Title, v. 1–29: Journal of the Parliaments of the Empire. Pub: Issued under the authority of the Commonwealth Parliamentary Assn. (General Council). *Q.*

Journal of the State Bar of California. *See* State Bar of California.. Journal.

Judge Advocate Journal. Washington, D. C. 2 v. June 1944–Sept. 1945. Pub: Judge Advocates Assn.

Judgment in Suits for Damages for Defamation. Bengal, Calcutta, India. Repr. from Legal Companion, 1883.

Judicature Quarterly Review. London. 1 no. Jan. 1896.

Judicial Laymen's Association, Inc. Bulletin. Mount Vernon, N. Y. 2 v. Jan. 1937–Ap. 1941.

Judicial Settlement of International Disputes. Baltimore. 29 nos. 1910–17. Pub: American Society for Judicial Settlements of International Disputes. *Q.*

Juridical Register. (Scotland). 1 v. 1829.

Juridical Review. Edinburgh and London. 64 v. 1889–Dec. 1952* 3 issues a year (*Q.* through vol. 53).

Juridical Society. Law Cases and Speculative Questions for Discussion. Edinburgh. 1817–94.

Juridical Society. Papers. London. 4 v. 1855–1874.

Jurisprudent. Boston. 1 v. July 10, 1830–July 23, 1831. *W.*

Jurist. London. 30 v. 1837–67. O. S. 18 v. Jan. 14, 1837–Jan. 6, 1855; N .S. 12 v. Jan. 13, 1855–Jan. 5, 1867 (N. S. 1–12 called also v. 19–30) *W.*

Jurist. London. 5 v. 1887–91. Merged into Law Students' Journal. *M.*

Jurist. Washington, D. C. 12 v. Jan. 1941–Oct. 1952* Pub: School of Canon Law, Catholic University of America. *Q.*

Jurist or Quarterly Journal of Jurisprudence and Legislation. London. 4 v. Mar. 1827–Feb. 1833. Vol. 4: 1 pt.

Justice. Boston. 1929–30. Pub: Boston Legal Aid Society. *Q.* (*Irreg.*)

Justice. India. 3 v. 1930–32. Vol. 3: 1 no.

Justice. Lahore. 3 v. Jan. 1934–Dec. 1937. *M.* (Irreg.: v. 1, 12 nos.; v. 2, 3 nos.; v. 3, 9 nos.)

Justice Library Review. Washington, D. C. 2 v. Jan. 1940–Sept. 1941. Pub: Library of U. S. Dept. of Justice. *Bi-M.* (v. 2, 5 nos.)

Justice of the Peace. Strasburg, Pa. 8 v. Dec. 1899–Oct. 1907. None pub. Ap. 1906 through May, 1907. *M.*

Justice of the Peace and Local Government Review. London. 116 v. Jan. 28, 1837–Dec. 27, 1952* Reports pub. in conjunction with this, beginning v. 67, 1903. *W.* (*Bi-W.* 1937).

Justinian. Brooklyn, N. Y. 14 v. Dec. 2, 1931–Ap. 1945. Pub: Brooklyn Law School, St. Lawrence University. *M.* (during school year; *Irreg.*)

Juvenile Court Judges Journal. Pittsburgh, Pa. 3 v. Sept. 1949–Oct. 1952* Pub: National Council of Juvenile Court Judges. *Q.*

Kansas Barletter. Topeka. 1 v. 1951?–1952* Pub: Bar Assn. of the State of Kansas. Current information service to member lawyers. Mimeo. *M.*(?)

Kansas City Bar Bulletin. *See* Kansas City Bar Journal.

Kansas City Bar Journal. Kansas City. 27 v. 1924–1952* Title, v. 1–25: Kansas City Bar Bulletin. *M.* (*Irreg.*)

Kansas City Bar Monthly. Kansas City, Mo. 19 v. Nov. 1895–1917. Pub: Official organ, Kansas City Bar Assn. v. 19, 3 nos.

Kansas City Law Reporter. Kansas City, Mo. 1 v. (7 nos.) June 22–Aug. 10, 1888.

Kansas City Law Review. *See* University of Kansas City Law Review.

Kansas City Lawyers Association News. *See* Lawyers Association of Kansas City.

Kansas Law Journal. Topeka. 5 v. Feb. 1885–Feb. 1887. *W.* (v. 5, 2 nos.)

Kansas Lawyer. Lawrence. 18 v. Mar. 21, 1895–1911. Title, v. 1–2: Kansas University Lawyer. *Bi-W.* and *M.*

Kansas University Lawyer. *See* Kansas Lawyer.

Kappa Beta Pi Quarterly. Cedar Rapids, Iowa. 32 v. Dec. 1916?–Dec. 1948*.

Kashmir Law Journal. Lahore. v. 1, pt. 1–2. Ap.–May 1929.

Kelly's Bar Examination Papers, Questions and Answers. London. 14 v. 1901–14. Title, v. 1–17: Bar Examination Papers, Questions and Answers. *A.*

Kentucky Law Journal. Louisville. 2 v. July, 1881–Jan. 1882. Merged into Kentucky Law Reporter. *M* (v. 2, 7 nos.)

Kentucky Law Journal. Lexington. 40 v. Jan. 1912–1951/52* Pub: University of Kentucky College of Law. Official pub. of Kentucky State Bar Assn. *Q.* (*Irreg; M.* during academic year, v. 1–6).

Kentucky Law Reporter. Frankfort. 33 v. July 1880–Oct. 15, 1908. Absorbed Kentucky Law Journal, Mar. 1883. Title varies. *Irreg.* (*M*, 1880–June 1887; *Semi-M*, July 1887–Sept. 1908; *W*, Oct. 1908).

Kentucky State Bar Journal. Frankfort. 16 v. Dec. 1936–1951/52* Pub: Kentucky State Bar Assn. *Q*.

Khulasa Nazair (Fatehqarh). India. 1876.

King's Bench Observer. (England) 1 v. 1829–30. "Lists of those imprisoned for debt. No legal articles or reports."

King's Counsel. Leominster, London. 11 nos. Mar. 1936–Feb. 1953* None pub. 1940–47 incl. and 1949. Beginning Ap. 1950, each issue numbered consecutively. Pub: Faculty of Laws, Society of King's College, London. *A* (1936–1939, 1948; *Irreg.* 1950–).

Kings County Criminal Bar Association. *See* Pleader.

King's Law Varthamani (in Telegu). 5 v. 1931–1935*?

Knight's Official Advertiser. *See* Local Government Chronicle.

Kosmodike: Periodical for International Law Matters. London. 3 v. 1898–1900. Pub. also in German.

Labor Law Journal. Chicago. 3 v. Oct. 1949–Dec. 1952* Pub. Commerce Clearing House. *M*.

Labor Relations Reporter. Washington, D. C. 17 v. Sept. 6, 1937–Ap. 1946. Continued by Labor Relations Reference Manual. Pub: Bureau of National Affairs. *W* (Current issues keep Labor Relations Manual up to date).

Labour Law Journal. Madras. v. 1. Ap. 1949*?

Lackawanna Bar. Scranton, Pa. 1 v. (9 nos.) Aug. 31–Oct. 26, 1878. *W*.

Lahore College Law Journal. Lahore. 26 v. 1921–June 1946. Title, v. 1–17: Law College Journal. Pub: University of the Punjab. *Q* (v. 26, 2 nos.)

Lahore Law Journal. Lahore. 12 v. 1919–30. *M* (v. 1, 1 no.)

Lahore Law Times. Lahore. 18 v. 1922–May 1939. Preliminary volume, (1921) not numbered. *M*.

Lancaster Bar. Lancaster, Pa. 15 v. June 5, 1869–Nov. 17, 1883. *W* (v. 15, 25 nos.)

Land Economics; a Quarterly Journal of Planning, Housing & Public Utilities. Madison, Wis. 28 v. Jan. 1925–Nov. 1952* Title, 1925–47: Journal of Land & Public Utility Economics. Pub: University of Wisconsin.

Latin-American Advisor: Legal, Commercial and Financial Information. New York. 1 v. (4 nos.) Ap.–July 1926. *M*.

Latin American Journal on Politics, Economics, and Law. Buenos Aires, Argentina. v. 1, no. 1. Jan.–Mar. 1950*.

Latin-American Official Gazettes Bulletin. New York. 1 v. 1932. Loose-leaf index containing sheets supplied weekly. Ceased at end of 6 months. Pub: W. L. Finn. *W*.

Law. Chicago. 2 v. (14 nos.) Sept. 1889–Oct. 1890. *M* (v. 1, nos. 1–12, v. 2, nos. 13–14).

Law. London. 2 v. Nov. 1874–July 1875. *M* (v. 1, 6 nos.; v. 2, 3 nos.)

Law. (St. Louis). *See* Law and Commerce.

Law, a Magazine Devoted to Legal Lore. Oklahoma City. 1 v. (2 nos.) June–Sept. 1901.

Law Advertiser. London. 9 v. Mar. 13, 1823–Dec. 29, 1831. Issued as supp. to Law Journal. *W*.

Law Amendment Journal. London. 3 v. 1855–58. Pub: Law Amendment Society. *W* (v. 2, 30 nos.)

Law and Commerce. St. Louis and New York. 7 v. Sept. 15, 1905–1909. Title, 1905–07: Law. *W*.

Law and Commercial Daily Remembrancer. (England). 1833.

Law and Contemporary Problems. Durham, N. C. 18 v. Dec. 1933–Dec. 1953* Pub: School of Law, Duke University. *Q*.

Law and Labor. New York. 14 v. Jan. 1919–May 1932. Pub: League for Industrial Rights. *M*. (v. 1–13), *Bi-M.* (v. 14; v. 14, 3 nos.)

Law and Land. London. 2 nos. Feb.–Mar. 1903.

Law and Social Action. New York. 5 v. Jan. 1946–June 1950* Pub: Commission on Law and Social Action, American Jewish Congress. *Irreg.* (v. 5, 3 nos.)

Law Book Adviser; a Journal of Legal Bibliography. Washington, D. C. 11 nos. Feb. 1893–Oct. 1897. Pub: John Byrne.

Law Book Broker. *See* Lawyers' Review.

Law Book Bulletin. Boston. 68 nos. 1878–Nov. 1925. Title varies: no. 1–8, May 1878–Oct. 1881, Quillets of the Law; no. 9–32, Mar. 1882–Dec. 1901, Little, Brown & Company's Law Book Bulletin. *Irreg.*

Law Book News. Philadelphia. 4 nos. Oct. 1888–Nov. 1890.

Law Book News. St. Paul, Minn. 2 v. Jan. 1894–Dec. 1895. *M.*

Law Book Record. Cincinnati. 3 nos. Jan.–Dec. 1890.

Law Book Review Digest and Current Legal Bibliography. Philadelphia. 1 v. (4 nos.) Oct. 1931–Jan. 1932. *M* (except Aug.–Sept.)

Law Budget. London. 8 nos. 1894.

Law Budget. London. 1 v. 1903.

Law Bulletin. San Francisco. 1870–71. *Q.*

Law Bulletin. Washington, D. C. 43 nos. Nov. 10, 1928–Oct. 12, 1937. Supersedes Washington Service Bulletin. Superseded by N. A. M. Law Digest. Pub: National Assn. of Manufacturers. Law Dept.

Law Bulletin and Brief. London. 4 v. 1903–06.

Law Bulletin of the State University of Iowa. Iowa City. 42 nos. Oct. 1891–Dec. 1901. Superseded by Iowa Law Bulletin which merged into Iowa Law Review. *Bi-M.*

Law Central. Washington, D. C. 3 nos. Aug.–Oct. 1881. *M.*

Law Chronicle (Edinburgh). *See* Law Chronicle or Journal of Jurisprudence.

Law Chronicle. London. 63 nos. Oct. 1811–Dec. 1812.

Law Chronicle. London. 5 v. June 1854–Dec. 1858. Continues Law Students' Magazine. Continued by Law Chronicle and Law Students' Magazine. *M.*

Law Chronicle. Transvaal, Union of South Africa. 1908–1909.

Law Chronicle, a Legal Newspaper. Sydney. 7 v. 1892–99. Continues Articled Clerks' Journal.

Law Chronicle and Auction Register. London. 25 v. June 17, 1813–1837. Title varies: v. 1–3, no. 146: Auction Register and Law Chronicle; v. 3, no. 147–v. 8, no. 448: Law Chronicle and Estate Advertiser; v. 8, no. 449–v. 20: Law Chronicle, Commercial and Bankruptcy Register. *W.*

Law Chronicle and Students' Magazine. London. 2 v. 1859–60. Continues Law Chronicle, 1854–58. Continued by Law Students' Examination Chronicle.

Law Chronicle or Journal of Jurisprudence. Edinburgh. 5 v. Ap. 29, 1829–1833. Title, v. 1, nos. 1–4: Scots Law Chronicle. Deas and Anderson's Reports were issued with this periodical. Contains Reports of Appeals from Scottish Courts. *M.*

Law Clerk and Municipal Assistant. London. 7 v. March, 1906–Jan. 1913. *M* (v. 6, 3 nos.; v. 7, 9 nos.)

Law Clerk Record. London. 5 nos. 1910–11.

Law Clerks' Magazine. *See* Weekly Law Magazine and Law Clerks' Magazine.

Law Coach. London. 6 v. June 1920–Sept. 1928. Suspended Nov. 1924–Oct. 1926. *M* (*Irreg.*)

Law College Journal. *See* Lahore Law College Journal.

Law College Magazine. Bombay. 21 v. Feb. 1930–Mar. 1952* Pub: Government Law College. 2 nos. a year. (v. 5, no. 2 not pub.)

Law College Magazine. Poona City, India. 14 v. Jan. 1939–1953* *Irreg.*

Law Department Bulletin, Union Pacific Railroad. *See* Union Pacific Railroad Law Dept. Bulletin.

Law Digest and Recorder. Madras. 6 v. 1896–1901. New Series v. 1, 1902, published at Madura.

Law Examination Journal and Law Student's Magazine. London. 4 v. 1869–85.

Law Examination Reporter. London. 2 v. (15 nos.) 1866–69.

Law Gazette. London. 1146 nos. Aug. 15, 1822–Dec. 23, 1847.

Law Gazette. London. 8 v. May 22, 1890–Ap. 14, 1894. *W.*

Law Gazette. Brisbane, Queensland. 2 v. Oct. 1930–Sept. 1932. Pub: Queensland Law Students Assn.

Law Gazette. San Francisco. 1867. *W* (No more information available).

Law Institute Journal. Melbourne. 26 v. July 1, 1927–Dec. 1952* Pub: Law Institute of Victoria and Queensland Law Society, Inc. *M* (v. 1, 6 nos.)

Law Intelligencer. London. 4 nos. Jan. 7–28, 1843.

Law Intelligencer (U. S.). *See* United States Law Intelligencer and Review.

Law Journal. London. 102 v. Jan. 1866–Dec. 26, 1952* Title varies. In conjunction with this are issued Law Journal Reports. *W*.

Law Journal, Irish Supplement. 4 v. (195 pts.) May 9, 1931–Dec. 29, 1934.

Law Journal (Morgan and Williams). London. 2 v. Mar. 1, 1803–Jan. 1, 1804. Vol. 1 of Law Journal (Smith) was begun as v. 3 of Morgan and Williams. *M*.

Law Journal (Smith). London. 3 v. 1804–06. Vol. 1 was begun as v. 3 of Law Journal (Morgan and Williams) v. 3, 3 pts.

Law Journal. Valletta, Malta. 3 v. Oct. 1944–Feb. 1952* Pub: University Students Law Society, Royal University of Malta. *Irreg*.

Law Journal of the Student Bar Association of Ohio State University. *See* Ohio State Law Journal.

Law Librarian. San Francisco. 3 v. Nov. 1887–Nov. 1890. Vol. 1, Nov. 1887–Nov. 1888; Ser. 2, v. 1–2, Feb. 1889–Nov. 1890. *Q*.

Law Library. Milwaukee. v. 1, no. 1. 1892.

Law Library. London. 10 nos. Jan. 1892–Mar. 1893.

Law Library Bulletin, Duke University. Durham, N. C. 1 v. Oct. 1930–June 1931. Issued in 2 series: n. s. v. 1, no. 1–5, 7–10, Oct. 1930–June 1931 (omits no. 6); Accessions series, no. 1–7, Nov. 1930–May 1931. Continued by Law School Bulletin, Duke University. *M* during college year.

Law Library Bulletin, University of Southern California. Los Angeles . 3 v. Feb. 1930–Mar. 1934. *M* (*Irreg.*)

Law Library Bulletin, University of Washington. Seattle. 11 v. Nov. 1, 1930–Jan. 1942. Title, v. 1, Bulletin of Principal Accessions, University of Washington Law Library. *Q* (v. 1–3 *M*, *Irreg.*; v. 11, 2 nos.)

Law Library Journal. New York. 45 v. 1908–Nov. 1952* Pub: American Assn. of Law Libraries. For a complete check list of numbers isued, see Law Library Journal, v. 31, p. 72–76, Mar. 1938. Beginning Sept. 1937, Law Library News combined with the Journal. *Q* (*Irreg*; 5 times a year v. 30–39).

Law Library News. Minneapolis. 10 v. Nov. 1927–June 1937. Combined with Law Library Journal, Sept. 1937. Vol. 1–5 mimeo. and pub. in Rochester, N. Y. *M* (*Irreg.*; v. 10, 8 nos.)

Law Library Reporter. Washington, D. C. Jan. 15–Dec. 15, 1941*? Ed. by Libraries of U. S. Dept. of the Interior. *Fortn*.

Law Magazine and Review. London. 131 v. June 1828–Aug. 1915. Vol. 1–31, June 1828–May 1844; v. 32–55 (n.s.v. 1–24) Dec. 1844–Feb. 1856; 3d ser. v. 1–32, May 1856–Nov. 1871; New 4th ser., v. 1–4, Feb. 1872–Aug. 1875; 5th ser., v. 1–40, Nov. 1875–Aug. 1915 (v. 1–23 called 4th ser. v. 1–23). Absorbed Law Review, May 1856. Title varies. *Q* (*M* Feb. 1872–Aug. 1875).

Law News. St. Louis, Mo. 2 v. 1872–73. *W* (v. 1), *M* (v. 2).

Law Notes. Cleveland, Ohio. 1 no. Mar. 1940. Pub: Western Reserve Law School. Continued as Western Reserve Law Notes.

Law Notes. London. 71 v. Jan. 1882–Dec. 1952* Title, v. 1 and some nos. of v. 2–3: Gibson's Law Notes. *M*.

Law Notes. Northport, N. Y. 50 v. April 1897–Feb. 1946. Combined with Lawyer to form Lawyer and Law Notes. *Q* (*M* Ap. 1897–Mar. 1932).

Law Notes' Yearbook. London. 9 v. 1921–32. None pub. 1926–28.

Law Observer. India. 1 v. 1872.

Law Quarterly Review. London. 69 v. (228 nos.) Jan. 1885–Oct. 1953* *Q*.

Law Record. India. 2 v. 1911–12.

Law Recorder. Dublin. 10 v. 1827–1838. Title, some nos. of v. 1: Irish Law Recorder. 1st ser., 4 v., 1827–31; 2d ser. 6 v., 1833–38. Continued as Irish Equity Reports and Irish Law Reports.

Law Register. Chicago. 29 v. 1880–1909. Title, v. 1–17: Legal Adviser. *W* (*M* 1909).

Law Reporter. (Boston). *See* Monthly Law Reporter.

Law Reporter (England). 2 v. 1821–22.

Law Reporter: Journal de Jurisprudence. Montreal. 1 v. Jan.–Oct. 1854. *M*.

Law Review. Albany. v. 1, no. 1, July 1866.

Law Review and Quarterly Journal of British and Foreign Jurisprudence. London. 23 v. Nov. 1844–Feb. 1856. Merged into Law Magazine and Review.

Law Review of the Law Department of the University of Detroit. *See* University of Detroit Bimonthly Law Review.

Law School Bulletin, Duke University. Durham, N. C. 10 v. Sept. 1931–June 1941* *Irreg.* Mimeo.

Law School News. Minneapolis. 6 v. Ap. 1948–Ap. 1953* Pub: West Pub. Co. A single mimeographed sheet containing news about U. S. Law Schools. *Irreg.*

Law Society Journal. Boston. 13 v. May 1929–Feb. 1949. Title, v. 1, no. 1: Law Society of Massachusetts Journal. Dec. 1949 issue called "The Massachusetts Law Society Journal, 20th Anniversary Edition," vol. 20. *Q.*

Law Society's Gazette. London. 49 v. 1903–Dec. 1952* Pub: Incorporated Law Society of the United Kingdom. *M.*

Law Society's Gazette. Regina, Saskatchewan. 3 v. June 1929–Dec. 1935. Contains Proceedings of the Law Society. Beginning v. 3, no. 6, included in Saskatchewan Bar Review. *Q* (v. 3, 5 nos.)

Law Student. Brooklyn, N. Y. 20 v. Oct. 1923–May 1943. Pub: American Law Book Co. *Q* (*Irreg.*; v. 20, 3 nos.)

Law Student. London. 3 v. Jan. 1947–Mar. 1949. Pub: Law Students' Tutorial College. *M* (v. 3, 3 nos.)

Law Student: a Journal Serving the Interests of the Law Students of America. Chicago. v. 1, no. 1. March 1898?

Law Student Monthly. New York. 1 no. Ap. 1920. Pub: Students of Columbia Law School.

Law Students' Debating Society's Journal. London. 4 nos. 1865–66.

Law Student's Examination Chronicle. London. 8 v. 1861–68. Supersedes Law Chronicle and Law Students' Magazine. *M.*

Law Student's Helper. Detroit. 23 v. Jan. 1893–Dec. 1915. Merged into American Legal News. *M.*

Law Students' Journal. London. 39 v. Jan. 1879–Dec. 1917. Absorbed Jurist. *M.*

Law Students' Journal (Lucknow). India.

Law Students' Magazine. London. 12 v. Aug. 1844–June 1854. O. S. 6 v., Aug. 1844–Dec. 1848; N. S. 6 v., Jan. 1849–June 1854. v. 1–3 (N. S.) each in 5 parts, also issued with altered title-page as "Legal Practitioner, N. S." Superseded by Law Chronicle. *M.*

Law Students' Monthly. Philadelphia. 1 v. Oct. 1889–1890.

Law Students' Review. London. 1 v. 1886.

Law: the Lawyers Magazine. New York. v. 1, no. 1. Ap. 1932? *M.*

Law Times. London. 214 v. Ap. 1843–Dec. 26, 1952* Title varies. In conjunction with this are issued Law Times Reports. *W.*

Law Times. Scranton, Pa. 13 v. Oct. 31, 1873–Feb. 20, 1885. Title, Oct. 1873–Nov. 20, 1874: Scranton Law Times; v. 5–6, 1877–78 have caption title: Luzerne Law Times. O. S. 6 v. (v. 6, 34 nos,), Oct. 31, 1873–Dec. 1878; N. S. 7 v. (v. 7, 8 nos.) Jan. 3, 1879–Feb. 20, 1885. *W.*

Law Times Legal Circular. *See* Legal Circular

Law Weekly. Mylapore, Madras. 65 v. 1914–Dec. 27, 1952*.

Laws of India. 1 v. 1926.

Lawyer. Ahmedabad, Bombay. 21 v. 1899–1920. *M.*

Lawyer. Brooklyn, N. Y. 9 v. Sept. 1937–June 1946. Title, v. 1, no. 1–2: American Lawyer. Pub: American Law Book Co. Combined with Law Notes to form Lawyer and Law Notes. *Q* (v. 3, 3 nos.)

Lawyer. London. 1 no. Jan. 26, 1833.

Lawyer. London. 7 nos. Nov. 1–Dec. 14, 1900.

Lawyer (Madras). No information available.

Lawyer (in Tamil). India. 1911.

Lawyer and Banker, and Central Law Journal. New Orleans, La. 27 v. Jan. 1909–
Feb. 1934. Title varies: Jan. 1909–Oct. 1913, Lawyer and Banker and Bench and Bar
Review; Nov. 1913–Dec. 1926, Lawyer and Banker and Southern Bench and Bar
Review. Absorbed Central Law Journal, 1927. *Bi-M* (v. 1, *Q;* v. 27, 1 no.)

Lawyer and Credit Man. New York. 10 v. 1892–Sept. 1899. United with Mercantile Adjuster, Nov. 1899. *M* (v. 10, 3 nos.)

Lawyer and Magistrate. London. 6 nos. Dec. 1898–June 1899.

Lawyer and Law Notes. Brooklyn, N. Y. 5 v. Oct. 1946–Winter 1951/52* Continues
Law Notes and Lawyer. Pub: American Law Book Co. and Edward Thompson Co.
3 issues a year.

Lawyer, or Jurisprudential Record. London. 6 nos. May–Nov. 1948. *M.*

Lawyers and Bankers Quarterly of St. Louis. 25 v. 1903–1928*? Title, v. 1–24:
Flugel's List.

Lawyer's and Magistrate's Magazine. Dublin. 6 v. 1790–94. Subtitle: In Which is
Included an Account of Every Important Proceeding in the Courts of Westminster
. . . with the Decisions of the Judges. Binder's title: Lawyer's Magazine.

Lawyers Association of Kansas City, News and Announcements. Kansas City, Mo.
2 v. Dec. 7, 1939–May 9, 1941*? *M (Irreg.)*

Lawyers Association of St. Louis. Official Publication. Continues Bench and Bar:
Official Publication of Lawyers' Association of Eighth Judicial Circuit of Missouri.
No information available.

Lawyers' Club Docket. Los Angeles. 3 v. Jan. 1937–Mar. 1939. *Irreg.* (v. 1, 4 nos.;
v. 2–3, 1 no each).

Lawyers Guild Monthly. Chicago. N. S. 7 v. Ap. 1944–1950* Pub: Chicago Chapter
of National Lawyers Guild. vol. 5, no. 1–2 and vol. 6, never pub., instead there
appeared Chicago Guild Review, v. 1, no. 1, Feb. 1949.

Lawyers' Guild Review. Washington & New York. 12 v. Oct. 1940–Fall 1952*
Succeeds National Lawyers' Guild Quarterly. *Q.*

Lawyers' Journal. Manila, P. I. 18 v. Jan. 1933–Dec. 1953* Pub: Lawyers' League
of Philippine Islands. Title, v. 1–3, Lawyers' League Journal. Beginning v. 4, pub:
Vicente J. Francisco. *Fortn* (v. 1–3, *M*).

Lawyers' League Journal. *See* Lawyers' Journal.

Lawyer's Magazine. Dublin. 3 v. 1792–94.

Lawyers' Magazine. London. 2 v. 1761–62. Vol. 1, 4 terms; v. 2, Hilary and Easter
terms.

Lawyers' Magazine or General Repository of Practical Law. London. 3 v. 1773–
76. For full bibliographical information see 27 Law Library Journal p. 45, Ap. 1934.

Lawyers' Monthly. New York. v. 1, no. 1. Jan. 1913.

Lawyers News. New York. 2 v. Mar.–Oct. 1934. v. 1, 5 nos.; v. 2, 2 nos. Vol. 1,
Mar.–Aug. 1934 as Lawyers' News Monthly.

Lawyers News Monthly. *See* Lawyers News.

Lawyers' Post. London. 14 nos. c.1716. Subtitle: An Express to the Practitioners and
Clients as well as to the Students and Professors of Law, Equity and good conscience
both in and out of the Third University of England. The 14 numbers are entirely
concerned with the history and bibliography of legal books.

Lawyers' Review. Seattle. 3 v. June 1915–June 1921. Title, v. 1, no. 1–4: Law Book
Broker. Pub. suspended June–Sept. 1916, Jan. 1917–Aug. 1919. *Irreg.*

Lawyers' Scrap Book. New York. 2 v. 1909–12. *M.*

Legal Advertiser. London. 68 nos. Oct. 1881–Dec. 1887. Title, no. 22–50: Monthly
Legal Advertiser (contains advertisements only). From Jan. 1883 to Dec. 1884 there
were issued monthly supps. containing points of practice, etc. *M.*

Legal Adviser. Chicago, 1880–1909. *See* Law Register.

Legal Adviser. Chicago. 61 v. 1861–1920.

Legal Adviser. Denver. 6 v. Aug. 1897–1902. *W (M,* v. 1–2; v. 6, 10 nos.)

Legal Adviser. India. 1910. Possibly never published.

Legal Advisor. Denver. 2 v. 1888–89.

Legal Aid Brief Case. Rochester, N. Y. 11 v. Nov. 1942–June 1953* Title varies:
Brief Case; N. A. L. A. O. Brief Case. Pub: National Legal Aid Assn. 5 times a year.

Legal Aid News Letter. Rochester, N. Y. 15 v. 1927?–Nov. 1941*? Pub: National Assn. of Legal Aid Organizations. *Irreg.*

Legal Aid Review. New York. 50 v. Ap. 1903–Oct. 1952* Pub: Legal Aid Society. *Q.*

Legal and Insurance Reporter. Philadelphia. 40 v. Dec. 31, 1859–1899. Original title: Insurance Reporter. *Semi-M.*

Legal Bibliography. Boston. 5 v. Nov. 1881–Mar. 1913. O. S. 12 nos. Nov. 1881–Jan. 1890; N. S. (1) 15 nos. and supp. to no. 15, Nov. 1894–Jan. 1903; v. 2, 15 nos. and supp. to nos. 4, 8, 12, Ap. 1903–Oct. 1906; v. 3, 12 nos. and supp. to nos. 5, 9, Jan. 1907–Oct. 1909; v. 4, 12 nos. Jan. 1910–Mar. 1913. *Q.*

Legal Bibliography. Boston. 5 nos. Mar–June 1923, Jan. 1924. Pub: Chipman Law Pub.Co.

Legal Bulletin, American Life Convention. *See* American Life Convention. Legal Bureau. Legal Bulletin.

Legal Center News. Dallas, Tex. v. 1–3 # 1. Mar. 1, 1948–Mar. 1953* Title, vol. 1–v. 2 # 4: Southwestern Legal Center. Pub: Southwestern Legal Foundation, Southern Methodist University School of Law.

Legal Chatter. Baltimore. 2 v. July 1937–June 1939. *M (Irreg.* v. 2, 10 nos.)

Legal Chronicle. London. 12 nos. Jan. 20–Ap. 6, 1844. *W.*

Legal Circular. London. 3 v. 1855–57. Individual nos. have title: Law Times Legal Circular. *W.*

Legal Companion. Konnagar, India. 1873.

Legal Companion. Serampore, Calcutta. 16 v.

Legal Companion. Vizagapatam, India. 11 nos. Feb.–Nov. 1933.

Legal Counselor. Chicago. 2 v. Sept. 1897–Ap. 1898. v. 2, 4 nos.

Legal Digest and Journal. New South Wales. 1 part. Nov. 1899.

Legal Examiner. London. 3 v. Nov. 5, 1831–1833. Continued by Legal Examiner and Law Chronicle. *W.*

Legal Examiner. London. 35 nos. 1862–68.

Legal Examiner. New York. 1 v. 1850.

Legal Examiner and Law Chronicle. London. 5 v. Mar. 13, 1833–1835. Supersedes Legal Examiner (1831–33). Superseded by Westminster Hall Chronicle and Legal Examiner. *W.*

Legal Examiner and Medical Jurist. London. 2 v. Jan. 10, 1852–1853. Title, v. 1: Legal Examiner, Weekly Reporter, and Journal of Medical Jurisprudence.

Legal Gazette. Huntington, Tenn. v. 1, no. 1. Jan./Feb. 1900.

Legal Gazette. Philadelphia. 8 v. July 1869–May 1876. *W* (v. 8, 21 nos.)

Legal Guide. London. 9 v. Nov. 1838–1843. *W.* (v. 9, 12 nos.)

Legal Information Bulletin. Washington, D. C. 7 v. Jan. 1924–Aug. 1932. Pub: American Foundation of Labor, Legal Information Bureau, no. 1–11 (v. 1) as the Bureau's Bulletin. *Irreg.*

Legal Information Quarterly. Howell, Mich. 3 v. Ap. 1900–Oct. 1902. vol. 3, 3 nos.

Legal Inquirer. London. 14 nos. 1869–72. *Q.*

Legal Intelligencer. Philadelphia. 128 v. 1843–June 30, 1953* Title, v. 1–3: Philadelphia Legal Intelligencer. *D.* (except Sat. & Sun.)

Legal Journal. New South Wales. 4 v. May 1924–July 1924.

Legal Literature. London. 22 nos. 1899–1911.

Legal Miscellany and Review. India, 12 nos. 1915–16.

Legal Monthly Digest. Melbourne, Australia. 6 v. July 1947–Dec. 1952*.

Legal News. Montreal. 20 v. Jan. 5, 1878–Dec. 15, 1897. *W* (1878–91); *Semi-M* (1892–97).

Legal News. Sunbury. Pa. 1 v. (69 nos.) Aug. 25, 1888–Dec. 14, 1889. Vol. 1, no. 1 as Northumberland County Legal News; v. 1, no. 2–11 without title, dates or numbering; no. 67–69 undated. *W.*

Legal News, the Toledo Legal News, and the Ohio Legal News. *See* Ohio Legal News.

Legal Notes on Local Government. New York. 6 v. Mar. 1936–July 1941. Pub: Section of Municipal Law, American Bar Assn.; ed. by Legal Research Bureau, New York University School of Law. Continued by American Municipal Law Review. For periodicity see American Municipal Law Review.

Legal Observer and Solicitors' Journal. London. 52 v. Nov. 6, 1830–Dec. 1856. Title varies: v. 1–32, Legal Observer, or Journal of Jurisprudence; v. 33–47, Legal Observer Digest, or Journal of Jurisprudence. Continued by Solicitors Journal. *W.*

Legal Observer, or Record of Jurisprudence. London. 2 v. Jan. 1831–Oct. 1832. Issued as supp. to Legal Observer and Solicitors' Journal. *M.*

Legal Opinion. Harrisburg, Pa. 5 v. Nov. 5, 1870–Oct. 11, 1873. *W.*

Legal Practice. New York. v. 1, no. 1. Jan./Feb. 1934. Ed. W. H. Crow.

Legal Practitioner and Solicitors' Journal. London. 4 v. Nov. 1846–1851. O. S. 1 v. Nov. 1846–Aug. 1847; N. S. 3 v. 1849–51. *See* Note to Law Students' Magazine.

Legal Record. Detroit. 16 v. Oct. 5, 1933–Sept. 1941* Pub: Michigan Legal Record Pub. Co. *W.*

Legal Recreations. London. 1 v. 1792–93.

Legal Recreations. San Francisco. 9 v. 1876–85. v. 5–9 unnumbered.

Legal Register. London. 134 nos. 1807–08. *W.*

Legal Remembrancer. Calcutta. 4 nos. June–Aug. 1864. *Bi-M* (no. 1–2); *W* (no. 3–4).

Legal Remembrancer, N.-W.-P. Mirzapur, Allahabad. 3 v. July 1879–Oct. 1882.

Legal Reporter. Dublin. 3 v. Nov. 1840–Ap. 1843. *W* (v. 3: 26 nos.)

Legal Review. London. 1 v. Nov. 1812–July 1813. 3 times a year.

Legal Reviews: Concerning Legal Decisions, State and Federal Legislation. New York. 5 nos. May 1941–Sept. 1941. *M.*

Legal Service Bulletin. New York. 2 nos. Ap. 20–June 25, 1926. Pub: American Bankers' Assn.

Legal Skill. Los Angeles. 2 v. 1915–17. Undated. v. 1, 4 nos.; v. 2, 2 nos.

Legal Tit-Bits. London. 1 no. June 1931.

Legal World. Parvatipuram, Madras. 2 v. Jan. 1, 1920–Jan. 1921.

Legal Year Book. London. 3 v. 1849–51.

Legislation of Poland. Warsaw. 3 v. 1949–June 1950* Sub-title (with variations) selection of the most important acts published in the Journal of Laws of the Republic of Poland, along with excerpts from motivations and shorthand reports. Absorbed Review of Polish Law, Dec. 1950. *Bi-A.*

Legislative Report. Washington, D. C. Feb. 1947–Aug. 1951* 1947, 4 nos. & 1 Supp.; 1950, 7 nos.; 1951, 10 nos.; Pub: Bureau of Labor Standards. Subtitle, A Current Summary on Labor Legislation.

Legislator. *See* State Government.

Legist. London. 6 nos. 1851.

Legist. New York. 1 v. Feb.–June 1941. News-letter of Law Library Assn. of Greater New York. Mimeo. *Irreg.*

Leguleian. London. 59 nos. 1851–65. Title, no. 1–22: Examinations of Articled Clerks. Issued in manuscript.

Leguleian. N. S. London. 1 v. Aug. 1850–Oct. 1851. *M.*

Lens. Boston. 41 v. 1923–Nov. 1952* Pub: Massachusetts Civic League. *Irreg.*

"Lex." the Lawyers' Magazine. Toronto. 3 v. Nov. 1949–1952* *Bi-M.*

Lex Mercatorium. London. 8 nos. 1866.

Lincoln Law Review. Buffalo. 6 v. Oct. 1927–Oct. 1932. Pub: Lincoln Club. *Q* (v. 6, 1 no.)

Little Brown & Company's Law Book Bulletin. *See* Law Book Bulletin.

Liverpool Law Students' Magazine. Liverpool. 6 v. 1908–13. Superseded by Woolsack.

Livingston's Monthly Law Magazine. New York. 4 v. Jan. 1853–Jan. 1856. Continues United States Monthly Law Magazine. *M* (v. 4, 1 no.)

Local Association Bulletin. Columbus, Ohio. 5 v. Aug. 4, 1948–May 9, 1953* Pub: Ohio State Bar Assn., Committee on Local Bar Assn. Activities. *Irreg.*

Local Courts' and Municipal Gazette. Toronto. 8v . Jan. 1865–Dec. 1872. Pre-

ceded by Upper Canada Law Journal and Local Courts' Gazette, which was divided
in 1865 into Local Courts' and Municipal Gazette, and Upper Canada Law Journal
(N. S.) *M.*

Local Government Chronicle and Magisterial Reporter. London. 97 v. 1855–
1952* Title, 1855–May 1872, Knight's Official Advertiser.

Local Government Review. London. 9 v. Nov. 1909–Mar. 1916. Merged into Municipal Engineering and the Sanitary Record. *M.*

London Quarterly of World Affairs. *See* World Affairs.

Los Angeles Bar Bulletin. Los Angeles. 26 v. Sept. 1925–Aug. 1951* Title varies:
v. 1–5, # 7: Bar Association Bulletin; v. 5 # 8–v. 13 # 7: Los Angeles Bar Association
Bulletin; v. 13 # 8–v: Bar Bulletin. *M.*(*Semi-M* v. 1, no. 1–v. 3).

Los Angeles Law Review. Los Angeles. 1 v. (2 nos.) Mar.–Ap. 1934. Ed. by C. F.
Cable. Mimeo.

Loss and Damage Review. Fowler, Ind. 20 v. May, 1917–July 1940. Suspended
1926–27. v. 20, 1 no.

Louisiana Bar, Official Publication of Louisiana State Bar Association. New
Orleans. 12 v. Jan. 1942–Oct. 1952* *Q.*

Louisiana Law Journal. New Orleans. 4 nos. May 1841–Ap. 1842. *Q.*

Louisiana Law Journal. New Orleans. 6 nos. 1875–76.

Louisiana Law Review. University, La. 13 v. Nov. 1938–May 1953* Pub: Louisiana
State University Law School. *Q.*

Louisiana Legal News. New Orleans. v. 2, no. 21. May 22, 1923?

Lower Canada Jurist. Montreal, Quebec, Canada. 35 v. 1848–91.

Lower Canada Law Journal. *See* Canada Law Journal.

Loyola Law Journal. New Orleans. 13 v. 1929–Ap. 1932. Pub: Loyola University
School of Law. *Q* (v. 13, 2 nos.)

Loyola Law Review. New Orleans. 6 v. May 1941–1952* Pub: School of Law,
Loyola University. Continues Loyola Law Journal. *A.*

Luzerne Law Journal. Scranton, Pa. 1 no. Nov. 17, 1871.

Luzerne Law Times. *See* Law Times (Scranton, Pa.)

Luzerne Legal Observer. Scranton, Pa. 4 v. Oct. 31, 1860–1864. *W.*

McGill Law Journal. Montreal. v. 1, no. 1. Autumn 1952* Pub: Law Undergraduate
Society, McGill University.

Madras Jurist. Madras. 11 v. 1866–76. Superseded by Indian Jurist. *M.*

Madras Law College Magazine. Madras, India. No more information available.

Madras Law Journal and Reports. Mylapore, Madras. 74 v. 1891–June 1938; 1939–
1941*? *M.* (Beginning 1939, 2 vols. a year).

Madras Law Reporter. Madras. 4 nos. 1876–77.

Madras Law Review. Madras. 5 nos. Nov. 1932–Mar. 1933. *M.*

Madras Law Times (1906-28). *See* Indian Law Times.

Madras Legal Companion. *See* Civil and Criminal Law Notes.

Madras Revenue Register. Madras. 11 v. 1867–76.

Madras Weekly Notes. Madras. 38 v. 1910–1938*?

Magazine Articles Dealing with Questions of War and Peace. *See* Selected List
of Recent Articles on International Affairs.

Magistrate. London. 3 nos. May–July 1825.

Magistrate; the Bulletin of the Magistrates' Association. London. 8 v. July 1922–
Dec. 1949* *Bi-M.* (*Irreg.* July 1922–Feb. 1929).

Magistrate. Sydney. 10 v. 1905–1914. Superseded by J. P. Contains notes of cases.
no t.-p. v. 10, 2 pts.

Magistrate and Constable. Lebanon, Pa. 8 nos. Mar. 21–May 9, 1895. *W.*

Magistrate and Municipal and Parochial Lawyer. London. 5 v. Sept. 1848–Mar.
1853. Preceded by New Magistrates' and Municipal Corporations' Cases. Superseded
by Handbook for Magistrates. *M* (v. 5: 69 pages).

Magistrate: Official organ of Justices' Association of Western Australia, Inc.
Perth, W. A. 38 v. 1916–Dec. 1952* numbering skips from vol. 14 no. 10 to vol. 16,
no. 11. *M.*

Magistrates National Magazine.   Camden, N. J. 4 v. Nov. 1923–July 1927? Vol. 4, 1 no.

Maine Law Review.   Bangor. 13 v. Ap. 1908–June 1920. Pub: University of Maine College of Law. Imprint varies. *M.* (during academic year).

Malabar Law Quarterly.   Ernakulam. 1 v. 1906–07. In 3 pts., each with separate pagination: (1) Journal; (2) Cochin Law Reports; (3) Travancore Law Reports.

Malayan Law Journal.   Singapore. 9 v. July 1932–Dec. 1940*? Vol. 2 contains Straits Settlements Law Reports. *M* (v. 1, 6 nos.)

Man of Business, or Every Man's Law Book.   Greensborough, N. C. 2 v. July 1833–Oct. 1835.

Manchester Law Students' Chronicle.   Manchester. 26 v. 1901–1935*?

Manchester Law Students' Journal.   Manchester, Eng. v. 1, no. 1. 1926.

Manitoba Bar News.   Winnipeg. 24 v. Oct. 1928–Dec. 1952* Pub: Manitoba Bar Association. *Bi-M.* (v. 1, 7 nos.; v. 2–13 *M.* (*Irreg.*))

Manitoba Law Journal.   Winnipeg. 2 v. 1884–85. *M.*

Maritime Notes and Queries.   London. 14 v. Mar. 1873–1900. *Q.* (*Irreg.*)

Marquette Law Review.   Milwaukee. 36 v. Dec. 1916–Spring 1953* Pub: Students of Marquette University School of Law. *Q.*

Maryland Law Journal and Real Estate Record.   Baltimore. 19 v. Aug. 31, 1878–Mar. 27, 1889. Title, v. 1–17: Maryland Law Record. *W* (v. 19, 13 nos.)

Maryland Law Record.   *See* Maryland Law Journal and Real Estate Record.

Maryland Law Reporter.   Baltimore. 1 v. 1872.

Maryland Law Review.   Baltimore. 2 v. Dec. 1901–June 1903. Pub: Baltimore Law School. *M.*

Maryland Law Review.   Baltimore. v. 1–13, no. 1–2. Dec. 1936–Spring 1953* Pub: Maryland Law Review, Inc., in cooperation with Maryland State Bar Assn., Bar Assn. of Baltimore City, Junior Bar Assn. of Baltimore City, University of Maryland School of Law. None pub. during 1952 (Fall 1951–Winter 1953) *Q.*

Massachusetts Law Quarterly.   Boston. 37 v. Nov. 1915–Dec. 1952* Pub: Massachusetts Bar Association. For a complete check list of numbers issued see Law Library Journal, v. 31, p. 158–161, July 1938. *Q.* (*Irreg.*)

Massachusetts Law Reporter.   Boston. 7 v. 1877–84. Merged into Banker and Tradesman.

Medico-Legal and Criminological Review.   *See* Medico-Legal Journal.

Medico-Legal Bulletin.   Fort Wayne, Ind. 5 v. 1903–09.

Medico-Legal Journal.   (Incorporating the Transactions of the Medico-Legal Society). London. 20 v. Jan. 1933–1952* Title, 1933–46, Medico-Legal and Criminological Review. *Q.*

Medico-Legal Journal.   New York. 50 v. June 1883–June 1933. Pub: Medico-Legal

Medico-Legal Society.   Transactions. London, Cambridge. 26 v. Nov. 3, 1902–1931/32. Continued by Medico-Legal and Criminological Review, later Medico-Legal Journal. *A.* (except 1902/04 and 1915/17).

Memorandum (Law Dept., Southern Railway Co.).   Washington, D. C. 3 v. Sept. 1915–July 1918. *M.*

Memphis Law Journal.   Memphis. 2 v. 1878–79. Merged into Southern Law Journal. *M.* (v. 1 *Q.* and *M.*)

Mercantile Adjuster and the Lawyer and Credit Man.   New York. May 1886–1903. Absorbed Lawyer and Credit Man, Nov. 1899. *M.*

Mercantile Law Journal.   New York. 5 nos. 1884.

Mercantile Law Journal.   Madras. 2 v. Jan. 8, 1911–Dec. 1913. *W.* (v. 1); *M.* (v. 2.)

Mercer Beasley Law Review.   Newark, N. J. 5 v. Jan. 1932–Jan. 1936. Merged with New Jersey Law Review to form University of Newark Law Review. *Semi-A.* (v. 5, 1 no.)

Mercer Law Review.   Macon, Ga. 4 v. Fall 1949–Spring 1953* Pub: Walter F. George School of Law, Mercer University. *Semi-A.*

Metropolitan Police College Journal.   London. 5 v. 1935–Mar. 1939.

Meyers' Minutes. New York. 4 v. Aug. 1930–May 1934. *M.* (v. 4, 10 nos.).

Miami Law Quarterly. Coral Gables, Fla. 7 v. Mar. 1947–June 1953* Pub: School of Law, University of Miami; Dade County Bar Assn.

Miami Lawyer. Miami, Fla. 5 v. Nov. 1948–June 1952* Title, Nov. 1948–June 1949, and cover-title Nov. 1948 to date, University of Miami Lawyer. *A.*

Michigan Law Journal. Detroit. 7 v. Feb. 1892–Dec. 1898. Vols. 1–3 contain Proceedings of Michigan State Bar Assn., 1892–94. *M.*

Michigan Law Review. Ann Arbor. 51 v. June 1902–June 1953* Pub: University of Michigan Law School. *M.* (Nov.–June).

Michigan Lawyer. Detroit. 4 v. Oct. 1875–June 1879. *Q.*

Michigan Legal News. Detroit. 1 no. 1886.

Michigan State Bar Journal. Lansing. 31 v. Nov. 1921–Dec. 1952* Vol. 15, 1935–36 issued as Michigan Section, a supp. to Michigan Law Review. Ed. under direction of State Bar Assn. of Michigan. *M.* (*Irreg.*)

Middle Eastern Affairs. New York. 3 v. Jan. 1950–Dec. 1952* Pub: Council for Middle Eastern Affairs. *M.*

Militia Reporter. Boston. 1 v. 1810. Contains reports of four trials.

Milwaukee Bar Association Gavel. Milwaukee, Wis. 14 v. Jan. 1938–June 1953* Title, v. 1, no. 1: The Gavel. *Irreg.* (v. 1–2, 3 nos. each; v. 3, 7 nos.)

Minnesota Law Journal. St. Paul. 5 v. May 1893–Dec. 1897. Superseded by Minnesota District Court Reporter (1 no. only, Jan. 1898). *M.*

Minnesota Law Review. Minneapolis. 37 v. Jan. 1917–June 1953* Pub: University of Minnesota Law School. In 1922 became Official publication of Minnesota Bar Assn., Proceedings of which are issued as suppl. number of the Review. *M.* (Dec.–June).

Mississippi Law Journal. University. 23 v. July 1928–Oct. 1952* Pub: University of Mississippi Law School and Mississippi State Bar Assn. *Q.* (*Irreg.*)

Mississippi Law Review. University. 5 nos. Nov. 1922–Ap. 1923. Pub: Blackstone Law Club of University of Mississippi. *M.* (Nov.–June).

Missouri Bar. Jefferson City. 15 nos. 1879. *W.*

Missouri Bar Journal. Kansas City, Mo. 15 v. Jan. 1930–Oct. 1944. Superseded by Journal of the Missouri Bar. Official pub. of Missouri Bar Assn. *M.* (*Irreg.*)

Missouri Law Review. Columbia, Mo. 17 v. Jan. 1936–Nov. 1952* Pub: School of Law, University of Missouri. Supersedes University of Missouri Bulletin, Law Series. *Q.*

Missouri. Lawyers' Association of the Eighth Judicial Circuit. *See* Bench and Bar.

Mitchell's Maritime Register. London. 28 v. 1856–83.

Modern Law List and Weekly Gazette of Politics and Literature, with a picture of the English Bar. v. 1, nos. 1 and 2. Jan. 19 and 26, 1828. 32 pages.

Modern Law Review. London. 15 v. June 1937–Oct. 1952* *Q.*

Montana Law Review. Missoula. 14 v. Spring, 1940–Spring, 1953* Pub: Law School Assn. of Montana State University. *A.* (v. 2 not numbered).

Monthly Criminal Law Journal. Patna City. 5 v. 1905–10.

Monthly Digest of Tax Articles. Albany. 2 v. Oct. 1950–Sept. 1952* *M.*

Monthly Journal of Law. Washington, D. C. 7 nos. Jan.–May 1881.

Monthly Jurist. *See* Weekly Jurist.

Monthly Law Digest and Reporter. Quebec, Canada. 1 v. 1892–93.

Monthly Law Journal. Washington, D. C. 1 v. 1881.

Monthly Law Magazine. London. 10 v. Feb. 1838–May 1841. Title, Feb. 1838–May 1840, Monthly Law Magazine and Political Review. Imprint varies.

Monthly Law Magazine. New York. 3 v. 1853–55.

Monthly Law Magazine. Reuben Vose's New Lawyer. New York. v. 1, no. 1, 1858.

Monthly Law Reporter. Boston. 27 v. Mar. 10, 1838–May 1866. Vols. 11–20 also called New Series v. 1–10. Title, v. 1–10, Mar. 1838.–Ap. 1848: Law Reporter. vol. 27, 7 nos.

Monthly Law Review of the Law Department of the University of Detroit. *See* University of Detroit Bi-monthly Law Review.

Monthly Legal Advertiser. *See* Legal Advertiser.

Monthly Legal Examiner. New York. 2 nos. May–June 1850.

Monthly Summary of the International Labour Organization. London. 12 v. Jan. 1927–Dec. 1938. Pub. on the responsibility of International Labour Organization, Geneva. Superseded by I.L.O. Month by Month, Jan. 1939.

Monthly Western Jurist. *See* Weekly Jurist.

Montreal Legal News. Montreal. 20 v. 1878–97.

Moot Court Bulletin. Urbana, Ill. 20 v. Oct. 1902–Jan. 25, 1926. Pub: University of Illinois College of Law. *Bi-W.* (during 2d semester of college year; vol. 20, 7 nos.)

Motion Picture Law Review. West Los Angeles, Calif. 4 v. June 1938–Oct. 1941. Pub: Dennis Hartman. *M.* (*Irreg.*; v. 4, 5 nos.)

Municipal Corporations Circular. London. 51 v. 1878–1929. Continued as Municipal Review.

Municipal Court Review. v. 1, no. 1. Jan. 1904?

Municipal Law Journal. Washington, D. C. 17 v. Jan. 1936–Dec. 1952* Pub: Institute of Municipal Law Officers. *M.* (v. 1, 10 nos.)

Municipal Law Service Letter, news and comments on local government law. Chicago. v. 1, no. 1. Jan. 1951*? Pub: Section of Municipal Law, American Bar Assn.

Municipal Law Survey. Chicago. 6 nos. Mar.–Oct. 1942. Supplementing American Municipal Law Review. Loose-leaf monthly review of case law, legislation, administrative regulations and legal literature.

Municipal Legislative Bulletin. *See* Municipal Ordinance Review.

Municipal Ordinance Review. Washington, D. C. 6 v. July 1948–Ap. 1953* Pub: National Institute of Municipal Law Officers. Title, v. 1–5: Municipal Legislative Bulletin. *M.*

Municipal Review. London. 23 v. 1930–1952* *M.*

Municipal Review of Canada. Montreal, etc. 47 v. 1905–June 1951.

Mysore Law Journal. Bangalore City. 19 v. 1923–1941*? Contains reports.

NACCA Law Journal. Boston. 10 v. May 1948–Nov. 1952* Pub: National Assn. of Claimants Compensation Attorneys. *Semi-A.*

N. A. L. A. O. Brief Case. *See* Legal Aid Brief Case.

N. A. M. Law Digest; analysis of laws, legislation and decisions. New York. 14 v. Nov. 1937–Sept. 1952* Supersedes National Association of Manufacturers Law Bulletin (Law Dept.) *Q.* (*M.* Sept. to June, to Jan. 1941).

Nagpur Law Journal. Nagpur. 29 v. 1918–1946*? Title, v. 1 # 1: Nagpur University of Law Magazine. Beginning v. 18, 1935, volumes not numbered.

Nagpur Law Notes. Central Provinces, India. 14 nos. 1938–39.

Nagpur University College of Law Magazine. *See* University College of Law Journal.

Nassau County Bar Association Bulletin. *See* Bar Association of Nassau County. Bulletin.

Natal Law Journal. Durban. 3 v. 1905–07. United with Natal Law Quarterly to form Natal Law Magazine.

Natal Law Magazine. Durban. 2 v. 1908–09. Pub: Incorporated Law Society of Natal. Formed by union of Natal Law Quarterly and Natal Law Journal.

Natal Law Quarterly. Durban. 6 v. Mar. 1902–Dec. 1907. v. 3 never pub. United with Natal Law Journal to form Natal Law Magazine.

National Association of Manufacturers' Law Bulletin. *See* Law Bulletin.

National Association of Referees in Bankruptcy. Journal. Winona, Minn. 26 v. Dec. 1926–Oct. 1952* Contains Proceedings of the Conference. *Q.* (v. 1–2 *Semi-A.*)

National Bankruptcy News and Reports. Detroit. 4 v. Dec. 1, 1898–Dec. 15, 1901. Merged with American Bankruptcy Reports. *Semi-M.* (v. 4, 2 nos.)

National Bankruptcy Register. New York. 19 v. June 1867–1882. Title, v. 1–3: Bankrupt Register. Reprinted later with comments limited to reports of decisions, and continued in the same way, under title: National Bankruptcy Register Reports. *Semi-M.* (*W.* Jan.–June 1868).

National Bar Journal. St. Louis, Mo. 9 v. July 1941–Mar. 1951. Pub: National

Bar Assn., Inc. Suspended pub. Nov. 1941–June 1944. Vol. 1, 2 nos.; v. 2, 3 nos.; v. 3–5, 4 nos. each.; v. 6, 3 nos.; v. 7, 4 nos.; v. 8, 1 no.; v. 9, 1 no.

National Commission News. *See* U. S. National Commission for the United Nations Educational, Scientific and Cultural Organization. News.

National Coroner. Milwaukee, Wis. 4 nos. Oct. 1927–Jan. 1928. Pub: National Assn. of Coroners. *M.*

National Corporation Reporter. Chicago. 125 v. Sept. 1890–Dec. 19, 1952* *W.*

National Income Tax Magazine. *See* Taxes.

National Insurance Gazette and Sickness Societies Review. London. 26 v. May 11, 1912–1942*? Title varies.

National Journal of Legal Education. Chicago. 3 v. Feb. 1937–Ap. 1940*? Organ of National Assn. of Law Schools. *A.* (1939 not issued).

National Law Enforcement Review. Chicago. July 1946*?

National Law Reporter. New York. v. 1, no. 1. 1857.

National Law Review. Philadelphia. 11 nos. 1888. Ed. N. M. Taylor. *M.*

National Lawyers Guild. News-Letter. Washington, D. C. 4 v. June 1937–May 1940. *Irreg.* (v. 1, 4 nos.; v. 2, 2 nos.; v 3, 1 no.; v. 4, 2 nos.)

National Municipal Review. New York. 41 v. 1912–Dec. 1952* Place of publication varies. Pub: National Municipal League. *M.*

National Recovery Administration Bulletin. Washington, D. C. 7 nos. June 16, 1933–Jan. 22, 1934.

National Tax Journal. Lancaster, Pa. 5 v. Mar. 1948–Dec. 1952* Pub: National Tax Assn. *Q.*

National Tax Magazine. *See* Taxes.

National Titleman. New York. 40 nos. Nov. 1926–June 1933. *Bi-M.*

National University Law Review. Washington, D. C. 11 v. 1921–Jan. 1931. Pub: National University Law School. Twice during academic year (v. 11, 1 no.)

Nebraska Law Bulletin. *See* Nebraska Law Review.

Nebraska Law Journal. Lincoln. 1 v. 1890–91.

Nebraska Law Review. Lincoln. 32 v. July 1922–May 1953* Title, v. 1–19: Nebraska Law Bulletin. Pub: University of Nebraska College of Law. Official organ of Nebraska State Bar Assn. *Q.*

Nebraska Legal News. Lincoln. 59 v. 1892–Mar. 19, 1939. *W.* (v. 59, 28 nos.)

Nebraska Supreme Court Journal. Lincoln. 13 v. Oct. 1931–Dec. 1944. Pub: Gant Publishing Co.

Nevada State Bar Journal. Reno. 17 v. Jan. 1936–Oct. 1952* Pub: State Bar of Nevada. Contains annual proceedings. *Q.*

New Brunswick University Law Journal. *See* University of New Brunswick Law Journal.

New Commonwealth Quarterly. *See* World Affairs.

New Constitution. Columbus, Ohio. 26 nos. May 5–Nov. 17, 1849. *W.*

New Haven County Bar Association Bulletin. New Haven, Conn. 23 nos. Mar. 1926–Mar. 1939. *Irreg.*

New Irish Jurist and Local Government Review. *See* Irish Jurist and Local Government Review.

New Jersey Law Journal. Plainfield and Newark. 75 v. Jan. 1878–Dec. 25, 1952* Absorbed New Jersey State Bar Association Quarterly with v. 58, no. 5. Some issues of v. 58, 1935 as New Jersey Law News. *W.* (*M.* 1878–Mar. 1935; 1935 *Irreg.*)

New Jersey Law News. See New Jersey Law Journal.

New Jersey Law Review. Newark. 2 nos. May 1915, June 1916. Pub: New Jersey Law School.

New Jersey Law Review. Newark. 2 v. Jan. 1935–Jan. 1936. Pub: New Jersey Law School. Merged with Mercer Beasley Law Review to form University of Newark Law Review. *Semi-A.* (v. 2, 1 no.)

New Jersey Lawyer. Paterson. 2 v. Feb. 1935–1936. Pub. New Jersey Lawyer Pub. Co. vol. 1, 4 nos.; v. 2, 2 nos.

New Jersey Legal Record. Newark. 15 v. Oct. 1931–Dec. 16, 1932. *D.* (v. 15, 12 nos.)

New Jersey Realty Title News. Newark. v. 1, no. 1. June 1944*? Pub: New Jersey Realty Title Insurance Co.

New Jersey State Bar Association Quarterly. Trenton. 4 v. Jan. 1934–Oct. 1937.

New Mexico State Bar. Secretary's Letter. Santa Fe. 3 v. July 1941–July 1944. *Irreg.*

New Pacific Coast Law Journal. Pasadena, Calif. 3 v. Jan. 15, 1924–July 1926. *M.* (v. 3, 7 nos.)

New South Wales Weekly Notes. Sydney. 69 v. July 26, 1884–1952* Separate nos. issued as Weekly Notes. Absorbed New South Wales Bankruptcy Cases, 1899.

New York City-Hall Recorder. New York. 6 v. Jan. 1816–Jan. 1822. Daniel Rogers, Reporter.

New York City-Hall Recorder. New York. 3 nos. 1823.

New York County Lawyers Association. Bar Bulletin. *See* Bar Bulletin, New York County Lawyers Association.

New York Daily Law Gazette. New York. 66 nos. (1 v.) 1858.

New York Daily Transcript. New York. 28 v. July, 1859–1872. Superseded by Daily Register. O. S. 11 v., July 1859–1868; N. S. 17 v., 1868–1872.

New York Guild Lawyer. New York. 10 v. Sept. 1943–Dec. 1952* Continues Guild Lawyer. *M.*

New York Judicial Repository. New York. 6 nos. Sept. 1818–Mar. 1819. *M.*

New York Law Book News, Published for the Information of the New York Bar. Northport. v. 1, no. 1. May 1926.

New York Law Journal. New York. 128 v. Mar. 26, 1888–Dec. 31, 1952* *D.*

New York Law Review. Ithaca. 1 v. Jan.–July 1929. Merged with American Law Review to form United States Law Review, v. 74 of which is again entitled New York Law Review. *M.* (v. 7, 5 nos.)

New York Law School Review. New York. 1 v. Dec. 1928–Jan. 1930. *Q.* (during academic year).

New York Legal Observer. New York. 12 v. Oct. 1, 1842–Dec. 1854. Publication suspended June 1844–Feb. 1845. Signature 21 of v. 6 omitted. *Irreg.* (v. 1, *W.*; v. 2, *W.* and *Semi-M.*; v. 3, *Irreg.*; v. 4–12, *M.*)

New York Monthly Law Bulletin. New York. 5 v. Dec. 1878–Dec. 1883.

New York Monthly Law Record. New York. 3 v. Jan. 1896–1898. Supersedes New York Monthly Law Bulletin.

New York State Bar Association Bulletin. Albany. 24 v. Mar. 1928–Dec. 1952* *Bi-M.* (*Irreg.*)

New York State Bar Association Circular. Albany. 108 nos. Jan. 8, 1936–Ap. 1945; N. S. #1–73, ?1945–Ap. 27, 1953* No. 1–15 autographed from typewritten copy. *M.* (*Irreg.*)

New York State Bar Association Lawyer Service Letter. Albany. 174 nos. Oct. 12, 1936–Ap. 24, 1953* Supersedes Onondaga County Bar Association Research Committee Circular Letter. Every three weeks.

New York State Bureau of Criminal Investigation. Bulletin. *See* Bulletin of the Bureau of Criminal Investigation.

New York State Industrial Commission. Bulletin. Albany. 6 v. Oct. 1915–Aug. 1921. Continued by Industrial Bulletin. *M.*

New York State Police Bureau of Criminal Investigation. Bulletin. *See* Bulletin of the Bureau of Criminal Investigation.

New York University Law Review. New York. 27 v. Ap. 1924–Nov. 1953* Title varies: v. 1, Annual Review of Law School of New York University; v. 2–7, New York University Law Review; v. 8–24, New York University Law Quarterly Review; None pub. June 1942–Ap. 1944. 5 times a year (with variations: v. 1, 1 no.; v. 2, 2 nos.; v. 3, 2 nos., v. 4, 2 nos., v. 5, 2 nos.)

New York University School of Law. Social Meaning of Legal Concepts. *See* Social Meaning of Legal Concepts.

New Yugoslav Law. Belgrade. 2 v. 1950–1952* Pub: Assn. of Jurists of Federative People's Republic of Yugoslavia. *Q.*

New Zealand Jurist. Dunedin. 2 v. Jan. 1873–1875.

New Zealand Jurist Reports. Dunedin. N. S. 4 v. 1875–78. vol. 4: 7 pts.

New Zealand Justice of the Peace. New Zealand. 1876–77.

New Zealand Law Journal. Wellington. 28 v. Mar. 3, 1925–Dec. 16, 1952* Title, v. 1–3: Butterworth's Fortnightly Notes. *Fortn.*

Newark Law Review. *See* University of Newark Law Review.

News From Behind the Iron Curtain. New York. 1 v. Jan. 1952–Dec. 1952*. Pub: National Committee for a Free Europe. *M.*

News Letter (Washington University). *See* Washington University School of Law News Letter.

News-Reporter. Newark. v. 1, no. 1–3. Mar.–May 1, 1953* *M.*

Newsletter (Yale). *See* Yale Law School Association. Newsletter.

Nigeria Gazette. Lagos. 37 v. to Ap. 1950*?

Nigeria Law Quarterly Review. Lagos. 2 v. Ap. 1946–Jan. 1947. Pub: Nigeria Bar Assn. Vol. 1 # 3 and v. 2 # 1, Oct. 1946–Jan. 1947 is a combined issue.

Nigerian Law Journal. Lagos. 5 v. 1921–26.

North Carolina Journal of Law. Chapel Hill. 2 v. Jan. 1904–Dec. 1905. Pub: North Carolina University School of Law. *M.*

North Carolina Law Journal. Tarboro. 2 v. Mar. 1900–1902. Pub: State Bar Assn. of North Carolina. Imprint varies. *M.* (v. 2, 11 nos.)

North Carolina Law Review. Chapel Hill. 31 v. June 1922–June 1953* Pub: University of North Carolina School of Law. *Q.*

North Dakota Bar Briefs. *See* North Dakota Law Review.

North Dakota Law Review. Bismarck. 28 v. Dec. 1924–Oct. 1952* Title, 1924—Jan. 1948, Bar Briefs; Ap. 1948–Oct. 1950, North Dakota Bar Briefs. Pub: State Bar Assn. of North Dakota in cooperation with North Dakota School of Law. Contains proceedings. *M.*

Northeastern Law Review. Boston. no. 1. May 1951.

Northern Ireland Legal Quarterly. Belfast. 9 v. Nov. 1936–May 1952* Journal of Incorporated Law Society of Northern Ireland.

Northumberland County Legal News. *See* Legal News (Sunbury, Pa.)

Northwest Law Journal. Fargo, N. D. 1 v. 1896.

Northwest Law Journal. Seattle, Wash. 18 nos. June 10, 1891–Feb. 25, 1892.

Northwestern Law Journal, and Real Estate Reporter. Portland, Ore. 27 nos. 1881.

Northwestern Law Review. Chicago. 4 v. 1893–1896. Pub: Students of Northwestern University Law School. *M.* during school year.

Northwestern University Law Review. Chicago. 47 v. May 1906–Feb. 1953* Through v. 46 ed. jointly by Law Schools, University of Chicago, University of Illinois and Northwestern University. Beginning v. 47, ed. by Northwestern University School of Law. Absorbed Illinois Law Quarterly, Nov. 1924. Title, v. 1–46: Illinois Law Review. 6 times a year.

Notaries' Journal. New York. 6 v. Feb. 1877–1883. *Q.*

Notes on Legal Education. Denver, Colo. Title varies: vol. 1, no. 1, American Bar Association. Standards; v. 1, no. 2, The Bulletin. Only first 2 nos. have volume numbering. Pub: Council of Section of Legal Education and Admissions to the Bar of American Bar Association. *Irreg.*

Notre Dame Law Reporter. South Bend, Ind. 2 v. Ap.–Nov. 1920. v. 2, 1 no.

Notre Dame Lawyer. Notre Dame, Ind. 27 v. Nov. 1925–Summer 1952* Pub: Notre Dame Law Students. *Q.* (*M.* during college year, Nov. 1925–May 1930).

Nu Bate. Chicago. 6 v. 1938–Ap. 1943. Pub: Nu Beta Epsilon Law Fraternity. Vol. 6, 1 no.

Obiter Dicta. Canada. 27 v. 1927–1953*.

Observateur. *See* Examiner.

Official Circular. *See* Parish and District Councils Association. Official Circular.

Ohio Bar. Columbus. 25 v. Ap. 1928–Dec. 26, 1952* Title, v. 1–21, #36, Ohio State Bar Association Report (which continued Ohio State Bar Association Bulletin) *W.*

Ohio Law Bulletin. Norwalk. 66 v. Feb. 1876–May 2, 1921. Title varies: Feb. 1876–Feb. 1879, Cincinnati Weekly Law Bulletin; Feb. 10, 1879–July 2, 1883, Weekly Cincinnati Law Bulletin; July 9, 1880–Dec. 31, 1884, Weekly Law Bulletin; Jan. 1, 1885–Dec. 30, 1901, Weekly Law Bulletin and Ohio Law Journal; Jan. 6, 1902–May 2, 1921, Ohio Law Bulletin. Absorbed Ohio Law Journal, Jan. 5, 1885 and Ohio Legal News, Jan. 1902. Merged into Ohio Law Reporter, May 9, 1921. *W.*

Ohio Law Journal. Columbus. 6 v. Aug. 1880–1884. Merged into Weekly Law Bulletin, later Ohio Law Bulletin. *W.*

Ohio Law Reporter, and Weekly Law Bulletin. Cincinnati. 50 v. Nov. 5, 1934–June 22, 1953* Continues Ohio Law Reporter; a Weekly Journal. Sometimes cited as v. 41– of the earlier publication. Published with official advance sheets for Ohio Opinions. *W.* (3 volumes each year).

Ohio Legal News. Norwalk. 9 v. Ap. 1894–1902. Title, v. 1: Legal News, the Toledo Legal News and the Ohio Legal News. Continued by Ohio Law Bulletin and Reporter. *W.*

Ohio State Bar Association. Local Association Bulletin. *See* Local Association Bulletin.

Ohio State Bar Association Bulletin. Columbus. 4 v. Oct. 21, 1924–Mar. 27, 1928. Title, v. 1, no. 1: Bar Association Paragraph Digest; v. 1, nos. 2–6, Bar Association Bulletin. Continued by Ohio State Bar Association Report. *W.* (v. 4, 24 nos.)

Ohio State Bar Association Report. *See* Ohio Bar.

Ohio State Law Journal. Columbus. 13 v. Jan. 1935–Autumn 1953* Title, v. 1–8: Law Journal of the Student Bar Association of Ohio State University. Suspended 1942–1947. *Q.* (3 times a year 1935–1942).

Oil and Gas Law Review. Los Angeles. no. 1. Nov. 1939. Superseded by Oil and Gas and Filling Station Law Review.

Oil and Gas Reporter. Dallas, Texas. 1 v. 1952–1953* Pub: Southwestern Legal Foundation. *Q.*

Oil and Gas Tax Quarterly. New York. 2 v. Oct. 1951–July 1953* Pub: Matthew Bender.

Oklahoma Law Journal. Stillwater. 14 v. June 1902–1916. *M.*

Oklahoma Law Review. Norman. 5 v. May 1948–Nov. 1952* *Q.*

Oklahoma Lawyer. Coalgate. 1 v. 1908. *M.*

Oklahoma State Bar Association. Journal. Oklahoma City. 23 v. Ap. 1, 1930–Dec. 1952* Title, v. 1–10: Oklahoma State Bar Journal. Imprint varies. Pub: Oklahoma State Bar Assn. *W.* (v. 1–9 *M.*)

Old Bailey Chronicle. London. 7 v. 1763–1786. 3 v., 1763–1770; 4 v., 1783–1786.

Olwine's Law Journal. Philadelphia. 21 nos. Dec. 20, 1849–May 18, 1850. *W.*

Onondaga County Bar Association. Research Committee. Circular Letter. Albany. 35 nos. Oct. 1933–June 12, 1936. Continued by New York State Bar Association Lawyer Service Letter.

Ontario Legal News. Ontario, Canada. 1 v. 1947–48.

Opinion. Buffalo, N. Y. v. 2 #3–v. 3 #3. Feb. 1951–Feb. 1952*.

Oregon Law Review. Eugene. 32 v. Ap. 1921–June 1953* Pub: University of Oregon School of Law. *Q.* (v. 1, 6 nos.)

Oregon Law School Journal. Salem. 9 nos. Sept. 1902–Dec. 1903. New Series, v. 1 not pub.; v. 2 (4 nos., Feb.–Nov. 1915); v. 3 (4 nos. Feb.–Nov. 1916); v. 4 (1 no., Feb. 1917).

Oregon State Bar Bulletin. Portland. 13 v. July 1941–Sept. 1953* *M.*

Osaka University Law Review. Osaka, Japan. no. 1, 1952*.

Otago Police Gazette. New Zealand. 1861–64.

Oudh Law Journal. United Provinces, India. 13 v. 1914–1926.

Oudh Weekly Notes. 28 ? v. 1924–1947*.

Overseas Official Publications (Royal Empire Society). London. 5 v. Dec. 1926–Jan. 1932. *Q.*

Owl of Sigma Nu Phi. Washington, D. C. 30 v. July 1916–Sept. 1952* Publication suspended Jan. 1918–Oct. 1919. Imprint varies. *Q.* (*Bi-M.* Nov. 1921–May 1924).

Pacific Coast International. Portland, Ore. 13 v. 1934–Jan. 1946. Title v. 1–5, Traffic

Police. Pub: Pacific Coast International Assn. of Law Enforcement Officials; District Attorneys' Assn. of the State of Oregon; Washington Assn. of Chiefs of Police; Oregon State Sheriffs' Assn; Idaho Peace Officers' Assn; Oregon Assn. of City Police Officers. *M.*

Pacific Coast Law Journal. San Francisco. 12 v. Mar. 2, 1878–Dec. 29, 1883. Continues San Francisco Law Journal. Superseded by West Coast Reporter. *W.*

Pacific Law Magazine. San Francisco. 1 v. (6 nos.) Jan.–June 1867. *M.*

Pacific Law Reporter. San Francisco. 14 v. Dec. 5, 1870–1877.

Pacific Legal News. Seattle. v. 1, no. 1. Jan. 1911.

Pakistan Law Review. Karachi. v. 1, no. 1. Aug. 1952* Pub: Sind Muslim Law College.

Pan American News. Washington, D. C. 2 v. Feb. 1, 1940–Dec. 18, 1941. Merged with Inter-American Quarterly to form Inter-American. *Bi-W.*

Panel. New York. 23 v. June 1924–June 1945. Pub: Assn. of Grand Jurors of New York County. *Irreg.*

Paper Book. Menasha, Wis. 57 v. 1905?–Dec. 1952* Pub: Delta Theta Phi Law Fraternity. *Q.*

Parish and District Councils Association. Official Circular. London? 19 nos. (2 v.) 1911–12. Afterwards issued as part of Local Government Review.

Parish Councils Journal. *See* Councils Journal.

Patent and Trade Mark Review. New York. 51 v. Oct. 1902–Sept. 1953* *M.*

Patent Law Review. Washington, D. C. 5 nos. 1879–1880.

Patent Office Society. Journal. Washington, D. C. 34 v. Sept. 1918–Dec. 1952* *M.*

Patna Law Journal. Bankipore. 6 v. Ap. 25, 1916–Aug. 1921. *A or Semi-A.*

Patna Law Reporter. 3 v. 1923–25.

Patna Law Times. Patna. 31 v. Jan. 27, 1920–1950* *W.*

Patna Law Weekly. Calcutta. 5 v. 1917–18.

Peabody Law Review. Portland, Maine. Ap. 1936–Feb. 1941. Pub: Peabody Law School. *Q.*

Pennsylvania Bar Association Quarterly. Philadelphia. 24 v. June 1929–June 1953* *Q.*

Pennsylvania Law Journal. Lancaster, Pa. 7 v. 1842–June 1848. Vol. 6–7 also called New Series v. 1–2. Continued as American Law Journal, N. S. *M.*

Pennsylvania Law Record. Philadelphia. 3 v. June 3, 1879–June 29, 1880. *W* (v. 3, 4 nos.)

Pennsylvania Law Review. *See* University of Pennsylvania Law Review.

Pennsylvania Law Series. Philadelphia. 3 v. Nov. 1894–1896. *M.*

Peoples Law Journal. New York. 3 nos. Dec. 1927–Feb. 1928. *M.*

People's Lawyer. (England?) 3 v. 1885–86.

People's Legal Adviser and Law Reformer. Utica, N. Y. v. 1, no. 1. 1858.

Personal Injury Law Journal. New York. 2 v. July 1910–June 1911. A set of law reports. *M.*

Phax; a Magazine Devoted to the Review of Important Tax and Corporation Information. New York. 2 v. Sept. 1926–May 1928. v. 2, 2 nos.

Phi Alpha Delta Quarterly. *See* Reporter.

Phi Delta Delta. Menasha, Wis. 31 v. 1923–May 1953* Pub: Phi Delta Delta Legal Fraternity. *Bi–M* (Nov.–May).

Phi Delta Phi. *See* Brief: a Legal Miscellany.

Phi Pi Counsellor. Lebanon, Tenn. v. 1, no. 1. June 1924. Pub: National Council of the Phi Pi Legal Fraternity.

Philadelphia Legal Intelligencer. *See* Legal Intelligencer.

Philippine Law Journal. Manila. 27 v. Jan. 1914–Dec. 1952* Suspended Dec. 1919–Aug. 1927. Pub: University of the Philippines College of Law. *M.*

Philippine Law Review. Manila. 6 v. 1911–Ap. 1919. Pub: Philippine Bar Assn. *M.* (v. 6, 4 nos.)

Pittsburgh Law Review. *See* University of Pittsburgh Law Review.

Pittsburgh Legal Journal. Pittsburgh. 100 v. 1853–Dec. 26, 1952* *W.*

Pleader. Brooklyn, N. Y. 6 v. Jan. 1938–1951* Pub: Kings County Criminal Bar Assn. *Irreg.*

Polamerican Law Journal. Chicago. 4 v. June 1938–Aug. 1941. Pub: National Assn. of the Polish Bar. *Semi-A.* (v. 1, 1 no.)

Police Journal. London. 26 v. Jan. 1928–Oct. 1953* *Q.*

Political Science Quarterly. New York. 67 v. Mar. 1886–Dec. 1952* Pub: Academy of Political Science, Columbia University.

Poor Law and Local Government Magazine. Glasgow. 72 v. Sept. 1858–1930. O. S. v. 1–9, Sept. 1858–Aug. 1867; N. S. v. 1–5, Oct. 1867–Sept. 1872; Ser. 3, v. 1–18, 1873–1890; N. S. v. 1–40, 1891–1930. *M.*

Popular Government. Chapel Hill, N C. 19 v. Jan. 1931–June 1953* Pub: Institute of Government. *M.* (Sept.–June).

Popular Monthly Law Tracts. London. 2 v. (16 nos.) 1877–78.

Portland University Law Review. Portland, Maine. 2 v. 1949–1952* *A* (1 vol. in 2 years).

Practice Points. London. 2 v. 1910–Ap. 1912. v. 2, 5 pts.

Practitioner. Baltimore. 18 nos. 1890. *W.*

Preliminary Examination Journal. London. 1871–75.

Progress Report. Washington, D. C. 5 v. 1947–1951. Pub: U. S. Bureau of Prisons. Mimeo. *Q.* (v. 5, 1 no.)

Property Lawyer. London. 15 v. Jan. 1826–Dec. 1830. O. S. 12 v. Jan. 1826–Dec. 1829; N. S. 3 v. Jan.–Dec. 1830. *M.*

Public Administration Review. Crawfordsville, Ind. 13 v. Autumn 1940–Autumn 1953* Pub: American Society for Public Administration. *Q.* (v. 1, 5 nos.)

Public Relations Bulletin. Chicago. v. 1, no. 1–2. Jan.–Mar. 1953* Pub: American Bar Association Standing Committee on Public Relations. 5 times a year.

Public Utilities Fortnightly. Washington, D. C. 51 v. 1928–May 1953* Vol. 1–2 consist of editorial section of advance sheets of Public Utilities Reports. Imprint varies.

Pump Court. London. 13 v. June 1883–Oct. 31, 1891. *M.* (v. 13, 1 no.)

Quarterly Bulletin published by the Illinois State Bar Association. *See* Illinois Bar Journal.

Quarterly Journal of Inter-American Relations. *See* Inter-American Quarterly.

Quarterly Journal of Science, Religion, Philosophy. *See* World Affairs Interpreter.

Quarterly Law Journal. Richmond, Va. 4 v. Jan. 1856–Oct. 1859. With each no. were issued two supps. with separate paging: 1. Selections from reports of revisors of the statutes of Virginia; 2. A general index of Grattan's Virginia Reports. Continued by Quarterly Law Review.

Quarterly Law Review. Richmond, Va. 2 v. Ap. 1860–Jan. 1861. Continues Quarterly Law Journal. v. 2, 1 no.

Quarterly Research Survey. Ithaca, N. Y. July 1947?–Jan. 1949. Each issue has also separate title. Pub: Pacifist Research Bureau.

Queens Bar Bulletin. Jamaica, N. Y. 16 v. Jan. 1928–May 1953* Title, v. 1–10: Queens County Bar News; v. 11–13: Queens County Bar Association Bulletin. None pub. July 1940–Sept. 1950. *M.* (Oct.–May.).

Queens County Bar Association Bulletin. *See* Queens Bar Bulletin.

Queensland Justice of the Peace and Local Authorities' Journal. Brisbane. 46 v. Jan. 1907–1952* Continues Queensland Criminal Reports. *M.*

Queensland Law Reporter and Weekly Notes. Queensland, Australia. 45 v. 1908–1952*.

Queensland University Law Journal. *See* University of Queensland Law Journal.

Quill. London. 9 v. 1890–93. vol. 7, 1 no., Jan. 1898. v. 8 begins Nov. 1900.

Quillets of the Law. Boston. *See* Law Book Bulletin.

Railway and Corporation Law Journal. New York. 12 v. Jan. 1887–Dec. 1892. *W.*

Railway Law and Legislation. Washington, D C. 3 nos. Sept.–Oct. 1891.

Rangoon Criminal Law Journal. Vizagapatam, Madras. 1 v. Jan.–Dec. 1931. *M.*

Rating and Income Tax. London. 35 v. 1924–1942*? *W.*

Reading Guide. Charlottesville, Va. 7 v. Jan. 1946–Dec. 1952* Pub: Law Library, University of Virginia. 6 issues a year.

Record (Denver Bar Association). *See* Dicta.

Record of the Association of the Bar of the City of New York. 7 v. Feb. 1946–Dec. 1952* *M.* (except July–Aug.)

Recorder, or Judicial and Magisterial Magazine. London. 3 nos. Feb.–Ap. 1816.

Reporter: Official Publication of Phi Alpha Delta Law Fraternity. Los Angeles. 25 v. 1914?–Dec. 1940*? Title, v. 1–18: Phi Alpha Delta Quarterly. *Q.*

Reports of Proceedings in Edinburgh Police Court. Edinburgh. 2 v. Feb.–Dec. 1829. *D.*

Res Adjudicata. Newark, N. J. 4 nos. Jan.–Ap. 1938. Pub.: Student Council of Law School, University of Newark. v. 1, no. 1 without title. *Irreg.*

Res Ipsa Loquitur. Washington, D. C. 2 v. Nov. 1936–Dec. 1941. Pub: Georgetown University Law School Alumni Assn. Supersedes Hoya: Law School Number. v. 1, 3 nos.; v. 2, 1 no.

Res Judicatae. Melbourne, Victoria. 6 v. Sept. 1935–July 1952* Pub: Law Students' Society of Victoria. *A.*

Rescript of Gamma Eta Gamma. Harrisburg, Pa. 26 v. Sept. 1912–Mar. 1942*? Imprint varies. *Q.*

Revenue and Criminal Law Journal. United Provinces, India. 12 v. 1915–26.

Revenue, Civil, and Criminal Reporter. Calcutta. 6 v. Jan. 3, 1866–July 3, 1868. Known as Wyman's Reports.

Revenue, Judicial, and Police Journal. Calcutta. 5 v. Sept. 1863–Nov. 1865. *M.*

Review and Record: Banker and Tradesman. *See* Banker and Tradesman.

Review of Polish Law. Warsaw. 4 v. Nov. 1947–Dec. 1950. Merged into Legislation of Poland. Pub: Ministry of Justice.

Review of the International Juridical Association. Berlin. 4 nos. Ap.–June 1930. Pub. also in French and German. *M.*

Revista de Legislacion y Jurisprudencia de la Asociacion de Abogados de Puerto Rico. San Juan. 5 v. Jan. 1914–Ap. 1919. Publication suspended 1918. *Bi-M.* (*M.* v. 1–2; v. 5, 2 nos.)

Revista Juridica de la Universidad de Puerto Rico. San Juan. 20 v. Mar. 1932–May 1951* Pub: Faculty of Law, University of Puerto Rico. *Q.*

Revue Critique de Legislation et de Jurisprudence du Canada. Montreal. 3 v. 1871–75.

Revue de Jurisprudence, ou, Recueil de Decisions des Divers Tribunaux de la Province de Quebec. Montreal. 48 v. 1895–Dec. 1942. *M.*

Revue de Legislation et de Jurisprudence. Quebec. 3 v. Oct. 1845–Sept. 1848. *M.*

Revue du Barreau de la Province de Quebec. Quebec. 12 v. Jan. 1941–Dec. 1952* *M.* (except Aug.–Sept.)

Revue du Droit. Quebec. 17 v. Sept. 1922–June 1939. *M.* (except July–Aug.)

Revue du Notariat. Quebec. 54 v. Aug. 15, 1898–July 1952* Title, v. 1–19: Revue du Notariat, Journal Publie Avec le Concours des Notaries de la Province de Quebec. *M.*

Revue Internationale de Legislation et de Jurisprudence Mussulmanes. Cairo. 1 v. 1895–96. 384 pages, no general t.–p.

Revue Judiciaire de l'Ile Maurice (Bruzaud). 24 pts. June 1, 1843–May 15, 1844. Said to have continued another year by M. Savy, but no copy is known to exist.

Revue Legale. Montreal. 22 v. 1869–92. N. S. 58 v. 1895–Dec. 1952* *M.*

Rhode Island Bar Journal. Providence. v. 1, no. 1–8. Oct. 1952–May 1953* *M.*

Rocky Mountain Law Review. Boulder, Colo. 24 v. Dec. 1928–June 1952* Pub: University of Colorado School of Law. *Q.*

Rosenberger's Pocket Law Journal. Chicago. 7 v. 1894–1900. Title varies: v. 1, Business Law Weekly; v. 2–4, Business Law; v. 5, Rosenberger's Law Monthly.

Round the Courts. New York. v. 1, no. 1. Aug. 1915.

Royal Canadian Mounted Police Quarterly. Ottawa. 17 v. July 1933–1952*.

Royal Institute of International Affairs. Journal. *See* International Affairs.

Rural District Councils Association Circular. London. 41 v. 1895–1935*?

Rutgers Law Center Development Committee. News-Reporter. *See* News-Reporter.

Rutgers University Law Review. Newark, N. J. 7 v. Spring 1947–Spring 1953* Absorbed New Jersey Law Review, Mercer Beasley Law Review, University of Newark Law Review. 3 issues a year.

St. John's Law Review. New York. 27 v. Dec. 1926–May 1953* Pub: St. John's University Law Students, Brooklyn. *Semi–A.*

St. Louis Law Review. *See* Washington University Law Quarterly.

Saint Louis University Law Journal. St. Louis, Mo. 1 v. May 1949–Winter 1951* Title, v. 1, no. 1, Intramural Law Review of St. Louis University; no. 2–3, Intramural Law Review.

Sales Tax Cases; a Journal of the Law of Sales Tax of India. Madras. ?1953* Pub: Company Law Institute of India.

San Francisco Bar. San Francisco. 6 v. Feb. 1937–Dec. 1943. Pub: Bar Assn. of San Francisco. *Bi-M.* (v. 6, 2 nos. Dec. 1943 number called "Special Edition.")

San Francisco Law Journal. San Francisco. 1 v. Sept. 1, 1877–Feb. 23, 1878. Continued by Pacific Coast Law Journal and California Legal Record. *W.*

San Francisco Legal News. San Francisco. 4 v. 1892–95. *W.*

Saskatchewan Bar Review. Regina. 17 v. Mar. 1936–Dec. 1952* Pub: Law Society of Saskatchewan. Incorporates Law Society's Gazette, v. 3, no. 6. *Q.* (v. 5, 5 nos.)

School Law Review. Los Angeles. 3 nos. Mar.–July 1941.

School of Law Review. Canada. 10 v. 1942–1952*

Scots Law Chronicle. *See* Law Chronicle, or Journal of Jurisprudence.

Scots Law Times. Edinburgh. 58 v. May 20, 1893–Dec. 1952* Unnumbered after v. 16, 1908. Title varies. Absorbed Scottish Law Reporter, Oct. 1924. *W.*

Scottish Jurist. Edinburgh. 46 v. 1829–73. Titles and imprints vary. After v. 46, pt. 5 merged in Session Cases, Fourth Series.

Scottish Law Gazette. Edinburgh. # 1. Mar. 1933. Pub: Official organ of Law Agents. Not issued for sale.

Scottish Law Journal and Sheriff Court Record. *See* Scottish Law Magazine and Sheriff Court Reporter.

Scottish Law Reporter. Edinburgh. 61 v. Nov. 1, 1865–Oct. 1924. Incorporated in Scots Law Times.

Scottish Law Review and Sheriff Court Reports. Glasgow. 68 v. Jan. 1885–Dec. 1952* *M.*

Scranton Law Times. *See* Law Times (Scranton, Pa.)

Scraps. New York. 15 v. July 1925–Jan. 1939. Pub: Office of United States Attorney, Southern District of New York. *Irreg.*

Search. New York. v. 1, #1–2. Jan./Feb.–Mr./Ap. 1953* Pub: City Title Insurance Co. *Bi-M.*

Searchlight. New York. 39 v. May 16, 1911–1949* Pub: Citizens Union of New York. *Irreg.*

Selden Society Yearbook. Columbia, S. C. 9 v. Mar. 1937–June 1948. Pub: Selden Society of the University of South Carolina School of Law. Superseded by South Carolina Law Quarterly. *Semi-A.*

Selected List of Recent Articles on International Affairs. Washington, D. C. 107 nos. Oct. 1923–Oct. 1932. Title varies: Oct.–Nov. 1923, Magazine Articles Dealing with Questions of War and Peace; Nov. 1923–Feb. 1924: International Relations as Presented in Recent Periodicals, Books and Pamphlets; Feb. 1924–Jan. 1931, International Affairs as Presented . . . Pub: National Council for Prevention of War. *M.*

Seminar; Annual Extraordinary Number of The Jurist. Washington, D. C. 10 v. 1943–1952* Pub: Catholic University of America. *A.*

Shingle. Philadelphia. 15 v. Jan. 1938–Dec. 1952* Pub: Philadelphia Bar Assn. *M.* (Oct.–June).

Shome's Law Reporter. India. 4 v. 1877–81.

Si-De-Ka Quarterly. Menasha, Wis. 33 v. 1917–Mar. 1947*? Pub: Sigma Delta Kappa. Following issues never published: v. 8, nos. 3–4; v. 9, nos. 1 and 3; v. 10, no. 4; v. 11, nos. 2–4; v. 12, nos. 1–4; v. 13, nos. 2–4; v. 14, nos. 3–4; v. 15, nos. 3–4; v. 16, nos. 3–4.

Sigma Delta Kappa. *See* Si-Di-Ka Quarterly.

Sigma Nu Phi. *See* Owl.

Sittings Review. Halifax. 2 v. (5 nos.) Michaelmas, 1920–Michaelmas, 1921. Incorporates Student's Companion and Articled Clerk's Annual. v. 1, 4 nos.; v. 2, 1 no.

Social Meaning of Legal Concepts; an Annual Conference. New York. 5 nos. 1948–1953* Pub: New York University School of Law.

Social Science Abstracts. Menasha, Wis. 5 v. Mar. 1929–Jan. 1933. v. 5, 1 no.

Social Security. New York and Washington, D. C. 17 v. April 1937–June 1943*? Information Service for members of National Assn. of Manufacturers. *Fortn.*

Social Security Analyst, Weekly Reports for Minimizing Payroll Taxes. Chicago. 34 nos. Jan.–Nov. 1, 1937. Title varies. *M.* (Jan.–Mar.) *W.* (Ap.–Nov.)

Society of Clerks-At-The-Table in Empire Parliaments. Journal. Guildford, England. 9 v. 1932–1940*? *A.*

Society of Comparative Legislation. Journal. *See* Journal of Comparative Legislation and International Law.

Society of Public Teachers of Law. Journal. London. 1924–1952* Suspended publication between 1938 and 1947. New Series begins 1947 and is numbered as follows: v. 1 no 1 (in 2 pts.) 1947; no. 2, 1948; no. 3, 1949; no. 4, 1950; no. 5, 1951; v. 2 no. 1, 1952. *A.*

Solicitor. London. 19 v. Jan. 1934–Dec. 1952* *M.*

Solicitors' Clerks Gazette. London. 1921–July 1940.

Solicitors' Journal. London. 96 v. Jan. 1857–Dec. 1952* Continues Legal Observer and Solicitors' Journal. Absorbed Weekly Reporter, 1906. *W.*

Somerset Legal Journal. Somerset, Pa. 15 v. Mar. 1, 1920–Mar. 1, 1952* Pub: Somerset County Bar Assn.

South African Law Journal. Capetown and Johannesburg. 69 v. 1884–Nov. 1952* Title, v. 1–17: Cape Law Journal. Pub: Law Society of Cape of Good Hope. *Q.*

South African Law Times. Johannesburg. 5 v. Jan. 1932–Dec. 1936. Pub: Incorporated Law Society of the Transvaal. *M.*

South Carolina Law Quarterly. Columbia, S. C. 5 v. Sept. 1948–June 1953* Pub: South Carolina Bar Assn. and Faculty and Students of University of South Carolina School of Law. Continues Selden Society Yearbook. Supplement, special issue on water law, Dec. 1952, v. 5 #2–A. *Q.*

South Dakota Bar Journal. Pierre. 21 v. July 1932–Ap. 1953* Pub: State Bar of South Dakota. *Q.*

South Eastern Affairs: Quarterly Review for the History of South Eastern Europe (Central Europe and the Balkan Peninsula). Budapest. 10 v. Jan. 1931–1940. Pub: Hungarian Society for Foreign Affairs.

South Jersey Law School Dictum. Camden. Sept. 1928–Dec. 1930? 3 or 4 issues each school year.

Southern Bench and Bar Review. Jackson, Miss. 1 v. 1913. Merged with Lawyer and Banker. *Bi-M.*

Southern California Law Review. Los Angeles. 26 v. Nov. 1927–July 1953* Pub: School of Law, University of Southern California. *Q.* (*Irreg.*)

Southern City; official organ of North Carolina League of Municipalities. Raleigh. 4 v. 1949–1952* *M.*

Southern Law Journal and Reporter. Tuscaloosa, Nashville, Tenn. 4 v. 1878–Nov. 1881.

Southern Law Quarterly. *See* Tulane Law Review.

Southern Law Review. Atlanta, Ga. 1 v. June 1901–May 1902. *M.*

Southern Law Review. St. Louis, Mo. 11 v. Jan. 1872–Feb. 1883. Title, Jan. 1872–Oct. 1874: Southern Law Review and Chart of the Southern Law and Collection Union. Merged into American Law Review, 1883. O. S. v. 1–3, Jan. 1872–Oct. 1874; N. S. v. 1–8, Ap. 1875–Feb. 1883. *Q.* (1872–June 1877); *Bi-M.* (Aug. 1877–1883.)

Southern Law Times. Chattanooga. 2 v. 1885–86. v. 2, 26 nos.

Southern Lawyer. Milledgeville, Ga. 2 nos. Jan., Ap. 1937.

Southwestern Law Journal. Dallas, Tex. 6 v. Spring 1947–Fall 1952* Title, v. 1: Texas Law and Legislation. Pub: Southern Methodist University School of Law and Southwestern Legal Foundation. *Q.* (*Irreg.*)

Southwestern Law Journal and Reporter. Nashville. 1 v. 1844.

Southwestern Law Review. Los Angeles. 2 v. June 1916–June 1918. Pub: Southwestern University School of Law. *Q.* (*Irreg.*)

Southwestern Legal Center. Dallas, Texas. 2 v. Mar. 1, 1948–Dec. 1952* Pub: Southwestern Legal Foundation at Southern Methodist University. *Irreg.*

Soviet Press Translations. Seattle. 8 v. Oct. 31, 1946–Mar. 15, 1953. Pub: Far Eastern & Russian Institute, University of Washington. *Bi-W.* (except August; v. 8, 6 nos.)

Standards. American Bar Association Section on Legal Education. *See* Notes on Legal Education.

Stanford Intramural Law Review. Stanford, Calif. 2 nos. Ap.–June 1948. Pub: Board of Trustees, Leland Stanford Junior University. Superseded by Stanford Law Review.

Stanford Law Review. Stanford, Calif. 5 v. Nov. 1948–July 1953* Supersedes Stanford Intramural Law Review. 4 issues a year.

State Bar Association of Wisconsin. Bulletin. *See* Wisconsin Bar Bulletin.

State Bar of California. Journal. San Francisco. 27 v. Aug. 1926–Dec. 1952* Title, v. 1–17 # 2 (Feb. 1942): State Bar Journal. 6 issues a year, every 2 months combined in 1 issue (earlier *M.*)

State Bar Review. Seattle. 2 v. Oct. 1934–July 1936. Pub: Washington State Bar Assn. Merged with Washington Law Review to form Washington Law Review and State Bar Journal. *Q.*

State Government. Chicago. 25 v. Jan. 1926–Dec. 1952* Title varies: v. 1, no. 1: American Legislator; v. 1, no. 2 through v. 2: Legislator. Suspended Oct. 1926–Feb. 1929. v. 1–3 pub. at Denver. *M.* (no number issued July 1926).

State Tax Review. Chicago. 13 v. Jan. 1941–Dec. 31, 1952* Supersedes Tax Legislation Bulletin. Pub: Commerce Clearing House. *W.* (v. 1–9 *Irreg.*)

Straits Law Journal and Reporter. Singapore. 5 v. June 1888–June 1892. With v. 5 were issued Straits Law Reports. For complete collation of each volume see Carswell checklist, 3d ed., 1937, p. 100. *M.*

Student Law Review. New York. 1 v. Fall 1951–Summer 1952* Pub: New York Law School.

Student Lawyer. New Orleans. 2 v. 1951–1952* Pub: American Law Students Assn. An introductory issue was pub. Dec. 1940.

Students' Companion. London. 5 v. 1910–15. Title, pt. 1–4, Companion Class Notes. Later incorporated with Sittings Review.

Students' Law Exchange. *See* Washington Law Exchange.

Students' Law Journal. Brooklyn, N. Y. 2 nos. Feb.–Ap. 1934. Pub: Students' Law Pub. Co.

Studies in International Affairs. Boston. 2 v. 1951?–June 1952* Pub: Harvard University.

Subpoena. San Antonio, Texas. 7 v. Feb. 1938–July 18, 1946* 6 v., Feb. 1938–Oct. 22, 1943; N. S. v. 1, July 18, 1946. Pub: San Antonio Bar Assn. *M.* (*Irreg.*)

Summons. Melbourne. 12 v. 1891–1902. *M.* (v. 12, 3 nos.)

Summons. Pittsburgh, Pa. 18 v. 1926?–Nov. 1944*? Pub: Tau Epsilon Rho. *Irreg.*

Summons. San Francisco. 2 v. May 1920–Autumn 1931. *Irreg.* (v. 1, 24 nos.; v. 2, 10 nos.)

Supreme Court Journal. Mylapore, Madras. 14 v. Jan. 1937–Dec. 1951. Contains reports of proceedings of Federal Court of India, ed. by A. N. Aiyar. Title varies: 1937–43, Federal Law Journal of India; 1944–49, Federal Law Journal. Place of Pub. varies. *M.*

Surrogate. New York. 10 nos. Jan.–Dec. 1891. *M.*

Susquehanna Legal Chronicle. Montrose, Pa. 12 nos. Ap. 1, 1878–Mar. 1879. *M.*

Sutherland's Weekly Reporter. India. 26 v. 1864–77; Supplements, 3 v. 1868–75. vol. 26, 4 nos. For description see Carswell checklist, 3d ed., 1937, p. 89.

Syllabi. St. Paul. 26 nos. 1876–77.

Syllabus. Houston, Texas. v. 2, no. 1. Ap. 1938. Pub: Houston Bar Assn.

Syracuse Law Review. Syracuse, N. Y. 4 v. Spring 1949–Spring 1953* *Semi-A.* (Fall, Spring).

Tamil All India Law Journal. 6 v. 1929–35.

Tau Epsilon Rho. *See* Summons.

Tax Administrators News. Chicago. 5 v. Oct. 1937–Dec. 1941*? Pub: Federation of Tax Administrators. *M.*

Tax Bulletin to Members of the Canadian Tax Foundation. Toronto. 2 v. 1951?–Oct. 1952* *Bi-M.*

Tax Law Reporter. Bay City, Mich. 2 v. Mar. 1884–Aug. 1890. *M.* (v. 2, 11 nos.)

Tax Law Review. New York. 8 v. Oct. 1945–May 1953* Pub: New York University School of Law. *Q.*

Tax Legislation Bulletin. New York. 8 v. Jan. 16, 1933–Nov. 27, 1940. Pub: Commerce Clearing House. Superseded by State Tax Review.

Tax Magazine. *See* Taxes.

Taxation. London. 50 v. 1927–1953*

Taxes. Chicago. 30 v. Feb. 1923–Dec. 1953* Title varies: Feb. 1923–Aug. 1930, National Income Tax Magazine; Sept.-Oct. 1930, National Tax Magazine; Nov. 1930–Dec. 1938, Tax Magazine. Pub: Commerce Clearing House. *M.*

Taxpayer. South Africa. v. 1 #1. 1951* *M.*

Telegram. (England). 24 nos. 1859–64. "Examination questions with answers."

Telegu Law Journal. India. 1 v. 1911.

Templar. London. 2 v. Jan. 1788–Jan. 1789. *M.*

Temple Law Quarterly. Philadelphia. 26 v. Mar. 1927–Spring 1953* Pub: Temple University School of Law. 4 times during school year.

Tennessee Law Review. Knoxville. 22 v. Nov. 1922–June 1953* Official publication Bar Assn. of Tennessee. Pub. by University of Tennessee College of Law. *Q.* (v. 1, 2 nos.; none for Jan., May, 1923 and May 1925).

Texas Bar Journal. Austin. 15 v. Jan. 1938–Dec. 1953* Pub: Texas Bar Assn. *M.*

Texas Law and Legislation. *See* Southwestern Law Journal.

Texas Law Journal. Austin. 5 v. June 22, 1882–June 22, 1896. *W.*

Texas Law Journal. Tyler. 5 v. Aug. 22, 1877–Ap. 19, 1882. *W.*

Texas Law Reporter. Austin. 3 v. 1882–85. v. 3, 9 nos.

Texas Law Review. Austin. 6 v. Jan. 6, 1883–86. Imprint varies. *W.*

Texas Law Review. Austin. 31 v. Dec. 1922–June 1953* Pub: Texas Lawyers and University of Texas School of Law. *Q.*

Texas Southern University Law Review. Houston. v. 1, no. 1 will not appear before April 1953. (As of July, 1953, not yet pub.)

Texas University School of Law, News Sheet. Austin. 14 nos. Mar. 1945–Aug. 1945.

Themis: Revue de Legislation, de Droit et de Jurisprudence. Montreal. 5 v. Feb. 1879–Jan. 1884. *M.*

Title News. Mount Morris, Ill. 31 v. 1922–Dec. 1952* Pub: American Title Assn. Includes its proceedings. *Irreg.*

To Wit. Hartford, Conn. 12 v. Nov. 1929–June 1941*? Official broadside of Hartford Bar Library. *Irreg.*

Toronto Law Journal. *See* University of Toronto Law Journal.

Trade Mark Record. New York. 38 v. (1261 nos.) 1886–1914. *M.*

Trade Mark Reporter. New York. 42 v. June 1911–Dec. 1952* Absorbed Bulletin of United States Trade-Mark Assn., 1941. Pub: United States Trade-Mark Assn. (*M.* except July–Aug.)

Trade Marks Journal. London. 65 v. May 3, 1876–Dec. 1941*? *W.*

Trade Regulation Review. New York. 2 v. Dec. 1936–Winter, 1938. Pub: Reinhold Wolff. Mimeo. v. 1, 7 nos.; v. 2, 4 nos.

Traffic Law Letter. Fowler, Ind. 19 nos. 1924–Oct. 1935. Pub: H. C. Lunt. *Irreg.*

Travancore Law Journal. Trivandrum. 37 v. Oct. 1910–1947. With this are issued Travancore Law Reports. v. 37 # 8 last issued.

Travancore Law Times. Trivandrum. 12 v. Aug. 1926–1938*?

Trust Companies. *See* Trusts and Estates.

Trusts and Estates. New York. 91 v. Mar. 1904–Dec. 1952* Title, v. 1–67, Trust Companies. *M.*

Tulane Law Review. New Orleans, La. 27 v. Jan. 1916–June 1953* Title, v. 1–3: Southern Law Quarterly. Pub. suspended Nov. 1918–Dec. 1929. 4 times a year.

U. C. L. A. Intramural Law Review. Los Angeles, Calif. 2 nos. June 1952–Mar. 1953*.

UNESCO Copyright Bulletin. Paris. 5 v. July 1948–1952* July–Dec. 1948 as the Organization's Copyright Bulletin. *Q.*

U. P. Law Times. *See* United Provinces Law Times.

Unauthorized Practice News. Chicago. 18 v. Dec. 1934–Dec. 1952* Pub: Committee on Unauthorized Practice of the Law, American Bar Assn. *Bi-M.* (*Irreg.* v. 1–4, *M.*; v. 5, 9 nos.; v. 6, 5 nos.)

Unchristened Notes of the Colorado Bar Association. *See* Jealous Mistress.

Union Law Review. Johannesburg, Transvaal. 2 v. Mar. 1910–Nov. 1911. v. 2, 577 p.

Union Pacific Railroad. Law Department Bulletin. Omaha. 17 v. Dec. 1911–Nov. 1929. Title, v. 4–6, Union Pacific Law Department Bulletin. *M.* (v. 17, 9 nos.)

United Nations Bulletin. New York. 14 v. Aug. 3, 1946–June 15, 1953* Title, Aug. 3, 1946–Dec. 23, 1947, United Nations Weekly Bulletin. *Semi-M.*

United Nations Documents Index. Lake Success, N. Y. 3 v. Jan. 1950–Dec. 1952* *M.*

United Nations Review. New York. 5 v. Jan. 1941–Dec. 1945. Pub: United Nations Information Office. Title varies: v. 1–2, no. 12, 1941–Dec. 15, 1942, Inter-Allied Review. *Irreg.*

United Nations Weekly Bulletin. *See* United Nations Bulletin.

United Nations World. New York. 6 v. Feb. 1947–Dec. 1952* Formed by merger of Asia, Inter-American, and Free World. *M.*

United Provinces Law Reporter. Allahabad. 4 v. in 12. 1919–1922. A few numbers of a periodical with this title may have been issued in 1912. *Irreg.* (v. 1, 2 pts.; v. 2–4, 3 pts. each; Current digest, 1 v.)

United Provinces Law Times; a Monthly Journal of Legislation. Lucknow, India. 17 v. 1937–Dec. 1953* Contains current legislation relating to the United Provinces of Agra and Oudh. *M.*

United States Daily. Washington, D. C. 8 v. Mar. 4, 1926–May 13, 1933. vol. 8, 10 nos. (2–10 pub. once for every six days of government action with title: United States Daily, Weekly Composite Issue.) Superseded by United States News and United States Weekly Law Journal.

United States Daily's Law Journal. *See* United States Weekly Law Journal.

U. S. Department of State Bulletin. Washington, D. C. 28 v. (731 nos.) July 1, 1939–June 29, 1953* Replaces Press Releases and Treaty Information Bulletin which were discontinued with the June 1939 issues. *W.*

U. S. Department of State. Documents and State Papers. 15 nos. Ap. 1948–June 1949. Combined with Dept. of State Bulletin.

United States Judge Advocate General (Army) Bulletin. Washington, D. C. 10 v. Jan. 1942–June 1951* *M.*

United States Jurist. Washington, D. C. 3 v. Jan. 1871–Oct. 1873. *M.* (v. 1); *Q.* (v. 2–3).

United States Law Intelligencer and Review. Providence and Philadelphia. 3 v. Jan. 1829–Dec. 1831. *M.*

United States Law Journal and Civilian's Magazine. New Haven and New York. 2 v. (6 nos.) June 30, 1822–Ap. 1826. Suspended pub. Ap. 1823–Jan. 1826. *Q.*

United States Law Review. New York. 74 v. Oct. 1866–Dec. 1940. Title, v. 1–63, no. 2: American Law Review; v. 74, New York Law Review. Absorbed Southern Law Review, 1883; Western Jurist, 1884; and New York Law Review, 1929. *Irreg.*

United States Law Week. Washington, D. C. 20 v. Sept. 5, 1933–June 1952* Pub: Bureau of National Affairs, Inc. Supersedes United States Weekly Law Journal.

United States Monthly Law Magazine. New York. 6 v. Jan. 1850–Dec. 1852. Continued by Livingston's Monthly Law Magazine. Title varies.

United States. National Commission for the United Nations Educational, Scientific and Cultural Organization. News. Washington, D. C. v. 1–5 #10. June 15, 1947–May 1952. Title, v. 1–2: National Commission News. Superseded by its Newsletter. *M.*

United States. National Commission for the United Nations Educational, Scientific & Cultural Organization. Newsletter. Washington, D. C. 20 nos. June 26, 1952–Ap. 8, 1953* Supersedes Its News. *Bi-W.*

United States Trade-Mark Association. Bulletin. New York. 35 v. Nov. 1887–Dec. 1940. Merged with Trade-Mark Reporter Jan. 1941. *Irreg.*

United States Weekly Law Journal. Washington, D. C. 25 nos. Mar. 14–Aug. 29, 1933. Title, Mar. 14–May 16, United States Daily's Law Journal. Supp. to United States Daily. Pub: United States News Pub. Corp. Superseded by United States Law Week.

University College of Law Journal. Nagpur. 9 v. Nov. 1933–1941. Title, v. 1–2: Nagpur University College of Law Magazine; v. 3: College of Law Journal. *Semi-A.*

University Law Review. New York. 3 v. Nov. 1893–Aug. 1897. Publication suspended Mar. 1896–Jan. 1897. Pub: University of the City of New York. Continues Intercollegiate Law Journal. *M.* (during academic year).

University of British Columbia Legal Notes. No information available.

University of Chicago Law Review. Chicago. 20 v. May, 1933–Summer 1952* *Q.* (v. 1, 5 nos.)

University of Chicago Law School Record. 1 v. 1952(?)* Pub: For the Alumni of University of Chicago Law School. *Q.*

University of Cincinnati Law Review. Cincinnati. 21 v. Jan. 1927–Nov. 1952* Suspended publication 1943–47. *Q.*

University of Detroit Bi-Monthly Law Review. Detroit. 14 v. Nov. 1916–June 1931. Title, v. 1: Monthly Law Review: v. 2: Law Review; 3–10: Bimonthly Law Review. Suspended June 1918–Sept. 1919. Continued by University of Detroit Law Journal.

University of Detroit Law Journal. Detroit. 16 v. Nov. 1931–May 1953* Publication suspended Feb. 1933–Nov. 1939. Supersedes University of Detroit Bimonthly Law Review. *Q.*

University of Florida Law Review. Jacksonville. 5 v. Spring 1948–Winter 1952* *Q.*

University of Illinois Law Bulletin. *See* Illinois Law Quarterly.

University of Illinois Law Forum. Urbana. Spring 1949–Winter, 1952* no volume numbering. Pub: College of Law, University of Illinois. *Q.*

University of Kansas City Law Review. Kansas City, Mo. 21 v. Nov. 1932–Summer 1953* Title, v. 1–6, Kansas City Law Review. *Q.* (v. 1–4 *M.* Nov.–June).

University of Kansas Law Journal. 10 nos. Sept. 1912–June 1913. *M.* (except July and Aug.)

University of Kansas Law Review. Lawrence. 1 v. Nov. 1952–May 1953* 3 times a year.

University of Miami Lawyer. *See* Miami Lawyer.

University of Missouri Bulletin, Law Series. Columbia, 50 nos. 1913–1935. Superseded by Missouri Law Review. *Irreg.*

University of New Brunswick Law Journal. St. John, N. B. 5 v. 1948–1952* Twice a year.

University of Newark Law Review. Newark, N. J. 7 v. May 1936–June 1942. Absorbed New Jersey Law Review and Mercer Beasley Law Review. *Semi-A.* (v. 1, 1 no.; v. 4–5, *Q.*)

University of Omaha Night School of Law Bulletin. Omaha, Neb. 3 v. Mar. 1923–Jan. 1927. *Irreg.* (v. 1, 2 nos., March., Oct. 1923; v. 2: 2 nos. May 1924, Oct. 1925; v. 3: 1 no., Jan. 1927).

University of Pennsylvania Law Review. Philadelphia. 101 v. Nov. 1852–June 1953* Title, v. 1–55, American Law Register, (1852–1907). Volume numbers irreg. from Jan. 1908 to Oct. 1910; v. 56–59 also called N. S. v. 47–50. *M.* (during academic year; Dec. 1917–May 1925, *Bi-M.*)

University of Pittsburgh Law Review. Pittsburgh, Pa. 14 v. Mar. 1935–Summer 1953* Publication suspended May 1942–Oct. 1947. *Q.*

University of Queensland Law Journal. Brisbane. 3 nos. Dec. 1948–Sept. 1951* v. 1 #1, Dec. 1948; #2, Aug. 1950; #3, Sept. 1951.

University of Toronto Law Journal. Toronto. 9 v. 1935–1952* *A.* (2 nos. to a vol.)

University of Washington Alumni News Bulletin. Seattle. no. 1. Aug. 1951* Pub: School of Law.

Upper Canada Jurist. Toronto. 2 v. 1844–48.

Upper Canada Law Journal. *See* Canada Law Journal (Toronto).

Urban District Councils' Association Official Circular. London. 45 v. 1890–1935*.

Utah Bar Bulletin: Official Organ of Utah State Bar. Salt Lake City. 22 v. Oct. 1931–Dec. 1952* *M.*

Utah Law Review. Salt Lake City. 3 v. 1949–1952* None pub. 1951. *Semi-A.* (*A.* 1949–1950).

Vanderbilt Law Review. Nashville, Tenn. 5 v. Dec. 1947–Ap. 1952* *Q.*

Victoria Law Journal. Melbourne. 2 v. Feb. 1932–Ap. 1933. *M.* (v. 1, no. 1 not pub.; v. 2, 4 nos.)

Victoria Law Times and Legal Observer. Melbourne. 2 v. May 10, 1856–Sept. 26, 1857. *W.* (May-Oct. 1856); *Irreg.* (Nov. 1856–Sept. 1857).

Videlicet, the Librarian's Now and Then Letter. Indianapolis. 5 v. Oct. 1936–June 1941*? Pub: Indianapolis Bar Association Library. 3 issues a year.

Virginia Bar Weekly. Richmond. 3 v. Jan. 21, 1941–Jan. 4, 1944. Pub: Daily Record Co. *W.* (v. 3, 46 nos.)

Virginia Law Digest: A Synopsis of the Decisions of the Supreme Court of Appeals. Richmond. 6 v. Jan. 1928–Dec. 1933. Pub: Under Auspices of Virginia State Bar Assn. *M.*

Virginia Law Journal. Richmond. 17 v. Jan. 1877–Sept. 14, 1893. Imprint varies. *M.* (v. 1–13); *W.* (v. 14–17).

Virginia Law Register. Charlottesville. May 1895–Ap. 1928. Merged into Virginia Law Review. O. S. v. 1–20, May 1895–Ap. 1915; N. S. v. 1–13, May 1915–Ap. 1928. Vol. 1–10 pub. Lynchburg by J. P. Bell Co. *M.*

Virginia Law Review. Charlottesville. 38 v. Oct. 1913–Dec. 1952* Pub: University of Virginia Law School. Absorbed Virginia Law Register May 1928. *M.* (during academic year).

Virginia Law Weekly. Charlottesville. 5 v. May 23, 1948–1953* Pub: Dept. of Law, University of Virginia.

Virginia Law Weekly; Dicta; a compilation of the Virginia Law Weekly. Charlottesville. 3 v. 1948/49–50/51* Each issue on a separate topic. *A.*

Wage and Hour Reporter; News and the Law of Wage Hour Regulation. Washington, D. C. 9 v. Oct. 24, 1938–Ap. 29, 1946. Absorbed by Labor Relations Reporter. v. 9, 17 nos.

War and Peace. *See* International Review.

Washington and Lee Law Review. Lexington, Va. 9 v. 1939–1952* Suspended publication 1942–Oct. 1946. *Semi-A.*

Washington Law Exchange. Washington, D. C. 2 v. 1890–91. Title, v. 1: Students' Law Exchange.

Washington Law Reporter. Washington, D. C. 79 v. Jan. 13, 1874–Dec. 1951* Title varies. For a complete checklist of numbers issued to 1938 see Law Library Journal, v. 31, p. 369–376, Sept. 1938. *W.*

Washington Law Review and State Bar Journal. Seattle. 27 v. Ap. 1919–Nov. 1952* Pub: University of Washington Law School; official organ of Washington State Bar Assn. Absorbed State Bar Review, Oct. 1936. Suspended publication May 1919–Sept. 1925. *Q.*

Washington State Bar News. Seattle. 5 v. Mar. 1947–1951* Pub: State Bar Assn.

Washington University Law Library Bulletin. *See* Law Library Bulletin.

Washington University Law Quarterly. St. Louis, Mo. 31 v. Dec. 1915–1952* Title, v. 1–21, St. Louis Law Review. Volume numbering discontinued after v. 28, 1949. Publication suspended 1943–Sept. 1949. 1949, 1 issue.

Washington University School of Law News Letter. St. Louis, Mo. 34 nos. Nov. 1937–Ap. 1953* Pub: Law Library Staff of Washington University. Mimeo. *Irreg.*

Wayne County Legal News. Detroit. 1 v. (52 nos.) Ap. 1894–Ap. 1895.

Weekly Jurist. Bloomington, Ill. 7 v. May 1874–1881. Title, v. 1–3, 1874–1877: Monthly Western Jurist; v. 4–5 (1877–79): Monthly Jurist. v. 4–5 also issued as [Ser. 2] v. 1–2; v. 6–7 also issued as [Ser. 3] v. 1–2.

Weekly Law and Bank Bulletin. *See* Weekly Law Gazette.

Weekly Law Bulletin and Ohio Law Journal. *See* Ohio Law Bulletin.

Weekly Law Gazette. Cincinnati. 5 v. 1858–June 30, 1860. Title, v. 1: Weekly Law and Bank Bulletin.

Weekly Law Magazine and Law Clerks' Magazine. London. 2 v. (52 nos.) Oct. 1, 1842–1843.

Weekly Law Reports. London. 1 v. 1953* Supplementary to Law Reports. Supersedes Weekly Notes.

Weekly Law Review. San Francisco. 3 nos. 1885.

Weekly Notes. London. 84 v. 1866–1952. Superseded by Weekly Law Reports.

Weekly Notes (New South Wales.) *See* South Wales Weekly Notes.

Weekly Reporter. London. 54 v. 1852–Oct. 27, 1906. Absorbed by Solicitors' Journal.

Weekly Transcript. New York. 1 v. (11 nos.) Jan 5–Mar. 16, 1861.

West Coast Reporter. San Francisco. 10 v. Jan. 3, 1884–May 6, 1886. Supersedes Pacific Coast Law Journal. Merged with Pacific Reporter. v. 4–10 include also decisions of U. S. Circuit and District courts of Alaska. *W.* (v. 10, 6 nos.)

West Publishing Co.'s Docket. *See* Docket, West Publishing Co.

West Virginia Law Quarterly. *See* West Virginia Law Review.

West Virginia Law Review. Morgantown. 54 v. Mar. 1894–June 1952* Publication suspended June 1943–Dec. 1946. Title varies: Mar. 1894–Dec. 1895, West Virginia Bar; Jan. 1896–July 1917 (v. 24) The Bar . . .; v. 25–31, 1917–1925, West Virginia Law Quarterly and The Bar; v. 32–51, 1925–1949, West Virginia Law Quarterly. 3 nos. a year (*M.*, 1894–1901; *M.*, Oct.–May, *Bi-M.*, June–Sept., 1902–1917; 4 nos. a year, 1917–1951).

Western Australia Annual Law Review. *See* Annual Law Review.

Western Jurist. Des Moines. 17 v. Feb. 1867–1883. Contains Court reports. Merged into American Law Review after Dec. 1883. *M.* (*Bi-M.*, 1867–Ap. 1870).

Western Law Journal. Cincinnati. 10 v. Oct. 1843–Oct. 1853. Imprint varies. Vol. 6–10 also numbered N. S. v. 1–5. *M.*

Western Law Monthly. Cleveland. 5 v. Jan. 1859–Ap. 1863. Vol. 5, 4 nos.

Western Law Review. San Francisco. 1 v. 1885.

Western Legal News. Lincoln, Neb. 4 nos. 1887.

Western Legal Observer. Quincy, Ill. 12 nos. 1849. *M.*

Western Political Quarterly. Salt Lake City, Utah. 5 v. Mar. 1948–1952*

Western Reserve Law Journal. Cleveland. 7 v. Feb. 1895–May, 1901. Pub: Faculty and Students of Franklin T. Backus Law School of Western Reserve University. *M.* (*Irreg.*)

Western Reserve Law Notes. Cleveland. 2 v. 1941–1942. Preceded by Law Notes, March, 1940. Superseded by Western Reserve Law Review. *A.*

Western Reserve Law Review. Cleveland. 4 v. June 1949–Winter 1953* Supersedes Western Reserve Law Notes. Twice a year.

Westminster Hall Chronicle and Legal Examiner. London. 2 v. Nov. 1835–July 1836. Supersedes Legal Examiner and Law Chronicle. *W.*

Willamette Series of Legal Handbooks. Salem, Oregon. #1–16. 1948–July 1952* devoted to "Instructions to Juries as Commented upon by the Supreme Court of Oregon." Pub: College of Law, Willamette University. *Irreg.*

William & Mary Review of Virginia Law. Williamsburg (intramural law review published by students of Dept. of Jurisprudence, College of William & Mary) v. 1, no. 1–4. May 1949–May 1952* *A.*

Wisconsin Bar Bulletin. Madison. 25 v. Sept. 1927–Dec. 1952* Title, 1927–May 1948, Bulletin of the State Bar Association of Wisconsin; August–November 1948, Bulletin of the Wisconsin Bar Association. *Bi-M.* (*Q.* through 1951).

Wisconsin Bench and Bar. 14 nos. Ap.–June 1898.

Wisconsin Law Review. Madison. 27 v. Oct. 1920–July 1953* Volume numbering discontinued after v. 12, 1937. Pub: University of Wisconsin Law School. *Q.* (during academic year).

Wisconsin Legal News. Milwaukee. 6 v. Oct. 1878–1884. *W.*

Wisconsin State Bar Association Bulletin. *See* Wisconsin Bar Bulletin.

Women Lawyers' Journal. Washington, D. C. 38 v. May 1911–Fall 1952* Pub: National Assn. of Women Lawyers. *Q.* (*Irreg.*)

Woolsack. Liverpool. 16 pts. 1923–1938.

Workmen's Compensation Bulletin. *See* Association of Casualty and Surety Executives. Bulletin.

Workmen's Compensation Law Journal. New York. 10 v. Jan. 1918–Oct. 1922.

World Affairs. London. v. 1–12 #3. April 1935–Oct. 1946; N. S. 5 v. Jan. 1947–Oct. 1951. Title varies: v. 1–8, Ap. 1935–Ap. 1943, New Commonwealth Quarterly; v. 9–12, July 1943–Oct. 1946, London Quarterly of World Affairs. Pub: Under auspices of London Institute of World Affairs, formerly New Commonwealth Institute. *Q.*

World Affairs Interpreter. Los Angeles. 23 v. Spring 1930–Jan. 1953* Title, v. 1–3, #1: Quarterly Journal of Science, Religion, Philosophy. Pub: Los Angeles University of International Relations. *Q.*

World Federation — Now. Winnetka, Ill. 3 v. Ap. 1939–Dec. 1941*? Official organ of Campaign for World Government. *Irreg.*

World Politics; a Quarterly Journal of International Relations. New Haven, Conn. 5 v. Oct. 1948–July 1953* Pub: Yale Institute of International Studies. *Q.*

World Today. London. 8 v. July 1945–Dec. 1952* Continues Bulletin of International News. Pub: Royal Institute of International Affairs. *M.*

World Trade Law Journal. Chicago. 1 v. Jan.–Oct. 1946. Pub: Commerce Clearing House.

Wyoming Law Journal. Laramie. 6 v. Dec. 1946–Summer 1952* Pub: joint auspices of University of Wyoming College of Law and Wyoming State Bar. *Q.*

Yale Law Journal. New Haven, Conn. 61 v. Oct. 1891–Nov. 1952* *M.* (with many variations).

Yale Law School Association. Alumni Newsletter. New Haven. 5 v. Dec. 1948–April 1953* Supersedes Yale Law School Association Newsletter. *Irreg.*

Yale Law School Association. Newsletter. New Haven. v. 1, no. 1–2. July 1947–Jan. 1948. Superseded by Yale Law School Association. Alumni Newsletter.

Yale Political Journal. New Haven. v. 1, no. 1–3. Feb. 1947–Spring 1948.

Yale Reporter. New Haven. 1946*? 1946 called Supplement. Revival of an annual known as Yale Shingle, pub. from 1893 to 1912. Pub: Student Assn. of School of Law, Yale University.

Yearbook of School Law. Washington, D. C. 10 v.; 2d Ser. 3 v. 1933–1942; 1950–1952* Suspended 1943–1949. Imprint varies.

Young Lawyer. Chicago. 8 v. Jan. 1945–Feb. 1953* Pub: Junior Bar Conference, American Bar Assn. *Irreg.*

STANDARD FORM OF APPELLATE BRIEF [1]

[COVER TITLE.]

No. 387

Supreme Court of the United States

October Term, 1951

Jones & Company, *Petitioner,*

v.

Smith Corporation, *Respondent*

ON WRIT OF CERTIORARI TO THE UNITED STATES COURT OF APPEALS FOR THE EIGHTH CIRCUIT

BRIEF FOR PETITIONER

John Jones Smith,
Attorney for Petitioner

---

[1]This form is reprinted here by permission of a prominent law firm. It is the form supplied to its own attorneys for use by them in writing briefs. It is, of course, only an outline of a complete brief.

INDEX

CITATIONS

[FIRST PAGE OF BRIEF]

Supreme Court of the United States

OCTOBER TERM, 1951

No. 387

JONES & COMPANY, *Petitioner,*

v.

SMITH CORPORATION, *Respondent*

ON WRIT OF CERTIORARI TO THE UNITED STATES COURT OF APPEALS FOR THE EIGHTH CIRCUIT

BRIEF FOR PETITIONER

OPINIONS BELOW

The opinion of the District Court (R. 202) is unreported. The opinion and dissenting opinion in the Court of Appeals (R. 276) are reported at 182 F.2d 841.

JURISDICTION

This is an action for breach of contract, brought in the District Court of the United States for the Western District of Missouri. The District Court had jurisdiction under 28 U. S. Code Sec. 1332, the plaintiff Smith Corporation being organized under the laws of the State of Missouri (R. 36), the defendant Jones & Company being a partnership all of whose members are citizens of the State of Oklahoma (R. 48), and the matter in controversy exceeding the sum of $3,000 exclusive of interest and costs (R. 171).

The final judgment of the District Court, in favor of the plaintiff for the sum of $4,325.76 and costs, was entered on January 16, 1949 (R. 204). Notice of appeal to the United States Court of Appeals for the Eighth Circuit was filed on March 3, 1949 (R. 207), that Court having jurisdiction of the appeal under 28 U. S. Code Sec. 1291.

The final judgment of the Court of Appeals affirming the judgment of the District Court was entered on August 24, 1951 (R. 282). The petition for a writ of certiorari was filed on October 14, 1951, and was granted on November 20, 1951. The jurisdiction of this Court rests on 28 U. S. Code Sec. 1254(1).

QUESTIONS PRESENTED

*   *   *   *

STATUTE INVOLVED

The pertinent provisions of the Missouri Sale of Goods Law, Missouri Revised Code, Sections 4226-4240 (1936), are set out in full in Appendix A to this brief, pp. i-iii, *infra.*

*   *   *   *

STATEMENT

*   *   *   *

History of the Litigation

*   *   *   *

Findings of Fact and Judgment

*   *   *   *

SPECIFICATION OF ERRORS TO BE URGED

*   *   *   *

SUMMARY OF ARGUMENT

*   *   *   *

ARGUMENT

* * * *

I

THIS CASE "INVOLVES OR GROWS OUT OF A LABOR DISPUTE" AND THEREFORE IS GOVERNED BY THE NORRIS-LAGUARDIA ACT

Section 1 of the Norris-LaGuardia Act is plain and un-ambiguous:

> "... no court of the United States ... shall have juris-diction to issue any restraining order or temporary or permanent injunction in a case involving or growing out of a labor dispute, except in a strict conformity with the provisions of this Act. ..."

The "labor dispute" involved in this case consists pri-marily of three fundamental issues, etc., etc., etc.

* * * *

A. VIOLENCE AGAINST CUSTOMERS IS NEITHER CHARGED, PROVED NOR FOUND

* * * *

1. THE FINDING THAT THE POLICE WERE UNABLE AND UNWILLING TO FURNISH ADEQUATE PROTECTION MUST BE SET ASIDE

* * * *

a. Upon This Record the District Court Was Clearly Wrong in Finding that any Effort by Plaintiffs to Settle the Dispute Would Have Been Impossible, Useless, or Unreasonable, and upon the Basis of this Finding, in Excusing the Making of any Effort

* * * *

II

ALL CLAUSES OF THE DECREE ENJOINING USE OR THREATS OF FRAUD MUST BE REVERSED

* * * *

A. DISCRIMINATION AGAINST THE INTERNATIONAL

* * * *

1. FINDINGS REQUIRED BY SECTION 7(a)

* * * *

a. Speed-up System

* * * *

CONCLUSION

Wherefore, it is respectfully submitted that the judgment of the court below should be reversed and the cause remanded with instructions to grant the motion to dismiss the complaint.

August 1, 1953

Respectfully submitted,

JOHN JONES SMITH,
Attorney for Petitioner

APPENDIX A

Pertinent Provisions of Statutes

1. AGRICULTURAL ADJUSTMENT ACT OF MAY 12, 1933, C. 25, 48 STAT. 31, AS AMENDED, 48 STAT. 676, 49 STAT. 48, 770, 1739, 7 U.S.C. § 617 (1946)

Sec. 17. (a) Upon the exportation to any foreign country (and/or to the Philippine Islands, the Virgin Islands, American Samoa, the Canal Zone, and the island of Guam) of any product processed wholly or partly from a commodity with respect to which product or commodity a tax has been paid or is payable under this title, the tax due and payable or due and paid shall be credited or refunded. Under regulations prescribed by the Commissioner of Internal Revenue, with the approval of the Secretary of the Treasury, the credit or refund shall be allowed to the consignor named in the bill of lading under which the product is exported or to the shipper or to the person liable for the tax provided the consignor waives any claim thereto in favor of such shipper or person liable for the tax. In the case of rice, a tax due under this title which has been paid by a tax-payment warrant shall be deemed for the purposes of this subsection to have been paid; and with respect to any refund authorized under this section, the amount scheduled by the Commissioner of Internal Revenue. . . .

* * * *

2. INTERNAL REVENUE CODE, § 1112

In any proceeding involving the issue whether the petitioner has been guilty of fraud with intent to evade tax, the burden of proof in respect of such issue shall be upon the Commissioner.

* * * *

APPENDIX B

Legislative History

1. REPORT OF THE HOUSE COMMITTEE ON WAYS AND MEANS, H. REPT. NO. 2475, 74TH CONG., 2D SESS. (1934), p. 13.

It is the purpose of Section 601 of Title IV to reenact into law certain sections of the Agricultural Adjustment Act.

MEMORANDUM OF LAW [1]

Question Presented

Under the terms of a will governed by Rhode Island law, does a gift in trust to the testator's daughter for life with a testamentary power of appointment and a gift to "her own right heirs, of my blood" in default of appointment mean that the daughter's heirs take *per stirpes* or *per capita* upon the death of the daughter failing to exercise the power of appointment?

Conclusion

The Rhode Island cases indicate that the gift would be construed to require a stirpital division.

Facts

Joseph Paul Jones died a resident of the State of Rhode Island, and his will was proved on February 15, 1911. By the terms of his will, the testator after making certain specific bequests gave the residue of his estate to trustees in trust. He directed that the corpus be divided into five equal shares, one such share to be held in trust for each of his two sons and each of his two daughters, and one share to be held in trust for his wife. The share for each daughter was to be held for her for life, and upon her death, as she might appoint by her will, and in default of such appointment, "to her own right heirs, of my blood." One of the daughters of Joseph Paul Jones died failing to exercise the power of appointment. The question arises, do the heirs of the daughter take *per stirpes* or *per capita*.

Applicable Statutes

The applicable provisions of the Rhode Island statute of descent and distribution are found in Rhode Island General Laws 1938, ch. 567.

Course of Descent.

§ 1. Whenever any person having title to any real estate or inheritance shall die intestate as to such estate, it shall descend and pass, in equal portions to his kindred, in the following course:

First. To his children or their descendants, if any there be.

---

[1] An important function of the junior attorneys in a law firm is to submit memoranda of law to seniors, on request. The one here reproduced is an actual memorandum from such a junior to his senior, reproduced here by permission. It shows the form and style desired, though it is somewhat shorter and simpler than most memoranda. Note that the conclusion is given immediately following the statement of the problem, not at the end of the memorandum. The same form and techniques may profitably be employed by law students in their written work.

Second. If there be no children nor their descendants, then to the parents in equal shares, or to the surviving parent of such intestate.

Third. If there be no parent, then to the brothers and sisters of such intestate, and their descendants, or such of them as there be.

(As amended by ch. 1283, Public Laws 1943.)

Section 2 of ch. 567 makes provisions for the event that there be no parent nor brother nor sister.

Inheritance by Descendants.

§ 5. The descendants of any person deceased shall inherit the estate which such person would have inherited had such person survived the intestate, subject to the express provisions of these canons of descent.

Distribution of Surplus Property Not Bequeathed.

§ 9. The surplus of any chattels or personal estate of a deceased person, not bequeathed, after the payment of his just debts, funeral charges, and expenses of settling his estate, shall be distributed by order of the probate court which shall have granted administration in manner following:

First. — The sum of $3,000.00 from said surplus and one-half of the remainder to the widow or surviving husband forever, if the intestate died without issue.

Second. — One-half of said surplus to the widow or surviving husband forever, if the intestate died leaving issue.

Third. The residue shall be distributed among the heirs of the intestate in the same manner real estates descend and pass by this chapter but without having any respect to the life estate and discretionary allowance provided by section 4 of this chapter. (As amended by ch. 1283, Public Laws 1943.)

Case Law

From this it can be seen that the statute itself provides in section 7 for stirpital provision. The descendants are to inherit the share which their deceased ancestor would have taken. However, this statutory direction can be overcome if the will of the person making a gift to "heirs" indicates an intent that the division be *per capita.* For example, in *Oulton v. Kidder,* ....R. I..............., 128 Atl. 674 (1925), where a testatrix gave the residue of her estate to her brother for life, and upon his death "to Helen E. Oulton and my legal heirs," it was held that Helen Oulton and the legal heirs of the testatrix took *per capita* and not *per stirpes.* The Court said, at 128 Atl. 675,

The general rules controlling whether a gift to 'legal heirs' is to be distributed per capita or per stirpes had been considered at length in Branch v. DeWolf, 38 R.I. 395, 95 A. 857, and Turbitt v. Carney, 43 R.I. 582, 114 A. 134. The court said: 'heirs at law' commonly not only designated the beneficiaries as those who would inherit in case of intestacy but the quantum of interest each should take. This is determined per stirpes and not per capita, unless a contrary intention appears. If Helen E. Oulton had not been interjected into the residuary clause, there would be good ground for the application of the usual rules calling for a per stirpes distribution. Does the will show any facts indicating a contrary intention?

The Court answers its own question in the affirmative, and finds that the testatrix intended the distribution to be *per capita.* Helen E. Oulton received a specific gift under a separate clause of the will, and the Court found no intention to prefer her, through a stirpital division of the residue, to other nephews and nieces.

Another case in which a gift to "heirs" was held to require a *per capita* division is *Dodge* v. *Slate*, 71 R. I. 191, 43 A.2d 242 (1945). The testator left his entire estate to "my heirs now living, share and share alike." The Court says at 43 A.2d 244,

> In both sentences which constitute clause "First" of the will, the testator leaves the estate to his "heirs." Although there are decisions to the contrary, it is generally held that, in the absence of language in the will indicating a different intention, a devise or bequest to a testator's "heirs," without qualification, designates not only the persons who are to take, but also the manner in which the estate shall be distributed, both being in accordance with the statute of intestate succession. The determining issue on this point therefore is whether the testator intended a distribution to his estate to be different from the one prescribed by such statute.

By singling out the words "share and share alike" and "equally among the heirs," the Court finds an intention that the estate be distributed to the heirs *per capita*. Great stress is laid on the word "among" as indicative of an intention that the distribution be *per capita*.

The will of Joseph Paul Jones appears to contain not the slightest hint of an intention that the distribution to the heirs of his daughter should be other than that provided by the statute, that is, stirpital. It is assumed, that at the time the will was executed, the daughters of the testator were unmarried and childless, consequently it cannot be argued that there were any particular individuals in mind when he used the word "heirs." It would seem that here, the general rule of a *per stirpes* provision should apply. No significance can be attached to the word "right" or the words "of my blood" used in the phrase "to her own right heirs, of my blood." These words in no way connote a *per capita* provision. The words "right heirs" are synonymous with "legal heirs," or just "heirs," *Starrett* v. *Botsford*, 64 R. I. 1, 9 A.2d 871 (1931). The cases of *Oulton* v. *Kidder, supra*, and *Dodge* v. *Slate, supra*, which found an intention that there be a *per capita* distribution are clearly distinquishable on their facts from the situation at hand.

A recent case, *Powers* v. *Dossett*,................R. I................, 81 A.2d 275 (1951), held that a gift to heirs at law required a *per stirpes* distribution. In this case a testatrix established by her will a trust for her father-in-law and mother-in-law for life, and upon the death of the survivor directed her trustee "to pay over to my heirs at law all [the] trust estate." In a construction proceeding, the Court said,

> In construing the meaning of heirs at law as used in the instant will, we find nothing therein to show clearly that the testatrix intended that those answering such description should be determined at a time other than at her death. We therefore apply the general rule to the will before us and decide that the testatrix' heirs at law are those to whom her estate and property would pass immediately upon her death by operation of law under the statutes of descent and distribution of this state. It follows that our answer to the first question is that the balance of the trust estate should be distributed among the heirs at law of the testatrix *per stirpes*.

As previously said, no intention can be found in the will of Joseph Paul Jones that the distribution to the heirs of his daughter should be other than *per stirpes*. His daughter's heirs will naturally be ascertained at the time of her death.

February 10, 1953

ABBREVIATIONS COMMONLY USED IN
ANGLO-AMERICAN LAW.[1]

Scope of Definitions.

The definitions in this list do not aim at bibliographical completeness, but for the most part such further information as is needed may be found by using the list as a point of reference to other tables in this Bibliographical Manual. For example, American law reports are listed and described in Appendix I; British in Appendix II; and Anglo-American legal periodicals are listed and described in Appendix III. In looking up references to English reports prior to 1865, it should be remembered that nearly all of these were reprinted in the *English Reports — Full Reprint.* In most libraries a chart is posted by the *Reprint,* listing all included reports and reporters by name, and their location in the respective volumes of the *Reprint.*

Although this list of abbreviations aims at substantial completeness for practical purposes, no attempt is made to list each possible variation of an abbreviated title. On the other hand, for many titles there are three or four different forms of abbreviation.

Alphabetical Arrangement. In order to follow the forms of abbreviations as found in the literature, the abbreviations are listed herein in three different sequences for each initial letter.

1. Abbreviations composed entirely of single letters, or of which the *first* element is a single letter and the *second* element is not an ampersand (&). Thus:

A.B.C.	A.R.R.	A.Ins.Co.	A.T.& T.Co.

2. Next come abbreviations of which the *first* element is a single letter and the *second* is an ampersand Thus:

A.& B.	A.& E.	A.& E.Pat.Cas.

3. Last come abbreviations, the *first* element of which is composed of two or more letters, as:

Ab.Eq.Cas.	Am.L.Rev.	Ad.& El.

Abbreviations Employed in the Definitions. In the definitions themselves in this list, certain standard abbreviations are employed, among which are the following:

Adm.	Admiralty	Cas.	Cases
Admin.	Administration	Ch.	Chancery
Aus	Australia	Com.Pl.	Common Pleas
B.C.	Bail Court	Comm.	Commission
Bk. or Bkc.	Bankruptcy	Cr.Cas.	Crown Cases
Can	Canada	Ct.	Court

---

[1] This list was compiled by the authors from a wide variety of publishers' lists, library catalogs, digests, old legal dictionaries, and periodical indexes. By permission of Mr. Frederick C. Hicks it was then checked and compared with the list in his *Materials and Methods of Legal Research* (3d. rev. ed. 1942). This latter list was originally compiled by Mr. Lawrence H. Schmehl, Librarian of the New York County Lawyers' Association, who has kindly permitted the authors to consult his own annotated copy, by which he has kept it up to date.

Div.	Division	N.P.	Nisi Prius
Ecc.	Ecclesiastical	P.C.	Privy Council
Eq.	Equity	Pr.R.	Practice Reports
Ex.	Exchequer	Q.B.	Queen's Bench
H.L.	House of Lords	R.C.	Rolls Court
Ir	Ireland	Reg.Cas.	Registration Cases
K.B.	King's Bench	Rep.	Reports
Mag.Cas.	Magistrates' Cases	UN	United Nations

A. Abbott
Alabama
American
Arkansas
Atlantic Reporter
Indian Reports, Allahabad Series
Louisiana Annuals
AAA Agricultural Adjustment Admin.
U.S.
A.B. Anonymous Rep. at end of Benloe
Eng
A.B.A.J[o]. American Bar Assn.
Journal
A.B.A.Rep. American Bar Assn.
Reports
A.B.C. Australian Bankruptcy Cases
A.B.R[ep]. American Bankruptcy
Reports
A.B.Rev. American Bankruptcy
Review
A'B.R.J.N.S.W. A'Beckett Reserved
Judgments [Eq.], New South
Wales *Aus*
A'B.R.J.P.P. A'Beckett Reserved
Judgments, Port Philip, New
South Wales *Aus*
A.C. Advance California Reports
Appeal Cases, Ceylon
Buchanan, Cape Colony Ct. of Appeal
Rep.
Law Reports, Appeal Cases *Eng*
ACA Administrator of Civil Aeronau-
tics
A.C.A. Advance California Appellate
Rep.
ACAA Agricultural Conservation &
Adjustment Admin.
A.C.C. Allahabad Criminal Cases *India*
American Corporation Cases, by
Withrow
A.C.L.J. Amerian Civil Law Journal
A.C.M. Court-Martial Rep. Air Force
Cases
A.C.M.S. Special Court-Martial, U. S.
Air Force
A.C.R. American Criminal Reports,
Hawley
Appeal Court Reports, Ceylon

A.Cr.C. Allahabad Criminal Cases
India
A.D. Agriculture Decisions
American Decisions
New York Sup. Ct. Appellate Div.
Rep.
S. African Law Rep., Appellate Div.
AEC Atomic Energy Commission *U.S.*
A.E.C. American Electrical Cases
A.E.L.R. All England Law Reports
A.F.Rep. Alaska Federal Reports
AFTR American Federal Tax Reports
(P-H)
A.G. Attorney General, Opinions
AGO Adjutant General's Office
A.G.O. Attorney General, Opinions
A.I.R. All India Law Reporter
[Usually followed by a province
abbreviation, (as A.I.R. All., for
Allahabad), Bom. for Bombay,
Dacca for Dacca, H.P. for
Himachal Pradesh, Hyd. for Hy-
derabad, etc.]
A.Ins.R. American Insolvency Reports
A.J. American Jurist
British Guiana Sup. Ct., Appellate
Juris.
A.J.R. Australian Jurist Reports
A.Jur.Rep. Australian Jurist Reports
A.K.Marsh. A. K. Marshall (v. 8-10
Ky.)
A.L.C. (or ALC) American Labor
Cases (P-H)
American Leading Cases
A.L.J. Albany Law Journal
Allahabad Law Journal *India*
American Law Journal
Australian Law Journal
A.L.J.N.S. American Law Journal,
N.S.
A.L.M. American Law Magazine
A.L.R. Alberta Law Reports *Canada*
American Labor Cases (P-H)
American Law Reports, Annotated
Argus Law Reports, Victoria *Aus*
A.L.R.(C.N.) Argus Law Rep.
Current Notes

A.L.Rec. American Law Record
A.L.Reg. American Law Register
A.L.Rep. American Law Reporter
A.L.Rev. American Law Review
A.L.T. American Law Times
Australian Law Times
A.L.T.Bankr. American Law Times,
Bankruptcy Rep.
A.L.T.R. American Law Times
Reports
AMA Agricultural Marketing Admin.
U.S.
AMS Agricultural Marketing Service
U.S.
A.M.& O. Armstrong, Macartney &
Ogle N.P. *Ir*
A.M.C. American Maritime Cases
A.M.L.J. Ajmer-Merwara Law Journal
India
A.M.S.,P.& S. Agricultural Marketing
Service, P.& S. Docket *U.S.*
A.Moo. A. Moore Rep., in 1 Bosanquet
& Puller *Eng*
A.N.C. Abbott's New Cases *N.Y.*
American Negligence Cases
A.N.R. American Negligence Reports
AO Administrative Order
A.P. Annual Practice *Eng*
APC Alien Property Custodian *U.S.*
A.P.D. Alien Property Div. (Justice
Dept.) *U.S.*
A.P.S.C. Alabama Public Service
Commission Dec.
A.R. American Reports
Army Regulations *U.S.*
Atlantic Reporter
Argus Reports *Aus*
Industrial Arbitration Rep.,
N.S.Wales
Ontario Appeal Reports
ARA Agricultural Research Admin.
U.S.
ARC American Red Cross
A.R.C. American Railway Cases
American Ruling Cases
A.R.M. Internal Revenue Bureau
Committee on Appeals & Review,
Memorandum *U.S.*
A.R.(N.S.W.) Industrial Arbitration
Rep., New South Wales
A.R.(Ont) Ontario Appeal Reports
A.R.R. American Railway Reports
Internal Revenue Bureau Committee
on Appeals & Review, Recom-
mendation *U.S.*
A.Rep. American Reports
Atlantic Reporter

ASB Air Safety Board *U.S.*
ASPR Armed Services Procurement
Regulation
A.S.R. American State Reports
ASRB Armed Services Renegotiation
Bd. *U.S.*
A.T. Alcohol & Tobacco Tax Div.,
Internal Revenue Bureau *U.S.*
A.T.C. Annotated Tax Cases *Eng*
A.W. Articles of War
A.W.N. Allahabad Weekly Notes
India
A.& E. Admiralty & Ecclesiastical
Adolphus & Ellis, Q.B. Reports *Eng*
A.& E. Ann.Cas. American & English
Annotated Cases
A.& E.Corp.Cas. American & English
Corporation Cases
A.& E.Ency.Law American & English
Encyclopedia of Law
A.& E.N.S. Adolphus & Ellis, Q.B.
Rep.N.S. *Eng*
A.&E.Pat.Cas. American & English
Patent Cas.
A.& E.R.Cas. American & English
Railroad Cas.
A.& E.R.Cas.N.S. *Same*, New Series
A.& H. Arnold & Hodges, Q.B.
Reports *Eng*
A.& N. Alcock & Napier, K.B. Rep. *Ir*
Ab. Abstracts of Treasury Decisions
U.S.
Ab.Eq.Cas. Equity Cases Abridged
Eng
Abb. Abbott, Circuit & District Ct.
Rep. *U.S.*
Abb.Adm. Abbott, Admiralty Reports
U.S.
Abb.App.Dec. Abbott Ct. of Appeals
Dec. *N.Y.*
Abb.C.C. Abbott's Circuit Court Rep.
U.S.
Abb.Ct.App. Abbott Ct. of Appeals
Dec. *N.Y.*
Abb.Dec. Same as above.
Abb.N.Cas. Abbott's New Cases *N.Y.*
Abb.N.Y.App. Abbott Ct. of Appeals
Dec. *N.Y.*
Abb.Pr. Abbott, Practice Reports *N.Y.*
Abb.Pr.N.S. *Same*, New Series
Abb.U.S. Abbott, Circuit Ct. Reports
U.S.
Abbrev.Plac. Placitorum Abbreviatis,
Record Commissioner *Eng*
A'Beck.Judg.Vict. A'Beckett, Reserved
Judgments, Victoria *Aus*

Abr.Cas. Crawford & Dix, Abridged
Cas.   *Ir*

Abr.Cas.Eq. Equity Cases Abridged
                                        Eng

Acad.Pol.Sci.Proc. Academy of Political Science Proceedings   *U.S.*

Acct.L.Rep. Accountant Law Reports
                                        Eng

Act.Ass. Acts of the General Assembly,
Church of Scotland 1638-1842

Act.Can. Acta Cancellariae, by
Monroe   *Eng*

Act.Cur.Ad.Sc. Acta Curiae
Admiralatus Scotiae (Wade)

Act.Lawt.Ct. Acts of Lawting Court
                                        Scot

Act.Ld.Aud.C. Acts of Lords
Auditors of Causes   *Scot*

Act.Ld.Co. C.C. Acts of Lords of
Council in Civil Causes 1478-1501
                                        Scot

Act.Ld.Co.Pub.Aff. Acts of the Lords
of Council in Public Affairs *Scot*

Act.P.C. Acts of the Privy Council
(Dasent)   *Eng*

Act.P.C.N.S. Same as above, New
Series   *Eng*

Act.Pr.C. Acton's reports, Prize Cases
                                        Eng

Act.Pr.C.Col.S. Acts of the Privy
Council, Colonial Series   *Eng*

Ad. Addams' Ecclesiastical Reports
                                        Eng

Ad.& El. Adolphus & Ellis' K. B. Rep.
                                        Eng

Ad.& El. N. S. Same as above, New
Series

Adam Adam's Justiciary Reports *Scot*

Adams Adam's Reports (41, 42 Maine)
Adams' Reports (1 New Hampshire)

Add. Addams' Ecclesiastical Reports
                                        Eng
Addison's Reports (Pa. Supreme
Court)

Addams Addams' Ecclesiastical
Reports   *Eng*

Add.E.R. Same as above

Add.Pa. Addison's County Court
Reports   *Pa*

Adm.& Ecc. Law Reports, Admiralty
& Ecclesiastical   *Eng*

Admin.Dec. Administrative Decision

Adol.& El. Adolphus & Ellis' Q. B.
Rep.   *Eng*

Adol.& El.N.S. Same as above, New
Series

Adv.Chron. Advocates' Chronicle
                                        India

Adv.Rep.N.J. New Jersey Advance
Reports & Weekly Review

Advocate Advocate (B. C.)   *Canada*

Agra F.B. Agra High Court, Rep. Full
Bench   *India*

Agra H.C. Agra High Court Reports
                                        India

Aik. Aiken's Reports (Vermont
1825-28)

Air L.R. Air Law Review

Aiyar Aiyar's Company Cases   *India*

Aiyar C.C. Same as above

Aiyar L.P.C. Aiyar's Leading Privy
Council Cases   *India*

Aiyar Unrep.D. Aiyar's Unreported
Decisions   *India*

Ajmer-Merwara L.J. Ajmer-Merwara
Law Journal   *India*

Al. Alabama
Aleyn, King's Bench Reports   *Eng*

Al.Kada Native Tribunals' Reports
                                        Egypt

Al.& Nap. Alcock & Napier, K.B. Rep.
                                        Ir

Al.Ser. Indian Law Reports, Allahabad
Ser.

Ala. Alabama Supreme Court
Minor's Alabama Reports 1820-26

Ala.App. Alabama Appeals Reports

Ala.L.J. Alabama Law Journal

Ala.L.Rev. Alabama Law Review

Ala.Law. Alabama Lawyer

Ala.N.S. Alabama Reports, N.S.,
1840-date

Ala.S.BA. Alabama State Bar Assn.

Ala.Sel.Cas. Alabama Select Cas. (and
in 37-39 Alabama)

Ala.St.Bar Assn. Alabama State Bar
Assn.

Alaska Alaska Reports

Alaska Fed. Alaska Federal Reports

Alb.Arb. Albert Arbitration (Cairns
Dec.)   *Eng*

Alb.L.J. Albany Law Journal

Alb.L.Q. Alberta Law Quarterly

Alb.L.R. Alberta Law Reports

Alb.L.Rev. Albany Law Review

Alb.L.S.Jour. Albany Law School
Journal

Alc. Alcock, Registry Cases   *Ir*

Alc.& N. Alcock & Napier, K.B.& Ex.
Rep.   *Ir*

Alc.Reg.Cas. Alcock's Registry Cases
                                        Ir

Ald. Alden's Condensed Reports   *Pa*

Alexander Alexander's Reports (66-72 Miss.)

Aleyn Aleyn's King's Bench Reports *Eng*

All. Indian Law Reports, Allahabad Series

Allen, *infra* *India*

All.Cr.Cas. Allahabad Criminal Cases

All.E.R. All England Law Reports (formerly All England Law Reports Annotated)

All Ind.Cr.R. All Indian Criminal Reports

All Ind.Cr. T. All India Criminal Times

All Ind.Rep. All India Reporter

All Ind.Rep.N.S. Same as above, New Series

All.L.J.& Rep. Allahabad Law Journal Reports *India*

All.L.T. Allahabad Law Times *India*

All.N.B. Allen's New Brunswick Rep. *Canada*

All.Tel.Cas. Allen's Telegraph Cases

All.W.N. Allahabad Weekly Notes (and Supplement) *India*

All.W.R. Allahabad Weekly Reporter *India*

Allen Allen's Reports (83-96 Mass.)

Allen's Reports (6-11 New Brunswick) *Can*

Allen's Reports (1-2 1854-1885 Washington Terr.)

Allin. Allinson's Pa. Super & District Court Reports

Alta.L.Q. Alberta Law Quarterly *Canada*

Alta.L.R. Alberta Law Reports *Canada*

Alves Dampier & Maxwell's British Guiana Reports

Allwood Allwood's Appeal Cases under the Weights & Measures Act *Eng*

Am.B.A. American Bar Association

Am.B.R. American Bankruptcy Reports

Am.B.R.N.S. *Same*, New Series

Am.Bank.Rev. American Bankruptcy Review

Am.Bar Ass.J. American Bar Assn. Journal

Am.C.L.J. American Civil Law Journal

Am.City The American City

Am.Civ.L.J. American Civil Law Journal

Am.Consul.Bul. American Consular Bulletin

Am.Corp.Cas. American Corporation Cases

Am.Cr.Rep. American Criminal Rep., Hawley

Am.Dec. American Decisions

Am.Dig. American Digest

Am.Econ.Rev. American Economic Review

Am.Electl.Cas. American Electrical Cases

Am.Fed.Tax R. American Federal Tax Rep. (P-H)

Am.Ins.Rep. American Insolvency Reports

Am.J. Comp.Law American Journal of Comparative Law

Am.J.Int.L. American Journal of International Law

Am.Jud.Soc. American Judicature Society (Bulletins or Journal)

Am.Jur. American Jurisprudence American Jurist

Am.L.Cas. American Leading Cases

Am.L.J. American Law Journal (Philadelphia or Columbus, Ohio)

Am.L.J.N.S. *Same*, New Series

Am.L.M. American Law Magazine

Am.L.Rec. American Law Record

Am.L.Rev. American Law Review

Am.L.S.Rev. American Law School Review

Am.L.T. American Law Times

Am.L.T.Bankr. American Law Times Bankruptcy Reports

Am.L.T.R. American Law Times Reports

Am.L.T.R.N.S. *Same*, New Series

Am.Lab.Cas. American Labor Cases (P-H)

Am.Lab.Arb.Cas. American Labor Arbitration Cases (P-H)

Am.Lab.Leg.Rev. American Labor Legis. Review

Am.Law Mag. American Law Magazine

Am.Law Rec. American Law Record

Am.Law Reg. American Law Register

Am.Law Rev. American Law Review

Am.Law S.Rev. American Law School Review

Am.Lawy. American Lawyer

Am.Lead.Cas. American Leading Cases.

Am.Leg.N. American Legal News

Am.Mar.Cas. American Maritime Cases

Am.Neg.Cas. American Negligence Cases

Am.Neg.Rep. American Negligence Reports

Am.Pol.Sci.Rev. American Political Science Review

Am.Prob.Rep. American Probate Reports

Am.R.Ca. American Railway Cases

Am.R.R.& C.Rep. American Railroad & Corporation Reports

Am.R.R.Cas. American Railway Cases

Am.Rail.Cas. American Railway Cases

Am.Rep. American Reports (Ann. Cases System)

Am.Ry.Ca. American Railway Cases

Am.Ry.Rep. American Railway Reports

Am.St.P. American State Papers

Am.St.Rep. American State Reports (Annotated Cases System)

Am.St.Ry.Dec. American Street Railway Dec.

Am.Taxp.Q. American Taxpayers' Quarterly

Am.Them. American Themis

Am.Tr.M.Cas. American Trade Mark Cases (Cox)

Am.U.Int.L.Rev. American University, Intramural Law Review

Am.& Eng.Corp.Cas. American & English Corporation Cases

Am.& Eng.Dec.in Eq. American & English Decisions in Equity

Am.& Eng.Encyc.Law American & English Encyclopaedia of Law

Am.& Eng.Pat.Cas. American & English Patent Cases

Am.& Eng.R.Cas. American & English Railr.Cas.

Am.& Eng.R.Cas.N.S. *Same*, New Series

Amb. Ambler's Reports, Chancery *Eng*

Amer. American

Amerman's Reports (111-115 Pa.)

Amer.Fed.Tax Rep. American Federal Tax Rep. (P-H)

Amer.Jur. American Jurist

Amer.Lawy. American Lawyer

Amer.Law Reg.(N.S.) American Law Register, New Series

Amer.Law Reg.(O.S.) *Same*, Old Series

Amer.& Eng.Enc.Law. American & English Encyclopaedia of Law

Ames Ames' Reports (1 Minnesota)

Ames' Reports (4-7 Rhode Island)

Ames,K.& B. Ames, Knowles & Bradley (8 R.I.)

An. Anonymous, at end of Benloe Reports 1661

And. Anderson's Com. Pleas Rep. *temp*. Eliz.

Anderson's Agriculture Cases   *Scot*

Andrews' K.B. Reports   *Eng*

Andrews' Reports (63-73 Conn.)

Andr. Andrews' K.B. Reports   *Eng*

Ang. Angell's Rhode Island Reports

Angell & Durfee Reports (1 Rhode Island)

Ang.& Dur. *See* above

Ann. Cunningham's Rep. temp. Hardwicke, K. B., 7-10 Geo.II

Ann.Cas. American & English Annotated Cases

American Annotated Cases

New York Annotated Cases

Ann.Cong. Annals of Congress

Ann.L.Rep. Annotated Law Reporter 1932-35   *India*

Ann.Law Reg. Annual Law Register   *U.S.*

Ann.Leg.Forms Mag. Annotated Legal Forms Mag.

Ann.Tax Cas. Annotated Tax Cases 1922-date   *Eng*

Annals Annals of American Academy of Political & Social Science

Annaly Lee's K.B. Reports *temp*. Hardwicke. Annaly edition. *Eng*

Anst. Anstruther's Reports, Exchequer   *Eng*

Anth. Anthon's New York N.P. Reports

Anth.N.P. Same as above

Ap.Bre. Breese's Illinois Rep., Appendix

App. Appleton's Reports (19, 20 Maine)

Ohio Appellate Reports

App.Bd.O.C.S. Office of Contract Settlement, Appeal Board Decisions.   *U.S.*

App.Ca. Buchanan, Reports, Ct. of Appeal, Cape Colony   *S.Af.*

App.Cas. Law Reports, Appeal Cases   *Eng*

App.Cas.Beng. Sevestre & Marshall, Bengal Rep.

App.Ct.Rep. Appeal Court Reports
New Zeal.
Bradwell's Illinois Appeal Ct. Reports

App.D. South African Law Rep.,
Appellate Div.

App.D.C. Appeal Cases, District of
Columbia

App.Div. Appellate Div. Rep., N.Y.
Sup. Ct.

App.Fish.Com. Appeals from Fisheries
Commission 1861-93 *Ir*

App.N.Z. Appeal Reports, New
Zealand

App.Rep. Ontario Appeal Reports
Canada

App.Tax Serv. Appeals Relating to
Tax on Servants 1781 *Eng*

Appleton Appleton's Reports (19, 20
Maine)

Arabin Arabin's Decisions *Eng*

Arb.J. Arbitration Journal
Arb.J.N.S. *Same,* New Series
Arbitration *Eng*

Arbuth. Arbuthnot Select Crim. Cas.
Madras

Arch.L.R. Architects Law Reports
Eng

Arch.P.L.Cas. Archbold's Poor Law
Cas. *Eng*

Archer Archer's Reports (2 Florida)

Archer & Hogue Archer & Hogue
(2 Florida)

Architects'L.R. Architects' Law Rep.
Eng

Arg.Mo. Moore's King's Bench Reports
(Arguments of Moore) *Eng*

Arg.Rep. Argus Reports *Aus*

Arg.L.R. Argus Law Reports *Aus*

Ariz. Arizona

Ark. Arkansas
Arkley, Justiciary Reports *Scot*

Ark.B.A. Arkansas Bar Association

Ark.L.J. Arkansas Law Journal

Ark.L.Rev. Arkansas Law Review

Ark.R.C. Arkansas Railroad
Commission

Arkl[ey]. Arkley's Justiciary Reports
Scot

Armour Manitoba Q.B. Rep. *temp.*
Wood *Canada*

Arms.Br.P.Cas. Armstrong's Breach of
Privilege Cases. *N.Y.*

Arms.Con.El. Armstrong Contested
Election Cas. *N.Y.*

Arms.M.& O. Armstrong, Macartney,
& Ogle Civil & Criminal Rep. *Ir*

Arn. Arnold's Reports, Common Pleas
Eng
Arnot's Criminal Trials *Scot*

Arn.El.Cas. Arnold's Election Cases
Eng

Arn.& H. Arnold & Hodges' Q.B.
Reports *Eng*

Arn.& H.B.C. Arnold & Hodges' Bail
Ct. Rep. *Eng*

Arn.& Hod. Arnold & Hodges' Q.B.
Rep. *Eng*

Arn.& Hod.P.C. Arnold & Hodges'
Practice Cases *Eng*

Arnot Cr.C. Arnot's Criminal Cases
Scot

Ash[m]. Ashmead Pa. Reports 1808-41

Ashe Ashe's Tables to the Year Books,
Coke's Reports, or Dyer's Reports

Ashurst Manuscript Reports in 2
Chitty *Eng*

Asp. Aspinall's Maritime Cases *Eng*

Asp.Cas. Same as above

Asp.M.C. Aspinall's Maritime Cases
Eng

Asp.M.L.C. Aspinall's Maritime Law
Cas. *Eng*

Ass. Book of Assizes, Liber Assissarum,
pt. 5 of Year Books

Ast.Ent. Aston's Entries 1673. *Eng*

Atch. Atchison's Navigation & Trade
Rep. *Eng*

Atch.E.C. Atcheson's Election Cases.
Eng

Atk. Atkyn's Chancery Reports *Eng*
Atkinson's Quarter Sessions Records,
Yorkshire *Eng*

Atl. Atlantic Reporter

Atty.Gen.Op. Attorney General's
Opinions

Atw[ater] Atwater's Reports (1
Minnesota)

Auch. Auchinleck Manuscript Cas., Ct.
Of Session. *Scot*

Auct.Reg.& L.Chron. Auction
Register & Law Chronicle

Ault. Court Rolls of Ramsey Abbey
1928 *Eng*

Aust. Austin's County Court Cases *Eng*
Australia

Aust.K.A. Austin's Kandran Appeals
Ceylon

Aust.Jur. Australian Jurist

Aust.L.J. Australian Law Journal

Aust.L.T. Australian Law Times

Austin Austin's Reports *Ceylon*

Austin C.C. Austin's County Court
Cases *Eng*

Austr.B.C. Australian Bankrupts' Cases

Austr.C.L.R. Australia, Commonwealth Law Rep.

Austr.Jur. Australian Jurist

Austr.L.T. Australian Law Times

Austr.Tax D. Australian Tax Decisions

Auto.C. Automobile Cases (C.C.H.)

Aviation Q. United States Aviation Quarterly

Ayr. Ayr's Registration Cases   *Scot*

Ayr & Wig. Ayr & Wigton's Registration Cases   *Scot*

B. Barber's Gold Law   *S.Af.*
Barbour's N. Y. Reports
Beavan's Rolls Court Reports   *Eng*
Indian Law Reports, Bombay Series
Weekly Law Bulletin (Ohio)

B.A.Bull.L.A. Bar Assn. Bulletin, Los Angeles

BAE Bureau of Agricultural Economics   *U.S.*

B.A.I. Bureau of Animal Industry Docket   *U.S.*

B.Bar Bench & Bar

B.C. Bail Court
Bankruptcy Cases
British Columbia Reports

B.C.A. Board of Contract Appeals Dec.   *U.S.*

B.C.C. Bail Ct. Cases (Lowndes & Maxwell.)
Brown's Chancery Cases   *Eng*

BCD Bituminous Coal Division (Interior)   *U.S.*

BCLB Bituminous Coal Labor Board   *U.S.*

B.C.R. Bail Court Rep. Lowndes & Maxwell   *Eng*
Bail Court Rep., Saunders & Cole *Eng*
British Columbia Reports

B.Ch. Barbour's Chancery Reports   *N.Y.*

B.D.& O. Blackham, Dundas & Osborne N.P.   *Ir*

BEC Bureau of Employees' Compensation   *U.S.*

BEPQ Bureau of Entomology and Plant Quarantine

BEW Board of Economic Welfare   *U.S.*

B.G.L.R. British Guiana Law Reports (Old & New Series)

B.H.C. Bombay High Court Reports   *India*

BIS Bank for International Settlements

B.L.J. Burma Law Journal   *India*

B.L.R. Bahamas Law Reports
Barbados Law Reports
Bengal Law Reports, High Court   *India*
Bermuda Law Reports

B.L.R.A.C. Bengal Law Rep. Appeal Cases

B.L.R.P.C. Bengal Law Rep. Privy Council

B.L.R.Supp.Vol. Bengal Law Rep., Supplementary Volume

BLS Bureau of Labor Statistics   *U.S.*

B.L.T. Baltimore Law Transcript
Burma Law Times

B.M. Burrow's Reports *temp.* Mansfield   *Eng*

B.Mon. Ben Monroe Rep. (40-57 Ky.)

B.Moore Moore Com. Pl. Reports *Eng*

B.N.A. Bureau of National Affairs (Unofficial)

B.N.C. Bingham's New Cases, Com. Pl.   *Eng*
Brook's New Cases, K.B.   *Eng*
Busbee's Reports (44, 45 N.C.)

B.P.C. Brown's Parliamentary Cases   *Eng*

B.P.L. Pott's Poor Law Cases   *Eng*

B.P.N.R. Bosanquet & Puller, New Reports, Common Pleas   *Eng*

B.P.R. Brown's Parliamentary Reports   *Eng*

B.R. Bancus Regis [King's Bench]
Bankruptcy Reports
Bankruptcy Register
Board of Review, U.S. Army

B.R.A. Butterworth's Rating Appeals   *Eng*

B.R.C. British Ruling Cases

B.R.H. Cases *temp.* Hardwicke, K.B.   *Eng*

B.Reg. Bankrupt Register

B.T.A. Board of Tax Appeals   *U.S.*

B.T.A.C.C.H. Board of Tax Appeals Dec. (CCH)

B.T.A.P.H. Board of Tax Appeals Dec. (P-H)

B.T.R. Brewing Trade Review Licensing Law Rep.   *Eng*

B.U.L.Rev. Boston University Law Review

B.W.C.C. Butterworth's Workmen's Compensation Cases   *Eng*

B.& A. Banning & Arden Patent Rep.   *U.S.*
Barnewall & Adolphus' K.B. Reports   *Eng*

Barnewall & Alderson's K.B. Reports
Eng

Barron & Arnold's Election Cases *Eng*

B.& Ad. Barnewall & Adolphus K.B.
Rep.   *Eng*

B.& Ald. Barnewall & Alderson K.B.
Rep.   *Eng*

B.& Arn. Barron & Arnold Election
Cas.   *Eng*

B.& Aust. Barron & Austin El. Cases
Eng

B.& B. Ball & Beatty Chancery
Reports   *Ir*
Bench & Bar
Bowler & Bowers Comptroller's Dec.
U.S.
Broderip & Bingham's Com. Pl.
Reports   *Eng*

B.& Bar Bench & Bar

B.& C. Barnewall & Cresswell's K.B.
Rep.   *Eng*

B.& C.Pr.Cas. British & Colonial Prize
Cases   *Eng*

B.& C.R. Reports of Bankruptcy &
Companies Winding-Up Cases
Eng

B.& D. Benloe & Dalison's C.B. Rep.
Eng

B.& F. Broderick & Freemantle Eccl.
Cas.   *Eng*

B.& G. Brownlow & Goldesborough
N.P. Rep.   *Eng*

B.& H. Blatchford & Howland Dist.
Ct. Rep.   *U.S.*

B.& I. Bankruptcy & Insolvency Cases
Eng

B.& L. Browning & Lushington's
Admiralty Rep.   *Eng*

B.& M[acn]. Browne & Macnamara's
Repts.   *Eng*

B.& P. Bosanquet & Puller Com.Pl., Ex.
& H.L. Reports   *Eng*

B.&P.N.R. Bosanquet & Puller, New
Rep.   *Eng*

B.& S. Best & Smith's Q.B. Reports
Eng
Beven & Siebel's Reports   *Ceylon*

B.& V. Beling & Vanderstraaten's Rep.
Ceylon

Ba.& Be. Ball & Beatty Ch. Reports *Ir*

Bac.Abr. Bacon's Abridgement   *Eng*

Bac.Chanc. Bacon's Chancery Cases
Eng

Bac.Rep. Bacon's Decisions (Ritchie)
Eng

Bach Bach's Reports (19-21 Montana)

Bagl. Bagley's Reports (16 California)

Bagl.& Har. Bagley & Harman Rep.
(17-19 Calif)

Bah.L.R. Bahamas Law Reports

Bai[l]. Bailey's Law Reports   *S.C.*

Bai[l].Eq. Bailey's Equity Rep.   *S.C.*

Bail Ct.Cas. Bail Ct. Cases (Lowndes
& Maxwell)   *Eng*

Bail Cr.Rep. Bail Ct. Cases (Lowndes
& Maxwell or Saunders & Cole)
Eng

Bail. Bailey's Equity or Law Reports
S.C.

Baild. Baildon's Select Cases in Ch.
Eng

Bailey Bailey's Equity or Law Reports
S.C.

Bal. Balasingham's Reports   *Ceylon*

Bal.R.D. Baldeva Ram Dave, P.C.
Judg.   *India*

Balas. Balasingham's Supreme Court
Reports   *Ceylon*

Balas.N.C. Balasingham's Notes of
Cases   *Ceylon*

Bald[w]. Baldwin's Reports, Circuit
Ct.   *U.S.*

Bald.App. Appendix to 11 Peters *U.S.*

Bald.C.C. Baldwin's Circuit Ct. Rep.
U.S.

Bald.Pat.Cas. Baldwin's Patent, Copyright, Trade-Mark Cases   *U.S.*

Baldev.P.C. Baldev Ram Dave's Privy
Council Cases   *India*

Balf.Pr. Balfour's Practice   *Scot*

Ball. Ballard's Somerton Court Rolls
(Oxford Arch. Soc. No. 50) *Eng*

Ball & B. Ball & Beatty's Ch. Cases *Ir*

Balt.C.Rep. Baltimore City Reports

Balt.L.Tr. Baltimore Law Transcript

Ban.& A. Banning & Arden, Patent
Cas.   *U.S.*

Bang.L.R. Bangala Law Reporter
India

Bank.Ct.Rep. American Law Times
Bankruptcy Reports
Bankrupt Court Reporter

Bank.Gaz. Bankruptcy Gazette

Bank.L.J. Banking Law Journal

Bank.Mag. Bankers' Magazine

Bank.Reg. Bankruptcy Register

Bank.Rep. American Law Times
Bankruptcy Rep.

Bank & Ins.R. Bankruptcy &
Insolvency Rep.   *Eng*

Banker's L.J. Banker's Law Journal

Bankr.& Ins.R. Bankruptcy &
Insolvency Rep.   *Eng*

Banks Banks' Reports (1-5 Kansas)

Bann. Bannister's Com. Pl. Reports
Eng

Bann.Br. Bannister's O. Bridgman's
Com. Pl. Rep. *Eng*

Bann.& A[rd]. Banning & Arden's
Patent Cas. *U.S.*

Bar. Barbour, New York Reports
Barnardiston, Ch. & K. B. Reports *Eng*

Bar Bull.(N.Y.County L.A.) Bar
Bulletin, New York County
Lawyers' Association

Bar Ex.Jour. Bar Examination Journal

Bar Exam. Bar Examiner

Bar.N. Barnes' Notes, Com. Pl. Rep.
Eng

Bar Re. Bar Reports in all Courts *Eng*

Bar.& Ad. Barnewall & Adolphus K.B.
Rep. *Eng*

Bar.& Al. Barnewall & Alderson K.B.
Rep. *Eng*

Bar.& Arn. Barron & Arnold's El.
Cases *Eng*

Bar.& Au[st]. Barron & Austin's
Election Cases *Eng*

Bar.& Cr. Barnewall & Cresswell K.B.
Rep. *Eng*

Bar & Leg.W. Bar & Legal World *Eng*

Bar Rep. Bar Reports (*see* Law Times
Reports, v. 1-12)

Barb. Barber's Gold Law *S.Af.*
Arkansas Reports (14-42 Arkansas)
Barbour's N. Y. Supreme Court
Reports
Barbour's Chancery Cases (Contracts)
Eng

Barb.Abs. Barbour's Abstracts of
Chancellor's Decisions *N.Y.*

Barb.Ch. Barbour's New York
Chancery Rep.

Barb.L.R. Barbados Law Reports

Barb.S.C. Barbour's New York Sup.
Ct. Rep.

Barber Barber's Reports (14–42
Arkansas)

Barn. Barnardiston K.B. & Ch. Reports
Eng
Barnes' Common Pleas Reports *Eng*

Barn.Ch. Barnardiston's Chancery
Rep. *Eng*

Barn.K.B. Barnardiston's K.B. Reports
Eng

Barn.No. Barnes' Notes of Cases, C.P.
Eng

Barn.& A[dol]. Barnewall & Adolphus
K.B. Rep. *Eng*

Barn.& A[ld]. Barnewall & Alderson,
K.B. Rep. *Eng*

Barn.& Cr. Barnewall & Cresswell
K.B. Rep. *Eng*

Barnes Barnes' Notes of Cases, Com.
Pl. *Eng*

Barnet Barnet's Central Criminal
Courts Reports *Eng*

Barnf.& S. Barnfield & Stiness' Rep.
(20 R.I.)

Baroda L.R. Baroda Law Reports
India

Barr. Barr Reports (1-10 Pa. State)
Barrows' Reports (18 Rhode Island)
The Barrister

Barr.Mss. Barradall's Manuscript Rep.
Va

Barr.& Arn. Barron & Arnold El.
Cases *Eng*

Barron Barony of Urie Court Records
1604-1747 *Scot*

Bart.El.Cas. Bartlett, Congressional
Election Cases

Bartholoman Bartholoman's Reports,
Yorkshire Lent Assize, March 9,
1911 *Eng*

Bates Bate's Delaware Chancery
Reports

Bateson Leicester Records (Municipal
Courts 1103-1603) *Eng*

Batt. Batty's K. B. Reports *Ir*

Bax[t]. Baxter's Reports (60-68
Tennessee)

Bay Bay's Reports (1-3, 5-8 Missouri)
Bay's South Carolina Reports

BaylorL.Rev. Baylor Law Review

Bea.Ord. Beames' Orders in Chancery
Eng

Beasl. Beasley's New Jersey Equity
Reports

Beat. Beatty's Chancery Reports *Ir*

Beav. Beavan's Rolls Court Reports
Eng

Beav.R.& C.Cas. Railway & Canal
Cases *Eng*

Beav.& Wal.Ry.Cas. Beavan &
Walford's Railway Parliamentary
Cases *Eng*

Beaw. Beawes' Lex Mercatoria *Eng*

Beck Beck's Colorado Reports
(Supreme Court and Court of
Appeals)

Bedell Bedell's Reports (163-191 N.Y.)

Bee Bee's District Court Reports *U.S.*

Bee Alm. Bee's District Court Reports
U.S.

Bee C.C.R. Bee's Crown Cases
Reserved *Eng*

Behari Revenue Reports of Upper
Provinces *India*
Bel. Beling's Ceylon Reports
Bellasis' Bombay Reports
Bellewe's K.B. Reports *Eng*
Bel.Ca.t. H.VIII. Bellewe's Cases
temp. Henry VIII (Brooke's
New Cases) *Eng*
Beling Beling's Ceylon Reports
Beling & Van. Beling & Vander-
straaten's Rep. *Ceylon*
Bell. Bell's Appeal Cases *Scot*
Bell's Crown Cases Reserved *Eng*
Bell's Session Cases *Scot*
Bell's Calcutta Reports *India*
Bellasis' Bombay Reports *India*
Bellewe's K. B. Reports *Eng*
Bellinger's Reports (4-8 Oregon)
Bell App.Cas. Bell's House of Lords
Appeal Cases *Scot*
Bell C.C. T.Bell's Crown Cases
Reserved *Eng*
Bellasis' Bombay Civil & Criminal
Cases *India*
Bell C.H.C. Bell's Reports, Calcutta
High Court *India*
Bell Cas. Bell's Cases, Court of Session
Scot
Bell.Cas.t.H.VIII. Brooke's New
Cases *Eng*
Bell.Cas.t.R.II. Bellewe's K.B.
Reports *Eng*
Bell Cr.Cas. Bell's Crown Cases Res.
Eng
Bellasis' Criminal Cases, Bombay *India*
Bell Ct. of Sess. R. Bell's Decisions,
Court of Session. *Scot*
Bell Dict.Dec. Bell's Dictionary of
Decisions, Court of Session *Scot*
Bell fol. Bell's folio Reports, Ct. of
Session *Scot*
Bell H.C. Bell's Reports, High Court
of Calcutta *India*
Bell H.L. Bell's House of Lords Cases
Eng
Bell H.L.Sc. Bell's House of Lords
Cases, Scotch Appeals
Bell Med.L.J. Bell's Medico Legal
Journal
Bell.(Or.) Bellinger's Oregon Reports
Bell P.C. Bell's Cases in Parliament:
Scotch Appeals
Bell Sc.App. S.S. Bell's Scotch Appeals
Bell Ses.Cas. Bell's Court of Session
Cases *Scot*
Bellas. Bellasis' Criminal or Civil
Cases, Bombay *India*

Bellasis Bellasis' Bombay Reports
Bellewe Bellewe's Cases *temp.* Rich.II
Eng
Bellewe t.H.VIII Brooke's New Cases
Eng
Bellinger Bellinger's Reports (4-8
Oregon)
Belt Bro. Brown's Ch. Cases, by Belt
Eng
Belt's Sup. Belt's Supplement to Vesey
Sen., Chancery *Eng*
Belt Ves.Sen. Vesey's Senior's
Chancery Reports, Belt's Edition
Eng
Ben. Benedict's District Court Reports
U.S.
Bengal Law Reports
Benloe's Com. Pl. & K.B. Reports *Eng*
Ben.Monroe Ben Monroe's Reports
(40-57 Ky.)
Ben.& Dal. Benloe & Dalison's C.P.
Rep. *Eng*
Bench & Bar Bench and Bar (*see* List
of Anglo-American Legal
Periodicals)
Bench & Bar.N.S. *Same*, New Series
Bendl. *See* Benloe
Bened. Benedict's District Ct. Reports
U.S.
Benefit Series U.C.I.S. Social Security
Board Unemployment Compensa-
tion Interpretation Service, Bene-
fit Series *U.S.*
Beng.L.R. Bengal Law Reports *India*
Beng.L.R.App.Cas. *Same*, Appeal
Cases
Beng.L.R.P.C. *Same*, Privy Council
Cases
Beng.S.D.A. Bengal Sadr Diwani
Adalat Cases *India*
Benj. Benjamin's Annotated Cases
N.Y.
Benl. *See* Benloe
Benl.in Keil. Benloe in Keilway Rep.
Eng
Benl.New Benloe's K.B. & Com. Pl.
Rep. 1661 ed. *Eng*
Benl.Old Benloe & Dalison Com. Pl.
Rep. *Eng*
Benl.& Dal. Benloe & Dalison's Com.
Pl. Rep. *Eng*
Benloe Benloe's K.B. & Com. Pl. Rep.
Eng
Benn. Bennett's Reports (1 California)
Bennett's Reports (1 Dakota)
Bennett's Reports (16-21 Missouri)
Benne. Modern Reports, v.7 *Eng*

Bennett *See* Benn., *supra*

Bent. Bentley's Chancery Reports *Ir*

Beor. Queensland Law Reports *Aus*

Ber. Berton's New Brunswick Reports *Can*

Berar Berar Law Journal *India*

Berks. Berks County Law Journal *Pa*

Bern.Ch.Cas. Bernard's Church Cases *Ir*

Berry Berry's Reports (1-28 Missouri Appeals)

Bert. Berton's New Brunswick Reports *Can*

Best & Sm. Best & Smith's Q.B. Reports *Eng*

Betts.Dec. Blatchford & Howland Dist. Ct. Reports *U.S.*
Olcott's District Ct. Reports *U.S.*

Bev[en]. Beven's Reports *Ceylon*

Bev.Pat. Bevill's Patent Cases *Eng*

Bev.& M. Beven & Mills' Reports *Ceylon*

Bev.& Sieb. Beven & Siebel's Reports *Ceylon*

Bi-Mo.L.Rev. Bi-Monthly Law Review, University of Detroit

Bibb. Bibb's Reports (4-7 Kentucky)

Bick. Bicknell & Hawley's Rep. (10-20 Nevada)
Bicknell's Reports *India*

Bick.& Hawl. Bicknell & Hawley's Rep. (10-20 Nevada)

Bid. Bidder's Locus Standi Reports *Eng*
Bidder's Court of Referees Reports *Eng*

Big. Bignell's Reports *India*

Big.Cas. Bigelow's Cases, Wm.I to Richard I *Eng*

Big.Ov.Cas. Bigelow's Overruled Cases *U.S., Eng, Ir*

Big.Plac. Bigelow's Placita Anglo-Normanica. *Eng*

Bign. Bignell's Reports (Bengal) *India*

Bih.Rep. Bihar Reports *India*

Bi-Mo.L.Rev. Bi-Monthly Law Review, University of Detroit

Bin. Binney's Reports (Pa. 1799-1814)

Bing. Bingham's Common Pleas Rep. *Eng*

Bing.N.C. Bingham's New Cases, Com. P. *Eng*

Binn. Binney's Reports, Pennsylvania

Birdw. Birdwood's Printed Judgments *India*

Birk.J. Birkenhead's Judgments (H.L. 1919–22) *Eng*

Bis[s]. Bissell's Circuit Court Rep. *U.S.*

Biss.& Sm. Bissett & Smith's Digest *S.Af.*

Bitt. Bittleston's Chamber Reports *Eng*

Bitt.Ch. Bittleston's Chamber Reports *Eng*

Bitt.P.C. Bittleston's Practice Cases under Judicature Acts *Eng*

Bitt.Rep.in Ch. Bittleston's Reports in Chambers, Q.B. Div. *Eng*

Bitt.W.& P. Bittleston, Wise & Parnell Rep. 2 & 3 New Practice Cases *Eng*

Bk. Black (66, 67 U. S. Reports)

Bl. Black's U.S. Supreme Court Rep. (66, 67 U.S.)
Blackford's Indiana Rep. (1817-47)
Blackstone's Commentaries
Henry Blackstone's Com. Pleas Rep. *Eng*
William Blackstone's K. B. Reports *Eng*
Blatchford's Circuit Court Reports *U.S.*

Bl.C.C. Blatchford's Circuit Ct. Rep. *U.S.*

Bl.Comm. Blackstone's Commentaries on the Law of England

Bl.D.& O. Blackham, Dundas & Osborne's Rep., Practice & Nisi Prius *Ir*

Bl.H. Henry Blackstone's Com. Pl. Rep. *Eng*

Bl.N.S. Bligh's H.L. Reports, New Ser. *Eng*

Bl.Pr.Cas. Blatchford's Prize Cases *U.S.*

Bl.R. William Blackstone's K. B. Rep. *Eng*

Bl.W. William Blackstone's K. B. Rep. *Eng*

Bl.& H. Blake & Hedges' Reports (2, 3 Ind.)
Blatchford & Howland Dist. Ct. Rep. *U.S.*

Bl.& How. Blatchford & Howland's Admiralty Rep. *U.S.*

Bla.Ch. Bland's Chancery Reports *Md*

Bla.H. Henry Blackstone's Comm. Pl. Rep. *Eng*

Bla.W. Wm. Blackstone's K.B. Reports *Eng*

Black. Black's Reports (30-53 Indiana)
Black's Supreme Court Rep. (66, 67 U.S.)
Blackerby's Magistrates Reports *Eng*
Blackford's Reports (Indiana 1817-47)

H.Blackstone's Com. Pl. Reports *Eng*

W.Blackstone's K. B. Reports *Eng*

Blackstone's Rep., K. B., *temp.* Geo. II & III; Com. Pl., Geo. III *Eng*

Black.Cond.Rep. Blackwell's Condensed Rep. *Ill*

Black.D.& O. Blackham, Dundas, & Osborne's N.P. Reports *Ir*

Black.H. H. Blackstone's Com. Pl. Rep. *Eng*

Black.Jus. Blackerby's Justices' Cas. *Eng*

Black.R. *See* Black., *supra*

Black.W. Wm. Blackstone's K. B. Rep. *Eng*

Blackf. Blackford's Rep. (Indiana 1817-47)

Blackst. Blackstone's Reports, K. B., *temp.* Geo. II, III; Com. Pl., Geo. III *Eng*

Blackw.Cond. Blackwell's Condensed Rep. *Ill*

Blair Co.L.R. Blair County Law Rep. *Pa*

Blake Blake's Reports (1 Montana)

Blake & H. Blake & Hedges' Montana Reports

Blan.& W.Lead.Cas. Blanchard & Weeks' Leading Cases, Mines

Bland Bland's Ch. Rep. (Maryland 1811-32)

Blatch. Blatchford's Circuit Ct. Rep. *U.S.*

Blatch.Pr.Cas. Blatchford's Prize Cas. *U.S.*

Blatch.& H. Blatchford & Howard's District Court Rep. *U.S.*

Bleck[ley]. Bleckley's Rep. (34, 35 Georgia)

Bli. Bligh's Reports, House of Lords *Eng*

Bli.N.S. *Above*, New Series *Eng*

Bligh. *See* Bli., *supra*

Bliss. Delaware County Reports *Pa*

Bloom.Man. Bloomfield's Manumission Cas. *N.J.*

Bloom.Neg. Bloomfield's Negro Cas. *N.J.*

Bluett Bluett's Isle of Man Cases

Bohun Bohun's Election Cases *Eng*

Bolland Select Bills in Eyre (Selden Society Pub. v. 30) *Eng*

Bom. Bombay High Court Reports *India*

Bom.A.C. Bombay Rep., Appellate Juris. *India*

Bom.Cr.Cas. Bombay Rep., Crown Cases *India*

Bom.L.J. Bombay Law Journal *India*

Bom.O.C. Bombay Rep., Original Civil Jurisdiction *India*

Bombay Reports, Oudh Cases *India*

Bomb. Indian Law Reports, Bombay Ser. *India*

Bomb.Cr.Rul. Bombay High Ct., Criminal Rulings *India*

Bomb.H.C. Bombay High Ct. Reports *India*

Bomb.Sel.Cas. Bombay Select Cases, Sadr Diwani Adalat *India*

Bomb.Ser. Indian Law Reports, Bombay Series *India*

Bond Bond's Circuit Court Reports *U.S.*

Bond Md.App. Proceedings of Court of Appeal of Maryland (in American Legal Records, v. 1)

Boor[aem] Booraem's Rep. (6–8 Calif.)

Booth Chester Palatine Courts 1811 *Eng*

Borr. Borradaile's Rep., Bombay *India*

Bos. Bosworth's Superior Court Rep. *N.Y.*

Bos.& P[u]. Bosanquet & Puller's Com. Pl. Rep. *Eng*

Bos.& Pul.N.R. Bosanquet & Puller's New Reports Com. Pl. *Eng.*

Bost.Law Rep. Boston Law Reporter

Bost.Pol.Rep. Boston Police Court Reports

Bost.U.L.Rev. Boston University Law Review

Bosw. Boswell's Ct. of Session Rep. *Scot*

Bosworth's New York Superior Court Rep.

Bott.P.L.Cas. Bott's Poor Law Cases *Eng*

Bouln. Boulnois Bengal Sup. Court Rep. *India*

Bourke Bourke's Rep., Calcutta High Ct. *India*

Bourke P.P. Bourke's Parliamentary Precedents *Eng*

Bov.Pat.Ca. Bovill's Patent Cases

Bow. Bowler & Bowers (U.S. Comptroller's Dec., v. 2, 3.)

Bowler's London Session Records 1605-85 *Eng*

Boyce Boyce's Reports (24-30 Delaware)

Br. Bracton; Bradford; Bradwell; Brayton; Breese; Brevard; Brewster; Bridgman; British; Brockenbrough; Brooke; Brown; Browne; Brownlow;

Br.Abr. Brooke's Abridgment   *Eng*

Br.Bro. Brooke; Brown; Brownlow

Br.C.C. British Crown Cases
Brown's Chancery Cases   *Eng*

Br.Cr.Ca. British Crown Cases

Br.N.B. Bracton's Note Book   *Eng*

Br.N.C. Brook's New Cases, K. B. *Eng*

Br.P.C. Brown's Chancery Cases *Eng*

Br.R. Browne's Reports   *Ceylon*

Br.Rul.Cas. British Ruling Cases

Br.Sup. Brown's Supplement to Morison's Dictionary of Session Cases   *Scot*

Br.Syn. Brown's Synopsis of Decisions, Court of Session   *Scot*

Br.& B. Broderip & Bingham's Com. Pl. Rep.   *Eng*

Br.& Col.Pr.Cas. British & Colonial Prize Cas.

Br.& Fr. Broderick & Freemantle Ecc. Cas.   *Eng*

Br.& G[old]. Brownlow & Goldesborough's Com. Pl. Rep.   *Eng*

Br.& L[ush]. Browning & Lushington's Admiralty Rep.   *Eng*

Br.& R. Brown & Rader's Rep. (137 Mo.)

Bra. Bracton's De Legibus Angliae

Bract. Same as above

Brad. Bradford's Reports (Iowa 1838-41)
Bradford's New York Surrogate Reports
Bradford's Somerset Star Chamber
Bradwell's Reports (1-20 Ill. App.)
Cases (Somerset Record Society No. 27)   *Eng*

Bradb. Bradbury's Pleading & Practice Rep.   *N.Y.*

Bradf. *See* Brad., *supra*

Bradw. Bradwell's Illinois Appellate Rep.

Brain.L.P. Brainard's Legal Precedents in Land & Mining Cases   *U.S.*

Braith. Braithwaite's Jamaica Law Reports

Brame Brame's Reports (66-72 Mississippi)

Branch Branch's Reports (1 Florida)

Brant. Brantley's Reports (80–116 Md.)

Brayt. Brayton's Reports (Vermont 1815–19)

Breese Breese's Reports (1 Illinois)

Brev. Brevard's Reports (2, 3 South C.)

Brew[er]. Brewer's Reports (19-26 Md.)

Brew[st]. Brewster's Rep. (Pa. 1856-73)

Brew.(Md). Brewer's Maryland Reports

Bridg.J. J. Bridgman's Com. Pl. Rep.   *Eng*

Bridg.O. O. Bridgman's Com. Pl. Rep.   *Eng*

Brief Brief of Phi Delta Phi

Brief Case Brief Case, National Legal Aid Association

Bright. Brightly's Nisi Prius Rep. *Pa*

Bright. Brightly's N.P. Rep. (Pa. 1809-51)

Bright N.P. Same as Bright, *supra*.

Brisbin Brisbin's Rep. (in 1 Minnesota)

Brit.Cr.Cas. British Crown Cases (reprint)

Brit.Y.B.Int.L. British Year Book of International Law

Brit.& Col.Pr.Cas. British & Colonial Prize Cases

Bro. Brooke (which *see*, below)
Brown's English Chancery Reports
Brown's Parliamentary Cases   *Eng*
Brown's Michigan Nisi Prius Reports
Brown's Reports (53-65 Missouri)
Brown's Reports (80-136 Missouri)
Browne's Reports (Pa. 1801-14)
Browne's Reports 1872-1902   *Ceylon*

Bro.Ab. Brooke's Abridgment   *Eng*

Bro.A.& R. Brown's District Court (Admiralty & Revenue) Reports   *U.S.*

Bro.Adm. Brown's Admiralty Reports   *U.S.*

Bro.C.C. W. Brown's Chancery Cases   *Eng*

Bro.Ch. Brown's Chancery Reports *Eng*

Bro.Ecc. Brooke's Ecclesiastical Rep., Privy Council.   *Eng*
Brooke's Six Judgments in Eccles Cas.   *Eng*

Bro.Ent. Brownlow's Entries 1693 *Eng*

Bro.N.B.Cas. Browne's National Bank Cas.   *U.S.*

Bro.N.C. R. Brooke's New Cases, K. B.   *Eng*

Bro.N.P. Brown's Michigan Nisi Prius Rep.

Bro.P.C. J. Brown's Cases in Parliament   *Eng*

Bro.Pa. Browne's Pennsylvania Rep. 1801-14

Bro.Parl.Cas. Brown's Cases in Parliament

Bro.Sup.to Mor. Brown's Supplement to Morison's Dictionary of Decisions *Scot*

Bro.Synop. Brown's Synopsis of Decisions, Ct. of Session *Scot*

Bro.& Fr. Broderick & Freemantle's Eccles. Cases. *Eng*

Bro.& G. Brownlow & Goldesborough Com. Pl. Reports *Eng*

Bro.& H. Brown & Hemingway's Rep. (53–65 Mississippi)

Bro.& L[ush]. Browning & Lushington's Admiralty Cases *Eng*

Bro.& M[ac]. Browne & Macnamara's Railway Cases *Eng*

Brown & McCall's Yorkshire Star Chamber (Yorkshire Arch. Soc. Record, Series 44, 45, 51, 70)

Brock. Brockenbrough's Marshall's Decisions, U. S. Circuit Court

Brock. Cas. Brockenbrough's Virginia Cases

Brock.& H[ol]. Brockenbrough & Holmes Virginia Cases

Brod. Broderick & Freemantle's Ecc. Cas. *Eng*

Brod.& Bing. Broderip & Bingham's Com. Pl. Rep. *Eng*

Brod.& F[r.] Broderick & Freemantle's Eccles. Reports, Privy Council *Eng*

Brodix Am.& Eng.Pat.Cas. Brodix's American & English Patent Cases

Brooke Brooke's Ecclesiastical Cases *Eng*

Brooke's New Cases, King's Bench *Eng*

Brooke Eccl.Judg. Brooke's Six Ecclesiastical Judgments *Eng*

Brooke N.C. Brooke's New Cases, K.B. *Eng*

Brooke (Petit) Brooke's New Cases, K.B. *Eng*

Brooke Six Judg. Brooke's Six Ecclesiastical Judgments *Eng*

Brookl.Bar. Brooklyn Barrister Brooklyn Bar Association

Brookl.L.Rev. Brooklyn Law Review

Brookl.Rec. Brooklyn Record

Brooks Brooks' Reports (106-119 Mich.)

Broun Broun's Justiciary Reports *Scot*

Brown Brown's District Court Reports *U.S.*

Brown's Chancery Reports *Eng*

Brown's Reports (Michigan Nisi Prius)

Brown's Reports (53-65 Mississippi)

Brown's Reports (4-25 Nebraska)

Brown's Parliamentary Cases *Eng*

Brownlow & Goldesborough's C. P. Rep. *Eng*

Brown A.& R. Brown's District Ct. Reports (Admiralty & Revenue Cases) *U.S.*

Brown Adm. Brown's Admiralty Reports *U.S.*

Brown C. Brown's Chancery Cas. *temp.* Lord Thurlow *Eng*

Brown N.P. Brown's Michigan Nisi Prius Rep.

Brown Sup. Brown's Supplement to Morison's Dictionary, Session Cases *Scot*

Brown Syn. Brown's Synopsis of Decisions, Court of Session *Scot*

Brown.& Gold. Brownlow & Goldesborough's Com. Pl. Rep. *Eng*

Brown & H. Brown & Hemingway's Reports (53-58 Mississippi)

Brown & Lush. Browning & Lushington's Rep., Admiralty *Eng*

Browne Browne's Reports *Ceylon*

Brown's Reports (97-109 Massachusetts)

Browne's Civil Procedure Reports *N.Y.*

Browne's Reports (Pa. 1801-14)

Browne Bank.Cas. Browne's National Bank Cas.

Browne N.B.C. Same as above

Browne & Gray Browne & Gray's Rep. (110-114 Mass.)

Browne & Macn. Browne & Macnamara's Ry. & Canal Cas. *Eng*

Brownl. Brownlow & Goldesborough's Com. P. Rep. *Eng*

Bru[ce] Bruce's Dec., Ct. of Session *Scot*

Brun.Col.Cas. Brunner's Collected Cas. *U.S.*

Brun.Sel.Cas. Brunner's Selected Cases. *U.S.*

Bruns.L.C. Brunskill's Land Cases *Ir*

Buch. Buchanan's Reports, Cape Colony *S.Af.*

Buchanan's Reports, Cape of Good Hope *S.Af.*

Buchanan's Reports, (71-85 N.J.Eq.)

Buchanan's Reports, Court of Session
   & Justiciary   *Scot*

Buch.A.C. Buchanan's Rep. Appeal
   Court   *S.Af.*

Buch.Cas. Buchanan, Remarkable
   Criminal Cases   *Scot*

Buch.Ct.Ap.Cape G.H. *See* Buch,
   supra

Buchan. *See* Buch., *supra*

Buchanan *See* Buch., *supra*

Buck Buck's Cases in Bankruptcy *Eng*
   Buck's Reports (7-8 Montana)

Buck Cas. Buck's Cases in Bankruptcy
                 Eng

Buck.Cooke Bucknill's Cooke's Cases
   of Practice, Common Pleas   *Eng*

Buck.Dec. Buckner's Decisions (in
   Freeman's Mississippi Chancery
   Reports 1839-43)

Buff.L.Rev. Buffalo Law Review

Buff.Super.Ct. Buffalo (N.Y.)
   Superior Court Reports, Sheldon

Bull. Bulletin
   Weekly Law Bulletin, Ohio

Bull.JAG Bulletin of Judge Advocate
   General of Army   *U.S.*

Bull.N.P. Buller's Nisi Prius   *Eng*

Bull.Nat.Tax Assn. Bulletin, National
   Tax Association

Bull.O. Weekly Law Bulletin, Ohio

Bulst. Bulstrode's King's Bench
   Reports   *Eng*

Bunb. Bunbury's Exchequer Reports
                 Eng

Bur. Burnett's Reports (Wisconsin
   1841-43)
   Burnett's King's Bench Reports *Eng*

Bur.L.J. Burma Law Journal   *India*

Bur.L.R. Burma Law Reports *India*

Bur.L.T. Burma Law Times   *India*

Bur.M. Burrow's Reports *temp.*
   Mansfield   *Eng*

Bur.S.C. Burrow's Settlement Cases
                 Eng

Burf. Burford's Reports (6-18
   Oklahoma)

Burgess Burgess' Reports (46-51 Ohio
   State)

Burke Tr. Burke's Celebrated Trials

Burks Burks' Reports (91-98 Virginia)

Burm.L.R. Burma Law Reports *India*

Burm.L.T. Burma Law Times   *India*

Burn High Commission Court 1865
                 Eng
   Star Chamber Proceedings   *Eng*

Burnet Burnet's Manuscript Decisions,
   Court of Session   *Scot*

Burnett Burnett's Reports (Wisconsin
   1841-43)

Burr. Burrow's K.B. Rep. *temp.*
   Mansfield   *Eng*

Burr.S.C. Burrow's Settlement Cases
                 Eng

Burr.T.M. Burrow's Rep. *temp.*
   Mansfield   *Eng*

Burrell. Burrell's Admiralty Reports
                 Eng

Burrnett. Burrnett's Reports (20-22
   Oregon)

Burt.Cas. Burton's Cases & Opinions
                 Eng

Bus.L.J. Business Law Journal

Busb. Busbee's Law Reports (44
   N.C.)

Busb.Eq. Busbee's Equity Reports (45
   N.C.)

Bush. Bush's Reports (64-77
   Kentucky)

Butt.Rat.App. Butterworth's Rating
   App.   *Eng*

Butt's Sh. Butt's Shower's K. B, Rep.
                 Eng

Buxton Buxton's Reports (123-29
   N.C.)

C. Cowen's New York Reports
   Indian Law Reports, Calcutta Series
                India

C.A. Court of Appeal; Courts of
   Appeals.
   Court of Appeals Reports *New Zeal.*
   Customs Appeals Reports   *U.S.*
   U.S. Court of Appeals

CA CCH Standard Federal Tax
   Reporter

C.A.A. Civil Aeronautics Administra-
   tion   *U.S.*
   Civil Aeronautics Authority   *U.S.*
   Civil Aeronautics Authority Reports
                 U.S.

C.A.A.J. Civil Aeronautics Journal

C.A.A.Op. Civil Aeronautics Authority Opinions   *U.S.*

C.A.B. (*or* **CAB**) Civil Aeronautics
   Board   *U.S.*

C.A.D. Canadian Annual Digest

CAJR New York State Commission on
   Administration of Justice, Report

C.A.L.Bull. Association of the Bar,
   City of New York, Committee on
   Amendment of the Law, Bulletin.

CAM Civil Aeronautics Manual

CAP Civil Air Patrol *U.S.*

C.A.P.A. Comisión Aeronaútica Permanente Americana

CAR Civil Air Regulations ("Safety Regulations") *U.S.*

C.A.R. Commonwealth Arbitration Rep. *Aus*
Criminal Appeal Reports *Eng*

C.App.R. Criminal Appeal Reports *Eng*

C.B. Common Bench Reports (Manning, Granger, & Scott) *Eng*
Cumulative Bulletin, Internal Revenue Bureau *U.S.*

C.B.N.S. Common Bench Rep., New Series *Eng*

C.B.R. Canadian Bankruptcy Reports
Cour du Banc de la Reine, Quebec

C.C. Cases in Chancery *Eng*
Coleman's New York Cases
County Council
Ohio Circuit Court Reports

C.C.A. Circuit Court of Appeals, prior to Sept. 1, 1948 *U.S.*
County Court Appeals
Court of Criminal Appeal *Eng*

C.C.C. Canadian Criminal Cases
Central Criminal Court (Old Bailey) *Eng*
Choyce Cases in Chancery *Eng*
Cox's Criminal Cases *Eng*

CCC Civilian Conservation Corps. *U.S.*
Commodity Credit Corporation *U.S.*

C.C.C. Sess.Pap. Central Criminal Court Session Paper *Eng*

C.C.C.Bull. Bulletin, Committee on Criminal Courts' Law & Procedure, Assn. of the Bar, City of New York

C.C.Chr. Chancery Cases Chronicle *Canada*

C.C.Ct.Cas. Central Criminal Court Cas. *Eng*

C.C.E. Caine's Cases in Error *N.Y.*
Caines' New York Term Reports

C.C.F. Contract Cases Federal (CCH) *U.S.*

C.C.H. Commerce Clearing House

C.C.N.S. Circuit Court Reports, N.S. *Ohio*

C.C.P.A. Court of Customs & Patent App. *U.S.*

C.C.R. Circuit Court Reports
City Courts Reports
County Courts Reports
Crown Cases Reserved

C.C.Rep. County Courts Reporter (in Law Journal, London)

C.C.Supp. City Court Reports, Supplement *N.Y.*

C.D. Century Digest or Current Digest, in American Digest System
Chancery Division
Circuit Decisions
Commissioner's Decisions, U. S. Patent Office
Customs Court Decisions *U.S.*
Customs Decisions (U.S. Treasury Dept.)

C.E.A. Council of Economic Advisers *U.S.*

CEA Commodity Exchange Authority

C.E.D. Canadian Encyclopedic Digest

C.E.Gr. Green's Reports (16–27 N. J. Eq.)

C.E.S. Court of Exchequer *Scot*

C.F.R. Code of Federal Regulations *U.S.*

C.G.O. Comptroller General's Opinion *U.S.*

CGCM Court Martial Reports, Coast Guard Cases *N.Y.*

CGCMM Coast Guard Court-Martial Manual (1949) *U.S.*

CGCMS Special Court-Martial, Coast Guard *U.S.*

C.G.O. Comptroller General's Opinion *U.S.*

CGR Coast Guard Regulations *U.S.*

CGSMCM Coast Guard Supplement to Manual for Courts-Martial *U.S.*

C.H.& A. Carro, Hamerton & Allen's New Session Cases *Eng*

C.H.Rec. City Hall Recorder *N.Y.*

C.H.Rep. City Hall Reporter *N.Y.*

CIA Central Intelligence Agency *U.S.*

C.I.C. Current Indian Cases, Old Ser. *India*

CITEJA International Technical Committee of Aerial Legal Experts

C.J. Corpus Juris

C.J.C. Couper's Judiciary Cases *Scot*

C.J.Can. Corpus Juris Canonici

C.J.Civ. Corpus Juris Civilis

C.L. Common Law Reports

C.L.Ch. Common Law Chamber Rep. *Ontario*

C.L.J. Calcutta Law Journal
Canada Law Journal
Cape Law Journal
Central Law Journal
Chicago Law Journal
Colonial Law Journal Reports
Criminal Law Journal *India*

C.L.J.N.S. Canada Law Journal, New Series

C.L.J.O.S. Canada Law Journal, Old Series

C.L.L.R. Crown Lands Law Reports *Aus*

C.L.N. Chicago Legal News

C.L.Q. Crown Land Reports, Queensland

C.L.R. Calcutta Law Reporter
Canada Law Reports
Cape Law Reports *S.Af.*
Ceylon Law Reports
Cleveland Law Record
Columbia Law Review
Common Law Reports *Eng*
Commonwealth Law Reports *Aus*
Crown Lands Reports, Queensland
Current Law Reports *Palestine*
Cyprus Law Reports

C.L.R. Aust. Commonwealth Law Rep. *Aus*

C.L.R.Can. Canada Law Reports
Common Law Reports (Canada)

C.L.T. Canadian Law Times

C.L.T.Occ.N. Canadian Law Times Occasional Notes

CM Court Martial Rep. Army Cases *U.S.*

CMC Collective Measures Commission *UN*

C.M.-E.T.O. Court-Martial, European Theater of Operations *U.S.*

C.M.J. Canadian Municipal Journal

C.M.O. U.S. Judge-Advocate-General (Navy) Compilation of Court-Martial Orders

CMP Reg. Controlled Materials Plan Regulation (National Production)

CMR Court-Martial Reports, Judge Advocates General of the Armed Forces and the United States Court of Military Appeals

CMR (AF) Court-Martial Reports, Air Force

C.M.&R. Crompton, Meeson & Roscoe's Ex. Reports *Eng*

C.N.Conf. Cameron & Norwood's Conference Reports *NC*

C.N.J.F.D.C. Notices of Judgments, Cosmetics, U. S. Food & Drug Administration

C.N.P.C. Campbell's Nisi Prius Cases *Eng*

C. of S.Ca. Court of Session Cases (in four series) *Scot*

C.P. Common Pleas Reports, Upper Canada Law Reports, Common Pleas Series *Eng*

C.P.C.[oop]. C.P. Cooper's Practice Cas. *Eng*

C.P.C.t.Br. C. P. Cooper's Ch. Rep. *temp.* Brougham *Eng*

C.P.C.t.Cott. C. P. Cooper's Ch. Rep. *temp.* Cottenham *Eng*

C.P.D. Cape Provincial Division Rep. *S.Af.*
Commissioner of the Public Debt
Law Reports, Common Pleas Division *Eng*
South African Law Rep., Cape Provincial Division *S.Af.*

C.P.L.R. Central Provinces Law Reports *India*

C.P.R. Canadian Patent Reporter

CPR Ceiling Price Regulation

C.P.Rept. Common Pleas Reporter *Pa*

C.P.U.C. Upper Canada Com. Pl. Reports

C.R. Canadian Reports, Appeal Cases
Chancery Reports *temp.* Car.I to Queen Anne
Central Reporter
Code Reporter
Criminal Reports *Canada*

C.R. [date] A.C. Canadian Appeal Cases

C.R.C. Canadian Railway Cases
Criminal Reports (Canada)

C.R.N.S. Code Reports, New Series *N.Y.*

C.R.T.C. Canadian Railway & Transport Cases

C.Rob. Robinson's Admiralty Reports *Eng*

C.S. Court of Session *Scot*
Supreme Court Reports, *Quebec*
Camden Society *Eng*

CSAB Contract Settlement Appeal Board *U.S.*

C.S.A.B. Civil Service Arbitration Awards

C.S.C. Court of Sessions Cases *Scot*
Civil Service Commission *U.S.*

C.S.C.R. Cincinnati Superior Court Reporter

CSJAG Opinion of Judge Advocate General, U. S. Army

CSJAGA Military Affairs Div., Judge Advocate of U. S. Army

CSJAGE Assistant Judge Advocate General for Procurement (Army); Contract Div., Off. of Judge Advocate Gen. of Army

C.S.T. Capital Stock Tax Ruling, Internal Revenue Bureau *U.S.*

C.S.U.C. Consolidated Statutes, Upper Canada

C.S.& J. Cushing, Storey & Joselyn's Election Cases *Mass*

C.S.& P. Craiger, Stewart & Paton App. Cas. *Scot*

C.T.C. Canada Tax Cases

C.Tax C. Canadian Tax Cases

C.T.C.L.R. Cape Times Common Law Rep. *S.Af*

C.T.R. Cape Times Supreme Court Reports, Cape of Good Hope *S.Af.*

C.t.K. Macnaghten's Select Chancery Cases *temp.* King *Eng*

C.t.N. Eden's Chancery Reports *temp.* Northington *Eng*

C.t.T. Cases *temp.* Talbot, Chancery *Eng*

C.W.Dud. Dudley's South Carolina Reports

C.W.N. Calcutta Weekly Notes *India*

CYC Cyclopedia of Law and Procedure *U.S.*

CZO Canal Zone Order

C.Z.Rep. Canal Zone Reports *U.S.*

C.& A. Cooke & Alcock's K.B. Reports *Ir*

C.& C. Case and Comment
Coleman & Caines' New York Cases

C.& D. Corbett & Daniell's Elec. Cases *Eng*
Crawford & Dix Circuit Cases *Ir*

C.& D.A.C. Crawford & Dix Abridged Cas. *Ir*

C.& D.C.C. Crawford & Dix Circuit Cases *Ir*

C.&E. Cababé & Ellis Queen's Bench Rep. *Eng*

C.& F. Clark & Finnelly's H. L. Cases *Eng*

C.& H.Elec.Cas. Clarke & Hall, Cases of Contested Elections in Congress, 1789–1834 *U.S.*

C.& J. Crompton & Jervis Ex. Reports *Eng*

C.& K. Carrington & Kirwan's N.P. Rep. *Eng*

C.& L. Connor & Lawson's Chancery Rep. *Ir*

C.& L.C.C. Cane & Leigh's Crown Cases *Eng*

C.& M. Carrington & Marshman's N.P. Rep. *Eng*
Crompton & Meeson Exchequer Reports *Eng*

C.& Marsh. Carrington & Marshman's N.P. Rep. *Eng*

C.& N. Cameron & Norwood's Conference Rep. *NC*

C.& O.R.Cas. Carrow & Oliver's English Railway & Canal Cases

C.& P. Carrington & Payne's N. P. Rep. *Eng*
Craig & Phillips' Chancery Reports *Eng*

C.& R. Cockburn & Rowe's Election Rep. *Eng*

C.& S. Clark & Scully's Drainage Cases *Can*
Clifford & Stephen's Locus Standi Cas. *Eng*

Ca. Celeb. Causes Celebres, Quebec

Ca.temp.F. Cases *temp.* Finch. *Eng*

Ca.temp.H. Cases *temp.* Hardwicke *Eng*

Ca.temp.Holt Cases *temp.* Holt *Eng*

Ca.temp.K. Cases in Chancery *temp.* King *Eng*

Ca.temp.Talb. Cases in Chancery *temp.* Talbot *Eng*

Cab.& E. Cababé & Ellis Rep., Q.B.D. *Eng*

Cab.Lawy. Cabinet Lawyer by John Wade *Eng*

Cadwalader Cadwalader's Dist. Ct. Cases, Eastern District of Pennsylvania *U.S.*

Cai. Caines' New York Term Reports; Cases in Error

Cai.Cas. Caine's Cases in Error *N.Y.*

Cai.T.R. Caines' Term Reports *N.Y.*

Cairns' Dec. Cairns' Dec., Albert Assurance Arbitration *Eng*

Cal. Calcutta Series, Indian Law Reports
Caldecott's King's Bench Reports *Eng*
California Law Reports
Calthrop King's Bench Reports *Eng*

Cal.App. California Appeals Reports

Cal.App.Sup. California Superior Court, Appellate Department (with California Appeals)

Cal.Ch. Calendar of Proceedings in Chancery

Cal.Dec. California Decisions

Cal.I.A.C.Dec. California Industrial Accident Decisions

Cal.Jur. California Jurisprudence

Cal.L.J. Calcutta Law Journal Rep. *India*

California Law Journal

Cal.L.Rev. California Law Review

Cal.Leg.Adv. Calcutta Legal Adviser *India*

Cal.Leg.Obs. Calcutta Legal Observer *India*

Cal.Leg.Rec. California Legal Record

Cal.P.Ch. Calendar of Proceedings in Chancery. *Eng*

Cal.R.C.Dec. California Railroad Comm. Dec.

Cal.Rep. California Reports

Calthrop's King's Bench Reports *Eng*

Cal.S.D.A. Calcutta Sadr Diwani Adalat Rep. *India*

Cal.Ser. Indian Law Reports, Calcutta Ser.

Cal.Sup. California Superior Court, Reports of Cases in Appellate Departments

Cal.Unrep. California Unreported Cases

Cal.W.R. Calcutta Weekly Reporter *India*

Calc.L.J. Calcutta Law Journal *India*

Calc.W.N. Calcutta Weekly Notes *India*

Cald. Caldecott's Magistrates' and Settlement Cases *Eng*

Caldwell's Reports (25–36 West Va.)

Cald.J.P. Caldecott's Magistrates' Cas. *Eng*

Cald.Mag.Cas. Same as above

Cald. S.C. Caldecott's Settlement Cases *Eng*

Calif.L.Rev. California Law Review

Calif.S.B.J. California State Bar Journal

Call Call's Reports (5–10 Virginia)

Calth. Calthrop's City of London Cases, K.B. *Eng*

Calthrop's King's Bench Reports *Eng*

Cam. Cameron's Reports, Upper Canada

Cam.Cas. Cameron's Supreme Court Cases *Can*

Cam.Op. Cameron's Legal Opinions *Canada*

Cam.Prac. Cameron's Supreme Ct. Pract. *Can*

Can.S.C. Reports Hitherto Unpublished, Supreme Court of Canada (Cameron)

Cam.Scacc. Camera Scaccarii (Exchequer Chamber) *Eng*

Cam.Stell. Camera Stellate (Star Chamber) *Eng*

Cam.& N[or]. Cameron & Norwood's North Carolina Conference Reports

Camb.L.J. Cambridge Law Journal

Cameron *See* Cam., *supra*

Camp. Camp's Reports (1 North Dakota)

Campbell's Nisi Prius Reports *Eng*

Campbell's Reports (26–58 Nebraska)

Camp.Dec. Taney's U. S. Circuit Court Decisions, by Campbell

Camp.N.P. Campbell's Nisi Prius Reports *Eng*

Campbell Campbell's Legal Gazette (27–58 Nebraska)

Campbell's Nisi Prius Reports *Eng*

Taney's Circuit Court Decisions, by Campbell *U.S.*

Can.Abr. Canadian Abridgment

Can.B.J. Canada Bar Journal

Can.B.R. Canadian Bar Review

Can.Bank.R. Canadian Bankruptcy Reports

Can.Bar.Rev. Canadian Bar Review

Can.C.C. Canada Crim. Cas. Annotated

Can.Com.Cas. Commercial Law Reports *Canada*

Can.Com.L.R. Canadian Commercial Law Rep.

Can.Com.R. Canadian Commercial Reports

Can.Crim.Cas. Canadian Criminal Cases, Ann.

Can.Exch. Reports, Exchequer Court *Canada*

Can.Gaz. Canadian Gazette

Can.L.J. Canada Law Journal, Montreal

Canada Law Journal, Toronto

Can.L.R. Canada Law Reports, Exchequer & Supreme Court, in two series

Can.L.Rev. Canadian Law Review

Can.L.T. Canadian Law Times

Can.L.T.Occ.N. Canadian Law Times, Occasional Notes

Can.Mun.J. Canadian Municipal Journal

Can.R.A.C. Canadian Reports, Appeal Cases

Can.R.C. Railway Commission of Canada

Can.Ry.Cas. Canada Railway Cases

Can.S.C.Rep. Canada Supreme Court Reports

Can.Sup.Ct. Canada Supreme Court Reports

Can.Tax Cas. Canada Tax Cases

Canal Zone Sup.Ct. Canal Zone Supreme Court Reports

Candy Sind Judgments, Candy & Birdwood *India*

Cane & L. Cane & Leigh's Crown Cas. Res. *Eng*

Cantwell Cases on Tolls & Customs *Ir*

Cape L.J. Cape Law Journal

Cape T.Div. Cape Provincial Div. Rep. *S.Af.*

Cape T.R. Cape Times Reports, Supreme Court, Cape of Good Hope *S.Af.*

Car.H.& A. Carrow, Hamerton, & Allen Session Cases *Eng*

Car.L.J. Carolina Law Journal

Car.L.Rep. Carolina Law Repository (4 N.C.)

Car.O.& B. Railway Cases, Carrow, etc. *Eng*

Car.& Kir. Carrington & Kirwan's N.P. Reports *Eng*

Car.& Mar. Carrington & Marshman's N.P. Reports *Eng*

Car.& Ol. Railway & Canal Cases, Carrow etc. *Eng*

Car.& P. Carrington & Payne's N.P. Rep. *Eng*

Carey.M.R. Carey's Manitoba Reports *temp.* Wood *Canada*

Carl. Carleton's New Brunswick Rep. *Canada*

Carp.P[at].C[as]. Carpmael's Patent Cas. *Eng*

Carpenter Carpenter's Reports (52, 53 Calif)

Carr.Cas. Carrau's Summary Cases *India*

Carr.Ham.& Al. Carrow, Hamerton & Allen's New Sessions Cases *Eng*

Carrau Carrau's Summary Cases *India*

Carsh. Carshaltown's Court Rolls *Eng*

Cart. Carter's Reports, Common Pleas *Eng*

Carter's Reports (1, 2 Indiana)
Cartwright's Cases on British North America Act *Can*

Carter Carter's Com. Pl. Reports *Eng*
Carter's Reports (1, 2 Indiana)

Carth. Carthew's King's Bench Reports *Eng*

Cartm. Cartmell's Trade Mark Cases *Eng*

Cartw.C.C. Cartwright's Constitutional Cases *Canada*

Cary Cary's Chancery Reports *Eng*

Cas. Casey's Reports (25–36 Pa. State)

Cas.App. Cases of Appeal to House of Lords

Cas.Arg.& Dec. Cases Argued & Decreed in Chancery *Eng*

Cas.B.R. Cases Banco Regis *temp.* Wm. III (12 Modern Reports)

Cas.B.R.Holt Cases & Resolutions of Settlements *Eng*

Cas.C.L. Cases in Crown Law *Eng*

Cas.C.R. Cases *temp.* Wm. III (12 Modern)

Cas.Ch. (or Cas. in Ch.) Cases in Chancery 1660–88 *Eng*
Cases in Chancery 1660–97 *Eng*
Select Cases in Chancery *Eng*
Cases in Chancery *temp.* Car. II *Eng*

Cas.Eq. Gilbert's Cases in Equity *Eng*

Cas.L.Eq. Cases in Law & Eq. (10 Modern) *Eng*

Cas.Eq.Abr. Cases in Equity, Abridged *Eng*

Cas.F.T. Cases in Chancery, *temp.* Talbot, by Forester *Eng*

Cas.H.L. Cases in the House of Lords *Eng*

Cas.in Ch. *See* Cas.Ch., *supra*

Cas.K.B. Cases in King's Bench (8 Modern)

Cas.K.B.t.H. Cases *temp.* Hardwicke (Kelynge's K. B. Reports) *Eng*

Cas.Prac.C.P. Cases of Practice, Com. Pl. *Eng*

Cas.Op. Burton's Cases & Opinions *Eng*

Cas.P. Cases in Parliament *Eng*

Cas.Pr.C.P. Cooke's Reports of Cases of Practice in Common Pleas *Eng*

Cas.Pr.K.B. Cases of Practice, K.B. *Eng*

Cas.R. Casey's Reports (25–36 Pa. State)

Cas.S.M. Cases of Settlement, K. B. *Eng*

Cas.Sett. Cases of Settlements & Removals *Eng*

Cas.Six Cir. Cases on Six Circuits *Ir*

Cas.*t*.Ch.II Reports in Chancery,
Cases *temp*. Charles II   *Eng*

Cas.*t*.F. Chancery Cases *temp*. Finch
Eng

Cas.*t*.Geo.I. Chancery Cas. *temp*
George I (8, 9 Modern Reports)
Eng

Cas.*t*.H. King's Bench Cases *temp*.
Hardwicke
Chancery Reports *temp*. Hardwicke
(West)
King's Bench Reports *temp*. Holt
(7, 11 Modern Reports)   *Eng*

Cas.*t*.K. Chancery Cases *temp*. King
Eng
Chancery Reports *temp*. King
(Mosley)   *Eng*

Cas.*t*.Lee Cases *temp*. Lee, Ecclesiastical (Phillimore)   *Eng*

Cas.*t*.Mac[cl]. Cases *temp*. Macclesfield (10 Modern Reports)   *Eng*

Cas.*t*.Nap. Drury's Ch. Cas. *temp*.
Napier   *Ir*

Cas.*t*.North. Cases *temp*. Northington
Eng

Cas.*t*.Plunk. Cases *temp*. Plunkett
(Lloyd & Gould Chancery)   *Ir*

Cas.*t*.Q.Anne (11 Modern Rep.) *Eng*

Cas.*t*.Sugd. Cases *temp*. Sugden,
Chancery   *Ir*

Cas.*t*.Talb. Ch. Cases *temp*. Talbot
Eng

Cas.*t*.Wm.III Cases *temp*. Wm.III (12
Modern)

Cas.*temp*. *See* Cas.*t*., *supra*

Cas.Wm.I Cases, Wm.I to Richard I
(Bigelow)   *Eng*

Cas.& Op. Cases & Opinions of
Eminent Counsel   *Eng*

Case & Com. Case and Comment

Cases in Ch. Select Cases in Chancery
Eng

Casey Casey's Reports (25–36 Pa.
State)

Cass.L.G.B. Casson's Local Govt. Bd.
Dec.   *Eng*

Cates Cates' Reports (109–127
Tennessee)

Catholic U.L.R. Catholic University
Law Rev.

Cent[r].Crim.C.Cas. Central
Criminal Court Cases (Sessions
Papers)   *Eng*

Cent[r].Crim.C.R. Central Criminal
Court Reports   *Eng*

Cent.Dig. Century Digest

Cent.L.J. Central Law Journal

Cent.L.Mo. Central Law Monthly

Cent.Prov.L.R. Central Provinces
Law Reports   *India*

Cent.Rep. Central Reporter

Cert. Certiorari

Ceyl.Cr.App.R. Ceylon Criminal
Appeal Rep.

Ceyl.L.J. Ceylon Law Journal

Ceyl.L.R. Ceylon Law Recorder

Ceyl.L.Rev. Ceylon Law Review

Ceyl.Leg.Misc. Ceylon Legal
Miscellany

Ch. Chalmers' Colonial Opinions
Law Reports, Ch. Div. Since 1890 *Eng*

Ch.App. Law Reports, Chancery
Appeals   *Eng*

Ch.App.Cas. Law Reports, Chancery
Appeals

Ch.Cas. Cases in Chancery 1660–88
Eng
Select Cases in Chancery *temp*. King
Eng

Ch.Cas.in Ch. Choyce Cases in
Chancery   *Eng*

Ch.Ch. Upper Canada Chancery
Chambers Rep.

Ch.Cham. *Same* as above

Ch.Col.Op. Chalmers' Colonial
Opinions   *Eng*

Ch.D.[iv]. Law Reports, Chancery
Div.   *Eng.*

Ch.K. Charter K, Home Loan Bank
Board   *U.S.*

Ch.Pre. Precedents in Chancery *Eng*

Ch.R. Chitty's King's Bench Reports
Eng
Reports in Chancery 1615–1712 *Eng*
Upper Canada Chancery Chambers
Reports
Irish Chancery Reports

Ch. Rep. *See* Ch.R., *supra*

Ch.R.M. Charlton's Reports (Georgia
1811–37)

Ch.Rob. Robinson's Admiralty
Reports   *Eng*

Ch.Sent. Chancery Sentinel   *U.S.*

Ch.T.U.P. T. U. P. Charlton's Reports
Ga

Ch.& Cl.Cas. Cripps' Church & Clergy
Cases   *Eng*

Chal.Op. Chalmers' Opinions, Const.
Law   *Eng*

Cham. Chambers' Upper Canada
Reports

Chamb.Rep. Chambers' Ch. Rep.,
Ontario

Champ. Champion's Cases, Wine &
Beer-Houses Act *Eng*
Chan. Chaney's Reports (37–58 Mich.)
Chand. Chandler's Reports (20, 38–44
N.H.)
Chandler's Reports (Wisconsin 1849–
52)
Chaney Chaney's Reports (37–58
Michigan)
Char.Cham.Cas. Charley's Chamber
Cases *Eng*
Char.Pr.Cas. Charley's New Practice
Rep. *Eng*
Charl.R.M. R.M.Charlton's Georgia
Reports
Charl.T.U.P. T.U.P.Charlton's
Georgia Rep.
Chase Chase's Circuit Court Decisions
U.S.
Chest.Co.Rep. Chester County Rep.
Pa
Chetty Sudder Dewanny Adawlut
Cases, Madras *India*
Chev. Cheves' Reports (S.C. 1839–40)
Chev.Ch. Cheves' Equity Rep. (S. C.
1839–40)
Chi.B.Rec. Chicago Bar Record
Chi-Kent L.Rev. Chicago-Kent Law
Review
Chi.L.B. Chicago Law Bulletin
Chi.L.J. Chicago Law Journal
Chi.L.R. Chicago Law Record
Chi.Leg.N. Chicago Legal News
China L.Rev. China Law Review
Chip. Chipman's Reports, New Bruns-
wick
Chipman's Reports (Vermont 1789–
1824)
Chip.D. D. Chipman's Vermont
Reports
Chip.Ms. Chipman's Manuscript
Reports, New Brunswick
Chip.N. N. Chipman's Vermont
Reports
Chit. Chitty's Bail Court Reports *Eng*
Chitty's K. B. Practice Reports *Eng*
Chit.B.C. Chitty's Bail Court Decisions
Eng
Chit.F. Chitty's King's Bench Forms
Eng
Chit.R. Chitty's Bail Court Reports
Eng
Chit.Stat. Chitty's Statutes *Eng*
Chitt. Same as Chit., *supra*
Chitt.& Pat. Chitty & Patell's Supreme
Court Appeals *India*

Cho.Ca.Ch. Choyce Cases in Chancery
Eng
Chr.Rep. Chambers' Reports, Upper
Canada
Chr.Rob. Robinson's Admiralty
Reports *Eng*
Cin.Law Bul. Cincinnati Law Bulletin
Cin.L.Rev. University of Cincinnati
Law Rev.
Cin.Mun.Dec. Cincinnati Municipal
Decisions
Cin.Rep. Cincinnati Superior Ct.
Reports
Cin.S.C.Rep. Same as above
Cir.Ct.Dec. Ohio Circuit Court
Decisions
Cit. The Citator; Reports of Indian
Cases & Statutes
City Ct.R.Supp. New York, City
Court Reports Supplement
City Ct.Rep. New York, City Court
Reports
City H.Rec. New York, City Hall
Recorder
City H.Rep. City Hall Reporter
(Lomas, N.Y.)
City Rec. New York, City Record
Civ.Pr.Rep. Civil Procedure Reports
N.Y.
Civ.& Cr.L.S. Civil & Criminal Law
Series *India*
C.L.J. Cape Law Journal
Cl. Rotulus Clausarum (Close Roll)
Eng
Clark
Clarke
Cl.App. Clark's H. L. Appeal Cases
Eng
Cl.Ch. Clarke's Chancery Reports
N.Y.
Cl.Home Clerk Home's Session Cases
Scot
Cl.& Fin. Clark & Finnelly's H.L. Cas.
Eng
Cl.& Fin.N.S. Clark's H. L. Cases *Eng*
Cl.& H. Clarke & Hall's Contested
Elections in Congress *U.S.*
Cl.& Sc.Dr.Cas. Clark & Scully's
Drainage Cases *Canada*
Clark Clark's House of Lords Cases
Eng
Clark's Reports (58 Alabama)
Jamaica Supreme Ct. Judgments
(Clark)
Clark (Pa.) Clark's Pennsylvania Law
Journal Reports
Clark & Fin. *See* Cl. & Fin., *supra*

Clarke   Clarke's Notes of Bengal Cases
India
Clarke's New York Chancery Reports
Clarke's Reports (19–22 Michigan)
Clarke's Reports (Pa. 1842–52)
Clarke Ch.   Clarke's New York Chancery Rep.
Clarke Not.   Clarke's Notes of Cases, Bengal
Clarke & H. Elec. Cas.   Clarke & Hall's Contested Elections in Congress   *U.S.*
Clay.   Clayton's Rep. & Pleas of Assizes at York, 1631–50   *Eng*
Clayton   Same as above
Cleary R.C.   Cleary's Registration Cases   *Eng*
Clem.   Clemens' Reports (57–59 Kansas)
Clerk Home   Decisions, Court of Sess.
Scot
Clev.L.Rec.   Cleveland Law Record
Clev.L.Reg.   Cleveland Law Register
Clev.L.Rep.   Cleveland Law Reports
Ohio
Clev.-Mar.L.Rev.   Cleveland-Marshall Law Review
Clif.El.   Clifford's Southwark El. Cas.
Eng
Clif.& Ri[ck].   Clifford & Rickard's Locus Standi Reports   *Eng*
Clif.& St.   Clifford & Stephen's Locus Standi Reports   *Eng*
Cliff.   Clifford's First Circuit Reports
U.S.
Cliff.El.Cas.   Clifford's Southwark El. Cas.   *Eng*
Clift   Clift's Entries 1719   *Eng*
Clk.Mag.   Clerk's Magazine, London
Rhode Island Clerk's Magazine
Co.   Coke's Institutes   *Eng*
Coke's King Bench Reports   *Eng*
Co.A.   Cook's Lower Canada Admiralty Cas.
Co.Ct.Cas.   County Court Cases   *Eng*
Co.Ct.Chr.   County Courts Chronicle
Co.Ct.I.L.T.   Irish Law Times, County Courts
Co.Ct.Rep.   County Courts Reports
Eng
Pennsylvania County Court Reports
Co.Cts.   Coke's Courts (4th Institute)
Eng
Co.Ent.   Coke's Entries   *Eng*
Co.G.   G. Coke's Practice Reports *Eng*
Cooke's Practice Reports   *Eng*
Co.Inst.   Coke's Institutes   *Eng*

Co.L.J.   Cochin Law Journal
Colonial Law Journal   *New Zealand*
Co.Litt.   Coke on Littleton   *Eng*
Co.on Courts   Coke's 4th Institute *Eng*
Co.P.C.   Coke's Pleas of the Crown
Eng
Co.R.   Code Reporter   *N.Y.*
Co.R.N.S.   Code Reporter, New Series
N.Y.
Co.Rep.   Code Reporter
Coke's King's Bench Reports   *Eng*
Cob.St.Tr.   Cobbett's (Howell's) State Trials   *Eng*
Cobb.   Cobb's Reports (121 Alabama) (4–20 Georgia)
Cobb.St.Tr.   Cobbett's (Howell's) State Trials   *Eng*
Coch.   Cochran's Nova Scotia Reports
Coch.Ch.Ct.   Chief Court of Cochin, Select Decisions
Cochin   Cochin Law Reports
Cochin L. J.   Cochin Law Journal
Cochr.   Cochran's Nova Scotia Reports
Cochran's Reports (3–10 North Dakota)
Cochran   Same as Coch., *supra*
Cockb.& R[owe].   Cockburn & Rowe's Election Cases   *Eng*
Cocke   Cocke's Reports (16–18 Ala.) (14, 15 Florida)
Code Rep.   New York Code Reporter
Code Rep.N.S.   New York Code Reporter, N.S. [Reporter]
Coffey.   Coffey's Probate Dec. (California)
Coke   *See* Co., *supra*
Col.   Coldwell's Reports (41–47 Tennessee)
Coleman's Reports (Alabama)
Colorado Reports
Colonial
Columbia
Col.App.   Colorado Appeals Reports
Col.C.C.   Collyer's Chancery Cases
Eng
Col.Cas.   Coleman's Practice Cases *N.Y.*
Col.L.J.   Colonial Law Journal
New Zealand
Col.L.Rep.   Colorado Law Reporter
Col.L.Rev.   Columbia Law Review
Col.N.P.   Colorado Nisi Prius Decisions
Col.& Cai.Cas.   Coleman & Caines' Cases   *N.Y.*
Cold.   Coldwell's Reports (41–47 Tennessee)

Cole. Coleman's Reports (Alabama)

Colem.Cas. Coleman's Cases *N.Y.*

Coll.C.R. Collyer's Chancery Reports *Eng*

Coll.Jurid. Collectanea Juridica *Eng*

Coll.P.C. Colles' Parliamentary Cases *Eng*

Coll.& E.Bank. Collier & Eaton's American Bankruptcy Reports

Colles. Colles' Cases in Parliament *Eng*

Colly. Collyer's Vice-Chancellors' Rep. *Eng*

Colo. Colorado

Colo.App. Colorado Appeals Reports

Colo.B.A. Colorado Bar Association

Colo.Dec. Colorado Decisions

Colo.Dec.Fed. Colorado Decisions, Federal

Colo.Dec.Supp. Colorado Decisions Supplement

Colo.I.C. Colorado Industrial Comm. Report

Colo.L.Rep. Colorado Law Reporter

Colo.N.P.Dec. Colorado Nisi Prius Decisions 1900–02

Colo.S.R.C. Colorado State Railroad Comm.

Colq. Colquit's Reports (1 Modern) *Eng*

Colt. Coltman's Registration Cases *Eng*

Colum.Jur. Columbia Jurist

Colum.L.Rev. Columbia Law Review

Colum.L.T. Columbia Law Times

Colvil Colvil's Manuscript Decisions, Court of Session *Scot*

Com. Blackstone's Commentaries
Comberbach's Reports, King's Bench *Eng*
Comstock's Reports (1–5 New York)
Comyns' Reports, K.B., Com. Pl. Ex. *Eng*

Com.B. Common Bench Reports 1845–65 *Eng*

Com.B.N.S. Common Bench Reports, New Ser. *Eng*

Com.Cas. Commercial Cases *Eng*

Com.Dig. Comyn's Digest *Eng*

Com.Jour. House of Commons Journal *Eng*

Com.L.J. Commercial Law Journal

Com.L.L.J. Commercial Law League Journal

Com.L.R. Common Law Reports 1853–55 *Eng*

Com.L.Rep. Same as above

Com.Pl. Common Pleas

Com.Pl.Div. Law Reports, Com. Pl. Div. *Eng*

Com.Pl.Rep. Common Pleas Reporter *U.S.*

Com.& Leg. Rep. Commercial & Legal Reporter

Comb. Comberbach's K. B. Reports *Eng*

Comm.Journ. House of Commons Journal *Eng*

Comm.L.R. Commercial Law Reports *Canada*
Commonwealth Law Reports *Aus*

Commw.L.R. Commonwealth Law Reports *Aus*

Comp.Dec. Comptroller of the Treasury Dec. *U.S.*

Comp.Gen. Comptroller General's Dec. *U.S.*

Comp.Rev. Compensation Review

Company Cases *India*

Comst. Comstock's Reports (1–4 N.Y.)

Comyns Comyns' King's Bench Reports *Eng*

Con. Conover's Reports (16–153 Wisconsin)
Connoly's Criminal Reports *N.Y.*

Con.Cus. Conroy's Custodian Reports *Eng, Ir.*

Con.Sur. Connoly's Surrogate's Rep. *N.Y.*

Con.& Law. Connor & Lawson's Ch. Rep. *Ir*

Cond.Ch.R. Condensed Chancery Reports *Eng*

Cond.Eccl. Condensed Ecclesiastical Rep. *Eng*

Cond.Ex.R. Condensed Exchequer Reports *Eng*

Cond.H.C. Conders Highway Cases

Cond.Rep.U.S. Condensed U. S. Rep. (Peters)

Conf. North Carolina Conference Reports (Cameron & Norwood)

Conf.Pers.Fin.L.Q.R. Conference on Personal Finance Law, Quarterly Report

Cong.Deb. Congressional Debates *U.S.*

Cong.Dig. Congdon's Digest *Canada*

Cong.El.Cas. Congressional Election Cas. *U.S.*

Cong.Rec. Congressional Record *U.S.*

Conn. Connecticut [Reports]
Connolly's New York Surrogate's Reports

Conn.B.J. Connecticut Bar Journal

Conn.Comp.Com. Connecticut Compensation Commissioners, Compendium of Awards

Conn.Comp.Dec. Connecticut Workmen's Compensation Decisions

Conn.Dec. Connecticut Decisions

Conn.R.C. Connecticut Railroad Commissioners

Conn.S. Connecticut Supplement

Connolly Connolly's Surrogate's Rep.
N.Y.

Connor.& L. Connor & Lawson Ch.
Rep. *Ir*

Conover Conover's Reports (16–153 Wis.)

Conr. Conroy's Custodian Reports *Ir*

Consist [Rep.] Haggard's Consistory
Rep. *Eng*

Const. Bott's Poor Laws, by Const *Eng*
Constitutional Reports by Harper,
Mill, Treadway (South Carolina)

Const.N.S. Same as above, New Series

Const.R.S.C. Constitutional Rep. of
South Carolina, by Treadway

Const.Rep. Constitutional Reports *SC*

Const.Rev. Constitutional Review

Const.S.C. South Carolina Constitutional Reports, N.S.

Cont.El. Controverted Elections
Judgts. *Eng*

Cont.L.Rev. Contemporary Law
Review *India*

Convey. Conveyancer

Convey.N.S. Conveyancer & Property
Lawyer

Co.& Al. Cooke & Alcock's K. B. Rep.
Ir

Cook V.Adm. Cook's Vice-Admiralty
Rep. *Can*

Cooke Cooke's Cases of Practice, Com.
P. *Eng*
Cases under Sugden's Act, 1838 *Eng*
Cooke's Reports (3 Tennessee)

Cooke C.P. Cooke's Common Pleas
Rep. *Eng*

Cooke Pr.Cas. Cooke's Practice Rep.,
Com. Pl. *Eng*

Cooke Pr.Reg. Cooke's Practical
Register of the Common Pleas
Eng

Cooke & Al. Cooke & Alcock's K.B.
Rep. *Ir*

Cooley Cooley's Reports (5–12
Michigan)

Coop. Cooper's Chancery Reports *Eng*
Cooper's Chancery Rep. *temp.*
Cottenham *Eng*

Cooper's Practice Cases, Chancery
Eng

Cooper's Reports (21–24 Florida)

Cooper's Tennessee Chancery Reports

Coop.C.C. Cooper's Chancery Cases
temp. Cottenham *Eng*

Coop.C.& P.R. Cooper's Chancery &
Practice Reporter, Upper Canada

Coop.Ch. Cooper's Tennessee
Chancery Rep.

Coop.Ch.Pr. Cooper's Chancery
Practice Rep. *Eng*

Coop.G. G. Cooper's Chancery
Reports *Eng*

Coop.Pr.Cas. C.P. Cooper's Ch.
Practice Cases *Eng*

Coop.Sel.Ca. Cooper's Select Cases
temp. Eldon. *Eng*

Coop.Sel.E.C. Cooper's Select Early
Cases *Scot*

Coop.t.Br. Cooper's Cases *temp.*
Brougham *Eng*

Coop.t.Cott. Cooper's Chancery Cases
temp. Cottenham *Eng*

Coop.t.Eld. Cooper's Rep. *temp.*
Eldon *Eng*

Coop.*temp.* See Coop.*t.*, *supra*

Coop.Ten.Chy. Cooper's Tennessee
Ch. Rep.

Cooper Cooper's Tennessee Chancery
Reports

Cope Cope's Reports (63–73
California)

Copp Min.Dec. Copp's Mining
Decisions *U.S.*

Cor. Coryton's Reports (Bengal)
India

Cor.Cas. American & English Corporation Cas.

Cor.Jud. Correspondances Judiciaires
Can

Cor.Soc.Cas. Coroner's Society Cases
Eng

Corb.& D[an]. Corbett & Daniell's
Election Cases *Eng*

Cornell L.Q. Cornell Law Quarterly

Corp.J. Corporation Journal

Corp.Prac.Rev. Corporate Practice
Review

Corp.Rep. Pennsylvania Corporation
Reporter

Correspondances Jud. Correspondances Judiciaires *Can*

Coryton Coryton's Rep., Calcutta
India

Cou. Couper's Justiciary Reports
Scot

Counsellor The Counsellor

Count.Cts.Chron. County Courts Chronicle

County Co.Cas. County Council Cases *Scot*

County Cts.& Bankr.Cas. County Courts & Bankruptcy Cases

Coup[er] Couper's Justiciary Reports *Scot*

Cour.& Macl. Courtenay & Maclean's Scotch Appeals (6 & 7 Wilson & Shaw)

Court Cl. Court of Claims *U.S.*

Court J.& Dist.Ct.Rec. Court Journal & District Court Record

Court Sess. Ca. Court of Session Cases *Scot*

Cout. Coutlee's Unreported Cases *Canada*

Cout.S.C. Notes of Unreported Cases, Supreme Court of Canada (Coutlee)

Cow. Cowen's New York Reports 1823–29

Cowper's King's Bench Reports *Eng*

Cow.Cr.Rep. Cowen's Criminal Reports *N.Y.*

Cowp. Cowper's King's Bench Reports *Eng*

Cox Cox's Chancery Reports *Eng*

Cox's Criminal Cases *Eng*

Cox's Reports (25–27 Arkansas)

Cox Am.T.M.Cas. Cox's American Trade Mark Cases

Cox C.C. Cox's County Court Cases *Eng*

Cox's Criminal Law Cases *Eng*

Cox C.L.Pr. Cox's Common Law Practice *Eng*

Cox Ch. Cox's Chancery Cases *Eng*

Cox Ch.Pr. Cox's Chancery Practice *Eng*

Cox Cr.Ca. Cox's Criminal Cases *Eng*

Cox Cty.Ct.Ca. Cox's County Court Cas. *Eng*

Cox.Eq.Cas. S.C. Cox's Equity Cases *Eng*

Cox Jt.Stk. Cox's Joint Stock Co. Cas. *Eng*

Cox M.C. Cox's Magistrates' Cases *Eng*

Cox M.&H. Cox, Macrae & Hertslet's County Court Cases & Appeals *Eng*

Cox P.W. Cox's ed. of Peere Williams' Rep. *Eng*

Cox Tr.M.Ca. Cox's American Trade Mark Cas.

Cox & Atk. Cox & Atkinson's Registration Appeal Cases *Eng*

Coxe Coxe's Reports (1 New Jersey Law)

Cr. Cranch's Reports (5–13 U. S.) Cranch's Circuit Court Reports *U.S.*

Cr.App.Rep. Cohen's Criminal Appeal Rep. *Eng*

Cr.Cas.Res. Crown Cases Reserved *Eng*

Cr.L. Criminal Lawyer *India*

Cr.M.& R. Crompton, Meeson & Roscoe Rep. *Eng*

Cr.Pat.Dec. Cranch's Decisions on Patent Appeals *U.S.*

Cr.R. Criminal Reports *India*

Cr.Rg. Criminal Rulings, Bombay *India*

Cr.S.& P. Craigie, Stewart & Paton's Appeal Cases *Scot*

Cr.& Dix Crawford & Dix Circuit Ct. Cas. *Ir*

Cr.& Dix Ab.Cas. Crawford & Dix Abridged Cases *Ir*

Cr.& J. Crompton & Jervis Ex. Reports *Eng*

Cr.& M. Crompton & Meeson's Ex. Rep. *Eng*

Cr.& Ph. Craig & Phillips Chancery Rep. *Eng*

Cr.& St. Craigie & Stewart H. L. Rep. *Scot*

Crabbe Crabbe's District Court Rep. *U.S.*

Craig & Ph. Craig & Phillips Ch. Rep. *Eng*

Craig.& St. Craigie, Stewart & Paton's Appeal Cases *Scot*

Cranch Cranch's Supreme Ct. Rep. (5–13 U.S.)

Cranch C.C. Cranch's Circuit Court Rep. U.S.

District of Columbia App. Cas. (v.1–5)

Cranch D.C. District of Columbia App. Cas., v.1–5

Cranch Pat.Dec. Cranch's Patent Dec. *U.S.*

Crane Crane's Reports (22–29 Montana)

Crane.C.C. Cranenburgh's Criminal Cases *India*

Craw. Crawford's Reports (53–69, 72–101 Ark.)

Craw.& D.Abr.Cas. Crawford & Dix's Abridged Cases *Ir*

Craw.& Dix Crawford & Dix's Circuit
Cases   *Ir*
Creasy Creasy's Ceylon Reports
Cress.Ins.Ca. Cresswell's Insolvency
Cas.   *Eng*
Crim.App.Rep. Cohen's Criminal
App. Rep.   *Eng*
Crim.L.J.I. Criminal Law Journal of
India
Crim.L.Mag. Criminal Law Magazine
Crim.L.Rec. Criminal Law Recorder
Crim.L.Rep. Criminal Law Reporter
Crim.Rec. Criminal Recorder,
Philadephia
Criminal Recorder, London
Criminal Recorder (1 Wheeler's New
York Criminal Reports)
Cripps Cripps' Church & Clergy Cases
Eng
Critch. Critchfield's Reports (5–21
Ohio St.)
Cro. Croke's King's Bench Reports
Eng
Keilway's King's Bench Rep. 1496–
1531   *Eng*
Cro.Car. Croke's K. B. Rep. *temp.*
Car. I   *Eng*
Cro.Eliz. Croke's Rep. *temp.* Elizabeth
Eng
Cro.Jac. Croke's K. B. Rep. *temp.*
James I   *Eng*
Crockford Crockford's Maritime Law
Rep.   *Eng*
Croke *See* Cro., *supra*
Crom.[p.] Crompton's Star Chamber
Cases   *Eng*
Cromp.Ex.R. Crompton's Exchequer
Rep.   *Eng*
Cromp.M.& R. Crompton, Meeson &
Roscoe's Exchequer Rep.   *Eng*
Cromp.& Jerv. Crompton & Jervis'
Ex. Rep.   *Eng*
Cromp.& Mees. Crompton & Meeson's
Ex. Rep.   *Eng*
Crosw.Pat.Cas. Croswell's Patent
Cases   *U.S.*
Crown L.C. Crown Land Cases,
N.S.W.   *Aus*
Crounse Crounse's Reports (3
Nebraska)
Crowther Crowther's Ceylon Reports
Crumrine Crumrine's Reports (116–
146 Pa.)
Pittsburgh Reports, ed. Crumrine
Ct.App.N.Z. Court of Appeals Rep.
New Zeal
Ct.Cl. Court of Claims   *U.S.*

Ct.Cl.N.Y. Court of Claims Reports
N.Y.
Ct.Cls. Court of Claims   *U.S.*
Ct.Com.Pl. Court of Common Pleas
Ct.Crim.App. Court of Criminal
Appeal   *Eng*
Ct.Errors & App. Court of Errors &
Appeals
Ct.Just. Court of Justiciary
Ct.Sess.Cas. Court of Session Cases
Scot
Cum.Bull. Cumulative Bulletin, In-
ternal Revenue Bureau, Treasury
Department
Cummins Cummins' Reports (Idaho
1866–67)
Cun. Cunningham's K. B. Reports
Eng
Cur. Curtis' Circuit Court Reports *U.S.*
Cur.Com. Current Comment & Legal
Miscellany
Cur.Dec. Curtis's Edition, U. S.
Supreme Court Reports
Cur.Ind.Cas. Current Indian Cases
Cur.Leg.Thought Current Legal
Thought
Cur.Ov.Ca. Curwen, Overruled Cases
Ohio
Cur.Reg.R. Curia Regis Rolls   *Eng*
Curry Curry's Reports (6–19
Louisiana)
Curt. Curtis' Circuit Court Reports
U.S.
Curtis' Edition, U. S. Supreme Court
Rep.
Curteis' Ecclesiastical Reports   *Eng*
Curt.C.C. Curtis' Circuit Court
Reports   *U.S.*
Curt.Cond. Curtis' Edition, U. S.
Supreme Court Reports
Curt.Dec. Same as above
Curt.Ecc. Curteis' Ecclesiastical
Reports   *Eng*
Curtis Curtis' Circuit Court Reports
U.S.
Curtis' Edition, U. S. Supreme Court
Rep.
Curw.Ov.Cas. Curwen's Overruled
Ohio Cases
Cush. Cushing's Reports (55–66 Mass.)
Cush.Elec.Cas. Cushing's Election
Cases   *Mass.*
Cushing Cushing's Reports (55–66
Mass.)
Cushman Cushman's Reports (23–29
Miss.)

Cust.Rep. Custer's Ecclesiastical Rep. *Eng*

Cut.Pat.Cas. Cutler's Trademark & Patent Cases

Cyc. Cyclopedia of Law and Procedure

Cyprus L.R. Cyprus Law Reports

D. Dallas' U. S. & Pennsylvania Reports

  Delaware Reports

  Denio's Reports   *N.Y.*

  Denison's Crown Cases   *Eng*

  Dictionary

  Dunlop, Bell, & Murray Reports *Scot*

  Duxbury

  Digest, Justinian's

  Dowling, *which see*

  Dunlop, Bell & Murray's Reports *Scot*

  Duxbury's High Court Reports *S.Af.*

  Dyer's Reports   *Eng*

  Disney's Ohio Superior Court Reports

DATA Defense Air Transportation Admin.   *U.S.*

D.B. Domesday Book

DC Disarmanent Commission   *UN*

D.C. District Court; District of Columbia; Treasury Department Circular   *U.S.*

D.C. (no.) Bull.Memo. United States Internal Revenue Bureau, Cumulative Bulletin, Treasury Dept. Circular

D.C.A. Dorion's Queen's Bench Rep. *Canada*

D.C.App. District of Columbia Appeals Rep.

DCCA District of Columbia Compensation Act

D.C.Lab.S. Dominion of Canada Labour Service (C.C.H.)

D.Chip. D.Chipman's Rep. (Vt.1789–1824)

D.Ct. District Court (usually U. S.)

D.D.N.J.F.D.C. Food & Drug Admin. Notices of Judgment   *U.S.*

D.Dec. Dix's School Law Decisions *N.Y.*

DEPA Defense Electric Power Admin. *U.S.*

DFA Defense Fisheries Administration *U.S.*

DFO Defense Food Order (Production & Marketing Adm.)   *U.S.*

DFO,SO Defense Food Order, Sub-Order   *U.S.*

D.F.& J. DeGex, Fisher & Jones' Ch. Rep.   *Eng*

D.F.& J.B. DeGex, Fisher & Jones' Bankruptcy Reports   *Eng*

D.G. DeGex's Bankruptcy Reports *Eng*

D.H.L. Dunlop's Session Cas., House of Lords   *Scot*

D.J.& S. DeGex, Jones & Smith's Ch. Rep.   *Eng*

D.J.& S.B. DeGex, Jones & Smith's Bankruptcy Rep.   *Eng*

DLC Disaster Loan Corporation *U.S.*

D.L.R. Dominion Law Reports *Canada*

  Dominion Law Reporter   *India*

  (usually with a Province abbreviation, as D.L.M. (A.M.), Ajmer-Merwara)

DMA Defense Manpower Administration   *U.S.*

DMB Defense Mobilization Board *U.S.*

DMEA Defense Materials Exploration Agency   *U.S.*

DMO Defense Mobilization Order *U.S.*

DMP Defense Materials Procurement Agency   *U.S.*

D.M.& G. DeGex, Macnaghten & Gordon Ch. Rep.   *Eng*

D.M.& G.B. DeGex, Macnaghten & Gordon Bankruptcy Rep. *Eng*

D.N.S. Dow, New Series (House of Lords Cases)   *Eng*

  Dowling's Bail Court Rep. N.S. *Eng*

DPA Defense Production Adm. *U.S.*

DPC Displaced Persons Comm. *U.S.*

D.P.R. Porto Rico Reports (Spanish ed.)

DR Distribution Regulation (Office of Price Stabilization)   *U.S.*

D.R. Dacca Reports   *India*

  De-rating and Rating Appeals *Scot, Eng*

DRC Defense Relocation Corporation *U.S.*

D.R.S. Dominion Report Service (CCH)   *Canada*

DSB Drug Supervisory Body   *UN*

DSFA Defense Solid Fuels Administration   *U.S.*

DSM Designation of Scarce Materials *U.S.*

DTA Defense Transport Administration   *U.S.*

D.& B. Dearsley & Bell's Crown Cases *Eng*

  Devereux & Battle's Reports (18–20 N.C.)

D.& C. District & County Reports *Pa*
Dow & Clark's Parliamentary Cases
Eng
D.& Ch. Deacon & Chitty's
Bankruptcy Rep. *Eng*
D.& E. Durnford & East's K. B. Rep.
(Term Reports) *Eng*
D.& F. Divisional & Full Court
Judgments *Gold Coast*
D.& G. Diprose & Gammon's Reports
of Law Affecting Friendly
Societies *Eng*
D.& J. DeGex & Jones' Chancery
Reports *Eng*
D.& J.B. DeGex & Jones' Bankruptcy
Rep. *Eng*
D.& L. Dowling & Lowndes' Bail Ct.
Rep. *Eng*
D.& M. Davison & Merivale's Q. B.
Rep. *Eng*
D.& P. Dearsley & Pearce's Crown
Cases *Eng*
D.& R. Dowling & Ryland's K. B. Rep.
Eng
D.& R.M.C. Dowling & Ryland's
Magistrates Cases *Eng*
D.& R.N.P. Dowling & Ryland's N. P.
Cas. *Eng*
D.& S. Deane & Swabey's Ecc. Reports
Eng
Doctor and Student
Drewry & Smale's Chancery Reports
Eng
D.& W. Drury & Walsh's Chancery
Rep. *Ir*
Drury & Warren's Chancery Reports
Ir
Dady. Dadyburjar's Small Court
Appeals *India*
Dai.Reg. New York Daily Register
Daily Trans. New York Daily Tran-
script, Old and New Series
Dak. Dakota
Dak.Law Rev. Dakota Law Review
Dal. Dalison's Common Pleas Reports
Eng
Dallas' United States Reports (1–4
U.S.)
Dallas' Pennsylvania Reports 1754–
1806
Dalrymple's Session Cases *Scot*
Dale Dale's Reports (2–4 Oklahoma)
Dale Ecc. Dale's Ecclesiastical Rep.
Eng
Dale Leg.Rit. Dale's Legal Ritual *Eng*
Dall. Dallam's Texas Supreme Court
Decisions

Dallas' United States Reports (1–4
U.S.)
Dallas' Pennsylvania Reports 1754–
1806
Dall.(Tex.) Dallam's Texas Decisions
Dall.Dec. Dallam's Texas Decisions,
from Dallam's Digest
Dall.in Keil. Dallison's Reports in
Keilway's K. B. Reports *Eng*
Dall.S.C. Dallas' U. S. Reports (1–4
U.S.)
Dallas *See* Dall. *supra*
Dalr. Dalrymple's Decisions, Ct. of
Session *Scot*
Daly Daly's New York Common Pleas
Reports
Dan. Dana's Reports (31–39 Ky.)
Daniels' Compendium Compensation
Cases *Eng*
Daniell's Excheq. in Equity Rep. *Scot*
Danner's Reports (42 Alabama)
Dan.& Ll. Danson & Lloyd's Mercan-
tile Cases *Eng*
Dana Dana's Reports (31–39
Kentucky)
Dann. Dann's Reports (1 Arizona)
Dann's Reports (in 22 California) 2d
ed. 1871
Danner's Reports (42 Alabama)
Danner Danner's Reports (42
Alabama)
Danquah Cases in Gold Coast Law
Dans.& LL. Danson & Lloyd's Mer-
cantile Cases *Eng*
Danv. Danvers' Abridgment *Eng*
Das. Common Law Reports, v.3 *Eng*
Dasent's Bankruptcy & Insolvency
Rep. *Eng*
Dasent Acts of Privy Council, ed.
Dasent *Eng*
Dasent's Bankruptcy & Insolvency
Rep. *Eng*
Dauph.Co.Rep. Dauphin County Rep.
Pa
Dav. Davies' District Court Reports
U.S.
Davies' K. B. & Exchequer Reports *Ir*
Davies' Patent Cases *Eng*
Davis' Hawaiian Reports
Davis' Abridgment of Coke's Reports
Eng
Dav.Coke Davis' Abridgment of
Coke's Rep. *Eng*
Dav.Ir. (Dav.Ir.K.B.) Davis or
Davy's or Davies K. B. Reports *Ir*
Dav.Pat.Cas. Davies' Patent Cases *Eng*

Dav.Rep. Davies' King's Bench
  Reports   *Ir*
Dav.& Mer. Davison & Merivale's Q.B.
  Rep.   *Eng*
Dav.(U.S.) Daveis District Court Rep.
  (v.2 of Ware)   *U.S.*
Daveis (U.S.) Daveis' District Court
  Rep. (v.2 of Ware)   *U.S.*
  Daveis, Davis, Davy's K. B. Reports
                                        Ir
Davis Davies, Davis, Davy's K. B.
  Rep.   *Ir*
  Davis' Hawaiian Reports
  Davis (Sir John) Reports   *Eng*
Davis L.Ct.Cas. Davis Land Court
  Decisions 1898–1908
Davis Rep. Davis' Hawaiian Reports
  (Sandwich Islands)
Day Day's Election Cases   *Eng*
  Day's Reports, Connecticut 1802–13
Dayton Dayton (Laning) Reports
                                        Ohio
  Dayton Superior & Common Pleas
  Rep.   *Ohio*
DeCol. De Colyar's County Ct. Cases
                                        Eng
De G. *See* De Gex
DeG.F.& J. DeGex, Fisher & Jones Ch.
  Rep.   *Eng*
DeG.J.& J.By. DeGex, Fisher & Jones
  Bankruptcy Appeals   *Eng*
DeG.J.& S. DeGex, Jones & Smith
  Chancery Rep.   *Eng*
DeG.M.& G. DeGex, Macnaghten, &
  Gordon Chancery Rep.   *Eng*
DeG.M.& G.By. DeGex, Macnaghten,
  & Gordon Bankruptcy Appeals
                                        Eng
DeG& J. DeGex & Jones' Chancery
  Reports   *Eng*
DeG.& J.By. DeGex & Jones' Bank-
  ruptcy Appeals   *Eng*
DeG.& Sm. DeGex & Smale's Chan-
  cery Rep.   *Eng*
DeGex DeGex' Bankruptcy Reports
                                        Eng
  See also DeG., *supra*
DeKrets. DeKretser's Matara Appeals
                                        Ceylon
DePaul L.Rev. De Paul Law Review
DeWitt De Witt's Reports (24–42
  Ohio State)
Dea. Deady's Circuit & District Court
  Reports   *U.S.*
Dea.& Ch. Deacon & Chitty's Bank-
  ruptcy Rep.   *Eng*

Dea.& Sw. Deane & Swabey's Ecc.
  Reports   *Eng*
Deac. Deacon's Bankruptcy Reports
                                        Eng
Deac.& Ch. Deacon & Chitty's Bank-
  ruptcy Reports   *Eng*
Deady Deady's Circuit & District
  Court Reports   *U.S.*
Deane Deane's Reports (24–26
  Vermont)
  Deane & Swabey's Ecc. Reports *Eng*
  Deane & Swabey's Probate & Divorce
  Rep.   *Eng*
  Deane's Blockade Cases   *Eng*
Deane Ecc.Rep. Deane & Swabey's
  Ecclesiastical Reports   *Eng*
Deane & Sw. Deane & Swabey's
  Ecclesiastical Reports   *Eng*
Dears.C.C. Dearsly's Crown Cases
                                        Eng
Dears.& B.C.C. Dearsley & Bell's
  Crown Cases   *Eng*
Deas & And. Deas & Anderson's Decis.
                                        Scot
Dec.Ch. Decisions from the Chair
  (Parliamentary)   *Eng*
Dec.Dig. American Digest System,
  Decennial Digests
Dec.O. Ohio Decisions
Dec.Rep. Ohio Decisions, Reprint
Dec.S.D.A. Bengal Sadr Diwani Adalat
  Dec.
Dec.*t*.H.& M. Admiralty Decisions
  temp. Hay & Marriott   *Eng*
Del. Delane's Revision Cases   *Eng*
  Delaware Reports
Del.Ch. Delaware Chancery Reports
Del.Civ.Dec. Delhi Civil Decisions
                                        India
Del.Co.R. Delaware Co.(Pa.) Reports
Del.Cr.Cas. Houston's Criminal Cas.
                                        Del.
Del.El.Cas. Delane's Election Revision
  Cases   *Eng*
Delane Delane's Revision Courts Dec.
                                        Eng
Delehanty New York Miscellaneous
  Reports
Dem. Demarest's Surrogate Reports
                                        N.Y.
Den. Denio's New York Reports
  Denis' Reports (32–46 La. Annual)
  Denison's Crown Cases Reserved *Eng*
Den.C.C. Denison's Crown Cas.
  Reserved   *Eng*
Den.& P. Denison & Pearce 's Crown
  Cas.   *Eng*

Denio Denio's New York Reports

Denis Denis' Reports (32–46 La. Annual)

Denver L.J. Denver Law Journal

Denver L.N. Denver Legal News

Dept.Dec. Departmental Decisions 1905-date *Eng*

Dept.R. Department Reports, State Dept. *N.Y.*

Des. Desaussure's Eq. Reports *S.C.*

Desaus.Eq. Same as above

Det.Law Detroit Lawyer (Detroit Bar Association)

Det.Leg.N. Detroit Legal News

Dev. Devereux' Reports (N.C. Law & Equity)

Devereux' Court of Claims Reports *U.S.*

DeVilliers Reports, Orange Free State *S.Af.*

Dev.Ct.Cl. Devereux' Court of Claims Rep. *U.S.*

Dev.Eq. Devereux' Reports (16, 17 N.C. Eq.)

Dev.L. Devereux' Reports (12–15 N.C. Law)

Dev.& Bat. Devereux & Battle's Reports (17–20 N.C. Law)

Dev.& Bat.Eq. Devereux & Battle's Reports (21, 22 N.C. Eq.)

Dew. Dewey's Reports (60–70 Kansas)

Dewey's Kansas Court of Appeals Reports

Di Dyer's King's Bench Reports *Eng*

Dice Dice's Reports (71–99 Indiana)

Dick. Dickens' Chancery Reports *Eng*

Dickinson's Reports (46–66 N.J. Eq.)

Dick.L.R. Dickinson Law Review

Dicta Dicta of the Denver Bar Association

Dill. Dillon's Circuit Court Reports *U.S.*

Dirl. Dirleton's Ct. of Session Dec. *Scot*

Disn. Disney's Ohio Superior Court Reports

Div.Ct. Divisional Court

Selected Judgments, Divisional Courts of the Gold Coast Colony

Dix Dec. Dix' School Law Decisions *N.Y.*

Docket The Docket

Doct.& St. Doctor & Student *Eng*

Dod[s]. Dodson's Admiralty Reports *Eng*

Dom.Boc. Domesday Book

Donaker Donaker's Reports (154 Indiana)

Donn. Donnell's Land Cases *Ir*

Donnelly's Chancery Reports *Eng*

Donnelly Donnelly's Chancery Reports *Eng*

Dorion Dorion's Queen's Bench Rep. *Quebec*

Doug. Douglas' Election Cases *Eng*

Douglas' King's Bench Reports *Eng*

Douglas' Reports (Michigan 1843–47)

Doug.El.Cas. Douglas' Election Cases *Eng*

Doug.K.B. Douglas' King's Bench Reports *Eng*

Dow. Dow's House of Lords Reports *Eng*

Dowling's Practice Cases *Eng*

Dow N.S. Dow & Clark's H. of L. Cases *Eng*

Dow.P.C. Dowling's Practice Cases *Eng*

Dow & Cl. Dow & Clark's H. of L. Cas. *Eng*

Dow.& L. Dowling & Lowndes Bail Ct. Rep. *Eng*

Dow.& Ry. Dowling & Ryland's K. B. Rep. *Eng*

Dowling & Ryland's Nisi Prius Cases *Eng*

Dow.& Ry.K.B. Dowling & Ryland's K.B. Rep. *Eng*

Dow.& Ry.M.C. Dowling & Ryland's Magistrates' Cases *Eng*

Dow.& Ry.N.P. Dowling & Ryland's N.P. Rep. *Eng*

Dowl. Dowling's Bail Court Cases *Eng*

Dowl.N.S. Dowling's Q. B., Practice Cases, & Bail Court Rep., New Series *Eng*

Dowl.P.R. Dowling's Practice Reports *Eng*

Dowl.& Lownd. Dowling & Lowndes Practice Cases *Eng*

Dowl.& Ryl. *See* Dow.& Ry., *supra*

Down.& Lud. Downton & Luder's El. Cas. *Eng*

Dr. Drewry's Vice-Chancellors' Reports *Eng*

Drury's Reports *temp.* Napier *Ir*

Drury's Reports *temp.* Sugden *Ir*

Dr.& Sm. Drewry & Smale's Vice-Chancellors' Reports *Eng*

Dr.&Wal. Drury & Walsh's Ch. Rep. *Ir*

Dr.& War. Drury & Warren's Ch. Rep. *Ir*

Dra[per] Draper's K. B. Reports
Canada
Drake L.Rev. Drake Law Review
Drew. Drew's Reports (13 Florida)
Drewry's Vice-Chancellors' Reports
Eng
Drew.& Sm. Drewry & Smale's Ch.
Rep. *Eng*
Drink. Drinkwater's Common Pleas
Rep. *Eng*
Dru. Drury's Chancery Rep. *t.* Sugden
Ir
Dru.*t*.Nap. Drury's Ch. Rep. *t.*
Napier *Ir*
Dru.*t*.Sug. Drury's Ch. Rep. t. Sugden
Ir
Dru.& Wal. Drury & Walsh's Chan-
cery Rep. *Ir*
Dru.& War. Drury & Warren's Ch.
Rep. *Ir*
Drury *See* Dru., *supra*
Dud. Dudley's Georgia Reports 1830–
35
Dud.Ch. Dudley's S. C. Equity Rep.
1837–38
Dud.L. Dudley's S. C. Law Rep. 1837–
38
Duer Duer's Superior Ct. Reports *N.Y.*
Dug.Orig. Dugdale's Origines
Juridiciales
Dugd. Same as above
Duke B.A.Jo. Duke Bar Association
Journal
Duke B.J. Same as above
Dulck. Dulcken's Eastern District
Reports, Cape Colony *S.Af.*
Dunc.Ent.Cas. Duncan's Entail Cases
Scot
Dunc.Merc.Cas. Duncan's Mercantile
Cas. *Scot*
Dunl. Dunlop's Ct. of Session Cases
Scot
Dunl.Abr. Coke's Reports, Dunlap's
Abridgment *Eng*
Dunlop B.& M. Dunlop, Bell, &
Murray's Reports, Session Cases,
2d Series *Scot*
Dunn. Dunning's King's Bench Rep.
Eng
Durf[ee] Durfee's Reports (2 Rhode
Island)
Durie Durie's Ct. of Session Decisions
Scot
Durn.& E. Durnford & East's (Term)
Rep. *Eng*
Dutch. Dutcher's Reports (25–29 N. J.
Law)

Duv. Duvall's Reports (62, 63
Kentucky)
Duvall's Supreme Court Reports
Canada
Dwight Dwight's Charity Cases *Eng*
Dy. Dyer's King's Bench Reports *Eng*
Dyer Dyer's King's Bench Reports *Eng*
E. East's Reports *Eng*
E.A.C.A. East Africa Court of Appeal
Reports
E.A.L.R. East Africa Law Reports
E.A.Prot.L.R. East Africa Protec-
torate Law Reports
E.B.& E. Ellis, Blackburn, & Ellis' Rep.
Eng.
E.C. Election Cases; English Chancery
ECA Economic Cooperation
Administration *U.S.*
ECAFE Economic Commission for
Asia & the Far East *UN*
ECE Economic Commission for
Europe *UN*
ECITO European Inland Transport
Organization
E.C.L. English Common Law Reports
Reprint
ECLA Economic Commission for
Latin America *UN*
EGOSAC Economic & Social Council
UN
E.D. Exchequer Division
E.D.C. Eastern District Court Reports,
Cape of Good Hope *S.Af.*
E.D.L. South African Law Reports,
Eastern Districts Local Division
S.Af.
E.D.Smith E. D. Smith's Com. Pl.
Rep. *N.Y.*
E.E. Equity Exchequer
E.E.R. English Ecclesiastical Reports
Reprint
E.L.& Eq. English Law & Equity Rep.
Reprint
E.L.R. Eastern Law Reporter *Canada*
E.O. Presidential Executive Order *U.S.*
E.P.C. East's Pleas of the Crown *Eng*
Excess Profits Tax Council Ruling or
Memorandum, Internal Revenue
Bureau *U.S.*
Roscoe's Prize Cases *Eng*
EPU European Payments Union
E.R. East's King's Bench Reports *Eng*
Election Reports *Ontario*
English Reports, Full Reprint
ER Economic Regulations (CAB)
ERP European Recovery Program
E.R.A. English Reports Annotated

E.R.C. English Ruling Cases

E.S.A. Economic Stabilization Agency *U.S.*

E.T. Estate & Gift Tax Ruling (U.S. Internal Revenue Bureau)

E.W.T. Eastern War Time

E.& A. Eccles. & Admiralty Rep. (Spinks) *Eng*
Upper Canada Error & Appeal Reports

E.& A.R. Upper Canada Error & Appeal Rep.

E.& A.W.C. Grant's Error & Appeal Rep. *Ontario*

E.& B. Ellis & Blackburn's Q. B. Rep. *Eng*

E.& E. Ellis & Ellis' Q. B. Reports *Eng*

E.& I.App. Law Reports, English & Irish Appeals (House of Lords)

E.& Y. Eagle & Younge's Tithe Cases *Eng*

Ea. East's King's Bench Reports *Eng*

Eag.& Y. Eagle & Younge's Tithe Cases *Eng*

Earw. Earwalker's Manchester Court Leet Records *Eng*

East East's King's Bench Reports *Eng*
Eastern Reporter

East Af. East Africa Court of Appeals Reports

East D.C. Eastern District Court Rep. *S.Af.*

East D.L. Eastern Districts, Local Division, South African Law Reports

East.L.R. Eastern Law Reporter *Canada*

East P.C. East's Pleas of the Crown *Eng*

East.Rep. Eastern Reporter

Ebersole Ebersole's Reports (59–80 Iowa)

Ec.& Mar. Notes of Cases, Ecclesiastical & Maritime Courts *Eng*

Eccl.& Ad. Spinks' Eccl. & Admiralty Reports *Eng*

Eccl.R. English Ecclesiastical Rep. Reprint

Ed. Eden's Chancery Reports *Eng*

Ed.Bro. Brown's Chancery Rep. (Eden ed.) *Eng*

Ed.C.R. Edwards' Chancery Reports *N.Y.*

Ed.L.J. Edinburgh Law Journal

Eden Eden's Chancery Reports *Eng*

Edg. Edgar's Ct. of Session Decisions *Scot*

Edinb.L.J. Edinburgh Law Journal

Edm.Sel.Cas. Edmons' Select Cases *N.Y.*

Edw. Edwards' Admiralty Reports *Eng*
Edwards' New York Chancery Reports
Edwards' Reports (2, 3 Missouri)
Edwards' Chester Palatine Courts *Eng*

Edw.Abr. Edwards' Abridgment, Prerogative Court Cases *Eng*

Edw. Edwards' Admiralty Reports *Eng*

Edw.Ch. Edward's Chancery Reports *N.Y.*

Edw.Lead.Dec. Edwards' Leading Decisions in Equity (Edwards' Admiralty Rep.) *Eng*

Edw.P.C. Edwards' Prize Cases *Eng*

Edw.Pr.Ct.Cas. Edwards' Abridgment Prerogative Court Cases *Eng*

Edw. (Tho.) Edwards' Admiralty Reports *Eng*

Efird Efird's Reports (46–51 S. C.)

El. Elchies' Court of Session Dec. *Scot*

El.B.& E. Ellis, Blackburn, & Ellis' Queen's Bench Reports *Eng*

El.Cas. Ontario Election Cases

El.Dict. Elchies' Dictionary of Decisions, Court of Session *Scot*

El.& Bl. Ellis & Blackburn's Q. B. Rep. *Eng*

Elchies Elchies' Ct. of Session Dec. *Scot*

Elchies' Dict. *See* El.Dict, *supra*

Elect.Cas.N.Y. Armstrong's New York Election Cases

Elect.Rep. Ontario Election Cases

Ell.& Bl. *See* El. & Bl., *supra*

Ell.& Ell. Ellis & Ellis' Q. B. Rep. *Eng*

Ell.B.& S. Ellis, Best & Smith's Q. B. Rep. *Eng*

Ell.Bl.& Ell. Ellis, Blackburn, & Ellis' Q.B. Rep. *Eng*

Els.W.Bl. Blackstone's K. B. Rep. Elsley's edition *Eng*

Ency.L.& P. American & English Encyclopedia of Law & Practice

Ency. of Forms Encyclopaedia of Forms & Precedents

Ency.P.& P. Encyclopedia of Pleading & Pract.

Eng. English; English Reports (Moak edition)
English's Reports (6–13 Arkansas)

Eng.C.C. English Crown Cases (American Reprint)

Eng.Ch. English Chancery; English Chancery Reports Reprint

Eng.C.L. English Common Law Reports Reprint

Eng.Eccl. English Eccles. Reports Reprint

Eng.Exch. English Exchequer Reports Reprint

Eng.Hist.Rev. English Historical Review

Eng.Judg. Court of Session Cases, decided by English Judges *Scot*

Eng.L.& Eq. English Law & Equity Reports Reprint

Eng.Pr.Cas. Roscoe's English Prize Cases

Eng.Rep. English Reports, Full Reprint

English Reports (Moak's Amer. Reprint)

English's Reports (6–13 Arkansas)

Eng.R.R.Ca. English Railway & Canal Cases

Eng.Ru.Cas. English Ruling Cases

Eng.Sc.Ecc. English & Scotch Eccles. Rep.

Eng.& Ir.App. Law Reports, English & Irish Appeal Cases

English English's Reports (6–13 Arkansas)

Eq.Ab. Abridgment of Cases in Equity *Eng*

Eq.Cas. Equity Cases in 9, 10 Modern Reports *Eng*

Eq.Cas.Abr. Abridgment, Cases in Equity *Eng*

Eq.Judg. A'Beckett's Equity Judgments *N.S.W.*

Eq.Rep. Equity Reports 1835–55 *Eng*

Gilbert's Equity Reports *Eng*

Harper's Reports (S. C. Equity 1824)

E.R. English Reports; English Reports, Full Reprint

Erck Erck's Ecclesiastical Register 1608–1825 *Eng*

Erie Co.L.J. Erie County Law Journal *Pa*

Err.& App. Error & Appeals Reports, Upper Canada (Grant)

Ersk.Dec. Erskine's U.S. Circuit Court Decisions (in 35 Georgia)

Esp. Espinasse's Nisi Prius Reports *Eng*

Estee Estee's District Ct. of Hawaii Reports *U.S.*

Eur.Ass.Arb. European Assurance Arbitration

Evans Lord Mansfield's Decisions *Eng*

Everybody's L.M. Everybody's Law Magazine

Ex. Exchequer Reports 1848–56 *Eng*

Ex.C.R. Canada Exchequer Court Reports

Canada Law Reports (Ex. Court)

Ex.D. Law Reports, Exchequer Division *Eng*

Ex.Div. Law Reports, Exchequer Div. *Eng*

Exam. The Examiner

Exch. Law Reports, Exchequer Division *Eng*

Exchequer Reports (Welsby, Hurlstone, & Gordon) *Eng*

Exch.C. Canada Law Reports, Exchequer Court

Exch.C.R. Exchequer Court Reports *Canada*

Exch.Can. Exchequer Reports *Canada*

Exch.Cas. Exchequer Cases *Scot*

Exch.Div. Law Reports, Exchequer Div. *Eng*

Exch.Rep. English Exchequer Reports Reprint

Exchequer Reports (Welsby, Hurlstone, & Gordon) *Eng*

Exec.Order Presidential Executive Order *U.S.*

Exter.Ca. Lobingier's Extraterritorial Cases, U. S. Court for China

Extra.Ca. Same as above

Eyre Eyre's K. B. Rep. *temp.* Wm. III *Eng*

F. Faculty Collection, Ct. of Session *Scot*

Foord's Cape of Good Hope Reports *S.Af.*

Fraser's Court of Session Cases *Scot*

Federal Reporter *U.S.*

F.2d Federal Reporter, Second Series *U.S.*

F.A.D. Federal Anti-Trust Decisions

FAO Food & Agriculture Organization *UN*

F.B.C. Fonblanque's Bankruptcy Cases *Eng*

F.B.I. Federal Bureau of Investigation *U.S.*

Full Bench Decisions *India*

F.B.R. Full Bench Rulings, Bengal *India*

F.B.R.N.W.P. Full Bench Rulings, Northwest Provinces *India*

F.C. Faculty Collection (Session Cas.) *Scot*

Federal Cases *U.S.*

Accra & Gold Coast Full Court, Selected Judgments

F.C.A. Farm Credit Administration

F.C.C.(or FCC) Federal Communications Comm. *U.S.*

FCDA Federal Civil Defense Admin.

FCU Federal Credit Union *U.S.*

FDA Food & Drug Administration *U.S.*

FDC Food, Drug and Cosmetic Docket

FDIC Federal Deposit Insurance Corp. *U.S.*

F.Dict. Kames & Woodhouselee's Dictionary, Court of Session Cases *Scot*

FEA Foreign Economic Administration *U.S.*

FEB Fair Employment Board

FEC Far Eastern Commission

FFMC Federal Farm Mortgage Corp. *U.S.*

FHA or F.H.A. Farmers' Home Administration *U.S.*

Federal Housing Administration *U.S.*

F.H.L. Fraser's House of Lords Rep. *Scot*

F.H.L.B.A. Federal Home Loan Bank Act

F.J.C. Fraser's Justiciary Ct. Rep. *Scot*

F.L.J. Canada Fortnightly Law Journal

F.L.R. Fiji Law Reports

FLSA Fair Labor Standards Act *U.S.*

FM Field Manual, U. S. Army

FMB Federal Maritime Board *U.S.*

FMCS Federal Mediation & Conciliation Service *U.S.*

F.M.S.L.R. Federated Malay States Reports

F.Moore Moore's King's Bench Reports *Eng*

F.N.B. Fitzherbert's Natura Brevium *Eng*

F.N.D. Finnemore's Notes & Digest *Natal*

FNMA Federal National Mortgage Assn. *U.S.*

F.P.C. Federal Power Commission

F.R. Federal Register *U.S.*

FRB Federal Reserve Board *U.S.*

FRC Federal Radio Commission *U.S.*

F.R.D. Federal Rules Decisions

F.R.S. Federal Reserve System *U.S.*

F.Supp. Federal Supplement

F.S.A. Federal Security Agency *U.S.*

FSA Farm Security Adm.

F.S.L.I.C. Federal Savings and Loan Insurance Corp.

FTC Federal Trade Commission *U.S.*

F.U.R.A. Federal Utility Regulations Ann.

F.& C.C. Fire & Casualty Cases (CCH)

F.& F. Foster & Finlason's N. P. Rep. *Eng*

F.& Fitz. Falconer & Fitzherbert's Election Cases *Eng*

F.& S. Fox & Smith's King's Bench Rep. *Ir*

Fac. Faculty of Advocates, Court of Session, Decisions *Scot*

Fac.Coll. Faculty of Advocates, Collection of Decisions, Court of Session *Scot*

Fairchild Fairchild's Reports (10–12 Maine)

Falc. Falconer's Court of Session Dec. *Scot*

Falc.Co.Cts. Falconer's County Ct. Cas. *Eng*

Falc.& Fitz. Falconer & Fitzherbert Election Cases *Eng*

Fam.Cas.Cir.Ev. Phillips' Famous Cases of Circumstantial Evidence

Far. Farresley (7 Modern Reports) *Eng*

Farresley Farresley's Reports (7 Modern Reports) *Eng*

Holt's King's Bench Reports (Farresley Cases) *Eng*

Fawc. Fawcett's Ct. of Referees Rep. *Eng*

Fed. Federal Reporter *U.S.*

The Federalist

Fed.2d Federal Reporter, Second Series *U.S.*

Fed.Alc.Adm. Federal Alcohol Administration

Fed.Anti-Tr.Dec. Federal Anti-Trust Decisions

Fed.B.A.J[o]. Federal Bar Assn. Journal

Fed.B.J. Federal Bar Journal

Fed.Carr.Cas. Federal Carrier Cases (1940-date)

Fed.Cas. Federal Cases *U.S.*

Fed.Com.B.J. Federal Communications Bar Journal

Fed.L.J.Ind. Federal Law Journal of India

Fed.L.Q. Federal Law Quarterly

Fed.Prob. Federal Probate, Washington, D.C.

Fed.R.D. Federal Rules Decisions *U.S.*

Fed.Rep. Federal Reporter *U.S.*

Fed.Stat.Ann. Federal Statutes Annotated

Fed.Supp. Federal Supplement *U.S.*

Fed.Tr.Rep. Federal Trade Reporter

Fent. Fenton's Important Judgments *New Zeal*

Fenton's Reports *New Zeal*

Fent.Imp.Judg. Fenton's Important Judgments *New Zeal*

Ferg. Fergusson's Consistorial Dec. *Scot*

Fergusson Fergusson's Consistorial Dec. *Scot*

Fergusson's Session Cases *Scot*

Fid.L.Chron. Fiduciary Law Chronicle

Fiji L.R. Fiji Law Reports

Fin. Finch's Chancery Reports *Eng*

Finlay's Irish Digest

Fin.H. H. Finch's Chancery Reports *Eng*

Fin.Pr. T. Finch's Precedents in Ch. *Eng*

Fin.T. T. Finch's Precedents in Ch. *Eng*

Fin.& Dul. Finnemore & Dulcken's Natal Law Reports

Finch Finch's Chancery Reports *Eng*

Finch's Precedents in Chancery *Eng*

Finl.Dig. Finlay's Irish Digest

Fire & Cas.Cas. Fire & Casualty Cases (CCH 1939–date)

First Bk.Judg. First Book of Judgments 1655 *Eng*

Fish. Fisher's Prize Cases, District Courts *U.S.*

Fisher's Patent Cases *U.S.*

Fish.Pat.Cas. Fisher's Patent Cases *U.S.*

Fish.Pat.Rep. Fisher's Patent Reports *U.S.*

Fish.Pr.Cas. Fisher's Prize Cases, District Courts *U.S.*

Fits.Nat.Brev. Fitzherbert's Natura Brevium

Fitzg. Fitzgibbon's King's Bench Rep. *Eng*

Fitzgibbon's Land Reports *Ir*

Fitzgibbon's Registration Appeals *Ir*

Fitzh.Abr. Fitzherbert's Abridgment *Eng*

Fitzh.N.B. Fitzherbert's New Natura Brevium

Fl. Fleta *Eng*

Fl.& K. Flanagan & Kelly's Rolls Ct. Rep. *Ir*

Fla. Florida

Fla.L.J. Florida Law Journal

Fla.S.B.A.Jo. Florida State Bar Assn. Jour.

Fla.Supp. Florida Supplement

Flan.& Kel. Flanagan & Kelly's Rolls Court Reports *Ir*

Flip. Flippin's Circuit Court Reports *U.S.*

Fogg Fogg's Reports (32–37 N. Hampshire)

Fol. Foley's Poor Law Cases *Eng*

Fol.Dict. Kames & Woodhouselee's Dictionary, Court of Session. *Scot*

Fol.P.L.Cas. Foley's Poor Law Cases *Eng*

Fonbl. Fonblanque's Bankruptcy Rep. *Eng*

Fonbl.N.R. Fonblanque's Cases in Ch. *Eng*

Food Drug Cosmetic L.J. Food, Drug, & Cosmetic Law Journal

Foord Foord's Sup. Ct. Rep., Cape Colony *S.Af.*

For. Forrest's Exchequer Reports *Eng*

Forrester's Ch. Rep. *temp.* Talbot *Eng*

For.Aff. Foreign Affairs

For.Tax L.W.Bull. Foreign Tax Law Weekly Bulletin

Forb. Forbes' Court of Session Dec. *Scot*

Forbes' Cases in St. Andrews Bishop's Court *Scot*

Fordh.L.Rev. Fordham Law Review

Forman Forman's Reports (1 Scammon, 2 Illinois)

Forr. Chancery Cases *temp.* Talbot *Eng*

Forrest's Exchequer Reports *Eng*

Fors.Cas.& Op. Forsyth's Cases & Opinions on Constitutional Law *Eng*

Fort. Fortescue's King's Bench Reports *Eng*

Fort.de Laud. Fortesque, De Laudibus Legum Angliae

Fortes Rep. Fortescue's King's Bench Rep. *Eng*

Fortn.L.J. Fortnightly Law Journal

Forum Forum: Bench & Bar Review

Forum Law Review

Forum, Dickinson School of Law

Fost. Foster's Crown Cases   *Eng*
Foster's Legal Chronicle Rep.   *Pa*
Foster's Reports (21–31 N.
Hampshire)
Foster's Reports (5,6,8 Hawaii)
Fost.& Fin. Foster & Finlason's Nisi
Prius Reports   *Eng*
Fount. Fountainhall's Ct. of Session
Dec.   *Scot*
Fox Fox's Patent, Trade Mark, Design
& Copyright Cases   *Canada*
Fox's Circuit & District Ct. Decisions
U.S.
Fox's Registration Cases   *Eng*
Fox Pat.Cas. Fox's Patent, Trade
Mark, Design & Copyright Cases
Canada
Fox & S.Ir. Fox & Smith's King's
Bench Rep.   *Ir*
Fox & S.Reg. Fox & Smith's Registra-
tion Cases   *Eng*
Fox & Sm. Fox & Smith's King's Bench
Rep.   *Ir*
Fox & Smith's Registration Cases *Eng*
Fr. Freeman's K. B. & Ch. Reports *Eng*
Fr.Chy. Freeman's Chancery Reports
Eng
Fr.E.C. Freeman's Election Cases *Eng*
Franc.Judg. Francillon's County
Court Judgments   *Eng*
France France's Reports (3–11
Colorado)
Fras. Fraser's Election Cases   *Eng*
Fraser Fraser's Election Cases   *Eng*
Fraser's Session Cases, 5th Series *Scot*
Fraz. Frazer's Admiralty Cases   *Scot*
Free. Freeman's Chancery Reports *Eng*
Freeman's King's Bench Reports *Eng*
Freeman's Reports (31–96 Illinois)
Free.Ch. Freeman's Chancery Reports
Eng
Freeman's Reports (Miss. Ch. 1839–
43)
Freem.C.C. Freeman's Chancery Cases
Eng
Freem.Ch. Freeman's Chancery
Reports   *Eng*
Freem.(Ill.) Freeman's Reports (31–
96 Ill.)
Freem.K.B. Freeman's King's Bench &
Common Pleas Reports   *Eng*
Freem.(Miss.) Freeman's Mississippi
Chancery Reports
French French's Reports (6 New
Hampshire)

Full B.R. Bengal Full Bench Rulings
(North-Western Provinces)
India
Fuller Fuller's Reports (59–105 Mich.)
Fulton Fulton's Bengal Supreme Ct.
Rep.
G. Georgia
Gale's Exchequer Reports   *Eng*
Gregorowski's Orange Free State
High Court Reports   *S.Af.*
GA General Assembly   *UN*
G.A. General Appraisers' Decision *U.S.*
G.A.O. General Accounting Office
U.S.
GATT/CP General Agreement
Tariffs & Trade, Contracting
Parties   *U.S.*
G.C.Div.Ct. Gold Coast Divisional
Courts, Selected Judgments
G.C.F.C. Gold Coast Full Court
Selected Judgments
G.C.M. General Counsel's Memoran-
dum, Internal Revenue Bureau
U.S.
GCPR General Ceiling Price
Regulation
G.Coop. G. Cooper's Chancery
Reports   *Eng*
GFR General Flight Rules (CAB) *U.S.*
G.Gr. G.Green's Reports (Iowa 1847–
54)
GLO General Land Office (Interior
Dept.)   *U.S.*
G.L.R. Gazette Law Reports
New Zeal
G.M.Dud. Dudley's Reports (Ga.
1830–33)
GO DPT General Order Defense
Transport Administration   *U.S.*
GOR General Overruling Regulation
(Office of Price Stabilization) *U.S.*
GRASR General Railroad and Airline
Stabilization Reg.   *U.S.*
GSA General Services Administration
U.S.
GSO General Salary Order   *U.S.*
GSSR General Salary Stabilization Reg.
U.S.
G.W.D. South African Law Reports,
Griqualand West Local Division
G.W.L. South African Law Reports,
Griqualand West Local Division
(Kitchin)
G.W.L.D. South African Law Reports,
Griqualand West Local Division
G.W.R. General Wage Regulation *U.S.*
Griqualand High Court Reports

GWSR General Wage Stabilization
Reg. *U.S.*

G.& D. Gale & Davison's Q. B. Reports
Eng

G.& G. Goldsmith & Guthrie's Reports
(36–67 Mo. App.)

G.& J. Gill & Johnson's Reports *Md*
Glyn & Jameson's Bankruptcy Reports
Eng

G.& R. Geldert & Russell's Nova
Scotia Rep.

Ga. Georgia
General Appraisers' Decisions *U.S.*

Ga.App. Georgia Appeals Reports

Ga.B.A. Georgia Bar Association

Ga.B.J. Georgia Bar Journal

Ga.Dec. Georgia Decisions

Ga.L. Georgia Lawyer

Ga.L.J. Georgia Law Journal
Georgetown Law Journal

Ga.L.Rep. Georgia Law Reporter

Ga.L.Rev. Georgia Law Review

Ga.Lawyer Georgia Lawyer

Ga.R.C. Georgia Railroad Commission

Ga.Supp. Lester's Supplement to 33
Georgia

Gal.& Dav. Gale & Davison's Q. B.
Rep. *Eng*

Galb.& M. Galbraith & Meek's
Reports (12 Fla.)

Galbraith Galbraith's Reports (9–12
Florida)

Gale Gale's Exchequer Reports *Eng*
Gale's New Forest Decisions *Eng*

Gale & Dav. Gale & Davison's Q. B.
Rep. *Eng*

Gall. Gallison's Circuit Ct. Reports
U.S.

Gall.Cr.Cas. Gallick's Reports of
French Criminal Cases

Ganatra Ganatra's Criminal Cases
India

Gane Eastern District Court Reports,
Cape Colony *S.Af.*

Gard.N.Y.Rep. Gardenier's New York
Reporter

Gardenhire Gardenhire's Rep. (14,
15 Mo.)

Gaspar Gaspar's Small Cause Court
Rep. *Bengal*

Gay.(La.) Gayarre's Reports (25–28
La. Annual)

Gayarre Same as above

Gaz. Weekly Law Gazette, Cincinnati

Gaz.Bank. Gazette of Bankruptcy
Eng

Gaz.L.R. New Zealand Gazette Law
Reports

Gaz.& B.C.Rep. Gazette & Bankrupt
Court Reporter

Geld.& Ox. Geldert & Oxley's Nova
Scotia Dec.

Geld.& R. Geldert & Russell's Nova
Scotia Reports

Geldart Geldart & Maddock's Ch. Rep.
(6 Maddock) *Eng*

Gen.Dig. General Digest

Geo. Georgia

Geo.Coop. G. Cooper's Ch. Cas. *temp.*
Eldon *Eng*

Geo.Dec. Georgia Decisions

Geo.L.J. Georgetown Law Journal

Geo.Wash.L.Rev. George Washington Law Rev.

George George's Reports (30–39
Mississippi)

Georget.L.J. Georgetown Law
Journal

Gib.Cod. Gibson's Codex Juris
Ecclesiastici Anglicani

Gib.Dec. Gibson's Decisions *Scot*

Gibbons Gibbons' Surrogate's Reports
N.Y.

Gibbs Gibbs' Reports (2–4 Michigan)

Giff. Giffard's Chancery Reports *Eng*

Giff.& H. Giffard & Hemming's Ch.
Rep. *Eng*

Gil. Gilbert's Cases in Law & Equity
Eng
Gilbert's Chancery Reports *Eng*
Gilman's Reports (6–10 Illinois)
Gilmer's Reports (21 Va.)
Gilmour's Reports, Ct. of Session *Scot*

Gilb. Gilbert's Cases in Law & Equity
Eng

Gilb.Cas. Gilbert's Cases in Law &
Equity

Gilb.Ch. Gilbert's Ch. & Ex. Reports
Eng

Gilb.Eq.Rep. Gilbert's Ch. & Eq. Rep.
Eng

Gilb.Rep. Gilbert's Chancery Reports
Eng

Gilchr. Gilchrist's Local Government
Cases

Gildersleeve Gildersleeve's Rep. (1–10
N.Mex.)

Gilfillan. Minnesota Reports, Gilfillan
ed.

Gill. Gill's Reports (Md. Ct. of
Appeals)

Gill Pol.Rep. Gill's Police Court
Reports, Boston, Mass.

Gill & Johns. Gill & Johnson's Maryland Rep.

Gilm. Gilman's Reports (6–10 Illinois)
Gilmer's Reports (21 Virginia)
Gilmour's Court of Session Reports
Scot

Gilm.& Falc. Gilmour & Falconer's Court of Session Reports   *Scot*

Gilmer Gilmer's Reports (21 Virginia)

Gilp. Gilpin's District Court Reports
U.S.

Gl.& J. Glyn & Jameson's Bankruptcy Rep.   *Eng*

Glanv. Glanville's De Legibus et Consuetudinibus Regni Angliae

Glanv.El.Cas. Glanville's Election Cas.
Eng

Glas. Glascock's Irish Court Reports

Glascock Same as above

Glenn Glenn's Reports (16–18 La. Annual)

Glyn.& Jam. Glyn & Jameson's Bankruptcy Reports   *Eng*

Goldb. Goldbolt's King's Bench, Common Pleas, and Exchequer Reports   *Eng*

Godson Godson's Mining Commissioner's Cases   *Ontario*

Goebel Goebel's Ohio Probate Cases

Gold. Goldesborough's King's Bench Rep.   *Eng*

Gold Coast Judgments (Full Court, Privy Council, Divisional Courts)

Gold.& G. Goldsmith & Guthrie's Reports (36, 37 Missouri Appeals)

Good.Pat. Goodeve's Abstract of Patent Cases   *Eng*

Good.& Wood. Goodeve & Woodman's Bengal Full Bench Rulings

Gord.Tr. Gordon's Treason Trials

Gordon. Gordon's Reports (24–26 Colorado)
Gordon's Reports (10–13 Colorado Appeals)

Gosf. Gosford's Manuscript Reports, Court of Session   *Scot*

Gottschall Gottschall's Dayton (Ohio) Superior Court Reports

Gould Sten.Rep. Gould's Stenographic Reporter (Monographic Series Albany, N. Y.)

Gouldsb. Gouldsborough's K. B. Reports   *Eng*
Gouldsborough's Q. B. Reports   *Eng*

Gour. Gourick's Patent Digest 1889–91

Gow Gow's Nisi Prius Reports   *Eng*

Gr. Grant's Upper Canada Chancery Reports
Grant's Pennsylvania Cases 1814–63
Green's Reports (N. J. Law & Equity)
Greenleaf's Reports (1–9 Maine)

Gr.Eq. Green's Reports (16–27 N. J. Equity)

Gra. Graham's Reports (98–139 Georgia)

Granger Granger's Reports (22, 23 Ohio St.)

Grant Grant's Jamaica Reports
Grant's Upper Canada Chancery Reports
Grant's Pennsylvania Cases 1814–63

Grant Cas. Grant's Pennsylvania Cases

Grant Ch. Grant's Upper Canada Chancery Rep.

Grant E.& A. Grant's Ontario Error & Appeal Reports

Grant (Pa.) Grant's Pennsylvania Cases

Grant U.S. Grant's Upper Canada Ch. Rep.

Grat. Grattan's Reports (42–74 Virginia)

Graves Proceedings in King's Council 1392–93   *Eng*

Gray Gray's Reports (67–82 Massachusetts)
Gray's Reports (112–22 North Carolina)

Graya Graya (a periodical)

Green Green's Reports (N. J. Law & Equity)
Green's Reports (1–9 Maine)
Green's Reports (1 Oklahoma)
Green's Reports (11–17 Rhode Island)

Green Bag Green Bag, Boston

Green C.E. Green's Reports (16–27 N. J. Eq.)

Green Ch. H. W. Green's Rep. (2–4 N. J. Eq.)

Green Cr.L.Rep. Green's Criminal Law Rep.   *Scot*

Green L. Green's Rep. (13–15 N. J. Law)

Green R.I. Green's Reports (11–17 R. I.)

Green Sc.Cr.Cas. Green's Criminal Cas.   *Scot*

Greene Greene's Iowa Reports 1847–54
Greene's Reports (7 N. Y. Ann. Cas.)

Greenl. Greenleaf's Reports (1–9 Maine)

Greenl.Ov.Cas. Greenleaf's Overruled Cas.

Greer Greer's Land Cases *Ir*

Greg. Gregorowski's Orange Free State High Court Reports

Gren [ier] Grenier's Ceylon Reports

Gretton Oxford Quarter Sessions Records (Oxford Record Soc. 16)

Grif.P.L.Cas. Griffith's London Poor Law Cas.

Griff.Pat.Cas. Griffin's Patent Cases *Eng*

Griffith Griffith's Reports (117–32 Indiana)

Griffith's Reports (1–5 Indiana Appeals)

Grisw [old] Griswold's Reports (14–19 Ohio)

Gro. Gross' Select Cases Concerning the Law Merchant (Selden Society)

Guild Law. Guild Lawyer, National Lawyers' Guild, N. Y. Chapter

Guild Q. National Lawyers' Guild Quarterly

Gunby Gunby's District Court Reports (La. 1885)

Guth.Sh.Cas. Guthrie's Sheriff Ct. Cas. *Scot*

Guthrie Guthrie's Reports (33–83 Mo. Appeals)

Guthrie's Sheriff Court Cases *Scot*

Gwill. Gwillim's Tithe Cases *Eng*

H. Hare's Chancery Reports *Eng*

Hertzog's High Court Reports *S.Af.*

Hill New York Reports 1841–44

Howard Supreme Court Rep. (42–65 U.S.)

H.B. House [of Representatives] Bill

H.B.R. Hansell's Rep., Bankruptcy & Companies Winding Up Cases *Eng*

H.Bl. H. Blackstone's Com. Pleas Rep. *Eng*

H.C. Griqualand West High Court Rep. *S.Af.*

H.C.A. High Court of Australia

H.C.G. Griqualand High Court Reports *S.Af.*

H.C.R. High Court Reports *India*

H.C.R.N.W.P. North West Provinces High Court Reports *India*

H.Con.Res. House of Representatives Concurrent Resolution

H.Doc. House of Representatives Document

H.E.C. Hodgin's Ontario Election Cas. *Canada*

HHFA Housing & Home Finance Agency *U.S.*

H.H.L. Court of Session Cases, House of Lords *Scot*

HICOG High Commissioner for Germany *U.S.*

H.J.Res. House of Representatives Joint Res.

H.K.L.R. Hong Kong Law Reports

H.L. House of Lords

Clark's House of Lords Cases *Eng*

HLBB Home Loan Bank Board *U.S.*

H.L.Cas. Clark's House of Lords Cases *Eng*

H.L.J. Hindu Law Journal

H.L.R. Harvard Law Review

HOLC Home Owners' Loan Corporation *U.S.*

H.P.C. Hale's Pleas of the Crown *Eng*

H.R. House of Representatives Bill; House Roll *U.S.*

H.R.Rep. House of Representatives Report

H.Rept. House of Representatives Report

H.Res. House of Representatives Resolution

H.W.Gr. H. W. Green's Reports (2–4 N. J. Eq.)

H.& B. Hudson & Brooke's K. B. Rep. *Ir*

H.& C. Hurlstone & Coltman's Ex. Rep. *Eng*

H.& D. Lalor's Supplement to Hill & Denio's New York Reports

H.& G. Harris & Gill's Md. Rep. 1826–29

Hurlstone's & Gordon's Reports *Eng*

H.& H. Harrison & Hodgin's Upper Canada Municipal Reports

Horn & Hurlstone's Exchequer Reports *Eng*

H.& J. Harris & Johnson's Reports (Md. App.)

Hayes & Jones Exchequer Reports *Ir*

H.& M. Hemming & Miller's Vice-Chancellor's Reports *Eng*

Hening & Munford's Reports (11–14 Va.)

H.& McH. Harris & McHenry's Maryland Rep.

H.& N. Hurlstone & Norman's Excheq. Rep. *Eng*

H.& P. Hopwood & Philbrick's Elect. Cas. *Eng*

H.& R. Harrison & Rutherford's Com. Pl. Reports *Eng*

H.& R.Bank. Hazlitt & Roche's Bankruptcy Rep.

H.& S. Harris & Simrall's Rep. (49–52 Miss.)

H.& T. Hall & Twell's Chancery Reports *Eng*

H.& W. Harrison & Wollaston's K. B. Rep. *Eng*

Hazzard & Warburton's Prince Edward Island Reports

Hurlstone & Walmsley's Exchequer Rep. *Eng*

Ha. Hare's Vice-Chancellors' Reports *Eng*

Ha.App. Appendix to volume 10 of Hare's Vice-Chancellor's Reports *Eng*

Ha.& Tw. Hall & Twell's Chancery Reports *Eng*

Had. Hadley's Reports (45–48 New Hampshire)

Haddington Haddington's Court of Session Rep. *Scot*

Hadley Hadley's Reports (45–48 N. Hampshire)

Hag. Hagans' Reports (1–5 West Virginia)

Haggard's Admiralty Reports *Eng*

Hag.Adm. Haggard's Admiralty Reports *Eng*

Hag.Con. Haggard's Consistory Reports *Eng*

Hag.Ecc. Haggard's Ecclesiastical Rep. *Eng*

Hagan Hagan's Reports (1,2 Utah)

Hagans Hagans' Reports (1–5 West Viriginia)

Hagn.& Mill. Hagner & Miller's Rep. (2 Md. Ch.)

Hailes Hailes Ct. of Sessions Dec. *Scot*

Hal.Law Halsted's Reports (6–12 N. J. Law)

Halc. Halcomb's Mining Cases *Eng*

Hale Hale's Reports (33–37 California)

Hale Cr.Prec. Hale's Precedents in Criminal Cases *Eng*

Hale Ecc. Hale's Ecclesiastical Causes *Eng*

Hale P.C. Hale's Pleas of the Crown *Eng*

Hale Prec. Hale's Ecclesiastical Precedents *Eng*

Hall Hall's Reports (56, 57 New Hampshire)

Hall's New York Superior Court Rep. (1,2)

Hallett's Reports (1, 2 Colorado)

Hall A.L.J. Hall's American Law Journal

Hall Jour.Jur. Journal of Jurisprudence (Philadelphia)

Hall L.J. Hall's American Law Journal

Hall N.H. Hall's Reports (56, 57 New Hamp.)

Hall & Tw. Hall & Twell's Chancery Cas. *Eng*

Hallett Hallett's Reports (1, 2 Colorado)

Hals. Halsted's Reports (6–12 N. J. Law)

Hals.Ch. Halsted's Reports (5–8 N. J. Eq.)

Ham. Hamilton's Court of Session Rep. *Scot*

Hammond's India & Burma Election Cases

Hammond's Reports (1–9 Ohio State)

Ham.A.& O. Hammerton, Allen, & Otter's Magistrates' Cases (New Sessions Cas. v.3) *Eng*

Hamilton Haddington's Manuscript Cas., Court of Session *Scot*

Hamilton's American Negligence Cases

Hamlin Hamlin's Reports (81–99 Maine)

Hammond Hammond's Reports (36–45 Georgia)

Hammond's Reports (1–9 Ohio)

Hammond & Jackson Hammond & Jackson's Reports (45 Georgia)

Hamps.Co.Cas. Hampshire County Court Rep. *Eng*

Han. Handy's Ohio Reports (12 Ohio Dec.)

Hannay's Reports (12, 13 New Brunswick)

Hand. Hand's Reports (40–45 New York)

Handy Handy's Ohio Reports (12 Ohio Dec.)

Hanf. Hanford's Entries 1685

Hanmer Hanmer's ed., Kenyon's Notes of King's Bench Reports *Eng*

Hann. Hannay's Reports (12, 13 New Brunswick)

Hans.Deb. Hansard's Parliamentary Debates *Eng*

Hansb. Hansbrough's Reports (76–90 Virginia)

Har.App. Hare's Ch. Reports, Appendix to v. X *Eng*

Har.Del. Harrington's Reports (1–5 Delaware)

Har.St.Tr. Hargrave's State Trials *Eng*

Har.& Gil. Harris & Gill's Rep. (1826–29 Md.)

Har.& John. Harris & Johnston's Rep. (Md.App.)

Har.& McH. Harris & McHenry (Md. Gen'l. Court)

Har.& Ruth. Harrison & Rutherfurd's Com. Pl. Rep. *Eng*

Har.& Woll. Harrison & Wollaston's K. B. & Bail Court Rep. *Eng*

Harc. Harcarse's Court of Session Dec. *Scot*

Hard. Hardin's Reports (3 Kentucky)
Hardres' Exchequer Reports *Eng*
Kelyngs (W.), Chancery Reports *Eng*

Hardes. Hardesty's Reports (Delaware Term)

Hardw. Cases *temp.* Hardwicke, Lee's *Eng*

Cases *temp.* Hardwicke, Ridgeway's *Eng*

Hare Hare's Vice-Chancellors' Reports *Eng*

Hare App. Appendix to volume 10 of Hare's Vice-Chancellors' Reports *Eng*

Hare & W. Hare & Wallace's American Leading Cases

Harg. Hargrave's State Trials *Eng*
Hargrove's Reports (68–75 N. C.)

Hargrove Hargrove's Reports (68–75 N. C.)

Hari Rao Indian Income Tax Decisions

Harland Manchester Court Leet Records

Harm. Harmon's Reports (13–15 California)
Harmon's Upper Canada Com. Pl. Reports

Harp.Con.Cas. Harper's Md. Conspiracy Cases

Harp.Eq. Harper's Reports (1824 S. C. Eq.)

Harp.L. Harper's Reports (1823–30 S. C. Law)

Harr. Harrington's Reports (1–5 Delaware)

Harrington's Chancery Rep. (Mich. 1836–42)

Harris' Reports (13–24 Pa. State)

Harrison's Reports (15–17, 23–29 Indiana)

Harrison's Reports (16–19 N. J. Law)

Harr.Ch. Harrington's Michigan Ch. Reports

Harr.Con.La.R. Harrison's Condensed Louisiana Reports

Harr.N.J. Harrison's Reports (16–19 N. J. Law)

Harr.& G. Harris & Gill's Rep. (Md. 1826–29)

Harr.& Hodg. Harrison & Hodgin's Upper Canada Municipal Reports

Harr.& J. Harris & Johnson's Reports (Md. 1800–26)

Harr.& Ruth. Harrison & Rutherfurd's Com. Pl. Reports *Eng*

Harr.& Sim. Harris & Simrall's Rep. (49–52 Miss.)

Harr.& Woll. Harrison & Wollaston's King's Bench & Bail Court Reports *Eng*

Harring. Harrington's Reports (1–5 Delaware)
Harrington's Michigan Chancery Reports

Harris Harris' Reports (13–24 Pa. State)

Harris & Sim. Harris & Simrall's Reports (49–52 Mississippi)

Harrison Harrison's Rep. (15–17, 23–29 Ind.)
Harrison's Reports (16–19 N. J. Law)

Hartley Hartley's Reports (4–10 Texas)

Hartley & Hartley Reports (11–21 Texas)

Harv.Bus.Rev. Harvard Business Review

Harv.L.Rev. Harvard Law Review

Harv.L.S.Bull. Harvard Law School Bulletin

Hask. Haskell's Reports for U. S. Courts in Maine (Fox's Decisions)

Hast. Hastings' Reports (69, 70 Maine)

Hast.L.J. Hastings Law Journal

Hats.Pr. Hatsell's Parliamentary Precedents

Hav.Ch.Rep. Haviland's Ch. Reports, Prince Edward Island

Hav.P.E.I. Same as above

Haw. Hawkins' Pleas of the Crown
                      Eng
  Hawkins' Reports (19–24 La. Annual)
  Hawaii (Sandwich Islands) Reports
  Hawley's Reports (10–20 Nevada)
Haw.Cr.Rep. Hawley's American
    Criminal Reports
Hawaii Hawaii (Sandwich Islands)
    Reports
Hawarde Hawarde's Star Chamber
    Cases   *Eng*
Hawarde St.Ch. Same as above
Hawk.P.C. Hawkins' Pleas of the
    Crown   *Eng*
Hawkins Hawkins' Pleas of the
    Crown   *Eng*
  Hawkins' Reports (19–24 La. Annual)
Hawks Hawks' Reports (8–11 North
    Carolina)
Hawl.Cr.R. Hawley's American
    Criminal Rep.
Hawley Hawley's American Criminal
    Reports
  Hawley's Reports (10–20 Nevada)
Hay. *See also* Hayes, Haynes, *infra*
  Hay's Calcutta High Court Reports
                   India
  Hayes' Exchequer Reports   *Ir*
  Haywood's Reports (4–6 Tennessee)
  Haywood's Reports (2–3 North
    Carolina)
Hay.P.L. Hay's Poor Law Decisions
                   Eng
Hay.& J. Hayes & Jones' Ex. Rep. *Ir*
Hay & M. Hay & Marriott's
    Admiralty Rep.   *Eng*
Hayes Hayes' Exchequer Reports *Ir*
Hayes Exch. Same as above
Hayes & Jo. Hayes & Jones Ex.
    Reports   *Ir*
Hayw. Haywood's Reports (2–3
    North Carolina)
  Haywood's Reports (4–6 Tennessee)
Hayw.L.R. Hayward's Law Register
Hayw.N.C. Haywood's Reports (2–3
    N. C.)
Hayw.Tenn. Haywood's Reports (4–6
    Tennessee)
Hayw.& H. Hayward & Hazelton's
    District of Columbia Reports
    1840–63
Haz.P.Reg. Hazard's Pennsylvania
    Register
Haz.U.S.Reg. Hazard's United States
    Register
Head Head's Reports (38–40
    Tennessee)

Hearnshaw Southampton Court Leet
    Records
Heath Heath's Reports (36–40 Maine)
Hedges Hedges' Reports (2–6
    Montana)
Heisk. Heiskell's Reports (48–59
    Tennessee)
Helm Helm's Reports (2–9 Nevada)
Hem.& M. Hemming & Miller's Ch.
    Reports   *Eng*
Heming. Hemingway's Reports (53–
    65 Miss.)
Hemmant Hemmant's Select Cases in
    Exchequer Chamber (Selden
    Society Pub. v. 51)
Hemp. Hempstead's Circuit Court
    Reports   *U.S.*
Hen.Bl. H. Blackstone's Com. Pl.
    Reports   *Eng*
Hen.Man.Cas. Henry's Manumission
    Cases
Hen.& Mun. Hening & Munford's
    Rep. (11–14 Va.)
Hennepin Law. Hennepin Lawyer
Hepb. Hepburn's Reports (3–4
    California)
Hermand Hermand's Consistorial
    Dec. (Stair Society, v.6) *Scot*
Hertzog Hertzog's Transvaal High
    Court Rep.
Het. Hetley's Common Pleas Reports
                   Eng
Hibb. Hibbard's Reports (67 New
    Hampshire)
Higgins Higgins Reports (Tenn. Civil
    Appeals)
Hight Hight's Reports (57–58 Iowa)
Hill. Hill's New York Reports 1841–
    44
  Hill's Reports (S. C. Law 1833–37)
Hill & Den. Hill & Denio Supplement
    (Lalor) 1842–44   *N.Y.*
Hill Eq. Hill's Reports (S. C. Equity)
Hill S.C. Hill's Reports (S. C. Law or
    Equity)
Hillyer Hillyer's Reports (20–22
    California)
Hilt. Hilton's New York Com. Pl.
    Reports
Hind.L.J. Hindu Law Journal
Hind.L.Q. Hindu Law Quarterly
Hines Hines' Reports (83–98 Ky.)
Ho.L.Cas. Clark's House of Lords
    Cases   *Eng*
Hob. Hobart's King's Bench Reports
                   Eng

Hodg. Hodges' Common Pleas Reports
      Eng

Hodg.El.Cas. Hodgins' Election Cases
      Ontario

Hoff. Hoffman's New York Chancery
  Reports

Hoff.Ch. Hoffman's New York
  Chancery Reports

Hoff.L.C. Hoffman's Land Cases, U. S.
  Dist. Ct.

Hoff.N.Y. Hoffman's New York
  Chancery Rep.

Hoffm.Ch. Same as above

Hog. Hogan's Rolls Court Reports *Ir*
  Harcarse's Session Cases   *Scot*

Hog.St.Tr. Hogan's State Trials   *Pa*

Hogue Hogue's Reports (1–4 Florida)

Holl. Hollinshead's Reports (1 Minn.)

Holm. Holmes' Circuit Court Reports
      U.S.
  Holmes' Reports (15–17 Oregon)

Holt Holt's Equity Reports   *Eng*
  Holt's King's Bench Reports   *Eng*
  Holt's Nisi Prius Reports   *Eng*

Holt Adm. W. Holt's Rule of the
  Road Cases (Admiralty)   *Eng*

Holt Eq. W. Holt's Equity Reports
      Eng

Holt K.B. John Holt's King's Bench
  Rep.   *Eng*

Holt.N.P. F. Holt's Nisi Prius Rep.
      Eng

Home Home's Manuscript Decisions,
  Court of Session   *Scot*

Home (Clk.) Clerk Home's Ct. of
  Session Rep.   *Scot*

Home Ct. of Sess. Same as above

Hong Kong L.R. Hong Kong Law
  Reports

Hong Kong U.L.Jo. Hong Kong University Law Journal

Hook. Hooker's Reports (25–62
  Conn.)

Hoonahan Hoonahan's Sind Reports
      India

Hop. Hopkins

Hop.& C. Hopwood & Coltman's
  Registration Cas.   *Eng*

Hop.& Colt. Same as above

Hop.& Ch. Hopwood & Philbrick's
  Regis. Cas.

Hope Manuscript Decisions, Ct. of
  Sessions   *Scot*

Hopk.Adm. Hopkinson's Judgments
  in Admiralty (Pa. 1779–89)

Hopk.Adm.Dec. Hopkinson's Admiralty Decisions (*see* Gilpin's U. S.
  District Ct. Rep.)

Hopk.Ch. Hopkins' New York
  Chancery Reports

Hopw.& Colt. Hopwood & Coltman's
  Registration Cases   *Eng*
  Hopwood & Coltman's Registration
  Appeal Cases   *Eng*

Hopw.& Phil. Hopwood & Philbrick's
  Registration Appeal Cases   *Eng*

Horn & H. Horn & Hurlstone's Ex.
  Rep.   *Eng*

Horner Horner's Reports (11–28 S.
  Dak.)

Hosea Hosea's Reports (Ohio)

Hoskins Hoskins' Reports (2 North
  Dakota)

Hough V.-Adm. Reports of Cases in
  Vice-Admiralty of Province of
  New York 1715–88 (1925 reprint)

Houghton Houghton's Reports (97
  Alabama)

Houst. Houston's Reports (6–14
  Delaware)

Houst.Cr.Cas. Houston's Delaware
  Criminal Cases 1856–79

Hov.Sup. Hovenden's Supplement to
  Vesey Jun.'s Chancery Reports
      Eng

How. Howard's Reports (2–8
  Mississippi)
  Howard's New York Practice Reports
  Howard's Reports (42–65 U. S.)
  Howell Reports (22–26 Nevada)

How.App. Howard's Appeal Cases
  (N. Y. 1847–48)

How.Cas. Howard's Appeal Cases
  (N. Y. 1847–48)
  Howard's Popery Cases   *Ir*

How.Ch.P. Howard's Chancery
  Practice   *Ir*

How.Cr.Tr. Howison's Criminal
  Trials (Va. 1850–51)

How.E.E. Howard's Equity
  Exchequer Rep.   *Ir*

HowN.S. Howard's New York Practice Rep.   *N.S.*

How.Po.Ca. Howard's Property Cases
      Ir

How.Pr. Howard's New York Practice
  Reports

How.St.Tr. Howell's State Trials *Eng*

How.& Beat. Howell & Beatty's
  Nevada Reports

Howard S.C. United States Reports,
  v.42–65

Howell N.P. Howell's Nisi Prius Cas. (Michigan 1868–84)

Hu. Hughes

Hubbard Hubbard's Reports (45–51 Maine)

Hud.& B. Hudson & Brooke's K. B. & Ex. Reports *Ir*

Hugh. Hughes' Circuit Court Reports *U.S.*

Hughes' Reports (1 Kentucky)

Hugh.Abr. Hughes' Abridgment *Eng*

Hugh.Ent. Hughes' Entries 1659

Hum. Humphrey's Reports (20–30 Tennessee)

Hume Hume's Court of Session Decisions *Scot*

Humph. Humphrey's Reports (20–30 Tennessee)

Hun New York Supreme Court Reports

Hun's New York Appellate Division Reports

Hunt. Hunt's Annuity Cases *Eng*

Hunter's Torrens Cases *Canada*

Hunt Ann.Cas. Hunt's Annuity Cases *Eng*

Hurl.& Colt. Hurlstone & Coltman's Exchequer Reports *Eng*

Hurl.& Gord. Hurlstone & Gordon's Reports (10, 11 Exchequer Reports) *Eng*

Hurl.& Nor. Hurlstone & Norman's Ex. Rep.

Hurl.& Walm. Hurlstone & Walmsley's Ex. Rep. *Eng*

Hut. Hutton's Common Pleas Reports *Eng*

Hutton's Court of Requests *Eng*

Hutch. Hutcheson's Reports (81 Alabama)

Hutt. Hutton's Common Pleas Reports *Eng*

Hux.Judg. Huxley's Second Book of Judgments *Eng*

Hy.Bl. Henry Blackstone's Com. Pl. Rep. *Eng*

Hyde Hyde's Bengal Reports *India*

I.A. Law Reports, Indian Appeals

IABD Inter-American Defense Board

IATA Inter-Allied Reparation Agency

IBRD International Bank for Reconstruction & Development *UN*

I.C. Indian Cases

ICAC International Cotton Advisory Committee

ICAN International Commission for Air Navigation *UN*

ICAO International Civil Aviation Organization *UN*

I.C.C. Indian Claims Commission *U.S.*

Interstate Commerce Commission *U.S.*

I.C.C.Pract.J. I.C.C. Practitioners' Journal

ICEF International Children's Emergency Fund *UN*

ICITO Interim Commission for International Trade Organization *UN*

ICJ International Court of Justice

I.C.L.R. Irish Common Law Reports

ICNAF International Commission for Northwest Atlantic Fisheries

I.C.R. Irish Chancery Reports

Irish Circuit Reports

I.C.Rep. Interstate Commerce Comm. Rep. *U.S.*

I.Ch.R. Irish Chancery Reports

I.D. Interior Department Decisions *U.S.*

ID Indian Div. Bureau of Indian Affairs *U.S.*

IEFC International Emergency Food Council

I.Eq.R. Irish Equity Reports

IGC Inter-Governmental Committee on Refugees

IIA International Institute of Agriculture

I.J. Indian Jurist, Old Series

Irish Jurist

I.J.C. Irvine's Justiciary Cases *Scot*

I.J.N.S. Irish Jurist, New Series

I.L. Fitzgibbon's Land Reports *Ir*

ILC International Law Commission *UN*

ILO International Labor Organization *UN*

I.L.Q. Indian Law Quarterly

I.L.R. Indian Law Reports

Insurance Law Reporter *Canada*

Irish Law Reports

I.L.R.All. Indian Law Reports, Allahabad Series

I.L.R.Bom. Indian Law Reports, Bombay Ser.

I.L.R.Calc. Indian Law Rep., Calcutta Ser.

I.L.R.Kar. Indian Law Reports, Karachi Ser.

I.L.R.Lah. Indian Law Reports, Lahore Ser.

I.L.R.Luck. Indian Law Reports, Lucknow Ser.

I.L.R.Mad. Indian Law Reports, Madras Ser.

I.L.R.Nag. Indian Law Reports, Nagpur Ser.

I.L.R.Pat. Indian Law Reports, Patna Ser.

I.L.R.Ran. Indian Law Reports, Rangoon Ser.

I.L.T. Irish Law Times

I.L.T.Jo. Irish Law Times Journal

IMC International Materials Conference

IMCO Inter-Governmental Maritime Consultative Organization *UN*

IMF International Monetary Fund *UN*

IMO International Meteorological Organization *UN*

IPPC International Penal & Penitentiary Commission *UN*

I.R. Indian Rulings
Internal Revenue Decisions (U.S. Treasury Department)
Irish Law Reports, since 1893

I.R.All. Indian Rulings, Allahabad Ser.

I.R.B. Internal Revenue Bulletin *U.S.*

I.R.Bom. Indian Rulings, Bombay Series

I.R.C. Internal Revenue Code *U.S.*

I.R.Cal. Indian Rulings, Calcutta Series

I.R.C.L. Irish Reports, Common Law Series

I.R.Comrs. Inland Revenue Commissioners *Eng*

I.R.Eq. Irish Reports, Equity Series

I.R.Fed.Ct. Indian Rulings, Federal Court

I.R.Lah. Indian Rulings, Lahore Series

I.R.Mad. Indian Rulings, Madras Series

I.R.Nag. Indian Rulings, Nagpur Ser.

IRO International Refugee Organization *UN*

I.R.Oudh Indian Rulings, Oudh Series

I.R.Pat. Indian Rulings, Patna Series

I.R.Pesh. Indian Rulings, Peashawar Ser.

I.R.Pr.C. Indian Rulings, Privy Council Ser.

I.R.R. Internal Revenue Record

I.R.Ran. Indian Rulings, Rangoon Series

I.R.Rep. Inland Revenue Commissioners Rep. *Eng*

I.R.R.& L. Irish Reports, Registry Appeals in Court of Exchequer Chamber, and Appeals in Court for Land Cases Reserved

I.R.Sind Indian Rulings, Sind Series

I.T. Income Tax Division Ruling (U. S. Internal Revenue Bureau)

I.T.C. Spinivasan's Reports of Income Tax Cases *India*

I.T.D.A. Australian Income Tax Decisions

I.T.Info. Income Tax Information Release *U.S.*

I.T.L.J. Income Tax Law Journal *India*

ITO International Trade Organization *UN*

I.T.R. Income Tax Reports *India*
Irish Term Reports (Ridgeway, Lapp & Schoales)

ITS International Trading Service

ITU International Telecommunication Union *UN*

IWC International Wheat Council

I.& N. Immigration & Nationality Laws Administrative Decisions (Justice Dept.) *U.S.*

I.& N.S. Immigration & Naturalization Service *U.S.*

Ia. Iowa

Ia.L.Rev. Iowa Law Review

Id.L.J. Idaho Law Journal

Ida. Idaho

Ida.I.A.B. Idaho Industrial Accident Board Reports

Idaho Idaho Reports

Iddings T.R.D. Iddings' Dayton (Ohio) Term Reports

Ill. Illinois

Ill.App. Illinois Appellate Court Reports

Ill.B.J. Illinois Bar Journal

Ill.C.C. Illinois Commerce Commission Opinions & Orders

Ill.Ct.Cl. Illinois Court of Claims

Ill.L.B. Illinois Law Bulletin

Ill.L.Q. Illinois Law Quarterly

Ill.L.Rec. Illinois Law Record

Ill.L.Rev. Illinois Law Review

Ill.Leg.N. Illustrated Legal News *India*

Ill.P.U.C.Ops. Illinois Public Utilities Commission Opinions & Orders

Ill.R.& W.C. Illinois Railroad & Warehouse Commission Reports

Ill.R.& W.C.D. Illinois Railroad & Warehouse Commission Decisions

Ill.S.B.A. Illinois State Bar Assn. Reports

Ill.W.C.C. Illinois Workmen's Compensation Cases

Inc.Tax Cas. Reports of Cases on Income Tax 1875　*Eng*

Inc.Tax L.J. Income Tax Law Journal *India*

Inc.Tax R. Income Tax Reports *India*

Ind. India; Indiana

Ind.App. Indiana Appellate Court Reports

Law Reports, Indian Appeals

Ind.Awards Industrial Awards Recommendations *New Zealand*

Ind.Cas. Indian Cases　*India*

Ind.Court Aw. Industrial Court Awards　*Eng*

Ind.Jur. Indian Jurist (Calcutta or Madras)

Ind.Jur.N.S. Indian Jurist, New Series

Ind.L.J. Indiana Law Journal

Ind.L.Mag. Indian Law Magazine

Ind.L.R. Indian Law Reports (East)

Ind.L.R.All. Indian Law Reports, Allahabad Ser.

Ind.L.R.Bomb. Same, Bombay Series

Ind.L.R.Calc. Same, Calcutta Series

Ind.L.R.Kar. Same, Karachi Series

Ind.L.R.Lah. Same, Lahore Series

Ind.L.R.Luck. Same, Lucknow Series

Ind.L.R.Mad. Same, Madras Series

Ind.L.R.Nag. Same, Nagpur Series

Ind.L.R.Pat. Same, Patna Series

Ind.L.R.Ran. Same, Rangoon Series

Ind.L.Reg. Indiana Legal Register

Ind.L.Rep. Indian Law Reporter

Ind.L.Rev. Indian Law Review

Ind.L.T. Indian Law Times

Ind.P.S.C. Indiana Public Service Comm.

Ind.R.C. Indiana Railroad Commission

Ind.S.B.A. Indiana State Bar Assn. Reports

Ind.Super. Wilson's Indiana Superior Court Reports 1871–74

Ind.T. Indian Territory

Ind.U.C.D. Indiana Unemployment Compensation Division, Selected Appeal Tribunal Dec.

Ind.& L.Rel.Rev. Industrial & Labor Relations Review

Indian L.Rev. Indian Law Review

Indust.Ct.Aw. Industrial Court Awards　*Eng*

Indust.L.Rev.Q. Industrial Law Review Quarterly

Ing.Ves. Vesey, Jun., Reports, Ingraham ed.

Ins.Counsel J. Insurance Counsel Journal

Ins.L.J. Insurance Law Journal

Ins.Mon. Insurance Monitor

Ins.Rep. Insurance Reporter

Inst. Coke's Institutes　*Eng*

Justinian's Institutes

Inst.Com.Com. Interstate Commerce Comm.　*U.S.*

Inst.Fed.Tax. Institute of Federal Taxation

Int.Cas. Rowe's Interesting Cases *Eng., Ir*

Int.Com.Rep. Interstate Commerce Commission Reports　*U.S.*

Int.L.Notes International Law Notes *Eng*

Int.L.Q. International Law Quarterly

Int.Rev.Rec. Internal Revenue Record

Int.& Comp.L.Q. International & Comparative Law Quarterly

Inter.Am. Inter-American Quarterly

Internat. L.N. International Law Notes

Interst.Com.R. Interstate Commerce Commission Reports　*U.S.*

Intra.L.Rev.(N.Y.U.) Intramural Law Review, New York University

Intra.L.Rev.(St.L.U.) Intramural Law Review, St. Louis University

Intra.L.Rev.(U.C.L.A.) Intramural Law Review, University of California at Los Angeles

Iowa Iowa Reports

Iowa L.Bull. Iowa Law Bulletin

Iowa L.Rev. Iowa Law Review

Iowa R.C. Iowa Railroad Commissioners Rep.

Iowa St.B.A.Q. Iowa State Bar Assn. Quarterly

Iowa Univ.L.Bull. Iowa University Law Bull.

Iowa W.C.S. Iowa Workmen's Compensation Comm. Reports

Ir. Ireland; Irish

Iredell's Law or Equity Rep.　*NC*

Ir.C.L. Irish Common Law Reports

Ir.Ch. Irish Chancery Reports

Ir.Ch.Rep. Irish Chancery Reports

Ir.Cir. Cases on the Six Circuits　*Ir*

Ir.Cir.Rep. Reports of Irish Circuit Cases

Ir.Com.L.Rep. Irish Common Law Reports

Ir.Eccl. Irish Ecclesiastical Rep. (Milward)

Ir.Eq. Irish Equity Reports

Ir.Jur. Irish Jurist

Ir.L. Law Reports, Ireland
Ir.L.N.S. Irish Common Law Reports
Ir.L.J. Irish Law Journal
Ir.L.Rec.1st Ser. Law Recorder *Ir*
Ir.L.Rec.N.S. Law Recorder, New Series *Ir*
Ir.L.T. Irish Law Times
Ir.L.T.J. Irish Law Times Journal
Ir.Law & Ch. Irish Common Law & Chancery Reports, New Series
Ir.Law & Eq. Irish Law & Equity Reports, Old Series
Ir.Law Rec. Irish Law Recorder
Ir.Law Rep. Irish Law Reports
Ir.Law Rep.N.S. Irish Common Law Reports
Ir.Law T. Irish Law Times
Ir.Pet.S.J. Irish Petty Sessions Journal
Ir.R. Irish Law Reports
Ir.R.C.L. Irish Reports, Common Law Series
Ir.R.Ch. Irish Reports, Chancery
Ir.R.Eq. Irish Equity Reports 1866–78
Ir.R.Reg.App. Irish Reports, Registration Appeals
Ir.R.Reg.& L. Irish Reports, Registry & Land Cases
Ir.Rep.Ch. Irish Reports, Chancery
Ir.Rep.N.S. Irish Common Law Reports
Ir.Rep.V.R. Irish Reports, Verbatim Reprint
Ir.St.Tr. Ridgeway's Irish State Trials
Ir.T.R. Irish Term Reports (Ridgeway, Lapp, Schoales)
Ir.W.C.C. Irish Workmen's Compensation Cas.
Ir.W.L.R. Irish Weekly Law Reports
Ired. Iredell's Reports (23–35 N. C. Law)
Ired.Eq. Iredell's Reports (36–43 N. C. Eq.)
Irish L.T. Irish Law Times
Irv. Irvine's Justiciary Reports *Scot*
J. Johnson's Cases or Reports *N.Y.*
Justiciary Cases *Scot*
Juta's South African Reports
Scottish Jurist
J.Account. Journal of Accountancy
JAGA Military Affairs Division, Office of Judge Advocate General, U. S. Army
JAGT Procurement Division, Judge Advocate General, U. S. Army
J.Air L. Journal of Air Law
J.Am.Bankers' Assn. Journal of American Bankers Association

J.Am.Jud.Soc. Journal of American Judicature Society
J.Am.Soc.C.L.U. Journal of American Society of Chartered Life Underwriters
J.B.A.D.C. Journal of Bar Assn. of the District of Columbia
J.B.A.Kan. Journal, Bar Assn. of Kansas
J.B.Moo. J.B. Moore's Common Pleas Rep. *Eng*
J.Bridg. J. Bridgman's Comm. Pl. Rep. *Eng*
J.C. Johnson's Cases or Reports *N.Y.*
Justiciary Cases *Scot*
J.Ch. Johnson's Chancery Reports *N.Y.*
J.C.L.& I.L. Journal of Comparative Legislation & International Law
J.C.R. Judicial Council Reports
J.Comp.Leg. Journal of Society of Comparative Legislation
J.Comp.Leg.& Int.Law Journal of Comparative Legislation & International Law
J.Conat.Law Journal of Conational Law
J.Crim.L. Journal of American Institute of Criminal Law & Criminology
J.D.R. Juta's Daily Reporter *S.Af.*
J.H. Journal, House of Representatives *U.S.*
J.J.Mar. Marshall's Reports (24–30 Ky.)
J.Kel. John Kelyng's Crown Cases *Eng*
J.L.R. Jamaica Law Reports
Johore Law Reports *India*
J.Land & Pub.Util.Econ. Journal of Land & Public Utility Economics
J.Legal Ed. Journal of Legal Education
J.Mo.B. Journal of the Missouri Bar
J.N.A.Referees Bank. Journal of the National Assn. of Referees in Bankruptcy
J.of Account. Journal of Accountancy
J.of Air Law Journal of Air Law
J.of Business Journal of Business
J.P. Justice of the Peace
J.P.Jo. Justice of the Peace & Local Government Review
Justice of the Peace (Weekly Notes of Cases)
J.P.L. Journal of Planning Law
Journal of Public Law

J.P.N.S.W. Justice of the Peace, New South Wales

J.P.O.S. Journal of the Patent Office Society

J.P.Sm. J. P. Smith's King's Bench Rep. *Eng*

J.Pol.Econ. Journal of Political Economy

J.Pl.L. Journal of Planning Law

J.Pub.L. Journal of Public Law

J.R. Johnson's Reports *N.Y.* Jurist Reports *New Zeal*

J.R.N.S. Jurist Reports, New Ser. *New Zeal*

J.R.N.S.C.A. Jurist Reports, New Series, Court of Appeal *New Zeal*

J.R.N.S.M.L. Jurist Reports, New Series, Mining Law Cases *New Zeal*

J.R.N.S.S.C. Jurist Reports, New Series, Supreme Court *New Zeal*

J.Radio L. Journal of Radio Law

J.S. Jury Sittings, Faculty Cases *Scot*

J.S.Gr. J. S. Green's Reports (13–15 N. J. L.)

J.Shaw J. Shaw's Justiciary Reports *Scot*

J.Soc.Pub.Teach.Law Journal of the Society of Public Teachers of Law

J.Soc.Pub.Teach.Law N.S. Same, New Series

J.& H. Johnson & Hemming's Vice-Chancery Reports *Eng*

J.& La.T. Jones & La Touche's Ch. Rep. *Ir*

J.& S. Jones & Spencer's Reports (33–61 New York Superior)

J.&S.Jam. Judah & Swan's Jamaica Reports

J.& W. Jacob & Walker's Chancery Rep. *Eng*

Jac. Jacob's Chancery Reports *Eng*

Jac.& W. Jacob & Walker's Chancery Rep. *Eng*

Jack.Tex.App. Jackson's Reports (1–29 Court of Appeals Reports)

Jackson Jackson's Reports (46–58 Georgia) Jackson's Reports (1–29 Texas App.)

Jackson & Lumpkin Jackson & Lumpkin's Reports (59–64 Georgia)

James James' Reports (2 Novia Scotia)

James Sel.Cas. James' Select Cases (Nova Scotia)

James & Mont. Jameson & Montagu's Bankruptcy Reports (2 Glyn & Jameson) *Eng*

Jay W. Jaywardine's Appeal Cases *Ceylon*

Jebb. Jebb's Crown Cases *Ir*

Jebb C.C. Jebb's Crown Cases *Ir*

Jebb Cr.& Pr.Cas. Jebb's Crown & Presentment Cases *Ir*

Jebb & B. Jebb & Bourke's Q. B. Rep. *Ir*

Jebb & S. Jebb & Symes' Q. B. Rep. *Ir*

Jeff. Jefferson's Reports (Va. General Ct.)

Jenk. Jenkins' Reports 1220–1623 *Eng* Jenkins' Exchequer Reports *Eng*

Jenk.Cent. Jenkins' Exchequer Reports *Eng*

Jenk.& Formoy Jenkinson & Formoy's Select Cases in the Exchequer of Pleas. (Selden Society Publication, v.48)

Jenks Jenks' Reports (58 New Hampshire)

Jenn. Jennison's Reports (14–18 Michigan)

Jo.Ex.Ir. Jones' Exchequer Reports *Ir*

Jo.Ex.Pro.W. Jones' Exchequer Proceedings Concerning Wales 1939

Jo.Jur. Journal of Jurisprudence

Jo.Radio Law Journal of Radio Law

Jo.T. T. Jones' King's Bench Reports *Eng*

Jo.& Car. Jones & Carey's Ex. Rep. *Ir*

Jo.& La T. Jones & La Touche Ch. Rep. *Ir*

John [s]. Johnson's Reports (Md. Chancery) Johnson's Reports (New York Supreme or Chancery) Chase's Circuit Court Decisions, edited by Johnson *U.S.* Johnson's Vice-Chancery Reports *Eng*

John Marsh.L.Rev. John Marshall Law Review

John.& H. Johnson & Hemming Ch. Rep. *Eng*

Johns.Cas. Johnson's Cases (N.Y. 1799–1803)

Johns.Ch. Johnson's Maryland Chancery Dec.

Johnson's Chancery Reports (N.Y. 1814–23)

Johnson's Vice-Chancery Reports *Eng*

Johns.Ct.Err. Johnson's Reports (New York Court of Errors)

Johns.Dec. Johnson's Chancery Dec. *Md*

Johns.Eng.Ch. Johnson's Chancery Reports *Eng*

Johns.Rep. Johnson's Reports (New York Supreme or Chancery)

Johns.U.S. Chase's Circuit Court Decisions, edited by Johnson *U.S.*

Johns.V.C. Johnson's Vice-Chancery Rep. *Eng*

Johns.& Hem. Johnson & Hemming's Ch. Rep. *Eng*

Johnst.N.Z. Johnston's Reports *New Zeal*

Jon. T. Jones' K. B. & Com. Pl. Rep. *Eng*

W. Jones' B. & Com. Pl. Reports *Eng*

Jones' Irish Exchequer Reports *Ir*

Jones Jones' Reports (43–48, 52–57, 61, 62 Alabama)

Jones' Reports (22–30 Missouri)

Jones' Reports (11, 12 Pennsylvania)

Jones' Reports (N. C. Law or Equity)

Jones' Irish Exchequer Reports

Jones' Upper Canada Common Pleas Reports

Jones 1 W. Jones' King's Bench Reports *Eng*

Jones 2 T. Jones' King's Bench Reports *Eng*

Jones,Barclay,& Whittlesey (Reports 31 Mo.)

Jones Eq. Jones' Reports (54–59 N. C. Eq.)

Jones Exch. T. Jones' Exchequer Reports *Ir*

Jones Ir. Jones' Exchequer Reports *Ir*

Jones N.C. Jones' Reports (46–53 N. C. Law)

Jones Pa. Jones' Reports (11, 12 Pa. State)

Jones T.(*or* 2) T. Jones' K. B. Rep. *Eng*

Jones U.C. Jones' Upper Canada Com. Pl. Rep.

Jones W.(*or* 1) W. Jones' K. B. Reports *Eng*

Jones & C. Jones & Cary's Exchequer Rep. *Ir*

Jones & La T. Jones & La Touche Ch. Rep. *Ir*

Jones & McM. Jones & McMurtrie's Pennsylvania Supreme Court Reports

Jones & Sp. Jones & Spencer's Reports (33–61 N. Y. Superior)

Jos. Joseph's Reports (21 Nevada)

Jour.Jur. Hall's Journal of Jurisprudence

Jour.Jur.Sc. Journal of Jurisprudence & Scottish Law Magazine

Jour.Juris. Hall's Journal of Jurisprudence

Jour.Law Journal of Law

Jour.Ps.Med. Journal of Psychological Medicine & Medical Jurisprudence

Jud.Chr. Judicial Chronicle

Jud.Coun.N.Y. Judicial Council, New York, Annual Reports

Jud.G.C.C. Judgments, Gold Coast Colony

Jud.Rep. New York Judicial Repository

Jud.& Sw. Judah & Swan's Reports *Jamaica*

Judd Judd's Reports (4 Hawaii)

Judg.U.B. Judgments of Upper Bench *Eng*

Jug.et Délib. Jugements et Délibérations du Conseil Souverain de la Nouvelle France

Jur. The Jurist (*see* List of Anglo-American Periodicals)

Jurist Reports *Eng*

Jur.N.S. The Jurist, New Series

Jurist Reports, New Series *Eng*

Jur.Rev. Juridical Review

Jur.Soc.P. Juridical Society Papers, London

Jurid.Rev. Juridical Review

Jurispr. The Jurisprudent

Just.L.R. Justices' Law Reporter (Pa. 1902–18)

Just.Peace Justice of the Peace

Juta Juta's Cape of Good Hope Reports *S.Af.*

Juta's Daily Reporter *S.Af.*

Juta's Prize Cases *S.Af.*

K. Keyes' Court of Appeals Rep.
(40–43 N. Y.)

Kenyon's King's Bench Reports *Eng*

Kotze's Reports, Transvaal High
Court   *S.Af.*

K.B. Law Reports, King's Bench *Eng*

Law Reports, King's Bench Division
Eng

K.B.U.C. Upper Canada King's Bench
Reports

K.C.R. Reports *temp.* King   *Eng*

K.L.R. Kathiawar Law Reports *India*

K.L.T. Kerala Law Times   *India*

K.& B. Kotze & Barber Transvaal
Reports (Supreme or High
Court)

K.& F.N.S.W. Knox & Fitzhardinge's
Reports, N. S. W.   *Aus*

K.& G. Keane & Grant's Registration
Appeal Cases   *Eng*

K.& J. Kay & Johnson's Chancery
Reports   *Eng*

K.& O. Knapp & Ombler's Election
Cas.   *Eng*

Kam. Kames' Dictionary of Decisions,
Court of Session   *Scot*

Kam.Rem.Dec. Kames' Remarkable
Decisions, Court of Sessions *Scot*

Kam.Sel.Dec. Kames' Select Decisions
Scot

Kames *See* Kam., *supra*

Kan. Kansas

Kan.App. Kansas Appeals Reports

Kan.C.L.Rep. Kansas City Law
Reporter

Kan.C.L.& I.W.C. Kansas Commission of Labor & Industry Workmen's Compensation Dept.
Reports

Kan.Jud.Council Bul. Kansas Judicial
Council Bulletin

Kan.L.J. Kansas Law Journal

Kan.L.Rev. University of Kansas Law
Review

Kan.P.S.C. Kansas Public Service
Commission

Kan.P.U.C. Kansas Public Utilities
Comm.

Kan.R.C. Kansas Railroad Commission

Kan.S.C.C. Kansas State Corporation
Commission Reports

Kan.U.Lawy. Kansas University
Lawyer

Kans.App. Kansas Appeals Reports

Kans.S.B.A. Kansas State Bar Association

Kay Kay's Chancery Reports   *Eng*

Kay & John. Kay & Johnson's Vice-
Chancellors' Reports   *Eng*

Ke. Keen's Rolls Court Reports *Eng*

Keane & Gr. Keane & Grant's
Registration Cases   *Eng*

Keb. Keble's King's Bench Reports
Eng

Keen Keen's Rolls Court Reports *Eng*

Keil. Keilway's King's Bench Reports
Eng

Keilw. Same as above

Keith Ch.Pa. Registrar's Book, Keith's
Court of Chancery   *Pa*

Kel. John Kelyng's Crown Case Rep.
Eng

Kel.1(or J.) John Kelyng's Crown
Cases   *Eng*

Kel.2(or W.) W. Kelynge's Chancery
Rep.   *Eng*

Kel.Ga. Kelly's Reports (1–3
Georgia)

Kel.J. Same as Kel. 1, *supra*

Kel.W. Same as Kel. 2, *supra*

Kellen Kellen's Reports (146–55
Mass.)

Kelly Kelly's Reports (1–3 Georgia)

Kelly & Cobb Kelly & Cobb's Rep.
(4, 5 Ga.)

Kelyng J. Kelyng's Crown Cases *Eng*

Ken. Kenyon's King's Bench Reports
Eng

Ken.Dec. Kentucky Decisions, Sneed
(2 Ky.)

Ken.L.Re. Kentucky Law Reporter

Ken.Opin. Kentucky Opinions 1864–
1886

Kenan Kenan's Reports (76–91
N. C.)

Keny. Kenyon's King's Bench Reports
Eng

Kenyon's Notes of King's Bench Rep.
Eng

Keny.Ch. Chancery Cases (v.2 of
Notes of King's Bench Cases) *Eng*

Keny.Chy.(3 Keny.) Chancery
Reports, at end of 2 Kenyon *Eng*

Kenya L.R. Kenya Law Reports

Kern. Kern's Reports (100–116
Indiana)

Kernan's Reports (11–14 New York)

Kerr Kerr's Reports (3–5 New
Brunswick)

Kerr's Reports (18–22 Indiana)

Kerr's Reports (27–29 N. Y. Civil
Procedure Reports)

Kerse Kerse's Manuscript Decisions, Court of Session *Scot*

Key. Keyes' Reports (40–43 New York)

Keyl. Keilway's English Bench Reports *Eng*

Kilb. Kilburn's Magistrates' Cases *Eng*

Kilk. Kilkerran's Court of Session Dec. *Scot*

King King's Reports (5, 6 La. Annual) Eastern District Court Reports, Cape Colony *S.Af.*

King Select Cases *temp.* King, Chancery *Eng*

King's Conf.Ca. King's Conflicting Cases (Texas 1840–1911)

Kir. Kirby's Reports & Supplement (Conn. 1785–89)

Kitchen Griqualand West Reports, Cape Colony *S.Af.*

Kn. Knapp's Privy Council Cases *Eng*

Kn.A.C. Knapp's Appeal Cases (Privy Council) *Eng*

Kn.L.G.R. Knight's Local Government Rep. *Eng*

Kn.N.S.W. Knox's New South Wales Reports

Kn.P.C. Knapp's Privy Council Cases *Eng*

Kn.& Moo. 3 Knapp's Privy Council Rep. *Eng*

Kn.& Omb. Knapp & Ombler's Election Cas. *Eng*

Knapp Knapp's Privy Council Reports *Eng*

Knowles Knowles' Reports (3 Rhode Island)

Knox Knox's Reports (N.S.W.) *Aus*

Knox & Fitz. Knox & Fitzhardinge's Reports (N.S.W.) *Aus*

Koch. Koch's Supreme Court Decisions *Ceylon*

Konst.Rat.App. Konstam's Reports of Rating Appeals *Eng*

Konst.& W.Rat.App. Konstam & Ward's Reports of Rating Appeals *Eng*

Kotze Kotze's Transvaal High Court Reports

Kotze & Barber Transvaal Court Reports

Kreider Kreider's Reports (1–23 Washington)

Kress Kress's Reports (166–194 Pa. State)

Kress's Reports (2–12 Pa. Superior)

Kulp Kulp's Luzerne Legal Register Reports *Pa*

Ky. Kentucky

Ky.Dec. Sneed's Kentucky Decisions (2 Ky.)

Ky.L.J. Kentucky Law Journal

Ky.L.Rep. Kentucky Law Reporter

Ky.L.Rev. Kentucky Law Review

Ky.Op. Kentucky Court of Appeals Opinions

Ky.R.C. Kentucky Railroad Commission

Ky.S.B.A. Kentucky State Bar Association

Ky.S.B.J. Kentucky State Bar Journal

Ky.W.C.Dec. Kentucky Workmen's Compensation Board Decisions

L. Lansing's Select Cases in Chancery (N. Y. 1824, 1826)

Lawson's Notes of Registration Dec. *Eng*

L.5 Long Quinto (Year Books, pt. X) *Eng*

LA Labor Relations Reporter: Labor Arbitration & Disputes Settlement (B.N.A.)

L.A.B. Los Angeles Bar Bulletin

LABPR Local Advisory Board Procedural Regulation (Office of Rent Stabilization. Economic Stabilization Agency) *U.S.*

L.Abr. Lilly's Abridgment *Eng*

L.B.R. Lower Burma Rulings *India*

L.C. Lord Chancellor

L.C.A. Leading Cases Annotated

L.C.C. Land Court Cases (N.S.W.) *Aus*

L.C.C.N.S.W. Same as above

L.C.D. Ohio Lower Court Decisions

L.C.Eq. White & Tudor's Leading Cases in Equity *Eng*

L.C.G. Lower Courts Gazette, Ontario

L.C.J. Lower Canada Jurist

L.C.L.J. Lower Canada Law Journal

L.C.R. Lower Canada Reports

L.C.& M.Gaz. Lower Courts & Municipal Gazette *Canada*

L.D. Land Office Decisions *U.S.*

L.E.C. Landed Estates Courts Commission *Eng*

L.Ed. Lawyers' Edition, U. S. Supreme Court Reports

L.G.R. Local Government Reports (N.S.W.) *Aus*

Local Government Rep. (Knight) *Eng*

LHA Lanham Housing Act   *U.S.*
L.I. Legal Intelligencer   *Pa*
L.Inst.J. Law Institute Journal   *Aus*
L.J. Law Journal
 Hall's Law Journal
 House of Lords Journal
 New York Law Journal
L.J.Adm. Law Journal Reports,
 Admiralty   *Eng*
L.J.App. Law Journal Reports, New
 Series, Appeals
L.J.Bcy. Law Journal Reports,
 Bankruptcy   *Eng*
L.J.C. Law Journal Reports, New
 Series, Common Pleas   *Eng*
L.J.C.C. Law Journal, County Courts
 Reporter
L.J.C.C.R. Law Journal Reports, New
 Series, Crown Cases Reserved
     Eng
L.J.C.P. Law Journal Reports,
 Common Pleas   *Eng*
L.J.C.P.D. Law Journal Reports, New
 Series, Common Pleas Decisions
     Eng
L.J.Ch. Law Journal Reports, N. S.
 Chancery   *Eng*
L.J.Ch.(O.S.) Law Journal Reports,
 Chancery, Old Series   *Eng*
L.J.D.& M. Law Journal Reports,
 New Series, Divorce &
 Matrimonial   *Eng*
L.J.Eccl. Law Journal, Ecclesiastical
 Cases   *Eng*
L.J.Exch. Law Journal Reports, New
 Series, Exchequer   *Eng*
L.J.Ex.D. Law Journal Reports, New
 Series, Exchequer Division   *Eng*
L.J.Ex.Eq. Law Journal, Exchequer in
 Equity   *Eng*
L.J.H.L. Law Journal Reports, New
 Series, House of Lords   *Eng*
L.J.K.B. Law Journal Reports, King's
 or Queen's Bench   *Eng*
L.J.L.C. Law Journal, Lower Canada
L.J.M.C. Law Journal Reports, New
 Series, Magistrates' Cases   *Eng*
L.J.M.P.A. Law Journal Reports,
 Matrimonial, Probate and
 Admiralty   *Eng*
L.J.M.& W. Morgan & Williams' Law
 Journal
L.J.Mat.Cas. Law Journal Reports,
 New Series, Divorce & Matri-
 monial   *Eng*
L.J.N.C. Law Journal, Notes of Cases
     Eng

L.J.N.C.C.A. Law Journal News-
 paper, County Court Appeals *Eng*
L.J.N.S. Law Journal, New Series *Eng*
L.J.O.S. Law Journal, Old Series *Eng*
L.J.P. Law Journal Reports, New
 Series, Privy Council   *Eng*
 Law Journal Reports, Probate,
 Divorce, Admiralty   *Eng*
L.J.P.C. Law Journal Reports, Privy
 Council   *Eng*
L.J.P.C.N.S. Law Journal Reports,
 New Series, Privy Council *Eng*
L.J.P.D.& A. Law Journal Reports,
 New Series, Probate, Divorce, and
 Admiralty   *Eng*
L.J.P.M.& A. Law Journal Reports,
 New Series, Probate, Matrimonial,
 & Admiralty   *Eng*
L.J.P.& M. Law Journal, Probate &
 Admiralty Cases   *Eng*
L.J.Q.B. Law Journal Reports, New
 Series, Queen's Bench   *Eng*
L.J.Q.B.D. Law Journal Reports, New
 Series, Queen's Bench Division
     Eng
L.J.R.[ep.] Law Journal Reports *Eng*
L.J.Rep.N.S. Law Journal Reports,
 New Series (from 1831)   *Eng*
L.J.(Sm.) Smith's Law Journal
L.J.U.C. Law Journal of Upper
 Canada
L.Jo. Law Journal Newspaper   *Eng*
L.L.J. Lahore Law Journal   *India*
 Law Library Journal
L.L.R. Leader Law Reports   *S.Af.*
L.L.T. Lahore Law Times   *India*
L.Lib.J. Law Library Journal
L.M. Law Magazine
L.M.& P. Lowndes, Maxwell, & Pol-
 lock's Rep., Bail Court & Practice
     Eng
L.Mag.& Rev. Law Magazine &
 Review
L.N. Law Notes, London or North-
 port   *N.Y.*
 Legal News   *Canada*
 Liber Niger (Black Book)
 League of Nations
L.O. Legal Observer
 Solicitor's Law Opinion (U. S.
 Internal Revenue Bureau)
L.Q.Rev. Law Quarterly Review
 Law Reporter (*see* List of Anglo-
 American Legal Periodicals)
 Law Reporter (Law Times Reports,
 N. S.)
 Law Reports

L.R. Law Recorder (Irish)
Louisiana Reports
L.R.A. Lawyers' Reports Annotated
L.R.A.C. Law Reports, Appeal Cases
Eng
L.R.A.& E. Law Reports, Admiralty
& Ecclesiastical Cases *Eng*
L.R.App. Law Reports, Appeal Cases,
House of Lords *Eng*
L.R.A.N.S. Lawyers' Reports
Annotated, New Series
LRB Loyalty Review Board *U.S.*
L.R.B.G. Law Reports, British Guiana
L.R.Burm. Law Reports, British
Burma
L.R.C.A. Law Reports, Court of
Appeals *N.Z.*
L.R.C.C.R. Law Reports, Crown Cases
Reserved *Eng*
L.R.C.P. Law Reports, Common Pleas
Eng
L.R.C.P.D. Law Reports, Comm. Pl.
Div. *Eng*
L.R.Ch. Law Reports, Chancery App.
Cas. *Eng*
L.R.Ch.D. Law Reports, Chancery
Div. *Eng*
L.R.E.& I.App. Law Reports, House
of Lords (English & Irish Appeals)
L.R.Eq. Law Reports, Equity *Eng*
L.R.Ex. Law Reports, Exchequer *Eng*
L.R.Ex.Div. Law Reports, Exchequer
Div. *Eng*
L.R.H.L. Law Reports, English &
Irish Appeals & Peerage Claims,
House of Lords *Eng*
L.R.H.L.Sc. Law Reports, Scotch &
Divorce Appeal Cases *Eng*
L.R.Ind.App. Law Reports, Indian
Appeals
L.R.Ind.App.Supp. Law Reports,
Indian Appeals Supplement
L.R.Ir. Law Reports, Ch. & Common
Law *Ir*
L.R.K.B. Law Reports, King's Bench
Div. *Eng*
L.R.Misc.D. Law Reports, Miscel-
laneous Div. *Eng*
L.R.N.S. Law Recorder, New Series
Nova Scotia Reports *Ir*
L.R.N.S.W. Law Reports, New South
Wales Supreme Court, 1880–1900
L.R.N.Z. Law Reports, New Zealand
L.R.P. Law Reports Probate Division
Eng
L.R.P.C. Law Reports, Privy Council
Eng

L.R.P.Div. Law Reports, Probate,
Divorce, & Admiralty Div. *Eng*
L.R.P.& D. Law Reports, Probate,
Divorce *Eng*
L.R.P.& M. Law Reports, Probate,
Matrimonial *Eng*
L.R.Q.B. Law Reports, Queen's
Bench *Eng*
Quebec Reports, Queen's Bench
Canada
L.R.Q.B.D. Law Reports, Q. B.
Division *Eng*
LRR Labor Relations Reporter
(B.N.A.) *U.S.*
LRRM Labor Relations Reporter:
Labor-Management Relations
L.R.S.A. Law Reports, South
Australia
L.R.S.C. Law Reports, New Zealand
Supreme Court
L.R.Sc.Div.App. Law Reports,
Scotch Appeals
L.R.Sc.& D. Law Reports, Scotch &
Irish Appeals, House of Lords
Eng
L.R.Sess.Cas. Law Reports, Session
Cases *Eng*
L.R.Stat. Law Reports, Statutes *Eng*
L.Rec.O.S. Law Recorder, Old Series
Ir
L.Rep.Mont. Law Reporter, Montreal
L.Repos. Law Repository
L.Rev. The Law Review *Eng*
L.Rev.U.Detroit. Law Review,
University of Detroit
L.Rev.& Quart.J. Law Review &
Quarterly Jour.
L.Soc.J. Law Society Journal
L.Stu.Mag.N.S. Law Student's
Magazine, New Series
L.T. Law Times (Luzerne Law
Times)
Law Times Reports
L.T.B. Law Times Bankruptcy
Reports *U.S.*
L.T.Jo. Law Times Journal (a
Newspaper) *Eng*
L.T.N.S. Law Times Reports, New
Series *Eng*
L.T.O.S. Law Times Reports, Old
Series *Eng*
L.T.R. Law Times Reports *Eng*
L.Th. La Themis *Canada*
L.V.R. Land and Valuation Court
Rep. *N.S.W.*
L.V.Rep. Lehigh Valley Law
Reporter (Pa. 1885–87)

L.W. Law Weekly, Madras   *India*

L.& A. Leembruggen & Asirvatham's Appeal Court Reports   *Ceylon*

L.& B. Leadam & Baldwin's Select Cases before the King's Council   *Eng*

L.& B.Bull. Daily Law & Bank Bulletin   *Ohio*

L.& C. Lefroy & Cassel's Pract. Cas.   *Canada*

Leigh & Cave's Crown Cases Reserved   *Eng*

L.& E. English Law & Equity Reports Reprint

L.& E.Rep. Law & Equity Reporter   *N.Y.*

L.& G.*t*.Plunk. Lloyd & Goold's Chancery Reports *temp.* Plunkett   *Ir*

L.& G.*t*.Sugd. Lloyd & Goold's Chancery Reports *temp.* Sugden   *Ir*

L.& M. Lowndes & Maxwell's Pract. Cases   *Eng*

L.& T. Longfield & Townsend's Ex. Cases   *Ir*

L.& W. Lloyd & Welsby's Mercantile Cas.   *Eng*

L.& Welsb. Lloyd & Welsby's Commercial & Mercantile Cases   *Eng*

La. Lane's Exchequer Reports   *Eng*

Louisiana

La.A. Louisiana Court of Appeals (Orleans)

Louisiana Annual Reports

La.Ann. Louisiana Annual Reports

La.App. Louisiana Courts of Appeal Reports

La.App.(Orleans) Orleans Court of Appeals Reports, by Teissier (Louisiana 1903–17)

La.B.A. Louisiana Bar Association

La.L.J. Louisiana Law Journal

La.L.Rev. Louisiana Law Review

La.P.S.C. Louisiana Public Service Commission Reports

La.R.C. Louisiana Railroad Commission

La.T.R. Louisiana Term Rep. (Martin)

La Them.L.C. La Themis, Lower Canada

Lab. Labatt's District Court Reports (California 1857–58)

Labor L.J. Labor Law Journal

Lac.Jur. Lackawanna Jurist   *Pa*

Lack.Leg.N. Lackawanna Legal News   *Pa*

Lack.Leg.R. Lackawanna Legal Record   *Pa*

Ladd. Ladd's Reports (59–64 New Hampshire)

Lah.Cas. Lahore Cases   *India*

Lah.L.J. Lahore Law Journal   *India*

Lah.L.T. Lahore Law Times   *India*

Lalor Lalor's Supplement to Hill & Denio's New York Reports

Lamar Lamar's Reports (25–42 Florida)

Lamb Lamb's Reports (103–105 Wisconsin)

Lanc.Bar Lancaster Bar (Pa. 1869–83)

Lanc.L.Rev. Lancaster Law Review (Pa., 1883-date)

Land App.Ct.Cas. Land Appeal Court Cases, N.S.W.   *Aus*

Land Com.Rep. Land Reports, by Roche, Dillon, & Kehoe   *Ir*

Land.Est.C. Landed Estate Court   *Eng*

Lane Lane's Exchequer Reports   *Eng*

Lans. Lansing's Supreme Ct. Rep. (N. Y. 1869–73)

Lans.Ch. Lansing's Select Cases, Chancery (N. Y. 1824, 1826)

Lans.Sel.Cas. Same as above

Lap.Dec. Laperriere's Speaker's Dec.   *Canada*

Lat. Latch's King's Bench Reports   *Eng*

Lath [rop] Lathrop's Reports (115–145 Mass.)

Lauder Fountainhall's Session Cases   *Scot*

Laur.H.C.Ca. Lauren's High Court Cases   *S.Af.*

Law The Law (*see* List of Anglo-American Legal Periodicals)

Law Am.Jour. Law Amendment Journal

Law Bk.Rev.Dig. Law Book Review Digest & Current Legal Bibliography

Law Bul. Law Bulletin

Law Bul.& Br. Law Bulletin & Brief

Law Bul.Ia. Law Bulletin, State University of Iowa

Law Cas.Wm.I. Law Cases, William I to Richard I   *Eng*

Law Chr. Law Chronicle

Law Chr.& Auct.Rec. Law Chronicle & Auction Record

Law Chr.& Jour.Jur. Law Chronicle & Journal of Jurisprudence

Law Cl. Law Clerk (*see* List of Anglo-American Legal Periodicals)

Law.Dept.Bull. Law Department Bulletin, Union Pacific Railroad Co.

Law.Ed. Lawyers' Edition, United States Supreme Court Reports

Law Ex.J. Law Examination Journal

Law Ex.Rep. Law Examination Reporter

Law Gaz. Law Gazette

Law.Guild Rev. Lawyers' Guild Review

Law Inst.J. Law Institute Journal

Law J. Law Journal (*see* List of Anglo-American Legal Periodicals)

Law J. Law Journal Reports (for various series, *see* L. J., *supra*)

Law Jour. Law Journal Reports (for various series, *see* L. J., *supra*)

Law Lib.J. Law Library Journal

Law Lib.N. Law Library News

Law Mag. Law Magazine

Law Mag.& R. Law Magazine & Review

Law N. Law Notes (London or Northport, N. Y.)

Law Notes Same as above

Law Q.Rev. Law Quarterly Review

Law Rec. Law Recorder   *Ir*

Law Reg. Law Register, Chicago American Law Register, Philadelphia

Law Reg.Cas. Lawson's Registration Cases   *Eng*

Law Rep. Law Reports (*see* abbreviations under L.R.)

Law Reporter (for various periodicals, *see* List of Anglo-American Legal Periodicals)

Law Rep.N.S. Monthly Law Reporter

Law Rep. Law Reporter (Ramsey & Morin)   *Can*

Law Reporter   *Eng*

Law Repos. Carolina Law Repository

Law Rev. Law Review (*see* List of Anglo-American Legal Periodicals)

Law Rev.Comm. Law Revision Commission

Law Rev.U.Det. Law Review University of Detroit

Law Rev.& Qu.J. Law Review & Quarterly Jour.

Law Soc.Jo. Law Society of Massachusetts, Journal

Law Soc.Gaz. Law Society's Gazette (London or Regina)

Law.Stu. Law Student (*see* List of Anglo-American Legal Periodicals)

Law.Stu.H. Law Students' Helper

Law Stud.Mag. Law Students' Magazine

Law Times (London, Eng.; Scranton, Pa.)

Law T.Rep.N.S. Law Times Reports, New Series

Law T.Rep.O.S. Law Times Reports, Old Series

Law W. Law Weekly

Law.& Bank. Lawyer & Banker (New Orleans)

Lawyers' & Bankers' Quarterly (St. Louis)

Law & Contemp.Prob. Law & Contemporary Problems

Law.& L.N. Lawyer & Law Notes   *Eng*

Law.& Mag. Lawyers' & Magistrates' Magazine

Lawyer & Magistrate

Lawrence Lawrence's Reports, High Court of Griqualand   *S.Af.*

Lawrence's Reports (20 Ohio)

Lawrence Comp.Dec. Lawrence's Comptroller's Decisions   *U.S.*

Lawy. Lawyer or Lawyers' (*see* List of Anglo-American Legal Periodicals)

Lawyer Lawyer or Lawyers' (*see* above)

Lay Lay's Chancery Reports   *Eng*

Ld.Birk. Lord Birkenhead's Judgments, House of Lords   *Eng*

Ld.Ken. Lord Kenyon's King's Bench Rep.   *Eng*

Ld.Raym. Lord Raymon's K. B. & Com. Pl. Rep.

Le.& Ca. Leigh & Cave's Crown Cases Reserved   *Eng*

Lea. Lea's Reports (69–84 Tennessee)

Leach Leach's Crown Cases   *Eng*

Leach Cl.Cas. Leach's Club Cases *Eng*

Lead. Leader Law Reports   *Ceylon*

Lead.Cas.Am. Hare & Wallace's American Leading Cases

Lead.Cas.Eq. White & Tudor's Leading Cases in Equity

Leadam Leadam's Select Cases before King's Council in the Star Chamber (Selden Society Publications, v. 16, 25)

Leadam Req. Leadam's Select Cases in the Court of Requests (Selden Society Publications, v.12)

Lee Lee's Ecclesiastical Judgments *Eng*

Lee's Reports (9–12 California)

Lee G. George Lee's Ecclesiastical Rep. *Eng*

Lee *t*.Hard. Lee's Cases *temp*. Hardwicke, in K. B. & Chancery *Eng*

Leese Leese's Reports (26 Nebraska)

Lef.Dec. Lefevre's Parliamentary Decisions, by Bourke *Eng*

Lefroy Lefroy's Railroad & Canal Cas. *Eng*

Legal Adv. Legal Advertiser (Chicago)

Legal Adviser (Chicago or Denver)

Leg.Aid Rev. Legal Aid Review

Leg.Bib. Legal Bibliography (Boston)

Leg.Chron. Legal Chronicle (Foster's Pa. Rep.)

Leg.Exam. Legal Examiner (London or N. Y.)

Leg.Exam.N.S. Legal Examiner, N. Ser. *Eng*

Leg.Exam.W.R. Legal Examiner Weekly Reporter

Leg.Exam.& L.C. Legal Examiner & Law Chronicle (London)

Leg.Exam.& Med.J. Legal Examiner Medical Jurist (London)

Leg.Exch. Legal Exchange (Des Moines, Ia.)

Leg.G. Legal Guide

Leg.Gaz. Legal Gazette

Leg.Gaz.Rep. [Campbell's Legal Gazette Reports (Pa. 1869–71)]

Leg.Inf.Bul. Legal Information Bulletin

Leg.Int. Legal Intelligencer (Philadelphia)

Leg.Misc.& Rev. Legal Miscellany & Review *India*

Leg.News Legal News (Montreal; Sunbury, Pa; Toledo, Ohio)

Leg.Notes Legal Notes on Local Government (New York)

Leg.Obs. Legal Observer (London)

Legal Observer & Solicitors' Journal (London)

Leg.Op. Legal Opinion (Harrisburg, Pa.)

Leg.Rec. Legal Record (Detroit, Mich.)

Leg.Rec.Rep. Legal Record Reports (1–2 Schuykill Co. (Pa.) Legal Record Reports)

Leg.Rem. Legal Remembrancer (Calcutta)

Leg.Rep. Legal Reporter *Ir*

Leg.Rev. Legal Review

Leg.Y.B. Legal Year Book *Eng*

Leg.& Ins.Rep. Legal & Insurance Reporter (Pa. 1859–67)

Legg. Leggett's Reports, Sind *India*

Legge Legge's Reports *Aus*

Leguleian (a periodical) *Eng*

Lehigh Co.L.J. Lehigh (Pa.) Law Journal

Lehigh Val.L.Rep. Lehigh Valley (Pa.) Law Reporter

Leigh Leigh's Reports (28–39 Virginia)

Leigh & C. Leigh & Cave's Crown Cases *Eng*

Leo. Leonard's King's Bench Reports *Eng*

Leon. Leonard's K. B., Com. Pl. Exchequer Reports *Eng*

Lest.P.L. Lester's Public Land Decisions *U.S.*

Lester Lester's Reports (31–33 Georgia)

Lester Supp. Supplement to 33 Georgia Rep.

Lev. Levinz's K. B. & Com. Pl. Rep. *Eng*

Lev.Ent. Levinz's Entries *Eng*

Lew. Lewin's Crown Cases Reserved *Eng*

Lewis' Reports (29–35 Missouri Appeals)

Lewis' Reports (1 Nevada)

Lew.C.C. Lewin's Crown Cases Reserved *Eng*

Lewis Lewis' Reports (1 Nevada)

Lewis' Reports (29–35 Mo. Appeals)

Kentucky Law Reporter

Lex Man. Lex Maneriorum (Wm. Nelson)

Lex Merc.Red. Lex Mercatoria Rediviva (Beawes)

Ley Ley's King's Bench Reports *Eng*

Ley's Court of Wards Reports *Eng*

Lib.Ass. Liber Assisarum, Year Books, 1–51 Edw. III *Eng*

Lib.Int. Liber Intrationum (Book of Entries)

Lib.Reg. Register Books *Eng*

Life & Acc.Ins.R. Bigelow's Life & Accident Insurance Reports

Life C.   Life Cases, Including Health & Accident (CCH)

Lil.   Lilly's Assize Reports   *Eng*

Lill.Ent.   Lilly's Entries   *Eng*

Lilly   Lilly's Cases in Assize   *Eng*

Lincoln L.Rev.   Lincoln Law Review (Buffalo)

Lit.   Littell's Reports (11–15 Kentucky)

Littleton's Common Pleas Reports
Eng

Lit.Brooke   Brooke's New Cases, K. B.
Eng

Litt.   Littleton's Common Pleas Reports   *Eng*

Littell   Littell's Reports (11–15 Kentucky)

Little Brooke   Brooke's New Cases
Eng

Liv.Cas.   Livingston's Cases in Error
N.Y.

Liv.Jud.Op.   Livingston's Judicial Opinions   *N.Y.*

Liv.L.Mag.   Livingston's Monthly Law Magazine

Liv.L.Reg.   Livingston's Law Register

Liz.Sc.Exch. Lizar's Exchequer Cases
Scot

Ll.L.Pr.Cas.   Lloyd's List Prize Cas.
Eng

Ll.L.Rep.   Lloyd's List Law Reports
Eng

Ll.List. L.R.   Lloyd's List Law Reports   *Eng*

Ll.& G.*t*.P.   Lloyd & Goold's Ch. Rep. *temp.* Plunkett   *Ir*

Ll.& G.*t*.S.   Lloyd & Goold's Ch. Rep. *temp.* Sugden   *Ir*

Ll.& W[els].   Lloyd & Welsby's Mercantile Cases   *Eng*

Lloyd,L.R.   Lloyd's List Law Reports
Eng

Lloyd List   Lloyd's List   *Eng*

Lloyd's Pr.Cas.   Lloyd's Prize Case Rep.   *Eng*

Lloyd's Rep.   Lloyd's List Law Reports   *Eng*

Lobin.   Lobingier's Extraterritorial Cases, U. S. Court for China

Loc.Ct.Gaz.   Local Courts & Municipal Gazette (Toronto)

Loc.Govt.Chr.& Mag.Rep.   Local Government Chronicle & Magisterial Reporter (London)

Lock.Rev.Cas.   Lockwood's Reversed Cas.   *N.Y.*

Locus Standi   Locus Standi Reports
Eng

Lofft   Lofft's King's Bench Reports
Eng

Lofft Max.   Maxims, in appendix to Lofft's Reports

Lond.Gaz.   London Gazette

Lond.Jur.   London Jurist Reports
Eng

Lond.Jur.N.S.   London Jurist, New Series

Lond.L.M.   London Law Magazine

Long.Q.   Long Quinto (Year Books, Part X)

Long.& T.   Longfield & Townsend's Ex. Rep.   *Ir*

Lor.& Russ.   Loring & Russell's Election Cases (Mass.)

Lords Jour.   Journals, House of Lords
Eng

Lorenz   Lorenz's Ceylon Reports

Lorenz.App.R.   Lorenz's Appeal Reports   *Ceylon*

Los Angeles B.A.B.   Los Angeles Bar Association Bulletin

Los Angeles L.Rev.   Los Angeles Law Review

Loss & Dam.Rev.   Loss & Damage Review

Lou.   Louisiana (*see* La.)

Lou.L.Jour.   Louisiana Law Journal

Lou.L.Rev.   Louisiana Law Review

Lou.Leg.N.   Louisiana Legal News

Low.   Lowell's District Court Reports (U.S., Mass. District)

Low.C.Seign.   Lower Canada Seignorial Rep.

Low.Can.   Lower Canada Reports

Low.Can.Jur.   Lower Canada Jurist

Low.Can.L.J.   Lower Canada Law Journal

Low.Can.Rep.   Lower Canada Reports

Low.Can.Rep.S.Q.   Lower Canada Reports, Seignorial Questions

Lowell   Lowell's District Court Reports (U. S., Mass. District)

Lower Ct.Dec.   Ohio Lower Court Decisions

Lownd.& M.   Lowndes & Maxwell's Bail Ct. Reports   *Eng*

Lownd.M.& P.   Lowndes, Maxwell, & Pollock's Bail Court Reports *Eng*

Loyola L.J.   Loyola Law Journal

Loyola L.Rev.   Loyola Law Review

Luc.   Lucas' Reports (Modern Reports, Part X)

Lucas   Same as above

Luck.Ser. Indian Law Reports, Lucknow Ser.

Lud.E.C. Luder's Election Cases *Eng*

Ludden Ludden's Reports (43, 44 Maine)

Lum.P.L.C[as]. Lumley's Poor Law Cases   *Eng*

Lumpkin Lumpkin's Reports (59–77 Georgia)

Lush. Lushington's Admiralty Reports *Eng*

Lut. E. Lutwyche's Entries & Reports, Common Pleas   *Eng*

Lut.Elec.Cas. Lutwyche's Election Cas.   *Eng*

Lut.Reg.Cas. A. J. Lutwyche's Registration Cases   *Eng*

Lutw. *see* Lut., *supra*

Luz.L.J. Luzerne Law Journal   *Pa*

Luz.L.T. Luzerne Law Times   *Pa*

Luz.Leg.Obs. Luzerne Legal Observer *Pa*

Luz.Leg.Reg. Luzerne Legal Register *Pa*

Luz.Leg.Reg.Rep. Luzerne Legal Register Reports   *Pa*

Lynd. Lyndwood, Provinciale   *Eng*

Lyne Lyne's Chancery Cases (Wallis) *Ir*

M. Indian Law Reports, Madras Series
Macpherson's Session Cases   *Scot*
Maine; Manitoba; Maryland; Massachusetts; Michigan; Minnesota; Mississippi; Missouri; Montana
Menzies's Cape Colony Supreme Ct. Rep.
Miles' Pennsylvania Reports
Morison's Dictionary of Sessions *Scot*
New York Miscellaneous Reports

M' *See* Mac and Mc

MA Maritime Administration   *U.S.*

M.A. Missouri Appeals Reports
Munitions Tribunals Appeals, Great Britain High Court of Justice

MAP Military Assistance Program

M.B. Miscellaneous Branch, Internal Revenue Bureau   *U.S.*
Morrell's Bankruptcy Reports   *Eng*
Munitions Board   *U.S.*

M.C. Magistrates' Cases   *Eng*
Matara Cases   *Ceylon*
Mayor's Court

M.C.C. Interstate Commerce Commission Reports, Motor Carrier Cases   *U.S.*
Martin's Mining Cases, British Columbia

Mining Commissioner's Cases *Canada*
Moody's Crown Cases Reserved *Eng*

M.C.Cas. Municipal Corporation Cases Annotated

MCM 1928 Manual for Courts-Martial, U.S.A.

MCM 1949 Manual for Courts-Martial, U.S.A. or U.S.A.F.

MCM 1951 Manual for Courts-Martial *U.S.*

M.C.R. Magistrates' Courts Reports *New Zeal*
Montreal Condensed Reports

M.Cr.C. Madras Criminal Cases

M.D.& D.(or DeG.) Montagu, Deacon, & DeGex's Bankruptcy Reports   *Eng*

M.G.& S. Manning, Granger, & Scott's Common Pleas Reports   *Eng*

M.H.C. Madras High Court Reports *India*

M.H.C.R. Madras High Court Reports   *India*

M.H.L. Scotch Session Cases, House of Lords

M.I.A. Moore's Indian Appeals

ML Military Laws of the United States (Army) Annotated

MLB Maritime Labor Board   *U.S.*

M.L.Dig.& R. Monthly Law Digest & Reporter   *Canada*

M.L.J. Madras Law Journal   *India*
Malayan Law Journal
Memphis Law Journal

M.L.Q. Malabar Law Quarterly

M.L.R. Maryland Law Record
Montreal Law Reports
Modern Law Review

M.L.R.Q.B. Montreal Law Reports, Q. B.

M.L.R.S.C. Montreal Law Reports, Superior Court

M.L.T. Madras Law Times   *India*

M.L.W. Madras Law Weekly   *India*

M.M.C. Martin's Reports, Mining Cases   *Can*

M.M.R. Mitchell's Maritime Register *Eng*

MO Mineral Order (Defense Minerals Exploration Administration, Dept. of the Interior)   *U.S.*

MO-JAGA Memorandum Opinions, Judge Advocate General of the Army   *U.S.*

M.P.C. Moore's Privy Council Cases *Eng*

M.P.R. Maritime Provinces Reports
Canada

M.R. Manitoba Law Reports
Mauritius Decisions (or Reports)
Master of the Rolls   *Eng*

MSA Mutual Security Agency   *U.S.*

MSC Military Staff Committee   *UN*

MT Miscellaneous Branch Ruling,
Internal Revenue Bureau   *U.S.*

M.U.R. Montana Utilities Reports

M.W.N. Madras Weekly Notes *India*

M.W.N.C.C. Madras Weekly Notes,
Criminal Cases   *India*

M.& A. Montagu & Ayrton's Bankruptcy Rep.   *Eng*

M.& B. Montagu & Bligh's Bankruptcy
Rep.   *Eng*

M.& C. Montagu & Chitty's Bankruptcy Rep.   *Eng*
Mylne & Craig's Chancery Reports
                            Eng

M.& G. Macnaghten & Gordon's
Chancery Rep.   *Eng*
Maddock & Geldart's Chancery Rep.
                            Eng
Manning & Granger's Com. Pl. Rep.
                            Eng

M.& Gel. Maddock & Geldart's Ch.
Rep.   *Eng*

M.& Gord. Macnaghten & Gordon's
Ch. Rep.   *Eng*

M.& H. Murphy & Hurlstone's Ex.
Reports   *Eng*

M.& K. Mylne & Keen's Chancery
Reports   *Eng*

M.& M. Montagu & Macarthur's
Bankruptcy Reports   *Eng*
Moody & Malkin's Nisi Prius Reports
                            Eng

M.& M'A. Montagu & Macarthur's
Bankruptcy Reports   *Eng*

M.& P. Moore & Payne's Com. Pl.
Reports   *Eng*

M.& R. Maclean & Robinson's Appeal
Cas.   *Scot*
Manning & Ryland's King's Bench
Rep.   *Eng*
Moody & Robinson's Nisi Prius
Reports   *Eng*

M.& R.M.C. Manning & Ryland's
Magistrates Cases   *Eng*

M.& Rob. Maclean & Robinson's
Appeal Cases   *Scot*
Moody & Robinson's Nisi Prius Rep.
                            Eng

M.& S. Manning & Scott's Reports (9
Common Bench)   *Eng*

Maule & Selwyn's King's Bench Rep.
                            Eng
Moore & Scott's Common Pleas Rep.
                            Eng

M.& Scott Moore & Scott's Com. Pl.
Rep.   *Eng*

M.& W. Meeson & Welsby's
Exchequer Rep.   *Eng*

M.& W.Cas. Mining & Water Cases
Annotated   *U.S.*

M.& Y. Martin & Yerger's Reports
(8 Tenn.)

Mac. *See* also M'., Mc.
Macassey's New Zealand Reports

Mac.N.Z. Macassey's New Zealand
Reports

Mac.P.C. Macrory's Patent Cases *Eng*

Mac.Pat.Cas. Macrory's Patent Cases
                            Eng

Mac.& G. Macnaghten & Gordon's
Ch. Rep.   *Eng*

Mac.& H. Macrae & Hertslet's
Insolvency Cases   *Eng*

Mac.& Rob. Maclean & Robinson's
Appeal Cases   *Scot*

Macall. McAllister's Circuit Court
Rep.   *U.S.*

MacArth. MacArthur's Reports (8–
10 District of Columbia)

MacArth.Pat.Cas. MacArthur's
Patent Cas.   *U.S.*

MacArth.& M. MacArthur &
Mackey's Reports (11 D.C.)

MacCarthy MacCarthy's Land Cases
                            Ir

Macas. Macassey's New Zealand
Reports

M'Cle. M'Cleland's Exchequer
Reports   *Eng*

M'Cle.& Yo. M'Cleland & Younge's
Exchequer Reports   *Eng*

Maccl. Macclesfield's Rep. (Modern
Reports, pt. X)   *Eng*

Macd.Jam. Macdougall's Jamaica
Reports

MacDev. MacDevitt's Land Cases *Ir*

Macf. Macfarlane's Jury Trials, Court
of Session   *Scot*

Mac G.C.C. MacGillivray's Copyright
Cases   *Eng*

Mackey Mackey's Reports (12–20
D. C.)

Macl. McLean's Circuit Court Reports
                            U.S.
MacLaurin's Remarkable Cases *Scot*

MacL.& Rob. Maclean & Robinson's
Appeals, House of Lords   *Scot*

M'Laur. M'Laurin's Judiciary Cases
1774   *Scot*
Macn. Macnaghten's Reports   *India*
Macnaghten's Select Cases in Chancery
temp. King   *Eng*
Macn.Fr. Francis Macnaghten's
Bengal Rep.
Macn.N.A.Beng. Macnaghten's
Nizamut Adalut Reports   *India*
Macn.S.D.A.Beng. (W. H.) Mac-
naghten's Sadr Diwani Adalat
Reports   *India*
Macn.Sel.Cas. Macnaghten's Select
Cases in Chancery *temp.* King
                                      Eng
Macn.& G. Macnaghten & Gordon's
Ch. Rep.   *Eng*
Macph. Macpherson's Court of
Session Cases   *Scot*
Macpherson, Lee, & Bell's Session
Cases   *Scot*
Macq. Macqueen's Appeal Cases,
House of Lords   *Scot*
Macq.H.L.Cas. Same as above
Macr. Macrory's Patent Cases   *Eng*
Macr.& H. Macrae & Hertslet's
Insolvency Cases   *Eng*
Macr.Pat.Cas. Macrory's Patent Cases
                                      Eng
Mad. Indian Law Reports, Madras
Series
Maddock's Chancery Reports   *Eng*
Maddock's Reports (9–18 Montana)
Madras High Court Reports   *India*
Mad.Exch. Madox's History of the
Exchequer
Mad.H.C. Madras High Court
Reports   *India*
Mad.L.J. Madras Law Journal *India*
Mad.L.Rep. Madras Law Reporter
                                      India
Mad.L.T. Madras Law Times (Indian
Law Times)
Mad.S.D.A.R. Madras Sadr Diwani
Adalat Reports   *India*
Mad.Sel.Dec. Madras Select Decrees
                                      India
Mad.Ser. Indian Law Reports, Madras
Series
Mad.W.N. Madras Weekly Notes
Mad.& B. Maddox & Bach's Reports
(19 Mont.)
Mad.& Gel. Maddock & Geldart's
Chancery Reports   *Eng*
Madd. Maddock's Chancery Reports
                                      Eng
Maddox's Reports (9–18 Montana)

Madd.& G. Maddock & Geldart's Ch.
Rep.   *Eng*
Madox Madox's Formulare
Anglicanum
Madox's History of the Exchequer
Madr. Madras. *See* entries under Mad.
Mag. Magistrate (*see* List of Anglo-
American Legal Periodicals)
Magistrate & Municipal & Parochial
Lawyer
Mag.Cas. Magistrates' Cases;
Magisterial Cases
Bittleston, Wise, & Farnell's
Magistrates' Cases   *Eng*
Mag. Magruder's Reports (1, 2 Mary-
land)
Mag.& M.& P.L. Magistrate and
Municipal & Parochial Lawyer
Magruder Magruder's Reports (1, 2
Maryland)
Maine Maine Reports
Maine L.Rev. Maine Law Review
Maine P.U.R. Maine Public Utilities
Commission Reports
Maine S.B.A. Maine State Bar
Association
Mait. Maitland's Select Pleas of the
Crown
Mait.Gl. Maitland's Pleas of the
Crown, County of Gloucester
Maitland *See* also Mait., *supra*
Maitland's Manuscript Session Cases
                                      Scot
Maitland's Pleas of the Crown 1221
                                      Eng
Maitland's Select Pleas of the Crown
                                      Eng
Mallory Mallory's Chancery Reports
                                      Ir
Malone Heiskell's Reports (6, 9, 10
Tennessee)
Man. Manitoba
Manning Reports, Revision Court *Eng*
Manning Reports (1 Michigan)
Manson's Bankruptcy Cases   *Eng*
Man.Bar News Manitoba Bar News
Man.Cas. Bloomfield's Manumission
Cases   *N.J.*
Man.El.Cas. Manning's Court of
Revision Cases   *Eng*
Man.Gr.& S. Manning, Granger, &
Scott's Common Bench Reports,
Old Series   *Eng*
Man.L.J. Manitoba Law Journal
                                   Canada
Man.L.R. Manitoba Law Reports
                                   Canada

Man.R. Manitoba Law Reports
        Canada

Man.R.*t*.Wood Manitoba Reports,
 temp. Wood   *Canada*

Man.Unrep.Cas. Manning's Unreported Cases (Louisiana)

Man.& G. Manning & Granger's Com.
 Pl. Rep.   *Eng*

Man.& Ry. Manning & Ryland's K. B.
 Rep.   *Eng*

Man.& Ry.Mag.C. Manning &
 Ryland's Magistrates' Cases *Eng*

Man.& Sc. Manning & Scott's Common Bench Reports, Old Series
          Eng

Manb.Coke Manby's Abridgment of
 Coke's Rep.   *Eng*

Manitoba *See* Man., *supra*

Mann. Manning's Reports
 (1 Michigan)
 Manning's Revision Court Reports
          Eng

Manning Manning's Reports
 (1 Michigan)

Manning (La.) Manning's Unreported Cases (Louisiana)

Mans. Mansfield's Reports (49–52
 Arkansas)
 Manson's Bankruptcy & Company
 Cases   *Eng*

Manum.Cas. Bloomfield's Manumission Cases   *N.J.*

Mar. Maritime
 March's King's Bench Reports *Eng*
 Martin Reports (Louisiana 1809–30)
 Martin's Reports (1 N. C.)
 Marshall's Circuit Court Reports *U.S.*
 Marshall's Reports *Bengal*
 Marshall's Reports *Ceylon*
 Marshall's Reports (24–30 Kentucky)

Mar.Br. March's Brooke's New Cases
          Eng

Mar.Cas. Maritime Law Cases *Eng*

Mar.L.C. Maritime Law Reports
 (Crockford)

Mar.L.C.N.S. Maritime Law Cases,
 N.S., by Aspinall   *Eng*

Mar.L.J. Maryland Law Journal &
 Real Estate Record

Mar.L.Rec. Maryland Law Record

Mar.L.Rev. Maryland Law Review

Mar.(La.) Martin's Reports
 (Louisiana)

Mar.N.C. Martin's Reports (1 N. C.)
 March's New Cases, K. B. *Eng*

Mar.N.S. Martin's Reports, New
 Series   *La*

Mar.N.& Q. Maritime Notes &
 Queries

Mar.R. Maritime Law Reports

Mar.Reg. Mitchell's Maritime Register
          Eng

March. March's K. B. & Com. Pl.
 Reports   *Eng*
 March's Brooke's New Cases, K. B.
          Eng

March.N.C. March's New Cases,
 K.B. & Com. Pl.   *Eng*

Marine Ct.R. Marine Court Reporter
 (McAdam)   *N.Y.*

Marks & Sayre Marks & Sayre's Rep.
 (108 Ala.)

Marq.L.Rev. Marquette Law Review

Marr. Hay & Marriott's Admiralty
 Dec.   *Eng*
 Marrack's European Assurance Cases
          Eng

Mars. Marsden's Select Pleas in the
 Court of Admiralty (Selden
 Society Publications, v. 6, 11)

Marsh. Marshall's Reports, Bengal
         India
 Marshall's Circuit Court Decisions
          U.S.
 Marshall's Reports *Ceylon*
 Marshall's Common Pleas Reports
          Eng
 Marshall's Reports (8–10, 24–30 Ky.)
 Marshall's Reports (4 Utah)

Marsh.A.K. A. K. Marshall's Reports
 (8–10 Ky.)

Marsh.Beng. Marshall's Reports,
 Bengal   *India*

Marsh.C.P. Marshall's Common Pleas
 Rep.   *Eng*

Marsh.Calc. Marshall's Reports,
 Calcutta   *India*

Marsh.Dec. Marshall's Circuit Court
 Decisions, by Brockenbrough *U.S.*

Marsh.J.J. J. J. Marshall's Rep.
 (24–30 Ky.)

Marsh.Op. Marshall's Constitutional
 Opinions

Marshall Marshall's Reports, Bengal
         India

Mart.Ark. Martin's Decisions in
 Equity   *Ark*

Mart.Cond.La. Martin's Condensed
 Reports   *La*

Mart.Dec. (1 North Carolina; contains U. S. Circuit Court reports
 for N. C.)

Mart.Ga. Martin's Reports (21–30
 Georgia)

Mart.Ind. Martin's Reports (54–70 Indiana)

Mart.La. Martin's Reports (Louisiana, Old and New Series)

Mart.M.C. Martin's Mining Cases, B.C.   *Canada*

Mart.N.C. Martin's Reports (1 N. C.)

Mart.N.S. Martin's Louisiana Rep., New Ser.

Mart.O.S. Martin's Louisiana Rep., Old Ser.

Mart.U.S.C.C. Martin's Circuit Court Reports, in 1 North Carolina

Mart.& Yerg. Martin & Yerger's Rep. (8 Tenn.)

Martin. *See also* entries under Mart., *supra*

  Martin's Reports (21–30 Georgia)
  Martin's Reports (54–70 Georgia)
  Martin's Reports (La., 1809–30)
  Martin's Reports (1 N. C.)

Marvel Marvel's Reports (15, 16 Delaware)

Maryland Maryland Reports

Mas. Mason's Circuit Court Reports   *U.S.*

Mass. Massachusetts Reports

Mass.App.Div. Massachusetts Appellate Division Reports 1935-date

Mass.B.C.& A. Massachusetts Board of Conciliation & Arbitration Reports

Mass.B.T.A. Massachusetts Board of Tax Appeals

Mass.Elec.Ca. Massachusetts Election Cases

Mass.G.& E.L.C. Massachusetts Board of Gas & Electric Light Commissioners

Mass.I.A.B. Massachusetts Industrial Accident Board Reports of Cases

Mass.L.Q. Massachusetts Law Quarterly

Mass.L.R. Massachusetts Law Reporter

Mass.L.R.C.Dec. Massachusetts Labor Relations Commission Decisions

Mass.P.S.C. Massachusetts Public Service Commission

Mass.P.U.R. Massachusetts Public Utility Commission Reports

Mass.R.C. Massachusetts Board of Railroad Commissioners

Mass.St.B.C.& A. Massachusetts State Board of Conciliation & Arbitration Reports

Mass.U.C.C.Op. Massachusetts Unemployment Compensation Commission Opinions

Mass.U.C.Ops. Massachusetts Division of Unemployment Compensation Opinions

Mass.W.C.C. Massachusetts Workmen's Compensation Cases

Mast. Master's Supreme Court Reports   *Canade*

Math. Mathieu's Quebec Reports

Matson Matson's Reports (22–24 Connecticut)

Matthews Matthews' Reports (75 Virginia)
  Matthews' Reports (6–9 West Virginia)

Mau.& Sel. Maule & Selwyn's K. B. Rep.   *Eng*

Maur.Dec. Mauritius Decisions

May.L.R. Mayurbhanj Law Reporter   *India*

Mayn. Maynard's Reports, Exchequer Memoranda of Edw. I, & Year Books of Edw. II   *Eng*

Mc. *See also* Mac.

M'Cl. McCleland's Exchequer Reports   *Eng*

M'Cl.& Y. McCleland & Younge's Ex. Rep.   *Eng*

McCl.& Y. McCleland & Younge's Ex. Rep.   *Eng*

M'F.R. MacFarlane's Jury Court Rep.   *Scot*

M'Mul.Ch.S.C. M'Mullan's Equity Rep. (S. C. 1840–42)

M'Mul.L.S.C. M'Mullan's Law Reports (S. C. 1840–42)

Mc.Al. McAllister's Circuit Court Reports   *U.S.*

McAll. McAllister's Circuit Court Rep.   *U.S.*

McCah. McCahon's Reports (Kansas 1858–68)

McCahon Same as above

McCart. McCarter's Reports (14, 15 N. J. Eq.)
  McCarty's New York Civil Procedure Reports

McCl. McCleland's Exchequer Rep.   *Eng*

McCl.& Y. McCleland & Younge's Ex. Rep.   *Eng*

McClel. *See* McCl. *supra*

McCook McCook's Reports (1 Ohio State)

McCord   McCord's Reports (S. C. Law 1821–28)

McCord Ch.   McCord's Reports(S. C. Eq. 1825–27)

McCord Eq.   Same as above

McCorkle   McCorkle's Reports (65 N. C.)

McCr.   McCrary's Circuit Court Reports   *U.S.*

McDonnell   McDonnell's Sierra Leone Reports

McFar.   McFarlane's Jury Court Rep.   *Scot*

McGill   McGill's Manuscript Decisions, Court of Session *Scot*

McGl.   McGloin's Court of Appeal Rep.   *La*

Mc.L.   McLean's Circuit Court Reports   *U.S.*

McL.& R.   McLean & Robinson's Appeal Cas.   *Scot*

Mc M.Com.Cas.   McMaster's Commercial Cases   *U.S.*

McMul.   McMullan's Rep. (S. C. Law 1840–42)

McMul.Eq.   McMullan's Rep. (S. C. Eq. 1840–42)

McNagh.   McNaghten, under Macn., *supra*

McPherson   McPherson, Lee, & Bell's Session Cases   *Scot*

McQ.   McQueen's Scottish Appeals Cases

McWillie   McWillie's Reports (73–76 Miss.)

Md.   Maryland

Md.Ch.   Maryland Chancery Reports (*see* American Law Reports by States and Territories, Appendix I

Md.L.Rec.   Maryland Law Record

Md.L.Rev.   Maryland Law Review

Md.P.S.C.   Maryland Public Service Commission

Md.W.C.C.   Maryland Workmen's Compensation Cases

Me.   Maine

Me.P.U.C.   Maine Public Utilities Commission

Me.R.C.   Maine Railroad Commissioners

Med.Leg.& Crim.Rev.   Medico-Legal & Criminological Review

Med.Leg.Bul.   Medico-Legal Bulletin

Med.Leg.J.   Medico-Legal Journal

Meddaugh   Meddaugh's Reports (13 Michigan)

Mees.& Ros.   Meeson & Roscoe's Ex. Rep.   *Eng*

Mees.& Wels.   Meeson & Welsby's Ex. Rep.   *Eng*

Meg.   Megone's Companies Acts Cases   *Eng*

Meigs   Meigs' Reports (19 Tennessee)

Mem.L.J.   Memphis Law Journal

Memo.   Memorandum (Law Department, Southern Railway)

Men.   Menzie's Cape of Good Hope Reports

Menken   Menken's Reports (9 New York Civil Procedure Reports)

Menz.   Menzie's Cape of Good Hope Reports

Mer.   Merivale's Chancery Reports   *Eng*

Merc.Ad.& Law.& Credit Man   Mercantile Adjuster & Lawyer & Credit Man

Merc.L.J.   Mercantile Law Journal (New York or Madras)

Mercer B.L.Rev.   Mercer Beasley Law Review

Mercer L.Rev.   Mercer Law Review

Met [c].   Metcalf's Reports (42–54 Mass.)

   Metcalf's Reports (3 Rhode Island)
   Metcalfe's Reports (58–61 Kentucky)

Metc.Ky.   Metcalfe's Reports (58–61 Kentucky)

Metc.Mass.   Metcalf's Reports (42–54 Mass.)

Mews   The Reports (1893–95)   *Eng*
   Mews' Digest of English Case Law

Miami L.Q.   Miami Law Quarterly

Mich.   Michigan; Michaelmas Term

Mich.C.C.R.   Michigan Circuit Court Reporter

Mich.Jur. Michigan Jurisprudence

Mich.L.   Michigan Lawyer

Mich.L.J.   Michigan Law Journal

Mich.L.Rev.   Michigan Law Review

Mich.N.P.   Brown's or Howell's Michigan Nisi Prius Reports or Cases

Mich.P.U.C.Ops.   Michigan Public Utilities Commission Opinions

Mich.R.C.Dec.   Michigan Railroad Comm. Dec.

Mich.S.B.A.Jo.   Michigan State Bar Assn. Jour.

Mich.S.B.J.   Michigan State Bar Journal

Mich.W.C.C. Michigan Industrial Accident Board, Workmen's Compensation Cases

Mil.Rep. Militia Reporter

Miles Miles' District Court Reports (Philadelphia 1825–41)

Mill Mill's Constitutional Rep. *S.C.*

Mill. Miller's Reports (1–5 Louisiana) Miller's Reports (3–18 Maryland)

Mill Const. Mill's South Carolina Constitutional Reports

Mill.Dec. Miller's Circuit Court Decisions (Woolworth's) *U.S.* Miller's U. S. Supreme Court Decisions (condensed, continuation of Curtis)

Mill.La. Miller's Reports (1–5 Louisiana)

Mill.Md. Miller's Reports (3–18 Maryland)

Mill.Op. Miller's Circuit Court Decisions (Woolworth) *U.S.*

Miller Miller's Reports (1–5 Louisiana) Miller's Reports (3–18 Maryland)

Mills Mills' Surrogate Reports *N.Y.*

Mills'Surr.Ct. Mills' Surrogate Rep. *N.Y.*

Milw. Milward's Ecclesiastical Reports *Ir*

Milw.B.A.G. Wilwaukee Bar Assn. Gavel

Mim. Commissioner's Mimeographed Letter (Internal Revenue Bureau) *U.S.*

Min. Minor's Reports (Alabama 1820–26)

Minn. Minnesota

Minn.Ct.Rep. Minnesota Court Reporter

Minn.L.J. Minnesota Law Journal

Minn.L.Rev. Minnesota Law Review

Minn.R.& W.C. Minnesota Railroad & Warehouse Commission

Minn.S.B.A. Minnesota State Bar Association

Minn.W.C.D. Minnesota Workmen's Compensation Decisions

Minor Minor's Institutes Minor's Reports (Alabama 1820–26)

Mirch.D.& S. Mirchall's Doctor & Student

Misc. Miscellaneous Reports (N. J., N. Y.)

Misc.Dec. Ohio Miscellaneous Decisions (Gottschall 1865–73)

Miss. Mississippi

Miss.Dec. Mississippi Decisions

Miss.L.J. Mississippi Law Journal

Miss.L.Rev. Mississippi Law Review

Miss.R.C. Mississippi Railroad Commission

Miss.S.B.A. Mississippi State Bar Assn.

Miss.St.Ca. Morris' Mississippi State Cases (1818–72)

Mister Mister's Reports (17–32 Mo. Appeals)

Mitch.M.R. Mitchell's Maritime Register *Eng*

Mo. Missouri
Modern Reports 1669–1732 *Eng*
Moore's Privy Council Reports *Eng*
Moore's Common Pleas Reports *Eng*
Moore's Indian Appeal Cases
Moore's King's Bench Reports *Eng*

Mo.App. Missouri Appeals Reports

Mo.App.Rep. Missouri Appeals Reports

Mo.Bar Missouri Bar

Mo.Bar J. Missouri Bar Journal

Mo.Dec. Missouri Decisions

Mo.F. Francis Moore's King's Bench Rep. *Eng*

Mo.I.A. Moore's Indian Appeals

Mo.J.B. J. B. Moore's Com. Pl. Rep. *Eng*

Mo.Jur. Monthly Jurist

Mo.L.Mag. Monthly Law Magazine (*see* List of Anglo-American Legal Periodicals)

Mo.L.Rev. Missouri Law Review

Mo.Law Rep. Monthly Law Reporter

Mo.Leg.Exam. Monthly Legal Examiner

Mo.P.C. Moore's Privy Council Reports *Eng*

Mo.P.S.C.R. Missouri Public Service Commission Reports

Mo.R.& W.C. Missouri Railroad & Warehouse Commission

Mo.R.C. Missouri Railroad Commissioners

Mo.W.Jur. Monthly Western Jurist

Mo.& P. Moore & Payne's Com. Pl. Rep. *Eng*

Mo.& R. Moody & Robinson's N. P. Rep. *Eng*

Mo.& S. Moore & Scott's Com. Pl. Rep. *Eng*

Moak Eng.Rep. Moak's English Reports

Mob[1]. Mobley's Contested Election Cases, House of Representatives 1882–89

Mod. Modern Reports 1669–1732 *Eng*
Style's King's Bench Rep. 1646–55
Eng
Mod.Cas. Modern Cases (6 Modern Reports)
Mod.Cas.L.& Eq. Modern Reports, pts. 8, 9
Mod.Cas.per Far.(*t*.Holt) Modern Cases *temp.* Holt, by Farresby (6, 7 Modern Reports)
Mod.L.Rev. Modern Law Review
Mod.Rep. Modern Reports 1669–1732
Eng
Style's King's Bench Rep. 1646–55
Eng
Mol. Molloy's Chancery Reports *Ir*
Moll. Molloy's Chancery Reports *Ir*
Molloy's De Jure Maritimo
Moly. Molyneaux's Reports *temp.*
Car. I *Eng*
Mon. Monaghan's Unreported Cas. (Pa. Super.)
T. B. Monroe's Reports (17–23 Kentucky)
Montana
Mon.B. Monroe's Reports (40–57 Kentucky)
Mon.Law Mag. Monthly Law Magazine
Mon.Law Rep. Monthly Law Reporter
Mon.L.Rev.,Univ.of Detroit
Monthly Law Review of University of Detroit
Mon.T.B. T. B. Monroe's Reports (17–23 Ky.)
Mon.W.J. Monthly Western Jurist
Monag. Monaghan's Reports (147–65 Pa. St.)
Monaghan's Reports (Pa. 1888–90)
Monr. Monroe *See* Mon., *supra*
Monro Monro's Acta Cancellariae *Eng*
Mont. Montagu's Bankruptcy Reports
Eng
Montana
Montrion's Bengal Reports *India*
Mont.B.C. Montagu's Bankruptcy Rep. *Eng*
Mont.Cas. Montrion, Cases in Hindoo Law
Mont.Cond.Rep. Montreal Condensed Reports
Mont.D.& DeG. Montagu, Deacon, & DeGex, Bankruptcy Reports *Eng*
Mont.L.R. Montreal Law Reports
Mont.L.Rev. Montana Law Review

Mont.Leg.News Montreal Legal News
Mont.R.C. Montana Railroad Commission
Mont.& A[yr]. Montagu & Ayrton's Bankruptcy Reports *Eng*
Mont.& B.[1]. Montagu & Bligh's Bankruptcy Reports *Eng*
Mont.& Ch. Montagu & Chitty's Bankruptcy Reports *Eng*
Mont.& M. Montagu & MacArthur's Bankruptcy Reports *Eng*
Mont.Co.L.Rep. Montgomery County (Pa.) Law Reporter
Month.J.L. Monthly Journal of Law
Month.Jur. Monthly Jurist
Month.L.M. Monthly Law Magazine
Month.L.Rep. Monthly Law Reporter
Month.Leg.Ex. Monthly Legal Examiner
Month.West.Jur. Monthly Western Jurist
Montreal L.R.Q.B. Montreal Law Rep. Q. B.
Montreal L.R.S.C. Montreal Law Rep. Superior Court
Moo. Moody's Crown Cases Reserved
Eng
F. Moore's King's Bench Reports
J. B. Moore's Common Pleas Reports
Eng
Moo.A. Moore's Rep. (1 Bosanquet & Puller after p.470) *Eng*
Moo.C.C. Moody's Crown Cases Reserved *Eng*
Moo.C.P. J. B. Moore's Com. Pl. Reports *Eng*
Moo.Cr.C. Moody's Crown Cases Reserved *Eng*
Moo.F. F. Moore's King's Bench Reports *Eng*
Moo.Ind.App. Moore's Indian Appeal Cases
Moo.J.B. J. B. Moore's Com. Pl. Rep.
Eng
Moo.K.B. Moore's King's Bench Reports *Eng*
Moo.P.C. Moore's Privy Council Cases *Eng*
Moo.P.C.C. Moore's Privy Council Cases *Eng*
Moo.P.C.C.N.S. Moore's Privy Council Cases, New Series *Eng*
Moo.& Mal. Moody & Malkin's Nisi Prius Rep. *Eng*

Moo.& P [ay]. Moore & Payne's Com. Pl. Rep. *Eng*

Moo.& Rob. Moody & Robinson's Nisi Prius Reports *Eng*

Moo.& S. Moore & Scott's Com. Pl. Rep. *Eng*

Mood. Moody's Crown Cases Reserved *Eng*

Mood.C.C. Moody's Crown Cases Reserved *Eng*

Mood.& M [alk]. Moody & Malkin's Nisi Prius Reports *Eng*

Mood.& R. Moody & Robinson's Nisi Prius Rep. *Eng*

Moon Moon's Reports (133–144 Indiana; 6–14 Indiana Appeals)

Moore *See also* Moo., *supra*
Moore's Common Pleas Reports *Eng*
Moore's King's Bench Reports *Eng*
Moore's Privy Council Reports *Eng*
Moore's Reports (67 Alabama)
Moore's Reports (28–34 Arkansas)
Moore's Reports (22–24 Texas)

Moore.A. Moore's Reports (1 Bosanquet & Puller, after p.470) *Eng*

Moore C.P. Moore's Common Pleas Reports *Eng*

Moore E.I. Moore's East Indian Appeals

Moore G.C. Moore, Gorham Case (Privy Council) *Eng*

Moore Ind.App. Moore's Indian Appeals

Moore K.B. F. Moore's K. B. Reports *Eng*

Moore P.C. Moore's Privy Council Rep. *Eng*

Moore P.C.N.S. Moore's Privy Council Rep., New Series *Eng*

Moore Q.B. F. Moore's Queen's Bench Rep. *Eng*

Moore & P. Moore & Payne's Com. Pl. Rep. *Eng*

Moore & S. Moore & Scott's Com. Pl. Rep. *Eng*

Moore & Walker Moore & Walker's Rep. (22–24 Texas)

Moot Ct.Bull. University of Illinois Moot Court Bulletin

Mor. Morison's Dictionary of Court of Session Decisions *Scot*

Mor.Dic.or Dict. Same as above

Mor.Ia. Morris' Reports (Iowa 1839–46)

Mor.Miss. Morris' Reports (43–48 Miss.)

Mor.St.Ca. Morris' State Cases (Miss. 1818–72)

Mor.Supp. Morison's Dictionary, Court of Session Decisions, Supplement *Scot*

Mor.Syn. Morison's Synopsis, Session Cases

Morg.& W.L.J. Morgan & Williams Law Journal

Morr. Morrell's Bankruptcy Reports *Eng*
Morris' Reports (Iowa 1839–46)
Morris' Reports (5 California)
Morris' Reports *Jamaica*
Morris' Reports (23–26 Oregon)
Morris' Reports, Bombay *India*

Morr.B.C. Morrell's Bankruptcy Reports *Eng*

Morr.Bomb. Morris' Reports, Bombay *India*

Morr.Cal. Morris' Reports (5 California)

Morr.Jam. Morris' Reports *Jamaica*

Morr.M.R. Morrison's Mining Reports *U.S.*

Morr.Min.R. Same as above

Morr.Miss. Morris' Reports (43–48 Miss.)

Morr.St.Cas. Morris' State Cases (Miss.)

Morris. Morris' Reports (5 California)
Morris Reports (Iowa 1839–46)
Morris' Reports, Bombay *India*
Morris' Reports *Jamaica*
Morris' Reports (23–26 Oregon)
Morrissett's Reports (80, 98 Alabama)

Morris & Har. Morris & Harrington's Reports, Bombay *India*

Morse Exch.Rep. Morse's Exchequer Rep. *Can*

Morton Morton's Rep. Calcutta Sup. Ct. *India*

Mos. Moseley's Chancery Reports *Eng*

Moyle Moyle's Criminal Circulars *India*
Moyle's Entries 1658 *Eng*

Ms. Manuscript Reports or Decisions

Ms.D. Manuscript Decisions, Commissioner of Patents *U.S.*
Manuscript Decisions, Comptroller Gen. *U.S.*

Mu.Corp.Ca. Municipal Corporation Cases *U.S.*

Mu.Corp.Cir. Municipal Corporation Circular *Eng*

Mu.L.J. Municipal Law Journal

Mumf. Mumford's Reports   *Jamaica*

Mun. Munford's Reports (15–20 Virginia)

Mun.App. Munitions Appeals Reports   *Eng*

Mun.App.Rep. Same as above

Mun.App.Sc. Munitions of War Acts, Appeal Reports   *Scot*

Mun.Corp.Cas. Municipal Corporation Cases   *U.S.*

Mun.L.R. Municipal Law Reporter (Pa. 1909–)

Municipal Law Reports   *Scot*

Mun.Rep. Municipal Reports *Canada*

Mun.& El.Cas. Municipal & Election Cases   *India*

Munf. Munford's Reports (15–20 Virginia)

Munic.& P.L. Municipal & Parish Law Cases   *Eng*

Mur. Murphey's Reports (5–7 N. C.)

Murray's Reports   *Ceylon*

Murray's Reports New South Wales   *Aus*

Murray's Jury Court Reports   *Scot*

Mur.& Hurl. Murphy & Hurlstone's Ex. Rep.   *Eng*

Murd.Epit. Murdoch's Epitome *Canada*

Murph. Murphey's Reports (5–7 N. C.)

Murph.& H. Murphy & Hurlstone's Ex. Rep.   *Eng*

Murr. Murray's Reports   *Ceylon*

Murray's Jury Court Reports   *Scot*

Murray's Reports, New South Wales   *Aus*

Murr.Over.Cas. Murray's Overruled Cases   *U.S.*

Murray *See* Murr., *supra*

Mut. Mutukisna's Reports   *Ceylon*

My.& Cr. Mylne & Craig's Ch. Reports   *Eng*

My.& K. Mylne & Keen's Chancery Reports   *Eng*

Myer's Fed.Dec. Myer's Federal Dec.   *U.S.*

Myl.& Cr. Mylne & Craig's Ch. Reports   *Eng*

Myl.& K. Mylne & Keen's Chancery Rep.   *Eng*

Myr. Myrick's Probate Rep. (Cal. 1872–79)

Myr.Prob. Same as above

Mys.Ch.Ct. Mysore Chief Court Reports   *India*

Mys.H.C.R. Mysore High Court Reports   *India*

Mys.L.J. Mysore Law Journal

Mys.L.R. Mysore Law Reports   *India*

Mysore *See* Mys., *supra*

N. Nebraska; Nevada

Northern Ireland Law Reports

N.A. Nizamut Adalut Reports   *India*

N.A.C. Native Appeal Cases   *S.Af.*

NACA National Advisory Committee for Aeronautics   *U.S.*

NACCA Law Journal, National Assn. of Claimants' Compensation Attorneys

N.A.C.& O. Cape & Orange Free State Native Appeal Court, Selected Decisions

N.A.& D.T.& N. Transvaal & Natal Native Appeal & Divorce Court Decisions

N.A.M.L.Dig. National Association of Manufacturers Law Digest

N.A.So.Rhod. Southern Rhodesia Native Appeal Court, Reports

NATO North Atlantic Treaty Organization

N.B. New Brunswick

New Benloe (or Bendloe) K. B. Reports   *Eng*

N.B.Eq. New Brunswick Equity Reports

N.B.Eq.Ca. New Brunswick Equity Cases

N.B.Eq.Rep. New Brunswick Equity Reports

N.B.J. National Bar Journal

N.B.L.R. North Borneo Law Reports

N.B.N.R. National Bankruptcy News & Reports

N.B.R. New Brunswick Reports

National Bankruptcy Register Reports   *U.S.*

N.B.R.All. Allen's New Brunswick Reports

N.B.R.Ber. Berton's New Brunwsick Reports

N.B.R.Carl. Carleton's New Brunswick Reports

N.B.R.Chip. Chipman's New Brunswick Reports

N.B.R.Han. Hannay's New Brunswick Reports

N.B.R.Kerr Kerr's New Brunswick Reports

N.B.R.P.& B. Pugsley & Burbridge's New Brunswick Reports

N.B.R.P.& T. Pugsley & Trueman's New Brunswick Reports

N.B.R.Pug. Pugsley's New Brunswick
Reports
N.B.R.Tru. Trueman's New Brunswick Reports
N.B.Rep. New Brunswick Reports
N.B.S. National Bureau of Standards
          U.S.
N.B.V.Ad. New Brunswick Vice-Admiralty Rep.
N.Benl. New Benloe's King's Bench
Rep.   *Eng*
N.C. Notes of Cases (Eccles. &
Maritime)   *Eng*
 Notes of Cases (Australian Jurist)
 Notes of Cases, T. Strange, Madras
          India
 North Carolina Reports
N.C.& B. Naval Courts and Boards
          U.S.
N.C.C. New Chancery Cases (Younge
& Collyer)   *Eng*
N.C.C.A. Negligence & Compensation
Cases, Annotated
N.C.C.C. North Carolina Corporation
Comm.
N.C.Conf. North Carolina Conference
Rep.
N.C.Ecc. Notes of Cases in Ecclesiastical & Maritime Courts *Eng*
N.C.F.A. National Consumers'
Finance Assn. Law Bulletin
N.C.J.of L. North Carolina Journal of
Law
N.C.L.Rep. North Carolina Law
Repository
N.C.L.Rev. North Carolina Law
Review
N.C.Law Repos. North Carolina Law
Repository
NCM Navy Board of Review
Decisions   *U.S.*
 Court-Martial Reports, Navy Cases
N.C.Str. Strange's Notes of Cases,
Madras
N.C.T.Rep. North Carolina Term
Rep. (4 N. C.)
N.C.U.C. North Carolina Utilities
Commission Reports
N.Car. North Carolina
N.Ch.R. Nelson's Chancery Reports
         Eng
 H. Finch's Chancery Reports 1673–81
         Eng
N.Chip. N. Chipman's Reports (Vt.
1789–91)
N.D. North Dakota
NDA National Defense Act   *U.S.*

NDB Navy Department Bulletin *U.S.*
N.D.B.B. North Dakota Bar Brief
N.D.L.Rev. North Dakota Law
Review
N.E. North Eastern Reporter,
National Reporter System
N.E.2d Same as above, Second Series
N.E.C. Notes of Ecclesiastical Cases
         Eng
N.Eng.Rep. New England Reporter
N.F. Newfoundland
NFLA National Farm Loan Association   *U.S.*
NGR National Guard Regulation
N.H. New Hampshire
NH Act National Housing Act
N.H.C. Native High Court Reports
         S.Af.
N.H.L.Rep. New Hampshire Law
Reporter
N.H.R. New Hampshire Reports
N.H.& C. Railway & Canal Cases
 1835–55   *Eng*
N.Hamp.S.B.A. New Hampshire
State Bar Assn.
N.I. Northern Ireland Law Reports
N.I.J. New Irish Jurist
N.I.J.R. New Irish Jurist Reports
N.I.R.A National Industrial Recovery
Act
N.I.T.M. National Income Tax
Magazine
N.J. New Jersey
N.J.Eq. New Jersey Equity Reports
N.J.F.D. Notices of Judgment, U. S.
Food & Drug Administration
N.J.L.J. New Jersey Law Journal
N.J.L.Rev. New Jersey Law Review
N.J.L[aw] New Jersey Law Reports
N.J.Misc. New Jersey Miscellaneous
Reports
N.J.Re.Tit.N. New Jersey Realty
Title News
N.J.S.B.A. New Jersey State Bar
Association
N.J.S.B.T.A.Ops. New Jersey State
Board of Tax Appeals, Opinions
N.J.Super. New Jersey Superior
Court Reports
NL Lutwych's Com. Pl. Rep.
(Nelson)   *Eng*
N.L.G.Q. National Lawyers' Guild
Quarterly
N.L.J. Nagpur Law Journal *India*
N.L.R. Nagpur Law Reports *India*
 Natal Law Reports   *S.Af.*
 New Law Reports   *Ceylon*

N.L.R.B. National Labor Relations
Board *U.S.*

N.L.Rev. Northeastern Law Review

N.M. New Mexico

NMB National Mediation Board

N.M.S.B.A. New Mexico State Bar
Assn.

N.Mag.Ca. New Magistrates' Cases
Eng

N.of Cas. Notes of Cases, Ecclesiastical
& Maritime Courts *Eng*
Notes of Cases, Madras, by T. Strange

N.P. Nisi Prius

NPA National Production Authority
U.S.

N.P.C. Nisi Prius Cases *Eng*

N.P.D. South African Law Reports,
Natal Provinces Division

N.P.N.S. Ohio Nisi Prius Rep., New
Series

N.P.Ohio Ohio Nisi Prius Reports

N.P.R. Nisi Prius Reports

N.R. Bosanquet & Puller's New
Reports *Eng*
The New Reports 1862–65 *Eng*
Natal Reports *S.Af.*

NRA National Recovery Administration *U.S.*

N.R.A.B. National Railroad Adjustment Awards

N.R.B.P. Bosanquet & Puller's New
Reports *Eng*

N.S. New Series; Nova Scotia

N.S.A. National Shipping Authority
U.S.

N.S.C. National Security Council *U.S.*
New Session Cases *Scot*

N.S.Dec. Nova Scotia Decisions

N.S.L.R. Nova Scotia Law Reports

NSMCM Naval Supplement, Manual
for Courts-Martial, 1951 *U.S.*

N.S.R. Nova Scotia Reports

N.S.R.B. National Security Resources
Board *U.S.*

N.S.R.Coh. Cohen's Nova Scotia
Reports

N.S.R.G.& O. Nova Scotia Reports,
Geldert & Oxley

N.S.R.G.& R. Nova Scotia Reports,
Geldert & Russell

N.S.R.James James' Nova Scotia
Reports

N.S.R.Old. Oldbright's Nova Scotia
Reports

N.S.R.R.&C. Russell & Chesley's Nova
Scotia Reports

N.S.R.R.& G. Russell & Geldert's
Nova Scotia Reports

N.S.R.Thom. Thomson's Nova Scotia
Reports

N.S.W. New South Wales

N.S.W.Adm. New South Wales Rep.,
Admiralty

N.S.W.B.(or Bktcy.Cas.) New South
Wales Reports, Bankruptcy Cases

N.S.W.C.RD. New South Wales
Court of Review Decisions

N.S.W.Eq. New South Wales Equity
Reports

N.S.W.Ind.Arbtn.Cas. New South
Wales Industrial Arbitration
Cases

N.S.W.L.R. New South Wales Law
Reports

N.S.W.Land App.Cts. New South
Wales Land Appeal Courts

N.S.W.C.Eq. New South Wales
Reports, Equity

N.S.W.C.R.L. New South Wales Law
Reports (Supreme Court)

N.S.W.S.C.R.N.S. Same as above,
New Series

N.S.W.St.R. New South Wales State
Reports

N.S.W.W.N. New South Wales
Weekly Notes

N.Sc.Dec. Nova Scotia Decisions

N.T.Rep. New Term Reports,
Queen's Bench *Eng*

N.W. North Western Reporter
(National Reporter System)
North-Western Provinces, High
Court Reports *India*

N.W.Law Rev. Northwestern Law
Review

N.W.P. North-Western Provinces
High Court Reports *India*

N.W.P.H.C. North-Western
Provinces, High Court Reports
India

N.W.T.R[ep]. North-West Territories Reports *Canada*

N.W.U.L.Rev. Northwestern University Law Review

N.Y. New York

N.Y.Anno.Cas. New York Annotated
Cases

N.Y.App.Dec. New York Court of
Appeals Decisions
New York Appellate Division
Decisions

N.Y.C.B.A.Bull. Bulletin of the Association of the Bar of the City of New York

N.Y.Cas.Err. Caines' New York Cases in Error

NY.Ch.Sent. New York Chancery Sentinel

N.Y.City Ct.Rep. New York City Court Rep.

N.Y.City H.Rec. New York City Hall Recorder

N.Y.Civ.Proc.R. New York Civil Procedure Rep.

N.Y.Civ.Proc.R.N.S. Same as above, New Ser.

N.Y.Code Reptr. New York Code Reporter

N.Y.Code Reptr.N.S. Same as above, New Ser.

N.Y.Cond. New York Condensed Reports 1881–82

N.Y.Cr.R. New York Criminal Reports 1878–1924

N.Y.Ct.App. New York Court of Appeals (highest court)

N.Y.Daily Tr. New York Daily Transcript, Old and New Series

N.Y.E.T.R. New York Estate Tax Reports (P–H)

N.Y.El.Cas. New York Contested Election Cases (Armstrong, Baxter)

N.Y.Jud.Rep. New York Judicial Repository

N.Y.Jur. New York Jurist

N.Y.L.J. New York Law Journal

N.Y.L.R.B. New York State Labor Relations Board and Decisions

N.Y.L.Rev. New York Law Review

N.Y.L.S.Rev. New York Law School Review

N.Y.L.S.Stud.L.Rev. New York Law School Student Law Review

N.Y.Law Gaz. New York Law Gazette

N.Y.Law J. New York Law Journal

N.Y.Law Rev. New York Law Review

N.Y.Leg.N. New York Legal News 1880–82

N.Y.Leg.Obs. New York Legal Observer

N.Y.Leg.Reg. New York Legal Register 1850

N.Y.Misc. New York Miscellaneous Reports

N.Y.Mo.L.Bul. New York Monthly Law Bulletin

N.Y.Mo.L.Rec. New York Monthly Law Record

N.Y.Mun.Gaz. New York Municipal Gazette

N.Y.Off.Dept.R. New York Official Department Reports

N.Y.Pr. New York Practice Reports (various reporters)

N.Y.Rec. New York Record

N.Y.Reg. New York Daily Register 1872–89

N.Y.Rep. New York Reports (Court of Appeals)

N.Y.Reptr. New York Reporter (Gardenier 1820)

N.Y.S. New York State Reporter New York Supplement

N.Y.S.B.A.Bull. New York State Bar Assn. Bul.

N.Y.S.B.Bull. New York State Bar Assn. Bul.

N.Y.S.D.R. New York State Department Rep.

NY.Spec.Term.Rep. Howard's Practice Rep.

N.Y.St.R. New York State Reporter 1886–96

N.Y.Super.Ct. New York Superior Court Reports (various reporters)

N.Y.Supp. New York Supplement

N.Y.Supr.Ct. New York Supreme Court Reports

N.Y.Tax Cas. New York Tax Cases (CCH)

N.Y.T.R. New York Term Reports (Caines)

N.Y.Trans. New York Transcript 1861

N.Y.Trans.Rep. New York Transcript Reports

N.Y.Trans.N.S. New York Transscript Rep. N. S.

N.Y.U.L.Qu.Rev. New York University Law Quarterly Review

N.Y.U.L.Rev. New York University Law Review

N.Y.Week.Dig. New York Weekly Digest

N.Z. New Zealand

N.Z.App.Rep. New Zealand Appeal Reports

N.Z.Col.L.J. New Zealand Colonial Law Jour.

N.Z.Gaz.L.R. New Zealand Gazette Law Rep.

N.Z.Ind.Arb. New Zealand Industrial Arbitration Awards

N.Z.Jur. New Zealand Jurist

N.Z.Jur.N.S. Above, New Series

N.Z.L.J. New Zealand Law Journal

N.Z.L.J.M.C. New Zealand Law Journal, Magistrates' Court Decisions

N.Z.L.R. New Zealand Law Reports

N.Z.L.R.C.A. New Zealand Law Reports, Court of Appeal

N.Z.P.C.C. New Zealand Privy Council Cases

N.Z.Rep. New Zealand Reports, Court of Appeals

N.& H. Nott & Huntington's Reports (1–7 U. S. Court of Claims)

N.& Hop. Nott & Hopkins' Reports (8–29 U. S. Court of Claims)

N.& M. Nevile & Manning's K. B. Reports   *Eng*

N.& Mc. Nott & McCord's Rep. (S. C. Law)

N.& M.Mag. Nevile & Manning's Magistrates' Cases   *Eng*

N.& P. Nevile & Perry's K. B. Reports   *Eng*

N.& S. Nicholls & Stops' Reports   *Tasmania*

N.Bruns. New Brunswick Reports

N.Ch.R. Nelson's Chancery Reports   *Eng*

Nacca L.J. Nacca Law Journal: National Assn. of Claimants' Compensation Attorneys

Nag.L.J. Nagpur Law Journal *India*

Nag.L.R. Nagpur Law Reports *India*

Napton Napton's Reports (4 Missouri)

Narr.Mod. Narrationes Modernae (Style's K. B. Reports 1646–55)   *Eng*

Nat.B.C. National Bank Cases *U.S.*

Nat.B.J. National Bar Journal

Nat.B.R. National Bankruptcy Register   *U.S.*

Nat.Bar.J. National Bar Journal

Nat.Corp.Rep. National Corporation Reporter

Nat.Inc.Tax Mag. National Income Tax Mag.

Nat.J.Leg.Ed. National Journal of Legal Education

Nat.L.R. Natal Law Reports

Nat.L.Rep. National Law Reporter

Nat.L.Rev. National Law Review

Nat.Law Guild Q. National Lawyers' Guild Quarterly

Nat.Mun.Rev. National Municipal Review

Nat.Rept.Syst. National Reporter System

Nat.Tax.J. National Tax Journal

Nat.Tax Mag. National Tax Magazine

Nat.U.L.Rev. National University Law Review

Nd. Newfoundland

Neb. Nebraska

Neb.Bd.R.C. Nebraska Board of Railroad Commissioners

Neb.Bd.Trans. Nebraska Board of Transportation

Neb.L.B. Nebraska Law Bulletin

Neb.L.Rev. Nebraska Law Review

Neb.Leg.N. Nebraska Legal News

Neb.S.R.C. Nebraska State Railway Comm.

Neb.Unoff. Nebraska Unofficial Rep. 1901–04

Neb.W.C.C. Nebraska Workmen's Compensation Court Bulletin

Need. Needham's Annual Summary of Tax Cases   *Eng*

Neg.C. Negligence Cases (CCH)

Neg.Cas. Bloomfield's Manumission (or Negro) Cases   *N.J.*

Nel. Nelson's Chancery Reports *Eng* H. Finch's Chancery Reports   *Eng*

Nel.C.R. Nelson's Chancery Reports   *Eng*

Nell Nell's Reports   *Ceylon*

Nels. Nelson's Chancery Reports *Eng* H. Finch's Chancery Reports   *Eng*

Nels.Fol.Rep. H. Finch's Chancery Reports, by Nelson   *Eng*

Nev. Nevada

Nev.P.S.C.Op. Nevada Public Service Commission Opinions

Nev.R.C. Nevada Railroad Commission

Nev.S.B.J. Nevada State Bar Journal

Nev.& M.K.B. Nevile & Manning's K. B. Rep.

Nev.& M.M.C. Nevile & Manning's Magistrates' Cases   *Eng*

Nev.& P. Nevile & Perry's K. B. Rep.   *Eng*

Nevile & Perry's Magistrates' Cases   *Eng*

Nev.& Mac. Neville & Macnamara's Railway Cases   *Eng*

Nev.& Man. Nevile & Manning's K. B. Reports

Nev.& Man.Mag.Cas. Nevile & Manning's Magistrates' Cases *Eng*

Nev.& McN. Neville & McNamara's Railway Cases   *Eng*

New. Newell's Reports (48–90 Illinois App.)

New B.Eq.Ca. New Brunswick Equity Cases

New Benl. Benloe's K. B. Rep. 1531–1628   *Eng*

New Br. New Brunswick Reports

New Cas. Bingham's New Cases, Com. Pl.   *Eng*

New Cas.Eq. New Cases in Equity (8, 9 Modern Reports)   *Eng*

New Mag.Cas. New Magistrates' Cases (Bittleston, Wise, Parnell)   *Eng*

New Ir.Jur. New Irish Jurist & Local Government Review

New Jersey L.J. New Jersey Law Journal

New Jersey L.Rev. New Jersey Law Review

New Jersey Leg.Rec. New Jersey Legal Record

New Jersey S.B.A.Qu. New Jersey State Bar Association Quarterly

New Mag.Cas. New Magistrates' Cases (Bittleston, Wise, Parnell)   *Eng*

New Pr.Cas. New Practice Cases 1844–48   *Eng*

New Rep. New Reports 1862–65 *Eng* Bosanquet & Puller's New Reports (4, 5 Bosanquet & Puller)   *Eng*

New Sess.Cas. New Sessions Cases (Carrow, Hamerton, Allen) *Eng*

New Term.Rep. New Term Reports (East)   *Eng* Dowling & Tyland's King's Bench Rep.   *Eng*

New York *See* N. Y., *supra*

New Zeal.Jur.R. New Zealand Jurist Reports

New Zeal.L.J. New Zealand Law Journal

New Zeal.L.R. New Zealand Law Reports

Newark L.Rev. University of Newark Law Rev.

Newb. Newberry's Admiralty Reports   *U.S.*

Newbon Newbon's Private Bills Reports   *Eng*

Newbyth Newbyth's Manuscript Decisions, Session Cases   *Scot*

Newell Newell's Reports (48–90 Illinois App.)

Newf. Newfoundland

Newf.Sel.Cas. Newfoundland Select Cases

Newfld.L.R. Newfoundland Law Reports

Newfoundl.R. Newfoundland Reports

Nfld.L.R. Newfoundland Law Reports

Ni

Nic.H.& C. Nicholl, Hare & Carrow's English Railway & Canal Cases

Nicholson Nicholson's Manuscript Decisions, Session Cases   *Scot*

Nicolas Proceedings & Ordinances of the Privy Council, ed. Harry Nicolas

Nig.L.J. Nigerian Law Journal

Nigeria L.R. Nigeria Law Reports

Nisbet Dirleton's Decisions, Court of Session 1665–77   *Scot*

No.Ca.Ecc.& Mar. Notes of Cases, Ecclesiastical & Maritime   *Eng*

No.Ca.S.B.A. North Carolina State Bar Assn.

Noble Noble's Current Court Decisions   *N.Y.*

Nol. Nolan's Magistrates' Cases *Eng* Nolan's Settlement Cases   *Eng*

Nonacq.(or NA) Nonacquiescence by Commissioner in a Tax Court or Board of Tax Appeals decision   *U.S.*

Norc. Norcross' Reports (23, 24 Nevada)

Norris Norris' Reports (82–96 Pa. State)

North. Eden's Chancery Reports *Eng* Reports *temp.* Northington, by Eden   *Eng*

North.Co.Rep. Northampton County Reporter   *Pa*

North & G. North & Guthrie's Reports (68–80 Missouri Appeals)

Northam. Northampton Law Reporter   *Pa*

Northam.L.Rep. Same as above

Northum. Northumberland County Legal News   *Pa*

Northum.Co.Leg.N. Same as above

Northumb.L.N. Northumberland Legal Journal   *Pa*

Northw.L.J. Northwestern Law Journal

Northw.L.Rev. Northwestern University Law Review

Northw.Pr. North-West Provinces *India*

Not.Cas. Notes of Cases, Ecclesiastical & Maritime *Eng*
Notes of Cases at Madras, T. Strange *India*

Not.Cas.Ecc.& M. Notes of Cases, Ecclesiastical & Maritime *Eng*

Not.J. Notaries' Journal

Notes of Cases Notes of Cases, Ecclesiastical & Maritime *Eng*

Notre Dame Law. Notre Dame Lawyer

Nott & Hop. Nott & Hopkins' Reports (8–15 U. S. Court of Claims)

Nott & Hunt. Nott & Huntington's Reports (1–7 U. S. Court of Claims)

Nott & McC. Nott & McCord's Rep. (S. C. Law)

Nov.Sc. Nova Scotia

Nov.Sc.Dec. Nova Scotia Decisions

Nov.Sc.L.R. Nova Scotia Law Reports

Noy Noy's King's Bench Reports *Eng*

Ny.L.R. Nyasaland Law Reports *S.Af.*

Nye Nye's Reports (18–21 Utah)

O. Ohio; Oregon; Ontario
Otto's Reports (91–107 U. S.)
Solicitor's Law Opinion (U. S. Internal Revenue Bureau)

O.A. Oudh Appeals *India*

O.A.G. Opinions of Attorney General *U.S.*

OAP Office of Alien Property

O.A.R. Ontario Appeal Reports
Ohio Appeals 1913–date

OAS Organization of American States *UN*

O.B. Official Bulletin, International Commission for Air Navigation

O.B.S.P. Old Bailey Session Papers *Eng*

O.B.& F. Ollivier, Bell, & Fitzgerald's Court of Appeal Reports *New Zealand*

O.Bar. Ohio State Bar Assn. Reports

O.Ben. Old Benloe Common Pleas Reports *Eng*

O.Bridg. Carter's Reports *temp.* Bridgman, Common Pleas Reports *Eng*
Orlando Bridgman's Common Pleas Rep. *Eng*

O.C. Oudh Cases *India*
Ordres du Conseil *Jersey*

O.C.A. Ohio Courts of Appeal Rep. 1915–22

O.C.C. Ohio Circuit Reports or Decisions

O.C.C.N.S. Ohio Circuit Court Reports, New Series 1903–17

O.C.D. Ohio Circuit Court Decisions 1901–18

OCF Office, Chief of Finance, Army *U.S.*

O.Cr.C. Oudh Criminal Cases *India*

O.C.S. Office of Contract Settlement *U.S.*

O.D. Office Decision (U. S. Internal Revenue Bureau)
Ohio Decisions 1894–1920

ODC Office of Domestic Commerce *U.S.*

O.D.C.C. Ohio Decisions, Circuit Court

ODM Office of Defense Mobilization *U.S.*

O.Dec.Rep. Ohio Decisions Reprint

O.Dep.Rep. Ohio Department Reports

O.E.C. Ontario Election Decisions

OEEC Organization of European Economic Cooperation

OEM Office for Emergency Management *U.S.*

O.F.D. Ohio Federal Decisions

O.F.S. Orange Free State High Court Rep. *S.Af.*

O.G.(or O.G.Pat.Off.) Official Gazette, U. S. Patent Office

OIT Office of International Trade *U.S.*

O.Jur. Ohio Jurisprudence

O.L.Abs. Ohio Law Abstract

O.L.B. Ohio Law Bulletin

O.L.D. Ohio Lower Court Decisions

O.L.J. Ohio Law Journal
Oudh Law Journal *India*

O.L.N. Ohio Legal News

O.L.R. Ontario Law Reporter
Ontario Law Reports
Oudh Law Reports *India*

O.L.Rep. Ohio Law Reporter

O'M.& H. O'Malley & Hardcastle's Election Petitions Reports *Eng*

OMGUS Office of Military Gov't., U. S. Zone, Germany

O.N.P. Ohio Nisi Prius Reports 1894–1901

O.N.P.N.S. Ohio Nisi Prius Rep. New Series 1903–1913

OPA Office of Price Administration *U.S.*

O.P.D. South African Law Reports, Orange Free State Provincial Division

O.P.R. Ontario Practice Reports

O.P.S. Office of Price Stabilization *U.S.*
Official Public Service Reports *N.Y.*

O.R. Official Reports, South Africa Ontario Reports

O.R.C. Orange River Colony High Ct. Rep. *S.Af.*

ORS Office of Rent Stabilization *U.S.*

O.R.S.A.R. Official Reports, South African Republic

O.S. Ohio State Reports
Upper Canada Queen's Bench Rep., Old Ser.

O.S.C.D. Ohio Supreme Court Decisions, Unreported Cases

O.S.L.J. Law Journal of Student Bar Assn., Ohio State University

OSS Office of Strategic Services *U.S.*

O.St. Ohio State Reports

O.Supp. Ohio Supplement

O.S.U. Ohio Supreme Court Decisions, Unreported Cases

O.U.U.I. Office of the Umpire Decisions, Out-of-Work Claims, Unemployment Insurance *Eng*

O.U.U.I.B.D. Benefit Decisions of the British Umpire

O.U.U.I.D. Umpire Decisions, Benefit Claims *Eng*

O.U.U.I.S.D. Benefit & Donation Claims, Selected Decisions of Umpire *Eng*

OWM Office of War Mobilization *U.S.*

O.W.N. Ontario Weekly Notes
Oudh Weekly Notes *India*

O.W.R. Ontario Weekly Reporter

O'Brien O'Brien's Upper Canada Reports

O'Mal.&H. O'Malley & Hardcastle's Election Cases *Eng*

Occ.N. Occasional Notes, Canada Law Times

Odeneal Odeneal's Reports (9–11 Oregon)

Off.Gaz.Pat.Off. Official Gazette, U. S. Patent Office

Off.Jl.Pat. Official Journal of Patents *Eng*

Off.Rep. Transvaal High Court Official Rep.

Officer Officer's Reports (1–9 Minnesota)

Ogden Ogden's Reports (12–15 Louisiana)

Ohio App. Ohio Appeals 1913–date

Ohio Bar Ohio State Bar Assn. Report

Ohio C.C. Ohio Circuit Court Reports

Ohio C.C.Dec. Ohio Circuit Court Decisions

Ohio C.C.N.S. Ohio Circuit Court Rep., N. S.

Ohio Cir.Ct.N.S. Same as above

Ohio Cir.Ct.R. Ohio Circuit Court Reports

Ohio Cir.Dec. Ohio Circuit Court Decisions

Ohio Dec. Ohio Decisions 1894–1920

Ohio L.B. Ohio Law Bulletin

Ohio L.J. Ohio Law Journal

Ohio L.R. Ohio Law Reporter

Ohio L.R.&Wk.Bul. Ohio Law Reporter & Weekly Bulletin

Ohio Leg.N. Ohio Legal News

Ohio Misc.Dec. Ohio Miscellaneous Decisions

Ohio N.P. Ohio Nisi Prius Reports

Ohio N.P.N.S. Ohio Nisi Prius Reports N. S.

Ohio Op. Ohio Opinions

Ohio P.S.C. Ohio Public Service Comm.

Ohio P.U.C. Ohio Public Utilities Comm.

Ohio Prob. Ohio Probate Reports by Goebel

Ohio R.C. Ohio Railroad Commission

Ohio R.Cond. Ohio Reports Condensed

Ohio S.B.A. Ohio State Bar Association

Ohio S.L.J. Ohio State Law Journal

Ohio St. Ohio State Reports

Ohio Sup.& C.P.Dec. Ohio Superior Common Pleas Decisions

Ohio Unrept.Cas. Ohio Unreported Cases (Pollack)

Oil & Gas Tax.Q. Oil & Gas Tax Quarterly

O'Keefe Ord. O'Keefe's Orders in Ch. *Ir*

Okla.Ap.Ct.Rep. Oklahoma Appellate Court Reporter

Okla.B.A.J. The Journal, Oklahoma Bar Assn.

Okla.C.C. Oklahoma Corporation
Commission

Okla.Crim. Oklahoma Criminal
Reports

Okla.I.C.R. Oklahoma Industrial
Commission Reports

Okla.L.J. Oklahoma Law Journal

Okla.L.Rev. Oklahoma Law Review

Olc. Olcott's District Reports
(Admiralty) *U.S.*

Olc.Adm. Same as above

Old. Oldright's Reports (5, 6 Nova
Scotia)

Old Bailey Chr. Old Bailey Chronicle

Old Ben. Benloe in Benloe & Dalison's
Common Pleas Reports *Eng*

Old.S.C. Old Select Cases (Oudh)
India

Oliv.B.& L. Oliver, Beavan, &
Lefroy's Reports (Railway &
Canal Cas. 5–7) *Eng*

Oll.B.&F. Olliver, Bell, & Fitzgerald's Reports *New Zealand*

O'M.& H. O'Malley & Hardcastle's
Election Cases *Eng*

Ont. Ontario *Canada*

Ont.App. Ontario Appeal Reports

Ont.Dig. Digest of Ontario Case Law

Ont.El.Cas. Ontario Election Cases

Ont.L.Rep. Ontario Law Reports

Ont.Pr.Rep. Ontario Practice Reports

Ont.R. Ontario Reports

Ont.Wkly.Rep. Ontario Weekly
Reporter

Op.CCCG. Opinion, Chief Counsel,
U. S. Coast Guard

Op.GCT Opinion, General Counsel,
U. S. Treasury Department

Op.JAGAF. Opinion, Judge Advocate
General, U. S. Air Force

Op.JAGN. Opinion, Judge Advocate
General, U. S. Navy

Ops.A.G. Opinions, Attorney General

Ops.J.A.G. Opinions, Judge Advocate
General, U. S. Army

Or. Oregon

Or.R.C. Oregon Railroad Commission

Or.T.Rep. Orleans Term Reports
(Martin, La.)

Ord.Con.Jer. Ordes du Conseil
Enregistrés à Jersey

Oreg. Oregon

Oreg.L.Rev. Oregon Law Review

Orl.Bridgman Orlando Bridgman's
Common Pleas Reports *Eng*

Orl.T.R. Martin's Orleans Term
Reports *La*

Ormond Ormond's Reports (19–107
Alabama)

Otto Otto's Supreme Court Rep.
(91–107 U. S.)

Oudh L.R. Oudh Law Reports *India*

Oudh Wkly.N. Oudh Weekly Notes
India

Out. Outerbridge's Rep. (97–110 Pa.
St.)

Over. Overton's Reports (1–2
Tennessee)

Ow. New South Wales Reports, v.1–3
Aus

Owen's King's Bench Reports *Eng*

Owen's Common Pleas Reports *Eng*

Oxley Young's Vice-Admiralty
Decisions, ed. Oxley *Nova Scotia*

P. Law Reports, Probate, Divorce, &
Admiralty, since 1890 *Eng*

Pacific Reporter

Pennsylvania

Peters' (26–41 U. S. Reports)

Pickering (18–41 Massachusetts)

P&S Production & Subsistence *U.S.*

PAD Petroleum Administration for
Defense *U.S.*

P.A.D. Peters' Admiralty Decisions
U.S.

PASO Pan-American Sanitary
Organization

PAU Pan-American Union

P.B.S. Public Buildings Service *U.S.*

P.C. Pleas of the Crown; Parliamentary
Cases; Patent Cases; Practice
Cases; Prize Cases; Privy Council;
Probate Court; Precedents in
Chancery

Price Control Cases 1942–date

P.C.A. Acts of the Privy Council *Eng*

P.C.App. Law Reports, Privy Council
Appeals *Eng*

P.C.C. Privy Council Cases *Eng*

Privy Council Cases

Peters' Circuit Court Reports *U.S.*

P.C.I. Privy Council Decisions *India*

PCIJ Permanent Court of International Justice

P.C.Int. Pacific Coast International

P.C.L.J. Pacific Coast Law Journal

PCOB Permanent Central Opium
Board *UN*

P.C.R. Parker's Criminal Reports *N.Y.*

Pennsylvania Corporation Reporter

P.C.Rep. Privy Council Reports *Eng*

P.Cas. Prize Cases 1914–22 *Eng*

Prize Cases (Trehearn, Grant) *Eng*

P.D. Law Reports, Probate Division
Eng

P.D.A. Probate, Divorce, & Admiralty
Eng

PDC Price Decontrol Board *U.S.*

P.E.I. Prince Edward Island Reports
Canada

P.F.S. P. F. Smith's Rep. (51–81 Pa.
State)

P.-H. Prentice-Hall
Prentice-Hall Weekly Reports
Prentice-Hall Legal Service

PHA Public Housing Administration
U.S.

P.H.C.C. Punjab High Court Cases
India

P.-H.Cas. American Federal Tax
Reports (P-H)

P.-H.N.Y.E.T.R. Prentice-Hall New
York Estate Tax Reports

PHS Public Health Service *U.S.*

P.-H.Unrep.Tr.Cas. Prentice-Hall
Unreported Trust Cases

P.I.C.A.O. Provisional International
Civil Aviation Organization *UN*

P.J. Bombay High Court, Printed
Judgments

P.J.L.B. Lower Burma, Printed
Judgments

P.Jr.& H. Patton, Jr., & Heath's
Reports (Va. Special Court of
Appeals)

P.L. Public Law

P.L.J. Patna Law Journal *India*

PLO Public Land Order *U.S.*

P.L.R. Pennsylvania Law Record
Private Legislation Reports *Scot*
Punjab Law Reporter *India*

P.L.R.J.& K. Punjab Law Reporter,
Jammu & Kashmir Section *India*

P.L.T. Patna Law Times *India*
Punjab Law Times *India*

PMA Production & Marketing Admin.
U.S.

P.N.P. Peake's Nisi Prius Cases *Eng*

P.O.Cas. Perry's Oriental Cases,
Bombay

P.O.G. Official Gazette, U. S. Patent
Off.

P.O.R. Patent Office Reports

PPR Price Procedural Regulation *U.S.*

P.Q.W. Placita de Quo Warranto,
Record Commission *Eng*

P.R. Ontario Practice Reports
Pacific Reporter (Nat. Reporter
System)

Parliamentary Reports *Eng*

Pennsylvania Reports (Penrose &
Watts)

Philadelphia Reports (Pa. 1850–51)

Philippine Island Reports

Pittsburgh Reports (Pa. 1853–73)

Press Release (U. S. Gov't.
Departments)

Probate Reports

Punjab Record *India*

Pyke's Reports *Canada*

Porto Rico (*now* Puerto Rico)

P.R.C.P. Practical Register, Com. P.
Eng

P.R.Ch. Practical Register in Chancery
Eng

P.R.Fed. Porto Rico Federal Reports
(*now* Puerto Rico)

P.R.R. Porto Rico Supreme Court
Reports (*now* Puerto Rico)

P.R.S.C.R. Porto Rico Supreme Court
Reports (*now* Puerto Rico)

P.R.U.C. Upper Canada Practice
Reports

P.R.& D. Power, Rodwell, & Dew El.
Cas. *Eng*

P.S.C. Public Service Commission

P.S.C.U.S. Peters' Reports (26–41
U. S.)

P.S.R. Pennsylvania State Reports

P.T. Processing Tax Division, U. S.
Internal Revenue Bureau

P.T.B.R. Processing Tax Board of
Review Decisions U. S. Internal
Revenue Bureau

P.U.R. Public Utilities Reports *U.S.*

P.W. Peere Williams' Ch. & K. B.
Rep. *Eng*

P.Wms. Same as above

PWA Public Works Administration
U.S.

P.W.N. Patna Weekly Notes *India*

P.W.R. Punjab Weekly Reporter
India

P.& B. Pugsley & Burbidge's New
Brunswick Reports

P.& C. Prideaux & Cole's Reports
(New Session Cases, v.4)

P.& D. Perry & Davison's Q. B.
Reports *Eng*
Law Reports, Probate & Divorce Ser.
Eng

P.& F. Pike & Fischer's Administrative
Law
Pike & Fischer's Federal Rules Service
Pike & Fischer's OPA Price Service

P.& H. Patton (Jr.) & Heath's Reports (Va. Special Court of Appeals)

P.& K. Perry & Knapp's Election Cases   *Eng*

P.& M. Law Reports, Probate & Matrimonial Cases   *Eng*
Pollock & Maitland's History of Eng. Law

P.& M.H.E.L. Pollock & Maitland's History of English Law

P.& R. Pigott & Rodwell's Election Cas.   *Eng*

P.& T. Pugsley & Trueman's New Brunswick Rep.

P.& W. Penrose & Watts' Reports (Pa. 1829–32)

Pa. Paine's Circuit Court Rep. *U.S.*
Pennsylvania; Pennsylvania State Reports

Pa.B.A. Pennsylvania Bar Assn. Reports

Pa.B.A.Q. Pennsylvania Bar Assn. Quarterly

Pa.C.Dec.W.C.C. Pennsylvania Courts, Decisions in Workmen's Compensation Cases

Pa.Co.Ct.R. Pennsylvania Corporation Reporter

Pa.Corp.Rep. Pennsylvania Corporation Reporter

Pa.D.& C. Pennsylvania District & County Reports (1921–date)

Pa.Dep.L.& I.Dec. Pennsylvania Department of Labor & Industry Decisions

Pa.Dep.Rep. Pennsylvania Department Rep.

Pa.Dist.R. District Reports (Pa. 1892–1921)

Pa.Dist.& C.Rep. District & County Reports (Pa. 1921–date)

Pa.L.J. Pennsylvania Law Journal
Pennsylvania Law Journal Reports (1842–52)

Pa.L.Rec. Pennsylvania Law Record

Pa.L.Ser. Pennsylvania Law Series

Pa.Law J. Pennsylvania Law Journal

Pa.N.P. Brightly's Nisi Prius Rep. *Pa*

Pa.P.S.C. Pennsylvania Public Service Comm.

Pa.Rep. Pennsylvania Reports

Pa.St. Pennsylvania State Rep. (1845–date)

Pa.Super.Ct. Pennsylvania Superior Ct. Rep.

Pa.W.C.Bd.Dec. Pennsylvania Work-

men's Compensation Board Decisions

Pac. Pacific Reporter (Nat. Reporter System)

Pac.Coast L.J. Pacific Coast Law Journal

Pac.Law Mag. Pacific Law Magazine

Pac.Law Reptr. Pacific Law Reporter

Pac.Leg.N. Pacific Legal News

Page Page's Three Early Assize Rolls, County of Northumberland (Surtees Society Publications, v. 88)

Pai. Paige's New York Chancery Reports
Paine's Circuit Court Reports   *U.S.*

Pai.Ch. Paige's New York Chancery Reports

Paine C.C. Paine's Circuit Court Reports   *U.S.*

Pak.L.R. Pakistan Law Reports *India*

Pal[m]. Palmer's King's Bench Reports   *Eng*
Palmer's Reports (53–60 Vermont)
Palmer's Assizes at Cambridge *Eng*

Palgrave Palgrave's Rotuli Curiae Regis

Palmer Palmer's Assizes at Cambridge   *Eng*
Palmer's King's Bench Reports *Eng*
Palmer's Reports (53–60 Vermont)

Panel The Panel, Association of Grand Jurors of New York County Bar

Papy Papy's Reports (5–8 Florida)

Par. Parker's Exchequer Reports *Eng*
Parker's New York Criminal Cases 1823–68

Par.Dec. Parsons' Decisions (from 2–7 Mass.)

Par.Eq.Cas. Parson's Select Equity Cases (Pa. 1842–51)

Park. Parker's Exchequer Reports   *Eng*
Parker's New York Criminal Cases 1823–68
Parker's New Hampshire Reports

Park.Exch. Parker's Exchequer Reports   *Eng*

ParkN.H. Parker's New Hampshire Reports

Park.Rev.Cas. Parker's Exchequer Reports (Revenue Cases) *Eng*

Parker Parker's Exchequer Reports   *Eng*
Parker's New Hampshire Reports
Parker's New York Criminal Cases

Parl.Cas. Parliamentary Cases (House of Lords)   *Eng*

Parl.Deb. Parliamentary Debates (Cobbett, Hansard)

Parl.Reg. Parliamentary Register *Eng*

Pars.Dec. Parsons' Decisions (from 2–7 Mass.)

Pars.Eq.Cas. Parsons' Select Equity Cases (Pa. 1842–51)

Pasc. Paschal or Easter Term
Paschal's Reports (Supp. to 25; 28–31 Texas)

Paschal Same as above

Pat. Indian Law Reports, Patna Series
Paterson's Scotch Appeals, House of Lords
Paton's Scotch Appeals, House of Lords

Pat.App. Paton's Scotch Appeals, H. of L.

Pat.App.Cas. Paterson's Scotch Appeals
Paton's Scotch Appeals, House of Lords

Pat.Copyright & T.M.Cas. Patent, Copyright & Trade Mark Cases (Baldwin)   *U.S.*

Pat.Dec. Decisions, Commissioner of Patents

Pat.H.L.Sc. Paton's or Paterson's Scotch Appeals

Pat.L.J. Patna Law Journal   *India*

Pat.L.R. Patna Law Reports   *India*

Pat.L.Reptr. Patna Law Reporter   *India*

Pat.L.T. Patna Law Times   *India*

Pat.L.W. Patna Law Weekly   *India*

Pat.Off.Gaz. Official Gazette, U. S. Patent Office

Pat.Ser. Indian Law Reports, Patna Series

Pat.& H. Patton, Jr., & Heath's Reports (Va. Special Court of Appeals)

Pat.& Mur. Paterson & Murray's Rep. N.S.W.

Pater. Paterson's Scotch Appeals

Pater.App. Same as above

Paton Paton's Scotch Appeals, House of Lords

Patr.Elec.Cas. Patrick's Contested Elections Cases (Ontario) *Canada*

Patt.& H. Patton, Jr., & Heath's Reports (Va. Special Court of Appeals)

Pea. Peake's Nisi Prius Reports   *Eng*

Pea.Add.Cas. Peake's Nisi Prius Reports (v. 2 of Peake)

Peake N.P. Peake's Nisi Prius Reports   *Eng*

Pearce C.C. Pearce, in Dearsly's Crown Cases   *Eng*

Pears. Pearson's Reports (Pa. 1850–80)

Peck. Peck's Reports (24–30 Illinois)
Peck's Reports (7 Tennessee)
Peckwell's Election Cases   *Eng*

Peeples Peeples' Reports (78, 79 Georgia)

Peeples & Stevens (80–97 Georgia)

Peere Wms. Peere Williams' Chancery & King's Bench Cases   *Eng*

Pelham Pelham's South Australia Rep.   *Aus*

Pen. Pennington's Reports (2, 3 N. J. Law)

Pen.Dec. Pension Decisions, U. S. Interior Department

Pen.N.J. Pennington's Rep. (2, 3 N. J. Law)

Pen.& W. Penrose & Watts' Reports (Pa. 1829–32)

Penn. Pennsylvania (*see also* entries under "Pa.")
Pennington's Reports (2, 3 N. J. Law)
Pennypacker's Reports (Pa. 1881–84)

Penn.B.A. Pennsylvania Bar Association

Penn.B.A.Q. Pennsylvania Bar Ass. Quarterly

Penn.Co.Ct.Rep. Pennsylvania County Court Reports

Penn.Corp.Rep. Pennsylvania Corporation Reporter

Penn.L.G. Pennsylvania Legal Gazette
Pennsylvania Legal Gazette Reports (Campbell)

Penn.L.J. Pennsylvania Law Journal

Penn.L.J.R. Pennsylvania Law Journal Reports (Clark 1842–52)

Penn.Law Jour. Pennsylvania Law Journal

Pennewill Pennewill's Reports (17–23 Del.)

Penning. Pennington's Reports (2, 3 N. J. Law)

Penny. Pennypacker's Reports (Pa. Unreported, or Colonial Cases)

Penr.& W. Penrose & Watts' Rep. (Pa. 1829–32)

Per. Perera's Select Decisions   *Ceylon*

Per.C.S. Perrault's Conseil Superieur   *Canada*

Per.Or.Cas. Perry's Oriental Cases
Bombay
Per.P. Perrault's Prévosté de Quebec
Per.& Dav. Perry & Davison's Q. B.
Rep.   *Eng*
Per.& Kn. Perry & Knapp's Election
Cas.   *Eng*
Perrault Perrault's Quebec Reports
Perrault's Conseil Superieur *Canada*
Perrault's Prévosté de Quebec
Perry Ins. Perry's Insolvency Cases
Eng
Perry O.C. Perry's Oriental Cases
Bombay
Perry & D. Perry & Davison's Q. B.
Rep.   *Eng*
Perry & Kn. Perry & Knapp's Elect.
Cas.   *Eng*
Pershad Privy Council Judgments
1829–69   *India*
Pet. Peters
Peters' Admiralty Reports, Dist. Ct.
U.S.
Peters' Circuit Court Reports   *U.S.*
Peters' Supreme Court Reports
(26–41 U. S.)
Peters' Prince Edward Island Reports
Can
Pet.Adm. Peters' Admiralty Reports,
U. S. District Courts
Pet.Br. Brooke's New Cases (Petit
Brooke)
Bellewe's Cases *temp.* Hen. VIII *Eng*
Pet.C.C. Peters' Circuit Court Rep.
U.S.
Pet.Cond. Peters' Condensed Reports,
U. S. Supreme Court
Pet.S.C. Peters' Supreme Ct. Rep.
(26–41 U S)
Peters Adm. Peters' Admiralty
Reports, U. S. District Courts
Peters C.C. Peters' Circuit Court Rep.
U.S.
Petit Br. Brooke's New Cases 1515–58
Eng
Ph. Philipps' Chancery Reports *Eng*
Phillimore's Ecclesiastical Reports
Eng
Pheney Rep. Pheney's New Term
Reports   *Eng*
Phi Delta Delta Phi Delta Delta
(periodical)
Phil. Phillimore's Ecclesiastical Rep.
Eng
Phillips' Chancery Reports   *Eng*
Phillips' Election Cases   *Eng*

Phillips' Reports (152–245 Illinois)
Philipps' Reports (61–64 North
Carolina)
Philippine Reports
Phil.Ecc.R. Phillimore's Eccles. Rep.
Eng
Phil.El.Cas. Phillips' Election Cases
Eng
Phil.Eq. Phillips Reports (62 N. C.
Eq.)
Phil.Jud. Phillimore's Eccles.
Judgments   *Eng*
Phil.L.J. Philippine Law Journal
Phil.L.Rev. Philippine Law Review
Phil.Law. Phillips' Law Reports
(61 N. C.)
Phil.N.C. Phillips' Law Reports
(61 N. C.)
Phil.St.Tr. Phillipps' State Trials
Phila. Philadelphia Reports (Pa. 1850–
91)
Phila.Leg.Int. Philadelphia Legal
Intelligencer
Phill. (*See* Phil., *supra*)
Phillim. Phillimore's Eccles. Reports
Eng
Phillips *See* Phil., *supra*
Phip. Phipson's Digest, Natal Reports
S.Af.
Phipson's Reports, Natal Supreme Ct.
S.Af.
Phipson Same as above
Pick. Pickering's Reports (18–41
Mass.)
Pickle Pickle's Reports (85–108
Tenn.)
Pig.& R. Pigott & Rodwell's Registra-
tion Cases   *Eng*
Pike Pike's Reports (1–5 Arkansas)
Pike & F.Adm.Law Pike & Fischer's
Administrative Law
Pike & F.Fed.Rules Service Pike &
Fischer's Federal Rules Service
Pin[n]. Penney's Reports (Wis.
Reprint)
Piston Piston's Mauritius Reports
Pitc. Pitcairn's Criminal Trials   *Scot*
Pitts.L.J. Pittsburgh Legal Journal
Pitts.L.Rev. University of Pittsburgh
Law Review
Pitts.Rep. Pittsburgh Reports (Pa.
1853–73)
Pittsb. *See* Pitts., *supra*
Pl. Plowden's Commentaries 1550–80
Eng
Pl.Com. Same as above

Pl.C. Placita Coronae (Pleas of the Crown)

Pl.& Pr.Cas. Pleading & Practice Cas. *Eng*

Pla.Par. Placita Parliamentaria *Eng*

Plaxton Plaxton's Constitutional Dec. *Canada*

Plow. Plowden's Reports (and Queries) *Eng*

Pol. Pollexfen's King's Bench Reports *Eng*

Pol.J. Police Journal *Eng*

Polam.L.J. Polamerican Law Journal

Poll. Pollexfen's King's Bench Reports *Eng*

Pollack's Ohio Unreported Judicial Decisions Prior to 1823

Pop. Popham's King's Bench Reports *Eng*

Pop.Govt. Popular Government

Poph. Popham's King's Bench Reports *Eng*

Poph.(2) Cases at end of Popham's Reports

Port. Porter's Reports (Alabama 1834–39)

Porter Porter's Reports (Alabama 1834–39)

Porter's Reports (3–7 Indiana)

Port.U.L.Rev. Portland University Law Rev.

Porto Rico Fed.Rep. Porto Rico Federal Rep.

Posey Unrep.Cas. Texas Unreported Cases (1879–84)

Post Post's Reports (23–26 Michigan)

Post's Reports (42–64 Missouri)

Potter Potter's Reports (4–7 Wyoming)

Pow.R.& D. Power, Rodwell, & Dew El. Cas. *Eng*

Powers Powers' New York Surrogate Ct. Rep.

Pr. Practice Reports (various jurisdictions)

Price's Exchequer Reports *Eng*

Pr.C.K.B. Practice Cases, King's Bench *Eng*

Pr.Ca. Great War Prize Cases (Evans) *Eng*

Pr.Ch. Precedents in Chancery (Finch) *Eng*

Pr.Dec. Kentucky Dec. (Sneed, 2 Kentucky)

Pr.Div. Law Reports, Probate Division *Eng*

Pr.Edw.I. Prince Edward Island Rep. *Canada*

Pr.Exch. Price's Exchequer Reports *Eng*

Pr.Falc. President Falconer's Court of Session Cases *Scot*

Pr.R. Practice Reports (various jurisdictions)

Practice Reports (Ontario)

Practice Reports (Quebec)

Pr.Reg.C.P. Practical Register, Com. Pl. *Eng*

Pr.Rep.B.C. Lowndes, Maxwell, & Pollock's Bail Court Practice Cases *Eng*

Pr.& Div. Law Reports, Probate & Divorce *Eng*

Pract. Practitioner, Baltimore

Pract.Reg. Practical Register of Common Pleas *Eng*

Pratt Pratt's Contraband of War Cases

Pre.Ch. Precedents in Chancery 1689–1722 *Eng*

Pres.Falc. President Falconer's Court of Session Cases *Scot*

Pri. Price's Exchequer Reports *Eng*

Price's Mining Commissioners' Cases *Eng*

Price Same as above

Price Notes P.C. Price's Notes of Practice Cases in Exchequer *Eng*

Price Notes P.P. Price, Notes of Points of Practice, Exchequer Cases *Eng*

Price & St. Price & Stewart's Trade Mark Cas.

Prickett Prickett's Reports (1 Idaho)

Prid.& C. Prideaux & Cole's Reports (4 New Sessions Cases)

Prin.Dec. Kentucky Decisions (Sneed, 2 Ky.)

Priv.C.App. Privy Council Appeals *Eng*

Priv.C.D.I. Indian Privy Council Decisions

Prob. Law Reports, Probate Division *Eng*

Prob.Ct.Rep. Probate Court Reports

Prob.Div. Law Reports, Probate Division *Eng*

Prob.Rep. Probate Reports

Prob.Rep.Annot. Probate Reports Annotated *N.Y.*

Prob.& Adm.Div. Law Reports, Probate & Admiralty Division *Eng*

Prob.& Div. Law Reports, Probate &
Divorce Division *Eng*
Prob.& Mat. Probate & Matrimonial
Cases *Eng*
Proc. Proclamation
Prop.Law. Property Lawyer
Prop.Law.N.S. Property Lawyer,
New Series
Proudf.Land Dec. United States Land
Decisions (Proudfit)
Prouty Prouty's Reports (61–68
Vermont)
Prt.Rep. Practice Reports
Psych.& M.L.J. Psychological &
Medico-Legal Journal
Pub.Adm.Rev. Public Administration
Review
Pub.Health U. S. Public Health
Service, Court Decisions
Pub.Manag. Public Management
Pub.Util.Fort. Public Utilities
Fortnightly
Pug[s]. Pugsley's Rep. (14–16 New
Brunswick)
Pugs.& Bur. Pugsley & Burbidge
Reports (17–20 New Brunswick)
Pulsifer Pulsifer's Reports (35–68
Maine)
Punj.Rec. Punjab Record *India*
Py.R. Pyke's Lower Canada Reports,
K. B .
Pyke Same as above
Q. Year Books Part IV
Quebec
Queensland
Q.B. Queen's Bench
Adolphus & Ellis' Q. B. Reports, New
Series
Law Reports, Queen's Bench, from
1891
Queen's Bench Reports, Quebec
Queen's Bench Reports, Upper Canada
Q.B.D[iv]. Queen's Bench Division
Law Reports, Queen's Bench Division
Eng
Q.B.L.C. Queen's Bench Reports,
Lower Canada
Q.B.R. Queen's Bench Reports
(Adolphus & Ellis, New Series)
Q.B.U.C. Queen's Bench Reports,
Upper Canada
Q.C.L.L.R. Crown Lands Law
Reports (Queensland) *Aus*
Q.C.R. Queensland Criminal Reports
Aus
Q.J.P. Queensland Justice of the Peace
Rep.

Q.L.J. Queensland Law Journal
Queensland Law Journal Reports
Q.L.R. Quebec Law Reports
Queensland Law Reports *Aus*
Q.L.Beor Beor's Queensland Law
Rep. *Aus*
Q.P.R. Queensland Practice Reports
Q.R. Quebec Official Reports
Q.R.K.B.(*or* Q.B.) Quebec King's
(*or* Queen's) Bench Reports
Rapports Judiciaires de Québec, Cour
du Banc du Roi
Q.R.S.C. Rapports Judiciaires de
Québec, Cour Supérieure
Q.S.C.R. Queensland Supreme Ct.
Rep. *Aus*
Q.S.R. Queensland State Reports *Aus*
Q.W.N. Weekly Notes, Queensland
Aus
Qu.Jour.Int-Amer.Rel. Quarterly
Journal of Inter-American
Relations
Qu.L.J. Quarterly Law Journal
Qu.L.Rev. Quarterly Law Review
Quadr. Year Books, Part IV *Eng*
Que.K.B.(*or* Q.B.) Quebec King's (*or*
Queen's) Bench Reports
Que.S.C. Quebec Superior Court
Reports
Queb.K.B. Quebec King's Bench
Reports
Queb.L.R. Quebec Law Reports
(Queen's Bench or Superior
Court)
Queb.Pr. Quebec Practice Reports
Queens B.Bull. Queens Bar Bulletin
Queens C.B.A.Bull. Queens County
Bar Association Bulletin
Queens.J.P.& Loc.Auth.Jo. Queens-
land Justice of the Peace & Local
Authorities' Journal
Queens.L.J. Queensland Law Journal
Queens.L.R. Queensland Law Reports
Aus
Queens.St.R. Queensland State
Reports *Aus*
Quin. Quincy (Mass.) Superior Court
of Judicature Reports
Quinti,Quinto Year Book 5 Henry V
Eng
R. Rawle's Reports (Pa. 1828–35)
Rettie's Court of Session Reports, 4th
Series *Scot*
The Reports (1893–95) *Eng*
Roscoe's Cape of Good Hope Reports
S.Af.
Kentucky Law Reporter (1880–1908)

R.A.   Registration Appeals

R.A.C.   Ramsay's Appeal Cases *Canada*

RB   Renegotiation Board   *U.S.*

R.B.G.   British Guiana Reports of
Opinions

R.C.   Revue Critique de Législation
et de Jurisprudence de Canada
Ruling Cases

R.C.L.   Ruling Case Law (an
encyclopedia)

R.C.& C.R.   Revenue, Civil & Criminal
Reporter

R.D.   Indian Revenue Decisions

R.D.B.   Research & Development
Board   *U.S.*

R.de D.   Revue de Droit (Quebec)

R.de J.   Revue de Jurisprudence
Canada

R.de L.   Revue de Législation et de
Jurisprudence   *Canada*

REA   Rural Electrification Administration   *U.S.*

R.E.D.   New South Wales Reserved
Eq. Dec.
Ritchie's Equity Decisions (Russell)
Can

RFC   Reconstruction Finance
Corporation   *U.S.*

R.G.   Regulae Generales of Ontario

R.H.   Rotuli Hundredorum, Record
Commission   *Eng*

R.H.L.   Rettie's Session Cases, H. L.
Scot

R.I.   Rhode Island

R.J.   New South Wales, Port Phillip
District Judgments   *Aus*

R.J.Q.   Rapports Judiciaires, Quebec

R.J.R.   Quebec Revised Reports
(Mathieu)

R.J.R.Q.   Quebec Revised Reports
(Mathieu)

R.J.& P.J.   Revenue, Judicial & Police
Journal, Calcutta   *India*

R.L.   Revue Légale   *Canada*

R.L.N.S.   Revue Légale, New Series
Canada

R.L.O.S.   Revue Légale, Old Series
Canada

R.L.Q.B.   Revue Légale Reports,
Queen's Bench   *Canada*

R.L.S.C.   Revue Légale Reports,
Supreme Court   *Canada*

R.L.& S.   Ridgeway, Lapp, &
Schoales's King's Bench Reports
Ir

R.L.W.   Rajasthan Law Weekly *India*

R.L.& W.   Robert, Leaming & Wallis
County Court Reports   *Eng*

R.M.Ch.   P. M. Charlton's Rep.
(Ga. 1811–37)

RP   Rent Regulation (Office of Price
Stabilization, Economic Stabilization Agency)   *U.S.*

R.P.   Rotuli Parliamentorum 1278–1553
Eng

R.P.C.   Real Property Cases 1843–48
Eng
Reports of Patent Cases   *Eng*
Reports of Patent, Design & Trade
Mark Cases   *Eng*
Real Property Commissioners' Report,
1832   *Eng*

R.P.C.Rep.   Real Property Commissioners' Report, 1832   *Eng*

RPR   Rent Procedural Regulation (Office of Rent Stabilization Economic Stabilization Agency) *U.S.*

R.P.& W.   Rawle, Penrose & Watts'
Reports (Pa. 1828–40)

RR   Rural Rehabilitation   *U.S.*

RR   Rent Regulation (Office of Rent
Stabilization, Economic Stab.
Agency.)   *U.S.*

R.R.   Revised Reports   *Eng*
Pike & Fischer's Radio Regulations

RRB   Railroad Retirement Board *U.S.*

R.R.& Can.Cas.   Railway & Canal
Cases   *Eng*

R.S.   Revised Statutes (various jurisdictions); Rolls Series

R.S.C.   Revised Statutes of Canada
Rules of the Supreme Court   *Eng*

R.S.C.O.   Rules of the Supreme Court,
Order Number   *Eng*

R.t.F.   Reports *temp.* Finch, Chancery
Eng

R.t.H.   Reports *temp.* Hardwicke *Eng*
Ridgway's Chancery & K. B. Reports,
temp. Hardwicke   *Eng*
Reports of Cases Concerning Settlements, *temp.* Holt   *Eng*

R.t.Q.A.   Reports *temp.* Queen Anne
(11 Modern)   *Eng*

R.t.W.   Manitoba Reports *temp.* Wood

R.& C.   Russell & Chesley's Nova
Scotia Rep.

R.&C.Ca.   Railway & Canal Cases *Eng*

R.& C.Tr.Cas.   Railway & Canal
Traffic Cases (Neville)   *Eng*

R.& G.   Russell & Geldert's Nova
Scotia Rep.

R.& G.N.Sc.   Same as above

R.& I.T. Rating & Income Tax
Reports   *Eng*

R.& J. Rafique & Jackson's Privy
Council Decisions   *India*

R.& M. Russell & Mylne's Chancery
Rep.   *Eng*
Ryan & Moody's Nisi Prius Reports
                                Eng

R.& M.C.C. Ryan & Moody's Crown
Cases Reserved   *Eng*

R.& M.N.P. Ryan & Moody's Nisi
Prius Rep.   *Eng*

R.& My. Russell & Mylne's Chancery
Rep.   *Eng*

R.& R. Russell & Ryan's Crown Cas.
Res.   *Eng*

R.&R.C.C. Same as above

Rader Rader's Reports (138–163
Missouri)

Rail.& Can.Cas. Railway & Canal
Cases   *Eng*
Railway & Canal Traffic Cases *Eng*

Railw.Cas. Railway Cases

Railw.& Corp.L.J. Railway & Corporation Law Journal

Raj. Rajaratnam Revised Reports
                             Ceylon

Ram. Ramsey's Quebec Appeal Cases
Ramanathan's Reports   *Ceylon*

Ram.S.C. Ramanathan's Supreme Ct.
Rep.   *Ceylon*

Ram.& Mor. Ramsey & Morin's
Montreal Law Reporter

Rand. Randall's Reports (62–71 Ohio
State)
Randolph's Reports (21–56 Kansas)
Randolph's Reports (7–11 Louisiana)
Randolph's Reports (22–27 Virginia)

Raney Raney's Reports (16–20
Florida)

Rang.Cr.L.J. Rangoon Criminal Law
Journal

Rang.Dec. Rangoon Decision
(Sparks)

Rang.L.R. Rangoon Law Reports
                              India

Rap.& L. Rapalje & Lawrence's
American & English Cases

Rast. Rastell's Entries & Statutes *Eng*

Rast.Ent. Same as above

Rat.Sel.Cas. Rattigan's Select Cases in
Hindu Law

Rat.Unrep.Cr. Rataanlal's Unreported
Criminal Cases   *India*

Raw [le] Rawle's Reports (Pa. 1828–
35)

Rate Res. Rate Research (a
periodical)

Rawle Rawle's Reports (Pa. 1828–35)

Rawle Pen.& W. Rawle, Penrose, &
Watts' Reports (Pa. 1828–40)

Raym.Ent. Lord Raymond's Entries
                                Eng

Raym.Ld. Lord Raymond's K. B.
Reports   *Eng*

Raym.Sir T. T. Raymond's K. B.
Reports   *Eng*

Raymond Raymond's Reports (81–99
Iowa)

Rayn. Rayner's Tithe Cases   *Eng*

Re.de L. Revue de Législation et de
Jurisprudence, Montreal

Real Est.Rec. Real Estate Record,
New York

Real Pr.Cas. Real Property Cases *Eng*

Reapp.Dec. Reappraisement
Decisions, U. S. Treasury

Rec.Comm. Record Commission *Eng*

Rec.Dec. Vaux' Recorders Dec. (Pa.
1841–45)

Record. Record, Association of the
Bar, City of New York

Red. Redfield's New York Surrogates'
Rep.
Redington's Reports (31–35 Maine)

Red.Am.R.Cas. Redfield's American
Railway Cases

Redf. Redfield's New York Surrogate
Rep.

Redf.Am.Railw.Cas. Redfield's
American Railway Cases

Redf.Surr. Redfield's New York
Surrogate Reports

Redington Redington's Reports (31–
35 Maine)

Reeves H.E.L. Reeves' History of
English Law

Ref.J. Referees' Journal   *Eng*

Reg. Daily Register, New York

Reg.App. Registration Appeals   *Eng*

Reg.Cas. Registration Cases   *Eng*

Reg.Deb. Gales & Seaton's Register of
Debates in Congress, 1824–37

Reg.Pl. Regula Placitandi   *Eng*

Reilly E.A. Reilly's European Arbitration (Lord Westbury's
Decisions)

Rem.Cr.Tr. Remarkable Criminal
Trials

Remy Remy's Reports (145–162
Indiana; 15–33 Indiana Appellate)

Ren. Renner's Reports   *Gold Coast*

Rep. Report or Reports
Coke's King's Bench Reports (commonly known as "The Reports")   *Eng*
Reporter (Boston, Los Angeles, New York, Washington)
Knapp's Privy Council Reports   *Eng*

Rep.Ass.Y. Clayton's Reports, Assizes of York

Rep.Cas.Eq. Gilbert's Chancery Reports   *Eng*

Rep.Cas.Pr. Cooke's Practice Cases   *Eng*

Rep.Ch. Reports in Chancery 1615–1710   *Eng*

Rep.Ch.Pr. Reports on Chancery Practice   *Eng*

Rep.Com.Cas. Reports of Commercial Cas.   *Eng*

Rep.Const.Ct. South Carolina Constitutional Court Reports

Rep.Cr.L.Com. Reports of Criminal Law Commissioners   *Eng*

Rep.Eq. Gilbert's Reports in Equity   *Eng*

Rep.in C.of A. Reports, Courts of Appeal   *New Zealand*

Rep.Jur. Repertorium Juridicum *Eng*

Rep.Pat.Cas. Reports of Patents, Designs and Trade-Mark Cases   *Eng*

Rep.Q.A. Reports *temp.* Queen Anne (11 Modern Reports)

Rep.*t*.Finch Finch's Chancery Reports   *Eng*

Rep.*t*.Hard. Lee's Reports *temp.* Hardwicke, King's Bench   *Eng*

Rep.*t*.Holt Settlement Cases, Reports *temp.* Holt   *Eng*

Rep.*t*.O.Br. Common Pleas Reports *temp.* O. Bridgman, by Carter   *Eng*

Rep.*t*.Q.A. Reports *temp.* Queen Anne (11 Modern Reports)   *Eng*

Rep.*t*.Talb. Chancery Reports *temp.* Talbot   *Eng*

Rep.*t*.Wood Manitoba Reports *temp.* Wood

Rep.York.Ass. Clayton's Pleas of Assize at York   *Eng*

Reports Coke's King's Bench Reports   *Eng*

Reptr. The Reporter (Boston, Los Angeles, New York, Washington)

Res. Resolution (of a legislative body)

Res.Cas. Reserved Cases   *Ir*

Res.& Eq.Jud. Reserved & Equity Judgments N.S.W.   *Aus*

Res.Gamma Eta Gamma Rescript of Gamma Eta Gamma

Res.Jud. Res Judicatae (periodical)   *Aus*

Reserv.Cas. Reserved Cases   *Ir*

Rettie Rettie's Court of Session Cases, 4th Series   *Scot*

Rev.C.& C.Rep. Revenue, Civil, & Criminal Reporter, Calcutta *India*

Rev.Cas. Revenue Cases

Rev.Crit. Revue Critique, Montreal

Rev.Crit.de Légis.et.Jur. Revue Critique de Législation et de Jurisprudence, Montreal

Rev.de Jur. Revue de Jurisprudence, Quebec

Rev.de Leg. Revue de Législation et de Jurisprudence, Montreal

Rev.du B. Revue du Barreau de la Province de Québec

Rev.du Dr. Revue du Droit, Quebec

Rev.du Not. Revue du Notariat, Quebec

Rev.Gen.Reg. Revised General Regulation, General Accounting Office   *U.S.*

Rev.J.& P.J. Revenue, Judicial, & Police Journal   *Bengal*

Rev.Jur.U.P.R. Revista Jurídica, Universidad de Puerto Rico

Rev.Leg. Revue Légale, Montreal

Rev.Rep. Revised Reports (Reprint)   *Eng*

Rev.Stat. Revised Statutes (various jurisdictions)

Rice Rice's Reports (S. C. Law 1838–39)
Records of the Court of General Sessions of the Peace, Worcester County, Mass., 1731–37

Rice Eq. Rice's Reports (S. C. Eq. 1838–39)

Rich. Richardson's Reports (S. C. Law)
Richardson's Reports (3–5 New Hampshire)
Richardson's Reports (18 U. S. Ct. Claims)

Rich.Ch. Richardson's Reports (S. C. Equity)

Rich.Ct.Cl. Richardson's Reports (18 U. S. Court of Claims)

Rich.Eq. Richardson's Reports (S. C. Equity)

Rich.Law Richardson's Reports (S. C. Law)

Rich.N.H. Richardson's Reports (3–5 N. H.)

Rich.N.S. Richardson's Reports, New Series (S. C. Law & Equity 1850–68)

Rich.P.R.C.P. Richardson's Practical Register of Common Pleas *Eng*

Rich.Pr.Reg. Same as above

Rich.& H. Richardson & Hook's Street Railway Decisions

Rich.& S. Richardson & Sayles' Select Cases of Procedure without Writ (Selden Soc. Pub. 60)

Rich.& W. Richardson & Woodbury's Reports (2 New Hampshire)

Rick.& M. Rickards & Michael's Locus Standi Reports *Eng*

Rick.& S. Rickards & Saunders' Locus Standi Reports *Eng*

Ridg. Ridgeway's Reports *temp.* Hardwicke, Chancery & King's Bench *Eng*

Ridg.Ap. Ridgeway's Appeal Cases *Ir*

Ridg.Cas. Ridgeway's Reports *temp.* Hardwicke, Chancery & King's Bench *Eng*

Ridg.L.& S. Ridgeway, Lapp, & Schoales' Irish Term Reports

Ridg.P.C. Ridgeway's Appeal Cases *Ir*

Ridg.Pr.Rep. Ridgeway's Appeal (or Parliamentary) Cases *Ir*

Ridg.*t*.H[ard]. Ridgeway's Reports *temp.* Hardwick, Ch. & K. B. *Eng*

Ridg.& Hard. Same as above

Ried. Riedell's Reports (68, 69 N. H.)

Rigg Select Pleas, Starrs, and other Records from the Rolls of the Exchequer of the Jews, ed. J. M. Riggs (Selden Society Publication, v. 15)

Ril[ey] Riley's Reports (Law & Equity)

Riley's Reports (37–42 West Virginia)

Ril.Harp. Harper's Reports (S. C. Law & Equity), ed. Riley

Rin. Riner's Reports (2 Wyoming)

Ritch.Eq.Rep. Ritchie's Equity Reports, Nova Scotia

Ro. Rolle's Abridgment *Eng*

Ro.Abr. Same as above

Ro.Rep. Rolle's King's Bench Reports *Eng*

Robards' Conscript Cases (Texas 1862–65)

Rob. Robards' Reports (12, 13 Missouri)

Roberts' Reports (29–31 La. Annual)

Robertson's Ecclesiastical Reports *Eng*

Robertson's Reports (1 Hawaii)

Robertson's Reports (24–30 N. Y. Superior)

Robertson's Scotch Appeal Cases

Robinson's Admiralty Reports *Eng*

Robinson's Reports (38 California)

Robinson's Reports (2–9, 17–23 Colo. App.)

Robinson's Reports (1–4 La. Annual; Supreme Court La. 1841–46)

Robinson's Scotch Appeals, House of Lords

Robinson's Reports (1 Nevada)

Robinson's Reports (40, 41 Virginia)

Robinson's Reports (1–8 Ontario)

Robinson's Upper Canada Reports

Rob.Adm. C. Robinson's Admiralty Rep. *Eng*

W. Robinson's Admiralty Reports *Eng*

Rob.App. Robinson's Appeal Cases, House of Lords *Scot*

Rob.Cal. Robinson's Reports (38 California)

Rob.Cas. Robertson's Scotch Appeal Cases

Rob.Chr. Chr. Robinson's Admiralty Rep. *Eng*

Rob.Colo. Robinson's Reports (2–9, 17–23 Colorado App.)

Rob.Consc.Cas. Robards' Texas Conscript Cases

Rob.Eccl. Robertson's Ecclesiastical Rep. *Eng*

Rob.Hawaii Robinson's Reports (1 Hawaii)

Rob.Jun. Wm. Robinson's Admiralty Rep. *Eng*

Rob.L.& W. Roberts, Leeming, & Wallis New County Court Cases *Eng*

Rob.La. Robinson's Reports (1–4 La. Annual; La. Supreme Court 1841–46)

Rob.Mo. Robards' Reports (12, 13 Missouri)

Rob.Nev. Robinson's Reports (1 Nevada)

Rob.N.Y. Robertson's Reports (24–30 N. Y. Superior Court)

Rob.Ont. Robinson's Reports (1–8 Ontario)

Rob.S.I. Robertson's Sandwich Island Reports (1 Hawaii)

Rob.Sc.App. Robinson's Scotch Appeal Cases

Rob.Super.Ct. Robertson's Reports (24–30 New York Superior Court)

Rob.U.C. Robinson's Reports (Upper Canada)

Rob.Va. Robinson's Reports (40, 41 Va.)

Rob.Wm.Adm. Wm. Robinson's Admiralty Reports   *Eng*

Rob.& J. Robards' & Jackson's Reports (26, 27 Texas)

Robards Robards' Reports (12, 13 Missouri)
Robards' Conscript Cases (Texas 1862–65)

Robards & Jackson Texas Reports, v. 26, 27

Robb. Robbins' Reports (67–70 N. J. Eq.)

Robb Pat.Cas. Robb's Patent Cases   *U.S.*

Robert.App. Robertson's House of Lords Appeals   *Scot*

Roberts Roberts' Reports (29–31 La. Annual)

Robertson *See also* Rob., *supra*
Robertson's Ecclesiastical Reports *Eng*
Robertson's Reports   *Hawaii*
Robertson's Reports, New York Marine Ct.
Robertson's Rep. (24–30 N. Y. Superior)
Robertson's Scotch Appeal Cases

Robin.App. Robinson's House of Lords Appeals   *Scot*

Robinson Chr. Robinson's Admiralty Rep.   *Eng*
W. Robinson's Admiralty Reports   *Eng*
Robinson's Reports (38 California)
Robinson's Reports (17–23 Colorado)
Robinson's Reports (La. 1841–46)
Robinson's Reports (1 Nevada)
Chr. Robinson's Reports   *Ontario*
J.L. Robinson's Upper Canada Reports
Robinson's House of Lords Appeals   *Scot*
Robinson's Reports (40–41 Virginia)

Robt. Robertson, *supra*

Roche D.& K. Roche, Dillon, Kehoe, Land Reports   *Ir*

Rocky Mt.Law Rev. Rocky Mountain Law Review

Rodm. Rodman's Reports (78–82 Kentucky)

Rog.C.H.R. Rogers' City Hall Recorder (New York 1816–22)

Rog.Rec. Rogers' New City Hall Recorder

Rogers Rogers' Reports (47–51 La. Annual)

Rol[1]. Rolle's Abridgment   *Eng*
Rolle's King's Bench Reports   *Eng*

Roll.Rep. Rolle's King's Bench Reports   *Eng*

Rolle Same as above

Rolls Ct.Rep. Rolls Court Reports

Rom. Romilly's Notes of Chancery Cases   *Eng*

Root Root's Reports (Connecticut 1774–89)

Rosc.Jur. Roscoe's Jurist   *Eng*

Rosc.P.C. Roscoe's Prize Cases   *Eng*

Roscoe *See also* Rosc., *supra*
Roscoe's Cape Colony Supreme Ct. Rep.

Rose. Rose's Bankruptcy Reports Eng

Rose's Notes Rose's Notes on United States Reports

Rosenberger Pock.L.J. Rosenberger's Pocket Law Journal

Ross L.C. Ross's Leading Cases in Commercial Law   *Eng*

Rot.Cur.Reg. Rotuli Curiae Regis 1194–99

Rot.Parl. Rotuli Parliamentorum 1278–1553

Rowe Rowe's Interesting Cases 1798–1823   *Eng*
Rowe's Reports   *Eng, Ir*

Rowe's Rep. Rowe's Reports *Eng, Ir*

Rowell Rowell's Contested Election Cases, U. S. House of Representatives
Rowell's Reports (45–52 Vermont)

Rt.Law Rep. Rent Law Reports *India*

Rucker Rucker's Reports (43–46 West Va.)

Ruff. Statutes at Large, Ruffhead's Ed.   *Eng*
Ruffin & Hawks' Reports (8 N. C.)

Ruff.& H. Ruffin & Hawks' Reports (8 N. C.)

Rul.Cas. Campbell's Ruling Cases *Eng*

Runn. Statutes at Large, Runnington Ed.   *Eng*
Runnell's Reports (38–56 Iowa)

Runnell Runnell's Reports (38–56 Iowa)

Rus. *See* Russ., *infra*

Rus.E.C. Russell's Election Reports
Canada
Russell's Election Cases *Mass*
Russ. Russell's Chancery Reports *Eng*
Russell's Election Cases *Canada*
Russell's Election Cases *Mass*
Rus.Eq.Rep. Russell's Equity
Decisions *Nova Scotia*
Russ.t.Eld. Russell's Chancery Cases
temp. Eldon *Eng*
Russ.& Ches. Russell & Chesley's
Reports (10–12 Nova Scotia)
Russ.& Geld. Russell & Geldert's
Reports (13–27 Nova Scotia)
Russ.& Jap.P.C. Russian & Japanese
Prize Cas.
Russ.& M. Russell & Mylne's Chancery
Rep. *Eng*
Russ.& Ry. Russell & Ryan's Crown
Cases Reserved *Eng*
Russell N.S. Russell's Nova Scotia
Equity Decisions
Rutg.L.Rev. Rutgers Law Review
Ry.Cas. Reports of Railway Cases *Eng*
Ry.Corp.Law Jour. Railway & Cor-
poration Law Journal
Ry.& Can.Cas. Railway & Canal Cases
Eng
Ry.& Can.Traf.Cas. Railway & Canal
Traffic Cases *Eng*
Ry.& M. Ryan & Moody's Nisi Prius
Rep. *Eng*
Ry.& M.N.P. Same as above
Ryde Rat.App. Ryde's Rating Appeals
Eng
Ryde & K.Rat.App. Ryde & Kon-
stam's Reports of Rating Appeals
Eng
Ryl.Plac.Parl. Ryley's Placita Parlia-
mentaria 1290–1307 *Eng*
S. Senate Bill
Searle's Cape of Good Hope Reports
S.Af.
Shaw's Court of Session Cases *Scot*
Shaw, Dunlop, & Bell's Court of
Session Reports *Scot*
New York Supplement (Nat. Reporter
System)
Quebec Supreme Court Reports
S.A.I.R. South Australian Industrial
Reports
S.A.L.J. South African Law Journal
S.A.L.R. South African Law Reports
South Australian Law Reports
S.A.L.T. South African Law Times
S.A.L.R.,S.W.A. South African Law
Reports, South West African
Reports

S.A.R. South African Republic High
Court Reports
South Australian Reports
S.A.S.R. South Australian State
Reports
S.A.Tax Cas. South African Tax Cases
S.App. Shaw, House of Lords Cases
Scot
S.B. Senate Bill (in state legislation)
Supreme Bench
Special Bulletin, N. Y. Dept. of Labor
S.C. Cape of Good Hope Reports *S.Af.*
Court of Session Cases *Scot*
Same Case
Superior Court
Supreme Court
Select Cases (Oudh) *India*
South Carolina
Supreme Court Reporter (Nat.
Reporter System)
United Nations Security Council
SCAP Supreme Commander, Allied
Powers
S.C.Bar Assn. South Carolina Bar
Association
S.C.C. Select Chancery Cases *Eng*
Select Cases in Chancery *temp.* King,
ed. Macnaghten *Eng*
Small Cause Court *India*
Cameron's Supreme Court Cases
Canada
S.C.D.C. Supreme Court Reports,
District of Columbia
S.C.D.C.N.S. Same, New Series
S.C.Eq. South Carolina Equity Reports
S.C.H.L. Court of Session Cases, House
of Lords *Scot*
S.C.(J.) Court of Justiciary Cases *Scot*
S.C.J.B. Jamaica Supreme Court Judg-
ment Books
S.C.L. South Carolina Law Reports
S.C.L.Q. South Carolina Law
Quarterly
S.C.Oudh. Oudh Select Cases *India*
S.C.R. Canada Supreme Court Reports
Canada Law Reports, Supreme Court
Cape Colony Supreme Court Reports
South Carolina Reports
S.C.R.N.S.W. New South Wales
Supreme Court Reports
S.C.U.C.C.Dec. South Carolina Un-
employment Compensation Com-
mission Decisions
S.Car. South Carolina
S.Con.Res. Senate Concurrent
Resolution

S.Ct. Supreme Court; Supreme Court Reporter

S.D. South Dakota
Sadr Diwani Adalat Court, Bengal *India*

S.D.A. Special Disbursing Agent, Bur. of Indian Affairs *U.S.*

S.D.A. Sadr Diwani Adalat Court Reports *India*

S.D.B.Jo. South Dakota Bar Journal

S.D.K. Si De Ka Quarterly

S.D.R. New York State Department Reports

S.D.& B. Shaw, Dunlop, & Bell's Session Reports *Scot*

S.D.& B.Supp. Supplement to above, with House of Lords decisions

S.Dak. South Dakota

S.Doc. Senate Document

SDPA Small Defense Plants Administration *U.S.*

S.E. South Eastern Reporter (Nat. Reporter System)

S.E.C. Securities and Exchange Commission *U.S.*

S.E.C.Jud.Dec. Securities & Exchange Commission Judicial Decisions 1934–39 *U.S.*

SFO Defense Solid Fuels Order *U.S.*

SHAPE Supreme Headquarters, Allied Powers in Europe

S.J. Solicitors' Journal

S.J.L.B. Selected Judgments, Lower Burma

S.J.Res. Senate Joint Resolution

S.Just. Shaw's Justiciary Cases *Scot*

S.L.C. Scottish Land Court Reports

S.L.C.App. Lower Canada Appeal Cas. (Stuart)

S.L.C.R. Scottish Land Court Reports

S.L.F.C. Sierra Leone Full Court Reports

S.L.J. Scottish Law Journal

S.L.L.R. Sierra Leone Law Recorder

S.L.R. Saskatchewan Law Reports
Scottish Law Reporter
Scots Law Review
Scottish Land Reports
Sind Law Reporter *India*
Southern Law Review

S.L.R.B. State Labor Relations Board

S.L.Rev. Scottish Law Review & Sheriff Court Reports

S.L.T. Scots Law Times; Scots Law Times Reports

S.L.T.Sh.Ct. Scots Law Times Reports, Sheriff Court

S.M. Solicitor's Memorandum, U. S. Internal Revenue Bureau

S.N. Session Notes *Scot*

S.N.A. Sadr Nizamat Adalat Reports *India*

S.O.L.Rev. School of Law Review *Canada*

SPC South Pacific Commission *UN*

S.P.R. Porto Rico Reports, Spanish edition

S.Q.T. Queensland State Reports *Aus*

S.R. Solicitor's Recommendation, U. S. Internal Revenue Bureau
Special Regulation, U. S. Army
New South Wales State Reports
New York State Reporter
Supreme Court of Quebec, Reports
Southern Rhodesia High Court Reports

SRA Service & Regulatory Announcement, Dept. of Agric. *U.S.*

S.R.C. Stuart's Lower Canada Reports

SRM Ship Repairs Maintenance Order, Nat'l. Shipping Authority Maritime Adm. *U.S.*

S.R.N.S.W. New South Wales State Reports

S.R.Q. Queensland State Reports

S.R.R. Scots Revised Reports

S.R.& O. Statutory Rules & Orders *Eng*

S.Rept. Senate Report

S.Res. Senate Resolution

S.S. Selden Society
Silvernail's New York Supreme Court Reports
Synopsis Series, U. S. Treasury Decisions

SSA Social Security Administration *U.S.*

SSB Salary Stabilization Board *U.S.*

S.S.C. Sanford's Superior Court Reports, New York City
Sarawak Supreme Court Reports
Scotch Session Cases

S.S.C.R. Sind Sadr Court Reports *India*

S.S.L.R. Straits Settlements Law Reports

S.S.R. Social Security Tax Ruling, U. S. Internal Revenue Bureau

SSS Selective Service System *U.S.*

S.T. Sales Tax Branch, U. S. Internal Revenue Bureau
Sales Tax Rulings, U. S. Internal Revenue Bureau

S.T.C. State Tax Cases (CCH)

S.T.D. Synopsis Decisions, U. S. Treasury

S.Teind Shaw's Teind Cases *Scot*

S.V.A.R. Stuart's Vice-Admiralty Rep. *Can*

S.W. South Western Reporter (Nat. Reporter System)

S.W.A. South-West Africa Law Reports

S.W.L.Rev. Southwestern Law Review

S.W.L.J. Southwestern Law Journal & Reporter

S.W.Pol.Sci.Q. Southwestern Political Science Quarterly

S.& B. Smith & Batty's King's Bench Rep. *Ir*

S.&C. Saunders & Cole's Bail Court Rep. *Eng*

S.& D. Shaw, Dunlop, & Bell, Court of Session Reports *Scot*

S.& G. Smale & Giffard's Vice-Chancery Reports *Eng*

Stone & Graham's Court of Referees Reports *Eng*

Stone & Graham's Private Bills Reports *Eng*

S.& L. Schoales & Lefroy's Chancery Rep. *Ir*

S.& M. Shaw & Maclean's House of Lords Cas.

Smedes & Marshall's Reports (9–22 Miss.)

Smedes & Marshall's Chancery Rep. *Miss*

S.& M.Ch. Smedes & Marshall's Chancery Reports *Miss*

S.& Mar. Smedes & Marshall's Rep. (9–22 Miss.)

S.& R. Sergeant & Rawles' Reports (Pa. 1824–28)

S.& S. Sausse & Scully's Rolls Ct. Rep. *Ir*

Simons & Stuart's Vice-Chancery Rep. *Eng*

S.& Sm. Searle & Smith's Probate & Divorce Reports *Eng*

S.& T. Swabey & Tristram's Probate & Divorce Reports *Eng*

Sachse N.M. Sachse's Minutes, Norwich Mayoralty Court

Sad.Pa.Cas. Sadley's Cases (Pa. 1885–88)

Sal. Salinger's Reports (88–117 Iowa)

Salk. Salkeld's King's Bench Reports *Eng*

San. Sanford's Reports (59 Alabama)

San Fr.L.B. San Francisco Law Bulletin

San Fr.L.J. San Francisco Law Journal

Sand. Sandford's Reports (3–7 N. Y. Superior)

Sand.Ch. Sandford's Reports (N. Y. Chancery 1843–47)

Sand.I.Rep. Sandwich Islands (Hawaiian) Reports

Sandf. Sandford's Rep. (3–7 N. Y. Superior)

Sandf.Ch. Sandford's Rep. (N. Y. Chancery)

Sanf. Sanford's Reports (59 Alabama)

Sar. Sarswati's P. C. Judgments *India*

Sar.Ch.Sen. Saratoga Chancery Sentinel *N.Y.*

Sarbah Sarbah, Fantti Law Reports *Gold Coast*

Sarbah F.C. Sarbah, Fantti Customary Laws *Gold Coast*

Sask. Saskatchewan *Canada*

Sask.B.Rev. Saskatchewan Bar Review

Sask.Gaz. Saskatchewan Gazette

Sask.L.R. Saskatchewan Law Reports *Canada*

Sau.L.R. Saurastra Law Reports *India*

Sau.&Sc. Sausse & Scully's Rolls Court Reports *Ir*

Sauls. Reports time of Saulsbury (5–6 Delaware)

Saund. Saunders' King's Bench Reports *Eng*

Saund.& A. Saunders & Austin's Locus Standi Reports *Eng*

Saund.& B. Saunders & Bidder's Locus Standi Reports *Eng*

Saund.& C. Saunders & Cole's Bail Court Reports *Eng*

Saund.& M. Saunders & Macrae's County Courts & Insolvency Cases (County Courts Cases & Appeals, v. II–III) *Eng*

Sausse & Sc. Sausse & Scully's Rolls Court Reports *Ir*

Sav. Savile's Common Pleas Reports *Eng*

Saw. Sawyer's Circuit Court Reports *U.S.*

Sax. Saxton's Reports (1 N. J. Equity)

Say. Sayer's King's Bench Reports *Eng*

Sayles Sayles' Select Cases in the Court of King's Bench (Selden Society Publications, v. 55, 57, 58)

Sc. Scammon's Reports (2–5 Illinois)

Scott's Common Pleas Reports *Eng* Scotch

Sc.Jur. Scottish Jurist

Sc.L.J. Scottish Law Journal & Sheriff Court Record

Sc.L.M. Scottish Law Magazine and Sheriff Court Reporter

Sc.L.R. Scottish Law Reporter
Scottish Law Review & Sheriff Court Reports

Sc.L.T. Scots Law Times

Sc.La.R. Scottish Land Court Reports

Sc.La.Rep. Scottish Land Court Reports

Sc.La.Rep.Ap. Scottish Land Court Report Appendices

Sc.Mun.App.Rep. Scotch Munitions Appeals Reports

Sc.N.R. Scott's New Reports, Com. Pl.   *Eng*

Sc.R.R. Scots Revised Reports

Sc.Rev.Rept. Scots Revised Reports

Sc.Sess.Cas. Scotch Court of Session Cases

Sc.& Div.App. Law Reports, Scotch & Divorce Appeals

Scam. Scammon's Reports (2–5 Illinois)

Sch.& Lef. Schoales & Lefroy's Ch. Rep.   *Ir*

Schalk Schalk's Jamaica Reports

Scher. Scherer's Reports (22–47 N. Y. Misc.)

Schm.L.J. Schmidt's Law Journal

Schuyl.Leg.Rec. Schuylkill Legal Record   *Pa*

Sco. Scott's Common Pleas Reports   *Eng*

Sco.N.R. Scott's New Reports, Com. Pl.   *Eng*

Scot. Scotland; Scots; Scottish

Scot.App.Rep. Scottish Appeal Reports

Scot.Jur. Scottish Jurist

Scot.L.J. Scottish Law Journal & Sheriff Court Record

Scot.L.M. Scottish Law Magazine & Sheriff Court Reporter

Scot.L.R. Scottish Law Reporter Scottish Law Review

Scot.L.Rev. Scottish Law Review

Scot.L.T. Scots Law Times

Scott Scott's Common Pleas Reports   *Eng*
Scott's Reports (25, 26 N. Y. Civil Pro.)

Scott N.R. Scott's New Common Pleas Rep.   *Eng*

Scr.L.T. Scranton (Pa.) Law Times

Sea.& Sm. Searle & Smith's Probate & Divorce Reports   *Eng*

Searle & Sm. Same as above

Sec.Bk.Judg. Second Book of Judgments (Huxley)   *Eng*

Sec.& Ex.C. Securities & Exchange Commission

Sec.Int. Secretary of the Interior   *U.S.*

Secd.pt.Edw.III Year Books, Part III   *Eng*

Secd.pt.H.VI Year Books, Part VIII   *Eng*

Seign.Rep. Lower Canada Seigniorial Reports

Sel.Cas. Select Cases Central Provinces   *India*

Sel.Cas.Ch. Select Cases in Chancery   *Eng*

Sel.Cas.D.A. Select Cases Sadr Diwani Adalat   *India*

Sel.Cas.Ev. Select Cases in Evidence (Strange)   *Eng*

Sel.Cas.K.B.Edw.I. Select Cases in K. B. under Edward I (Sayles)   *Eng*

Sel.Cas.N.F. Select Cases, Newfoundland

Sel.Cas.N.W.P. Select Cases, Northwest Provinces   *India*

Sel.Cas.N.Y. Yates' Select Cases (N. Y. 1809)

Sel.Cas.S.D.A. Select Cases Sadr Diwani Adalat (Bengal, Bombay)   *India*

Sel.Cas.*t*.King Select Cases in Chancery *temp*. King   *Eng*

Sel.Cas.*t*.Nap. Select Cases *temp*. Napier   *Ir*

Sel.Ch.Cas. Select Cases in Chancery *temp*. King, ed. Macnaghten   *Eng*

Sel.Col.Cas. Select Collection of Cases   *Eng*

Sel.Dec.Bomb. Select Cases Sadr Diwani Adalat, Bombay   *India*

Sel.Dec.Madr. Select Decrees, Sadr Adalat, Madras   *India*

Seld. Selden's Reports (5–10 N. Y.)

Seld.Notes Selden's Notes, N. Y. Court of Appeals

Seld.Soc. Selden Society

Seld.Soc.Yrbk. Selden Society Yearbook   *U.S.*

Selden *See* Seld., *supra*

Selw.& Barn. Barnewall & Alderson's K. B. Reports, 1st part   *Eng*

Seminar (Annual extraordinary number of the Jurist, Catholic University of America)

Sen.Doc. Senate Document

Sen.Jo. Senate Journal

Sen.Rep. Senate Report

Serg.& Lowb. English Common Law Reports, ed. Sergeant & Lowber

Serg.& Rawl. Sergeant & Rawle's Reports (Pa. 1814–28)

Sess.Ca. Scotch Court of Session Cases

Sess.Cas. Scotch Court of Session Cases
Sessions Cases, King's Bench *Eng*
Sessions Settlement Cases, K. B. *Eng*

Sess.Cas.K.B. Sessions Settlement Cases, King's Bench *Eng*

Sess.Cas.Sc. Scotch Court of Session Cases

Sess.N. Session Notes *Scot*

Sess.Pap.C.C.C. Central Criminal Court Session Papers *Eng*

Sess.Pap.O.B. Old Bailey Session Papers

Sett.Cas. Settlements & Removals, Cases in King's Bench *Eng*
Burrow's Settlement Cases *Eng*

Sett.& Rem. Same as above

Sev.H.C. Sevestre's Bengal High Court Rep. *India*

Sev.S.D.A. Sevestre's Sadr Diwani Adalat Reports, Bengal *India*

Sevestre Calcutta Reports of Cases in Appeal

Seych.L.R. Seychelles Law Reports

Sh. Shadforth's Reserved Judgments *Aus*
Shand's Reports (11–41 South Carolina)
Shaw's Appeal Cases *Scot*
Shaw's Session Cases *Scot*
Shaw's Scotch Justiciary Cases
Shaw's Teind Court Reports *Scot*
G.B. Shaw's Reports (10, 11 Vermont)
W. G. Shaw's Reports (30–35 Vermont)
Sheil's Cape Times Law Reports *S.Af.*
Sheldon's Reports (Buffalo, N. Y. Superior Court)
Shepherd's Alabama Reports
Shepley's Reports (13–18, 21–30 Maine)
Shipp's Reports (66, 67 North Carolina)
Shirley's Reports (49–55 New Hampshire)
Shower's King's Bench Reports *Eng*
Shower's Parliamentary Cases *Eng*

Sh.App. Shaw's House of Lords App. Cas. *Scot*

Sh.Crim.Cas. Shaw's Justiciary Court, Criminal Cases . *Scot*

Sh.Ct.of Sess. Shaw's Court of Session Cases *Scot*

Sh.Ct.Rep. Sheriff Court Reports *Scot*

Sh.Dig. Shaw's Digest of Decisions *Scot*

Sh.Just. P. Shaw's Justiciary Decisions *Scot*

Sh.Sc.App. P. Shaw's Scotch Appeals

Sh.Teind.Ct. P. Shaw's Teind Court Dec. *Scot*

Sh.W.& C. Shaw, Wilson, & Courtenay's Scotch Appeals Reports

Sh.& Dunl. Shaw & Dunlop's Court of Session Reports, 1st Series *Scot*

Sh.& Macl. Shaw & Maclean's Scotch Appeal Cases

Shad. Shadforth's Reports, Victoria *Aus*

Shale Decrees & Judgments in Federal Anti-Trust Cases *U.S.*

Shan. Shannon's Unreported Cases *Tenn.*

Shand Shand's Reports (11–41 N. C.)

Shaw Shaw's Scotch Appeal Cases
Shaw's Court of Session Cases, 1st Ser.
Shaw's Justiciary Cases *Scot*
Shaw's Teind Court Reports *Scot*
G. B. Shaw's Reports (10, 11 Vermont)
W. G. Shaw's Reports (30–35 Vermont)

Shaw App. Shaw's Appeal Cases, H. L.: Appeals from Scotland

Shaw Dec. Shaw's Court of Session Decisions, 1st Series *Scot*

Shaw Dig. Shaw's Digest of Decisions *Scot*

Shaw Dunl.& B. Shaw, Dunlop, & Bell's Session Cases, 1st Series *Scot*

Shaw H.L. Shaw's House of Lords Appeal Cases *Scot*

Shaw Jus. J. Shaw's Justiciary Cases *Scot*

Shaw T.Cas. Shaw's Teind Court Cases *Scot*

Shaw (Vt.) G. B. Shaw's Reports (10, 11 Vt.)
W. G. Shaw's Reports (30–35 Vermont)

Shaw (W.G.) W. G. Shaw's Reports (30–35 Vt.)

Shaw,W.& C. Shaw, Wilson, & Courtenay's Scotch Appeals Reports, House of Lords

Shaw & Dunl. Shaw & Dunlop's Court of Session Reports, 1st Series *Scot*

Shaw & Macl. Shaw & Maclean's
Appeal Cases, House of Lords
Scot

Sheil Sheil's Cape Times Law Reports
S.Af.

Sheld. Sheldon's Reports (Buffalo,
N. Y., Superior Court)

Shep. Shepherd's Reports, Alabama
Select Cases (in 37–39 Ala.)
Shepley's Reports (13–18, 21–30
Maine)

Shep.Touch. Sheppard's Touchstone
Eng

Shepley Shepley's Reports (13–18,
21–30 Me.)

Sher.Ct.Rep. Sheriff Court Reports
Scot
Sheriff Court Reporter *Scot*

Shill.W.C. Shillman's Workmen's
Compensation Cases *Ir*

Shingle The Shingle, Phila. Bar Assn.

Ship.Gaz. Shipping Gazette *Eng*

Shipp. Shipp's Reports (66, 67 N. C.)

Shirley Shirley's Reports (49–55
N. H.)

Shome L.R. Shome's Law Reporter
India

Show. Shower's King's Bench Reports
Eng
Shower's Parliamentary Cases *Eng*

Show.K.B. Shower's King's Bench
Reports *Eng*

Show.P.C. Shower's Cases in Parliament *Eng*

Show.Parl.Cas. Same as above

Sick. Sickels' Reports (46–85 N. Y.)

Sick.Min.Dec. Sickels' U. S. Mining
Laws & Decisions

Sid. Siderfin's K. B., Com. Pl., & Ex.
Rep.

Silv. Silvernails Reports (N. Y. 1886–
92)
Silvernail's Reports (9–14 N. Y.
Criminal Reports)
Silvernail's Supreme Ct. Rep. (N. Y.
1889–90)

Sim. Simmons' Reports (99 Wisconsin)
Simons' Chancery Reports *Eng*

Sim.N.S. Simons' Chancery Rep. New
Ser. *Eng*

Sim.& C. Simmons & Conover's Rep.
(99–100 Wis.)

Sim.& St. Simons & Stuart's Ch.
Reports *Eng*

Sinclair Sinclair's Manuscript
Decisions, Scotch Session Cases

Sir J.S. Sir John Strange's Reports *Eng*

Sir T.J. Sir Thomas Jones' Reports,
King's Bench & Common Pleas
Eng

Sir T.Ray. T. Raymond's K. B.
Reports *Eng*

Six Circ. Cases on the Six Circuits *Ir*

Skill.Pol.Rep. Skillman's N. Y. Police
Rep.

Skin. Skinner's King's Bench Reports
Eng

Skinker Skinker's Reports (65–79
Missouri)

Slade Slade's Reports (15 Vermont)

Sloan Leg.Reg. Sloan's Legal Register
N.Y.

Sm. Smith

Sm.C.C.M. Smith's Circuit Courts-
Martial Reports, Maine *U.S.*

Sm.Cond.Ala. Smith's Condensed
Alabama Rep.

Sm.E.D. E. D. Smith's Common Pleas
Rep. *N.Y.*

Sm.Eng. Smith's King's Bench Reports
Eng

Sm.Ind. Smith's Reports (In 1–4
Indiana)

Sm.K.B. Smith's King's Bench Reports
Eng

Sm.L.J. Law Journal (Smith) *Eng*

Sm.Me. Smith's Reports (61–84
Maine)

Sm.& B.R.R.Cas. Smith & Bates'
American Railway Cases

Sm.& Bat. Smith & Batty's K. B.
Reports *Ir*

Sm.& G. Smale & Giffard's Chancery
Rep. *Eng*
Smith & Guthrie's Reports (81–101 Mo.
App.)

Sm.& M. Smedes & Marshall's Rep.
(Mississippi Chancery 1840–43)
Smedes & Marshall's Reports (9–22
Miss.)

Sm.& M.Ch. Same as above

Sm.& S. Smith & Sager's Drainage Cases
Can

Smed.& M. Smedes & Marshall's
Reports (Mississippi Chancery
1839–43, or 9–22 Mississippi)

Smed.& M.Ch. Smedes & Marshall's
Mississippi Chancery Reports

Smi.& Bat. Smith & Batty's K. B. Rep.
Ir

Smith. J. P. Smith's King's Bench
Reports *Eng*

Smith's Registration Cases *Eng*
Smith's Reports (54–62 California)
Smith's Reports (In 1–4 Indiana)
Smith's Reports (61–64 Maine)
Smith's Reports (81–101 Missouri App.)
Smith's Reports (N. H. 1796–1816)
E. D. Smith's Reports (N. Y. Com. Pl.)
E. P. Smith's Reports (15–27, 147–62 N. Y.)
Smith's Reports (51–81 Pa. State)
Smith's Reports (2–4 South Dakota)
Smith's Reports (7, 12 Tennessee)
Smith's Reports (1–11 Wisconsin)
Smith,E.D. E. D. Smith's Reports (N. Y. Common Pleas)
Smith,J.P. J. P. Smith's K. B. Reports *Eng*
Smith K.B. Same as above
Smith L.C. Smith's Leading Cases *Eng*
Smith Lead.Cas. Same as above
Smith Me. Smith's Reports (61–64 Maine)
Smith N.H. Smith's Reports (N. H. 1796–1816)
Smith N.Y. E. P. Smith's Reports (15–27, 147–62 N. Y.)
Smith, P.F. P. F. Smith's Rep. (51–81 Pa. St.)
Smith Reg.Cas. C. L. Smith's Registration Cases *Eng*
Smith Wis. Smith's Reports (1–11 Wisconsin)
Smith & B.R.R.C. Smith & Bates, American Railway Cases
Smith & G. Smith & Guthrie's Reports (81–101 Missouri Appeals)
Smoult Notes of Cases in Smoult's Collection of Orders, Calcutta *India*
Smy. Smythe's Common Pleas Reports *Ir*
Smy.& B. Smythe & Bourke's Marriage Cas. *Ir*
Smythe Smythe's Common Pleas Reports *Ir*
Sneed Sneed's Kentucky Decisions (2 Ky.)
Sneed's Reports (33–37 Tennessee)
Sneed Dec. Sneed's Kentucky Decisions (2 Ky.)
Snow Snow's Reports (3 Utah)
So. Southern Reporter (Nat. Reporter System)
So.Afr.L.J. South African Law Journal
So.Afr.L.R. South African Law Reports
So.Afr.L.T. South African Law Times

So.Afr.Prize Cas. South African Prize Cases (Juta)
So.Aust.L.R. South Australian Law Reports
So.Calif.L.Rev. Southern California Law Rev.
So.Car. South Carolina
So.Car.Const. South Carolina Constitutional Reports, by Treadway, Mill, or Harper
So.Car.L.J. South Carolina Law Journal
So.Dak.B.Jo. South Dakota Bar Journal
So.East.Rep. South Eastern Reporter
So.Jersey L.S.Dictum South Jersey Law School Dictum
So.L.J. Southern Law Journal & Reporter
So.L.R. Southern Law Review
So.L.R.N.S. Southern Law Review, New Series
So.L.T. Southern Law Times
So.Rep. Southern Reporter
So.West.L.J. Southwestern Law Journal
So.West.Rep. South Western Reporter
Sol. The Solicitor
Soloman's Court of Request Appeals *Ceylon*
Sol.J. Solicitors' Journal
Sol.J.& R. Solicitors' Journal & Reporter
Sol.Op. Solicitors' Opinion (especially of Internal Revenue Bureau) *U.S.*
Som.L.J. Somerset Legal Journal (Pa. 1920–date)
Sm.Pl. Somersetshire Pleas Civil & Criminal, ed. Chadwyck-Healey and Landon (Somerset Record Society Publications, v. 11, 36, 41, 44)
South. Southern Reporter (National Reporter System)
South Aus.L.R. South Australian Law Reports
South.L.J. Southern Law Journal
South.L.J.& Rep. Southern Law Journal & Reporter
South.L.Rev. Southern Law Review
South.L.Rev.N.S. Same as above, New Series
Southard Southard's Reports (4–5 N. J. Law)
Southw.L.J. Southwestern Law Journal & Reporter
Southwestern L.J. Southwestern Law Journal

Sp. Spear's Reports (S. C. Law 1842–44)

Spinks' Ecclesiastical & Admiralty Reports *Eng*

Sp.CM Special Court-Martial (U. S. Navy)

Sp.Eq. Spear's Reports (S. C. Equity)

Sp.Pr.Cas. Spinks' Prize Cases *Eng*

Sp.& Sel.Cas. Special & Selected Law Cases *Eng*

Sparks Sparks' British Burma Reports

Spaulding Spaulding's Reports (71–80 Me.)

Spears Spears' Reports (S. C. Law or Equity)

Spears Eq. Spears' Reports (S. C. Equity)

Speers Alternate spelling of above

Spencer Spencer's Reports (10–20 Minn.)

Spencer's Reports (20 N. J. Law)

Spens Sel.Cas. Spens' Select Cases, Bombay *India*

Spinks Spinks' Ecclesiastical & Admiralty Reports *Eng*

Spinks P.C. Spinks' Prize Court Cases *Eng*

Spooner Spooner's Reports (12–15 Wisconsin)

Spott.Eq.Rep. Spottiswoode's Equity Rep. *Eng*

Spottis. R. Spottiswoode's Court of Session Reports *Scot*

Spottis.C.L.& Eq.Rep. Spottiswoode's Common Law & Equity Reports *Eng*

Spr. Sprague's District Court & Admiralty Decisions *U.S.*

St. Stair's Decisions, Court of Session *Scot*

Story's Circuit Court Reports *U.S.*

Stuart, Milne, & Peddie's Session Cases *Scot*

St.Ab. Statham's Abridgment *Eng*

St.Cas. Stillingfleet's Eccles. Cas. *Eng*

St.Ch.Cas. Star Chamber Cases *Eng*

St.Eccl.Cas. Stillingfleet's Ecclesiastical Cases *Eng*

St.Inst. Statutory Instruments *Eng*

St.John's L.Rev. St. John's Law Review

St.L.U.Intra.L.Rev. St. Louis University Intramural Law Review

St.Louis L.Rev. St. Louis Law Review

St.M.& P. Stuart, Milne, & Peddie's Session Cases *Scot*

St.P. State Papers

St.Pl.Cr. Staundford's Pleas of Crown *Eng*

St.Pr.Reg. Style's Practical Register *Eng*

St.R.Q. Queensland State Reports *Aus*

St.R.Qd. Same as above

St.Rep. State Reports

State Reporter (Montana Supreme Court Advance Sheets)

New York State Reporter

St.Ry.Rep. Street Railway Reports *U.S.*

St.Tr. Howell's State Trials *Eng*

St.Tr.N.S. Macdonell's State Trials *Eng*

Stafford Stafford's Reports (69–71 Vt.)

Stair Stair's Court of Session Reports *Scot*

Stanford Staundford's Pleas of the Crown *Eng*

Stanford L.Rev. Stanford Law Review

Stanton Stanton's Reports (11–13 Ohio)

Star. Starkie's Nisi Prius Reports *Eng*

Star Ch.Ca. Star Chamber Cases *Eng*

Stark. Starkie's Nisi Prius Reports *Eng*

Stark.N.P. Same as above

Stat. Statutes; Statutes at Large; Statutes Revised

Stat.at L. Statutes at Large

Stat.Realm Statutes of the Realm *Eng*

State Tr. State Trials (Howell) *Eng*

State Tr.N.S. State Trials, New Series, ed. Macdonell *Eng*

Staund.Pl. Staundford's Pleas of Crown *Eng*

Staundforde Same as above

Stenton Stenton, Rolls of the Justices in Eyre for Lincolnshire & Worcestershire (Selden Society Publication, v. 53)

Stenton G. Stenton, Rolls of the Justices in Eyre for Gloucestershire & Staffordshire (Selden Society Publication, v. 59)

Stenton Y. Stenton, Rolls of the Justices in Eyre for Yorkshire (Selden Society Publication, v. 56)

Stephens J. E. R. Stephens' Supreme Court Decisions, Jamaica, & Privy Council Decisions

Stevens & G. Stevens & Graham's Reports (98–139 Georgia)

Stew. Stewart's Reports (Alabama 1827–31)
Stewart's Reports (28–45 N. J. Equity)
Stewart's Reports (1–10 South Dakota)
Stewart's Nova Scotia Admiralty Reports

Stew.Adm. Stewart's Nova Scotia Admiralty Reports

Stew.Eq. Stewart's Reports (28–45 N. J. Eq.)

Stew.N.Sc. Stewart's Nova Scotia Admiralty Reports

Stew.V.A. Same as above

Stew.& P. Stewart & Porter's Reports (Alabama 1831–34)

Stewart *See* Stew., *supra*

Stewart-Brown Stewart-Brown Lancashire & Cheshire Cases, Star Chamber *Eng*

Sth.Af.Rep. South African High Court Rep.

Stiles Stiles' Reports (22–29 Iowa)

Still.Eccl.Cas. Stillingfleet's Ecclesiastical Cases *Eng*

Stiness Stiness' Reports (20–34 Rhode Is.)

Sto. Story's Circuit Court Reports *U.S.*

Sto.C.C. Same as above

Sto.& G. Stone & Graham's Private Bills Decisions *Eng*

Stock. Stockton's Vice-Admiralty Rep. *Can*
Stockton's Reports (9–11 N. J. Equity)
Stockton's New Brunswick Reports (Berton)

Stock.Adm. Stockton's Vice-Admiralty Reports *Canada*

Stockett Stockett's Reports (27–79 Md.)

Stockt.Ch. Stockton's Rep. (9–11 N. J. Eq.)

Stockton *See* Stock., *supra*

Story Story's Circuit Court Reports *U.S.*

Str. Strange's King's Bench Reports *Eng*
Strange's Cases of Evidence *Eng*

Str.N.C. T. Strange's Notes of Cases *Madras*

Stra. Strange; *see* Str., *supra*

Strahan Strahan's Reports (19 Oregon)

Stran. Strange; *see* Str., *supra*

Strange *See* Str., *supra*

Strange Madras Strange's Notes of Cases

Stratton Stratton's Rep. (12–14, 19 Oregon)

Street Ry.Rep. Street Railway Reports

Stringfellow Stringfellow's Rep. (9–11 Mo. App.)

Strob. Strobhart's Reports (S. C. Law)

Strob.Eq. Strobhart's Reports (S. C. Equity)

Struve Struve's Reports (Washington Territory 1854–88)

Stu.Adm. Stuart's Lower Canada Vice-Admiralty Reports

St.Adm.N.S. Stuart's Lower Canada Vice-Admiralty Reports, New Series

Stu.Ap. Stuart's Lower Canada King's Bench Reports, Appeal Cases

Stu.K.B. Stuart's Lower Canada K. B. Rep.

Stu.M.& P. Stuart, Milne, & Peddie's Court of Session Reports *Scot*

Stuart *See* Stu., *supra;* Stuart's Session Cases *Scot*

Stuart Adm.N.S. Stuart's Lower Canada Vice-Admiralty Reports, New Series

Stuart K.B. Stuart's Lower Canada King's Bench Reports

Stubbs Sel.Ch. Stubbs' Select Charters

Sty. Style's King's Bench Reports *Eng*

Su.Ct.Cir. Supreme Court Circular *Ceylon*

Sud.Dew.Ad. Sudder Dewanny Adawlut Rep. *India*

Sud.Dew.Rep. Sudder Dewanny Reports, N. W. Province *India*

Sum. Sumner's Circuit Court Reports *U.S.*
Hale's Summary of Pleas of the Crown *Eng*

Sum.Dec. Summary Decisions, Bengal *India*

Summerfield Summerfield's Rep. (21 Nevada)

Sumn. Sumner's Circuit Court Reports *U.S.*

Sumn.Ves. Vesey's Reports, Sumner Edition

Sup.Ct. Supreme Court
Supreme Court Reporter (National Reporter System)

Super. Superior Court

Super.Ct.Rep. Superior Court Reports (New York, Pennsylvania, *etc.*)

Supp.Ves.Jun. Supplement to Vesey, Jr. Rep.

Susq.L.C. Susquehanna Law Chronicle *Pa*

Suth. Sutherland's Calcutta Reports *India*

Suth.Bengal Sutherland's Bengal High
Court Reports   *India*
Suth.F.B.R. Sutherland's Bengal Full
Bench Reports   *India*
Suth.Mis. India Weekly Reporter,
Miscellaneous Appeals
Suth.P.C.A. Sutherland Privy Council
Appeals
Suth.P.C.J. Sutherland Privy Council
Judgments (same as above)
Suth.W.R. Sutherland's Weekly
Reporter   *India*
Sw. Swabey's Admiralty Reports *Eng*
Swan's Reports (31, 32 Tennessee)
Swanston's Chancery Reports   *Eng*
Sweeney's N. Y. Superior Court
Reports
Swinton's Scotch Justiciary Cases
Sw.& Tr. Swabey & Tristram's Probate
& Divorce Reports   *Eng*
Swab. Swabey's Admiralty Reports
Eng
Swan. Swan's Reports (31, 32
Tennessee)
Swanston's Chancery Reports   *Eng*
Swan.Ch. Swanston's Chancery
Reports   *Eng*
Swans. Same as above
Sween. Sweeny's N. Y. Superior Court
Rep.
Sweet M.Sett.Cas. Sweet's Marriage
Settlement Cases   *Eng*
Swin. Swinton's Justiciary Reports
Scot
Swin.Reg.App. Swinton's Registration
Appeal Cases   *Scot*
Swint. Same as Swin., *supra*
Syd.App. Sydney Appeals   *Aus*
Syl. The Syllabi (legal periodical)
Syme Syme's Justiciary Reports *Scot*
Syn.Ser. Synopsis Series, Treasury
Decisions   *U.S.*
Syracuse L.Rev. Syracuse Law Review
T. Tappan's Common Pleas Reports
Ohio
Tobacco Tax Ruling, Internal Revenue
Bureau   *U.S.*
TAB Technical Assistance Board *UN*
T.B.M. Advisory Tax Board Memor-
andum (Internal Revenue Bureau)
U.S.
T.B.Mon. T. B. Monroe's Reports
(17–23 Ky.)
T.B.R. Advisory Tax Board Recom-
mendation (Internal Revenue
Bureau)   *U.S.*
T.B.& M. Tracewell, Bowers, & Mit-
chell's U. S. Comptroller's
Decisions

T.C. Tax Court of the United States
Reports of Tax Cases   *Eng*
Trade Cases (CCH)
T.C. U. N. Trusteeship Council
TCM Tax Court Memorandum
Decisions (CCH)
T.C.Memo. Tax Court Memorandum
Decisions (P–H)
T.C.R. Transit Commission Reports
N.Y.
T.D. Treasury Decisions (U. S.
Treasury Dept.)
T.H. Reports of the Witwatersrand
High Court (Transvaal)   *S.Af.*
TICER Temporary International
Council for Educational Recon-
struction
T.T.S. Tea Inspection Service   *U.S.*
T.Jo. T. Jones' King's Bench &
Common Pleas Reports   *Eng*
T.Jones (2 Jones) Same as above
T.L. Reports of the Witwatersrand
High Court (Transvaal)   *S.Af.*
T.L.J. Travancore Law Journal *India*
T.L.R. Tasmanian Law Journal
Reports   *Aus*
Times Law Reports   *Eng*
Travancore Law Reports   *India*
T.L.T. Travancore Law Times *India*
T.M. National Income Tax Magazine
Technical Manual, U. S. Army
T.M.Bull. Trade Mark Bulletin, New
Series
T.M.Rep. Trade Mark Reporter
T.P. Transvaal Supreme Court Reports
S.Af.
T.P.D. South African Law Reports,
Transvaal Provincial Division
S.Af.
T.R. Taxation Reports   *Eng*
Term Reports (Durnford & East) *Eng*
Caine's Term Reports   *N.Y.*
T.R.N.S. Term Reports, New Series
(East)   *Eng*
T.Raym. T. Raymond's King's Bench
Rep.   *Eng*
T.S. Transvaal Supreme Court Reports
S.Af.
T.U.P.Charlt. T. U. P. Charlton's
Reports   *Ga*
TVA Tennessee Valley Authority *U.S.*
T.& B. Taylor & Bell's Calcutta
Supreme Court Reports   *India*
T.& G. Tyrwhitt's & Granger's Ex.
Rep.   *Eng*
T.& M. Temple & Mew's Criminal
Appeal Cases   *Eng*
Temple & Mew's Crown Cases   *Eng*

T.& P. Turner & Phillips' Chancery
Rep.   *Eng*
T.& R. Turner & Russell's Chancery
Rep.   *Eng*
T.& T.Supp. Trinidad & Tobago
Supreme Court Judgments
Tait Tait's Manuscript Decisions,
Scotch Session Cases
Tal [b] Chancery Cases *temp.* Talbot
Eng
Tam. Tamlyn's Rolls Court. Reports
Eng
Tamb. Tambyah's Reports   *Ceylon*
Taml. Tamlyn's Rolls Court Reports
Eng
Tan. Taney's Circuit Court Reports
U.S.
Tan.L.R. Tanganyika Territory Law
Reports
Tanner Tanner's Reports (8–14
Indiana)
Tanner's Reports (13–17 Utah)
Tapp. Tappan's Ohio Common Pleas
Reports
Tarl.Term R. Tartleton's Term
Reports, N.S.W.   *Aus*
Tas.L.R. Tasmanian Law Reports
Aus
Taun. Taunton's Common Pleas
Reports   *Eng*
Tax Cas. Tax cases   *Eng**
See also TC
Tax L.Rep. Tax Law Reporter
Tax L.Rev. Tax Law Review
Tax Rev. Tax Review
Taxes Taxes — The Tax Magazine
Tay. Taylor
Taylor's King's Bench Reports *Canada*
Taylor's Reports (1 North Carolina)
Tay.J.L. J. L. Taylor's Reports
(1 N. C.)
Tay.N.C. Same as above
Tay.&B. Taylor & Bell's Bengal Rep.
India
Tayl.N.C. Taylor's Reports (1 N. C.)
Taylor Taylor's King's Bench Rep.
Canada
Taylor's Reports, Bengal   *India*
Taylor's Reports (1 North Carolina)
Tem. The Templar   *Eng*
Temp.Geo.II Cases in Chancery *temp.*
George II   *Eng*
Temp.L.Q. Temple Law Quarterly
Temp.Wood Manitoba Reports *temp.*
Wood

_____
* The American ones are not referred to
as Tax Cases

Temp.& M. Temple & Mew's Crown
Cases   *Eng*
Temple L.Q. Temple Law Quarterly
Tenn. Tennessee
Tenn.App. Tennessee Civil Appeals
Reports
Tenn.B.A. Tennessee Bar Association
Tenn.C.C.A. Tennessee Court of Civil
Appeals
Tenn.Cas. Shannon's Unreported
Cases (Tenn. 1847–94)
Tenn.Ch. Tennessee Chancery Rep.
(Cooper)
Tenn.Ch.App. Tennessee Chancery
Appeals (Wright)
Tenn.L.Rev. Tennessee Law Review
Tenn.Leg.Rep. Tennessee Legal
Reporter
Tenn.R.C. Tennessee Railroad
Commission
Term. Term Rep. (Durnford & East
K. B.)   *Eng*
Term.N.C. Term Reports (Taylor,
4 N. C.)
Term.Rep. Term Reports (Durnford
& East)   *Eng*
Terr. Terrell's Reports (52–71 Texas)
Terr.L.R. Territories Law Reports
Canada
Terr.& Walk. Terrell & Walker's
Reports (38–51 Texas)
Tex. Texas
Tex.App. Texas Criminal Appeals
Reports
Tex.B.J. Texas Bar Journal
Tex.Cr.R. Texas Criminal Reports
Tex.Ct.Rep. Texas Court Reporter
1900–08
Tex.Dec. Texas Decisions
Tex.Jur. Texas Jurisprudence
Tex.L.J. Texas Law Journal
Tex.L.Rev. Texas Law Review
Tex.R.C. Texas Railroad Commission
Tex.Supp. Supplement to 25 Texas
Reports
Tex.Unrep.Cas. Texas Unreported
Cases (Posey)
Th.C.C. Thacher's Criminal Cases
(Mass. 1823–42)
Th.& C. Thompson & Cook's Rep.
(N. Y. Supreme 1873–75)
Thac.Cr.Cas. Thacher's Criminal
Cases (Mass. 1823–42)
Thayer Thayer's Reports (18 Oregon)
The Rep. The Reporter, Phi Alpha
Delta
The Reports, Coke's Reports   *Eng*

Thém. American Thémis *N.Y.*
La Thémis, Montreal, Quebec

Thes. Thesawaleme *Ceylon*

Thom. Thomas' Reports
(1 Wyoming)
Thomson's Nova Scotia Reports

Thom.Dec. Thomson's Decisions
(1 Nova Scotia)

Thom.Rep. Thomson's Reports
(3 Nova Scotia)

Thom.& Fr. Thomas & Franklin's
Reports (1 Maryland Chancery)

Thomas Thomas' Reports
(1 Wyoming)

Thomp.Cal. Thompson's Reports
(39, 40 Calif.)

Thomp.N.B.Cas. Thompson's
National Bank Cas.

Thomp.Tenn.Cas. Thompson's Unreported Cases (Tenn. 1847–69)

Thomp.& C. Thompson & Cook's
New York Supreme Court
Reports

Thompson Thompson's Reports
(39, 40 Calif.)

Thor. Thorington's Reports
(107 Alabama)

Thorn. Notes of Cases Ecclesiastical &
Maritime (Thornton) *Eng*

Thorpe Thorpe's Reports (52 La.
Annual)

Tiffany Tiffany's Reports (28–39
N. Y.)

Tillman Tillman's Reports (68, 69, 71,
73, 75 Alabama)

Times L.R. Times Law Reports *Eng*
Times Law Reports *Ceylon*

Tinw. Tinwald's Reports, Court of
Session *Scot*

Title News Title News

Tob. Tobacco Branch, U. S. Internal
Revenue Bureau

Tobey Tobey's Reports (9, 10 Rhode
Island)

Toml. Tomlin's Election Cases *Eng*

Toml.Supp.Br. Tomlins' Supplement
to Brown's Parliamentary Cases
Eng

Tot. Tothill's Chancery Reports *Eng*

Toth. Tothill's Chancery Reports *Eng*
Tothill's Transactions in Chancery
Eng

Town St.Tr. Townsend's Modern
State Trials *Eng*

Tr. Tristram's Consistory Judgments
Eng

Tr.App. Transcript Appeals (N. Y.
1867–68)

Tr.Ch. Tothill's Reports, Transactions
of the High Court of Chancery
Eng

Tr.Consist.J. Tristram's Consistory
Judgments *Eng*

Tr.& Est. Trusts & Estates

Trace.& M. Tracewell & Mitchell's
U. S. Comptroller's Decisions

Trans.Ap. Transcript Appeals (N. Y.
1867–68)

Trade-Mark Rep. Trade-Mark
Reporter

Traff.Cas. Railway, Canal, & Road
Traffic Cases *Eng*

Trav.L.J. Travancore Law Journal
India

Trav.L.R. Travancore Law Reports
India

Trav.L.T. Travancore Law Times
India

Tread. Treadway's Reports (S. C.
Constitutional)

Tred. Tredgold's Cape Colony Reports

Trehern British & Colonial Prize Cases
v. 1

Trem. Tremaine's Pleas of the Crown
Eng

Trem.P.C. Tremaine's Pleas of the
Crown *Eng*

Trin. Trinity Term

Tripp Tripp's Reports (5, 6 Dakota)

Trist. Tristram's Consistory Judgments
Eng
Supplement to 4 Swabey & Tristram's
Probate & Divorce Reports *Eng*

Tru. Trueman's New Brunswick
Reports

Tru.Railw.Rep. Truman's American
Railway Rep.

True. Trueman's New Brunswick
Reports

Trust Bull. Trust Bulletin, American
Bankers Association

Trusts & Est. Trusts & Estates

Tuck. Tucker's Reports (District of
Columbia)
Tucker's Reports (156–175
Massachusetts)
Tucker's N. Y. Surrogate Reports
Tucker's Select Cases, Newfoundland

Tuck.Sel.Cas. Tucker's Select Cases,
Newfoundland

Tuck.Surr. Tucker's New York
Surrogate Rep.

Tuck.& Cl. Tucker & Clephane's Rep.
(21 D. C.)

Tud.Cas.Merc.Law Tudor's Leading
Cases on Mercantile Law *Eng*

Tul.L.Rev. Tulane Law Review

Tulane L.Rev. Tulane Law Review

Tup.App. Tupper's Appeal Reports
                      Ontario

Tupper Tupper's Appeal Reports
                      Ontario

  Tupper's Upper Canada Practice
  Reports

Tur.& Rus. Turner & Russell's Ch.
  Rep.   *Eng*

Turner Turner's Reports (35–48
  Arkansas)

  Turner's Reports (99–101 Kentucky)

  Turner Select Pleas of the Forest
  (Selden Society Publication, v. 13)

Tuttle Tuttle's Reports (23–32, 41–51
  Calif.)

Tuttle & Carp. Tuttle & Carpenter's
  Reports (52 Calif.)

Tyl. Tyler's Reports (Vt. 1800–1803)

Tyng Tyng's Reports (2–17
  Massachusetts)

Tyr. Tyrwhitt's Exchequer Reports
                     Eng

Tyr.& Gr. Tyrwhitt & Granger's Ex.
  Rep.   *Eng*

Tyrw. Tyrwhitt, Tyr., *supra*

U. Utah

U.B.C.Legal N. University of British
  Columbia Legal Notes

U.B.R. Upper Burma Rulings   *India*

U.C.App. Upper Canada Appeal
  Reports

U.C.C.P. Upper Canada Common
  Pleas Reports

U.C.C.P.D. Upper Canada Common
  Pleas Div.

U.C.C.R. Upper Canada Court
  Records (of Ontario Bureau of
  Archives)

U.C.Ch. Upper Canada Chancery
  Reports

U.C.Cham. Upper Canada Chambers
  Reports

U.C.Chan. Upper Canada Chancery
  Reports

U.C.E.& A. Upper Canada Error &
  Appeal Rep.

U.C.Jur. Upper Canada Jurist

U.C.K.B. Upper Canada King's Bench
  Reports, Old Series

U.C.L.J. Upper Canada Law Journal

U.C.L.J.N.S. Upper Canada Law
  Journal, N. S.

U.C.L.J.O.S. Upper Canada Law
  Journal, O. S.

UCMJ Uniform Code of Military
  Justice   *U.S.*

U.C.O.S. Upper Canada King's (or
  Queen's) Bench Reports, Old
  Series

U.C.P.R. Upper Canada Practice
  Reports

U.C.Pr. Upper Canada Practice
  Reports

U.C.Q.B. Upper Canada Queen's
  Bench Reports

U.C.Q.B.O.S. Same as above, Old
  Series

U.C.R. Upper Canada Reports

U.Chi.L.Rev. University of Chicago
  Law Rev.

U.Cin.L.Rev. University of Cincinnati
  Law Review

U.Det.L.Rev. University of Detroit
  Law Review

U.Fla.L.Rev. University of Florida
  Law Rev.

U.I.D. Selected Decisions by Umpire
  for Northern Ireland, respecting
  Claims to Benefit

U.Ill.L.F. University of Illinois Law
  Forum

U.Iowa L.Rev. University of Iowa
  Law Review

U.Kan.City L.Rev. University of Kansas City Law Review

U.L.A. Uniform Laws Annotated

UN United Nations

UNAC United Nations Appeal for
  Children

UNCIP United Nations Commission
  for India and Pakistan

UNCOK United Nations Commission
  on Korea

UNCURK United Nations Commission for Relief & Rehabilitation of
  Korea

UNESCO United Nations Educational,
  Scientific & Cultural Organization

UNICEF United Nations International
  Children's Emergency Fund

UNKRA United Nations Korean
  Reconstruction Agency

UNRPR United Nations Relief for
  Palestine Refugees

UNRRA United Nations Relief &
  Rehabilitation Administration

UNRWAPR United Nations Relief &
  Works Agency for Palestine
  Refugees in the Near East

UNSCCUR United Nations Scientific
  Conference on the Conservation &
  Utilization of Resources

UNSCOB United Nations Special
  Committee on the Balkans

UNSCOP United Nations Special Committee on Palestine

UNTCOK United Nations Temporary Commission on Korea

U.of M.L.B. University of Missouri Law Bul.

U.of Omaha Bull. Night Law School Bulletin, University of Omaha

U.of P.L.Rev. University of Pennsylvania Law Review

U.P.U. Universal Postal Union

U.Pa.L.Rev. University of Pennsylvania Law Review

U.Pitts.L.Rev. University of Pittsburgh Law Review

U.S. United States or United States Reports

USAAF U. S. Army Air Force

U.S.Ap. United States Appeals (Circuit Courts, or Courts of Appeals)

U.S.App. Same as above

U.S.App.D.C. U. S. Court of Appeals for District of Columbia beginning with v. 75

U.S.Av.R. United States Aviation Reports

U.S.C. United States Code

U.S.C.A. United States Code Annotated

U.S.C.C.A. United States Circuit Court of Appeals Reports

USCG United States Coast Guard

USCMA Official Reports, United States Court of Military Appeals

U.S.Ct.Cl. United States Court of Claims

USDA U. S. Dept. of Agriculture

U.S.Daily United States Daily, Washington, D. C.

U.S.Dist.Ct.Haw. District Court. Hawaii *U.S.*

USES United States Employment Service

USHA United States Housing Authority

USIS U. S. Indian Service

U.S.Jur. United States Jurist

U.S.L.Ed. Lawyers' Edition, United States Supreme Court Reports

U.S.L.Rev. United States Law Review

U.S.Law Int. United States Law Intelligencer & Review

U.S.Law Jour. United States Law Journal

U.S.Law Mag. United States Law Magazine

U.S.M.C. United States Marine Corps United States Maritime Commission

U.S.Month.Law Mag. United States Monthly Law Magazine

U.S.P.Q. United States Patents Quarterly

U.S.R.R.Lab.Bd. United States Railroad Labor Board

U.S.Reg. United States Register

U.S.Rep. United States Reports

U.S.Rep.(L.Ed.) United States Reports, Lawyers' Edition

U.S.S.B. United States Shipping Board [Decisions]

U.S.S.B.B. United States Shipping Board Bureau Decisions 1919–36

U.S.S.C.Rep. United States Supreme Court Reports

U.S.St.Tr. United States Trials (Wharton)

U.S.Sup.Ct.(L.Ed.) United States Reports, Lawyers' Edition

U.S.Sup.Ct.Rep. United States Supreme Court Reporter

U.S.T. United States Treaties & Other International Agreements 1950–date

USTC United States Tax Cases (CCH)

U.S.Treas.Reg. United States Treasury Regulations

U.S.Treaty Ser. United States Treaty Series

U.Toronto L.J. University of Toronto Law Journal

U.West.Aust.Ann.L.Rev. University of Western Australia Annual Law Review

Udal Udal's Fiji Law Reports

Ug.L.R. Uganda Law Reports *Africa*

Ug.Pr.L.R. Uganda Protectorate Law Reports *Africa*

Ulm.L.Rec. Ulman, Lawyers' Record *N.Y.*

Un.Trav.Dec. Unreported Travancore Decisions

Union Pac.L.D.B. Union Pacific Law Department Bulletin

Unrep.N.Y.Est.T.C. Unreported New York Estate Tax Cases (P–H)

Unrep.Wills Cas. Unreported Wills Cases (P–H)

Up.Ben.Pr. Upper Bench Precedents *temp.* Car. I *Eng*

Utah B.Bull. Utah Bar Bulletin

Utah I.C.Bull. Utah Industrial Commission Bulletin

Utah L.Rev. Utah Law Review

Utah P.U.C. Utah Public Utilities Commission Reports

Utah S.B.A. Utah State Bar Association

V. Vermont; Victoria; Virginia
Victorian Law Reports *Aus*

VA Administrator of Veterans' Affairs

V.A.D. Veterans' Affairs Decisions, Appealed Pension & Civil Service Retirement Cases *U.S.*

V.B. Veterans' Bureau *U.S.*

V.C.Rep. Vice-Chancellor's Reports (English; Canadian)

V.L.R. Victorian Law Reports *Aus*

V.N. Van Ness' Prize Cases *U.S.*

V.R. Vermont (or Victorian, or Virginia) Reports

V.R.Adm. Victorian Reports, Admiralty *Aus*

V.R.L. Victorian Law Reports *Aus*

V.R.(Law) Victorian Reports (Law) *Aus*

Va. Virginia [Reports]

Va.B.A. Virginia Bar Association

Va.Cas. Virginia Cases (Brockenbrough & Holmes)
Virginia Criminal Cases (3, 4 Virginia)

Va.Ch.Dec. Wythe's Chancery (Va. 1788–99)

Va.Col.Dec. Virginia Colonial Decisions (Randolph & Barradall)

Va.Dec. Virginia Decisions (Unreported)

Va.I.C.Ops. Virginia Industrial Commission Opinions

Va.L.Dig. Virginia Law Digest

Va.L.J. Virginia Law Journal

Va.L.Reg. Virginia Law Register

Va.L.Reg.N.S. Same as above, New Series

Va.L.Rev. Virginia Law Review

Va.L.Wk.Dicta Comp. Virginia Law Weekly Dicta Compilation

Va.R. Virginia Reports

Va.S.C.C. Virginia State Corporation Comm.

Val.Rep.I.C.C. Valuation Reports, Interstate Commerce Commission

Vand.L.Rev. Vanderbilt Law Review

Vanderstr. Vanderstraaten's Reports *Ceylon*

Van K. Van Koughnet's Reports (15–21 Upper Canada Common Pleas Reports)

Van N. Van Ness' Prize Cases, U. S. District Court, District of New York

Vaugh. Vaughan's Common Pleas Reports *Eng*

Vaux Vaux's Recorder's Decisions (Pa. 1841–45)

Ve. *See* Ves., below

Vea. *See* Ves., *below*

Ve.& B. Vesey & Beames' Chancery Rep. *Eng*

Veazey Veazey's Reports (36–44 Vermont)

Vent. Ventris' Com. Pl. & K. B. Reports *Eng*

Ver. Vermont

Verm. Vermont

Vern. Vernon's Chancery Reports *Eng*

Vern.& Scr. Vernon & Scriven's King's Bench Reports *Ir*

Ves. Vesey, Senior's, Chancery Reports *Eng*

Ves.Jr. Vesey, Junior's, Chancery Rep. *Eng*

Ves.Jun.Supp. Hovenden's Supplement to Vesey, Junior's, Reports *Eng*

Ves.Sen. Vesey, Senior's, Chancery Rep. *Eng*

Ves.&Bea. Vesey & Beames' Chancery Rep. *Eng*

Vez. Vezey's Chancery Reports *temp.* Hardwicke *Eng*

Vict.L.J. Victorian Law Journal *Aus*

Vict.L.R. Victorian Law Reports *Aus*

Vict.L.R.Min. Victorian Mining Law Reports *Aus*

Vict.L.T. Victorian Law Times *Aus*

Vict.Rep. Victorian Reports *Aus*

Vict.St.Tr. Victorian State Trials *Aus*

Vid. Vidian's Entries 1684 *Eng*

Vilas Vilas' Reports (1–5 N. Y. Criminal Rep.)

Vin.Abr. Viner's Abridgement of Law & Equity

Vin.Supp. Supplement to above

Vir.L.J. Virginia Law Journal

Virg. Virginia
Virginia Cases (Brockenbrough & Holmes)

Virgin Virgin's Reports (52–60 Maine)

Vr. Vroom's Reports (30–85 N. J. Law)

Vt. Vermont

Vt.P.S.C. Vermont Public Service Commission

Vt.R.C. Vermont Railroad Commission

W. Watt's Pennsylvania Reports
Watermayer's Reports, Supreme Court, Cape of Good Hope
Wendell's Reports (New York 1826–41)

Wheaton's Reports (14–25 United States)

Wisconsin Reports

Wright's Ohio Reports (1831–1834)

Wyoming Reports

WAA   War Assets Adm.   *U.S.*

W.A.C.A.   West African Court of Appeal, Selected Judgments

W.A.'B.&W.   Webb, A'Beckett, & Williams' Victorian Reports   *Aus*

W.A.L.R.   Western Australian Law Reports

W.Bl.   William Blackstone's K. B. Rep.   *Eng*

W.C.C.   Washington's Circuit Court Rep.   *U.S.*
Workmen's Compensation Cases (Minton-Senhouse)

W.C.L.J.   Workmen's Compensation Law Journal

W.C.Ops.   Workmen's Compensation Opinions, U. S. Dept. of Commerce

W.C.R.N.S.W.   Workers' Compensation Commission Reports of Cases, New South Wales   *Aus*

W.C.&I.Rep.   Workmen's Compensation & Insurance Reports   *Eng*

W.Coast Rep.   West Coast Reporter

W.Ct.S.A.   Union of South Africa Water Courts Decisions

W.Ent.   Winch's Book of Entries

WFO   War Food Order   *U.S.*

W.H.   Wage & Hour Cases (BNA)

W.H.C.   South African Law Reports, Witwatersrand High Court

W.H.Cas.   Wage & Hour Cases (BNA)

W.H.Chron   Westminster Hall Chronicle   *Eng*

WHO   World Health Organization   *UN*

W.H.&G.   Welsby, Hurlstone, & Gordon's Exchequer Reports *Eng*

W.H.R.   Wage & Hour Reporter (BNA)

W.H.R.Man.   Wage & Hour Reference Manual (BNA)

W.I.S.A.Law Rep.   West India States Agency Reports

W.J.   Western Jurist   *U.S.*

W.Jo.   William Jones' King's Bench Rep.   *Eng*

W.Kel.   William Kelynge's Chancery Rep.   *Eng*

W.L.D.   South African Law Reports, Witwatersrand Local Division

W.L.Gaz.   Western Law Gazette   *U.S.*

W.L.Jour.   Western Law Journal   *U.S.*

W.L.M.   Western Law Monthly   *U.S.*

W.L.R.   Washington Law Reporter (D. C.)   *U.S.*
Western Law Reporter   *Canada*

W.L.T.   Western Law Times   *Canada*

W.M.O.   World Meteorological Organization   *UN*

W.N.   Calcutta Weekly Notes   *India*
Weekly Notes (of English Law Reports)

W.N.Cas.   Weekly Notes of Cases (Pa. 1874–99)

W.N.N.S.W.   Weekly Notes, New South Wales

W.P.Cas.   Wollaston's Bail Court (Practice) Cases   *Eng*

W.P.R.   Webster's Patent Reports *Eng*

W.R.   Sutherland's Weekly Reporter   *India*
War Risk Insurance Decisions   *U.S.*
Weekly Reporter, Bengal   *India*
Weekly Reporter   *Eng*
Weekly Reporter, Cape Provincial Division   *S.Af.*
Wendell's Reports (N. Y. 1826–41)
West's Chancery Reports   *Eng*
Wisconsin Reports

W.R.C.R.   Wisconsin Railroad Commission Rep.

W.R.Calc.   Sutherland's Weekly Reporter   *India*

W.Rep.   West's Reports *temp.* Hardwicke   *Eng*

W.Rob.   W. Robinson's Admiralty Reports   *Eng*

W.T.B.R.   War Trade Board Rulings   *U.S.*

W.T.R.   Weekly Transcript Reports   *N.Y.*

W.Ty.R.   Washington Territory Rep. 1854–88

W.Va.   West Virginia

W.Va.L.Q.   West Virginia Law Quarterly

W.Va.L.Rev.   West Virginia Law Review

W.Va.P.S.C.   West Virginia Public Service Commission Decisions

W.Va.P.U.R.   West Virginia Public Utility Commission Reports

W.W.Harr.Del.   W. W. Harrington's Reports (31–39 Delaware)

W.W.R.   Western Weekly Reports   *Canada*

W.W.&A'B.Eq. Wyatt, Webb, & A'Beckett's Victoria Equity Reports *Aus*

W.W.&D. Willmore, Wollaston, & Davison's Queen's Bench Reports *Eng*

W.W.&H. Willmore, Wollaston, & Hodges' Queen's Bench Reports *Eng*

W.&C. Wilson & Courtenay's Appeal Cas. *Scot*

W.&D. Wolferstan & Dow's Election Cas. *Eng*

W.&M. Woodbury & Minot's Circuit Court Reports *U.S.*

W.&S. Watts & Sergeant's Rep. (Pa. 1841–45)

W.&S.App. Wilson & Shaw's Scotch Appeal Cases (H. L.)

W.&W. de Witt & Weeresinghe's Appeal Court Reports *Ceylon*
White & Wilson's Texas Civil Cases, Court of Appeals
Wyatt & Webb's Victorian Reports *Aus*

Wa. Watts' Reports (Pa. 1832–40)

Wal. Wallace; usually abbreviated as Wall.

Wal.by L. Wallis' Irish Chancery Reports, by Lyne

Walk. Walker

Walk.Ch. Walker's Michigan Chancery Reports

Walk.Mich. Walker's Michigan Chancery Rep.

Walk.Miss. Walker's Reports (1 Mississippi)

Walk.Pa. Walker's Reports (Pa. 1855–85)

Walk.Tex. Walker's Reports (22–25, 38–51, 72–88 Texas; 1–10 Civil Appeals Texas)

Walker Walker's Reports (96, 109 Alabama)
Walker's Michigan Chancery Reports
Walker's Reports (1 Mississippi)
Walker's Reports (Pa. 1855–85)
Walker's Reports (22–25, 38–51, 72–88 Texas; 1–10 Civil Appeals Texas)

Wall. Wallace; Wallis
Philadelphia Reports (Pa. 1855–85)
Wallace's Reports (68–90 U. S.)
Wallace's Circuit Court Reports *U.S.*
Wallis' Irish Chancery Reports

Wall.C.C. Wallace's Circuit Court Rep. *U.S.*

Wall.Jr. J. W. Wallace's Circuit Court Reports *U.S.*

Wall.Lyn. Wallis' Irish Chancery Reports by Lyne

Wall.Rep. Wallace, The Reporters (treatise)
Wallace's Reports (68–90 U. S.)

Wall.S.C. Wallace's Reports (68–90 U. S.)

Wall.Sen. J. B. Wallace's Circuit Court Reports *U.S.*

Wallis by L. Wallis' Irish Chancery Reports, by Lyne

Walsh Walsh's Registry Cases *Ir*

Walter (14–16 New Mexico)

War Dept.B.C.A. U. S. War Department, Decisions of Board of Contract Adjustment

War Trade Reg. War Trade Regulations *U.S.*

Ward. Warden's Reports (2, 4 Ohio State)

Warden Warden's Reports (2, 4 Ohio State)

Warden & Smith (3 Ohio State Reports)

Ware Ware's District Court Reports *U.S.*

Wash. Washburn; Washington
Washington's Reports (16–23 Vermont)
Washington's Reports (1, 2 Virginia)
Washington's Circuit Court Reports *U.S.*
Washington Territory or State Reports

Wash.C.C. Washington's Circuit Court Reports *U.S.*

Wash.Co.R. Washington County Reports *Pa*

Wash.Jur. Washington Jurist

Wash.L.Rep. Washington Law Reporter *D.C.*

Wash.L.Rev. Washington Law Review

Wash.Terr. Washington Territory Opinions 1854–64
Washington Territory Reports 1854–88

Wash.Ter.N.S. Allen's Washington Territory Reports, New Series

Wash.Ty. *See* Wash. Terr., *supra*

Wash.U.L.Rev. Washington University Law Review

Wash.Va. Washington's Reports (1, 2 Va.)

Wash.& Haz.P.E.I. Washburton & Hazard's Reports, Prince Edward Island *Canada*

Wash.& Lee L.Rev. Washington & Lee Law Review

Washburn Washburn's Reports (18–23 Vt.)

Wat.C.G.H. Watermeyer's Reports, Cape of Good Hope *S.Af.*

– **Watermeyer** Same as above

Watson Watson's Bristol Pleas of the Crown *Eng*

Watts Watts' Reports (Pa. 1832–40) Watts' Reports (16–24 West Virginia)

Watts & Serg. Watts & Sergeant's Reports (Pa. 1841–45)

We. West's Chancery Reports *Eng* West's Reports, House of Lords *Eng* Western Tithe Cases *Eng*

Web.Pat.Cas. Webster's Patent Cases *Eng*

Webb Webb's Reports (6–20 Kansas) Webb's Reports (11–20 Texas Civil Appeals)

Webb,A'B.& W. Webb, A'Beckett, & Williams' Victorian Reports *Aus*

Webb,A'B.& W.Eq. Webb, A'Beckett, & Williams' Victorian Equity Reports *Aus*

Webb,A'B.& W.I.P.& M. Webb, A'Beckett, & Williams' Insolvency, Probate & Matrimonial Reports, Victoria *Aus*

Webb,A'B & W.Min. Webb, A'Beckett & Williams' Victorian Mining Cases *Aus*

Webb & Duval Webb & Duval's Reports (1–3 Tex.)

Webs. Webster's Patent Cases *Eng*

Week.Cin.L.B. Weekly Cincinnati Law Bulletin

Week.Dig. New York Weekly Digest 1876–88

Week.Jur. Weekly Jurist

Week.L.Gaz. Weekly Law Gazette

Week.L.Rev. Weekly Law Review

Week.Law Bull. Weekly Law Bulletin and Ohio Law Journal

Week.No. Weekly Notes of Cases (Law Reports)

Week.No.Cas. Weekly Notes of Cases (Pa. 1874–99)

Week.Reptr. Weekly Reporter (London or Bengal)

Week.Trans.Repts. Weekly Transcript Reports (N. Y. 1861)

Weekly Notes Weekly Notes (of Law Reports) *Eng*

Weer. Weerakoon's Appeal Court Rep. *Ceylon*

Weight.Med.Leg.Gaz. Weightman's Medico-Legal Gazette

Wel. *See* Welsh, *infra*

Welsb.H.& G. Welsby, Hurlstone, & Gordon's Exchequer Reports *Eng*

Welsh Welsh's Irish Cases at Sligo Welsh's Irish Registry Cases

Wend. Wendell's Reports (N. Y. 1826–41)

Wendt Wendt's Reports of Cases *Ceylon*

Wenz. Wenzell's Reports (60–72 Minnesota)

Wes.Res.Law Jo. Western Reserve Law Journal

West.Res.Law Rev. Western Reserve Law Review

West. West's Chancery Reports *Eng* West's Reports, House of Lords *Eng* Westbury, European Arbitration (Reilly) Western's London Tithe Cases *Eng* Weston's Reports (11–14 Vermont)

West.Chy. West's Chancery Reports, *temp.* Hardwicke *Eng*

West Co.Rep. West Coast Reporter

West *t.*H. West's Chancery Reports, *temp.* Hardwicke *Eng*

West H.L. West's Reports, House of Lords *Eng*

West.Jur. Western Jurist

West.L.J. Western Law Journal

West.L.Mo. Western Law Monthly

West.L.R. Western Law Reporter *Canada*

West.L.T. Western Law Times *Canada*

West.Leg.Obs. Western Legal Observer

West.Rep. Western Reporter

West.Tithe Cas. Western's London Tithe Cases *Eng*

West Va. West Virginia

West Va.B.A. West Virginia Bar Association

West.Week.N. Western Weekly Notes *Canada*

Westmoreland Co.L.J. Westmoreland County Law Journal (Pa. 1911–date)

Weston Weston's Reports (11–14 Vermont)

Weth.U.C. Wethey's Reports, Upper Canada Queen's Bench

Wh. Wharton's Reports (Pa. 1835–41) Wheaton's Reports (14–25 U. S.)

Wh.Cr.Cas. Wheeler's Criminal Cases *N.Y.*

Wh.& T.L.C. White & Tudor's Leading Cases in Equity *Eng*

Whar. Wharton's Reports (Pa. 1835–41)

Whar.St.Tr. Wharton's U. S. State Trials

Whart.Pa. Wharton's Reports (Pa. 1835–41)

Wheat. Wheaton's Reports (14–25 U. S.)

Wheel. Wheelock's Reports (32–37 Texas)

Wheeler's Criminal Cases *N.Y.*

Wheel.Cr.Cas. Wheeler's Criminal Cases *N.Y.*

Wheel.Cr.Rec. Wheeler's Criminal Recorder (1 Wheeler's Criminal Cases) *N.Y.*

Whit.Pat.Cas. Whitman's Patent Cases *U.S.*

White White's Justiciary Court Rep. *Scot*

White's Reports (31–44 Texas Appeals)

White's Reports (10–15 West Virginia)

White & T.L.Cas. White & Tudor's Leading Cases in Equity *Eng*

White & W. White & Willson's Reports (Texas Civil Cases of Court of Appeals)

White & W.Civ.Cas.Ct.App. Same as above

Whitm.Lib.Cas. Whitman's Massachusetts Libel Cases

Whitm.Pat.Cas. Whitman's Patent Cases *U.S.*

Whitm.Pat.Law Rev. Whitman's Patent Law Review

Whittlesey Whittlesey's Reports (32–41 Mo.)

Wight. Wightwick's Exchequer Reports *Eng*

Wight El.Cas. Wight's Election Cases *Scot*

Wightw. Wightwick's Exchequer Reports *Eng*

Wil. Williams, abbreviated as Will. Wilson, abbreviated as Wils.

Wilc.Cond.Rep. Wilcox's Condensed Reports (1–7 Ohio, Reprint)

Wilcox Wilcox's Reports (10 Ohio) Wilcox's Lackawanna County (Pa.) Reports

Wilk. Wilkinson's Reports, Texas Court of Appeals & Civil Appeals Wilkinson's Reports *Aus*

Wilk.P.& M. Wilkinson, Paterson, & Murray's Reports, New South Wales *Aus*

Wilk.& Ow. Wilkinson, Owen, Patterson, & Murray's Reports, New South Wales *Aus*

Will. Willes' Common Pleas Reports *Eng*

Will.Ann.Reg. Williams' New York Annual Register

Will.-Bund St.Tr. Willis-Bund, Cases from State Trials

Will.Mass. Williams' Reports (1 Mass.)

Will.P. Peere Williams' Chancery Reports *Eng*

Will.Saund. Williams' Notes to Saunders' Reports *Eng*

Will.Vt. Williams Reports (27–29 Vermont)

Will.Woll.& D. Willmore, Wollaston, Davison's Queen's Bench Rep. *Eng*

Will.Woll.& Hodg. Willmore, Wollaston, & Hodges' Queen's Bench Rep. *Eng*

Willes Willes' Common Pleas Reports *Eng*

Williams Peere Williams' Chancery Rep. *Eng*
Williams' Reports (1 Massachusetts)
Williams' Reports (10–12 Utah)
Williams' Reports (27–29 Vermont)

Williams P. Peere Williams' Ch. Reports *Eng*

Williams Saund. Williams' Notes to Saunders Reports *Eng*

Willm.W.& D. Willmore, Wollaston, Davison's Queen's Bench Rep. *Eng*

Willm.W.& H. Willmore, Wollaston, & Hodges' Queen's Bench Rep. *Eng*

Willson Willson's Reports, Texas Appeals

Willson Civ.Cas.Ct.App. White & Willson's Civil Cases of Texas Court of Appeals

Wilm. Wilmot's Notes of Opinions, King's Bench *Eng*

Wilm.Op. Same as above

Wils. G. Wilson's Reports, King's Bench & Common Pleas *Eng*

Wils.Ch. Wilson's Chancery Reports *Eng*

Wils.Ent. Wilson's Entries & Pleading (3 Lord Raymond's King's Bench & Common Pleas Reports) *Eng*

Wils.Exch. Wilson's Exchequer *Eng*

Wils.Ind. Wilson's Reports, Indiana Superior Court

Wils.K.B. Wilson's King's Bench Reports

Wils.Minn. Wilson's Reports (48–59 Minn.)

Wils.Oreg. Wilson's Reports (1–3 Oregon)

Wils.& Court *See* Wils. & S., *infra*

Wils.& S. Wilson & Shaw's Scotch Appeals, House of Lords

Wils.& Sh. Same as above

Wilson Wilson's Chancery Reports *Eng*

Wilson's King's Bench & Common Pleas Reports *Eng*

Wilson's Exchequer in Equity Reports *Eng*

Wilson's Reports, Indiana Superior Court

Wilson's Reports (48–59 Minnesota)

Wilson's Reports (1–3 Oregon)

Win. Winch's Common Pleas Reports *Eng*

Winer's Unreported Opinions (N. Y. Supreme Court, Erie County)

Winston's Reports (60 North Carolina)

Win.Eq. Winston's Reports (60 North Carolina)

Winch Winch's Common Pleas Reports *Eng*

Winst. Winston's Reports (60 North Carolina)

Wis. Wisconsin

Wis.B.A.Bull. Wisconsin State Bar Association Bulletin

Wis.B.Bull. Wisconsin Bar Bulletin

Wis.I.C. Wisconsin Industrial Commission (Workmen's Compensation Reports)

Wis.L.R.Bd.Dec. Wisconsin Labor Relations Board Decisions

Wis.L.Rev. Wisconsin Law Review

Wis.Leg.N. Wisconsin Legal News

Wis.P.S.C. Wisconsin Public Service Commission Reports

Wis.P.S.C.Ops. Wisconsin Public Service Commission Opinions & Decisions

Wis.R.C.Ops. Wisconsin Railroad Commission Opinions & Decisions

Wis.S.B.A. Wisconsin State Bar Association

With.Corp.Cas. Withrow's American Corporation Cases

Withrow Withrow's American Corporation Cases

Withrow's Reports (9–21 Iowa)

Wkly.Dig. New York Weekly Digest

Wkly.Law Bul. Weekly Law Bulletin & Ohio Law Journal

Wkly Law Gaz. Weekly Law Gazette

Wm.Bl. William Blackstone's K. B. Rep. *Eng*

Wm.Rob. William Robinson's Admiralty Rep. *Eng*

Wms. Williams, commonly abbreviated as Will.

Wms.Mass. Williams' Reports (1 Mass.)

Wms.Notes Williams' Notes to Saunders' Reports *Eng*

Wms.Peere Peere Williams' Chancery Rep. *Eng*

Wms.Saund. Williams' Notes to Saunders' Reports *Eng*

Wms.Vt. Williams' Reports (27–29 Vermont)

Wol. Wolcott's Reports (7 Delaware Chancery)

Wollaston's Bail Court Reports *Eng*

Wolf.& B. Wolferstan & Bristow's Election Cases *Eng*

Wolf.& D. Wolferstan & Dew's Election Cases *Eng*

Woll. Wollaston's Bail Court Reports *Eng*

Women L.Jour. Women's Law Journal

Wood Wood's Tithe Cases *Eng*

Wood Decr. Wood's Tithe Cases *Eng*

Wood H. Hutton Wood's Decrees in Tithe Cases *Eng*

Wood.& M. Woodbury & Minot's Circuit Court Reports *U.S.*

Woodman Cr.Cas. Woodman's Reports of Thacher's Criminal Cases *Mass.*

Woods Wood's Circuit Court Reports *U.S.*

Woods C.C. Same as above

Wood's R. Wood's Manitoba Reports 1875–83

Woodw.Dec. Woodward's Decisions (Pa. 1861–74)

Wool. Woolworth's Circuit Court Reports *U.S.*

Wool.C.C. Same as above

Woolsack Woolsack (a periodical) *Eng*

Woolw. Woolworth's Circuit Court Rep. *U.S.*

Woolworth's Reports (1 Nebraska)

Words.Elect.Cas. Wordsworth's Election Cases   *Eng*

Wright Wright's Reports (Ohio 1831–34)

Wright's Reports (37–50 Pa. State)

Wright Ch. Wright's Reports (Ohio 1831–34)

Wright N.P. Wright's Nisi Prius Rep.   *Ohio*

Wy. Wythe's Chancery Reports (Va. 1788–99)

Wyoming Reports

Wy.Dick. Dickens' Chancery Reports, by Wyatt   *Eng*

Wy.Pr.R. Wyatt's Practical Register in Chancery   *Eng*

Wyatt,W.& A'B. Wyatt, Webb, & A'Beckett's Victorian Equity Reports   *Aus*

Wyatt,W.& A'B.Eq. Same as above

Wyatt,W.& A'B.I.P.& M. Wyatt, Webb, & A'Beckett's Victorian Insolvency, Probate, & Matrimonial Reports   *Aus*

Wyatt,W.& A'B.Min. Wyatt, Webb, & A'Beckett's Victorian Mining Cases   *Aus*

Wyatt & W.Eq. Wyatt & Webb's Victorian Equity Reports   *Aus*

Wyatt & W.I.P.& M. Wyatt & Webb's Insolvency, Probate, & Matrimonial Reports, Victoria *Aus*

Wyatt & W.Min. Wyatt & Webb's Victorian Mining Cases   *Aus*

Wyatt & Webb Wyatt & Webb's Reports, Victoria   *Aus*

Wyman Wyman's Civil & Criminal Rep.   *India*

Wynne Bov. Wynne, Bovill's Patent Cases

Wyo. Wyoming

Wyo.B.A. Wyoming Bar Association

Wyo.L.J. Wyoming Law Journal

Wyo.T. Wyoming Territory

Wythe Wythe's Chancery Reports (Va. 1788–99)

Y. Yeates Reports (Pa. 1791–1808)

Y.A.D. Young's Vice-Admiralty Dec.   *Canada*

Y.B. Year Books. The Year Books are usually cited by the year of each King's reign, the initial letter of his name, and the folio and number of the *placita, e.g.,* 34 H. VI, 25.3.

Y.B.Ames Year Books, Ames Foundation

Y.B.(Rolls Ser.) Year Books, Rolls Series

Y.B.(Sel.Soc.) Year Books, Selden Society

Y.L.R. York Legal Record (Pa. 1880–date)

Y.& C. Younge & Collyer's Chancery or Exchequer Equity Reports *Eng*

Y.& C.Ex. Younge & Collyer's Exchequer in Equity Reports *Eng*

Y.& J. Young & Jervis' Exchequer Rep.   *Eng*

Yale L.J. Yale Law Journal

Yates Sel.Cas. Yates' Select Cases (N. Y. 1809)

Yea. Yeates' Reports (Pa. 1791–1808)

Year Books *See* Y. B., *supra*

Yeates Same as yea, above

Yel. Yelverton's King's Bench Reports   *Eng*

Yelv. Same as above

Yerg. Yerger's Reports (9–18 Tennessee)

Yo. Younge's Exchequer Equity Reports   *Eng*

York Leg.Rec. York Legal Record (Pa. 1880–date)

Yorke Ass. Clayton's Reports, Yorke Assizes

You. Younge's Exchequer Equity Reports   *Eng*

You.& Coll.Ch. Younge & Collyer's Chancery Reports   *Eng*

You.& Coll.Ex. Younge & Collyer's Exchequer Equity Reports   *Eng*

You.& Jerv. Younge & Jervis' Exchequer Reports   *Eng*

Young Young's Reports (21–47 Minn.)

Young Adm.Dec. Young's Nova Scotia Vice-Admiralty Decisions

Young M.L.Cas. Young's Maritime Law Cases   *Eng*

Young V.A.Dec. Young's Nova Scotia Vice-Admiralty Decisions

Younge Younge's Exchequer Reports   *Eng*

Younge & Coll.Ch. Younge & Collyer's Chancery or Exchequer Equity Reports   *Eng*

Younge & Coll.Ex. Younge & Collyer's Exchequer Equity Reports   *Eng*

Younge & Jerv. Younge & Jervis' Exchequer Reports   *Eng*

Z.L.R. Zanzibar Law Reports

Zab. Zabriskie's Reports (21–24 N. J. Law)

Zane Zane's Reports (4–9 Utah)

Zanzib.Prot.L.R. Zanzibar Protectorate Law Reports   *East Africa*

Zilla C.D. Zilla Court Decisions (Bengal, Madras, North West Provinces)   *India*

Zululand Zululand Commissioner's Court Cases

INDEX